BIOSECURITY LAW & POLICY

Victoria Sutton, M.P.A., Ph.D., J.D.

PAUL WHITFIELD HORN PROFESSOR
DIRECTOR, CENTER FOR BIODEFENSE, LAW AND PUBLIC POLICY
TEXAS TECH UNIVERSITY SCHOOL OF LAW

ISBN-10:0983802491
ISBN-13:978-0-9838024-9-5

LCCN

Vargas Publishing
P.O. Box 6801
Lubbock, TX 79401
Phone: (806) 797-0022
FAX: (806) 797-3102

Printed in the United States of America

To Summer and Remington

TABLE OF CONTENTS

**Chapter Twelve   The Future of Law and Biosecurity,
                      Biodefense and Bioterrorism**

TABLE OF CASES

FOREWORD

The Anthrax attacks in the fall of 2001 did not leave us where they found us. At the same time, epoch-making discoveries in biology are charting a course for a society that will likely be astonishingly different a century from now. The increase, speed and pace of international travel has permitted newly emerging infectious diseases to travel and spread to humans at unpreceded rates in human history. That biosecurity law and policy would become an essential way for civil society to address these changes should come as no surprise. This book takes a look at the foundation for these changes and the legal and regulatory framework that has evolved. Taking legal methods and exploring scientific and global health problems with breadth and depth is the goal of this text for law students, public health students, national security students and public health students as well as practitioners in almost any area of law who need to have a starting point for understanding this emerging framework of biosecurity law and regulation.

This book, updates and adds many new areas of law and regulation of *Law and Bioterrorism* (2003, Carolina Academic Press). As the field has evolved from its early focus on criminal law and bioterrorism to more prospective biosecurity laws, so has this book's contents.

Your thoughts and insights are welcome and you may contact me at vickie.sutton@ttu.edu.

Victoria Sutton
Lubbock, TX

ABOUT THE AUTHOR

Prof. Victoria Sutton, Paul Whitfield Horn Professor, Texas Tech University is both a scientist and a lawyer, pursuing interdisciplinary research and teaching interests. She is a graduate of American University, Washington College of Law with a Juris Doctorate degree *magna cum laude*; Old Dominion University with a Master's Degree in Public Administration and The University of Texas at Dallas with a Doctorate of Philosophy in Environmental Sciences. Her undergraduate degrees are a Bachelor of Science in Zoology and a Bachelor of Science in Animal Science, *cum laude*, from North Carolina State University. established the Center for Biodefense, Law and Public Policy in 2002, serving as the founding Director. Since that time, the Center has doubled its funding, receiving support from the National Institutes of Health, NIAID through the federal funding program for biodefense researchers, the national Regional Centers of Excellence for Biodefense and Emerging Infectious Diseases.

Prof. Sutton is Director of the Center for Biodefense, Law and Public Policy and Professor of Law, Texas Tech University School of Law, and also has an appointment in the Texas Institute for Environmental and Human Health, Texas Tech University. She served as the first Chief Counsel of the Research and Innovative Technology Administration of the U.S. Department of Transportation in the Pres. George W. Bush Administration and previously served in the George H.W. Bush Administration from 1989 to 1993 first in the U.S. Environmental Protection Agency and then as Assistant Director of the Office of Science and Technology Policy, Executive Office of the President. Following her White House service, she was the Executive Director of The Ronald Reagan Institute for Emergency Medicine, George Washington University; then Research Associate Professor at the Uniformed Services University for the Health Sciences in Bethesda, Maryland.

Prof. Sutton has provided legal and policy advice on biosafety and biosecurity law to departments and agencies of the federal government as well as the White House Homeland Security Council. She has also served as a consulting attorney on several high profile biosafety and biosecurity cases involving criminal, civil and administrative processes.

The Center supports a national Hotline for Biosafety and Biosecurity Law questions and established the Journal of Biosecurity, Biodefense and Bioterrorism Law, the only journal to focus in this scholarly area of law. The Center also supports the annual student Symposium on Biosecurity Law.

She has published more than thirty articles, and several casebooks: Law and Science (Carolina Academic Press, 2001); Law and Bioterrorism (Carolina Academic Press, 2003); Law and Biotechnology (Carolina Academic Press, 2009); and Nanotechnology Law and Policy (Carolina Academic Press, 2010). Her work has been cited by the National Institute of Medicine.

In international work, she has provided advice to the Biological Weapons Convention Assembly, and has served in an advisory capacity and given talks on biosecurity law at conferences in Europe, Africa, the South Pacific and the Middle East.

In 2010, Prof. Sutton's research was cited by the White House Science Office in support of Pres. Obama's Executive Order to review the biosafety and biosecurity regulatory program. http://www.whitehouse.gov/blog/2010/07/02/presidential-order-balances-security-and-scientific-enterprise .

Prof. Sutton is a member of the American Microbiology Association and the American Biological Safety Association and currently serves as a member of the ABSA Task Force on Biosafety Regulation. She has testified before Committees of the National Academies, Institute of Medicine on biosecurity.

Professor Sutton is a member of the District of Columbia Bar and of the Federal Circuit Bar.

ACKNOWLEDGMENTS

I want to acknowledge D. Allan Bromley, Ph.D. (deceased), Sterling Professor of the Sciences, Yale University, and most importantly, my husband, for sharing his insights into international bioterrorism, security in research practices, and his review and comments on numerous drafts of the book which preceded this one. I also appreciate his encouragement to continue this line of research well before September 11th when many thought that law and bioterrorism was not an issue.

I would also like to thank Richard Rosen, Professor of Law, Texas Tech University for his advice on military and vaccination law issues.

For her research and persistence in finding and obtaining difficult documents, I am grateful to Sharon Blackburn, Research Librarian, Texas Tech University School of Law. I am also indebted to Michele Thaetig, who assisted with many aspects of the preparation process. My thanks also go to, now, Professor Brie Sherwin, who worked on publication permissions and general management of the book project and many issues with regard to biosecurity law.

A special thanks is due students in my course, Law and Bioterrorism, in 2002, 2003, 2004, 2007, 2008, 2009 and 2010. I would like to particularly thank Jill Berry (JD, 2004) students, who tirelessly assisted in editing and cite checking; Brandon Gaines (J.D., 2008) for his research of the John Warner Act of 2007 and the Act of God defense; and Whitney Boatright (J.D., 2007) and Sara Thornton (J.D., 2007) for the First Amendment and Publication research.

Thanks for research on many issues important to this work is due Center for Biodefense Fellows: Jeff Mustin (J.D., 2012); James Garrett (J.D., 2012); Arslan Umarov J.D., 2011); Laci Lawrence (J.D., 2011); Marshall Maringola (J.D., 2012); Austin Franklin (J.D., 2013); Austin Carrizales (J.D., 2013); Heather Carson (J.D., 2013); Cory Davenport (Ph.D., 2013) and Joel Aldrich (J.D., 2015).

For the use of their materials in the development of this book, I acknowledge the following authors and publishers:

Albert, Ostheimer, Breman, "The Last Smallpox Epidemic in Boston and the Vaccination Controversy, 1901–1903," N. Engl. J. Med 2001; 344(5) 375–379 (Feb. 1, 2001). [Chapter Three].

Breuer, Marten, "Law and Medicine: Notes on the Meeting of German-Speaking Public Law Assistants in Vienna, 7 German Law Journal No. 4 (1 April 2006) at http://www.germanlawjournal.com/article.php?id=722 . [Chapter 11]

Gould, Chandre and Peter Folb, United Nations, *Project Coast: Apartheid's Chemical and Biological Warfare Programme,* UNIDIR/2002/12 (2002). [Chapter 11]

Guillemin, Jeanne, *Anthrax—An Investigation of a Deadly Outbreak* 113–4 (1999). [Chap. 8, Section 8.1 graphic and Section 8.3.4. quotation]

Kellman, Barry. "Biological Terrorism: Legal Measures for Preventing Catastrophe," 24 Harv. J.L. & Pub. Pol'y 417 (Spring 2001) [Chapter One].

Mccollough, Jason E., *State Tort Liability for Failure to Protect Against Bioterrorism*, 8 Drake J. Agric. L. 743, at 768-781 (Fall 2003). [Chapter Five].

National Conference of State Legislatures, http://www.ncsl.org/programs/press/2001/ freedom/bioterrorism01.htm, (website visited Aug. 13, 2002).

Root-Bernstein, Robert S. "Infectious Terrorism," 267 *The Atlantic Monthly* 44–50 (May 1991) can be found at http://www.theatlantic.com/issues/91may/rootbernstein.htm. [Chap Two. Resource for Chapter Two, Role of EPA, Water Supply].

Rothstein, Mark A., J.D., Director; M. Gabriela Alcalde, M.P.H., Nanette R. Elster, J.D., M.P.H., Mary Anderlik Majumder, J.D., Ph.D., Larry I. Palmer, LL.B., T. Howard Stone, J.D., LL.M., Institute for Bioethics, Health Policy and Law, University of Louisville School of Medicine; Richard E. Hoffman, M.D., M.P.H., Denver, Colorado, Consultant, *QUARANTINE AND ISOLATION: LESSONS LEARNED FROM SARS: A Report to the Centers for Disease Control and Prevention* (November 2003). [Chapter 11]

Sargent, Ben, Universal Press Syndicate, "Bill of Rights" political cartoon (Sept. 18, 2001).[Chap. 7].

Sutton, Victoria. "It will be too late for Congress to act after bioterrorism attack is launched," op-ed, *Lubbock Avalanche Journal* (Saturday, Sept. 22, 2001)
Sutton, Victoria. "A Precarious 'Hot Zone'—The President's Plan to Combat Bioterrorism," 164 *The Military Law Review* 135 (2000). This article is reprinted from *The Military Law Review*, Department of the Army Pamphlet 27-100-164, at 135 (2000). The opinions and conclusions expressed herein are those of the individual author, and do not necessarily represent the views of The Judge Advocate General's School, United States Army, or any other governmental agency.

Sutton, Victoria. Bioterrorism Preparation and Response Legislation—The Struggle to Protect States' Sovereignty While Preserving National Security, 6 *The Georgetown Public Policy Review* 93 (Spring 2001)

Sutton, Victoria. "Bioterrorism—A Change in Our Way of Life, and a Change in our Legal Framework, op-ed, *The Texas Lawyer* (Monday, Nov. 5, 2001)

Sutton, Victoria. "Legal Impediments to Surveillance for Biological Threats and Countering Terrorism," *BTR 2002 Proceedings*, Sandia Laboratories Conference, March 16, 2002.

Zilinskas, Raymond A., "Cuban Allegations of U.S. Biological Warfare, False Allegations and Their Impact on Attribution," from *Terrorism, War, or Disease?: Unraveling the Use of Biological Weapons*, edited by Anne L. Clunan, Peter R. Lavoy and Susan B. Martin (2008). [Chapter 11]

Zöller, Verena, "Liberty Dies by Inches: German Counter-Terrorism Measures and Human Rights, Part 1 of 2, and Part 2 of 2," *German Law Journal* Vol. 5 No. 5 - 1 May 2004 at http://www.germanlawjournal.com/print.php?id=424 and http://www.germanlawjournal.com/print.php?id=425 . [Chapter 11]

Biosecurity Law & Policy

Chapter One
Introduction to Biosecurity Law

Biosecurity law is broadly defined here as laws and regulations intended to limit, control, penalize or to make safe biological activities products and biological events, which are naturally emerging or intentionally planned, that cause injury or death to humans, plants or animals, in the context of warfare, domestic terrorism, or other human or environmental activities. The term also encompasses civil penalties, criminal codes and penalties, and other forms of social controls in response to violations of these laws and regulations. Biosecurity law includes U.S. domestic law, domestic laws of other countries and regions, and international approaches to law and biosecurity. Laws concerning bioterrorism and agroterrorism, and countermeasures for bioterrorism, agroterrorism, and emerging infectious diseases are also encompassed in the term biosecurity law. Additionally, laws and regulations concerning the use, possession, and storage of certain biological agents, and laws and regulations concerning the facilities in which they are used, are also within the scope of biosecurity law.

Other areas of law that are examined as important sources of law within biosecurity law include constitutional law, international law, state law and tribal law, emergency public health law, public health law, environmental law, administrative law, criminal law, tort law, human rights law, refugee law, and disaster law.

1.1. History of Law and Biosecurity, Biodefense and Bioterrorism

The use of law to control bioterrorism did not begin until its first mention in the Hague Convention in 1899, which addressed the rules of warfare to prohibit biological agents in the section entitled, "with Respect to the Laws and Customs of War on Land," declaring that "it is especially prohibited...To employ poison or poisoned arms."[1] The Geneva Protocol of 1925 included "bacteriological" warfare with chemical prohibitions. Mentions of bioterrorism in documents prior to this time tended more to describe events in medical terms, and provided military strategists with information on what was acceptable warfare until 1925. While natural law and morality have provided the basis for laws in civil societies, the development of the prohibition against bioterrorism did not develop until very recent history, although the existence of biological warfare is known from the earliest times. The moral basis of law and the development of a bioethic led to the very recent proscriptions against the use of bioterrorism in war against troops or against civilians in war or peacetime.

The ancient era of biological warfare.

The ancient Hammurabi code of law, where the "eye for an eye" code is found, suggests a policy of return with biological attack if attacked, but perhaps not a first strike policy.

The Hippocratic Oath was the first bioethical commitment on the part of the profession of medicine, and would have prohibited physicians from researching, experimenting or participating in biological warfare. The oath in its entirety reads as follows, with bold print added for emphasis:

> I swear by Apollo Physician and Sclepius and Hygieia and Panaceia and all the gods and goddesses, making them my witnesses, that I will fulfill according to my ability and judgment this oath and this covenant:
>
> To hold him who has taught me this art as equal to my parents and to live my life in partnership with him....
>
> I will apply dietetic measures for the benefit of the sick according to my ability and judgment; I will keep them from harm and injustice.
>
> **I will neither give a deadly drug to anybody if asked for it, nor will I make a suggestion to this effect.** [Emphasis added]. Similarly, I will not give to a woman an abortive remedy. In purity and holiness I will guard my life and my art.
>
> I will not use the knife, not even on sufferers from stone, but will withdraw in favor of such men as are engaged in this work.
>
> Whatever houses I may visit, I will come for the benefit of the sick, remaining free of all intentional injustice, of all mischief and in particular of sexual relations with both female and male persons, be they free or slaves.
>
> What I may see or hear in the course of the treatment or even outside of the treatment in regard to the life of men, which on no account one must spread abroad, I will keep to myself holding such things shameful to be spoken about.
>
> If I fulfill this oath and do not violate it, may it be granted to me to enjoy life and art, being honored with fame among all men for all time to come; if I transgress it and swear falsely, may the opposite of all this be my lot.

In 67 B.C., the first intentional use of a biological agent by one army against another has been proposed concerning the armies of Roman general Pompey and King Mithridates of Pontus. King Mithridates was very educated himself, and had as his chief advisor Kateuas, a Greek physician, who supposedly advised the King on biological warfare strategy. Kateuas is often mentioned as the first herbalist. King Mithridates had retreated in battle to the Black Sea coast of Turkey, and historians believe it may have been a strategic plan. Kateuas was aware of a battle that had taken place 300 years earlier in 401 B.C. when Xenophon recorded that his Greek soldiers retreated from Babylon to the same area of the Black Sea coast, where they consumed honeycombs. The result was the complete collapse of the troops from the effects of a toxin present in honey produced by bees gathering nectar from laurels and rhododendrons: grayanotoxin. Pompey's troops were led into the trap, consumed the honeycombs and were slaughtered by the awaiting King Mithridates troops.[2]

Between 43 B.C. and A.D. 17, Ovid was quoted giving the simplest of guidance for disease outbreaks: "Act, before disease becomes persistent through long delays," which might be considered the first public health guidance to thwart public health emergencies.[2A]

In 1346–47, the Tartars first used plague as a biological weapon when they catapulted plague-infected corpses over the walls in Kaffa, forcing the Genoans to evacuate the city.[3, 4]
De Mussis, a notary who observed the attacks, described the approach:

> [the Tartars], fatigued by such a plague and pestiferous disease, stupefied and amazed, observing themselves dying without hope of health ordered cadavers placed on their hurling machines and thrown into the city of Caffa, so that by means of these intolerable passengers the defenders dies widely.[5]

The Romans used dead animals to contaminate the water supply of the enemy by throwing the diseased carcasses into the flowing waters.

The New World engaged in its own brand of biological warfare in the attempt to eradicate the American Indian population in the seventeenth century. In 1633, the Narragansetts were struck by a smallpox epidemic, which they surmised had been deliberately transmitted to them by gifts from Captain John Oldham, an officer for the Massachusetts Colony. For this, the Narragansetts captured Oldham, tried him before the tribal council and executed him. This is said to have led to King Philips's War and the almost complete annihilation of the Pequots, who were blamed for Oldham's execution. Suspicion gave way to proof some one hundred and fifty years later when Sir Jeffrey Amherst took blankets from smallpox hospitals and gave them to the Indians in ceremonial exchanges with the Ottawas and Lenni Lanapes Tribes. Amherst wrote a letter to his subordinate, Colonel Henry Bouquet, about his plan and in one exchange Amherst wrote: "You will do well to [infect] the Indians by means of blankets as well as to try every other method that can serve to extirpate this [execrable] race." From a journal entry by Captain Ecuyer of the Royal Americans, he noted, "...we gave them two blankets and a handkerchief out of the smallpox hospital. I hope it will have the desired effect."[6] This resulted in the complete genocide of many East Coast tribes, many of whom lost up to 90% of their populations. More than 100,000 were killed among the indigenous population. Smallpox was an ideal biological agent for the European population because many had some immunity to the disease, while the American Indian population had none.[7]

In 1710, the Germans were alleged to have used plague-infected corpses to attack Swedes.[7]

During the U.S. Civil War, the U.S. War Department issued General Order 100, mandating that the "use of poison in any manner, be it to poison wells, or foods, or arms, is wholly excluded from modern warfare."[8] Dr. Luke Blackburn attempted to infect clothing with smallpox and yellow fever, which was intended for sale to the Union troops. The Confederates in their retreat from Mississippi deposited dead animals in the wells and ponds to putrefy the water supplies for advancing Union troops.[9]

The modern era of biological warfare.

World War I marks the first use of biological weapons against the United States in the modern era of biological warfare. A German veterinarian in the United States and other German agents infected cattle and horses with anthrax (*Bacillus anthracis*) and glanders (*pseudomonas pseudomallei*) before sending them to Allied Forces in Europe as food and transportation.[10] A German agent responsible for infecting 4,500 mules with glanders was arrested in Mesopotamia in 1917.[11]

The flu pandemic of 1918 raised suspicions that the flu had been purposefully inflicted on the shores of the United States. Lieutenant Colonel Philip S. Doane of the Health Sanitation Section of the Emergency Fleet Corporation stated on the first page of *The Philadelphia Inquirer* on September 21, 1918 that the Germans had come into Boston Harbor on U-boats, walked ashore carrying vials of the plague germs with them, and then released them into theaters and crowds.[12]

The Soviets also had a biological weapons program underway, and used a weaponized tularemia against the Germans in World War I. The significant number of deaths and infections in the local population, far above the expected number, indicated an intentional use of the biological agent. Not until 1998 did this event become public knowledge when Ken Alibek, a former administrator and scientist, who had defected from the Soviet Union Biopreparat, disclosed this occurrence.

The use of these biologics most certainly raised worldwide concern, which led to the negotiation of the Geneva Convention of 1925. The Geneva Protocol for the Prohibition of the Use in War of Asphyxiating, Poisonous or Other Gases, and of Bacteriological Methods of Warfare, provided rules of warfare. However, neither the United States nor Japan signed the Protocol.[13]

The Japanese biological weapons program began in 1937 in Manchuria, and was named Unit 731. During the course of this program tens of thousands of prisoners were used in experiments, including United States prisoners of war.[14] Their first use of these weapons was in 1939, when they poisoned a Soviet water supply with typhoid bacteria at the Mongolian border. The next year, the Japanese used air-drops of rice and wheat over China and Manchuria as delivery devices for plague-infected fleas, which were mixed with the grains.

The United States biological weapons program began in secrecy around 1941,[15] with the purpose of researching and producing an array of biological agents for offensive use.

In 1941, there is some suspicion that the Russians used a weaponized tularemia on German soldiers on the German-Soviet front, shortly before the Battle of Stalingrad. Ken Alibek reported that he researched the History of Soviet Military Medicine in *The Great Patriotic War: 1941–1945* and other scientific journals, and determined that the vast difference between hundreds of thousands of occurrences during the war, compared to tens of thousands of cases both before and after the battle, suggested that an intentional dissemination was responsible.[16]

In December 1949 the commander in Chief of the Japanese Kwantung Army was tried by a Soviet military tribunal in Khabarovsk, USSR for preparing and using biological weapons, and experimenting with them on prisoners of war. Former head of Unit 731, Major General Kawashima, testified that no fewer than 600 prisoners were killed yearly at Unit 731. The total estimate of those prisoners killed is more than 3,000, and no prisoner left Unit 731 alive.[17]

From about 1949 through the 1960s scientists conducted tests by dispersing innocuous biological agents in the Greyhound bus terminal in the District of Columbia and the Pentagon.[18]

In 1969, President Richard M. Nixon ended the nation's biologic weapons program, and converted the work to a defensive program, which led to the first world treaty to end the research and proliferation of biological weapons. He stated:

"*I have decided that the United States of America will renounce the use of any form of deadly biological weapons that either kill or incapacitate. Our bacteriological programs in the future will be confined to research in biological defense on techniques of immunization and on measures of controlling and preventing the spread of disease. I have ordered the Defense Department to make recommendations about the disposal of the existing Stocks of bacteriological weapons.*"

The Biological Weapons Convention of 1972 was ratified by 140 states as of May 1997, and prohibits the possession or use of biological weapons. This international treaty began our international agreements to cease the production of biological weapons. The former Soviet Union was among the signatories to the 1972 Convention.

Also, in 1969, in recognition of the growing transportation of diseases, the World Health Organization issued the first International Health Regulations to assist the organization in carrying out its mission to control the spread of diseases in the world. This was the first major internationally binding agreement to enforce controls on the spread of diseases worldwide, and was binding for member countries of the WHO.

In April and May of 1979, the Soviet city of Sverdlovsk experienced a wave of deaths from pulmonary anthrax. In 1980, the United States demanded an explanation from the Soviets, to which they received an explanation that the deaths were a result of the consumption of contaminated black-market meat.

From the late 1970s to the early 1990s, South Africa had a documented Chemical and Biological Weapons Program, called Project Coast, led by Dr. Walter Basson, who had a background as a former Special Forces Army Brigadier. He also served as a personal physician for former President P.W. Botha. The purported purpose of Project Coast was a purely defensive one, providing detection and protection capabilities to the South African Military; however, it is now undisputed that there was an offensive program.

The offensive program in South Africa was pursuing the development of chemical and biological weapons, targeting specifically black villages and towns. The biological weapons included efforts to disperse an infertility toxin to secretly sterilize the black population, skin-absorbing poisons for clothing, and poisons in food and cigarettes. There were also specific acts of bioterrorism when the Project Coast used cholera in water resources of particular South African villages with black populations, and provided cholera and anthrax to the government military of Zimbabwe (formerly Rhodesia) during the late 1970s. In Rhodesia, 1979 marks the largest outbreak of anthrax in the world, where 82 people were killed and thousands were made ill by anthrax. When President F.W. de Klerk took office in the early 1990s, he investigated the program and fired many scientists in the Project. However, the South African government took the official position that an offensive program never existed.[19] Walter Basson was charged with killing 16 people, conspiracy to murder and allegedly supplying poison to kill 200 members of a rebel group that fought South African rule in what is now neighbouring Namibia. The defense sought to dismiss the case because the crimes allegedly occurred outside the jurisdiction of South Africa[19A]. In May 2002, the South African court acquitted Basson on all 46 counts.[19B]

In 1980, the WHO declared that smallpox, the most deadly human disease, had been eradicated from the world.

In September 1984, the Oregon cult led by Bhagwan Shree Rajneesh cultivated Salmonella bacteria with which its members contaminated salad bars in restaurants, sickening about 750 people.[20] This was a modern shock to a vulnerable United States to find that it was susceptible to such activities.

There is a likelihood that the Soviet Union used biological weapons in its war with Afghanistan in 1989. Ken Alibek, defector from the Soviet Biopreparat, reported that a senior officer in the Fifteenth Directorate leaked that the Soviet Union used glanders in at least one attack between 1982 and 1984, disseminated by Ilyushin-28 planes from military airfields in Russia.[21]

During this time, in the United States two major laws aimed at preventing the acquisition and use of chemical or biological weapons were passed by Congress: (1) The Biological Weapons Act of 1989, which made it a federal crime to develop, manufacture, transfer, or possess any biological agent, toxin, or delivery system for use as a weapon; and (2) The Chemical and Biological Weapons Control Act of 1991, which established a system of economic and export controls designed to prevent export of goods or technologies used in the development of chemical and biological weapons to designated nationals.

In 1992 the Soviet Union was dissolved and it was discovered that a massive biological production program, Biopreparat, was underway, although the Soviets had signed the Biological Weapons Convention of 1972. Yeltsin admitted in May 1992 that the Sverdlovsk incident was the result of military activities. From 1992 to 1993 a joint team of United States and Russian scientists conducted an investigation and determined that 68 civilians had died from an accidental release of aerosolized anthrax bacteria from a military biological weapons facility in Sverdlovsk. This team was a U.N. temporary mechanism since the 1972 Convention provided no inspection protocol.

In March 1995, the Aum Shinrikyo cult attacked subway riders with a release of sarin gas, but had been working on developing the release of biological agents as well. A failed attempt to release anthrax from the roof of a building in Tokyo was among their exploits with anthrax. Japan revived a 1952 statute to disband such groups. These activities led the U.S. to include the Aum Shinrikyo group on a list that excluded such groups under the Anti-Terrorism and Death Penalty Act of 1996.

Just a few months later, in May 1995, Larry Wayne Harris of Lancaster, Ohio, ordered three vials of *Yersinia Pestis* (plague), from the American Type Culture Collection (ATCC) in Maryland. The ATCC routinely supplies thousands of biological cultures each year to laboratories around the world. However, the ATCC became suspicious when Harris made repeated telephone inquiries, and they discovered that the laboratory he identified as his organization did not exist. Harris, when questioned, said he feared an invasion of super germ-laden mice from Iraq, and he planned to do research with the bacteria to discover a "plague antidote." Harris was a member of the American Society for Microbiology and a lab technician, and had the knowledge needed to cultivate the bacteria. Had Harris not lied about the laboratory he claimed to have, there would have been no criminal conviction for any of Harris' activities. Under those circumstances, he was convicted for wire fraud and received a six-month suspended sentence. His lack of a criminal intent made it impossible to obtain a conviction under the Biological Anti-Terrorism Act of 1989.

Also in 1995, the World Health Organization General Assembly asked that the 1969 International Health Regulations be substantially updated in Resolution WHA48.7.

As a result of the Harris case, Congress passed the Anti-Terrorism and Effective Death Penalty Act of 1996, which expanded the government's powers under the CBWCA to cover individuals or groups who attempt or even threaten to develop or use a biological weapon. It broadened the definition of biological agent to include new or modified agents produced by biotechnology. Further, it delegated to the CDC the task of creating and maintaining a list of biological agents that potentially pose a severe threat to public health and safety, and requiring that supply laboratories check the identities of those researchers making requests for such materials.

Another statute, the Defense Against Weapons of Mass Destruction Act of 1996, addressed the federal, state and local government capabilities. This law directs the Secretary of Defense to take immediate actions to both enhance the capability of the federal government to respond to terrorist incidents, and to support improvements in the capabilities of state and local emergency response agencies.

Then on April 24, 1997 at the B'nai B'rith Society in Washington, D.C., a package was received marked "anthrachs." The package was determined to be nothing more than harmless bacteria; however, the building was evacuated and several streets were closed for much of the day in Washington, D.C.

The Nunn-Lugar-Domenici amendment to the Defense Authorization Act of 1997 (PL 104-201) authorized $100 million to establish a military rapid response unit to implement programs providing advice and training for major cities.

The Executive Office of the President created the Presidential Decision Directive (PDD-39)(1995) which addresses the responsibilities of federal agencies, the Presidential Decision Directive (PDD-62) Combating Terrorism (1998) and the Presidential Decision Directive (PDD-63) Critical Infrastructure Protection (1998) to address federal logistical and jurisdictional issues.

Cuba has developed its own bioweapons program in the 1980s, according to Ken Alibek, defector from the Soviet's Biopreparat program. From 1962 through 1997, Cuba accused the United States of conducting biological attacks on its livestock and crops. In 1997, Cuba filed a claim under Article 5 of the Biological Weapons Convention of 1972 that the United States had disseminated *Thrips palmi*, a crop insect pest, with crop-dusting airplanes. The United States responded that the planes were taking pesticides for the coffee plantations in Columbia.[22]

In February 1998, Harris was arrested a second time, now for possession of veterinary anthrax vaccine, a harmless strain. His probation from the 1995 arrest was at issue, but little could be done for a further conviction, since he did not possess a biological agent that fit the definition of the statute, nor was there evidence of the requisite intent to use it for other than peaceful purposes.

The new era of biological warfare

The attack on the United States by Osama bin Laden in the September 11, 2001 destruction of the World Trade Center and the Pentagon resulted in the deaths of more than 6,000 civilians, the largest terrorism attack in the history of the United States. The days that followed unfolded a chain of events that revealed that a biological attack had begun around that same time. Letters containing anthrax spores were mailed to media and Congressional offices, as well as to almost every federal governmental department in Washington, D.C. The first death was that of a media employee in Florida, which resulted in the finding of anthrax spores in the office. Some two weeks later, two postal workers died of pulmonary anthrax in Washington, D.C. from handling letters at the Brentwood postal facility that served the Congressional offices. Late attention to these postal workers gave rise to concerns that there was racial and class discrimination when the Congressional employees were given immediate attention while the postal workers were told to continue working in the postal facilities, and the facilities were not quarantined until the two workers died. A fourth death resulted from pulmonary anthrax from an unknown exposure to a hospital worker in New York City. Then the fifth death resulted in the case of a woman in rural Connecticut contracting a fatal case of pulmonary anthrax, potentially infected from ripping her "junk" mail before discarding it. Countless cases of cutaneous anthrax were also treated, and tens of thousands of exposed civilians were treated with antibiotics.

As a result of this anthrax attack, dozens of hoaxes ensued, which spurred the U.S. Attorney General to declare a campaign against prosecuting hoaxers. However, the available criminal statutes made prosecutions difficult. The Anti-Hoax Terrorism Act of 2001 passed the House of Representatives, but failed to move forward in the U.S. Senate.

In May 23, 2005, the fifty-eighth assembly of the World Health Organization issued the new International Health Regulations, which became effective on June 15, 2007.

In July 2008, the United States Department of Justice announced that the Amerithrax case was closed following the suicide of a suspect, Dr. Bruce Ivins, a career biodefense researcher at USAMRIID. The U.S. Federal District Court made available the evidence against Dr. Ivins through opening some of the court documents for public access, but questions still remain about whether the perpetrator was Dr. Ivins.

————————

Notes

1. For a succinct history of biological warfare, see Medical Aspects of Chemical and Biological Warfare (1997) at http://www.bordeninstitute.army.mil/published_volumes/chemBio/chembio.html.

2. The use of biological weapons is at least as old if not older than chemical warfare, and predates nuclear and radiological warfare by more than a millennia, yet the biotechnology revolution has brought with it greater accessibility and utilization of biotechnologies, thereby increasing the attractiveness of biological weapons as tools of warfare. In fact, they are so inexpensive to produce, the term "the poor man's weapon" has been used to describe biological weapons. For example, the use of conventional weapons would cost an estimated $2,000 per square kilometer, nuclear weapons $800, chemical weapons $600, and biological weapons would only cost an estimated $1 per square kilometer. How does this suggest that regulatory approaches to protect against bioterrorism will be more difficult with biological weapons compared to other weapons of mass destruction?

3. The U.S. Department of Justice's investigation of the anthrax attacks following 9-11 was named "Amerithrax." Dr. Barbara Rosenberg, Chair of the Working Group on Biological Weapons of the Federation of American Scientists, proposed that the FBI knew the perpetrator, and "he" was a former employee of the United States biological weapons defense program. The reason, she argued, that the FBI had not arrested that person was because they feared he had so much classified information on the United States program that he would be a national security threat. This discussion was previously posted at this address, http://fas.org/bwc/news/anthraxreport.htm, but has subsequently been removed. During the investigation, the U.S. Department of Justice named Dr. Stephen Hatfil a "person of interest," an undefined and controversial label, and made his name publicly known through media outlets, which led to defamation litigation against the United States and the media outlets. After more than four years, Dr. Hatfil reached a settlement with the U.S. Department of Justice of approximately $5 million. Just a little over two months later, Dr. Bruce Ivins, another biodefense researcher from USAMRIID, died by suicide during grand jury hearings that may have led to his indictment. If the FBI's statements are true, that there are no other perpetrators, what signal does this send to other potential perpetrators? Does it discourage them or has this investigation sensationalized the use of biological weapons, making them more attractive?

4. What legal codes, ethical codes or other mechanisms are available for protecting against biological terrorism that are not currently in existence?

————————

1.2.   Biological Agents as Potential Weapons

Excerpts from an article by Barry Kellman, "Biological Terrorism: Legal Measures for Preventing Catastrophe," 24 Harv. J.L. & Pub. Pol'y 417 (Spring 2001) provide a brief overview of issues in biological weapons:

> Biological terrorism is a truly despicable subject, raising nightmares of primal fear. Disease—plague, smallpox, and other decimating maladies—is dire trauma embedded in humanity's collective consciousness. Now, when the threat of thermonuclear holocaust may be ebbing, a few zealots or criminals can kill thousands (or more) and destabilize social order by revealing that no government, even that of superpower America, can protect its citizenry. A biological attack means that everyone is vulnerable. This is terrorism nonpareil....
>
> The agenda here is also overt. Law's contribution to preventing bioterrorism...is crucial. And time, unfortunately, is not on the side of the angels. This Article, therefore, is a call to action....

I. Understanding Bio-terrorism

> Because a catastrophic bioterrorism attack has not yet happened, trying to understand the phenomenon entails some speculation based on reasonable extrapolations both from the scientific understanding of pathogens and from the social science understanding of terrorist behavior. There has been only one notable effort to develop and employ biological capabilities for terrorist purposes, which was by the Japanese cult Aum Shinrikyo.
>
> Aum devoted vast sums of money, time, and considerable expertise to the task of making biological weapons, but it was not successful. Before puncturing bags of sarin nerve gas on Tokyo subway trains on March 20, 1995, killing twelve people and injuring more than 5,000, the cult had sought to acquire a wide range of weapons, including biological weapons. In April 1990, Aum attempted to attack the Japanese parliament with botulinum toxin aerosol. In 1992, Aum sent a mission to Zaire to assist in the treatment of Ebola victims in order to find a sample of the Ebola strain to take back to Japan for culturing purposes. In June 1993, the cult tried to release poison at the wedding of the crown prince. Later that month, Aum attempted to spray anthrax spores from the roof of a building in Tokyo. All these attacks were unsuccessful and resulted in no casualties. The consequences might have been drastically different had the weapons been properly disseminated.
>
> The cult built weapons under the guidance of well-trained biologists and chemists. They created a sophisticated biological research facility without attracting the attention of the Japanese or other governments. When Japanese officials investigated Aum's compound after the 1995 attack, they found large amounts of equipment indispensable to cultivating bacteria and viruses, peptone (a substance used to cultivate bacteria), and books and materials on the production of botulism, cholera, and dysentery. At Aum's site in Naganohara, officials found a four-story concrete facility equipped with a "clean room" with specialized ventilation systems and a sealed room to protect cultivated bacteria from leaking. In connection with these operations, Aum produced illegal drugs for their own use and for sale to others.
>
> In January 1995, an Oregon company sold Aum molecular modeling software that simulates molecular experimentation without the need for actual laboratory experimentation. This software is covered by export restrictions to countries such as China but not to Japan. Aum could have used this software to test theoretical designs for toxins. In March 1995, Aum supporters contacted a Missouri company that produces computer software for use in designing new therapeutic drugs but that can also be used to research and develop biological toxins. Although it harbored suspicions, the Missouri company installed software on a computer provided by Aum. Five days before the Tokyo gas attack, authorities discovered three attache cases containing a small tank to hold liquid, a small motorized fan, a vent, and a battery. The cult

had at least two radio controlled drone aircraft, and they were seeking hundreds of small fans as well as thousands of small serum bottles.

The Aum Shinrikyo experience raises several questions addressed in the remainder of this Part. First, why would a terrorist use biological weapons? Second, what pathogens could or would likely be used? And third, could an attack be concocted?

A. Why Attack with Biological Weapons?

Why would anyone use disease to cause mass death? How difficult is it to use biological agents as weapons, assuming the motivation to do so? If biological weapons are used, what casualties can be reasonably expected?

Biological weapons have three advantages from a terrorist's perspective. First, they (as well as chemical weapons) offer an optimal death to cost ratio. Second, they are virtually undetectable and can be handled with relative ease by properly trained and inoculated persons. Third, they offer the potential for mass panic that may uniquely serve a terrorist's purposes.

1. Inflicting Casualties

If a terrorist wants to kill thousands of people, biological weapons merit serious consideration. A nuclear weapon, by comparison, can certainly create far more devastation, but making a nuclear weapon is far more difficult and expensive, and smuggling it poses a far greater risk of detection. At the other end of the weapons spectrum, firearms are inexpensive and readily available, but they have the capacity to kill only a few dozen people before being stopped. Explosives present more technical obstacles than firearms, but offer the potential for inflicting far greater casualties. The failed attempt to blow up the World Trade Center building and kill thousands illustrates the difficulties inherent in this tradeoff. The calculus of terrorism, therefore, leads inexorably to biological and chemical weapons. Comparatively, while chemical weapons are easier to make and use, biological weapons are less detectable, less dangerous to the terrorist, and—except in a few scenarios—have greater killing capability.

Estimates vary widely as to the numbers of dead and sick from a bioterrorist attack. Projected seven-figure casualty estimates, based on multiplying the quantity of pathogen necessary to kill an individual, are flawed. Under this methodology, for example, a lethal dose of Type-A botulina toxin can be prepared in concentrations of ten billion micro-organisms per gram; accordingly, eight ounces is enough to kill every living creature on Earth. This arithmetic misleadingly assumes that these doses will be equally and effectively disseminated. But most pathogens disseminated among a large population would not be ingested at all and would die harmlessly from natural causes. The pathogens that are ingested would tend to be concentrated in a fraction of that population, and even some of these persons would, for various reasons, not get sick.

Nonetheless, there are reasonable scenarios involving dissemination of pathogens in confined spaces that predict over ten thousand casualties; in extraordinary circumstances, casualties in excess of 100,000 are not fanciful.

2. Non-Detectability and Manageability

Besides their capability to cause mass casualties, there are other good reasons (from a terrorist's perspective) to use biological weapons. Pathogens are undetectable or nearly so. Lethal pathogens may be attractive to foreign terrorist organizations or even rogue States seeking to cause catastrophic injury to the United States without exposing themselves to reprisal. Pathogens can be brought into the country by a single individual and can be smuggled through airports or customs checks. Once here, they can be propagated into enormous quantities. Even their use is initially undetectable. An epidemic can be initiated, and it may be days before symptoms are manifest; even then, the attack may be mistaken for a natural outbreak. Terrorists could easily have sufficient time to flee the scene of the attack, and perhaps the jurisdiction altogether, before law enforcement officials learn that a crime has been committed. The time-lag between release and effect on humans thus reduces the risks of a perpetrator being apprehended. Another contribution to anonymity is that dissemination of pathogens need not leave identifying markers that could be traced back to the perpetrators. No other weapon offers a comparable capability to inflict catastrophic disruption anonymously.

Despite their disease-causing capabilities, some pathogens can be produced and handled safely by persons who are properly equipped, knowledgeable of the risks, and perhaps inoculated against the disease. Starting with a small seed culture, terrorists could easily generate a stockpile and can work with it, carry it, and distribute it without undue risk. Some, but not all, pathogens have the ability to reproduce in the target population. If sufficiently contagious, an attack would only have to be against a small group (perhaps at an airport) who would then do the terrorists' work for them by carrying it out to a wider population. No other weapon offers similar capabilities to spread itself. Therefore, the problems of dissemination (discussed below) can be overcome to some degree by creating a more potent agent.

3. Panic Potential

Arguably the greatest advantage of biological weapons is their ability to cause mass panic. Bombing a large and heavily populated building is terrifying, as is releasing chemical weapons in a confined space such as a subway, but these attacks are geographically limited. A biological attack makes everyone vulnerable, and this insecurity is the terrorists' primary motivation. Moreover, even if not empirically justifiable, humanity fears disease not only for its ability to kill but for the horrifying way in which it kills. While we have no experience with a catastrophic terrorist attack, memories of past epidemics incite fears of future outbreaks. Thus, even if a biological attack kills only a relatively small number, it is likely to generate panic. This shredding of the fabric of the community and exposure of society's vulnerability, perhaps on a global scale, is the incentive for committing such heinous crimes.

Pathogens may appeal to domestic terrorists who have an anarchic or mystical sense that the modern era is corrupt, excessively regimented, or materialistic. For those with a profound sense of alienation or those motivated by a distorted sense of religious faith, disease has a unique Biblical history suggesting that God has often inflicted a scourge on the sinful. Inflating the death toll may be seen as performing a sacramental act, manifesting divine retribution that morally justifies mass murder.

B. What Pathogens Might Be Used?

The Centers for Disease Control (CDC) lists thirty-six pathogenic agents, including seven bacteria, thirteen viruses, three rickettsiae, one fungus, and twelve toxins. Bio-engineered variations of these agents, or development of new agents altogether, could expand this list.

1. Likely Pathogens

This Section briefly describes the agents most often cited as potentially weaponizeable and briefly explains their relevant characteristics. It must be noted that no agent is perfect; a terrorist must therefore choose among various characteristics, including:

. Pathogenicity of the agent (how likely the agent is to kill its victim): Agents can be chosen to sicken, incapacitate, or kill; to spread from person to person or to affect only those initially exposed; and to be susceptible or resistant to medical treatment.

. Degree to which the agent is contagious or infectious: The infectiousness of the agent is directly correlated with the mode of weaponization. If the terrorist intends to spray dust an area and infect via an aerosol cloud, then the likelihood of successful delivery is less than direct injection. Therefore, a more infectious agent would be more desirable.

. Process of contagion and resistance to protective measures or cures: The terrorist will also choose an agent that is known to be transferable or containable, depending once again on the terrorist's targeted group. For instance, if the intent is to cause a widespread outbreak, an agent that can be transmitted by coughing or contact with others would be more favorable than one that cannot be transmitted by human to human contact. Further, agents have variable lengths of incubation periods, some allowing ample time for vaccination once an outbreak has been identified. Also, agents differ in the length of time between the onset of symptoms and death.

. Degree of lethality (how many people are likely to be affected): In choosing the appropriate agent to execute the mission, the terrorist likely would consider the lethality of the agent. For instance, agents differ in incubation stages, some acting on their hosts quickly and others not showing signs for several days. Moreover, agents differ in their contagion capabilities. Therefore, when the intent is to indiscriminately pass the illness to a large number of people over a period of time, a less lethal but highly infectious agent may be chosen.

. Potential risk to the terrorist himself: The terrorist, through his knowledge of the agents and their production methods, may consider the risks of handling that the agent poses to his health in all the steps until it is disseminated. Those whose scientific proficiency bolsters their confidence in handling pathogenic agents may be more willing to weaponize highly pathogenic agents as compared to those who are wary of the unknown. It may be very important that there is an available vaccine with which the terrorist may vaccinate himself.

a. Smallpox

The smallpox virus is among the most dangerous organisms that might be used by bioterrorists. It is virulently contagious, often fatal, and spread through inhalation. Smallpox was responsible for hundreds of millions of fatalities before widespread vaccinations were thought to have eradicated it. In 1986, the Executive Committee on Smallpox of the World Health Organization unanimously decided to destroy the last strains of smallpox left in the world except for two samples in Moscow and Atlanta. However, unsubstantiated but highly disturbing reports from Russia suggest new concerns. This is especially frightening because health authorities, believing the disease to have been virtually eradicated, have discontinued vaccination programs, leaving current populations highly vulnerable to a terrorist attack using smallpox.

b. Anthrax

Anthrax (Bacillus anthracis) is often mentioned as the biological agent of choice. Anthrax is a spore that, if inhaled even in extremely low quantities, is nearly always fatal unless the patient is quickly given huge quantities of antibiotics. Ingestion leads to fatigue, coughing, fever, and chest pains; death comes within twenty-four to thirty-six hours. Anthrax has important virtues from a terrorist perspective. It occurs naturally in the soil. Herbivorous animals such as sheep or goats ingest spores while grazing. Seed cultures of the spores can be taken from samples of the wool or skin; taking more samples increases the likelihood of success. Only small samples would be needed, perhaps no larger than a postage stamp. Although anthrax is more common among Caribbean and Eastern Mediterranean countries, it is not impossible to find infected animals in the United States. As a weapon, the primary virtue of anthrax is its lethality; some experts assert that as little as a single gram, efficiently distributed, could kill more than one-third of the United States population. Another advantage is that it is an endospore and thus highly resistant to humidity, pressure, or temperature. Moreover, anthrax can be easily propagated. For these and perhaps other reasons, anthrax has been by far the most often pathogen allegedly used in the United States, although most if not all of these alleged uses were hoaxes.

Anthrax, however, has various disadvantages as a weapon. The fact that it is a spore and hence large relative to other agents means that it is difficult to aerosolize for weapons purposes, and, once released, falls rapidly to the ground, thereby diminishing the opportunity for inhalation. Furthermore, anthrax is not contagious except by direct contact. To kill many people would therefore require widespread dissemination. There is a licensed vaccine which, although the subject of considerable controversy in connection with its use during the Gulf War, can be effective if administered soon after exposure. This vaccine would, of course, enable a potential terrorist to handle anthrax without risk of infecting himself.

c. The Plague

Plague (Yersinia pestis) is a contagious bacterium. Only slightly less lethal than anthrax, it is also naturally available and can be scraped from dead animals. In North America, plague is found in certain animals and in their fleas from the Pacific Coast to the Great Plains, and from southwestern Canada to Mexico. It is more difficult to grow than anthrax, requiring a blood agar, but not so difficult as to preclude its potential weaponization. A licensed vaccine that would allow a terrorist to protect himself is available. However, this vaccine is used in animal experiments and will provide no protection against the aerosol exposure; a terrorist who chooses an aerosol route of dissemination would have to immediately take the antibiotic doxycycline. Unlike anthrax, plague is highly communicable; an infected individual may spread infection by coughing. Its capability to lead to an epidemic may be an advantage to someone seeking to generate mass havoc, but it may be a disadvantage to someone planning a more strategic strike. In contrast to anthrax, plague bacteria have the disadvantage of being subject to environmental stress, complicating dissemination.

d. Haemorrhagic Fevers

Rift Valley Fever (RVF) is a viral disease prevalent among livestock. The virus is spread by mosquitoes to animals. Infected animals then become new hosts for other mosquitoes that in turn become additional vectors for transmission. These mosquitoes can then infect humans. RVF victims tend to experience symptoms associated with a mild illness such as fever, dizziness, and back pain. In some people, the illness can progress into hemorrhagic fever, encephalitis, or ocular disease, but most patients recover from exposure within a few days. A terrorist's mishandling may lead to unintentional exposure, with no known treatment.

Marburg Hemorrhagic Fever affects humans and other primates in very localized areas. Like the plague, the virus is highly infectious. Humans can contract the disease from handling monkeys, from droplets of body fluids, or contact with contaminated people or other sources of infectious blood or tissues. Symptoms appear five to ten days after exposure. Death ensues rapidly. This virus may appeal to the potential terrorist for its 25% mortality rate, but knowledge of the virus and proper handling are necessary to prevent risk to oneself.

The ebola virus is known for its horrific symptoms: vomiting, chest pain, and bleeding from virtually every orifice. The disease is spread through close personal contact with an infected victim. Transmission has also been known to take place through hypodermic needles. The ebola virus is similar to the Marburg virus but has a lower infection rate. Humans are susceptible to several different strains; the more lethal strains are the less contagious.

e. Tularemia

Tularemia (Francisella tularensis) is an extremely lethal bacterium spread by insect bites from rodents to humans. A virulent form (fatality rate of approximately 5%) is endemic in much of North America and can be obtained from dead animals; a pneumonic form, which would result from an intentional release, would likely have a greater mortality rate. Propagation would require special media as tularemia does not typically grow in standard blood cultures. It is not transmitted person-to-person, eliminating the possibility of epidemic. Treatment is typically effective by common antibiotics within seven to fourteen days of infection, making treatment and containment by public health authorities possible. Moreover, like plague, it is subject to environmental stresses.

f. Venezuelan Equine Encephalitis

Venezuelan Equine Encephalitis (VEE) is a mosquito-borne virus. A large controlled mosquito population could feed on an infected animal and become the vector to transfer the virus to humans. Susceptibility to this disease is nearly 100%; however, its mortality rate is less than 1%, making it an unlikely choice for a weapon. An infected human remains infectious for mosquitoes for at least seventy-two hours after symptoms, enabling secondary spread of the disease. Infected individuals who do not seek treatment may progress into encephalitis, which is marked by convulsion, coma and paralysis. A human vaccine is available through USAMRIID.

g. Ricin

Ricin is an inanimate protein toxin that may be readily produced from castor beans. It acts as a cellular poison that is lethal either through inhalation or through epidermal absorption. A tiny quantity on the skin rapidly causes death. Ricin may be used to poison water or foodstuffs or lace injectiles. Ricin has a long record of use by assassins because the victim need only be poked by an object coated with the toxin. If ricin is inhaled, fever, coughing, and nausea occur within eight hours and death ensues within thirty-six to seventy-two hours. Notably, there is no treatment; once a victim is poisoned, death will follow. There is no vaccine, so a terrorist would have to be extremely sophisticated to avoid suicide. Since it is non-contagious, it has no ability to provoke an epidemic, yet it may be the most easily disseminated pathogenic agent and therefore one of the most effective means of committing murder.

2. Choosing the Appropriate Pathogen

No single agent is ideal for terrorism. A terrorist must make choices depending on what he is trying to accomplish as well as his level of technical knowledge and equipment.

If the goal is to murder an individual or small group of people, ricin may be uniquely suitable. Ricin is easily produced from widely available castor beans. Because it kills by epidermal contact, it is likely that the murderer will remain anonymous. However, there is no shortage of guns, knives, conventional poisons etc. available to the terrorist who wishes only to kill a small number of people; producing ricin may not be worth the time and risk.

If the terrorist's goal is mass murder, anthrax deserves its reputation as perhaps the most feared biological weapon. It is readily available. Disseminated in a closed, positive air pressure environment, anthrax could get into the lungs of most people in that environment. By the time symptoms become obvious, it would be difficult, even with a full commitment of health care resources, to prevent a high number of deaths. In other settings, however, the difficulties of suspending anthrax outdoors and the unlikelihood of it spreading from one victim to another render it a poor open-air, urban-devastating weapon.

If the terrorist's goal is contagion, plague is almost as readily available as anthrax and is contagious, although it is less resilient to environmental stresses and more difficult to cultivate. More esoteric are viruses including encephalitis or any of the extremely deadly hemorrhagic fevers. These viruses are far more difficult to obtain, and the knowledge of how to propagate them safely is far more limited. Moreover, as these viruses are not available domestically, the terrorist would have to go to some other part of the globe and bring at least some agent through customs, thereby risking detection. The organisms of brucellosis are difficult to grow, but are highly infectious and relatively stable for aerosolization. The tularemia organism is also extremely infectious; however, it is difficult to grow and is delicate when disseminated.

If the terrorist's goal is a weapon of mass destruction, smallpox has attributes of contagion and lethality that are unmatched by any other natural agent. However, smallpox is available, if at all, only from unsecured Russian laboratories. To obtain and transport it into the United States would entail an organized conspiracy more akin to an act of war than an act of terrorism. Sophisticated bio-engineered agents, whether animate or toxin, are similarly effective but require foreign assistance in order to be obtained. The good news here is that using biological agents as a weapon of mass destruction seems to be well beyond the capabilities of domestic hate groups or the likes of a Tim McVeigh or Ted Kaczynski ("The Unabomber").

C. Devising the Attack

How difficult it is to make biological weapons and how much sophistication is required are matters in sharp dispute. According to some experts, medical or microbiology students could prepare an agent without endangering themselves. But making that agent into a weapon by aerosolizing it requires considerably greater sophistication. Many experts believe that the difficulties of executing a mass biological attack explain why such a successful catastrophic attack has not yet occurred. Persons having extraordinary technical knowledge may be able to overcome problems of deficient resources and equipment, but there is a negative correlation between capability to use pathogens and a motivation to cause mass casualties.

1. Means of Acquisition

A seed culture could be obtained from a legitimate facility either by purchasing it or stealing it, from the natural environment, or by importing it. Purchase of pathogens was once not difficult, but controls have recently been significantly tightened, as will be discussed at length below. As discussed below, the stealing of agents raises serious problems, including alerting law enforcement authorities to the risk of an attack. Therefore, access to these agents may require the services of someone affiliated with the laboratory or facility.

The most likely means of acquiring pathogens are from a natural or a foreign source. Either of these means, as distinct from buying or stealing pathogens, is virtually unstoppable. Within the United States, agents such as anthrax and plague and tularemia as well as variety of toxins, can be obtained from dead animals or vegetable matter. Resort to this method minimizes the risks of detection as well as the financial cost. However, identifying a strain that can be effectively weaponized and then proceeding to weaponize it requires considerable sophistication as well as equipment. Procurement from a foreign source is a virtually foolproof solution to the task of acquisition, although smuggling the material into the United States poses risks of detection. Unless the agent is already weaponized (which would increase the danger and detectability of smuggling it), it would have to be weaponized here. In that respect, obtaining an agent from a foreign source poses problems similar to obtaining it from a natural source, although the agent is likely to be of a higher quality.

2. Means of Production

Once the agent has been obtained, it must be cultured. The difficulty in producing enough of the agent to create a weapon may present an important limitation to terrorism, because some methods may be too advanced for terrorists. Moreover, agents are fragile; production would require favorable conditions. For instance, the terrorist would need the appropriate media, the right temperature, pressure and atmospheric conditions, and the ability to maintain this environment for the necessary time for the particular agent. For bacteria, growth and production imply taking a small isolate (perhaps a test tube) and growing a large quantity that can be used in a weapon. The actual quantity of material required to produce an effective weapon depends on many factors, not least of which is the strain's virulence. Although some organisms are known to cause disease when infected with fewer than 100 cells (Pseudomonas), higher concentrations increase the chance of infection. Therefore, large volumes of highly concentrated material are required for a biological weapon.

The scientific proficiency required to culture an agent is a factor in agent selection. Growth and media requirements and techniques for production for pathogenic microorganisms are easily researched. The pathogenesis of these organisms has led to intensive study of growth characteristics and requirements, which are now well understood and published. However, obtaining the growth media used in traditional research, as well as the clinical setting, presents a significant hurdle in creating a biological weapon. For instance, Yersinia pestis, the bacterium that causes plague, is difficult to grow on any media other than blood agar.

3. Means of Dissemination

The means of delivery will depend on the number of people the terrorist seeks to reach and his ability to successfully weaponize the agent. For instance, dissemination by aerosolization, as opposed to delivering a sealed box of dry powder agent leading to infection if inhaled, requires knowledge and skill with regard to how to minimize the particle size of the agent and spread it in a fine cloud. Yet the requisite technology, laboratory facilities, and aerosolization devices are within the grasp of even the weakest countries.

Commentators differ as to the difficulty of disseminating biological agents. Biological agents can be disseminated individually through inanimate objects such as sticks, dusters, or projectiles. But if one seeks to spread disease to many people, the more common methods of dissemination of biological agents include aerosol delivery, dry-powder delivery, spraying, infecting food and water supplies, and introducing insect or animal vectors. The bioterrorist must choose an agent that has infectious capabilities but does not kill its host quickly. The fragile nature of the agents themselves can impede any dissemination effort; preparing and preserving the agent before dissemination can affect its ability to survive spraying and cause disease. Mechanical stresses and exposures to air, humidity, and ultraviolet light rapidly kill many microorganisms.

These considerations, in turn, will also contribute to the chosen route of dissemination. For instance, living microorganisms may enter the human body by an aerosol route, where they invade the respiratory tract, enter the bloodstream and lymphatic system, and then initiate infection; anthrax is not really infectious except by the aerosol route. By contrast, toxins affect people through direct exposure; they have no infectious characteristics but rather must be ingested, injected or inhaled.

a. Injection or Direct Poisoning

Almost all of the known incidents of hostile use of pathogens or toxins have involved direct injection or poisoning of an individual. This method of dispersion, referred to as "point source," occurs where the enemy spews a biological agent directly on the target. Ricin-tipped umbrellas have been used for clandestine espionage and counter-intelligence, and popular novels have illuminated the implications of murder-by-biology. These incidents are cited as evidence of how easy it is to make lethal biological agents, but there are prodigious technical differences between homicide and mass catastrophe. As earlier stated, guns are remarkably easier and cheaper to obtain and use.

b. Contamination of Foodstuffs or Potable Liquids

The easiest way to distribute pathogens is to spread them on foodstuffs. Most examples of successful biological terrorism have involved spreading food-borne diseases (e.g., salmonella) on openly accessible food sources such as salad bars. This type of attack is virtually impossible to prevent once the terrorist has developed the agent and has obtained access to the food source. Yet this type of attack is not likely to cause a catastrophic number of injuries; indeed, experience with this type of attack suggests that casualties are more likely to number in the dozens than the thousands. The most infamous known event of this type was in 1984 when the Rajneesh cult outside of Antelope, Oregon, poisoned 750 people with salmonella at local salad bars. Attacks through bulk foodstuffs or beverages have been discussed, but most experts believe that such a mass attack is unlikely.

Contamination of water supplies is considerably more difficult in countries which have efficient water purification systems (such as the United States) because of the extraordinary quantities of pathogens necessary and because filtration and chlorinated purification systems would likely kill the agent. Notably, Chicago-area neo-Nazis were arrested in 1972 with thirty to forty kilograms of typhoid bacteria for use against water supplies. That a few college students could cultivate this disease in a school laboratory provoked considerable concern, but their selected organism would have been readily destroyed by normal chlorination. This distribution method, however, could be effective in less-developed regions.

c. Aerosol Delivery

A terrorist employing biological weapons for a large-scale attack with many casualties will most likely distribute pathogens as an aerosol through airborne transmission. Experts differ as to how difficult aerosolization is likely to be. While most experts recognize the ready availability of aerosolization equipment (discussed below), there is considerable difference of opinion as to the level of expertise needed to produce an aerosol generator capable of weaponizing pathogens.

Outside aerosol delivery highlights contrasting opinions. An effective delivery system must have two major attributes. First, the delivery system needs to expel the agent efficiently from its container so that it will travel to potential targets. Second, assuming the agent attacks through the respiratory system, the delivery system must produce small particles that will be retained on inhalation. Ranges of one to ten microns are required because larger particles settle out of the atmosphere rapidly and are not inhaled. Paint spray devices are ineffective because of their large particle size. Also because of the necessity of small particle size, a terrorist employing agricultural spraying as his method of dissemination will have to address the problem of decreasing the particle size. Agricultural sprayers expel droplets of a size range that will fall onto the crops. By contrast, smaller particle sizes are necessary to produce an aerosol cloud which will suspend above the surface level.

Even if the terrorist can accomplish this successfully, a hardy agent is still required to survive the expulsion from a sprayer long enough to infect the intended targets. Outdoor aerosol delivery of biological weapons is acutely sensitive to weather conditions, the quality of the dispersal system, and the characteristics of the agent used, making aerosol dissemination of all but a few hardy species technologically challenging. The stress of the aerosolization process itself can kill a large portion of the pathogen; atmospheric conditions such as moisture, sunlight, smog, and temperature changes can take an enormous toll. A nighttime dissemination under stable meteorological conditions would improve chances of success. A cloud released to drift over a densely populated urban area during a mild winter night would probably be most effective; a light wind to prevent the aerosol from settling and an inversion layer to confine the cloud to lower altitudes would aid dissemination.

Somewhat more effective is aerosol dissemination in an indoor setting such as by gaining access to the air circulation system of an office building or public arena. The U.S. Army demonstrated the effectiveness of this delivery system by releasing harmless bacteria into New York City subways.

d. Animal and Insect Vectors

Vectors are normally insects that carry a host of different infectious agents, but a vector can be any creature that transmits an infectious agent to humans when it bites or touches a person. The infectious agent may be injected with the insect's salivary fluid when it bites, or an insect may regurgitate material or deposit feces on the skin that enter a person's body, typically through a bite wound or skin broken by scratching or rubbing. Once the agent is within the vector animal, an incubation period follows during which the agent grows or reproduces, or both, depending on the type of agent. Only after this phase is over does the vector become infectious.

A highly contagious pathogen could be propagated in a dead animal, and then large numbers of insects could be exposed to that carcass in a confined space, collected, and then released in a population center. Allegedly, the Soviet Union had researched this dissemination method, but there is scant evidence that terrorists have mastered it. More recently, Cuba accused the United States of committing a biological attack by distributing disease-carrying insects from aircraft.

Using insect vectors overcomes the difficulties of aerosolizing pathogens, but the use of insects is necessarily unreliable. Significantly, because only a few pathogens (notably the tropical viruses) are transmittable through this method, a terrorist would reduce options by using insects. To be effective, a highly contagious pathogen must be selected, raising the risk of self-contagion.

4. Assessing the Risk

It would verge on pure speculation to assert that the risk of a particular biological attack is significant or not. Conversations with U.S. government officials suggest that staging a biological attack is far easier than using a nuclear device, even a crude one. But there is no way to confirm or measure this risk. Decisions on appropriate policies must be made, therefore, in a condition of some uncertainty. Yet it should be noted that the direction of biological understanding renders current estimates somewhat irrelevant as to future capabilities. Even sophisticated biologists in the 1980s would have been hard pressed to predict the quality and magnitude of today's bio-engineering; implementation of policies to address threats are likely to follow a somewhat slower progress.

1.3.   Potential Biothreats from Emerging Infectious Diseases

Emerging infectious diseases hold an increasing threat for humanity with increasing resistance to antibiotics, exponential increases in human travel around the globe, and humans living in a more densely populated world. All of these factors, coupled with a decaying public health system worldwide, have created a substantial biothreat to the world's population. It is only a matter of time before we are faced with a pandemic influenza, which in its cyclic occurrence is likely to appear first in Asia and then quickly spread around the globe. This pandemic influenza as an emerging infectious disease is not the typical seasonal influenza, but a much more virulent form from the H5N1 strain, rather than the usual. Other strains are responsible for the 1918 H1N1 Spanish flu, and the 1956 Hong Kong Influenza, H2N1 pandemic; thus H1, H2, H3, and now the H5 and H7 strains have been associated with the more deadly forms of influenza. [22A] The Pandemic Influenza Act of 2006 was passed by the U.S. Congress with the intent of continuing preparations for such an event.

Predictions of emerging infectious diseases disasters are outlined in Laurie Garrett's *The Coming Plague* (Hyperion, 2000), in which her interviews with scientists predict worldwide epidemics and crises, much the result of crumbling public health infrastructures, both locally and globally. These threats have been recognized and new policy considerations are including addressing biothreats. Rand Corporation has examined the global biothreats of emerging infectious diseases in *The Global Threat of New and Reemerging Infectious Diseases, Reconciling U.S. National Security and Public Health Policy* (Rand, 2003), and the World Health Organization has initiated a new effort addressing security through global health; its policy is articulated in the report titled, "A Safer Future: global public health security in the 21st century," at http://www.who.int/whr/2007/en/index.html.

1.4.   Potential Biothreats from Global Climate Change

The changing climate has produced shifts in animal and insect populations, which has caused a movement of the diseases they carry with them into previously cooler climates. This is one of the effects of climate change that has been predicted by the United Nations' International Panel on Climate Change through their scientific reporting bodies. In addition to the ecological changes causing the shift in disease, the migration of people from flooding as a result of climate change will potentially produce large population shifts, including refugee populations. The Hurricane Katrina incident with millions of refugees from the devastated region is indicative of the kind of event that may be triggered by climate change. These kinds of events that produce dramatic disasters demonstrate the way that climate change takes place, rather than the gradual warming that is evident from a graphic which depicts a hundred-year trend. These changes occur as a series of spikes in events, such as rising sea level or flooding of regions. These events have led to more attention to another area of law, refugee law.

The Associated Press in March 2007 reported a surge in hemorrhagic dengue fever, a particularly dramatic form of the tropical disease, commonly referred to as "bone break fever" because of the intense bone pain from the disease. The reason, some experts say, is the increasing temperature brought on by climate change, which is causing dengue-carrying mosquitoes to move further north, coupled with the eradication failures, particularly after the banning of DDT, a very effective insecticide. The United Nations' International Panel on Climate Change, through their scientific reports, have predicted an increase in dengue in North America due to climate change.

Hemorrhagic dengue fever surges in Mexico with climate changes, migration, urbanization

By Mark Stevenson
ASSOCIATED PRESS , 1:14 p.m. March 30, 2007

MEXICO CITY – The deadly hemorrhagic form of dengue fever is increasing dramatically in Mexico, and experts predict a surge throughout Latin America fueled by climate change, migration and faltering mosquito eradication efforts. Overall dengue cases have increased by more than 600 percent in Mexico since 2001, and worried officials are sending special teams to tourist resorts to spray pesticides and remove garbage and standing water where mosquitoes breed ahead of the peak Easter Week vacation season. Even classic dengue – known as "bonebreak fever" – can cause severe flu-like symptoms, excruciating joint pain, high fever, nausea and rashes. More alarming is that a deadly hemorrhagic form of the disease, which adds internal and external bleeding to the symptoms – is becoming more common. It accounts for one in four cases in Mexico, compared with one in 50 seven years ago, according to Mexico's Public Health Department.

While hemorrhagic dengue is increasing around the developing world, the problem is most dramatic in the Americas, according to the Centers for Disease Control and Prevention. Like a poster child for the downside of humanity's impact on the planet, dengue is driven by longer rainy seasons some blame on climate change, as well as disposable plastic packaging and other trash that collects water. Migrants and tourists – including the many thousands of Americans expected for spring break this year – carry new strains of the virus across national borders, where mosquitoes can spread the disease.

The CDC says there's no drug to treat hemorrhagic dengue, but proper treatment, including rest, fluids and pain relief, can reduce death rates to about 1 percent. Latin America's hospitals are ill-equipped to handle major outbreaks, and officials say the virus is likely to grow deadlier, in part because tourism and migration are circulating four different strains across the region. A person exposed to one strain may develop immunity to that strain – but subsequent exposure to another strain makes it more likely the person will develop the hemorrhagic form. This dengue spread "is one of the primordial public health problems the country faces," said Mexico's Public Health Department, which has sent hundreds of workers to the resorts of Puerto Vallarta, Cancun and Acapulco to try to avert outbreaks ahead of the Easter week vacation. "We are working intensively, both the federal and state governments, on (these) three sites that we want to keep under control, so that it doesn't become a risk for tourists," said Pablo Kuri, head of Mexico's National Center for Epidemiology and Disease Control.

The Canadian Embassy in Mexico City issued an alert about dengue after five Canadians were sickened in Puerto Vallarta earlier this year. Acapulco, a city of 700,000, has documented 549 cases of classic and hemorrhagic dengue in the first two months of 2007, up from just 86 for the same period last year.

Dengue is mostly a problem in tropical slums, where trash collection and sanitation are not as good as in tourist areas. In January and February, Mexico's dry season, there were 1,589 cases of both types of dengue nationwide, up 380 percent from the same period in 2006, Kuri said. And last year was also bad for dengue: Mexico documented 27,000 infections overall – including 4,477 hemorrhagic cases and 20 deaths – compared with 1,781 cases overall in 2001.

Dengue has been found along the U.S.-Mexico border, where 151 classic and 46 hemorrhagic cases were recorded last year in the Gulf state of Tamaulipas, south of Texas. Historically, the United States hasn't been immune from dengue – a 1922 outbreak in Texas infected a half-million people. And according to the CDC, dengue returned to southern Texas in 1980 after a 35-year absence. Occasional cases since then have included hemorrhagic dengue.

The Intergovernmental Panel on Climate Change, made up of the world's leading climate scientists, predicted in March that global warming and climate change would cause an upsurge in dengue. In Mexico, officials say longer rainy seasons already are leading to more cases. "It used to be seasonal, in the hottest, wettest months, and now in some regions we are seeing it practically all year," said Joel Navarrete, an epidemiologist with the Mexican Social Security Institute. The global solution to dengue outbreaks is mosquito control, and faltering eradication efforts, together with climate change, probably share blame for dengue's rise in the Americas, Kuri said. A successful eradication program in Latin America in the 1960s sent the disease into remission, but economic crises and government downsizing sapped those efforts over the next two decades. Some countries reported severe outbreaks in the 1980s, and by the 1990s, dengue began a regional resurgence.

Paraguay declared a state of emergency in March after 17 people died of hemorrhagic dengue and an estimated 400,000 were infected with the milder "classic" form of the disease. The government sent soldiers into the streets in an emergency campaign to spray insecticides and clean up stagnant water. At least 24 people died of hemorrhagic dengue in the Dominican Republic last year.

"It's part of globalization," Kuri said. "Someone can be in Paraguay, where there is a big outbreak, with type-one virus, and six hours later be in Mexico."

1.5.   Why Examine Biosecurity Law?

The study of law and biosecurity, biodefense and bioterrorism examines the societal and governmental actions that form a legal and policy framework to address biological threats to individuals, the public and to the military resources, whether these threats are intentional or naturally occurring. This study presents unique challenges to incorporating new and emerging areas of biological and engineering sciences with law and regulatory processes and methodologies. This study incorporates sciences at the local levels as well as national and international levels. But why should we study biosecurity law?

First, the study of biotechnologies for scientists throughout the world involves the utility of sharing research and publications, which contributes to the same issues and research of all scientists. However, the study of law stops at jurisdictional boundaries among lawyers and scholars because laws in one state may have no application in another state, and even less so in other countries. Only in the academic area of comparative law would the issue arise to compare their features. The study of biosecurity law must be harmonized across jurisdictional boundaries to be effective against biological agents, which do not recognize or stop at such human-designed jurisdictional boundaries.

Second, the study of biosecurity law among administrators and military strategists was historically combined with all other weapons of mass destruction: chemical, radiological, and nuclear. The preparation against threats of chemical, radiological, and nuclear weapons employed similar approaches, and the differences between chemical, radiological, and nuclear compared to biological were indistinguishable for the military strategists. The problem of combining all weapons of mass destruction with the same planning and response activities is that it fails to account for the very different delivery systems, fragility, and self-propagating characteristics of biological weapons. For example, in the event of a chemical or nuclear incident, it is very evident immediately that there has been an attack. In contrast, should a biological attack take place, it could be days or weeks before the attack is evident.

Third, the study of biosecurity law is a new and important area for lawyers as they enter the profession of practicing law in the 21st Century. The regulatory and policy changes have been dramatic since 2001; for example, this author was the first to propose in an article written in 2002 [23] that biological weapons of mass destruction were very different from other weapons of mass destruction, and that biological weapons should not be managed by the same agencies as nuclear and chemical weapons. This recommendation was made on the heels of an influential discussion from the Kennedy School of the threat of weapons of mass destruction, encapsulated in a book entitled, *America's Achilles Heel—Nuclear, Biological and Chemical Terrorism and Covert Attack,* published in 1998,[24] which did not seek to distinguish approaches to biological threats. Over the past decade, new laws and regulatory programs have increased dramatically, requiring governments, the private sector, and individuals to keep pace with these rapid demands to be current with regulatory requirements.

Fourth, in addition to the simple increase in the number of laws and regulations concerning biothreats, the federalism relationship between states and the federal government in the United States has demonstrated significant changes. In the spring of 2001, in *The Georgetown Public Policy Review,* an article by this author challenged the status quo of public health law, proposing that a shift in federalism, consistent with the U.S. Constitution, was occurring in our legal jurisprudence.[25] Concurrently, the National Association of Governors began to address the concern of antiquated public health laws and emergency powers under state public health authority.

Finally, it is important that we learn from historical experiences using legal constraints and mandates to protect public health in times of emergencies, as well as make efforts to protect national security and homeland security from biothreats during times of conflict and war.

In summary, our examination of biosecurity law can be further illuminated by consideration of some salient statements from other legal scholars who have raised concerns that our legal framework is not sufficient for addressing biothreats:

"Vague and contradictory laws, overlapping jurisdictions, and a public health system grown slow and ponderous with complacency might well cripple the response to an act of biological warfare or terrorism in the precious few hours between detection and spread..."[26]

"Catastrophic terrorist threats have received far more attention than have the legal rules that are appropriate to a response. This suggests either that officials planning responses to terrorism are callous about those responses' legal implications or that answers are being formulated without overt public discussion involving the larger legal community. In either event, the very real risks of catastrophic terrorism are being compounded, unnecessarily, by the risk that a crisis will evoke an inefficient and/or repressive reaction."[27]

"Can anything be done to provide more legal guidance to officials in making the critical on-scene decisions that may be thrust upon them when faced with the possibility of a terrorist attack?....Our greatest dangers...are complacency, failure to anticipate the contingencies, and the constant assumption that someone else must be taking care of the problem."[28]

Then thinking began to evolve to distinguish the threats of biological weapons from other weapons of mass destruction:

"What is often neglected in thinking about the threats bioweapons pose to public health is the foundation that law provides for effective public health activities. Focusing on the link between public health and the law reveals that bioterrorism would also constitute a grave threat to the role law plays in regulating public and private behavior in the United States."[29]

"Vague and contradictory laws, overlapping jurisdictions, and procedural and professional divides among law enforcement, national security and public health officials have created a confusing set of laws that do not conform easily to the needs of first responders."[30]

In the study of law and bioterrorism, it is important to involve a public dialogue in order to reach a satisfactory legal structure to address the threat of bioterrorism. This requires the dialogue to expand to include public health officials, medical professionals, political and government officials from all departments, state and diplomatic officials, and lawyers and legal scholars. The interdisciplinary nature of bioterrorism requires not only legal, health sciences, policy, and public health interaction, but also the social sciences and environmental sciences as essential areas key to addressing this threat.

ENDNOTES

CHAPTER ONE pp. 1-31

---

[1] League of Nations, "Hague Convention (II) with Respect to the Laws and Customs of War on Land," July 29, 1899 (http://www.yale.edu/lawweb/avalon/lawofwar/hague02.htm) (site visited Apr. 4, 2002); *Encyclopedia of Bioethics* 2545 (2000).

[2] Strabo, *The Geography of Strabo* (The Loeb Classical Library ed., 1967); Adrienne Mayor, "Mad Honey!" 48 Archaeology 32–40 (Nov/Dec 1995); suggested as a bioterrorism event by Robert S. Root-Bernstein, "Infectious Terrorism," 267 *The Atlantic Monthly* 44–50 (May 1991) at http://www.theatlantic.com/issues/91may/rootbernstein.htm.

[2A] Laurie Garrett, The Coming Plague, Hyperion Publishers, New York (2000), p. 1.

[3] United States Army Medical Research Institute of Infectious Diseases (USAMRIID), "Medical Defense Against Biological Warfare Agents Course: History of Biological Warfare" *Encyclopedia of Bioethics* 2545.

[4] Robert O'Connell, *Of Arms and Men: A History of War, Weapons, and Aggression* 171 (1989).

[5] De Mussis G. *Historica de Morbo s. Mortalitate quae fuit Anno Dni MCCCXLVIII* cited by Derbes V.J., "DeMussis and the great plague of 1348: A forgotten episode of bacteriological warfare," 196 JAMA 179–182 (1966) cited by *Medical Aspects of Chemical and Biological Warfare*, Edward M. Eitzen, Jr. et.al., Chapter 18 "Historical Overview of Biological Warfare," *Medical Aspects of Chemical and Biological Warfare* (1994).

[6] E. Wagner Stearn and Allen E. Stearn, *The Effects of Small pox on the Destiny of the Amerindian* 44–45 (1945).

[7] USAMRIID.

[8] War Department, General Order 100 (1863).

[9] Jeffery K. Smart, M.A., "History of Chemical and Biological Warfare: An American Perspective," Chapter 2, *Medical Aspects of Chemical and Biological Warfare* 12–13 (2000).

[10] George W. Christopher, USAF, MC; Theodore J. Cjeslak et. al., "Biological Warfare: A Historical Perspective," *Journal of the American Medical Association* 278 (Aug. 6, 1997).

[11] Geissler, E., ed. *Biological Weapons Today* (1986).

[12] Gina Kolata, *Flu: The Story of the Great Influenza Pandemic of 1918 and the Search for the Virus that Caused It* 3–4 (1999).

[13] See http://state.gov/www/global/arms/treaties/geneva1.html.

[14] Hal Gold, *Unit 731 Testimony* 64 (?).

[15] Stockholm International Peace Research Institute (SIPRI), *The Problem of Chemical and Biological Warfare*, Vol. I, 111–119 (1971).

[16] Ken Alibek, *Biohazard* 30 (1999).

[17] *See* S. H. Harris, *Factories of Death* (1994).

[18] David Snyder, "On the Front Line of Anthrax War," *The Washington Post*, B01 (Tuesday, November 6, 2001).

[19] Frontline, "What Happened in South Africa?" at http://www.pbs.org/wgbh/pages/frontline/shows/plague/sa/.

[19A] CNN, October 4, 1999 at http://ospiti.peacelink.it/anb-bia/week_99/991007 .

[19B] Commey, Pusch, "Dr. Death Walks Free," The New African (May 1, 2002) at http://www.thefreelibrary.com/'Dr+Death'+walks+free.+(South+Africa)-a085881522 .

[20] Thomas J. Torok et. al., "A Large Community Outbreak of Salmonellosis Caused by Intentional Contamination of Restaurant Salad Bars," 278 J. Amer. Med. Assoc. 389–395 (August 6, 1997).

[21] Ken Alibek, *Biohazard* 268 (1999).

[22] Ken Alibek, *Biohazard* 274 (1999).

[22A] R. J. Russell1, D. J. Stevens1, L. F. Haire1, S. J. Gamblin1 and J. J. Skehel1, "Avian and human receptor binding by hemagglutinins of influenza A viruses," Glycoconjugate Journal, Publisher Springer Netherlands, ISSN 0282-0080 (Print) 1573-4986 (Online)

[23] Sutton, "A Precarious 'Hot Zone'—The President's Plan to Combat Bioterrorism," 164 *The Mil. Law Rev.* 135 (2000).

[24] Richard A. Falkenrath, Robert D. Newman and Bradley A. Thayer, *America's Achilles Heel: Nuclear, Biological and Chemical Terrorism and Covert Attack* (1998).

[25] Sutton, "Bioterrorism Preparation and Response Legislation—The Struggle to Protect States' Sovereignty While Preserving National Security," 6 *The Georgetown Public Policy Review* 93 (Spring 2001).
Issue Volume 23, Numbers 1-2 / February, 2006.

[26] Kristin Choo, "A Plague in the Making—US Lacks Legal Structure to Fight Bioterrorism, critics say," *ABA Journal* 18–20 (December 1999).

[27] Barry Kellman, "Catastrophic Terrorism—Thinking Fearfully, Acting Legally," 20 Mich. J. Int'l L. 537 (Spring 1999).

[28] Ronald J. Sievert, "Meeting the Twenty-First Century Terrorist Threat Within the Scope of Twentieth Century Constitutional Law," 37 Hous. L. Rev. 1421 (Winter 2000).

[29] David P. Fidler, "The Malevolent Use of Microbes and the Rule of Law: Legal Challenges Presented by Bioterrorism," Clinical Infectious Diseases 2001; 33:686–689 (30 July 2001).

Chapter Two
The Role of the Federal Government in Biodefense

2.1. Introduction

The U.S. Constitution provides for a national defense to be led by the federal government, and this national security responsibility has been defined as including the expectation that preparation is needed before times of emergency or attack in order to defend the nation. This federal responsibility requires a national policy that includes a coordinated surveillance and response system throughout the nation. The anthrax attacks of the fall of 2001 brought to the forefront the shortcomings of a coordinated federal system of biodefense among local, state, and federal response and surveillance activities. The events that followed Hurricane Katrina in Louisiana, Mississippi, and Texas again brought to national attention the necessary balance between state and federal emergency powers to respond to public health disasters. An examination of constitutional federalism is necessary to better define and explain the role of the federal, state, and local governments in planning for and participating in emergency public health matters. The need to utilize the resources and expertise of the federal government coupled with the need to utilize state and local experience in their own regions to optimally respond to biothreats has resulted in incremental shifts in the federalism relationship with public health governmental responsibilities in biosecurity and biosafety matters.

This chapter addresses the federalism aspects of balancing a need for a federal system of defense, while preserving the interests of state sovereignty in the area of public health emergencies. This chapter will examine the role of the federal government agencies and departments in a national biodefense framework, which has changed in significant ways, including the creation of a new cabinet level department, the Department of Homeland Security, the complete reorganization of the intelligence community, and the significantly evolving roles of the Centers for Diseases Control and Prevention (CDC), the Department of Health and Human Services (DHHS), and the military.

2.2. The Federal Organization— The Executive, Legislative and Judicial Roles

Congress reflects the will of the voters by passing laws to respond to the most important concerns. The concern of bioterrorism was heightened in the United States after the anthrax attacks of the fall of 2001, and Congress responded. Since 2001, Congress has increased spending for biodefense, biosecurity, and biosafety, and by 2005 had spent more than $14 billion, as shown in this chart:

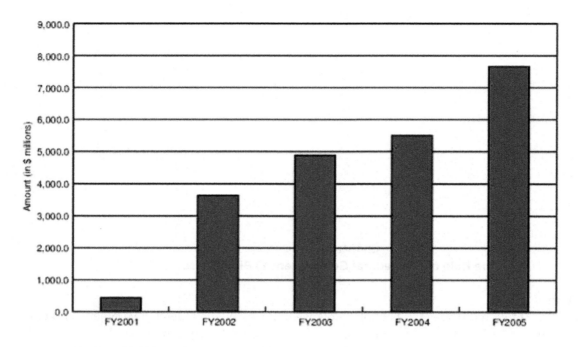

Fig. 2-1. Federal Expenditures in Biodefense. More than $14 billion has been invested in biodefense by the federal government from 2001-2005. Ari Schuler, "Billions for Biodefense: Federal Agency Biodefense Funding, FY2001–FY2005," *Biosecurity and Bioterrorism*, 2004;2(2):86-96.

New statutes specifically addressing five areas in bioterrorism, biosecurity, and biodefense have been passed since the fall of 2001: organizational, vaccines and countermeasures, pandemic influenza preparedness, public health responses, and bioterrorism crimes. Here are the major statutes in these categories:

Organizational:
The Homeland Security Act of 2002
http://fl1.findlaw.com/news.findlaw.com/hdocs/docs/terrorism/hsa2002.pdf

Vaccines and Countermeasures:
The Support Anti-Terrorism by Fostering Effective Technologies Act
(SAFETY Act) of 2002
Project Bioshield Act of 2004
The Public Readiness and Emergency Preparedness Act (PREPA) of 2005
Pandemic and All-Hazards Preparedness Act (PAHPA) of 2006

Public Health Responses:
The Smallpox Emergency Personnel Protection Act of 2003, Public Law 108-20, 117 Stat. 638 at http://www.hrsa.gov/smallpoxinjury/
Public Health Security and Bioterrorism Preparedness and Response Act of 2002, 116 Stat. 594, P.L. 107–188, JUNE 12, 2002.

Bioterrorism Crimes:
USA PATRIOT Act of 2001, §817, 1013

2.3 A Legal History of the Executive Branch approach to Biothreats 1998 to the present

The recent modern history of biothreats begins with the discovery in 1992 that the USSR had been engaged in the most massive offensive bioweapons program in the history of the world, seemingly triggered by the agreement to the Biological Weapons Convention in 1972. Two key defectors from the USSR disclosed details of the program. The claims of the expansiveness and technological descriptions that were provided by the defectors caught the U.S. intelligence by surprise. One of the defectors, Ken Alibek (formerly Ken Alibekov), described his work in the program named Biopreparat in his book, *Biohazard*, published in 2001.

With the collapse of the USSR, the thousands of bioweapons scientists who had been employed by the expansive Biopreparat program were looking for jobs. The expertise in the USSR that had been a secret for so long was now on the market to the highest bidder with the USSR collapse. With this security threat, the United States began to make some preparations for the possibility of a bioterrorism attack.

The following article excerpt examines the plan for combating bioterrorism during the Clinton Administration (1992-2000).

A Precarious 'Hot Zone'— The President's Plan to Combat Bioterrorism
164 *The Military Law Review* 135 (2000)

I. Introduction

The President, since taking office, has "made the fight against terrorism a top national security objective."[1] President Clinton announced on 22 May 1998 that he "is determined that in the coming century, we will be capable of deterring and preventing such terrorist attacks."[2] The President is also convinced that we must also have the ability to limit the damage and manage the consequences should such an attack occur."[3] With this most recent announcement, the President introduced Presidential Decision Directive 62 (PDD 62), which is to "create a new and more systematic approach to fighting the terrorist threat of the next century"[4] and to clarify the roles of agencies and departments to ensure a coordinated approach to planning for such terrorist induced emergencies. However, as yet no formal procedure exists for coordinating federal, state, and local forces should we have a bioterrorism event, or an effective plan for participation of the nation's military forces in response to such an event.

While nuclear, chemical, and biological weaponry all fall within the general classification of WMD, until very recently, nuclear weaponry has dominated planning and discussion. Today, however, it is increasingly recognized that chemical and particularly biological weapons represent much more credible threats in the hands of terrorists than do nuclear ones. This follows for many reasons, for example, ease of maintaining secrecy in preparation of the weapons, ease of production and delivery of the weapons, ease of obtaining wide dispersal of the weapons—particularly in the case of biological weapons. It is also true that modern genetic engineering carries with it the specter of modification of familiar weapons species such as anthrax and smallpox into forms against which all our vaccines and other defenses would be worthless.

This current planning is directed against all weapons of mass destruction (WMD), which include technological as well as specifically chemical and biological activities. This article will focus on a plan for biological and chemical weapons that should be distinguished from the approach to a plan for all other technological threats. While the United States skills in planning to combat nuclear weapons and other technological weapons have been practiced throughout the cold war, our skills in beginning to comprehend and meet the threats of chemical and biological warfare on a domestic level have only recently begun to be developed fully.

Although PDD 62 is the most recent formal action, the planning for responses to domestic bioterrorism is shaped by prior presidential directives, statutes, and U.S. constitutional guidance. The planning for the prevention, detection, and actual encounters with bioterrorism now has actually begun, but as separate departmental missions under the auspices of individual agencies and departments. These initial planning and funding activities have been examined through a number of Government Account Office (GAO) investigatory reports at the request of Congress, criticizing the lack of coordination. The implementation of any emergency response capability, fortunately, has not been tested on a major scale as yet, and this article addresses the legal status of the coordination of federal agencies, the military, as well as state and local governments under the constraints of statutes, regulations, case law and the U.S. Constitution.

Richard Preston, a science thriller novelist, produced a response scenario to a bioterrorism event in his 1997 book, *The Cobra Event.*[5] *The New York Times* reported that "Mr. Clinton was so alarmed by...*The Cobra Event*...that he instructed intelligence experts to evaluate its credibility."[6] More alarming perhaps even than its suggested biological possibility, is the lack of statutory clarity that would be essential for effective implementing of a strategy for the United States in terms of preparedness and emergency responsiveness. This article examines the present status of federal, state, and local preparedness and proposes such changes to statutes and federal regulations and to the implementation of currently applicable statutes to enable our federal, state, and local resources to be effectively used in research, preparedness as well as in emergency responsiveness.

II. Who Is In Charge?

The President's strategy has been to combine threats of all WMD into a single framework for preparation and planned response.[7] The designation of a lead agency or department for coordination appears to fall within the responsibility of the newly created Office of the National Coordinator for Security Infrastructure Protection and Counter-Terrorism, working "within the National Security Council and reporting to the Assistant to the President for National Security Affairs."[8] This office is to give "advice on budgets...lead in the development of guidelines that might be needed for crisis management,...oversee the broad variety of relevant policies and programs included in such areas as counter-terrorism, [and oversee the] protection of critical infrastructure and preparedness and consequence management for [response to] [WMD]" under PDD 62.[9]

The separation of WMD between technological weapons on the one hand and chemical and biological weapons on the other is suggested in the introduction to this article. Moreover, a separation of leadership among preparedness, research, funding, and planning activities and the emergency response activities, matched with respective missions of the departments and agencies would provide the most effective use of our resources. Perhaps a lesson from the Cherokee tribal custom of designating a wartime chief and a peacetime chief, where, "war was decided upon, its conduct was turned over to the town war organization,"[10] should be considered in structuring the leadership for these two activities. That is, preparedness and research are very different activities and require very different skills as compared to the activities and skills of emergency response.

Whether the proposed separation is a workable plan is examined in the following sections.

A. Preparedness, Research, Funding and Planning—Who is in Charge?

Recent GAO testimony before Congress describes the scope of combating foreign-origin as well as domestic terrorism and makes recommendations for crosscutting and coordination management,[11] which repeats many of the same criticisms included in a GAO report issued just over a year earlier.[12]

The second report recommends that the Office of Management and Budget (OMB) conduct a crosscutting review, identify priorities and gaps and identify funding. However, the scope of the responsibility requires the staffer in OMB charged with this duty, to fully understand the scientific merit of programs spanning approximately twenty-two departments and agencies, as well as the legal and interagency constraints. In addition, this OMB staffer must compose a line-item budget for each agency identifying those items which fit into the comprehensive, government-wide program, which will probably be reviewed by dozens of congressional committees and subcommittees that claim departmental jurisdiction—not program jurisdiction.

Before the line-item, crosscutting coordination can be accomplished, as envisioned by the GAO, Congress must also agree to a joint appropriations hearing, with each department's and agency's appropriations committee coming together to receive a joint presentation of the coordinated budget. . . .

1. Federal Coordination and Leadership

The design of a plan to confront the threats of bioterrorism, with a logical division of leadership between the planning and the emergency response responsibilities could follow previous statutory designs having demonstrated efficacy. Current statutory mechanisms are currently in place that could provide a framework for the recommendations made by the GAO.

The GAO recommendation that these responsibilities be assigned to the OMB represents an overwhelming range of duties. The performance of such crosscutting, coordinated functions was, in fact, performed in a previous Administration by a well-coordinated assemblage of federal employees and appointees, meeting once a month over an annual planning period enabled by the Federal Coordinating Council for Science, Engineering and Technology (FCCSET) statute.[13] During the period from 1989 to 1992, the implementation of this statute required three Ph.D.-level staff from the Office of Science and Technology Policy, one staff member from the OMB, and two levels of coordination among staff and senior policy appointees from twelve or more agencies and departments involved in each of the crosscutting programs.[14]

The GAO has identified twenty-two departments and agencies that should be involved in the crosscutting, coordinated plan to combat terrorism.[15] . . . With obviously no alternatives, and a vital need to match resources with programmatic goals, the GAO was left to suggest that OMB itself carry out the entire crosscutting, coordination function. . . .

2. Intergovernmental Planning and Coordination

The threat of domestic terrorism demands an intergovernmental coordination system as well as a coordinated federal intra-governmental process. This issue was also addressed by the GAO report in its acknowledgment that the Attorney General was in the process of establishing a National Domestic Preparedness Office within the Federal Bureau of Investigation "to reduce state and local confusion over the many federal training and equipment programs necessary to prepare for terrorist incidents involving weapons of mass destruction."[16] This addresses the question of the availability of training resources for state and local governments, but fails to address the more comprehensive issue of ensuring that each state and local government is linked to a process which addresses the legal and public health responsibilities and expectations. The effort to create an accessible laundry list of training programs in the hope of preparing state and local governments is comparable to sending state and local governments out to a grocery store with a grocery list (but without money) to make a specific unique cuisine for which only the federal government has the recipe.

B. Emergency Response—Who's in Charge?

1. Federal Coordination and Leadership

Intragovernmental relationships are addressed by Presidential Decision Directive 39 (PDD 39), which identifies the Federal Bureau of Investigation (FBI) as the lead agency for domestic crisis response and the Federal Emergency Management Agency (FEMA) as the lead agency for consequence management. The National Security Council is charged with the lead for interagency terrorism policy coordination.[17] The most recently issued of the directives—PDD 62—designated an office of "National Coordinator for Security Infrastructure Protection and Counter-Terrorism"[18] charged with government-wide responsibility for the broad GAO mandate for accountability, as discussed above. The FBI or FEMA, under the Economy Act of 1932,[19] could then use the broad authority given by Congress to any executive department to place orders with the military (or any other department) for materials, supplies, equipment, work or—from the military—passive services (those not statutorily prohibited).[20] . . .

2. Intergovernmental Coordination and Leadership—Sovereignty Analysis

The authority for the federal government to intervene in state matters such as public health presents an issue of state sovereignty, and must be considered in any intergovernmental plan. Indian reservations, both those held in trust by the Department of Interior or held in fee simple by the tribes, do not have the same sovereignty issues as do states; because although they are separate governments, these reservations apply federal law in areas where states enjoy exclusive jurisdiction. The importance of Indian tribal governments and Indian reservations are critical, however, in part because there are at least nine reservations that have boundaries on international borders or international waters.[21] This requires a federal and tribal relationship focusing on national security against the entry of bioterroristic threats into the U.S. border-crossing agreements. While the federal government has made agreements with these tribes, special focus is required on the emerging issues of possible bioterrorism.

3. Constitutional Tenth Amendment State Sovereignty

The readiness of state and local governments to respond to domestic terrorism was assessed by RAND Corporation in 1995 through a grant from the U.S. Department of Justice, National Institute of Justice.[22] Although the sponsoring department's mission is the application of law, this effort failed to address or even to identify legal issues for state and local governments as one of import in analyzing readiness.[23]

The first step in the response protocol to bioterrorism must necessarily take place at the state and local levels. The CDC, in collaboration with the Council of State and Territorial Epidemiologists, have developed guidance for public health surveillance which—for the first time—established uniform criteria for state health departments in reporting diseases.[24] This provides for uniform identification of the occurrence of reportable diseases. Laws that mandate the reporting of specific diseases however are state laws which result in variation in multiple lists of varying reportable diseases. A list of nationally reportable diseases however has been identified in the CDC protocol applicable to all states.[25]

Because the myriad of state laws provide no uniformity for federal response, the effort to address public health through the federal level has been lead by associations of state professionals. This reporting protocol was developed in collaboration with the Council of State and Territorial Epidemiologists (CSTE) and approved by a full vote of the CSTE membership. It was also endorsed by the Association of State and Territorial Public Health Laboratory Directors (ASTPHLD). From this, CDC in collaboration with the Council of State and Territorial Epidemiologists have developed a "policy" that requires state health departments nationwide to report cases of the selected diseases to CDC's National Notifiable Diseases Surveillance System (NNDSS).[26] Interestingly, a recommendation was proposed to develop an "NBC Response Center" to respond to nuclear, biological, and chemical attacks as a part of an interagency effort to combine the FBI, FEMA, Department of Defense, Department of Health and Human Services, the EPA, the U.S. Marine

Corps, the Chemical and Biological Defense Command and the Department of Energy into a central group, modeled after the existing Counterterrorist Centers, another interagency effort led by the Central Intelligence Agency.[27] Although the NNDSS had been in existence for more than four years, at the time of the recommendation, it was never included in this analysis as a possible national reporting center. While the use of these agencies as the lead intelligence agencies avoids the immediate concern of public health and state sovereignty, it all but ignores the unique agency missions, training, and skills demanded in a public health epidemic crisis.

The responsibilities for developing the reporting protocol of the NNDSS have been set forth in federal regulations promulgated by the CDC, which address the interface between the state associations and the federal agencies.[28] This rather surprising reliance upon non-governmental support for systems to safeguard our nation against presumptively catastrophic biological risks has evolved because of Tenth Amendment[29] constitutional prohibitions against usurping states' authority in the area of public health.

4. Constitutional Non-Delegation of Authority or Ultra Vires Analysis

Further, the broad delegation of authority for rulemaking to these non-governmental organizations suggests that the non-delegation doctrine[30] may be quietly eroding under the pressure of urgent need for essential national components of our national security considered within a state sovereignty context. If, in fact, this is a delegation of federal legislative powers, what is the legislative source of those powers?

The more obscure *ultra vires* doctrine,[31] which does not permit an agency to go beyond the scope of its delegated authority, may be at the heart of this analysis. Indeed, absent a congressional mandate to carry out a federal public health response system to bioterrorism, the agency has no defined scope to exceed. In fact, the very activity of rulemaking to develop a national public health bioterrorism response system, something that Congress is itself prevented from doing, must be beyond the scope of authority for any agency—*ultra vires*.

5. Federal Laws Applicable to Nationwide Bioterrorism Preparedness and Response

Given these constitutional limitations on congressional and Executive authority to usurp states' sovereignty, the application of existing federal laws must necessarily be considered as a partial solution to the bioterrorism challenge.

Under the Posse Comitatus Act[32] the military cannot be used to enforce any laws against civilians. However, an exception to this use of the military is made where states make a request, or where there is no state request, to suppress any insurrection where it is "impracticable to enforce the laws of the U.S....by the ordinary course of judicial proceedings."[33] The only clear exception (in the absence of insurrection) here is that a state must make a request prior to the use of military enforcement. In addition, to activate this latter exception, the President must issue an order activating the military for that specific exception. Failure to do so can leave in question the authority under which the military might be acting, as was the case in the Wounded Knee incident.[34] Under the Posse Comitatus Act, however, the military can be used for the provision of materials and supplies, and certain other passive activities.[35]

An innovative and clearly viable intergovernmental emergency preparedness statute exists in the area of environmental emergency preparedness. The Emergency Planning and Community Right-to-Know Act of 1986[36] provided for the coordination of local emergency planning committees (LEPCs) with both state and federal emergency planning authorities.[37] By 1989, most states had appointed LEPCs primarily based upon county delineations in compliance with this statute.[38]

The LEPC has a statutorily prescribed membership which is "to include, at a minimum, representatives from each of the following groups or organizations: elected state and local officials; law enforcement; civil defense; firefighting; first aid; health; local environmental; hospital; and transportation personnel; broadcast and print media; community groups; and owners and operators of facilities subject to the requirements of this subchapter.[39]

The responsibilities of these LEPCs include the collection of release information from local toxic substance emitters, as well as the development of comprehensive emergency response plans.[40]

While there is no mandate for the federal government to avoid duplication of resources at the local level as the result of federal mandates, members of Congress are ultimately accountable for such overlaps. Amending the Emergency Planning and Community Right-to-Know Act to provide for the emergency planning for bioterrorism emergencies, using the LEPC resource, would accelerate the development of plans for bioterrorism response by at least one or two years.[41] While the LEPC plans are subject to review and approval by the National Response Team[42] under the National Contingency Plan of the Superfund statute;[43] the bioterrorism component should also be reviewable by the FBI, as well as FEMA under the current leadership designations. The Attorney General's establishment of a National Domestic Preparedness Office within the Federal Bureau of Investigation "to reduce state and local confusion over the many federal training and equipment programs to prepare for terrorist incidents involving weapons of mass destruction"[44] might also be used to review such emergency plans and to identify training needs.

The most important, recent legislation in this area which has been constructed to meet the threat of bioterrorism are the Defense Against Weapons of Mass Destruction Act of 1996[45] and the Combating Proliferation of Weapons of Mass Destruction Act of 1996[46] which finds that "the threat posed to the citizens of the United States by nuclear, radiological, biological and chemical weapons delivered by unconventional means is significant and growing."[47] On its face, the legislation attempts to approach the terrorist threat by combining biological with chemical and radiological—again, biological requiring significantly different personnel, skills and strategies than chemical and radiological threats.

The legislation also recognizes there are shortcomings in the coordination between federal, state, and local governments;[48] however, the legislation finds that the "sharing of the expertise and capabilities of the Department of Defense, which traditionally has provided assistance to federal, state, and local officials in neutralizing, dismantling, and disposing of explosive ordnance, as well as radiological, biological, and chemical materials"[49] can be a vital contribution against bioterrorism. Although, the Congress may have an expectation that the Department of Defense is coordinating "traditionally" with state and local governments, there is no evidence of such a system or policy. Traditional coordination with states and local governments is more likely to be the result of very long and tedious negotiations, cost allocations, budgetary planning and eventual execution of a coordinated approach to, for example, the disposing of explosive ordnance at a locally closed military base. In fact, the largest appropriation authorized by this legislation for fiscal year 1997 was for $ 16.4 million to establish a training program for state and local responders, which is the list of courses discussed earlier in this article that fail to present any coordinated effort to link local and state governments with the federal government.

The most significant contribution of this legislation is the money to assist the Public Health Service in establishing Metro Medical Strike Teams in major U.S. cities; however the token $ 6.6 million appropriated for this effort does not signal serious congressional support for such a plan.[50] Again, there is a "grab-bag" of solutions, under-funded, nestled in the most significant of legislation passed to date on the bioterrorism threat.

. . . . The passage of the first comprehensive food and drug bill languished for seventeen years in Congress primarily because of the constitutional position of many legislators that this was a matter to be legislated by state and local governments.[51] Federal jurisdiction for this statute and others[52] is the Commerce Clause of the U.S. Constitution and thus applies to interstate sales. But to regulate bioterrorism on the basis of interstate commerce would require that the pertinent biologics be sold in interstate commerce. With the further restriction of *United States v. Lopez*[53] requiring a "substantial effects" standard on commerce further doubt would be raised as to the reliability of a Commerce Clause basis for regulation of bioterrorism in state and local government—hardly making such legislation useful to deal with public health emergencies.

Whether such federal legislation to invoke federal jurisdiction in emergency preparedness and response activities comports with the Tenth Amendment of the U.S. Constitution also poses potential constitutional challenges to any such legislation. Congressional power to determine what should be regulated for states and local governments was articulated by the court in *Garcia v. San Antonio Metropolitan Transit Authority*[54] when the more restrictive test of "traditional governmental functions"[55] was abandoned as "unworkable."[56] However, dissenters find that the Court's reasoning, in the majority opinion, that federal political officials should be "the sole judges of the limits of their own power"[57] runs afoul of the principle that the federal judiciary is the sole determiner concerning the constitutionality of legislation.[58]

However, if the regulation of the intergovernmental process to combat bioterrorism is developed, leaving no state role, then the preemption doctrine could be applied to overcome challenges through state legislation. In one case where nuclear safety for the citizenry was argued by the state to be an issue of state interest, the court found it not to be fully preempted by federal law. But the court did not allow preemption of the federal regulations concerning safety, but on the basis of economic interests of the state, as those would not be preempted by the statute.[59] The Court seems here to find a way to protect the state's jurisdiction over the safety of its citizens, even if through means of an economic test.

The U.S. Supreme Court, in consideration of the Twenty-First Amendment[60] to the U.S. Constitution in *South Dakota v. Dole*, permitted the withholding of highway funds from a state that failed to make unlawful the possession or purchase of alcoholic beverages by a person less that twenty-one years of age.[61] The issue turned on whether this was a condition on a grant or a regulation. Finding a condition on a grant permitted the application of the Spending Power Clause[62] rather than a violation of the Twenty-First Amendment.

A statutory solution to maintaining telecommunications during a disaster, with state and local governments, illustrates another intergovernmental emergency situation; however, the field of telecommunications is traditionally a federal area, not a state and local government issue. The subsequent regulations to implement the statute[63] address an emergency plan for telecommunications in the event of a natural disaster or non-wartime disaster, providing for communications of federal officials with state and local officials. This regulation requires a management structure to include the "legal authority for telecommunications management" and "[a] control mechanism to manage the initiation, coordination and restoration of telecommunications services."[64]

Legislation should be structured such as that in *South Dakota v. Dole*. This would mean requiring state coordination with federal governments as a condition for the receipt of grant money related to the objective of preparing and responding to bioterrorism, preempting the field through the principles of *Pacific Gas*, and satisfying the dissenters in *Garcia* by making a narrow delineation of the control of state and local resources at the direction of federal officials, in time of emergency. This would seem to satisfy the constitutional requirements of such legislation.

III. The Current Federal Plan

        Current planning, research, and preparedness in the area of potential bioterrorism are accurately reflected in the GAO reports that document an absence of strong leadership and a failure to achieve a crosscutting, coordinated program matched with identified resources in the federal budget. Responses to the GAO report by the various departments identified in the reports were not encouraging and indicated more that the departments and agencies did not fully understand the scope of the problem they were purporting to address.

        The Office of Management and Budget identified meetings with representatives of the National Security Council, Departments of State, Defense, Justice and the Public Health Service, for implementing the National Defense Authorization Act,[65] in which they have been establishing methodologies to identify functions in the budgets, which is unfortunate, since there exists a Congressionally mandated methodology for such identification that would address a broader range of resources.[66] Further, the OMB states that it does not concur with the implementation of a formal crosscutting review process based upon its years of experience.[67] Interestingly, the author of this OMB response seems to be unaware of the existing statutory, formal, crosscutting review process, which was a major part of the OMB budget review process from 1989 to 1992.

        The Department of Defense concurred with the GAO recommendations and expressed concern that the Economy Act prevented its assistance to state and local law enforcement agencies without reimbursement. Such reimbursement requires statutory authority, and since PDD 39 is not a statute, it cannot provide the authorization to waive reimbursement.[68] This is clearly an issue, which must be addressed in any legislation directed toward coordination of federal, state, and local governmental services.

        The Department of State sought to establish that the terrorism function was thoroughly coordinated through their Interagency Coordinating Subgroup—although there was no "National Security Council or Office of Management and Budget active participation" in this subgroup.[69]

IV. Recommendations for a Bioterrorism Plan—Congressional Leadership is Essential

        Congressional jurisdiction recently has been established by the Committee on Government Reform through its Subcommittee on National Security, Veterans Affairs, and International Relations in the U.S. House of Representatives, in its hearing on terrorism.[70] In the U.S. Senate, the Committee on Health, Education, Labor and Pensions Committee through the Subcommittee on Public Health and Safety, chaired by Senator Frist, have recently held hearings on bioterrorism.[71]

        There is an immediate need to propose a statute, with a title such as the Bioterrorism Research, Preparedness and Responsiveness Program, constructed much on the model of the High Performance Computing and Communications Act[72] and the Global Climate Change Research Program[73] to provide for a coordinated, crosscutting effort to avoid gaps in vital areas, to avoid duplication of programs and research and to provide for optimum use of our resources through matching resources with programmatic needs. Further, and as an essential component of this program, a joint appropriations hearing must be agreed among the Congressional committees having jurisdiction for appropriations for the participating agencies and departments. While some of these committees may anticipate having small parts of the crosscutting budget, a Joint Appropriations Committee representing all appropriations for this program is essential. Otherwise, each line item identified for the program may be selected for elimination by the respective appropriations committees for those agencies with no regard to the effect upon the comprehensive program placed at risk by these eliminations.

        The inclusions of other amendments to existing legislation is essential to the success of such a program. An amendment of the exceptions[74] to the Posse Comitatus Act to include military responses not only for the exceptions of drug enforcement, immigration and tariff laws which were included in amendments of 1981 and 1988, but for bioterrorism-related activities, as well, should be included. An amendment of the Emergency Planning and Community Right-to-Know Act of 1986 to include the preparation of plans in coordination with FEMA and the FBI for bioterrorism prevention, preparedness and response, should also be specifically included to avoid any confusion of interpretation.

Federal leadership in the intragovernmental crosscutting and coordination area for bioterrorism, as distinguished from the broadly defined area of WMD, should be lodged with the Public Health Service, Surgeon General. While other forms of terrorism correspond with the missions of the FBI and FEMA, the mission of the Public Health Service, coupled with the statutory provision for its conversion to a military service,[75] provides the appropriate level of leadership to command both civilian and military resources in response to a bioterrorism event. The Public Health Service, although converted to a military service, is not subject to the Posse Comitatus Act according to the analysis in *United States v. Jaramillo* wherein the special unit of the U.S. Marshall's Office is not found to be subject to the Act[76] and military policy statements,[77] while the Army is regulated by the Posse Comitatus Act, and as a matter of military policy, the Act is also applicable to the Marines and Navy. The use of the Public Health Service in the top leadership role provides the best of both worlds for domestic use of the military, while avoiding the need for any legislative amendment to allow for other branches of the military to take a leadership role.

During the NATO visit to Washington, D.C., in May 1999, over seventy museums and all of the Washington Metro stations were closed, and federal government employees were told not to report to work because of fear of a terrorism event. Unfortunately, much of congressional action in the past has been only as a result of a disaster: The Biologics Act of 1906 was a response to the death of several children due to a vaccine infected with tetanus. The Comprehensive Environmental Response, Compensation, and Liability Act of 1980 was a result of the Love Canal environmental disaster; and the Emergency Planning and Community Right-to-Know Act of 1986 was a result of the Bhopal disaster.

The importance of enactment of legislation to address the unique legal, scientific and budgeting problems presented by the issue of bioterrorism is apparent in light of the potential magnitude of the threat to public safety in the United States. As discussed, prior environmental disasters gave rise to major legislative solutions; but a bioterrorism disaster could prove to be greater in magnitude by far, than the previous problems that gave rise to congressional action. The threat of bioterrorism simply cannot be left to languish under the crippled plan of the President. Congressional action should be taken before we as a nation, defenseless, face the disaster of a shattered domestic security, a country in panic, and a national future in jeopardy.

Notes

1. The preceding article suggests that the federal government should take a role in the peacetime public health system, which has been within the sovereign police powers of the states. Should states give up any part of their jurisdiction over public health?

2. Beginning in the 1990s, states took the lead in passing laws concerning genetics and genetic privacy because the U.S. Congress has failed to take any action to establish federal standards for the use of genetic information. What kind of action would you expect states to take if Congress fails to pass legislation that establishes a federal plan? It was not until 2008 that the U.S. Congress passed and the President signed the Genetic Information Nondiscrimination Act (GINA) of 2008, which has been called a "13-year legislative saga." Kathy L. Hudson, M.K. Holohan, and Frances S. Collins, "Keeping Pace with the Times --- The Genetic Information Nondiscrimination Act of 2008, *New England Journal of Medicine* at http://content.nejm.org/cgi/content/full/358/25/2661.

3. As described in the above article, Congress does not typically respond to problems unless there is a major triggering event, and no federally coordinated plan for a bioterrorism attack existed outside of one grant program to about one hundred local governments for more emergency equipment and training. The anthrax attacks of fall of 2001 provided such an impetus, and Congress rapidly passed legislation in 2001, 2002, 2003, 2004, 2005, and 2006. Further legislation was proposed in 2008.

This article suggests that the U.S. Congress should show leadership on this issue. If Congress fails to take action, should the President proceed with a plan to address biothreats? In 2005, the President did prepare a government-wide plan to combat pandemic influenza and an extensively coordinated implementation plan. How much can the President do without a mandate from Congress?

4. If the federal government creates a surveillance system in public health with regulations for its enforcement, should states be required to comply? How would states be forced to comply? See ***Martin v. Hunter's Lessee***, 14 U.S. (1 Wheat) 304 (1816) and ***Worcester v. Georgia***, 31 U.S. (6 Pet.) 515 (1832).

5. The article describes the Clinton Administration plan for combating domestic terrorism directed by PDD-39, which designates to the National Security Council responsibility for the lead for interagency terrorism policy coordination. The most recently issued of the directives—PDD 62—designated an office of "National Coordinator for Security Infrastructure Protection and Counter-Terrorism" specifically charged with government-wide responsibility for the broad GAO mandate for accountability. The appointee to this position was Richard Clarke, who lashed out at the Bush Administration after 9-11 for its failure in the first nine months of the Administration to take action to combat terrorism, even though he had held this position since 1998, during which time he was the federal government lead for developing such a plan. However, as demonstrated in the article, the Clinton Administration Plan was doomed to failure from the beginning because the responsibilities placed on Richard Clarke were far beyond what could be accomplished from his subordinate position in the National Security Council with no mandate to require Cabinet-level participation.

The federal plan for responding to domestic terrorism was contained in these Presidential Decision Directives, PDD-39 U.S. Policy on Counterterrorism at http://www.fas.org/irp/offdocs/pdd39.htm

In the Presidential Decision Directive 39 (PDD 39), the FBI is designated as the lead agency for "domestic crisis response" and FEMA as the lead agency for "consequence management" for all weapons of mass destruction.

PDD-62 Protection Against Unconventional Threats to the Homeland and Americans Overseas at http://www.fas.org/irp/offdocs/pdd-62.htm which states the following:

Presidential Decision Directive-62
The following is an unclassified abstract derived from Presidential Decision Directive-62 (PDD-62), "Protection Against Unconventional Threats to the Homeland and Americans Overseas," dated May 22, 1998.

The full text of PDD-62 is a CLASSIFIED document. State and local officials should understand that PDD-62 reaffirms PDD-39, "United States Policy on Counterterrorism," signed June 21, 1995. As such, the Federal Bureau of Investigation (FBI) will continue to serve as the Lead Federal Agency for "crisis management" and the Federal Emergency Management Agency (FEMA) will continue to serve as the Lead Federal Agency for "consequence management."

1. General

ROLE OF THE FEDERAL GOVERNMENT IN BIODEFENSE

It is increasingly likely that terrorist groups, or individuals with criminal intent, may use unconventional methods to disrupt the Nation's critical infrastructure or use weapons of mass destruction (WMD) against our citizens.

As these types of threats mature, it is necessary to prepare to deter them, prevent them from occurring, or, if need be, limit the damage to a minimum. Success is dependent upon possessing the capability for an integrated response, and in the case of critical infrastructure protection, having public/private partnerships.

2. Present Achievements and Current Challenges
Present Achievements:
An increased rate of apprehensions and convictions;
An increase in counterterrorism legislative authorities;
An increase in the funding for consequence management planning;
An increase in the importance of terrorism on the diplomatic agenda;
Growth of assistance to, and cooperation with, other democracies in combating terrorism; and
Improving and expanding a professionally trained interagency cadre.

Current Challenges:
Terrorist groups may choose asymmetrical attacks on our domestic and international vulnerabilities, through the use of WMD and/or cyber warfare;
Terrorist groups possess the knowledge, skills, and abilities to use WMD;
Former "cold war" civil defense programs have been downsized or dismantled, and cities are not prepared to deal with a large-scale event;
Improvements in technology will make it difficult for law enforcement agencies to detect and prevent terrorist acts; and
The Nation's critical infrastructure relies heavily on the use of computers, which are prone to cyber attacks.

3. Consequences Management
In the event of a terrorism incident, the Federal Government will respond rapidly, working with State and local governments, to restore order and deliver emergency assistance. FEMA, the Lead Federal Agency for consequence management, is responsible for preparing for and responding to the consequences of a WMD incident with participation of other departments and agencies including the Public Health Service (PHS), Environmental Protection Agency (EPA), and Department of Energy (DOE), as necessary. The Department of Justice (DOJ), through the FBI, is the Lead Federal Agency for crisis management and operational response to a weapon of mass destruction incident.

Domestically, key Federal agencies and Departments, through interagency efforts, will continue training and providing equipment to first responders to prepare them for response to WMD incidents. Emphasis will be placed on preparing those responders in the largest 120 cities.

The Department of Defense, in coordination with other Federal Departments and agencies, will provide training to metropolitan first responders and will maintain trained military units to assist State and local responders. One example is the National Guard concept of initially forming 10 Rapid Assessment and Initial Detection (RAID) teams in each FEMA Region. These teams are designed to provide rapid response to a WMD incident and assist State and local responders.

PHS, in the Department of Health and Human Services, is the Lead Federal Agency in planning and preparing for response to WMD-related medical emergencies. PHS will continue supporting State and local governments in developing Metropolitan Medical Strike Teams; maintaining the National Disaster Medical System; and, in conjunction with the Department of Veterans Affairs, stockpiling antidotes and pharmaceuticals in the event of a WMD incident.

4. Equipment
DOJ, in coordination with FEMA, will provide equipment to State and local emergency responders.

5. Critical Infrastructure
It is imperative that the United States be adequately prepared to deal with attacks on critical infrastructure and cyber systems. As such, the President reviewed the recommendations of the Presidential Commission on Critical Infrastructure Protection and has signed PDD-63, entitled Protecting America's Critical Infrastructures (PDD-63 is For Official Use Only). A white paper, entitled "The Clinton Administration's Policy on Critical Infrastructure Protection: Presidential Decision Directive-63," is available at www.whitehouse.gov/WH/EOP/NSC/htm/NSCSDoo3.html. This white paper outlines the Administration's program to deal with threats to our Nation's critical infrastructure.

2.4.   How 9/11 and Amerithrax Changed the Federal Plan

Less than nine months after President George W. Bush took office, the terrorists' attacks occurred on September 11, 2001. After the World Trade Center was attacked, the question of bioterrorism was immediately considered. Federal officials visited the immediate wreckage fully suited in biosafety gear and considered whether a bioterrorism attack may have also occurred. The following guest editorial was published on September 22, 2001, and addresses this possibility:

> The tragic and horrific terrorist attack against the United States on Sept. 11 has left most of America in shock and disbelief that it could have happened. Our trust in our intelligence services—the FBI, domestically, and the CIA, internationally—has given us an earned sense of security in the past.
>
> Terrorist cells were identified and stopped during Desert Storm, and many potential terrorist attacks against the United States were aborted, and lacking any information, the public developed an unwarranted sense of security.
>
> The seriousness of this attack is more profound than the effect it will have on our way of life on air transportation or on our sense of safety in New York City or the Nation's Capital area.
>
> It forebodes a kind of terrorism which we have never experienced in America.
>
> Our understanding of mass disaster, debris removal, emergency medical response, and burn and crush victim medical knowledge has been developed and shaped over the decades.
>
> Even the response to the World Trade Center disaster draws upon the experience gained following the bombing in the World Trade Center in 1993; in particular for New York City's Emergency Services and St. Vincent's Hospital.
>
> Our national response teams were also well-experienced following natural disasters and practiced with mass emergencies calling for temporary triage units and rapid response.

ROLE OF THE FEDERAL GOVERNMENT IN BIODEFENSE

What does not bode well for our future in America is the threat of bioterrorism and the potential for mass destruction with no political, legal, scientific or coordinated national medical response structure much less a practiced response yet in place.

What works well with disasters like those involving the World Trade Center and the Pentagon has little relevance to a bioterrorism event.

Our ability to respond differs greatly from that following the World Trade Center disaster simply in that we may not know when we have been attacked. The release of a biological agent may not become evident for a week or more, and the silence of the attack will belie its deadly consequences. The response, too, must be different. Instead of a contained disaster within a given locality, the evacuation area will be vague and arbitrary because of the uncertainty of exposure to the biological agent.

For example, had a biological agent been released in New York City at the World Trade Center at ground level or at the 100th floor, the exposure would potentially extend to anyone who walked by in the preceding hour, with subsequent movement onto the subway system and into the suburbs, and onto aircraft and trains to all parts of the nation.

Our medical response teams would be faced with questions of quarantine and rapid identification of biological agents present in human tissues. The likelihood of genetically engineered organisms, with no existing vaccine, greatly exacerbates the danger. But this is just the beginning of the emergency, according to the mandate of the U.S. Constitution; the time at which a biological event becomes an emergency is much too late in the context of a biological event.

It is during times of peace that the federal government must be involved in monitoring and tracking the existence of biological agents; but in issues of public health, the U.S. Constitution clearly reserves those powers to the states, and they are not within the powers of the federal government.

This leaves a disjointed, uncoordinated assemblage of state jurisdictions recognizing geographic boundaries which biological agents certainly will not. Furthermore, in the disaster scenario, medical personnel will be unable to quarantine groups of people exposed, or believed to have been exposed, to biological agents, because our civil rights protections ensure that each person will have a separate hearing before they can be confined in quarantine against their will.

It is however, within the power of the U.S. Congress to respond to these legal impediments by developing a system of surveillance and protection from the threat of biological agents in accordance with U.S. constitutional protections for state sovereignty and individual freedoms.

Unfortunately, the U.S. Congress tends to respond only to disasters—Superfund legislation was the result of the Love Canal disaster; the Emergency Planning and Community Right to Know Act was the result of the Bhopal, India, disaster.

I can only hope that if anything good can come from the 9-11 tragedy it will be a call to action on the part of the U.S. Congress to exert leadership in establishing and funding national coordinated medical response systems needed. We need a legal system that can return a sense of security and safety to the American people and that recognized fully that America is in war with international terrorism.

Victoria Sutton, "It will be too late for Congress to act after bioterrorism attack is launched," op-ed, *Lubbock Avalanche Journal* (Saturday, Sept. 22, 2001).

The new, modern area of bioterrorism was triggered by these attacks, and new legislative proposals were quickly developed. One of the most widely known statutes passed in the days immediately following the attacks was the USA PATRIOT Act, signed into law on October 6, 2001, less than a month after the air attacks.

The traditional key agencies involved in domestic security and international security were those which had little role in public health issues: the Federal Bureau of Investigation, the Department of State, the National Security Council, and the Federal Emergency Management Agency. Under the nomenclature of CBN and WMD, there was no apparent need to ask other agencies to share in the responsibility and authority for addressing the threat of bioterrorism in a distinct or unique approach. This era continued into the 1990s when the Clinton Administration began to consider biological terrorism to be a real threat, again. Some administrative actions were taken and a new agency was developed within the Department of Defense, primarily to fund new projects which addressed all types of terrorism, but there was no distinction made between threats of biological terrorism and other threats of weapons of mass destruction.

The anthrax attacks of September 2001, which immediately followed the 9-11 attacks on the Pentagon in Washington, D.C. and the World Trade Center in New York, triggered the traditional protocol for weapons of mass destruction, omitting the involvement of public health at critical points of the response, and making it vividly evident to policy makers that these biothreats required a distinctly unique planning and response effort.

In October 2001, President George W. Bush created the Office of Homeland Security and the Homeland Security Council by Executive Order (Oct. 8, 2001), and appointed a Director, Governor Tom Ridge of Pennsylvania. This office examined the need for governmental reorganization, and in June 2002, the President proposed the Cabinet-level Department of Homeland Security. In November 2002, Congress passed the Homeland Security Act of 2002, establishing a Cabinet-level department with a mission to protect homeland security. The creation of a department was the first since the establishment of the Department of Veterans Affairs by President Reagan in 1988. However, it is the largest reorganization of government since the establishment of the Department of Defense and implementation of the National Security Act of 1947.

In February 28, 2003, the President issued HSPD-5, a domestic response strategy for emergencies, which highlighted the relationship between state and local governments and national responses.

The President also took immediate action to develop a new approach to organizing the federal government to respond to domestic terrorism. His series of directives were called Homeland Security Presidential Directives (HSPDs).

HSPD-5 Management of Domestic Incidents at http://www.fas.org/irp/offdocs/nspd/hspd-5.html, was issued February 28, 2003, to address the NIMS or national incident management system as a domestic response strategy.

Homeland Security Presidential Directive/HSPD-5
Subject: Management of Domestic Incidents

Purpose

(1) To enhance the ability of the United States to manage domestic incidents by establishing a single, comprehensive national incident management system.

Definitions

(2) In this directive:

(a) the term "Secretary" means the Secretary of Homeland Security.

(b) the term "Federal departments and agencies" means those executive departments enumerated in 5 U.S.C. 101, together with the Department of Homeland Security; independent establishments as defined by 5 U.S.C. 104(1); government corporations as defined by 5 U.S.C. 103(1); and the United States Postal Service.

(c) the terms "State," "local," and the "United States" when it is used in a geographical sense, have the same meanings as used in the Homeland Security Act of 2002, Public Law 107-296.

Policy

(3) To prevent, prepare for, respond to, and recover from terrorist attacks, major disasters, and other emergencies, the United States Government shall establish a single, comprehensive approach to domestic incident management. The objective of the United States Government is to ensure that all levels of government across the Nation have the capability to work efficiently and effectively together, using a national approach to domestic incident management. In these efforts, with regard to domestic incidents, the United States Government treats crisis management and consequence management as a single, integrated function, rather than as two separate functions.

(4) The Secretary of Homeland Security is the principal Federal official for domestic incident management. Pursuant to the Homeland Security Act of 2002, the Secretary is responsible for coordinating Federal operations within the United States to prepare for, respond to, and recover from terrorist attacks, major disasters, and other emergencies. The Secretary shall coordinate the Federal Government's resources utilized in response to or recovery from terrorist attacks, major disasters, or other emergencies if and when any one of the following four conditions applies: (1)a Federal department or agency acting under its own authority has requested the assistance of the Secretary; (2) the resources of State and local authorities are overwhelmed and Federal assistance has been requested by the appropriate State and local authorities; (3) more than one Federal department or agency has become substantially involved in responding to the incident; or (4) the Secretary has been directed to assume responsibility for managing the domestic incident by the President.

(5) Nothing in this directive alters, or impedes the ability to carry out, the authorities of Federal departments and agencies to perform their responsibilities under law. All Federal departments and agencies shall cooperate with the Secretary in the Secretary's domestic incident management role.

(6) The Federal Government recognizes the roles and responsibilities of State and local authorities in domestic incident management. Initial responsibility for managing domestic incidents generally falls on State and local authorities. The Federal Government will assist State and local authorities when their resources are overwhelmed, or when Federal interests are involved. The Secretary will coordinate with State and local governments to ensure adequate planning, equipment, training, and exercise activities. The Secretary will also provide assistance to State and local governments to develop all-hazards plans and capabilities, including those of greatest importance to the security of the United States, and will ensure that State, local, and Federal plans are compatible.

(7) The Federal Government recognizes the role that the private and nongovernmental sectors play in preventing, preparing for, responding to, and recovering from terrorist attacks, major disasters, and other emergencies. The Secretary will coordinate with the private and nongovernmental sectors to ensure adequate planning, equipment, training, and exercise activities and to promote partnerships to address incident management capabilities.

(8) The Attorney General has lead responsibility for criminal investigations of terrorist acts or terrorist threats by individuals or groups inside the United States, or directed at United States citizens or institutions abroad, where such acts are within the Federal criminal jurisdiction of the United States, as well as for related intelligence collection activities within the United States, subject to the National Security Act of 1947 and other applicable law, Executive Order 12333, and Attorney General-approved procedures pursuant to that Executive Order. Generally acting through the Federal Bureau of Investigation, the Attorney General, in cooperation with other Federal departments and agencies engaged in activities to protect our national security, shall also coordinate the activities of the other members of the law enforcement community to detect, prevent, preempt, and disrupt terrorist attacks against the United States. Following a terrorist threat or an actual incident that falls within the criminal jurisdiction of the United States, the full capabilities of the United States shall be dedicated, consistent with United States law and with activities of other Federal departments and agencies to protect our national security, to assisting the Attorney General to identify the perpetrators and bring them to justice. The Attorney General and the Secretary shall establish appropriate relationships and mechanisms for cooperation and coordination between their two departments.

(9) Nothing in this directive impairs or otherwise affects the authority of the Secretary of Defense over the Department of Defense, including the chain of command for military forces from the President as Commander in Chief, to the Secretary of Defense, to the commander of military forces, or military command and control procedures. The Secretary of Defense shall provide military support to civil authorities for domestic incidents as directed by the President or when consistent with military readiness and appropriate under the circumstances and the law. The Secretary of Defense shall retain command of military forces providing civil support. The Secretary of Defense and the Secretary shall establish appropriate relationships and mechanisms for cooperation and coordination between their two departments.

(10) The Secretary of State has the responsibility, consistent with other United States Government activities to protect our national security, to coordinate international activities related to the prevention, preparation, response, and recovery from a domestic incident, and for the protection of United States citizens and United States interests overseas. The Secretary of State and the Secretary shall establish appropriate relationships and mechanisms for cooperation and coordination between their two departments.

(11) The Assistant to the President for Homeland Security and the Assistant to the President for National Security Affairs shall be responsible for interagency policy coordination on domestic and international incident management, respectively, as directed by the President. The Assistant to the President for Homeland Security and the Assistant to the President for National Security Affairs shall work together to ensure that the United States domestic and international incident management efforts are seamlessly united.

(12) The Secretary shall ensure that, as appropriate, information related to domestic incidents is gathered and provided to the public, the private sector, State and local authorities, Federal departments and agencies, and, generally through the Assistant to the President for Homeland Security, to the President. The Secretary shall provide standardized, quantitative reports to the Assistant to the President for Homeland Security on the readiness and preparedness of the Nation -- at all levels of government -- to prevent, prepare for, respond to, and recover from domestic incidents.

(13) Nothing in this directive shall be construed to grant to any Assistant to the President any authority to issue orders to Federal departments and agencies, their officers, or their employees.

Tasking

(14) The heads of all Federal departments and agencies are directed to provide their full and prompt cooperation, resources, and support, as appropriate and consistent with their own responsibilities for protecting our national security, to the Secretary, the Attorney General, the Secretary of Defense, and the Secretary of State in the exercise of the individual leadership responsibilities and missions assigned in paragraphs (4), (8), (9), and (10), respectively, above.

(15) The Secretary shall develop, submit for review to the Homeland Security Council, and administer a National Incident Management System (NIMS). This system will provide a consistent nationwide approach for Federal, State, and local governments to work effectively and efficiently together to prepare for, respond to, and recover from domestic incidents, regardless of cause, size, or complexity. To provide for interoperability and compatibility among Federal, State, and local capabilities, the NIMS will include a core set of concepts, principles, terminology, and technologies covering the incident command system; multi-agency coordination systems; unified command; training; identification and management of resources (including systems for classifying types of resources); qualifications and certification; and the collection, tracking, and reporting of incident information and incident resources.

(16) The Secretary shall develop, submit for review to the Homeland Security Council, and administer a National Response Plan (NRP). The Secretary shall consult with appropriate Assistants to the President (including the Assistant to the President for Economic Policy) and the Director of the Office of Science and Technology Policy, and other such Federal officials as may be appropriate, in developing and implementing the NRP. This plan shall integrate Federal Government domestic prevention, preparedness, response, and recovery plans into one all-discipline, all-hazards plan. The NRP shall be unclassified. If certain operational aspects require classification, they shall be included in classified annexes to the NRP.

(a) The NRP, using the NIMS, shall, with regard to response to domestic incidents, provide the structure and mechanisms for national level policy and operational direction for Federal support to State and local incident managers and for exercising direct Federal authorities and responsibilities, as appropriate.

(b) The NRP will include protocols for operating under different threats or threat levels; incorporation of existing Federal emergency and incident management plans (with appropriate modifications and revisions) as either integrated components of the NRP or as supporting operational plans; and additional operational plans or annexes, as appropriate, including public affairs and intergovernmental communications.

(c) The NRP will include a consistent approach to reporting incidents, providing assessments, and making recommendations to the President, the Secretary, and the Homeland Security Council.

(d) The NRP will include rigorous requirements for continuous improvements from testing, exercising, experience with incidents, and new information and technologies.

(17) The Secretary shall:

(a) By April 1, 2003, (1) develop and publish an initial version of the NRP, in consultation with other Federal departments and agencies; and (2) provide the Assistant to the President for Homeland Security with a plan for full development and implementation of the NRP.

(b) By June 1, 2003, (1) in consultation with Federal departments and agencies and with State and local governments, develop a national system of standards, guidelines, and protocols to implement the NIMS; and (2) establish a mechanism for ensuring ongoing management and maintenance of the NIMS, including regular consultation with other Federal departments and agencies and with State and local governments.

(c) By September 1, 2003, in consultation with Federal departments and agencies and the Assistant to the President for Homeland Security, review existing authorities and regulations and prepare recommendations for the President on revisions necessary to implement fully the NRP.

(18) The heads of Federal departments and agencies shall adopt the NIMS within their departments and agencies and shall provide support and assistance to the Secretary in the development and maintenance of the NIMS. All Federal departments and agencies will use the NIMS in their domestic incident management and emergency prevention, preparedness, response, recovery, and mitigation activities, as well as those actions taken in support of State or local entities. The heads of Federal departments and agencies shall participate in the NRP, shall assist and support the Secretary in the development and maintenance of the NRP, and shall participate in and use domestic incident reporting systems and protocols established by the Secretary.

(19) The head of each Federal department and agency shall:

(a) By June 1, 2003, make initial revisions to existing plans in accordance with the initial version of the NRP.

(b) By August 1, 2003, submit a plan to adopt and implement the NIMS to the Secretary and the Assistant to the President for Homeland Security. The Assistant to the President for Homeland Security shall advise the President on whether such plans effectively implement the NIMS.

(20) Beginning in Fiscal Year 2005, Federal departments and agencies shall make adoption of the NIMS a requirement, to the extent permitted by law, for providing Federal preparedness assistance through grants, contracts, or other activities. The Secretary shall develop standards and guidelines for determining whether a State or local entity has adopted the NIMS.

. . . .[followed by technical amendments.]

On December 17, 2003, the President issued another HSPD to address federal preparedness and the relationship with state and local governments. The HSPD-8 National Preparedness is at http://www.ojp.usdoj.gov/odp/assessments/hspd8.htm, and appears below:

HSPD-8
Subject: National Preparedness

Purpose
(1) This directive establishes policies to strengthen the preparedness of the United States to prevent and respond to threatened or actual domestic terrorist attacks, major disasters, and other emergencies by requiring a national domestic all-hazards preparedness goal, establishing mechanisms for improved delivery of Federal preparedness assistance to State and local governments, and outlining actions to strengthen preparedness capabilities of Federal, State, and local entities.

Definitions

(2) For the purposes of this directive:

(a) The term "all-hazards preparedness" refers to preparedness for domestic terrorist attacks, major disasters, and other emergencies.

(b) The term "Federal departments and agencies" means those executive departments enumerated in 5 U.S.C. 101, and the Department of Homeland Security; independent establishments as defined by 5 U.S.C. 104(1); Government corporations as defined by 5 U.S.C. 103(1); and the United States Postal Service.

(c) The term "Federal preparedness assistance" means Federal department and agency grants, cooperative agreements, loans, loan guarantees, training, and/or technical assistance provided to State and local governments and the private sector to prevent, prepare for, respond to, and recover from terrorist attacks, major disasters, and other emergencies. Unless noted otherwise, the term "assistance" will refer to Federal assistance programs.

(d) The term "first responder" refers to those individuals who in the early stages of an incident are responsible for the protection and preservation of life, property, evidence, and the environment, including emergency response providers as defined in section 2 of the Homeland Security Act of 2002 (6 U.S.C. 101), as well as emergency management, public health, clinical care, public works, and other skilled support personnel (such as equipment operators) that provide immediate support services during prevention, response, and recovery operations.

(e) The terms "major disaster" and "emergency" have the meanings given in section 102 of the Robert T. Stafford Disaster Relief and Emergency Assistance Act (42 U.S.C. 5122).

(f) The term "major events" refers to domestic terrorist attacks, major disasters, and other emergencies.

(g) The term "national homeland security preparedness-related exercises" refers to homeland security-related exercises that train and test national decision makers and utilize resources of multiple Federal departments and agencies. Such exercises may involve State and local first responders when appropriate. Such exercises do not include those exercises conducted solely within a single Federal department or agency.

(h) The term "preparedness" refers to the existence of plans, procedures, policies, training, and equipment necessary at the Federal, State, and local level to maximize the ability to prevent, respond to, and recover from major events. The term "readiness" is used interchangeably with preparedness.

(i) The term "prevention" refers to activities undertaken by the first responder community during the early stages of an incident to reduce the likelihood or consequences of threatened or actual terrorist attacks. More general and broader efforts to deter, disrupt, or thwart terrorism are not addressed in this directive.

(j) The term "Secretary" means the Secretary of Homeland Security.

(k) The terms "State," and "local government," when used in a geographical sense, have the same meanings given to those terms in section 2 of the Homeland Security Act of 2002 (6 U.S.C. 101).

Relationship to HSPD-5

(3) This directive is a companion to HSPD-5, which identifies steps for improved coordination in response to incidents. This directive describes the way Federal departments and agencies will prepare for such a response, including prevention activities during the early stages of a terrorism incident.

Development of a National Preparedness Goal

(4) The Secretary is the principal Federal official for coordinating the implementation of all-hazards preparedness in the United States. In cooperation with other Federal departments and agencies, the

Secretary coordinates the preparedness of Federal response assets, and the support for, and assessment of, the preparedness of State and local first responders.

(5) To help ensure the preparedness of the Nation to prevent, respond to, and recover from threatened and actual domestic terrorist attacks, major disasters, and other emergencies, the Secretary, in coordination with the heads of other appropriate Federal departments and agencies and in consultation with State and local governments, shall develop a national domestic all-hazards preparedness goal. Federal departments and agencies will work to achieve this goal by:

(a) providing for effective, efficient, and timely delivery of Federal preparedness assistance to State and local governments; and

(b) supporting efforts to ensure first responders are prepared to respond to major events, especially prevention of and response to threatened terrorist attacks.

(6) The national preparedness goal will establish measurable readiness priorities and targets that appropriately balance the potential threat and magnitude of terrorist attacks, major disasters, and other emergencies with the resources required to prevent, respond to, and recover from them. It will also include readiness metrics and elements that support the national preparedness goal including standards for preparedness assessments and strategies, and a system for assessing the Nation's overall preparedness to respond to major events, especially those involving acts of terrorism.

(7) The Secretary will submit the national preparedness goal to me through the Homeland Security Council (HSC) for review and approval prior to, or concurrently with, the Department of Homeland Security's Fiscal Year 2006 budget submission to the Office of Management and Budget.

Federal Preparedness Assistance

(8) The Secretary, in coordination with the Attorney General, the Secretary of Health and Human Services (HHS), and the heads of other Federal departments and agencies that provide assistance for first responder preparedness, will establish a single point of access to Federal preparedness assistance program information within 60 days of the issuance of this directive. The Secretary will submit to me through the HSC recommendations of specific Federal department and agency programs to be part of the coordinated approach. All Federal departments and agencies will cooperate with this effort. Agencies will continue to issue financial assistance awards consistent with applicable laws and regulations and will ensure that program announcements, solicitations, application instructions, and other guidance documents are consistent with other Federal preparedness programs to the extent possible. Full implementation of a closely coordinated interagency grant process will be completed by September 30, 2005.

(9) To the extent permitted by law, the primary mechanism for delivery of Federal preparedness assistance will be awards to the States. Awards will be delivered in a form that allows the recipients to apply the assistance to the highest priority preparedness requirements at the appropriate level of government. To the extent permitted by law, Federal preparedness assistance will be predicated on adoption of Statewide comprehensive all-hazards preparedness strategies. The strategies should be consistent with the national preparedness goal, should assess the most effective ways to enhance preparedness, should address areas facing higher risk, especially to terrorism, and should also address local government concerns and Citizen Corps efforts. The Secretary, in coordination with the heads of other appropriate Federal departments and agencies, will review and approve strategies submitted by the States. To the extent permitted by law,

adoption of approved Statewide strategies will be a requirement for receiving Federal preparedness assistance at all levels of government by September 30, 2005.

(10) In making allocations of Federal preparedness assistance to the States, the Secretary, the Attorney General, the Secretary of HHS, the Secretary of Transportation, the Secretary of Energy, the Secretary of Veterans Affairs, the Administrator of the Environmental Protection Agency, and the heads of other Federal departments and agencies that provide assistance for first responder preparedness will base those allocations on assessments of population concentrations, critical infrastructures, and other significant risk factors, particularly terrorism threats, to the extent permitted by law.

(11) Federal preparedness assistance will support State and local entities' efforts including planning, training, exercises, interoperability, and equipment acquisition for major events as well as capacity building for prevention activities such as information gathering, detection, deterrence, and collaboration related to terrorist attacks. Such assistance is not primarily intended to support existing capacity to address normal local first responder operations, but to build capacity to address major events, especially terrorism.

(12) The Attorney General, the Secretary of HHS, the Secretary of Transportation, the Secretary of Energy, the Secretary of Veterans Affairs, the Administrator of the Environmental Protection Agency, and the heads of other Federal departments and agencies that provide assistance for first responder preparedness shall coordinate with the Secretary to ensure that such assistance supports and is consistent with the national preparedness goal.

(13) Federal departments and agencies will develop appropriate mechanisms to ensure rapid obligation and disbursement of funds from their programs to the States, from States to the local community level, and from local entities to the end users to derive maximum benefit from the assistance provided. Federal departments and agencies will report annually to the Secretary on the obligation, expenditure status, and the use of funds associated with Federal preparedness assistance programs.

Equipment

(14) The Secretary, in coordination with State and local officials, first responder organizations, the private sector and other Federal civilian departments and agencies, shall establish and implement streamlined procedures for the ongoing development and adoption of appropriate first responder equipment standards that support nationwide interoperability and other capabilities consistent with the national preparedness goal, including the safety and health of first responders.

(15) To the extent permitted by law, equipment purchased through Federal preparedness assistance for first responders shall conform to equipment standards in place at time of purchase. Other Federal departments and agencies that support the purchase of first responder equipment will coordinate their programs with the Department of Homeland Security and conform to the same standards.

(16) The Secretary, in coordination with other appropriate Federal departments and agencies and in consultation with State and local governments, will develop plans to identify and address national first responder equipment research and development needs based upon assessments of current and future threats. Other Federal departments and agencies that support preparedness research and development activities shall coordinate their efforts with the Department of Homeland Security and ensure they support the national preparedness goal.

Training and Exercises

(17) The Secretary, in coordination with the Secretary of HHS, the Attorney General, and other appropriate Federal departments and agencies and in consultation with State and local governments, shall establish and maintain a comprehensive training program to meet the national preparedness goal. The program will identify standards and maximize the effectiveness of existing Federal programs and financial assistance and include training for the Nation's first responders, officials, and others with major event preparedness, prevention, response, and recovery roles. Federal departments and agencies shall include private organizations in the accreditation and delivery of preparedness training as appropriate and to the extent permitted by law.

(18) The Secretary, in coordination with other appropriate Federal departments and agencies, shall establish a national program and a multi-year planning system to conduct homeland security preparedness-related exercises that reinforces identified training standards, provides for evaluation of readiness, and supports the national preparedness goal. The establishment and maintenance of the program will be conducted in maximum collaboration with State and local governments and appropriate private sector entities. All Federal departments and agencies that conduct national homeland security preparedness-related exercises shall participate in a collaborative, interagency process to designate such exercises on a consensus basis and create a master exercise calendar. The Secretary will ensure that exercises included in the calendar support the national preparedness goal. At the time of designation, Federal departments and agencies will identify their level of participation in national homeland security preparedness- related exercises. The Secretary will develop a multi-year national homeland security preparedness-related exercise plan and submit the plan to me through the HSC for review and approval.

(19) The Secretary shall develop and maintain a system to collect, analyze, and disseminate lessons learned, best practices, and information from exercises, training events, research, and other sources, including actual incidents, and establish procedures to improve national preparedness to prevent, respond to, and recover from major events. The Secretary, in coordination with other Federal departments and agencies and State and local governments, will identify relevant classes of homeland-security related information and appropriate means of transmission for the information to be included in the system. Federal departments and agencies are directed, and State and local governments are requested, to provide this information to the Secretary to the extent permitted by law.

Federal Department and Agency Preparedness

(20) The head of each Federal department or agency shall undertake actions to support the national preparedness goal, including adoption of quantifiable performance measurements in the areas of training, planning, equipment, and exercises for Federal incident management and asset preparedness, to the extent permitted by law. Specialized Federal assets such as teams, stockpiles, and caches shall be maintained at levels consistent with the national preparedness goal and be available for response activities as set forth in the National Response Plan, other appropriate operational documents, and applicable authorities or guidance. Relevant Federal regulatory requirements should be consistent with the national preparedness goal. Nothing in this directive shall limit the authority of the Secretary of Defense with regard to the command and control, training, planning, equipment, exercises, or employment of Department of Defense forces, or the allocation of Department of Defense resources.

(21) The Secretary, in coordination with other appropriate Federal civilian departments and agencies, shall develop and maintain a Federal response capability inventory that includes the performance parameters of the capability, the timeframe within which the capability can be brought to bear on an incident, and the readiness of such capability to respond to domestic incidents. The Department of Defense will provide to

the Secretary information describing the organizations and functions within the Department of Defense that may be utilized to provide support to civil authorities during a domestic crisis.

Citizen Participation

(22) The Secretary shall work with other appropriate Federal departments and agencies as well as State and local governments and the private sector to encourage active citizen participation and involvement in preparedness efforts. The Secretary shall periodically review and identify the best community practices for integrating private citizen capabilities into local preparedness efforts.

Public Communication

(23) The Secretary, in consultation with other Federal departments and agencies, State and local governments, and non-governmental organizations, shall develop a comprehensive plan to provide accurate and timely preparedness information to public citizens, first responders, units of government, the private sector, and other interested parties and mechanisms for coordination at all levels of government.

Assessment and Evaluation

(24) The Secretary shall provide to me through the Assistant to the President for Homeland Security an annual status report of the Nation's level of preparedness, including State capabilities, the readiness of Federal civil response assets, the utilization of mutual aid, and an assessment of how the Federal first responder preparedness assistance programs support the national preparedness goal. The first report will be provided within 1 year of establishment of the national preparedness goal.

(25) Nothing in this directive alters, or impedes the ability to carry out, the authorities of the Federal departments and agencies to perform their responsibilities under law and consistent with applicable legal authorities and presidential guidance.

(26) Actions pertaining to the funding and administration of financial assistance and all other activities, efforts, and policies in this directive shall be executed in accordance with law. To the extent permitted by law, these policies will be established and carried out in consultation with State and local governments.

(27) This directive is intended only to improve the internal management of the executive branch of the Federal Government, and it is not intended to, and does not, create any right or benefit, substantive or procedural, enforceable at law or in equity, against the United States, its departments, agencies, or other entities, its officers or employees, or any other person.

GEORGE W. BUSH

From 2003 until 2007, these directives provided guidance about biothreats and emergencies for coordination of the federal government. However, during this period of time, the SARS outbreak occurred in the international community, followed by the possibility of a pandemic influenza. By 2005, the federal government had developed a federal government-wide plan to address the possibility of a pandemic influenza and published the National Strategy for Combating Pandemic Influenza (2005) at http://www.whitehouse.gov/homeland/nspi.pdf. The federal government's lead on this plan was the Department of Health and Human Services. This was followed by specific steps with the Implementation Plan for the National Strategy for Combating Pandemic Influenza (2006).

These plans followed the HSPDs in terms of responsibilities and coordination.

Then, in 2006, the National Strategy for Combating Terrorism http://www.fas.org/irp/threat/nsct2006.pdf, was released by the White House. The strategy can be summarized as a two-prong strategy, with long-term and a short-term components:

Long-term approach: Advancing effective democracy
Short-term approach:
    Four priorities of action.
    1. Prevent attacks by terrorist networks
    2. Deny WMD to rogue states and terrorist allies who seek to use them
    3. Deny terrorists the support and sanctuary of rogue states
    4. Deny terrorists control of any nation they would use as a base and launching pad for terror

The strategy does not specifically address the threat of biological weapons or biothreats, but instead broadly considers all weapons of mass destruction.

The most sweeping HSPD by far, issued by President George W. Bush, is HSPD-21 National Strategy for Public Health and Medical Preparedness at http://www.upmc-biosecurity.org/website/resources/commentary/2007-10-23-summaryof_HSPD-21.html. This directive requires changes to intragovernmental and intergovernmental relationships.

Homeland Security Presidential Directive
HOMELAND SECURITY PRESIDENTIAL DIRECTIVE/HSPD-21
Subject: Public Health and Medical Preparedness

Purpose
(1) This directive establishes a National Strategy for Public Health and Medical Preparedness (Strategy), which builds upon principles set forth in Biodefense for the 21st Century (April 2004) and will transform our national approach to protecting the health of the American people against all disasters.

Definitions

(2) In this directive:
(a) The term "biosurveillance" means the process of active data-gathering with appropriate analysis and interpretation of biosphere data that might relate to disease activity and threats to human or animal health – whether infectious, toxic, metabolic, or otherwise, and regardless of intentional or natural origin – in order to achieve early warning of health threats, early detection of health events, and overall situational awareness of disease activity;

(b) The term "catastrophic health event" means any natural or manmade incident, including terrorism, that results in a number of ill or injured persons sufficient to overwhelm the capabilities of immediate local and regional emergency response and health care systems;

(c) The term "epidemiologic surveillance" means the process of actively gathering and analyzing data related to human health and disease in a population in order to obtain early warning of human health events, rapid characterization of human disease events, and overall situational awareness of disease activity in the human population;

(d) The term "medical" means the science and practice of maintenance of health and prevention, diagnosis, treatment, and alleviation of disease or injury and the provision of those services to individuals;

(e) The term "public health" means the science and practice of protecting and improving the overall health of the community through disease prevention and early diagnosis, control of communicable diseases, health education, injury prevention, sanitation, and protection from environmental hazards;

(f) The term "public health and medical preparedness" means the existence of plans, procedures, policies, training, and equipment necessary to maximize the ability to prevent, respond to, and recover from major events, including efforts that result in the capability to render an appropriate public health and medical response that will mitigate the effects of illness and injury, limit morbidity and mortality to the maximum extent possible, and sustain societal, economic, and political infrastructure; and

(g) The terms "State" and "local government," when used in a geographical sense, have the meanings ascribed to such terms respectively in section 2 of the Homeland Security Act of 2002 (6 U.S.C. 101).

Background

(3) A catastrophic health event, such as a terrorist attack with a weapon of mass destruction (WMD), a naturally-occurring pandemic, or a calamitous meteorological or geological event, could cause tens or hundreds of thousands of casualties or more, weaken our economy, damage public morale and confidence, and threaten our national security. It is therefore critical that we establish a strategic vision that will enable a level of public health and medical preparedness sufficient to address a range of possible disasters.

(4) The United States has made significant progress in public health and medical preparedness since 2001, but we remain vulnerable to events that threaten the health of large populations. The attacks of 9-11 and Hurricane Katrina were the most significant recent disasters faced by the United States, yet casualty numbers were small in comparison to the 1995 Kobe earthquake; the 2003 Bam, Iran, earthquake; the 2004 Sumatra tsunami; and what we would expect from a 1918-like influenza pandemic or large-scale WMD attack. Such events could immediately overwhelm our public health and medical systems.

(5) This Strategy draws key principles from the National Strategy for Homeland Security (October 2007), the National Strategy to Combat Weapons of Mass Destruction (December 2002), and Biodefense for the 21st Century (April 2004) that can be generally applied to public health and medical preparedness. Those key principles are the following: (1) preparedness for all potential catastrophic health events; (2) vertical and horizontal coordination across levels of government, jurisdictions, and disciplines; (3) a regional approach to health preparedness; (4) engagement of the private sector, academia, and other nongovernmental entities in preparedness and response efforts; and (5) the important roles of individuals, families, and communities.

(6) Present public health and medical preparedness plans incorporate the concept of "surging" existing medical and public health capabilities in response to an event that threatens a large number of lives. The assumption that conventional public health and medical systems can function effectively in catastrophic health events has, however, proved to be incorrect in real-world situations. Therefore, it is necessary to transform the national approach to health care in the context of a catastrophic health event in order to enable U.S. public health and medical systems to respond effectively to a broad range of incidents.

(7) The most effective complex service delivery systems result from rigorous end-to-end system design. A critical and formal process by which the functions of public health and medical preparedness and response are designed to integrate all vertical (through all levels of government) and horizontal (across all sectors in communities) components can achieve a much greater capability than we currently have.

(8) The United States has tremendous resources in both public and private sectors that could be used to prepare for and respond to a catastrophic health event. To exploit those resources fully, they must be organized in a rationally designed system that is incorporated into pre-event planning, deployed in a coordinated manner in response to an event, and guided by a constant and timely flow of relevant information during an event. This Strategy establishes principles and objectives to improve our ability to respond comprehensively to catastrophic health events. It also identifies critical antecedent components of this capability and directs the development of an implementation plan that will delineate further specific actions and guide the process to fruition.

(9) This Strategy focuses on human public health and medical systems; it does not address other areas critical to overall public health and medical preparedness, such as animal health systems, food and agriculture defense, global partnerships in public health, health threat intelligence activities, domestic and international biosecurity, and basic and applied research in threat diseases and countermeasures. Efforts in those areas are addressed in other policy documents.

(10) It is not possible to prevent all casualties in catastrophic events, but strategic improvements in our Federal, State, and local planning can prepare our Nation to deliver appropriate care to the largest possible number of people, lessen the impact on limited health care resources, and support the continuity of society and government.

Policy

(11) It is the policy of the United States to plan and enable provision for the public health and medical needs of the American people in the case of a catastrophic health event through continual and timely flow of information during such an event and rapid public health and medical response that marshals all available national capabilities and capacities in a rapid and coordinated manner.

Implementation Actions
(12) Biodefense for the 21st Century provides a foundation for the transformation of our catastrophic health event response and preparedness efforts. Although the four pillars of that framework – Threat Awareness, Prevention and Protection, Surveillance and Detection, and Response and Recovery – were developed to guide our efforts to defend against a bioterrorist attack, they are applicable to a broad array of natural and manmade public health and medical challenges and are appropriate to serve as the core functions of the Strategy for Public Health and Medical Preparedness.

(13) To accomplish our objectives, we must create a firm foundation for community medical preparedness. We will increase our efforts to inform citizens and empower communities, buttress our public health infrastructure, and explore options to relieve current pressures on our emergency departments and emergency medical systems so that they retain the flexibility to prepare for and respond to events.

(14) Ultimately, the Nation must collectively support and facilitate the establishment of a discipline of disaster health. The specialty of emergency medicine evolved as a result of the recognition of the special considerations in emergency patient care, and similarly the recognition of the unique principles in disaster-

related public health and medicine merit the establishment of their own formal discipline. Such a discipline will provide a foundation for doctrine, education, training, and research and will integrate preparedness into the public health and medical communities.

Critical Components of Public Health and Medical Preparedness

(15) Currently, the four most critical components of public health and medical preparedness are biosurveillance, countermeasure distribution, mass casualty care, and community resilience. Although those capabilities do not address all public health and medical preparedness requirements, they currently hold the greatest potential for mitigating illness and death and therefore will receive the highest priority in our public health and medical preparedness efforts. Those capabilities constitute the focus and major objectives of this Strategy.

(16) Biosurveillance: The United States must develop a nationwide, robust, and integrated biosurveillance capability, with connections to international disease surveillance systems, in order to provide early warning and ongoing characterization of disease outbreaks in near real-time. Surveillance must use multiple modalities and an in-depth architecture. We must enhance clinician awareness and participation and strengthen laboratory diagnostic capabilities and capacity in order to recognize potential threats as early as possible. Integration of biosurveillance elements and other data (including human health, animal health, agricultural, meteorological, environmental, intelligence, and other data) will provide a comprehensive picture of the health of communities and the associated threat environment for incorporation into the national "common operating picture." A central element of biosurveillance must be an epidemiologic surveillance system to monitor human disease activity across populations. That system must be sufficiently enabled to identify specific disease incidence and prevalence in heterogeneous populations and environments and must possess sufficient flexibility to tailor analyses to new syndromes and emerging diseases. State and local government health officials, public and private sector health care institutions, and practicing clinicians must be involved in system design, and the overall system must be constructed with the principal objective of establishing or enhancing the capabilities of State and local government entities.

(17) Countermeasure Stockpiling and Distribution: In the context of a catastrophic health event, rapid distribution of medical countermeasures (vaccines, drugs, and therapeutics) to a large population requires significant resources within individual communities. Few if any cities are presently able to meet the objective of dispensing countermeasures to their entire population within 48 hours after the decision to do so. Recognizing that State and local government authorities have the primary responsibility to protect their citizens, the Federal Government will create the appropriate framework and policies for sharing information on best practices and mechanisms to address the logistical challenges associated with this requirement. The Federal Government must work with nonfederal stakeholders to create effective templates for countermeasure distribution and dispensing that State and local government authorities can use to build their own capabilities.

(18) Mass Casualty Care: The structure and operating principles of our day-to-day public health and medical systems cannot meet the needs created by a catastrophic health event. Collectively, our Nation must develop a disaster medical capability that can immediately re-orient and coordinate existing resources within all sectors to satisfy the needs of the population during a catastrophic health event. Mass casualty care response must be (1) rapid, (2) flexible, (3) scalable, (4) sustainable, (5) exhaustive (drawing upon all national resources), (6) comprehensive (addressing needs from acute to chronic care and including mental health and special needs populations), (7) integrated and coordinated, and (8) appropriate (delivering the correct treatment in the most ethical manner with available capabilities). We

must enhance our capability to protect the physical and mental health of survivors; protect responders and health care providers; properly and respectfully dispose of the deceased; ensure continuity of society, economy, and government; and facilitate long-term recovery of affected citizens.

(19) The establishment of a robust disaster health capability requires us to develop an operational concept for the medical response to catastrophic health events that is substantively distinct from and broader than that which guides day-to-day operations. In order to achieve that transformation, the Federal Government will facilitate and provide leadership for key stakeholders to establish the following four foundational elements: Doctrine, System Design, Capacity, and Education and Training. The establishment of those foundational elements must result from efforts within the relevant professional communities and will require many years, but the Federal Government can serve as an important catalyst for this process.

(20) Community Resilience: The above components address the supply side of the preparedness function, ultimately providing enhanced services to our citizens. The demand side is of equal importance. Where local civic leaders, citizens, and families are educated regarding threats and are empowered to mitigate their own risk, where they are practiced in responding to events, where they have social networks to fall back upon, and where they have familiarity with local public health and medical systems, there will be community resilience that will significantly attenuate the requirement for additional assistance. The Federal Government must formulate a comprehensive plan for promoting community public health and medical preparedness to assist State and local authorities in building resilient communities in the face of potential catastrophic health events.

Biosurveillance

(21) The Secretary of Health and Human Services shall establish an operational national epidemiologic surveillance system for human health, with international connectivity where appropriate, that is predicated on State, regional, and community-level capabilities and creates a networked system to allow for two-way information flow between and among Federal, State, and local government public health authorities and clinical health care providers. The system shall build upon existing Federal, State, and local surveillance systems where they exist and shall enable and provide incentive for public health agencies to implement local surveillance systems where they do not exist. To the extent feasible, the system shall be built using electronic health information systems. It shall incorporate flexibility and depth of data necessary to respond to previously unknown or emerging threats to public health and integrate its data into the national biosurveillance common operating picture as appropriate. The system shall protect patient privacy by restricting access to identifying information to the greatest extent possible and only to public health officials with a need to know. The Implementation Plan to be developed pursuant to section 43 of this directive shall specify milestones for this system.

(22) Within 180 days after the date of this directive, the Secretary of Health and Human Services, in coordination with the Secretaries of Defense, Veterans Affairs, and Homeland Security, shall establish an Epidemiologic Surveillance Federal Advisory Committee, including representatives from State and local government public health authorities and appropriate private sector health care entities, in order to ensure that the Federal Government is meeting the goal of enabling State and local government public health surveillance capabilities.

Countermeasure Stockpiling and Distribution

(23) In accordance with the schedule set forth below, the Secretary of Health and Human Services, in coordination with the Secretary of Homeland Security, shall develop templates, using a variety of tools and including private sector resources when necessary, that provide minimum operational plans to enable communities to distribute and dispense countermeasures to their populations within 48 hours after a decision to do so. The Secretary of Health and Human Services shall ensure that this process utilizes current cooperative programs and engages Federal, State, local government, and private sector entities in template development, modeling, testing, and evaluation. The Secretary shall also assist State, local government, and regional entities in tailoring templates to fit differing geographic sizes, population densities, and demographics, and other unique or specific local needs. In carrying out such actions, the Secretary shall:

(a) within 270 days after the date of this directive, (i) publish an initial template or templates meeting the requirements above, including basic testing of component distribution mechanisms and modeling of template systems to predict performance in large-scale implementation, (ii) establish standards and performance measures for State and local government countermeasure distribution systems, including demonstration of specific capabilities in tactical exercises in accordance with the National Exercise Program, and (iii) establish a process to gather performance data from State and local participants on a regular basis to assess readiness; and

(b) within 180 days after the completion of the tasks set forth in (a), and with appropriate notice, commence collecting and using performance data and metrics as conditions for future public health preparedness grant funding.

(24) Within 270 days after the date of this directive, the Secretary of Health and Human Services, in coordination with the Secretaries of Defense, Veterans Affairs, and Homeland Security and the Attorney General, shall develop Federal Government capabilities and plans to complement or supplement State and local government distribution capacity, as appropriate and feasible, if such entities' resources are deemed insufficient to provide access to countermeasures in a timely manner in the event of a catastrophic health event.

(25) The Secretary of Health and Human Services shall ensure that the priority-setting process for the acquisition of medical countermeasures and other critical medical materiel for the Strategic National Stockpile (SNS) is transparent and risk-informed with respect to the scope, quantities, and forms of the various products. Within 180 days after the date of this directive, the Secretary, in coordination with the Secretaries of Defense, Homeland Security, and Veterans Affairs, shall establish a formal mechanism for the annual review of SNS composition and development of recommendations that utilizes input from accepted national risk assessments and threat assessments, national planning scenarios, national modeling resources, and subject matter experts. The results of each such annual review shall be provided to the Director of the Office of Management and Budget and the Assistant to the President for Homeland Security and Counterterrorism at the time of the Department of Health and Human Services' next budget submission.

(26) Within 90 days after the date of this directive, the Secretary of Health and Human Services shall establish a process to share relevant information regarding the contents of the SNS with Federal, State, and local government health officers with appropriate clearances and a need to know.

(27) Within 180 days after the date of this directive, the Secretary of Health and Human Services, in coordination with the Secretaries of State, Defense, Agriculture, Veterans Affairs, and Homeland Security, shall develop protocols for sharing countermeasures and medical goods between the SNS and other

Federal stockpiles and shall explore appropriate reciprocal arrangements with foreign and international stockpiles of medical countermeasures to ensure the availability of necessary supplies for use in the United States.

Mass Casualty Care

(28)   The Secretary of Health and Human Services, in coordination with the Secretaries of Defense, Veterans Affairs, and Homeland Security, shall directly engage relevant State and local government, academic, professional, and private sector entities and experts to provide feedback on the review of the National Disaster Medical System and national medical surge capacity required by the Pandemic and All-Hazards Preparedness Act (PAHPA) (Public Law 109-417) . Within 270 days after the completion of such review, the Secretary shall identify, through a systems-based approach involving expertise from such entities and experts, high-priority gaps in mass casualty care capabilities, and shall submit to the Assistant to the President for Homeland Security and Counterterrorism a concept plan that identifies and coordinates all Federal, State, and local government and private sector public health and medical disaster response resources, and identifies options for addressing critical deficits, in order to achieve the system attributes described in this Strategy.

(29)   Within 180 days after the date of this directive, the Secretary of Health and Human Services, in coordination with the Secretaries of Defense, Veterans Affairs, and Homeland Security, shall:

(a) build upon the analysis of Federal facility use to provide enhanced medical surge capacity in disasters required by section 302 of PAHPA to analyze the use of Federal medical facilities as a foundational element of public health and medical preparedness; and

(b) develop and implement plans and enter into agreements to integrate such facilities more effectively into national and regional education, training, and exercise preparedness activities.

(30)   The Secretary of Health and Human Services shall lead an interagency process, in coordination with the Secretaries of Defense, Veterans Affairs, and Homeland Security and the Attorney General, to identify any legal, regulatory, or other barriers to public health and medical preparedness and response from Federal, State, or local government or private sector sources that can be eliminated by appropriate regulatory or legislative action and shall, within 120 days after the date of this directive, submit a report on such barriers to the Assistant to the President for Homeland Security and Counterterrorism.

(31)   The impact of the "worried well" in past disasters is well documented, and it is evident that mitigating the mental health consequences of disasters can facilitate effective response.   Recognizing that maintaining and restoring mental health in disasters has not received sufficient attention to date, within 180 days after the date of this directive, the Secretary of Health and Human Services, in coordination with the Secretaries of Defense, Veterans Affairs, and Homeland Security, shall establish a Federal Advisory Committee for Disaster Mental Health. The committee shall consist of appropriate subject matter experts and, within 180 days after its establishment, shall submit to the Secretary of Health and Human Services recommendations for protecting, preserving, and restoring individual and community mental health in catastrophic health event settings, including pre-event, intra-event, and post-event education, messaging, and interventions.

Community Resilience

(32)   The Secretary of Health and Human Services, in coordination with the Secretaries of Defense, Veterans Affairs, and Homeland Security, shall ensure that core public health and medical curricula and training developed pursuant to PAHPA address the needs to improve individual, family, and institutional public health and medical preparedness, enhance private citizen opportunities for contributions to local, regional, and national preparedness and response, and build resilient communities.

(33)   Within 270 days after the date of this directive, the Secretary of Health and Human Services, in coordination with the Secretaries of Defense, Commerce, Labor, Education, Veterans Affairs, and Homeland Security and the Attorney General, shall submit to the President for approval, through the Assistant to the President for Homeland Security and Counterterrorism, a plan to promote comprehensive community medical preparedness.

Risk Awareness

(34)   The Secretary of Homeland Security, in coordination with the Secretary of Health and Human Services, shall prepare an unclassified briefing for non-health professionals that clearly outlines the scope of the risks to public health posed by relevant threats and catastrophic health events (including attacks involving weapons of mass destruction), shall coordinate such briefing with the heads of other relevant executive departments and agencies, shall ensure that full use is made of Department of Defense expertise and resources, and shall ensure that all State governors and the mayors and senior county officials from the 50 largest metropolitan statistical areas in the United States receive such briefing, unless specifically declined, within 150 days after the date of this directive.

(35)   Within 180 days after the date of this directive, the Secretary of Homeland Security, in coordination with the Attorney General, the Secretary of Health and Human Services, and the Director of National Intelligence, shall establish a mechanism by which up-to-date and specific public health threat information shall be relayed, to the greatest extent possible and not inconsistent with the established guidance relating to the Information Sharing Environment, to relevant public health officials at the State and local government levels and shall initiate a process to ensure that qualified heads of State and local government entities have the opportunity to obtain appropriate security clearances so that they may receive classified threat information when applicable.

Education and Training

(36)   Within 180 days after the date of this directive, the Secretary of Health and Human Services, in coordination with the Secretary of Homeland Security, shall develop and thereafter maintain processes for coordinating Federal grant programs for public health and medical preparedness using grant application guidance, investment justifications, reporting, program performance measures, and accountability for future funding in order to promote cross-sector, regional, and capability-based coordination, consistent with section 201 of PAHPA and the National Preparedness Guidelines developed pursuant to Homeland Security Presidential Directive-8 of December 17, 2003 ("National Preparedness").

(37)   Within 1 year after the date of this directive, the Secretary of Health and Human Services, in coordination with the Secretaries of Defense, Transportation, Veterans Affairs, and Homeland Security, and consistent with section 304 of PAHPA, shall develop a mechanism to coordinate public health and medical disaster preparedness and response core curricula and training across executive departments and agencies, to ensure standardization and commonality of knowledge, procedures, and terms of reference within the Federal Government that also can be communicated to State and local government entities, as well as academia and the private sector.

(38) Within 1 year after the date of this directive, the Secretaries of Health and Human Services and Defense, in coordination with the Secretaries of Veterans Affairs and Homeland Security, shall establish an academic Joint Program for Disaster Medicine and Public Health housed at a National Center for Disaster Medicine and Public Health at the Uniformed Services University of the Health Sciences. The Program shall lead Federal efforts to develop and propagate core curricula, training, and research related to medicine and public health in disasters. The Center will be an academic center of excellence in disaster medicine and public health, co-locating education and research in the related specialties of domestic medical preparedness and response, international health, international disaster and humanitarian medical assistance, and military medicine. Department of Health and Human Services and Department of Defense authorities will be used to carry out respective civilian and military missions within this joint program.

Disaster Health System

(39) Within 180 days after the date of this directive, the Secretary of Health and Human Services shall commission the Institute of Medicine to lead a forum engaging Federal, State, and local governments, the private sector, academia, and appropriate professional societies in a process to facilitate the development of national disaster public health and medicine doctrine and system design and to develop a strategy for long-term enhancement of disaster public health and medical capacity and the propagation of disaster public health and medicine education and training.

(40) Within 120 days after the date of this directive, the Secretary of Health and Human Services shall submit to the President through the Assistant to the President for Homeland Security and Counterterrorism, and shall commence the implementation of, a plan to use current grant funding programs, private payer incentives, market forces, Center for Medicare and Medicaid Services requirements, and other means to create financial incentives to enhance private sector health care facility preparedness in such a manner as to not increase health care costs.

(41) Within 180 days after the date of this directive, the Secretary of Health and Human Services, in coordination with the Secretaries of Transportation and Homeland Security, shall establish within the Department of Health and Human Services an Office for Emergency Medical Care. Under the direction of the Secretary, such Office shall lead an enterprise to promote and fund research in emergency medicine and trauma health care; promote regional partnerships and more effective emergency medical systems in order to enhance appropriate triage, distribution, and care of routine community patients; promote local, regional, and State emergency medical systems' preparedness for and response to public health events. The Office shall address the full spectrum of issues that have an impact on care in hospital emergency departments, including the entire continuum of patient care from pre-hospital to disposition from emergency or trauma care. The Office shall coordinate with existing executive departments and agencies that perform functions relating to emergency medical systems in order to ensure unified strategy, policy, and implementation.

National Health Security Strategy

(42) The PAHPA requires that the Secretary of Health and Human Services submit in 2009, and quadrennially afterward, a National Health Security Strategy (NHSS) to the Congress. The principles and actions in this directive, and in the Implementation Plan required by section 43, shall be incorporated into the initial NHSS, as appropriate, and shall serve as a foundation for the preparedness goals contained therein.

Task Force and Implementation Plan

(43) In order to facilitate the implementation of the policy outlined in this Strategy, there is established the Public Health and Medical Preparedness Task Force (Task Force). Within 120 days after the date of this directive, the Task Force shall submit to the President for approval, through the Assistant to the President for Homeland Security and Counterterrorism, an Implementation Plan (Plan) for this Strategy, and annually thereafter shall submit to the Assistant to the President for Homeland Security and Counterterrorism a status report on the implementation of the Plan and any recommendations for changes to this Strategy.

(a) The Task Force shall consist exclusively of the following members (or their designees who shall be full-time officers or employees of the members' respective agencies):

(i) The Secretary of Health and Human Services, who shall serve as Chair;
(ii) The Secretary of State;
(ii) The Secretary of Defense;
(iii) The Attorney General;
(iv) The Secretary of Agriculture;
(v) The Secretary of Commerce;
(vi) The Secretary of Labor;
(vii) The Secretary of Transportation;
(viii) The Secretary of Veterans Affairs
(ix) The Secretary of Homeland Security;
(x) The Director of the Office of Management and Budget;
 (xi) The Director of National Intelligence; and
(xii) such other officers of the United States as the Chair of the Task Force may designate from time to time.

(b) The Chair of the Task Force shall, as appropriate to deal with particular subject matters, establish subcommittees of the Task Force that shall consist exclusively of members of the Task Force (or their designees under subsection (a) of this section), and such other full-time or permanent part-time officers or employees of the Federal Government as the Chair may designate.

(c) The Plan shall:

(i) provide additional detailed roles and responsibilities of heads of executive departments and agencies relating to and consistent with the Strategy and actions set forth in this directive;

(ii) provide additional guidance on public health and medical directives in Biodefense for the 21st Century; and

(iii) direct the full examination of resource requirements.

(d) The Plan and all Task Force reports shall be developed in coordination with the Biodefense Policy Coordination Committee of the Homeland Security Council and shall then be prepared for consideration by and submitted to the more senior committees of the Homeland Security Council, as deemed appropriate by the Assistant to the President for Homeland Security and Counterterrorism.

General Provisions

(44) This directive:

(a)   shall be implemented consistent with applicable law and the authorities of executive departments and agencies, or heads of such departments and agencies, vested by law, and subject to the availability of appropriations and within the current projected spending levels for Federal health entitlement programs;

(b)   shall not be construed to impair or otherwise affect the functions of the Director of the Office of Management and Budget relating to budget, administrative, and legislative proposals; and

(c)   is not intended, and does not, create any rights or benefits, substantive or procedural, enforceable at law or in equity by a party against the United States, its departments, agencies, instrumentalities, or entities, its officers, employees, or agents, or any other person.

Federal Government Leadership in Bioterrorism—Who's in Charge?

The admitted shortcomings of the FBI include domestic bioterrorism, preparedness, and response as well as lack of expertise with respect to all weapons of mass destruction, its limited experience in counter-intelligence within governmental agencies, and its lack of skills crucial to the investigation and apprehension of extra-governmental counterintelligence agents involved in bioterrorism events. For example, Senator Feinstein remarked after testimony from FBI Director –Mueller, during the first week in November in 2002, "I was really taken aback by how little they seem to know." In October, the FBI was consulted about the destruction of more than 100 vials of different anthrax strains collected by the Iowa State University in Ames, and even after discovery that the Florida incident of anthrax was a result of terrorism, the FBI approved the destruction of this vital collection and data base collection. This more than illustrates the absolute lack of understanding and training on the part of the FBI in comprehending that the anthrax collection could have provided invaluable evidence in identifying the source of the anthrax, by comparing the DNA of the anthrax found in Florida with that of strains in the collection. But training alone is not sufficient for an agency that lacks the ability to make a culture shift. Just in November, after at least six weeks for the FBI to become familiar with anthrax investigations, the FBI still was not trained for basic investigations of anthrax threats.

In early November, the Congress approved an additional $250 million increase to the FBI, raising its budget to almost $3.5 billion.

2.5.   Reorganization in Response to 9/11 and Amerithrax: An Examination of the Roles of the Federal Departments and Agencies

The following sections address the roles based in enabling legislation and implementation of legislation of each federal agency and department in respect to biosecurity, bioterrorism, and emerging infectious disease emergencies:

2.5.1. The Department of Homeland Security

The Department of Homeland Security was created by the Homeland Security Act of 2002, and utilized existing federal authorities, bringing together under one department programs and components of other departments and agencies.

ROLE OF THE FEDERAL GOVERNMENT IN BIODEFENSE

Organization of the Department of Homeland Security

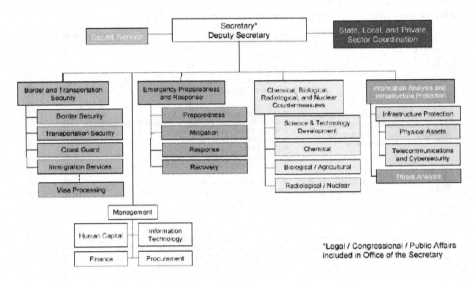

Fig. 2.2   President's Proposal for the Organization of the Department of Homeland Security

The review of the President's plan for a Department of Homeland Security shows that biological threats are in an office focused on countermeasures and combined with agricultural. The main aspect of a biodefense in this organization is through the "state, local and private sector coordination," which maintains state sovereignty over public health affairs, whereas the agricultural and biological threats could be managed by the Department through existing federal authorities, such as food safety and inspection statutes and regulations.

Department of Homeland Security

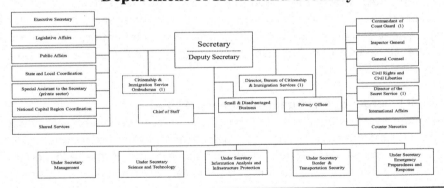

Fig. 2.3 The Homeland Security Act of 2002, resulted in this initial organization of the Department of Homeland Security, effective March 1, 2003

In 2003, the first organization of the Department of Homeland Security (Fig. 2.3) utilized the "state and local coordination" function as a link to the Office of the Security, and biological threats were addressed solely through the science and technology office of the undersecretary as a research and development function, rather than assuming any responsibility for planning or responding to biological threats.

A Single Roof for Homeland Security

The Department of Homeland Security would absorb the operations of a large portion of the executive branch.

COMPONENT	MISSION	OPERATIONS ABSORBED	MOVED FROM
Border and transportation security	Bring the major border security and transportation operations under one roof.	■ Immigration and Naturalization Service ■ Customs Service ■ Animal and Plant Health Inspection Service (part) ■ Coast Guard ■ Federal Protective Service ■ Transportation Security Administration	Justice Treasury Agriculture Transportation GSA Transportation
Emergency preparedness and response	Oversee domestic distaster preparedness training and coordinate government disaster response.	■ Federal Emergency Management Agency ■ Chemical, Biological, Radiological and Nuclear Response Assets ■ Domestic Emergency Support Team ■ Nuclear Incident Response ■ Domestic emergency support teams ■ Federal Law Enforcement Training Center ■ National Domestic Preparedness Office	(Independent) HHS (Interagency) Energy Justice Treasury FBI
Science and Technology	Lead federal government's efforts to prepare for and respond to terrorist threats involving weapons of mass destruction, including agroterrorism.	■ Civilian Biodefense Research Programs ■ Lawrence Livermore National Laboratory (part) ■ National BW Defense Analysis Center ■ Plum Island Animal Disease Center	HHS Energy (New) Agriculture
Information analysis and infrastructure protection	Analyze homeland intelligence from other agencies involving threats to homeland security. Evaluate vulnerabilities of the nation's infrastructure.	■ Critical Infrastructure Assurance Office ■ Federal Computer Incident Response Center ■ National Communications System ■ National Infrastructure Protection Center ■ National Infrastructure Simulation and Analysis Center	Commerce GSA Defense FBI Energy
Secret Service	The Secret Service reports directly to the secretary of homeland security. It would remain intact, and its primary mission remains the protection of the president and other government leaders.		Treasury
Coast Guard	The Coast Guard would report directly to the secretary of homeland security. It would remain intact, and its primary mission would remain securing the nation's waters and ports.		Transportation

Department of Homeland Security

SOURCE: Department of Homeland Security Book, courtesy of The White House (www.whitehouse.gov)   THE WASHINGTON POST

Fig. 2.4 Components of other agencies and departments transferred to the Department of Homeland Security with the Homeland Security Act of 2002.

Transfers of authorities from other departments and agencies are illustrated in Fig. 2.4. The Federal Emergency Management Agency, previously an independent agency, was transferred under the Secretary of the Department of Homeland Security. Similarly, the Immigration and Naturalization Service was reorganized and transferred from the Department of Justice to the Department of Homeland Security.

2.5.1.1. Federal Emergency Management Agency (FEMA)

The Federal Emergency Management Agency (FEMA) as an independent agency was charged with responding to natural and manmade disasters and was identified in the Presidential Decision Directives, prior to the establishment of the Department of Homeland Security, as the lead agency for domestic emergency response, while the FBI was designated the lead in investigative response. The FEMA's experience in disaster training and response with its national network of regional offices brought this nationwide framework for a federal response to the Department of Homeland Security.

2.5.1.2. Immigration and Naturalization Service (INS) to USCIS, ICE and CBP

The enabling statute for the Immigration and Naturalization Service is the Immigration and Nationality Act, created in 1952. Although immigration has been regulated by the federal government since the first statute's passage in 1790, the McCarran-Walter bill of 1952, Public Law No. 82-414, codified existing laws and reorganized the structure of immigration law.

The Homeland Security Act of 2002 transferred some of the functions of INS from the Department of Justice. The INS has two major functions: (1) to provide for immigration and naturalization services for citizenship and (2) to enforce violations and initiate deportment for violators. The INS has been criticized by the Bush Administration as ineffective, which was underscored by the highly publicized grant of student visas by the INS in March 2002 to two of the deceased Saudi Arabian hijackers, Mohammad Atta and Marwan Al-Shehhi, who participated in the 9-11 attacks.[78]

The Department of State performs the original grant of visa applications and the issuance process, while the INS has the implementation function, including notification of approval to applicants.

The INS is responsible for the U.S. Border Patrol, which exists as a uniformed branch of the Immigration and Naturalization Service. The mission of the Border Patrol is the "detection and prevention of smuggling and illegal entry of aliens into the United States, with primary responsibility between the Ports-of-Entry."[79]

The United States' international boundaries cover approximately 8,000 miles, which are patrolled by the Border Patrol through the use of automobile, boat, aircraft, horseback, snowmobile, motorcycle, bicycle, and foot.

Inspections is another uniformed branch of the INS, which is responsible for the inspection of all persons seeking admission to or transiting through the United States by air, land, or sea, and enforcing and administering the immigration laws. The Inspectors determine if the applicants qualify for admission and, if so, under what status. Inspectors look for fraudulent documents, previous overstays, question applicants under oath, and search without a warrant the applicant and effects. The Inspectors are charged with intercepting terrorists, alien and narcotic smugglers, impostors, false claims to U.S. citizenship, criminals, and undocumented aliens seeking admission.

The Inspection program also pre-inspects passengers arriving from five countries to the United States and works with foreign governments and carriers to assist them in identifying undocumented and/or unauthorized passengers before they board an aircraft to the United States.[80]

The Investigations Division is the interior enforcement arm of the service charged with investigating violations of the criminal and administrative provisions of law. The Investigations division seeks to: identify and remove criminal aliens, counter alien smuggling, counter immigration fraud, enforce employer provisions of the INA, and respond to community complaints regarding illegal criminal alien activity.

The INS also engages in detention and removal of illegal aliens.

In March 1, 2003, the INS was eliminated and replaced with the U.S. Citizenship and Immigration Services (USCIS), U.S. Immigration and Customs Enforcement (ICE), and U.S. Customs and Border Protection (CBP).

2.5.1.3.   Chief Medical Officer

The Department of Homeland Security four years after its establishment sought to extend its influence and role in biodefense and worked with Congress on legislation to create a new Office of Chief Medical Officer in DHS. The Homeland Security Appropriations Act of 2007, H.R. 5441 was signed by the President on October 4, 2006 and the office was created.

The legislation provides that the Chief Medical Officer would be appointed by the President with the advice and consent of the Senate; that the qualifications of the Chief Medical Officer would be "a demonstrated ability in knowledge of medicine and public health"; that the responsibilities would give primary responsibility within the Department for medical issues related to "natural disasters, acts of terrorism, and other man-made disasters including (1) serving as principal advisor to the secretary and Administrator on medical and public health issues; and (2) coordinating the biodefense activities of the Department; (3) ensuring internal and external coordination of all medical preparedness and response activities of the Department. . . ; and (4) serving as the point of contact for other departments and agencies "on medical and public health issues;" and (5) states and tribal governments; and (6) working Project Bioshield.

2.5.2. The Role of the FBI

The Federal Bureau of Investigation was formed by President Herbert Hoover to investigate racketeering and terrorism in the early 20th century. The mission of the agency was to investigate and prosecute criminals, and to enforce federal criminal laws.

> The mission of the Federal Bureau of Investigation is defined as: *(1) uphold the law through the investigation of violations of federal criminal statutes; (2) protect the United States from hostile intelligence efforts; (3) provide assistance to other federal, state and local law enforcement agencies; and (4) perform these responsibilities in a manner that is faithful to the Constitution and the laws of the United States.*[81]

This mission is an agency policy statement. Statutory authority provides for powers of the Federal Bureau of Investigation in arrests, for example:

> *The Director, Associate Director, Assistant to the Director, Assistant Directors, inspectors and agents of the Federal Bureau of Investigation of the Department of Justice may carry firearms, serve warrants and subpoenas issued under the authority of the United States and make arrests without warrant for any offense against the United States committed in their presence, or for any felony cognizable under the laws of the United States if they have reasonable grounds to believe that the person to be arrested has committed or is committing such felony.*[82]

The Federal Bureau of Investigation is part of the Department of Justice, which has undergone a reorganization. On November 8, 2001, the Federal Bureau of Investigation announced a "wartime reorganization,"[83] suggesting that Attorney General John Ashcroft intends to maintain the FBI in its current role in the plan to respond to bioterrorism under the current PDD 39. While the role of apprehension of a bioterrorist within the domestic territory of the United States is clearly within the scope of the mission of the FBI, the complexity of the threat belies what seems to be a simple decision for leadership. In Congressional testimony, in October 2001, the FBI confirmed their leadership role in crisis management with FEMA's leadership role in consequence management and, together, the coordination of the overall federal government response.[84] The response from the FBI testified,

> *begins with a threat assessment coordinated by the Weapons of Mass Destruction Operations Unit (WMDOU). This is initiated when the FBI receives notification of an incident or threat. WMDOU immediately notifies subject matter experts and federal agencies with relevant authorities to conduct a real-time assessment and determine the credibility of the threat. Based on the credibility and scope of the threat, WMDOU will coordinate an appropriate and tailored response by federal assets and the owners and operators of the facility to meet the requirements of the on-scene responders, and will oversee the investigation to its successful conclusion.*

About one month later, in November 2001, in Congressional testimony, the FBI presented their approach to the bioterrorism threat in terms of a coordinated approach. The FBI official presented the bioterrorism threat as one of either an overt attack or a covert attack, the overt attack being "an announced release of an agent, often with some type of articulated threat," such as an envelope containing anthrax with an announcement that the recipient has been exposed to anthrax, and the covert threat being one that is a release "not accompanied by any articulated or known threat."[85] The difference, the FBI testifies, is that the FBI takes the lead in both types of attacks, but in the covert attack the public health community is the first to detect the attack, and once it is known as an attack, the FBI assumes the lead.

In addressing biological threats, the FBI divides the response into two areas: the local and the federal. The division is made between coordination at the local level and a separate coordination approach at the federal level. State or local public health officials work with the local FBI WMD Coordinator, of which there is one in every FBI office, but at the federal level, the FBI and CDC work together.

The FBI also testified to the coordination with other federal agencies. After the threat assessment is made, the FBI determines the credibility of the threat, the immediate concerns involving health and safety of the responding personnel, and the requisite level of response warranted by the federal government. Then input from:

"the necessary federal agencies with an interest in the particular incident. In a biological event, representatives from Centers for Disease Control and Prevention (CDC), Department of Health and Human Services (DHHS), United States Department of Agriculture (USDA) and Food and Drug Administration (FDA) are the key agencies called upon to assist FBI personnel in assessing the particular threat. Based upon the assessment, a determination is made as to the level of response necessary to adequately address the particular threat, which could range from a full federal response if the threat is deemed credible to collection of the material in an effort to rule out the presence of any biological material if the threat is deemed not credible."

After the threat assessment is made, the FBI alone determines the level of response, which may include the determination of biological factors. Throughout this process, the FBI is acting without input from other agencies.

The collection of any biological material is also within the jurisdiction of the FBI under PDD 39 and 62, and the FBI follows their protocol for hazardous materials used by local HAZMAT teams. The FBI's Hazardous Material Response Unit (HMRU) protocols are followed.

These protocols, recognized and followed by state and local Hazmat teams, are necessary to ensure that sufficient evidentiary samples are collected, screened, and over-packed according to scientific safety guidelines for transportation to the appropriate testing facility. More than 85 state health laboratories perform this analysis on behalf of CDC and belong to a coordinated collection of facilities known as the Laboratory Response Network (LRN). Once the testing is completed, results are provided to the FBI for dissemination in the appropriate manner. The results of the analysis are then disseminated to the exposed person or persons, local first responders, and the local public health department. Additionally, results will be forwarded to the Centers for Disease Control and Prevention (CDC) in Atlanta, GA.

Although the CDC network of laboratories perform the tests, they are not sent to the CDC, but rather to the FBI for dissemination to the CDC. This, again, excludes the public health community from the decision-making process.

From testimony in 1999 and in 2001, the following data indicates the number of biological threats compared to all other threats of weapons of mass destruction that were cases lodged with the FBI. As a proportion of all threats, biological ones now comprise the majority of threats.

The organizational changes published on November 8, 2001 do not account for the range of expertise required for biological threats, but instead focus on intelligence and investigation, which are roles in the process, but certainly not the elements necessary to take the lead for the national security plan to combat bioterrorism.

The website for bioterrorism that included the protocols for a bioterrorism event in 2000 published the "Interim Recommended Notification Procedures for Local and State Public Health Department Leaders in the Event of a Bioterrorist Incident." The protocol specified that the first step is to "notify the FBI and notify local law enforcement."[86] Only after notifying these groups is the local public health authority notified, then the state, then the CDC.

The FBI maintains a website with information about the anthrax investigation[87] and contact information, in a cooperative effort with the U.S. Postal Service to develop protocols and offer a reward for the mailers of the four envelopes containing anthrax.

Notes

1. In January 2002, an FBI official informally asked an academic institution to review a physicians report concerning a black lesion on the calf of Al Haznawi, one of the hijackers responsible for the airline crashes on 9-11, and for the inquiry about the crop dusting that is a delivery method for biological weapons. The suspicion that the black lesion was indicative of anthrax would have linked the September 11, 2001 attacks to the anthrax attacks. However, the Chair of the American Academy of Dermatology's bioterrorism task force remarked that it was "highly unlikely" for someone to contract cutaneous anthrax on his lower leg, while the academic institution, Johns Hopkins University, believed that a black lesion would likely lead to the diagnosis of anthrax.[88] The FBI rejected the case as suspicious. The conclusion from this public debate indicates that the confidence in the FBI and their ability to investigate a matter which includes medical clues is extremely low, even from within the organization.

2. In November 2001 it was reported that the Ames Laboratory at Iowa State University made an inquiry to the FBI office in Omaha, Nebraska to determine if they could destroy their anthrax culture collection, which consisted of approximately 100 vials of anthrax strains collected over a period of seven decades. The Omaha office contacted the Miama office and advised the Omaha office that "the Ames strain was so widespread that it had no investigative or evidentiary value." Martin E. Hugh-Jones, an anthrax expert at Louisiana State University, stated to *The New York Times* that "if those cultures were still alive," they could have helped in "clearing up the muddy history."[89]

Based on these and other problems, experts have commented that the FBI "traditionally has had trouble understanding the language, and the demands, of science." There's a chasm between what's going on in the courtroom and forensic area," and that the flow of data "just does not seem to make it" into criminal investigations.

What coordination process might be helpful in providing necessary expertise at critical junctures of the investigative process that do not currently exist under the PDDs or other protocols?

3. Kris Kolesnik, director of the National Whistleblower Center, specializes in FBI issues. He commented in *The Washington Post* in November 2001 that "they [FBI] are not geared up for prevention of anything. They are geared up to arrest someone after a crime has been committed."[90] Sen. Dianne Feinstein (D-Calif.) held hearings on the anthrax investigation, and was quoted in one interview as saying, "I was really taken aback by how little they seem to know."[91] Bill Tobin, a former FBI metallurgist, was quoted as saying, "It's just unrealistic to ask 7,000 agents to overnight become sufficiently knowledgeable about bioterrorist agents and possible means of theft of those items and how they might be disseminated lethally to an American populace."[92] With the overwhelming concern that the FBI does not have the necessary expertise to address biological threats or investigations, should the policy be to work at training FBI agents about microbiology and epidemiology, or should an agency already trained in these fields be given the lead in the investigations? Or should there be a co-leadership established between the FBI and the CDC or USAMRIID (the U.S. Army biological weapons defense laboratory)?

4. The mission of the FBI is to uphold the law by investigating violations of federal law, providing assistance to state and local law enforcement agencies and protecting the U.S. against hostile intelligence efforts. Yet in testimony before the U.S. Congress on November 6, 2001, the Deputy Assistant Director of the Counterterrorism Division of the FBI stated, "...the primary mission of law enforcement and the public health community is saving lives."[93] Attorney General Ashcroft stated in a speech to the Justice Department managers in early November 2001 that the FBI "is at the center of our Counterterrorism effort." He cited the USA PATRIOT Act as a "mandate for fundamental change" and ordered the FBI "to put

the prevention of terrorism" ahead of all other priorities.[94] Does changing the mission of the FBI signal business as usual? While the stated mission makes terrorism a priority, how do their protocols address their mission?

5. The FBI has testified before Congress that the agency is utilizing the HAZMAT protocols for collecting samples. In at least one FBI office, the discovery of white powder in their own elevator in December 2001 prompted their own collection protocol, which involved using adhesive tape pressed against the powder and then delivering it to the appropriate public health laboratory. The public health laboratory suggested that the appropriate collection protocol for the powder would have been to use a cotton swab and place it in a glass vial. The adhesive made it virtually impossible to remove what might have proved to be spores in order to proceed with the testing procedure. Several years later, the FBI and CDC successfully collaborated on a protocol for collection and handling, including chain of custody requirements for use in biological incidents that are investigated as potential crimes.

2.5.3   The Role of the Department of Health and Human Services

Since the Amerithrax attacks, there are three national strategies for the Nation's CBRN defense, which specifically identify the Department of Health and Human Services (DHHS) as the lead agency with responsibility within the Federal government for the protection of the civilian population against the adverse health effects of chemical, biological, radiological, and nuclear (CBRN) threats. These strategies are the *National Strategy to Combat Weapons of Mass Destruction* (December 2002), *Biodefense for the 21st Century* (April 28, 2004), and *Medical Countermeasures Against Weapons of Mass Destruction* (HSPD-18, January 31, 2007). The DHHS' role is to implement through its research and development the acquisition and deployment of effective medical countermeasures.
(See http://www.hhs.gov/aspr/barda/phemce/index.html) .

2.5.3.1 National Institute of Allergies and Infectious Diseases (NIAID)

The National Institute of Allergies and Infectious Diseases (NIAID), a component of the National Institute of Health (NIH), has played a primary role in the research conducted on emerging infectious diseases. In 2005, the NIH was given the task of developing medical countermeasures for the civilian population against CBRN threats, and since NIAID had extensive expertise in developing countermeasures, it was assigned the role of coordinating these efforts.[95] NIAID conducts research in each of the areas of CBRN threats.   Biological countermeasures research has included research geared toward better understanding of the human immunological systems and how pathogens interact with human hosts.[96] For example, researchers working in this area are investigating the use of antibodies that can block the actions of toxins produced by the anthrax bacterium, as well as botulinum toxin.[97] In the areas of radiological and nuclear countermeasures research, NIAID was asked in 2004 to develop a research program to accelerate the development of countermeasures ionizing radiation in a civilian population.[98] NIAID also drafted a strategic plan to identify chemical attack scenarios and appropriate medical countermeasures for chemicals including neurotoxic chemicals such as organophosphates, and metabolic poisons such as cyanide.[99]

2.5.3.2.   Public Health Service (PHS)

The U.S. Public Health Service is provided with quarantine and inspection powers when communicable diseases may spread into the United States or from one state to another in 42 U.S.C. §264 et. al., and 42 C.F.R. §70.1-73.0 (2002). *Communicable disease means illnesses due to infectious agents or their toxic products, which may be transmitted from a reservoir to a susceptible host either directly as from an infected person or animal or indirectly through the agency of an intermediate plant or animal host, vector, or the inanimate environment.* (42 C.F.R. §70.1(a)(2002)).

The Presidential Decision Directives provide only a supporting role for the Public Health Service in addressing a bioterrorism attack. Rather, agencies having no expertise in public health have been designated the lead agency. In the recent anthrax attacks, the FBI, as designated by the PDDs, lead the investigation and decision-making process. The U.S. Congress recently noted the importance of the Public Health Service in a national security role. The U.S. House of Representatives in October 2001 introduced H.R. 3255, which provided in Sec. 127 Public Health Representation on the NSC. "It is the sense of the congress that the Surgeon General of the Public Health Service should serve as a member of the National Security Council."

2.5.3.3. Indian Health Service (HIS)

The Indian Health Service (IHS) is a component of the Public Health Service. The stated mission, goal, and foundation of the IHS is:

Our Mission...to raise the physical, mental, social, and spiritual health of American Indians and Alaska Natives to the highest level.

Our Goal...to assure that comprehensive, culturally acceptable personal and public health services are available and accessible to American Indian and Alaska Native people.

Our Foundation...to uphold the Federal Government's obligation to promote healthy American Indian and Alaska Native people, communities, and cultures and to honor and protect the inherent sovereign rights of Tribes.

(http://www.ihs.gov/AboutIHS/IHSintro.asp, site visited Aug. 8, 2002).

In the spring of 1993, the Indian Health Service was the lead partner in an investigation of an outbreak of hanta virus, which had begun mysteriously killing young, healthy adults, beginning with flu-like symptoms and ending with the victim drowning as a consequence of their lungs filling with their own bodily fluids. Tom Brokaw and Peter Jennings on NBC and ABC, respectively, described the virus as the "Navajo mystery virus" and speculation as to the cause of the deaths included many theories.

The example of the hanta virus outbreak is a true success story, which can be attributed in large part to the federal expertise that was immediately available because this was a community served by a federal system, rather than a local and state public health system. Delays of days or weeks may have resulted if the protocol of notification had been followed—first from the county to the state, and then, upon request only, to the CDC. In the Indian Health System, which is federal, the resources of the CDC and USAMRIID were immediately available. The Indian Health Service utilized the services of the Navajo Nation, the New Mexico Department of Health, the CDC, and also the Los Alamos National Laboratory and the Sandia National Laboratory.

It was the Navajo physician and CDC employee, Dr. Ben Muneta, who consulted a medicine man, which provided the break in discovering the cause of the outbreak. Dr. Muneta consulted with Andy Natonabah, a *htaalii* (medicine man), who told Muneta that the illness was due to the increased rainfall, which, in turn, had caused an unusually large crop of pinon nuts from the pinion trees. The pinion nuts created an explosion in the deer mouse population, which was the vector for the hanta virus. Oral tradition and historical sandpaintings of mice supported the idea that the source of the virus was a result of nature out of balance.

See Lori Arviso Alvord, MD and Elizabeth Cohen Van Pelt, *The Scalpel and the Silver Bear, The First Navajo Woman Surgeon Combines Western Medicine and Traditional Healing* 120–27 (1999).

2.5.3.4. Office of Preparedness and Response

The Office of the Assistant Secretary for Preparedness and Response, was reorganized from its former designation, the Office of Public Health Emergency Preparedness. This Assistant Secretary is the principle advisor to the Secretary for matters relating to bioterrorism and other public health emergencies. This office also coordinates the interagency, state, and local activities in its responsibility for civilian safety.

This Office has five components: the Biomedical Advanced Research and Development Authority (BARDA), the Office of Preparedness and Emergency Operations (OPEO), the Office of Medicine, Science, and Public Health (OMSPH), the Office of Policy and Strategic Planning (OPSP), and the Office of Resources, Planning, and Evaluation. In addition, the Office is responsible for the interagency, coordinated program for medical countermeasures, PHEMCE. (See http://www.hhs.gov/aspr/index.html .)

2.5.3.4.1.   Biomedical Advanced Research and Development Authority (BARDA)

BARDA was created by the Pandemic and All-Hazards Preparedness Act (PAHPA), P.L. 109-417, Title IV when signed into law on December 19, 2006. The Biomedical Advanced Research and Development Authority (BARDA) was established within the Department of Health and Human Services (HHS). The purpose of this new authority is "to facilitate the research, development, and acquisition of medical countermeasures for chemical, biological, radiological, and nuclear (CBRN) agents and emerging infectious diseases, including pandemic influenza, that threaten the U.S. civilian population." (See http://www.hhs.gov/aspr/barda/phemce/enterprise/strategy/bardaplan.html .)

BARDA's development is intended to facilitate the development and acquisition of medical countermeasures created through the NIH/NIAID biodefense and emerging infection diseases research programs, as well as other promising private sector research. These countermeasures include vaccines, therapeutics, diagnostics, and devices.

2.5.3.4.2.   Public Health Emergency Medical Countermeasures Enterprise (HHS PHEMCE)

The website for the interagency, coordinated program within the Office of Preparedness of DHHS describes their mission as follows (At http://www.hhs.gov/aspr/barda/phemce/index.html.):

The Public Health Emergency Medical Countermeasures Enterprise (PHEMCE) is a coordinated interagency effort by the Office of the Assistant Secretary for Preparedness and Response (ASPR) and includes three primary HHS internal agencies: the Centers for Disease Control and Prevention (CDC), the Food and Drug Administration (FDA), and the National Institutes of Health (NIH). The mission of the PHEMCE is to:

Define and prioritize requirements for public health emergency medical countermeasures; Integrate and coordinate research, early- and late-stage product development, and procurement activities addressing the requirements; and Set deployment and use strategies for medical countermeasures held in the Strategic National Stockpile (SNS).

The PHEMCE considers medical countermeasures to address CBRN, as well as naturally emerging infectious diseases and pandemic threats, including pandemic influenza.

2.5.3.5. The Centers for Disease Control and Prevention (CDC)

The role of the Centers for Disease Control and Prevention is limited in scope and recognizes the sovereignty of states in the regulation of public health, with some emergency powers. The federal statute that grants authority to the CDC outlines the relationship between the federal government and the states:
42 USCS §243 (2001)
§243. General grant of authority for cooperation (a) Enforcement of quarantine regulations; prevention of communicable diseases. The Secretary is authorized to accept from State and local authorities any assistance in the enforcement of quarantine regulations made pursuant to this Act

which such authorities may be able and willing to provide. The Secretary shall also assist States and their political subdivisions in the prevention and suppression of communicable diseases and with respect to other public health matters, shall cooperate with and aid State and local authorities in the enforcement of their quarantine and other health regulations, and shall advise the several States on matters relating to the preservation and improvement of the public health.

(b) Comprehensive and continuing planning; training of personnel for State and local health work; fees. The Secretary shall encourage cooperative activities between the States with respect to comprehensive and continuing planning as to their current and future health needs, the establishment and maintenance of adequate public health services, and otherwise carrying out public health activities. The Secretary is also authorized to train personnel for State and local health work. The Secretary may charge only private entities reasonable fees for the training of their personnel under the preceding sentence.

(c) Development of plan to control epidemics and meet emergencies or problems resulting from disasters; cooperative planning; temporary assistance; reimbursement of United States.

(1) The Secretary is authorized to develop (and may take such action as may be necessary to implement) a plan under which personnel, equipment, medical supplies, and other resources of the Service and other agencies under the jurisdiction of the Secretary may be effectively used to control epidemics of any disease or condition and to meet other health emergencies or problems. The Secretary may enter into agreements providing for the cooperative planning between the Service and public and private community health programs and agencies to cope with health problems (including epidemics and health emergencies).

(2) The Secretary may, at the request of the appropriate State or local authority, extend temporary (not in excess of six months) assistance to State or localities in meeting health emergencies of such a nature as to warrant Federal assistance. The Secretary may require such reimbursement of the United States for assistance provided under this paragraph as he may determine to be reasonable under the circumstances. Any reimbursement so paid shall be credited to the applicable appropriation for the Service for the year in which such reimbursement is received.

The CDC protocol for reporting bioterrorism events optimistically directs the public health community as follows: *The public health sector has important responsibilities related to BT detection, response, and control of health consequences, but the public health response will be most effective if the overall response by all sectors—pre-hospital and hospital care, law enforcement, public safety, etc.—is coordinated by the FBI.*[100]

Further, CDC maintains their directed role under the Presidential Decision Directive 39 and 62, but suggests that the state health departments should voluntarily contact the CDC, as well—but only on a voluntary basis: *State health Department notifies CDC. CDC requests that all incidents of apparent or threatened bioterrorism be voluntarily reported to CDC by State public health officials, immediately following notification of the FBI and local law enforcement agencies.*[101] The scope of statutory power of the CDC is only to respond if contacted by the states, and does not include directing the states to report to the CDC.

However, on June 12, 2002, the U.S. Congress recognized that the CDC mission did not fit the new demands of bioterrorism and amended the scope of the work of CDC in the Public Health Security and Bioterrorism Preparedness and Response Act of 2002:

§247d-4. Revitalizing the Centers for Disease Control and Prevention

(a) Facilities; capacities. (1) Findings. Congress finds that the Centers for Disease Control and Prevention has an essential role in defending against and combating public health threats and requires secure and modern facilities, and expanded and improved capabilities related to bioterrorism and other public health emergencies, sufficient to enable such Centers to conduct this important mission.

(2) Facilities.

(A) In general. The Director of the Centers for Disease Control and Prevention may design, construct, and equip new facilities, renovate existing facilities (including laboratories, laboratory support buildings, scientific communication facilities, transshipment complexes, secured and isolated parking structures, office buildings, and other facilities and infrastructure), and upgrade security of such facilities, in order to better conduct the capacities described in section 319A [42 USCS §247d-1], and for supporting public health activities.

(B) Multiyear contracting authority. For any project of designing, constructing, equipping, or renovating any facility under subparagraph (A), the Director of the Centers for Disease Control and Prevention may enter into a single contract or related contracts that collectively include the full scope of the project, and the solicitation and contract shall contain the clause "availability of funds" found at section 52.232-18 of title 48, Code of Federal Regulations.

(3) Improving the capacities of the Centers for Disease Control and Prevention. The Secretary, taking into account evaluations under section 319B(a) [42 USCS §247d-2(a)], shall expand, enhance, and improve the capabilities of the Centers for Disease Control and Prevention relating to preparedness for and responding effectively to bioterrorism and other public health emergencies. Activities that may be carried out under the preceding sentence include—

(A) expanding or enhancing the training of personnel;

(B) improving communications facilities and networks, including delivery of necessary information to rural areas;

(C) improving capabilities for public health surveillance and reporting activities, taking into account the integrated system or systems of public health alert communications and surveillance networks under subsection (b); and

(D) improving laboratory facilities related to bioterrorism and other public health emergencies, including increasing the security of such facilities.

The CDC's powers were extended to making it a regulatory agency for the possession, use, and transportation of select agents, a role that was new for the Center and changed the previously cooperative and advisory relationship with their constituencies to a much more adversarial one. Chapter Ten is devoted to this new framework of the regulation of biosafety and the biosecurity of laboratories and researchers who use biological agents listed as "select agents."

2.5.3.5.1. *Federal Quarantine Powers*

The CDC has Congressionally mandated authority to impose quarantines when there is a threat of interstate transmission of a communicable disease in 42 U.S.C. §264 (2002), from which regulations were promulgated at 42 C.F.R. §70.2 (2002):

§70.2 Measures in the event of inadequate local control.

Whenever the Director of the Centers for Disease Control and Prevention determines that the measures taken by health authorities of any State or possession (including political subdivisions thereof) are insufficient to prevent the spread of any of the communicable diseases from such State or possession to any other State or possession, he/she may take such measures to prevent such spread of the diseases as he/she deems reasonably necessary, including inspection, fumigation, disinfection, sanitation, pest extermination, and destruction of animals or articles believed to be sources of infection.

However, that quarantine is limited to the detention of individuals for a list of specific communicable diseases:

§70.6 Apprehension and detention of persons with specific diseases.

Regulations prescribed in this part are not applicable to the apprehension, detention, or conditional release of individuals except for the purpose of preventing the introduction, transmission, or spread of the following diseases: Anthrax, chancroid, cholera, dengue, diphtheria, granuloma inguinale, infectious encephalitis, favus, gonorrhea, leprosy, lymphogranuloma venereum, meningococcus meningitis, plague, poliomyelitis, psittacosis, relapsing fever, ringworm of the scalp, scarlet fever, streptococcic sore throat, smallpox, syphilis, trachoma, tuberculosis, typhoid fever, typhus, and yellow fever.

The CDC published the first comprehensive document to address a strategic plan for anti-bioterrorism. In 1998, the CDC completed a plan to address emerging diseases and a plan for prevention with *Preventing Emerging Infectious Disease: A Strategy for the 21st Century*, which focused on four areas: surveillance and outbreak responsel; applied research in diagnostic tests, drugs, and vaccines; infrastructure and training; and disease prevention and control.

In 1999, a CDC representative testified before Congress that in their bioterrorism coordination, they worked closely with the Department of Justice, including the FBI and the National Domestic Preparedness Office, with the Food and Drug Administration, the National Institutes of Health, the Department of Defense, and the Federal Emergency Management Agency.[102]

On September 11, 2001, the CDC sent an alert to state and local governments entitled, "Terrorist Activity Response Health Advisory," alerting the health departments that "CDC is on heightened alert status to monitor for any possible unusual disease patterns associated with today's events, including chemical and biological agents."[103] There was an immediate effort to respond to the possibility of a biological attack as well as the use of the airlines for attacks.

In the months following the anthrax attacks, the CDC was clearly the agency possessing the expertise necessary to respond to the attacks. However, the federal organization under PDD 39 gives CDC only a supporting role to the FBI and FEMA. While this works well for chemical or nuclear threats or bombs, this organization fails to match the challenges of a biological event.

The CDC has implemented a number of systems to carry out their mission for surveillance and response to bioterrorism.[104]

In arrangements with the state, the CDC has developed these programs:

2.5.3.5.2.   *Metropolitan Medical Response Systems*

Metropolitan Medical Response Systems (MMRS). Through contractual relationships the MMRS uses existing emergency response systems—emergency management, medical and mental health providers, public health departments, law enforcement, fire departments, EMS and the National Guard—to provide an integrated, unified response to a mass casualty event. As of September 30, 2001, OEP has contracted with 97 municipalities to develop MMRSs. The FY 2002 budget includes funding for an additional 25 MMRSs (for a total of 122).

MMRS contracts require the development of local capability for mass immunization /prophylaxis for the first 24 hours following an identified disease outbreak; the capability to distribute material deployed to the local site from the National Pharmaceutical Stockpile; local capability for mass patient care, including procedures to augment existing care facilities; local medical staff trained to recognize disease symptoms so that they can initiate treatment; and local capability to manage the remains of the deceased.[105]

2.5.3.5.3.   *Epidemiologic and Laboratory Capacity (E.C.) Program*

The CDC has implemented this system with more than 75 public health professionals (including 24 Epidemiologists and 25 laboratorians) as part of the training effort to assist state and large local health departments in acquiring the skills and resources to address infectious diseases.

2.5.3.5.4.   *Emerging Infections Program (EIP)*

The CDC has established EIP sites by entering into agreements with selected state health departments and in collaboration with local academic, government, and private sector organizations to establish sites that conduct active, population-based surveillance for selected diseases, as well as for unexplained deaths and severe illnesses in previously healthy people.

2.5.3.5.5. Strategic National Stockpile (SNS)

No longer named the National Pharmaceutical Stockpile Program (NPSP), the new Strategic National Stockpile (SNS) is intended to provide broader inventories of supplies beyond pharmaceuticals. The CDC had developed a stockpile of vaccines, drugs and anti-toxins that could reach the victims anywhere in the continental U.S. within 12 hours prior to the establishment of the Department of Homeland Security, and it continues to manage the program under the new name, SNS. The MMRS program, as discussed above, contracts with local entities for distribution of the pharmaceuticals when the demand is made.

2.5.3.5.6. National Notifiable Disease Surveillance System (NNDSS)

Before 9-11 this program was called the National Electronic Disease Surveillance System (NEDSS), but has subsequently been updated and renamed the National Notifiable Disease Surveillance System (NNDSS) with an expanded list of notifiable diseases. This is a system for public health surveillance that supports automated collection, transmission, and monitoring of disease data from multiple sources (clinicians' offices, laboratories, etc.) from local to state health departments to the CDC. The NNDSS reviews the list of notifiable diseases annually with the professional association of CSTE. Reporting to the CDC by the states is voluntary, and each state may designate which diseases are notifiable and may pass state legislation mandating reporting at the state level. States are only required by law to report the federally quarantinable diseases. http://www.cdc.gov/ncphi/disss/nndss/PHS/infdis2008.htm

2.5.3.5.7. The Epi-X Project

This system is a secure, moderated, web-based exchange for public health officials to rapidly report and discuss disease outbreaks and other health events that may indicate a bioterrorism event. The system is staffed with real-time expertise to assure rapid contact with state and local officials and to provide accurate information.[106]

2.5.3.5.8. The Epidemic Intelligence Service (EIS)

The Epidemic Intelligence Service was created in 1951 in response to concerns about biological warfare during the Cold War.

The program is a two-year post-graduate program of service for health professionals who want to pursue careers in public health. Each year, the CDC selects 60 to 80 candidates to enter the EIS and to experience on-the-job training in epidemiology. Qualifications for the appointment require that physicians have at least one year of clinical training and a Ph.D. Dr.Ph or MD in epidemiology, biostatistics, the social or behavioral sciences, and the nutrition sciences dentists, physician assistants, and nurses have an MPH or equivalent degree, and that veterinarians have an MPH or equivalent degree or relevant public health experience.[107]

The EIS is organized to work across CDC programs, including infectious diseases and maternal health. In January 2002, the EIS was comprised of a total of 130 EIS officers,[108] but by April 2002, the EIS reported that their numbers had increased to 146.[109] Each year, the EIS addresses approximately 100 investigations requested by states and other countries, and 500 studies or consultations each year.

The EIS sent 35 members to New York City immediately after the attacks on the World Trade Center to assist the New York City Health Department in the ongoing monitoring of public health issues. Secretary Thompson is quoted as saying, "The CDC workers will supplement local efforts in this regard and provide expertise in matters relating to public health. We're responding as rapidly as possible to any needs for resources the city and state need."[110] By April 2002, the EIS had mobilized 136 officers from Atlanta for assignments related to terrorism. Before this event, the largest single deployment in EIS history was 46 officers, responding to the fear that Korean soldiers had returned to the United States, possibly infected with biological agents.[111]

The EIS was also called upon to investigate the first cases of hantavirus, Legionnaire's Disease, West Nile virus outbreak, and ebola outbreaks in Uganda and Zaire. *The New Yorker* reported that the CIA asked the CDC to investigate the outbreak of West Nile Fever in New York City, which had killed six people and sickened two dozen others. Analysts at the CIA, reacting to information from an Iraqi defector, were concerned that Saddam Hussein may have developed a West Nile-like encephalitis and launched a bioterrorism attack.[112] http://www.cdc.gov/eis/

2.5.3.5.9.   A New Role for the CDC as Regulator of Biosafety and Biosecurity of Laboratories: The Select Agent Program

The CDC was given the implementation authority with the USDA to implement statutory mandates to regulate biological agents that are identified as "select agents." This program is one of the most significant statutory changes made in biosafety and biosecurity since 9-11 and because it has taken on such a broad role, it is addressed in a separate chapter, Chapter Ten, *supra*.

2.5.3.5.10.   CDC Partnerships with Professional Organizations

The CDC has also initiated programs in cooperation with professional organizations:

(1) The National Health Alert Network (HAN)

The CDC is implementing this national system in partnership with the National Association of County and City Health Officials (NACCHO), the Association of State and Territorial Health Officials (ASTHO), and other health organizations. The HAN will assist in communications, information, distance-learning, and organizational infrastructure to address the threat of bioterrorism, and will link all public health agencies at the local, state, and federal levels by continuous high-speed connection to the Internet, broadcast communications, and satellite and web-based distance-learning.

(2) The Laboratory Response Network (LRN)

The fundamental goal of the Laboratory Response Network for Bioterrorism (LRN) is to enhance laboratory capacity for preparedness and response to an act of bioterrorism by providing a collaborative network to facilitate rapid detection and analysis of chemical and biological agents. The LRN is a joint project supported by the CDC and the Association of Public Health Laboratories (APHL).[113]

In the aftermath of the anthrax attacks, the concern for a smallpox attack resulted in pressure on the CDC to develop a plan to address this threat. On November 21, 2001, the CDC distributed the CDC "Interim Smallpox Response Plan and Guidelines" to state and local health departments.

Notes

1. Recall note 2 in Section 2.5.1, which discussed the destruction of the anthrax culture collection at the University of Iowa. Under regulations promulgated for the Antiterrorism and Effective Death Penalty Act of 1996, the CDC was directed to develop regulations for the destruction of biological agents. In Congressional testimony in 1999, a CDC representative testified that under these regulations "CDC must be notified of the disposal or complete consumption of a select agent." Anthrax is one of the select agents. Why was the FBI notified and not the CDC for permission to destroy the anthrax collection? PDD 39 and 62 making the FBI the lead in bioterrorism events does not suspend the application of the regulations.

2. The CDC was the last federal agency among about a dozen to receive the report of a series of experiments performed in the spring of 2001 involving simulated anthrax-containing letters.[114] These

experiments were performed in Ottawa and Alberta and showed that the possibility of exposure was much greater than previously expected. The Alberta research had been presented on May 31 through October 17. The October 17th meeting was at the Canadian Embassy in Washington, DC, approximately three blocks from the U.S. Capitol, two days after the Sen. Daschle letter was opened. The Ottawa research was presented in mid-May in Canberra, Australia at a meeting of civil defense experts, which U.S. experts attended. FEMA contacted the Public Health Service and the U.S. Environmental Protection Agency. The State Department passed the research on to the FBI, Secret Service, and the U.S. Capitol Police. But the CDC did not hear about it until a professor in epidemiology sent the research to a contact in the CDC in November, about the time the anthrax threat was ending. Bradley A. Perkins, the CDC's lead anthrax investigator, noted that "It would have been good to have that information." How might this problem of leaving CDC out of the decision-making process be corrected, since the agency is responsible for the formulation of the nation's public health response?

2.5.4. The Roles of the Intelligence Agencies – the Office of the Director of National Intelligence

A new agency was created to coordinate the intelligence agencies to ensure that intelligence would be shared in such a way that the best possible intelligence could be made available to the President and policymakers. The Intelligence Reform and Terrorism Prevention Act of 2004 amended the National Security Act of 1947, with the goal of unifying the intelligence agencies and resources, and was signed into law on December 17, 2004. In the National Intelligence Strategy, October 2005, at http://www.globalsecurity.org/intell/library/policy/national/nis-usa october2005.pdf, it is recognized that biological weapons require different approaches than other weapons of mass destruction: ". . . Intelligence Community efforts must focus aggressive and innovative collection techniques to close knowledge gaps related to these technologies and associated weapons programs, particularly in the area of bioterrorism, to identify the methods of conveyance, and to prevent them from reaching our shores."

The Office of the Director of National Intelligence brought together the intelligence activities of sixteen federal organizations:

Central Intelligence Agency
Defense Intelligence Agency
Department of Energy (Office of Intelligence and Counterintelligence)
Department of Homeland Security (Office of Intelligence and Analysis)
Department of State (Bureau of Intelligence and Research)
Department of Treasury (Office of Intelligence and Analysis)
Drug Enforcement Administration (Office of National Security Intelligence)
Federal Bureau of Investigation (National Security Branch)
National Geospatial-Intelligence Agency
National Reconnaissance Office
National Security Agency/Central Security Service
US Air Force
US Army
US Coast Guard
US Marines
US Navy

The Intelligence Reform and Terrorism Prevention Act of 2004 also established the National Counterterrorism Center, National Counterproliferation Center, National Intelligence Centers, and Joint Intelligence Community Council.

2.5.4.1.   *National Security Agency*

The National Security Agency was created as a result of the growing needs of intelligence following the World War II code-breaking efforts and agencies responsible for that intelligence. In 1951, an investigation into security breaches and the conduct of intelligence activities was ordered by President Truman, which ultimately led to the formation of the National Security Agency. In 1952, President Truman met with members of the National Security Council and the State Department in an off-the-record meeting, issuing a highly secret order that reorganized the intelligence gathering agencies into the National Security Agency. On November 4, 1952, the National Security Agency was implemented and President Dwight D. Eisenhower was elected President of the United States. [See James Bamford, "Body of Secrets—Anatomy of the National Security Agency 30–31 (2002)].

2.5.4.2. The Central Intelligence Agency (CIA)

The Central Intelligence Agency is the independent agency that was rooted in the first organized intelligence office, the Office of Strategic Services (OSS), during World War II. The National Security Act of 1947 established the CIA, and it mandated that the CIA coordinate the nation's intelligence activities and correlate, evaluate, and disseminate intelligence affecting national security. (See www.cia.gov)

The Intelligence Reform and Terrorism Prevention Act of 2004, signed by President George W. Bush on December 17, 2004, abolished the positions of Director of Central Intelligence (DCI) and Deputy Director of Central Intelligence (DDCI), and created the position of Director of the Central Intelligence Agency (D/CIA). The Strategic Intent --- 2007-2011 plan includes in its core understandings that "the possession and proliferation of weapons of mass destruction threaten international stability and the safety of our homeland." Further, "our adversaries in the long war on terrorism are dispersed across the globe; they are resilient, ruthless, patient and committed to the mass murder of our citizens." (See https://www.cia.gov/about-cia/strategic_intent.pdf) This indicates that core capabilities of the CIA will be focused on weapons of mass destruction, including biological weapons.

2.5.5.   The Role of the Food and Drug Administration

The Food and Drug Administration (FDA) has a very specific role in biodefense, which is to oversee the safety and efficacy of countermeasures for bioterrorism through their oversight of clinical testing, processing, manufacturing, and stockpiling. The website states the role in biodefense as follows (at http://www.fda.gov/cber/cntrbio/cntrbio.htm):

The President's initiative on Countering Bioterrorism is comprised of a number of essential elements for which CBER plays an integral role. One such element is the expeditious development and licensing of products to diagnose, treat or prevent disease following exposure to pathogens that have been identified as bioterrorist agents. These products must be reviewed and approved prior to the large-scale productions necessary to create and maintain a stockpile. Staff must guide the products through the regulatory process, including the manufacturing process, pre-clinical testing, clinical trials, and the licensing and approval process. Experts in these areas are needed to expedite the licensing and approval process for these products. This process is extremely complex and early involvement by staff is crucial to the success of the expedited review process.

Preparedness for and response to an attack involving biological agents are complicated by the large number of potential agents (most of which are rarely encountered naturally), their sometimes long incubation periods and consequent delayed onset of disease, and their potential for secondary transmission. In addition to naturally occurring pathogens, agents used by bioterrorists may be genetically engineered to resist current therapies and evade vaccine-induced immunity. Pathogens that have been identified as potential biological warfare agents include those that cause smallpox, anthrax, plague, botulism, tularemia, and hemorrhagic fevers.

2.5.6.   **The Roles of the Department of Agriculture and the Food and Drug Administration**

Within the Department of Agriculture, Food Safety, Animal and Plant Health Inspection Service (APHIS), Agricultural Research Service (ARS), and the Forest Service serve in various roles that can be helpful in the federal anti-terrorism strategies. Particularly, inspections of imported foods at the border is a critical role for the Department of Agriculture, and monitoring food safety throughout the entire cycle of food production in the United States would address concerns of agro-terrorism.

The Food and Drug Administration works with the Department of Agriculture on food safety issues within the manufacturing phase. Inspections for food safety are a critical part of our ability to monitor bioterrorism attacks. After September 11, 2001 the Food and Drug Administration proposed new guidelines urging tamper-resistant packaging and other security measures, while the Department of Agriculture continues to contemplate regulations. The FDA's proposal to require tamper-resistant packaging on fruits and vegetables has been met with industry resistance, and the costs associated with the increased rot and temperature is projected by the industry to cost millions.[115]

The Public Health Security and Bioterrorism Preparedness Act of 2002 included a new title on "agroterrorism," and required both the USDA and the FDA to work to develop a new food safety program that ensured that food that reached the United States could be traced back to its origins, often referred to as "farm to fork." This new program required registration of facilities outside of the United States, as well as domestic producers, and a paper trail documenting the chain of custody of food to the point of purchase by consumers. The new law also instituted federal crimes and penalties, including the death penalty for agroterrorism crimes. Agroterrorism crimes are based on economic damages, as well as any cause of death in the course of committing the acts considered criminal as defined by this law. Chapter Four in 4.5.1 addresses the new federal crime of agroterrorism.

2.5.7. The Role of the Department of Defense

The Department of Defense was created at the request of President Harry Truman, who in December 1945 asked Congress to combine the War and Navy Departments into a single department. The National Security Act of 1947 consolidated the separate military departments into the Department of Defense. In large part, the proposed department was intended to address the Cold War.

After September 11, 2001 the Biosurveillance Program was created and Admiral John Poindexter was appointed to be its Director. This office is intended to carry out the collection of public health information and other sources of data to create an early detection system for any biological attack.

The Defense Threat Reduction Agency was created in 1998 by President Clinton in response to his reading *The Cobra Event* by Richard Preston. The first director, Jay Davis, was asked by the President to read the bioterroristic novel. The threat of such events that unfolded in the novel clearly raised concerns of the President for the safety of the American public. The Agency combined various parts of the Department of Defense to make grants and implement training programs for preparation and protection against weapons of mass destruction.

The DARPA was created to explore creative and new technologies which could be used for the national defense. The DARPA has played a major role in the exploration of surveillance technologies and biosensing technology.

The Agriculture Bioterrorism Act of 2002, incorporated into the Public Health Security Act of 2002, gives the Department of Agriculture regulatory authority over biological agents and toxins that can harm plants or animals.[116]

The Food and Drug Administration in the Public Health Security Act of 2002 is given the authority to expand powers for inspections and regulation of imported foods.[117]

2.5.7.1.   **The Role of the Military**

The role of the military in civilian biodefense is primarily that of providing resources and personnel to utilize equipment and resources. However, within the Department of Defense, the U.S. Army is the Material Command and the Medical Command, which includes weapons of mass destruction research and response activities. Within the Medical Command is the U.S. Army Medical Research Institute of Infectious Diseases (USAMRIID), which houses the medical defense program of the United States.

2.5.7.1.1.   *Civilian Contact:* **Posse Comitatus**

Posse comitatus is defined by *Black's Law Dictionary* (4th ed. rev., 1968) to be "the power or force of the county. The entire population of a county above the age of fifteen, which a sheriff may summon to his assistance in certain cases; as to aid him in keeping the peace in pursuing and arresting felons, etc." The use of this power was derived from the Judiciary Act of 1789 (1 Stat. 73), wherein the U.S. Marshals called upon the militia as a posse comitatus. In 1867, the U.S. Congress passed The Reconstruction Act, which established martial law in the southern states, which had seceded in the U.S. Civil War, 1860–1864. The Posse Comitatus Act was signed into law on June 18, 1878, in response to abuses of military control over the south after the U.S. Civil War during Reconstruction. Thereafter, the United States declared that the military should never have enforcement powers against civilians, except in a declared state of emergency.

Over its 124-year history, the Posse Comitatus Act has been amended by Congress to address changing needs for resources. In 1968, a separate statutory exception was created to provide assistance to the Secret Service in carrying out its protective duties. [H.J.R. 1292, P.L. No. 90-331, 82 Stat. 170 (1968)]. In 1969, the federal governmental departments developed an interdepartmental plan for civil disturbances in order to address overlapping jurisdictions and the use of the military ("Interdepartmental Action Plan for Civil Disturbances" (Apr. 1, 1969)). The Department of Defense articulated a policy directive to address terrorist incidents as either a civil disturbance or a criminal act, and how the incident was defined would give rise to the legal framework within which it was analyzed.[118]

In 1973, members of the Lakota Sioux Indian Nation occupied a building within the jurisdiction of the tribal reservation. The National Guard and the U.S. Army, among other local law enforcement agencies, participated in ending the occupation. The involvement of the military in evidence gathering was challenged in a criminal case against members of the Indian nation, who were charged with obstructing law enforcement officials. In this case, the court specifically excluded evidence that might have been collected during any illegal activity on the part of the military and law enforcement officials. (See *United States v. Red Feather*, 392 F. Supp. 916 (D.C.S.D 1975)). This use of the military in Wounded Knee, South Dakota, received nationwide attention in part because of its use against Native Americans, and its reminder to the Nation of the last incident at Wounded Knee in 1891, which utilized the military in a slaughter of women, children and elders, in what is considered the last battle in the United States' war against the Indians. This further raised the public concern of any use of the military in a civilian law enforcement role.

Following the public concern and litigation from the Wounded Knee incident in 1981, an amendment was made to the Act, which did little more than codify the existing relationship between the military and civilian law enforcement agencies. This led to increased cooperation through specific provision of intelligence (10 U.S.C. § 371) facilities, including materials not reasonably available from another source that is "any material or expertise of the Department of Defense appropriate for use in preparing for or responding to an emergency involving chemical or biological agents," such as biosensors, protective clothing, antidotes (10 U.S.C. § 372), training and advice (10 U.S.C. §373), and assistance in the operating and maintaining of military equipment to monitor air and sea traffic (10 U.S.C. § 374(b)). The Act provides that the military may "monitor, contain, disable, or dispose of the weapon involved or elements of the weapon" (10 U.S.C. § 382(c)). In the case of biological weapons, the military may not directly participate in arrest, search, or seizure of evidence or intelligence gathering for law enforcement purposes, unless it is necessary to save human life and civilian authorities are unable to do so (10 U.S.C. § 382(d)). The involvement is also limited in time and scope to addressing only the specific biological incident (10 USC §382(d)).

But the 1981 Amendment added additional prohibitions for the use of the military, including any use that would adversely affect military preparedness for national defense (10 USC §376), as well as the proviso that the use of military resources may be contingent upon reimbursement by the local or state governments or other federal agency (10 USC §377).

Following the 1981 Amendment, the interdepartmental plan was formalized with a Memorandum of Understanding between the Department of Justice, the Federal Bureau of Investigation, and the Department of Defense in 1983, which provided for responsibilities in the event of a domestic terrorist attack (Memorandum of Understanding, 5 Aug. 1983). The agreement gives guidance for permitted uses of the military:

> *Although the Posse Comitatus Act does not permit military personnel to actively engage in the law enforcement mission unless expressly authorized, the Act does not prohibit military observers form reporting to the Department of Defense; nor does it generally prohibit the preparation of contingency plans for lawful military intervention; advice to civilian officials, sharing intelligence information collected during the normal course of military operations, including operations relating to the incident; the loan of specialized equipment or weaponry; the use of military personnel to deliver and maintain equipment for civilian use, provided those personnel do not operate that equipment; or the use of military personnel to train civilian law enforcement officials in the operation and maintenance of military equipment (See 10 USC §371–378).*

In 1988, another amendment was made once again, codifying further clarifications, but also adding the allowance of the use of the military for drug interdictions, and formally giving the Department of Defense lead authority for advising civilian law enforcement agencies concerning the types of equipment and assistance available (10 USC §380).

Under the Posse Comitatus Act, the military cannot be used to enforce laws against civilians in the United States. There are constitutional exceptions to this act, as well as exceptions statutorily provided. The constitutional exceptions are Presidential powers in emergency authority and the protection of federal property and operations. The act provides for exceptions for when it is "impracticable to enforce the laws of the U.S....by the ordinary course of judicial proceedings," (18 USC §1385) and for the use of the military by the President to control an insurrection (10 USC §331–333). Otherwise, the use of the military requires that a state's governor make such a request, and the President must issue an order to activate the military for that purpose. The failure to have the President formally issue an order can raise questions with use of the military under the Posse Comitatus Act, as in the Wounded Knee incident.[119] However, specific passive activities have been held to be compliant with the Act, which include, for example, reconnaissance missions.[120]

In summary, there are six exceptions to the Posse Comitatus Act: two constitutional exceptions and four statutory and regulatory exceptions. The President's emergency powers to respond to insurrection and the protection of federal property and governmental functions are the constitutional exceptions. The Congressionally granted powers to the President include a national emergency involving civil disturbances (10 USC §331–334 (2000) and DOD Dir. No. 3025.12), rebellions that make it impracticable to enforce federal laws (10 USC §332 (2000) and DOD Dir. No. 3025.12), and any insurrection or violence that impedes the state's ability to protect citizens and/or when the state is unable or unwilling to protect those rights (10 USC §333 (2000) and DOD Dir. No. 5525.5).

2.5.7.1.2. The John Warner National Defense Authorization Act of 2006

On October 17, 2006 President Bush signed into law the John Warner National Defense Authorization Act ("Warner Act").[121] The law is a codification of the interpretation of the U.S. Constitution and the powers of state and federal governments. The Congressional finding that the Federal government should have clear direction for assisting states when the state has been overwhelmed by a disaster. The disaster that triggered this legislation was Hurricane Katrina.[122] The act amends the Insurrection Act, which affords Congress the power to call forth the military, suppress insurrections and repel invasions.[123]

The Warner Act acknowledges the executive power of the President to deploy federal troops to respond to natural disasters and other domestic emergencies without the consent of the states involved.[124] This is a departure from the traditional state and federal government interplay during a public health disaster and what led to the deadly delays in a federal response to Hurricane Katrina. This provision became law despite the objection of all fifty state governors who claimed it subverts state sovereignty. [125]

The law codifies the constitutional federal power that already existed before the law was passed. Since the use of the federal power to deploy federal troops was often uncertain as to when this power was triggered, the Warner Act clarifies these powers, most notably, when the Federal government's power is triggered.[126] This power only arises when a catastrophic event has overwhelmed state and local governments.[127] Congress may also properly exercise its Constitutional legislative powers to authorize the Federal government to take charge. This power includes the deployment of federal troops to a state or city without the consent of local and state governments.[128] The Posse Comitatus Act still prohibits the use of the military to enforce domestic law except where it is expressly authorized by the Constitution or Act of Congress.[129]

2.5.7.2. USAMRIID

The USAMRIID is the biological defense laboratory housed within the U.S. Army division of the Department of Defense.

The stated mission of the USAMRIID is:

> *The U.S. Army Medical Research Institute of Infectious Diseases (USAMRIID) conducts research to develop strategies, products, information, procedures, and training programs for medical defense against biological warfare threats and naturally occurring infectious diseases that require special containment. USAMRIID, an organization of the U.S. Army Medical Research and Materiel Command (USAMRMC), is the lead medical research laboratory for the U.S. Biological Defense Research Program. The Institute plays a key role in national defense and in infectious disease research as the largest biocontainment laboratory in the Department of Defense for the study of hazardous diseases.* http://www.usamriid. army.mil/general/index.html (site visited Aug. 8, 2002).

The USAMRIID focuses on the development of countermeasures to sustain the fighting ability of the military, and is also engaged in response to worldwide emerging diseases in investigation and response activities with the CDC.

The military and civilian staff includes approximately 450 physicians, veterinarians, microbiologists, pathologists, chemists, molecular biologists, physiologists, pharmacologists, and the support staff. The staff includes approximately 70 Medical Research Volunteer Subjects (MRVS), highly trained laboratory technicians who have requested to participate in clinical trials of vaccines and drugs developed at the USAMRIID, which comprises the first phase of human testing in the vaccine and drug development protocol. The staff also includes teams trained to deploy to combat zones to establish diagnostic laboratories, to respond to a disease outbreak anywhere in the world, and to evaluate patients under the most stringent containment conditions (Biological Containment Level 4).

The USAMRIID reports that current work includes improving vaccines for anthrax, Venezuelan equine encephalitis, plague, and botulism, and developing new vaccines for toxins such as staphylococcal enterotoxins and ricin. Work is also being conducted for medical countermeasures to viral hemorrhagic fevers and arboviral illnesses. Significant effort is also devoted to developing diagnostic tools for identifying the presence of biological agents or endemic disease threats. It is the department most analogous to the former Soviet Union's Biopreparat, military division, except that the USAMIIRD has no offensive program.

2.5.7.3. National Guard Bureau

The National Guard Bureau is a division of Personnel with Reserve Affairs in the Department of Defense, and provides federal coordination and administration for the army and air national guards. It serves as liaison for the U.S. Army, the U.S. Air Force, and the 54 National Guard units in the states and territories. The responsibilities of the National Guard include: contracting for supplies and services; managing supply operations and movements; preparing and distributing meals; purifying, storing, and removing waste; repairing vehicles and equipment; constructing life support centers; and removing debris.[130]

2.5.8.   The Department of Energy

The Department of Energy is responsible for the work of its national laboratories. Sandia National Laboratories, a U.S. Department of Energy National Laboratory, works closely with the U.S. Department of State in the Biological Engagement Program, which works internationally to assist and collaborate with biological scientists.

2.5.9.   The Expanding Role of the Environmental Protection Agency

The U.S. EPA in February 1998 issued a Fact Sheet (EPA 55-F-98-014), wherein the Agency outlined its role in counter-terrorism. The Agency is one of six federal agencies and departments involved in response training for weapons of mass destruction: U.S. EPA, DOD, DOE, FBI, FEMA and PHS.

The U.S. EPA published a second Fact Sheet in July 1998, which described its role in the national anti-terrorism effort, as required by Presidential Decision Directives 39, 62, and 63. The supporting role is implemented by (1) helping state and local responders plan for emergencies; (2) coordinating with key Federal Partners; (3) training first responders; and (4) providing resources in the event of a terrorist incident. Within the U.S. EPA, the Office of Emergency and Remedial Response (OERR), the Chemical Emergency Preparedness and Prevention Office (CEPPO), the Office of Radiation and Indoor Air (ORIA), and the National Enforcement investigations Center (NEIC) are the critical components involved in the planning and response activities.

Legal authority for the U.S. EPA's involvement includes the National Oil and Hazardous Substances Pollution Contingency Plan (NCP), the Comprehensive Emergency Response, Compensation, and Liability Act (CERCLA), the Emergency Planning and Community Right-to-Know Act (EPCRA), and the Resources Conservation and Recovery Act (RCRA). These provide for potential response authority when there is an imminent and substantial threat to human health or the environment. The Safe Drinking Water Act (SDWA) and the Clean Water Act (CWA) are also important statutes for addressing threats to water systems and represent the preventive component of EPA's responsibility. The U.S. EPA is also a participant in the Domestic Preparedness Program, part of the Nunn-Lugar-Domenici Act. (http://www.epa.gov/ceppo/ct-epro.htm)

President Clinton gave the U.S. EPA authority for these parts of counter-terrorism activity:

(1)   *Assisting the FBI in determining what sort of hazardous substance may be or has been, released in a terrorist incident.*

(2)   *Following an incident, assisting with environmental monitoring, decontamination efforts, and long-term site cleanup operations.*

(www.epa.gov/swercepp/)

After the anthrax attacks, the U.S. Congress responded with a number of proposals that would include support from the U.S. EPA. Recognizing the role that the EPA could assume in the war on terror, on October 17, 2001 the U.S. Senate introduced S. 1560, the Biological Agent—Environmental Detection Act of 2001 (107th Cong., S. 1560), which provided for strengthening the United States' capabilities in environmental detection and the monitoring of biological agents.

Sec. 2. Findings. Congress makes the following findings:

(1) The threat of bioterrorism depends on the ability to produce and distribute biological agents that cause illness or death. A bioterrorism attack, once executed, requires containment and treatment that relies on primary-care provider capabilities as well as information and communication infrastructure.

(2) Early detection of a biological threat will minimize the number of people exposed to the agent and the extent that the agent or disease will spread.

(3) Preventative measures that consider production, processing, and distribution of biological or chemical agents could significantly reduce the threat of bioterrorism.

(4) New tools capable of detecting small quantities of infectious agents in food, water, air, and other vectors are needed, as well as a library of the genomic signatures of unique agents.

Sec. 3 Novel Detection and Surveillance Tools

(a) In General. The Secretary of Health and Human Services, in conjunction with the Secretary of Defense, the Secretary of Energy, the Director of the National Science Foundation, the Administrator of the Environmental Protection Agency, and representatives from industry, shall form an interagency research task force to encourage non-duplicative, public-private research relating to environmental monitoring and detection tools with respect to biological agents.

These novel suggested methods include appropriations for the encouragement of cooperative agreements between the government and the private sector in detecting common pathogens, new technologies for and approaches to identifying clandestine laboratories, the investigation and development of technologies to identify possible biological or chemical attacks using atmospheric remote detection technologies, and establishing a means of testing and calibration of new detection and surveillance tools.

Although this is a proposal which may never materialize, the Congress is interested in redefining the cooperative nature of the work between these agencies, including the U.S. Environmental Protection Agency.

2.5.9.1. Decontamination

The utilization of the U.S. EPA throughout the anthrax attacks was in the decontamination phase of response. This role was part of the national plan, and the expertise of the EPA in cleaning hazardous waste sites was transferred to the decontamination of the Hart Senate Building and other federal buildings contaminated during the anthrax attacks of the fall of 2001.

The President's Budget for FY 2003 requested $124 million in new funding for a total EPA investment of $133.4 million in homeland security, with more than half dedicated to decontamination activities:

$75 million to conduct research on better technologies and assessments to clean up buildings contaminated with biological and chemical agents;

$19 million to maintain security contracts and continue upgrades at EPA facilities as initiated by the Emergency Supplemental Appropriation Act;

$16.9 million to conduct drinking water system vulnerability assessments on small to mid-sized systems;

$13.2 million for continued operation of the West Coast Environmental Response Team;

$5 million for grants to the states to enhance homeland security coordination;

$3.8 million for special agents who will provide environmental crimes expertise; and

$0.5 million to enhance outreach for the Agency's Homeland Security efforts to the public.

2.5.9.2. Protection of the Nation's Water Supply

An incident of intentional water supply contamination was identified in a 1991 article in *The Atlantic Monthly*.

> Giardiasis is a diarrheal illness caused by the microorganism Giardia Lamblia. It can be spread by means of fecal contamination of water or food, or anal-oral contact. It is often diagnosed in travelers to countries having inadequate sanitation, but several waterborne outbreaks appear every year in the United States as well. In the outbreak in question four unrelated people, none of whom had left Britain or had contact with the others, but all of whom lived in the same block of apartments in Edinburgh [Scotland], developed giardiasis in June of last year. The confluence of cases immediately suggested to C.N. Ramsay, M.D., and J. Marsh, M.D. of the Lothian Health Board, that some common source of infection must exist. Investigation revealed that all the apartments were supplied with water from tanks on the roof, which were accessible through inspection hatches. Analysis of the water and the tanks demonstrated the presence of fecal matter containing Giardia cysts. The contamination, which eventually sickened nine people, was found to have been deliberate.

> Fortunately, Giardia infection is rarely serious in otherwise healthy individuals, and it is usually easy to treat. But Ramsay and Marsh were not sanguine in their appraisal of this case. "Had the perpetrator been excreting a more dangerous organism," they warned—typhus or typhoid fever, for example—"the consequences could have been grave." They went on: "This incident highlights a potential danger to public health from malicious interference with communal water supplies." Ramsay and Marsh pointed out that other waterborne epidemics of giardiasis, stemming from accidental contamination of water supplies by sewage or by workers unknowingly infected with the organism, have been documented in the United Kingdom and the United States. Other illnesses, such as cryptosporidiosis and dysentery, can be spread in similar ways, and can be difficult to eliminate from the water supply once introduced. "In view of the potential for deliberate contamination of water at any point in the distribution system," Ramsay and Marsh concluded," and in order to prevent recurrence of incidents like that described here, we suggest there is a need for relevant authorities to protect supplies from interference."[131]

The U.S. Congress amended the Safe Drinking Water Act with the Public Health Security and Bioterrorism Preparedness and Response Act of 2002 on June 12, 2002:

Sec. 402. OTHER SAFE DRINKING WATER ACT AMENDMENTS.

The Safe Drinking Water Act (title XIV of the Public Health Service Act) is amended by inserting the following new sections after section 1433 (as added by section 401 of this Act):

"Sec. 1434. CONTAMINANT PREVENTION, DETECTION AND RESPONSE.

"(a) In General.—The Administrator, in consultation with the Centers for Disease Control and, after consultation with appropriate departments and agencies of the Federal Government and with State and local governments, shall review (or enter into contracts or cooperative agreements to provide for a review of) current and future methods to prevent, detect and respond to the intentional introduction of chemical, biological or radiological contaminants into community water systems and source water for community water systems, including each of the following:

"(1) Methods, means and equipment, including real time monitoring systems, designed to monitor and detect various levels of chemical, biological, and radiological contaminants or indicators of contaminants and reduce the likelihood that such contaminants can be successfully introduced into public water systems and source water intended to be used for drinking water.

"(2) Methods and means to provide sufficient notice to operators of public water systems, and individuals served by such systems, of the introduction of chemical, biological or radiological

contaminants and the possible effect of such introduction on public health and the safety and supply of drinking water.

"(3) Methods and means for developing educational and awareness programs for community water systems.

"(4) Procedures and equipment necessary to prevent the flow of contaminated drinking water to individuals served by public water systems.

"(5) Methods, means, and equipment which could negate or mitigate deleterious effects on public health and the safety and supply caused by the introduction of contaminants into water intended to be used for drinking water, including an examination of the effectiveness of various drinking water technologies in removing, inactivating, or neutralizing biological, chemical, and radiological contaminants.

"(6) Biomedical research into the short-term and long-term impact on public health of various chemical, biological and radiological contaminants that may be introduced into public water systems through terrorist or other intentional acts.

"(b) Funding.—For the authorization of appropriations to carry out this section, see section 1435(e).

"Sec. 1435. SUPPLY DISRUPTION PREVENTION, DETECTION AND RESPONSE.

"(a) Disruption of Supply or Safety.—The Administrator, in coordination with the appropriate departments and agencies of the Federal Government, shall review (or enter into contracts or cooperative agreements to provide for a review of) methods and means by which terrorists or other individuals or groups could disrupt the supply of safe drinking water or take other actions against water collection, pretreatment, treatment, storage and distribution facilities which could render such water significantly less safe for human consumption, including each of the following:

"(1) Methods and means by which pipes and other constructed conveyances utilized in public water systems could be destroyed or otherwise prevented from providing adequate supplies of drinking water meeting applicable public health standards.

"(2) Methods and means by which collection, pretreatment, treatment, storage and distribution facilities utilized or used in connection with public water systems and collection and pretreatment storage facilities used in connection with public water systems could be destroyed or otherwise prevented from providing adequate supplies of drinking water meeting applicable public health standards.

"(3) Methods and means by which pipes, constructed conveyances, collection, pretreatment, treatment, storage and distribution systems that are utilized in connection with public water systems could be altered or affected so as to be subject to cross-contamination of drinking water supplies.

"(4) Methods and means by which pipes, constructed conveyances, collection, pretreatment, treatment, storage and distribution systems that are utilized in connection with public water systems could be reasonably protected from terrorist attacks or other acts intended to disrupt the supply or affect the safety of drinking water.

"(5) Methods and means by which information systems, including process controls and supervisory control and data acquisition and cyber systems at community water systems could be disrupted by terrorists or other groups.

"(b) Alternative Sources.—The review under this section shall also include a review of the methods and means by which alternative supplies of drinking water could be provided in the event of the destruction, impairment or contamination of public water systems.

"(c) Requirements and Considerations.—In carrying out this section and section 1434—

"(1) the Administrator shall ensure that reviews carried out under this section reflect the needs of community water systems of various sizes and various geographic areas of the United States; and

"(2) the Administrator may consider the vulnerability of, or potential for forced interruption of service for, a region or service area, including community water systems that provide service to the National Capital area.

"(d) Information Sharing.—As soon as practicable after reviews carried out under this section or section 1434 have been evaluated, the Administrator shall disseminate, as appropriate as determined by the Administrator, to community water systems information on the results of the project through the Information Sharing and Analysis Center, or other appropriate means.

"(e) Funding.—There are authorized to be appropriated to carry out this section and section 1434 not more than $ 15,000,000 for the fiscal year 2002 and such sums as may be necessary for the fiscal years 2003 through 2005."

2.5.9.3. National Biowatch Airmonitoring Program

In 2003, the U.S. Environmental Protection Agency was initially the agency that hosted the new National Biowatch airmonitoring program through retrofitting existing air monitoring devices used for monitoring air pollutants for compliance with the Clean Air Act. Initially, about 300 monitors were retrofitted with sensors with the capability of detecting smallpox, anthrax, and tularemia in the ambient air. One of the first incidents was the detection of tularemia in the Houston area, which is discussed in the article below. While the detection was indeed a true positive result, it was determined that the tularemia detected was naturally occurring in the area. Samples were processed for these potential bioweapons using TaqMan™-based PCR assays designed to test the sample collected in the monitor. According to the EPA, there have been no false positives of the millions of samples. (See http://www.globalsecurity.org/security/systems/biowatch.htm)

In 2005, President Bush requested $118 million to continue the development of the Biowatch program. By 2007, the cost of the monitors was disclosed at $100,000 and were labor- intensive, requiring state and local governments to conduct daily monitoring of the devices, which involved physically visiting the site, removing the filter, and processing it in the laboratory.

The Department of Homeland Security, once established, now has the lead responsibility for the BioWatch program, but also works cooperatively with the U.S. EPA and the CDC in its implementation.

Congress and others have questioned whether this approach to monitoring for bioweapons is a cost-effective and sound strategy that is useful in addition to disease monitoring.

Environment and Public Health in a Time of Plague

Victoria Sutton[†]

I.   Introduction

The environment and public health goals hold a common value of healthy populations. The threat of bioterrorism requires a partnership of both, building upon the long history of the link between public health and the environment. This existing relationship is key to an effective system of biodefense for the nation, because the use of biological weapons through every environmental pathway poses a potential threat. Contamination of water, growing crops, grazing cattle, air through inhalation, dermal absorption, or consumption of food or water in the human environment are potential delivery methods. For these risks of bioterrorism in the environment, there is an existing federal regulatory and statutory framework upon which the relationship between the environment and public health can be strengthened and shaped. We took a narrower approach to public health priorities in the environment in 1962 with the publication of *Silent Spring*,[132] which shifted the direct public health effects regulation to a broader environmental protection policy, which took a more comprehensive, holistic approach to human health.

This Article examines two important features of change in the post-9-11 relationship between public health, public health law, and environmental law. The first is an immediate change in the expansion of environmental laws to address biodefense activities of surveillance and response through either executive action or congressional amendment.[133] The second and most pervasive change is the indication of a shift in federalism in public health law, in a way analogous to the development of federal environmental law in the last half of the twentieth century. This Article begins with an examination of the indications of a shift in federalism in public health, and then turns to the changing role of the U.S. Environmental Protection Agency ("EPA") and the application of existing environmental laws to new problems and controversies in bioterrorism.

II. THE SHIFT IN FEDERALISM AS A COURSE TOWARD AN EFFECTIVE BIODEFENSE

Because modern federal environmental law has a well-established existing regulatory structure, shaped by more than three decades of experience, this framework can present major contributions to a national homeland defense built around federal environmental law expanding on the original effort to protect public health.

A. Shifting Federalism and Environmental Law

The role today of the federal government in environmental protection is the product of the shift from state power over property law and water law,[134] to federal power because of the substantial effect on interstate commerce from environmental pollution control and remediation, which has preempted these areas for state control. An example of this shift in federalism can be observed in the area of regulation of water pollution.

The first action by Congress involving the effects of dumping trash and materials into rivers was through the regulation of "navigable waters" in the U.S. Rivers and Harbors Act of 1899[135] and the Refuse Act of 1899.[136] The primary purpose was to protect the rivers for navigation and to avoid impeding navigation traffic with trash or lumber and wood floating in the rivers obstructing shipping.[137] The Water Pollution Control Act of 1948[138] was the first comprehensive act to address the growing concern for water pollution but did little more than underscore states' responsibilities for water. This Act was replaced by the Water Pollution Control Act Amendments of 1956[139] which were intended to "extend and strengthen" the 1948 Act, and emphasized the continuing responsibilities of the state in controlling water pollution.[140] The House Report from the Committee on Public Works stated that:

> The bill as reported reemphasizes the policy of the Congress to recognize, preserve, and protect the primary rights and responsibilities of the States in controlling water pollution . . . . Regulatory authority at the Federal level should be limited to interstate pollution problems and used on a standby basis only for serious situations and which are not resolved through State and interstate collaboration.[141]

The Act specified that "nothing in this act shall be construed as impairing or affecting any right or jurisdiction of the States with respect to their waters."[142] The Public Health Service was designated as the lead agency with the goal of determining the "impact of new pollutants on public health and other vital water uses, and to find more practical and economically feasible abatement measures."[143] The Surgeon General was given authority to develop comprehensive programs to implement and enforce this Act, but was at the same time prevented from issuing any regulations without the prior agreement of the states.[144] The states were given grants to implement programs developed by the Surgeon General.[145]

In that same year, 1956, President Eisenhower vetoed the Rivers and Harbors Act of 1956[146] because, among other reasons, it lacked the provision of state participation in the bill.[147] In his veto message he stated that "vital water resources can best be conserved and utilized in the public interest if the Federal Government cooperates with State and local governments."[148]

The inability to control water pollution by the federal government, because of the policy of leaving regulation to the states, was exacerbated by the reorganization of the federal oversight mechanism. Although the 1956 Act designated the Public Health Service as the agency charged with implementation, the Refuse Act of 1965[149] changed the control to one of joint authority by the Public Health Service and the Commission appointed under the Federal Water Pollution Control Administration.[150] The states were given the charge to develop standards for water quality within their jurisdictions.[151] In 1966, the Federal Water Pollution Control Commission was moved to the Department of Interior,[152] keeping administration of the program in a state of instability.

The public pressure to address the growing problem of environmental pollution, which was not improving under states' control, culminated in the first Earth Day in 1970 with the signing of the National Environmental Policy Act,[153] the first major federal environmental statute, and the creation of the U.S. Environmental Protection Agency.[154] A growing environmental movement exploded in 1970 with this first Earth Day, marked by marches, celebrations, and a nationwide wave of determination to reverse the trend of polluting the environment and return the nation to its previous condition.[155] Although prior to 1970, Congress had passed statutes which directed states to give attention to limiting the pollution in their water and air, such rules could be avoided by the polluting industries by leaving any state with the tough regulations and seeking a more hospitable—and profitable—state.[156] This phenomenon became known as the "race to the bottom" with each state hoping to be the most attractive to businesses and factories which would bring employment and tax revenues to the state, and the way to attract them was to compete with other states, promulgating the least onerous regulations.[157]

Water quality standards were to be promulgated by the states, as required under the 1965 legislation, and the Committee Report described the process for that development: "[t]he States have first responsibility for enforcement of their standards. When approved by the Environmental Protection Agency, however, the standards for interstate navigable waters become Federal-State standards."[158]

A long history of litigation between states for polluting waterways[159] and air[160] further gave rise to the interstate commerce clause basis for federal environmental regulation.[161] Property law and water law, within the sovereign power of states, were areas among the "mass of legislation"[162] which has never been surrendered by the states. However, the federalism relationship between the states and the national government was not intended to be unchanging, but rather flexible enough to accommodate the interests of the people. James Madison wrote in The Federalist Papers No. 46: "If, therefore . . . the people should in future become more partial to the federal than to the State government, the people ought not to be precluded from giving most of their confidence where they may discover it to be most due . . . ."[163] The great pressure from the public with the groundswell of concern for the environment shifted the task to the federal government to overcome the interstate problems of air and water pollution as well as hazardous waste.[164] The model has been identified as one of cooperative federalism.

In 1972, Congress enacted the Federal Water Pollution Control Act[165] which established a national permit system to control all discharges of pollutants into surface waters to be implemented by the new federal agency, EPA.[166]

B. SHIFT IN FEDERALISM IN PUBLIC HEALTH LAW

Bioterrorism and emerging infectious diseases threaten the public health in a way we have not seen in almost a century.[167] States have had sovereignty in the area of public health since colonial existence, and preemption exists where food and drugs enter interstate commerce.[168] Federal regulation of food and drugs began with the turn of the twentieth century and was intended to regulate risks to the public health.[169] However, new threats of bioterrorism and emerging infectious diseases are regulated through the sovereign powers of states, not federal powers.[170] But after the anthrax attacks in the Fall of 2001, the public expected the federal government to provide a defense against bioterrorism as a matter of national security.[171] Consistent with the shifting federalism concept of the U.S. Constitution, interpreted through The Federalist's principle that "If . . . the people should in future become more partial to the federal than to the State government, the people ought not to be precluded from giving most of their confidence where they may discover it to be most due,"[172] a cooperative federalism model in public health is evidently emerging, in much the same manner as federal environmental law.[173] The following developments in the area of biodefense and public health law are illustrative of the shift in federalism analogous to that of federal environmental law.

As outlined above, in 1956 states were given grants to begin to develop standards for water quality on a state-by-state basis. The failure of the states to use grants for consistent regulation from state to state, which would have ensured a uniform approach to environmental regulation, gave rise to state-shopping by polluting industries to find the state with the least regulation.[174] Each state developed their own standards, leading to as many standards as there were states.

Just as grants to states to develop environmental water quality standards resulted in further creating a disjointed and uncoordinated state-by-state approach, the same approach has begun in preparation for bioterrorism. The Public Health Security and Bioterrorism Preparedness and Response Act of 2002[175] provides for grants to states to develop plans for biodefense dispersed through the Centers for Disease Control and Prevention ("CDC") to the state departments of public health.[176] A state-by-state approach to biodefense fails to encompass the overarching priority of national coordination in the event of an attack or the spread of an emerging infectious disease, which could spread much like the interstate nature of water and air pollution. Grants were also provided as a means to prepare for a bioterrorism attack through the Nunn-Lugar-Domenici Act,[177] to provide funding to purchase new equipment and to attend training in biodefense, beginning well before 9-11 in the mid-1990s.[178] The General Accounting Office ("GAO") cautioned against simply providing grants to the states for training and equipment, warning that "federal officials should be alert to the potential for these governments to use grants to substitute for their own resources in these programs, essentially converting a targeted federal grant into a general revenue sharing initiative."[179] Indeed, state and local governments, long neglected budget priorities, needed funding to obtain basics such as fax machines. Urging that national preparedness must hinge on the federal government's ability to form effective partnerships with nonfederal entities, the GAO argued that "federal initiatives should be conceived as national, not federal in nature," engaging not only local and state governments in partnerships, but also private partners.[180]

The triggering event for a movement in federalism occurred for federal environmental law in 1970 with the culmination of public demand for the federal government to address the growing problem of environmental pollution. The triggering event for a shift in federalism in public health law occurred with the anthrax attacks of the Fall of 2001, when the public demanded that the federal government provide the needed defense and response to the attacks.[181] The role of CDC, however, as stated in its mission, is merely to respond to the needs and requests of states for support and advice in public health matters.[182] The public demanded more, and the Public Health Security and Bioterrorism Preparedness and Response Act of 2002[183] provided a token expansion of CDC authority finding that "the Centers for Disease Control and Prevention has an essential role in defending against and combating public health threats and requires secure and modern facilities, and expanded and improved capabilities related to bioterrorism and other public health emergencies, sufficient to enable such Centers to conduct this important mission."[184] A closer examination of the section reveals only that an increase in facilities and training is mandated,[185] rather than an expansion of their mission to fulfill this role of biodefense. However, the provision for the establishment of a system of public health alert communications and surveillance networks between federal, state, and local public health officials through the use of grants and cooperative agreements is a move away from exclusive state power and control to a more cooperative federalism. The use of surveillance of public health has always been a power of the states, and states are not, therefore, compelled to report any symptoms or diseases other than those reportable communicable diseases required by federal law.[186]

Just as the precipitating event of Earth Day began the shift in federalism in pollution control in environmental law, the precipitating event of the anthrax attacks of the Fall of 2001 has begun a shift in federalism in public health law. The federal government first identified the Public Health Service as the lead agency, followed by the creation of a Federal Water Pollution Control Commission to join with the Public Health Service in administration of water quality.[187] Pollution control responsibilities were located first in the Public Health Service, then the Commission was made a part of the Department of Health, Education and Welfare.[188] Finally, the water pollution control authority was transferred to Department of Interior[189] and then to the U.S. Environmental Protection Agency with its formation by Executive Order in 1970 by President Nixon.[190] President Nixon created a new agency with a mission to implement federal environmental law, rather than to risk a "business-as-usual" response by the Department of Interior to the new duties of federal environmental law.[191]

The same reorganization strategy to combine effective federal offices within the Department of Homeland Security parallels the development of federal environmental law, in the shifting federalism responsibilities. President George W. Bush signaled three shifts in federalism in his proposal for the formation of the Department of Homeland Security. First, "the Department would set national policy and establish guidelines for state and local governments;"[192] second, the proposal makes the Department of Homeland Security "the lead agency preparing for and responding to . . . biological . . . terrorism," which takes part of the states' public health agencies' responsibility as described in the CDC biodefense plan;[193] and third, the proposal directs that "The new Department would ensure that local law enforcement entities—and the public—receive clear and concise information from their national government,"[194] which again, takes part of the states' public health agencies' responsibility in originating their own public health information.

Figure 1 notes significant events in the evolution of federal environmental law, and the parallel with public health law.

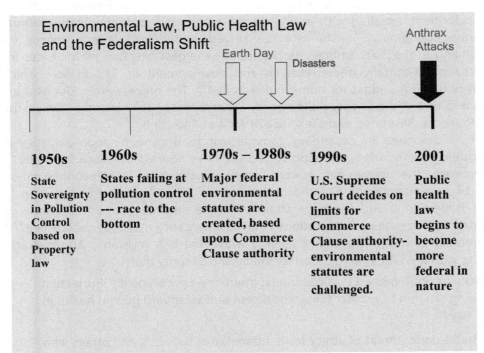

Fig. 1. Timeline of the development of federal environment law with recent developments in public health law.

III. ENVIRONMENTAL LAW AND HOMELAND DEFENSE

A. THE CHANGING ROLE OF EPA

After the anthrax attacks of 2001, EPA Administrator Christine Todd Whitman announced that the agency would seek more authority to protect water supplies and to manage contaminated sites, saying, "[I]t's not about turf . . . [I]t's about the best way to respond and use all the resources we have available to us to meet our responsibilities in responding to biological attacks."[195]

The role of the Environmental Protection Agency has been interpreted within its stated mission in 1997 "to protect human health and to safeguard the natural environment—air, water, and land—upon which life depends."[196] The mission was simplified in EPA's 2003 Strategic Plan: "Our mission statement is clear: to protect human health and the environment."[197] In February 1998, the EPA issued a Fact Sheet[198] outlining their responsibilities for responses to terrorism, followed by a further directive in July 1998 which described the role in the Presidential Decision Directives 39, 62, and 63.[199] These stipulated that the EPA was to be a supporting agency by: (1) helping state and local responders plan; (2) coordinating with key federal partners; (3) training first responders; and (4) providing resources in the event of a terrorist incident.[200] It further stipulated that "[b]ecause of [EPA's] inherent role in protecting human health and the environment from possible harmful effects of certain chemical, biological, and nuclear materials, EPA is actively involved in counter-terrorism planning and response efforts."[201]

The Nunn-Lugar-Domenici Act, which was among the first to address terrorism through providing grants for training for first responders at the local level, included EPA as a participant in this Domestic Preparedness Program.[202]

The President can provide direction of the operations of the Executive Branch through directives, which may be classified. In Presidential Decision Directives ("PDD") 39, 62, and 63 the responsibilities of each federal agency for terrorism events is outlined.[203] In these directives which have been redacted and declassified, the responsibilities of the U.S. Environmental Protection Agency include: "Assisting the FBI in determining what sort of hazardous substance may be, or has been, released in a terrorist incident; and following an incident, assisting with environmental monitoring, decontamination efforts and long-term site cleanup operations."[204] The EPA has served as the lead federal agency for decontamination in responding to the 2001 anthrax attacks and their largest new budget increases for FY 2003 were in the area of decontamination research and development at $75 million, which comprised more than half of the EPA budget for homeland security.[205] The offices within EPA who are assigned counter-terrorism roles are: the Chemical Emergency Preparedness and Prevention Office; the Office of Emergency and Remedial Response; and the Office of Air and Radiation.[206]

The 2004 Strategic Plan describes an expanding commitment to decontamination activities in response to terrorism including bioterrorism, planning for a budget to address five such incidents.[207] The Strategic Plan describes the movement toward more preparation for decontamination responsibilities because of expectations of EPA from the nation: "The Agency's crucial role in responding to the World Trade Center and Pentagon attacks, and the decontamination of anthrax at Capitol Hill, have further defined the nation's expectations of EPA's emergency response capabilities."[208]

Is an expanded environmental role in homeland security within the EPA mission? Administrator Whitman wrote in her letter with the EPA Strategic Plan for Homeland Security that:

> The terrorist attacks of September 11, 2001, transformed the Environmental Protection Agency's long-standing mission to protect the environment and safeguard human health in new and important ways. . . .

> With the United States under threat of attack from international terrorists and others who seek to do our country harm, EPA's traditional mission has expanded to include protecting our country against the environmental and health consequences of acts of terrorism.[209]

The role of EPA in Homeland Security is within EPA's stated mission, and the future of EPA's role is vital to the federal coordination of an effective biodefense. However, Administrator Whitman cautions "while the missions we are prepared to carry out are indispensable elements of any national effort to secure the homeland, there may, over time, be other federal departments or agencies better suited or able to carry out certain aspects of those missions."[210] However, with another passing year, and the intervening organization of the Department of Homeland Security, these EPA functions in biodefense are still vital, and unique to EPA's capabilities.

The Environmental Protection Agency was criticized for both its increasing role in homeland security, as well as its handling of the World Trade Center cleanup effort. In response to this criticism for its changing role and the criticism that it might have neglected its criminal enforcement duties as a result of the reallocation of resources, EPA issued a statement entitled "Correcting the record: EPA's Role in Homeland Security, Enforcement . . ." in April 2003. EPA stated "Since September 11, 2001 our government has experienced an enormous increase in the need to protect its citizens from acts of terrorism. . . . EPA responded immediately and continues to play a critical role in homeland protection. EPA's strategic plan for homeland security was held up as a model for other Agencies and Departments. . . . EPA's focus since September 11 has been to support our nation's effort at combating domestic threats while at the same time ensuring that enforcement of environmental crimes continues."[211]

B. TRADITIONAL NATIONAL SECURITY EXCEPTIONS

Major federal environmental laws address issues of national security through national security exemptions. The Endangered Species Act ("ESA"),[212] the Clean Water Act,[213] the Clean Air Act,[214] the Resource Conservation and Recovery Act ("RCRA"),[215] and the Toxic Substances Control Act[216] all provide for a national security exemption. The National Environmental Protection Act ("NEPA") has been interpreted to allow for environmental impact statements to be classified for national security reasons.[217] These exemptions and interpretations can be important to homeland security priorities, although their primary effect is to conserve resources.

C. EXECUTIVE ACTIONS THAT DO NOT REQUIRE AMENDMENTS TO EXISTING STATUTES

The use of environmental laws in homeland security capitalizes on an existing, mature framework of federal environmental law. In the EPA's Strategic Plan, the agency committed to the goal of protecting critical infrastructure through "manage[ment of] its federal civil, and criminal enforcement programs to meet our homeland security, counter-terrorism, and anti-terrorism responsibilities under [the] Presidential Decisional Directives . . . and environmental, civil and criminal statutes."[218] These Executive Branch actions operate within the delegated authority of Congress to the President through EPA.

1. Biowatch

Legislation was introduced after 9-11, to develop a system of biosensors for biological agents using "atmospheric remote detection technologies,"[219] but it remained in committee during the congressional session. However, by January 2003, such a system had been developed by EPA, on executive authority—not congressional authority.

On January 22, 2003, the White House announced that there would be a deployment of environmental biosensors for surveillance of any presence of biological disease agents,[220] in a program named "Biowatch." The more than 3,000 air quality monitors utilized in the monitoring of pollutants in the air comprise the network supporting Biowatch.[221] Air quality monitors in undisclosed major cities have been fitted with air filters that are analyzed on a daily basis by one of 120 laboratories around the United States.[222]

On October 4, 2003, Biowatch received its first "hit." In Houston, the air monitors retrofitted with the Biowatch filters utilizing a daily collection process detected tularemia[223] at two different air monitor sites on the east side of Houston.[224] Again, on Sunday, October 5, 2003 and Monday, October 6, 2003 the detection of tularemia was confirmed for the monitors.[225] The daily collection of paper-thin filters for crushing and analysis showed the presence of fragments of DNA of tularemia.[226] The days that followed resulted in negative reads, and on October 9, 2003 the Houston Department of Health and Human Services, in co-authorship with Harris County Public Health and Environmental Services, issued a press release disclosing the discovery.[227]

The response to the discovery of the DNA fragments permits an examination of the federalism relationship between the state and federal government in a newly cooperative federalism area of surveillance of biological agents through a federal environmental statute. The Department of Energy, the CDC, and the EPA all collaborated in the development of Biowatch. EPA coordinated the location of the filters, and arranged for collection of the filters by contractors.[228] It was estimated that the collection and processing of these filters would cost about one million dollars per year for each city.[229] The monitors are overseen by the Texas Commission on Environment Quality ("TCEQ"), and upon discovery of the indication of tularemia, TCEQ notified the FBI, and the appropriate official was alerted.[230] Concurrently, the confirmation process was underway, with samples being sent to CDC to confirm that the DNA fragments were tularemia and not a false positive.[231]

This new, and major, biosurveillance role for EPA is being assumed through state programs which have been delegated program authority under the Clean Air Act.[232] Because of this, the state TCEQ and not the local EPA office, was engaged in the process. A reassessment of the federal agency's role in homeland security began at EPA headquarters to question whether EPA should have a greater role.[233] As announced on September 30, 2003 in the pre-publication copy of EPA's Strategic Plan, EPA was made the lead agency for the Biowatch system by the former Office of Homeland Security.[234]

The EPA Strategic Plan for Homeland Security, released in September 2002, made bold and sweeping commitments to its role in homeland security, yet its more recent Strategic Plan, released in September 2003, does little more than mention homeland security[235]—no components of EPA were moved to the newly created Department of Homeland Security.[236] Any second EPA strategic plan for homeland security is very likely to show a significant withdrawal from the duties of homeland security, in part due to the lack of supporting congressional appropriations for the earlier, bolder commitments to homeland security by EPA.[237]

2. FIFRA

The Federal Insecticide, Fungicide, and Rodenticide Act ("FIFRA")[238] provides that the EPA may "exempt any Federal or State agency from any provision of this subchapter if the Administrator determines that emergency conditions exist which require such exemption."[239] An act of bioterrorism meets the requirements for an "emergency condition."[240] The conditions for a crisis exemption exist when there is no time for review by EPA, and a temporary crisis exemption may be issued, effective for fifteen days.[241] Crisis exemptions have been issued by EPA for the use of ethylene oxide application to decontaminate the congressional offices and the Department of Justice building;[242] hydrogen peroxide and dimethylbenzyl ammonium chlorides were exempted for use on contaminated personal property;[243] chlorine dioxide gas for use in the Hart Senate Office Building[244] and methyl bromide was exempted for application in a vacant mobile home on the premises of the University of Florida.[245] This emergency authority provides a framework to ensure that certain safety precautions are observed.

3. Local Emergency Planning Committees

The utilization of an existing national system of local emergency planning committees ("LEPCs"), mandated by the Emergency Planning and Community Right-to-Know Act,[246] can provide at least a two-year savings in time[247] for the implementation of any similar program for biodefense.

Another agency action which has the effective of bolstering the role of EPA in homeland defense was guidance issued in February 1998, for utilizing the LEPCs through expanding the local role in hazardous chemical emergencies to weapons of mass destruction emergencies.[248] The guidance urged LEPCs to expand their current role of information collection and dissemination to the community to include biological agents and threats of bioterrorism, as well as threats of releases of hazardous substances.[249] EPA issued guidance again in August 2001, for addressing terrorism activities in the local emergency plan, stating that "Local emergency planning committees should consider the possibility of terrorist events as they review existing pans and consider how to incorporate counter-terrorism ("CT") measures into their plans. CT planning and preparedness is often an extension of existing activities rather than a totally new effort."[250] Although the statute specifically directs the professional expertise of the membership of the LEPCs,[251] the guidance urges that the committees include additional members who may have expertise in biological agents "(e.g., the coroner, morticians, chemistry and biology labs, university experts.)"[252] The logical extension of the LEPCs to include the disclosure to the public[253] of the presence of biological agents in the community falls within a mission to provide residents with information about hazards that exist in their communities.

The statute also includes the provision of public information of inventories of chemicals in the community, as well as emergency plans,[254] which has been of concern since 9-11, yet objections from public interest groups in support of openness rejected any move to amend the statute.[255]

But contrast this proposed concern to know what biological agents are in the community with the movement to remove chemical "worst-case-scenario" information from the Internet. Due to increased concerns about chemical information available on the Internet,[256] EPA revised the rule which makes data about the kinds and amounts of hazardous materials, plans and most importantly, an estimation of the impact of a release on the surrounding communities including human health impacts, commonly referred to as the "worst-case-scenarios." The statutory requirement to make this information available to the public was modified by action from EPA which removed the material from the Internet, and made it available in reading rooms with some restrictions on access.[257] A proposed rule is expected to be final in 2004.

4. Decontamination Is Led by EPA

Prior to the anthrax attacks in the Fall of 2001, the EPA was designated as the lead agency in decontamination activity for any response to a biological terrorist event during the Clinton Administration.[258] This role was utilized during the anthrax decontamination of the Hart Senate Office Building and other government buildings.[259] The largest single budget item in homeland security for EPA in the following budget year was for decontamination activities to conduct research on technologies to decontaminate buildings which have been contaminated with a biological agent.[260]

Decontamination also includes the disposal of wastewater used to hose down workers after exiting a contaminated building.[261] After decontamination of the American Media building in Boca Raton, Florida, EPA developed a protocol with the Agency for Toxic Substances and Disease Registry in October 2001 for treatment of the wastewater before disposal.[262] The wastewater was used to water golf courses, Florida Atlantic University, and some of the city's southeastern neighborhoods.[263]

D. AMENDMENTS TO EXISTING STATUTES

The Public Health Security and Bioterrorism Preparedness and Response Act of 2002,[264] in Title V, amended the Safe Drinking Water Act to require systems subject to regulation under the act to develop safety plans to counter the threat of terrorism.[265] Upon receipt of the plan by the EPA Administrator, it is protected from disclosure to the public, not through the national security exemption[266] of the Freedom of Information Act ("FOIA"),[267] but through a specific exemption from the requirements of FOIA.[268] It does not protect the plans from local and state open records or "sunshine" acts.[269] All fifty states have some form of a FOIA-type statute,[270] which rely upon judicial determinations or provide for access to state information through their state constitution.[271] EPA has urged states to amend their statutes with regard to disclosure of security plans for water systems.[272]

E. JUDICIAL INTERPRETATION OF EXISTING FEDERAL ENVIRONMENTAL LAW TO INCLUDE BIOLOGICAL THREATS

1. Cleanup Actions in Response to Bioterrorism: RCRA and CERCLA

During the anthrax attacks, a circuit court was asked to issue an injunction to examine the U.S. Postal Service's cleanup plan for the Morgan Processing Center in New York.[273] The plaintiffs asked for the injunction using two federal environmental statutes, RCRA and the Comprehensive Environmental Response, Compensation, and Liability Act ("CERCLA"),[274] which provides for citizen action to require a plan for cleanup that meets the standards of the National Contingency Plan.[275] In the first case, the U.S. Postal Service took the position that anthrax did not meet the definition of "solid waste" as required to trigger a RCRA cleanup.[276] Solid waste is defined as, "any garbage, refuse sludge from a waste treatment plant, water supply treatment plant, or air pollution control facility and other discarded material, including solid, liquid, semisolid, or contained gaseous material resulting from industrial, commercial, mining, and agricultural operations, and from community activities."[277] CERCLA defines "pollutant or contaminant" as "any element, substance, compound, or mixture, including disease-causing agents, which after release into the environment and upon exposure, ingestion, inhalation, or assimilation into any organism, either directly from the environment or indirectly by ingestion through food chains will or may reasonably be anticipated to cause death [or] disease."[278] In order to trigger a RCRA cleanup, however, the definition of solid waste had to be met, and the U.S. Postal Service argued that anthrax was not a "solid waste" triggering the citizen suit.[279] However, the action was filed again several months later, and the Postal Service changed their position—anthrax was a solid waste.[280] The Postal Service made this concession with a caveat: "[T]he Government does not maintain that anthrax, *per se*, is a 'solid waste' under RCRA, or that RCRA applies in every context in which anthrax may be present. Whether RCRA applies in every context in any case involving anthrax requires a fact-specific analysis, which in turn considers whether the anthrax at issue has been discarded."[281]

2. Eradication of Smallpox, NEPA, and the ESA

Although no litigation has been initiated to prevent the eradication of the remaining smallpox virus, as planned by the World Health Organization, federal environmental laws most applicable to this consideration are NEPA and the ESA.[282]

Examining NEPA, the statutory mandate requires that an environmental impact statement be made for "any major federal action significantly affecting the quality of the human environment."[283] The CDC, which holds one of the U.S. samples of smallpox, might be required to examine the applicability of this statute. Although the effect on the human environment may be positive, courts have interpreted "effects" to include both positive and negative effects on the environment, requiring only a human alteration of the environment.[284]

The ESA protects fish or wildlife and excludes any insect that might be considered a pest, presenting an "overwhelming and overriding risk to man."[285] A virus is not included in the protections of the ESA, and it is inconceivable that Congress would intend to eradicate an insect that might be a pest while preserving a virus that was a serious public health threat.

IV. EMERGING DISEASES AND THE ENVIRONMENT

The problem of emerging infectious diseases in the world has become evident, and the role of the changing environment as either a natural cycle or as a human-created phenomenon has been a contributing factor to this change in environment.

Cycles of hantavirus,[286] occurring during especially wet spring seasons, evident from the historical sand paintings and the oral histories of the Navajos predating U.S. governmental records, are an example of increasing rains as a trigger for a disease cycle.[287] However, evidence of meningitis epidemics in South Africa, occurring with dry seasons, low humidity, and dusty conditions, and disappearing with the onset of the rains, indicates that it is not only wetter climate patterns that can trigger epidemics. [288]

Infectious pathogens are being affected by climate and weather patterns.[289] Natural disasters also occur as a result of shifts in climate and weather patterns, which often lead to disruption of communities and the development of temporary shelters, which inevitably provide a natural setting for the transmission of diseases in a densely populated community of displaced victims of these natural disasters.[290]

V. FUTURE ROLE OF THE U.S. EPA

A. MOSQUITOES AND WETLANDS REGULATION

On August 15, 2003, President George W. Bush signed into law the Mosquito Abatement for Safety and Health Act,[291] authorizing grants through CDC for mosquito control and to prevent mosquito-borne diseases and for other purposes.[292] The act requires EPA to consider the use of pesticides and what impact that use will have on public health.[293]

Could it be possible that we have come full circle in the management of wetlands? Wetlands have not always been seen as useful. One of the first appropriations of the Continental Congress was for $300 to purchase quinine for protection of the troops from malaria.[294] An important U.S. policy for land development included draining wetlands in order to reduce mosquito populations and the malaria they brought.[295] Some believe that protecting wetlands is inconsistent with public health, and argue that we cannot protect both wetlands and public health.[296]

Two centuries later, the Clean Water Act provided for the protection of wetlands, based on the Commerce Clause authority over navigable waters, and charging EPA with environmental oversight.[297] Should West Nile fever, or other mosquito-borne disease, become such a hazard that it requires drastic destruction of mosquitoes and other natural hosts and vectors, EPA might be balancing the risk of broad applications of pesticides which will be sure to harm other parts of the ecosystem, verses draining wetlands which could reduce the population of mosquitoes. Could EPA find that, on balance, the loss of wetlands is less costly to public health than the eradication of mosquitoes? Should EPA take on the role of balancing the interests of environmental protection and public health?

B. EPA AND INTERNATIONAL EXPERIENCE

EPA has been at the center of international negotiations for environmental protection, including such important agreements as the Montreal Protocol, an international approach to reduce and reverse ozone depletion,[298] and the development of the Kyoto Protocol for global climate change responses.[299] The need to begin to develop an international public health agreement has been evident with the recent SARS outbreak, which originated in China. An international protocol for addressing the important needs of communicating information about public health to the world community and the development of protocols for preventing the kind of spread of SARS that resulted from the delay in addressing the outbreak through the World Health Organization ("WHO") is a next step response to this event, and should involve the participation of EPA, because of their expertise and international experience in areas involving the impact on public health in the context of the environment. EPA should play a major role in the development of public health protocols with WHO.

VI. CONCLUSION

Environmental protection and public health have been common goals for a healthy population. The new threat of bioterrorism demands that we utilize existing federal environmental law systems through the role of the U.S. Environmental Protection Agency; amendments to existing federal environmental laws; application of existing federal environmental laws to new issues in bioterrorism; and judicial interpretations of these laws in the context of bioterrorism-related controversies. The evolution of public health law is following a pattern of development of cooperative federalism, seen in the last half century with the development of federal environmental law. In conclusion, the post 9-11 world will demand that public health be addressed through the environmental law system, and become more like the federal environmental law system.

The relationship of environmental law and public health law has historically been interdependent and promises to continue to be so in the context of bioterrorism. The use of the U.S. Environmental Protection Agency in cooperation with the Department of Homeland Security will enable the utilization of existing human resources in enforcement and in the shaping of environmental programs which also include elements of biodefense, through executive branch responses within the mission of EPA. Where amendments to existing federal environmental laws can enhance the ability to provide for homeland security, such as the Safe Drinking Water Act Amendments of 2002, they also provide for not only the utilization of existing resources for homeland security in an economical sense, but it also speed the development of institutional mechanisms to use for homeland security needs.

Public health law, an area of traditional state sovereignty, is shifting to more federal or national authority, as suggested in recent legislation and the announcements of President George W. Bush in his organizational plan for a Department of Homeland Security.[300] In fact, the shift in federalism is analogous to that of environmental law, an area of traditional state sovereignty in property, specifically using water as an example.

Former Administrator Christine Todd Whitman, signed a strong plan for homeland security in 2002, and this is no time—in a time of plague[301]—to reverse that strong course that has been set in motion.

2.5.10. Department of Veterans Affairs

The Department of Veterans Affairs manages a system of hospitals throughout the United States, which serve qualified military veterans throughout their lives. The system of hospitals provides an opportunity for a federal presence in communities to create a national biodefense system, ensuring training military medical personnel are within communities throughout the U.S.

2.5.11. The Role of the Federal Trade Commission

The Federal Trade Commission is a rulemaking agency and is responsible for "the protection of consumers from fraudulent, deceptive and unfair business practices in the marketplace and to provide information to help consumers spot, stop and avoid them."[302] During the anthrax attacks, the FTC, in conjunction with the FDA and the CDC, utilized the internet to warn consumers of internet vendors selling Ciprofloxacin (Cipro), the antibiotic recommended for the treatment of anthrax. The FTC warned against buying the drug without a prescription and without consulting the list of approved pharmacies produced by the Association of Boards of Pharmacy. The warning read, in part:

> The recent reports of anthrax exposure have spawned numerous websites and emails selling Ciprofloxacin (Cipro) and other antibiotics for treatment. The Federal Trade Commission (FTC) warns that fraudsters often follow the headlines, tailoring their offers to prey on consumers' fears and vulnerabilities.
>
> If you are wondering whether to buy products online from sellers who claim that their products will protect from biological threats, the FTC, as well as the Centers for Disease Control and Prevention (CDC) and the Food and Drug Administration (FDA) have news for you:
>
> Talk to your health-care professional before you use any medications...
>
> Know that some websites may sell ineffective drugs...
>
> Know who you are buying from...

2.6   Judicial Branch Role

The role of the Judiciary has been active and important in the review of legislation and the review of actions of the Executive Branch in the post-9/11 world. Reviewing legislation and executive actions to ensure consistency with the U.S. Constitution remains as important today as when the U.S. Supreme Court established their role in this process in *Marbury v. Madison*. While much of the Supreme Court's attention has been on issues in the context of privacy and detentions civil liberties, other cases in lower courts have addressed criminal and civil matters involved with potential biological weapons and the risks that they may pose to public health and national security. The remainder of this book will address some of the analysis provided by the judicial branch in these matters.

CHAPTER TWO ENDNOTES

1 The White House, Office of the Press Secretary, Fact Sheet: Combating Terrorism: Presidential Decision Directive 626, Annapolis, Md. (May 22, 1998) [hereinafter Combating Terrorism].

2 *Id.*

3 *Id.*

4 *Id.*

5 RICHARD PRESTON, THE COBRA EVENT (1997).

6 *See* Interview by *New York Times* with President Bill Clinton (Jan. 21, 1999).

7 *See* Presidential Decision Directive 62 (May 1998).

8 Combating Terrorism, *supra* note 2.

9 *Id.*

10 V. Richard Persico, Jr., *Early Nineteenth-Century Cherokee Political Organization, in* THE CHEROKEE INDIAN NATION (Duane H. King ed., 1979).

11 *Testimony of Henry L. Hinton, Jr., Assistant Comptroller General, National Security and International Affairs Division, before the Subcomm. on Nat'l Security, Veterans Affairs, and Int'l Relations, Committee on Government Reform,* U.S. House of Representatives, GAO/T-NSIAD/GGD-99-107 (March 11, 1999) [hereinafter Testimony of Henry L. Hinton, Jr.].

12 U.S. GENERAL ACCOUNTING OFFICE, REPORT TO CONGRESSIONAL REQUESTERS, COMBATING TERRORISM: SPENDING ON GOVERNMENT WIDE PROGRAMS REQUIRES BETTER MANAGEMENT AND COORDINATION, GAO/NSIAD-98-39 (Dec. 1997).

[13] 42 U.S.C.S. §6651 (LEXIS 2000).

[14] OFFICE OF SCIENCE AND TECHNOLOGY POLICY, FCCSET HANDBOOK (March 1991).

[15] U.S. General Accounting Office, GAO/NSIAD-98-39, app. I (Dec. 1997).

[16] *Testimony of Henry L. Hinton, Jr., supra* note 12, at 2.

[17] Presidential Decision Directive 39 (June 1995).

[18] Presidential Decision Directive 62 (May 1998).

[19] 31 U.S.C.S. §686 (LEXIS 2000).

[20] U.S. v. Jaramillo, 380 F. Supp. 1375, 1379 (D. Neb. 1974).

[21] Telephone Interview with Ron Andrade, former-President, National Congress of American Indians (Nov. 30, 1999) (identifying the following international border reservations: Tohona O'Dum, Cocopah, Ft. Huoma, Blackfeet, Red Lake Chippewa, Portage, Sue St. Marie, St. Regis, and Maloceet).

[22] KEVIN JACK RILEY ET AL., DOMESTIC TERRORISM—A NATIONAL ASSESSMENT OF STATE AND LOCAL PREPAREDNESS 1–4 (1995).

[23] *Id.*

[24] Centers for Disease Control, Case Definitions for Public Health Surveillance, MMWR 1997; 46 (No. RR-10): [p.57].

[25] *Id.* at 1.

[26] *Id.* at 1–2.

[27] FALKENRATH ET AL., *supra* note 25, at 274–76.

[28] 64 Fed. Reg. 17,674 (Apr. 12, 1999).

[29] U.S. CONST. art. X.

[30] The source of the non-delegation doctrine is found in the U.S. Constitution, Article I, §1, which provides that "all legislative powers herein granted shall be vested in a Congress of the Unites States," and in the Constitution, Article I, §8 which provides that Congress has the power "to make all laws which shall be necessary and proper for carrying into execution" the other powers in Article I. Therefore, Congress cannot delegate its legislative powers, but can delegate authority to promulgate rules to carry out those legislative powers.

[31] 5 U.S.C.S. §706(2)(C) (LEXIS 2000) (allowing judicial review to determine whether an agency has acted "in excess of statutory jurisdiction, authority, or limitations, or short of statutory right").

[32] 18 U.S.C.S. §1385 (LEXIS 2000).

[33] 10 U.S.C.S. §333 (LEXIS 2000).

[34] United States v. Jaramillo, 380 F. Supp. 1375, 1379 (1974).

[35] United States v. Red Feather, 392 F. Supp. 916 (DCSD 1975). This case sets forth a number of examples of passive activities under the Act to include, reconnaissance missions, but specifically includes advice from the military as participatory and non-passive.

[36] 42 U.S.C.S. §11001–11050 (LEXIS 2000).

[37] *Id.* §11001(b).

[38] *See generally* Vickie V. Sutton, Perceptions of Local Emergency Planning Committee Members Responsibility for Risk Communication and a Proposed Model Risk Communication Program for Local Emergency Planning Committees Under SARA, Title III (1989) (unpublished Ph.D. dissertation, University of Texas at Dallas) (on file with author) (providing information on the formation of the LEPCs).

[39] 42 U.S.C.S. §11001(c).

40 *Id.* §11003(a).

41 The appointment of the LEPCs took more than one year, and an additional year to resolve a conflict with the state of Georgia concerning the delineation of planning districts. A similar delay could be anticipated for a bioterrorism planning network for state and local governments.

42 42 U.S.C.S. §11003(g).

43 *Id.* §9605.

44 *Testimony of Henry L. Hinton, Jr., supra* note 12, at 2.

45 50 U.S.C.S. §2301–2363 (LEXIS 2000) (as amended by the Defense Against Weapons of Mass Destruction Act of 1998).

46 *Id.* §2351, 2366.

47 *Id.* §2301(13).

48 *Id.* §2301(19)–(26).

49 *Id.* §2301(25).

50 FALKENRATH ET AL., *supra* note 25, at 262.

51 PETER B. HUTT & RICHARD A. MERRILL, FOOD AND DRUG LAW 8 (1991). The Federal Food and Drugs Act of 1906 was enacted after legislation was first introduced in 1879.

52 The Biologics Act of 1902, 32 Stat. 728.

53 514 U.S. 549 (1995).

54 469 U.S. 528 (1985).

55 National League of Cities v. Usery, Secretary of Labor, 426 U.S. 833, 852 (1976).

56 *Id.* at 864.

57 *Id.*

58 *Id.* (referring to *Marbury v. Madison*).

59 Pacific Gas & Elec. Co. v. State Energy Res. Cons. & Devel. Comm'n, 461 U.S. 190 (1983).

60 U.S. CONST. art. XXI.

61 South Dakota v. Dole, 483 U.S. 203 (1987).

62 U.S. CONST. art. XVI.

63 42 U.S.C.S. §6611 (LEXIS 2000).

64 47 C.F.R. §202.0 (2000).

65 GAO Report, GAO/NSIAD-98-39, App. III (Dec. 1997).

66 42 U.S.C.S. §6651 (LEXIS 2000).

67 GAO Report, GAO/NSIAD-98-39, App. III (Dec. 1997).

68 *Id.*

69 *Id.*

70 11 March 1999.

71 25 March 1999.

72 15 U.S.C.S. §5511 (LEXIS 2000).

73 *Id.* §2921–2961.

74 10 U.S.C.S. §371–380 (LEXIS 2000).

75 42 U.S.C.S. §217 (LEXIS 2000).

[76] United States v. Jaramillo, 380 F. Supp. 1375 (1974).

[77] U.S. DEP'T OF NAVY, SECRETARY OF THE NAVY INSTR. 5820.7 (15 May 1974).

[78] News Advisory, U.S. House of Representatives, Comm. on the Judiciary, Mar. 18, 2002 at http://www.house.gov/judiciary/news031802 (site visited Apr. 1, 2002).

[79] http://www.ins.usdoj.gov/graphics/lawenfor/index.htm (site visited Aug. 8, 2002).

[80] http://www.ins.usdoj.gov/graphics/lawenfor/index.htm (site visited Aug. 8, 2002).

[81] http://www.fbi.gov/contact/fo/sandiego/missstat.htm

[82] 18 U.S.C. §3052 (2002).

[83] David Johnson, "Ashcroft Plan Would Recast Justice Dept. in a War Mode," *The New York Times* (Nov. 9, 2001).

[84] Ronald L. Dick, Deputy Assistant Director, Counter Terrorism Division and Director, National Infrastructure Protection Center, Federal Bureau of Investigation, Subcommittee on Water Resources and Environment, House Committee on Transportation and Infrastructure, "Terrorism: Are America's Water Resources and Environment at Risk," (Oct. 10, 2001).

[85] J.T. Caruso, Deputy Assistant Director, Counterterrorism Division, Federal Bureau of Investigation, "Bioterrorism," Senate Judiciary Subcommittee on Technology, Terrorism and Government Information (Nov. 6, 2001).

[86] http://www.bt.cdc.gov/protocols.asp (Site visited May 26, 2000).

[87] http://www.fbi.gov/majcases/anthrax/amerithraxlinks.htm (Site visited April 25, 2002).

[88] Steve Fainaru and Ceci Connolly, "Memo on Florida Case Roils Anthrax Probe, Experts Debate Theory Hijacker Was Exposed," A03 *The Washington Post* (Fri., Mar. 29, 2002).

[89] William J. Broad, David Johnston, Judith Miller and Paul Zielbauer, "Experts See FBI Missteps Hampering Anthrax Inquiry," *The New York Times* (Nov. 9, 2001).

[90] Dan Eggen and Jim McGee, "FBI Rushes to Remake Its Mission, Counterterrorism Focus Replaces Crime Solving," A01 *The Washington Post* (Mon., Nov. 12, 2001).

[91] Id.

[92] William J. Broad, David Johnston, Judith Miller and Paul Zielbauer, "Experts See FBI Missteps Hampering Anthrax Inquiry," *The New York Times* (Nov. 9, 2001).

[93] J.T. Caruso (Nov. 6, 2001).

[94] Eggen and McGee (Mon., Nov. 12, 2001).

[95] Fauci, Anthony S., "The Role NIH Biomedical Research in Responding to Threats of Chemical, Biological, Radiological and Nuclear Terrorism (CBRN)", Testimony Before the Committee on Government Reform Subcommittee on National Security, Emerging Threats, and International Relations. June 14, 2005.

[96] *Id.*

[97] *Id.*

[98] *Id.*

[99] *Id.*

[100] http://www.bt.cdc.gov/EmContact/Determine.htm (Website visited Nov. 4, 2001).

[101] http://www.bt.cdc.gov/EmContact/Notify1.htm (Website visited Nov. 4, 2001).

[102] Testimony of Scott Lillibridge, National Center for Infectious Diseases, Centers for Disease Control and Prevention, "Enhancing National Public Health Capacity to Respond to Bioterrorism," Subcommittee on National Security, Veterans Affairs, and International Relations, Committee on Government Reform, U.S. House of Representatives (Sept. 22, 1999).

[103] City of Lubbock, "SUBJECT: ALERT: Terrorist Activity Response Health Advisory," (Sept. 11, 2001).

[104] http://www.bt.cdc.gov/DocumentsApp/ImprovingBioDefense/ImprovingBioDefense.asp (Website visited Oct. 24, 2001).

[105] Dr. Scott R. Lillibridge, M.D., Special Assistant to the Secretary of HHS for National Security and Emergency Management, "A Review of Federal Bioterrorism Preparedness Programs from a Public Health Perspective," Subcommittee on Oversight and Investigations, Committee on Energy and Commerce, U.S. House of Representatives (Oct. 10, 2001).

[106] CDC, "National Bioterrorism Preparedness and Response Initiative," (May 8, 2000).

[107] http://www.cdc.gov/eis/abouteis/factsheet.htm (Website visited Mar. 17, 2002).

[108] http://www.cdc.gov/eis/abouteis/factsheet.htm (Website visited Mar. 17, 2002).

[109] M.A.J. McKenna, "War on Terrorism: CDC enlists 146 disease detectives; Unit works in epidemic intelligence," 12A *The Atlanta Constitution* (Thurs., Mar. 7, 2002).

[110] U.S. Department of Health and Human Services, "HHS Sends 35 Members of Centers for Disease Control and Prevention EIS Team to NYC," Press Release at www.hhs.gov/news (Sept. 14, 2001).

[111] M.A.J. McKenna, "War on Terrorism: CDC enlists 146 disease detectives; unit works on epidemic intelligence," 12A *The Atlantic Constitution* (Thurs., Mar. 7, 2002).

[112] http://cbsnews.com/now/story/0,1597,65855-412,00.shtml October 1999 (Website visited Oct. 26, 2001).

[113] CDC, "National Bioterrorism Preparedness and Response Initiative," (May 8, 2000).

[114] David Brown, "Agency With Most Need Didn't Get Anthrax Data, CDC Unaware of Canadian Study Before Attacks," A03 *The Washington Post* (Mon., Feb. 11, 2002).

[115] "Produce Industry Balks at Food Security Guidelines, Regulation: Firms say FDA proposals to protect against bioterrorism are ineffective and costly," Business, Part 3; P. 1, *Los Angeles Times*, Thursday, March 28, 2002.

[116] H.R. 3448, §211 et. seq. (2002).

[117] H.R. 3448, §301 et. seq. (2002).

[118] Dept. of Defense, Directive No. 3025.12 Employment of Military Resources in the Event of Civil Disturbances (Aug. 19, 1971).

[119] *United States v. Jaramillo*, 380 F. Supp. 1375, 1379 (1974).

[120] *United States v. Red Feather*, 392 F. Supp. 916 (D.C.S.D., 1975).

[121] John Warner National Defense Authorization Act, 2007, Pub. L. No. 109-364, 120 Stat. 2083 (2007).

[122] *A Failure of Initiative: Final Report of the Select Bipartisan Committee to Investigate the Preparation for and Response to Hurricane Katrina*, http://www.gpoaccess.gov/serialset/creports/katrina.html.

[123] U.S. Const. art. I, §8, cl. 15.

[124] John Warner National Defense Authorization Act for Fiscal Year 2007 §1076(a)(1), 120 Stat. 2404-05 (amending 10 U.S.C. §333).

[125] *Governors Association Opposes Senate Authorization Measure*, Inside the Army, Sept. 4, 2006, at 35

[126] *Id.*

[127] Press Release, FEMA, *Joint State/Federal Transportation Exercise Tests Response Plans* (May 5, 2005), available at http://www.fema.gov/news/newsrelease.fema?id=17420.

[128] U.S. Dep't of Homeland Sec., *National Response Plan* (Dec. 2004), available athttp://www.dhs.gov/xlibrary/assets/NRPbaseplan.pdf.

[129] 18 U.S.C. §1385 (2006).

130 The Memorial Institute for the Prevention of Terrorism, Barry Kellman, *Managing Terrorism's Consequences: Legal Issues* 26 (March 2002).

131 Robert S. Root-Bernstein, "Infectious Terrorism," 267 *The Atlantic Monthly* 44–50 (May 1991) can be found at http://www.theatlantic.com/issues/91may/rootbernstein.htm.

†   Victoria Sutton is Professor of Law and Director of the Center for Biodefense, Law and Public Policy, Texas Tech University, Ph.D. Environmental Sciences, J.D. She is the author of LAW AND SCIENCE: CASES AND MATERIALS (2001), LAW AND BIOTERRORISM (2003), and numerous articles. She is the former Assistant Director of the White House Office of Science and Technology Policy and White House EPA Liaison (1990-1993, during the George H.W. Bush Administration).

132 RACHEL CARSON, SILENT SPRING (1962).

133 *See* Victoria Sutton, *Bioterrorism Preparation and Response Legislation–The Struggle to Protect States' Sovereignty While Preserving National Security*, 6 GEO. PUB. POL'Y REV. 93 (2001).

134 See Richard L. Revesz, Federalism and Environmental Regulation: A Public Choice Analysis, 115 HARV. L. REV. 553, 578-83 (2001); Sutton, *supra* note 133, at 95.

135 33 U.S.C. § 401-467 (2000).

136 33 U.S.C. § 407 (2000).

137 Paul Boudreaux, *Federalism and the Contrivances of Public Law*, 77 ST. JOHN'S L. REV. 523, 552-53 (2003).

138 Water Pollution Control Act of 1948, Pub. L. No. 80-845, 62 Stat. 1155 (1948) (codified as amended at 33 U.S.C. § 1251-1376).

139 Water Pollution Control Act Amendments of 1956, Pub. L. No. 84-660, 70 Stat. 498 (1956) (codified as amended at 33 U.S.C. § 1251-1376).

140 Water Pollution Control Act Amendments of 1956, H.R. REP. NO. 1446, at 2 (1956), *reprinted in* 1956 U.S.C.A.A.N. (70 Stat. 498) 3023, 3023-24.

141 *Id.* at 3024.

142 *Id.* at 3026.

143 *Id.* at 3025.

144 *Id.*

145 *Id.*

146 H.R. 12080, 84th Cong. (1956).

147 President's Memorandum of Disapproval of Rivers and Harbors Act for 1956 (Aug. 10, 1956), *reprinted in* 1956 U.S.C.C.A.N. 4828.

148 *Id.*

149 33 U.S.C. § 1361 (1965).

150 Water Pollution Control Act Amendments of 1956, Pub. L. No. 84-660, § 10, 12, 70 Stat. 498 (1956), *reprinted in* 1956 U.S.C.C.A.N. 560, 570-71.

151 *Id.*

152 Federal Water Pollution Control Act Amendments of 1972, S. REP. NO. 92-414 (1972), *reprinted in* 1972 U.S.C.C.A.N. 3668, 3669-70.

153 42 U.S.C. § 4321-4370a (2000) (signed into law by President Nixon on Jan. 1, 1970).

154 Exec. Order No. 11,548, 35 Fed. Reg. 11,677 (July 20, 1970).

155 *See* John N. Hanson, *The Impact of the United States' Environmental Regulations on Innovation*, 21 CAN.-U.S. L.J. 229, 229 (1995); Robert V. Percival, *Separation of Powers, the Presidency, and the Environment*, 21 J. LAND RESOURCES & ENVTL. L. 25, 34 (2001).

156A circuit court described this phenomenon as the "Tragedy of the Commons" which "might result if jurisdictions can compete for industry and development by providing more liberal limitations than their neighboring states." National Resources Defense Council, Inc. v. Costle, 568 F.2d 1369, 1378 (C.A.D.C. 1975).

157 *See* Kirsten H. Engel, *State Environmental Standard Setting: Is There a "Race" and Is It "to the Bottom"?*, 48 HASTINGS L.J. 271, 274-76 (1997); Franz Xaver Perrez, *The Efficiency of Cooperation: A Functional Analysis of Sovereignty*, 15 ARIZ. J. INT'L & COMP. L. 515, 538-42 (1998).

158S. REP. NO. 92-414, at 4-5 (1971), *reprinted in* 1972 U.S.C.C.A.N. 3668, 3671-72.

159*See, e.g.*, Illinois v. City of Milwaukee, 406 U.S. 91 (1972); New York v. New Jersey, 256 U.S. 296 (1921); Missouri v. Illinois, 200 U.S. 496 (1906).

160 *See, e.g.*, Pennsylvania v. West Virginia, 262 U.S. 553 (1923); Connecticut v. Long Island Lighting Co., 535 F. Supp. 546 (E.D.N.Y. 1982).

161 Hodel v. Virginia Surface Mining & Reclamation Ass'n, 452 U.S. 264, 282 (1981).

162Gibbons v. Ogden, 22 U.S. 1, 203 (1824).

163James Madison, *No. 46: Relative Strength of the Federal and State Governments*, in THE ENDURING FEDERALIST 203, 204 (Charles A. Beard ed., 1948).

164*See* Resource Conservation and Recovery Act of 1976 ("RCRA"), 42 US.C. § 6901-6991i (2000) (providing a federal statutory scheme for regulating hazardous waste); Comprehensive Environmental Response Compensation and Liability Act of 1980 ("CERCLA"), 42 U.S.C. § 9601-9675 (2000) (providing a federal statutory scheme for cleaning up pollution cites).

165The Federal Water Pollution Control Act of 1972 ("FWOPCA" or "CWA"), 33 USC § 1251-1376 (2000).

166 *Id.*

167A smallpox epidemic in 1900 in Massachusetts, a Plague epidemic in San Francisco in 1900, the Flu Pandemic of 1918, and the polio epidemic of the 1940s mark some of the most devastating diseases in the past century.

168 *See* James G. Hodge, Jr., *The Role of New Federalism and Public Health Law*, 12 J.L. & HEALTH 309 (1998).

169 *Id.* at 332.

170 *See* Wendy E. Parmet, *After September 11: Rethinking Public Health Federalism*, 30 J.L. MED. & ETHICS 201, 202-03 (2002); Victoria Sutton, *Bioterrorism Preparation and Response Legislation–The Struggle to Protect States' Sovereignty While Preserving National Security Federalsim*, 6 GEO. PUB. POL'Y REV. 2 (2001).

171 *See* Richard L. Berke & Janet Elder, *Survey Shows Doubts Stirring on Terror War*, N.Y. TIMES, Oct. 30, 2001, at A1, B6.

172Madison, *supra* note 163, at 204.

173 *See* Adam Babich, *Our Federalism, Our Hazardous Waste, and Our Good Fortune*, 54 MD. L. REV. 1516, 1532 (1995); Victoria Sutton, *Biodefense–Who's in Charge?*, 13 HEALTH MATRIX 117 (2003).

174 William L. Andreen, *The Evolution of Water Pollution Control in the United States–State, Local, and Federal Efforts, 1789-1972: Part II*, 22 STAN. ENVTL. L.J. 215, 229-30 (2003).

175 Public Health Security and Bioterrorism Preparedness and Response Act of 2002, Pub. L. No. 107-188, 116 Stat. 694 (2002) (codified in scattered sections of 42 U.S.C.).

176 *Id.*

177 Pub. L. No. 104-201, 110 Stat. 2718 (1996) (codified as amended at 50 U.S.C. § 2312 (2000)).

178 *Id.*

179 U.S. GENERAL ACCOUNTING OFFICE, PUB. NO. GAO-02-886T, HOMELAND SECURITY: PROPOSAL FOR CABINET AGENCY HAS MERIT, BUT IMPLEMENTATION WILL BE PIVOTAL TO SUCCESS 28 (2002).

180 *Id.* at 27.

181 U.S. GENERAL ACCOUNTING OFFICE, PUB. NO. GAO-04-152, BIOTERRORISM: PUBLIC HEALTH RESPONSE TO ANTHRAX INCIDENTS OF 2001 4-5 (2003).

182 CENTERS FOR DISEASE CONTROL AND PREVENTION, CENTERS FOR DISEASE CONTROL AND PREVENTION MISSION, *at* http://www.cdc.gov/maso/agency.htm (last reviewed Aug. 27, 2003).

183 Pub. L. No. 107-188, 116 Stat. 594 (2002) (codified in scattered sections of 42 U.S.C.).

184 *Id.*

185 *Id.*

186 *See* Exec. Order No. 13,295, 68 Fed. Reg. 17,255 (Apr. 4, 2003); 42 U.S.C. § 264 (2000).

187 Andreen, *supra* note 174, at 222-42.

188 *See id.* at 242-43; Robert F. Blomquist, *Senator Edmund S. Muskie and the Dawn of Modern American Environmental Law: First Term, 1959-1964*, 26 WM. & MARY ENVTL. L. & POL'Y REV. 509, 546 (2002).

189 Reorg. Plan No. 2 of 1966, 80 Stat. 1608 (1966).

190 Reorg. Plan No. 3 of 1970, 84 Stat. 2086, 2087, 2089 (1970).

191 John C. Whitaker, *Earth Day Recollections: What It Was Like When the Movement Took Off*, EPA JOURNAL (July/Aug. 1988), *at* http://www.epa.gov/history/topics/earthday/10.htm.

192 OFFICE OF HOMELAND SECURITY, NATIONAL STRATEGY FOR HOMELAND SECURITY 2 (2002), *available at* http://www.whitehouse.gov/homeland/book/index.html.

193 *Id.*

194 *Id.* at 5.

195 *Whitman Says EPA May Seek More Control Over Water Security, Bioterrorism Response*, 32 BNA ENV'T REP. 2405 (Dec. 14, 2001).

196 OFFICE OF THE CHIEF FINANCIAL OFFICER, U.S. ENVIRONMENTAL PROTECTION AGENCY, PUB. NO. EPA/190-R-97-002, EPA STRATEGIC PLAN 7 (1997), *available at* http://www.epa.gov/ocfo/plan/plan.htm.

197 U.S. ENVIRONMENTAL PROTECTION AGENCY, 2003-2008 EPA STRATEGIC PLAN: DIRECTION FOR THE FUTURE 1 (2003), *available at* http://www.epa.gov/ocfo/plan/plan.htm [hereinafter 2003-2008 EPA STRATEGIC PLAN].

198 OFFICE OF SOLID WASTE AND EMERGENCY RESPONSE, U.S. ENVIRONMENTAL PROTECTION AGENCY, PUB. NO. EPA 550-F-98-014, EPA'S ROLE IN COUNTER-TERRORISM ACTIVITIES: FACTSHEET (1998), *available at* http://yosemite.epa.gov/oswer/ceppoweb.nsf/content/ct-publ.htm [hereinafter EPA FACTSHEET].

199 Presidential Decision Directive No. 39 (June 21, 1995), *available at* http://www.fas.org/irp/offdocs/pdd39.htm [hereinafter PDD No. 39]; Presidential Decision Directive No. 62 (May 22, 1998), *available at* http://www.fas.org/irp/offdocs/pdd-62.htm [hereinafter PDD No. 62]; Presidential Decision Directive No. 63 (May 22, 1998), *available at* http://www.fas.org/irp/offdocs/pdd/pdd-63.htm [hereinafter PDD No. 63].

200 *Id.* at 2.

201*Id.* at 1.

202U.S. ENVIRONMENTAL PROTECTION AGENCY, EPA'S ROLE AND AUTHORITY IN COUNTER TERRORISM, *at* http://www.epa.gov/ceppo/ct-epro.htm (last modified Oct. 17, 2002) [hereinafter EPA'S ROLE AND AUTHORITY].

203   PDD No. 39; PDD No. 62; PDD No. 63.

204EPA FACTSHEET, *supra* note 198, at 2.

205BUDGET OF THE UNITED STATES GOVERNMENT, FISCAL YEAR 2003 15 (2003).

206EPA'S ROLE AND AUTHORITY, *supra* note 202.

2072003-2008 EPA STRATEGIC PLAN, *supra* note 197, at 113-14.

208OFFICE OF SOLID WASTE AND EMERGENCY RESPONSE, U.S. ENVIRONMENTAL PROTECTION AGENCY, FY 2004 PERFORMANCE PRIORITIES FOR THE REGIONS § 3 (2004), *available at* http://www.epa.gov/ocfo/npmguidance/oswer/fy04performancepriorities.pdf.

(3) Performance Priority: Homeland Security

Responding to small and large-scale disasters is one of EPA's traditional responsibilities. The Agency's crucial role in responding to the World Trade Center and Pentagon attacks, and the decontamination of anthrax at Capitol Hill, have further defined the nation's expectations of EPA's emergency response capabilities. The Agency will continue to play a unique role in responding to and preparing for future terrorist incidents, which could possibly be more devastating in scale and nature than those of September 11, 2001, and could include bioterrorism or "dirty" bombs that affect the lives of millions of Americans and devastate the economy.

Performance Expectations for Regions: The FY 2004 budget provides additional resources for equipment, training, and establishment of a "Decontamination Team." We are facing FTE limitations, including a reduction of 55 FTE, from the level provided in the FY 2002 Counter-Terrorism Supplemental. OSWER Headquarters will work with the Regions and OCFO to address this shortfall. At the same time we face this challenge, we must continue to improve our readiness and response capabilities. The FY 2004 budget makes a commitment to establish a baseline for Agency preparedness in FY 2003, and formally report on that measure in FY 2004. Also, the Agency is striving to establish and maintain the capability to respond to simultaneous large-scale incidents, although, the resources in FY 2004 may not support the goal of responding to five such incidents as stated in the Agency's Homeland Security Strategic Plan.

209U.S. ENVIRONMENTAL PROTECTION AGENCY, STRATEGIC PLAN FOR HOMELAND SECURITY (2002), *available at* http://www.epa.gov/epahome/downloads/epa_homeland_security_strategic_plan.pdf [hereinafter SECURITY STRATEGIC PLAN].

210*Id.*

211 Office of Inspector General, Environmental. Protection Agency, Rep. No. 2003-P-00012, EPA's Response to the World Trade Center Collapse: Challenges, Successes, and Areas for Improvement, (2003), available at http://www.epa.gov/oig/reports/2003/WTC report 20030821.pdf.

212Endangered Species Act of 1973, 16 U.S.C. § 1536(j) (2000).

21333 U.S.C. § 1323, 1316, 1317 (2000).

21442 U.S.C. § 7418(b) (2000).

21542 U.S.C. § 6001.

[216]15 U.S.C. § 2621 (2000).

[217]Weinberger v. Catholic Action of Hawaii/Peace Education Project, 454 U.S. 139, 144 (1981).

[218]2003-2008 EPA STRATEGIC PLAN, *supra* note 197, at 162.

[219]Biological Agent-Environmental Detection Act of 2001, S. 1560, 107th Cong. § 3 (2001).

[220]Laura Meckler, *Nationwide Monitoring System Planned for Detecting Bioterror Attack*, AP NEWSWIRE, Jan. 22, 2003.

[221] *Id.*

[222]Judith Miller, *U.S. Deploying Monitor System for Germ Peril*, N.Y. TIMES, Jan. 22, 2003, at A1, A10.

[223] Tularemia is a potentially serious illness that occurs naturally in animals and because tularemia can spread to humans through airborne pathogens, the CDC has listed it as a bioterrorism agent. Centers for Disease Control and Prevention, *Key Facts About Tularemia*, *at* http://www.bt.cdc.gov/agent/tularemia/facts.asp (last modified Oct. 7, 2003).

[224] *See* Houston Department of Health and Human Services & Harris County Public Health and Environmental Services, *News Release–Officials Following Up on Bacteria Detection*, *at* http://www.ci.houston.tx.us/departme/health/bacteria%20detection.htm (Oct. 9, 2003) [hereinafter *News Release*].

[225] *Id.*

[226] *Id.*

[227] *Id.*

[228] *See* John Mintz, *U.S. Provides a Peek at Air Sensor Program*, WASH. POST, Nov. 15, 2003, at A3.

[229] *See id.*

[230]*See News Release*, *supra* note 224.

[231] *Id.*

[232] 42 U.S.C. § 7407, 7410 (2000).

[233] 2003-2008 EPA Strategic Plan, *supra* note 197, at 162.

[234]*Id.* "[A]s a result of EPA's experience with air monitoring and indoor air quality issues, the then-Office of Homeland Security at the White House gave the Agency the lead for the Biowatch system. This system is being implemented in cities across the country to monitor for airborne release of certain biological contaminants." *Id.*

[235] 2003-2008 EPA Strategic Plan, *supra* note 197, at 161-64.

[236] U.S. Department of Homeland Security, *DHS Organization: Who Will Be Part of the New Department?*, *at* http://www.dhs.gov/dhspublic/interapp/editorial/editorial_0133.xml (last accessed June 24, 2004).

[237]*See* BUDGET OF THE UNITED STATES GOVERNMENT, FISCAL YEAR 2003 (2003).

[238] 7 U.S.C. § 136-136y (2000).

[239]*Id.* § 136p.

[240] *See* 40 C.F.R. § 166.3 (2003).

[241] *Id.* § 166.2(c), 166.45.

[242]Pesticide Emergency Exemptions; Agency Decisions and State and Federal Agency Crisis Declarations, 67 Fed. Reg. 6707 § III.B (Feb. 13, 2002) (exemption issued Dec. 7, 2001, expiring in one year).

[243]*Id.* (exemption issued Nov. 16, 2001, expiring in one year).

244*Id.* (exemption issued Nov. 30, 2001, expiring in one year).

245 U.S. Environmental Protection Agency, *Pesticides: Topical & Chemical Fact Sheets— Methyl Bromide* 20, *at* http://www.epa.gov/pesticides/factsheets/chemicals/ methylbromide_factsheet.htm (last updated Aug. 11, 2003).

246Emergency Planning and Community Right-To-Know Act of 1986 ("EPCRA"), 42 U.S.C. § 11001 (2000).

247Victoria V. Sutton, *A Precarious "Hot Zone"—The President's Plan To Combat Bioterrorism*, 164 MIL. L. REV. 135, 147 (2000); *see also* Vickie V. Sutton, Perceptions of Local Emergency Planning Committee Members Responsibility for Risk Communication for Risk Communication and a Proposed Model Risk Communication Program for Local Emergency Planning Committees Under SARA, Title III (1989) (unpublished Ph.D. dissertation, University of Texas at Dallas) (on file with author) (providing information on the formation of the LEPCs; the designation of the LEPCs took one year, and an additional year to resolve a dispute concerning the delineation of planning districts).

248EPA FACTSHEET, *supra* note 198.

249 *Id.*

250OFFICE OF SOLID WASTE AND EMERGENCY RESPONSE, U.S. ENVIRONMENTAL PROTECTION AGENCY, PUB. NO. EPA 550-F-01-005, LEPCS AND DELIBERATE RELEASES: ADDRESSING TERRORIST ACTIVITIES IN THE LOCAL EMERGENCY PLAN (2001), *available at* http://yosemite.epa.gov/oswer/ ceppoweb.nsf/content/sta-loc.htm [hereinafter LEPCS AND DELIBERATE RELEASES].

251EPCRA, 42 U.S.C. § 11001(c).

252LEPCS AND DELIBERATE RELEASES, *supra* note 250, at 1.

25342 U.S.C. § 11044.

254*Id.* (plans, material safety data sheets); *id.* § 11022(e) (chemical inventories).

255 Kara Sissell, *Right-to-Know Activists Consider Lawsuit Over RMP Data*, CHEMICAL WEEK, April 28, 2004, at 13.

256U.S. GENERAL ACCOUNTING OFFICE, HOMELAND SECURITY: EPA'S MANAGEMENT OF CLEAN AIR ACT CHEMICAL FACILITY DATA, Rep. No. GAO-03-509R (Mar. 14, 2003).

25765 Fed. Reg. 48108 (Aug. 4, 2000).

258PDD No. 39, *supra* note 203; PDD No. 62, *supra* note 203; PDD No. 63, *supra* note 203.

259 *See* Rafael Lorente, *Congressman Mocks Plan to Buy AMI Building Closed by Anthrax*, S. FLA. SUN-SENTINEL, Feb. 11, 2003, *at* A1; U.S. Environmental Protection Agency, *Hart Senate Office Decontamination Progressing*, at http://www.epa.gov/epahome/headline_120301.htm (Dec. 3, 2001).

260The President's 2003 budget requested $124 million in new funding for a total EPA investment of $133.4 million for homeland security. Of the total EPA budget, $75 million was dedicated to decontamination activities. BUDGET OF THE UNITED STATES GOVERNMENT, FISCAL YEAR 2003 (2003).

261 *See* Kathy Bushouse, *AMI Test Water Was Cleaned, Dumped: Officials Say Waste Had Been Made Safe*, S. FLA. SUN-SENTINEL, Sept. 20, 2002, at B1.

262*Id.*

263*Id.*

264Pub. L. No. 107-188, 116 Stat. 633 (2002).

26542 U.S.C. § 300i-2 (2000).

2665 U.S.C. § 552(b)(1) (2000).

267*Id.* § 552.

[268]Public Health Security and Bioterrorism Preparedness and Response Act of 2002, Pub. L. No. 107-188, 116 Stat. 633, sec. 401 (2002).

[269] Association of Metropolitan Water Agencies, State FOIA Laws: A Guide To Protecting Sensitive Water Security Information (2002), available at http://www.amwa.net/security/.

[270]*Id.*

[271]*See, e.g.,* MONT. CONST. art. II, § 9.

[272]*Bush Signs Anti-Terrorism Bill Into Law Requiring Drinking Water Threat Assessments*, 1332 BNA ENV'T. REP. (June 14, 2002).

[273] Smith v. Potter, 187 F. Supp. 2d 93 (S.D.N.Y. 2001).

[274] Comprehensive Environmental Response, Compensation, and Liability Act of 1980, Pub. L. No. 96-510, 94 Stat. 2767 (1980) (codified in scattered sections of 42 U.S.C. and 26 U.S.C.).

[275] 42 U.S.C. § 9659 (2000).

[276]*Smith*, 187 F. Supp. 2d at 98.

[277]42 U.S.C. § 6903(27) (2000).

[278]*Id.* § 9601(33).

[279] *Smith*, 187 F. Supp. 2d at 98.

[280] Smith v. Potter, 208 F. Supp. 2d 415, 418 (2002).

[281]*Id.* at 418 n.2.

[282]*See* DAVID A. KOPLOW, SMALLPOX: THE FIGHT TO ERADICATE A GLOBAL SCOURGE 124-36 (2003).

[283] 42 U.S.C. § 4332 (2000).

[284]Douglas County v. Babbitt, 48 F.3d 1495, 1505 (9th Cir. 1995). "NEPA procedures do not apply to federal actions that do nothing to alter the natural physical environment," and the court explains, "when a federal agency takes an action that prevents human interference with the environment, it need not prepare an EIS." *Id.* at 1506.

[285]16 U.S.C. § 1532(6) (2000).

[286] Hantavirus is a deadly disease transmitted by infected rodents through urine, droppings, or saliva which humans can contract when they breathe in aerosolized virus. National Centers for Infectious Diseases, Centers for Disease Control and Prevention, *All About Hantaviruses*, at http://www.cdc.gov/ncidod/diseases/hanta/hps/ (last reviewed May 13, 2004).

[287]*See* LORI ARVISO ALVORD & ELIZABETH COHEN VAN PELT, THE SCALPEL AND THE SILVER BEAR 120-27 (1999).

[288]*See* Anna M. Molesworth et al., *Environmental Risk and Meningitis Epidemics in Africa*, 9 EMERGING INFECTIOUS DISEASES 1287 (2003).

[289]Paul R. Epstein, *Enhanced: Climate and Health*, 285 SCIENCE 347 (1999).

[290]M. Lechat, The Epidemiology of Health Effects of Disasters, 12 EPIDEMIOLOGICAL REV. (1990).

[291]Mosquito Abatement for Safety and Health Act of 2003, Pub.L. No. 108-75, 117 Stat. 898 (2003).

[292]*Id.*

[293] *Id.*

[294] ROBERT S. DESOWITZ, THE MALARIA CAPERS: MORE TALES OF PARASITES AND PEOPLE, RESEARCH AND REALITY (1991).

[295] THOMAS E. DAHL, U.S. DEPT OF INTERIOR, FISH & WILDLIFE SERVICE, WETLANDS LOSSES IN THE UNITED STATES, 1780 TO 1980s (1990).

296 *Saving the Ecosystem . . . for the Mosquitoes*, 8 DOCTORS FOR DISASTER PREPAREDNESS NEWSL. (1991), *at* http://www.oism.org/ddp/ddpnews/ddpnov91.html.

297 33 U.S.C. § 1251 (2000).

298 UNITED NATIONS ENVIRONMENT PROGRAMME, MONTREAL PROTOCOL ON SUBSTANCES THAT DEPLETE THE OZONE LAYER (2002), *available at* http://www.unep.org/ozone/Publications/6iv_publications%20others.asp.

299 KYOTO PROTOCOL TO THE UNITED NATIONS FRAMEWORK CONVENTION ON CLIMATE CHANGE, *available at* http://unfccc.int/resource/convkp.html (last visited June 23, 2004).

300 *See infra* Part II.B.

301 The origin of this phrase is not certain, but this author first identifies it from a letter (*circa* 1620) from Sir Drummond, a Scottish poet and author to Sir Robert Ker in response to a duel, won by Sir Ker: "Ye are too good for these times, in which, as in a time of plague, men must once be sick, and that deadly, ere they can be assured of any safety." A portion of this letter is available at http://www.electricscotland.com/history/other/drummond_william.htm (last visited June 23, 2004).

302 http://www.ftc.gov/bcp/conline/pubs/alerts/bioalrt.htm (site visited 12/8/01).

Chapter Three
Federalism and Biodefense, Bioterrorism,
Biosecurity, and other Public Health Emergencies

3.1.   Historical Federalism and Public Health Emergencies

The Constitution provides for powers for the federal government and the Tenth Amendment stipulates that "those powers not delegated to the United States by the Constitution, nor prohibited by it to the states, are reserved to the states . . . ." The U.S. Supreme Court in *Gibbons v. Ogden* (supra., Section 5.1) in a case about whether a field of regulation fell to the federal government or the state government in 1824 wrote that such laws as public health laws were reserved to the states. However, the Constitution is very clear that national security is one of the most important powers of the federal government. Bioterrorism and pandemics that may be so catastrophic that they are a threat or may be a threat to national security present a hybrid situation. Some sharing or shifting of those powers of state and federal government would be required, particularly when states become overwhelmed and are no longer effective in protecting its citizens. The events of September 11, 2001 brought this issue to the forefront, as well as the disaster on the Gulf Coast with Hurrican Katrina in 2005.

Grounded in the colonial period, the states have historically first implemented quarantine laws then other public health laws, not the federal government. Because of this historical jurisdiction, as well as state sovereignty over such areas of law as public health, states continue to have the primary responsibility to protect their citizens in a bioterrorism attack or emerging infectious disease emergency. In October 2001, in the midst of the Anthrax attacks which occurred in several states, it was estimated of the nation's 3,000 public health agencies that only 20% have plans to address bioterrorism events, and at least 10% do not have email capability.[1] Nevada surveyed its local health agencies to assess preparedness for a biological weapons attack and found that 50% lacked high-speed internet access, 94% lacked adequate emergency preparedness training for bioterrorism incidents, 46% did not have broadcast facsimile capabilities for emergency notifications, and 77% did not have an emergency response plan for a bioterrorist incident.[2]

During Hurricane Katrina in the fall of 2005, the struggle between federal and state authorities regarding who should respond and whether authority should be given to the federal government by the respective governors unfolded during the days when an emergency response was most urgent. Political differences made the Democrat Governor of Louisiana reluctant to cede authority to a federal government led by a Republican President, causing days of deadly delays. The public was furious and people suffered as a result of the delay. The federalism issues raised led to a broader dialogue about how disasters should be handled in our constitutional federalism framework. Then in 2006, the Warner Act was signed into law which gave clearer guidelines as to when the federal government could intervene in a disaster without waiting for a state's governor to make the request for federal aid.

The question of federalism is such a difficult political one that Congress has been reluctant to resolve it with regard to bioterrorism and pandemics. Rather, the Executive Branch has been left to work through the relationship between the federal government and the state governments, and has repeatedly cautioned states that they must be prepared and that they should not expect the federal government to respond for them to a bioterrorism attack or an emerging infectious disease emergency. This leaves the state with the need to be legally prepared to address quarantine and vaccination powers, emergency powers, and liability issues. The federal government through the CDC continues its role as advisory only.

A weak advisory role challenges the responsibility of the federal government to protect all of its citizens when the state may disagree with the federal approach. A classic study of this relationship is the plague epidemic in San Francisco at the turn of the twentieth century. The following excerpt from Marilyn Chase's *The Barbary Plague* (Random House, 2003) provides a historical narrative of the acts of the governments during that epidemic. It is not unlikely that the same political, power and sovereignty discourse between the federal government and state government in the twenty-first century might repeat itself in an epidemic event.

>   While plague once traveled on the wind that drove sailing ships, it now migrated at twentieth-century speed aboard new coal-fired steamships. . . .
>
>   Plague's only mercy was its speedy end. When buboes were the main symptom, plague killed in five days. If a victim was spitting up blood, a symptom of plague in the lungs, death came in two or three days. So-called pneumonic plague was the rarest and deadliest form of the disease. It was also the only form now known to be contagious, spread from person to person by saliva as the coughing victims helplessly infected caretakers and family. Bubonic or pneumonic, it all started from the same germ, the bacteria known, variously, as Bacillus pestis and Yersinia pestis.. . .Daniel Defoe, writing of seventeenth-century London n his 1722 work, A Journal of the Plague Year, said that the terror of the epidemic prompted "knavery and collusion" in infected towns where officials falsified burial records and fearful people hid the sick and the dead.
>
>   . . . [A]ll that could conceal their distempers did it, to prevent their neighbors shunning and refusing to converse with them, and also to prevent authority shutting up their houses; which though it was not yet practiced, yet was threatened, and people were extremely terrified at the thoughts of it.
>
>   . . . But to the San Francisco citizen of 1900 --- even to most practicing physicians --- the new bacteriology was still a form of black magic: mysterious, dimly understood, untrustworthy, and inferior to the laying on of hands and the observation of symptoms at the bedside. . . .
>
>   . . . Daily headlines [in San Francisco] declared it a fraud. The Plague a Phantom: More Bouffe Business by the Health Board, the Chronicle railed on March 13 [1900]. The next day, the paper proclaimed: "No Plague is Found." By St. Patrick's Day, with the town in a holiday mood, the paper concluded: "Bubonic Scare Has Collapsed."
>
>   In a counterpoint to the drumbeat of denial, a careful listener could hear the hammers in the coffin shops of Chinatown. On March 15 . . . a twenty-two-year-old laborer died on Sacramento Street. The next victim was a thirty –five-year-old cook, who died on March 17 on Dupont Street. The day after that, a middle-aged workingman collapsed and died on the tiny crooked alley called Oneida Place. All three had the plague stigmata on them.

FEDERALISM AND BIODEFENSE

The politicians, the merchants, and the Chinese all had good reasons for denying the diagnosis. No one wanted to see the yellow flag of pestilence flying over the portal to the Golden State. It would tarnish tourism and trade. It would turn Chinatown into a quarantine zone and subject the Chinese to the interventions of white doctors with their dissection tools, chemicals, and fire. To the Chinese, who were not unacquainted with epidemics, the cure must have seemed far worse than the disease.. . .

News of San Francisco's misfortune became impossible to contain, and dispatches reached other states and countries both north and south of the border. Westbound trains traveled empty, abandoned by those afraid of contracting the deadly bacteria. Vacationers favored safer destinations where the greatest concern was sunburn or overeating.

Trading partners began to balk at receiving the city's infected goods. The Canadian government ordered all steamers from San Francisco quarantined until further notice. And the outbound steamer Curacao was quarantined in Mazatlan by the government of Mexico. San Francisco businessmen remembered how quarantine had paralyzed Hawaiian sugar shipments after Honolulu's plague struck. A sickening vision of California wheat stranded on the docks, and its fruit rotting, rose before their eyes.

Editorial pages of the city's major dailies called it an outrage that the city was being branded a pestilential plague spot rather than the golden vision of health and pleasure they wanted to promote.

. . . de Young's Chronicle and Spreckels's Call found themselves on the same side of an issue. Both papers relentlessly ridiculed the plague campaign of Kinyoun as a fraud. Ironically, the only newspaper of the big three dailies to engage in serious coverage of the outbreak was that fount of yellow journalism Hearst's Examiner. To be sure, the so-called saffron sheet pursued the plague story less for its public health import than for its sensational ingredients of death and intrigue. But in the city, its coverage stood alone. Now, however, other city papers charged the Examiner with journalistic treason against San Francisco. Henrot's New York Journal spread news of the city's shame, declaring: "Black Plague Creeps Into America."

. . . As the rhetoric mounted, furious merchants converged on City Hall. They vowed the yellow flag of plague would never fly over San Francisco and demanded that the mayor repair the damage to the city's image.

Mayor Phelan had no choice. He dispatched telegrams to forty American cities, insisting --- falsely --- that there had been just one isolated case, adding that Chinatown was purged and purified. "There is no future danger," he promised.

Over the page one story, Call unfurled a banner headline: "City Plague Scare A Confessed Sham."

As City Hall capitulated to the merchants and newspapers, Kinyoun confirmed three new plague deaths. Word by word, the public health service expanded its codebook. In it, San Francisco's beleaguered health board acquired a code name that captured the style of the whole town --- "Burlesque."

. . . Back East, wire service stories about San Francisco's plague cases were now seeping into the press. With a major news event brewing out West, the dean of New York medical reporters decided to investigate. Dr. George F. Shrady, the burly, bearded medical correspondent for the New York Herald, boarded a train west to determine once and for all whether bubonic plague really existed in San Francisco.

The surgeon general got wind of the reporting trip. Fretting about bad publicity, he commanded Kinyoun to call upon the influential journalist at this hotel and brief him on the plague situation. . . . Kinyoun suspected that Shrady's real agenda was to deny plague had existed before his arrival and then to "discover" it during his stay and plant the Herald's flag on the story. . . But Kinyoun duly briefed Shrady on the plague cases diagnosed so far, and invited him to view an autopsy. . . .Kinyoun and Kellogg learned of a new suspicious death in Chinatown. They invited Shrady to attend the postmortem. . . . Kinyoun nursed hopes that this reporter, for all his arrogance, might yet help the plague campaign by writing truthful dispatches. It looked as if that might come to pass. Then, suddenly, Shrady turned from alarmist to apologist.

Shrady's conversion followed a banquet thrown in his honor by Mayor Phelan at the post Pacific Union Club.. . .Later that night, who should drop by Shrady's hotel for a chat but California's governor, Henry T. Gage.

. . . After being entertained, Shrady published a finale to his plague series, in which he withdrew any concern he'd earlier expressed:

"After having visited every section of Chinatown under the escort of the police and of the health authorities, both Federal and local, I have come to the conclusion that this plague scare in San Francisco is absolutely unwarranted," Shrady wrote. "I am thoroughly convinced that there really was no danger of the plague and that virtually it did not exist in this city."

"The rumor that plague threatens San Francisco is ridiculous and unfounded," he concluded.

. . . With the city's trade and prestige at stake, the Call pleaded "in the name of humanity" for Chinatown to be burned. "so long as it stands, so long will there be the menace of the appearance in San Francisco of every form of disease, plague and pestilence which Asian filth and vice generate," the paper said in its May 31 editorial: "Clear the foul spat form San Francisco and give its debris to the flames."

With a rising sense of panic, he [Kinyoun] urged the surgeon general to build detention camps to hold plague suspects at the state border, using War Department tests. . . .

Kinyoun also fired off warning letters to the health boards of Louisiana, Texas, Kansas, Nevada, Oregon, Colorado, Arizona, New Mexico, and Washington, urging that they stay on the look out for any infected passengers of freight from the Golden State.

The explosion was predictable. California's commercial and political powers erupted in fury: At stake was a bumper crop of California fruit worth $40 million and fortunes in transportation and tourism revenues --- all paralyzed by Kinyoun's sweeping new decree. Their wrath echoed in a banner headline in the Call on June 17, 1900:

"California is subjected to an unparalleled outrage: Dr. J.J. Kenyoun Strikes a Serious Blow to the State by Arbitrarily and Without Cause Placing it Under Federal Quarantine."

"The indignation of the people of California is beyond expression," said the Republican State Central Committee. A delegation led by the Call's publisher, John D. Spreckels, took the protest to the door of the White House.

President McKinley didn't take long to overrule Kinyoun's travel ban. Vindicated San Franciscans rejoiced, viewing the president's act as not just a green light for travel, but a clean bill of health for the city.

In the wake of the president's order, Kinyoun was charged with contempt of court. But the governor had an even more nefarious more effective plan to bury the quarrelsome quarantine officer for good. Gage unveiled a conspiracy theory that would discredit Kinyoun, while offering a convenient way to explain the existence of bacteria in his state.

Gage told the press that Kinyoun had imported cultures of bubonic plague bacteria for use in his laboratory on Angel Island, then suggested that, by spilling the bacteria, Kinyoun had created the catastrophe himself.

Kinyoun, captain of a sinking ship, was summoned to court for a hearing before Judge Morrow on the contempt charge. By turns meek and belligerent, Kinyoun gave assurances that he hadn't intended to violate any court order. The Call called Kinyoun "insolent and dangerous" and an "injudicious meddler" in state affairs.

Kinyoun got cold comfort from his government-appointed attorney, Frank Coombs, who told the quarantine officer he was going to have a hard time keeping him out of jail.

. . .Around the customs house, it was whispered that California's congressmen were lobbying for Kinyoun's transfer "as far away from San Francisco as possible."

San Francisco's Chamber of Commerce president, Charles Nelson, called Kinyoun "a menace to our trade and commerce." . . . The San Francisco Chronicle, in its year-end editorial, demanded the quarantine officer's expulsion. Headlined "The Doom of Kinyoun," the column declared: "Kinyoun is to go . . . The official acts of Kinyoun have been outrageous, and have fully warranted the public indignation . . .It is grossly improper for his Federal superiors to say that such a man must not be removed ;'under fire.'". . .

In Sacramento, Governor Henry T. Gage exalted his attacks. In his year-end address ---- a rhetorical volcano that spouted twenty thousand words and covered fifty-four sheets of foolscap --- he took his plague conspiracy theory to new and gothic heights. Now instead of just spilling the germs, he insinuated, Kinyoun spread them intentionally.

"Could it have been possible," said Gage, "that some dead body of a Chinaman had innocently or otherwise received a post-mortem inoculation in a lymphatic region by some one possessing the imported plague bacilli, and that honest people were thereby deluded?"

. . . To defend the state from such demonic experiments, Gage proposed making it a felony to import plague bacteria, to make slides or cultures from it, or to inoculate animals with it. He also proposed making it a felony for newspapers to publish "any false report on the presence of bubonic plague."

Rallying around the governor, the legislature passed a joint resolution on January 23 asking President McKinley to remove Kinyoun from West Coast duty. Fearing exile was too mild a punishment, the bill's author added that Kinyoun should be hanged.

. . . After eighteen months of toil and family sacrifice on Angel Island, Kinyoun was denounced as a fraud. He wired the surgeon general, asking to be avenged for the slander.

But Kinyoun got a vote of no confidence from his boss. With federal-state relations in San Francisco frayed past repair, Wyman sent in a new man to manage the crisis. Joseph H. White was a veteran who had fought cholera in Hamburg and leprosy in Hawaii. The day after New Year's , White set down his suitcase at the Occidental Hotel on Sutter Street and set to work.

. . . Confronting a hopeless impasse, Joseph White took a decisive step. He asked the Surgeon General Wyman to send a panel of independent experts to determine once and for all whether plague existed in San Francisco. Meanwhile, White kept a discreet distance from the embattled Kinyoun.

. . . Their grim task completed, and their lips sealed about their findings, the expert panel trio prepared to leave for home. But a trickle of leaks about the plague report in the Sacramento Bee alerted Governor Gage to impending trouble. He demanded an audience at the Palace Hotel.

Billing his visit as a courtesy call, Gage brought a delegation and prepared to lobby the scientist to head off any threat to his state. The plague commissioners, in no mood to be bullied, gave it to him straight: The state had the plague, and they intended to report it to the surgeon general. The governor retreated to Sacramento to plot his next move.

. . . On a train bound for Washington, D.C., the governor's men vowed to defend the Golden State in a deal that was pure brass. Having failed to deny the plague at home, they hoped to strike a bargain with federal officials to cover up the proof of its existence. The delegates --- men from the Chronicle, the Examiner, the Union Iron Works, and the Southern Pacific Railroad --- agreed with the Governor Henry Gage that only secrecy could save California from the ruin of a nationwide trade embargo.

Senators George C. Perkins and Thomas R. Bard of California acted as midwives to the plan. They had wired all the parties --- from Governor Gage and the newspapers to the surgeon general's bosses at the Treasury Department --- to make sure everyone was on board.

When the delegates arrived in Washington, they headed straight for a conference with Surgeon General Wyman and his bosses at the Treasury Department. California would clean up San Francisco, they promised, in exchange for a news blackout. There was no need to publicize the matter. Discretion was the key to gaining Governor Gage's cooperation with federal public health programs.

At the White House, the California delegation met with President McKinley to discuss more pleasant matters, specifically his upcoming trip to the Golden State. San Francisco had planned a lavish reception. The president and Mrs. McKinley would be guests at the Pacific Heights mansion of one of the delegates, Henry Scott, head of the Union Iron Works. McKinley would receive tributes from the state's Republicans. He would launch one of Scott's ships. The presidential presence would advertise the state as a mecca of commerce, culture, and health. Everyone would win.

Kinyoun tried to get word to the surgeon general warning him not to trust Gage's delegates. But the sales job was a brilliant success. Surgeon General Wyman not only agreed, he asked his special plague commissioners to sign on with the plan. They acquiesced, sharing Wyman's hope that quiet diplomacy would work better than public disclosure to improve the health of San Francisco.

Wyman went further, appealing to Victor Vaughan , dean of the University of Michigan Medical School, to use his influence to discourage the Associated Press from publishing anything about the plague report. The surgeon general was worried that the wire service would break the news nationwide, and only a perfect "seal of silence" could appease the California's governor, he explained.

. . . On March 6, the same day that the governor's men started for Washington, the Bee ran a banner headline on page one to trumpet the news of the federal panel's findings to its readers in the state capital: "Bubonic Plague exists in San Francisco . . ."

But the Bee wasn't finished leaking plague news. In yet another page on headline, the paper next exposed the deal struck between California and the surgeon general:

"Infamous Compact Signed by Wyman: Makes Agreement with Gage Not to Let Facts Become Known Contrary to Federal Law"

The story charged that the secrecy pact violated an 1893 quarantine law requiring the surgeon general to publish regular reports on the health status of U.S. ports. Concealing plague in the port of San Francisco was clearly illegal.

But Washington officials were too busy endorsing San Francisco's health to worry much. "I would feel as safe living in San Francisco as in Washington," said a top Treasury Department official. "Traveling and business can continue as safely with San Francisco today as a year ago."

Kinyoun sent Wyman a telegram arguing against the compromise and predicting that the delegation from California would "promise everything and do nothing" to purge the plague. When he read Kinyoun's warning wire, Wyman brusquely put the quarantine officer in his place. The deal was done, he said. Kinyoun's desire for public vindication "must be subordinated to maintain attitude of nonpublication," Wyman added. "The Department and its Officers will maintain this attitude until further orders."

The lame duck quarantine officer was now muzzled as well.

But Kinyoun wasn't alone in protesting the gag order. The man who had come to replace him agreed that silence was a bad idea.

"if the facts are kept secret now," wrote Joe White to the surgeon general, "they will rise up to damn us in the future . . . "

"I am at a lost to know what you want me to do," he told the surgeon general. "This is a most peculiar situation --- as I understand it, I am to say nothing about plague and yet supervise the disinfection for it," he said. But, he asked, "when I recommend moving the Chinese out of a given house and they say as they always do, 'What for?' what possible answer can be given?"

. . . Kinyoun wired the surgeon general, asking for a couple of weeks' leave to restore his health and visit his family.

Instead of a vacation, Kinyoun received a blow. "You are hereby directed to transfer the public property under your charge to Assistant surgeon L. L. Lumsden, who has been directed to relieve you . . . You will proceed to Detroit, Michigan, and assume charge of the Service at that station. . ."

He was given three weeks to pack up his family and get to Detroit. No thanks, no acknowledgment of service under difficult conditions --- nothing was offered to soften the blow.

. . . Wyman shipped [Rupert] Blue his orders to leave Milwaukee station and proceed at once to San Francisco.

While Blue was en route, pressure was building from outside the state for action. Texas health chief, W.F. Blunt demanded a copy of the plague commission's report. Colorado health chief G.E. Tyler declared, "Concealment of contagious diseases is an unpardonable sin in public health work." Newspapers in New York City and Washington State were beginning to sound alarms about California's cover-up.

. . . .Dr. W.P. Matthews, secretary of the state health board, burst into the Merchant Street lab, loudly declaring that the federal doctors had no authority to practice medicine in California. If they kept on diagnosing plague, he threatened, he'd cut off their access to patients.

. . . The federal doctors did not pull out, however. The federal public health mission was, in fact, broadening its scope. Under Walter Wyman, the name of the U.S. Marine Hospital Service was changed to the U.S. Public Health and Marine Hospital Service. Just as the plague campaign had broadened from shipboard inspection to investigation of an urban outbreak, so the service was evolving now from a corps of doctors treating sick seamen to a public health service fighting epidemics all over the country.

. . the leaders of the State and Provincial Health Boards of North America were fighting to get the facts about San Francisco's plague. As they gathered for their annual conference in New Haven, Connecticut, members had read dispatches from San Francisco in the New York newspapers. News of the unchecked epidemic, which ran counter to official state denials, infuriated the conferees. They moved plague to the top of their agenda and immediately passed a resolution condemning California. The plague was "a matter of grave national concern," they declared, branding the state's inaction an "irretrievable disgrace."

The San Francisco Board of Supervisors monitored the meeting with trepidation. The board sent frantic appeals to Governor Gage's ranch in Downey, where the lame duck governor had gone in the waning days of his administration. They implored Gage to come to the city and acknowledge the outbreak. Gage refused.

. . . In January 1903, state health chiefs convened at the Willard Hotel in Washington, D.C. They were even more irate than they had been in New Haven. Once again, they censured California for its gross neglect and Governor Gage for denial that imperiled the country at large.

Radicals among the state health chiefs wanted to do more than censure; they wanted to quarantine California. They also wanted the secretary of war to move the military's Pacific Coast transit service out of San Francisco. San Francisco had long feared losing military business to its rival Seattle. A quarantine and military pullout would cost San Francisco untold millions. The moderate state health chiefs just managed to defeat the measures --- for the time being.

. . . California's negligence had made the state a national pariah. Now, as the infection seeped south of the border, its unpopularity spread. Mexico blamed a plague outbreak in Mazatlan on rats in vegetable crates form San Francisco. Ecuador barred all vessels from California.

. . . The city was now in its fifth year of a smoldering plague.

3.2   The Federalists and Biodefense. An Originalist Approach

The relationship between the federal government, states, and tribes in bioterrorism requires an examination of our traditional federalism relationship in the area of public health. The following article discusses the issues of shifting to a federal responsibility in peace time for the protection of public health.

Sutton, "Bioterrorism Preparation and Response Legislation—The Struggle to Protect States' Sovereignty While Preserving National Security, " 6 *The Georgetown Public Policy Review* 93 (Spring 2001).

Bioterrorism Preparation and Response Legislation— The Struggle to Protect States' Sovereignty While Preserving National Security
"The means of security can only be regulated by the means and danger of attack. They will, in fact, be determined by these rules and by no others."
—James Madison, Federalist Paper No. 41

I. Introduction

The security of the United States has been a source of national pride and controversy since the founding of the nation. As a nation, we have enjoyed the protection and peace of mind which comes with having the most powerful military in the world. Today, not one living citizen of the United States, can personally remember a war being fought on American soil. However, the threat of biological attack[3]—as distinct from chemical and nuclear attacks—has raised new concerns about our national security.

The coordination of traditional emergency response mechanisms within the Constitutional framework are those which are clearly defined and practiced. However, the coordination of peacetime preparations for bioterrorist action is not so clearly defined and remains a vulnerable position for the United States. Where emergency response to natural disasters dictates clear intergovernmental relationships and practiced response operations, a bioterrorism event would be an ongoing disaster with casualties increasing geometrically during the response. In contrast, the casualties in a natural disaster are most likely to have peaked before the response and be in a sharp decline or at zero when the response begins. Preparation and surveillance are most critical to a threat of bioterrorism, and the only way to fulfill the Constitutional mandates for the federal government to provide adequate national security.

The question is now whether our governmental, administrative and legal infrastructure is designed to meet the critical need for our national security system to adequately prepare for, and defend against, such an attack.[4]

At the heart of the issue of bioterrorism is the balance between state and federal powers for public health regulation. Although the provision of national security falls squarely into the powers of the federal government, the use of these powers has been almost exclusively in the international arena for intelligence gathering for defense, and for military responses on other shores. Never before has the threat to national security originated so pervasively from within the United States' borders. Part of the threat stems from the ability to develop in a relatively small space; that commonly used equipment can easily be converted to use for the production of biological agents; and that the surveillance to prevent such an attack is certainly as important—if not more critical—than the response to such a threat. Because of the characteristics unique to a biological threat, our legal foundations of federalism—the division between federal and state powers—are directly challenged.

While it seems that no citizen would object to protection by the federal government, it is equally important to note that erosion of state powers can be threatening to the stability of state sovereignty, particularly in times of peace. The federal government cannot impose on that sovereignty, except, where interstate commerce is affected—the constitutional basis for federal environmental laws as well as the Food, Drug and Cosmetic Act. Other areas such as public health and safety are clearly powers of the states, originating such states' actions as quarantine laws. The Tenth Amendment assures us that states can protect the public health of their citizens as they see fit. The doctrine of preemption provides that the federal government can regulate where the government has so completely taken over the field that there is no room for state law, and state law is thereby preempted. But the U.S. Supreme Court has held that preemption cannot apply where Congress has no authority to regulate in the first place.[5]

Power between state and federal governments can be shared. Where there are conflicts, if that power is not reserved to the states, then the federal government may preempt the issue. Some scholars suggest that the Supremacy Clause of the Constitution is the source of that power; others suggest it is the Necessary and Proper Clause.[6]

Another approach to federal control involves a cooperative federalism model which establishes national standards based on the authority of federal legislation. States may choose to assume administration of the programs, such as some of the environmental statutes, i.e., the Clean Water Act, the Clean Air Act, and the Safe Drinking Water Act. Again, Congress is limited to regulating that which they have authority to regulate, and such environmental laws are based on Congress' authority to regulate commerce between the states.

However, the demarcation between federal and state powers has been clear in some areas. The regulation of public health has traditionally been a police power of the states, arising from the regulation of contagion and disease during colonial times. Quarantine laws have historically fallen under state powers, as have other areas of public health law; the regulation of national security has been exclusively given to the Congress through the Constitution.

Thus, bioterrorism has given rise to a new conflict with federalism where national security, the province of the federal government, becomes a matter of public health, an area traditionally regulated by the states. This conflict suggests that federalism should give way to the constitutionally delegated powers of the United States to preserve national security, even though it would mean the regulation of state public health systems in order to achieve that goal. The systematic communication and surveillance as well as reporting functions essential to preparation for and response to a bioterrorism event require federal coordination. However, any expansion of the federal government into the area of public health must be sufficiently narrow to avoid the erosion of the states' constitutionally preserved sovereignty.

The modern interpretation of federalism suggests that there is a shift from the New Deal era of federal regulation to recognizing powers reserved to the states, particularly in the area of public health. The suggestion that national public health goals must be implemented through state political processes rather than Congressional legislation[7] is troublesome because the essence of our defense against bioterrorism will be federal coordination of planning, preparedness and response. States are constitutionally prohibited from regulating such activities.[8] Traditional cooperative federalism with the necessary flexibility for states self-governance does not lend itself to a precise system designed to operate uniformly with sensitivity and rapid response.

It is established that states have the police powers to quarantine, balanced by the protection of Constitutional due process through the Fourteenth Amendment. In the 1824 landmark case, *Gibbons v. Ogden*,[9] the Supreme Court interpreted state police powers to be reserved to the states through the Tenth Amendment. States have regulated public health through quarantine, sanitation laws, control of water and air pollution, vaccination and the regulation of medical professionals. However, it is clearly established that the federal government does not have police powers to do so, except in a narrower circumstance where "in cases of rebellion or invasion the public safety may require it."[10] It is also very clear that in times of emergency and foreign invasion the federal government has the Constitutional authority to declare a state of emergency and respond to both invasions and domestic disasters. James Madison, the fourth President of the United States, has described the shared powers of the state and federal governments to mean that the federal government is best to govern during "times of war" and state government is best in "times of peace".[11]

However, the threat of bioterrorism is uniquely incapable of fitting neatly within these established Constitutional boundaries. When preparing for war, the federal government continually trains and recruits military troops and conducts international surveillance and intelligence gathering operations in preparation for defense. However, the preparation for action against bioterrorism requires a system of surveillance and preparation which will by necessity involve the state, county, and city governments as logical points in the matrix of national communication, surveillance and preparedness.

There is a vital need to create a mandatory system for epidemiological information, critical to the detection of biological attacks, on a nationwide basis. The battlefield is not traditional: it may be the winds, the mass transit systems, or a crowded gathering. State boundaries become meaningless where the attack media, a disease agent, can travel from any one point on the globe to another in under thirty-six hours.[12]

Whether the federal government adequately addresses the unique threat of bioterrorism during times of peace and times of war within the constraints of the U.S. Constitution involves a narrow set of circumstances. In order to effectively address national security concerns, it is necessary to decide whether a public health model exists, or whether other areas of law, such as federal environmental law may be used to design an effective preparation and response system to bioterrorism.

An analysis of the Federalist Papers raises the question as to whether Madison, Hamilton and Jay, authors of the Federalist Papers, may have contemplated the kind of national security issues raised by the threat of domestic bioterrorism.[13]

II. In times of war and peace

The authority and power of the United States is clearly a federal power in times of "war and danger" as interpreted by James Madison:

> "The operations of the federal government will be most extensive and important in times of war and danger; those of the State governments in times of peace and security...The more adequate, indeed, the federal powers may be rendered to the national defense, the less frequent will be those scenes of danger which might favor their ascendancy over the governments of the particular states."[14]

Herein, Madison suggested that the more adequate our national defense, the less frequently the question of power over state governments will arise.

In the matter of bioterrorism, our national defense from the foreign perspective is indeed formidable; however, domestically, the "scenes of danger" do not diminish proportionately with the strength of our national defense envisioned by Madison.

Contemplated are "scenes of danger"[15] which "might favor"[16] the "ascendancy"[17] of the federal government over the states. The "scenes of danger"[18] are those arising from releases of biologic agents, capable of widespread infection in a matter of hours. The "adequacy" of the national defense may have little or no effect on these kinds of attacks. The kinds of attacks contemplated by Madison were likely those by countries having inferior weapons and troops. In a visionary statement concerning national security, Madison suggested that with the rise of new means of inducing danger and attack on our national security, regulation must necessarily adapt and be shaped to respond to whatever new threat evolves. Madison further wrote that this rule is determining, and must be considered supreme relative to any other rules: "The means of security can only be regulated by the means and the danger of attack. They will, in fact, be ever determined by these rules and by no others."[19] Here, the characteristics of the weaponry and attack is the controlling standard—not the "means of security".[20] The "means of security", suggest federal or state powers to provide such security as dictated by the "means and the danger of attack."[21]

Referring to the threat of disease, one court has held that "drastic measures for the elimination of disease are not affected by constitutional provisions, either of the state or national government."[22] The case of a bioterrorism event involves "drastic measures" called upon in an emergency situation, which clearly finds power in the federal government in times of emergency. This case, however, would not give authority to the federal government where the elimination of a disease was not at issue. Surveillance, reporting and preparation for any response to a bioterrorism attack must necessarily come long before *elimination*[23] of disease becomes necessary.

In the same writing concerning national security, Madison, further suggested that threats can come from within the boundaries of the United States as well as foreign concerns: "In America, the miseries springing from her internal jealousies, contentions, and wars would form a part only of her lot."[24] It was not unforeseeable that internal strife and political rebellions of various degrees would continue to plague the nation.[25]

This relationship of the power vested in the federal government is directly proportional to the exigency which the United States faces, evidenced in Madison's discourse on the powers which should be held by the federal government. Here, again, Madison wrote that it is the exigency[26] that controls the proportional amount of federal power required. In the last sentence of his paper, Madison asserted that this question is the same as that of the continued existence of the Union, itself,[27] forcing the unequivocal conclusion that the federal government thereby possesses power to avert destruction of its "continued existence"[28]

The dangers discussed in Federalist No. 44 considered with the exigencies in Federalist No. 41, indicate that the ascendancy of the federal government may be favored where the exigency demands such a response and the existence of the Union is thus dependent upon such action. Thus, a limited ascendance of the federal government is not only required, but demanded by the constitutional context of national security. However, in times of peace, when the threat exists but does not rise to the level of an exigency, the federal government cannot act where the state has sovereign power. While we are certain that a bioterrorism threat exists, the exigency required by the Constitution to invoke federal powers means there must be an imminent threat to national security.

In this same context, the use of military obviously required the nation to address the use of military in peace-time in order to be prepared in the event of a national security threat. The Federalist Papers address some of the objections raised concerning the federal government power for "keeping them [military troops] up" in "a season of tranquility". Speaking to the timing which would evoke federal powers, Hamilton asked:

> "What time shall be requisite to ascertain the violation? Shall it be a week, a month, or a year? Or shall we say they may be continued as long as the danger which occasioned their being raised continues? This would admit that they might be kept up in time of peace, against threatening or impending danger, which would be at once to deviate from the literal meaning of the prohibition and to introduce an extensive latitude of construction. Who shall judge of the continuance of the danger?[29]

Alexander Hamilton described a scenario that has historically justified the maintenance of a military during times of peace, supported the draft, and other national defense preparations. Therein, Hamilton raises the specter of the consequences of a nation which does not have the ability to be prepared for national defense describing "a nation incapacitated by its Constitution to prepare for defense before it was actually invaded."[30]

The Founders cautioned against the strictest construction of the Constitution which would leave the nation "to prepare for defense before it was actually invaded."[31] This warning which is clearly analogous to the preparations and surveillance systems necessary to avoid becoming incapacitated by the convention of the strictest construction of state powers in public health and safety.

> "As the ceremony of a formal denunciation of war has of late fallen into disuse, the presence of an enemy within our territories must be waited for as the legal warrant to the government to begin its levies of men for the protection of the State. We must receive the blow

before we could even prepare to return it. All that kind of policy by which nations anticipate distant danger and meet the gathering storm must be abstained from, as contrary to the genuine maxims of a free government."[32]

This reference to the "distant danger"[33] and the "gathering storm"[34] is an appropriate analogy to the threat of bioterrorism. The caution that avoiding "[A]ll that kind of policy…"[35] suggests an aggressive national security policy should be implemented to address such anticipated dangers. This discussion indicates where the Federalists might stand on a national approach to a bioterrorism threat during peacetime—the raising of a "bioterrorism militia" would clearly be in order.

III. Where the federal government can be more effective than state governments

"The protection and preservation of the public health is among the most important duties of state government."[36] However, Madison observed that "…State legislatures will be unlikely to attach themselves sufficiently to national objects…"[37]

> "If, therefore, as has been elsewhere remarked, the people should in future become more partial to the federal than to the State government, the people ought not to be precluded from giving most of their confidence where they may discover it to be most due; but even in that case the State government could have little to apprehend, because it is only within a certain sphere that the federal power can, in the nature of things be advantageously administered."[38]

The Founders anticipated the need for the nation to have the flexibility to shift long-held powers of the states to the federal government, but only where the people have the highest "confidence" in the federal government, i.e, to respond to the threat of bioterrorism. But is there a legal mechanism to shift the long held powers of public safety from the states to the federal government in the case of bioterrorism, if each state elected to enact a uniform surveillance system which interfaces neatly with that of each and all of the other states would this be sufficient to address the needs of a national security response and preclude the need for more invasive uses of federal powers into the area of public health? The specter of a national security threat led by fifty leaders with fifty different sets of priorities is not only foolish but a failure of the role of the federal government in the "continued existence"[39] of the nation.

B. Public safety in times of rebellion

"The privilege of the writ of habeaus corpus shall not be suspended, unless when in cases of rebellion or invasion the public safety may require it,"[40] referring to the Constitutional provision for protection against being confined.[41] This specifically identifies a time of public safety as appropriate for the suspension of the writ of habeaus corpus, perhaps providing the Constitutional authority to invoke quarantine when the timing is such that public safety is at risk. However, the state has police powers for quarantine, its use contingent upon the public safety. In general, "probable cause"[42] that the subject is infectious, is all that is required by a state to quarantine.

Therefore, the federal government does have the Constitutional power to quarantine, but only on a much more limited and narrow precept than do the states. The quarantine power of the federal government is an untried power in this context; and the limited use of this power, coupled with the Constitutional due process requirements[43] of individual hearings for each individual makes its practical application in an emergency practically useless to address the exposure of thousands or more to a bioterrorism agent.

The ability of the states to muster state militias was a contentious issue when the Articles of Confederation were discussed during the construction of the Constitution. Alexander Hamilton addressed the issue of separate state militias and cautioned against the separate possession of military forces: "The framers of the existing [Articles of] Confederation, fully aware of the dangers to the Union from the separate possession of military forces by the States, have in express terms prohibited them from having either ships or troops, unless with the consent of Congress."[44] The use of military forces are an important component of a well-planned defense in preparation for a bioterrorism event, and the possibility of fifty different militias in a national response without one overall leader, again presents a threat to national security and a failure of the federal government to protect the "continued existence"[45] of the nation.

IV. "for the common defense or general welfare"[46]

The interpretation of the General Welfare Clause has been incontestably limited to the authority of Congress to tax since the time of The Federalist Papers. The interpretation given to the Clause was essentially narrowed to one of use as a "general phrase" followed by qualifications of the general meaning,[47] thereby narrowly applying the Clause to the ability for Congress to levy taxes. This limitation precludes the use of the General Welfare Clause as a basis for Congress to legislate on the basis of broad purposes of the general welfare of the nation.

In spite of such sweeping mandates to act for the general welfare, such as: "The prevention of disease or disability and the promotion of health, within reasonable resource constraints, provides the preeminent justification for the government to act for the welfare of society,"[48] Nevertheless, the General Welfare Clause bestows no power on Congress to act other than to tax in order to carry out these broad mandates.

E. A Contemporary Tenth Amendment Analysis[49]

The original powers used by the states during the colonial era were police powers which include the regulation of health, safety and welfare, later reserved to the states through the Constitution. During that time, states had the exclusive authority for the regulation of public health.[50] However, in 1870, the Surgeon General of the Public Health Service, General Woodworth, made an effort to establish quarantine as a federal responsibility. The resulting backlash of states' rights objections, argued that the matter of quarantine was better left to the states, as it was the historical pattern. General Woodworth argued that the regulations were inconsistent from state to state and the spread of disease was not relevant to states' borders. After the 1877 outbreak of yellow fever, General Woodworth worked for a national quarantine system which resulted in the Quarantine Act of 1878.[51] The Act stipulated that federal quarantine regulations must not conflict with or impair those of state and municipal authorities, and was to be administered by the precursor agency of the Public Health Service.[52] The use of a federal quarantine system would be an integral part of a national security plan against the threat of bioterrorism.

The test for Tenth Amendment distinctions between federal powers and state powers is articulated in *Hodel v. Virginia Surface Mining Reclamation Ass'n*.[53] First, the challenged statute must regulate "states as states"; second, the statute must involve matters strictly "attributes of state sovereignty"; and third, the state's compliance with the federal statute would impair the state's ability to "structure integral operations in areas of traditional functions." *Garcia v. San Antonio Metropolitan Transit Authority*[54] qualified the "states as states" criteria as "one of process rather than one of result," and overruled *National League of Cities v. Ussery*[55] where the standard of "traditional governmental functions" failed to articulate a clear principle as to what it means. In *Garcia*, the dissent of Justices O'Connor, Powell and Rehnquist saw this decision as ignoring the Tenth Amendment restraints on the Commerce Clause and leaving little to restrain Congress from passing legislation encroaching on state activities.[56] Instead of Tenth Amendment restraints, the majority in *Garcia* expected that the "built-in restraints that our system provides through state participation in federal governmental action" and the "political process" will "ensure[s] that laws that unduly burden the states will not be promulgated."[57]

The most recent teaching from the U.S. Supreme Court on the protections of the Tenth Amendment was articulated in *New York v. United States*[58] In *New York*, the Court sought to confine Congress' authority to "commandeer" states in the regulation of the disposal of radioactive wastes.[59] Rather the states were to be given a choice between regulating or to be preempted by federal legislation, or to attach conditions under the spending power of Congress to encourage states to regulate. This further limited Congressional reaches into state legislative choices, thereby introducing Tenth Amendment protections not recognized previously in the *Garcia* decision.

The most recent case to address state health and safety regulation in this line of cases is *Pacific Gas & Elec. Co. v. State Energy Res. Cons. & Devel. Comm'n*[60] wherein the court sought to avoid preemption of state public health and safety laws by preempting state law only where it conflicts with federal law. The subject of health and safety here, was nuclear safety, and the courts have consistently found that nuclear power and nuclear safety is an area where the federal government has clearly preempted state law. However, the dissent suggests that where safety of the state's citizens are at issue, the state should have the sovereign power to prohibit the construction of a nuclear power facility.[61] Again, the recognition of the power of states to protect its citizens is affirmed and the role of states in the federalist system gains establishment in case law.

The construction of federal legislation concerning a mandatory role for the states in what must be a precisely executed system of surveillance and response to any threat of bioterrorism, does not fit within the Tenth Amendment protection standard articulated by Justice O'Connor in *New York*. Here, the requirement that states be given the option to regulate or be preempted may work for the facts of *New York*, but in a system where coordination and uniformity are essential to a surveillance and response system, there is no room for options such as these.

VI. Police powers, the Commerce Clause, the Supremacy Clause and preemption
The police power

"[a]ims directly to secure and promote the public welfare by subjecting to restraint or compulsion the members of the community. It is the power by which the government abridges the freedom of action or the free use of property of the individual in order that the welfare may not be jeopardized."[62]

Since the Constitution does not expressly grant Congress the power to enact legislation for national public health, there exists a presumption that Congress does not have the power to do so—rather the states have that power. The Constitutional Convention considered numerous resolutions to give Congress such power, but all were rejected.

The Court extended the reach of the Commerce Clause in *Hoke v. United States*[63]—wherein the Mann Act[64] was found to be constitutional—just short of granting police powers, to that of regulations having the "quality of police regulations."[65] The Court limited Congress' police powers because the Commerce Clause gave the federal government power to regulate "among the states" and "that Congress, as incident to it, may adopt not only means necessary but convenient to its exercise, and the means may have the quality of police regulations."[66]

According to a scholar from the 1920s, James Tobey, the "Government is, in fact, organized for the express purpose, among others, of conserving the public health and cannot divest itself of this important duty,"[67] in reference to the police power. The use of police power by the federal government is a basis on which a federal approach to the threat of bioterrorism might be established.

A bioterrorism event would affect interstate commerce. Spreading rapidly from state to state it could bring death to those involved in commerce, inhibiting business trade and commerce. However, the relatively recent litigation of Congressional power to legislate in traditional areas of state power in *United States v. Lopez*[68] suggests that reliance on the Commerce Clause for federal bioterrorism legislation might exceed the shrinking reach of Congress' Commerce Clause powers. More recently, the U.S. Supreme Court, again, limited the reach of the standard for affecting commerce, in the review of the migratory bird rule,[69] by striking down a regulation which extended federal power beyond Constitutional limits into an area of state police powers.

Bioterrorism regulation based upon the doctrine of preemption could be proposed as a basis. Stating the doctrine: state law is deemed preempted by federal constitutional or statutory law either by express provision,[70] by a conflict between federal and state law,[71]; or by implication where "Congress so thoroughly occupies a legislative field 'as to make reasonable the inference that Congress left no room for the States to supplement it."[72] In public health law, Congress, however, has not preempted the field, as for example, as it has in the area of nuclear power.[73] Further, the trend in federalism suggests a trend toward more power for states—not less....

VIII. Conclusion and Recommendations

The enactment of federal legislation on the basis of the Commerce Clause, extending the character of those regulations to the "quality of police regulations,"[74] is an available federal approach to national security. In a reading of The Federalist Papers in the context of the new threat of bioterrorism, it is evident that the Constitution was intended to permit any shift of powers from the state to the federal government when the people's confidence shifted to the federal government. With the threat of bioterrorism, people are likely to expect federal preparedness for a national security threat, which ultimately involves extensive peacetime activities. Conversely, they may be unaware that the long-held powers of the states' governments which have so ably protected the public since colonial times may well prove to be an impediment to the effective role of the federal government, "or in other words, whether the Union itself shall be preserved."[75]

Legislation tailored to meet the narrow purpose of national defense against the threat of bioterrorism is an essential responsibility of our federal government. Recognition of the importance of constructing and approving such legislation prior to a bioterrorism disaster, requires that Congress face the constitutional challenge of taking national leadership in our national defense, and begin the political debate surrounding such legislation, sooner than later. There will be no opportunity to have the deliberative debate of state and national powers that are raised in this article, and that are essential to properly construct so as to protect our system of federalism, should a bioterrorism threat become a reality.

3.3   The Military and Domestic Emergencies
3.3.1.   *Posse Comitatus*, 18 U. S. C. §1385
The Posse Comitatus Act reads as follows:
> *Use of Army and Air Force as posse comitatus*

> *"Whoever, except in cases and under circumstances expressly authorized by the Constitution or Act of Congress, willfully uses any part of the Army or the Air Force as a posse*

comitatus or otherwise to execute the laws shall be fined under this title or imprisoned not more than two years, or both."

The Posse Comitatus Act prohibits the enforcement of laws by the military against citizens of the United States. Enacted at the end of Reconstruction as a result of the abuses of military control of the southern United States at the end of the U. S. Civil War, the Posse Comitatus Act is intended to protect its citizens against such governmental actions. Under the U.S. Constitution, the federal government must preserve the public order and protect federal property and functions. In such an emergency, the President may declare such a state and military control may be utilized.[76] For a state, the governor must request that the President declare such an emergency in order to engage military enforcement of the laws.[77] Congress has provided by law that the military may be used. One such instance is when the President declares a state of emergency through a formal proclamation to enforce federal law because of rebellion against the authority of the United States, rendering state enforcement means unworkable.[78] When domestic violence or conspiracy hinders execution of state or federal law, and a state will not or cannot protect the constitutional rights of its citizens, the President may declare an emergency and use military enforcement of the law.[79] More recently, a statutory provision permitting the Secret Service to request assistance from all departments of the government in carrying out responsibilities was enacted to protect government officials and major political candidates.[80]

3.3.2. John Warner National Defense Authorization Act, 2007, Pub. L. No. 109-364, 120 Stat. 2083 (2007)

This law amends the Insurrection Act, 10 U.S.C. §331-335 (2006), which implements Congressional authority and power to call forth the military, suppress insurrections, and repel invasions.[81] The Insurrection Act is thereby exempt from the prohibitions of the Posse Comitatus Act.

On October 17, 2006, President Bush signed into law the John Warner National Defense Authorization Act ("Warner Act"), P.L. 90-331, 82 Stat. 170 (2007), in response to the need to clarify military deployments in domestic emergencies and the Congressional finding [82] that the federal government should be better prepared to respond with federal resources.

The Warner Act specifies that the President has the authority to deploy federal troops when responding to natural disasters and other domestic emergencies without the consent of the states involved.[83] This is the most significant change in federalism between the federal government and state governments since 9-11 in the context of public health disasters. It explicitly changed the federalism relationship and garnered the objection of all fifty state governors who objected to the subversion of state sovereignty. [84]

The Warner Act has codified the constitutional power of the federal government to deploy troops in time of an emergency, specifically when a catastrophic event has overwhelmed state and local governments.[85] This deployment of federal troops may be initiated without the request or consent of local and state governments.[86]

(*Also see*, supra, section 2.5.7.1.2.)

3.4   First Amendment publication of research: The Dual-Use Dilemma

The First Amendment right to free speech encompasses a right to freely publish. However, when national security is a concern, some restraints may be Constitutionally acceptable. The first case to address the problem of scientific research and a risk of national security was the attempt to stop the publication of the description of the triggering mechanism for the H-Bomb. The article was eventually published in *The Progressive* in November 1979.[87] But before it was published, the federal government initially successfully obtained a temporary injunction against its publication, giving rise to the "born secret" doctrine. However, in *United States v. Progressive, Inc.*, 467 F. Supp. 990 (W.D. Wis. 1979), 610 F.2d 819 (7th Cir. 1979), the case was dismissed since the information had already been published elsewhere.

The Progressive magazine attempted to publish an article by a freelance writer with no scientific training entitled "The H-Bomb Secret: How We Got It, Why We're Telling It." The article sought to show that the key information surrounding atomic weapons is not really secret, by demonstrating how much a layperson could piece together through reading physics textbooks, scientific reference books, magazine articles, unclassified government publications, and through visiting nuclear production facilities and talking with Department of Energy personnel.[88] *The Progressive* argued that the article contained information already in the public domain that could be found by anyone.[89] The government argued that much of the information in the article had not ever been in the public domain, and that the core information of the article had never been previously published.[90] The court found that some concepts in the article were outside the public domain, that these concepts were vital to the operation of the hydrogen bomb, and that the author had to have some level of expertise or skill in order to fashion the article.[91] The court also found that the article was not a "do-it-yourself guide for the hydrogen bomb" and that it "could possibly provide sufficient information to allow a medium size nation to move faster in developing a hydrogen weapon."[92] Thus, because of the possibility of a foreign power to use this article to develop a weapon faster than it otherwise could, and because of the devastating risk posed by this, the court framed the case as a choice between the preservation of civil liberties and the preservation of life, and thus granted the injunction.[93] One thing present in *The Progressive* that was missing in *The Pentagon Papers* was a statute authorizing prior restraints: the Atomic Energy Act,[94] which authorized suits to enjoin restricted information.[95]

Based upon the decision in *The Progressive*, it seems that the government could enjoin publications of dual use research if it can show that the information: (1) was not already present in the public domain, (2) that the information could aid or hasten the process of a foreign power in developing a weapon, and (3) that the threat rises to such a degree that it becomes a choice between the preservation of liberty and the preservation of life. It is clear that some dual use research could meet these requirements.

After the anthrax attacks of 2001, concern about scientific information that could be helpful to terrorists, coupled with the actual possession of scientific articles by terrorists groups, made the question of prior restraint and publications again an issue. However, three research articles sparked specific concerns, bringing these issues once again to the forefront of national security concerns. In summary, these three articles were the mousepox experiment in Australia, the botulism contamination of the milk supply article, and the reassembly of the polio virus publication, which are discussed below.

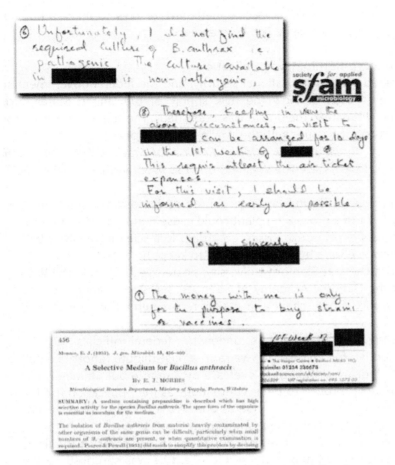

Fig. 3.1. Notes and an article on anthrax, found in a terrorist location.

3.4.1. The immunodeficient mouse research publication

In early 2001, pre-9/11, a group of Australian researchers conducted an experiment that exemplifies the dual use dilemma. The researchers were trying to suppress the mouse pox plagues that were disrupting Australian agriculture, and in doing so "inserted the gene for a mouse egg protein into the mouse pox genome in the hope of infecting the mice and creating an antibody response that would reduce mouse proliferation."[96] The response was not as good as expected, so the team added the gene for cytokine interleukin 4 (IL-4) into the mouse pox in an attempt to create an effective contraceptive.[97] This worked, but with unexpected consequences. The researchers created a highly lethal form of mouse pox, which shut down the mouse immune system, and as a result all of the mice died.[98] The group then inoculated a more resistant strain of mice and found that those mice also contracted the super strain and died.[99] These experiments and their subsequent publication left policymakers in fear that someone might try this strategy on smallpox, which is in the same family of viruses, and create a lethal agent with no effective vaccine.[100] At no stage is the risk of dual use of research greater than at the publication stage, because publication is the widest vehicle for dissemination and provides an opportunity for research to end up in the hands of terrorists.[101] The experiment generated information not previously available to the public, which could have probably aided a country in the development of a bioweapon. If terrorists could use that information to create a highly lethal strain of smallpox, then it would definitely cause the court to make a choice between preservation of liberty and preservation of life. However, it could be argued that it is not as certain that the mouse pox experiment would aid a foreign power in the way that the article in *The Progressive* would because it is not known that the same process used to make the highly lethal strain of mousepox would work for smallpox. However, with other dual use research, for example, any research that would inadvertently tell how to make a vaccine ineffective or how to make a human virus more lethal would be more analogous to the article in *The Progressive*.

3.4.2.   Botulinum toxin milk contamination publication

Another article was considered a threat to national security, and the federal government sought to block its publication. This article described how the milk supply of the United States might be contaminated with botulinum toxin. Ultimately, the article was published. The following article from the Washington Post describes the effort and the issues with the article's publication.

Rick Weiss, *Report Warns of Threat to Milk Supply, Release of Study Citing Vulnerability to Bioterrorism Attack Was Opposed by U.S. Officials*, The Washington Post, Wednesday, June 29, 2005; A08.

> About a third of an ounce of botulism toxin poured by bioterrorists into a milk truck en route from a dairy farm to a processing plant could cause hundreds of thousands of deaths and billions of dollars in economic losses, according to a scientific analysis that was published yesterday despite efforts by federal officials to keep the details secret.
>
> The analysis by researchers at Stanford University, posted yesterday on the Web site of the Proceedings of the National Academy of Sciences, seeks to quantify security weaknesses in the nation's milk-supply chain and makes recommendations for closing those gaps.
>
> Although some suggested changes are underway, federal officials felt the material had enough potential for misuse to warrant a last-minute effort to halt publication. That effort, which delayed the report's release by a month but ultimately did not keep it from becoming public, proved to be as contentious as the publication itself. It has assured the report's place in the scientific canon as one of the first test cases of how to balance scientific freedom and national security in the post-Sept. 11 era.
>
> Study leader Lawrence M. Wein, whose previous research had forecast the likely effects of terrorist attacks involving anthrax and smallpox, said he was surprised by the government's push to block publication, which involved a flurry of phone calls and meetings with officers of the National Academies. The organization advises the federal government on matters of science and publishes the journal.
>
> Last fall, Wein said, he briefed high-ranking officials of the departments of Homeland Security and Health and Human Services, along with dairy industry representatives, on his work.
>
> "It was clear the dairy people were nervous about this paper coming out," Wein said. But when federal officials did not follow up, he said, he assumed they had concluded -- as had every reviewer at the National Academies -- that the information in the article was publicly available and easily obtained through a Google search.
>
> Bill Hall, a spokesman for HHS, said yesterday that his department still opposes publication but was not in a position to block release of the data, which are not classified.
>
> "We don't see eye to eye on this," Hall said. "If this ends up being the wrong decision down the road, the consequences could be quite severe and HHS will have to deal with it, not the National Academies."
>
> The analysis by Wein and graduate student Yifan Liu considered what might happen if terrorists poured into a milk tanker truck a couple of gallons of concentrated sludge containing as much as 10 grams of botulinum toxin, a potent bacterial nerve poison now popular in low doses as a wrinkle eraser.
>
> Because milk from many sources is combined in huge tanks holding hundreds of thousands of gallons, the toxin would get widely distributed in low, but potentially lethal,

concentrations and within days be consumed by about 568,000 people, the report concludes.

The researchers acknowledge that their numbers are very rough. But depending on how thoroughly the milk was pasteurized (which partially inactivates toxins) and how promptly the outbreak was detected and supplies recalled, about 400,000 people would be likely to fall ill, they conclude.

Symptoms of botulism food poisoning arise within hours and progress from cramps, nausea and vision problems to paralysis and death by asphyxiation. Although only 6 percent of victims would generally be expected to die, the death rate could easily hit 60 percent, they conclude, because there would not be nearly enough mechanical ventilators or doses of antitoxin to treat so many victims.

Children could be hit first and hardest, because milk goes directly from processing plants to schools, avoiding the grocery-distribution system.

"They'd be the canaries," Wein said.

The report concludes that the most efficient ways to reduce such risks are to insist that latches on tanker trucks have locks; improve pasteurization processes; and develop tests that can detect contamination before milk is delivered to outlets -- changes, the team concludes, that are likely to cost just a few pennies per gallon.

Publication was scheduled for the week of May 30, but was abruptly postponed days before that date when HHS officials contacted the National Academies with concerns that the paper might inadvertently aid terrorists, according to an accompanying editorial written by Bruce Alberts, president of the Academies.

Those concerns were discussed in detail on June 7, after which the Academies decided to publish. By then, a preprint of the article had been widely distributed to journalists as part of the journal's standard procedures, and the New York Times had published a summary by Wein in an opinion piece.

Barry R. Bloom, dean of the Harvard School of Public Health, who oversaw an independent review of the paper earlier this spring, said he is convinced that the report did more good than harm by quantifying the risks posed at each point in the milk-delivery system -- a difficult job that now allows the industry and regulators to concentrate security efforts where they are most needed.

"This paper didn't just slip in with no one thinking about it," Bloom said. "But science depends on openness and the free exchange of ideas. And being aware of threats gives us a better chance of protecting against them than not being aware of them and having only the terrorists aware of them."

A national security directive signed by President Ronald Reagan and still in force demands that fundamental scientific information remain openly accessible unless it is formally classified.

Chris Galen, a spokesman for the National Milk Producers Federation in Arlington, criticized the Academies' decision, saying the information "could inform someone with malicious designs on food safety, even just as a prank."

The need for improved pasteurization "is something that has already been addressed" by the industry, he said, as has the need to keep locks on truck latches.

He acknowledged, however, that those improvements, encouraged by the Food and Drug Administration in recent years, are not mandatory. And although he said the newer standards are being "widely followed," he conceded he had no data to indicate what proportion of dairies and milk processors are adhering to the tougher recommendations.

3.4.3.   Building the polio virus research publication

An article describing polio virus synthesis was published in *Science* magazine in 2002, which raised questions about not only whether this research should be published, but whether this kind of research should be done, at all. The researchers were interested in whether they could synthesize a virus and their success signaled to the community that once the article was published which would make public the techniques and materials with which to do this, that it would pose a threat to national security. However, the bar for burdening free speech under the First Amendment is very high, and after much public debate, the article was published.

Then in 2011, a scientific article on the successful engineering of the H5N1 virus so that it is transmissible to mammals from its benign state to mammals caused another debate. Why would the researchers do such a potentially dangerous and deadly experiment and to what purpose? The researchers wanted to learn how this virus could change into one humans could contract, in order to understand how to combat it, should it evolve in nature, into a bird flu that would became transmissible to humans, potentially causing a global pandemic.

3.4.4.   NSABB role in reviewing scientific articles

The NSABB was created by the PAHPAct in 2005 as a federal advisory committee with members from the public. It was chartered in 2007 and renewed in 2012. Its charter states that the purpose or the NSABB is:

". . . to provide, as requested, advice, guidance, and leadership regarding biosecurity oversight of dual use research, defined as biological research with legitimate scientific purpose that may be misused to pose a biologic threat to public health and/or national security. The NSABB will provide advice on and recommend specific strategies for the efficient and effective oversight of federally conducted or supported dual use biological research, taking into consideration both national security concerns and the needs of the research community to foster continued rapid progress in public health and agricultural research."

In 2011, the scientific articles sought publication in *Science* and *Nature*, two leading scientific publications. The National Academy of Sciences reviewed the articles and generated a report. The NSABB whose role was to provide review and oversight to dual use activities of which this research was a part then took on the task. They recommended not publishing in its entirety and withholding details. Later, the World Health Organization convened a similar group of experts and came to the opposite conclusion – no speech should be prohibited. This caused the NSABB to reconsider its stand, and on March 30, 2012, the *ScienceInsider* led with an article by David Malakoff beginning with the headline, "Breaking News: NSABB Reverses Position on Flu Papers."[102]

All of the articles were eventually published --- the standard for prior restraint on free speech under our constitution is a high one, that none of these articles reached that level where the right of free speech could be burdened. The following sections discusses the constitutional doctrine which explains the position the NSABB eventual had to take.

3.4.5. History of the clear and present danger doctrine

This exception was first articulated by Supreme Court Justice Holmes in *Schenck v. United States*, 249 U.S. 47 (1919). *Schenck* involved an officer of the Socialist party who, while the United States was fighting in World War I, circulated pamphlets to recently drafted men that encouraged insubordination and obstructed the recruiting and enlisting service of the United States Military.[103] Schenck was convicted under the Espionage Act of 1917[104] for circulating these pamphlets.[105] Schenck argued that the pamphlet was protected by the First Amendment to the Constitution, but the Court upheld Schenck's conviction stating that "in ordinary times the defendants in saying all that was said in the circular would have been within their constitutional right. . .but the character of every act depends upon the circumstances in which it is done."[106] The Court went on to state that:

> The question in every case is whether the words used are used in such circumstances and are of such a nature as to create a clear and present danger that they will bring about the substantive evils that Congress has a right to prevent. It is a question of proximity and degree. When a nation is at war many things that might be said in time of peace are such a hindrance to its effort that their utterance will not be endured so long as men fight and that no Court could regard them as protected by any constitutional right.[107]

The Court went on to note that if the pamphlets had been successful and had caused obstruction of the recruiting service, then liability for those pamphlets would be a given; the Court saw no reason that the defendant's liability under the Espionage Act should depend on the success of the crime.[108] What can be taken from this case is that the circumstances of wartime permit greater restrictions on freedom of speech then might be permitted during peace.[109]

Important to note about *Schenck* is that the law at issue was not a prior restraint on speech, but rather a law prohibiting people from obstructing military recruitment.[110] However, subsequent cases have shown that the clear and present danger doctrine is applicable to prior restraints on speech as well as subsequent punishments.[111] Under the *Schenck* test it would seem that a prior restraint against publication of dual use research would be upheld based on the clear and present danger test, but as the next section will show, the test has become more speech protective since *Schenck*.

The modern clear and present danger test

The clear and present danger test has undergone a transformation since *Schenck*.[112] The original *Schenck* test was thought to be a weak test, meaning that it was not highly protective of speech.[113] Over time the Supreme Court began to apply the test more strictly and it became very speech-protective.[114] Although weakened during the Cold War era, it was strengthened in *Brandenburg v. Ohio*.[115] Under the current test, the only consideration is the consequences of the speech, and thus the only elements to take into consideration are the imminence and gravity of harm that the speech may cause.[116] Imminence of harm is a threshold requirement for upholding a prior restraint of speech under the doctrine, and because it is so hard to satisfy, it makes the test very speech-protective.[117] The gravity of the harm part of the test is not well-defined and is inconsistently applied.[118] The Court has stated that while violence definitely satisfies the gravity element, breach of the peace, interference with fair administration of justice, and restraint of trade could also satisfy the requirement.[119]

It is difficult to know whether the court would uphold a prior restraint on dual use research under the clear and present danger doctrine. Since *Schenck*, many of the cases dealing with meeting the elements of the clear and present danger doctrine involve verbal threats to incite violence or to advocate against something.[120] In other words, the dual use dilemma is not what the Supreme Court had in mind when it proscribed the current clear and present danger doctrine, so it is difficult to analyze whether a court would hold that publication of dual use research creates a clear and present danger. Under the current test it would probably be extremely difficult to uphold a prior restraint under the clear and present danger doctrine. The imminence requirement would most likely be too attenuated. The government would have to identify an organization that would have access to and plan to use research published by U.S. researchers to try to harm the U.S. Considering that terrorist organizations are by nature secretive, this would be almost impossible. The harm, a threat to national security, would surely be satisfied.

For the reasons set out in this part, probably none of the recognized exceptions to validate a prior restraint apply in the case of dual use research. However, some think that the Supreme Court case *Near v. Minnesota*, 283 U.S. 697 (1931) might have planted the "seeds of what might be called a 'national security exception' to the rule against prior restraints."[121]

The possible national security exception

Near dealt with a statute that provided for abatement, as a public nuisance, of any "malicious, scandalous, or defamatory newspaper, magazine, or other periodical."[122] A man publishing a newspaper that accused public officials, including a county attorney and chief of police, of some very unsavory things was enjoined from publishing the paper under the statute.[123] The Supreme Court overturned the decision and held that the statute was unconstitutional.[124]

However, the Court in its analysis stated that prior restraints could be constitutional under exceptional circumstances and that "no one would question but that a government might prevent actual obstruction to its recruiting service or the publication of the sailing dates of transports or the number and location of troops."[125] According to one commentator, this statement has raised many questions.

> Was the exception applicable only during times of war? What types of information could qualify as equivalent to the 'obstruction of its recruiting service,' the 'sailing dates of transports', or the 'number and location of troops?' Could the exception be applied to any state secret, or only secrets which the lives of troops and private citizens were directly imperiled? Would a court have inherent power to issue such an injunction at the request of the executive branch, or would such an order be permissible only pursuant to specific statutory authorization by Congress? What would be the burden of proof on the government in justifying such an order?[126]

These questions have yet to be answered, but in *New York Times Co. v. United States*, 403 U.S. 713 (1971) the court made clear that the dicta in *Near* would be narrowly construed.[127] In *New York Times*, also called the Pentagon Papers case, the United States was trying to enjoin the *New York Times* from publishing the contents of a classified forty-seven volume Pentagon study entitled "History of U.S. Decision Making On Viet Nam Policy."[128] When seeking the injunction in the lower courts in New York and Washington D.C., the government had urged that publication of the papers would cause irreparable injury to the national defense, but were unsuccessful.[129] The Supreme Court, in a *per curiam* opinion, simply stated that prior restraints come with a heavy presumption against invalidity and that it agreed with the lower courts that government had failed to meet its burden in overcoming that presumption.[130]

3.4.6. Prior restraints in general

Prior restraints impose advance limits upon the right to publish or speak.[131] A prior restraint seeks to suppress speech because of its content.[132] Not all regulations regarding speech are prior restraints; regulations that merely impose a time, place, or manner restriction on speech are not prior restraints.[133] A prior restraint can be effected through the use of a temporary restraining order, a permanent injunction, censorship, or the requirement of a license.[134] In order to determine whether a law is a prior restraint, the purpose and effect must be considered.[135] For instance, in *Paper Back Mart v. City of Anniston*, 407 F. Supp. 376 (N.D. Ala. 1976) the court held that a municipal ordinance forbidding the distribution of obscene materials was not a prior restraint because the *purpose* of the ordinance was to gather evidence in a criminal action to punish dissemination of *unprotected materials* and the ordinance did not impose any continuing restriction upon dissemination.[136] Likewise if the *effect* of the law is only to indirectly or minutely regulate speech, then it is not a prior restraint.[137]

When are prior restraints constitutionally valid?

Prior restraints carry a heavy presumption of invalidity.[138] However, they are not considered unconstitutional *per se* and can be valid under certain extreme circumstances.[139] In order to be found constitutionally valid, the restriction must fit within one of the certain exceptions carved out by the Supreme Court.[140] The exceptions are:

> (1) where the speech or activity restrained is not protected by the First Amendment; (2) where, although the speech is of a kind ordinarily protected, the agency applying the restraint is exempt from the strictures of the guaranty of freedom of speech and press; (3) where the restraint is reasonably incidental to the achievement of another valid governmental purpose; and (4) where the activity restrained poses a serious and imminent threat to some protected competing public interest, or will irreparably damage a private interest.[141]

The first and second exceptions do not apply to regulation of dual use research by the government.

The first exception does not apply because scientific research does not fall under the category of unprotected speech, which generally includes speech that is obscene, libelous, profane, or that incites to violence or a breach of the peace.[142] The second exception does not apply because the federal government is obviously not exempt from the strictures of the first amendment, since it is not a private citizen or corporation.[143]

The third exception

The third exception requires that the restraint be reasonably incidental to achieving another valid governmental purpose, which is a very general statement and requires further qualification. The third circuit held in *NJ Lottery Comm'n v. U.S.* that *Veterans and Reservists for Peace in Vietnam v. Regional Commissioner*[144] was an example of a court upholding a prior restraint based on this exception.[145] In *Veterans* the plaintiff claimed that the Trading with the Enemy Act[146] and the Foreign Assets Control Regulations[147] violated the First Amendment by "prohibiting the receipt of unsolicited publications unless the addressee obtains a license, submits to a permanent record his desire to receive the proscribed publications, and proves he has made no payment."[148] In this case, the plaintiff, an unincorporated association, received a letter from the Regional Commissioner of Customs that a shipment of Red Chinese literature from North Vietnam had been received and would not be released until the plaintiff procured a license.[149] The plaintiff claimed that the publications were unsolicited copies of an English language newspaper for which the plaintiff did not intend to compensate anyone, and in lieu of applying for a license, sued for an injunction and summary judgment.[150] The defendant cross-moved for summary judgment and won.[151]

On appeal, the plaintiff urged that the regulatory scheme was overbroad and that it constituted a prior restraint in violation of the first amendment; the plaintiff complained particularly of the licensing procedure.[152] The court held that when deciding whether congress had adopted a means of carrying out a legitimate governmental objective, it is necessary to balance the legitimate objective against the specific prohibitions of the first amendment.[153] The court held that a compelling governmental interest can justify limitations on first amendment freedoms.[154] The court noted that the governmental objective underlying the regulatory scheme, which was to prevent countries such as North Vietnam and China from deriving any economic benefit from transactions with United States citizens, was compelling.[155] The court went on to state that in light of the U.S.-North Vietnam relationship, and taking into consideration that money is a powerful weapon in an international struggle, the constitutional objective underlying the Act was "wholly proper."[156] The court stated that the statute did not *directly* regulate speech protected by the first amendment, nor did it grant discretion to a delagatee to determine whether particular items of expression may be prohibited on the basis of their *content*, and thus it did not trigger the overbreadth doctrine.[157] Next, the court addressed the plaintiff's contention that the licensing procedure was an unlawful prior restraint.[158] Having already found the governmental objective legitimate, all that was left to decide was whether the means of achieving the purpose violated the first amendment.[159]

The court looked at four factors in evaluating the licensing procedure: (1) the weight of the burden on the applicant and the length of the delay in receiving the license; (2) whether the government has unlimited discretion to deny the license; (3) the loss of anonymity of the applicant; and (4) the burden of proof required to obtain a license.[160] The court evaluated the licensing procedure under the factors and found the burden on the applicant not unreasonable.

It is easy to make a comparison between the compelling governmental objective in *Veterans*, which was to keep enemy countries from receiving American funds,[161] and the governmental objective in preventing publication of dual use research, which is to ensure that the U.S. does not show its enemies how to destroy it through a biological weapon. However, a prior restraint based on this objective would most likely not be found valid as in *Veterans* because of the focus on prohibiting the publication based on *the contents* of the speech. In *Veterans*, the court held that the regulatory scheme was saved from the application of the overbreadth doctrine because it did not directly regulate speech or expression, nor did it grant discretion to a delagatee to determine whether particular items of expression may be prohibited on the basis *of their content*.[162] Any regulation or licensing procedure would necessarily directly regulate protected[163] speech based on its content because the content of the speech is the source of the problem that creates the compelling governmental interest. In *Veterans* the goal of the scheme was not to prohibit receiving documents based upon their contents; it was merely to ensure that enemy sovereigns were not being financially compensated by American citizens.[164] Any prior restraint on dual use research based on this exception would necessarily be geared towards the content of the speech and thus does not fall within the "reasonably incidental to the achievement of another valid governmental purpose" exception.[165]

The fourth exception

The fourth exception to the general rule that prior restraints are invalid is when the speech poses a "serious and imminent threat to some protected competing public interest, or will irreparably damage a private interest."[166] Since a threat to national security, which is the issue with dual use research, is not a private interest, that part of the exception is inapplicable. In order for a prior restraint to be valid on the basis of a threat to the public, it must be shown that there exists a clear and present danger that rises far above public inconvenience, annoyance, or unrest.[167]

One case, which is more factually related to the dual use issue, where a court has actually issued a prior restraint based on national security, is *United States v. Progressive, Inc*,[168] mentioned in the introduction to this section.

If a prior restraint could issue, should it?

As stated in Section III, the official policy of the United States government is that the only mechanism for restricting fundamental research is classification.[169] However, as discussed above, a prior restraint against publication of dual use research could probably be upheld on the basis of national security. Thus, all the government would need to do is enact legislation similar to the Atomic Energy Act,[170] allowing for an injunction to issue against the publication of dual use life science research that threatens national security. This raises a question: just because the government could use a prior restraint to prevent dissemination of dual use research, should it? This question might have been answered in 2002, when a draft of the U.S. Department of Defense (DoD) regulation was proposed, which would have required researchers to "obtain DoD approval to discuss or publish findings of all military-sponsored unclassified research."[171] This regulation would have allowed the United States government to prevent biological research that it considered sensitive from becoming available to the public, thus allowing the research to be secret.[172] The constitutional validity of this regulation was never tested because public criticism from the scientific community for this proposal was great and it was withdrawn.[173] The following section describes many other reasons, besides the disquietude of the scientific community, why prior restraints restricting dissemination of scientific research with dual use capabilities is not a good mechanism for combating the dual use dilemma.

Problems with prior restraints

Prior restraints raise many concerns because information exchange is pivotal in scientific advancement.[174] Specifically, prior restraints have the potential to impede scientific researchers' ability to stay up on potential threats and effective countermeasures because of the restriction on the flow of information.[175]

Also problematic would be how a prior restraint would control the great mass of dual use research already in the public domain and research not funded by the government.[176]

Another issue is that any prior restraint on dual use research would necessarily cover a broad range of disciplines,[177] making the task more large and onerous.[178] It would be incredibly difficult to identify every piece of research with dual use capabilities that poses a real threat to national security.

Other problems with prior restraints include doubts about effectiveness[179] and the historically open research culture of the life sciences.[180]

This section has shown that it is possible that the government could have a prior restraint against publication of dual use research using the national security exception. For the reasons articulated above, the government should not depend on this route to combat the dual use dilemma. There are rare instances when a prior restraint might be necessary, such as books, articles, etc. that describe "recipes" for making and delivering weapons.[181] For the most part, however, the above problems associated with prior restraints and dual use research, paired with the U.S. policy to only restrict fundamental research through classification, point to the conclusion that most likely a prior restraint will not be issued to bar publication of dual use research.

3.4.7. NSDD-189

The policy embodied in NSDD-189,[182] issued by President Reagan on September 21, 1985, continues to be the official U.S. governmental policy for controlling the flow of science, technology, and engineering information produced in federally funded fundamental research at academic institutions, governmental and nongovernmental facilities, and private laboratories receiving federal funds.[183] On November 1, 2001, Condoleeza Rice, then the Assistant to the President for National Security Affairs, affirmed in a letter to Harold Brown of the Center for Strategic and International Studies that NSDD-189 would continue as the official policy until the administration updated the appropriate export control policies that effect basic research in the United States.[184] This also been reaffirmed by the Director of the Office of Science and Technology Policy, John Marburger, in 2003, and a number of recent publications and statements by other organizations have shown support for NSDD-189.[185] NSDD-189 states that "to the maximum extent possible, the products of fundamental research remain unrestricted" and that if control is needed for national security reasons, "the mechanism for control of information generated during federally-funded fundamental research in science, technology and engineering at colleges, universities and laboratories is classification."[186] Recently there have been some changes to the current classification system in the United States that may have a negative impact on the free exchange of biological research.[187] For instance, classification authority was recently extended to agencies not traditionally involved in these matters, such as the U.S. Department of Agriculture, the Environmental Protection Agency, and the U.S. Department of Health and Human Services.[188] These changes have raised the issue of how federally funded research might be scrutinized for classification.[189] Currently, in most agencies the tasks of applying classification standards to information is so great that authority is delegated to thousands of government officials.[190] While there are detailed guidelines for classifying information, these become less useful when the subject matter and associated risks are less defined and/or understood, and subjective judgment becomes more involved.[191] However, a recent publication and the newly created National Science Advisory Board for Biosecurity provide hope for guidance.

NAS Report on the Dual Use Dilemma 2004

In 2004, a committee of the National Research Council came out with a report addressing the dual-use dilemma.[192] The report was in response to the "increasing attention being paid by scientists to the potential for misuse of biotechnology by hostile individuals or nations and to the policy proposals that could be applied to minimize of mitigate those threats."[193] The three purposes of the report were to:

(1) review the current rules, regulations, and institutional arrangements and processes in the United States that provide oversight of research on pathogens and potentially dangerous biotechnology research, within government laboratories, universities and other research institutions, and industry; (2) assess the adequacy of the current rules, regulations, and institutional arrangements and processes to prevent the destructive application of biotechnology research; and (3) recommend changes in these practices that could improve U.S. capacity to prevent the destructive application of biotechnology research while still enabling legitimate research to be conducted."[194]

The authors stated that while the USA PATRIOT Act of 2001[195] and the Public Health Security and Bioterrorism Preparedness and Response Act of 2002[196] provided statutory and regulatory bases for protecting biological materials from inadvertent misuse, there were no guidelines or regulations for addressing potential misuse of biological research for terrorist purposes[197] Furthermore, the committee found that no national or international review body currently had the "legal authority or self-governance responsibility to evaluate a proposed research activity prior to its conduct to determine whether the risks associated with the proposed research, and its potential for misuse, outweigh its potential benefits."[198] The committee proposed that the current (non-existent) regulatory system of dual use research be overhauled to adequately address bioterrorism/dual use concerns, while still enabling vital research to go forward, and the committee provided several recommendations for doing so.[199]

The committee recognized that the publication of dual research provided for the greatest dissemination, including to those who would use the research for terrorist purposes.[200] The committee recommended total reliance on voluntary self-regulation of the scientific community instead of formal governmental regulations.[201] The eschew of governmental regulation was explained by the great controversy among the scientific community and publishers over censorship of research, because open communication is powerful in scientific advancement.[202]

However, the committee did not give any specific recommendations for how the scientific community should implement self-regulation beyond encouraging continued discussion among editors, publishers, and the scientific community.[203] Another recommendation by the committee was for the

Department of Health and Human Services (HHS) to create a National Science Advisory Board for Biodefense.[204] In 2006, Congress created the National Science Advisory Board for Biosecurity (NSABB). [205]

3.4.8.   The NSABB the dual use dilemma

The NSABB's authority comes from 42 U.S.C. § 217(a), section 222 of the Public Health Service Act, as amended.[206] The NSABB was created by Congress to provide guidance to the federal government regarding dual-use research by recommending specific strategies for efficient and effective oversight of federally conducted or supported dual use research, which balance national security issues with the needs of the scientific community.[207] The board consists of 25 members appointed by the secretary of HHS and 18 ex-officio members from various governmental agencies that have an interest in life science research.[208] These members are made up of experts in the life science, law, and security fields.[209] The board meets twice a year, and can be convened on an as needed basis.[210] The board does not approve or disapprove of specific experiments; they only advise on national policies governing institutional review and approval of dual use research.[211] The board plans to develop criteria and processes for institutions to refer classes of research or specific experiments for guidance.[212] Upon referral, the NSABB can review and give guidance on experiments that present a novel category of dual use research requiring additional guidance from the board.[213] The NSABB will also advise how to interpret and apply federal guidelines on dual use research in instances when the institution seeks additional advice.

The NSABB's Slow Start

The NSABB, while a step in the right direction, is perhaps not as strong a response to the dual use dilemma as might be needed. The first possible perceived weakness is that the NSABB does not appear to do all that much thus far. Their revised charter was issued in March of 2006 and according to their website, they have only conducted one meeting.[214] Also disconcerting is the small size of the board and the infrequency of meetings; two meetings a year and less than 50 members does not seem likely to have much of an impact on an entire field of research. In addition, the board only advises federally funded and/or conducted research, leaving out all privately done dual use research, which has the potential to be just as helpful to terrorists. Also, the board is simply advisory and thus those seeking the advice are under no legal obligation to follow the board's recommendations. However, the board has come up with a comprehensive proposal to serve as a framework for the federal government for overseeing research with dual use potential, which will be discussed in Section VI.

Although the NSABB may not be the ideal response to the dual use dilemma, on the other hand there is the more extreme response, censorship.

Could the government restrict a biodefense researcher's right to publish through use of a prior restraint?

Although any discussions to move seriously in this direction on the NSABB have not been made public, if there are such conversations, it remains only a partial solution to preventing publication of sensitive biological research. One of the obstacles that would have to be hurdled to address the dual use issue is the fear of censorship of scientific research through restrictive regulations.[215] There are two ways this could be done, through a prior restraint or through law that punishes publication or speech after the fact.

Prior Restraint v. Punishment after Publication: A constitutional perspective?

A prior restraint is any governmental regulation that forbids or limits future dissemination of constitutionally protected speech.[216] It is important to distinguish a prior restraint, which restricts dissemination, from a law that punishes the publication.[217] It has been argued that the distinction between the two is insignificant from the perspective of the speaker, since both have a chilling effect on speech.[218] Although prior restraints may seem no less deterrent than subsequent punishment for speech, they are considered more repugnant to a free society.[219] The following quote from the *Southeastern Promotions* case illustrates the Supreme Court's disdain for prior restraints:

> Behind the distinction is a theory deeply etched in our law: a free society prefers to punish the few who abuse rights of speech after they break the law than to throttle them and all others beforehand. It is always difficult to know in advance what an individual will say, and the line between legitimate and illegitimate speech is often so finely drawn that the risks of freewheeling censorship are formidable.[220]

It is more fitting with free society to punish after the fact, either criminally or civilly, than to use a prior restraint because penalties come with the protection of full trial, complete with a right to a jury.[221] It has even been argued that "prior restraints...tend to *encourage* indiscriminate censorship in a way that subsequent punishment does not."[222] The proponent of this argument reasons that groundless fears of consequences of dissemination, public opinion pressures, fear of not being able to undo damage, and the likelihood that judges will uphold speech once it has issued rather than permitting speech to issue because the consequences are already known cause prior restraints to encourage more censorship.[223]

Effectiveness: a prior restraint or a punishment?

A prior restraint would be more effective than a law punishing publication because once dual use research has been published, the harm is done. In other words, the fear is that the research will be used by terrorists, and once dual use research has been published, the information is already widely available and has had an opportunity to fall into the wrong hands. While a sanction for publication would deter future publication of dual use research, it would be less effective for combating the issue of dual use research; thus, this section will only discuss the use of prior restraints as a means of restricting publication of dual use research.

[The preceding analysis was first written by Whitney Boatright (JD, 2007) and Sarah Thornton (JD, 2007)]

3.5.   First Amendment Right of Association

The Anti-Terrorism and Death Penalty Act of 1996 provides that the federal government may identify groups that are known to conduct terrorist activities and exclude their members from entering the United States. The following case is a challenge to this statute, but the court does not address whether this would deprive American citizens who may be members of any of these designated groups of the constitutional right of association.

People's Mojahedin Organization of Iran, Petitioner v. United States Department of State
182 F.3d 17 (D.C. Cir. 1999)

OPINION

The Antiterrorism and Effective Death Penalty Act conferred upon the Secretary of State the power to designate "foreign terrorist organizations." 8 U.S.C. §1189. By order effective October 8, 1997, Secretary of State Madeline K. Albright so designated the People's Mojahedin Organization of Iran and the Liberation Tigers of Tamil Eelam. See Designation of Foreign Terrorist Organizations, 62 Fed. Reg. 52,650 (1997). Both groups have brought petitions for judicial review of their designations pursuant to 8 U.S.C. §1189(b)(1).

...The statute before us is unique, procedurally and substantively. On the basis of an "administrative record," the Secretary of State is to make "findings" that an entity is a foreign organization engaging in terrorist activities that threaten the national security of the United States....

[n6 Because the issue is not before us, we do not decide whether s 1189 deprives those in the United States of some constitutional right if they are members of, or wish to donate money to, an organization designated by the Secretary.]

...We also believe that the record, as the Secretary has compiled it, not surprisingly contains "substantial support" for her findings that the LTTE and the MEK engage in "terrorist activities" within the meaning of 8 U.S.C. s 1182(a)(3)(B). We have already recounted, above, enough of the record to show that the Secretary had before her information that each of the organizations engaged in bombing and killing in order to further their political agendas. Any one of the incidents attributed to the LTTE and to the MEK would have sufficed under the statute.

We therefore refuse to set aside either designation.

3.6   Fourth Amendment

The protection from unreasonable searches and seizures[224] requires in criminal surveillance (i.e., search and seizure) that "probable cause"[225] be found.

Searches in public health law have recognized a "special needs" exception for states: "special needs beyond the normal need for law enforcement" warrant that the probable cause requirement may not be applicable.[226] Compulsory screening requires limitations when persons must be "suspected" of having an infection or when persons must be "exposed" to bloodborn infections, before they may have samples taken.[227]

The critical zone doctrine has extended the ability of the government to take blood samples when the person is in the critical zone of the event. In establishing that doctrine, the court stated that "Society's judgment [is] that blood tests do not constitute an unduly extensive imposition on an individual's privacy and bodily integrity."[228]

The critical zone is another exception to the unreasonable search and seizure protection. When the subject is in a critical zone, for example on our international borders or in the airports as an airline passenger, the need for searches is much broader, and less protections are afforded to individuals.[229]

The critical zone doctrine might also be extended to the areas surrounding a smallpox case, for example. Critical zone analysis is not required for the surveillance of those who are "suspected" and those who have been "exposed." But in the CDC smallpox plan, which takes a concentric circle approach to the treatment of the contacts, in the outer circle there are contacts designated as "presumptive contacts,"[230] which include no known contact or exposure.

National security as a governmental interest, along with the risk of biological terrorism, will alter the balancing test against that of the private information interest.

In the case of emergency searches, the need for immediacy has been suggested as a basis for upholding a search without a warrant. These searches may be upheld when there are exigent circumstances and the common law doctrine of necessity.[231]

A recent concern has arisen that requires compulsory screening and surveillance of citizens who receive xenotransplantations. The risk of xenotransplantation is that viruses will be transmitted or changed when organs are transplanted from animals to humans. The need for surveillance and testing is imperative to avoid a public health risk of epidemics. The proposal for this protection would require compulsory screening and behavior modification, which should be monitored under a surveillance scheme with no "opt-out" provision. But because the risk is unquantifiable yet undeniable to the public health, insufficient basis for public health law to compel screening may exist as long as the patients are asymptomatic.[232]

The U.S. Supreme Court delivered their opinion in *Kyllo v. United States*[233] on June 11, 2001, overturning four Circuit Courts decisions to allow the new technology—thermal heat detection—to be used without a warrant. Justice Scalia, who delivered the opinion for the court, was seeking a rule for the case as well as for the rapid advances in technology. He wrote, "While the technology used in the present case was relatively crude, the rule we adopt must take account of more sophisticated systems that are already in use or in development."[234]

3.6.1. The law of "expectation of privacy" in searches

The law on the expectation of privacy begins with the Fourth Amendment, which reads, "the right of the people to be secure in their persons, houses, papers and effects against unreasonable searches and seizures."

In one of the first cases to address the warrantless gathering of information without a physical trespass, the court in *Olmstead v. United States* (1928) held that overheard conversations did not meet the criteria of trespass. Therefore, the court held, the existence of a search is dependent upon whether there is a physical trespass under local property law. For example, a microphone against the wall is not a search, whereas a microphone fed through the wall is a search because it is a physical trespass. The Supreme Court moved to a test based upon privacy interests, largely because of changes in technology.

In *Katz v. United States*, a listening device against a telephone booth was utilized to enable the FBI to detect illegally transmitted wagering information across state lines without a search warrant. Here, the technology detected vibrations in the glass of the phone booth, which set the standard for against the wall, rather than through the wall, tests. In that case, Justice Harlan articulated the "reasonable expectation of privacy" test and replaced the property concept of search to some degree with a two-prong test: (1) expectation of privacy; and (2) that the expectation of privacy be reasonable.

Then in *Dow Chemical*, the court held, about the changing technology, that "the effect of modern life, with its technological and other advances, serves to eliminate or reduce a person's justified expectation of privacy..." Using the *Katz* analysis: there *was* a subjective expectation of privacy; however, it was *not* reasonable because anyone could have taken those pictures. Also in *Dow*, the court determined that when an act is observable by the general public, it is unreasonable to expect privacy in that act.

Then in *California v. Greenwood* (1988), the court found no reasonable expectation of privacy when garbage bags left on the curb before pickup were readily accessible "to scavengers, snoops and other members of the public."

The continuing criticism of the *Katz* two-prong test has been that it is a circular argument: the Supreme Court protects only those expectations that are reasonable, while the only expectations that are reasonable are those that the Supreme Court is willing to protect.

Circuits holdings on thermal imaging devices

The Fifth,[235] Eighth,[236] Ninth,[237] and Eleventh[238] circuits have held that thermal image detection was not a "search" within the meaning of the Fourth Amendment. No Circuit Court has held a conflicting opinion with these Circuits, except for a short period when the Tenth Circuit in *United States v. Cusumano*, 67 F.3d 1497 (10th Cir. 1995) found thermal imaging a search, but the opinion was vacated. A rehearing en banc resulted in that issue not being decided.[239]

Some of the high technological surveillance tools

Is the Kyllo test workable with the next generation of surveillance tools?
1. Thermal heat detection
2. Gas chromatography and mass spectrometry are used to analyze samples taken from the bodies of drug smuggling suspects. A device that looks like a large flashlight is used in areas surrounding

his or her body. It is then inserted into a larger machine, which heats the samples and through high-speed gas chromatography separates the chemicals compounds contained there, including those found in cocaine, heroin, and other narcotics. "The senator" can detect traces of cocaine smaller than one billionth of a gram. HIV drug residue could also be detected, raising a suggestion of technology that is too intrusive to use without a search warrant.

3. Concealed weapons detectors such as "millivision," a new surveillance device that has been described as giving the police something akin to Superman's x-ray vision. These are not yet in the hands of law enforcement personnel. They will measure the electromagnetic radiation emitted by all objects, analyze it, and convert those readings into a visible form. Concealed weapons detectors are capable of revealing any item carried on the person, including those made of metal, liquid, ceramics, plastic, and powder, regardless of the number of layers of clothing, etc., and can be read through walls. This technology is far more precise than thermal heat detection.

3.6.2. The *Kyllo* test

The criteria used in *United States v. Ishmael*[240] for the use of technology without a warrant in an "open field" must meet certain criteria: it must be passive, it must be non-intrusive, it must include no "intimate details," and it must have no "intrusion on privacy."[241] It appears that the court was listening when, Lerner, the attorney for Kyllo, cautioned in oral argument, "The government's test is really going to lead down a difficult road for this court....when will information become...specific enough that it should be protected?"[242]

The U.S. Supreme Court in Kyllo did away with the "intimate details" test of *California v. Ciralo.*[243] In *Ciralo*, the court found that "modern technology" might become "invasive" if aerial searches showed the "intimate associations, objects or activities otherwise imperceptible to police or fellow citizens." The court in *Kyllo* simply said the focus on *Ciralo* should not have been on the intimate details criteria, but rather should have been on the "otherwise-imperceptibility."[244] Here, the court rejected a test that would require a rule for identification of objects of a certain size, or the development of a list of activities that would be considered "intimate."

Secondly, the court used as a factor whether the technology is "in general public use." The court held that "[w]here, as here, the Government uses a device that is not in general public use, to explore details of the home that would previously have been unknowable without physical intrusion, the surveillance is a 'search' and is presumptively unreasonable without a warrant."

The majority chose to focus on "sense-enhancing" technology in its search for a standard. The court said, "We have previously reserved judgment as to how much technological enhancement of ordinary perception from such a vantage point, if any is too much. While we upheld enhanced aerial photography of an industrial complex in *Dow Chemical*, we noted that we found it important that this is not an area immediately adjacent to a private home, where privacy expectations are mot heightened."[245] Rather than creating a standard simply for "sense-enhancing" technology, the court has inextricably connected the standard with whether the observation is near a private home, leaving intact the standard of *Dow Chemical*.

The rule, however, which does not find a search when a sniffing dog detects only the presence or absence of narcotics, appears to be broadened by the court's new rule. New technologies to replace the sniffing dog would be permitted and not limited to just the detection of illegal substances under the court's rule if the device is in the general public use.

The dissent's standard

The dissent was delivered by Justice Stevens and joined by Chief Justice Rehnquist, Justice O'Connor and Justice Kennedy. The standard, the dissent wrote, should not be changed.

The dissent relied on the standard that considers whether the technology is the "functional equivalent of actual presence in the area being searched." In addition, the dissent suggested that another factor should be whether the homeowner would even care if anybody noticed.

Much of the dissent's criticism of the majority was the focus on the "yet-to-be-developed technology that might allow 'through-the-wall surveillance.'"[246]

The workability of the *Kyllo* standard

If using the standard that the technology must be in the general use of the public, then instead of a dictionary, the court will be referring to the commercial "spy" catalogs to determine which technology might fit the definition of in the "general public use." If the technology is in the general public use, such as the monitors that were being commercially sold through technology chain stores to monitor cellular telephone conversations, but they are subsequently made illegal—as they were—does that meet the Kyllo test for in the "general public use"? Or will the test become not one of the availability of technology, but in the "general public use" if Congress *permits* it to be in the public use?

As the dissent aptly pointed out, "the contours of its new rule are uncertain because its protection apparently dissipates as soon as the relevant technology is 'in general public use.' Yet how much use is general public use is not even hinted at by the Court's opinion, which makes the somewhat doubtful assumption that the thermal imager used in this case does not satisfy that criterion."[247] The record describes the device as "readily available to the public" for commercial, personal, or law enforcement purposes, and is just an 800-number away from being rented from "half a dozen national companies by anyone who wants one."[248]

Kyllo was decided in the summer prior to the 9-11 attacks on the United States, and was intended to be protective of privacy; however, if the standard is measured by the availability to the public, it is assured that the expectation will be rapidly changing as technology races forward. Had Kyllo been heard after 9-11, the decision probably would have been less protective of privacy.

3.7.   Fourth Amendment Search and Seizure
3.7.1.   Domestic Application

The Fourth Amendment provides that "the right of the people to be secure in their persons, houses, papers, and effects, against unreasonable searches and seizures, shall not be violated, and no Warrants shall issue, but upon probable cause, supported by Oath or affirmation, and particularly describing the place to be searched, and the persons or things to be seized." U.S. CONST. amend. IV.

The following cases raise search and seizure issues in the context of bioterrorism and are cases that are applicable to bioterrorism activities.

United States v. Gill
280 F.3d 923 (9th Cir., 2002)

Investigators may inspect mail as they wish without any Fourth Amendment curtailment, so long as the inspection does not amount to a "search," and so long as it is conducted quickly enough so that it does not become a seizure by significantly delaying the date of delivery.[249] Inspectors without more may choose a particular package to detain in order to examine the addressee or return address and investigate further, as Officer Jaworowski did here. See United States v. Choate, 576 F.2d 165 (9th Cir. 1978) (holding that looking at information contained on the outside of mail does not implicate the Fourth Amendment).

Postal authorities may also use scientific methods, such as x-rays, irradiation, or other processes, to detect or eradicate materials in the mail that may pose a grave risk to society.[250] Authorities could, for example, irradiate all the mail in a particular facility, because this will not delay delivery beyond any other piece of mail sent from that location, and because irradiation may be the only means by which to achieve certain objectives. See Camara v. Municipal Court, 387 U.S. 523, 537, 18 L. Ed. 2d 930, 87 S. Ct. 1727 (1967) (upholding building inspections because "it is doubtful that any other canvassing technique would achieve acceptable results").

Only if the delivery date becomes delayed should reasonable suspicion be required to continue the detainment or inspection. Here, Officer Jaworowski had reasonable suspicion initially to detain the package. But he did not at all need it for the minimal intrusion that occurred. He kept the package in his office and investigated the addresses, phone numbers, and names on the outside of the package. He mailed the package that same day to Inspector Erdahl in Seattle, the package's destination area. The post office was able to deliver the package the next day. Only if the package was likely to miss its anticipated Friday delivery date by a significant degree would Jaworowski and Erdahl need to show "a reasonable and articulable suspicion of criminal activity."

United States v. Larry Wayne Harris
961 F. Supp. 1127 (S.D. Ohio, 1997)
Opinion by: Joseph P. Kinneary, UNITED STATES DISTRICT JUDGE

This matter is before the Court on the Defendant Larry Wayne Harris's ("Harris") motion to suppress statements, motion to suppress evidence, and motion to dismiss the indictment. The Court held hearings on these motions on April 1, 1997 and April 9, 1997. The Court DENIES Harris's motions.

I. Findings of Fact

Harris is charged in an indictment with wire fraud and mail fraud. The indictment alleges that Harris used fraudulent misrepresentations to mail order three vials of yersinia pestis, the bacteria that causes bubonic plague, from a Maryland company known as American Type Culture Collection ("ATCC").

The Court begins with the government's version of the facts. At approximately 4:15 p.m. on May 11, 1995, Forrest Smith of the Ohio Department of Health called Edward Sachs of the Lancaster Health Department, and informed Sachs that Harris, a resident of Lancaster, Ohio, had ordered and received vials of yersinia pestis. Smith added that Harris was not qualified to possess the bacteria. Around 5:20 p.m., Sachs contacted Captain Lutz of the Lancaster police department and together they investigated these allegations by confirming some of the details and by calling various health officials at both the state and federal level. Later that evening, Captain Lutz obtained a warrant from a state court to search Harris's residence at 266 Cleveland Avenue, Lancaster, Ohio.

At approximately 1:40 a.m., May 12, 1995, the Lancaster police arrived at Harris's residence to execute the search warrant. The search team included public health officials, members of the Fairfield County hazardous materials team, and a hazardous materials truck full of equipment and gear. Some of the officers and members of the hazardous materials team were dressed in hazardous material suits.

Captain Lutz and Lieutenant Regan approached the house in their regular uniforms. Lutz went to the door and lured Harris out of his residence by telling him his car had been involved in a hit-skip accident. After Harris stepped out of his residence, Captain Lutz walked him over to Harris's car where Regan was standing; Lutz and Regan then handcuffed Harris over the hood of his car. While they were handcuffing Harris, Harris spontaneously told them "if this is about the pestis, it's in the car." Regan asked Harris's permission to search the car, which Harris granted; Harris told the officers that his keys were in his pocket. Lutz and Bill Bropst of the Fairfield County hazardous materials team searched the car while Regan read Harris his rights. Harris was very talkative during this period, and told various officers and health agents that the pestis was safe to handle. Regan had to ask Harris to quit talking so that Regan could finish reading his rights. After the vials were found in the car, Harris was placed in the back of a police vehicle and eventually transported to the Lancaster police station where he was held for questioning. Lutz and Regan returned to the police station separately and interrogated Harris.

The police interrogated Harris at the Lancaster police station at around 2:40 a.m. The officers taped the interrogation with Harris's knowledge. Harris did not tell the officers that he wanted an attorney either before or during this interrogation. After the interrogation, Harris was returned to his residence.

Later on May 12, the Lancaster police contacted the Federal Bureau of Investigation ("FBI") and Special Agent Roger Wilson was assigned to the case. When Wilson arrived at the police station, the police briefed him on the case. Sometime that morning, the Chief of Police told Wilson that, during a phone conversation with Harris about Harris's impounded car, Harris asked the Chief whether the Chief thought that Harris needed an attorney. The Chief responded "that's up to you." Harris was at his residence at the time of the phone call.

While Wilson contacted his superiors, the police used information gathered during the first search and interrogation to obtain an arrest warrant for Harris and a warrant to search his house again. That afternoon, Lieutenant Michael Rosser went to Harris's residence to serve the arrest warrant on Harris. Rosser asked Harris to step outside, Rosser read Harris the warrant and then placed Harris under arrest. Rosser read Harris his Miranda rights at this time. Harris did not say anything about an attorney to Officer Rosser. Patrolman Gardner then cuffed Harris and transported him to the Lancaster Police Department. Harris did not say anything at all on the ride to the station.

Special Agent Wilson interrogated Harris at the police station. Wilson testified that when he introduced himself to Harris, Harris "immediately indicated to me that he wanted to tell me his side of the story regarding having the bubonic plague." Wilson then handed Harris a waiver form and read from a copy of the form as Harris followed along. Wilson proceeded with the interrogation after Harris signed the waiver form. Harris did not ask Wilson for an attorney nor did he mention to Wilson that he had called an attorney.

For the most part, Harris does not dispute the facts as stated above. However, he takes several crucial exceptions. First, Harris contends that no one read him his Miranda rights until the arrest warrant was executed. Second, Harris claims that he never consented to the search of his car or informed the officers that his keys were in his pocket. Third, Harris claims that in addition to telling the police chief over the phone that he had contacted an attorney, he also told the arresting officer and Special Agent Wilson that he had contacted his attorney.

Resolving these factual disputes is crucial to the decision of whether to grant or deny Harris's motions. Given the conflicting testimony, the resolution of these factual disputes depends upon whom the Court finds more credible. After observing the demeanor of the government witnesses and of Harris, the Court finds the government witnesses more credible than Harris. The Court doubts Harris's trustworthiness for three reasons.

First, Harris's testimony at the April 1 hearing is inconsistent with his statements at the first interrogation at the police station. When asked at the hearing whether he had a laboratory in his home, Harris testified:

> I most certainly do, most definitely do....I have, by all practical purposes, a very fine laboratory, very well equipped laboratory, even backup microscopes, backup equipment, and do extensive research.

Despite Harris's emphatic certainty, this testimony is directly contradicted by a number of Harris's earlier statements. ("I've been wanting to accumulate enough laboratory equipment so that I can build my own laboratory"); ("Once I got my lab together."); ("Once I get the laboratory going I can go ahead"); ("I do not have, in my possession, the necessary equipment at this time to carry out the experiment."); ("once I got my lab going").) Similarly, Harris testified that he "most definitely did not consent to the search of the vehicle." Yet, Harris admitted during the initial interrogation that he volunteered the information about the location of the pestis and of his car keys to the officers. Harris explained the inconsistency by saying that he was half asleep at the time he volunteered the information. This explanation, however, does not dispel the inconsistency.

Second, Harris spoke with certainty throughout his testimony when referring to events that were favorable to him. ("[Lutz] most definitely did not advise me of my rights"); ("most definitely" tried to call attorney"); ("most definitely" advised officers of call to attorney); Yet, when asked about events that were less favorable to him, Harris seemed uncertain and somewhat incoherent. ("I did not see [the waiver of attorney clause]"; "I did not understand it"; "I did not understand the fullest context of it.")

Third, the collective testimony of the government witnesses tells a consistent, coherent story of the events that occurred that night. Harris, on the other hand, provided little or no evidence to corroborate his testimony and his testimony was incoherent at times.

In sum, based on the above three reasons and on the Court's observation of Harris's demeanor at the hearing, the Court finds that Harris's version of the facts is unreliable. The Court therefore adopts, for the purpose of resolving Harris's motions, the facts as stated in the testimony of the government witnesses.

II. Analysis
A. The First Warrant

Harris raises numerous challenges to the state court's finding of probable cause to support the first warrant. The government argues that there was probable cause for the first warrant. The Court agrees with the government.

"The test for probable cause is simply whether 'there is a fair probability that contraband or evidence of a crime will be found in a particular place.'" United States v. Padro, 52 F.3d 120, 123 (6th Cir. 1995) (quoting Illinois v. Gates, 462 U.S. 213, 238, 76 L. Ed. 2d 527, 103 S. Ct. 2317 (1983)). Thus, the issuing judge must "make a practical, common sense decision whether, given all the circumstances set forth in the affidavit before him, including the 'veracity' and 'basis of knowledge' of persons supplying hearsay information," probable cause exists. A reviewing court, in turn, must give great deference to the decision of the issuing judge. The role of the reviewing court is limited to ensuring that the issuing judge had a "'substantial basis for...concluding' that a search would uncover evidence of wrongdoing." (quoting Jones v. United States, 362 U.S. 257, 271, 4 L. Ed. 2d 697, 80 S. Ct. 725 (1960)).

The affidavit supporting the first warrant was prepared by Captain Lutz and Ed Sachs. In the affidavit, Captain Lutz traces the official lines of communication from ATCC, who sent the bacteria to Harris and then became suspicious of his credentials, through the Center for Disease Control ("CDC") and the Ohio Department of Health, to Ed Sachs at the Lancaster Department of Health. Lutz states that a call by the CDC to Harris corroborated ATCC's initial concern; Harris told a CDC official that he was conducting research with the bacteria to counteract an "imminent invasion from Iraq of super-germ-carrying rats." Lutz confirmed with the delivery company the exact time and date of the delivery of the bacteria to Harris's residence. Lutz also confirmed the allegations that Harris may have misrepresented to ATCC both that he had an Environmental Protection Agency certification number and that he had a small animals laboratory. Captain Lutz concluded that "Larry Wayne Harris probably used deception" to obtain the bacteria. The Court finds that this affidavit provided a substantial basis for the issuing judge's finding of probable cause to support the first search warrant.

Probable cause for a search warrant does not require certainty that a crime has been committed or that the evidence will be present in the residence to be searched. On the date of the warrant, Captain Lutz had information that Harris had ordered the bacteria and had misrepresented himself to ATCC, and that the bacteria had been delivered to his residence earlier that day. The issuing Court therefore had a sufficient basis on which to conclude that an offense had been committed and that the bacteria was probably in Harris's residence. Contrary to Harris's assertions, the use of the term "probably" in the affidavit, and the presence of hearsay in the affidavit, do not undermine the issuing judge's finding of probable cause for the warrant. ("Finding probable cause based upon an affidavit that included the statements that incriminating evidence "could be" and "may be" present in a suspect's residence); (a substantial basis for crediting hearsay evidence exists where a government officer is the declarant of the hearsay.)

Harris also asserts that the warrant was overbroad and did not adequately describe the property to be searched for and seized. The Fourth Amendment requires a warrant "to particularly describe the place to be searched, and the persons or things to be seized." U.S. Const. amend. IV. The warrant must enable a searcher to reasonably ascertain and identify the things which are authorized to be seized. This requirement eliminates the danger of unlimited discretion in the executing officer's determination of what is subject to seizure. The search warrant in this case satisfies this standard. The search warrant provides in part as follows:

> As Judge of the Above Court of record, I command you [Captain Lutz]...to search...the person and/or place of: The residence of Larry Wayne Harris, 266 Cleveland Avenue, Lancaster, Ohio. Property which is the subject to search and seizure, to wit: Three vials of yersinia pestis (Bubonic Plague Virus [sic]), any and all records concerning the purchase and use of hazardous cultures.

The Court concludes that this description reasonably identifies the three vials of yersinia pestis and the files authorized to be seized and properly limits the discretion of the executing agent. Therefore, the first warrant was validly issued by the state court.

B. The First Search
1. Harris's challenges to all of the evidence seized.

Harris moves to suppress all of the evidence seized during the first search on the ground that the execution of the warrant was illegal because (1) the officers failed to knock and announce their identity and purpose; (2) the officers used a ruse to get Harris to leave his house; and (3) the officers illegally detained Harris. The government denies that the police acted illegally when they executed the search warrant.

First, the "knock and announce" rule to which Harris refers is inapplicable here because the officers did not make a forced entry into Harris's home. United States v. Gatewood, 60 F.3d 248, 250 (6th Cir. 1995)(holding that neither the Fourth Amendment nor the knock and announce statute, 18 U.S.C. §3109, are implicated where there is no evidence of forcible entry).

Second, the officers' use of a ruse—telling Harris his car was in a hit-skip accident to lure him outside his residence—was valid in light of the circumstances. Courts have upheld the use of ruses when police officers have deceived suspects so that the officers may gain consent to enter the suspect's home and conduct a warrantless search. Lewis v. United States, 385 U.S. 206, 17 L. Ed. 2d 312, 87 S. Ct. 424 (1967) (agent posed as customer to enter drug dealer's home without a warrant); United States v. Baldwin, 621 F.2d 251 (6th Cir. 1980)(agent posed as chauffeur for six months to observe cocaine distribution); United States v. Stevens, 635 F. Supp. 1356 (W.D. Mich. 1986). In addition, the First Circuit has upheld the use of a ruse by government agents to get suspects to leave a motel room so that the agents could, without a warrant, arrest them and search their room. The ruse in this case was far less intrusive than the ruses in the above mentioned cases. Unlike the law enforcement personnel in those cases, the police officers in this case had a properly issued warrant to search the premises, they did not use the ruse to gain entrance into Harris's home, and the ruse did not last more than a few moments. Therefore, the Court holds that the police officer's use of a ruse to lure Harris from his home was not invalid.

Finally, the Court holds that the officer's detention of Harris while they conducted their search was also valid. When police obtain a warrant to search a residence they also obtain the right to detain persons on the premises and take other such reasonable action that is necessary to protect themselves during the execution of the search. In this case, the use of the ruse and subsequent detention of Harris were reasonable actions necessary for the protection of the officers. When the officers approached Harris's residence, they did not know Harris's motivations or the specific dangers that they would face; this was a new situation for them and it involved a potentially deadly pathogen. Therefore, both the ruse and detention were justified.

2. Statements made during the search.

Harris moves to suppress all of his statements made during the search on the ground that any statements he made were the result of police interrogation, while he was in custody, and before he had been read his Miranda rights. See Miranda v. Arizona, 384 U.S. 436, 16 L. Ed. 2d 694, 86 S. Ct. 1602 (1966). Harris also moves to suppress any evidence found by the officers in reliance on those statements. The government argues that the police did not interrogate Harris before they read him his Miranda rights, or in the alternative, that the "public safety" exception to Miranda applies.

The Supreme Court has found that, in certain circumstances, concern for public safety justifies an officer's failure to provide Miranda warnings before asking questions devoted to locating a dangerous instrumentality. New York v. Quarles, 467 U.S. 649, 657, 81 L. Ed. 2d 550, 104 S. Ct. 2626 (1984). The Quarles Court held that the Fifth Amendment, as interpreted in Miranda, does not require the exclusion of a defendant's voluntary statements about the location of his gun, or the gun itself, when an officer asked the defendant where the gun was located while the defendant was in custody and before the officer read the defendant his rights. The Court stated that in a "kaleidoscopic situation...in which spontaneity rather than adherence to a police manual is necessarily the order of the day," the officers need not read a suspect his Miranda rights prior to asking questions reasonably prompted by a concern for public safety. The Court finds that the public safety exception to Miranda applies here. This investigation presented circumstances in which spontaneity rather than adherence to a police manual was the order of the day. Captain Lutz testified that no one in Lancaster had participated in a search for a deadly bacteria and, without assistance from someone who had, the officers had to "fly by the seat of our pants." The evidence shows that the officers were motivated by a concern for public safety when they questioned Harris prior to reading his rights; indeed, concern for public safety motivated this whole investigation as indicated by the presence of the hazardous materials team and the precautions taken by the officers. As in Quarles, the officers asked Harris only the questions needed to locate the dangerous instrumentality; Regan then read Harris his rights. In hindsight, it is possible to say that the immediate risk to the public posed by the freeze-dried bacteria was not as significant as the officers thought at the time. At the time the officers were faced by these circumstances, however, it was reasonable for them to anticipate danger from this bacteria and to have serious concern for the safety of the community and for their own safety. Therefore, the Court holds that the public safety exception to the Miranda rule applies here. As a result, any statements made by Harris before Lieutenant Regan read him his rights, and any evidence recovered in reliance on those statements, is admissible for purposes of trial.

3. The search of the car.

Harris argues that anything found in his car should be suppressed because the search of the car was outside the scope of the search warrant and no exception to the rule precluding warrantless searches applies in this case. The Government argues that the officers were entitled to search the car for two reasons: first, Harris consented to the search; and second, they had probable cause to believe the vials were in the car.

The Court holds that evidence found in the car is admissible because the search of the car was valid on a number of alternative theories. First, the Court holds that the warrant authorized the search. A warrant to search a residence at a particular address confers authority to search a vehicle parked in the driveway if the officers executing the warrant reasonably believe that the objects of the search might be located in the vehicle. United States v. Gottschalk, 915 F.2d 1459, 1461 (10th Cir. 1990)(search of car in driveway); United States v. Asselin, 775 F.2d 445 (1st Cir. 1985)(search of car next to carport); United States v. Napoli, 530 F.2d 1198 (5th Cir. 1976) (search of camper in driveway). The warrant in this case describes the premises to be searched as a residence at a particular address. Harris's car was parked in his driveway in front of a car port. Given the size of the vials, the officers could reasonably believe that the vials might be in the car. Moreover based on Harris's statement that the pestis was in the car, the officers had reason to believe that the vials were in the car. Therefore, the officers were authorized by the warrant to search the car. The officers were authorized to open the locked glove box because vials are small enough to fit in that compartment.

Second, the officers were justified in searching the car because Harris's statement that the pestis is in the car provided the officers with probable cause to search the car.

Finally, the Court finds that the police were justified in searching the car because Harris consented to the search of his car. See Schneckloth v. Bustamonte, 412 U.S. 218, 227, 36 L. Ed. 2d 854, 93 S. Ct. 2041 (1973). Harris voluntarily told the officers that the pestis was in the car and that his car keys were in his pocket. Harris claims that he took sleeping pills and was asleep when the officers arrived; however, in his interrogation answers, Harris provided details and descriptions of his motivations and research that are inconsistent with a drug impaired or sleep deprived mind. Therefore, the Court finds that the consent was knowing and intelligent. The officers were justified in searching Harris's car based on Harris's consent to search.

C. The First Interrogation

Harris moves to suppress any statement he made during the first interrogation because he claims he was not advised of his Miranda rights and did not waive those rights prior to the interrogation. The government claims that Harris was advised of his rights and voluntarily waived his rights before making any statements to law enforcement officers.

This Court has already found that Lieutenant Regan read Harris his Miranda rights after Regan handcuffed him and while Lutz was searching the car. Moreover, the Court has found that any statement Harris made to the officers at his residence was not coerced or involuntary. The only remaining issue, therefore, is whether Harris voluntarily waived his rights prior to the interrogation.

Harris's answers to the officer's interrogation at the police station were the result of a voluntary and intelligent waiver of his rights. Harris was very talkative and very willing to discuss his case to the officers during the interrogation. Harris provided long rambling answers in which he describes in extensive detail his research and motivations. Also, Harris admitted in the interrogation that the officers treated him decently and fairly and that the police made no threat against him. Given Harris's age, education and the detail and description provided in his answers during the interrogation, the Court concludes that Harris voluntarily and intelligently waived his rights prior to the first interrogation.

D. The Second Warrant

Harris challenges the validity of the second warrant on the grounds that it was supported by information obtained during the execution of the first warrant and that the first warrant was invalid. This argument fails because the Court has already held that the first warrant was valid.

E. The Second Interrogation

Harris moves to suppress any statement he made during the second interrogation because he claims he invoked his right to an attorney and the officers interrogated him without his attorney present anyway. Moreover, Harris asserts that the second interrogation was the product of the first interrogation which was itself illegal. This latter argument fails because the Court has already found that the first interrogation was valid.

With respect to the former argument, the only issue is whether Harris's statement to the Chief of the Lancaster Police, "do you think I need an attorney," was sufficient to invoke Harris's right to an attorney under the rule of Edwards v. Arizona, 451 U.S. 477, 68 L. Ed. 2d 378, 101 S. Ct. 1880 (1981). Edwards states that when an accused has invoked his right to have counsel present during custodial interrogation, no further interrogation is permitted until either his right is satisfied or the accused himself initiates further interrogation. The Edwards rule applies, however, only if the accused invokes his right to an attorney while in custody. ("Edwards held that once a person in custody has expressed his desire to deal with the police only through counsel, the police violate his or her rights if they initiate further questioning"). The Edwards rule does not apply here because Harris was at his home and not in custody, when he asked the police chief: "do you think I need an attorney?"

The government, nevertheless, still bears the burden of showing that Harris waived his right to counsel, along with his other Miranda rights, prior to the second interrogation. The government introduced a waiver of rights form signed by Harris. The government also introduced the testimony of Special Agent Wilson who stated that he read this form to Harris and that Harris was very willing to tell his side of the story. This evidence satisfies the government's burden to show that Harris voluntarily and intelligently waived his rights.

F. The Arrest

Harris claims that the criminal complaint was filed without probable cause and that, therefore, his arrest was unlawful. In particular, Harris asserts that the complaint charges him with receiving stolen property and that there is no evidence that the vials were obtained through the commission of a theft offense. The Court disagrees. Probable cause to arrest is sufficient if there are facts and circumstances within the issuing judge's knowledge that are sufficient to allow a reasonably prudent person to believe that a suspect has committed an offense. This standard is satisfied here. The Lutz affidavit and the results of the search provided the issuing judge with evidence that Harris used deception to receive the vials from ATCC. The theft element of the crime of receiving stolen property is satisfied by theft by deception. Therefore, the criminal complaint and the warrant to arrest Harris for receiving stolen property were supported by probable cause.

III. Conclusion

Upon consideration and being duly advised, the Court DENIES Harris's motion to suppress statements, DENIES Harris's motion to suppress evidence, and DENIES Harris's motion to dismiss the indictment.

IT IS SO ORDERED.

3.7.2. Foreign Application of Fourth Amendment Protections

United States v. Usama Bin Laden
126 F. Supp.2d 264 (SDNY, 2000)

Sand, District Judge.

The Defendants are charged with numerous offenses arising out of their alleged participation in an international terrorist organization led by Defendant Usama Bin Laden and that organization's alleged involvement in the August 1998 bombings of the United States Embassies in Nairobi, Kenya and Dar es Salaam, Tanzania. Presently before the Court are Defendant El-Hage's motions which seek the following: suppression of evidence seized from the search of his residence in Nairobi, Kenya in August 1997 and suppression of evidence obtained from electronic surveillance, conducted from August 1996 to August 1997, of four telephone lines in Nairobi, Kenya.

BACKGROUND

The charges currently pending against each of the Defendants in this case arise from their alleged involvement with an international terrorist organization known as "al Qaeda" or "the Base." Since its emergence in 1989, al Qaeda is alleged to have planned and financed (both independently and in association with other terrorist groups) numerous violent attacks against United States personnel and property abroad. The United States Attorney's Office in the Southern District of New York has been investigating al Qaeda since at least 1996. In the spring of 1996, Bin Laden, the founder and leader of al Qaeda was identified by the United States Government as "a serious threat to national security".

Among other things, the Government alleges that al Qaeda coordinates the activities of its global membership, sends its members to camps for military and intelligence training, obtains and transports weapons and explosives, and explicitly provides Muslims with religious authority for acts of terrorism against American citizens. In August 1996, Bin Laden "effectively declared a war of terrorism against all members of the United States military worldwide." In February of 1998, this declaration was expanded to include attacks on American civilians. Al Qaeda, which has at different points in its history been headquartered in Afghanistan, Pakistan and the Sudan, has maintained an international presence through "cells" (and al Qaeda personnel) located in a number of countries including Kenya, Tanzania, the United Kingdom, Canada and the United States.

By the late spring of 1996, the United States intelligence community ("Intelligence Community") became aware that persons associated with Bin Laden's organization had established an al Qaeda presence in Kenya. In addition, the Intelligence Community had isolated and identified five telephone numbers which were being used by persons associated with al Qaeda. All five of these phone lines were monitored by the Intelligence Community from August 1996 through August 1997. One of these phone lines was located in an office in the same building where the Defendant, El-Hage, and his family resided. (El-Hage, an American citizen, and his family lived in Nairobi from 1994 to 1997. Another of the phone lines, was a cellular phone used by El-Hage and others.

ANALYSIS

The Defendant seeks suppression of the evidence which was seized during the warrantless search of his home in Kenya and the fruits thereof. In addition, he seeks the suppression of evidence derived from electronic surveillance of several telephone lines over which his conversations were recorded, including the telephone for his Nairobi residence and his cellular phone. The Defendant also asks that the Court hold a hearing with respect to the validity of the surveillance and the search.

El-Hage bases his challenge to the evidence on the Fourth Amendment and asserts that the search and the electronic surveillance were unlawful because they were not conducted pursuant to a valid warrant. If the Court accepts the Government's argument that no warrant was required, El-Hage argues, in the alternative, that the searches were unreasonable. In its response to the Defendant's motion, the Government asserts that the searches were primarily conducted for the purpose of foreign intelligence collection and are, therefore, not subject to the Warrant Clause of the Fourth Amendment. As a result, it is the Government's position that the aforementioned evidence should not be suppressed. In addition, the Government claims that no hearing is necessary.

I. Application of the Fourth Amendment Overseas

Before proceeding to that Fourth Amendment analysis, it is necessary to ascertain whether the Amendment applies in this situation. El-Hage is an American citizen and the searches at issue were conducted in Kenya. The Defendant argues that the protection of the Fourth Amendment "does not dissolve once a United States citizen leaves the borders of the United States." The Government seems to concede the general applicability of the Fourth Amendment to American citizens abroad, but asserts that the particular searches contested in this case (which were conducted overseas to collect foreign intelligence) call for a more limited application of the Amendment.

The Supreme Court cases on point suggest that the Fourth Amendment applies to United States citizens abroad....Thus, this Court finds that even though the searches at issue in this case occurred in Kenya, El-Hage can bring a Fourth Amendment challenge. However, the extent of the Fourth Amendment protection, in particular the applicability of the Warrant Clause, is unclear

II. An Exception to the Warrant Requirement for Foreign Intelligence Searches

The Government urges that the searches at issue in this case fall within an established exception to the warrant requirement. According to the Government, searches conducted for the purpose of foreign intelligence collection which target persons who are agents of a foreign power do not require a warrant. The Defendant asserts that such an exception does not exist and should not be recognized by this Court.

The Supreme Court has acknowledged but has not resolved this issue.

The question, for this Court, is twofold. First, it is necessary to evaluate whether there is an exception to the warrant requirement for searches conducted abroad for purposes of foreign intelligence collection. Second, if such an exception exists, the Court must evaluate whether the searches conducted in this case properly fall within the parameters of that exception.

A. The Constitutional and Practical Bases for the Exception

Because the Second Circuit has not confirmed the existence of a foreign intelligence exception to the warrant requirement and because no other court has considered the applicability of such an exception overseas, the factors which call for the adoption of the exception are reviewed here.

1. The President's Power Over Foreign Affairs

In all of the cases finding an exception to the warrant requirement for foreign intelligence collection, a determinative basis for the decision was the constitutional grant to the Executive Branch of power over foreign affairs. On numerous occasions, the Supreme Court has addressed the constitutional competence of the President in the field of foreign affairs.

Warrantless foreign intelligence collection has been an established practice of the Executive Branch for decades.

2. The Costs of Imposing a Warrant Requirement

It is generally the case that imposition of a warrant requirement better safeguards the Fourth Amendment rights of citizens in the Defendant's position. But several cases direct that when the imposition of a warrant requirement proves to be a disproportionate and perhaps even disabling burden on the Executive, a warrant should not be required.

3. The Absence of a Warrant Procedure

The final consideration which persuades the Court of the need for an exception to the warrant requirement for foreign intelligence collection conducted overseas is that there is presently no statutory basis for the issuance of a warrant to conduct searches abroad. In addition, existing warrant procedures and standards are simply not suitable for foreign intelligence searches. The Defendant, nevertheless, argues strenuously that "if the government insists on exercising jurisdiction over conduct occurring extra-territorially, it must also abide by constitutional limitations on its own conduct in pursuing criminality in those same foreign locales."

Several factors counsel against overseas application of the warrant requirement including: "the absence of local judges or magistrates available to issue warrants, the differing and perhaps unascertainable conceptions of reasonableness and privacy that prevail abroad, and the need to cooperate with foreign officials"); Verdugo, 494 U.S. at 279 (Stevens, J., concurring) (concluding that the Warrant Clause does not apply to overseas searches of noncitizen's homes because of the powerlessness of American magistrates to authorize such searches).

B. Adoption of the Foreign Intelligence Exception to the Warrant Requirement

In light of the concerns outlined here, the Court finds that the power of the Executive to conduct foreign intelligence collection would be significantly frustrated by the imposition of a warrant requirement in this context. Therefore, this Court adopts the foreign intelligence exception to the warrant requirement for searches targeting foreign powers (or their agents) which are conducted abroad. As has been outlined, no court, prior to FISA, that was faced with the choice, imposed a warrant requirement for foreign intelligence searches undertaken within the United States. With those precedents as guidance, it certainly does not appear to be unreasonable for this Court to refuse to apply a warrant requirement for foreign intelligence searches conducted abroad.

At the same time, the Court is mindful of the importance of the Fourth Amendment interests at stake. In keeping with the precedents reviewed above, the warrant exception adopted by this Court is narrowly drawn to include only those overseas searches, authorized by the President (or his delegate, the Attorney General), which are conducted primarily for foreign intelligence purposes and which target foreign powers or their agents. The protection of individual rights in this context is not a significant departure from that which is envisioned by the Fourth Amendment. All warrantless searches are still governed by the reasonableness requirement and can be challenged in ex post criminal or civil proceedings.

C. Application of the Exception

Before the Court can find that the exception applies to this case, it is necessary to show, first, that Mr. El-Hage was an agent of a foreign power; second, that the searches in question were conducted "primarily" for foreign intelligence purposes; and finally, that the searches were authorized by the President or the Attorney General.

1. Agent of a Foreign Power

It is clear from the Court's review of the evidence contained in the classified DCI declaration and in the materials considered by the Attorney General in issuing authorization for the post-April 4, 1997 surveillance and the August 21, 1997 search of El-Hage's residence that there was probable cause to suspect that El-Hage was an agent of a foreign power. The Court is also persuaded that al Qaeda was properly considered a foreign power. In reaching this conclusion, the Court relies on the definitions of "foreign power" and "agent of a foreign power" which were incorporated by Congress into FISA.

2. Primarily for Foreign Intelligence Purposes

This exception to the warrant requirement applies until and unless the primary purpose of the searches stops being foreign intelligence collection. If foreign intelligence collection is merely a purpose and not the primary purpose of a search, the exception does not apply. See id. Similarly, if a reviewing judge finds that the Government officials were "looking for evidence of criminal conduct unrelated to the foreign affairs needs of a President, then he would undoubtedly hold the surveillances to be illegal and take appropriate measures."

The Government's submissions establish persuasively that the purpose, throughout the entire electronic surveillance of El-Hage and during the physical search of his Nairobi residence, was primarily the collection of foreign intelligence information about the activities of Usama Bin Laden and al Qaeda. There was no FBI participation in the electronic surveillance that took place. Although there was an FBI agent present during the search of El-Hage's residence, the Court does not find that foreign intelligence collection ceased to be the primary purpose of that search. The Court's determination about the purpose of the residential search is, in part, dependent upon the Government's classified submissions. For that reason, further analysis of this question is included in Classified Appendix A. The Court hereby directs the Government to institute proceedings to declassify Appendix A.

The Court acknowledges that the combination of Verdugo and the incidental interception cases outlined above would permit the surveillance if the Government had not been aware of El-Hage's identity or of his complicity in the enterprise. Extension of the doctrine to a case such as this, however, where El-Hage was suspected of involvement with al Qaeda and was a known and contemplated interceptee of electronic surveillance of his home and cellular phones (even if he was not officially deemed a target), is significantly more problematic.

Recognizing this, the Government urges the Court to adopt a broader definition of "incidental." To that end, the Government relies on several cases for the proposition that incidental does not necessarily mean unanticipated. But these cases address the collection of evidence of crimes which were "incidental" to those specified in the wiretap order and do not apply that definition of incidental to new persons exposed by the surveillance. To expand the definition of an "incidental" interceptee past what has been adopted by previous decisions is not appropriate in this case. It is the Court's view that, given the Government's suspicions about El-Hage's connection to al Qaeda, to say that al Qaeda was the target is merely to say that El-Hage was one of many targets of the surveillance.

Ultimately, the Court holds that with respect to the electronic surveillance of the home and cellular phones, El-Hage was not intercepted "incidentally" because he was not an unanticipated user of those telephones and because he was believed to be a participant in the activities being investigated. The Court finds that El-Hage had a reasonable expectation of privacy in his home and cellular phones[251] and the Government should have obtained approval from either the President or the Attorney General before undertaking the electronic surveillance on those phone lines in August 1996.

III. The Exclusionary Rule

Despite the fact that this electronic surveillance was unlawful, the Court finds that exclusion of this evidence would be inappropriate because it would not have the deterrent effect which the exclusionary rule requires and because the surveillance was undertaken in good faith. Many of the facts upon which the Court's conclusions are based involve presently classified material. This section outlines the legal precedents and the general conclusions which form the basis of the Court's decision.

B. Good Faith

One offshoot of the deterrence analysis has been the development of an exception to the exclusionary rule that is derived from the "good faith" of the officials involved in a particular search.

IV. The Reasonableness Requirement

Even if the Government was not required to secure a warrant in advance of the searches, the Fourth Amendment still requires that the searches be reasonable. El-Hage argues that the search of his home was unreasonable because of the "paramount Fourth Amendment interests in the sanctity of the home." In addition, he asserts that the electronic surveillance was unreasonable because it was conducted "continuously and without interruption" for a full year. These allegations are considered in turn.

A. The Physical Search of the Residence

Although the Defendant suggests that courts only permit warrantless residential searches in cases of exigency, several cases have permitted home entries, without warrants, where a special need of the government is shown. For these reasons, the Court finds that the foreign intelligence exception to the warrant requirement applies with equal force to residential searches. El-Hage's argument that the search of his residence was per se unreasonable is therefore rejected.

In addition, the limited scope and overall nature of the search indicate that the search was executed in a reasonable manner and was not, as El-Hage alleges "conducted as if pursuant to a 'general warrant.'" The Government and the Defendant both state that the search was conducted during the daytime, an inventory of the items seized was left at the residence and that an American official was present for the search (and "identified himself...in true name"). The scope of the search was limited to those items which were believed to have foreign intelligence value and retention and dissemination of the evidence acquired during the search were minimized. Therefore, the items seized during the physical search of El-Hage's Kenya residence are not suppressed.

The most significant factual question centered on the nature of the searches (whether they were conducted for foreign intelligence purposes or law enforcement purposes). This question was not overly complex and its resolution required that the Court review a limited (and manageable) number of documents. See Alderman, 394 U.S. at 183–84 (explaining that "the need for adversary inquiry is increased by the complexity of the issues presented for adjudication"). All of the other issues that required consideration were legal questions which, thoroughly briefed by the parties, did not require an adversary hearing. Based on Government's assertion that disclosure of the ex parte materials would jeopardize the ongoing investigation of al Qaeda and in light of the limited factual inquiry that was necessary to resolve the issues presented, the Court determined that a hearing was unnecessary.

CONCLUSION

For the foregoing reasons, El-Hage's motion to suppress evidence from the physical search of his Kenya residence and electronic surveillance is denied without a hearing.

Declassified Appendix A

As outlined in the opinion, the Court finds that the search of El-Hage's residence was undertaken primarily for the purpose of foreign intelligence collection. The mere fact that FBI Agent Coleman [redacted] was present during the residential search does not mean that law enforcement displaced foreign intelligence collection as the primary purpose of the search. Coleman's presence was intended to ensure that "if anything of evidentiary value for law enforcement was found, [he] could testify to a chain of custody without involving covert [redacted] employees." ([Name redacted] Decl. P 65.) Although [redacted] has, at times, "attempted to accommodate law enforcement...the primary focus has been collection, disruption, and dissemination of intelligence" on Bin Laden and his organization. The intelligence objective, [redacted] was at all times overriding, It was also believed that evidence gleaned from El-Hage's computer would provide [redacted] "insight into the Bin Laden infrastructure." (Id.) The Government's assertion that [redacted] actions were primarily for the purpose of foreign intelligence collection is reinforced by the fact that foreign intelligence collection against Bin Laden and al Qaeda "continues today." As is clear from the [name redacted] Declaration, the search of El-Hage's residence yielded important intelligence information about Bin Laden's organization. Finally, in disseminating the information discovered during the search, [redacted] followed minimization procedures.

3.8.   Fifth and Fourteenth Amendments: Equal Protection
3.8.1.   Equal protection in public health

The implementation of quarantine must be determined to be so important to a state interest of protecting public health that it may burden, although in the narrowest way, individual rights. Any disparate impact on a protected class of persons will almost certainly be unconstitutional. In the historic

FEDERALISM AND BIODEFENSE

San Francisco plague epidemic in 1900, the understanding of the science of plague was rudimentary, and the San Francisco government was convinced that it was occurring in an area of the city called Chinatown. The following excerpt of the historical narrative from Marilyn Chase, *The Barbary Plague* (Random House, 2003), vividly demonstrates the infringement on individual rights during this public health crisis when government officials used their legal powers to focus on Chinatown as the source of the plague.

But to the San Francisco citizen of 1900 --- event to most practicing physicians --- the new bacteriology was still a form of black magic: mysterious, dimly understood, untrustworthy, and inferior to the laying on of hands and the observation of symptoms at the bedside. Fevers and swollen glands could signify anything from strep to syphilis, they said. Many practicing physicians in town dismissed the bacteriologist Kinyoun . .

No one was more skeptical that Ng Poon Chew, the Presbyterian miniter who founded and edited Chinatown's leading newspaper, the Chung Sai Yat Po, or East-West Daily. In his story announcing the results of the plague test, he spoke for an entire community that feared not so much that they would die from plague, but that they would be ruined by it:

The Monkey is Dead

. . . Alas, why should Chinatown's good name depend on the life and death of a monkey? If this monkey lived, then Chinatown would be exempt from fear and the Chinese would rejoice at the news. We don't know the implications of the English-language press commentary, and whether they are rooting for Chinatown or the monkey. We don't know whether luck will favor the physician or Chinatown. But this morning, the monkey was reported to be dead. In the view of this newspaper, the monkey's death was not caused by plague. Alas, the monkey's death was due to starvation --- a result of its unlucky encounter with this physician.

But down at City Hall, San Francisco's mayor indulged the health board. James Duval Phelan was a democratic reformer sandwiched between corrupt and boss-ridden mayors, but he was also an arch-enemy of Chinese immigration. And as the Chinese Exclusion Act of 1882 was coming up for renewal, the plague scare gave him another reason to sound off on the yellow peril . . . Chinese labor had been sweet enough to railroad tycoons during the building of the transcontinental railroad, but with the dawn of the new century, a labor surplus frayed California's welcome mat. Phelan viewed Asian workers as a threat to the sons of the Golden State, even though many were native-born San Franciscans. Phelan would later run for the U.S. Senate under the slogan "Keep California White."

So when Chinese consult Ho Yow threatened to sue the city for $500,000 to recover Chinatown's damages from the quarantine, Phelan's true feelings erupted:

"As to objections and suits by the Chinese, I desire to say that they are fortunate, with the unclear habits . . .and their filthy hovels, to be permitted to remain within the corporate limits of any American city," the mayor exploded. "In an economic sense, their presence has been , and is, a great injury to the working classes, and in a sanitary sense, they are a constant menace to the public health." . . .

. . . Invoking the Quarantine Act of 1890, Wyman was authorized by President William McKinley to issue a sweeping order --- not just halting travel by plague patients, but forbidding train or boat travel by all "Asiatics and other races particularly liable to the disease." Now railroad and shipping companies refused to sell tickets to Asian passengers. No Asian could leave the state without a health certificate issue by Kinyoun. . . .

It was Kinyoun's job to enforce the order. The travel ban covered both Chinese and Japanese people. Clusters of Japanese lived and worked near the borders of Chinatown, but as yet no single case of plague had been found in a Japanese resident of San Francisco. It was a clear case of quarantine by color.

Challenges to the ban came quickly. After merchants like Louis Quong were barred from boarding the Oakland ferry, a class-action lawsuit was filed in federal court. Wong Wai, a buisinessman associated with the Chinese Six Companies, filed the suit charging Kinyoun with the board of health with illegally imprisoning twenty-five thousand Chinese inside San Francisco . . . The lawsuit charged that the travel restrictions were unconstitutional and demanded that Kinyoun and the health board be enjoined from requiring vaccination or barring their travel.

Left to untangle the snarl of competing federal and local health and civil rights claims was Judge William W. Morrow. Before he ascended the bench, the silver-haired jurist had been a three-term Republican member of Congress. As a lawmaker, Morrow wasn't known for his love of the Chinese, whom he once labeled "destitute of moral qualities." As a judge hearing exclusion-law cases, he often sided with the government.

But on May 28, Judge Morrow ruled in favor of the Chinese.. . . Thus the whole program ---- travel restrictions and vaccine --- discriminated against Chinese residents, deprived them of liberty in violation of the equal protection clause of the Fourteenth Amendment of the Constitution.

. . . In a surprise move, it [the California State Health Board] ordered the city to restore the quarantine and threatened to quarantine the entire city form the rest of the state of California if it did not comply. . . . D.D. Crowley of the California State Health Board. . . had his own preference, and that was to burn Chinatown to the ground. But if he couldn't use the torch, a fence would do. "Gentlemen," he ordered at the close of the May 28 meeting, "you must have Chinatown quarantined this evening." With Sacramento holding a gun to its head, the San Francisco Board of Supervisors passed a resolution empowering the health board to quarantine Chinatown for a second time.

Once again, 159 police officers descended on Chinatown. They guarded the district twenty-four hours a day in three shifts, sealing of the rectangle bounded by Stockton, Kearny, California and Broadway... Now the quarantine zone was enlarged by one block to the north. But again, it zigzagged to exempt white institutions, including the redbrick steeple of St. Mary's Church at California and Dupont Streets.

Chinatown churned in helpless frustration as the normal ebb and flow of business between whites and Asians was interrupted. A white woman on Stockton tried to pass garments to a Chinese tailor, but a police officer blocked the exchange. A Chinese man tried to mail a letter outside the zone, but guards spun him around and hustled him back to his quarter. A laundryman staggered up to the rope line under a heap of clean clothes for delivery outside the zone. An officer halted the shipment.

The first time, it was a penetrable quarantine made of flimsy ropes, but this time, the barricades were hardened with wooden fence posts and barbed wire. A persistent buzz in the neighborhood said the quarantine was a mere prelude to imprisonment. Wyman and Kinyoun were exchanging telegrams discussing a proposal for the mass relocation of the Chinese to plague detention camps on Angle Island near the quarantine station , or on Mission Rock, a tiny, desolate speck of land in the bay near the waterfront warehouses. The news shot a new bolt of fear through the Chinese. Detention camps were a throwback to the medieval lazarettos, isolation hospitals or pesthouses.

. . . But as the second quarantine stretched on, hunger afflicted the residents of Chinatown more than the plague did. There was nothing to buy and no money to buy it. The Chinese Six Companies asked the city for 25 cents a day to feed the hungry. But a city health board member vetoed the request as too high; the almshouse, he said, fed its inmates for 8 cents a day.

. . . a few Chinese took their anger to court. Jew Ho, a grocer on Stockton Street, was incenses to discover that the cordons encircling his store curved to exclude a white plumber and coal dealer next door. Starved of business, he filed a lawsuit on June 5, charging that the quarantine violated his constitutional guarantee of equal protection under the law. He demanded that Caucasian physicians not be barred from crossing the quarantine line to attend their Chinese patients.

Like other lawsuits before it, the heart of Jew Ho's claim was that there was no plague in San Francisco. But even if there were plague, the suit argued, a mass quarantine didn't protect the Chinese but heightened their risk by sealing them up inside an infected district. The complaint asked the court to end the quarantine and restrict isolation to only the infected homes and shops. . . .

In court, the Chinese relentlessly pounded away at the theme that the quarantine was an act of racial bias, not public health. "Real prison has iron bars," said the counsel for the Chinese Six Companies, a former judge names James Maguire. "But when you surround the area with ropes and hurdles and restrict the freedom of the people, it is also imprisonment," he said. "Do they want to starve 10,000 Chinese to death? . . .

Judge John J. De Haven chiseled the first legal chip off the quarantine by granting a habeas corpus petition. He ordered the release of a Chinese cook who lived with his white employers on Bush Street but who got trapped in the quarantine zone while visiting friends in Chinatown. Judge De Haven forbade the health board from restricting the liberty of anyone --- Asian or white --- who wasn't in direct contact with plague.

In Washington, the Chinese minister Wu Ting-Fang sent the U.S. government a bill for $30,000 for each day his subjects were incarcerated in Chinatown. . . .

On June 15, the courtroom was packed to hear arguments in the Jew Ho lawsuit. Consul Ho Yow was there, as were forty Christian missionaries and about a hundred Chinese spectators. Ng Poon Chew, the crusading editor of the Chung Sai Yat Po, took furious notes.

Jew Ho called a parade of expert medical witnesses, who gave sworn testimony that there was no plague. Physician Minnie Worley asserted that the young maid Chin Moon had died of typhoid fever. Judge Morrow listened attentively from the bench. It if were the court's job to rule on the truth of the diagnosis, Judge Morrow said, "I think upon such testimony as that given by these physicians I should be compelled to hold that the plague did not exist and has not existed in San Francisco."

Though it wasn't the court's job to settle matters of science, Judge Morrow threw the quarantine out on legal grounds. It lumped all Chinese homes and businesses together, while exempting white-occupied buildings. It didn't distinguish between homes of plague-infected and homes of health Chinese, but confined them all together, increasing risk of transmission. It forbade the Chinese from access to physicians of their choice. For all these reasons, said Judge Morrow, echoing the U.S. Supreme Court in a prior discrimination case, the San Francisco quarantine was imposed with "an evil eye and unequal hand."

"This quarantine," he went on, "cannot be continued by reason of the fact that it is unreasonable, unjust, and oppressive . . . discriminating in its character [and] contrary to the provisions of the Fourteenth Amendment of the Constitution of the United States."

Within hours of Judge Morrow's ruling, the city health board repealed the quarantine. . . That afternoon, a police wagon pulled up to the intersection of Kearny and Clay. A captain in civilian clothes jumped out, broke down the fences, and rolled up the barbed wire.

After reading the narrative above, a reading of the published opinion below should make for a deeper appreciation for Judge Morrow's task.

Jew Ho v. Williamson, et. al.
103 F. 10 (N.D. Cal. 1900)

Before MORROW, Circuit Judge, and DE HAVEN, District Judge.MORROW, Circuit Judge.

Having reached a conclusion as to the disposition to be made of the order to show cause in this case, I deem the circumstances of such a character as to justify an announcement of that conclusion at this time, without the delay incident to the preparation of a written opinion, which will be filed hereafter. On the 28th day of May, 1900, the board of health of the city and county of San Francisco adopted the following resolution:"Resolved, that it is the sense of this board that, in consequence of the discoveries in the district bounded by Broadway, Stockton, California, and Kearney streets, of nine deaths due to bubonic plague, which were verified by microscopical and animal inoculation tests, this board fears that there is still danger of the spread of this disease over a larger area, and therefore requests the board of supervisors to declare said district infected, and authorize the board of health to quarantine said district."Thereafter, on the said 28th day of May, 1900, said resolution was filed in the office of the board of supervisors, and thereupon the board of supervisors passed the following ordinance:

"Be it ordained by the people of the city and county of San Francisco, as follows:"Section 1. The board of health of this city and county is hereby authorized and empowered to quarantine persons, houses, places, and districts within this city and county, when in its judgment it is deemed necessary to prevent the spreading of contagious or infectious diseases."

This ordinance was approved by the mayor of the city, and thereafter transmitted to the board of health; and immediately thereafter, on the 29th day of May, 1900, at a special meeting of the board of health, a resolution was passed, which, after stating the passage by the board of supervisors of the foregoing ordinance, provided as follows:

"And whereas, after a careful and minute investigation had during a period of three months last past, and from the result of investigation made by Drs. Kellogg, bacteriologist to the board of health, Montgomery, of the University of California, Ophulf, of the Cooper Medical College, and J. J. Kinyoun, of the U.S. marine hospital service, each and all of whom have reported to this board that bubonic plague has existed in the district hereafter mentioned, and that nine deaths have occurred within said period within said district from said disease; and whereas, this board has reason to believe and does believe that danger does exist to the health of the citizens of the city and county of San Francisco by reason of the existence of germs of the said disease remaining in the district hereafter mentioned: Now, therefore, be it resolved: That the health officer be and is hereby instructed to place in quarantine until further notice that particular district of the city bounded north by Broadway, northeast by Montgomery avenue, east by Kearney, south by California, and west by Stockton streets; and that the chief of police is hereby requested to furnish such assistance as may be necessary to establish and maintain said quarantine. These lines may be modified by the health officer, or the chief of police, health board to be notified of the same. This resolution to take effect immediately."

Thereafter, on May 31, 1900, the board of supervisors passed another ordinance, which, after reciting the filing in the office of the resolution of the board of health of May 28, 1900, provided for the establishment of quarantine regulations in the district named, and directed the chief of police to furnish such assistance as might be necessary to establish and maintain this quarantine.

The complainant in this case, Jew Ho, alleges, among other things, that he resides at No. 926 Stockton street, within the limits of said quarantined district, and is engaged in the business of conducting a grocery store, as the proprietor and manager thereof, at his said place of residence, and that a great number of the patrons and customers of his said business reside at various places in the city and county of San Francisco outside the boundaries of said quarantined district, and are now, and ever since the 29th day of May, 1900, have been, prevented and prohibited by the defendants from visiting, patronizing, and dealing with the complainant in his said grocery store; that the complainant has been prevented and prohibited since the said 29th day of May, 1900, from selling his goods, wares, and merchandise, and from otherwise carrying on the business in which he is engaged. The complainant also alleges that although the said resolutions of the board of supervisors and the defendant board of health are in general terms, and purport to impose the same restrictions, burdens, and limitations upon all persons within the said quarantined district, the said resolution is enforced against persons of the Chinese race and nationality only, and not against persons of other races. In this behalf it is alleged that all stores, residences, and other buildings within the quarantined district as described in the resolution, occupied by persons of races other than Chinese, are not subjected to any of the restrictions or limitations provided for by said resolution, whereas those occupied by Chinese are subjected to said restrictions. It is also alleged that wanton and willful discrimination against the Chinese residents of said district by the defendants is shown by the exclusion from the limits of said districts of all physicians employed by Chinese residents, and by the free permission to other residents of said district to select physicians of their own choice, and the permission to all such physicians to enter and depart from all buildings occupied by persons of races other than Chinese within said quarantined district. The complainant alleges that there is not now, and never has been, any case of bubonic plague within the limits of said quarantined district, nor any germs or bacteria of bubonic plague, and that other diseases caused the illness and death of the persons claimed by defendants to have died of the bubonic plague within the 30 days next preceding the filing of this complaint. It is further alleged that the defendants have failed and neglected to quarantine the houses alleged to be so infected from the remainder of said quarantined district, and have wholly failed and neglected to quarantine or otherwise isolate from the other residents of said quarantined district the persons alleged to have been so exposed to the danger of contagion, and therefore likely to transmit the germs of said bubonic plague to others, but have included in said quarantined district an unreasonably large and populous district, namely, 12 blocks, containing a population of more than 15,000 persons, thereby increasing rather than diminishing the danger of contagion and epidemic, both to the people of said district and to the people of San Francisco generally, if there should be any epidemic disease existing in said district; that within said quarantined district are several blocks in which it is not claimed or asserted by the defendants that any case of bubonic plague has existed for 40 days and more next preceding the filing of the complaint, and in which there is not now, and never has been, any danger of contagion or infection. The complainant alleges that he has never had or contracted said bubonic plague; that he has never been at any time exposed to the danger of contracting it, and has never been in any locality where said bubonic plague, or any germs or bacteria thereof, has or have existed; that the action of the defendants in confining and imprisoning the complainant and other Chinese residents within the limits of said quarantined district is a purely arbitrary, unreasonable, unwarranted, wrongful, and oppressive interference with the personal liberty of the complainant and the said Chinese residents, and with their right to the pursuit of their lawful business; that said resolution providing for the said quarantine, and designating said quarantine district, is wholly unauthorized, invalid, and void, and contrary to the constitution and laws of the United States, and contrary to and in violation of the laws of the state of California; that it is not enforced against other residents of said district than those of the Chinese race; and that by its enforcement the said Chinese residents of said district are deprived of the equal protection of the laws, and of their rights and liberties under the constitution of the United States, and the laws and treaties passed and adopted in pursuance thereof. The complainant brings this suit in behalf of the Chinese residents of said quarantine district, to the number of 10,000 and upward, as well as in his own behalf. The prayer of the bill is that an injunction be granted, enjoining and restraining the defendants from interfering with the personal rights and privileges of the complainant.

Upon the filing of this bill of complaint, together with affidavits supporting the allegations therein contained, the court issued an order to the defendants to show cause why an injunction should not issue to restrain them from committing the acts and carrying into execution the threats set forth in the bill of complaint. To this order, return has been made by answer. In this answer the defendants allege the organization of the board of health, the provisions of the charter of San Francisco, the authority of the board of health, and the authority of the board of supervisors, as derived from the provisions of the charter. They allege that the board of supervisors have passed certain resolutions, to which I have already referred, and that they have acted in pursuance of the authority conferred by the charter, and that in establishing this quarantine district the defendants have been acting under the authority of the resolutions passed by the board of supervisors, and their own resolution in pursuance thereof. As the answer was originally framed, it denied that the complainant was within the quarantine limits as prescribed. But by oral amendment to the answer it is alleged that the particular place of residence of the complainant is included within the quarantined district. The defendants deny that they or any of their agents, in the enforcement of said quarantine regulations, exempt or relieve from all or any restrictions of quarantine all or any store or residence or other building whatever within said district. With regard to the averment that the complainant has never had or contracted the bubonic plague, the defendants state that they have not knowledge, information, or belief sufficient to enable them to answer, but they deny that the complainant has never at any time been exposed to the danger of contracting said bubonic plague, and that he has never been in any locality where said plague, or any germs or bacteria thereof, has or have existed. On the contrary, the defendants state their belief that the complainant is a Chinese person, and a resident within said quarantined district, where said plague has had its existence.

To this answer the complainant excepted orally on the ground that it did not respond to the equities of the bill, in this: that, with respect to the charges of detention and restriction of the complainant, the defendants' answer is that they have no information or belief with respect to the matters upon which the restraint is made or effected. It is contended that, the defendants having failed to answer fully and directly as to the cause of restraining the complainant of his liberty, the bill must be taken as confessed. The bill of complaint is not a bill of discovery, and cannot be treated in that light. It is true that, after stating the matters of complaint, it concludes with the prayer that a subpoena issue, and that the defendants be required to make full, true, direct, and perfect answer to the matters therein contained. But, under the equity practice, it is not required that the defendants in such a case shall do more than deny or answer the bill of complaint. They are not called upon to make a discovery, or to make specific disclosures concerning the matters therein contained. Moreover, the bill waived an answer under oath, but for the purpose of being used as an affidavit the answer is verified. In that form it has been introduced as a part of the return, in response to the order to show cause. There is some objection to the form of the answer as an affidavit, because, as an affidavit, it should be specific in reply to the matters charged in the bill of complaint. The equities of the bill are that the complainant is being unlawfully restrained of his liberty, and illegally deprived of the use of his property. The substantial answer to that charge is that the complainant is being restrained of his liberty and deprived of the use of his property by reason of certain quarantine regulations, and that, as to whether or not he has so exposed himself as to render himself personally subject to the restrictions of quarantine regulations, the defendants have no information or belief. Under the strict rules of equity practice, this answer, as an affidavit, would not be sufficient to meet the equities of the bill. But the court must take notice of the whole case, and it is evident therefrom that the answer of the defendants, averring that they have no knowledge or information or belief concerning the exposure of this complainant to this disease, is a difficulty or weakness that is inherent in the case, and not alone in the pleadings. We find from other portions of the pleadings that there are in this quarantined district some 10,000 people or more. It is quite likely that, with respect to such a large number, in a district of that character, there would be a great number, and perhaps the great majority, concerning which the defendants would have no knowledge, information, or belief. They could have no information concerning individuals upon which to found any belief, and therefore they have made denial in accordance with the circumstances of the case. Considering the pleading as dealing with a single case or a single fact, it would, of course, be insufficient. But, when it comes to dealing with a large population, -- 10,000 or more, -- the court must recognize that the lack of information on the part of the defendants in an infirmity that belongs to their case on the merits. The court will therefore not sustain the objection to the answer upon the ground that there is a defect in the showing made in the answer, but will consider that the case is inherently weak in this respect upon the actual facts alleged.

The next objection that has been interposed by the complainant to the sufficiency of the answer is that it does not appear therefrom that the ordinance has been passed with the formality required by the charter. I have examined the evidence that has been furnished to the court by these affidavits, and I am unable to find any evidence sufficient to justify the court in holding that this ordinance has not been passed with the requisite formalities. It may be that the requirements of the charter have not been complied with in every particular in the enactment of the ordinance upon which the complaint is founded. But that fact does not appear from the evidence submitted to the court, and the allegations are such that the court must indulge the presumption that the ordinance has been passed with the requisite formalities.

The next objection interposed on the part of the defendants is that this court has no authority to examine into the questions in controversy; that, it appearing from this return that a duly-constituted department of the municipality of San Francisco has made inquiry as to the situation attending an alleged epidemic of a contagious disease, and has adopted resolutions and taken such steps as it deemed necessary, such action is an adjudication on the part of a department having exclusive jurisdiction and authority over the subject, and this court has no jurisdiction to inquire into the reasonableness or propriety of the acts of the defendants. That objection I understand counsel to make not only to this court as a court of general jurisdiction, but also to this court as a court having jurisdiction to determine federal questions. I will consider the federal aspect of the objection first, namely, the jurisdiction of this court to determine other than federal questions.

The complainant alleges that he is an alien. He invokes the jurisdiction of this court on the ground of diverse citizenship. Where a cause is brought into this court upon that ground, the court has a concurrent jurisdiction with the state court to determine all the questions involved in the case. It has the same jurisdiction as the superior court of the state. It may inquire into the regularity and legality of proceedings of a municipality, or in any locality, precisely as would a state court. The cases to which counsel for defendants referred, wherein the federal court denied itself the right to inquire into the legislation of states or municipalities, have arisen where the jurisdiction of the federal court has been invoked on the sole ground that the controversy involved a federal question. In such cases the complainant states the federal question as the matter to be determined. If, for instance, in this case a citizen of the state of California should come into this court and invoke its jurisdiction on the ground that this action of the board of supervisors involved a federal question, and that it was contrary to the fourteenth amendment of the constitution, an allegation of that character would state the ground of jurisdiction and subject of controversy, and it would be the only question this court would be called upon to examine. The court would not, in such a case, enter into the question of whether or not the action of the board of supervisors was in conformity with the constitution of the state, or whether it was beyond the municipal powers of the city under its charter. All such questions would in that case be foreign to the investigation, and the court would be confined to the question as to whether or not it was contrary to the provisions of the fourteenth amendment to the constitution of the United States. But in the case at bar the complainant comes into court as an alien, and invokes the jurisdiction of the court on the ground of diverse citizenship, and presents also the federal question. The court is therefore not restricted in its jurisdiction to the federal question, but may inquire into all matters relating to the legality of the restraint imposed upon the complainant.

It is next contended that the acts of the defendants in establishing a quarantine district in San Francisco are authorized by the general police power of the state, intrusted to the city of San Francisco. The defendants rely upon a number of cases in support of this asserted jurisdiction and authority, -- among others, the case of *Mugler v. Kansas*, 123 U.S. 623, 8 Sup. Ct. 273, 31 L. Ed. 205. In that case it appears that the constitution of Kansas provided "that the manufacture and sale of intoxicating liquors shall be forever prohibited in this state, except for medical, scientific and mechanical purposes." The legislature of the state enacted a statute to carry this constitutional provision into effect. Mugler, the proprietor of a brewery, was indicted in one of the courts of the state for violation of this statute, and was tried and convicted and sentenced to pay a fine. The case was appealed to the supreme court of the state, and there affirmed. A writ of error took the case to the supreme court of the United States. The question was whether the prohibition by the state of Kansas, in its constitution and laws, of the manufacture or sale within the limits of the state of intoxication liquors for general use in the state as a beverage, was fairly adapted to the end of protecting the community against the evils which result from excessive use of ardent spirits, and whether it was subject to the objection that under the guise of police regulations the state was aiming to deprive the citizen of his constitutional rights. The court, in passing upon this question, said:

"Power to determine such question, so as to bind all, must exist somewhere; else, society will be at the mercy of the few, who, regarding only their own appetites or passions, may be willing to imperil the peace and security of the many, provided only they are permitted to do as they please. Under our system that power is lodged with the legislative branch of the government. It belongs to that department to exert what are known as the 'police powers' of the state, and to determine primarily what measures are appropriate or needful for the protection of the public morals, the public health, or the public safety."

But the court did not stop with this declaration. It went further, and explained that the legislative authority was subject to limitations, and that it was for the courts to determine whether such limitations were exceeded when such legislative acts were called in question. The court said:

> "It does not at all follow that every statute enacted ostensibly for the promotion of these ends is to be accepted as a legitimate exertion of the police powers of the state. There are, of necessity, limits beyond which legislation cannot rightfully go. While every possible presumption is to be indulged in favor of the validity of a statute (Sinking-Fund Cases, 99 U.S. 700, 718, 25 L. Ed. 496), the courts must obey the constitution, rather than the lawmaking department of government, and must, upon their own responsibility, determine whether, in any particular case, these limits have been passed. 'To what purpose,' it was said in Marbury v. Madison, 1 Cranch. 137, 176, 2 L. Ed. 60, 'are powers limited, and to what purpose is that limitation committed to writing, if these limits may at any time be passed by those intended to be restrained? The distinction between a government with limited and unlimited powers is abolished, if those limits do not confine the persons on whom they are imposed, and if acts prohibited and acts allowed are of equal obligation.' The courts are not bound by mere forms, nor are they to be misled by mere pretenses. They are at liberty -- indeed, are under a solemn duty -- to look at the substance of things, whenever they enter upon the inquiry whether the legislature has transcended the limits of its authority. If, therefore, a statute purporting to have been enacted to protect the public health, the public morals, or the public safety, has no real or substantial relation to those objects, or is a palpable invasion of rights secured by the fundamental law, it is the duty of the courts to so adjudge, and thereby give effect to the constitution."

And in the case of *Chy Lung v. Freeman*, 92 U.S. 275, 280, 23 L. Ed. 550, the same court, speaking of the right of a state, in the absence of legislation by congress, to protect herself by necessary and proper laws, said:

"Such a right can only arise from a vital necessity for its exercise, and cannot be carried beyond the scope of that necessity."

In Ex parte Whitwell, 98 Cal. 73, 78, 32 Pac. 870, 19 L.R.A. 727, the petitioner was imprisoned by the sheriff of San Mateo county upon a charge of maintaining within the boundaries of that county a hospital for the treatment of insane persons, without having procured a license so to do, as required by an ordinance adopted by the board of supervisors of that county March 16, 1892. The ordinance referred to purported to be one –

"To license for purpose of regulation and revenue, the business of keeping * * * within the county of San Mateo * * * hospitals, asylums, homes, retreats or places for the care or treatment of insane persons or persons of unsound mind, or inebriates, or persons affected by or suffering from any mental or nervous disease, or who are suffering from the effects of the excessive use of alcoholic liquors."

The ordinance made it unlawful to maintain within the county of San Mateo any hospital, asylum, or place for the care or treatment, for reward, of any insane person, or persons belonging to either of the classes mentioned in the title of the ordinance, unless the keeper of such hospital or asylum should have first procured a license therefore. The ordinance provided, however, that no license should be granted unless the board was satisfied that the building was fireproof, by reason of being constructed of brick and iron or stone and iron; that the building should not be more than two stories in height, and that the same, and the land used in connection therewith, or such part of said land as any of the patients were to have access to, was surrounded by a brick or stone wall not less than 18 inches in thickness and not less than 12 feet in height, and in which wall there was to be one opening, which opening should be closed by a solid iron door, so constructed and fitted into said wall as that the same might be securely fastened by a combination lock, and said door furnished with a combination lock. The petitioner was a physician and surgeon, and directed his attention to the treatment of persons afflicted as described in the ordinance. He had purchased a tract of land in San Mateo County, and erected a building thereon, prior to the passage of this ordinance, for the accommodation of such persons during treatment, but this building was not of the character designated and required by the ordinance. It was claimed by the petitioner that the ordinance imposed unreasonable restrictions upon his right to prosecute a lawful business and to devote his property to a lawful use, and that such provisions were in conflict with the constitution of the United States and of the state of California, and for that reason void. Upon the other hand, it was contended that the ordinance was a police regulation, and that the court was not authorized to declare it invalid because in its judgment the ordinance might be deemed unreasonable. Discussing this question, the supreme court, speaking through Mr. Justice De Haven, said:

> "The police power -- the power to make laws to secure the comfort, convenience, peace, and health of the community -- is an extensive one, and in its exercise a very wide discretion as to what is needful or proper for that purpose is necessarily committed to the legislative body in which the power to make such laws is vested. *Ex parte Tuttle*, 91 Cal. 589, 27 Pac. 933. But it is not true that, when this power is exerted for the purpose of regulating a business or occupation which in itself is recognized as innocent and useful to the community, the legislature is the exclusive judge as to what is a reasonable and just restraint upon the constitutional right of the citizen to pursue such business or profession. As the right of the citizen to engage in such a business or follow such a profession is protected by the constitution, it is always a judicial question whether any particular regulation of such right is a valid exercise of legislative power. Tied. Lim. §85, 194; *Pennsylvania Railroad Co. v. Mayor, etc., of Jersey City*, 47 N.J. Law, 286; *Com. v. Robertson*, 5 Cush. 438; *Austin v. Murray*, 16 Pick. 121. * * * And this necessary limitation upon the power of the legislature to interfere with the fundamental rights of the citizen in the enactment of police regulations was recognized by this court in *Ex parte Sing Lee*, 96 Cal. 354, 31 Pac. 245, 24 L.R.A. 195, in which case we said that the personal liberty of the citizen and his rights of property cannot be invaded under the disguise of a police regulation. This power of the courts, however, to declare invalid what they may deem an unreasonable legislative regulation of a business or occupation which the citizen has the constitutional right to follow, although undoubted, must, from the nature of the power, be exercised with the utmost caution, and only when it is clear that the ordinance or law so declared void passes entirely beyond the limits which bound the police power, and infringes upon rights secured by the fundamental law. The true rule upon this subject is thus expressed by the supreme court of the state of Missouri in the case of *City of St. Louis v. Weber*, 44 Mo. 547: 'In assuming, however, the right to judge of the reasonableness of an exercise of corporate power, courts will not look closely into mere matters of judgment, where there may be a reasonable difference of opinion. It is not to be expected that every power will always be exercised with the highest discretion, and when it is plainly granted a clear case should be made to authorize an interference upon the ground of unreasonableness.'"

It was held that the ordinance was unreasonable and void, and could not be sustained under the police power of the state.

In the case of *Health Department of City of New York v. Rector, etc., of Trinity Church*, 145 N.Y. 32, 39 N.E. 833, the question was with respect to the regulations concerning the introduction of water into tenement houses. The decision is by Judge Peck ham, now of the supreme court of the United States. The ordinance was sustained by the court, but in doing so the court declared very clearly the limitation upon the police power of the state, as follows:

> "It has frequently been said that it is difficult to give any exact definition which shall properly limit and describe such power. It must be exercised subject to the provisions of both the federal and state constitutions, and the law passed in the exercise of such power must tend, in a degree that is perceptible and clear, towards the preservation of the lives, the health, the morals, or the welfare of the community, as those words have been used and construed in many cases heretofore decided," -- citing a number of cases.

In the case of *In re Smith*, 146 N.Y. 68, 40 N.E. 497, 28 L.R.A. 820, there was involved the quarantine of a house in which a person was charged with being exposed to the smallpox. There the court said:

> "I think no one will dispute the right of the legislature to enact such measures as will protect all persons from the impending calamity of a pestilence, and to vest in local authorities such comprehensive powers as will enable them to act competently and effectively. That those powers would be conferred without regulating or controlling their exercise is not to be supposed, and the legislature has not relieved officials from the responsibility of showing that the exercise of their powers was justified by the facts of the case. The question here is not whether the legislature had the power to enact the provisions of section 24 of the health law, but whether the respondent has shown that a state of facts existed, warranting the exercise of the extraordinary authority conferred upon him. Like all enactments which may affect the liberty of the person, this one must be construed strictly, with the saving consideration, however, that, as the legislature contemplated an extraordinary and dangerous emergency for the exercise of the power conferred, some latitude of a reasonable discretion is to be allowed to the local authorities upon the facts of a case."

The case of *Lawton v. Steele*, 152 U.S. 133, 14 Sup. Ct. 499, 38 L. Ed. 385, had relation to a regulation concerning the fisheries. The court said with respect to the police power of the state:

> "The extent and limits of what is known as the 'police power' have been a fruitful subject of discussion in the appellate courts of nearly every state in the Union. It is universally conceded to include everything essential to the public safety, health, and morals, and to justify the destruction or abatement by summary proceedings of whatever may be regarded as a public nuisance. Under this power it has been held that the state may order the destruction of a house falling to decay, or otherwise endangering the lives of passers-by; the demolition of such as are in the path of a conflagration; the slaughter of diseased cattle; the destruction of decayed or unwholesome food; the prohibition of wooden buildings in cities; the regulation of railways and other means of public conveyance, and of interment in burial grounds; the restriction of objectionable trades to certain localities; the compulsory vaccination of children; the confinement of the insane or those afflicted with contagious diseases; the restraint of vagrants, beggars, and habitual drunkards; the suppression of obscene publications and houses of ill fame; and the prohibition of gambling houses and places where intoxicating liquors are sold. Beyond

this, however, the state may interfere wherever the public interests demand it; and in this particular a large discretion is necessarily vested in the legislature to determine, not only what the interests of the public require, but what measures are necessary for the protection of such interests. *Barbier v. Connolly*, 113 U.S. 27, 5 Sup. Ct. 357, 28 L. Ed. 923; *Kidd v. Prearson*, 128 U.S. 1, 9 Sup. Ct. 6, 32 L. Ed. 346. To justify the state in thus interposing its authority in behalf of the public, it must appear -- First, that the interests of the public generally, as distinguished from those of a particular class, require such interference; and, second, that the means are reasonably necessary for the accomplishment of the purpose, and not unduly oppressive upon individuals. The legislature may not, under the guise of protecting the public interests, arbitrarily interfere with private business, or impose unusual and unnecessary restrictions upon lawful occupations. In other words, its determination as to what is a proper exercise of its police powers is not final or conclusive, but is subject to the supervision of the courts."

This I find to be the law as established in the various states of the Union, as well as by the supreme court of the United States. These cases determine that this is a subject for judicial investigation, and the question therefore arises as to whether or not the quarantine established by the defendants in this case is reasonable, and whether it is necessary, under the circumstances of this case. As I had occasion to say in the former case (*Wong Wai v. Williamson* [C.C.]. 103 Fed. 1), this court will, of course, uphold any reasonable regulation that may be imposed for the purpose of protection the people of the city from the invasion of epidemic disease. In the presence of a great calamity, the court will go to the greatest extent, and give the widest discretion, in construing the regulations that may be adopted by the board of health or the board of supervisors. But is the regulation in this case a reasonable one? Is it a proper regulation, directed to accomplish the purpose that appears to have been in view? That is a question for this court to determine.

Affidavits have been filed on behalf of the complainant in this case, -- one of them by Dr. J. I. Stephen, to which I will refer. Dr. Stephen says:

"I am a regular physician and surgeon, licensed to practice medicine and surgery in the state of California. I obtained my medical education and diplomas in London, England, and in Dublin, Ireland. I have been in the active practice of medicine and surgery for the past twenty years, -- for several years, in London, England, where I held various official positions, such as surgeon to the police, medical officer of health, parish medical officer, and public vaccinator, and for the past thirteen years in the state of California. I have given much time and study to the literature of the bubonic plague, and am familiar with the nature, symptoms, and characteristics of said disease. The bubonic plague is a virulent, contagious disease, and under favorable conditions spreads with great rapidity. Those conditions are overcrowding and unsanitary surroundings. The above defendants claim to have discovered since the said month of March, 1900, at varying intervals, seven, eight, or nine dead bodies of Chinese whose death said defendants attribute to said bubonic plague. Bearing in mind the nature, symptoms, and characteristics of said disease, and the conditions generally prevailing in said district known as 'Chinatown,' and now under quarantine, it is impossible to believe that these persons died of such disease. If said disease had existed in the form and under the conditions claimed by said defendants, hundreds, perhaps thousands, of cases would have developed, and many deaths ensued therefrom; for I further aver that no proper or scientific precautions have been taken by said defendants to prevent the spread of said disease. Assuming that the said deceased persons died of said disease, it is my opinion, and I further aver, that said defendants have proceeded from erroneous theories to still more erroneous and unscientific practices and methods of dealing with the same; for, instead of quarantining the supposedly infected rooms or houses in which said deceased persons lived and died, and the persons who had been brought in contact with and been directly exposed to said disease, said defendants have quarantined, and are now maintaining a quarantine over, a large area of territory, and indiscriminately confining therein between ten and twenty thousand people, thereby exposing, and they are now exposing, to the infection of the said disease said large number of persons. Notwithstanding said lack of proper quarantining and said exposure of over ten to twenty thousand persons to infection during a period commencing in the early part of said month of March, 1900, there has not been found a single living case of said disease."

I read that affidavit for the purpose of showing the method adopted by the board of health for the suppressing of this so-called plague, namely, the quarantining of a large territory in the city of San Francisco, -- some 10 or 12 blocks, -- in which there are located about 10,000 people. It must necessarily follow that, where so many have been quarantined, the danger of the spread of the disease would not diminish. The purpose of quarantine and health laws and regulations with respect to contagious and infectious diseases is directed primarily to preventing the spread of such diseases among the inhabitants of localities. In this respect these laws and regulations come under the police power of the state, and may be enforced by quarantine and health officers, in the exercise of a large discretion, as circumstances may require. The more densely populated the community, the greater danger there is that the disease will spread, and hence the necessity for effectual methods of protection. To accomplish this purpose, persons afflicted with such diseases are confined to their own domiciles until they have so far recovered as not to be liable to communicate the disease to others. The same restriction is imposed upon victims of such diseases found traveling. The object of all such rules and regulations is to confine the disease to the smallest possible number of people; and hence when a vessel in a harbor, a car on a railroad, or a house on land, is found occupied by persons afflicted with such a disease, the vessel, the car, or the house, as the case may be, is cut off from all communication with the inhabitants of adjoining houses or contiguous territory, that the spread of the disease may be arrested at once and confined to the least possible territory. This is a system of quarantine that is well recognized in all communities, and is provided by the laws of the various states and municipalities: That, when a contagious or infectious disease breaks out in a place, they quarantine the house or houses first; the purpose being to restrict the disease to the smallest number possible, and that it may not spread to other people in the same locality. It must necessarily follow that, if a large section or a large territory is quarantined, intercommunication of the people within that territory will rather tend to spread the disease than to restrict it. If you place 10,000 persons in one territory, and confine them there, as they have been in prisons and other places, the spread of disease, of course, becomes increased, and the danger of such spread of disease is increased, sometimes in an alarming degree, because it is the constant communication of people that are so restrained or imprisoned that causes the spread of the disease. If we are to suppose that this bubonic plague has existed in San Francisco since the 6th day of March, and that there has been danger of its spreading over the city, the most dangerous thing that could have been done was to quarantine the whole city, as to the Chinese, as was substantially done in the first instance. The next most dangerous thing to do was to quarantine any considerable portion of the city, and not restrict intercommunication within the quarantined district. The quarantined district comprises 12 blocks. It is not claimed that in all the 12 blocks of the quarantined district the disease has been discovered. There are, I believe, 7 or 8 blocks in which it is claimed that deaths have occurred on account of what is said to be this disease. In 2 or 3 blocks it has not appeared at all. Yet this quarantine has been thrown around the entire district. The people therein obtain their food and other supplies, and communicate freely with each other in all their affairs. They are permitted to go from a place where it is said that the disease has appeared, freely among the other 10,000 people in that district. It would necessarily follow that, if the disease is there, every facility has been offered by this species of quarantine to enlarge its sphere and increase its danger and its destructive force. I need not enlarge upon this feature of the case. It is set forth fully by the affidavits in the case, by the original complaint, and by the opinions of the physicians who have furnished evidence to the court. The court cannot ignore this evidence and the condition it describes. The court cannot but see the practical question that is presented to it as to the ineffectiveness of this method of quarantine against such a disease as this. So, upon that ground, the court must hold that this quarantine is not a reasonable regulation to accomplish the purposes sought. It is not in harmony with the declared purpose of the board of health or of the board of supervisors.

But there is still another feature of this case that has been called to the attention of the court, and that is its discriminating character; that is to say, it is said that this quarantine discriminates against the Chinese population of this city, and in favor of the people of other races. Attention is called to the fact that, while the board of supervisors has quarantined a district bounded by streets, the operation of the quarantine is such as to run along in the rear of certain houses, and that certain houses are excluded, while others are included; that, for instance, upon Stockton street, in the block numbered from 900 to 1,000, there are two places belonging to persons of another race, and these persons and places are excluded from this quarantine, although the Chinese similarly situated are included, and although the quarantine, in terms, is imposed upon all the persons within the blocks bounded by such streets. The evidence here is clear that this is made to operate against the Chinese population only, and the reason given for it is that the Chinese may communicate the disease from one to the other. That explanation, in the judgment of the court, is not sufficient. It is, in effect, a discrimination, and it is the discrimination that has been frequently called to the attention of the federal courts where matters of this character have arisen with respect to Chinese. The case of *Yick Wo v. Hopkins*, 118 U.S. 356, 6 Sup. Ct. 1064, 30 L. Ed. 220, arose in this state, out of the operation of an ordinance of this city respecting Chinese laundries. The supreme court in that case had been discussing cases where there were simply opportunities for discrimination, not an actual discrimination. The court points this out as not being a case where there was not merely opportunity for discrimination, but where there was an actual discrimination. The court says:

> "In the present cases we are not obliged to reason from the probable to the actual, and pass upon the validity of the ordinances complained of, as tried merely by the opportunities which their terms afford of unequal and unjust discrimination in their administration; for the cases present the ordinances in actual operation, and the facts shown establish an administration directed so exclusively against a particular class of persons as to warrant and require the conclusion that, whatever may have been the intent of the ordinances as adopted, they are applied by the public authorities charged with their administration, and thus representing the state itself, with a mind so unequal and oppressive as to amount to a practical denial by the state of that equal protection of the laws which is secured to the petitioners, as to all other persons, by the broad and benign provisions of the fourteenth amendment to the constitution of the United States. Though the law itself be fair on its face and impartial in appearance, yet, if it is applied and administered by public authority with an evil eye and an unequal hand, so as practically to make unjust and illegal discriminations, between persons in similar circumstances, material to their rights, the denial of equal justice is still within the prohibition of the constitution."

In the case at bar, assuming that the board of supervisors had just grounds for quarantining the district which has been described, it seems that the board of health, in executing the ordinance, left out certain persons, members of races other than Chinese. This is precisely the point noticed by the supreme court of the United States, namely, the administration of a law "with an evil eye and an unequal hand." Wherever the courts of the United States have found such an administration of the law, although it may be, upon the face of the act or of the ordinance, such a lack of discrimination as to otherwise justify the ordinance or the law, still, if the court finds that, in its practical operation, -- in its enforcement by the state or the municipality, -- there is that opportunity, and that it is the purpose to enforce it "with an evil eye and an unequal hand," then it is the duty of the court to interpose, and to declare the ordinance discriminating in its character, and void under the constitution of the United States. Therefore the court must hold that this ordinance is invalid and cannot be maintained, that it is contrary to the provisions of the fourteenth amendment of the constitution of the United States, and that the board of health has no authority or right to enforce any ordinance in this city that shall discriminate against any class of persons in favor of another.

There is one other feature of this case, and that is as to whether or not the bubonic plague has existed in this city, and whether it does now exist. The complainant alleges in his bill of complaint that it does not exist in San Francisco or in this quarantined district, and the bill is supported by the affidavits of a number of reputable physicians. Dr. J. I. Stephen says in this regard:

"I am the regularly appointed physician of the Chinese Empire Reform Association, which numbers several thousand Chinese residents in the state of California, and in the performance of my professional duties have made frequent visits to that portion of said city and county commonly known as 'Chinatown,' and which is now under quarantine by order of the above defendants, and am well acquainted with the sanitary condition of said district, and with the people who reside therein. I am aware of the allegation of the above defendants that bubonic plague has existed within said quarantined district since the month of March, 1900, and am of the opinion, based upon my knowledge of said disease, and familiarity with said district and the people residing therein, that said allegation is based upon totally inadequate evidence. The said defendants have formed their diagnosis upon the alleged recognition of bacilli found in the tissues of certain deceased Chinese persons, and upon incomplete animal experimentations, and have entirely ignored the clinical history of the disease. I further state that the post mortem appearances that the said defendants claim to have found in their autopsies of said deceased persons, and which said defendants claim to be diagnostic of the presence of said disease, are found in many other diseases. I would further state that the said Chinese are particularly subject to enlarged glands due to syphilis and scrofula, and that the enlarged glands which are claimed to have been found in said deceased persons are not due to bubonic plague, but to the constitutional effects of either syphilis or scrofula. From these reasons, and facts hereinbefore stated, I draw the conclusion, and therefore aver, that said disease has not at any time since or during the said month of March existed, and that it does not now exist, within said district under quarantine, or elsewhere in the city and county of San Francisco."

Dr. E. S. Pillsbury, professor of pathology and bacteriology at the College of Physicians and Surgeons, states that he personally examined and diagnosed all bodies of deceased persons dying within the quarantined district between May 30th and June 7th, save one, and that he does not believe the bubonic plague now exists within the said district, or that it has existed there within the last four months. Dr. H. D'Arcy Power, employed by the Chinese Six Companies, visited the quarantined district during the 30th and 31st days of May and the 1st and 2d days of June, and saw all the sick persons and dead bodies then in said district. He states that none of the cases visited by him was a case of bubonic plague, and that he does not believe at the time of his visits there was a case of bubonic plague in said district, nor that one has since occurred. Dr. D. A. Hodghead testifies to the same effect. Dr. George L. Fitch states that he attended one of the Chinese persons said by the board of health to have died of the bubonic plague, but that in his opinion the said Chinese died of pneumonia. Dr. Fitch states that, from his knowledge, he does not believe there are now any cases of bubonic plague within the district of Chinatown. Dr. E. C. Atterbury was with him on this case, and gives the same testimony. Dr. Lydia J. Wyckoff states that she has practiced her profession during periods of epidemics of bubonic plague in other countries, and, from her knowledge of said disease, she is of the opinion that the cases which the board of health regard as having been bubonic plague were not in fact cases of true bubonic plague. Dr. George A. Cable testifies that he attended three of the cases in the quarantined district now suspicioned by the board of health to have been bubonic plague; that such cases were not, in his opinion, bubonic plague; and that, during the whole period of his practice within said district, he has never at any time seen a case resembling bubonic plague. He states it as his opinion that bubonic plague does not now exist, nor has it ever existed, within said Chinatown. Dr. Minnie G. Worley states that she attended the case of a Chinese girl on May 11th, who subsequently died, and which case the board of health have declared was bubonic plague; that she diagnosed the case as typhoid fever; that no other person, to her knowledge, has contracted the bubonic plague or any disease from the said case, and, in affiant's opinion, the girl did not die from bubonic plague.

The evidence of Dr. Stephen and these other physicians show that, at most, there have been 11 deaths in the quarantined district which on autopsy have disclosed some of the symptoms of the bubonic plague. But there has been no living case under the examination of the physicians from which a clinical history has been obtained, and it does not appear that there has been any transmission of the disease from any of those who have died. From all of which the court infers that the suspected cases were not contagious or infectious, or, if contagious and infectious, they were but sporadic in their nature, and had no tendency to spread or disseminate in the city. If it were within the province of this court to determine this issue, I think, upon such testimony as that given by these physicians, I should be compelled to hold that the plague did not exist and has not existed in San Francisco. But this testimony is contradicted by the physicians of the board of health. They have furnished the testimony of reputable physicians that the bubonic plague has existed, and that the danger of its development does exist. In the face of such testimony the court does not feel authorized to render a judicial opinion as to whether or not the plague exists or has existed in this city. Indeed, that is one of the questions that courts, under ordinary circumstances, are disposed to leave to boards of health to determine, upon such evidence as their professional skill deems satisfactory. If they believe, or if they have even a suspicion, that there is an infectious or contagious disease existing within the city, it is unquestionably the duty of such boards to act and protect the city against it, not to wait always until the matter shall be established to the satisfaction of all the physicians or all the persons who may examine into the question. It is the duty of the court to leave such question to be determined primarily by the authority competent for that purpose. So that in this case the court does not feel at liberty to decide this question, although, as I have said, personally the evidence in this case seems to be sufficient to establish the fact that the bubonic plague has not existed, and does not now exist, in San Francisco.

It follows from the remarks that I have made that this quarantine cannot be continued, by reason of the fact that it is unreasonable, unjust, and oppressive, and therefore contrary to the laws limiting the police powers of the state and municipality in such matters; and, second, that it is discrimination in its character, and is contrary to the provisions of the fourteenth amendment of the constitution of the United States. The counsel for complainant will prepare an injunction, which shall, however, permit the board to maintain a quarantine around such places as it may have reason to believe are infected by contagious or infectious diseases, but that the general quarantine of the whole district must not be continued, and that the people residing in that district, so far as they have been restricted or limited in their persons and their business, have that limitation and restraint removed. With respect to the examination of persons who have died, I have already issued a preliminary restraining order preventing the defendants from interfering with physicians attending upon persons claimed to be afflicted with this disease. It will result, probably, if other suspicious cases are found within San Francisco, in a quarantine immediately being imposed upon the proper locality or house or building. In such a case the physician who has been attending the person afflicted should be permitted to continue to attend, and, in case of a death, such physician as may be selected by the Chinese association mentioned in this case shall have a right to attend any autopsy that may be made. But, as before indicated to counsel, that privilege should not be abused. There should not be an effort on the part of everybody, out of curiosity and otherwise, to attend upon these autopsies. There should be some reasonable limit to such privilege. The board of health is charged with the responsibility of maintaining regulations for the protection of the health of this city, and there should be no unreasonable interference with its authority in matters of that kind. The board will have the right to maintain special quarantines in places suspected of having disease, and it has the right to enforce such regulations as it may deem proper, in order to secure an absolute exclusion of such places from the remainder of the community.

I am authorized to say that Judge DE HAVEN concurs in the conclusions here reached.

3.8.2. Equal protection in national security

A case which has been judicially narrowed and publicly discredited, yet not overruled, is the wartime case of *Korematsu v. United States*, involving the interment of citizens of Japanese descent. President Roosevelt signed Executive Order 9066 on February 19, 1942, which authorized military commanders to "prescribe military areas which any or all persons may be excluded, and with respect to which, the right of any person to enter, remain, or leave shall be subject to whatever restrictions Commander may impose in his discretion." On March 21, 1942, Congress thereafter made it a crime to violate an order issued by a military commander. On March 24, 1942, the western military defense command ordered the curfew of all persons of Japanese descent living on the west coast.

This order was challenged in *Hirabayashi v. United States*, and the constitutionality of the order for curfews was upheld by the U.S. Supreme Court.

In the following case, *Korematsu*, a U.S. citizen of Japanese descent was arrested for failure to leave his home as ordered by the military commander, and challenged the constitutionality of the order as to the removal of Korematsu from his home.

Korematsu v. United States
323 U.S. 214 (1944)

Opinion delivered by Justice Black:

It should be noted, to begin with, that all legal restrictions which curtail the civil rights of a single racial group are immediately suspect. That is not to say that all such restrictions are unconstitutional. It is to say that courts must subject them to the most rigid scrutiny. Pressing public necessity may sometimes justify the existence of such restrictions; racial antagonism never can.

In the light of the principles we announced in the *Hirabayashi* case, we are unable to conclude that it was beyond the war power of Congress and the Executive to exclude those of Japanese ancestry from the West Coast war area at the time they did. True, exclusion from the area in which one's home is located is a far greater deprivation than constant confinement to the home form 8 p.m. to 6 a.m. Nothing short of apprehension by the proper military authorities of the gravest imminent danger to the public safety can constitutionally justify either. But exclusion from a threatened area, no less than curfew, has a definite and close relationship to the prevention of espionage and sabotage. The military authorities, charged with the primary responsibility of defending our shores, concluded that curfew provided inadequate protection and ordered exclusion...

Here, as in the *Hirabayashi* case,

> ...we cannot reject as unfounded the judgement of the military authorities and of Congress that there were disloyal members of that population, whose number and strength could not be precisely and quickly ascertained. We cannot say that the war-making branches of the Government did not have ground for believing that in a critical hour such persons could not readily be isolated and separately dealt with, and constituted a menace to the national defense and safety, which demanded that prompt and adequate measures be taken to guard against it.

Like curfew, exclusion of those of Japanese origin was deemed necessary because of the presence of an unascertained number of disloyal members of the group, most of whom we have no doubt were loyal to this country. It was because we could not reject the finding of the military authorities that it was impossible to bring about an immediate segregation of the disloyal form the loyal that we sustained the validity of the curfew order as applying to the whole group. In the instant case, temporary exclusion of the entire group was rested by the military on the same ground. The judgment that exclusion of the whole group was for the same reason a military imperative answers the contention that the exclusion was in the nature of group punishment based on antagonism to those of Japanese origin. That there were members of the group who retained loyalties to Japan has been confirmed by investigations made subsequent to the exclusion. Approximately five thousand American citizens of Japanese ancestry refused to swear unqualified allegiance to the United States and to renounce allegiance to the Japanese Emperor, and several thousand evacuees requested repatriation to Japan.

We uphold the exclusion order as of the time it was made and when the petitioner violated it....we are not unmindful of the hardships imposed by it upon a large group of American citizens. But hardships are a part of war...Citizenship has its responsibilities as well as its privileges, and in time of war the burden is always heavier....But when under conditions of modern warfare our shores are threatened by hostile forces, the power to protect must be commensurate with the threatened danger...

It is said that we are dealing here with the case of imprisonment of a citizen in a concentration camp solely because of his ancestry, without evidence or inquiry concerning his loyalty and good disposition towards the United States. Our task would be simple, our duty clear, were this a case involving the imprisonment of a loyal citizen in a concentration camp because of racial prejudice. Regardless of the true nature of the assembly and relocation centers—and we deem it unjustifiable to call them concentration camps with all the ugly connotations that term implies—we are dealing specifically with nothing but an exclusion order. To cast this case into outlines of racial prejudice, without reference to the real military dangers which were presented merely confuses the issue. Korematsu was not excluded from the Military Area because of hostility to him or his race. He was excluded because we are at war with the Japanese Empire, because the properly constituted military authorities feared an invasion of our West Coast and felt constrained to take proper security measures...

Affirmed.

3.8.3. Equal protection and protective services

In *Amos v. City of Page, Arizona*, 257 F.3d 1086 (9th Cir. 2001), the court denied the defendant's motion to dismiss the plaintiff's §1983 claim for equal protection violation because of a racially discriminatory policy which selectively abandoned searches for Native Americans in automobile accidents. The court's opinion includes the following description of the policy:

Trustee next contends that the City violated the Equal Protection Clause by selectively withholding protective services from Amos because they believed he was a Native American. Trustee's complaint alleges that it is standard practice for the City of Page not to search for runaway drivers because the City believes that most runaway drivers are Native Americans who bolt to the Navajo Reservation after an accident and call the police shortly thereafter, reporting their car as stolen. Further, Trustee alleges that the City does search for runaway drivers when they have reason to believe that they are white. *Id.* at 1093.

3.9. Fifth Amendment Taking

Miller v. Horton
152 Mass. 540, 26 N.E. 100, (Mass., 1891)

OPINION: Holmes, J.

This is an action of tort for killing the plaintiff's horse. The defendants admit the killing, but justify as members of the board of health of the town of Rehoboth, under an order addressed to the board and signed by two of the three commissioners on contagious diseases among domestic animals, appointed under the St. of 1885, c. 378, and acting under the alleged authority of the St. of 1887, c. 252, §13. This order declared that it was adjudged that the horse had the glanders, and that it was condemned, and directed the defendants to cause it to be killed. The judge before whom the case was tried found that the horse had not the glanders, but declined to rule that the defendants had failed to make out their justification, and found for the defendants. The plaintiff excepted.

The language of the material part of §13 of the act of 1887 is: "In all cases of farcy or glanders, the commissioners, having condemned the animal infected therewith, shall cause such animal to be killed without an appraisal, but may pay the owner or any other person an equitable sum for the killing and burial thereof." Taken literally, these words only give the commissioners jurisdiction and power to condemn a horse that really has the glanders. The question is whether they go further by implication, so that, if a horse which has not the disease is condemned by the commissioners, their order will protect the man who kills it in a subsequent suit by the owner for compensation.

The main ground for reading into the statute an intent to make the commissioners' order an absolute protection is, that there is no provision for compensation to the owner in this class of cases, and therefore, unless the order is a protection, those who carry it out will do so at their peril. Such a construction when once known would be apt to destroy the efficiency of the clause, as few people could be found to carry out orders on these terms.

On the other hand, this same absence of any provision for compensation to the owner, even if not plainly founded on the assumption that only a worthless thing and a nuisance is in question, still would be an equally strong argument for keeping to the literal and narrower interpretation. If the Legislature had had in mind the possible destruction of healthy horses, there was no reason in the world why it should not have provided for paying the owners. Section 12 does provide for paying them in all cases where they are not in fault, unless this is an exception. When, as here, the horse not only is not to be paid for, but may be condemned without appeal and killed without giving the owner a hearing or even notice, the grounds are very [*543] strong for believing that the statute means no more than it says, and is intended to authorize the killing of actually infected horses only. If the commissioners had felt any doubt, they could have had the horse appraised under §12. Whether an action would have lain in that case we need not consider.

The reasons for this construction seem decisive to a majority of the court, when they consider the grave questions which would arise as to the constitutionality of the clause if it were construed the other way.

Section 13 of the act of 1887, by implication, declares horses with the glanders to be nuisances, and we assume in favor of the defendant that it may do so constitutionally, and may authorize them to be killed without compensation to the owners. But the statute does not declare all horses to be nuisances, and the question is, whether, if the owner of the horse denies that his horse falls within the class declared to be so, the Legislature can make the *ex parte* decision of a board like this conclusive upon him. That question is answered by the decision in *Fisher* v. *McGirr*, 1 Gray 1. It is decided there that the owner has a right to be heard, and, further, that only a trial by jury satisfies the provision of Article XII of the Declaration of Rights, that no subject shall be deprived of his property but by the judgment of his peers, or the law of the land.

In *Belcher* v. *Farrar*, 8 Allen 325, 328, it was said: "It would violate one of the fundamental principles of justice to deprive a party absolutely of the free use and enjoyment of his estate under an allegation that the purpose to which it was appropriated, or the mode of its occupation, was injurious to the health and comfort of others, and created a nuisance, without giving the owner an opportunity to appear and disprove the allegation, and protect his property from the restraint to which it was proposed to subject it." See also *Sawyer* v. *State Board of Health*, 125 Mass. 182; *Winthrop* v. *Farrar*, 11 Allen 398. Of course there cannot be a trial by jury before killing an animal supposed to have a contagious disease, and we assume that the Legislature may authorize its destruction in such emergencies without a hearing beforehand. But it does not follow that it can throw the loss on the owner without a hearing. If he cannot be heard beforehand, he may be heard afterward. The statute may provide for paying him in case it should appear that his property was not what the Legislature has declared to be a nuisance, and may give him his hearing in that way. If it does not do so, the statute may leave those who act under it to proceed at their peril, and the owner gets his hearing in an action against them.

An illustration, although not strictly an instance, of the former mode may be found in the statute authorizing fire-wards or engineers of fire departments to order houses to be pulled down in order to prevent the spreading of a fire, and making the town answerable to the house owner, except in certain cases in which the house is practically worthless because it would have been burned if it had not been destroyed. Pub. Sts. c. 35, §3–5. No doubt the order would be conclusive in its legislative capacity, or "so far as the *res* is concerned," as is said in *Salem* v. *Eastern Railroad*, 98 Mass. 431, 449, that is to say, that the house should be pulled down. But the owner is preserved his right to a hearing in a subsequent proceeding for compensation. On the other hand, a case where a party proceeds at his peril is when he pulls down a house for the same object without the authority of statute. It is said that if the destruction is necessary he is not liable. But by the common law as understood in this Commonwealth, "if there be no necessity, then the individuals who do the act shall be responsible." *Shaw*, C. J., in *Taylor* v. *Plymouth*, 8 Met. 462, 465. *Philadelphia* v. *Scott*, 81 Penn. St. 80, 87. See *Mitchell* v. *Harmony*, 13 HOW 115, 134, 135, 14 L. Ed. 75. This means that the determination of the individual is subject to revision by a jury in an action, and is not conclusive on the owner of the house.

So in *Blair* v. *Forehand*, 100 Mass. 136, where it was held that a statute might constitutionally authorize the killing of unlicensed dogs as nuisances, it was assumed, at page 143, that the question whether the particular dog killed was unlicensed was open in an action against the officer who killed it, and that if he killed a licensed dog he would be liable in tort; in other words, that he proceeded in that respect at his own risk, citing *Shaw*, C. J., in *Tower* v. *Tower*, 18 Pick. 262. It could have made no difference in that case if a board of three had been required to decide *ex parte* beforehand whether the dog was licensed.

In *Salem* v. *Eastern Railroad*, 98 Mass. 431, it was decided, in agreement with the views which we have expressed, that the decision of a board of health that a nuisance existed on certain premises, and the order of the board that it be removed at the expense of the owner, were not conclusive upon the owner in a subsequent action against him to recover the expense, he having had no notice or opportunity to be heard. The general rule is, that a judgment *in rem*, even when rendered by a regularly constituted court after the fullest and most formal trial, is not conclusive of the facts on which it proceeds against persons not entitled to be heard and not heard in fact, although, if the court has jurisdiction, the judgment does change or establish the status it deals with as against all the world, from the necessities of the case, and frequently by express legislation.

It is true that it is said in *Salem* v. *Eastern Railroad* that the board's determination of questions of discretion and judgment in the discharge of their duties would protect all those employed to carry such determinations into effect. The remark is *obiter*, and it is doubtful perhaps, on reading the whole case, whether it means that the determination would protect them in an action for damages, when the statute provides no compensation for property taken which is not a nuisance....We are not prepared to admit that a condemnation by the present board under §13 could be made conclusive in the present action of the fact that the plaintiff's horse had the glanders.

But we are led by the dictum in *Salem* v. *Eastern Railroad* to consider another possible suggestion. It may be said, suppose that the decision of the board is not conclusive that the plaintiff's horse had the glanders, still the Legislature may consider that self-protection requires the immediate killing of all horses which a competent board deem infected, whether they are so or not, and, if so, the innocent horses that are killed are a sacrifice to necessary self-protection, and need not be paid for.

In *Train* v. *Boston Disinfecting Co.* 144 Mass. 523, 11 N.E. 929, it was held that all imported rags might be required to be put through a disinfecting process at the expense of the owner. Of course, the order did not mean that the Legislature or board of health declared all imported rags to be infected, but simply that the danger was too great to risk an attempt at discrimination. If the Legislature could throw the burden on owners of innocent rags in that case, why could it not throw the burden on the owners of innocent horses in this? If it could order all rags to be disinfected, why might it not have ordered such rags to be disinfected as a board of three should determine, summarily, and without notice or appeal? The latter provision would have been more favorable to owners, as they would have had a chance at least of escaping the burden, and it would stand on the same ground as the severer law.

The answer, or a part of it, is this. Whether the motives of the Legislature are the same or not in the two cases supposed, it declares different things to be dangerous and nuisances unless disinfected. In the one it declares all imported rags to be so; in the other, only all infected rags. Within limits it may thus enlarge or diminish the number of things to be deemed nuisances by the law, and courts cannot inquire why it includes certain property, and whether the motive was to avoid an investigation. But wherever it draws the line, an owner has a right to a hearing on the question whether his property falls within it, and this right is not destroyed by the fact that the line might have been drawn so differently as unquestionably to include that property. Thus, in the first case, the owner has a right to try the question whether his rags were imported; in the second, whether they were infected. His right is no more met in the second case by the fact that the Legislature might have made the inquiry immaterial by requiring all imported rags to be disinfected, than it would be in the first by the suggestion that possibly the Legislature might require all rags to be put through the same process, whether imported or not. But if the property is admitted to fall within the line, there is nothing to try, provided the line drawn is a valid one under the police power. All that *Train* v. *Boston Disinfecting Co.* decided was that the line there considered was a valid one.

Still it may be asked, if self-protection required the act, why should not the owner bear the loss? It may be answered, that self-protection does not require all that is believed to be necessary to that end, or even all that reasonably is believed to be necessary to that end. It only requires what is actually necessary. It would seem doubtful, at least, whether actual necessity ought not to be the limit when the question arises under the Constitution between the public and an individual. Such seems to be the law as between private parties in this Commonwealth in the case of fires, as we have seen. It could not be assumed as a general principle, without discussion, that even necessity would exonerate a party from civil liability for a loss inflicted knowingly upon an innocent person, who neither by his person nor by his property threatens any harm to the defendant. It has been thought by great lawyers that a man cannot shift his misfortunes upon his neighbor's shoulders in that way when it is a question of damages, although his act may be one for which he would not be punished. *Gilbert* v. *Stone*, Aleyn, 35; *S. C.* Style, 72. *Scott* v. *Shepherd*, 2 W. Bl. 892, 896. See *Fairbanks* v. *Snow*, 145 Mass. 153, 155, 13 N.E. 596. Upon this we express no opinion.

It is enough to say, that in this case actual necessity required the destruction only of infected horses, and that was all that the Legislature purported to authorize. Again, there is a pretty important difference of degree, at least, (*Rideout* v. *Knox*, 148 Mass. 368, 372, 19 N.E. 390,) between regulating the precautions to be taken in keeping property, especially property sought to be brought into the State, and ordering its destruction. We cannot admit that the Legislature has an unlimited right to destroy property without compensation, on the ground that destruction is not an appropriation to public use within Article X. of the Declaration of Rights. When a healthy horse is killed by a public officer, acting under a general statute, for fear that it should spread disease, the horse certainly would seem to be taken for public use, as truly as if it were seized to drag an artillery wagon. The public equally appropriate it, whatever they do with it afterwards. Certainly the Legislature could not declare all cattle to be nuisances, and order them to be killed without compensation. *Watertown* v. *Mayo*, 109 Mass. 315, 319. *In re Jacobs*, 98 N.Y. 98, 109. It does not attempt to do so. As we have said, it only declares certain diseased animals to be nuisances. And even if we assume that it could authorize some trifling amount of innocent property to be destroyed as a necessary means to the abatement of a nuisance, still, if in this §13 it had added in terms that such healthy animals as should be killed by mistake for diseased ones should not be paid for, we should deem it a serious question whether such a provision could be upheld.

For these reasons, the literal, and as we think the true construction of §13, seems to us the only safe one to adopt, and accordingly we are of opinion that the authority and jurisdiction of the commissioners to condemn the plaintiff's horse under §13 was conditional upon its actually having the glanders. If this be so, their order would not protect the defendants in a case where the commissioners acted outside their jurisdiction. *Fisher* v. *McGirr*, 1 Gray 1, 45. The fact as to the horse having the disease was open to investigation in the present action, and on the finding that the horse did not have it, the plaintiff was entitled to a ruling that the defendants had failed to make out their justification.

In view of our conclusion upon the main question, we have not considered whether an order signed by two members of the board, upon an examination by one, satisfies the statute, or whether cases like *Ruggles* v. *Nantucket*, 11 Cush. 433, and *Parsons* v. *Pettingell*, 11 Allen 507, apply.

Exceptions sustained.

DISSENT: Devens, J.

I am unable to concur in the opinion of the majority of the court in the narrow and limited construction which they give to §13 of chapter 252 of the Acts of 1887, or in the view expressed of its constitutionality if otherwise construed. That construction holds that no power or jurisdiction was conferred upon the commissioners to order the killing of an animal which they adjudged to be affected by the farcy or glanders unless the same was actually thus infected. It would therefore follow, that in a subsequent proceeding, as in an action against the person who executed the order of the commissioners, if it were shown to the satisfaction of a jury that the animal was not thus diseased, the owner of the animal would be entitled to recover its value in damages. In §12 of the same chapter provision is made for the killing of certain animals upon the order of the commissioners, who are directed to have the same appraised at their fair value, except as provided for in §13, and provision is made for the payment thereof. The animals affected by the farcy or glanders, described in §13, when condemned by the commissioners as such, are to be killed without appraisal; no provision is made for payment therefor, although it is made for the expense of killing. When the two sections are read together, the fair result appears to be that it was the intention of the Legislature that the right of any servant or agent whom the commissioners employ should rest, not on the fact that the animal is actually affected by the glanders, but upon this condemnation. The constitutionality of the act must, therefore, be discussed.

The distinction between the exercise of the right of eminent domain and the power to make police regulations, by virtue of which the uses of property may be limited and controlled to the pecuniary disadvantage of the owner, or even property itself destroyed, is well recognized. Where property is appropriated to the public use, provision must be made for compensation to the owner. Declaration of Rights, Article X. But laws passed in the lawful exercise of the police power are not made unconstitutional because no provision is made for compensation to the individual whose property may be affected thereby. They are passed for the protection of the community against the ravages of fire, the spreading of pestilence, and the prevention of other serious calamities; and such property is not taken for any use by the public, within the meaning of the Constitution. The regulations in regard to quarantine, health, fire, and the laws for the abatement of existing and preservation of threatened nuisances, are instances of the exercise of this power. *Bancroft* v. *Cambridge*, 126 Mass. 438, and authorities cited. Their validity rests upon the necessity of providing for the public safety, and the individual is presumed to be compensated by the benefit which such regulations confer upon the community of which he is a member, or by which his property is protected. It is for the Legislature ordinarily to determine how, when, and through whom this police power is to be exercised, and all rights of property are held subject to such reasonable control as it may deem necessary for the prevention of injury to the rights of others, or for the protection of the public health and welfare. "In the exercise of this power," says Mr. Justice Gray "the Legislature may not only provide that certain kinds of property (either absolutely, or when held in such manner or under such circumstances as to be injurious, dangerous, or noxious) may be seized and confiscated upon legal process after notice and hearing; but may also, when necessary to insure the public safety, authorize them to be summarily destroyed by the municipal authorities without previous notice to the owner,—as in the familiar cases of pulling down buildings to prevent the spreading of a conflagration or the impending fall of the buildings themselves, throwing overboard decaying or infected food, or abating other nuisances dangerous to health." *Blair* v. *Forehand*, 100 Mass. 136, 139, and authorities. In that case it was held that a law by which any person was permitted to kill an unlicensed dog without any previous adjudication, was within the constitutional authority of the Legislature; and, while dogs have sometimes been said to be entitled to less protection than more necessary domestic animals, they are certainly entitled to as much as a horse sick with an infectious disease, which was alleged to be the animal destroyed by the defendants.

In the case at bar, the animal was killed after an adjudication by the cattle commissioners, by which it was determined that it was affected with the contagious disease known as the glanders, and no provision having been made by the law for payment to the owner in such case, it is contended that the law is wholly unconstitutional; and further, that, even if it should be held constitutional so far as it relates to animals actually infected with this disease, the plaintiff is entitled to show as against these defendants that the animal was not so infected, and to recover from them the value of the animal by reason of the fact that they executed the order of the commissioners.

The contention that the law is unconstitutional so far as animals actually infected are concerned cannot be maintained, unless it is true that every police regulation affecting the use of property or authorizing the destruction of property as dangerous to the community is unconstitutional except when it provides for payment to the owner. The law is a police regulation; the adjudication was made by a tribunal acting quasi judicially, of the same general character as boards of health, to which large powers have always been confided for the abatement of nuisances and the protection of the public health. It was for the Legislature to determine a particular disease to be such that the existence of the animal would be dangerous to public health; and the authorities are numerous and decisive, that for injuries to or diminution of value of property by reason of the operation of a police regulation the owner is not entitled to demand compensation. *Baker* v. *Boston*, 12 Pick. 184. *Belcher* v. *Farrar*, 8 Allen 325. *Bergin* v. *Hayward*, 102 Mass. 414. *Salem* v. *Eastern Railroad*, 98 Mass. 431. *Taunton* v. *Taylor*, 116 Mass. 254.

In regard to the plaintiff's second contention, it would perhaps be sufficient to say that the defendants acted by direction of a body to which the Legislature lawfully could and did confide the power of deciding whether the animal in question was affected with disease. As an officer is protected by his warrant if it issue from a court having jurisdiction, no matter what previous errors may have been made which led to the issuance of it, so the defendants, who simply executed the decree of a tribunal which was competent to deal with the subject and which the Legislature had created, cannot be made responsible for any error committed by it in its adjudication. *Chase* v. *Ingalls*, 97 Mass. 524. But as I am of opinion that the decision of the commissioners is conclusive, and can lawfully be made conclusive by the Legislature, it would be preferable to state briefly the reasons for this view.

The most frequent application of the police power is in the abatement of nuisances by the intervention of boards of health and similar tribunals. It cannot make any material difference that in these cases property is not always destroyed, and that more frequently the cases are those in which its uses are limited, or particular uses forbidden.

From the nature of the case...the *res* is an alleged "nuisance, source of filth, or cause of sickness," as an embankment by which running waters are stopped and filth accumulated, or like infected clothes from persons diseased, or rotting and putrescent meats on shipboard or in warehouses, or animals afflicted with contagious diseases, and many other noxious objects, action by boards of health must be prompt and summary. Powers to determine whether these objects should be removed or destroyed are undoubtedly very high powers, and they must of necessity be confided to boards of administration in order that the public safety may be guarded. Although of a quasi judicial nature, they must be exercised often without the delays which necessarily attend formal notices and formal trials; and where adjudications are fairly and honestly made, even if mistakes may sometimes occur, they should be held conclusive so far as the *res* with which they deal is concerned. Certainly no one would voluntarily undertake the heavy responsibilities of a board of health, or, as in the case at bar, of the cattle commissioners, if they were to be made responsible in damages for errors of judgment which they might commit. "Their determination," says Mr. Justice Wells, in speaking of the proceedings of boards of health, "of questions of discretion and judgment in the discharge of their duties is undoubtedly in the nature of a judicial decision; and, within the scope of the power conferred, and for the purposes for which the determination is required to be made, it is conclusive. It is not to be impeached or set aside for error or mistake of judgment; nor to be reviewed in the light of new or additional facts. The officer or board to whom such determination is confided, and all those employed to carry it into effect, or who may have occasion to act upon it, are protected by it, and may safely rely upon its validity for their defence. It is in this sense that such adjudications are often said to be conclusive against all the world; and they are so, so far as the *res* is concerned. The statute and the public exigency are sufficient to justify the omission of previous notice, hearing, and appeal." In those provisions of the statute...no provision is made for any appeal from the decision of the board of health adjudicating any objects to be nuisances, sources of filth, or causes of sickness, and ordering the removal or destruction of the same, including, when their order is not complied with, the removing or destroying the same themselves, nor for any compensation to those who may thus lose valuable private rights.....

They are the selectmen and board of health of the town of Rehoboth, whose duty it is to carry out the lawful regulations of the commissioners. The order addressed to them as such board of health is actually signed by a majority of the commissioners. It purports to state their examination of the animal, their adjudication that it had the contagious disease known as the glanders, their condemnation of it, and their direction that it should be killed forthwith. An order issued by the commissioners in a matter of which they had lawful jurisdiction would protect the defendants in the performance of it, even if its recitals were not in fact true.

FEDERALISM AND BIODEFENSE

Miller v. Schoene
276 U.S. 272 (1928)

Opinion by Justice Stone:

Acting under the Cedar Rust Act of Virginia, state entomologist ordered the plaintiffs in error to cut down a large number of ornamental red cedar trees growing on their property, as a means of preventing the communication of a rust or plant disease with which they were infected to the apple orchards in the vicinity. The plaintiffs in err [paid] $100 to cover the expense of removal of the cedars. Neither the judgment of the court nor the statute as interpreted allows compensation for the value of the standing cedars or the decrease in the market value of the realty caused by their destruction whether considered as ornamental trees or otherwise...

[Cedar] rust is an infectious plant disease in the form of a fungoid organism which is destructive of the fruit and foliage of the apple, but without effect on the value of the cedar. Its life cycle has two phases which are passed alternately as a growth on red cedar and on apple trees. It is communicated by spores from one to the other over a radius of at least two miles. It appears not to be communicable between trees of the same species but only from one species to the other, and other plants seem not to be appreciably affected by it. The only practicable method of controlling the disease and protecting apple trees from its ravages is the destruction of all red cedar trees, subject to the infection, located within two miles of apple orchards.

The red cedar, aside from its ornamental use, has occasional use and value as lumber. It is indigenous to Virginia, is not cultivated or dealt in commercially on any substantial scale, and its value throughout the state is shown to be small as compared with that of the apple orchards of the state. Apple growing is one of the principal agricultural pursuits in Virginia. The apple is used there and exported in large quantities. Many millions of dollars are invested in the orchards, which furnish employment for a large portion of the population, and have induced the development of attendant railroad and cold storage facilities.

On the evidence we may accept the conclusion of the Supreme Court of Appeals that the state was under the necessity of making a choice between the preservation of one class of property and that of the other wherever both existed in dangerous proximity. It would have been none the less a choice if, instead of enacting the present statute, the state, by doing nothing, had permitted serious injury to the apple orchards within its borders to go on unchecked. When forced to such a choice the state does not exceed its constitutional powers by deciding upon the destruction of one class of property in order to save another which, in the judgment of the legislature, is of greater value to the public. It will not do to say that the case is merely one of a conflict of two private interests and that the misfortune of apple growers may not be shifted to cedar owners by ordering the destruction of their property; for it is obvious that there may be, and that here there is, a preponderant public concern in the preservation of the one interest over the other. [Where] the public interest is involved preferment of that interest over the property interest of the individual, to the extent even of its destruction, is one of the distinguishing characteristics of every exercise of the police power which affects property.

We need not weigh with nicety the question whether the infected cedars constitute a nuisance according to the common law; or whether they may be so declared by statute. For where, as here, the choice is unavoidable, we cannot say that its exercise, controlled by considerations of social policy which are not unreasonable, involves any denial of due process.

[Case reversed.]

3.10. Statutory Requirements
Americans with Disabilities Act

The Americans with Disabilities Act includes communicable diseases and the protection against the prejudices and disabilities associated with them. The social stigma attached to diseases such as HIV or latent TB may be more disabling than the diseases themselves.

In *City of Newark v. J.S.*, (N.J. 1993), the Americans with Disabilities Act of 1990 (ADA), 42 U.S.C.S. §12101–12213 is a remedial statute intended to eliminate a long history of discrimination. Persons with HIV, alcoholism, epilepsy, and emotional illness are disabilities under the Act, in part because there are unfounded myths associated with those conditions. While a person currently using illegal drugs is not "disabled," once in a rehabilitation program or once rehabilitated, he or she is covered under the ADA. 42 U.S.C.A. §12114; 28 C.F.R. §35.131(a)(2)(i)–(iii)(1993). A person is covered if that person has a "record" of or is "regarded" as being disabled, even if there is no actual disability. 42 U.S.C.A. §12102(2)(B) and (C). Thus, a person who has no clinical symptoms but is discriminated against because of latent TB is nonetheless protected by the ADA. *School Board of Nassau County, Florida v. Arline*, 480 U.S. 273 at 281 (1987). In *City of Newark*, the court required that the most extreme confinement for a homeless individual with tuberculosis (TB) include a determination that due process requirements and the Americans with Disabilities Act of 1990 (ADA), 42 U.S.C.S. §12101–12213 standards were met. The ADA requires an evaluation of the nature of the risk, which in this case was based upon how TB was transmitted, the duration of the risk as to how long the defendant was infectious, the severity of the risk of potential harm to third parties, and the probability the disease would be transmitted.

CHAPTER THREE ENDNOTES

[1] *The Washington Post* A11 (Tues., Oct. 23, 2001)..

[2] (http://www.ncsl. org/programs/press/2001/freedom/bioterrorism01.htm).

[3] Bioterrorism may be defined as an overt release of a biological agent which is calculated to expose populations which result in immediate or delayed mortality or morbidity.

[4] *See* Victoria Sutton, "A Precarious 'Hot Zone'—The President's Plan to Combat Bioterrorism", 164 Mil. Law Rev. 135 (Spring 2000).

[5] The Supreme Court has found that federal environmental laws may preempt state law, but only so long as the federal government has authority to regulate under the Commerce Clause, *New York v. United States*, 505 U.S. 144, 167–168 (1992).

[6] See, Stephen Gardbaum, "The Nature of Preemption," 79 Cornell L. Rev. 767 (1994), "the most common and consequential error is the belief that Congress's power of preemption is closely and essentially connected to the Supremacy Clause" rather than the necessary and proper clause."

[7] James G. Hodge, Jr., J.D., LLM., "Implementing Modern Public Health Goals Through Government: An Examination of New Federalism and Public Health Law," 14 J. Contemp. JH.L. & Pol. 93 (Fall 1997).

[8] U.S. Const. Art. I, Sec. 10, Cl. 3, "No state shall, without the Consent of Congress, lay any duty of Tonnage, keep Troops, or Ships of War in time of Peace, enter into any Agreement or Compact with another State, or with a foreign Power, or engage in War, unless actually invaded, or in such imminent Danger as will not admit of delay."

[9] 22 U.S. 1 (1824).

[10] The Federalist No. 84, 511 (Alexander Hamilton)(Clifford Rossiter ed. 1961).

[11] The Federalist No. 44. 293 (James Madison)(Clifford Rossiter ed. 1961).

[12] David Satcher, M.D., Ph.D., "The History of the Public Health Service and the Surgeon General's Priorities," 54 Food Drug L.J. 13, 17 (1999).

13 The "germ theory" was not among the new knowledge, sweeping in during the Enlightenment era; however, the use of biological warfare should not have been unknown to the Founders. As early as 1385, the practice of catapulting the corpses of plague victims and the carcasses of diseased animals into cities under attack was in use. [Quoting Robert O-Connell, *Of Arms and Men: A History of War, Weapons, and Aggression* 171 (1989), in Ward Churchill, *A Little Matter of Genocide—Holocaust and Denial in the Americas 1492 to the Present* 151–152 (1997).] Clearly, at least a crude notion of how epidemiology works was known at that time. In 1663, Captain John Oldham, a diplomat for Massachusetts Colony, was believed to have deliberately infected the Narragansett Indians by gifting them with contaminated blankets. [Quoting Robert O-Connell, *Of Arms and Men: A History of War, Weapons, and Aggression* 171 (1989), in Ward Churchill, *A Little Matter of Genocide—Holocaust and Denial in the Americas 1492 to the Present* 152 (1997).] In 1763, the Founding Fathers must have certainly known about Lord Jeffrey Amherst's attempt at genocide when he ordered smallpox-infected blankets to be passed out to the Ottawa and Lenni Lanape Indians in order to accomplish his own quoted goal to 'extirpate this execrable race.' [See John Duffy, *Epidemics in Colonial America* (1953); E. Wagner Stearn and Allen E. Stearn, *The Effects of Smallpox on the Destiny of the Amerindian* (1945), footnoted in Ward Churchill, *A Little Matter of Genocide—Holocaust and Denial in the Americas 1492 to the Present* 153 (1997).] Whether the Founders contemplated the use of contagion as a possible threat to other than the American Indians is not clear.

14 The Federalist No. 44, 293 (James Madison)(Clifford Rossiter ed. 1961).

15 *Id.*

16 *Id.*

17 *Id.*

18 *Id.*

19 The Federalist No. 41, 257 (James Madison)(Clifford Rossiter ed. 1961).

20 *Id.*

21 *Id.*

22 *In re Caselli*, 204 P. 364, 364 (1922).

23 *Id.*

24 The Federalist No. 41, 258 (James Madison)(Clifford Rossiter ed. 1961).

25 Bernard Bailyn, et. al., *The Great Republic—A History of the American People* 306 4th ed. (1992). Rebellions, internal attacks and political factions forming threats to the new nation were probably freshly on the mind of Madison in 1787–1788, and with good reason. In 1787, in western Massachusetts, a group of farmers, unhappy with a threatened mass foreclosure of their farms, known as the Shays Rebellion, temporarily closed the courts and threatened a federal installation during the insurrection.

26 Exigency does not necessarily mean emergency, but rather urgency.

27 The Federalist No. 44, 288 (James Madison)(Clifford Rossiter ed. 1961), "The question, therefore, whether this amount of power shall be granted or not resolves itself into another question, whether or not a government commensurate to the exigencies of the Union shall be established; or in other words, whether the Union itself shall be preserved."

28 *Id.*

29 The Federalist No. 25, 164–165 (Alexander Hamilton)(Clifford Rossiter ed. 1961).

30 The Federalist No. 25, 165 (Alexander Hamilton)(Clifford Rossiter ed. 1961). The full quotation reads: "If, to obviate this consequence, it should be resolved to extend the prohibition to the raising of armies in

time of peace, the United States would then exhibit the most extraordinary spectacle which the world has yet seen—that of a nation incapacitated by its Constitution to prepare for defense before it was actually invaded."

31 *Id.*

32 The Federalist No. 25, 165 (Alexander Hamilton)(Clifford Rossiter ed. 1961).

33 *Id.*

34 *Id.*

35 *Id.*

36 *Jacobson v. Massachusetts*, 197 U.S. 11 (1905).

37 The Federalist No. 46, 298 (James Madison)(Clifford Rossiter ed. 1961).

38 The Federalist No. 46, 295 (James Madison)(Clifford Rossiter ed. 1961).

39 The Federalist No. 44, 288 (James Madison)(Clifford Rossiter ed. 1961).

40 The Federalist No. 84, 511 (Alexander Hamilton)(Clifford Rossiter ed. 1961).

41 U.S. Const. §9, cl. 2.

42 *Ex parte Martin*, 188 P.2d 287 (Cal. App. 1948).

43 U.S. Const. Amend. V.

44 The Federalist No. 25, 164 (Alexander Hamilton) (Clifford Rossiter ed. 1961).

45 The Federalist No. 44, 288 (James Madison)(Clifford Rossiter ed. 1961).

46 U.S. Const. Art. I, Sec. 8, Cl. 1, "The Congress shall have the Power To lay and collect Taxes, Duties, Imposts and Excises, to pay the Debts and provide for the common Defense and general welfare of the United States..."

47 The Federalist No. 41, 262–263, "It has been urged and echoed that the power 'to lay and collect taxes, duties, imposts, and excises, to pay the debts, and provide for the common defense and general welfare of the United States,' amounts to an unlimited commission to exercise every power which may be alleged to be necessary for the common defense or general welfare...Nothing is more natural nor common than first to use a general phrase, and then to explain nor qualify the general meaning and can have no other effect than to confound or mislead, is an absurdity..."

48 Lawrence O. Gostin, Symposium: Securing Health or Just Health Care? The Effect of the Health Care system on the Health of America, 39 St. Louis U.L.J. 7, 12 (1994).

49 U.S. Const., Amend X., "...Powers not delegated to the US by the constitution; nor prohibited by it to the States, are reserved to the States respectively, or to the people."

50 *Medtronic, Inc. v. Lohr*, 116 S. Ct. 2240, 2245 (1996).

51 20 Stat. 37 (1878).

52 David Satcher, M.D., Ph.D., "The History of the Public Health Service and the Surgeon General's Priorities," 54 Food Drug L.J. 13, 14 (1999).

53 452 U.S. 264 (1981).

54 469 U.S. 528 (1985).

55 426 U.S. 833 (1976).

56 The dissent wrote, "With the abandonment of *National League of Cities*, all that stands between the remaining essentials of state sovereignty and Congress is the latter's underdeveloped capacity for self-restraint."

---

[57] 469 U.S. 528 at ___ (1985).

[58] 505 U.S. 144 (1992).

[59] *New York v. United States*, 505 U.S. 144 (1992).

[60] 461 U.S. 190 (1983).

[61] *Id.*

[62] Robert Cushman, "The National Police Power Under the Commerce Clause of the Constitution," 3 Minn. L.Rev. 289, 290 (1919).

[63] 227 U.S. 308 (1913).

[64] The Mann Act prohibits the transportation of females across state lines for immoral purposes.

[65] Police powers include those regulating safety, health and welfare.

[66] 227 U.S. 308 (1913).

[67] James A. Tobey, Public Health and the Police Power, 4 N.Y.U. L. Rev. 126 (1927).

[68] 514 U.S. 549 (1995).

[69] *Solid Waste Agency of Northern Cook County v. United States Army Corp of Engineers*, 148 L.Ed.2d 576 (2001).

[70] *See e.g., Rice v. Santa Fe Elevator Corp.* 331 U.S. 216 (1947).

[71] *See Maryland v. Louisiana*, 451 U.S. 725 (1981); *New York State Conf. Of Blue Cross & Blue Shield Plans v. Travelers Ins. Co.*, 514 U.S. 645, 653 (1995).

[72] See *Fidelity Fed. Sav. And Loan Assn. V. De la Cuesta*, 458 U.S. 141 (1982), quoting *Rice v. Santa Fe Elevator Corp.*, 331 U.S. 218, 230 (1947); *Jones v. Rath Packing Co.*, 430 U.S. 519, 526 (1977).

[73] *See Vermont Yankee Nuclear Power Corp. v. Natural Resources Defense Council, Inc.*, 435 U.S. 519 (1978). Congress could decide to preempt the field but it should not be in an area of safety. Even in the area of nuclear power, the courts have held that Congress has preempted the field in nuclear power, but *not* in the area of nuclear safety where the concerns of the states' citizens are at issue.

[74] 227 U.S. 308 (1913).

[75] The Federalist No. 44, 288 (James Madison)(Clifford Rossiter ed. 1961).

[76] 32 C.F.R. 215.4(c)(1)(i). The emergency power: authorizes prompt and vigorous federal action, including use of military forces, to prevent loss of life or wanton destruction of property and to restore governmental functioning and public order when sudden and unexpected civil disturbances, disasters, or calamities seriously endanger life and property and disrupt normal governmental functions to such an extent that duly constituted local authorities are unable to control the situations.

[77] 10 U.S.C. §331 (implementing U.S. Const. art. IV, §4).

[78] 10 U.S.C. §332 (implementing U.S. Const. Art. II, §3).

[79] 10 U.S.C. §333 (implementing U.S. Const. Art., II, §3 & U.S. Const. Amend. XIV).

[80] 18 U.S.C. §3056

[81] U.S. Const. art. I, §8, cl. 15.

[82] *A Failure of Initiative: Final Report of the Select Bipartisan Committee to Investigate the Preparation for and Response to Hurricane Katrina*, http://www.gpoaccess.gov/serialset/creports/katrina.html.

[83] John Warner National Defense Authorization Act for Fiscal Year 2007 §1076(a)(1), 120 Stat. 2404-05 (amending 10 U.S.C. §333).

[84] *Governors Association Opposes Senate Authorization Measure*, Inside the Army, Sept. 4, 2006, at 35

[85] Press Release, FEMA, *Joint State/Federal Transportation Exercise Tests Response Plans* (May 5, 2005), available at http://www.fema.gov/news/newsrelease.fema?id=17420.

[86] U.S. Dep't of Homeland Sec., *National Response Plan* (Dec. 2004), available athttp://www.dhs.gov/xlibrary/assets/NRPbaseplan.pdf.

[87] http://www.progressive.org/images/pdf/1179.pdf.

[88] Smolla and Nimmer, Supra, at § 15: 21 (citing Franklyn Haim, Speech and Law in a Free Society 399-404 (1981)).

[89] *Progressive, Inc.*, 467 F. Supp. at 993.

[90] *Id.*

[91] *Id.*

[92] *Id.*

[93] Smolla and Nimmer, Supra, at § 15:21.

[94] 42 U.S.C. § 2011

[95] Smollla and Nimmer, *Supra*, at § 15:21.

[96] Brian Rappert, University of Exeter, Malcolm Dando, University of Bradford, *No Easy Answers: Balancing Security and Openness in Civilian Research* , (March 28, 2006) (report by Marilynn Larkin available at http://www.nyas.org/ebrief/miniEB.asp?ebriefID=531).

[97] *Id.*

[98] *Id.*

[99] *Id.*

[100] *Id.*

[101] Committee on Research Standards and Practices to Prevent the Destructive Application of Biotechnology, National Research Council, *Biotechnology Research in an Age of Terrorism: Executive Summary* 8 (2004).

[102] http://news.sciencemag.org/people-events/2012/03/breaking-news-nsabb-reverses-position-flu-papers .

[103] *Schenck*, 249 U.S. at 49

[104] 40 Stat. 217

[105] *Schenck*, 249 U.S. at 49.

[106] *Id.* at 52.

[107] *Id.*

[108] *Id.* (stating that the Act in § 4 punishes conspiracies to obstruct as well as actual obstruction).

[109] *See Id.*

[110] *See Id.*

[111] *Terminiello*, 337 U.S. at 4 ("freedom of speech is protected against censorship or punishment, unless shown likely to produce a clear and present danger..."); *Arcara v. Cloud Books, Inc.* 503 N.E.2d 492, 495, 68 N.Y.2d 553, 558, 510 N.Y.S.2d 844, 847 (N.Y. 1986) ("the government may not impose a prior restraint on freedom of expression to silence an unpopular view, absent a showing on the record that such expression will immediately and irreparably create public injury.");

[112] Tom Hentoff, Speech, Harm, and Self-Government: Understanding the Ambit of the Clear and Present Danger Test, 91 Colum. L. Rev. 1453, 1456 (1991) (stating that the clear and present danger doctrine has gone through three phases, and that the current reading of the clear and present danger doctrine is from *Brandenburg v. Ohio*, 395 U.S. 44 (1969)).

[113] Michael J. Mannheimer, The Fighting Words Doctrine, 93 Colum. L. Rev. 1527 (October 1993).

[114] *Supra* note 85, at 1531.

[115] *Supra* note 85, at 1531.

[116] *Supra* note 84, at 1457.

---

[117] *Supra* note 84, at 1457.

[118] *Supra* note 84, at 1458.

[119] *Supra* note 84, at 1458-1459.

[120] *See Supra* note 34, at 10:1-10:

[121] Smolla and Nimmer, *Supra*, at § 15:12.

[122] *Near*, 283 U.S. at 701.

[123] *Id.* at 704.

[124] *Id.* at 722-723.

[125] *Id.* at 715-716.

[126] Smolla and Nimmer, *Supra*, at § 15:12

[127] Smolla and Nimmer, *Supra*, at § 15: 13

[128] *New York Times Co.*, 403 U.S. at 714; Smolla and Nimmer, *Supra*, at § 15:14

[129] Smolla and Nimmer, *Supra*, at § 15:14

[130] *New York Times Co.*, 403 U.S. at 714.

[131] *Id.* (citing *State v. Haley*, 687 P.2d 305 (Alaska 1984); *Des Moines Register & Tribune Co. v. Osmundson*, 248 N.W.2d 493 (Iowa 1976); *State v. A Motion Picture Entitled "The Bet"*, 219 Kan. 64, 547 P.2d 760 (1976); *Cherne Indus., Inc. v. Grounds & Associates, Inc.*, 278 N.W.2d 81 (Minn. 1979); *City of Lincoln v. ABC Books, Inc.*, 238 Neb. 378, 470 N.W.2d 760 (1991); *In re Initiative Petition No. 341, State Question No. 627*, 1990 OK 53, 796 P.2d 267 (Okla. 1990); *In re Marriage of Suggs*, 152 Wash. 2d 74, 93 P.3d 161 (2004), as amended on denial of reconsideration, (Nov. 2, 2004).

[132] *State v. Kelly*, 249 Neb. 99, 108-109, 541 N.W.2d 645, 653 (1996).

[133] *State v. Coe*, 679 P.2d 353, 350, 101 Wash. 2d. 364, 373 (Wash. 1984).

[134] 16B C.J.S. Constitutional § 808 (2007) (citing .—*State ex rel. Wampler v. Bird*, 499 S.W.2d 780 (Mo. 1973); *State v. Hanna*, 901 So. 2d 201 (Fla. Dist. Ct. App. 5th Dist. 2005)).

[135] *Id.*(citing *Paper Back Mart v. City of Anniston*, 407 F. Supp. 376 (N.D. Ala. 1976); *Murray v. Lawson*, 649 A.2d 1253, 138 N.J. 206 (1994)).

[136] *Paper Back Mart*, 407 F. Supp. at 378.

[137] *Murray*, 649 A.2d at 223. (citing Laurence E. Tribe, *American Constitutional Law* § 12-36 at 1051 (2ed. 1988)).

[138] Smolla and Nimmer, *Supra*, at § 15:8.

[139] *Soutneastern Promotions, Ltd.* at 558 (citing *Bantam Books, Inc. v. Sullivan*, 372 U.S. 58, 70 n. 10 (1963)); *Nebraska Press Assn' v. Stuart*, 427 U.S. 539, 561 (1976).

[140] *Supra* note 43. (citing *Southeastern Promotions, Ltd*, 420 U.S. at 546 (1975); *Rosen v. Port of Portland*, 641 F.2d 1243 (9th Cir. 1981); *Bernard v. Gulf Oil Co.*, 619 F.2d 459, (5th Cir. 1980), judgment aff'd, 452 U.S. 89 (1981)).

[141] *Supra* note 43 (citing *Bernard v. Gulf Oil Co.*, 619 F.2d 459 (5th Cir. 1980), judgment aff'd, 452 U.S. 89 (1981); *Rodgers v. U.S. Steel Corp.*, 536 F.2d 1001 (3d Cir. 1976); *Curran v. Price*, 638 A.2d 93, 334 Md. 149 (1994); *J.Q. Office Equipment of Omaha, Inc. v. Sullivan*, 432 N.W.2d 211, 230 Neb. 397 (1988); *State ex rel. Haas v. Dionne*, 601 P.2d 894, 42 Or. App. 851 (1979); *CBS Inc. v. Young*, 522 F.2d 234 (6th Cir. 1975); *People ex rel. Arcara v. Cloud Books, Inc.*, 503 N.E.2d 492, 68 N.Y.2d 553, 510 N.Y.S.2d 844 (1986); *J.Q. Office Equipment of Omaha, Inc. v. Sullivan*, 432 N.W.2d 211, 230 Neb. 397 (1988); *K. D. v. Educational Testing Service*, 386 N.Y.S.2d 747, 87 Misc. 2d 657 (N.Y. Sup. Ct. 1976).

[142] *Collin v. Smith*, 447 F. Supp. 676, 689 (N.D. Ill. 1978).

[143] *Lloyd Corp. Ltd. v. Tanner*, 407 U.S. 551, 567 (1972) (holding that the first and fourteenth amendments protect the rights of free speech and assembly by limitations on *state* action, not on action by the owner of private property used non-discriminatorily for private purposes only).

[144] *Veterans and Reservists for Peace in Vietnam v. Regional Commissioner*, 459 F.2d 676 (3rd 1972).

[145] *NJ Lottery Comm'n v. U.S.*, 491 F.2d 219, 222 (3rd 1974).

[146] 50 USCS Appx § 5

[147] 31 C.F.R. Part 500

[148] *Veterans and Reservists for Peace in Vietnam*, 459 F.2d 676 (3rd 1972).

[149] *Id.*at 678-679.

[150] *Id.* at 679.

[151] *Id.*

[152] *Id.* at 681.

[153] *Id.* at 681.

[154] *Id.* at 682.

[155] *Id.* at 680.

[156] *Id.* at 680.

[157] *Id.* at 681.

[158] *Id.* at 681-682.

[159] *Id* at 680, 682.

[160] *Id.* at 682-683.

[161] *See Veterans and Reservist for Peace in Vietnam,*

[162] *Id.* at 681

[163] There is no case on point which states that scientific research is protected speech, but since it does not fall under any of the categories of unprotected speech at *supra* note 51, at 689 this paper assumes that it is protected.

[164] *Id.*

[165] *See supra* note 43.

[166] *See supra* note 43 (citing *CBS v. Young*, 522 F.2d 234 (6th Cir. 1975); *K.D. v. Educational Testing Serv.*, 386 N.Y.S.2d 747, 87 Misc. 2d 657 (N.Y. Sup. Ct. 1976).

[167] *Supra* note 43 (citing *Corocan v. Quirk*, 441 N.Y.S.2d 365, 109 Misc. 2d 996 (N.Y. Sup. Ct. 1981); *Terminiello v. City of Chicago*, 337 U.S. 1(1949)).

[168] *United States v. Progressive, Inc.*, 467 F. Supp. 990 (W.D. Wis. 1979).

[169] *See* Section III.

[170] The Atomic Energy Act of 1954, 42 USCA § 2280.

[171] *Supra*, note 97, at 220.

[172] *Supra*, note 97, at 220.

[173] *Supra*, note 97, at 220.

[174] *See Supra*, note 97, at 221.

[175] *Supra*, note 97, at 221.

[176] *Supra*, note 97, at 221. ("The U.S. classification system primarily applies to work done in government laboratories or that is funded by the federal government.")

[177] *Supra*, note 97, at 221 (examples include improved prevention, diagnosis, treatment of human and animal diseases, environmental remediation, enhanced production of food and energy, etc.). *See also Supra*, note 97, at 139-197.

[178] *Supra*, note 92, at 222.

[179] *Supra*, note 97, at 223. (Stating that the classification of dual use research could lead to a "black market" that could more difficult to oversee than an open market).

[180] *Supra*, note 97, at 224. (Stating that few biological research institutions have any experience with classification schemes).

[181] *Supra*, note 97, at 225.

---

[182] *See* National Security Decision Directive-189 (Sept. 21, 1985) in Institute of Medicine and National Research Council, Globalization, Biosecurity, and The Future of Life Sciences 227 (The National Academies Press 2006).

[183] Institute of Medicine and National Research Council, *Supra* note 8, at 226.

[184] Institute of Medicine and National Research Council, *Supra* note 8, at 226.

[185] Institute of Medicine and National Research Council, *Supra* note 8, at 227.

[186] *See* National Security Decision Directive-189 (Sept. 21, 1985) in Institute of Medicine and National Research Council, *Supra* note 8, at 227.

[187] Institute of Medicine and National Research Council, *Supra* note 8, at 219.

[188] Institute of Medicine and National Research Council, *Supra* note 8, at 220.

[189] Institute of Medicine and National Research Council, *Supra* note 8, at 220.

[190] Institute of Medicine and National Research Council, *Supra* note 8, at 220.

[191] Institute of Medicine and National Research Council, *Supra* note 8, at 220.

[192] Committee on Research Standards and Practices to Prevent the Destructive Application of Biotechnology, National Research Council, *supra* note 7, at 1.

[193] Committee on Research Standards and Practices to Prevent the Destructive Application of Biotechnology, National Research Council, *supra* note 7, at 1.

[194] Committee on Research Standards and Practices to Prevent the Destructive Application of Biotechnology, National Research Council, *supra* note 7, at 2.

[195] Uniting and Strengthening America by Providing Appropriate Tools Required to Intercept and Obstruct Terrorism (USA PATRIOT Act) Act of 2001, Pub. L. No. 107-56, 115 Stat. 272 (2001) [hereinafter Patriot Act] (codified in scattered titles of U.S.C).

[196] Cite this act

[197] Committee on Research Standards and Practices to Prevent the Destructive Application of Biotechnology, National Research Council, *supra* note 7, at 2-3.

[198] Committee on Research Standards and Practices to Prevent the Destructive Application of Biotechnology, National Research Council, *supra* note 7, at 3.

[199] Committee on Research Standards and Practices to Prevent the Destructive Application of Biotechnology, National Research Council, *supra* note 7, at 3.

[200] Committee on Research Standards and Practices to Prevent the Destructive Application of Biotechnology, National Research Council, *supra* note 7, at 8.

[201] Committee on Research Standards and Practices to Prevent the Destructive Application of Biotechnology, National Research Council, *supra* note 7, at 8.

[202] Committee on Research Standards and Practices to Prevent the Destructive Application of Biotechnology, National Research Council, *supra* note 7, at 8.

[203] *Id.*

[204] Committee on Research Standards and Practices to Prevent the Destructive Application of Biotechnology, National Research Council, *supra* note 7, at 9.

[205] Revised National Science Advisory Board for Biosecurity Charter *available at* http://www.biosecurityboard.gov/index.asp (click "charter" link at top).

[206] NSABB Charter, *supra* note 20.

[207] http://www.biosecurityboard.gov/faq.asp#2

[208] http://www.biosecurityboard.gov/faq.asp#8

[209] *Supra,* note 23.

[210] http://www.biosecurityboard.gov/faq.asp#11

[211] http://www.biosecurityboard.gov/faq.asp#15

[212] http://www.biosecurityboard.gov/faq.asp#15

[213] http://www.biosecurityboard.gov/faq.asp#15

[214] http://www.biosecurityboard.gov/meetings.asp

[215] Jennifer Granick, Will Bioterror Fears Spawn Science Censorship, available at http://www.wired.com/politics/onlinerights/commentary/circuitcourt/2007/04/circuitcourt_0425.

[216] *Fantasy Book Shop, Inc. v. Boston*, 652 F.2d 1115, 1120 (1st 1981) (citing *Se.Promotions, Ltd. v. Conrad*, 420 U.S. 546, 552-558 (1976).

[217] 16B C.J.S. Constitutional § 808 (2007).

[218] Rodney A. Smolla and Melville Nimmer, Smolla and Nimmer on Freedom of Speech, § 15:9 (3d ed. 1996)

[219] *Southeastern Promotions, Ltd. v. Conrad*, 420 U.S. 546, 559 (1975).

[220] *Id.*

[221] Smolla and Nimmer, Supra, at § 15:10

[222] Smolla and Nimmer, Supra, at § 15:10 (citing Vincent Blasi, Toward a Theory of Prior Restraint: The Central Linkage, 66 Minn. L. Rev. 11, 49-54 (1981)).

[223] Smolla and Nimmer, Supra, at § 15:10 (citing Vincent Blasi, Toward a Theory of Prior Restraint: The Central Linkage, 66 Minn. L. Rev. 11, 49-54 (1981)).

[224] U.S. Const., Amend IV.

[225] U.S. Const., Amend IV.

[226] *Schmerber v. California*, 384 U.S. 757, 767–68 (1966).

[227] Lawrence O. Gostin, *Public Health Law, Power, Duty, Restraint* 193 (2000).

[228] *Skinner v. Railway Labor Executives Ass'n*, 489 U;.S. 602 at 625 (1989) (Upholding drug tests following accident even without reasonable suspicion of impairment.) *See also*, Addie S. Ries, "America's Anti-hijacking Campaign—Will It Conform to Our Constitution?" footnote 14 N.C. J.L. & Tech. 123 (Fall 2001).

[229] *See* Addie S. Ries, "America's Anti-hijacking Campaign—Will It Conform to Our Constitution?" 3 N.C. J.L. & Tech. 123 (Fall 2001).

[230] Centers for Disease Control and Prevention, "Smallpox Response Plan, Guide A—Surveillance, Contact racing and Epidemiological Investigation," A-17 (November 21, 2001).

[231] A. L. DeWitt, "The Ultimate Exigent Circumstance, 5 Kan. J.L. Pub. Pol'y 169, 173–75 (1996)(justifying FBI activity).

[232] Patrik S. Florencio and Erik D. Ramanathan, "Are Xenotransplantation Safeguards Legally Viable?" 16 Berkeley Tech. L.J. 937, 958–59 (Summer 2001).

[233] 121 S. Ct. 2038, 150 L.Ed. 2d 94; 2001 LEXIS 4487, 69 U.S.L.W. 4431 (June 11, 2001).

[234] 121 S. Ct. 2038 at 2044.

[235] *States v. Ishmael*, 48 F.3d 850 (5th Cir. 1995).

[236] *States v. Pinson*, 24 F.3d 1056 (8th Cir. 1994).

[237] *States v. Kyllo,* 190 F.3d 1041 (9th Cir. 1999).

[238] *States v. Ford,* 34 F.3d 992 (11th Cir. 1994).

[239] See 83 F.3d 1247 (10th Cir. 1996).

[240] 48 F.3d 850 (5th Cir. 1995).

[241] *States v. Ishmael*, 48 F.3d 850 (5th Cir. 1995).

[242] Charles Lane, "Justices Hear Oregon Case on High-Tech Surveillance," *The Washington Post*, Wednesday, February 21, 2001, A03.

[243] 476 U.S. 207 at 215, n.3 (1986).

244 121 S. Ct. 2038 at 2043, n. 5 (2001).

245 121 S. Ct. 2038 at 2041 (2001).

246 121 S. Ct. 2038

247 121 S. Ct. 2038 (dissent).

248 121 S. Ct. 2038 n.5 (dissent).

249 If a search or a seizure has occurred, it may still be allowed, but only when it is "reasonable" under the Fourth Amendment. When one considers reasonableness, it requires consideration of the degree of cause for the search or seizure. And the level of required cause, such as probable cause for a search or reasonable suspicion for a "Terry" stop varies with the degree of intrusion by the government on the person's privacy and other interests protected by the Fourth Amendment. But none of these interests are implicated when postal inspectors, postal police, or other authorities examine the outside of an envelope or assess its characteristics without intruding on private communications. There is, for example, no reasonable expectation of privacy in the designated return address on a letter, and it may be freely investigated so long as the duration of investigation is sufficiently brief that no seizure occurs.

250 Despite (or some might say because of) advances of science, arts, law, and the cooperative efforts of many cultures, all is not safe in the world. Some persons may seek to use innocent mechanisms like the mails to harm others. Indeed, our society must consider the possibility that chemical or biological agents, including anthrax, sarin, or other toxins, and perhaps other weapons of mass destruction, may be transmitted by mail. No doubt there are limits, but as a general rule the Constitution does not bind the hands of postal authorities in a way that would prohibit them from taking reasonable and nonintrusive investigatory or curative steps to protect the public.

251 The Government suggests that El-Hage's expectation of privacy was not reasonable. The Government asserts that because El-Hage spoke cryptically in his phone calls and because one associate expressed concern that the phone was tapped, his expectation of privacy was reduced. (citing United States v. Hall, 488 F.2d 193, 198 (9th Cir. 1973)("It would be absurd to hold that one is constitutionally protected from untoward results when he makes statements at a time when he has reason to know that some third party is, or probably is, listening."). But see El-Hage Reply at 27 ("Mr. El-Hage's expectation of privacy in his telephone communications in Kenya was absolute in light of Kenya's complete prohibition on wiretapping."). It is also suggested that El-Hage's expectation of privacy was diminished because he lived in another country. Finally, the fact that El-Hage allowed al Qaeda associates to stay at his home is said to have reduced his expectation of privacy. But cf. Minnesota v. Olson, 495 U.S. 91, 109 L. Ed. 2d 85, 110 S. Ct. 1684 (1990) (affording Fourth Amendment protection to an overnight guest because he had a reasonable expectation of privacy in the residence that was searched). These considerations, while relevant, do not sway the Court's finding that El-Hage had a reasonable expectation of privacy in his home and cellular phones. See Katz v. United States, 389 U.S. 347, 361, 19 L. Ed. 2d 576, 88 S. Ct. 507 (1967). The conclusion that he did have a reasonable expectation of privacy seems unassailable, in light of both the doctrinal holding of Katz and its factual predicate—the defendant's telephone conversations (deemed worthy, by the Court, of Fourth Amendment protection) occurred in a public phone booth.

Chapter Four
Biodefense Countermeasures:
Liability, Compensation, Intellectual Property

4.1   Introduction

The tort law and liability model works well unless the manufacture of a product, if it causes injury, is far more economically risky than the potential economic gain from the sale of the product. Generally, the market system would control the decision for the manufacturer to stop manufacturing the product. This illustrates the complexity of the need to manufacture vaccines, in particular childhood vaccines, for the government interest of public health. A new liability and compensation model is required to compensate those who are injured, without economically driving the manufacturer out of the business of supplying these vital vaccines. In the case of biodefense and emerging infectious diseases, the governmental interest is not only about public health, but also potentially about national security.

This chapter will examine the foundations of vaccine injury and compensation, and move through the new statutes to address biological countermeasures after the anthrax attacks in the fall of 2001.

4.2. Foundations in Vaccine Injury Compensation
4.2.1. Polio Vaccine

Reyes v. Wyeth Laboratories, Inc.
498 F.2d 1264 (5th Cir. 1974)

JUDGES: Brown, Chief Judge and Wisdom and Ainsworth, Circuit Judges.
Opinion by Justice Wisdom:

This products liability case raises significant questions concerning the scope of a drug manufacturer's duty to warn ultimate consumers of dangers inherent in his product.

In May 1970, slightly more than two weeks after she had received a dose of Wyeth Laboratories' oral polio vaccine, eight-month-old Anita Reyes was diagnosed as having paralytic poliomyelitis. Epifanio Reyes, Anita's father, filed suit against Wyeth Laboratories, alleging that the live polio virus in the vaccine had caused Anita's polio and that Wyeth was liable for her injuries because it had failed to warn her parents of this danger. Wyeth contends that it is not liable for Anita Reyes's injuries under the products liability law of Texas. In addition, Wyeth raises numerous procedural and evidentiary questions. The case was tried to a jury. The jury answered special interrogatories and returned a verdict in favor of Reyes against Wyeth for the sum of $200,000.

I.

Twenty or thirty years ago poliomyelitis was a dread disease that especially attacked the very young. In 1952 alone, there were 57,879 reported cases of polio in the United States; 21,269 of these resulted in crippling paralysis to the victims. By 1970, when Anita Reyes contracted polio, the number of those stricken by polio had diminished dramatically; she was one of just 33 individuals to be afflicted during that year. Credit for this precipitous decline must go primarily to the medical researchers who discovered the viral nature of the disease, and were able to isolate and reproduce the virus in an inactivated or an attenuated form. But credit for this remarkable achievement must also be given to such laboratories as Wyeth, which processed the polio vaccine, and to massive federal-state public health programs for the administration of the vaccine.

On May 8, 1970, Anita Reyes was fed two drops of Sabin oral polio vaccine by eye-dropper at the Hidalgo County Department of Health clinic in Mission, Texas. The vaccine was administered to Anita by a registered nurse; there were no doctors present. Mrs. Reyes testified that she was not warned of any possible danger involved in Anita's taking the vaccine. Mrs. Reyes has a seventh grade education, but her primary language is Spanish. She signed a form releasing the State of Texas from "all liability in connection with immunization". The form contained no warning of any sort, and it is apparent from her testimony that she either did not read the form or lacked the linguistic ability to understand its significance. About fourteen days after the vaccine was administered, Anita Reyes became ill. On May 23, 1970, she was admitted to the McAllen (Texas) General Hospital, where her disease was diagnosed as Type I paralytic poliomyelitis. As a result of the polio, at the time of trial Anita was completely paralyzed from the waist down, her left arm had become atrophied, and she was unable to control her bladder or bowel movements.

The vaccine given Anita Reyes in the Mission clinic on May 8, 1970 was part of a "lot", No. 15509, prepared by Wyeth. Lot No. 15509 was trivalent oral polio vaccine that Wyeth had titered (mixed) from Types I, II, and III monovalent vaccine provided by Pfizer, Ltd. In response to an order placed by the Texas State Department of Health on December 23, 1969, Wyeth shipped 3500 vials of Lot No. 15509 vaccine to the State Health Department which in turn transferred 400 vials to the Hidalgo County Health Department. The jury found that vaccine from one of these vials was given to Anita Reyes. Included with every vial, each of which contained ten doses of vaccine, was a "package circular" provided by Wyeth which was intended to warn doctors, hospitals, or other purchasers of potential dangers in ingesting the vaccine. Mrs. Lenore Wiley, the public health nurse who administered the vaccine to Anita Reyes, testified that she had read the directions on this package insert, but that it was not the practice of the nurses at the Mission Health Clinic to pass on the warnings to the vaccines or to their guardians. She testified that she gave Mrs. Reyes no warning before she administered the vaccine to Anita....

Basically, Section 402A subjects to liability the seller or manufacturer of a product sold "in a defective condition unreasonably dangerous" to an ultimate user or consumer whose person or property is physically harmed by the product. n10 Moreover, one who places defective goods in the stream of commerce will be liable "to the user or consumer even though he has exercised all possible care in the preparation and sale of the product". Restatement (Second) of Torts, Section 402A, comment a. Yet imposition of liability is by no means automatic; the elements tacit or explicit in Section 402A's mandate must be demonstrated to the trial court's satisfaction before the burden of the consumer's loss will be imposed on the seller of the product:

> The plaintiff is faced with an arduous burden of proof. He must prove that: 1) the product in question was defective; 2) the defect existed at the time the products left the hands of the defendant; 3) that because of the defect the product was unreasonably dangerous to the user or consumer (plaintiff); 4) that the consumer was injured or suffered damages; 5) and that the defect (if proved) was the proximate cause of the injuries suffered.

All five elements, however, which constitute the Gravis requirements need not be discussed here. There can be no question that Anita Reyes was injured, so the fourth element is not in issue. Nor is the second, since the defect alleged, failure to warn by the manufacturer, is by definition the *manufacturer's* dereliction. Moreover, to find that the plaintiff proved the first element is to conclude that he proved the third, for properly understood, "defective condition" has no meaning independent of "unreasonably dangerous"; the two terms are essentially synonymous. Thus if a product is unreasonably dangerous as marketed, the manufacturer may be held liable for injuries proximately caused by what he has produced, whether or not it was manufactured exactly as intended, that is without a production "defect". We do not understand this approach to dispense with the principle that to prompt liability a product must reach the consuming public in a "defective condition". Rather, by rephrasing the defectiveness requirement in terms of "unreasonable danger", it becomes clear that the circumstances of marketing themselves can amount to a defect; the defect can be extrinsic to the product. All that we need determine here, then, is first, whether the vaccine was unreasonably dangerous, and second, whether the showing of proximate causation was sufficient under Texas law.

...a) Unreasonable Danger and the Duty to Warn

We begin the inquiry by asking whether the vaccine was unreasonably dangerous, that is, in a defective condition when Anita Reyes received it. It is clear, of course that the vaccine was not itself defective....

Although the living virus in the vaccine does not make the vaccine defective, it does make it what the Restatement calls an "unavoidably unsafe product", one which cannot be made "safe" no matter how carefully it is manufactured. Such products are not necessarily "*unreasonably* dangerous", for as this Court has long recognized in wrestling with product liability questions, many goods possess both utility and danger. Rather, in evaluating the possible liability of a manufacturer for injuries caused by his inevitably hazardous products, a two-step analysis is required to determine first, whether the product is so unsafe that marketing it at all is "unreasonably dangerous per se", and, if not, whether the product has been introduced into the stream of commerce without sufficient safeguards and is thereby "unreasonably dangerous as marketed". In either case, the applicable standard, as formulated in the Restatement, is as follows: In terms of the user's interests, a product is "unreasonably dangerous" only when it is "dangerous to an extent beyond that contemplated by the ordinary consumer"; or, to phrase it in terms of the seller's responsibility, "so dangerous that a reasonable man would not sell the product if he knew the risk involved"...

In determining whether placing a commodity on the market is "unreasonably dangerous per se", the reasonable man standard of the Restatement becomes the fulcrum for a balancing process in which the utility of the product properly used is weighed against whatever dangers of harm inhere in its introduction into commerce. Obviously, use of an unavoidably unsafe product always presents at least a minimal danger of harm, but only if the potential harmful effects of the product—both qualitative and quantitative—outweigh the legitimate public interest in its availability will it be declared unreasonably dangerous per se and the person placing it on the market held liable. Applying this standard here, the scales must tip in favor of availability. The evil to be prevented—poliomyelitis and its accompanying paralysis—is great. Although the danger that vaccines may contract polio is qualitatively devastating, it is statistically miniscule. On balance then, marketing the vaccine is justified despite the danger....

Since Sabin oral polio vaccine is not "unreasonably dangerous per se", we move to the second step of our analysis to determine whether it is "unreasonably dangerous as marketed", for to conclude that the maker of an unavoidably unsafe product did not act unreasonably in placing it on the market is not to relieve him of the responsibility to market it in such a way as to prevent unreasonable danger. In the case of a product such as Sabin oral polio vaccine, this translates into a duty to provide proper warnings in selling the product....

V.

In closing, we feel that we should comment on the important policy considerations raised in the briefs of the amici curiae, the American Academy of Pediatrics [AAP] and the Conference of State and Territorial Epidemiologists [CSTE]. Both insist that the holding we reached is "dangerous" to the nation's preventive medicine programs and contravenes a strong public policy favoring large-scale participation in immunization efforts to combat infectious disease. The crucial points of the argument are two: first, that any effort to warn vaccines will be futile and frightening, leading only to confusion, and second, that a warning is unnecessary once epidemiologists have reached a deliberate medical judgment that universal vaccination is necessary. These public health policy questions cut across the law. We realize their importance.

Citing a recent Texas statute which requires that all Texas schoolchildren receive polio vaccine, the AAP insists that this renders any warnings futile. This argument assumes, of course, that the only options available are to ingest the oral vaccine at the clinic or to eschew immunity. Obviously, however, one can choose to be inoculated with killed-virus Salk vaccine, either to provide complete immunity or as a precautionary prelude to ingesting oral vaccine. The AAP also insists that the warnings would be so complex or misleading as to confuse and frighten potential vaccines. This is possible. Yet we believe that a warning advising a patron of a public health clinic of the relative risk of contracting polio from a "wild" source against the slight chance of contracting it from the vaccine would not be terrifying or confusing. Some would be sufficiently concerned to take the Salk vaccine inoculation. Others, perhaps those who, like the plaintiff in Davis, have as great a chance of contracting polio from the vaccine as contracting it from a wild source, will undoubtedly be deterred from immunization. The AAP's answer to this problem is to warn no one. That is no answer.

This position raises a policy consideration scarcely less urgent than the need for mass immunization from disease; the right of the individual to choose and control what risk he will take, in the absence of an individualized medical judgment by a physician familiar with his needs and susceptibilities. Recognition of this right counters the argument advanced in the CSTE's brief that once an epidemiological balancing of the risks of immunization has been made, no warning is required. Clearly, the rationale excusing warnings to ultimate consumers of prescription drugs whose physicians have balanced the risk for them, cannot be extended to a medical determination that statistical probabilities justify universal immunization. In such cases, the test is that outlined in *Davis*:

When...the risk qualitatively (e.g., of death or major disability) as well as quantitatively, on balance with the end sought to be achieved, is such as to call for a true choice judgment, medical or personal, the warning must be given....the qualitative risk was great, the quantitative risk minute. The end sought to be achieved—immunization—is important both to the individual and society. Striking the balance in this case is difficult, but by adding two elements to the Davis calculus we conclude that a sufficient "true choice judgment" was involved here to lend strong policy support to our holding. First, the risk here was foreseeable statistically, although unknowable individually. Thus, unlike the abreaction cases, here there was a basis for rational choice. Second, a choice here, if given, had an opportunity to be efficacious, since reasonable alternatives to taking the oral vaccine were available. Therefore, the choice was not so clear cut that even offering the opportunity to choose was meaningless.

Moreover, there is a third policy factor at work here, overlooked by the amici:

Until Americans have a comprehensive scheme of social insurance, courts must resolve by a balancing process the head-on collision between the need for adequate recovery and viable enterprises....This balancing task should be approached with a realization that the basic consideration involves a determination of the most just *allocation of the risk of loss* between the members of the marketing chain.

Statistically predictable as are these rare cases of vaccine-induced polio, a strong argument can be advanced that the loss ought not lie where it falls (on the victim), but should be borne by the manufacturer as a foreseeable cost of doing business, and passed on to the public in the form of price increases to his customers.

Contrary to the assertions of the AAP and the CSTE, we feel strongly that our holding is in accord with public policy considerations. We recognize both the essential role the city health clinic and the rural county clinic play in the nation's public health scheme, and the dangers that their depersonalized medical treatment pose. We do not then, lay down an absolute duty to warn all who receive medication at public clinics. Instead, we hold that in the case of a prescription drug which is unavoidably unsafe, and as to which there is a certain, though small, risk throughout the population, there must be *either* a warning—meaningful and complete so as to be understood by the recipient—*or* an individualized medical judgment that this treatment or medication is necessary and desirable for this patient. Anita's parents received neither. Wyeth is therefore liable for the consequence of its failure to market its unavoidably unsafe product in such a way as to warn Anita's parents of its unreasonably dangerous condition.

The judgment is affirmed.

Cunningham v. Pfizer & Co., Inc.
532 P.2d 1377 (Okla. 1974)

Berry and Hodges, Lavender, Simms, Doolin, JJ., concur. Davison, C.J., and Irwin, Barnes, JJ., concur in result.

Opinion by Justice Berry :

Plaintiff brought this action to recover damages for injuries allegedly sustained from ingesting oral polio vaccine manufactured by Charles Pfizer & Company, Inc. [defendant].

The jury returned a verdict for plaintiff for $340,000 and the trial court entered judgment accordingly. Defendant appeals. For reasons hereinafter stated we conclude the judgment of the trial court must be reversed and remanded for a new trial.

The Sabin oral vaccine contains live attenuated polio virus. Producers of the vaccine, including defendant, are licensed by the United States Government.

There are three types of polio virus, Type I, Type II and Type III. There are three corresponding types of monovalent Sabin vaccine, Type I, Type II and Type III. One must take each vaccine in order to be immunized against all three polio viruses.

There is also a trivalent vaccine which contains all three types of attenuated viruses.

Prior to 1963 the Surgeon General appointed a committee to investigate cases of polio which might have been caused by the vaccine.

In 1963 the Tulsa County Medical Society and the Tulsa City-County Health Department sponsored a mass polio immunization clinic using Sabin oral polio vaccine manufactured by defendant.

A licensed doctor was available at each distribution point to answer questions.

It was stipulated that the vaccine furnished by defendant was produced and manufactured in accordance with U.S. Government specifications.

The evidence indicated members of the medical society sponsoring the program were aware of all existing information concerning any relationship between ingestion of the vaccine and the onset of polio. However, defendant made no effort to furnish this information to participants in the mass immunization program.

On January 20, 1963, plaintiff, who was 15 years old at the time, took Type I vaccine as a part of this program. Defendant gave no direct warning to plaintiff or his parents concerning possible untoward effects of the vaccine.

Within five weeks after he took the vaccine plaintiff contracted a paralytic disease.

Plaintiff's theory in the trial court was to the effect defendant failed to warn him, or his parents, of the risk of contracting polio from the polio vaccine, and this failure to warn rendered defendant liable for all damages plaintiff incurred as a result of taking the vaccine.

Defendant's theory in the trial court was to the effect plaintiff did not contract polio, that if he did, he did not contract it from defendant's vaccine, and defendant had no duty to warn ultimate consumers of risks involved in taking the vaccine, but only had a duty to warn members of the medical society sponsoring the program.

The trial court adopted plaintiff's theory. The court's instruction 7 set out this theory as follows:

"You are instructed that a manufacturer of polio vaccine has the duty to warn consumers of the risks involved in taking the vaccine or the vaccine is considered as being in an unfit condition, thereby being unreasonably dangerous, and subjecting the manufacturer to liability for physical harm caused to the consumer of the vaccine."

Defendant excepted to this instruction.

The remainder of the instructions indicate the only issues submitted to the jury were (1) whether plaintiff contracted polio (2) whether he contracted it from taking defendant's vaccine and (3) the amount of damages.

On appeal defendant first contends the trial court erred in applying the theory of strict liability in tort to this case. In Kirkland v. General Motors Corp., Okl., 521 P.2d 1353, we adopted the theory of strict liability in tort set out in Restatement of Torts, 2nd Ed. §402A. This principle is to the effect that one who sells a product in a defective condition unreasonably dangerous to the user or consumer or to his property is liable for physical harm thereby caused to the ultimate user or consumer or to his property (a) if the seller is engaged in the business of selling such a product and (b) it is expected to and does reach the user and consumer without substantial change in the condition in which it is sold.

In that case we stated:

"....we specifically hold that the law hereby established will be applied prospectively to all cases for trial from and after the date the mandate issues herein; and may likewise be applied by the appellate courts in cases which have been tried and are for decision on appeal where it would not prejudice the rights of the litigants."

Defendant contends the trial court erred in applying the theory in this case because this case was tried prior to the time the mandate issued in Kirkland v. General Motors Corp., supra.

If we were to reverse the trial court's judgment on this ground, the trial court could apply the principles of Kirkland in the new trial. Furthermore, we note defendant's theory at trial was that the case was governed by strict liability in tort but that theory did not impose liability upon defendant under the facts in this case. Therefore, we conclude the principles enunciated in Kirkland are applicable to this appeal.

Defendant next contends the evidence was insufficient to establish plaintiff contracted polio as a result of taking defendant's vaccine.

We note there was medical testimony which tended to establish plaintiff's injuries were sustained as a result of taking defendant's vaccine.

Defendant next contends the trial court erred in submitting the case to the jury because there was no proof of a defect in the vaccine.

Subsection k of the comments under §402A, supra, states:

"k. *Unavoidably unsafe products.*
"There are some products which, in the present state of human knowledge, are quite incapable of being made safe for their intended and ordinary use. These are especially common in the field of

drugs....Such a product, properly prepared, and accompanied by proper directions and warning, is not defective nor is it *unreasonably* dangerous. The same is true of many other drugs, vaccines, and the like, many of which for this very reason cannot legally be sold except to physicians, or under the prescription of a physician.....The seller of such products, again with the qualification that they are properly prepared and marketed, and proper warning is given, where the situation calls for it, is not to be held to strict liability for unfortunate consequences attending their use merely because he has undertaken to supply the public with an apparently useful and desirable product, attended with a known but apparently reasonable risk."

In applying §402A, supra, courts have construed this comment to mean that in certain circumstances a drug manufacturer has a duty to ensure consumers are warned of known risks involved in taking a drug and a failure to fulfill this duty renders the drug defective within the meaning of §402A.

Therefore, if a duty to warn existed in the present case, we conclude plaintiff was not required to establish the vaccine was otherwise defective.

Our research has led us to only three cases which have considered the duty of a manufacturer of polio vaccine to warn consumers of the risk of contracting polio from the vaccine. Davis v. Wyeth Laboratories, Inc., supra; Stahlheber v. American Cyanamid Company, Mo., 451 S.W. 2d 48; Reyes v. Wyeth Laboratories, 5th Cir., 498 F.2d 1264. All three of these cases held the manufacturer had a duty to warn of the risk of contracting polio from the vaccine.

At the time plaintiff herein took the vaccine defendant was aware of a report of the special advisory committee on oral poliomyelitis vaccine dated December 18, 1962. This report indicated the committee had considered 23 cases of polio associated with administration of Type I vaccine causation, six were inconclusive and ten were not compatible with vaccine causation. The report also indicates 31 million doses of Type I vaccine were given in non-epidemic areas during 1962.

Evidence in the record indicates the 1962 paralytic polio rate from all three types of polio was between 4.0–7.0 per million. There is no evidence indicating the incidence of Type I polio during this period.

There was testimony there were 12 cases of polio in Tulsa during October and November, 1962, and Oklahoma was an epidemic state prior to 1963.

A duty to warn of known potential risks of drugs had been found to exist even though the chances of the adverse reaction occurring are statistically small. Therefore, we conclude defendant had a duty to warn plaintiff or his parents of the risk of contracting polio from the vaccine and the failure to warn of this risk rendered the vaccine defective within the meaning of §402A, supra.

Defendant next contends the trial court erred in instructing the jury that defendant had a duty to warn plaintiff of risks involved in taking the vaccine rather than instructing that defendant's duty was limited to warning the members of the medical society under whose supervision the vaccination was given.

As a general rule it has been held that in cases involving prescription drugs the drug manufacturer has only a duty to warn the prescribing physician.

In Davis v. Wyeth Laboratories, Inc., supra, the court noted the reason for this rule to be as follows:

"....In such cases the choice involved is essentially a medical one involving an assessment of medical risks in the light of the physician's knowledge of his patient's needs and susceptibilities. Further it is difficult under such circumstances for the manufacturer, by label or direct communication, to reach the consumer with a warning. A warning to the medical profession is in such cases the only effective means by which a warning could help the patient."

However, with reference to a mass immunization program the court stated:

"Here....although the drug was denominated a prescription drug it was not dispensed as such. It was dispensed to all comers at mass clinics without an individualized balancing by a physician of the risks involved. In such cases (as in the case of over-the-counter sales of nonprescription drugs) warning by the manufacturer to its immediate purchaser will not suffice. The decision (that on balance and in the public interest the personal risk to the individual was worth taking) may well have been that of the medical society and not that of appellee...."We conclude that appellee did not meet its duty to warn.

"This duty does not impose an unreasonable burden on the manufacturer....means of communication such as advertisements, posters, releases to be read and signed by recipients of the vaccine, or oral warnings were clearly available and could easily have been undertaken or prescribed by appellee."

In the present case the vaccine was administered as part of a mass immunization program and the evidence does not indicate the doctor present at each center assessed medical risks in light of his knowledge of each patient's needs and susceptibilities. We conclude instruction 7 was not erroneous insofar as it stated defendant had a duty to warn plaintiff, rather than the medical society sponsoring the program, of the risks involved in taking the vaccine.

Defendant next contends the trial court erred in submitting the case to the jury because there was no evidence plaintiff would have refused to take the vaccine if he or his parents had been informed of risks involved in taking the vaccine.

In *Reyes v. Wyeth Laboratories*, supra, the court considered a similar contention. There the defendant requested the trial court to submit a special interrogatory to the jury concerning whether failure to warn was the proximate cause of a child's contracting polio in view of the fact that "even with warning they may have proceeded with immunization."

The trial court refused to give such an instruction.

The Court of Appeals held there are two causation issues in most products liability cases (1) was defendant's product the cause in fact of plaintiff's injuries and (2) did the plaintiff's injuries result from the alleged defect in the defendant's product [i.e., the failure to warn].

However, that court held failure to submit the latter question to the jury did not constitute reversible error in that case. In so doing the court stated:

"....Where a consumer, whose injury the manufacturer should have reasonably foreseen, is injured by a product sold without a required warning, a rebuttable presumption will arise that the consumer would have read any warning provided by the manufacturer, and acted so as to minimize the risks. In the absence of evidence rebutting the presumption, a jury finding that the defendant's product was the producing cause of the plaintiff's injury would be sufficient to hold him liable.

"....According to the test we have distilled above, we must assume in the absence of evidence to the contrary that Anita's parents would have acted on the warning, had it been given....."

We agree with defendant's contention that as part of plaintiff's cause of action plaintiff must establish he would have refused to take the vaccine if adequate warning had been given.

However, we conclude plaintiff was not required to present any direct evidence upon this point because he was entitled to a rebuttable presumption he would have heeded any warning which might have been given. Reyes v. Wyeth Laboratories, supra.

In the present case there was evidence which tended to overcome the presumption. This evidence indicates when plaintiff took the vaccine there was considerable risk of contracting polio from natural sources, there had been 12 cases of polio in Tulsa during October and November 1962, and Oklahoma was an epidemic state prior to 1963.

In these circumstances we conclude the issue of whether the plaintiff as a reasonably prudent person would have refused to take the vaccine if adequate warning had been given should have been submitted to the jury.

We further conclude the test applied should be an objective test, i.e., in light of all circumstances existing on the date plaintiff took the vaccine, would a reasonably prudent person in plaintiff's position have refused the vaccine if adequate warning of risks had been given.

Neither party requested such an instruction.

We conclude the trial court's failure to instruct the jury that defendant would be liable only if its failure to warn was the cause of plaintiff's injury constituted a failure to instruct upon a material issue and was fundamental error. Furthermore, we conclude instruction 7 was erroneous because it allowed the jury to find for plaintiff if no warning was given and the vaccine caused plaintiff's injuries, and did not require the jury to find the failure to warn caused the injury.

The judgment of the trial court is reversed and remanded with instructions to grant defendant a new trial.

4.2.2. Swine flu vaccine

The Swine Flu Liability Act was created to address injuries received up to two years after vaccination. In September 1977, 743 claims were filed for damages of $325,671,708 and 67 claims of wrongful death, 19 of which were due to Guillain-Barre syndrome, totaling damages of $32,948,179. According to testimony from Neil R. Peterson of the U.S. Department of Justice, the claims were being filed at a rate of about 20 per week, and he expected a total of 2,500 claims in all. However, by May 1980 there had been 3,917 claims filed, totaling $3.5 billion in damages.[1]

Sparks v. Wyeth Laboratories, Inc.
431 F. Supp. 411 (W.D. Okla. 1977)

Opinion by: Luther Bohanon, United States District Judge.

This is a civil action wherein the plaintiff, Donna J. Sparks, prays judgment against the defendant manufacturers jointly and severally for $6,675,210.00; and the intervenor defendant, United States of America, has filed certain motions which come on for hearing.

This case comes on before the court on two motions:

1. The United States has moved to substitute itself as sole party defendant in the place of the four defendants named by plaintiff (Wyeth Laboratories, Inc.; Merrill-National; Parke, Davis and Company; and Merck, Sharpe and Dohme Orthopedics, Inc. [hereinafter called "vaccine manufacturers"]). These four defendants are the sole manufacturers of so-called swine flu vaccine (Dr. David W. Berry Affidavit) under the National Swine Flu Immunization Program of 1976 (Public Law 94-380; 42 U.S.C. §247b(j)-(l) [hereinafter referred to as "Swine Flu Act"]). The motion to substitute is made pursuant to 42 U.S.C. 247b(k)(5)(A).

2. Assuming that the substitution is accomplished, the United States has moved to dismiss the action against it because of the failure of the plaintiffs to file an administrative claim as required by 28 U.S.C. §2675(a), a part of the Federal Tort Claims Act [hereinafter referred to as "Tort Act"].

Plaintiff opposes these dual motions on three grounds: 1) that the Swine Flu Act is unconstitutional because it violates the due process and equal protection clauses and the Seventh and Tenth Amendments; 2) that an injured party may still sue a vaccine manufacturer directly for negligence notwithstanding the provisions of the Swine Flu Act; and 3) that the claim procedures of the Tort Act may not be invoked in a suit against a manufacturer who is not an employee of the United States. Because this will be the seminal decision dealing with the Swine Flu Act, the Court deems it appropriate to express its reasoning on each of these issues in some detail.

Plaintiff allegedly received a swine flu immunization on November 24, 1976 at the office of a private physician and within six hours experienced a condition which has left her with "some paralysis in her body and loss of vision and ability to speak" (Complaint, paragraphs 7, 8, 9). The Court accepts this statement as true, without, of course, deciding whether there is any medical or legal causation between the inoculation and the purported condition, and, if so, whether the condition is compensable.

The Swine Flu Act became law on August 12, 1976 and was to apply in the instance of all swine flu inoculations given after September 30, 1976 (42 U.S.C. §247b(k)(2)(A)). Its provisions are simple. It applies to three categories of "program participants" as defined in 42 U.S.C. §247b(k)(2)(B):

1. Manufacturers or distributors of vaccine who make no profit on the vaccine;

2. Public or private agencies or organizations that provide an inoculation with informed consent and without charge to the recipient for the vaccine or its administration; and,

3. Medical or other health personnel who provided or assisted in providing an inoculation with informed consent and without charge to the recipient for the vaccine or its administration.

We are here concerned with only the first or manufacturers category, although what is said as to it would apply with equal validity to the other categories.

The Swine Flu Act does three basic and relevant things:

1. It creates a cause of action against the United States for any personal injury or wrongful death sustained as a result of a swine flu inoculation (42 U.S.C. §247b(k)(2)(A)).

2. Making that cause the exclusive remedy (42 U.S.C. §247b(k)(3)), it abolishes the cause of action against the manufacturer-program participant.

3. It makes the procedures of the Tort Act applicable to the suits against the United States (42 U.S.C. §247b(k)(2)(A)). However, the Swine Flu Act does not limit a plaintiff's theory of recovery to negligence alone as under the Tort Act (28 U.S.C. 1346(b), 2674), but rather specifies that the United States shall be liable upon any theory available against a program participant under the law of the place where the act or omission occurred, "including negligence, strict liability in tort, and breach of warranty" (42 U.S.C. 247b(k)(2)(A)(i)).

The Swine Flu Act does contain other provisions which are set forth only insofar as necessary to the discussion which follows.

The Swine Flu Act was generated and enacted by Congress in good faith haste. This is apparent both from the fact that the bill was not even referred formally to the House Judiciary Committee and the fact that no formal report of either chamber of Congress exists. In fact, such a report is contained only in the remarks of Representative Paul Rogers (Fla.) in the Congressional Record of August 26, 1976 which supplement his remarks during the August 10, 1976 debate on the bill. Congressman Rogers is Chairman of the House Subcommittee on Interstate and Foreign Commerce, the committee which drafted the bill and held applicable hearings. His remarks contain an exposition of the legislative history of the Swine Flu Act, its rationale, the alternatives considered and rejected by Congress, and a section-by-section analysis of the bill. They are set forth at pp. E 4695-4707 of the Congressional Record of August 12, 1976. Debate occurred in both chambers on August 10, 1976, that of the House appearing at Cong. Rec. H 8643-8655 and that of the Senate appearing at Cong. Rec. S 14108-14122.

It is sufficient to say that the bill was occasioned by the collapse of the commercial liability insurance market, both for the manufacturers and other program participants (Cong. Rec., *Liability*, E 4698-4699). Since the bill was generated by the House Interstate and Foreign Commerce Committee with some amendments by the Senate, it is natural that the legislative history would evidence such connection with the commerce clause was apparent. This was found in two areas. First, the economic cost of the last flu epidemic in the United States, the Hong Kong flu of 1968–69, was $3,900,000,000 with 33,000 excess deaths (Cong. Rec., E 4696), much of the economic loss being due to lost wages. As a corollary, flu was noted to be the one disease with the capacity to close plants (Ibid.). Second, the vaccine would not be available for distribution in interstate commerce unless the insurance-liability problem was solved.

The need for haste arose from the need to inoculate the population before the flu season began (Cong. Rec., E 4701, S 14110).

The collapse of the insurance market was occasioned by two factors:

1. The miniscule claims experience of insurers with prior flu vaccines was not a problem (Cong. Rec., E 4699). However, the significant problem was the potential for a large number of claims with the attendant costs of investigation and defense. Insurance company witnesses estimated that this cost alone could run into the billions of dollars (Cong. Rec., H 8648-9). Such claims were called frivolous or non-meritorious.

2. The recent cases of *Davis v. Wyeth Laboratories, Inc.*, 399 F.2d 121 (9th Cir., 1968) and *Reyes v. Wyeth Laboratories*, 498 F.2d 1264 (5th Cir., 1974) had held a manufacturer of polio vaccine liable on a non-negligence, strict liability in tort theory for failure to warn a vaccinee of the risks attendant upon the vaccine. Thus, while the manufacturers could insure themselves against negligence, they could not afford insurance premiums for the cost of defense of frivolous, non-meritorious claims or for attenuated theories of non-negligent liability (Cong. Rec., E 4698-9, 4700). Since the manufacturers could insure themselves for negligence liability, the manufacturers would thus be liable in a suit over by the United States on a negligence theory (42 U.S.C. §247b(k)(7)) if it has settled any claim or has been found liable on any theory and can make out a case of negligence against a manufacturer (Cong. Rec., E 4705).

It is apparent that both the text of the Swine Flu Act and the legislative history show that the statute passes any test of its constitutionality. But, the Court will deal with each of the plaintiff's contentions in order.

1. There is no question but that the Swine Flu Act comports with the due process clause of the Fifth Amendment. It is manifest that the statute, insofar as it abolishes a cause of action against a program participant, does so only prospectively. It does not suffer the infirmity of the cases cited by plaintiff in which abolitions of vested rights were found to be a due process violation. This is the teaching of *Keller v. Dravo Corporation*, 441 F2d 1239 (5th Cir., 1971). As has been stated by the Supreme Court:

A person has no property, no vested interest, in any rule of the common law. [*Mondou v. New York, New Haven & Hartford Railroad Co.*, 223 U.S. 1, 50, 32 S. Ct. 169, 56 L. Ed. 327 (1912)].

And again:

No person has a vested interest in any rule of law entitling him to insist that it shall remain unchanged for his benefit....[*New York Central R.R. Co. v. White*, 243 U.S. 188, 198, 61 L. Ed. 667, 37 S. Ct. 247 (1917)].

Moreover, while the prospective direct remedy of an injured person against a manufacturer has been abolished, an alternative, efficacious remedy against the United States is substituted. Such a replacement or substitution of remedies, while perhaps not technically necessary for due process, is nonetheless even more indicative of the satisfaction of due process requirements:

The abolition of non-vested rights is especially innocuous if, as here, one remedy is substituted for another.

The simple fact is that—

No one has a vested right in a given mode of procedure and so long as a substantial and efficient remedy is provided, due process of law is not denied by a change in remedy. [Swanson v. Bates, 170 F2d 648, 650-1 (10th Cir., 1948), citing *Crane v. Hahlo*, 258 U.S. 142, 147, 66 L. Ed. 514, 42 S. Ct. 214 (1922)].

This is precisely what the Congress has done with the Swine Flu Act. Nor does the fact that the alternative remedy against the United States here involves an administrative aspect render it constitutionally defective. This point was decided principally in *N.L.R.B. v. Jones & Laughlin Steel Corp.*, 301 U.S. 1, 81 L. Ed. 893, 57 S. Ct. 615 (1937), and inferentially in workmen's compensation decisions, since most such statutes entail administrative proceedings and remedies.

Not only does general constitutional law support what the Congress has done here, but the Court concurs that several of the examples cited by the United States of the abolition of prospective rights with or without substitution of another remedy are ample authority. The foremost example is that of several statutes which have amended the Tort Act to abolish a remedy against certain government employees and leave the injured person solely to his suit against the United States. See: 28 U.S.C. §2679(b) (the Federal Drivers Act); 38 U.S.C. §4116 (Veterans Administration medical personnel); 42 U.S.C. §233 (Public Health Service medical personnel); 22 U.S.C. §817(a) (State Department medical personnel); 10 U.S.C. §1089(a) (Armed Forces medical personnel). The Swine Flu Act is modeled precisely on these previous statutes, which have always been found to be constitutional when challenged (Cong. Rec., *The Tort Claims Approach,* E 4700-4701). Moreover, none of these statutes, dating back to 1961, substituted any alternative remedy since, in each case, the injured party was already entitled to sue the United States under the Tort Act. The contention that the abolition of one remedy by the Federal Drivers Act without the substitution of another violated due process was specifically rejected in *Carr v. United States,* 422 F2d 1007, 1010 (4th Cir., 1970).

Those statutes which substitute a remedy against the United States for a remedy an injured person formerly had against a government contractor. Thus, the Suits in Admiralty Act and its predecessor constitutionally immunized private operators of government vessels. Remember 28 U.S.C. §1498(a) constitutionally makes an action in the Court of Claims the exclusive remedy for any patent owner whose patent is infringed after the date of the statute by the actions of a government contractor. The importance of these statutes and cases lies in the fact that they immunize and abolish rights against government contractors as opposed to government employees. Thus, what Congress has done as to the government contractor-manufacturers under the Swine Flu Act is just another example of permissible legislation in areas "necessary and proper" to the fulfillment of federal constitutional responsibilities for the public welfare.

Without citation, other examples of the abolition of remedies consistent with due process include state workmen's compensation statutes, no-fault automobile insurance laws, the so-called "heart balm" statutes, and charitable immunity statutes.

The additional arguments made by plaintiff that the Swine Flu Act would contravene Rules 17 and 19 of the Federal Rules of Civil Procedure are simply not of sufficient magnitude to pose any constitutional infraction. If it were necessary to decide these contentions, the Court could as well note that the legislative history and the statute support the proposition that the United States is the real party in interest, that the non-joinder provisions were necessary to achieve the legislative intent and therefore that the substantive provisions of the Swine Flu Act control over the procedural devices of the Federal Rules, and that there will not be any infringement of plaintiff's discovery rights since the manufacturers are obligated to cooperate with the United States relative to discovery and the plaintiff can move to decertify them if they impede discovery.

2. There is no equal protection violation. The plain fact is that only the Fourteenth Amendment, which is not applicable to the federal government contains an equal protection clause. To be applied against the federal government, the equal protection clause must be incorporated as the equivalent of a due process violation under the Fifth Amendment. Thus, while a person attacking the constitutionality of a statute has the burden of proof and a heavy one, plaintiff here has a double burden. She must prove that not only is the classification in which she has been placed discriminatory, but that it is so arbitrary and injurious as to constitute a denial of due process.

3. The Swine Flu Act in no manner unconstitutionally constricts plaintiff's right to a jury trial in violation of the Seventh Amendment. We must begin with the proposition set out above that due process does not categorically prevent the abrogation of causes of action. The fact is that the alternative remedy, the Tort Act, proscribes jury trials. 28 U.S.C. §2402. This, claims plaintiff, violates the Seventh Amendment.

However, as a matter of logic, it is axiomatic that if a cause of action can be abolished, the jury trial of that action is also abolished. The elemental fact is that suits against the sovereign were unknown at common law. Thus, perforce, there was no right of trial by jury against the sovereign at common law. Hence, a jury trial need not be accorded where a sovereign waives its immunity, and the Seventh Amendment guarantee is inapplicable. This is the direct holding of the Supreme Court...and is the factor which distinguishes the Swine Flu Act from the cases cited by plaintiff where the sovereign was not involved....

The Court also notes in passing that the Seventh Amendment has never been held to be such a fundamental right that it was incorporated against the states under the Fourteenth Amendment. The Oklahoma Supreme Court has held that a state may abolish a right of jury trial. In fact, the Oklahoma State Constitution partially abrogates the common law jury trial right in two respects: trial by six rather than twelve jurors, and verdict by three-fourths of the jury in civil actions Thus, there could not even be an equal protection argument fashioned out of the denial of a jury trial here as plaintiff tries to do.

4. There is no Tenth Amendment violation. Plaintiff relies mainly upon cases declaring early pieces of New Deal legislation to be unconstitutional. However, the spirit if not the letter of those cases has been overruled in subsequent decisions. Thus, in a case practically dispositive of this one, the Supreme Court, in *Helvering v. Davis*, 301 U.S. 619, 81 L. Ed. 1307, 57 S. Ct. 904 (1937), held as follows:

Congress may spend money in aid of the "general welfare." Constitution, Art. I, section 8; *United States v. Butler,* 297 U.S. 1, 65, 80 L. Ed. 477, 56 S. Ct. 312; *Steward Machine Co. v. Davis, supra.* There have been great statesmen in our history who have stood for other views. We will not resurrect the contest. It is now settled by decision. *United States v. Butler, supra.*

Nor is the concept of the general welfare static. Needs that were narrow and parochial a century ago may be interwoven in our day with the well-being of the Nation. What is critical and urgent changes with the times.

The problem is plainly national in area and dimensions. Moreover, laws of the separate states cannot deal with it effectively. Congress, at least, had a basis for that belief.

When money is spent to promote the general welfare, the concept of welfare or the opposite is shaped by Congress, not the states. So the concept be not arbitrary, the locality must yield. Constitution, Art. VI, Par. 2. [301 U.S. at 640, 641, 644, 645].

Both *Helvering and Steward Machine Co. v. Davis,* 301 U.S. 548, 81 L. Ed. 1279, 57 S. Ct. 883 (1937) upheld portions of the Social Security Act against Tenth Amendment challenges. Steward held that Social Security was an area in which the states and the federal government could work together and that the legislation imposed no coercion on the states.

Such is plainly true of the Swine Flu Act, which amends the Public Health Service Act. The latter Act authorizes the Secretary of Health, Education and Welfare to make grants to the states and to assist states and their political subdivisions "to assist in meeting the costs of communicable and other disease control programs" (42 U.S.C. §247b(a)). This directive is in fulfillment of the general directive to the Secretary to "assist States and their political subdivisions in the prevention and suppression of communicable diseases" (42 U.S.C. §243(a)).

The Swine Flu Act calls for the participation of state and local health departments (42 U.S.C. 247b(j)(1)(c); Cong. Rec., E 4698). Moreover, Oklahoma law sanctions this very cooperation. It basically provides that the State Commissioner of Health, the Chief Administrative Officer of the State Board of Health, shall have authority to enter into agreements with the Federal Government on matters pertaining to public health (63 Okla. St. 1-106(b)(12)). These agreements may be for money, personnel, or property to promote the control of disease. The State Treasurer acts as the custodian of federal funds received to promote public health (63 Okla. St. 1-108). In addition, County Boards of Health are authorized to cooperate with the State Board of Health in matters of disease prevention and control (63 Okla. St. 1-201–1-218).

Not only does the State of Oklahoma authorize participation in such programs, but, as in *Steward Machine Co. v. Davis, supra,* 301 U.S. 548, 57 S. Ct. 883, 81 L. Ed. 1279, there is no coercion on the state. Nor is there coercion upon any individual to be inoculated in view of the consent requirements expressed in 42 U.S.C. §247b(j)(1)(F) (Cong. Rec., S 14118). Thus, contrary to plaintiff's assertion, state and individual participation are not forbidden, but mandated. How such a statute interferes with state sovereignty is something plaintiff has failed to explain. Certainly, it contains no ingredients of a Tenth Amendment violation.

5. The Swine Flu Act is applicable to all causes of action, including those sounding in negligence. Plaintiff has claimed that, since the statute says it was necessary to protect program participants from "other than their own negligence" (42 U.S.C. §247b(k)(1)(A)(i)), and since she is suing for negligence, this suit will lie. The Court simply cannot agree with this interpretation of the statute. 42 U.S.C. §247b(k)(2)(A)(i), an operative provision, says that the liability of the United States may be on any theory "including negligence", that this liability is exclusive (42 U.S.C. §247b(k)(3)), and that only the United States may sue over against a negligent program participant (42 U.S.C. §247b(k)(7)). This scheme effectuates the Congressional design to leave the program participants at risk for negligence only, since negligence was a risk which they could insure. Since the manufacturers could not protect themselves against the cost of defending meritless suits, it was necessary for Congress to both eliminate direct actions against them (many of which could be meritless) and obviate their joinder in what could otherwise be meritless suits.

6. Plaintiff claims that the Swine Flu Act cannot be applied to manufacturers as government contractors since only employees are covered by 28 U.S.C. §2671 of the Tort Act. This contention is in error because it wrongly assumes that the Congress amended the Tort Act (which, it should be noted, Congress could have done validly). In any event, the Swine Flu Act has its own definitional sections (42 U.S.C. §247b(k)(2)(B), and (1)) and merely incorporates the *procedures* of the Tort Act (42 U.S.C. §247b(k)(1)(B)). The Swine Flu Act applies to manufacturers.

Having determined the constitutionality and applicability of the Swine Flu Act, there remains only the relatively simple task of determining the motions of the United States before the Court. The United States is to be substituted in the place of the four manufacturers (42 U.S.C. §247b(k)(5)(A)). The requisite certification of the program participant status of the manufacturers is attached to the United States' Motion to Substitute and it is conclusive upon this Court (Cong. Rec., E 4704) for purposes of this motion.

One of the procedures specified by the Tort Act is the filing of an administrative claim (28 U.S.C. §2675(a)). This the plaintiff has not done. Since the filing of this claim is jurisdictional this action should be dismissed. Accordingly, a judgment of dismissal without prejudice accompanies this Memorandum Opinion.

Note

One of the first cases to test the new statute was that of Ms. Alvarez, who had received a swine flu vaccine. The case was the first to utilize Federal Rule of Evidence 706 in the appointment of a panel of experts to decide whether in each case the vaccine had caused the injuries. See *In re (Swine Flu Immunization) Products Liability Litigation; Alvarez v. United States,* 495 F. Supp. 1188 (D. Col. 1980).

4.2.3. The National Childhood Vaccine Injury Act of 1986

The previous cases demonstrate the background for the passage of the National Vaccine Injury Compensation Program (NVICP) in 1986. The public policy purpose is to provide "a less adversarial, less expensive and less time-consuming system of recovery than the traditional tort system that governs medical malpractice, personal injury and product liability cases."[2]

The National Vaccine Injury Compensation Program (NVICP), enabled by the National Childhood Vaccine Injury Act of 1986,[3] provides no-fault compensation for injury or death from the vaccines for polio, diphtheria, pertussis, tetanus, measles, mumps, rubella, hepatitis B, haemophilius influenza type B, varicella (chicken pox), rotavirus, and pneumoccocal 7-valent conjugate.[4] The development of new vaccines, including the anthrax vaccine and smallpox vaccine, for the broad vaccination program contemplated by the CDC for adults as well as children will make new legislation necessary. The manufacturer will be liable for vaccine injuries unless the new vaccines are indemnified by new legislation or amendment.

The program is jointly administered by the Department of Justice and the Department of Health and Human Services. Specific jurisdiction for hearing vaccine cases is the U.S. Court of Federal Claims, and for appeals, the U.S. Court of Appeals, Federal Circuit. It is required that a parent, guardian, or trustee file on behalf of a child, or, if of adult age, if incapacitated.[5] A claim must be filed within 36 months after the first symptoms appear in the case of injury, or within 48 months after the onset of symptoms in the case of death.[6]

In order to recover under the Act, a case must fall within the definition of a case as defined by a table of injuries,[7] which includes the time of onset and the symptoms for each vaccine. The petitioner must show that the injury occurred and that the vaccine was the cause of the disease or that the vaccine significantly exacerbated a pre-existing condition. Awards are set at a maximum of $250,000 for death, and injuries are not limited but have averaged $824,463. In the first 10 years of the program's existence (1988–1998), the National Vaccine Injury Compensation Program has paid almost $1 billion to more than 1,300 people.[8]

4.2.4. E.O. 13232, Indemnification of Defense Manufacturers

On October 20, 2001, President George W. Bush signed an Executive Order 13232, authorizing the Department of Health and Human Services to be added to the list of departments with contracting authority "in connection with national defense functions." 66 Fed.Reg. 53941 (Oct. 24, 2001). In accordance with the law, the agency must carry out its functions and vested authority and "such regulations shall, to the extent practicable, be uniform with the regulations prescribed or approved by the Secretary of Defense under the provisions of Part I of this order." 50 U.S.C.S. §1431 (2002). Those regulations in Part I (1A) provide that:

1A. (a) The limitation in paragraph 1 to amounts appropriated and the contract authorization provided therefor shall not apply to contractual provisions which provide that the United States will hold harmless and indemnify the contractor against any of the claims or losses set forth in subparagraph (b), whether resulting from the negligence or wrongful act or omission of the contractor or otherwise (except as provided in subparagraph (b)(2)). This exception from the limitations of paragraph 1 shall apply only to claims or losses arising out of or resulting from risks that the contract defines as unusually hazardous or nuclear in nature. Such a contractual provision shall be approved in advance by an official at a level not below that of the Secretary of a military department and may require each contractor so indemnified to provide and maintain financial protection of such type and in such amounts as is determined by the approving official to be appropriate under the circumstances. In deciding whether to approve the use of an indemnification provision and in determining the amount of financial protection to be provided and maintained by the indemnified contractor, the appropriate official shall take into account such factors as the availability, cost and terms of private insurance, self-insurance, other proof of financial responsibility and workmen's compensation insurance. Such approval and determination, as required by the preceding two sentences, shall be final.

(b)

(1) Subparagraph (a) shall apply to claims (including reasonable expenses of litigation and settlement) or losses, not compensated by insurance or otherwise, of the following types:

(A) Claims by third persons, including employees of the contractor, for death, personal injury, or loss of, damage to, or loss of use of property;

(B) Loss of, damage to, or loss of use of property of the contractor;

(C) Loss of, damage to, or loss of use of property of the Government;

(D) Claims arising (i) from indemnification agreements between the contractor and a subcontractor or subcontractors, or (ii) from such arrangements and further indemnification arrangements between subcontractors at any tier; provided that all such arrangements were entered into pursuant to regulations prescribed or approved by the Secretaries of Defense, the Army, the Navy, or the Air Force.

(2) Indemnification and hold harmless agreements entered into pursuant to this subsection, whether between the United States and a contractor, or between a contractor and a subcontractor, or between two subcontractors, shall not cover claims or losses caused by the willful misconduct or lack of good faith on the part of any of the contractor's or subcontractor's directors or officers or principal officials which are (i) claims by the United States (other than those arising through subrogation) against the contractor or subcontractor, or (ii) losses affecting the property of such contractor or subcontractor. Regulations to be prescribed or approved by the Secretaries of Defense, the Army, the Navy or the Air Force shall define the scope of the term "principal officials".

(3) The United States may discharge its obligation under a provision authorized by subparagraph (a) by making payments directly to subcontractors or to third persons to whom a contractor or subcontractor may be liable.

(c) A contractual provision made under subparagraph (a) that provides for indemnification must also provide for—

(1) notice to the United States of any claim or action against, or of any loss by, the contractor or subcontractor which is covered by such contractual provision; and

(2) control or assistance by the United States, at its election, in the settlement or defense of any such claim or action.

These broad indemnification powers embodied in the Executive Order potentially expose the federal government to unlimited claims for liability. Further, the legal authority for the Executive Order provides that the President can "authorize any department or agency...to enter into contracts...whenever he deems that such action would facilitate the national defense," (50 U.S.C. §1431) "*during a national emergency declared by Congress or the President...*"(50 U.S.C. §1435). This suggests that these types of indemnifications are very limited to only those contracts made during a declared national emergency. [See Bert Rein and Kristina R. Osterhaus, "Combating Bioterrorism: The Product Liability Threat," National Security White Papers, The Federalist Society, http://www.fed-soc.org/Publications/TErrorism/bioterrorism.htm] (Site visited on Aug. 16, 2002).

4.2.4.1. The Cipro™ Controversy in the Anthrax Attacks and Compulsory License under 28 U.S.C. §1498

During the anthrax attacks of 2001, the federal government began negotiations with Bayer, the owner of the patent on Cipro™ (the recommended drug for the treatment of anthrax), for supplying the National Pharmaceutical Stockpile with sufficient drugs for treatment of the American public. Controversy arose because more than one supplier was qualified to manufacture the drug. The patent was not to expire until December 2003 and the federal government had not exercised its compulsory license under 28 U.S.C. §1498.

Under 28 U.S.C. §1498, the federal government may use any patent or copyright without seeking a license or negotiating for its use. The owner of the patent is entitled to compensation, but cannot enjoin a third party. Any third party, such as a contractor, subcontractor, person, firm, or corporation, who is authorized by the federal government to produce a product pursuant to a patent cannot be sued for infringement.

Bayer had settled a challenge to the validity of its patent on Cipro™ in February 2001, when Mylan and Schein asked the U.S. District Court for New Jersey to grant a summary judgment, holding the patent invalid. The court denied their motion, but Bayer reached a settlement with the two companies as well as Barr Laboratories to end their challenges.

Upon publication of the Executive Order on October 24, 2001, which provided for indemnification for supply contracts procured by the Department of Health and Human Services under a national defense program, the contract was signed between Bayer and Secretary Thompson for the purchase of at total of 300 million tablets of Cipro™, with an initial order of 100 million tablets of Cipro™ at $0.95 per tablet. It is predicted that the first order will be ready by the end of 2001.

Rather than authorize a compulsory license for the Cipro™ patent, the federal government chose to contract with only one company for the drug instead of multiple companies licensed by FDA to produce the drug once the patent has expired. The federal government announced it would begin the process of contracting for the purchase of other antibiotics that are effective against anthrax, such as doxycycline. HHS Press Release (Oct. 24, 2001). The choice, however, to grant a compulsory license has been criticized as a political decision to protect its negotiating position at the then upcoming WTO meeting which was held on November 9–13 in Doha. It is anticipated that the compulsory licensing of drugs and imports will be a central issue for the United States in order to protect pharmaceutical companies in developing countries, where imports under a compulsory license to a country without production capacity would threaten the growth of that country's pharmaceutical industry.

4.2.4.2. Vaccines

If vaccines are purchased under a national defense program (i.e., the National Stockpile Program), provision for indemnification can be included in federal supply contracts with vaccine manufacturers in accordance with 50 U.S.C. §1431-35 (2002). This would provide an indemnification for vaccine manufacturers who provide vaccine under the National Stockpile Program pursuant to a national defense contract under this chapter, with the provision of an indemnification agreement in the contract with the manufacturer. A program would necessarily need to be established to meet the requirements in 50 U.S.C.§1431 (c)(1) to provide notice to the United States and a plan for the defense or settlement of the claim. The need to amend the National Childhood Vaccine Injury Act of 1986 may be replaced with executive action, rather than legislative action.

The Food and Drug Administration approves vaccines under the Federal Food, Drug, and Cosmetic Act, 21 U.S.C.S. §355 (a), which reads, "...No person shall introduce or deliver for introduction into interstate commerce any new drug, unless an approval of an application...is effective with respect to such drug."

The approval process required data to be obtained first from studies in animal species, as well as laboratory studies relating to safety and efficacy. This scientific information with an application for clinical trials must be evaluated and approved before clinical trials with human subjects may begin. The clinical trials proceed in three phases, with each phase requiring success before going on to the next phase. The first phase is a clinical trial with generally healthy human subjects to evaluate the safety of the drug or vaccine only. The second phase is a clinical trial with human subjects from among the intended population to measure the efficacy of the drug, (i.e., to determine whether it prevents the disease in the case of a vaccine). The third phase of the clinical trial is a test on a broader segment of the population to test both safety and efficacy.

The clinical trials make the testing of vaccines for bioweapons an impossibility because as a matter of public policy the United States does not allow such testing. Currently, much of clinical drug trials work is conducted outside of the United States because of the more readily available human subjects. The use of a primate model for substitution for the human subject clinical trials is currently being considered as a reasonable alternative that will still ensure safety and efficacy.

A vaccine that has not passed all of these testing phases is an "investigational new drug" (IND), and requires the informed consent of any individual receiving the vaccine. Such is the case of the smallpox vaccine, currently being produced for mass vaccination in the United States in the event of an occurrence of smallpox. It has been estimated that vaccinations would require four times the number of personnel where the informed consent requirements must be met for each individual. The informed consent process for INDs includes not only disclosure forms, but also individual counseling by medical personnel with the individual receiving the drug, in conjunction with a medical history that must also be compiled on each individual in order to conduct the counseling.

The rapid need for developing and producing vaccines in the event of a biological attack will require a legal framework in which safety and efficacy can be tested and ensured in the most efficient way possible.

4.2.4.3. Other Products and Product Liability

Although E.O. 13232 amending E.O. 10789 provides indemnity for contractors who contract with the federal government for a national defense program, and include such an indemnification clause in the contract, it leaves open the problem of private sector research and development in the field of homeland security where liability could be geometrically larger than typical markets. These provisions would not be applicable when a state or local government contracts with a private entity to develop or distribute priority countermeasures, or when a developer or distributor sells its countermeasures internationally and is sued by a foreign entity.

4.2.5   Private Insurance Liability

In the private sector, the risk management industry is part of a serious crisis that has arisen when insurance companies have dropped their coverage for risks and losses associated with terrorism. All 50 states and the District of Columbia received petitions to exclude coverage for terrorism claims by November 2001 in order to meet deadlines to notify insurees of major changes in coverage. Reinsurance companies who provide insurance to primary insurance companies have indicated that they will not cover terrorism claims after January 1, 2002. Because reinsurance companies are not regulated by states, they can exclude coverage without petitioning the state, and about 70% of their policies with primary insurers expired at the end of 2001. Airline companies, hotels, and transportation systems are most seriously impacted by this loss in coverage.

In June 2002, the Senate rejected a bill that would exclude punitive damages against businesses for losses due to terrorist attacks without a finding of criminal negligence. Insurance companies would be co-insured by the federal government for 80–90% of the claims amounts. As of July 27, 2002, the conferees were continuing to consider the terms, particularly the award of punitive damages. Currently, the language prohibits the award of punitive damages in excess of the defendant's direct proportion of responsibility for the plaintiff's physical harm. H.R. 3210, 107th Cong. (2002); S. 2600, 107th Cong. 2002.

4.3   Vaccine Liability Market Incentives and Biodefense Countermeasures
4.3.1.   The Support Anti-Terrorism by Fostering Effective Technologies Act (SAFETY Act) of 2002

This Act was created under the Homeland Security Act of 2002. Its purpose is to encourage the development of anti-terrorism technology that would protect this nation from terroristic attacks. The legislation protects certified manufacturers from tort liability in the event that their technologies do not prevent a terroristic attack. In order for a company to receive this protection, it must submit an application providing proof that the technology is safe and effective for the use of anti-terrorism. In order for a plaintiff to successfully bring suit against one of the certified companies, they must prove that the information submitted in the company's application had the willful disregard for the truth or was fraudulent.

4.3.2. The Smallpox Emergency Personnel Protection Act of 2003

This act gave the Secretary of Health and Human Services the power to create the Smallpox Injury Compensation program. There is a one in a million risk of death with the vaccine, so deaths were anticipated, requiring compensation. Another effect might be vaccinia which is a skin eruption in reaction to innoculation. This program was allocated $42 million dollars in order to provide "benefits and/or compensation to eligible individuals." Eligible persons for compensation under this statute include a personnel member who participated in a smallpox emergency response plan and was a smallpox vaccine recipient; someone who contracted vaccinia; "a survivor of a smallpox vaccine recipient or a vaccinia contact who died as a direct result of a medical condition that is covered by this [p]rogram;" and "a representative of an estate of a deceased smallpox vaccine recipient or vaccinia contact."

The National Academy reviewed the Smallpox Vaccination Program and reported on the implementation and ending of the program[9]:

> On December 13, 2002, President George W. Bush announced that the United States would begin two programs of smallpox vaccination: a military program, and a voluntary civilian program. The president stated:
>
> > "We know, however, that the smallpox virus still exists in laboratories, and we believe that regimes hostile to the United States may possess this dangerous virus. To protect our citizens in the aftermath of September the 11th, we are evaluating old threats in a new light. Our government has no information that a smallpox release is imminent. Yet it is prudent to prepare for the possibility that terrorists would kill indiscriminately—who kill indiscriminately would use diseases as a weapon." (White House, 2002).
>
> On January 22, 2003, CDC began shipping smallpox vaccine from its vaccine stockpiles to the 11 states that had requested it. On January 24, 2003, the secretary of Health and Human Services declared that the smallpox vaccination program could begin under the authority of an amendment to the Public Health Service Act by Section 304 of the Homeland Security Act[3] (DHHS, 2003a). The secretary's declaration marked the true beginning of the smallpox vaccination program, in that states, territories, and municipalities chose to defer program implementation until the protections conferred by the Homeland Security Act went into effect (Kemper, 2003a). . . .
>
> In late March 2003, three vaccinees—two civilian women and one man in the military program—died from myocardial infarction (heart attack) within 5, 6, and 22 days of smallpox vaccination, respectively. All three had a history of heart disease or risk factors, including smoking and hypertension, so it was not immediately clear whether their deaths were related to vaccination. Later study showed that the deaths were consistent with what would have been expected in the population, and there was no evidence that smallpox vaccination created a higher-than-expected risk of heart attacks. But their deaths, combined with concern about a newly identified cardiac adverse event, had a substantial chilling effect on the willingness of volunteers to receive the vaccine. . .

A total of 1,000 people were vaccinated in the first 2 weeks of the program (different jurisdictions began at different times). After that, the number of vaccinees grew at a relatively steady rate of roughly 3,000–5,000 every week. That changed with the appearance of cardiac adverse events at the end of March 2003, when the program slowed down to fewer than 1,500 per week. By the end of April 2003, only a few hundred volunteers were being vaccinated every week (Henderson, 2003b). The number of weekly vaccinations continued to decline and never recovered, reaching a handful of vaccinees weekly, then monthly. Between April 30, 2004, and July 31, 2004, 25 people received smallpox vaccination, and during August 2004, 5 people were vaccinated (CDC, 2004a, 2004b, 2004c). . . .

Concerns about program safety persisted. The present committee and the Association of State and Territorial Health Officials (ASTHO) recommended a pause between phases I and II to evaluate safety and ensure an adequate level of planning for expanded vaccination to a new population that required extensive communication and education for safety (for example, prevaccination screening and postvaccination site care). Phase III, intended to make the vaccine available to insistent members of the public, seemed even more problematic, in that it would pose public health threats, vast logistic challenges, and special and intensive communication requirements. Also, the final phase of the program would offer a potentially harmful vaccine in the context of an unknown risk, creating a philosophic conflict with health care and public health workers' injunction to "do no harm" (AAP, 2003; Libbey, 2002). . .

Military action in Iraq began on March 19, 2003. Both the events leading up to the war and the period after the declared end of major combat may have influenced public opinion and attitudes about and participation in the smallpox vaccination program. President Bush declared an end to major hostilities in Iraq in April 2003 (although military action continued). . . .

In April 2003, a compensation plan for people who experienced a smallpox vaccine injury was signed into law, largely addressing concerns about the adequacy of provisions available to protect people injured by smallpox vaccination and resolving some concerns about institutional liability in the event of inadvertent transmission of vaccinia. . . .

[In 2004,] CIA issues *Comprehensive Report of the Special Advisor to the Director of Central Intelligence on Iraq's WMD*. Report concludes that, although Iraq had capability to work with smallpox virus, there is "no direct evidence that Iraq either retained or acquired smallpox virus isolates or proceeded with any follow up smallpox related research" (CIA, 2004).

The program was halted as the threat became less threatening; however, CDC continued to acquire supplies of smallpox vaccine enough for everyone in the UUnited States in the event of a threat of a smallpox event and so that the program could be implemented, again.

4.3.3. Bioshield

The purpose of the Project Bioshield Act of 2004 is to encourage the development of countermeasures for chemical, biological, radiological, and nuclear (CBRN) agents. The Act authorized the appropriation of approximately $5.6 billion dollars over 10 years to the Department of Homeland Security to assist the government in purchasing and developing vaccines for smallpox, anthrax, and other biological threats to public health and safety. One of the problems encountered in countermeasure or vaccine development is the lack of market guarantee, primarily due to the fact that smallpox and/or anthrax outbreaks are not common. (Congressional Research Service Report for Congress at http://www.fas.org/sgp/crs/terror/RS21507.pdf)   The government is addressing this problem by purchasing vaccines and countermeasures after they have been approved for use in order to provide a market guarantee. In addition, this Act will help expedite the procedure for the development of countermeasures by shortening the time to process and approve grants for research and development. With development being expedited it will be easier to maintain an adequate supply of vaccines or countermeasures for at-risk persons. The Secretary of Health and Human Services, along with the help of the Secretary of the Department of Homeland Security, is now required under this Act to maintain a large enough stockpile of treatments and vaccines to treat children and other vulnerable populations if a bioterroristic attack occurred. If for some reason not enough approved treatments are available, this Act will allow the government to provide people with promising but not yet approved vaccines or countermeasures in emergency situations.

4.3.4.   Public Readiness and Emergency Preparedness Act of 2005 (PREPA)
42 USC §247d-6d

The purpose of PREPA is to protect vaccine manufacturers from lawsuits when the Secretary of Human and Health Services (Secretary) declares a public health emergency. This declaration is also not reviewable by any state or federal court. The Act provides these drug manufacturers with immunity from tort liability for the avian influenza clinical trials they conduct in order to produce vaccines. The Act eliminates the right to a jury trial by people injured by a vaccine covered by the Act, unless it can be proven that the injury is a direct result of "willful misconduct." There was considerable opposition to this legislation because it makes it nearly impossible for an injured party to collect damages from a drug company. However, those in favor of the legislation indicate the immense necessity for this protection to encourage drug companies to develop life saving vaccines and countermeasures.

4.3.5.   Pandemic and All-Hazards Preparedness Act of 2006 (PAHPA)

The purpose of the Pandemic and All Hazards Preparedness Act (PAHPA) of 2006 is to improve preparedness and response to all public health emergencies at local, state, and national levels of government. The Act is broken down into four different areas: National Preparedness and Response, Leadership, Organization, and Planning; Public Health Security Preparedness; All Hazards Medical Surge Capacity; and Pandemic and Biodefense Vaccine and Drug Development.

As part of the first area, the Act created the new leadership position of Assistant Secretary for Preparedness and Response. The Assistant Secretary is the principal advisor to the Secretary of Health and Human Services (Secretary) and carries out various duties as required to promote public health and medical preparedness for the nation, including but not limited to overseeing countermeasure research, coordinating preparedness and response activities at all levels of government, and promoting improvements in research, emergency medical services, and uniformity in database collection systems. Part of the planning requires the Secretary to review the stockpile annually and make modifications or changes as necessary to ensure there is a sufficient supply, while taking into consideration the needs of "at risk individuals" in a public health emergency. Starting in 2009 the Secretary is now also responsible for preparing a strategy and plan for public preparedness and response every four years, and presenting it to the relevant congressional committees.

The second area of PAHPA focuses on improving state and local public health security by encouraging the involvement of all levels of government in order to run an effective and efficient system. One way of bringing local and state governments together is by awarding cooperative grants. These grants are awarded to qualified entities, either states or political subdivisions of states that are working together by developing strategies to accomplish both preparedness and response to public health emergencies. The Secretary will further assist the improvement of state and local public health security by coordinating with states and local communities the tracking and distribution of influenza vaccines from wholesalers and distributors. Under this Act the Secretary will also be responsible for coordinating with local, state, and national governments to establish and maintain a Medical Reserve Corps, which will entail an adequate supply of volunteers available for service in public emergency situations.

In furtherance of its goal to improve preparedness and response to emergency situations, the third area of the Act moved the National Disaster Medical System from the Department of Homeland Security back to the Department of Health and Human Services. This change is believed to have been stimulated by Hurricane Katrina in 2005 and the poor response to the natural disaster. Aileen M. Marty, *Hurricane Katrina: A Deadly Warning Mandating Improvement to the National Response to Disasters*, 31 Nova L. Rev. 423. In an effort to assist the medical system's response to emergency situations, this Act proposed that the Secretary review and encourage the enhancement of medical surge capacity in local communities when feasible. One example of improving the surge capacity is by awarding grants to state and regional hospitals participating in partnerships.

The purpose of the fourth area is the improvement in the area of biomedical advanced research and development. This includes activities that would provide a longer shelf life for countermeasures, improving the manufacturing process, and improving the testing procedures. Under this area the Secretary also has the authority to expedite the peer review process for approving countermeasures and vaccines. The Secretary is also allowed to award grants, contracts, and payment prizes to encourage innovative development of countermeasures. To facilitate advanced research and development, the National Biodefense Science Board is created under this area; its function is to provide expert advice and guidance to the Department of Health and Human Services in the area of "present and future biological, chemical, nuclear, and radiological agents..."

4.3.5.1.Biomedical Advanced Research and Development Authority (BARDA)

BARDA was authorized in the PAHPA with a goal to move to the next step in a strategic plan to first, research new discoveries and applications in biodefense and then, second, to translate these into countermeasures. While scientific work is funded by the federal government, the anticipated fruits of this public investment are that at the right point in development, the private sector will acquire or partner on this investments and discoveries and turn them into marketable and valuable countermeasures. These might include sensors, diagnostic tools and devices, medicines or vaccines.

In 2011, BARDA requested proposals to build manufacturing surge capacity for vaccines and countermeasures. Three awards were made for all weapons of mass destruction countermeasures. Texas A&M University, College Station, Texas, was awarded funds in June 2012 of $176 million from BARDA with other contributions for a total of $285.6 million, according to their press release.[10] The project is described on their website as follows:

> The Texas A&M Center for Innovation in Advanced Development and Manufacturing is a public-private partnership with the U.S. Department of Health and Human Services that will bolster the nation's ability to respond to any attack or threat, known or unknown, including a novel, previously unrecognized, naturally occurring emerging infectious disease.
> The Center offers an innovative, integrated and comprehensive solution, providing surge capacity for domestically produced vaccines and medical countermeasures to chemical and biological events.[11]

CHAPTER FOUR ENDNOTES

[1] Gina Kolata, *Flu: The Story of the Great Influenza Pandemic of 1918 and the Search for the Virus that Cause It,* 175 (1999).

[2] http://www.usdoj.gov/opa/pr/1998/September/453civ.htm (Site visited Aug. 16, 2002).

[3] 42 USC 300(aa) (2001).

[4] http://www.cdc.gov/od/nvpo/fs_tableIV_doc1.htm (Site visited July 29, 2002).

[5] http:bhpr.hrsa.gov/vicp (Site visited August 16, 2002).

[6] *Id.*

[7] http://www.hrsa.gov/osp/vicp/table.htm (Site visited Aug. 16, 2002).

[8] http://www.usdoj.gov/opa/pr/1998/September/453civ.htm (Site visited Aug. 16, 2002).

[9] The Smallpox Vaccination Program: Public Health in an Age of Terrorism (2005) / 1 Smallpox and Smallpox Control in the Historical Context (National Academies, 2005).

[10] Texas A&M University, Press Release, March 26, 2013, http://ciadm.tamus.edu/news/tamus-gsk-receive-approval-vaccine-facility-in-texas/ .

[11] http://ciadm.tamus.edu/about/.

Chapter Five
State Laws and Biodefense, Biosecurity,
and other Public Health Emergencies

5.1.   States and Public Health Laws

As previously discussed, the implementation public health laws has typically resided with the states. Given the responsibilities of the state and the probability of a biological weapons incident with the current state of unpreparedness, examination of a legal framework to address quarantine and vaccination powers, emergency powers, and liability issues for states in the context of bioterrorism is the subject of this chapter.

5.2. Quarantine Powers

The federal government enacted the first quarantine law in 1796 to address a yellow fever epidemic, which provided the President with the power to assist states in their quarantine power (Act of May 27, 1796, 1 Stat. 474 (repealed 1799)). Thereafter, the Act was repealed and replaced with a maritime quarantine law, and moved away from conflicts with state powers.

The Surgeon General of the Public Health Service requested the power to quarantine from Congress in 1877 when there was an outbreak of yellow fever in New Orleans, Louisiana. The Congress passed the legislation in 1878, but by that time the yellow fever had spread to Mississippi. During the bubonic plague epidemic in San Francisco in 1900, another Surgeon General asked for quarantine power but the business community of San Francisco opposed the move. It was not until the disease had spread to all of California that Congress granted the power, and all of California had to be quarantined.

The first recognition of the quarantine powers of the states by the U.S. Supreme Court was in the opinion of Justice Marshall in the landmark case, below.

Gibbons v. Ogden
22 U.S. 1 (1824)

This doctrine of a general concurrent power in the States, is insidious and dangerous. If it be admitted, no one can say where it will stop. The States may legislate, it is said, wherever Congress has not made a plenary exercise of its power. But who is to judge whether Congress has made this plenary exercise of power? Congress has acted on this power; it has done all that it deemed wise; and are the States now to do whatever Congress has left undone? Congress makes such rules as, in its judgment, the case requires; and those rules, whatever they are, constitute the system.

All useful regulation does not consist in restraint; and that which Congress sees fit to leave free, is a part of its regulation, as much as the rest.

He thought the practice under the constitution sufficiently evinced, that this portion of the commercial power was exclusive in Congress. When, before this instance, have the States granted monopolies? When, until now, have they interfered with the navigation of the country? The pilot laws, the health laws, or quarantine laws; and various regulations of that class, which have been recognised by Congress, are no arguments to prove, even if they are to be called commercial regulations, (which they are not,) that other regulations, more directly and strictly commercial, are not solely within the power of Congress....

To sustain the interference of the State, in a high concern of maritime commerce, the argument adopts a principle which acknowledges the right of Congress, over a vast scope of internal legislation, which no one has heretofore supposed to be within its powers. But this is not all; for it is admitted, that when Congress and the States have power to legislate over the same subject, the power of Congress, when exercised, controls or extinguishes the State power; and, therefore, the consequence would seem to follow, from the argument, that all State legislation, over such subjects as have been mentioned, is, at all times, liable to the superior power of Congress; a consequence, which no one would admit for a moment. The truth was, he thought, that all these things were, in their general character, rather regulations of police than of commerce, in the constitutional understanding of that term. A road, indeed, might be a matter of great commercial concern. In many cases it is so; and when it is so, he thought there was no doubt of the power of Congress to make it. But, generally speaking, roads, and bridges, and ferries, though, of course, they affect commerce and intercourse, do not obtain that importance and elevation, as to be deemed commercial regulations. A reasonable construction must be given to the constitution; and such construction is as necessary to the just power of the States, as to the authority of Congress. Quarantine laws, for example, may be considered as affecting commerce; yet they are, in their nature, health laws. In England, we speak of the power of regulating commerce, as in Parliament, or the King, as arbiter of commerce; yet the city of London enacts health laws. Would any one infer from that circumstance, that the city of London had concurrent power with Parliament or the Crown to regulate commerce? or, that it might grant a monopoly of the navigation of the Thames? While a health law is reasonable, it is a health law; but if, under colour of it, enactments should be made for other purposes, such enactments might be void....

The quarantine laws further illustrate our position. The appellant's counsel says, these are to be considered merely as laws of police; they are laws of police, but they are also laws of commerce; for such is the nature of that commerce, which we are told must be regulated exclusively by Congress, that it enters into, and mixes itself with, almost all the concerns of life. But surely that furnishes an argument, showing the necessity that the States should have a concurrent power over it. Judge Tucker considers them as laws of commerce, when he says, "another consequence of the right of regulating foreign commerce, seems to be, the power of compelling vessels infected with any contagious disease, or arriving from places usually infected with them, to perform their quarantine. The laws of the respective States upon this subject, were, by some persons, supposed to have been virtually repealed by the constitution of the United States:" (and why must not that be the case, if the power of Congress regulating commerce be exclusive?) "but Congress have manifested a different interpretation of that instrument, and have passed several acts for giving aid and effect to the execution of the laws of the several States respecting quarantine." It will be recollected, that the first recognition by Congress of the quarantine laws, was in 1796; and that only directs the officers of the government to obey them; but does not pretend, or attempt, to legalize them. And, indeed, it could not do so, if the States had no concurrent power, and the regulation of commerce was exclusively delegated to Congress; for the power which is exclusively delegated to Congress, can only be exercised by Congress itself, and cannot be sub-delegated by it. It is, therefore, no reply to the force of the argument drawn from those laws, to say, that they have been ratified by Congress. Another answer to that observation is, that the supposed ratification by Congress did not take place until 1796; and that many of those laws were in active operation several years before. For instance, as few out of many: New Hampshire passed her quarantine laws first, February 3d, 1789, and again on the 25th of September, 1792. Connecticut passed hers in May, 1795. The laws of Maryland show the temporary continuation of those laws in that State, from 1784 to 1785, from 1785 to 1792, from 1792 to 1799, and so down to 1810; and the 2d vol. contains a law passed in November, 1793, giving to the Governor the strongest powers on the subject. The State of Virginia passed, 26th of December, 1792, "an act reducing into one the several acts to oblige vessels coming from foreign parts, to perform quarantine;" which act was amended on the 5th of December, 1793; and further amended on the 19th of December, 1795. Georgia passed her quarantine law December 17th, 1793. Undoubtedly those laws derive their efficacy from the sovereign authority of the States; and they expressly restrain, and indeed prohibit, the entry of vessels into part of the waters and ports of the States. They are all so similar, that one or two may suffice as examples. The quarantine law of Georgia, s. 1. prohibits the landing of persons or goods coming in any vessel from an infected place, without permission from the proper authority; and enacts, that the said vessels or boats, and the persons and goods coming and imported in, or going on board during the time of quarantine; and all ships, vessels, boats, and persons, receiving any person or goods under quarantine, shall be subject to such orders, rules and directions, touching quarantine, as shall be made by the authority directing the same. The law of Delaware, passed the 24th of January, 1797, s. 1. provides, that "no master of a ship bound to any part of that State, having on board any greater number of passengers than forty, or any person with an infectious disease, or coming from a sickly port, shall bring his ship, or suffer it to be brought, nearer than one mile to any port or place of landing; nor land such persons, or their goods, till he shall have obtained a permit." The law of Massachusetts, passed June 22d, 1797, s. 6. enacts, that "vessels passing the castle, in Boston harbour, may be questioned and detained; s. 12. that vessels at any other port than Boston, may be prevented from coming up, and brought to anchor where the select men shall direct; s. 4. empowers the select men of any town, bordering on either of the neighbouring States, to appoint persons to attend at ferries and other proper places, by or over which passengers may pass from such infected places, which persons have power to examine, stop and restrain such passengers from travelling, until licensed by a Justice of the peace, or the select men; and a fine of 100 pounds is enacted on the passenger presuming to travel onward; s. 5. gives power to seize and detain suspected goods coming from any other State," &c. By an act of June 20th, 1799, s. 10. "any master, &c. who shall enter the harbour of Boston after notice of a quarantine, for all vessels coming from the same place, &c., or who shall land, or suffer to be landed, and passenger or goods, without permission of the board of health, in subject to fine and imprisonment." These are all obviously direct regulations of trade, and so is the whole of every quarantine system....

The object of inspection laws, is to improve the quality of articles produced by the labour of a country; to fit them for exportation; or, it may be, for domestic use. They act upon the subject before it becomes an article of foreign commerce, or of commerce among the States, and prepare it for that purpose. They form a portion of that immense mass of legislation, which embraces every thing within the territory of a State, not surrendered to the general government: all which can be most advantageously exercised by the States themselves. Inspection laws, quarantine laws, health laws of every description, as well as laws for regulating the internal commerce of a State, and those which respect turnpike roads, ferries, &c., are component parts of this mass.

5.3. Vaccination Powers

An outbreak of smallpox in Boston, Massachusetts occurred in May 1901, and the city responded by initiating a voluntary vaccination program and free vaccinations. By December 1901, the smallpox epidemic was still raging, and the city began a house-to-house vaccination program in January 1902. Instructions to the physicians included, "No force to be used." Persons who refused the vaccine were subject to a $5 fine or a 15-day jail sentence.

A *Boston Globe* reporter who accompanied a vaccination squad described the scene: "Every imaginable threat from civil suits to cold-blooded murder when they got an opportunity was made by the writhing, cursing, struggling tramps who were operated upon, and a lot of them had to be held down in their cots, one big policeman sitting on their legs, and another on their heads, while the third held the arms, bared for the doctors...[one] fighting tramp...went down in a heap on the floor," the result of a policeman's club, and was vaccinated.[1]

The Anti-Compulsory Vaccination League, opponents to the forced vaccination program, believed that compulsory vaccinations were violations of civil liberties and that "from the standpoint of free citizenship no government should forcibly inflict on any individual enjoying all other rights of the nation, a disease [vaccine] loathsome in its origin, and not free from danger to life, and with, at all events, impairment of bodily health, at least of a temporary nature."[2] This led to legislation introduced in the Massachusetts legislature to repeal the compulsory vaccination laws in January 1902, but by February they had all been defeated.

This controversy led to the following landmark case and state powers to require compulsory vaccination.

Jacobson v. Massachusetts
197 U.S. 11 (1905)

JUDGES: Fuller, Harlan, Brewer, Brown, White, Peckham, McKenna, Holmes, Day

Opinion by Justice Harlan: Mr. Justice Harlan, after making the foregoing statement, delivered the opinion of the court.

We pass without extended discussion the suggestion that the particular section of the statute of Massachusetts now in question (§137, c. 75) is in derogation of rights secured by the Preamble of the Constitution of the United States. Although that Preamble indicates the general purposes for which the people ordained and established the Constitution, it has never been regarded as the source of any substantive power conferred on the Government of the United States or on any of its Departments. Such powers embrace only those expressly granted in the body of the Constitution and such as may be implied from those so granted. Although, therefore, one of the declared objects of the Constitution was to secure the blessings of liberty to all under the sovereign jurisdiction and authority of the United States, no power can be exerted to that end by the United States unless, apart from the Preamble, it be found in some express delegation of power or in some power to be properly implied there from.

We also pass without discussion the suggestion that the above section of the statute is opposed to the spirit of the Constitution. Undoubtedly, as observed by Chief Justice Marshall, speaking for the court, "the spirit of an instrument, especially of a constitution, is to be respected not less than its letter, yet the spirit is to be collected chiefly from its words." We have no need in this case to go beyond the plain, obvious meaning of the words in those provisions of the Constitution which, it is contended, must control our decision.

What, according to the judgment of the state court, is the scope and effect of the statute? What results were intended to be accomplished by it? These questions must be answered.

The Supreme Judicial Court of Massachusetts said in the present case: "Let us consider the offer of evidence which was made by the defendant Jacobson. The ninth of the propositions which he offered to prove, as to what vaccination consists of, is nothing more than a fact of common knowledge, upon which the statute is founded, and proof of it was unnecessary and immaterial. The thirteenth and fourteenth involved matters depending upon his personal opinion, which could not be taken as correct, or given effect, merely because he made it a ground of refusal to comply with the requirement. Moreover, his views could not affect the validity of the statute, nor entitle him to be excepted from its provisions. The other eleven propositions all relate to alleged injurious or dangerous effects of vaccination. The defendant 'offered to prove and show by competent evidence' these so-called facts. Each of them, in its nature, is such that it cannot be stated as a truth, otherwise than as a matter of opinion. The only 'competent evidence' that could be presented to the court to prove these propositions was the testimony of experts, giving their opinions. It would not have been competent to introduce the medical history of individual cases. Assuming that medical experts could have been found who would have testified in support of these propositions, and that it had become the duty of the judge to instruct the jury as to whether or not the statute is constitutional, he would have been obliged to consider the evidence in connection with facts of common knowledge, which the court will always regard in passing upon the constitutionality of a statute. He would have considered this testimony of experts in connection with the facts that for nearly a century most of the members of the medical profession have regarded vaccination, repeated after intervals, as a preventive of smallpox; that while they have recognized the possibility of injury to an individual from carelessness in the performance of it, or even in a conceivable case without carelessness, they generally have considered the risk of such an injury too small to be seriously weighed as against the benefits coming from the discreet and proper use of the preventive; and that not only the medical profession and the people generally have for a long time entertained these opinions, but legislatures and courts have acted upon them with general unanimity. If the defendant had been permitted to introduce such expert testimony as he had in support of these several propositions, it could not have changed the result. It would not have justified the court in holding that the legislature had transcended its power in enacting this statute on their judgment of what the welfare of the people demands."

While the mere rejection of defendant's offers of proof does not strictly present a Federal question, we may properly regard the exclusion of evidence upon the ground of its incompetency or immateriality under the statute as showing what, in the opinion of the state court, is the scope and meaning of the statute. Taking the above observations of the state court as indicating the scope of the statute—and such is our duty—we assume for the purposes of the present inquiry that its provisions require, at least as a general rule, that adults not under guardianship and remaining within the limits of the city of Cambridge must submit to the regulation adopted by the Board of Health. Is the statute, so construed, therefore, inconsistent with the liberty which the Constitution of the United States secures to every person against deprivation by the State?

The authority of the State to enact this statute is to be referred to what is commonly called the police power—a power which the State did not surrender when becoming a member of the Union under the Constitution. Although this court has refrained from any attempt to define the limits of that power, yet it has distinctly recognized the authority of a State to enact quarantine laws and "health laws of every description;" indeed, all laws that relate to matters completely within its territory and which do not by their necessary operation affect the people of other States. According to settled principles the police power of a State must be held to embrace, at least, such reasonable regulations established directly by legislative enactment as will protect the public health and the public safety. It is equally true that the State may invest local bodies called into existence for purposes of local administration with authority in some appropriate way to safeguard the public health and the public safety. The mode or manner in which those results are to be accomplished is within the discretion of the State, subject, of course, so far as Federal power is concerned, only to the condition that no rule prescribed by a State, nor any regulation adopted by a local governmental agency acting under the sanction of state legislation, shall contravene the Constitution of the United States or infringe any right granted or secured by that instrument. A local enactment or regulation, even if based on the acknowledged police power of a State, must always yield in case of conflict with the exercise by the General Government of any power it possesses under the Constitution, or with any right which that instrument gives or secures.

We come, then, to inquire whether any right given, or secured by the Constitution, is invaded by the statute as interpreted by the state court. The defendant insists that his liberty is invaded when the State subjects him to fine or imprisonment for neglecting or refusing to submit to vaccination; that a compulsory vaccination law is unreasonable, arbitrary and oppressive, and, therefore, hostile to the inherent right of every freeman to care for his own body and health in such way as to him seems best; and that the execution of such a law against one who objects to vaccination, no matter for what reason, is nothing short of an assault upon his person. But the liberty secured by the Constitution of the United States to every person within its jurisdiction does not import an absolute right in each person to be, at all times and in all circumstances, wholly freed from restraint. There are manifold restraints to which every person is necessarily subject for the common good. On any other basis organized society could not exist with safety to its members. Society based on the rule that each one is a law unto himself would soon be confronted with disorder and anarchy. Real liberty for all could not exist under the operation of a principle which recognizes the right of each individual person to use his own, whether in respect of his person or his property, regardless of the injury that may be done to others. This court has more than once recognized it as a fundamental principle that "persons and property are subjected to all kinds of restraints and burdens, in order to secure the general comfort, health, and prosperity of the State; of the perfect right of the legislature to do which no question ever was, or upon acknowledged general principles ever can be made, so far as natural persons are concerned." "The possession and enjoyment of all rights are subject to such reasonable conditions as may be deemed by the governing authority of the country essential to the safety, health, peace, good order and morals of the community. Even liberty itself, the greatest of all rights, is not unrestricted license to act according to one's own will. It is only freedom from restraint under conditions essential to the equal enjoyment of the same right by others. It is then liberty regulated by law." In the constitution of Massachusetts adopted in 1780 it was laid down as a fundamental principle of the social compact that the whole people covenants with each citizen, and each citizen with the whole people, that all shall be governed by certain laws for "the common good," and that government is instituted "for the common good, for the protection, safety, prosperity and happiness of the people, and not for the profit, honor or private interests of any one man, family or class of men." The good and welfare of the Commonwealth, of which the legislature is primarily the judge, is the basis on which the police power rests in Massachusetts.

Applying these principles to the present case, it is to be observed that the legislature of Massachusetts required the inhabitants of a city or town to be vaccinated only when, in the opinion of the Board of Health, that was necessary for the public health or the public safety. The authority to determine for all what ought to be done in such an emergency must have been lodged somewhere or in some body; and surely it was appropriate for the legislature to refer that question, in the first instance, to a Board of Health, composed of persons residing in the locality affected and appointed, presumably, because of their fitness to determine such questions. To invest such a body with authority over such matters was not an unusual nor an unreasonable or arbitrary requirement. Upon the principle of self-defense, of paramount necessity, a community has the right to protect itself against an epidemic of disease which threatens the safety of its members. It is to be observed that when the regulation in question was adopted, smallpox, according to the recitals in the regulation adopted by the Board of Health, was prevalent to some extent in the city of Cambridge and the disease was increasing. If such was the situation—and nothing is asserted or appears in the record to the contrary—if we are to attach any value whatever to the knowledge which, it is safe to affirm, is common to all civilized peoples touching smallpox and the methods most usually employed to eradicate that disease, it cannot be adjudged that the present regulation of the Board of Health was not necessary in order to protect the public health and secure the public safety. Smallpox being prevalent and increasing at Cambridge, the court would usurp the functions of another branch of government if it adjudged, as matter of law, that the mode adopted under the sanction of the State, to protect the people at large, was arbitrary and not justified by the necessities of the case. We say necessities of the case, because it might be that an acknowledged power of a local community to protect itself against an epidemic threatening the safety of all, might be exercised in particular circumstances and in reference to particular persons in such an arbitrary, unreasonable manner, or might go so far beyond what was reasonably required for the safety of the public, as to authorize or compel the courts to interfere for the protection of such persons....this court recognized the right of a State to pass sanitary laws, laws for the protection of life, liberty, health or property within its limits, laws to prevent persons and animals suffering under contagious or infectious diseases, or convicts, from coming within its borders. But as the laws there involved when beyond the necessity of the case and under the guise of exerting a police power invaded the domain of Federal authority and violated rights secured by the Constitution, this court deemed it to be its duty to hold such laws invalid. If the mode adopted by the Commonwealth of Massachusetts for the protection of its local communities against smallpox proved to be distressing, inconvenient or objectionable to some—if nothing more could be reasonably affirmed of the statute in question—the answer is that it was the duty of the constituted authorities primarily to keep in view the welfare, comfort and safety of the many, and not permit the interests of the many to be subordinated to the wishes or convenience of the few. There is, of course, a sphere within which the individual may assert the supremacy of his own will and rightfully dispute the authority of any human government, especially of any free government existing under a written constitution, to interfere with the exercise of that will. But it is equally true that in every well-ordered society charged with the duty of conserving the safety of its members the rights of the individual in respect of his liberty may at times, under the pressure of great dangers, be subjected to such restraint, to be enforced by reasonable regulations, as the safety of the general public may demand. An American citizen, arriving at an American port on a vessel in which, during the voyage, there had been cases of yellow fever or Asiatic cholera, although apparently free from disease himself, may yet, in some circumstances, be held in quarantine against his will on board of such vessel or in a quarantine station, until it be ascertained by inspection, conducted with due diligence, that the danger of the spread of the disease among the community at large has disappeared. The liberty secured by the Fourteenth Amendment, this court has said, consists, in part, in the right of a person "to live and work where he will," and yet he may be compelled, by force if need be, against his will and without regard to his personal wishes or his pecuniary interests, or even his religious or political convictions, to take his place in the ranks of the army of his country and risk the chance of being shot down in its defense. It is not, therefore, true that the power of the public to guard itself against imminent danger depends in every case involving the control of one's body upon his willingness to submit to reasonable regulations established by the constituted authorities, under the sanction of the State, for the purpose of protecting the public collectively against such danger.

It is said, however, that the statute, as interpreted by the state court, although making an exception in favor of children certified by a registered physician to be unfit subjects for vaccination, makes no exception in the case of adults in like condition. But this cannot be deemed a denial of the equal protection of the laws to adults; for the statute is applicable equally to all in like condition and there are obviously reasons why regulations may be appropriate for adults which could not be safely applied to persons of tender years.

Looking at the propositions embodied in the defendant's rejected offers of proof it is clear that they are more formidable by their number than by their inherent value. Those offers in the main seem to have had no purpose except to state the general theory of those of the medical profession who attach little or no value to vaccination as a means of preventing the spread of smallpox or who think that vaccination causes other diseases of the body. What everybody knows the court must know, and therefore the state court judicially knew, as this court knows, that an opposite theory accords with the common belief and is maintained by high medical authority. We must assume that when the statute in question was passed, the legislature of Massachusetts was not unaware of these opposing theories, and was compelled, of necessity, to choose between them. It was not compelled to commit a matter involving the public health and safety to the final decision of a court or jury. It is no part of the function of a court or a jury to determine which one of two modes was likely to be the most effective for the protection of the public against disease. That was for the legislative department to determine in the light of all the information it had or could obtain. It could not properly abdicate its function to guard the public health and safety. The state legislature proceeded upon the theory which recognized vaccination as at least an effective if not the best known way in which to meet and suppress the evils of a smallpox epidemic that imperiled an entire population. Upon what sound principles as to the relations existing between the different departments of government can the court review this action of the legislature? If there is any such power in the judiciary to review legislative action in respect of a matter affecting the general welfare, it can only be when that which the legislature has done comes within the rule that if a statute purporting to have been enacted to protect the public health, the public morals or the public safety, has no real or substantial relation to those objects, or is, beyond all question, a plain, palpable invasion of rights secured by the fundamental law, it is the duty of the courts to so adjudge, and thereby give effect to the Constitution."

Whatever may be thought of the expediency of this statute, it cannot be affirmed to be, beyond question, in palpable conflict with the Constitution. Nor, in view of the methods employed to stamp out the disease of smallpox, can anyone confidently assert that the means prescribed by the State to that end has no real or substantial relation to the protection of the public health and the public safety. Such an assertion would not be consistent with the experience of this and other countries whose authorities have dealt with the disease of smallpox. And the principle of vaccination as a means to prevent the spread of smallpox has been enforced in many States by statutes making the vaccination of children a condition of their right to enter or remain in public schools.

"It must be conceded that some laymen, both learned and unlearned, and some physicians of great skill and repute, do not believe that vaccination is a preventive of smallpox. The common belief, however, is that it has a decided tendency to prevent the spread of this fearful disease and to render it less dangerous to those who contract it. While not accepted by all, it is accepted by the mass of the people, as well as by most members of the medical profession. It has been general in our State and in most civilized nations for generations. It is generally accepted in theory and generally applied in practice, both by the voluntary action of the people and in obedience to the command of law. Nearly every State of the Union has statutes to encourage, or directly or indirectly to require, vaccination, and this is true of most nations of Europe...." A common belief, like common knowledge, does not require evidence to establish its existence, but may be acted upon without proof by the legislature and the courts.... "The fact that the belief is not universal is not controlling, for there is scarcely any belief that is accepted by everyone. The possibility that the belief may be wrong, and that science may yet show it to be wrong, is not conclusive; for the legislature has the right to pass laws which, according to the common belief of the people, are adapted to prevent the spread of contagious diseases. In a free country, where the government is by the people, through their chosen representatives, practical legislation admits of no other standard of action; for what the people believe is for the common welfare must be accepted as tending to promote the common welfare, whether it does in fact or not. Any other basis would conflict with the spirit of the Constitution, and would sanction measures opposed to a republican form of government. While we do not decide and cannot decide that vaccination is a preventive of smallpox, we take judicial notice of the fact that this is the common belief f the people of the State, and with this fact as a foundation we hold that the statute in question is a health law, enacted in a reasonable and proper exercise of the police power."

Since then vaccination, as a means of protecting a community against smallpox, finds strong support in the experience of this and other countries, no court, much less a jury, is justified in disregarding the action of the legislature simply because in its or their opinion that particular method was—perhaps or possibly—not the best either for children or adults.

Did the offers of proof made by the defendant present a case which entitled him, while remaining in Cambridge, to claim exemption from the operation of the statute and of the regulation adopted by the Board of Health? We have already said that his rejected offers, in the main, only set forth the theory of those who had no faith in vaccination as a means of preventing the spread of smallpox, or who thought that vaccination, without benefiting the public, put in peril the health of the person vaccinated. But there were some offers which it is contended embodied distinct facts that might properly have been considered, Let us see how this is.

The defendant offered to prove that vaccination "quite often" caused serious and permanent injury to the health of the person vaccinated; that the operation "occasionally" resulted in death; that it was "impossible" to tell "in any particular case" what the results of vaccination would be or whether it would injure the health or result in death; that "quite often" one's blood is in a certain condition of impurity when it is not prudent or safe to vaccinate him; that there is no practical test by which to determine "with any degree of certainty" whether one's blood is in such condition of impurity as to render vaccination necessarily unsafe or dangerous; that vaccine matter is "quite often" impure and dangerous to be used, but whether impure or not cannot be ascertained by any known practical test; that the defendant refused to submit to vaccination for the reason that he had, "when a child," been caused great and extreme suffering for a long period by a disease produced by vaccination; and that he had witnessed a similar result of vaccination not only in the case of his son, but in the case of others.

These offers, in effect, invited the court and jury to go over the whole ground gone over by the legislature when it enacted the statute in question. The legislature assumed that some children, by reason of their condition at the time, might not be fit subjects of vaccination; and it is suggested—and we will not say without reason—that such is the case with some adults. But the defendant did not offer to prove that, by reason of his then condition, he was in fact not a fit subject of vaccination at the time he was informed of the requirement of the regulation adopted by the Board of Health. It is entirely consistent with his offer of proof that, after reaching full age he had become, so far as medical skill could discover, and when informed of the regulation of the Board of Health was, a fit subject of vaccination, and that the vaccine matter to be used in his case was such as any medical practitioner of good standing would regard as proper to be used. The matured opinions of medical men everywhere, and the experience of mankind, as all must know, negative the suggestion that it is not possible in any case to determine whether vaccination is safe. Was defendant exempted from the operation of the statute simply because of this dread of the same evil results experienced by him when a child and had observed in the cases of his son and other children? Could he reasonably claim such an exemption because "quite often" or "occasionally" injury had resulted from vaccination, or because it was impossible, in the opinion of some, by any practical test, to determine with absolute certainty whether a particular person could be safely vaccinated?

It seems to the court that an affirmative answer to these questions would practically strip the legislative department of its function to care for the public health and the public safety when endangered by epidemics of disease. Such an answer would mean that compulsory vaccination could not, in any conceivable case, be legally enforced in a community, even at the command of the legislature, however widespread the epidemic of smallpox, and however deep and universal was the belief of the community and of its medical advisers, that a system of general vaccination was vital to the safety of all.

We are not prepared to hold that a minority, residing or remaining in any city or town where smallpox is prevalent, and enjoying the general protection afforded by an organized local government, may thus defy the will of its constituted authorities, acting in good faith for all, under the legislative sanction of the State. If such be the privilege of a minority then a like privilege would belong to each individual of the community, and the spectacle would be presented of the welfare and safety of an entire population being subordinated to the notions of a single individual who chooses to remain a part of that population. We are unwilling to hold it to be an element in the liberty secured by the Constitution of the United States that one person, or a minority of persons, residing in any community and enjoying the benefits of its local government, should have the power thus to dominate the majority when supported in their action by the authority of the State. While this court should guard with firmness every right appertaining to life, liberty or property as secured to the individual by the Supreme Law of the Land, it is of the last importance that it should not invade the domain of local authority except when it is plainly necessary to do so in order to enforce that law. The safety and the health of the people of Massachusetts are, in the first instance, for that Commonwealth to guard and protect. They are matters that do not ordinarily concern the National Government. So far as they can be reached by any government, they depend, primarily, upon such action as the State in its wisdom may take; and we do not perceive that this legislation has invaded by right secured by the Federal Constitution.

Before closing this opinion we deem it appropriate, in order to prevent misapprehension as to our views, to observe—perhaps to repeat a thought already sufficiently expressed, namely—that the police power of a State, whether exercised by the legislature, or by a local body acting under its authority, may be exerted in such circumstances or by regulations so arbitrary and oppressive in particular cases as to justify the interference of the courts to prevent wrong and oppression. Extreme cases can be readily suggested. Ordinarily such cases are not safe guides in the administration of the law. It is easy, for instance, to suppose the case of an adult who is embraced by the mere words of the act, but yet to subject whom to vaccination in a particular condition of his health or body, would be cruel and inhuman in the last degree. We are not to be understood as holding that the statute was intended to be applied to such a case, or, if it was so intended, that the judiciary would not be competent to interfere and protect the health and life of the individual concerned. "All laws," this court has said, "should receive a sensible construction. General terms should be so limited in their application as not to lead to injustice, oppression or absurd consequence. It will always, therefore, be presumed that the legislature intended exceptions to its language which would avoid results of that character. The reason of the law in such cases should prevail over its letter." Until otherwise informed by the highest court of Massachusetts we are not inclined to hold that the statute establishes the absolute rule that an adult must be vaccinated if it be apparent or can be shown with reasonable certainty that he is not at the time a fit subject of vaccination or that vaccination, by reason of his then condition, would seriously impair his health or probably cause his death. No such case is here presented. It is the case of an adult who, for aught that appears, was himself in perfect health and a fit subject of vaccination, and yet, while remaining in the community, refused to obey the statute and the regulation adopted in execution of its provisions for the protection of the public health and the public safety, confessedly endangered by the presence of a dangerous disease.

We now decide only that the statute covers the present case, and that nothing clearly appears that would justify this court in holding it to be unconstitutional and inoperative in its application to the plaintiff in error.

The judgment of the court below must be affirmed.

It is so ordered.

MR. JUSTICE BREWER and MR. JUSTICE PECKHAM dissent.

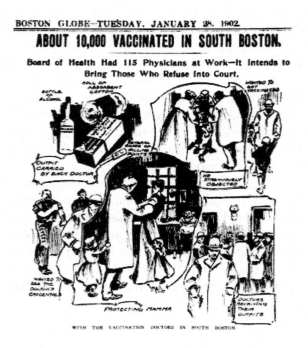

Fig. 5-2. Illustration from *The Boston Globe* of House-to-House Vaccination (Jan. 28, 1902) from N Engl J Med 2001; 344(5) 375–379.

Notes

1. From *Jacobson v. Massachusetts* in 1905, the court includes in a footnote the current state of vaccination regulation throughout the world:

State-supported facilities for vaccination began in England in 1808 with the National Vaccine Establishment. In 1840 vaccination fees were made payable out of the rates. The first compulsory act was passed in 1853, the guardians of the poor being entrusted with the carrying out of the law; in 1854 the public vaccinations under one year of age were 408,825 as against an average of 180,960 for several years before. In 1867 a new Act was passed, rather to remove some technical difficulties than to enlarge the scope of the former Act; and in 1871 the Act was passed which compelled the boards of guardians to appoint vaccination officers. The guardians also appoint a public vaccinator, who must be duly qualified to practice medicine, and whose duty it is to vaccinate (for a fee of one shilling and sixpence) any child resident within his district brought to him for that purpose, to examine the same a week after, to give a certificate, and to certify to the vaccination officer the fact of vaccination or of insusceptibility....Vaccination was made compulsory in Bavaria in 1807, and subsequently in the following countries: Denmark (1810), Sweden (1814), Wurtemburg, Hesse, and other German states (1818), Prussia (1835), Roumania (1874), Hungary (1876), and Servia (1881). It is compulsory by cantonal law in ten out of the twenty-two Swiss cantons; an attempt to pass a federal compulsory law was defeated by a plebiscite in 1881. In the following countries there is no compulsory law, but Government facilities and compulsion on various classes more or less directly under Government control, such as soldiers, state employes, apprentices, school pupils, etc.: France, Italy, Spain, Portugal, Belgium, Norway, Austria, Turkey....Vaccination has been compulsory in South Australia since 1872, in Victoria since 1874, and in Western Australia since 1878. In Tasmania a compulsory Act was passed in 1882. In New South Wales there is no compulsion, but free facilities for vaccination. Compulsion was adopted at Calcutta in 1880, and since then at eighty other towns of Bengal, at Madras in 1884, and at Bombay and elsewhere in the presidency a few years earlier. Revaccination was made compulsory in Denmark in 1871, and in Roumania in 1874; in Holland it was enacted for all school pupils in 1872. The various laws and administrative orders which had been for many years in force as to vaccination and revaccination in the several German states were consolidated in an imperial statute of 1874." 24 *Encyclopoedia Britannica*(1894), *Vaccination.*

2. Given the rise in smallpox cases in Massachusetts, in retrospect, at what point would compulsory vaccination be acceptable to protect the public health? In order to assess that point, consider the following graphic distribution of smallpox cases from 1901 to 1903.

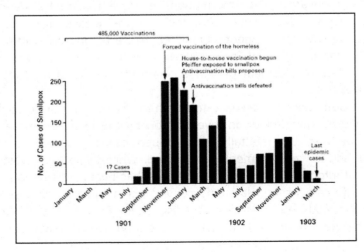

Fig. 5-2. Distribution of Smallpox Cases in Boston during the Epidemic of 1901–93 Data are from the annual reports of the Boston Health Department. [Source: N. Engl. J. Med. 2001; 344(5) 376]

3. A challenge was made by Dr. Durgin, the Chairman of the Boston Board of Health, to the anti-vaccinationists, to come forward and profess the sincerity of their beliefs by exposing themselves to smallpox. Dr. Immanuel Pfeiffer, a physician and Danish immigrant who recommended hypnotism and fasting instead of vaccination came forward. The Chairman took him to visit the Gallop Island smallpox hospital and they walked among the 100 smallpox patients on January 23, 1902. On February 8, 1902, Dr. Pfeiffer was observed to be critically ill in his home in Bedford, Massachusetts. Because the Boston Board of Health had failed to place Dr. Pfeiffer under any restrictions after his exposure at Gallop Island, and because Dr. Pfeiffer returned to his home in Bedford with the disease, the City of Bedford considered suing the City of Boston for importing smallpox to their city, charging that smallpox had been "imported because of the inexcusable negligence of the health authorities of Boston." [Albert, Ostheimer, Breman, "The Last Smallpox Epidemic in Boston and the Vaccination Controversy, 1901–1903," N. Engl. J. Med 2001; 344(5) 377, quoting "Bedford May Sue," Boston Globe (Feb. 17, 1902:1)]

What theories of recovery might the City of Bedford have proposed?

4. The United States ended smallpox vaccinations for school-age children in the 1970s. The federal government has proposed a smallpox vaccination program since the September 2001 anthrax attacks; it expects to begin with health care providers, but will eventually include all citizens. Exclusions will be made for those who are at risk, such as HIV patients, transplant patients, and pregnant individuals.

What legal issues might be raised in opposition to a smallpox vaccination program such as this based upon state powers versus federal powers? Could the federal government compel vaccination just as the states can compel vaccination within their police powers?

5.4. State Emergency Powers

The CDC created a list of state emergency powers needed by states in order to respond to a biological attack at the Cantingy Conference on State Emergency Health Powers and the Bioterrorism Threat on April 26–27, 2001 as part of its Bioterrorism Preparedness and Response Program.

5.4.1. Collection of Records and Data

The CDC list of emergency powers needed includes: reporting of diseases, unusual clusters, and suspicious events; access to hospital and provider records; data sharing with law enforcement agencies; veterinary reporting; reporting of workplace absenteeism; reporting from pharmacies.

5.4.4.1. Access to Records

The substantive due process right of privacy cannot be ignored in the disclosure of private health information. The Health Insurance Portability and Accountability Act of 1996 (HIPAA) provided for the protection of private health information. In implementing HIPAA, regulations were promulgated that created privacy standards, which do not permit the release of private health information to public health authorities or law enforcement personnel. However, in the context of an emergency, private health information can be released for purposes of payment or treatment of the individual (45 CFR §164.506). Neither can law enforcement personnel share the results of their investigations and interviews with the public health staff.

An outbreak of a sexually-transmitted disease in a state facility for the mentally and physically handicapped in Iowa led to an investigation by the local and state health departments to control the outbreak. Because the mentally handicapped cannot consent to sexual relations, sexual abuse was suspected, and law enforcement was notified. While these two investigations proceeded in parallel, little exchange of information occurred because public health was unable to share private health information with law enforcement, and law enforcement was unable to disclose the results of their interviews with public health authorities. Patricia Quinlisk, State Epidemiologist for the Iowa Department of Health, testified before Congress that the investigation would have benefited from the removal of legal constraints that prevented the sharing of information in the investigation. (Patricia Quinlisk, Testimony before the Committee on Government Reform, Subcommittee on National Security, Veterans Affairs, and International Relations, "Combating Terrorism: Federal Response to a Biological Weapons Attack," July 23, 2001.)

The consequences of disclosing private health information with consent from the patient can result in the loss of the license by the physician, civil or criminal punishment, or monetary damages. Other possible consequences include common law state tort actions for negligence, malpractice, privacy, implied breach of contract, breach of fiduciary duty, intentional or negligent infliction of emotional distress, and invasion of privacy. (Kellman, Barry, "Managing Terrorism's Consequences: Legal Issues," Quoting Footnote 119, Note: "Do Doctors Have a Constitutional Right to Violate Their Patients' Privacy?: Ohio's Physician Disclosure Tort and the First Amendment, 46 Vill. L. Rev. 141 (2001)).

5.4.4.2. Collection of Samples, Fourth Amendment Search, and Seizure Issues

Constitutional protections cannot be legislated away. For example, collection of samples may violate Fourth Amendment search and seizure constitutional requirements, unless there is probable cause to believe that the person has been exposed to a communicable disease or has a communicable disease. Without any reasonable suspicion, the routine collection of samples (for example, saliva samples at a roadblock) would likely be held as an unreasonable search. This can only be accomplished in a true emergency.

5.4.2. Control of Property

The CDC list of emergency powers needed includes: right of access to suspicious premises; emergency closure of facilities; temporary use of hospitals and ability to transfer patients; temporary use of hotel rooms and drive-through facilities; procurement or confiscation of medicines and vaccines; seizure of cell phones and other "walkie-talkie" type equipment; decontamination of buildings; and seizure and destruction of contaminated articles.

5.4.3. Management of Persons

The CDC list of emergency powers needed by a public health officer include: identification of exposed persons; mandatory medical examinations; collection of laboratory specimens and performance of tests; rationing of medicines; tracking and follow-up of persons; isolation and quarantine; logistical authority for patient management; enforcement authority through police or National Guard; suspension of licensing authority for medical personnel from outside jurisdictions; authorization of doctors to perform functions of medical examiner; and safe disposal of corpses.

5.4.3.1. Declaration of a State of Emergency

The governor has the authority to declare a state of emergency and issue executive orders. A declared state of emergency triggers the governor's emergency powers for a limited statutory period of time. The governor can order evacuations, utilize public schools and public school buses for evacuation facilities and evacuation transportation, respectively. Temporary housing obtained through leases, purchases, or other arrangements are also within the emergency powers of the governor. The governor can also issue executive orders initiating a quarantine or restriction of travel.

5.4.3.2. National Guard

The use of the National Guard is by request of either the governor or the President of the United States, in their dual roles. The U.S. Constitution, Art. I, §8, cl. 15-16, provides for a militia to execute the laws of the Union and for state control of the militia when it is not in the service of the National Guard.

In order to control a declared state of emergency, a governor has the authority to declare martial law and call upon its National Guard to suppress insurrection and disorder. (See *Moyer v. Peabody*, 212 U.S. 78, 83 (1909)].

5.4.3.3. Human Remains

State law applies to the rights to human remains and their disposition when the remains are located within the state's jurisdiction. However, when human remains as the result of an attack are located within federal jurisdiction, the military guidelines for human remains apply. For example, in the aftermath of the 9-11 attacks, jurisdiction for human remains in the World Trade Center was within that of the state of New York, while the jurisdiction over human remains in the Pentagon was within that of the U.S. military.

State law provides for a right for relatives to have the human remains, as well as an obligation to take possession of human remains of relatives. When human remains are contaminated with communicable diseases, the use of sealed body bags or sealed containers containing the remains can be returned to the families, according to military guidance. Short of an emergency situation, when the time and resources are available to prepare contaminated human remains for receipt by the family, refusal to release the human remains to the families would be contrary to the rights of the family to have the remains, as well as military guidance.

5.4.3.4. Professional Licensing Requirements

State law applies to professional licensing in the medical professions and other professions such as law, psychology, engineering, and architecture. In the event of a biological attack, medical professionals would likely arrive from various states, each with a license to practice medicine or nursing, for example, from their own states. This license does not entitle these professionals to practice in another state, and to do so would violate that state's licensing requirement.

It is not unforeseeable that litigation might arise from medical services administered in the context of a biological attack. The ability to temporarily suspend this requirement is necessary for a state to permit medical professionals to respond to an attack. Without this suspension authority, pursuing malpractice claims, filing complaints, and overseeing those medical professionals would be jeopardized. Further, particular requirements of the state would be unknown to these professionals and present the possibility of negligence claims for failure to provide informed consent in conformance with state law, without the ability to suspend the licensing requirement.

5.4.4. Access to Communication and Public Relations

The CDC list also includes needs for communication: identification of public health officers (e.g., badges); dissemination of accurate information, rumor control, and a 1–800 number; establishment of a command center; access to elected officials; access to experts in human relations and post-traumatic stress syndrome; and diversity training, cultural differences, and dissemination of information in multiple languages.

In the Public Health Security and Bioterrorism Preparedness and Response Act of 2002, enacted on June 12, 2002, provision for the needs for communication were included and provide a much broader role for the federal government, particularly in the event the state's communication systems are inadequate:

> *Study regarding communications abilities of public health agencies. Act June 12, 2002, P.L. 107-188, Title I, Subtitle A, §104(b), 116 Stat. 606, provides: "The Secretary of Health and Human Services, in consultation with the Federal Communications Commission, the National Telecommunications and Information Administration, and other appropriate Federal agencies, shall conduct a study to determine whether local public health entities have the ability to maintain communications in the event of a bioterrorist attack or other public health emergency. The study*

shall examine whether redundancies are required in the telecommunications system, particularly with respect to mobile communications, for public health entities to maintain systems operability and connectivity during such emergencies. The study shall also include recommendations to industry and public health entities about how to implement such redundancies if necessary.".

(3) Emergency Public Information and Communications Advisory Committee.

(A) In general. For purposes of paragraph (1), the Secretary shall establish an advisory committee to be known as the Emergency Public Information and Communications Advisory Committee (referred to in this paragraph as the "EPIC Advisory Committee").

(B) Duties. The EPIC Advisory Committee shall make recommendations to the Secretary and the working group under subsection (a) and report on appropriate ways to communicate public health information regarding bioterrorism and other public health emergencies to the public.

(C) Composition. The EPIC Advisory Committee shall be composed of individuals representing a diverse group of experts in public health, medicine, communications, behavioral psychology, and other areas determined appropriate by the Secretary.

(D) Dissemination. The Secretary shall review the recommendations of the EPIC Advisory Committee and ensure that appropriate information is disseminated to the public.

(E) Termination. The EPIC Advisory Committee terminates one year after the date of the enactment of Public Health Security and Bioterrorism Preparedness and Response Act of 2002 [enacted June 12, 2002].

(c) Strategy for communication of information regarding bioterrorism and other public health emergencies. In coordination with working group under subsection (a), the Secretary shall develop a strategy for effectively communicating information regarding bioterrorism and other public health emergencies, and shall develop means by which to communicate such information. The Secretary may carry out the preceding sentence directly or through grants, contracts, or cooperative agreements.

(d) Recommendation of Congress regarding official Federal Internet site on bioterrorism. It is the recommendation of Congress that there should be established an official Federal Internet site on bioterrorism, either directly or through provision of a grant to an entity that has expertise in bioterrorism and the development of websites, that should include information relevant to diverse populations (including messages directed at the general public and such relevant groups as medical personnel, public safety workers, and agricultural workers) and links to appropriate State and local government sites.

(42 USC §247d-6).

5.5. States and Territories Biodefense

5.5.1. State Legislatures

Prior to the anthrax attacks in the fall of 2001, several states had enacted legislation to amend old quarantine and isolation laws; however, immediately after the anthrax attacks in the fall of 2001, most states proposed a range of legislative initiatives in response to addressing public health emergencies and bioterrorism events.

5.5.2. State Executives: Governors' Powers

In six states, Governors have appointed task forces or commissions, or have created offices to examine the state's preparedness for biological attacks.

5.5.3. Pacts between States

In December 2001, North Carolina Governor Jim Hodges and South Carolina Governor Mike Easley signed a security pact for mutual assistance in the event of a terrorist attack.

The U.S. Constitution, however, prohibits the formation of pacts between states without Congressional approval. [Art. of Confed. and U.S. Const., Art. I, Sec. 10]

The following excerpt from Sutton, "Bioterrorism Preparation and Response Legislation—The Struggle to Protect States' Sovereignty While Preserving National Security," 6 *The Georgetown Public Policy Review* 93–106 (Spring 2001), discusses the prohibition of pacts between states in the bioterrorism context.

VII. "No state shall enter into any treaty, alliance, or Confederation"[3]

Madison discussed the prohibitions against alliances between the states, from the Articles of Confederation to the U.S. Constitution. He explained that "for reasons which need no explanation, [the prohibition against states entering into treaties...] is copied into the new Constitution [from the Articles]."[4] Although alliances and treaties may serve nationally important goals,[5] they are strictly prohibited without the authority of Congress.[6] Any formal alliances between states for purposes of bioterrorism preparation and response would be therefore strictly prohibited by the Constitution, without Congressional approval.

An informal alliance of state epidemiologists have filled the void where the federal government is unable, under current public health law, to provide a national uniform system of reporting diseases. These diseases include those biological agents that are commonly known to be among those used for bioterrorism. Without this alliance our coordination of state reporting would be so useless as to be non-existent. This alliance has articulated uniform standards for identifying and reporting of a list of selected diseases in order to maintain a national surveillance system. The Centers for Disease Control has adopted these standards and provides them as guidance.[7] However, this system has reached its maximum coordination and standard-setting powers as a volunteer organization. Without federal governmental powers, or a Congressionally authorized states compact, the system is doomed to collapse in times of emergency.

Establishing a network of state epidemiologists for the constitutionally narrow purpose of preparation and response to bioterrorism as part of federal legislation would institutionalize a successful working model. The result would be a coordinated national response to the threat of bioterrorism, otherwise impossible where forty-eight independent sovereigns are protecting their individual state interests, as they must, rather than the national interest.

The Supreme Court has established that a state's police powers are not absolute and could not be exercised outside a state's territory or in contravention of the federal Constitution.[8] The court specified that police powers authorize the state to legislate "all laws that relate to matters completely within its territory and which do not by their necessary operation affect the people of other States...[including] health laws of every description."[9] Therefore, while the state epidemiologist's alliance may act to create uniformity and compliance, it has no power to require any other state to do anything. It is conceivable that should one or more states choose to avoid reporting a disease cluster, the state epidemiologists—as well as the CDC—have no power to mandate their compliance, even for the health of the nation, or in the name of national security under the current regime of public health laws and case law.

5.5.4. The Model Act for Emergency State Powers

The development of a model public health act for states was commissioned by the Centers for Disease Control and Prevention, in collaboration with the National Governors Association (NGA), the National Conference of State Legislatures (NCSL), the National Association of Attorneys General (NAAG), the Association of State and Territorial Health Officials (ASTHO), and the National Association of City and County Health Officers (NACCHO), with financial support provided by the Centers for Disease Control and Prevention (CDC), the Sloan Foundation, and the Robert Wood Johnson Foundation.

A draft was developed in October 2001 when the need to accelerate the project became a concern after the September anthrax attacks. The draft was posted on the web by the Center for Law and the

Public's Health, a Center of both Georgetown and Johns Hopkins Universities. A second draft was produced on December 21, 2001 for consideration by state legislatures.

The Model Act is entitled "Model State Emergency Health Powers Act" and addresses planning, measures for detection and tracking public health emergencies, declaring a state of public health emergency, special powers during a state of public health emergency concerning both persons and property, public information regarding public health emergencies, and miscellaneous provisions such as liability, strict liability, constitutional taking, and other issues.

The proposal grants specific authority to the governor and public health department to empower states to protect the health and safety of its population in emergencies, and codifies the powers needed by authorities to respond in an emergency. The Act codifies powers that allow the collection of data and records in public health emergencies, control of property, and restriction of individual conduct in an emergency. The need for early detection of a biological terrorism event is addressed in the Model Act to include granting access to private individual health information. Provision for the use of property for the care, treatment, and housing of patients is also addressed in the Act. Finally, the Act addresses the use of vaccines and medications for infected or exposed persons and provides for a system of quarantine.

As of May 1, 2002, the Center for Law and the Public's Health at Georgetown and Johns Hopkins Universities reported that 33 state legislatures had introduced bills or resolutions based in whole or part on the Model Act, while 11 of those states have passed their bills. These 11 states are: Georgia, Hawaii, Maine, Maryland, New Hampshire, New Mexico, Oklahoma, South Dakota, Tennessee, Utah, and Virginia. [James G. Hodge, Jr., Project Director, email communication to the author, May 6, 2002]

The Department of Homeland Security, established in November of 2002, superseded several of the provisions of the Model Act, including the public information function of the state agencies. The state public health agencies would no longer be the lead in a biological attack, but rather, the Department of Homeland Security.

5.6. State Common Law and Potential Liabilities as a Result of a Public Health Emergency

States have sovereign immunity granted under the 11th Amendment of the U.S. Constitution, and must consent to being liable in an action in tort. There are four general exceptions to the general principle of state immunity: a state action can be compelled if action is required by federal or state law [*Edelman v. Jordan*, 415 U.S. 651 (1974)]; Congress may create causes of action against state officials to be heard in federal court, such as §1983 claims; state enacted tort claims acts embody their own exemptions; and during a declared state of emergency, state officials acting in an emergency are protected from liability if the state statute provides such immunity.

5.6.1. Good Samaritan Laws

The Good Samaritan laws are intended to encourage people to help others in emergency situations. However, these statutes vary from state to state in such substantial ways that it would be foolhardy to rescue someone or give assistance or emergency care to someone if you are in a state in which you have no familiarity. However, there are two states that make it a crime to *fail* to assist someone who is in an emergency situation if it can be done without your own harm or your responsibility to someone else.

The common law meaning of the Good Samaritan rule is explained in the Restatement of Torts (Second):

One who undertakes gratuitously or for consideration to render services to another which he should recognize as necessary for the protection of the other's person or things, is subject to liability to the other for physical harm resulting from his failure to exercise reasonable care to perform his undertaking, if(a) his failure to exercise such care increases the risk of such harm, or(b) the harm is suffered because of the other's reliance upon the undertaking. RESTATEMENT (SECOND) OF TORTS, Section 323.

Only when a response has started does an obligation attach to anyone who begins a rescue in 48 states.

If you are a private individual with none of the statutorily required health care training or certification in eight states, then you will have no protection from liability for being a Good Samaritan, even in good faith. Eight states provide no immunity to private individuals who do not meet certain qualifications of training or certification. These states are California, Connecticut, Illinois, Indiana, Kansas, Louisiana, Missouri, and Oregon.

Four states provide immunity to healthcare-related graduate students. Alabama requires the person to be an "intern or resident" in an AMA approved program, whereas Kansas includes all postgraduate students in any program that is state-approved in the healing arts. Louisiana provides immunity to an "intern or resident" in a public or private hospital or medical health care facility licensed by the state LSA-R.S. 37:1731 (2)(a). Michigan provides immunity to any student of an approved educational institution who is working in a clinical setting. M.C.L.A. 333.20965 (1)(k).

Two states caution that this section does not require someone to accept medical treatment if they object on religious grounds. Delaware and Maine [14 M.R.S.A. §164] caution that the statue should not be construed to give treatment to those who object on religious grounds.

Not all states specifically provide immunity for physicians who are licensed in any state in rendering emergency care in a hospital. To enjoy this immunity, the physician must be without expectation of remuneration. The standard for these acts would be one that would be appropriate in a public health emergency or in a field hospital in a bioterrorism event. The standard is "that standard of care expected of similar physicians under similar circumstances." HRS §663-1.5 (c)

Hawaii provides immunity to those who publish general first aid information.

For their immunity Idaho does not require physicians to be licensed, and the immunity is broad enough to cover any person who stops at the scene of an accident. ID St 5-330.

Some states require that the actions of the rescuer be gratuitous and without expectation of compensation. Iowa has statutorily defined gratuitous to include the receipt of nominal compensation to define this as "no compensation." I.C.A. §613.17.

Lifeguards are specifically granted immunity in only two states: Connecticut and Florida.

Assisting under the right conditions with the right qualifications is not enough to avoid liability if you fail to meet the standards established by the state in which the emergency occurs. Good faith is the lowest (or easiest) standard to meet with no other qualifications.   This would do the most to encourage emergency responses. There are eight states that have this lowest level of performance in an emergency to avoid liability for injuries or deaths. These states are Alabama, Arkansas, Massachusetts, New Jersey, Oklahoma, Virginia, West Virginia, and Wyoming.

Maryland also has a low standard, although a bit more difficult to meet than good faith. That is, the action must be done in a "reasonably prudent manner." Florida requires that the rescuer should be "acting as an ordinary, reasonable, prudent person under the same or similar circumstances," as the only standard for the actions taken.

The next standard of care, which is arguably just as low as these affirmative standards, is that the act should be immune from liability as long as the actions were not "willful and wanton," which is required in two states: Kentucky and Ohio. Minnesota adds "reckless" to the list, making the standard that much lower.

Very close to "willful and wanton" behavior is the requirement that the behavior be "intentionally" harmful. North Carolina has the lowest of these for the Good Samaritan to meet, requiring that the actions constitute not only gross negligence but also "intentional wrongdoing and wanton conduct."

Pennsylvania requires that the actions be "gross negligence" and "intentionally designed to cause harm," and North Dakota requires that the actions must both with "gross negligence and intentional misconduct."

The "good faith unless negligent" states

The next group of states require an affirmative proof that the actions were taken in "good faith" to be immune unless they are done with some level of negligence. Texas requires "good faith" unless the acts are "willful and wanton," while New Hampshire requires "good faith" unless the acts are "willful and wanton negligence." Significantly, New Hampshire is one of only two states that require you to stop and assist someone in an emergency, at a level of performance that does not rise to these levels of negligence!

Iowa requires "good faith" for immunity unless the acts are "reckless," and South Dakota requires almost the same standard, except it must be in addition to these standards, "willful and wanton." Similarly, four states require "good faith" unless there is "gross negligence and willful and wanton" acts: Colorado, Georgia, Mississippi, and Nevada. The more stringent level within this group of states is New Mexico, which requires "good faith" unless the acts rise to the level of "gross negligence."

The negligence states

The next group of states have no "good faith" requirement or mitigating behavior on the part of the Good Samaritan. The only standard is whether the acts were at some level of negligence, regardless of the motivation of the Good Samaritan. Topping the list in this category with the lowest standard of actions taken by the Good Samaritan while still receiving protection from liability are Delaware, Michigan, Montana, Nebraska, and Washington, which require the acts to be with "gross negligence and willful and wanton," and Delaware adds "reckless" to this list.

Alaska and Maine require the acts to be done with "gross negligence" and to be "reckless." For purposes of this discussion, "reckless" is considered to be a lower standard to meet than "willful and wanton," although it is interpreted on a state-by-state basis by that state's court.

The states that become particularly risky for the Good Samaritan begin at this point where these states use the standard of merely "gross negligence" to deny immunity to the rescuer, with no consideration of motivation. These states are Arizona, Hawaii, Idaho, New York, Tennessee, and Vermont.

Rhode Island sets a standard barely above "negligence" to nullify the immunity of any Good Samaritan by requiring that acts rise not only to "gross negligence and willful and wanton behavior," but also "not ordinary negligence," barely making this a Good Samaritan statute at all.

Some strange results arise when health care providers licensed only in that state are provided immunity unless gross negligence or wanton or willful acts cause injury, leaving the private individual category to a much lower standard of "good faith." But this individual category would include physicians who are licensed in other states, resulting in higher standards being placed on home-state Good Samaritans and lower standards being placed on out-of-state Good Samaritans. This is probably not a result that will encourage local physicians to help in emergencies. This is the case in Oklahoma, for example Oklahoma 76 OKL.ST.ANN. § 5(1)-(3). In Oregon, only team physicians licensed by the state of Oregon enjoy immunity for giving "emergency medical assistance" at athletic events. OR ST §30.800. Out-of-state teams with team physicians licensed from out of state do not have immunity while their teams are in Oregon, and emergency medical attention is required to be treated by their team physicians.

Ambulance drivers or drivers of other motor vehicles involved in a Good Samaritan action are treated differently by states. For example, South Dakota specifically includes anyone operating a motor vehicle in an emergency response within the immunity protections of the statute South Dakota (SDCL §20-9-4.1), whereas Ambulance drivers are specifically excluded from immunity in Pennsylvania (§8332(b)(1)).

The state with the least clarity of the Good Samaritan law is Texas. The state still relies upon common law for interpreting Good Samaritan defenses, but utilizes statutory definitions in Tex. Civ. Prac. & Rem. Code Ann. § 74.001(a) (Vernon Supp. 2002). The court interprets this statute as offering protection to individuals who voluntarily administer emergency care. The statute lowers the standard of care to encourage both certain medically-trained persons and laypersons to render aid in emergency situations.

For a more complete analysis and updates on this area, please go to www.goodsamaritanlawproject.com .

5.6.1.1. Immunity and Bioterrorism and Terrorism

Utah is the only state that provides immunity for responding to a bioterrorism event. The following statutory sections describe the extent of the immunity:

"(2)(a) implementation of measures to control the causes of epidemic and communicable diseases and other conditions significantly affecting the public health, or necessary to protect the public health . . ." and for (2)(b) investigating and controlling suspected bioterrorism and disease as set out in Title 26, Chap. 23b, Detection of Public Health Emergencies Act; and

(2)(c) responding to a national, state, or local emergency, a public health emergency as defined in Section 26-23b-102, or a declaration by the President of the United States or other federal official requesting public health-related activities when responding to an emergency declared by the President of the United States. Ut St U.C.A. 1953 §78-11-22 (2)(c).

Virginia provides immunity for health care workers who are involved in the smallpox vaccination program. Va. Code Ann. §8.01-225(E). In a detailed statute, the state provides immunity when there is an absence of gross negligence or willful misconduct for health care providers (E)(1) and workers (E)(2), and for the administration of the vaccinia (smallpox) vaccine or other smallpox countermeasure or any injuries sustained as a result of such other person coming into contact with the health care worker, either directly or indirectly. Immunity applies as long as the recommendations of the CDC were being utilized in the administration and monitoring of the actions.

Hazardous materials threatened or actual releases

Wisconsin provides immunity for those who are hazardous waste predictors and those who give advice and assistance in the event of a threatened or actual release of a hazardous substance. W.S.A. 895.48.

Wyoming provides immunity for those who give assistance or advice concerning actual or threatened releases of hazardous materials. Wyo. Stat. §1-1-120(c).

States that identify circumstances of illness that provide immunity are few. The statute in North Dakota provides immunity when people are "injured or are ill as the result of an accident or illness, or any mechanical, external or organic trauma." ND ST 32-03.1-02. Virginia provides for an "ill person."

Affirmative duties to rescue or assist

Several states have affirmative duties to assist someone in an emergency: Minnesota without penalty and Vermont includes a fine for failing to assist. Both states have similarly worded law. "A person at the scene of an emergency who knows that another person is exposed to or has suffered grave physical harm shall . . .give reasonable assistance to the exposed person." (1). Vermont provides that the individual "give reasonable assistance" and is provided immunity unless the acts constitute "gross negligence" or the individual receives or expects remuneration. Vermont 12 V.S.A. §519.

New Hampshire also has an affirmative duty: "Any person rendering emergency care shall have the duty to place the injured person under the care of a physician, nurse, or other person qualified to care for such person as soon as possible and to obey the instructions of such qualified person." N.H. Rev. Stat. §508:12

Change of rules in an emergency

Indiana, while creating one of the weakest Good Samaritan statutes in the fifty states by denying immunity for ordinary negligence, has provided for changing the rules in the event of a "disaster emergency" declared by the governor. This section, I.C. 16-31-6-4, applies to a disaster emergency declared by the governor "in response to an act that the governor in good faith believes to be an act of terrorism." Further, (2) incorporates any rules adopted by the state emergency services commission or in the occurrence of a disaster emergency declaration by the governor. The governor could include in his declaration the provision of immunity at any standard during this disaster.

Massachusetts is the only state to provide immunity from liability for a physician or nurse who administers a vaccination or immunization as part of a public health program, which could be critical in the event of a mass vaccination program in response to a threatened bioterrorism attack.

Many states, in order to provide immunity to physicians and surgeons, require that they be licensed in the state in which the emergency occurs. Maryland has the best approach to providing immunity to out-of-state physicians or physicians from other countries by requiring only that they provide assistance in a "reasonably prudent manner" and that they relinquish care when someone who is licensed in the state becomes available to take responsibility. MD Code §5-603 (C)(1)-(3).

Standards and their application to the Good Samaritan statutes

Good faith includes but is not limited to "a reasonable opinion that the immediacy of the situation is such that the rendering of care should not be postponed." HI St 663-1.5

Gross negligence is defined in Maryland to be only when there is infliction of injury intentionally or when it is so utterly indifferent to the rights of others that he acts as if such rights did not exist. Only extraordinary or outrageous conduct by a person giving assistance or medical care in an emergency or by a member of a fire company or rescue company can be termed gross negligence . . . mere recklessness is not enough, but must be reckless disregard for human life. *McCoy v. Hatmaker*, 763 A.2d 1233 (2000).

Michigan defines gross negligence as conduct so reckless as to demonstrate substantial lack of concern for whether injury results. *Jennings v. Southwood*, 521 N.W.2d 230, 446 Mich. 125 (1994).

North Dakota defines gross negligence in their statute to mean "acts or omissions falling short of intentional misconduct which nevertheless show a failure to exercise even slight care or any conscious interest in the predictable consequences of the acts or omissions" and "includes the failure of an aider to relinquish direction of the care of an injured or ill person when an appropriate person licensed or certified by this state or by any state or province to provide medical care or assistance assumes or attempts to assume responsibility for the care of the injured or ill person." ND ST 32-03.1-01.

Willful and wanton misconduct in Illinois is if it is "intentional or if it is committed under circumstances exhibiting a reckless disregard for the safety of others." *Ramirez v. City of Chicago*, 82 F.Supp.2d 836 (1999).

5.6.2. Failure to Prepare or Warn

Given the anthrax attacks in the fall of 2001, a biological attack is a foreseeable event that may give rise to a duty on the part of municipalities and states to prepare for such an event. The failure to warn of a potential danger from an attack could also give rise to a breach of duty to citizens.

The devastation to property and life after Hurricane Katrina reminded the United States that we were unprepared for responding to the public health needs in the wake of a major disaster, in addition to the property issues which arose. The incident gave rise to a developing area of law, disaster law, which focuses in part on recovery efforts and on public and private insurance legal issues. After Hurricane Katrina, state governments in hurricane-prone regions gave more policy consideration to the state's role in preparation, warning, planning, and responding to disasters.

The following excerpt uses an Iowa statute to examine state tort liability for failure to protect against bioterrorism injuries:

Jason E. Mccollough, *State Tort Liability for Failure to Protect Against Bioterrorism*, 8 Drake J. Agric. L. 743, at 768-781 (Fall 2003).

IV. Assigning Liability via the ITCA

A. Overview

The great hurdle to overcome in finding state liability for a bioterror attack is the requirement that the injury result from a negligent act or omission of the state. Thus, for this element of the claim to be present the four elements of negligence must also be present: (1) the state must have owed some duty to the injured person; (2) the state must have breached that duty; (3) there must be a causal connection between the injury and the breach of the duty; and (4) there must be actual damages. It is to finding these four elements that the analysis must turn if liability in tort is to be imposed upon the state.

B. State Negligence Analyzed

1. Is a Duty Owed?

It is first necessary to determine whether or not the state owes to its citizens a duty to protect them from bioterror attacks. The lack of case law on the subject, either inside or outside of Iowa, makes it extremely difficult to determine whether any duty is actually owed in this context, so the best that can be done is to reason by analogy. Any case presented to a court on this issue would be a matter of first impression for both courts and administrative agencies and decisions would likely be subject to further examination by appellate courts.

a. The "Public Duty" Doctrine. The general rule is that where the state's duty is to the public at large, the state is immune from liability to individual plaintiffs. This doctrine is perhaps the most important consideration in determining whether an act, or failure to act, by the state to protect against bioterrorism is actionable. Unless the public duty doctrine can be overcome in bioterrorism cases, the whole issue of assigning state liability is moot. Within Iowa courts, the public duty doctrine arguably lost favor in recent years, although it clearly still applies.

In 1979, the Iowa Supreme Court addressed, but failed to resolve, the question of the public duty doctrine in Iowa jurisprudence. The decision in Wilson v. Nepstad resulted from the consolidated decision of five separate cases. These cases alleged negligence on the part of the City of Des Moines in its execution of certain fire code and inspection provisions; fires within the allegedly negligently inspected occupancies had led to death of the occupants and destruction of property. The plaintiffs claimed both a common law duty of reasonable care and that various statutory duties had been breached. In responding to the allegations the city relied heavily on the public duty doctrine. The ultimate question the court reached in deciding the case was whether the common law duty was "owed to the plaintiffs or their decedents, victims of the fire?" It was determined that the public duty doctrine was inapplicable to this case for two reasons: (1) the common law duty established was not owed to the public generally, it benefits a limited class of persons; and (2) "the 'duty to all, duty-to-no-one' doctrine is really a form of sovereign immunity" which the court refused to expand de facto by applying the public duty doctrine.

A few years later the public duty doctrine was revisited by the Iowa Supreme Court. In the 1986 decision of Adam v. State, the court again refused to accept the public duty doctrine as a bar to liability. In Adam, the lower court found the state liable for negligent licensing and inspection of a grain elevator. Specific claims brought by the plaintiff "included negligent failure to inspect as often as required, negligent inspections, and negligent failure to adopt rules." To reach this conclusion, the court relied heavily on legislative intent, whether the legislature intended certain provisions to expand or constrict liability under the ITCA. The court stated that it makes no difference whether the state's duty is derived from common law or from statute; a breach from either derivation is sufficient to constitute actionable negligence. If the duty is created by statute, then the duty is breached when the state does not act in conformance with the statutory requirements. Finally, the court concluded that the plaintiff belonged to the specific class of individuals the duty was intended to protect.

Recently, however, the Iowa Supreme Court distinguished both Adam and Wilson. In its 2001 decision of Kolbe v. State, the court carefully noted that the public duty doctrine has not been specifically rejected in Iowa jurisprudence. It was merely the nature of the statutes under review in the earlier cases that had resulted in the inapplicability of the public duty doctrine. The Kolbe court held that the public duty doctrine is applicable because the statute under review in that case was designed to protect the public at large rather than any identifiable class of persons. Public policy considerations also played a substantial role in the court's application of the public duty doctrine.

Given the flux of the law, it is probably best if one can clearly avoid the applicability of the public duty doctrine in an ITCA suit. This is best accomplished when a special duty owed to a specific class of individuals can be shown; of course it will also be necessary for the claimant to fall within the protected class. A common law duty of reasonableness may be insufficient to hurdle the public duty doctrine. However, a statutory duty which clearly identifies a protected class of individuals, and which better yet specifically provides for recovery in the event of negligence will serve to open the widest door to enable ITCA recovery.

b. Establishing a Special Duty. There are two basic means of establishing a duty. The most usual method is through affirmative conduct on the part of the defendant. Another method of establishing liability is when an act is not done, although liability for omissions is somewhat dubious. The ITCA provides for causes of action when either an act or an omission leads to injury, so the state may be liable whether it acts in some way to cause the bioterror incident to come to fruition or whether its inaction is the ultimate cause of the injury.

The state's affirmative acts to create a duty to protect against bioterrorism are in the form of statutes and administrative regulations. Iowa has recognized the need for disaster management and established the emergency management division of the department of public defense "in order to insure that preparations of this state will be adequate to deal with . . . disasters, and to provide for the common defense and to protect the public peace, health and safety, and to preserve the lives and property of the people of the state." This department is also responsible for coordinating a plan with federal emergency management agencies to cope with a bioterror attack, should it ever occur. The Division of Emergency Management is also responsible for all homeland security activities. Given that "homeland security" is defined to include "the detection, prevention, preemption, deterrence of, and protection from attacks targeted at state territory, population, and infrastructure," as well as defining "disaster" to include attacks originating from within or without Iowa, Iowa has statutorily assumed the duty to protect its citizens and their property from bioterror attacks.

However, it seems unreasonable to assume that just because a bioterror attack occurs that Iowa must have breached its duty. This type of res ipsa loquitur analysis is disfavored in some courts. Despite the disfavor by some courts, this type of analysis is widely used in Iowa courts, even in cases where the state is a party in interest. It is not unreasonable to assume that a much stronger claim would be presented when actual negligence can be shown rather than by arguing that Iowa should be held liable because bioterror attacks do not occur unless someone is negligent. Before one can argue that Iowa has breached its duty it must first be firmly established exactly what the duty Iowa owes to its citizens is. Although the statutes establishing the Division of Emergency Management provide a general sense that the state has imposed a duty on itself to protect its citizens from bioterror attacks, it does little to tell us how far that duty extends.

To determine how far the duty of protection extends it is necessary to delve further into the Iowa Code and into the rules and regulations promulgated by state agencies. It is the responsibility of the Department of Public Health to maintain a statewide risk assessment of dangerous biological agents within the state. If, after inspection by an employee or agent of the department, certain premises are found to be unsafe, the director is authorized, but is not required, to implement any safeguards deemed appropriate. From an animal perspective, the Iowa Department of Agriculture and Land Stewardship ("Iowa Department of Agriculture") has been given, by the legislature, the task of suppressing and preventing the introduction and spread of infectious animal diseases within the state. Through these two entities and their promulgated rules the state has effectively created a duty of care which it must maintain if it is to escape ITCA liability in the event of a bioterror attack.

Even absent clear statutory or regulatory requirements creating the duty, it is possible that the advertent or inadvertent actions of the state may have created the duty. The applicable doctrine, commonly referred to as the "good Samaritan" doctrine, holds that where one undertakes to perform an act, thereby causing those affected to expect the act to be performed, one has a duty to perform the act in a reasonable fashion. For example, if a neighborhood parent walks his children to school every morning, and performs the function of a crossing guard for only his children, he owes to the other children no duty to perform the function. If he serves in his "crossing guard" capacity for other children, and the children come to rely on his presence to stop traffic, then he owes a duty to those children. The repercussions of this could be mixed. On one hand, a court might rule that the duty owed was the father's presence every day school was in session. It is more likely, however, that a court would rule that so long as he was performing his function, he owed a similar duty of care to all children. Thus, he owes the same standard of care to the children of his hated rival as he does to his own children.

In cases involving the Federal Tort Claims Act, the United States Supreme Court has found it appropriate to impose this type of reasoning in holding the federal government liable in tort. The case of Indian Towing Co. v. United States is a prime example. Much like the cautious father above or the federal government in Indian Towing, the state has undertaken to protect its citizens from the threats posed by bioterrorism and has thereby imposed upon itself a standard of care. Thus, although no duty may be explicitly stated in a single statute, the various statutes, taken as a whole, may be sufficient to establish a duty, the breach of which may cause the state to become liable under the ITCA.

2. What May Constitute a Breach?

The answer to this question is not as straightforward as it first appears. The ITCA does not go so far as to define what level of negligence is required, so presumably even slight negligence on the part of the state is sufficient to warrant a claim being filed. Thus, although logic holds that in order to breach the duty the state must have violated a duty, either by failing to take a required action or by taking action prohibited, there may be a grey area. The greyness comes from the fact that a court is unlikely to adopt a slight negligence standard given the fact that the state would be the defendant. There must be a duty owed to an individual and the injury must be foreseeable. In order to determine when a breach occurs, therefore, it is necessary to determine what steps taken can meet the ordinary or gross negligence standards and also to determine whether the "citizens" can be a specific individual to whom a duty can be owed. This issue is perhaps best explored through the following original hypothetical:

A rancher, Paul, raises cattle on his rural Iowa ranch. His goal is to get his stock to market as quickly as possible. He buys young steers and sells them after they mature and become more valuable. Paul has been in this business for several decades, since his father retired and transferred the business. During the course of his experience, he has never had a serious disease introduced from one of his purchased steers, so he has never thought it necessary to keep his purchased steers separated from the rest of his herds but rather has simply given his new head a series of shots and vaccines when they are tagged and then released.

One day in late Spring of 2002 Paul acquires several hundred young steers and introduces them into his herd as he always has. The next day Paul reads in the newspaper that several cattle throughout Iowa have been diagnosed with mad cow disease. There have not been reports of the disease outside Iowa. He contacts his seller, Sam, and inquires as to the origin of the cattle. Sam informs him that he purchased the cattle from a man who was passing through town and offered the cattle at a price that was "too good to pass up." Paul is now concerned that his entire herd may be infected with mad cow disease, and wishes to file a claim against the Iowa Department of Agriculture. He thinks that the state should have been monitoring the movement of cattle in and out of the state and wants the state to pay him to test his entire herd (several thousand head of cattle) and to replace any cattle required to be destroyed.

It is reasonably clear that based on the strictest interpretation of the Iowa Code, Iowa, or more specifically the Iowa Department of Agriculture, probably failed to meet its mandate. Because mad cow disease has been identified by the state to be a candidate for bioterrorism, the fact that its widespread presence has been shown in Iowa makes it unlikely that its introduction and release was natural or accidental. Yet, should the state be absolutely liable if an agent is introduced, or is a less strict interpretation of the Iowa Code appropriate for finding a breach? An absolutist reading of the various provisions would likely lead to liability on such a level that the state would be liable in tort every time a person or animal contracts an infectious disease. Consider, however, the following additional facts:

The Department of Agriculture issues a warning shortly after 9/11 indicating that Iowans should be on the lookout for suspect livestock that could be carrying biological agents. The warning is issued as part of the department's emergency preparedness strategy and is distributed through the news media as well as through the posting of flyers at rural veterinarians' offices throughout the state.

In this case, the state has clearly taken steps to warn the agricultural community that attacks could occur. Is this the type of care that an ordinarily prudent person would exercise in fulfilling its duty to protect against bioterror attacks? The act of warning the population at large of a general threat of an impending attack probably does little to curtail the attack. In the facts above, the state merely informed and perhaps educated the population for what to look for after the animals were sick. Although this may certainly help to contain a bioterror attack by keeping livestock owners from transporting or selling sick animals, it does little to keep the initial attack from happening. Still, an analysis of the various state departments' mission statements seems to indicate that the state agencies do not have such lofty goals as the legislature. Many agencies are dedicated to containment and isolation of outbreaks, as well as to education of those in contact with the animals so the diseases are diagnosed early.

It is a canon of tort law that there generally exists no duty to warn another of impending harm by a third party. However, where a special relationship exists between the defendant and either the third party or the plaintiff, then there exists a duty to warn. The Iowa Supreme Court has recognized that in certain circumstances there may exist a duty of the state to warn of injury by a third party. However, the court concluded that when victims had not been threatened or were not readily identifiable, no duty to warn was created. Despite reaching this conclusion, the court acknowledged that other cases have recognized the general duty to protect the public against foreseeable harm. It is certainly possible, therefore, that notwithstanding any statute or administrative rule requirement, the state's issuance of a warning was only "good Samaritan" in nature. Because the facts do not indicate that the state's warning was in some way lacking, the warning is probably sufficient to meet either an ordinary care or gross negligence standard if it was determined that the duty owed was simply based on "good Samaritan" principles rather than on black letter law. A final consideration is offered to complete the breach analysis:

Remember that Sam, the one who sold the infected animals to Paul, purchased the livestock from a man passing through town. Our terrorist, Tom, brought the cattle into the state from the Tulsa, Oklahoma stockyard. The day before the cattle crossed into Iowa, but after Tom had left the stockyard, the Tulsa stockyard is placed under quarantine. When Tom is stopped at the Iowa border, his cargo of livestock is inspected, but the agent inspecting the livestock is unaware, due to a miscommunication, that the Tulsa facility is now under quarantine. The miscommunication came as the result of the message simply being forgotten, and thus, the Iowa Department of Agriculture's staff had not distributed the message regarding the Tulsa facility. Therefore, rather than holding the livestock as he should have, The Border Inspector permits Tom to go about his business.

The key element to the final part of the hypothetical is the miscommunication. There were procedures adopted and in place which required all cattle leaving a quarantined facility to be further quarantined before entering the state. Had this border quarantine been conducted, the illness would have been discovered and the bioterror attack would not have entered Iowa, despite the fact that the attack on the Tulsa facility had already occurred. Because of the state's failure, however, animals throughout Iowa are now infected and the costs will likely be great.

Thus, the breach of the duty actually occurs regardless of whether the statutory duty or the "good Samaritan" duty is considered. In the former case, states adopting standards will generally be held liable when they fail to meet those self-imposed standards. In the later case, the fact that the state failed to do as it had always done--that is, to communicate with its employees effectively--indicates that it probably breached any non-statutory duty it owed to protect against bioterrorism. In this case, the facts indicate that the duty was probably breached whether an ordinary care or gross negligence standard was adopted.

In summary, the question of when a breach occurs depends on the negligence standard adopted by a court. Given the fact that waivers of sovereign immunity are to be construed narrowly, it is also most reasonable to assume that the level of care required by the state in order to meet its duty to protect Iowans and their property will be relatively low; a court is likely to consider the nature of sovereign immunity and infer from the ITCA a standard of gross negligence. Under the standard of gross negligence, therefore, a substantial failing on the part of the state will likely have to be shown before a court will conclude that the state breached its duty in failing to prevent a bioterror attack.

3. Does a Causal Relationship Exist?

The lack of case law in the context of terrorism and tort liability presents further problems in determining what type of causal relationship must exist in order for the state to be held liable under the ITCA. This notwithstanding: It is fundamental that negligence is not actionable unless it is a cause in fact of the harm for which recovery is sought. It need not, of course, be the sole cause. Negligence is a cause in fact of the harm to another if it was a substantial factor in bringing about that harm.

From the proximate cause analysis in Perkins v. Texas & New Orleans Railroad Co., it can be concluded that the state's conduct in causing an injury is a substantial factor if one can conclude that "but for" the state's conduct the injury would not have occurred. In reaching this conclusion, it is necessary to show that the causal chain between the state's negligence and the injuries suffered are probable, not just possible.

Using the same hypothetical presented in the previous subsection, it becomes difficult to show that the state's failure to effectively communicate the information regarding the Tulsa quarantine was the proximate cause of Paul's injury. Difficulty in such a showing comes from the possibility that the bioterror act was an intervening cause. Early English courts held that direct causation may be sufficient to sustain an action for negligence, regardless of the non-foreseeability of either the damage or the plaintiffs. American courts first rejected the direct causation analysis in the late 1920s and required a showing by the defendant that both the consequences and the injured party be the foreseeable result of the negligent act or omission in order to assign liability. The English rule was modified in the 1960s by the Wagon Mound cases to require that at least the consequences of the negligent act or omission must be foreseeable in order for the defendant to be held accountable for the injuries suffered. Thus, the foreseeability requirement is important in American jurisprudence, and has been adopted by courts of other nations.

It is unnecessary to devote many words to an analysis of whether Iowa, in the hypothetical above, was the proximate cause of Paul's injury if "but for" causation is applied. Clearly there is a connection between the inspector permitting the animals in and the spread of the disease. Had the inspector been properly notified, the livestock would not have been permitted into the state and the injury may have been averted. Based on this analytical framework the causation requirement is met. Furthermore, the less-strict "substantial factor" test from Yun is clearly met where the "but for" test is satisfied. After all, if the absence of a cause will entirely eliminate an effect, then the cause was clearly a "substantial factor" contributing to the effect.

Analysis under a foreseeability framework is somewhat more complex because both the injuries and the plaintiffs generally must have been the foreseeable result of the negligent act. Using the hypothetical already presented, there are at least two possible acts of negligence to consider. On the one hand, there could have been "negligent miscommunication" regarding the Tulsa quarantine. On the other hand, the act of letting Tom into the state with his infected cargo might have been negligent of the inspector. In order to meet the elemental requirements of a negligence claim, therefore, it is necessary to prove that it is foreseeable that one or both of these acts would have led to the foreseeable result of Paul's injuries.

At the time the infected livestock entered Iowa, the Iowa Department of Agriculture knew of the quarantine that had been imposed on the Tulsa stockyard. Although the agency may not have had a reason to suspect that a specific shipment would be infected, it certainly seems reasonable to assume that there is a possibility that a shipment of livestock could be en route from the Tulsa yard. Given this assumption, it is only a small logical step to assume that failure to communicate the possibility of infected animals entering the state would have the consequence of livestock already in-state becoming infected as well. This being established, in order to meet the Palsgraf standard, the plaintiffs must also be foreseeable. Given the direction that the Iowa agencies and legislature have taken regarding precisely whom they seek to protect, each and every livestock-owning citizen of the state is considered by the state to be a foreseeable plaintiff. These things considered, the state's communication failure was the proximate, although not the sole, cause of the injury suffered.

In considering whether the inspector himself acted negligently, it is relatively clear that the injury suffered was not foreseeable from his act of letting the infected livestock into the state. The inspector, given the facts, had no reason to suspect infection of the livestock. Given that he acted in accordance with agency rules and standards there is little room to hold the inspector negligent in the performance of his duty. This example is different than a Department of Transportation snow plow operator who "plows" into a parked car while performing his duties; it is foreseeable that if one negligently operates a snow plow that it may damage another vehicle. Furthermore, given courts' general reluctance to determine the merit of various legislative and administrative enactments, it seems unlikely that a court would find the rules and standards adopted by the Iowa Department of Agriculture to be negligently adopted.

In summary, proximate cause must be present in order for a claim of negligence to lie. Showing proximate cause requires that a relationship be shown between the negligent conduct and the foreseeable injury and foreseeable plaintiff. *780 In order for the state to be a proximate cause of a bioterror attack, its action must have been a substantial factor leading to the injury.

4. Can Damages Be Shown?

The issue of damages is relatively straightforward and does not require much attention. Based upon the hypothetical, the plaintiff's damages are those resulting from vaccination or destruction of cattle as a result of the state's negligence. Under the ITCA the claim for damages must be for money only, so the plaintiff cannot seek replacement of the cattle or delivery of the vaccine, but can only seek the value of the cattle or the costs incurred in vaccinating the livestock.

V. Conclusion; Public Policy; Solutions
A. Conclusion

Terrorism is a threat to America. Countries across the globe have been dealing with terrorism for decades. Until September 11, 2001, America had never been the victim of a major terrorist attack on its own soil. Until the anthrax scare of late 2001 and early 2002, America had never been seriously presented with the challenge of defending itself against chemical or biological terrorism. Federal and state agencies met the challenge with due diligence, and have since promulgated statutes and administrative regulations to further meet the challenge of defending our homeland against the bioterrorist threat. But this preparation comes with a price.

In formulating its statutes and regulations Iowa seems to have made itself a likely candidate for tort liability in many plausible bioterror scenarios. The public duty doctrine notwithstanding, the ITCA clearly provides for the state to be held accountable for injuries suffered by the classes of persons the statutes and regulations seek to protect. The formulation of many regulations has limited application to relatively small, identified classes of persons. The Iowa Department of Public Health and the Iowa Department of Agriculture have both adopted policies and regulations intended to prevent bioterror attacks against specific targets. The Department of Public Defense established a committee to prepare a report specifically detailing the strengths and weaknesses of very specific portions of Iowa's infrastructure.

It is precisely the specific tailoring of regulations and the identification of classes sought to be protected that may have made the public duty doctrine inapplicable. Furthermore, when the state undertakes to perform its functions and specific individuals rely on the performance of those functions, any negligent performance may be sufficient to create liability even where there is no duty established.

B. Public Policy Considerations

A final consideration on the issue of Iowa's liability for failing to protect against a bioterror attack is simply to ask whether such liability is actually in the public interest. Permitting state liability is certainly a double-edged sword. Those who would argue in favor of imposing tort liability on the state in the manner suggested above would likely claim that only when the state can be held accountable for its failure to act can its citizens ensure that the state is taking all the necessary steps to protect them against bioterrorism. On the other hand, opponents to liability would probably argue that it would only take one bioterror incident, for which the state was required to make an accounting, to ultimately bankrupt the state treasury. Neither of these options seems too appealing. If we do not assign liability to the state, then we ensure that the state's funds will not be depleted by the bioterror act of a third party. However, failing to assign liability may cause us to question whether the state really took all reasonable steps to prevent a bioterror attack should one occur.

5.6.2.1. Adequacy or Inadequacy of a Plan

Generally, governments are not held to be liable for officials' acts or omissions. However, when a hazard is foreseeable, the government may have a duty to prepare adequately with a plan. At least one court has held the government to be immune from suit. In *Bradley v. Board of County Commissioners of Butler County*, 890 P.2d 1228 (Kan. Ct. App. 1995), the victim of a tornado complained that the county was the only county in the state that did not have a disaster plan. The court held that "nowhere in all of the statutes of this state is there any mention that having an approved emergency plan on file is a prerequisite to immunity for emergency preparedness activities." (890 P.2d at 1291).

5.6.2.2. Failure to Warn of Potential Danger

The government has a duty to warn citizens of the potential danger of a natural disaster or disease if that warning is mandatory under a statute or regulation. However, the courts have held that if the government warned the public, but a specific plaintiff did not receive the warning, the government will not be liable. For example, in *Jasa v. Douglas County*, 510 N.W. 2d 281 (Neb. 1994), the warning for bacterial meningitis through the county policy and state regulations provided for notice to the daycare operators where the case had occurred, but not for notice to the parents. Further warnings, the court held, were a discretionary function of the department and therefore there was no liability.

The court has held that the duty runs to the public, not to specific entities or individuals within the public. For example, when a county received information of an approaching tornado but failed to warn a school where 30 children were killed or injured, the court held that the duty ran to the public, not to the school or the students. Further warnings fell within the discretionary functions of the county, and therefore the county was not held liable. *Litchhult v. County of Orange*, 583 N.Y.S. 2d 891 (La. 1989).

5.6.2.3. Failure to Maintain Emergency Systems

Governments are generally not held liable for failure to maintain their emergency systems. The misrouting of a 911 call, was held not to create liability for the county. Only willful or wanton conduct, constituting a "course of action which shows an actual or deliberate intention to cause harm or which, if not intentional, shows an utter indifference to or conscious disregard for the safety of others or their property," 745 ILCS 10/1 210 (West 1994), would result in liability.

5.6.2.4. Failure to Enter into a Mutual Aid Agreement

Governments may have mutual aid agreements that are made in accordance with statutes or regulations, which provide for the assistance of neighboring services. Most statutes provide for mutual aid agreements through the provision of aid to neighboring jurisdictions, which is voluntary and conditional on the availability of the resources. Failure to utilize an agreement does not give rise to liability where the statutory language gives discretion to the government.

5.6.3. Liability for Damage to Private Property
5.6.3.1. Act of God Defense

The plaintiffs in the litigation that followed Hurricane Katrina were faced with the "act of God defense." This defense allows governments to try to demonstrate that a force of nature occurred with such force that it constituted an intervening force or superseding cause, thus breaking the chain of causation linking the defendant to the injury (*Kimble v. Mackintosh Hemphill Co.*, 59 A.2d 68, 71 (Pa. 1948)).

Congress defines an act of God as "an unanticipated grave natural disaster or other natural phenomenon of an exceptional, inevitable, and irresistible character, the effect of which could not have been prevented or avoided by the exercise of due care or foresight." (33 U.S.C. § 2701(1) (1983)).   This defense is only available when it can be proven by a preponderance of evidence that the act of God was the sole cause of the injury, which has led many courts to reject the defense. (*United States v. Alcan Aluminum Corporation*, 990 F.2d 711 (2nd Cir. 1993)).

The act of God defense requires a showing of two factors. First, the plaintiff must show that the event was unforeseeable based on a reasonableness standard. Courts have historically found that an act of God is foreseeable when the event occurred in an area where such occurrences are normal, and that the event occurred during a time when they are expected.

Second, the act of God defense requires the absence of a human agency causing the damage. If a defendant can prove that the injury occurred exclusively because of natural causes and without human intervention, then the defendant can satisfy the second prong of the defense.

5.6.3.2. Public Necessity Doctrine

Governments take actions that damage or destroy property without liability when there is an imminent public danger. "[O]ne is privileged to enter land in possession of another if it is necessary for the purpose of averting an imminent public disaster." Restatement (Second) of Torts §196. The public necessity doctrine supersedes that of individual property rights when the action is necessary to preserve the public good. For example, destroying a building in order to prevent the spread of fire to other buildings was held by the court to be a public necessity, and therefore there was no liability for the government. *Surocco v. Geary*, 3 Cal. 69 (1853).

5.6.3.3. Public Nuisance

A public nuisance is defined by Restatement (Second) of Torts §821B, and directs courts to consider: (1) whether the conduct involves a significant interference with the public health, safety, comfort, or convenience; (2) whether the conduct is illegal; and (3) whether the conduct is of a continuing nature or has produced a long-lasting effect on the public right that the actor has reason to know will be significant.

There are both civil and criminal common law actions in public nuisance, and bioterrorism is an action that may be found by the court to be criminal public nuisance.

However, claims against the federal government will be governed by those torts available through the Federal Tort Claims Act, and any other theory of recovery in tort will be rejected, as in the following case involving anthrax contamination of a postal facility and efforts to compel expedited cleanup of the facility for the protection of the workers.

The following case uses the public nuisance as a common law action against the federal government in the aftermath of the anthrax attacks of 2001 challenging the cleanup standard for contamination for postal workers in the postal facility where anthrax spores had been detected. However, using the Federal Torts Claims Act, the plaintiffs were limited to money damages and could not get the relief of an injunction against returning to the contaminated facility, which they sought.

Smith v. Potter
2001 U.S. Dist. LEXIS 18625 (Nov. 16, 2001)

B. Public Nuisance Cause of Action

In its opposition papers, the USPS argues that sovereign immunity bars the Plaintiffs' public nuisance cause of action. The public nuisance claim centers on allegations that "actions and omissions of the USPS with respect to the handling of anthrax have created a public nuisance because of the potential exposure of the general public to a deadly bacteria" The USPS argues that the Court should consider this theory relative to the injunction, even though the plaintiffs have not urged it on the injunction aspect of the case.

Congress has waived the Postal Services' sovereign immunity by providing that the Postal Service may "sue or be sued." But the scope of the waiver under Section 401(1) is limited with respect to tort claims. Specifically...any tort claim against the Postal Service is subject to the remedies and restrictions of the Federal Tort Claims Act ("FTCA"). "[The FTCA] shall apply to tort claims arising out of the activities of the Postal Services."

Money damages are the only form of relief permitted under the FTCA. Accordingly, Congress has not waived the government's sovereign immunity for tort claims, like the plaintiffs' public nuisance claim, that seek injunctive relief against the USPS. As such, the circumstances here mean that injunctive relief is not appropriate based on a public nuisance theory.

CHAPTER FIVE ENDNOTES

[1]Albert, Ostheimer, Breman, "The Last Smallpox Epidemic in Boston and the Vaccination Controversy, 1901–1903," N Engl J Med 2001; 344(5) 375–379, quoting "Virus squad out," Boston Globe, (Feb. 5, 1902:4).

[2] N. Engl. J. Med. 2001; 344(5) 376, quoting Pratt C.M., "Disputed points in small-pox," Marit. Med. News 1907; 19:6–13.

[3] Art. of Confed., and U.S. Const. Art. I, Sec. 10.

[4] The Federalist No. 44, 281 (James Madison) (Clifford Rossiter ed. 1961).

[5] Interview with Joe G. Moore, Jr., former Director, Water Commission, Department of Interior, 1968–1970 (April 3, 1998). The Delaware River Basin Commission was proposed for the goal of cooperative use and protection of water resources in the 1960s, but opposition in Congress eventually led to its demise.

[6] Low Level Radioactive Waste Policy Act, 42 U.S.C. §2021b et.seq. The Southern Compact for the disposal of nuclear waste, is intended to allocate the burden of nuclear waste equally among the seven southern state members of the compact was authorized by Congress.

[7] Centers for Disease Control, Case Definitions for Public Health Surveillance, MMWR 1997; 46 (No. RR-10):[p.57].

[8] *Jacobson v. Massachusetts*, 197 U.S. 11 (1905).

[9] *Jacobson*, 197 U.S. at 25.

Chapter Six
Regulation of Biological Agents, Biological Safety Laboratories,
and Biodefense Research

6.1   Introduction

The rapid development of a regulatory framework for dangerous pathogens followed the events of 9-11 and the Amerithrax attacks, which were thought to have originated from a biological laboratory. Prior to these events, some existing statutes and regulations addressed the need to protect the public from accidents or intentional use of biological agents. These problems were addressed from the criminal aspect of using these agents as weapons, and from the safe-handling or biosafety aspect by the regulation of transportation of certain biological agents. The regulatory framework that was developed after the Amerithrax attacks closed gaps and was more far reaching into the culture of biological research than ever before.

6.2   The Development of the Regulatory Framework of Select Agents

The regulatory framework that requires the regulation of biological agents, which are potential bioweapons, was developed over a period of decades. The foundation provided by 9-11 and the anthrax attacks of the fall of 2001 was used to build a new generation of regulations. These regulations have been shaped as a result of incidents involving biological agents, which have moved Congress to act to address the threat.

The first domestic law to address bioterrorism, the Biological Weapons Act, was passed in 1989 and made it a crime when there was an "intent to use [biological agents] as a biological weapon." The law was passed in part as an international obligation under the Biological Weapons Treaty of 1972. However, the United States had already experienced its first modern biological attack in 1984, when a cult in Oregon poisoned salad bars in the community with *salmonella* bacteria, in an attempt to influence the outcome of an election. This law requires a criminal standard of intent to use any of a list of biologicals as weapons. Congress took care in the construction of the statute to make criminal only those who possessed biological agents "for other than peaceful purposes." This placed no limits on researchers who used these agents for typical research, and indeed, it was Congress's intent to avoid obstructing scientists in their work.

In 1995 and 1996, Larry Wayne Harris obtained plague bacteria from the American Type Culture Collection by using letterhead from a laboratory. This incident moved Congress to pass the Anti-Terrorism and Death Penalty Act of 1996, which added that not only must there be an "intent to use [biological agents] as a weapon. . .," but also included "attempts, threatens or conspires to do the same."[1]

In *United States v. Larry Wayne Harris*, 961 F. Supp. 1127 (S.D. Ohio, Eastern Div., 1997), the lack of intent to use the anthrax as a weapon, left prosecutors with only wire fraud in misrepresenting himself to obtain bubonic plague. He received only probation.

Larry Wayne Harris identified himself as a scientist,[2] which contributed to the concern that caused Congress to begin to regulate biological agents typically transferred by scientists in laboratories and academic institutions to other researchers, rather than merely making criminal the use or intent to use them as weapons. The gap between possession of these agents and the attempt to use them as weapons began to close when Congress created the select agent regulatory framework.[3]   The select agent framework "represents a legislative mandate to balance the regulatory oversight of agents and toxins that have the potential to pose a severe threat to public health and safety while maintaining availability of these agents and toxins for research and educational activities."[4] From 1996 until 2002, scientists could remain out of the reach of regulation of these agents, unless they chose to ship them, and then compliance with transportation labeling and notification requirements would be required. In the 1996 publication of the final rules, the CDC responded to concerns from scientists that mere possession would be governed by the regulations.   They responded that "this final rule and associated criminal penalties apply only to interstate and intrastate transfer of these agents. Possession of these agents is outside the scope of this final rule . . ."[5]

The anthrax attacks of 2001 following 9/11 moved Congress to close the gap between possession and criminal intent to use or attempt to use a biological weapon. The USA PATRIOT Act made criminal the possession of an agent "of a type or in a quantity that, under the circumstances, is not reasonably justified . . . ." The statute also added the expanded definition of weapon to include the development or possession of an agent "for other than peaceful purposes."[6]

The USA PATRIOT Act was effective immediately upon its passage in October 23, 2001. The first person was charged under the new rules in November 2001. Tomas Foral, a graduate student at the University of Connecticut, was charged in November 2001 for possession of an agent for no "reasonably justified" purpose. While a graduate student at the University of Connecticut, he was found in possession of anthrax from about October 27, 2001 until November 27, 2001. Foral was charged with "unlawfully retaining a portion of the anthrax that had been initially discovered October, 2001 at a University of Connecticut research laboratory in Storrs, Connecticut. The charge of unlawfully possessing a biological agent carries a maximum term of incarceration of 10 years and a fine of as much as $250,000."[7]

The second generation of the select agent rules was also set forth in the USA PATRIOT Act. The new regulations now imposed informational disclosures, security background checks, security plans for laboratories, and registration of facilities and personnel where select agents were housed. This second generation was an interim final rule in December 2002, and became effective on February 7, 2003.[8] These rules effectively changed the culture of biodefense research from one of fetterless freedom in the laboratory to one of controlled security and accountability to a regulatory authority.

Mere possession and criminal intent

In 1996 scientists feared that mere possession would make biological agents criminal, and indeed, Congress sought to limit the rules so as not to impede legitimate research of scientists. The CDC assured scientists that "[t]his final rule and associated criminal penalties apply only to interstate and intrastate transfer of these agents. Possession of these agents is outside the scope of this final rule; however, an individual in possession of a 'biological agent or toxin . . . for use as a weapon,' as defined in Title 18 of the U.S. Code, may be subject to separate criminal penalties (18 U.S.C. 175 et seq.)."[9] The gap between the regulation for movement of select agents and the intent to use them as weapons left many activities unregulated, ranging from the work of a clandestine scientist to the legitimate work of a government scientist.

In 1996 scientists were concerned about the inadvertent or unintentional mistake that could make criminals of scientists. In particular, the question was raised to make the required mental state very clear. The criminal state of mind required to be convicted under the rules governing select agents, the CDC explained, was found in two criminal statutes:

> Title 18, United States Code, Section 1001 applies to false statements made to the Federal Government in connection with the rule. Such false statements may be made in connection with a facility's application to become a registered entity, completion of CDC Form EA-101 for transfers of select agents, and in other circumstances. To constitute a criminal violation, Section 1001 requires that the false statement be made "knowingly and willfully." Other violations of the rule are covered under Title 42, United States Code, Section 271. This violation is classified as a misdemeanor and requires a "knowing" mental state by the defendant. Thus, both of these criminal statutes subject offenders to punishment for knowing conduct." [10]

In the post-§73, post-9/11 environment, the FBI and the Office of the U.S. Attorney in the northern district of New York investigated Associate Professor Steven Kurtz, an artist from State University at New York–Syracuse who depicts biotechnologies in artform, after they were informed of biological equipment in his home by 911 responders who had responded to a call concerning Professor Kurtz's wife. In 2004, Associate Professor Steven Kurtz was arrested for possession of bacteria in his home. It was discovered that Professor Robert Ferrell of the Department of Human Genetics at the University of Pittsburg had supplied the bacteria to Professor Kurtz, and was also charged by the FBI. Professor Kurtz had asked Professor Ferrell to order *serratia marcesens* and other bacteria, [11] which Ferrell did. However, since the bacteria was not a select agent, the federal prosecutor could not charge him under this law or the criminal statute. The case was dismissed by the Court in April 2008 after four years of litigation.

In a later case, Professor John K. Rosenberger of the University of Delaware, an expert in avian influenza, was charged with smuggling an avian flu virus into Maine and then to a laboratory in Delaware in 1998. Rosenberger pled guilty in September 2004 to violation of the select agent rules. Rosenberger is recognized as an international authority on avian influenza virus, but a felony conviction would permanently bar him from ever working with any select agent again.

In 2002 Congress passed the Public Health Security and Bioterrorism Preparedness and Response Act of 2002, 42 U.S.C. 262a, also known as the Bioterrorism Preparedness Act, which required the regulation of the possession of select agents. The USA PATRIOT Act of 2001 required security investigations of people who had access to select agents. These statutes were implemented in 42 CFR § 73, called the Select Agent Program, and implemented by the Centers for Diseases Control and Prevention.

The select agent rules and the bioweapons criminal statute have effectively closed the gap between the criminal and the mere possession of select agents and potentially subject biodefense researchers to one or both of these statutes, as illustrated in the preceding examples.

In addition to the select agent rules, the transportation of select agents continues to be an important part of tracking biological agents. The transportation requirements make criminal the failure to complete shipping papers, the failure to mark shipments, and the failure to affix a Class 6.2 label indicating a biohazard in shipments. Imports are controlled by U.S. Customs, and exports must be permitted by the Department of Commerce. It was the exportation of the plague bacteria that carried the longest prison sentence for Professor Thomas Butler of Texas Tech University. The unauthorized export of any commercially controlled item is criminal. One of the disturbing parts of the case was that although Thomas Butler had carried the plague onto a commercial airline on which he was a passenger, in what is commonly referred to as the "VIP" (vial-in-pocket) technique, there was no conviction for carrying plague in that manner because there is no civil or criminal penalty for this action under §72, since it is not put into interstate shipment. Although §73 was in a notice and comment period before becoming a final rule, the VIP issue was never addressed, and it remains an unclear violation of the interstate shipment regulations under another title. If the CDC wishes to proscribe this behavior, it should do so in an express rule that does not leave the regulated community unsure about its prohibition.

The prohibition against certain types of experiments is another section of the select agent program that attempts to limit the types of experiments that might be done on biological agents to make them more useful as weapons. NIH is charged with regulating experiments involving recombinant DNA, and the rDNA Guidelines have been used effectively to utilize at the local level the Institutional Biosafety Committees for approval in the first step, followed by the Recombinant DNA Advisory Committee (RAC) at the federal level, and final approval from NIH for such experiments.

The next section will examine the transportation of biological agents, regulated by Congress, based on the effect on interstate commerce, consistent with the power delegated to Congress through the Commerce Clause.

6.3   Transportation of Biological Agents
6.3.1.   42 CFR §72

The Centers for Diseases Control is delegated the responsibility to implement the regulation of the transportation of "select agents" or those biological agents and toxins determined to be dangerous along with other characteristics that were placed on a published "select agent list." These regulations were effective in 1996 and codified at 42 CFR §72.

On July 21, 2006, the Centers for Diseases Control published a notice in the Federal Register proposing to remove 42 CFR § 72 and transfer the responsibilities and regulation of infectious agent transportation to the Department of Transportation:

> HHS proposes to remove Part 72 of Title 42, Code of Federal Regulations, which governs the interstate shipment of etiologic agents, because the U.S. Department of Transportation (DOT) already has in effect a more comprehensive set of regulations applicable to the transport in commerce of infectious substances. DOT harmonizes its transport requirements with international standards adopted by the United Nations (UN) Committee of Experts on the Transport of Dangerous Goods for the classification, packaging, and transport of infectious substances. Rescinding the rule will eliminate duplication of the more current DOT regulations that cover intrastate and international, as well as interstate, transport. HHS replaced those sections of Part 72 that deal with select biological agents and toxins with a new set of regulations found in Part 73 of Title 42. HHS anticipates that removal of Part 72 will alleviate confusion and reduce the regulatory burden with no adverse impact on public health and safety.

The Department of Transportation (DOT) published the final rule, "Hazardous Materials: Infectious substances; Harmonization with the United Nations Recommendations" (71 FR 32244; June 2, 2006), about three weeks before the Centers for Diseases Control transferred responsibility of regulating transportation of infectious agents to the U.S. DOT. This new regulation changes the definition of an "infectious substance" from a risk group categorization to the World Health Organization system of categorization, which has two groups: Category A for high-risk substances, and Category B for all other agents and substances. Previous packaging regulations are also replaced by this rule and are regulated under the Hazardous Materials Regulations, 49 CFR Part 171-180, which the CDC and DOT consider to be more consistent with international transportation and packaging standards.

6.3.2. Biologics
Biologics, not otherwise hazardous, can be shipped in normal shipping services if labeled properly, and are not subject to the regulations in Section 6.3.3., infra. Human blood and samples not suspected of containing pathogens are exempt from the regulations except they must meet leak-proof packaging standards and include a label "Exempt human specimen" (IATA, 3.6.2.2.3.6)

Biological products are defined in the IATA Dangerous Goods Regulations as "those products derived from living organisms which are manufactured and distributed in accordance with the requirements of appropriate national authorities, which may have special licensing requirements, and are used either for prevention, treatment, ordiagnosis of disease in humans or animals or for development, experimental or investigational purposes related thereto. They include but are not limited to finished or unfinished products such as vaccines." (IATA, 3.6.2.1.2).

6.3.3. IATA Dangerous Goods Regulations
While not law, the IATA regulations are a compendium of regulations developed by each airline and collectively in the International Air Transport Association (IATA) for carrying hazardous materials including infectious substances and biologics. These have not been adopted as binding regulations by any government, but the penalty is the loss of an airline resource to transport your goods, so there is an incentive to comply.

Infectious substances are defined as "substances which are known or are reasonably expected to contain pathogens. Pathogens are defined as micro-organisms (including bacteria, viruses, rickettsiae, parasites, fungi and other agenst suc as prions, which can cause disease in humans or animals." (IATA, 3.6.2.1.1).

Infectious substances are divided into two categories. Category A infectious substances are defined as "An infectious substance which is transported ina form that, when exposure to it occurs is capable of causing permanent disability, life-threatening or fatal disease in otherwise healthy humans or animals. . . ." (IATA 3.6.2.2.2.1) Category B infectious substances are simply those that do not fall into the definition for Category A (IATA 3.6.2.2.2.2.)

The regulations are in a sourcebook the size of a major city phone book, and require an eight-hour course to understand where to find and apply the applicable regulations. Professional shippers often handle these infectious materials because of this complicated set of rules, driving up the cost of working in a field which requires this kind of transport.

6.4   Importation and Exportation of Biological Agents
Biological agents that are infectious agents, or "etiologic agents," are those microorganisms and toxins that cause disease or injury in humans, and include bacteria, bacterial toxins, viruses, fungi, rickettsiae, protozoans, and parasites, among other groups. Vectors are also regulated and are defined as arthropods and other organisms that transmit pathogens to animals as well as humans.

6.4.1. Importation permits
Etiological agents are defined as "hazardous materials" in the regulation of importation,

regulated by the U.S. Public Health Service, and require a permit. Import permits are required for etiological agents, biological agents, and hosts and vectors. The regulatory website describes these materials:

Etiologic agents
> *In general, an import permit is needed for any infectious agent known or suspected to cause disease in humans.*

Biological materials
> *Unsterilized specimens of human and animal tissues (such as blood, body discharges, fluids, excretions or similar material) containing an infectious or etiologic agent require a permit in order to be imported.*

Hosts and Vectors
> • *Animals. Any animal known or suspected of being infected with an organism capable of causing disease in humans may require a permit issued by CDC. Importation of live turtles of less than 4 inches in shell length and live nonhuman primates is regulated by the CDC, Division of Global Migration and Quarantine (www.cdc.gov/ncidod/dq/). Telephone (404) 498-1600 for further information.*

> • *Bats. All live bats require an import permit from the CDC and the U.S. Department of Interior, Fish and Wildlife Services. The application for a CDC import permit for live exotic bats is on this website.*

> • *Arthropods. Any living insect or other arthropod that is known or suspected of containing an etiologic agent (human pathogen) requires a CDC import permit.*

> • *Snails. Snail species capable of transmitting a human pathogen require a permit from the Centers for Disease Control. Importation permits are issued to an importer who is located in the United States. The importation permit must be cleared upon arrival to the United States through the U.S. Customs Service and the U.S. Division of Quarantine Personnel.*

The regulation of etiological agents is described in U.S. Public Health Service, regulation, 42 CFR Part 71, Foreign Quarantine, Part 71.54:
> *Etiologic agents, hosts, and vectors.*

> *(a) A person may not import into the United States, nor distribute after importation, any etiologic agent or any arthropod or other animal host or vector of human disease, or any exotic living arthropod or other animal capable of being a host or vector of human disease unless accompanied by a permit issued by the Director.*

> *(b) Any import coming within the provisions of this section will not be released from custody prior to receipt by the District Director of U.S. Customs Service of a permit issued by the Director (Centers for Disease Control and Prevention).*

The regulation also includes packaging guidelines for safe shipment of etiologic agents and is regulated by the U.S. Department of Transportation, 49 CFR part 173, which requires the "consultation" of the International Air Transport Association (IATA) Dangerous Goods Transportation guidance, discussed in Section 6.3.3., supra. The IATA Dangerous Goods Regulations are available at: http://www.iata.org/whatwedo/cargo/dangerous goods/infectious substances.htm.

Since these are guidelines adopted by reference to the regulations, they do not carry the force of law. However, in practice, the IATA will not allow the shipment of any materials not in compliance with these guidelines, and therefore, failure to comply with the guidance has great consequences in a commercial sense for noncompliance.

International shipping is also governed by the IATA guidance, and, by adoption, also includes the WHO guidance on regulations for the Transport of Infectious Substances 2007-2008 available at: http://www.who.int/csr/resources/publications/biosafety/WHO CDS EPR 2007 2cc.pdf This also includes reference to 49 CFR, Parts 100 - 185. Hazardous materials regulations by the Department of Transportation are available at: http://phmsa.dot.gov.

Other permits may also be required from the United States Department of Agriculture, Animal and Plant Health Inspection Service (USDA/APHIS) for animal material including tissue cultures, cell cultures, bovine growth stimulants, and other materials of livestock origin. Wildlife permits may also be required from the U.S. Fish and Wildlife Service for some live animals classified as "wild," such as bats.

6.4.2. Export permits
Exportation of infectious materials is regulated by the Department of Commerce through the application for an export permit. The export of not only biological agents, but also equipment involved in the handling and research of biological agents may also be regulated under the export licensing regulations.

Export License Applications for Chemical, Biological, Nuclear and Missile Technology Items are regulated by the Office of Chemical and Biological Controls and Treaty Compliance and the Office of Nuclear and Missile Technology Controls.

Specifically, the export license must address the following items about the biological materials; this guidance is used for completing the export permit application:

2. Microorganisms and Toxins
* Any alternative names for the organism: For example, Variola virus is the same as smallpox, Lyssa virus is the same as rabies.
* A summary of current research activities of the institution when the organism is intended for use in research.
* For individual researchers, provide their name, date & place of birth, academic background, work experience, summary of research history, and recent publications.
* The specific department in which the item will be used, i.e., biology, pathology, radiology, etc.

3. Chemical and Biological Equipment
* Specific type of equipment as defined in Category 2 of the Commerce Control List, Export Control Classification Numbers 2B350, 2B351 and 2B352

* Technical parameters to describe the equipment in terms of the ECCN For example, for reactors controlled under ECCN 2B350 include their "total internal (geometric) volume."

* Surface materials that come into direct contact with chemicals, i.e., nickel, glass, zirconium, etc.

* Brochures for the equipment or a description on your letterhead describing the functional characteristics of the equipment. Guidance available at http://www.bis.doc.gov/licensing/pdf/cbwmtcr2.pdf.

Exporting infectious substances without a permit is punishable by a criminal offense and potentially a felony offense. In *United States v. Thomas Butler* (W.Tex. 2003), Dr. Butler, a scientist who studied plague was prosecuted for exporting plague specimens to Tanzania without an export permit among other counts, but it was the violation of this export process which caused him to receive a two-year prison sentence.

6.5   Handling, Storage, and Use of Biological Agents, 42 CFR §73

§ 73.1 Definitions.

For purposes of this part:

Administrator means the Administrator, Animal and Plant Health Inspection Service, or any person authorized to act for the Administrator.

Animal and Plant Health Inspection Service (APHIS) means the Animal and Plant Health Inspection Service of the U.S. Department of Agriculture.

Attorney General means the Attorney General of the United States or any person authorized to act for the Attorney General.

Biological agent means any microorganism (including, but not limited to, bacteria, viruses, fungi, rickettsiae, or protozoa), or infectious substance, or any naturally occurring, bioengineered, or synthesized component of any such microorganism or infectious substance, capable of causing death, disease, or other biological malfunction in a human, an animal, a plant, or another living organism; deterioration of food, water, equipment, supplies, or material of any kind; or deleterious alteration of the environment.

CDC means Centers for Disease Control and Prevention of the Department of Health and Human Services.

Diagnosis means the analysis of specimens for the purpose of identifying or confirming the presence or characteristics of a select agent or toxin provided that such analysis is directly related to protecting the public health or safety, animal health or animal products, or plant health or plant products.

Entity means any government agency (Federal, State, or local), academic institution, corporation, company, partnership, society, association, firm, sole proprietorship, or other legal entity.

HHS means the Department of Health and Human Services.

HHS Secretary means the Secretary of the Department of Health and Human Services or his or her designee, unless otherwise specified.

HHS select agent and/or toxin means a biological agent or toxin included in § 73.3.

Overlap select agent and/or toxin means a biological agent or toxin listed in § 73.4 and 9 CFR part 121.4.

Principal investigator means the one individual who is designated by the entity to direct a project or program and who is responsible to the entity for the scientific and technical direction of that project or program.

Proficiency testing means the process of determining the competency of an individual or laboratory to perform a specified test or procedure.

Responsible Official means the individual designated by an entity with the authority and control to ensure compliance with the regulations in this part.

Select agent and/or toxin means unless otherwise specified, all of the biological agents or toxins listed in § 73.3 and 73.4.

Specimen means samples of material from humans, animals, plants or the environment or isolates or cultures from such samples for the diagnosis, verification, or proficiency testing.

State means any of the several States of the United States, the Commonwealth of the Northern Mariana Islands, the Commonwealth of Puerto Rico, the District of Columbia, Guam, the Virgin Islands of the United States, or any other territory or possession of the United States.

Toxin means the toxic material or product of plants, animals, microorganisms (including, but not limited to, bacteria, viruses, fungi, rickettsiae, or protozoa), or infectious substances, or a recombinant or synthesized molecule, whatever their origin and method of production, and includes any poisonous substance or biological product that may be engineered as a result of biotechnology, produced by a living organism; or any poisonous isomer or biological product, homolog, or derivative of such a substance.

United States means all of the States.

USDA means the United States Department of Agriculture.

Verification means the demonstration of obtaining established performance (*e.g.,* accuracy, precision, and the analytical sensitivity and specificity) specifications for any procedure used for diagnosis.

§ 73.2 Purpose and scope.

This part implements the provisions of the Public Health Security and Bioterrorism Preparedness and Response Act of 2002 setting forth the requirements for possession, use, and transfer of select agents and toxins. The biological agents and toxins listed in this part have the potential to pose a severe threat to public health and safety, to animal health, or to animal products. Overlap select agents and toxins are subject to regulation by both CDC and APHIS.

§ 73.3 HHS select agents and toxins.

(a) Except for exclusions under paragraphs (d) and (e) of this section, the HHS Secretary has determined that the biological agents and toxins listed in this section have the potential to pose a severe threat to public health and safety.

(b) HHS select agents and toxins:
Abrin
Cercopithecine herpesvirus 1 (Herpes B virus)
Coccidioides posadasii
Conotoxins
Crimean-Congo haemorrhagic fever virus
Diacetoxyscirpenol
Ebola viruses
Lassa fever virus
Marburg virus

Monkeypox virus
Ricin
Rickettsia prowazekii
Rickettsia rickettsii
Saxitoxin
Shiga-like ribosome inactivating proteins
South American Haemorrhagic Fever viruses
(Junin, Machupo, Sabia, Flexal, Guanarito)
Tetrodotoxin
Tick-borne encephalitis complex (flavi)
viruses (Central European Tick-borne
encephalitis, Far Eastern Tick-borne
encephalitis [Russian Spring and Summer
encephalitis, Kyasanur Forest disease,
Omsk Hemorrhagic Fever])
Variola major virus (Smallpox virus) and
Variola minor virus (Alastrim)
Yersinia pestis

(c) Genetic Elements, Recombinant Nucleic Acids, and Recombinant Organisms:

(1) Nucleic acids that can produce infectious forms of any of the select agent viruses listed in paragraph (b) of this section.

(2) Recombinant nucleic acids that encode for the functional form(s) of any of the toxins listed in paragraph (b) of this section if the nucleic acids:

(i) Can be expressed *in vivo* or *in vitro*, or

(ii) Are in a vector or recombinant host genome and can be expressed *in vivo* or *in vitro.*

(3) HHS select agents and toxins listed in paragraph (b) of this section that have been genetically modified.

(d) HHS select agents or toxins that meet any of the following criteria are excluded from the requirements of this part:

(1) Any HHS select agent or toxin that is in its naturally occurring environment provided the select agent or toxin has not been intentionally introduced, cultivated, collected, or otherwise extracted from its natural source.

(2) Non-viable HHS select agents or nonfunctional HHS toxins.

(3) HHS toxins under the control of a principal investigator, treating physician or veterinarian, or commercial manufacturer or distributor, if the aggregate amount does not, at any time, exceed the following amounts: 100 mg of Abrin; 100 mg of Conotoxins; 1,000 mg of Diacetoxyscirpenol; 100 mg of Ricin; 100 mg of Saxitoxin; 100 mg of Shiga-like ribosome inactivating proteins; or 100 mg of Tetrodotoxin.

(e) An attenuated strain of a HHS select agent or toxin may be excluded   from   the requirements of this part based upon a determination that the   attenuated strain does not pose a severe threat to public health and   safety.

(1) To apply for an exclusion, an individual or entity must submit a written request and supporting scientific information. A written decision granting or denying the request will be issued. An exclusion will be effective upon notification to the applicant. Exclusions will be published periodically in the notice section of the Federal Register and will be listed on the CDC Web site at *http://www.cdc.gov/.*

(2) If an excluded attenuated strain is subjected to any manipulation that restores or enhances its virulence, the resulting select agent or toxin will be subject to the requirements of this part.

(3) An individual or entity may make a written request to the HHS Secretary for reconsideration of a decision denying an exclusion application. The written request for reconsideration must state the facts and reasoning upon which the individual or entity relies to show the decision was incorrect. The HHS Secretary will grant or deny the request for reconsideration as promptly as circumstances allow and will state, in writing, the reasons for the decision.

(f) Any HHS select agent or toxin seized by a Federal law enforcement   agency will be excluded from the requirements of this part during the   period between seizure of the select agent or toxin and the transfer or   destruction of such agent or toxin provided that:

(1) As soon as practicable, the Federal law enforcement agency transfers the seized select agent or toxin to an entity eligible to receive such agent or toxin or destroys the agent or toxin by a recognized sterilization or inactivation process,

(2) The Federal law enforcement agency safeguards and secures the seized select agent or toxin against theft, loss, or release, and reports any theft, loss, or release of such agent or toxin, and

(3) The Federal law enforcement agency reports the seizure of the select agent or toxin to CDC or APHIS.

(i) The seizure of Ebola viruses, Lassa fever virus, Marburg virus, South American Haemorrhagic Fever virus (Junin, Machupo, Sabia, Flexal, Guanarito), Variola major virus (Smallpox virus), Variola minor (Alastrim), or *Yersinia pestis* must be reported within 24 hours by telephone, facsimile, or e-mail. This report must be followed by submission of APHIS/CDC Form 4 within seven calendar days after seizure of the select agent or toxin.

(ii) For all other HHS select agents or toxins, APHIS/CDC Form 4 must be submitted within seven calendar days after seizure of the agent or toxin.

(iii) A copy of APHIS/CDC Form 4 must be maintained for three years.

(4) The Federal law enforcement agency reports the final disposition of the select agent or toxin by submission of APHIS/CDC Form 4. A copy of the completed form must be maintained for three years.

§ 73.4 Overlap select agents and toxins.

(a) Except for exclusions under paragraphs (d) and (e) of this section, the HHS Secretary has determined that the biological agents and toxins listed in this section have the potential to pose a severe threat to public health and safety, to animal health, or to animal products.

(b) Overlap select agents and toxins:

Bacillus anthracis
Botulinum neurotoxins
Botulinum neurotoxin producing species of
Clostridium
Brucella abortus
Brucella melitensis
Brucella suis
Burkholderia mallei (formerly *Pseudomonas mallei*)
Burkholderia pseudomallei (formerly *Pseudomonas pseudomallei*)
Clostridium perfringens epsilon toxin

Coccidioides immitis
Coxiella burnetii
Eastern Equine Encephalitis virus
Francisella tularensis
Hendra virus
Nipah virus
Rift Valley fever virus
Shigatoxin
Staphylococcal enterotoxins
T–2 toxin
Venezuelan Equine Encephalitis virus

(c) Genetic Elements, Recombinant Nucleic Acids, and Recombinant Organisms:

(1) Nucleic acids that can produce infectious forms of any of the overlap select agent viruses listed in paragraph (b) of this section.

(2) Recombinant nucleic acids that encode for the functional form(s) of any overlap toxins listed in paragraph (b) of this section if the nucleic acids:

(i) Can be expressed *in vivo* or *in vitro*, or

(ii) Are in a vector or recombinant host genome and can be expressed *in vivo* or *in vitro*.

(3) Overlap select agents and toxins listed in paragraph (b) of this section that have been genetically modified.

(d) Overlap select agents or toxins that meet any of the following criteria are excluded from the requirements of this part:

(1) Any overlap select agent or toxin that is in its naturally occurring environment provided that the select agent or toxin has not been intentionally introduced, cultivated, collected, or otherwise extracted from its natural source.

(2) Non-viable overlap select agents or nonfunctional overlap toxins.

(3) Overlap toxins under the control of a principal investigator, treating physician or veterinarian, or commercial manufacturer or distributor, if the aggregate amount does not, at any time, exceed the following amounts: 0.5 mg of Botulinum neurotoxins; 100 mg of *Clostridium perfringens* epsilon toxin; 100 mg of Shigatoxin; 5 mg of Staphylococcal enterotoxins; or 1,000 mg of T–2 toxin.

(e) An attenuated strain of an overlap select agent or toxin may be excluded from the requirements of this part based upon a determination that the attenuated strain does not pose a severe threat to public health and safety, to animal health, or to animal products.

(1) To apply for an exclusion, an individual or entity must submit a written request and supporting scientific information. A written decision granting or denying the request will be issued. An exclusion will be effective upon notification to the applicant. Exclusions will be published periodically in the notice section of the **Federal Register** and will be listed on the CDC Web site at *http://www.cdc.gov/*.

(2) If an excluded attenuated strain is subjected to any manipulation that restores or enhances its virulence, the resulting overlap select agent or toxin will be subject to the requirements of this part.

(3) An individual or entity may make a written request to the HHS Secretary for reconsideration of a decision denying an exclusion application. The written request for reconsideration must state the facts and reasoning upon which the individual or entity relies to show the decision was incorrect. The HHS Secretary will grant or deny the request for reconsideration as promptly as circumstances allow and will state, in writing,

the reasons for the decision.

(f) Any overlap select agent or toxin seized by a Federal law enforcement agency will be excluded from the requirements of this part during the period between seizure of the select agent or toxin and the transfer or destruction of such agent or toxin provided that:

(1) As soon as practicable, the Federal law enforcement agency transfers the seized select agent or toxin to an entity eligible to receive such agent or toxin or destroys the agent or toxin by a recognized sterilization or inactivation process,

(2) The Federal law enforcement agency safeguards and secures the seized select agent or toxin against theft, loss, or release, and reports any theft, loss, or release of such agent or toxin, and

(3) The Federal law enforcement agency reports the seizure of the overlap select agent or toxin to CDC or APHIS.

(i) The seizure of Bacillus anthracis, Botulinum neurotoxins, Brucella melitensis, Francisella tularensis, Hendra virus, Nipah virus, Rift Valley fever virus, or Venezuelan equine encephalitis virus must be reported within 24 hours by telephone, facsimile, or e-mail. This report must be followed by submission of APHIS/CDC Form 4 within seven calendar days after seizure of the select agent or toxin.

(ii) For all other overlap select agents or toxins, APHIS/CDC Form 4 must be submitted within seven calendar days after seizure of the select agent or toxin.

(iii) A copy of APHIS/CDC Form 4 must be maintained for three years.

(4) The Federal law enforcement agency reports the final disposition of the overlap select agent or toxin by the submission of APHIS/CDC Form 4. A copy of the completed form must be maintained for three years.

§ 73.5 Exemptions for HHS select agents and toxins.

(a) Clinical or diagnostic laboratories and other entities that possess, use, or transfer a HHS select agent or toxin that is contained in a specimen presented for diagnosis or verification will be exempt from the requirements of this part for such agent or toxin contained in the specimen, provided that:

(1) Unless directed otherwise by the HHS Secretary, within seven calendar days after identification, the select agent or toxin is transferred in accordance with § 73.16 or destroyed on-site by a recognized sterilization or inactivation process,

(2) The select agent or toxin is secured against theft, loss, or release during the period between identification of the select agent or toxin and transfer or destruction of such agent or toxin, and any theft, loss, or release of such agent or toxin is reported, and

(3) The identification of the select agent or toxin is reported to CDC or APHIS and to other appropriate authorities when required by Federal, State, or local law.

(i) The identification of any of the following HHS select agents or toxins must be immediately reported by telephone, facsimile, or e-mail: Ebola viruses, Lassa fever virus, Marburg virus, South American Haemorrhagic Fever viruses (Junin, Machupo, Sabia, Flexal, Guanarito), Variola major virus (Smallpox virus), Variola minor (Alastrim), or Yersinia pestis. This report must be followed by submission of APHIS/CDC Form 4 within seven calendar days after identification.

(ii) For all other HHS select agents or toxins, APHIS/CDC Form 4 must be submitted within seven calendar days after identification.

(iii) Less stringent reporting may be required based on extraordinary circumstances, such as a widespread outbreak.

(iv) A copy of APHIS/CDC Form 4 must be maintained for three years.

(b) Clinical or diagnostic laboratories and other entities that possess, use, or transfer a HHS select agent or toxin that is contained in a specimen presented for proficiency testing will be exempt from the requirements of this part for such agent or toxin contained in the specimen, provided that:

(1) Unless directed otherwise by the HHS Secretary, within 90 calendar days of receipt, the select agent or toxin is transferred in accordance with § 73.16 or destroyed on-site by a recognized sterilization or inactivation process,

(2) The select agent or toxin is secured against theft, loss, or release during the period between identification of the select agent or toxin and transfer or destruction of such agent or toxin, and the theft, loss, or release of such agent or toxin is reported, and

(3) The identification of the select agent or toxin, and its derivative, is reported to CDC or APHIS and to other appropriate authorities when required by Federal, State, or local law. To report the identification of a select agent or toxin, APHIS/CDC Form 4 must be submitted within 90 calendar days of receipt of the select agent or toxin. A copy of the completed form must be maintained for three years.

(c) Unless the HHS Secretary issues an order making specific provisions of this part applicable to protect public health and safety, products that are, bear, or contain listed select agents or toxins that are cleared, approved, licensed, or registered under any of the following laws, are exempt from the provisions of this part insofar as their use meets the requirements of such laws:

(1) The Federal Food, Drug, and Cosmetic Act (21 U.S.C. 301 et seq.),

(2) Section 351 of the Public Health Service Act pertaining to biological products (42 U.S.C. 262),

(3) The Act commonly known as the Virus-Serum-Toxin Act (21 U.S.C. 151–159), or

(4) The Federal Insecticide, Fungicide, and Rodenticide Act (7 U.S.C. 136 et seq.).

(d) The HHS Secretary may exempt from the requirements of this part an investigational product that is, bears, or contains a select agent or toxin, when such product is being used in an investigation authorized under any Federal Act and additional regulation under this part is not necessary to protect public health and safety.

(1) To apply for an exemption, an individual or entity must submit a completed APHIS/CDC Form 5.

(2) The HHS Secretary shall make a determination regarding the application within 14 calendar days after receipt, provided the application meets all of the requirements of this section and the application establishes that the investigation has been authorized under the cited Act. A written decision granting or denying the request will be issued.

(3) The applicant must notify CDC or APHIS when an authorization for an investigation no longer exists. This exemption automatically terminates when such authorization is no longer in effect.

(e) The HHS Secretary may temporarily exempt an individual or entity from the requirements of this part based on a determination that the exemption is necessary to provide for the timely participation of the individual or entity in response to a domestic or foreign public health emergency. With respect to the emergency involved, the exemption may not exceed 30 calendar days, except that one extension of an additional 30 calendar days may be granted. To apply for an exemption or an extension of an exemption, an individual or entity must submit a completed APHIS/CDC Form 5 establishing the need to provide for the timely participation of the individual or entity in a response to a domestic or foreign public health emergency. A written decision granting or denying the request will be issued.

§ 73.6 Exemptions for overlap select agents and toxins.

(a) Clinical or diagnostic laboratories and other entities that possess, use, or transfer an overlap select agent or toxin that is contained in a specimen presented for diagnosis or verification will be exempt from the requirements of this part for such agent or toxin contained in the specimen, provided that:

(1) Unless directed otherwise by the HHS Secretary or Administrator, within seven calendar days after identification, the select agent or toxin is transferred in accordance with § 73.16 or 9 CFR part 121.16 or destroyed on-site by a recognized sterilization or inactivation process,

(2) The select agent or toxin is secured against theft, loss, or release during the period between identification of the select agent or toxin and transfer or destruction of such agent or toxin, and any theft, loss, or release of such agent or toxin is reported, and

(3) The identification of the select agent or toxin is reported to CDC or APHIS and to other appropriate authorities when required by Federal, State, or local law.

(i) The identification of any of the following overlap select agents or toxins must be immediately reported by telephone, facsimile, or e-mail: Bacillus anthracis, Botulinum neurotoxins, Brucella melitensis, Francisella tularensis, Hendra virus, Nipah virus, Rift Valley fever virus, or Venezuelan equine encephalitis virus. This report must be followed by submission of APHIS/CDC Form 4 within seven calendar days after identification.

(ii) For all other overlap select agents or toxins, APHIS/CDC Form 4 must be submitted within seven calendar days after identification.

(iii) Less stringent reporting may be required based on extraordinary circumstances, such as a widespread outbreak.

(iv) A copy of APHIS/CDC Form 4 must be maintained for three years.

(b) Clinical or diagnostic laboratories and other entities that possess, use, or transfer an overlap select agent or toxin that is contained in a specimen presented for proficiency testing will be exempt from the requirements of this part for such agent or toxin contained in the specimen, provided that:

(1) Unless directed otherwise by the HHS Secretary or Administrator, within 90 calendar days of receipt, the select agent or toxin is transferred in accordance with § 73.16 or 9 CFR part 121.16 or destroyed on-site by a recognized sterilization or inactivation process,

(2) The select agent or toxin is secured against theft, loss, or release during the period between identification of the select agent or toxin and transfer or destruction of such agent or toxin, and the theft, loss, or release of such agent or toxin is reported, and

(3) The identification of the select agent or toxin, and its derivative, is reported to CDC or APHIS and to other appropriate authorities when required by Federal, State, or local law. To report the identification of an overlap select agent or toxin, APHIS/CDC Form 4 must be submitted within 90 calendar days of receipt of the select agent or toxin. A copy of the completed form must be maintained for three years.

(c) Unless the HHS Secretary issues an order making specific provisions of this part applicable to protect public health and safety, products that are, bear, or contain listed select agents or toxins that are cleared, approved, licensed, or registered under any of the following laws, are exempt from the provisions of this part insofar as their use meets the requirements of such laws:

(1) The Federal Food, Drug, and Cosmetic Act (21 U.S.C. 301 et seq.),

(2) Section 351 of the Public Health Service Act pertaining to biological products (42 U.S.C. 262),

(3) The Act commonly known as the Virus-Serum-Toxin Act (21 U.S.C. 151–159), or

(4) The Federal Insecticide,Fungicide, and Rodenticide Act (7 U.S.C. 136 et seq.).

(d) The HHS Secretary, after consultation with Administrator, may exempt from the requirements of this part an investigational product that is, bears, or contains an overlap select agent or toxin, may be exempted when such product is being used in an investigation authorized under any Federal Act and additional regulation under this part is not necessary to protect public health and safety.

(1) To apply for an exemption, an individual or entity must submit a completed APHIS/CDC Form 5.

(2) The HHS Secretary shall make a determination regarding the application within 14 calendar days after receipt, provided the application meets all of the requirements of this section and the application establishes that the investigation has been authorized under the cited Act. A written decision granting or denying the request will be issued.

(3) The applicant must notify CDC or APHIS when an authorization for an investigation no longer exists. This exemption automatically terminates when such authorization is no longer in effect.

(e) The HHS Secretary may temporarily exempt an individual or entity from the requirements of this part based on a determination that the exemption is necessary to provide for the timely participation of the individual or entity in response to a domestic or foreign public health emergency. With respect to the emergency involved, the exemption may not exceed 30 calendar days, except that one extension of an additional 30 calendar days may be granted. To apply for an exemption or an extension of an exemption, an individual or entity must submit a completed APHIS/CDC Form 5 establishing the need to provide for the timely participation of the individual or entity in a response to a domestic or foreign public health emergency. A written decision granting or denying the request will be issued.

(f) Upon request of the Administrator, the HHS Secretary may exempt an individual or entity from the requirements of this part, for 30 calendar days if the Administrator has granted the exemption for agricultural emergency. The HHS Secretary may extend the exemption once for an additional 30 calendar days.

§ 73.7 Registration and related security risk assessments.

(a) Unless exempted under § 73.5, an individual or entity shall not possess, use, or transfer any HHS select agent or toxin without a certificate of registration issued by the HHS Secretary. Unless exempted under § 73.6 or 9 CFR part 121.6, an individual or entity shall not possess, use, or transfer overlap select agents or toxins, without a certificate of registration issued by the HHS Secretary and Administrator.

(b) As a condition of registration, each entity must designate an individual to be its Responsible Official. While most registrants are likely to be entities, in the event that an individual applies for and is granted a certificate of registration, the individual will be considered the Responsible Official.

(c)   (1) As a condition of registration, the following must be approved by the HHS Secretary or Administrator based on a security risk assessment by the Attorney General:

(i) The individual or entity,

(ii) The Responsible Official, and

(iii) Unless otherwise exempted under this section, any individual who owns or controls the entity.

(2) Federal, State, or local governmental agencies, including public accredited academic institutions, are exempt from the security risk assessments for the entity and the individual who owns or controls such entity.

(3) An individual will be deemed to own or control an entity under the following conditions:

(i) For a private institution of higher education, an individual will be deemed to own or control the entity if the individual is in a managerial or executive capacity with regard to the entity's select agents or toxins or with regard to the individuals with access to the select agents or toxins possessed, used, or transferred by the entity.

(ii) For entities other than institutions of higher education, an individual will be deemed to own or control the entity if the individual:

(A) Owns 50 percent or more of the entity, or is a holder or owner of 50 percent or more of its voting stock, or

(B) Is in a managerial or executive capacity with regard to the entity's select agents or toxins or with regard to the individuals with access to the select agents or toxins possessed, used, or transferred by the entity.

(4) An entity will be considered to be an institution of higher education if it is an institution of higher education as defined in section 101(a) of the Higher Education Act of 1965 (20 U.S.C. 1001(a)), or is an organization described in 501(c)(3) of the Internal Revenue Code of 1986, as amended (26 U.S.C. 501(c)(3)).

(5) To obtain a security risk assessment, an individual or entity must submit the information necessary to conduct a security risk assessment to the Attorney General.

(d) To apply for a certificate of registration that covers only HHS select agents or toxins, an individual or entity must submit the information requested in the registration application package (APHIS/CDC Form 1) to CDC. To apply for a certificate of registration that does not cover only HHS select agents or toxins (i.e., covers at least one overlap select agent and/or toxin, or covers any combination of HHS select agents and/or toxins and USDA select agents and/or toxins), an individual or entity must submit the information requested in the registration application package (APHIS/CDC Form 1) to CDC or APHIS, but not both.

(e) Prior to the issuance of a certificate of registration, the Responsible Official must promptly provide notification of any changes to the application for registration by submitting the relevant page(s) of the registration application.

(f) The issuance of a certificate of registration may be contingent upon inspection or submission of additional information, such as the security plan, biosafety plan, incident response plan, or any other documents required to be prepared under this part.

(g) A certificate of registration will be valid for one physical location (a room, a building, or a group of buildings) where the Responsible Official will be able to perform the responsibilities required in this part, for specific select agents or toxins, and for specific activities.

(h) A certificate of registration may be amended to reflect changes in circumstances (e.g., replacement of the Responsible Official or other personnel changes, changes in ownership or control of the entity, changes in the activities involving any select agents or toxins, or the addition or removal of select agents or toxins).

(1) Prior to any change, the Responsible Official must apply for an amendment to a certificate of registration by submitting the relevant page(s) of the registration application.

(2) The Responsible Official will be notified in writing if an application to amend a certificate of registration has been approved. Approval of the amendment may be contingent upon an inspection or submission of additional information, such as the security plan, biosafety plan, incident response plan, or any other documents required to be prepared under this part.

(3) No change may be made without such approval.

(i) An entity must immediately notify CDC or APHIS if it loses the services of its Responsible Official. In the event that an entity loses the services of its Responsible Official, an entity may continue to possess or use select agents or toxins only if it appoints as the Responsible Official another individual who has been approved by the HHS Secretary or Administrator following a security risk assessment by the Attorney General and who meets the requirements of this part.

(i) A certificate of registration will be terminated upon the written request of the entity if the entity no longer possesses or uses any select agents or toxins and no longer wishes to be registered.

(j) A certificate of registration will be valid for a maximum of three years.

§ 73.8 Denial, revocation, or suspension of registration.

(a) An application may be denied or a certificate of registration revoked or suspended if:

(1) The individual or entity, the Responsible Official, or an individual who owns or controls the entity is within any of the categories described in 18 U.S.C. 175b,

(2) The individual or entity, the Responsible Official, or an individual who owns or controls the entity as reasonably suspected by any Federal law enforcement or intelligence agency of:

(i) Committing a crime specified in 18 U.S.C. 2332b(g)(5),

(ii) Knowing involvement with an organization that engages in domestic or international terrorism (as defined in 18 U.S.C. 2331) or with any other organization that engages in intentional crimes of violence, or

(iii) Being an agent of a foreign power (as defined in 50 U.S.C. 1801).

(3) The individual or entity does not meet the requirements of this part, or

(4) It is determined that such action is necessary to protect public health and safety.

(b) Upon revocation or suspension of a certificate of registration, the individual or entity must:

(1) Immediately stop all use of each select agent or toxin covered by the revocation or suspension order,

(2) Immediately safeguard and secure each select agent or toxin covered by the revocation or suspension order from theft, loss, or release, and

(3) Comply with all disposition instructions issued by the HHS Secretary for the select agent or toxin covered by the revocation or suspension.

(c) Denial of an application for registration and revocation of registration may be appealed under § 73.20. However, any denial of an application for registration or revocation of a certificate of registration will remain in effect until a final agency decision has been rendered.

§ 73.9 Responsible Official.

(a) An individual or entity required to register under this part must designate an individual to be the Responsible Official. The Responsible Official must:

(1) Be approved by the HHS Secretary or Administrator following a security risk assessment by the Attorney General,

(2) Be familiar with the requirements of this part,

(3) Have authority and responsibility to act on behalf of the entity,

(4) Ensure compliance with the requirements of this part, and

(5) Ensure that annual inspections are conducted for each laboratory where select agents or toxins are stored or used in order to determine compliance with the requirements of this part. The results of each inspection must be documented, and any deficiencies identified during an inspection must be corrected.

(b) An entity may designate one or more individuals to be an alternate Responsible Official, who may act for the Responsible Official in his/her absence. These individuals must have the authority and control to ensure compliance with the regulations when acting as the Responsible Official.

(c) The Responsible Official must report the identification and final disposition of any select agent or toxin contained in a specimen presented for diagnosis or verification.

(1) The identification of any of the following select agents or toxins must be immediately reported by telephone, facsimile, or e-mail: Bacillus anthracis, Botulinum neurotoxins, Brucella melitensis, Francisella tularensis, Ebola viruses, Hendra virus, Marburg virus, Lassa fever virus, Nipah virus, Rift Valley fever virus, South American Haemorrhagic Fever viruses (Junin, Machupo, Sabia, Flexal, Guanarito), Variola major virus (Smallpox virus), Variola minor (Alastrim), Venezuelan equine encephalitis virus, or Yersinia pestis. The final disposition of the agent or toxin must be reported by submission of APHIS/CDC Form 4 within seven calendar days after identification. A copy of the completed form must be maintained for three years.

(2) To report the identification and final disposition of any other select agent or toxin, APHIS/CDC Form 4 must be submitted within seven calendar days after identification. A copy of the completed form must be maintained for three years.

(3) Less stringent reporting may be required based on extraordinary circumstances, such as a widespread outbreak.

(d) The Responsible Official must report the identification and final disposition of any select agent or toxin contained in a specimen presented for proficiency testing. To report the identification and final disposition of a select agent or toxin, APHIS/CDC Form 4 must be submitted within 90 calendar days of receipt of the agent or toxin. A copy of the completed form must be maintained for three years.

§ 73.10 Restricting access to select agents and toxins; security risk assessments.

(a) An individual or entity required to register under this part may not provide an individual access to a select agent or toxin, and an individual may not access a select agent or toxin, unless the individual is approved by the HHS Secretary or Administrator, following a security risk assessment by the Attorney General.

(b) An individual will be deemed to have access at any point in time if the individual has possession of a select agent or toxin (e.g., ability to carry, use, or manipulate) or the ability to gain possession of a select agent or toxin.

(c) Each individual with access to select agents or toxins must have the appropriate education, training, and/or experience to handle or use such agents or toxins.

(d) To apply for access approval, each individual must submit the information necessary to conduct a security risk assessment to the Attorney General.

(e) An individual's security risk assessment may be expedited upon written request by the Responsible Official and a showing of good cause (e.g., public health or agricultural emergencies, national security, or a short term visit by a prominent researcher). A written decision granting or denying the request will be issued.

(f) An individual's access approval will be denied or revoked if the individual is within any of the categories described in 18 U.S.C. 175b,

(g) An individual's access approval may be denied, limited, or revoked if:

(1) The individual is reasonably suspected by any Federal law enforcement or intelligence agency of committing a crime specified in 18 U.S.C. 2332b(g)(5), knowing involvement with an organization that engages in domestic or international terrorism (as defined in 18 U.S.C. 2331) or with any other organization that engages in intentional crimes of violence, or being an agent of a foreign power (as defined in 50 U.S.C. 1801), or

(2) It is determined such action is necessary to protect public health and safety.

(h) An individual may appeal the HHS Secretary's decision to deny, limit, or revoke access approval under § 73.20.

(i) Access approval is valid for a maximum of five years.

(j) The Responsible Official must immediately notify CDC or APHIS when an individual's access to select agents or toxins is terminated by the entity and the reasons therefore.

§ 73.11 Security.

(a) An individual or entity required to register under this part must develop and implement a written security plan. The security plan must be sufficient to safeguard the select agent or toxin against unauthorized access, theft, loss, or release.

(b) The security plan must be designed according to a site-specific risk assessment and must provide graded protection in accordance with the risk of the select agent or toxin, given its intended use. The security plan must be submitted upon request.

(c) The security plan must:

(1) Describe procedures for physical security, inventory control, and information systems control,

(2) Contain provisions for the control of access to select agents and toxins,

(3) Contain provisions for routine cleaning, maintenance, and repairs,

(4) Establish procedures for removing unauthorized or suspicious persons,

(5) Describe procedures for addressing loss or compromise of keys, passwords, combinations, etc. and protocols for changing access numbers or locks following staff changes,

(6) Contain procedures for reporting unauthorized or suspicious persons or activities, loss or theft of select agents or toxins, release of select agents or toxins, or alteration of inventory records, and

(7) Contain provisions for ensuring that all individuals with access approval from the HHS Secretary or Administrator understand and comply with the security procedures.

(d) An individual or entity must adhere to the following security requirements or implement measures to achieve an equivalent or greater level of security:

(1) Allow access only to individuals with access approval from the HHS Secretary or Administrator,

(2) Allow individuals not approved for access from the HHS Secretary or Administrator to conduct routine cleaning, maintenance, repairs, or other activities not

related to select agents or toxins only when continuously escorted by an approved individual,

(3) Provide for the control of select agents and toxins by requiring freezers, refrigerators, cabinets, and other containers where select agents or toxins are stored to be secured against unauthorized access (e.g., card access system, lock boxes),

(4) Inspect all suspicious packages before they are brought into or removed from the area where select agents or toxins are used or stored,

(5) Establish a protocol for intra-entity transfers under the supervision of an individual with access approval from the HHS Secretary or Administrator, including chain-of-custody documents and provisions for safeguarding against theft, loss, or release,

(6) Require that individuals with access approval from the HHS Secretary or Administrator refrain from sharing with any other person their unique means of accessing a select agent or toxin (e.g., keycards or passwords),

(7) Require that individuals with access approval from the HHS Secretary or Administrator immediately report any of the following to the Responsible Official:

(i) Any loss or compromise of keys, passwords, combination, etc.,

(ii) Any suspicious persons or activities,

(iii) Any loss or theft of select agents or toxins,

(iv) Any release of a select agent or toxin, and

(v) Any sign that inventory or use records for select agents or toxins have been altered or otherwise compromised, and

(8) Separate areas where select agents and toxins are stored or used from the public areas of the building.

(e) In developing a security plan, an entity or individual should consider, the document entitled "Laboratory Security and Emergency Response Guidance for Laboratories Working with Select Agents. Morbidity and Mortality Weekly Report December 6, 2002; 51:RR–19:1–6." The document is available on the Internet at: http://www.cdc.gov/mmwr.

(f) The plan must be reviewed annually and revised as necessary. Drills or exercises must be conducted at least annually to test and evaluate the effectiveness of the plan. The plan must be reviewed and revised, as necessary, after any drill or exercise and after any incident.

§ 73.12 Biosafety.

(a) An individual or entity required to register under this part must develop and implement a written biosafety plan that is commensurate with the risk of the agent or toxin, given its intended use. The biosafety plan must contain sufficient information and documentation to describe the biosafety and containment procedures.

(b) The biosafety and containment procedures must be sufficient to contain the select agent or toxin (e.g., physical structure and features of the entity, and operational and procedural safeguards).

(c) In developing a biosafety plan, an individual or entity should consider:

(1) The CDC/NIH publication, "Biosafety in Microbiological and Biomedical Laboratories", including all appendices. Copies may be obtained from the Superintendent of Documents, U.S. Government Printing Office, Post Office Box 371954, Pittsburgh, Pennsylvania, 75250–7954 or from the CDC Web site at http://www.cdc.gov/. Copies may be inspected at the Centers for Disease Control and Prevention, 1600 Clifton Road, Mail Stop E–79, Atlanta, Georgia.

(2) The Occupational Safety and Health Administration (OSHA) regulations in 29 CFR parts 1910.1200 and 1910.1450.

(3) The "NIH Guidelines for Research Involving Recombinant DNA Molecules," (NIH Guidelines). Copies may be obtained from the Centers for Disease Control and Prevention, 1600 Clifton Road, Mail Stop E–79, Atlanta, Georgia, 30333 or from the CDC Web site at http://www.cdc.gov/. Copies may be inspected at the Centers for Disease Control and Prevention, 1600 Clifton Road, Mail Stop E–79, Atlanta, Georgia.

(d) The plan must be reviewed annually and revised as necessary. Drills or exercises must be conducted at least annually to test and evaluate the effectiveness of the plan. The plan must be reviewed and revised, as necessary, after any drill or exercise and after any incident.

§ 73.13 Restricted experiments.

(a) An individual or entity may not conduct a restricted experiment with a HHS select agent or toxin unless approved by and conducted in accordance with any conditions prescribed by the HHS Secretary. In addition, an individual or entity may not conduct a restricted experiment with an overlap select agent or toxin unless approved by and conducted in accordance with any conditions prescribed by the HHS Secretary, after consultation with Administrator.

(b) Restricted experiments:

(1) Experiments utilizing recombinant DNA that involve the deliberate transfer of a drug resistance trait to select agents that are not known to acquire the trait naturally, if such acquisition could compromise the use of the drug to control disease agents in humans, veterinary medicine, or agriculture.

(2) Experiments involving the deliberate formation of recombinant DNA containing genes for the biosynthesis of select toxins lethal for vertebrates at an LD50 < 100 ng/kg body weight.

(c) The HHS Secretary may revoke approval to conduct any of the experiments in paragraph (b) of this section, or revoke or suspend a certificate of registration, if the individual or entity fails to comply with the requirements of this part.

(d) To apply for approval to conduct any of the experiments in paragraph (a) of this section, an individual or entity must submit a written request and supporting scientific information. A written decision granting or denying the request will be issued.

§ 73.14 Incident response.

(a) An individual or entity required to register under this part must develop and implement a written incident response plan.2 The incident response plan must be coordinated with any entity-wide plans, kept in the workplace, and available to employees for review.

(b) The incident response plan must fully describe the entity's response procedures for the theft, loss, or release of a select agent or toxin, inventory discrepancies, security breaches (including information systems), severe weather and other natural disasters, workplace violence, bomb threats, suspicious packages, and emergencies such as fire, gas leak, explosion, power outage, etc. The response procedures must account for hazards associated with the select agent and toxin and appropriate actions to contain such select agent or toxin.

(c) The incident response plan must also contain the following information:

(1) The name and contact information (e.g., home and work) for the individual or entity (e.g., responsible official, alternate responsible official(s), biosafety officer, etc.),

(2) The name and contact information for the building owner and/or manager, where applicable,

(3) The name and contact information for tenant offices, where applicable,

(4) The name and contact information for the physical security official for the building, where applicable,

(5) Personnel roles and lines of authority and communication,

(6) Planning and coordination with local emergency responders,

(7) Procedures to be followed by employees performing rescue or medical duties,

(8) Emergency medical treatment and first aid,

(9) A list of personal protective and emergency equipment, and their locations,

(10) Site security and control,

(11) Procedures for emergency evacuation, including type of evacuation, exit route assignments, safe distances, and places of refuge, and

(12) Decontamination procedures.

(d) The plan must be reviewed annually and revised as necessary. Drills or exercises must be conducted at least annually to test and evaluate the effectiveness of the plan. The plan must be reviewed and revised, as necessary, after any drill or exercise and after any incident.

§ 73.15 Training.

(a) An individual or entity required to register under this part must provide information and training on biosafety and security to each individual with access approval from the HHS Secretary or Administrator before he/she has such access.3 In addition, an individual or entity must provide information and training on biosafety and security to each individual not approved for access from the HHS Secretary or Administrator before he/she works in or visits areas where select agents or toxins are handled or stored (e.g., laboratories, growth chambers, animal rooms, greenhouses, storage areas, etc.). The training must address the particular needs of the individual, the work they will do, and the risks posed by the select agents or toxins.

(b) Refresher training must be provided annually.

(c) A record of the training provided to each individual must be maintained. The record must include the name of the individual, the date of the training, a description of the training provided, and the means used to verify that the employee understood the training.

§ 73.16 Transfers.

(a) Except as provided in paragraphs (c) and (d) of this section, a select agent or toxin may only be transferred to individuals or entities registered to possess, use, or transfer that agent or toxin. A select agent or toxin may only be transferred under the conditions of this section and must be authorized by CDC or APHIS prior to the transfer.

(b) A transfer may be authorized if:

(1) The sender:

(i) Has at the time of transfer a certificate of registration that covers the particular select agent or toxin to be transferred and meets all requirements in this part,

(ii) Meets the exemption requirements for the particular select agent or toxin to be transferred, or

(iii) Is transferring the select agent or toxin from outside the United States and meets all import requirements.

(2) At the time of transfer, the recipient has a certificate of registration that includes the particular select agent or toxin to be transferred and meets all of the requirements of this part.

(c) A select agent or toxin that is contained in a specimen for proficiency testing may be transferred without prior authorization from CDC or APHIS provided that, at least seven calendar days prior to the transfer, the sender reports to CDC or APHIS the select agent or toxin to be transferred and the name and address of the recipient.

(d) On a case-by-case basis, the HHS Secretary may authorize a transfer of a select agent or toxin, not otherwise eligible for transfer under this part under conditions prescribed by the HHS Secretary.

(e) To obtain authorization for transfer, APHIS/CDC Form 2 must be submitted.

(f) The recipient must submit a completed APHIS/CDC Form 2 within two business days of receipt of a select agent or toxin.

(g) The recipient must immediately notify CDC or APHIS if the select agent or toxin has not been received within 48 hours after the expected delivery time, or if the package containing select agents or toxins has been damaged to the extent that a release of the select agent or toxin may have occurred.

(h) An authorization for a transfer shall be valid only for 30 calendar days after issuance, except that such an authorization becomes immediately null and void if any facts supporting the authorization change (e.g., change in the certificate of registration for the sender or recipient, change in the application for transfer).

(i) The sender must comply with all applicable laws concerning packaging and shipping.

§ 73.17 Records.

(a) An individual or entity required to register under this part must maintain complete records relating to the activities covered by this part. Such records must include:

(1) Accurate, current inventory for each select agent (including viral genetic elements, recombinant nucleic acids, and recombinant organisms) held in long-term storage (placement in a system designed to ensure viability for future use, such as in a freezer or

lyophilized materials), including:

(i) The name and characteristics (e.g., strain designation, GenBank Accession number, etc.),

(ii) The quantity acquired from another individual or entity (e.g., containers, vials, tubes, etc.), date of acquisition, and the source,

(iii) Where stored (e.g., building, room, and freezer),

(iv) When moved from storage and by whom and when returned to storage and by whom,

(v) The select agent used and purpose of use,

(vi) Records created under § 73.16 and 9 CFR 121.16 (Transfers),

(vii) For intra-entity transfers (sender and the recipient are covered by the same certificate of registration), the select agent, the quantity transferred, the date of transfer, the sender, and the recipient, and

(viii) Records created under § 73.19 and 9 CFR part 121.19 (Notification of theft, loss, or release),

(2) Accurate, current inventory for each toxin held, including:

(i) The name and characteristics,

(ii) The quantity acquired from another individual or entity (e.g., containers, vials, tubes, etc.), date of acquisition, and the source,

(iii) The initial and current quantity amount (e.g., milligrams, milliliters, grams, etc.),

(iv) The toxin used and purpose of use, quantity, date(s) of the use and by whom,

(v) Where stored (e.g., building, room, and freezer),

(vi) When moved from storage and by whom and when returned to storage and by whom including quantity amount,

(vii) Records created under § 73.16 and 9 CFR part 121.16 (Transfers),

(viii) For intra-entity transfers (sender and the recipient are covered by the same certificate of registration), the toxin, the quantity transferred, the date of transfer, the sender, and the recipient,

(ix) Records created under § 73.19 and 9 CFR part 121.19 (Notification of theft, loss, or release), and

(x) If destroyed, the quantity of toxin destroyed, the date of such action, and by whom,

(3) A current list of all individuals that have been granted access approval from the HHS Secretary or Administrator,

(4) Information about all entries into areas containing select agents or toxins, including the name of the individual, name of the escort (if applicable), and date and time of entry,

(5) Accurate, current records created under § 73.9 and 9 CFR part 121.9 (Responsible Official), § 73.11 and 9 CFR part 121.11 (Security), § 73.12 and 9 CFR part 121.12 (Biosafety), § 73.14 and 9 CFR part 121. 14 (Incident response), and § 73.15 and 9 CFR part 121.15 (Training), and (6) A written explanation of any discrepancies.

(b) The individual or entity must implement a system to ensure that all records and data bases created under access, and that their authenticity may be verified.

(c) All records created under this part must be maintained for three years and promptly produced upon request.

§ 73.18 Inspections.

(a) Without prior notification, the HHS Secretary, shall be allowed to inspect any site at which activities regulated by this part are conducted and shall be allowed to inspect and copy any records relating to the activities covered by this part.

(b) Prior to issuing a certificate of registration to an individual or entity, the HHS Secretary may inspect and evaluate the premises and records to ensure compliance with this part.

§ 73.19 Notification of theft, loss, or release.

(a) Upon discovery of the theft or loss of a select agent or toxin, an individual or entity must immediately notify CDC or APHIS and appropriate Federal, State, or local law enforcement agencies. Thefts or losses must be reported even if the select agent or toxin is subsequently recovered or the responsible parties are identified.

(1) The theft or loss of a select agent or toxin must be reported immediately by telephone, facsimile, or e-mail. The following information must be provided:

(i) The name of the select agent or toxin and any identifying information (e.g., strain or other characterization information),

(ii) An estimate of the quantity lost or stolen,

(iii) An estimate of the time during which the theft or loss occurred,

(iv) The location (building, room) from which the theft or loss occurred, and

(v) The list of Federal, State, or local law enforcement agencies to which the individual or entity reported, or intends to report the theft or loss.

(2) A completed APHIS/CDC Form 3 must be submitted within seven calendar days.

(b) Upon discovery of a release of an agent or toxin causing occupational exposure or release of a select agent or toxin outside of the primary barriers of the biocontainment area, an individual or entity must immediately notify CDC or APHIS.

(1) The release of a select agent or toxin must be reported by telephone, facsimile, or e-mail. The following information must be provided:

(i) The name of the select agent or toxin and any identifying information (e.g., strain or other characterization information),

(ii) An estimate of the quantity released,

(iii) The time and duration of the release,

(iv) The environment into which the release occurred (e.g., in building or outside of building, waste system),

(v) The location (building, room) from which the release occurred,

(vi) The number of individuals potentially exposed at the entity,

(vii) Actions taken to respond to the release, and

(viii) Hazards posed by the release.

(2) A completed APHIS/CDC Form 3 must be submitted within seven calendar days.

§ 73.20 Administrative review.

An individual or entity may appeal a denial, revocation, or suspension of registration under this part. An individual may appeal a denial, limitation, or revocation of access approval under this part. The appeal must be in writing, state the factual basis for the appeal, and be submitted to the HHS Secretary within 30 calendar days of the decision. Where the denial, revocation, or suspension of registration or the denial, limitation, or revocation of an individual's access approval is based upon an identification by the Attorney General, the request for review will be forwarded to the Attorney General. The HHS Secretary's decision constitutes final agency action.

§ 73.21 Civil money penalties.

(a) The Inspector General of the Department of Health and Human Services is delegated authority to conduct investigations and to impose civil money penalties against any individual or entity in accordance with regulations in 42 CFR part 1003 for violations of the regulations in this part, as authorized by the Public Health Security and Bioterrorism Preparedness and Response Act of 2002 (Pub. L. 107–188). The delegation of authority includes all powers contained in section 6 of the Inspector General Act of 1978 (5 U.S.C. App.).

(b) The administrative law judges in, assigned to, or detailed to the Departmental Appeals Board have been delegated authority to conduct hearings and to render decisions in accordance with 42 CFR part 1005 with respect to the imposition of civil money penalties, as authorized by the Public Health Security and Bioterrorism Preparedness and Response Act of 2002 (Pub. L. 107–188). This delegation includes, but is not limited to, the authority to administer oaths and affirmations, to subpoena witnesses and documents, to examine witnesses, to exclude or receive and give appropriate weight to materials and testimony offered as evidence, to make findings of fact and conclusions of law, and to determine the civil money penalties to be imposed.

(c) The Departmental Appeals Board of the Department of Health and Human Services is delegated authority to make final determinations with respect to the imposition of civil money penalties for violations of the regulations of this part.

6.5.1 Civil Penalties for violations

The Office of Inspector General, in conjunction with the inspection power of the Centers for Diseases Control and Prevention's Select Agent Program, is empowered to assess and collect civil penalties of a maximum of $500,000 per violation. The civil penalties have been an active and often used enforcement mechanism of the Select Agent Program, and the magnitude of the penalties evidence this activity. From the OIG archives on enforcement actions in the Select Agent Program at http://oig.hhs.gov/fraud/enforcement/cmp/agents_toxins_archive.asp, the following civil penalties have been assessed since the establishment of the Select Agent Program.

08-16-2008

A Texas University agreed to pay $1 million to resolve its liability for numerous violations of the select agent regulations. OIG's allegations included the following: failure of the university's Responsible Official (RO) to apply for an amendment to the university's certificate of registration; failure of the RO to receive the necessary approval prior to university researchers conducting aerolization experiments with select agents; failure of the RO to be familiar with and ensure compliance with the requirements of the select agent regulations; failure of the RO to ensure that deficiencies identified during annual inspections were corrected; failure to obtain CDC approval to conduct restricted experiments with a select agent; allowing researchers, on multiple occasions, to have access to select agents without prior CDC approval and without having the appropriate education, training, and/or experience to handle or use select agents; failure to investigate whether elevated titers of three laboratory workers were caused by occupational exposure to a select agent; failure to ensure that appropriate biosafety and security plans were implemented; failure to ensure that laboratory personnel were trained in biosafety and security; failure to maintain a current list of individuals with access approval to select agents and toxins; failure to keep records of access to at least seven laboratory rooms where select agent work was conducted; failure to implement an accurate record keeping system for its select agent inventory; and failure to report occupational exposures to select agents.

10-02-2007

A Virginia corporation agreed to pay $50,000 to resolve its liability for an alleged violation of the select agent regulations. The OIG alleged that the corporation violated the select agent regulations in the following ways: (1) failing to meet biosafety and security standards appropriate for a select toxin; (2) storing packaged, regulated toxins to be shipped in an unsecured, unregistered location before shipping, which allowed unrestricted access to the toxins; (3) having an inadequate incident response plan; and (4) failing to provide and document the required annual select agent training.

09-24-2007

A California laboratory agreed to pay $450,000 to resolve its liability for an alleged violation of the select agent regulations. The OIG alleged that the laboratory transferred vials of a select agent to two laboratories located in Florida and Virginia. During the transfers, the select agent was released from the shipped vials. An investigation of the packaging for the shipments revealed several violations of regulations governing the shipment of the select agent. The OIG alleged that the laboratory violated the transfer requirements of the select agent regulations by failing to comply with the applicable shipping and packaging laws when transferring a select agent. In addition, the OIG also alleged that the laboratory failed to comply with security and access requirements by allowing an individual not authorized to have access to select agents to package the shipments of the select agent, and that the laboratory's Responsible Official failed to ensure compliance with the shipping and packaging requirements of the select agent regulations.

04-30-2007

A Missouri corporation agreed to pay $25,000 to resolve its liability for an alleged violation of the select agent regulations. The OIG alleged that the corporation violated the select agent regulations by making two unauthorized transfers of select agents. Specifically, the OIG alleged that the corporation sent a select agent to a university which was not registered with the CDC to possess, use, or transfer this select agent. In addition, the OIG alleged that the corporation sent the select agent to a laboratory without obtaining prior authorization from DSAT for the transfer.

02-27-2007

A California Institute agreed to pay $50,000 to resolve its liability for an alleged violation of the select agent regulations. The OIG alleged that the Institute violated the select agent regulations in the following ways: (1) synthesized and possessed a select agent before obtaining a certificate of registration from the Centers for Disease Control and Prevention, and (2) violated transfer requirements related to the Institute's possession of the select agent.

12-18-2006

A Florida corporation agreed to pay $15,000 to resolve its liability for an alleged violation of the select agent regulations. The OIG alleged that the corporation violated the select agent regulations by receiving a transfer of a select agent from another entity without first obtaining authorization from the Centers for Disease Control and Prevention (CDC) and by failing to provide necessary paperwork to the CDC within two business days of receiving the select agent.

10-10-2006

A South Carolina university agreed to pay $50,000 to resolve its liability for an alleged violation of the select agent regulations. The OIG alleged that the university violated the select agent regulations in the following ways: (1) failure of Responsible Official to apply for an amendment to the university's Certificate of Registration; (2) inadequate security plan; (3) inadequate biosafety plan; (4) inadequate incident response plan; (5) failure to maintain adequate training records; and (6) failure to maintain adequate inspection and inventory records.

12-05-2005

A Pennsylvania corporation agreed to pay $15,000 to resolve its liability for an alleged violation of the select agent regulations. The OIG alleged that the corporation violated the select agent regulations by possessing a select agent without filing for a certificate of registration with the Centers for Disease Control and Prevention.

11-07-2005

A Maryland institute agreed to pay $150,000 to resolve its liability for an alleged violation of the select agent regulations. The OIG alleged that the institute made an unauthorized transfer of a select agent to an unregistered entity. The unregistered entity, a research facility, had requested that the institute send it nonviable cells of the select agent. The preparations that the institute sent, however, contained viable spores of the select agent.

09-28-2005

A Colorado research center agreed to pay $20,000 to resolve its liability for an alleged violation of the select agent regulations. The OIG alleged that the research center made an unauthorized transfer of a select agent to a corporation, without first obtaining authorization from the Centers for Disease Control and Prevention.

05-23-2005

A Minnesota corporation agreed to pay $12,000 to resolve its liability for an alleged violation of the select agent regulations. The OIG alleged that the corporation possessed a select agent from March 12, 2003 until July 17, 2004. The OIG alleged that during this time, the corporation failed to submit application materials and failed to register with the Centers for Disease Control and Prevention.

7-26-2004

An Ohio corporation agreed to pay $50,000 to resolve its liability for an alleged violation of the select agent regulations. The OIG alleged that the corporation possessed a select agent from at least March 12, 2003 until March 4, 2004. The OIG alleged that during this time, the corporation failed to submit application materials, and failed to properly register, with the Centers for Disease Control and Prevention

6.5.2   Administrative process for appeals

The Select Agent regulations provide for an administrative appeal for suspension of the registration of a facility. However, there has been only one appeal for a suspension of a permit, and despite promises during the notice and comment period that the CDC did not need a time limit for a response to an administrative appeal, their response to this sole appeal took more than fourteen months, and they assessed fines and penalties before they filed their response.

6.5.3   USAMRIID and Military Regulation of Biological Containment Laboratories

The Amerithrax attacks attributed by the FBI and U.S. Department of Justice to Dr. Bruce Ivins, a research scientist at USAMRIID, the U.S. military biodefense research laboratory, has brought a focus on this individual as the only named suspect. Affidavits and witness testimony in a restraining order action just prior to his suicide in July 2008 indicate that he was having psychiatric problems, that he was under the care of a psychiatrist and a therapist, and that he was taking medications for these problems, which may have affected his behavior in his work as a research scientist specializing in anthrax research at USAMRIID.

The Select Agent regulations apply to military institutions, such as the U.S. Army Medical Research Institute of Infectious Diseases (USAMRIID), by adoption in their own directives. A DOD regulation temporarily issued (in interim) around the same time as the civilian regulations adopted the CDC requirements for FBI background investigations before the researcher can have "access" to the biological agents. In addition, the Department of Defense, which is responsible for USAMRIID, adopted its own, more extensive background investigation requirements.

The CDC background investigation regulation allows the denial or revocation of an investigator's access "to any select agent or toxin to an entity or individual identified by the Attorney General as a 'restricted person' under 18 U.S.C. 175b." In summary, a "restricted person" is someone who could not meet the requirements to obtain a gun permit: they cannot be under indictment for, or convicted of, a felony; be a fugitive from justice; be an unlawful user of a controlled substance; be unlawfully in the United States; be found mentally defective by a court; or have been dishonorably discharged.

However, for biodefense researchers like Dr. Ivins, the DOD background investigation requirement is much more extensive, has much higher threshold standards, and also adds the CDC and FBI background investigation requirement. Specifically, USAMRIID researchers must be "mentally and emotionally stable, trustworthy, and physically competent."   Mandatory disqualifying factors include "attempting or threatening suicide while currently enrolled" in the program as a researcher, or "individuals who have attempted or threatened suicide before entry into" the program and require the certifying official to revoke access to the researcher who meets any of those criteria. Even "inappropriate attitude or behavior," including "aberrant behavior such as impulsiveness, suicide threat, or threats toward other individuals" are mandatory factors for disqualification and barring the individual from work.

A civilian researcher has only to meet the requirements of a FBI background investigation that comprises nothing greater than meeting the requirements equivalent to those for a gun permit, while the DOD has these significantly greater additional military regulations for access.

6.5.4.   BMBL Guidance v. Regulation

Regulation is defined as the legally enforceable rules developed by federal agencies. The procedure of developing regulation is described in the Administrative Procedure Act (APA). Constitutional Due Process is the foundation for the APA requirement that a "notice and comment" rulemaking process is required, which means that the agency proposing the rulemaking must give notice, including the time, place, and nature of the public proceedings, in the *Federal Registrar* at least 30 days before taking effect. This "notice" period allows time for interested parties to "comment" on the proposed regulation before it becomes a final rule. A final regulation is then codified in the *Code of Federal Regulation* (C.F.R.).

Guidance, in contrast, is created with little public participation and is often immune from judicial review. Guidance is a less formal way for the agencies to communicate their position and is not legally enforceable. Guidance does not bind the agency or the public, and no legally enforceable rights or obligations are created through guidance. No statute requires specific procedures for agency guidance documents, aside from the FDA required procedures.

Treatment of Guidance:

Although guidance may not be legally binding, perceptions within the regulated entities and agency are still greatly impacted. Guidance issued by agencies, particularly since 2000, has contained suggestive language rather than binding, enforcement language to mirror its non-binding legal effect. Agencies, in general, see guidance as a way to "clarify and elaborate on regulations." Guidance is believed by agencies to be appreciated by the regulated entities because of the added clarification of the regulation. Because guidance is not legally enforceable, agencies cannot treat non-compliance with guidance as the sole tool of enforcement.

In practice, however, the regulated entities generally do not treat guidance differently than regulation. In most cases, guidance takes on the weight of the rule for the regulated entities. The regulated entities look to guidance for clarification and consistency, and the entities frequently state that they will make an effort to follow guidance even though guidance lacks any legal binding effect. Complying with guidance will often alleviate the possibility of the regulated entities being investigated by the agency for a possible violation, thus saving the regulated entities both time and money. The regulated entities' treatment of guidance as binding alleviates the agency's burden of enforcement.

Concerns of Guidance:

Since guidance is not subject to the same formal procedures as the APA requires for regulation, it is not legally binding. However, regulated entities treat guidance as if it is legally enforceable. Concern arises about whether the regulating agencies are also treating guidance as an enforceability tool, rather than a suggestive document.

SWANCC:

The Supreme Court has addressed the concern of guidance in *Solid Waste Agency of Northern Cook County v. United States Army Corps of Engineers* (SWAANC). In this case, the Army Corps of Engineers extended the definition of "navigable waters" under the Clean Water Act (CWA). The Army Corps of Engineers' extended definition included abandoned sand and gravel pits containing ponds used by migratory birds as their habitat. The Supreme Court held that these intrastate waters were not subject to the Corps' jurisdiction under the CWA. The court stated that, "where an administrative interpretation of a statue invokes the outer limits of Congress' power, we expect a *clear indication* that Congress intended that result."[12] "This requirement stems from . . . our *assumption that Congress does not casually authorize administrative agencies* to interpret a statute to push the limit of congressional authority."[13]

NIH Guidelines:

The NIH has written guidance for recombinant DNA molecules (rDNA). The *NIH Guidelines* were last updated in September 2009. "The purpose of the *NIH Guidelines* is to specify practices for constructing and handling: (i) recombinant deoxyribonucleic acid (DNA) molecules, and (ii) organisms and viruses containing recombinant DNA molecules."

The language of the guidelines state that "as a condition for NIH funding of recombinant DNA research, institutions shall ensure that such research conducted at or sponsored by the institution, irrespective of the source of funding, shall comply with the *NIH Guidelines*." The language suggests that regulated entities must comply with the guidelines provided by the NIH.

The language of the guidelines also lists the possible results from non-compliance. The NIH states, "Non-compliance may result in: (i) suspension, limitation, or termination of financial assistance for the noncompliant NIH-funded research project and of NIH funds for other recombinant DNA research at the institution, or (ii) a requirement for prior NIH approval of any or all recombinant DNA projects at the institution." This enforcement provision, in contrast, states that the non-compliance of guidance "may" result in (punishment). The language of this provision seems to suggest that guidance may not be used as an enforcement tool. One interpretation of the languages suggests that the regulated entity will not be subject to discipline for the sole reason of non-compliance with the guidelines. However, another interpretation of the language is that the regulating agency has discretion on whether to use guidance as a tool of enforcement upon the regulated entity.

BMBL Guidance:

The Select Agent Regulations, 42 C.F.R. § 73, sets forth the requirements for possession, use, and transfer of select agents as expressed in the provisions of the Public Health Security and Bioterrorism Preparedness and Response Act of 2002 (the "Bioterrorism Act"). The Department of Health and Human Services (HHS) created a list of select agents that is deemed a threat to public health. The Centers for Disease Control and Prevention (CDC) was designated as the HHS agency to provide guidance on this regulation.

Biosafety in Microbiological and Biomedical Laboratories (BMBL), 5th Edition, was published in February 2007. "The BMBL is both a code of practice and an authoritative reference." The self-proclaimed intent of the BMBL "is to establish a voluntary code of practice, one that all members of a laboratory community will together embrace to safeguard themselves and their colleagues, and to protect the public health and environment."

In a 2002 letter written by the U.S. Government Accountability Office (GAO) Director of Health Care to the Secretary of the Health and Human Services, Honorable Tommy G. Thompson, stated that "as part of the registration process, facilities must demonstrate in their applications that they meet the requirements delineated in *Biosafety in Microbiological and Biomedical Laboratories* (BMBL) for working with particular select agents."

On October 4, 2007, Dr. Richard Besser, Director of the Coordinating Office for Terrorism Preparedness and Emergency Response (COTPER) at the CDC, made a statement on Oversight of Select Agents by the CDC before the Committee on Energy and Commerce, Subcommittee on Oversight and Investigations United States House of Representatives. In the statement he said, "The BMBL provides recommendations for safely working with a variety of human pathogens and describes standard and special microbiological practices, safety equipment, and facilities (constituting Biosafety Levels 1-4). In the BMBL, there are agent summary statements that provide recommendations for the appropriate biosafety safety level to work with these agents. The BMBL also is offered as a guide and reference in the construction of new laboratory facilities and in the renovation of existing facilities."

42 CFR § 73.12(c) states that "in developing a biosafety plan, an individual Laboratories for Research or entity should consider" both the CDC/NIH publication, *Biosafety in Microbiological and Biomedical Laboratories* (BMBL), including all appendices, and the *NIH Guidelines Involving Recombinant DNA Molecules* (NIH Guidelines). The language of the statute references both the NIH Guidance and the BMBL Guidance. Although Dr. Besser first quotes the language of the regulation specifically stating that the regulated entities "should consider" the BMBL and NIH Guidelines, he continues by stating that the "CDC references the BMBL in the select agent regulations and requires select agent registered entities to comply with the BMBL guidelines or equivalent standards." Dr. Besser interpreted the "should consider" language of the regulation as requiring compliance by the regulating agencies. The strict language, however, only strongly suggests that regulated entities "consider" these guidance documents and does not suggest that either guidance should be treated as a binding enforcement provision.

"To ensure compliance with these requirements, the program established a goal of inspecting these facilities once during the 3-year registration period. Facilities may be inspected before and after registration, but there is no requirement that inspections be performed." The CDC offers compliance assistance through checklists that contain the BMBL recommendations, as well as checklists that contain the NIH Guidelines. The checklists are easily accessible through a "compliance assistance" link on the Select Agents web site. Dr. Besser stated that the CDC uses the specific checklists as a "guide" to its inspections.

According to Dr. Besser, "as of September 25, 2007, CDC has referred 37 entities to HHS-OIG for violation of the select agent regulations (such as for unauthorized transfers and entities that are not registered with the Select Agent Program in possession of select agents). HHS-OIG has levied $837,000 in civil monetary penalties against ten (10) of the entities." "HHS has not referred to DOJ any violations of the select agent regulations for criminal prosecution."

Expected Findings:

Comparing the strict language of the *NIH Guidelines* and the *BMBL*, the NIH guidance language suggests that it may be used more as a tool of enforcement rather than guidance. However, in practice, it appears that the BMBL language is interpreted as also being an enforcement tool.

[Memorandum on Guidance vs. Regulation by Mary Louden, 3L TTU.]

6.6   Biological Safety Laboratories and NEPA

Two National Laboratories for biological containment were planned by the NIH to meet the needs for biodefense and emerging infectious diseases research. In 2003, proposals were made to the NIH for the building of national biological containment laboratories. Two sites were selected: Galveston, Texas and Boston, Massachusetts.   The Galveston National Laboratory proceeded with support from the local community, with some opposition from special interest groups, in particular The Sunshine Group, primarily driven by a single individual who opposed the "proliferation" of biodefense laboratories.   The Galveston National Laboratory proceeded with appropriate environmental impact statements, building was commenced, and having beautifully survived Hurricane Ike in the fall of 2008, it was ceremoniously commissioned to begin operation in the spring of 2009.

The Boston National Laboratory was sited in an urban area of Boston, in contrast to the more remote, island location of the Galveston National Laboratory. From the beginning of the proposal, community opposition arose, primarily citing the risk of siting this facility in such a densely populated area as downtown Boston.

In 2005, after the initial risk assessments had been completed for the federal statute, NEPA in the development of the Environmental Impact Statement (EIS), the project was challenged both in federal and state court for compliance with the Massachusetts Environmental Impact Report (EIR) requirements.   The Massachusetts state court invalidated the Secretary's certification of the Massachusetts' EIR, and the Superior Court affirmed. Excerpts of both the federal and cases are included here, beginning with the federal case:

Allen v. Boston Redevelopment Authority, et. al.
DOCKET SJC-09960
September 5, 2007. - December 13, 2007.
Superior Court, County Suffolk.

The Supreme Judicial Court on its own initiative transferred the case from the Appeals Court.

SPINA, J. In the present case, we consider the planned development by University Associates Limited Partnership (University Associates)(3) of a project known as BioSquare Phase II, a biomedical research complex in the South End neighborhood of Boston, which will include the National Emerging Infectious Diseases Laboratory (Biolab). This laboratory will be a Biosafety Level 4 facility,(4) requiring the highest level of security, where medical research will be conducted on the most dangerous diseases and toxins, including, but not limited to, the Ebola virus, smallpox, anthrax, and botulism.(5) The plaintiff residents of Boston commenced an action in the Superior Court pursuant to G. L. c. 214, § 7A; G. L. c. 30, § 61; and G. L. c. 231A, challenging the adequacy of the environmental reviews of BioSquare Phase II pursuant to the Massachusetts Environmental Policy Act (MEPA), G. L. c. 30, § 61-62H, and the regulations promulgated thereunder, 301 Code Mass. Regs. § 11.00 (1998). In a thorough and well-reasoned memorandum of decision on the plaintiffs' motion for judgment on the pleadings, the judge concluded, as to Count II of the amended complaint, that the November 15, 2004, certification by the Secretary of the Executive Office of Environmental Affairs (Secretary) that the final environmental impact report (EIR) submitted by University Associates adequately and properly complied with MEPA was arbitrary and capricious. Accordingly, the judge vacated the Secretary's certification of the final EIR and remanded the matter to the Secretary for further administrative action.(6) University Associates, the trustees of Boston University, Boston Medical Center Corporation (BMC), and the Boston Redevelopment Authority (BRA) (collectively, the defendants) filed a petition, pursuant to G. L. c. 231, § 118, first par., for interlocutory relief from the judge's order.... A single justice of the Appeals Court granted the petition, and the case was transferred from the Appeals Court on our own motion. For the reasons that follow, we now affirm.

    1. Statutory and regulatory scheme. Before considering the specific facts in this case, we begin with a brief overview of MEPA, and the regulations promulgated thereunder, so as to put the proceedings here in context. General Laws c. 30, § 61, sets forth a broad policy of environmental protection in this Commonwealth by directing "[a]ll agencies, departments, boards, commissions and authorities" to "review, evaluate, and determine the impact on the natural environment of all works, projects or activities conducted by them and . . . use all practicable means and measures to minimize damage to the environment."(8) See 301 Code Mass. Regs. § 11.01. . . . The statute mandates that any determination made by a Commonwealth agency include "a finding describing the environmental impact, if any, of the project and a finding that all feasible measures have been taken to avoid or minimize said impact." G. L. c. 30, § 61. . . . The MEPA review process is "concerned with ensuring that relevant information [about potential environmental damage] is gathered before a project is allowed to proceed [to the permitting stage]." . . . .

    On August 31, 1999, University Associates submitted [notice] to the Executive Office of Environmental Affairs, proposing to commence the development of BioSquare Phase II, which would consist of two research buildings, a parking facility, and a helipad. . . . It made no mention of the Biolab.

    On October 8, 1999, the Secretary issued a certificate on the ENF, concluding that University Associates was required to prepare an EIR for BioSquare Phase II. . . .

    Before University Associates submitted a draft EIR to the Secretary in September, 2003, the National Institute of Allergy and Infectious Diseases, an agency within the National Institutes of Health, accepted a grant proposal jointly filed by the trustees of Boston University and the Boston University Medical Center to build and operate the Biolab. In light of this change to the proposed development of BioSquare Phase II, University Associates met with the assistant secretary to discuss whether the Secretary would require any changes to the scope of the draft EIR. . . . University Associates submitted its draft EIR to the Secretary on September 30, 2003. . . The draft EIR did not discuss the medical research that would take place within the Biolab, or consider the potential consequences of such work on the surrounding community. It merely stated that in order to accommodate the safety and security requirements of the Biolab, a parcel of land that originally had been designated for a hotel in BioSquare Phase I would be reallocated to other purposes in BioSquare Phase II. . . .

    After receiving public comments on the draft EIR,(12) the Secretary determined, in a certificate issued on December 1, 2003, that the draft EIR adequately and properly complied with MEPA and its implementing regulations. . . . In particular, she wrote, the final EIR should include more detail on the proposed use of the Biolab and any potential environmental impacts from such use, should address concerns raised about the safety of the Biolab, should discuss design features that the Biolab would employ to enhance safety, should document how the Biolab would meet any applicable State and Federal safety regulations, should evaluate a "worst case" safety event involving the loss of the physical integrity of the containment systems, should address safety considerations relating to the transportation of potentially hazardous biological agents to and from the Biolab, and should respond to the public comments received on the draft EIR, particularly a detailed comment letter submitted by a Roxbury organization, Alternatives for Community & Environment (ACE), requesting an analysis of, inter alia, alternative locations for the Biolab in a less densely populated area.

    On July 30, 2004, University Associates submitted its final EIR to the Secretary. BioSquare Phase II would consist of two medical research buildings, one of which would house the Biolab, and a parking garage. In its discussion of the Biolab's operational, safety, and security issues, University Associates analyzed the public health impacts of a "worst case scenario" involving the loss of the Biolab's containment systems. RWDI West Inc. (RWDI) was hired to perform the risk assessment. It assumed that dry purified anthrax stored in a container was dropped accidentally in the Biolab, releasing ten billion aerosolized anthrax spores. It further assumed that there would be a complete failure of all containment systems, resulting in anthrax spores being expelled from the building through the exhaust system over a period of approximately thirty minutes. Based on an analysis of this event, RWDI and University Associates determined that the risk of public harm was so minute as to be negligible.

The final EIR also discussed briefly other potential risk scenarios, including the risk of staff acquiring infections within the Biolab, the release of contaminated air through the exhaust system, the escape of an infected animal, the release of infectious materials during transportation, the unauthorized removal of biological materials from the containment area, and the threat of terrorism. University Associates concluded that, given the specialized precautions taken by the Biolab, the risk of harm from any of these scenarios was insignificant or negligible. In its responses to comments received from ACE, University Associates did not specifically address the issue of alternative locations for the Biolab. After receiving public comments on the final EIR, the Secretary issued a certificate on November 15, 2004, stating that the final EIR adequately and properly complied with MEPA and its implementing regulations. Consequently, the Secretary concluded that the plans for BioSquare Phase II could proceed to the State permitting agencies.

The plaintiffs then commenced the present action against the defendants in the Superior Court, alleging in Count II of their amended complaint, which is the focus of this interlocutory appeal, that the Secretary erred in concluding that the final EIR adequately and properly complied with MEPA. More specifically, the plaintiffs asserted that the final EIR analyzed only a single "worst case" scenario, one involving the hypothetical release of anthrax where the pathogen is transmitted by the inhalation of spores, and did not consider any risk scenario involving the release of a contagious pathogen, which can be transmitted through human contact from person to person. The plaintiffs further asserted that the final EIR failed to analyze alternative locations for the Biolab outside the densely populated neighborhood of the South End. . . .

Subsequently, the plaintiffs filed a motion for judgment on the pleadings . . . In his memorandum and order on the plaintiffs' motion, the judge found that the Secretary's certification on November 15, 2004, that the final EIR adequately and properly complied with MEPA and its implementing regulations was arbitrary and capricious. Given that BioSquare Phase II would include a Biosafety Level 4 laboratory, the judge concluded that the environmental reviews were inadequate because University Associates failed to analyze the risks posed by the potential release of a contagious disease from the Biolab, which could cause catastrophic harm, and because University Associates had not considered locations for the Biolab other than the South End. In the absence of such critical analysis, the judge opined, the Secretary's certification of the final EIR lacked a necessary rational basis. The judge pointed out that those governmental agencies whose permits and financing were necessary for the development of BioSquare Phase II should have the benefit of an EIR that properly evaluated the full extent of the environmental impacts of the Biolab, and considered whether such impacts would be different in another location. . . .

4. Consideration of "remote" contingencies. The defendants first contend that the judge's conclusion that the environmental reviews of the Biolab were inadequate was based on a fundamental misconstruction of MEPA. . . .[T]he scope of MEPA is limited to environmental consequences that are "actual," "probable," or "likely," not those that are highly remote. Consequently, the defendants argue that because the Secretary was not required to consider unlikely contingencies, such as the actual release of a pathogen from the Biolab, her certification

of the final EIR was proper, not arbitrary or capricious. Further, the defendants contend that even if remote contingencies were a necessary focus of the MEPA review process, the judge here substituted his own opinion for that of the Secretary with respect to what circumstances constituted a plausible "worst case" scenario for analyzing the environmental risks posed by the Biolab's operation. We disagree with the defendants' interpretation of MEPA and the Secretary's corresponding obligations thereunder in certifying the final EIR.

. . .

The Secretary's authority over the submission and scope of an EIR flows from G. L. c. 30, § 62A, which provides that "the secretary . . . shall . . . limit the scope of the report to those issues which by the nature and location of the project are likely to cause damage to the environment" (emphasis added). The regulations promulgated in accordance with MEPA further provide that "[t]he Secretary shall limit the Scope [of the EIR] to those aspects of the Project that are likely, directly or indirectly, to cause Damage to the Environment." 301 Code Mass. Regs. § 11.06(9)(a). The focus of this statutory and regulatory scheme is not, as the defendants seem to suggest, on whether the release of a pathogen from the Biolab is probable in the first instance. Rather, the focus is on whether, if such a release occurs, even if the chances are remote, it is "likely to cause damage to the environment." G. L. c. 30, § 62A.

The term "likely" is not defined in MEPA, nor is it understood to be a term of art requiring a specific and limited interpretation. Where a statutory term is not defined, it must be understood in accordance with its generally accepted plain meaning. See Lawrence v. Cambridge, 422 Mass. 406, 410 (1996). The dictionary defines "likely" as "having a better chance of existing or occurring than not," and as "having the character of a probability." Webster's Third New Int'l Dictionary 1310 (1993). "As commonly used and understood, 'likely' is a word that encompasses a range of probabilities depending on the specific context in which it is used. . . . [S]omething is 'likely' if it is reasonably to be expected in the context of the particular facts and circumstances at hand." Commonwealth v. Boucher, 438 Mass. 274, 276 (2002). Given that the nature of a Biosafety Level 4 facility is to conduct research on highly virulent and infectious pathogens, and given that the Biolab will be located in a densely populated urban area, the likelihood that the release of such a pathogen will cause damage to the environment is extraordinarily high. The fact that University Associates will take all necessary precautions to minimize the chances of a release at the Biolab does not diminish the potential for catastrophic environmental damage if such a release does occur.

The Secretary plainly recognized the inherent hazards associated with the operation of a Biosafety Level 4 facility in the South End because she specifically mandated that University Associates evaluate a "worst case" scenario in its final EIR. However, the Secretary's subsequent determination that the final EIR adequately and properly complied with MEPA, based, in part, on an assessment by University Associates that an accidental release of anthrax from the Biolab would result in negligible public harm, lacked a rational basis because the evaluation of the "worst case" scenario was significantly incomplete. The final EIR failed to analyze the likely damage to the environment caused by the release of a contagious pathogen, whether through laboratory accident, escape of an infected research animal, theft, terrorism, or transportation mishap, which is a critical consideration in a densely populated urban area. As was pointed out in the public comments on the final EIR, anthrax can be spread through the air and may be fatal if inhaled, but it is not a contagion that is transmitted from person to person.

We recognize that the Secretary has considerable discretion over the scope of an EIR given her expertise in environmental matters. At the same time, the purpose of MEPA and the regulations promulgated thereunder is "to provide meaningful opportunities for public review of the potential environmental impacts of Projects for which [State] Agency Action is required, and to assist each Agency in using . . . all feasible means to avoid Damage to the Environment or, to the extent Damage to the Environment cannot be avoided, to minimize and mitigate Damage to the Environment to the maximum extent practicable" (emphasis added). 301 Code Mass. Regs. § 11.01(1)(a). See G. L. c. 30, § 61. The release of a highly virulent and contagious pathogen from the Biolab would present numerous and unique challenges for State agencies, which those agencies likely would not confront if the release involved a noncontagious pathogen. The absence of any information in the final EIR about such a contingency, one likely to cause damage to the environment, was a substantial oversight. Accordingly, we conclude that the judge's determination that the Secretary's certification of the final EIR was arbitrary and capricious was warranted. The "worst case" scenario put forth by University Associates inadequately addressed the consequences of a release of contagious pathogens from the Biolab, potentially denying State agencies the opportunity for meaningful review of the environmental impact of such a release and consideration of the measures that would be necessary to mitigate environmental damage.

5. Consideration of alternative geographical locations. The defendants next contend that the judge erred in concluding that the Secretary should have required University Associates to analyze alternative locations for the Biolab. The defendants point out that, pursuant to G. L. c. 30, § 62A, the Secretary is vested with the authority to determine what "alternatives" should be included in a particular EIR, and nothing in MEPA or the regulations promulgated thereunder dictates that one such "alternative" must be the location of a proposed project. Consequently, they continue, the fact that the Secretary did not mandate such an analysis did not render her certification of the final EIR arbitrary and capricious. We disagree.

General Laws c. 30, § 62A, states, in pertinent part, that "[t]he secretary shall determine the form, content, level of detail and alternatives required for the [EIR]." . . .

We recognize, as did the judge below, that it is not clear from the statute, the regulations, or case law whether the "reasonable alternatives" that must be considered are simply those within the proposed site of BioSquare Phase II, such as a different physical design, or whether "reasonable alternatives" would encompass a different site location altogether. . . .

Here, the Secretary specifically informed University Associates that the final EIR should respond to public comments received on the draft EIR, particularly the detailed letter submitted by ACE, and should present additional narrative or technical analysis, as appropriate, to respond to substantive concerns. The letter from ACE repeatedly and pointedly emphasized that it was imperative for University Associates to address the issue of alternative locations for the Biolab. The Secretary's mandate with respect to the final EIR suggested that she regarded locations outside the South End neighborhood to be "reasonable alternatives" for consideration. However, University Associates never addressed this issue in its final EIR, even insofar as to explain that locations outside the South End would not, for whatever reasons, be feasible.

Accordingly, we conclude that the judge correctly determined that the Secretary's certification of the final EIR was arbitrary and capricious because the final EIR did not adequately and properly comply with MEPA where University Associates failed to consider alternative locations for the Biolab in response to the comment letter from ACE as directed by the Secretary.

6. Conclusion. The order of the Superior Court vacating the Secretary's certification of the final EIR is affirmed. This case is remanded to the Superior Court for further proceedings consistent with this opinion.

So ordered.

The following comment, made in 2006, examines the Programmatic Environmental

Impact statement, implementing the National Environmental Policy Act in an examination of the federal policy to develop more biological containment laboratory capacity, and, in particular, the Boston National Laboratory litigation.

David M. Shea , *The Project Bioshield Prisoner's Dilemma: An Impetus for the Modernization of Programmatic Environmental Impact Statements*, 33 B.C. Envtl. Aff. L. Rev. 695 (2006).

Biosafety level 4 (BSL-4) organisms, including Ebola and several other African, Asian, and South American viral hemorrhagic fevers, are those determined by the Department of Health and Human Services to be "[d]angerous/exotic agents which pose high risk of life-threatening disease, aerosol-transmitted lab infections; or related agents with unknown risk of transmission." While these pathogens cause the most dangerous diseases known to man, the amount of laboratory space devoted to their study is comparatively small. In the wake of the September 2001 terrorist attacks and the October 2001 anthrax letter scares, President George W. Bush announced a major initiative--Project BioShield--to swiftly fund additional BSL-3 and BSL-4 (BSL-3/4) laboratory space across the country.

In September 2003, Boston University Medical Center (BUMC) received $120 million toward the construction and operation of a BSL-3/4 research facility, after being selected as one of nine institutions to be awarded generous federal grants under Project BioShield. Many local politicians supported the proposed project, based partly on the government's assurance that the risk involved is "negligible." Despite this self-serving administrative assurance, recent media coverage has documented numerous scenarios involving non-negligible amounts of risk at existing BSL-3/4 laboratories, including: the potential spread of pathogens due to power loss; the release of pathogens inside a laboratory; the misplacement of pathogens; the release of pathogens during transit; and the accidental transmission of pathogens to laboratory workers. One can easily conceive of a disaster scenario in downtown Boston rivaling or surpassing the 2002 SARS epidemic in Southeast Asia. This Note does not take the radical view that accidents of this nature are certain to occur if the proposed BUMC laboratory is built; rather, it assumes that the siting of a BSL-3/4 laboratory in such a densely populated area would, contrary to the government's assertion, necessarily constitute some nontrivial amount of risk.

Two local groups--Alternatives for Community & Environment (ACE) and Safety Net-- share this assumption, including it among their claims in various response letters written during public comment periods throughout the federal and state environmental review processes. As of the date of publication, these groups were involved in an ongoing lawsuit challenging the final state environmental certification. This Note foregoes analysis of the local matters and focuses instead on the legal challenges surrounding the federal environmental certification once it becomes final, because these findings will be more relevant to other proposed laboratory sites. In addition, if the state litigation were to block the proposed BUMC BSL-3/4 laboratory, the analysis in this Note will remain relevant should the federal government choose to redirect its munificence.

While the local groups' missives offer a potential road map for future Project BioShield litigation, they also raise pertinent questions about the future of environmental review in general. In particular, one of the environmental plaintiffs' central claims--that the government failed to complete a programmatic environmental impact statement (PEIS) for Project BioShield as a whole before choosing specific locations for the proposed BSL-3/4 laboratories --is a frequent point of contention in environmental litigation. Indeed, uncertainties as to how and when to complete PEISs have recently led one government task force to call for their modernization, as some agencies "struggle[d]" with this "valuable decisionmaking tool[]."

This Note supports the need for PEIS modernization; the predictions made herein regarding the impending Project BioShield litigation also bolster the need for this Note's proffered remedies. Part I details the recent political events leading up to the present controversy. Part II establishes the foundation for the plaintiffs' "Failure to Complete a PEIS" claim by discussing the statutory and regulatory foundation behind PEISs, as well as related case law from the past three decades. Part III examines two relevant branches of plaintiffs' "Inadequate EIS" claim: failure to adequately consider project alternatives, and inadequate risk-assessment methodologies.. . .

I. Setting the Stage for Litigation

In order to prepare the United States for a potential bioterrorism attack, President George W. Bush has authorized a major funding initiative intended to increase the amount of research space dedicated to the study of potential bioterrorism agents. Due to the inherently dangerous nature of the bioterrorism agents, local siting disputes have arisen at several of the newly proposed laboratories.

A. Project BioShield and the Push for More BSL-3/4 Space

President Bush first mentioned Project BioShield during his January 2003 State of the Union Address. Shortly thereafter, details of the plan revealed that Project BioShield would consist of $6 billion in funding, a large part of which would be allocated for "research and development on bioterrorism threat agents." Eighteen months later President Bush signed into law the Project BioShield Act, stating, "Our goal is to translate today's promising medical research into drugs and vaccines to combat a biological attack in the future--and now we will not let bureaucratic obstacles stand in the way."

As a result of the President's initiative, the National Institutes of Health (NIH) has seen its prominence--and its funding--increase dramatically in the past four years. From an annual budget of almost $50 million for "anti-bioterrorism research" in fiscal year 2001, NIH has seen its coffers balloon to nearly $1.7 billion in estimated fiscal year 2005 funding for "biodefense research"--an increase of 3,400%.

Regardless of which public relations moniker is used, the research in question has traditionally been conducted by a specific branch of NIH: the National Institute for Allergy and Infectious Diseases (NIAID). Shortly after the September 11, 2001 terrorist attacks, and the October 2001 anthrax attacks that killed five people, NIAID convened a blue ribbon panel on "Bioterrorism and Its Implications for Biomedical Research," which concluded that "[a]ccess to [BSL-3/4] facilities ... is limited and must be expanded." Although this viewpoint has been disputed by some, the passage of the Project BioShield Act makes it clear that both the executive and legislative branches believe that there is an imminent public health threat that the swift proliferation of BSL-3/4 laboratories can help allay.

B. NIAID Responds, Amid Controversy

To this end, NIAID undertook two laboratory expansion initiatives with its new-found capital. First, it sought to enhance and upgrade the existing BSL-3/4 space as much as possible at its intramural laboratories--sites already under federal control. Believing that these improvements would not result in a large enough increase in laboratory capacity, NIAID also attempted to locate willing extramural institutional partners by issuing a Broad Agency Announcement (BAA) in late 2002. This document stated that any "Domestic (U.S.), Non-Federal, Public or Private Non-Profit Organizations that Support Biomedical Research [were] eligible to apply" for funding to run

"Regional Biocontainment Laboratories (RBL[s]) and National Biocontainment Laboratories (NBL[s])." Institutions selected to receive RBLs would build BSL-2 and BSL-3 space with one-time federal construction grants ranging from $7 to $21 million each, while institutions awarded NBLs would be required to build BSL-2, BSL-3, and BSL-4 space with grants of $120 million each.

On September 30, 2003, in what former Secretary of Health and Human Services Tommy G. Thompson hailed as "'a major step towards being able to provide Americans with effective therapies, vaccines and diagnostics for diseases caused by agents of bioterror,'" NIAID awarded nine RBLs and two NBLs to selected universities across the nation.

Not everyone shares the former Secretary's exuberance for the proposed BSL-3/4 laboratories, however. For a variety of reasons, protests have sprung up in a number of communities where laboratories--both intramural and extramural--have been proposed. In an effort to predict the outcomes of potential lawsuits, the following Parts discuss several of the major claims likely to be made by environmental plaintiffs.

II. Litigation Background: "Failure to Complete a PEIS" Claim

A December 2004 letter from two environmental groups, detailing the shortcomings of NIH's draft environmental review for the proposed BUMC NBL, articulates the environmental plaintiffs' first major claim: NIH's failure to complete a PEIS before proceeding with the site-specific EIS process. This topic is relevant to Project BioShield as a whole because initial completion of a PEIS would have rendered this claim moot nationwide.

Although the broad language of the nation's most important environmental law does not specifically mention PEISs, the Council on Environmental Quality (CEQ)--established to aid in the statute's interpretation--has recognized the existence of PEISs and has issued regulations defining their relevance. The courts, in turn, have validated CEQ's view that PEISs are legitimate undertakings, and have even stated that, under certain circumstances, PEISs are required. Although courts often defer to federal agencies' determinations regarding whether to prepare a PEIS, a line of cases indicates that research into nominally beneficial but potentially damaging new technology should require a PEIS.

A. Statutory Authority: The National Environmental Policy Act's "Broad Brush"

Upon its inception in 1969, the National Environmental Policy Act (NEPA) was considered "the most important and far-reaching environmental and conservation measure ever enacted by the Congress."

At that time, the legislative talk of a "comprehensive national [environmental] policy" was in part a reference to the scope of review that government agencies were henceforth required to conduct upon the proposal of any "major Federal actions significantly affecting the quality of the human environment." This broad review--known as an Environmental Impact Statement (EIS)--is a "detailed" report on, inter alia, "the environmental impact of the proposed action."

Although an EIS must be detailed, the language of NEPA itself remains purposefully vague, reflecting the legislators' intent to replace what had been a piecemeal approach among the agencies towards environmental planning with a more "rationalized, comprehensive system." NEPA's broad language does not specifically mention PEISs, leaving the interpretation of its provisions to the appropriate regulatory authority. Importantly, the federal government is directed to "use all practicable means, consistent with other essential considerations of national policy" in exercising their discretion with respect to environmental decisions.

B. Regulatory Authority: CEQ's PEIS Recommendations

CEQ was created by NEPA in 1969 and was charged with reviewing, investigating, and reporting back to the President on environmental issues. [FN59] Due to early confusion over how much weight agencies were required to give CEQ's guidelines, President Carter issued an Executive Order in 1977 empowering CEQ to interpret NEPA's procedural provisions and issue its findings as regulations. [FN60] These regulations became binding upon all federal agencies in November *706 1979, and have been interpreted by the U.S. Supreme Court to be entitled to "substantial deference." [FN61]

The CEQ regulations make numerous positive references to the overarching policy theory behind PEISs: if disparate federal actions are sufficiently related, a broad PEIS should be conducted if it will serve to "avoid duplication and delay" in the long run. Echoing NEPA's statutory language, the regulations list "systematic and connected agency decisions allocating agency resources to implement a specific statutory program or executive directive" as a recognized "Federal action[]." Once this threshold has been met, the regulations further state that an EIS "may be prepared, and [is] sometimes required" for the project as a whole --the very definition of a PEIS.

When preparing statements on these expansive actions, agencies are encouraged to consider preparing a PEIS for proposals which have "common timing, impacts, alternatives, methods of implementation, media, or subject matter." Similarly, and perhaps more relevant to Project BioShield, a PEIS on federal proposals that are at the same "stage of technological development including federal or federally assisted research ... for new technologies" may be required "before the program has reached a stage of investment or commitment to implementation likely to determine subsequent development or restrict later alternatives."

Lastly, CEQ regulations devote a subsection to the definition of "tiering": the discretionary process by which an agency may choose to file a PEIS discussing broad program objectives before following up with site-specific EISs referencing the general findings.

C. Case Law

NEPA is aptly described as a statute more concerned with looking at the forest than the trees. In spite of--or perhaps because of--its broad language and purpose, NEPA's legislative history has often *707 played a secondary role to case law in court decisions. At the highest level, the U.S. Supreme Court has been disappointingly silent on the applicability of PEISs, issuing its lone defining opinion on the matter--Kleppe v. Sierra Club-- three decades ago. Following the Supreme Court's lead, lower courts have generally refused to take a serious look at the PEIS issue in the context of NEPA's legislative history, leading one observer to note that "it is difficult to successfully challenge an agency's decision to forego a programmatic assessment." In one line of cases, however, a circuit court has held that PEISs are indeed required for certain national research programs.

1. Kleppe v. Sierra Club

One year before its precedential Kleppe decision, the U.S. Supreme Court decided Aberdeen & Rockfish Railroad Co. v. Students Challenging Regulatory Agency Procedures (SCRAP). In SCRAP, the Court paved the way for Kleppe by acknowledging the existence of different types of EISs corresponding in breadth to the type of proposed federal action. A regional or national federal action would therefore warrant an EIS of correspondingly regional or national scope: a PEIS.

Subsequently, the Court's decision in Kleppe specifically stated that PEISs of a national scope were indeed legitimate undertakings. Citing SCRAP, the Court observed that, although these PEISs would *708 likely "bear little resemblance" to site-specific local EISs, they would be valid in either case since the "bounds of the analysis are defined." Moreover, the Kleppe Court ruled that NEPA's "action forcing" EIS obligation "may require a [PEIS] in certain situations where several proposed actions are pending at the same time." In the words of Justice Powell, "[W]hen several proposals for ... actions that will have cumulative or synergistic environmental impact ... are pending concurrently before an agency, their environmental consequences must be considered together." The Court cited the statute's lofty policy objectives in determining Congress's original intention to require "'all agencies to assure consideration of the environmental impact of their actions in decisionmaking.'"

2. Reconciling Kleppe with a Deferential Standard of Review

Though Kleppe is still good law after thirty years, the Court's finding that a PEIS is required in certain circumstances has proven difficult to implement in lower courts. This is due in large part to the deferential "arbitrary or capricious" standard of review for agency actions. Indeed, in Kleppe itself, the Court stated that, for a plaintiff to prevail on a charge of failure to complete a PEIS, she "must show that [an agency has] acted arbitrarily in refusing to prepare one comprehensive statement on [an] entire region ...."

One year after Kleppe, a ruling of the U.S. District Court for the District of Columbia heralded the lower courts' frequent response to PEIS challenges. Environmental Defense Fund, Inc. v. Adams addressed a major revision of the National Airport System Plan that sought to upgrade public airports across the nation. Citing Kleppe, the district court found that the plan was indeed a "proposal for a major federal *709 action" with a national scope, and therefore required preparation of a PEIS. After stating its adherence to the Supreme Court's ruling, however, the lower court refused to impose its stated "requirement." Citing the fact that the agency had previously decided to prepare site-specific EISs, the court held that "there would be little sense in requiring an impact statement at the planning stage which would cover the same ground." Thus, despite ruling that a PEIS was required under Kleppe, the court deferred to the agency's decision not to prepare one.

In Churchill County v. Norton, the Ninth Circuit Court of Appeals reaffirmed the Adams holding nearly a quarter-century later. In holding that there is little courts can do if agencies do not act arbitrarily--even when a court finds a PEIS to be the preferred method of analysis--the Ninth Circuit stated:

The regulations and case law would support a decision by the [defendant agency] to prepare a programmatic EIS, had it decided to prepare one. Indeed, had we been charged with the decision, we may have elected to prepare a programmatic EIS first. The problem, of course, is that it was not our decision to make.

Finally, although it is often the function of courts to substantively balance and choose between polarized positions, the Supreme Court has interpreted NEPA as a strictly procedural statute since the 1980s. Thus, regardless of the conflicting policy arguments often present in environmental litigation, courts leave the NEPA-mandated balancing of interests up to the expertise of agencies.

3. New Technologies

One line of cases in the D.C. Circuit Court of Appeals discusses the implications of using PEISs for research into new technologies. These cases show that, despite courts' deference to agencies' decisions, research into a nominally beneficial but potentially damaging new technology should require a PEIS.

Scientists' Institute for Public Information, Inc. v. Atomic Energy Commission (SIPI) was decided before Kleppe in 1973. In an opinion by Judge Skelly Wright, a unanimous panel of the D.C. Circuit held that NEPA required a PEIS for concerted federal technology research and development initiatives. In a time of "growing demand for economical clean energy," the Atomic Energy Commission (AEC) had the support of both Congress and President Nixon in carrying out its Liquid Metal Fast Breeder Reactor (LMFBR) Program Plan. Despite this support and the public service potential of the research, the court ruled for the plaintiffs and stated that "[the AEC] takes an unnecessarily crabbed approach to NEPA in assuming that the impact statement process was designed only for particular facilities rather than for analysis of the overall effects of broad agency programs. Indeed, quite the contrary is true." Both the testimony of the AEC Chairman at a Senate Joint Hearing and a CEQ memorandum helped convince the court that it would "tread firm ground in holding that NEPA requires [PEISs] for major federal research programs ...."

One year after Kleppe, the D.C. Circuit again addressed the issue of PEISs in the context of technology development programs. In Concerned About Trident v. Rumsfeld, citizens' groups brought an action against the Secretary of Defense for his decision to locate a support facility for the new Trident nuclear submarine program in Bangor, Washington. The court distinguished its prior ruling in SIPI and found that no PEIS was necessary because unlike the LMFBR program, the Trident program did not involve "brand new technology with the possibility of unforeseen or unknown consequences." The court also stated that the Trident program did not come about as the result of any declared change to the national defense strategy. Implicit in these rulings is an idea central to the current Project BioShield disputes: the government's development of a new technology with unknown environmental consequences--if commenced in response to an asserted change in national defense strategy--would not fall under the SIPI exception carved out by Trident.

Twelve years after authoring the D.C. Circuit's opinion in SIPI, Judge Wright updated the court's views on whether a PEIS should be completed for a federal technology research program. In *Foundation on Economic Trends v. Heckler*, he wrote that the challenge is "to ensure that the bold words and vigorous spirit of NEPA are not ... lost or misdirected in the brisk frontiers of science." The current debates over Project BioShield's proposed BSL-3/4 expansions echo the arguments in Heckler twenty years earlier. There, as in the instant dispute, plaintiffs challenged an NIH decision not to produce a PEIS for an action taken in the name of public health: the planned release of a genetically engineered bacteria into the environment. The court stated that the potential for environmental damage was a "'low probability, high consequence risk; that is, while there is only a small possibility that damage could occur, the damage that could occur is great.'"

Although the court ultimately deferred to the agency's decision, it made a point of imposing a tangible obligation upon NIH. Citing SIPI, the court concluded that a failure to "at least consider" the advisability of a PEIS would likely "violate established principles of reasoned decisionmaking."

A concurring opinion by Senior Circuit Judge MacKinnon reiterated the D.C. Circuit's collective viewpoint that a PEIS was highly recommended prior to implementation of a broad research agenda for a new technology, "not only [to] ease lay concerns, but [to] facilitate review as well." Although Judge MacKinnon ultimately agreed with the majority that no PEIS was required in this specific case, the D.C. Circuit Court's reluctance to stay within the bounds of the Supreme Court's Kleppe ruling is evident.

4. Do Not Waste Agency Resources

The circuit court's ruling in Heckler is an example of a larger tendency: courts will not require a PEIS if the agency has decided to complete site-specific EISs instead. Environmental Defense Fund, Inc. v. Adams provides an early expression of this sentiment, where a district court stated that, "[s]ince, at the award stage, the Secretary has a specific application before him, ... there would be little sense in requiring an impact statement at the planning stage which would cover the same ground." Both Heckler and Adams articulate the view, also held by CEQ in its regulations, that agencies should only apply PEIS methods if they can do so while "avoid[ing] duplication and delay."

Mooreforce, Inc. v. United States Department of Transportation--a recent district court case refusing to mandate a PEIS-- illustrates the court's reluctance to require a PEIS when it may waste resources. In denying the plaintiffs' motion for a preliminary injunction to stop construction of a highway bypass, the Mooreforce court ruled that the plaintiffs were unlikely to prove that a PEIS was necessary. The court noted that the agency "could not accomplish the purpose of a PEIS because [it] had already completed an [EIS]."

Similarly, in *National Wildlife Federation v. Appalachian Regional Commission*, a circuit court held that "relevance at the planning stage is the measure of agency reasonableness for preparing EISs." In refusing to require a PEIS for construction of a highway system "well beyond the nascent stage," the court noted a good-faith requirement for an agency's postponement of its PEIS.

III. Litigation Background: "Inadequate EIS" Claim

The second major NEPA claim in environmental groups' comment letters on Project BioShield is that NIH's site-specific EIS, as completed, is inadequate. Because EISs are complex documents with various mandated components, a claim of this nature can fault a number of distinct aspects of an EIS. The two aspects of PEIS inadequacy most relevant to this Note's discussion are: (1) failure to adequately consider alternative locations; and (2) inadequate risk-assessment methodologies.

A. Failure to Adequately Consider Project Alternatives

In what the CEQ regulations characterize as the "heart" of an EIS, NEPA requires all federal agencies to consider possible alternatives to their proposed actions in an EIS. These alternatives may take two different forms--referred to as primary and secondary alternatives--between which courts do not discriminate when evaluating the adequacy of an EIS. NEPA requires agencies to consider these project alternatives in order to "insure the integrated use of ... the environmental design arts in planning and decisionmaking."

A CEQ regulation codifies the "rule of reason" set forth in a leading circuit court decision, stating that agencies are to "[r]igorously explore and objectively evaluate all reasonable alternatives, and for alternatives which were eliminated from detailed study, briefly discuss the reasons for their having been eliminated." In addition, agencies must "[d]evote substantial treatment to each alternative considered in detail including the proposed action so that reviewers may evaluate their comparative merits."

Importantly, agencies must state an underlying "purpose and need" to which they are responding when discussing proposed alternatives. The narrowness of these stated rationales can potentially limit the alternatives that an agency is required to take into account. Agencies have been criticized for intentionally propounding narrow project purposes, and two Circuit Courts of Appeals have *715 recently supported this assertion. However, the arbitrary or capricious standard of review applies to judicial review of an agency's stated purpose. Thus, notwithstanding these circuit court decisions, the majority of courts have found agencies' purpose and need statements to be reasonable.

If a reviewing court does not invalidate an EIS for having a purpose and need statement that is too narrow, it must then decide whether the agency's discussion of alternatives violates the "'rule of reason' which governs both 'which alternatives the agency must discuss' and 'the extent to which it must discuss them.'" The specific number of alternatives considered-- whether discussed in detail or only briefly--is not determinative; rather, an agency is charged with evaluating a "reasonable" number of alternatives for the particular situation. While courts have found to be reasonable agencies' choices to discuss varying numbers of alternatives, they have at times found unreasonable agencies' choices to discuss only a single alternative.

Another factor that makes it less likely for courts to rule in favor of plaintiffs is that agencies are not required to select the most environmentally*716 preferable option as their favored alternative. Thus, once reasonable alternatives receive procedural consideration, an agency is free to select whichever alternative it desires based on criteria of its choosing. A recent Ninth Circuit Court of Appeals decision gives certain agencies additional leeway by holding that an agency primarily concerned with conserving and protecting the environment is subject to less stringent requirements when choosing a range of alternatives to consider.

Acting as a judicial counterbalance, however, is the fact that courts will invalidate an EIS if the agency has neglected to fully analyze all of the reasonable alternatives. This requires a court hearing a challenge to an EIS to review both the reasonableness of an agency's choice to forego certain alternatives, and the reasonableness of the agency's level of review for its chosen alternatives. The Seventh Circuit Court of Appeal's conclusion in a 1997 case emphasizes this point succinctly:

If NEPA mandates anything, it mandates this: a federal agency cannot ram through a project before first weighing the pros and cons of the alternatives. In this case, the officials of [the agency] executed an end-run around NEPA's core requirement. By focusing on [one range of alternatives], [the agency] never looked at an entire category of reasonable alternatives and thereby ruined its environmental impact statement.

B. Inadequate Risk-Assessment Methodologies

Prior to 1986, CEQ regulations required agencies to conduct a worst-case analysis when completing an EIS. Then, in a move that had been forecast three years earlier, CEQ revoked the worst-case analysis requirement. The new regulations required only analysis of "reasonably foreseeable" events and a statement of any "incomplete or unavailable" relevant information. In 1989, the U.S. Supreme Court upheld the change, holding that requiring analysis of only "reasonably foreseeable" occurrences would focus public discussion on the issues of greatest relevance.

This change, coupled with a deferential standard of review, established a high bar for plaintiffs challenging agencies' decisions on whether, and how, to analyze certain environmental impacts. A one-sided battle over scientific methodologies often results, with plaintiffs charging agencies with cherry-picking scientific studies to match their desired outcomes, and courts in turn deferring to those studies.

It may still be possible, however, to invalidate an EIS for failure to consider low-probability, high-risk environmental consequences of an agency action. As defined in the regulations, "'reasonably foreseeable' includes impacts which have catastrophic consequences, even if their probability of occurrence is low, provided that the analysis of the impacts is supported by credible scientific evidence, is not based on pure conjecture, and is within the rule of reason." This language has led some observers to point out that courts may still be required to review the credibility of scientific opinions, if only to check for procedural compliance.

Despite the deferential standard of review and CEQ's revocation of the worst-case scenario requirement, courts do at times engage in this type of review. In a 1991 district court decision, the Department of Energy was required to fully examine the risks of transporting nuclear material:

> The Department's decision is akin to saying that some things just cannot happen. Yet the Department cannot deny that such accidents are possible .... Further, although the Department discounts the possibility of human intervention--either through error or sabotage, the risks remain. It is particularly important that a government agency be completely forthright about the risks of a program involving radioactive materials, which inspire great fear among many members of the public.

The court went on to note--perhaps sarcastically--that since the agency had already come up with a risk assessment methodology likely to show that its actions carried no risk, it had no reason to not apply its chosen method to each potential risk scenario.

IV. Analysis: Courts Are Unlikely to Mandate a PEIS for Project BioShield

Potential environmental plaintiffs can look to both regulatory language and case law to support their assertion that a PEIS is necessary for Project BioShield. However, the commonsense objective of not wasting government resources would counsel against requiring a PEIS, since site-specific EISs have already been undertaken. When called upon to balance the plaintiffs' claims with the conservation of government resources, a court will likely find that no PEIS is necessary for Project BioShield.

A. Plaintiffs' Argument: A PEIS Is Necessary

As evidenced by the fact that NIH has already prepared a Draft EIS (DEIS) for the proposed BUMC BSL-3/4 laboratory, that the nine proposed Project BioShield facilities constitute "major Federal actions significantly affecting the quality of the human environment" is not under debate. Courts will analyze regulatory language and case law to determine whether a PEIS is necessary. Here, both CEQ's guidelines and cases discussing the development of new technologies stand for the proposition that NIH should indeed conduct a PEIS.

1. Regulatory Language

Because NEPA does not directly mention PEISs reviewing courts will look to CEQ regulations for guidance, and will give "substantial deference" to CEQ's opinions. Interestingly, whether the CEQ provision most relevant to Project BioShield actually requires a PEIS is debatable. Section 1502.4(c) of the Code of Federal Regulations begins with the statement, "When preparing statements on broad actions ... agencies may find it useful to evaluate the proposal(s) in one of the following ways ...." Although this would seem to make the following subsections optional, subsection (c)(3)-- discussing PEISs for new technologies--contains the statement that PEISs "shall be prepared on such programs."

Environmental plaintiffs may make the argument that the word "shall" in subsection (c)(3) means that certain PEISs must be conducted for programs involving a certain "stage of technological development including federal or federally assisted research, development or demonstration programs for new technologies." Project BioShield fits in this category.

Similarly, the definition of "tiering" in the regulations appears directly applicable to Project BioShield. This term refers to "the coverage of general matters in broader environmental impact statements (such as national program or policy statements) with subsequent narrower statements ... (such as ... site-specific statements) incorporating by reference the general discussions." Although agencies may use tiering at their discretion, a reviewing court may read the inclusion of tiering in the regulations as an indication that CEQ intended for agencies to use it.

2. New Technology Cases

From the U.S. Supreme Court's *Kleppe v. Sierra Club* decision, it is clear that PEISs of a national scope are required in certain instances. To determine whether Project BioShield falls within the ambit of the Court's decision, further examination of the previously discussed line of cases involving new technologies is instructive. These cases suggest that reviewing courts may see Project BioShield as exactly the kind of "broad action" envisioned by CEQ when drafting its regulations.

Scientists' Institute for Public Information, Inc. v. Atomic Energy Commission (SIPI), has several remarkable similarities to the case at hand. SIPI involved the development of nuclear power technology; in that case, as with Project BioShield, a government agency had the support of both Congress and the President to begin a nationwide research initiative into a potentially beneficial, but also potentially dangerous, new technology. Environmental citizens' groups litigating the construction of BSL-3/4 laboratories would do well to quote Judge Skelly Wright's ruling that a court would "tread firm ground in holding that NEPA requires [PEISs] for major federal research programs."

Although the court did not find a PEIS necessary in *Concerned About Trident v. Rumsfeld*, the circumstances surrounding that case are distinguishable from those of Project BioShield. The court in Trident stated that the submarine modernization at issue did not involve any new technology with "the possibility of unforeseen or unknown consequences." In contrast, however, it could be argued that there are many unknowable aspects of Project BioShield's proposed widespread research into BSL-3/4 pathogens. Similarly, the Trident court declined to require a PEIS because there was "no shift in our defense policy." Rather, since the new Trident submarines were simply updated replacements for the outdated Polaris/Poseidon submarines, a PEIS was not required. Project BioShield, on the other hand, is clearly a major shift in the way the Bush administration intends to defend the country in the newly emerging "Time of Terror."

If a plaintiff were to use these cases addressing new technology to bolster the argument that a PEIS should be ordered for Project BioShield, however, Foundation on Economic Trends v. Heckler would have to be rationalized. In a case remarkably similar to the Project BioShield debate, the court noted that the agency had "'passed the point at which a [PEIS] is required by NEPA and the [CEQ]'s regulations,'" and ruled that a PEIS, though "helpful," was not required. With this language in mind, plaintiffs must argue that Project BioShield has not passed this point. Additionally, a plaintiff would want to argue that NIH never even considered completing a PEIS, as the court required in Heckler. Lastly, a plaintiff would want to quote the language of Senior Circuit Judge MacKinnon's concurrence, and assure the court that the lawsuit was not brought with "delaying tactics" in mind.

B. Agency's Argument: A PEIS Is Not Necessary

The deference that reviewing courts must give to agencies' decisions creates a significant hurdle for plaintiffs to clear before their claim will be heard. Adding to the plaintiffs' challenge is the fact that agencies have an entrenched policy argument they can use to counter plaintiffs' claims that a PEIS is necessary for Project BioShield: government agencies should not waste resources by reevaluating information that has already been analyzed.

Presumably in good faith, NIH made the decision to not prepare a PEIS for Project BioShield. Because of courts' deferential standard of review toward agencies' choices, NIH's decision alone might be enough for a court to refuse mandating a PEIS. Tipping the scales even further in favor of the agency is the fact that work has already begun on the EISs in question. NIH's current position is similar to that of the Department of Transportation in Mooreforce, Inc. v. U.S. Department of Transportation, where site-specific EISs were complete at the time of litigation. Similarly, two separate circuit court decisions have stated that a PEIS should only be prepared if it can be "forward-looking"--a quality that cannot exist when individual, site-specific EISs have already been prepared. Consequently, NIH can effectively argue that it should not have to prepare a PEIS, since imposing that requirement would "not accomplish the purpose of a PEIS," and would likely violate CEQ's directive to "avoid duplication and delay."

C. Prediction

Because of the deference NIH will receive from the court, plaintiffs must fully meet their burden in order to persuade a judge to mandate a PEIS. Although the CEQ regulations contain language that plaintiffs can cite with respect to new technologies and tiering, the regulations also support NIH's assertion that a PEIS should not be completed because it would cause "duplication and delay." Although the Circuit Court of Appeals for the District of Columbia has made a point of adhering to the exact regulatory language when interpreting new technology cases, it stands alone. Meanwhile, Supreme Court decisions interpreting NEPA have been conspicuously sparse, and those that exist have overwhelmingly upheld agency actions. Consequently, environmental plaintiffs are unlikely to convince a reviewing court to require NIH to prepare a PEIS for Project BioShield.

V. Case Study Analysis: Courts May Invalidate the BUMC EIS

In analyzing the likelihood of plaintiffs' claim that the site-specific EIS is inadequate as filed, each of the two issues detailed in Part III must be examined. Because NIH declined to prepare a PEIS, however, it is not possible to herein address the specifics of each individual EIS. As such, this Note analyzes these charges as they specifically apply to the EIS submitted by NIH for the BUMC site. The conclusions drawn may apply to other Project BioShield lawsuits, depending on the adequacy of the respective EISs. More important for the purposes of this Note, the potential inadequacy of the BUMC EIS raises significant questions about the future role of PEISs in general.

A. Consideration of Project Alternatives May Be Inadequate

A reviewing court could potentially invalidate the BUMC DEIS for any one of the following reasons: (1) an impermissibly narrow purpose and need statement; (2) failure to discuss in detail a reasonable number of alternatives; (3) failure to discuss in detail a reasonable alternative; and (4) disingenuous timing.

The BUMC DEIS's purpose and need statement reads in pertinent part: "The purpose of the Proposed Action is to fund the construction of the Boston-NBL at the BioSquare Research Park .... [The facility] would be located on the BUMC campus in Boston, MA ...." Admittedly a "slippery concept," NIH's definition of "purpose" in this instance appears to be "so slender as to define competing reasonable alternatives out of consideration (and even out of existence)." It is difficult to imagine a single alternative which would fit this purpose besides NIH's own predetermined choice. As the Tenth Circuit Court of Appeals recently noted, a reviewing court may conclude that "such a narrow definition of Project needs would violate NEPA."

Secondly, the BUMC DEIS provides a detailed discussion of only a single action alternative in addition to the requisite no action alternative, and briefly discusses three additional alternatives that NIH deemed unreasonable. While there is no mandated number of alternatives that must be discussed in detail, the "rule of reason" suggests that this number should be more than one. Similarly, an agency's decision to only analyze a single option in detail appears disingenuous in light of NEPA's mandate to foster informed decisionmaking.

Thirdly, the BUMC DEIS "considered and subsequently eliminated from further review" three alternatives which NIH determined "provided no environmental advantage over the

Proposed Action or No Action or [did] not meet the purpose and need of the Project." Two of these alternatives--locating the NBL in lower-density areas outside Boston and locating the NBL at other Boston University-owned sites--represent essentially the same view: a BSL-3/4 laboratory should not be built in a densely populated area. In declining to give these alternatives detailed analysis, NIH tautologously refers to benefits already present at the BUMC campus. The DEIS then summarily concludes the discussion by stating, "[f]inally, the alternative of a location outside Massachusetts or in a lower density area outside of Boston are not a feasible alternatives [sic] as they do not meet the purpose and need for the Project." A reviewing court could find this circular argument unreasonable and, following the lead of a recent holding by the Seventh Circuit Court of Appeals, invalidate the BUMC DEIS for failure to address reasonable alternatives.

Finally, and perhaps most poignantly, the DEIS states that "NIAID selected the BUMC ... based on multiple factors including review of environmental issues, but focused primarily on the scientific and technical merit of the application ... and on BUMC's ability to contribute to the overall NIAID biodefense research agenda."

In another feat of circular logic, the "review of environmental issues" that NIH speciously claims to have conducted prior to its site selection can only be seen as disingenuous, since the NEPA-mandated alternatives review was initiated after the selection was made. As such, a reviewing court could indeed find that NIH did not fulfill its statutory obligation to consider project alternatives in its decisionmaking process. As the Second Circuit Court of Appeals observed three decades ago, "the critical agency decision must, of course, be made ... in light of the alternatives, not before. Otherwise the process becomes a useless ritual, defeating the purpose of NEPA, and rather making a mockery of it."

Alternatively, a reviewing court may validate NIH's choices of alternatives if NIH effectively argues that the overall goal of Project BioShield is to conserve and protect the environment by creating vaccines for deadly diseases before terrorists have an opportunity to unleash them. Following the Ninth Circuit Court of Appeal's lead, a court could therefore decide that, given the "conservation and preventative goals" of the agency, NIH was not required to conduct in-depth analysis of certain alternatives. It is also to NIH's advantage that courts find agencies' purpose and need statements valid three times as often as they invalidate them. Additionally, some lower courts have previously validated EISs discussing in detail only a single alternative.

B. Risk-Assessment Methodologies May Be Inadequate

If a reviewing court does not invalidate the BUMC DEIS on the basis of inadequate consideration of project alternatives, it may still decide to invalidate it for using inadequate risk-assessment methodologies. First, NIH cites a study concluding that the proposed NBL presented a "negligible" risk to the public as a factor in determining that "locating the facility in a lower density area would not in any way reduce the risk to the public." Additionally, although CEQ regulations no longer require it, the BUMC DEIS discusses in detail what it claims to be a realistic worst-case scenario. Finally, the DEIS briefly discusses--and then dismisses-- five other potential risk scenarios as presenting "negligible" community risk.

Not surprisingly, there has been a backlash from environmental groups over NIH's choice of scientific methodologies. While plaintiffs have an uphill battle in proving that the agency did not properly analyze all "reasonably foreseeable" occurrences, the regulations do leave room for courts to find NIH's risk-assessment methodologies inadequate. It is possible that a reviewing court will see the BSL-3/4 laboratory materials as analogous to the spent nuclear fuel rods in *Sierra Club v. Watkins*-- potentially dangerous offshoots of a nominally beneficial public enterprise. In such an instance, the Watkins court's admonition that "[i]t is particularly important that a government agency be completely forthright about the risks of a program involving radioactive materials, which inspire great fear among many members of the public," would seem equally pertinent to the infectious disease materials in the present case. Thus, a reviewing court may indeed invalidate the BUMC DEIS for inadequate risk-assessment methodologies.

_____

The risk assessments developed by the NIH for the Boston University BSL were challenged. In fact, the National Institutes of Health's risk assessment was considered so inadequate, that the National Academies, National Research Council was asked by the Commonwealth of Massachusetts to establish an expert Committee to "provide technical input on the document Draft Supplementary Risk Assessments and Site Suitability Analyses for the National Emerging Infectious Diseases Laboratory, Boston University . . . (DSER)." The NAS was asked to "determine if the scientific analyses in NIH Study are sound and credible; to determine whether the proponent has identified representative worst case scenarios; and to determine, based on the study's comparison of risk associated with alternative locations." In November 2007, the Committee concluded that the scientific analyses were not sound and credible; that the DSER did not adequately identify and develop worst case scenarios; and that "the DSER [did] not contain the appropriate level of information to compare the risks associated with alternative locations." [Technical Input on the National Institutes of Health's Draft Supplementary Risk Assessments and Site Suitability Analyses for the National Emerging Infectious Diseases Laboratory, Boston University, A Letter Report (Nov. 29, 2007), at http://www.nap.edu/catalog/12073.html]

6.7   NBAF and NEPA

The research laboratory for animal and plant diseases has long been important to the United States. While the Soviet Union's offense biological weapons program was fully underway, they employed more than 2,000 scientists focused solely on agriculture bioweapons, compared to about 20 research experts in the United States, who were focused on biodefense of agricultural bioweapons.

However, the safety of these animal laboratories was called into question when, in the United Kingdom, the research laboratory was identified as a possible source for the Foot and Mouth Disease outbreak in the UK in 2005, which was responsible for significant monetary damages.

In the organization of the U.S. Department of Homeland Security, the U.S. Department of Agriculture research laboratory, Plum Island, was transferred to the new department. Over the next two years, the U.S. Department of Homeland Security made a decision to look for other operators of the research laboratory and possibly move its location. In 2007 and 2008, final selections of locations were made, and a Programmatic Environmental Impact Statement was developed to assess the impact of any of these new laboratories.

The Programmatic Environmental Impact Statement is developed as a result of triggering the application of the National Environmental Policy Act's requirement that an environmental assessment be done any time there is "a major federal action significantly affecting the human environment." The environmental assessment is a process to determine whether an environmental impact statement is needed, and for the NBAF proposal, a determination was made that a programmatic environmental impact statement should be done.

In 2008, the U.S. Department of Homeland Security recommended Kansas State University in Manhattan, Kansas to be the new home of the National Bioand Agro-Defense Facility, based on its proximity to existing research facilities and workforce, which includes its veterinary college, agricultural college and Biosecurity Research Institute. Additionally, almost all environmental impacts at this location were categorized in the "no impact" to "minor impact" category, making Kansas an attractive location.

6.8   State and Local Regulation of Biological Safety Laboratories

The Boston, Massachusetts Department of Public Health, well-known through legal jurisprudence as one of the parties in *Jacobson v. Massachusetts*, is actively seeking to regulate biological safety laboratories through local ordinance and inspection regulatory mechanisms. This ordinance would require registration and inspection, as well as a permit for biological containment laboratories, in addition to existing federal regulations.

Boston University experienced a tularemia infection incident when the laboratory researchers were working with a strain of tularemia that they believed was an attenuated, or harmless, strain of tularemia because it was ordered, packaged, and delivered to the laboratory with that description.   Over the course of a couple of months, as researchers became sick, it became apparent that this was a virulent strain of tularemia. Tularemia is an infectious agent, and is listed on the select agent list regulated by the CDC. As a result, the CDC conducted an investigation of the facility and the incident. In addition, the Occupational Health and Safety Administration (OSHA), which has jurisdiction in Massachusetts, unlike many other states where states have assumed occupational health jurisdiction, also conducted an investigation.

In March 2008, similar litigation was initiated against Columbia University for their plans to site a biological containment laboratory in Manhattan.   The news article describes the community's concerns:

Lawsuit: Columbia Expansion Poses 'Biohazard' Risk
by Duncan Meisel, March 27, 2008

The largest landowner threatened by Columbia's Manhattanville expansion has filed a suit against the school and city, alleging that the environmental review process for the expansion was insufficient. The process may have even ignored the risk for potential biohazard threats to the West Harlem community, the plaintiff's lawyer said.

"I think it's selfish for Columbia, it shows a level of uncaring for the people of West Harlem" said Nick Sprayregen, the owner of Tuck-It-Away Storage, the lead petitioner in the suit, which was filed Wednesday afternoon.

At issue is the construction of a massive underground "bathtub" structure that would extend about seven stories below ground throughout the development, a planned expansion that would include a research facility that the university calls a "biosafety" center, while the plaintiff calls it a "biohazard" center. According to the plaintiffs, the placement of such a structure on a geological fault in a flood zone poses a risk to the surrounding community. But according to Columbia, the research facilities will be built above grade and pose no risk.

"The rim of the bathtub is barely above the Hudson river, we believe it poses a risk of catastrophic failure" said Norman Siegel, Sprayregen's lawyer. He cited global warming and its connected risks as an issue of serious concern.

"There exists a likelihood of a storm surge that would come over the bulkhead and flood the bathtub" and "hazardous materials from these facilities could be washed out into the West Harlem community" he said.

The suit challenges whether the City Planning Commission took the required "hard look" at environmental hazards for the site. The suit claims that the planning commission "provided that the engineering issues raised during the environmental review process would be resolved at some later unspecified date."

However, "Neither the engineering consultants... nor Columbia University consultants outline in any detail what those solutions are, what the impact of carrying out those approaches might be" the suit claims in a quote from Jordi Reyes-Montblanc, the chairman of Community Board 9.

Columbia declined to comment on the pending litigation, but said in a statement: "We are confident that the extended public land use and environmental review processes were rigorous and comprehensive. They underscored that thriving universities are essential for New York City to remain a leader in attracting the talent that pursues new knowledge and creating the good, middle-income jobs for people who seek to improve their lives here."

A Columbia spokeswoman clarified the nature of the research facility, taking issue with the plaintiff's use of "biohazard." "There are no plans to put biosafety facilities below grade," said the spokeswoman La-Verna J. Fountain.

Sprayregen's concerns extend beyond the bathtub to the facility itself.

"It just boggles the mind why Columbia, supposedly an altruistic institution, would but a biohazard research center in Manhattan" he said. "I question the wisdom of placing, particularly after 9/11, a biohazard facility that sticks out like a sore thumb for any potential terrorists" in the city center.

"These are bio-safety rooms" Fountain said. "These are not whole buildings, just rooms."

No matter the result of this current suit, litigation about the Columbia expansion seems bound to continue. The suit filed yesterday is the fifth which Siegel has been involved in, and he sees the potential for at least one other suit. "If eminent domain is used, transferring private property to a private university, we will litigate that issue" he said.

The activist group Coalition to Preserve Community announced a protest for Monday at Columbia. Continued community resistance to the Manhattanville plans has been a driving force for the ongoing legal battle between landowners and the school, and both Sprayregen and Siegel cited community activists as a key factor in their decision to file suit.

"You need the community behind you on this" Siegel said. "Property owners have standing, but the community members were the heart and soul of this lawsuit."

6.9   Proposals to Review and Change the Select Agent Program

S.B. 3127, introduced on June 12, 2008, proposes to review the entire select agent program and proposes new mechanisms for biosafety and biosecurity of high-level containment laboratories. At the expiration of the session no action had been taken, given the election year absences from Congress and other issues, and the identical language was re-introduced on February 26, 2009 with H.R. 1225 and S.B. 485, the Select Agent Program and Biosafety Improvement Act of 2009. The following is an excerpt from a letter written with a general, as well as a sectional, analysis of S.B. 3127 from the Director of the Center for Biodefense, Law and Public Policy at Texas Tech University School of Law:

The bill continues to delegate implementation authority to two agencies: the Centers for Disease Control and Prevention (CDC) and the Animal and Plant Health Inspection Service (APHIS). In my opinion, this has presented some confusion to the regulated community, and I would like to see this bill expand its review of the program in Sec. 102 in its charge to the National Academies, to include consideration of this aspect of the Select Agent Program.

The bill is divided in two titles: the first title is the reauthorization of the select agent program and the second title is "biosafety improvements."

In the Title I, the reauthorization section, the Select Agent Program is reauthorized for the next five years --- 2009 through 2013. The current program was authorized from 2002 to 2007 and expired September 30, 2007.

Sec. 102 requires that the Secretaries of Health and Human Services and Agriculture contract with the National Academy of Sciences to conduct a review of the program, which is a wisely conceived priority for the Select Agent Program. The bill seeks a focus on the statutory goal of enhancing "biosecurity and biosafety in the United States," and how this program has impacted the work of researchers in "scientific advances" as well as "international scientific collaboration." The regulated community has been limited in their ability to work with select agents with their colleagues in other countries, often in the very countries where these diseases are endemic, because of regulatory barriers to collaboration. In the Survey, when researchers were asked what they considered to be the major problems or constraints in conducting international research on select agents and or Category A-C agents (which is a potential-use-as-bioweapons classification), 34% responded that one of the major problems or constraints was biosafety and security regulations pertaining to possessing, transporting, and working with select agents, including rules imposed on collaborating foreign institutions and investigators. This Sec. 102 is clearly responsive to the concerns and needs of the regulated researchers, and could go a long way in resolving this problematic feature of the Select Agent Program.

Sec. 103 of the bill requires the revision of the list of select agents to reflect current advances in science, without which, the originally conceived select agent definitions would become potentially marginalized and the rapidly growing field of research in genetically-modified-organisms and synthetically developed agents would quickly escape the scope of the Select Agent Program, leaving a gap in protecting public health and national security and homeland security. This bill adequately addresses that need and forestalls a public health risk by including these areas within the scope of the regulated select agents. Further, the bill addresses the consideration of listing agents which are "endemic" to the United States and provides that the status of "endemic" does not preclude their inclusion on the Select Agent lists. For example, this provision will inevitably address the issue of why hanta virus, a hemorrhagic fever virus endemic to the United States, is not on a Select Agent list, even though it appears on a list of agents that are potential bioweapons. This bill establishes in its rule of construction, that the fact that an agent is "endemic" to the U.S., should not be a reason for excluding it from the list. This provision adequately addresses those questions which should be considered in identifying select agents which should be listed.

Sec. 104 of the bill addresses sharing information with trusted state partners. This section of the bill addresses the need for sharing information in events requiring public health or criminal investigatory state partners. Similarly, it effectively reflects the need recognized in HIPAA, to reveal protected health information to investigatory government agencies in the event of a public health emergency. The same need may arise in the context of any Select Agents or registered institutions which may be the subject of a public health emergency. However, it is my opinion that without harmonizing state laws or a statement of preemption for any state law contrary to these provisions, in this bill, the implementation of this section may not achieve the goals sought.

Sec. 105 addresses needed improvements to the inventory and monitoring regulations currently in effect, and requires a gap in the lack of guidance to be filled. The implementation of this section alone, could be the most substantive and significant improvement to the Select Agent Program. While regulatory agency officials made determinations from one registered facility to the next, about inventories, none of these interpretations were shared with the regulated community except the one that they were given on an inspection visit. For example, should vials of select agents in inventories be counted once a week, once a month or once a year? If they are sealed in a styrene storage box with a taped seal, how often should they be recounted. On such inspection visits, only that one facility would hear the answer to the question, and other facilities were left in the dark about the regulating agencies' stated opinions. Guidance on these questions, or simply anecdotal letters illustrating the application of their interpretations, made available to the regulated community would provide predictability and more certainty in registered institutions and for biodefense researchers, who themselves have the burden of compliance with their particular questions. An example of an individual researcher, is whether a collection of 25,000 vials or a collection of 10 vials should be handled in the same manner? Again, this bill will require issued guidance, remedying many of the problems which have plagued the regulating community. While guidance does not have the force of law, as statutes and regulations; the courts have shown a strong interest in referring to or using agency guidance in the absence of statutory or regulatory language.

This section, Sec. 105 also requires a benefit-burden analysis which is a much needed component of any regulatory program, and fills this wide gap in regulatory development. The problem of "regulatory mismatch" discussed in the administrative law literature, can be effectively addressed through this requirement to consider the effectiveness of the regulation against the burden, thereby assuring that the goals of the regulatory program are actually achieved through the regulatory means selected.

Sec. 106 seeks to bring clarity to a vague definition for variola virus in 18 USC §175c and the Attorney General with the Secretary of HHS are charged with defining the scope of the existing definition and issuing guidance to interpret the scope of the definition. In section (d) of the statue, "the term 'variola virus' means a virus that can cause human smallpox or any derivative of the variola major virus that contains more than 85 percent of the gene sequence of the variola major virus or the variola minor virus." This statute is part of the criminal code. However, since variola virus is a listed select agent, it is critical to determine its precise definition, since experimentation and research is conducted on widely varying components of the virus, and without a precise definition, vagueness will lead to uncertainty.

Sec. 107 addresses the need for utilizing biocontainment laboratories for surge capacity needs in the event of a bioterrorism attack or a pandemic. These events may require testing exponentially increasing numbers of biological samples, in the days following an event, incident or cluster of illnesses, or agricultural event. In the days following the anthrax attacks in the fall of 2001, surge capacity for testing envelopes, packages alone, quickly overwhelmed existing public health facilities and many academic institutions with biocontainment facilities were called upon to assist in an unprecedented manner. This bill addresses that need, and calls upon all laboratories, not only biocontainment laboratories, to develop guidelines as part of the plan, for example CLIA laboratories which are otherwise excluded from the Select Agent Program. This bill recognizes the need to utilize laboratory capacity on a broad and inclusive scale, and insightfully identifies the scope necessary to adequately plan for surge events.

In Title II, addressing biosafety improvements, there are three parts: Sec. 201 for oversight of laboratories; Sec. 202 specifying training requirements; and Sec. 203 establishing an incident reporting system.

Sec. 201 defines a "high containment biological laboratory" as a BSL 3 or BSL 4, and requires an evaluation of the national need for such laboratories and an evaluation of the oversight of these laboratories. For this evaluation the bill requires the coordinated efforts of four cabinet level Departmental Secretaries: Health and Human Services, Agriculture, Defense and Homeland Security. The bill requires four specific considerations: (1) whether the construction of high containment biological laboratories, planned and in existence, "provide sufficient capacity for the needs of Government biodefense and infectious disease research"; (2) how lessons learned can be shared nationally and internationally; (3) whether guidance on laboratories is "adequate" and also how to improve and streamline the guidance; and (4) identify ways to streamline training and to provide minimum standards for training.

Part (1) addresses a question raised at an October 5, 2007 Congressional Committee Hearing, whether any Government agency or department knew how many biocontainment laboratories existed in the U.S. This bill, S.B. 3127, has explored and refined the question to seek an answer to what is the capacity need for the Government. A capacity need analysis will provide the foundation for other components of the bill, for example, planning for surge capacity.

Part (2) is vital and has been a missing part of the service needed to the regulated community. This part could be implemented through guidance much like other agencies, like EPA (guidance), the SEC (SEC letters) and the IRS which provide cases and their resolution or interpretation. Regulatory guidance has not been published by the regulating agencies, to date, another important component of a more mature regulatory program.

Part (3) addresses the adequacy of incorporating the BMBL guidance into the regulation which provides recommendations, but is used for enforcement purposes, circumventing an important Due Process principle of our government which would require providing notice of how a party will be regulated. This vagueness is evident in the regulatory text at 42 CFR § 73.12 (a) which reads, "In developing a biosafety plan, an individual or entity **should** consider: (1) he CDC/NIH publication . . . [emphasis added]." In the Survey of biodefense researchers, the question was asked whether different guidance was needed, and 32% of the respondents wanted "clearer standards", and 4% simply wanted to replace the BMBL guidance. (See Fig. 1, above).

Part (4) effectively stabs in the heart, the beast that prevents this Program from providing Biosafety, and would thwart its goal of achieving public safety and protecting national security and homeland security. Minimum training standards will now be an essential component and threshold requirement for individuals who work with Select Agents. The current regulation, 42 CFR § 73.15 which addresses the provision of training by the institution requires only that "An entity . . .must provide information and training on biosafety and security to each individual . . ." and 42 CFR § 73.10(c) provides that "Each individual with access to select agents or toxins must have the appropriate . . . education, training and/or experience. . " [emp added]. This bill gives CDC and APHIS the authority to move forward, with advice, in developing more predictable requirements for regulated institutions and researchers, and essential components for national biosafety.

Sec. 202 takes Sec. 201's evaluative consideration one step further by specifying that the Secretary of HHS in coordination with the Secretary of Agriculture "and scientific experts" . . . "shall develop minimum standards for laboratory biosafety and biosecurity training for relevant personnel of high containment biological laboratories. Registration of researchers will then require evidence of meeting these minimum training requirements.

In the Survey, when asked about specific areas of training for working in biocontainment laboratories; 85.1% said that BSL training should be required; 53.2 % said that emergency response training should be required; and 85.1% said that regulatory compliance training should be required. This bill in Sec. 201(4) and Sec. 202, responds directly to the need for training standards, which is clearly indicated as an area of high importance to the regulated community. This bill identifies and provides for filling that regulatory gap.

Sec. 203 establishes a "Biological Laboratory Incident Reporting System" for "voluntary reporting of biosafety or biosecurity incidents of concern", and statistics on these reports "may" be collected and characterized where trends exist in order to make improvements in biosafety *and biosecurity. The Secretaries (HHS and Agriculture) "shall contract with a public or private entity that does not regulate biological laboratories to administer the reporting system." The seven functions of this system are identified in the bill: "(1) receive and process incident reports; (2) analyze, interpret incident data, and identify incident trends, (3) issue alert messages; (4) disseminate reports; (5) not have authority to direct corrective action or to initiate enforcement action; (6) ensure anonymity of individuals reporting to the system, to the extent permitted by law; and (7) conduct other activities as requested by the Secretaries."*

The Survey analysis showed that there was a real desire on the part of the regulated community to have a resource for answering compliance questions without fear of civil or criminal prosecution. When asked whether they would use a hotline for anonymous compliance questions about the select agent regulations, 42.6% responded in the affirmative. This survey was conducted in the fall of 2007, during the widely publicized CDC suspension of the Texas A&M University registration to work with select agents, and this was a likely confounding external factor which contributed to this high, affirmative response.

This contract for providing compliance information must include attorneys who can offer the caller anonymity through protection through attorney-client privilege relationship, or anonymity cannot be assured, and the recipient of the call will be subject to subpoena or civil interrogation. However, the attorney-client privilege has its limits in law, and this is clearly addressed in the bill In response to the Survey results, the Center for Biodefense, Law and Public Policy has developed guidelines for such a call center, and is being made initially available to the NIAID supported Regional Centers of Excellence for Biodefense and Emerging Infectious Diseases Research.

In summary, the regulated community, biodefense researchers and biocontainment laboratories and other institutions, have been inordinately concerned about inadvertently violating the select agent regulations, which in large part, can be explained by the vagueness and unpredictable enforcement standards of the training requirements, the inventory requirements, the reporting requirements and the infrastructure requirements. This bill goes to the heart of these issues and establishes improvements and fills gaps in the Select Agent Program in a way that can prevent our national biodefense research enterprise from being unnecessarily steeped in a regulatory quagmire that may have failed the Constitutional Due Process test had the regulation been judicial reviewed and in large part failed to meet the very goals of the statute in protecting public health and national and homeland security, while not unnecessarily impeding scientific advances.

After attempts to pass legislation to amend the select agent program all failed, the President issued an Executive Order 13546 , July 2, 2010, "Optimizing the Security of Biological select Agents and Toxins in the United States," requiring a complete review of the program including hearings and input from the regulated community. The process took more than two years, and CDC published proposed regulations as the outcome from that process in October 2011.

6.10.   Biological Materials Not Regulated by the Select Agent Program

United States v. Steven Kurtz
Professor pleads guilty in bio-arts case
By CAROLYN THOMPSON, Associated Press Writer

8:06 PM EDT, October 11, 2007

BUFFALO, N.Y. A college researcher has admitted to illegally mailing bacteria to an avant-garde artist friend in a federal case that arts supporters see as an attack on artistic expression.

Dr. Robert Ferrell's attorney, who characterized the mailed material as "high school science bacteria," said the University of Pittsburgh genetics professor agreed to plead guilty to a misdemeanor count of "mailing an injurious article" because of his poor health.

"He's had a rough road," attorney Efrem Grail said in U.S. District Court Thursday.

Ferrell, 64, has had several recurrences of non-Hodgkin's lymphoma since being diagnosed in 1980 and has had a series of strokes since his arrest in 2004. He could face up to a year in prison and $100,000 in fines when he is sentenced in February.

Assistant U.S. Attorney William Hochul said Buffalo artist Steven Kurtz would ask Ferrell from time to time to order biological organisms for him because Kurtz could not order them on his own.

The men acknowledged in e-mail exchanges that the bacteria could be harmful to people with weakened immune systems, the prosecutor said.

Kurtz, a University at Buffalo arts professor and founding member of Critical Art Ensemble, "could not have gotten these organisms in any way, shape or form" from the Manassas, Va., laboratory that filled orders for university researchers and medical doctors, Hochul said.

Buffalo police noticed the bacteria and other laboratory equipment in Kurtz's home in May 2004 after Kurtz called 911 to report the death of his wife, Hope. Suspicious of bioterrorism, police alerted the Joint Terrorism Task Force, whose agents combed through Kurtz's home in biohazard suits.

An autopsy showed Hope Kurtz died of natural causes.

Authorities have never accused Kurtz or Ferrell of planning to use the bacteria for terrorism. A June 2004 indictment charged the men with felony mail and wire fraud.

The prosecution has provoked widespread outrage from artists, who say the government has used post-9/11 anti-terrorism powers to intimidate artists and others who are critical.

Kurtz's Critical Art Ensemble targets government policy on issues such as cloning and genetically modified food. The bacteria from Ferrell was to be used in an installation.

"I am appalled with the ferocity with which this case has been prosecuted," said Ed Cardoni, a member of the Critical Art Ensemble Defense Fund, established in support of Kurtz and Ferrell.

Ferrell declined to comment after pleading guilty to the lesser charge. His daughter, in a written statement, said her father agreed to settle the case out of "pure exhaustion."

"I remain unable to wrap my mind around the absurdity of the government's pursuit of this case," Gentry Ferrell wrote.

Federal prosecutors have said the prosecution is based on public safety concerns surrounding the illegal transfer of controlled bacteria.

One of the organisms "is used in biological warfare experiments" to "determine what anthrax would do," Hochul said.

Kurtz still faces trial on the felony charges. Supporters said he is not interested in a plea agreement. A trial date has not yet been set.

The federal district court on April 21, 2008 dismissed the case against Steven Kurtz, in an unusual action when a grand jury has indicted a defendant, and the prosecutor has proceeded to trial with the case. The core of the case involved the legal theory that Kurtz and Ferrell had committed mail and wire fraud when they misrepresented to the supplier, American Type Culture Collection, that they would comply with all the terms of the material safety transfer agreement, which described that the bacteria purchased would be handled in the laboratory of the purchaser, Ferrell. However, there was no money obtained, ATTC was not deprived of their payment, and the universities did not suffer any loss by the actions of Ferrell and Kurtz in the application of the mail and wire fraud statutes. Criminal cases, which appear to be more of a civil case of fraud, are always criticized by the courts as reaching too far into civil matters when they are brought as criminal matters. The judge in this case appeared to take this position when he dismissed the case.

Reading the mail fraud statute, below before reading the order in the *Kurtz* case will be helpful in reading this unusual opinion.

18 U.S.C. Section 1341 -- Elements of Mail Fraud

"There are two elements in mail fraud: (1) having devised or intending to devise a scheme to defraud (or to perform specified fraudulent acts), and (2) use of the mail for the purpose of executing, or attempting to execute, the scheme (or specified fraudulent acts)." *Schmuck v. United States*, 489 U.S. 705, 721 n. 10 (1989); *see also Pereira v. United States*, 347 U.S. 1, 8 (1954) ("The elements of the offense of mail fraud under . . . § 1341 are (1) a scheme to defraud, and (2) the mailing of a letter, etc., for the purpose of executing the scheme."); Laura A. Eilers & Harvey B. Silikovitz, *Mail and Wire Fraud*, 31 Am. Crim. L. Rev. 703, 704 (1994) (cases cited).

United States v. Kurtz
W.D.N.Y., Order 04-CR-0155A (April 21, 2008)

Introduction

On June 29, 2004, defendant Steven Kurtz was charged by indictment with two counts of mail fraud, in violation of 18 U.S.C. § 1341, and two counts of wire fraud, in violation of 18 U.S.C. § 1343. The indictment alleges that the defendant, a faculty member of the Art Department of the State University of New York at Buffalo, sought to acquire samples of certain biological materials from a supplier of such materials, American Type Culture Collection ("ATCC"), a not-for-profit organization located in Manassas, Virginia. ATCC had a policy, however, of selling biological materials only to approved businesses and institutions with a demonstrated need for such materials. Such businesses and institutions were required to submit an application and become registered customers of ATCC. Under its policy, ATCC did not sell biological materials to individual purchasers, such as the defendant.

The indictment alleges that the defendant circumvented ATCC's policy of not selling biological materials to individuals by entering into a scheme with Robert Ferrall, the principal investigator for the University of Pittsburgh ("UP") Human Genetics Laboratory, and Chairman of UP's Department of Human Genetics, to defraud ATCC. UP was a registered customer of ATCC. Under the scheme, Ferrell ordered the biological materials that the defendant wanted from ATCC using UP's ATCC account, and then once the materials were received by Ferrell, he provided them to the defendant.

This case was referred to Magistrate Judge H. Kenneth Schroeder, Jr., pursuant to 28 U.S.C. § 636(b)(1)(A), on July 13, 2004. On January 21, 2005, defendant filed an omnibus motion seeking, *inter alia*, dismissal of the indictment because it fails to allege that the victims were deprived of "property" within the meaning of the mail and wire fraud statutes, and because it fails to allege that the defendant intended to defraud ATCC and UP of any property. On January 12,

2006, Magistrate Judge Schroeder filed a Report and Recommendation, recommending, *inter alia*, that defendant's motion to dismiss be denied.

Defendant filed objections to the Report and Recommendation, and the government filed a response thereto. Oral argument on the objections was held on December 18, 2007 and January 28, 2008. Following oral argument, the Court requested further briefing, which was completed on March 14, 2008.

Pursuant to 28 U.S.C. 636(b)(1), this Court must make a *de novo* determination of those portions of the Report and Recommendation to which objections have been made. Upon a *de novo* review of the Report and Recommendation, and after reviewing the submissions from the parties and hearing argument from counsel, the Court declines to adopt the proposed findings of the Report and Recommendation. For the reasons stated herein, the Court grants the defendant's motion to dismiss the indictment.

Discussion

1. *Standard for Pretrial Motion to Dismiss*

Rule 12(b) of the Federal Rules of Criminal Procedure provides that a motion to dismiss may raise "any defense, objection, or request which is capable of determination without a trial of the general issue." A pretrial motion to dismiss an indictment under Rule 12 must satisfy "a high standard." United States v. Lazore, 90 F. Supp. 2d 202, 203 (N.D.N.Y. 2000).

> [A]n indictment is sufficient if it, first, contains the elements of the offense charged and fairly informs a defendant of the charge against which he must defend, and, second, enables him to plead an acquittal or conviction in bar of future prosecutions for the same offense. It is generally sufficient that an indictment set forth the offense in the words of the statute itself, as long as those words of themselves fully, directly, and expressly, without any uncertainty or ambiguity, set forth all the elements necessary to constitute the offence intended to be punished. Undoubtedly the language of the statute may be used in the general description of an offence, but it must be accompanied with such a statement of the facts and circumstances as will inform the accused of the specific offence, coming under the general description, with which he is charged.

Hamling v. United States, 418 U.S. 87, 117 (1974) (internal quotations and citations omitted). "[T]he sufficiency of the evidence is not appropriately addressed on a pretrial motion to dismiss an indictment," United States v. Alfonso, 143 F.3d 772, 777 (2d Cir.1998), therefore the court accepts as true the facts alleged in the indictment and determines only whether the indictment is "valid on its face." Costello v. United States, 350 U.S. 359, 363 (1956).

2. *Insufficiency of the Indictment*

Defendant argues that the indictment must be dismissed because it fails to allege that the victims were deprived of "property" within the meaning of the mail and wire fraud statutes, and because it fails to allege that the defendant intended to defraud ATCC and UP of any property. The Court agrees that, as written, the indictment is insufficient on its face.

The "essential elements of a mail or wire fraud violation are (1) a scheme to defraud, (2) money or property as the object of the scheme, and (3) use of the mails or wires to further the scheme." Fountain v. United States, 357 F.3d 250, 255 (2d Cir. 2004), cert. denied, 544 U.S. 1017 (2005) (quotation marks, citation, and brackets omitted). Because the mail fraud and the wire fraud statutes use the same relevant language, they are analyzed the same way. United States v.

Schwartz, 924 F.2d 410, 416 (2d Cir.1991). In the context of mail fraud and wire fraud, "the words 'to defraud' commonly refer 'to wronging one in his property rights by dishonest methods or schemes,' and 'usually signify the deprivation of something of value by trick, deceit, chicane or overreaching.'" McNally v. United States, 483 U.S. 350, 358 (1987) (quoting Hammerschmidt v. United States, 265 U.S. 182, 188 (1924)). It need not be shown that the intended victim of the fraud was actually harmed; it is enough to show the defendant contemplated doing actual harm, that is, something more than merely deceiving the victim. See United States v. Regent Office Supply Co., 421 F.2d 1174, 1180-81 (2d Cir.1970). As a consequence, the deceit practiced must be related to the contemplated harm, and that harm must be found to reside in the bargain sought to be struck. Id. at 1182.

Here, each count of the indictment alleges that as a result of the scheme to defraud, defendant obtained "property from ATCC and the University of Pittsburgh consisting of the biological agent . . . , and the rights, ownership and interest in such biological agent . . .." Thus, the government alleges that there were two victims of the alleged scheme to defraud, ATCC and UP, and that they were each deprived of two types of "property," the biological agent itself and the "rights, ownership and interest" in the biological agent.

With regard to ATCC as an alleged victim, the biological agent itself cannot, without more, constitute the "property" or thing of value of which ATCC was deprived, because ATCC was actually paid for the biological agents. ATCC was in the business of selling biological agents in exchange for money, and in this case it got what it bargained for. Ferrell, using the UP account, paid ATCC for the biological agents. Therefore, ATCC was not deprived of the biological agents–it simply sold them. In order for the indictment to allege a valid charge of mail or wire fraud under these circumstances, it must allege that ATCC was deprived of some property right beyond the actual biological agents themselves. See Schwartz, 924 F.2d at 420-21 (where the seller of goods (night vision goggles) was paid for such goods, wire fraud indictment must allege a deprivation of "property" beyond the goods themselves).

Nor is the allegation that ATCC was deprived of its "rights, ownership and interest" in the biological agents sufficient. It is not clear what this allegation even means. On its face, it would appear to be simply another way of saying that the defendant sought to obtain the biological agents from ATCC. In its submissions, the government states that this language refers to ATCC's "intellectual property rights" in the biological agents. Docket No. 128 at 9.   However, there is no allegation that the defendant intended to deprive ATCC of any intellectual property rights associated with the biological agents. For example, there is no claim that the defendant intended to reproduce the biological agents and sell them, or that he intended to resell them under a different trademark, etc.

With regard to UP as an alleged victim, the indictment is also insufficient. There is no allegation in the indictment that UP ever actually possessed the biological agents, or had any "right, ownership or interest," such as intellectual property rights, in such materials. In fact, there is no allegation that UP itself was ever even aware that the biological agents had been ordered or received by Ferrell. The indictment alleges that Ferrell ordered the biological agents, and that when he received them, he transferred them to the defendant. UP's real loss was the UP funds that Ferrell used to pay for the biological agents, not the biological agents themselves. Yet, the indictment contains no allegation regarding the money lost by UP.

Moreover, even if it were assumed that UP was deprived of "property" in the form of the biological agents, the indictment would still be insufficient because it does not allege any type of misrepresentation or fraudulent conduct directed toward UP, as opposed to ATCC, regarding the biological agents. For example, the indictment does not allege that Ferrell misrepresented to UP that the biological agents were to be used in the UP laboratory for official purposes when in fact

REGULATION OF BIOLOGICAL AGENTS, BIOLOGICAL SAFETY LABORATORIES

they were to be transferred to the defendant.

3. *No-Sale Theory*

Perhaps recognizing the potential insufficiency of the indictment, the government asserts, in its response to the motion to dismiss, a so-called "nosale" theory of fraud. The government argues that defendant's scheme to defraud induced ATCC to sell biological agents to Ferrell that it would not have sold had it know that Ferrell in fact intended to transfer such biological agents to the defendant, who was not a registered ATCC customer. In other words, the government argues that ATCC was denied the right to control to whom it sold its product.

The Second Circuit most recently discussed this "no-sale" theory of fraud in the case of United States v. Shellef, 507 F.3d 82 (2d Cir. 2007). In Shellef, the defendant allegedly misrepresented to the manufacturer of a regulated solvent that he was purchasing solvent for resale overseas, and thus was not subject to excise taxes. He instead sold the solvent domestically. The indictment charged him, *inter alia*, with wire fraud under the "no-sale" theory of fraud. The indictment alleged that the defendant's misrepresentations that he would sell the solvent overseas induced the manufacturer to sell solvent to him that it would not have sold had it known that he, in fact, intended to sell it domestically. The defendant was convicted, *inter alia*, of wire fraud and appealed.

The Second Circuit reversed the conviction, holding that the indictment was insufficient to allege a "no-sale" theory of wire fraud. As part of its analysis, the court discussed its prior cases involving the "no-sale" theory of fraud:

> Our cases have drawn a fine line between schemes that do no more than cause their victims to enter into transactions they would otherwise avoid-which do not violate the mail or wire fraud statutes-and schemes that depend for their completion on a misrepresentation of an essential element of the bargain-which do violate the mail and wire fraud statutes.
>
> In *United States v. Regent Office Supply Co.*, 421 F.2d 1174 (2d Cir.1970), the defendants sold stationery, id. at 1176. The defendants' scheme consisted of directing their sales personnel to misrepresent their identities to prospective customers so that the customers would be willing to entertain their offers. See id. (noting, as an example, that the sales personnel fraudulently claimed that they had been referred by a friend of the customer or an officer of the customer's firm). We concluded that no conviction under the mail fraud statute could stand where the misrepresentation was "not directed to the quality, adequacy or price of goods to be sold, or otherwise to the nature of the bargain." See id. at 1179.
>
> *United States v. Starr*, 816 F.2d 94 (2d Cir.1987), is similar. The defendants there collected bulk mailings from their customers and then sent them through the post office. See id. at 95-96. At the post office, however, they hid high-rate mail in low-rate mail packages, and paid the low-rate price for the entire shipments. Id. at 96. The defendants nonetheless charged their customers as if the mailings were high-rate, and produced and mailed false invoices to show that the high-rate price had in fact been paid. Id. We decided that "[t]he misappropriation of funds simply ha[d] no relevance to the object of the contract; namely, the delivery of mail to the appropriate destination in a timely fashion." Id. at 100. Because "[m]isrepresentations amounting only to a deceit are insufficient to maintain a mail or wire fraud prosecution," we concluded that such a charge can not apply to situations where the alleged victims "received exactly what they paid for" and "there was no discrepancy between benefits reasonably anticipated

and actual benefits received." Id. at 98-99 (internal quotation marks and citation omitted); cf. id. at 102 (Newman, J., concurring) ("An indictment for defrauding the Postal Service would have led to a conviction that would surely have been affirmed. However, the indictment for defrauding the customers has led to a conviction that must be reversed.")

In *Schwartz*, 924 F.2d 410, however, we were faced with the type of misrepresentation that *Regent Office* recognized might form the basis for a wire fraud prosecution-that is, one "directed to ... the nature of the bargain," id. at 1179. The defendants in Schwartz had purchased night-vision goggles from Litton Industries. Schwartz, 924 F.2d at 414. Because the Arms Export Control Act restricted the sale of these goggles to certain nations, Litton sought assurances, both in the contract and during the course of performance, that the defendants would not export to the restricted nations. Id. Though the defendants promised to abide by all applicable export regulations, they sold the goggles to nations that were prohibited from purchasing them. Id. at 414-16. We upheld their conviction for wire fraud under a no-sale theory because the "misrepresentations went to an essential element of the bargain between the parties and were not simply fraudulent inducements to gain access to Litton equipment." Id. at 421. The defendants had "deprived Litton of the right to define the terms for the sale of its property in that way," that is, that its product not be exported from this country illegally, and therefore "cost it, as well, good will." Id.

Shellef, 507 F.3d at 107-109.

Applying these cases to the case before it, the Second Circuit concluded:

As in *Starr,* the indictment here does not allege, pursuant to the government's "no-sale" theory, that there was a "discrepancy between benefits reasonably anticipated" and actual benefits received. And as in *Regent Office*, it fails to allege that [the defendant] misrepresented "the nature of the bargain." Instead, the indictment states only that [the defendant's] misrepresentation induced [the manufacturer] to enter into a transaction it would otherwise have avoided. Because it does not assert that [the defendant's] misrepresentation had "relevance to the object of the contract," we do not think it is legally sufficient.

Shellef, 507 F.3d at 109 (citations omitted).

The Second Circuit recognized that the facts in Shellef closely resembled the facts in Schwartz and that there might be sufficient evidence to prove a "no-sale" theory. However, because the Shellef indictment failed to plead sufficiently the "no-sale" theory, the fraud conviction based on a "no-sale" theory could not stand. Id.

Applying *Shellef* to the instant case, it is clear that the indictment does not sufficiently allege a "no-sale" theory of fraud. The indictment does not define the "property" of which the alleged victim was deprived as *the right to define the sale of its property*. Instead, the indictment alleges that the "property" was the biological agents themselves, which as discussed above, is insufficient. [FN1] In addition, there is no allegation that the defendant's scheme depended on a misrepresentation of an essential element of the bargain. Although the indictment does allege that the Material Transfer Agreement which accompanied each shipment provided that the purchaser not transfer the biological materials, it does not allege that this restriction on transfer was an essential element of the bargain or that the defendant's scheme depended on a misrepresentation regarding the transfer restriction. In fact, the indictment does not allege that either the defendant or Ferrell even knew about the transfer restriction.

The Court passes no judgment on whether the indictment could have been drafted in such a way, based on the facts and circumstances as they have been presented here, to allege sufficiently a "no-sale" theory of fraud. It simply finds that the indictment, as currently written, fails to allege such a theory.

Conclusion

For the reasons stated, the Court grants the defendant's motion to dismiss the indictment

SO ORDERED.

s/ *Richard J. Arcara*, Chief Judge, U.S. Dist. Ct., W.D.N.Y., April 21, 2008

[FN1] The *Schwartz* decision makes clear that the biological agents themselves cannot constitute the "property" that was the object of the scheme to defraud. In *Schwartz*, the Second Circuit recognized that because the defendant had paid for the night vision goggles, the "property" of which the victim manufacturer was deprived had to be something beyond the night vision goggles themselves for purposes of the fraud statutes. The court found that the "property" was the right to define the terms of the sale of the night vision goggles.

6.11.   **Human Subject Experimentation**

The use of human subjects in experimentation should be limited to those contexts in which the balance of its importance outweighs the risks of the individuals. This section will examine several cases that address the use of human subject experimentation for defense purposes.

The guidelines of human subject testing are grounded in the Nuremberg Code principles, which resulted from the court's findings in the Nazi trials following World War II and the atrocities of human experimentation in which the Nazi regime was engaged. Following this trial, the United States adopted similar guidelines in response to the Nuremberg trials, published by NIH as the "Handbook On The Utilization of Normal Volunteers In The Clinical Center," in 1961. The NIH guidelines are required for human subject testing with the award of NIH funding.

In *United States v. Stanley*, 483 U.S. 669 (1987), the U.S. Army administered LSD to an enlisted individual who was unaware of the administration of the drug or any of the risks. The U.S. Supreme Court (5-4) opined that the enlisted individual, Stanley, could not recover damages for injuries from the LSD simply because he was enlisted in the military, applying the Feres doctrine, which provides that members of the military cannot sue the U.S. government for damages due to injuries. Justice Scalia, in writing for the court, opined that allowing members of the military to sue the government "would call into serious question military discipline and decision-making." Justice O'Connor, dissenting, cited the Nuremberg Code for the proposition that due process guarantees human subjects of experiments the right to voluntary and informed consent.

6.11.1. The Operation White Coats

The USAMRIID has developed a unique corps of military personnel who comprise what is arguably the most well-informed corps of human subjects for testing ever comprised. Approximately seventy Medical Research Volunteer Subjects (MRVS) are utilized for the first phase of clinical trials in the testing of vaccines and drugs.

The following excerpt from *Medical Aspects of Biological Warfare* (Jeffrey E. Stephenson, Ph.D. and Arthur O. Anderson, M.D., *Medical Aspects of Biological Warfare*, Chap. 24, "Ethical and Legal Dilemmas of Biodefense Research" (2006) at http://www.bordeninstitute.army.mil/published_volumes/biological_warfare/BW-ch24.pdf) is a history overview of the Operation White Coats program:

The Army included the code in directive Cs-385, which required that informed consent must be in writing, excluded prisoners of war from participation, and included a method for DoD compensation for research-related injuries sustained by participants. In 1962 Cs-385 became AR 70-25, *Use of Volunteers as Subjects of Research*,13 which regulated Army research until 1983.

In 1952 the Armed Forces Medical Policy Council noted that nonpathogenic biological warfare simulations conducted at Fort Detrick and at various locations across the United States showed that the population was vulnerable to biological attack. Additionally, experiments with virulent disease agents in animal models attested to the incapacitating and lethal effects of these agents when delivered as weapons. However, there was doubt among the council members that extrapolation of animal data to humans was valid, and human studies appeared necessary. Ad hoc meetings of scientists, Armed Forces Epidemiology Board advisors, and military leaders occurred at Fort Detrick during the spring of 1953.14,15 Thorough consideration of the ethical and legal basis for human subjects research resulted in the design of several prototype research protocols and creation of the US Army Medical Unit (Figures 24-3 and 24-4). This unit heavily invested in animal experimentation but aimed at modeling human infectious diseases to study pathogenesis and response to vaccines and therapeutics. Later, the US Army Medical Unit became the US Army Medical Research Institute of Infectious Diseases (USAMRIID).

In 1955 military research studies using human participants began in a program called CD-22 (Camp Detrick–22) that included soldier participants in a project called Operation Whitecoat. The participants were mainly conscientious objectors who were Seventh-day Adventists trained as Army medics. The program was designed to determine the extent to which humans are susceptible to infection with biological warfare agents. The soldier participants were exposed to actual diseases such as Q fever and tularemia to understand how these illnesses affected the body and to determine indices of human vulnerability that might be used to design clinical efficacy studies. In keeping with the charge in the Nuremberg Code to protect study participants, the US Army Medical Unit, under the direction of the Army surgeon general, carefully managed the project. Throughout the program's history from 1954 to 1973, no fatalities or long-term injuries occurred among Operation Whitecoat volunteers.

Operation Whitecoat serves as a morally praiseworthy model for the conduct of biodefense research involving human subjects. The process of informed consent was successfully implemented from the inception of Operation Whitecoat. Each medical investigator prepared a protocol that was extensively reviewed and modified to comply with each of the elements of the Nuremberg Code. After a committee determined whether ethical requirements and scientific validity were met, Army officials approved the protocol. Then potential volunteers were briefed as a group regarding the approved protocol, and they attended a project interview with the medical investigator in which the potential volunteers could ask questions about the study. Informed consent documents (Figure 24-5) were signed after an obligatory waiting period that ranged from 24 hours to 4 weeks, depending on the risk involved in the study. Volunteers were encouraged to discuss the study with family members, clergy, and personal physicians before making a final decision. By allowing volunteers sufficient time and opportunity to ask questions about risks, potential benefits, and the conduct of the study, this multistage informed consent process ensured that participation was voluntary. Soldiers were told that their participation in the research was not compulsory. Approximately 20% of those soldiers approached for participation in Operation Whitecoat declined. Review of Operation Whitecoat records of interviews with many of the volunteers and investigators revealed that the researchers informed participants that the research was scientifically valid and potentially dangerous, and that any harm to the participants would be minimized.

Approximately 150 studies related to the diagnosis, prevention, and treatment of various diseases were completed during Operation Whitecoat, including research on Q fever and tularemia infections and staphylococcal enterotoxins. Vaccines to be used against Venezuelan equine encephalitis, plague, tularemia, Rocky Mountain spotted fever, and Rift Valley fever were tested for evidence of safety in humans. However, scientists conducted animal studies before human subjects research. For instance, researchers exposed Operation Whitecoat volunteers to aerosolized Q fever organisms only after completion of animal safety and efficacy studies. The first exposure occurred on January 25, 1955, with the use of a 1-million-liter stainless steel sphere at Fort Detrick known as the "Eight Ball." This research device was designed to allow exposure of animals and humans to carefully controlled numbers of organisms by an aerosol route.

Research conducted during Operation Whitecoat also contributed to the development of equipment and procedures that established the standard for laboratory biosafety throughout the world. The ethical commitment to the safety of laboratory workers engaged with dangerous toxins, viruses, and diseases was manifested by the development of biological safety cabinets with laminar flow hoods, "hot suites" with differential air pressure to contain pathogens, decontamination procedures, prototype fermentors, incubators, refrigerated centrifuges, particle sizers, and various other types of specially fabricated laboratory equipment. Many of the techniques and systems developed at Fort Detrick to ensure worker safety while handling hazardous materials are now used in hospitals, pharmacies, and various manufacturing industries.

The following informed consent document is used for participants in the program:

Fig. 6.1. Informed consent form for volunteers

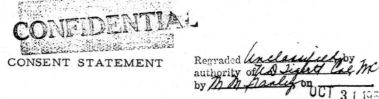

CONSENT STATEMENT

Regraded *unclassified* by
authority of *US Tigntt Col. MC*
by *M M Baaley* on OCT 3 1 1955

A program of investigation, sponsored by the United States Army, aimed toward determining the amount of a disease agent necessary to produce illness in man, has been explained to me. I understand that the only way in which this essential information can be obtained is by the exposure of volunteers to known amounts of the agent. I understand that such volunteers may become ill and that the program is not without hazard.

I further understand that the agent to be studied is Coxiella burnetii, which is the cause of Q fever. I understand that the organism(s) causing the disease will be suspended in air, and that by breathing this air I will expose myself to infection with this disease agent. I understand that within three (3) to twenty-one (21) days after the exposure I may become ill and that the expected symptoms are fever, headache, and generalized aching. I understand that the course of the disease may be from one (1) to three (3) weeks. I understand the decision as to appropriate treatment will be made by the attending physicians. I understand that such treatment, if employed, may have to be given in two (2) or more phases.

I further understand that I will be restricted to a single area for the period of this study, probably four (4) to six (6) weeks. I understand that various diagnostic procedures will be required.

There has been no exercise of force, fraud, deceit, duress, over-reaching, or other ulterior forms of constraint or coercion in order to obtain this consent from me.

Of my own free will, and after consideration for a period of more than four (4) weeks, I affix my signature hereto, indicating my willingness, as a soldier, to serve voluntarily as a subject for these studies, with the understanding that I will not be required to participate in studies which, in themselves, are contrary to my religious beliefs.

Signature _____

WITNESS: ASN _____

_____   Date   JUN 2 9 1955
                                        _____

CONFIDENTIAL

6.11.2. Radiation Experiments

During the Clinton Administration, the revelation was made that the United States had engaged in research involving the exposure of humans to radiation for purposes of examining the effects of military attacks involving radiation exposure on humans. These experiments are described in the decision below when, in 1995, the court found that these human subjects were entitled to recovery from the federal government, which led to a settlement from the United States to the victims and their families.

In re Cincinnati Radiation Litigation
874 F. Supp. 796 (S.D. Ohio, Western Div. 1995)

Cancer patient whom government and university physicians allegedly subjected to radiation experiments under guise that they were receiving cancer treatment sued physicians employed by Department of Defense, physicians employed by city university, city, and university, seeking recovery under § 1983 and 1985(3), alleging that patients were denied due process, equal protection, and access to courts, and that individual defendants engaged in conspiracy to deprive patients of their constitutional rights. Individual defendants moved to dismiss. The District Court, Beckwith, J., held that: (1) Department of Defense physicians were subject to personal jurisdiction; (2) individual defendants were not entitled to qualified immunity. . . (4) patients stated claim for violation of procedural due process; . . .(6) patients stated equal protection claim . .

Motions granted in part and denied in part.

OPINION and ORDER

BECKWITH, District Judge.

The Complaint in this much-publicized matter alleges that the Defendants engaged in the design and implementation of experiments from 1960 to 1972 to study the effects of massive doses of radiation on human beings in preparation for a possible nuclear war. The experiments utilized terminal cancer patients who were not informed of the consequences of their participation nor, indeed, informed of the existence or purpose of the experiments. The Complaint alleges that most of the patients selected were African-American and, in the vernacular of the time, charity patients. The Complaint further alleges that the various Defendants actively concealed the nature, purpose and consequences of the experiments. The allegations of the Complaint make out an outrageous tale of government perfidy in dealing with some of its most vulnerable citizens. The allegations are inflammatory and compelling, creating a milieu in which it is difficult to objectively examine the allegations for legal sufficiency or to apply a view of constitutional rights unilluminated by the legal evolution that has taken place since 1972 when the experiments at issue ended. The task is especially difficult in the constricted format afforded by Fed.R.Civ.P. 12(b)(1) and (6). The frequent lapses into factual disputes and arguments on all sides attest to the strong temptation to move beyond the four corners of Plaintiffs' Second Amended Complaint.

. . .

I. THE COMPLAINT

To follow the path of analysis prescribed by Fed.R.Civ.P. 12(b)(6), the Court must look first to the allegations contained in the Complaint. The Court will then examine each issue raised by the Defendants through the lens created by the allegations contained in the Complaint.

An overview of the Complaint reveals that the Plaintiffs allege that they were the unwitting subjects of Human Radiation Experiments conducted at Cincinnati General Hospital ("CGH") between 1960 and 1972. The Complaint alleges that the experiments were conducted under the auspices of the University of Cincinnati College of Medicine with funding and authorization from the United States Department of Defense's Nuclear Agency.

Plaintiffs allege that the Human Radiation Experiments were designed to study the effects of radiation on combat troops. Consequently, Plaintiffs allege they were exposed to doses of radiation at levels to be expected on a nuclear battlefield.

It is also alleged that the subjects of the radiation experiments all had inoperable cancer and were told that they were receiving treatment for their cancer. Plaintiffs allege that they were in fact never told that they were part of a medical experiment or that they were receiving radiation in doses ranging from 25 to 300 rads as a means of providing the Defense Department information about the effects of radiation on military personnel in the event of a nuclear attack. Thus, the principal thrust of the Complaint is that none of the subjects gave informed consent to participate in the Human Radiation Experiments.

The Plaintiffs claim they were denied substantive due process, procedural due process, equal protection, and access to courts under the Fourth, Fifth, and Fourteenth Amendments of the United States Constitution. The Plaintiffs also claim that the individual Defendants engaged in a conspiracy to deprive Plaintiffs of their constitutional rights and seek recovery under this theory pursuant to 42 U.S.C. § 1983 and 1985(3).

Finally, the Plaintiffs assert several Ohio common law claims including wrongful death, medical malpractice, negligence, intentional infliction of emotional distress, and negligent infliction of emotional distress. Plaintiffs also assert that the Price-Anderson Act, 42 U.S.C. § 2210(h)(2) independently permits this Court to exercise jurisdiction over these state law claims.

The individual Defendants are denominated as follows: Eugene L. Saenger, M.D. was employed by the Department of Radiology of the University of Cincinnati College of Medicine and was the lead researcher conducting the Human Radiation Experiments at Cincinnati General Hospital. Dr. Saenger is alleged to have designed, supervised and conducted the experiments that are the subject of this Complaint. . . .

Warren O. Kessler, M.D., and Myron I. Varon, M.D., were medical officers in the United States Navy and are alleged to have been the Project Officers charged with providing federal oversight of the Human Radiation Experiments. Because Drs. Kessler and Varon were federal officials, their conduct will be examined along with that of the other individual Defendants under the doctrine of qualified immunity and as regards Section 1985 and the Price-Anderson statute. However, the claims against Drs. Kessler and Varon will also be analyzed separately under the Bivens doctrine, which specifically permits claims against federal employees who violate constitutional law.

. .

The City, a municipality in Hamilton County, Ohio, is also a Defendant. The Complaint alleges that the City sanctioned, funded, and actively participated in the Human Radiation Experiments.

Finally, the University of Cincinnati ("University"), including its constituent College of Medicine and University Hospital (formerly Cincinnati General Hospital) is also named as a Defendant. The University, now a state-owned academic and research institution, is located in Cincinnati, Ohio. During the time of the Human Radiation Experiments, the Defendant University and its constituents were owned and operated by the Defendant City. The University's Board of Directors are also alleged to have controlled and directed the Human Radiation Experiments.

A. Factual Allegations

For purposes of the motions to dismiss, a detailed examination of the Complaint is necessary. Under the allegations of the Complaint, Plaintiffs tell the following story:

From 1960 to 1972 experiments were conducted at the University of Cincinnati College of Medicine and Cincinnati General Hospital on at least 87 people. The subjects of the experiments were exposed to total or partial body irradiation. The primary purpose of the experiments was to test the psychological and physical effects of radiation on humans. Indeed, a report prepared for the Department of Defense by the individual Defendants who conducted the Human Radiation Experiments during the period 1960 to 1966 indicated that the goal was "to develop a baseline for determining how much radiation exposure was too much, and to determine how shielding could decrease the deleterious effect of the radiation," and to determine what a single dose of whole or partial radiation could do to "cognitive or other functions mediated through the central nervous system."

Patients were selected to be subjects in the experiments because they had cancer. The patients were not, however, in the final stages of their disease, nor were they close to death. Each patient selected was deemed in reasonably good clinical condition. Further, Dr. Saenger is alleged to have noted that the patients selected had life expectancies of up to two years. Those patients selected were primarily indigent, poorly educated, and of lower than average intelligence. A majority of the patients selected were African-Americans.

The patients selected for the experiments were told that they were receiving radiation for their cancer, although the radiation tests were designed to benefit the Human Radiation Experiments rather than the patients. A 1961 report from the individual Defendants on the Human Radiation Experiments indicates that the patients were told that they were to receive treatment to help their sickness.

No consent forms were used for the first five years of the Human Radiation Experiments. Beginning in 1965, the Complaint alleges, consent forms were used but failed to state the real risk of the radiation exposure to the patients. Further, the Complaint alleges that the consent forms did not indicate to the Plaintiffs that they were part of experiments funded by the Department of Defense or that the primary purpose of the experiments was to test the effect of radiation on soldiers in the event that they would encounter a nuclear attack. Rather, the consent forms indicated only that the patients were participating in scientific experiments. Thus, the Plaintiffs allege, all risks and hazards of the Human Radiation Experiments were not made known and, indeed, were intentionally concealed from the Plaintiffs. Specifically, none of the consent forms indicated that there was a risk of death from bone marrow infection within 40 days of irradiation. Likewise, none of the consent forms indicated that nausea and vomiting would likely be experienced by the subjects following irradiation. Finally, the long-term carcinogenic and genetic hazards associated with massive doses of radiation were also concealed.

The Plaintiffs also allege that the subjects of the experiments were poorly educated and deemed to be of low intelligence, according to standardized tests. In light of the Plaintiffs' lack of sophistication, the Complaint alleges that the information provided by Defendants could not have been sufficient, in any event, to provide a basis for informed consent. In other words, voluntary and informed consent was impossible.

Plaintiffs also allege that they did not have reason to know the true dangers of the Human Radiation Experiments to which they were subjected because of Defendants' purposeful concealment of information. Because of the purposeful concealment, the Plaintiffs had no reason to know of their possible claims for relief until approximately January 1994, when press reports identified a few of the subjects in the Human Radiation Experiments for the first time by name.

Radiation exposure from the Human Radiation Experiments either led to the patients' death, seriously shortened their life expectancies, and/or led to radiation injury resulting in bone marrow failure or suppression, nausea, vomiting, burns on the patients' bodies, severe and permanent pain, and/or suffering and emotional distress.

The Plaintiffs allege that the Human Radiation Experiments were designed and conducted by Defendant Saenger and the other individual Defendants with callous indifference to the effects such experiments would have on the physical and mental health of the subjects, and with conscious disregard for the rights and safety of the subjects in situations where there was a great probability of causing substantial harm. The Human Radiation Experiments were also designed and conducted by Defendant Saenger and the other individual Defendants in direct contravention of the Helsinki Declaration Mandate regarding nontherapeutic clinical research. The Helsinki Declaration requires that the doctor "remain the protector of the life and health of that person on whom clinical research is being carried out." Instead, the Human Radiation Experiments were conducted recklessly and willfully without due regard for the rights of the subjects of the research under the United States Constitution and laws, the laws of the State of Ohio, and international law.

B. Legal Claims

Based upon the foregoing factual allegations, Plaintiffs set forth the following claims for relief:

(1) Plaintiffs' participation in the Human Radiation Experiments without informed consent resulted in a violation of their rights, privileges and immunities secured by the First and Fourteenth Amendments to the United States Constitution, including, but not limited to, the right of access to the courts, the rights to procedural and substantive due process of law, the right to equal protection under the law, and the right to privacy under 42 U.S.C. § 1983.

(2) The federal Defendants, Drs. Kessler and Varon, have, under color of law, deprived Plaintiffs of rights, privileges and immunities secured by the First and Fourteenth Amendments to the United States Constitution, including the right of access to the courts, the rights to procedural and substantive due process of law, the right to equal protection under the law, and the right to privacy under Bivens v. Six Unknown Federal Agents, supra.

(3) By conspiring with each other to choose African-Americans as subjects for the Human Radiation Experiments, the Defendants violated 42 U.S.C. § 1985 and the United States Constitution.

. . .

(5) The Defendants' program of nonconsensual Human Radiation Experiments constituted an abnormally dangerous activity, which caused harm to the Plaintiffs and for which they are strictly liable.

(6) Defendants University, City, and the individual Defendants committed medical malpractice by conducting the nonconsensual Human Radiation Experiments.

(7) The Defendants University and City, as well as the individual Defendants, acted negligently by authorizing, encouraging or carrying out the nonconsensual Human Radiation Experiments.

(8) As a result of the Defendants' negligent conduct, the Plaintiffs and/or their surviving family members have suffered severe emotional distress.

(9) The Defendants intentionally inflicted severe emotional distress by extreme and outrageous conduct, by conducting the nonconsensual Human Radiation Experiments.

(10) By intentionally exposing Plaintiffs or their decedents to harmful or fatal doses of radiation without informed consent, the Defendants committed a battery.

(11) By intentionally concealing from the Plaintiffs the full extent, potential consequences, and true purposes of the Human Radiation Experiments, the Defendants perpetrated a fraud upon Plaintiffs. . .

II. BIVENS ISSUES

. . .

B. Supervisory Liability

Plaintiffs also allege that Drs. Varon and Kessler, as Project Officers for the Human Radiation Experiments in the Defense Atomic Support Agency and/or the Defense Nuclear Agency of the Department of Defense, were responsible for federal oversight of the experimentation program. Specifically, they were to ensure that the research design was sound and that risks to subjects were minimized. Further, Plaintiffs assert that the Project Officers acted in supervisory capacities by implicitly authorizing, approving, or knowingly acquiescing in the Human Radiation Experiments.

Respondeat superior does not apply in this claim. Rather, in order to establish the liability of the Bivens Defendants, a plaintiff must allege and prove that the supervisors in question condoned, encouraged, or knowingly acquiesced in the alleged misconduct...A supervisor may be liable for violations of clearly established constitutional rights, even if the violations were directly carried out by others. . . . The Plaintiffs have sufficiently alleged the Bivens Defendants' own wrongful conduct, as the Project Officers who authorized, approved, or acquiesced in the Human Radiation Experiments. The Plaintiffs are entitled to discover whether the Bivens Defendants were in fact supervisors of the Human Radiation Experiments.

Accordingly, the Bivens Defendants' motion to dismiss is DENIED.

III. QUALIFIED IMMUNITY

Section 1983, enacted in 1871, provides a right of action for parties deprived of their constitutional or federal statutory rights by actions taken "under color of state law." [42 U.S.C. § 1983] Section 1983 thus holds public officials who violate an individual's rights under the Fourteenth Amendment liable for that violation.

42 U.S.C. § 1983 provides as follows:

Every person who, under color of any statute, ordinance, regulation, custom, or usage, of any State or Territory or the District of Columbia, subjects, or causes to be subjected, any citizen of the United States or other person within the jurisdiction thereof to the deprivation of any rights, privileges, or immunities secured by the Constitution and laws shall be liable to the party injured in an action at law, suit in equity, or other proper proceeding for redress. For the purposes of this section, any Act of Congress applicable exclusively to the District of Columbia shall be considered to be a statute of the District of Columbia.

. . .The defense, spurred in large measure by the rise of suits against public officials under Section 1983 is a judicially created doctrine. The text of Section 1983 does not suggest the availability of such a defense; rather, it derives from the common law doctrine of sovereign immunity, often stated as the maxim, "the king can do no wrong". . . .The qualified immunity defense operates as an affirmative defense protecting officials from liability for any damages caused by their performance of discretionary functions. Importantly, the defense is not effective when plaintiffs can demonstrate that an official's conduct violated a plaintiff's clearly established statutory or constitutional rights.

The qualified immunity defense is designed to accommodate two conflicting public policy concerns. On the one hand, the Supreme Court recognizes the need to defend constitutional rights. At the same time, the Court has sought to protect public officials from suits for every error in judgment, thereby diverting their attention from their public duties, preventing them from independently exercising their discretion because of fear of damages liability, and discouraging qualified persons from seeking public office. . . .

If the Plaintiffs do assert a valid constitutional claim, the Court must then make an additional two-step inquiry into the sufficiency of the Complaint. First, the Court must determine whether the constitutional rights alleged to have been violated were clearly established at the time of the alleged Human Radiation Experiments. . . .

The second inquiry is inextricably intertwined with the first. The Court must examine the allegations of the Complaint that relate to the alleged misconduct of the defendant officials; in the context of a motion to dismiss, the Court must accept these allegations as true. The Court must then ask and answer the following question: Would a reasonable official in defendant's position have known that what defendant did, as expressed in the allegations, violated plaintiffs' clearly established rights? If, upon the conclusion of this analysis, Plaintiffs have failed to allege sufficient facts to withstand the qualified immunity defense, this Court will grant the motions to dismiss.

IV. DUE PROCESS
A. Right to Bodily Integrity

The first step in deciding whether the individual and Bivens Defendants are entitled to qualified immunity is to determine whether the Constitution, through the Fourteenth Amendment's substantive due process component, protects an individual from nonconsensual invasive medical experimentation by state actors. Section 1983 imposes liability for violations of rights protected by the Constitution, not for violations of duties of care arising out of tort law. . . .To state a cause of action under Section 1983 for violation of the Due Process Clause, Plaintiffs must show that they have asserted a recognized liberty or property interest within the purview of the Fourteenth Amendment and that they were intentionally or recklessly deprived of that interest, even temporarily, under color of state law. . . . The Supreme Court has expanded the definition of "liberty" beyond the core textual meaning of that term to include not only the privileges expressly enumerated by the Bill of Rights but also the fundamental rights implicit in the concept of ordered liberty, deeply rooted in this nation's history and tradition under the Due Process Clause. . . .

The Due Process Clause of the Fourteenth Amendment provides that no state shall "deprive a person of life, liberty, or property without due process of law." . . .

The Plaintiffs' substantive due process claim in this case is grounded upon the premise that individuals have a liberty interest in their bodily integrity that is protected by the Due Process Clause of the Fourteenth Amendment, and particularly upon the premise that nonconsensual experiments involving extremely high doses of radiation, designed and supervised by military doctors and carried out by City hospital physicians violate that right.

The right to be free of state-sponsored invasion of a person's bodily integrity is protected by the Fourteenth Amendment guarantee of due process. In Albright v. Oliver, 510 U.S. 266, 114 S.Ct. 807, 127 L.Ed.2d 114 (1994), Chief Justice Rehnquist, writing for the Court, specifically noted that "the protections of substantive due process have for the most part been accorded to matters relating to marriage, family, procreation, and the right to bodily integrity." Citing Planned Parenthood v. Casey, 505 U.S. 833, ----, 112 S.Ct. 2791, 2804, 120 L.Ed.2d 674 (1992) (emphasis added). . .

As a threshold matter, the individual and Bivens Defendants raise the issue of voluntariness. Voluntariness pertains to this case on two levels. First is the question of whether the Plaintiffs were voluntary patients at Cincinnati General Hospital, and if so, what effect that voluntary presence has on their ability to assert this claim. Second, the Court must determine whether the Plaintiffs in this case sufficiently allege that they were involuntary participants in the Human Radiation Experiments, and, if so, what effect that involuntary participation has on their ability to assert this claim.

. . . The Court of Appeals held that "voluntary patients have no constitutionally protected right to refuse unwanted drugs because voluntary patients could simply leave the hospital if they did not want to be drugged. Voluntary patients can be forced to choose between leaving the hospital and accepting prescribed treatment." Thus, the Defendants argue that because Plaintiffs in this case "carried the key to the hospital exit" they chose to accept radiation treatment as a matter of free will and cannot claim that their liberty was in any way curtailed.

This argument fails at this stage of the litigation for several reasons. First, it is not at all clear that Plaintiffs were voluntary patients at Cincinnati General Hospital. The Plaintiffs in this case are all alleged to have been poor. Discovery may demonstrate that the only hospital in the city to treat indigent patients was Cincinnati General Hospital. If this is so, the Court would be reluctant to hold that a person with only one hospital from which to choose voluntarily enters that hospital when he becomes ill. Regardless of that factual uncertainty, Defendants argument still fails for the following reasons.

The Plaintiffs allege that they were purposefully misled in several respects. First, Plaintiffs allege that they were specifically not informed that the radiation they were receiving was for a military experiment rather than treatment of their cancer. Further, Plaintiffs allege that they were never informed that the amount of radiation they were to receive would cause burns, vomiting, nausea, bone marrow failure, severe shortening of life expectancy, or even death. When a person is purposefully misled about such crucial facts as these, he can no longer be said to exercise that degree of free will that is essential to the notion of voluntariness.

To manipulate men, to propel them toward goals which we see but they may not, is to deny their human essence, to treat them as objects without wills of their own, and therefore to degrade them. This is why to lie to men, or to deceive them, that is, to use them as means for our not their own, independently conceived ends, even if it is to their own benefit, is, in effect to treat them as sub-human, to behave as if their ends are less ultimate and sacred than our own.... For if the essence of men is that they are autonomous beings-authors of values, of ends in themselves ...-then nothing is worse than to treat them as if they were not autonomous but natural objects whose choices can be manipulated. [Isaiah Berlin, FOUR ESSAYS ON LIBERTY 136-37 (1969)].

Defendants assert that if Plaintiffs did not like what was being done to them they could have left the hospital at any time. Unfortunately for Plaintiffs, however, they allegedly never possessed knowledge sufficient to make that choice. The allegations in the Complaint indicate that the choice Plaintiffs would have been forced to make was one of life or death. If the Constitution protects "personal autonomy in making certain types of important decisions," Whelan v. Roe, infra, at 589, the decision whether to participate in the Human Radiation Experiments was one that each individual Plaintiff was entitled to make freely and with full knowledge of the purpose and attendant circumstances involved. Without actually seizing the Plaintiffs and forcing them to submit to these experiments, the individual and Bivens Defendants, agents of the state, accomplished the same feat through canard and deception, according to the allegations of the Complaint.

In 1990, the Supreme Court unequivocally held that the "forcible injection of medication into a nonconsenting person's body represents a substantial interference with that person's liberty." Washington v. Harper, 494 U.S. 210, 229, 110 S.Ct. 1028, 1041, 108 L.Ed.2d 178 (1990). . . .

Determining that a person has a "liberty interest" under the Due Process Clause does not end the inquiry; whether a person's constitutional rights have been violated must be determined by balancing his liberty interest against the relevant state interests. . . .Indeed, compulsory vaccinations, compelled blood tests and extractions of contraband material from the rectal cavity have sometimes been upheld on a showing of clear necessity, procedural regularity, and minimal pain. However, each of these cases has acknowledged that an aspect of fundamental liberty was at stake and that the government's burden was to provide more than minimal justification for its action. . . .

It bears repeating ... that we reach this judgment only on the facts of the present record. The integrity of the individual's person is a cherished value of our society. That we hold today that the Constitution does not forbid the state's minor intrusions into an individual's body under strictly limited conditions in no way indicates that it permits more substantial intrusions or intrusions under other conditions.

. . . These several cases indicate that in order to maintain an action under the Fifth Amendment, it is sufficient that a plaintiff demonstrate that an invasion of bodily integrity was deficient in procedural regularity, or that it was needlessly severe.

When an individual's bodily integrity is at stake, a determination that the state has accorded adequate procedural protection should not be made lightly. Since bodily invasions often cannot be readily remedied after the fact through damage awards in the way that most deprivations of property can, . . .the state must precede any deliberate invasion with formalized procedures. This is precisely what the Supreme Court held in Washington v. Harper, 494 U.S. at 210, 110 S.Ct. at 1030-31. In Washington, the Supreme Court held that the extent of a prisoner's right under the Due Process Clause to avoid the unwanted administration of an antipsychotic drug had to be defined within the context of the inmate's confinement. . . It was the procedural structure surrounding the nonconsensual administration of the medication that kept the state-sponsored invasion of bodily integrity within the boundaries of due process.

In applying the criterion of needless severity, the crucial factors are the presence of physical pain, the permanence of any disfigurement or ensuing complication, the risk of irreversible injury to health, and the danger to life itself. . . . However, an intrusion otherwise sufficiently minimal to pass this test is, nevertheless, beyond the boundaries of due process if less severe means could achieve the state's purpose with the same effectiveness. For example, the Supreme Court has unanimously held that compelling a suspect to submit to the surgical removal under general anesthesia of a bullet that authorities believed would link him to a crime violated the Constitution if the state already possessed substantial, independent evidence of the origin of the bullet.

The allegations in the Complaint indicate that procedural regularity was absent and that the invasion of bodily integrity was severe. In essence, the allegations in the Complaint amount to a claim that the individual Defendants blatantly lied to the Plaintiffs . . . the allegations give rise to the question of whether Plaintiffs were receiving medical treatment at all. This absence of procedural safeguards alone is sufficient to trigger the protections of the Due Process Clause. However, the allegations contained even more.

The allegations also indicate that the Plaintiffs received needlessly severe invasions of their bodily integrity. [T]he invasion Plaintiffs allege in this case was total and partial body radiation, which caused burns, vomiting, diarrhea and bone marrow failure, and resulted in death or severe shortening of life. These allegations are more than sufficient to trigger Fifth Amendment protection.

Thus, in accord with Barrett v. United States, 798 F.2d 565 (2nd Cir.1986), [FN15 Barrett involved a Plaintiff who had been the unwitting subject of a state-sponsored experiment with a mind altering drug. The experiment occurred in 1953, and when the Second Circuit Court of Appeals finally heard the case in 1986, the Court held that by sanctioning the experimental use of a deadly drug, the defendant officials were not exercising powers delegated to them by the government. Barrett is both factually and legally analogous to the instant case.] The Court is compelled to hold that the individual and Bivens Defendants may not assert the defense of qualified immunity. The qualified immunity defense is reserved to those officials who are sued for their exercise of discretionary responsibilities delegated to them by the government. There can be no doubt that the individual and Bivens Defendants' alleged instigation of and participation in the Human Radiation Experiments were acts far beyond the scope of their delegated powers. The individual and Bivens Defendants, many of whom were physicians, were not acting as physicians when they conducted experiments on unwitting subjects at Cincinnati General Hospital. Rather, the Defendants were acting as scientists interested in nothing more than assembling cold data for use by the Department of Defense. While many government officials are authorized to conduct research, the individual and Bivens Defendants were hired by the City to care for the sick and injured. The Constitution never authorizes government officials, regardless of their specific responsibilities, to arbitrarily deprive ordinary citizens of liberty and life.

Nevertheless, the Court will consider both prongs of the qualified immunity defense. First, the preceding analysis accepts, for purposes of this motion, the facts in the Complaint detailing state-sponsored experiments involving procedural due process irregularity, severe pain and death, and purposeful deception. These allegations are more than adequate to state a cause of action under the Due Process Clause of the Fourteenth Amendment.

B. Clearly Established Law

The Court must next determine whether the conduct alleged by Plaintiffs was clearly unconstitutional when the Human Radiation Experiments were performed. As the Court indicated previously, the right that Plaintiffs assert must have been sufficiently clear during the period between 1960 and 1972 that a reasonable official would have understood that his actions violated that right. See Anderson, 483 U.S. at 640, 107 S.Ct. at 3039. In order to gauge the clarity with which the claimed right has been established, this Court must look to the binding precedent of the Supreme Court, the Sixth Circuit Court of Appeals, and the District Court for the Southern District of Ohio. Due to the span of time between the acts alleged and the filing of this case, the Court is required to determine the state of the law three decades ago. Even more difficult is the fact that at this juncture of qualified immunity analysis, the Court is only concerned with the law as it stood between 1960 and 1972. If the Court concludes that a reasonable official would have known that the alleged conduct was unconstitutional-even if the analysis of that violation has changed in the ensuing decades-the Court will deny the individual and Bivens Defendants' qualified immunity defense on this claim.

The conduct attributed to the individual and Bivens Defendants-all representatives of government-strikes at the very core of the Constitution. Even absent the abundant case law that has developed on this point since the passage of the Bill of Rights, the Court would not hesitate to declare that a reasonable government official must have known that by instigating and participating in the experimental administration of high doses of radiation on unwitting subjects, he would have been acting in violation of those rights. Simply put, the legal tradition of this country and the plain language of the Constitution must lead a reasonable person to the conclusion that government officials may not arbitrarily deprive unwitting citizens of their liberty and their lives.

If the Constitution were held to permit the acts alleged in this case, the document would be revealed to contain a gaping hole. This is so in part because the alleged conduct is so outrageous in and of itself, and also because a constitution inadequate to deal with such outrageous conduct would be too feeble in method and doctrine to deal with a very great amount of equally outrageous activity. Indeed, virtually all of the rights that we as a nation hold sacred would be subject to the arbitrary whim of government.

Respect for an individual's right to bodily integrity is central to American constitutional history and tradition. The Constitution's Framers were heavily influenced by the enlightened views of popular sovereignty and limited government. For John Locke, the ideological father of the American Revolution, liberty was freedom from restraint, and the exercise of coercive power by the sovereign was always suspect. The function of the law, in Locke's view, was to protect individual liberty from restraint by government or others. A central principle in Locke's thinking was the essential need for a certain minimum area of personal freedom which must on no account be violated; for if it is overstepped, the individual will find himself in an area too narrow for even that minimum development of his natural faculties which alone make it possible to pursue, and even to conceive, the various ends which men hold good or right, or sacred. [Isaiah Berlin, FOUR ESSAYS ON LIBERTY 124 (1969)].

Indeed, this principle was reflected by Thomas Jefferson in the Declaration of Independence. [Garrett W. Sheldon, THE POLITICAL PHILOSOPHY OF THOMAS JEFFERSON, 9, 12 (1991)].

An individual's autonomy was, thus, the primary value in revolutionary idealism that led to colonial independence. Then, when the first ten amendments to the Constitution were ratified in 1791, six amendments made clear that the newly created national government was a government of limited authority. Our entire history has been a continuous effort to safeguard that concept of ordered liberty. Respect for individual autonomy by the government is a central principle within that ideal.

These principles of individual autonomy and liberty were absorbed into American legal theory and the doctrine of substantive due process. As indicated previously, while the common law understanding of the term "liberty" within the due process clause was initially limited to freedom from physical restraint, this concept has gradually expanded to include a variety of personal liberties. . . .

The Supreme Court has since construed the Due Process Clause of the Fourteenth Amendment not only to incorporate virtually all of the specific provisions of the Bill of Rights, but also to protect liberty interests not specifically enumerated in the Constitution itself. The Court has expressed the view that the Framers believed the full scope of the liberty guaranteed by the Due Process Clause could not be found in or limited by the precise terms of the specific guarantees elsewhere provided in the Constitution. Rather, in a constitution for free people, the meaning of liberty must be broad . . Like other constitutionally protected autonomy rights, the right to self-determination in matters of personal health is deeply rooted in our constitutional tradition. The right is an outgrowth of the "historic liberty interests in personal security and bodily integrity." . . .

The common law origins of the right of the individual to exercise control over health care decisions have also been recognized throughout this country's history. Almost 80 years ago, Justice Cardozo, then a Judge serving on the New York Court of Appeals, memorialized the right to make personal health decisions: "Every human being of adult years and sound mind has a right to determine what shall be done with his own body; and a surgeon who performs an operation without his patient's consent commits an assault for which he is liable in damages." Schloendorff v. Society of New York Hospital, 211 N.Y. 125, 105 N.E. 92, 93 (1914). Case law developing the informed consent doctrine as a device to protect patients' rights to refuse treatment is also grounded in the common law's deference to individual autonomy. . . .

Tort law has embraced this basic principle of informed consent in order to guard a patient's control over decisions affecting his or her own health. See Cruzan v. Director, Missouri Department of Health, 497 U.S. 261, 269, 110 S.Ct. 2841, 2846-47, 111 L.Ed.2d 224 (1990). Under the tort construct, absent an emergency or incompetency, the individual must voluntarily consent before medical treatment may be administered, and the physician is required to provide sufficient information so that the consent is informed. It is patently clear that the premise of the informed consent doctrine is the "concept, fundamental in American jurisprudence, that the individual may control what shall be done with his own body." Canterbury v. Spence, 464 F.2d 772, 780 (D.C.Cir.1972), cert. denied, 409 U.S. 1064, 93 S.Ct. 560, 34 L.Ed.2d 518 (1972).

Because of this historical protection by state tort law, the individual Defendants attempt to describe this case as one of "simple medical malpractice" or "an ordinary tort case" in order to circumvent Plaintiffs' Section 1983 claims. The individual and Bivens Defendants' argument is without merit, and the argument reveals an interpretation of the Constitution that would vitiate the fundamental constitutional principles just described. The distinction between this case and an ordinary tort case in not one of degree, but rather, of kind.

Government actors in cases such as this violate a different kind of duty from that owed by a private tort defendant. Individuals in our society are largely left free to pursue their own ends without regard for others, save a general duty not to harm others by negligent conduct. This is the "ordinary" tort case. The relationship between government and the individual is fundamentally different. In a free society, government is neither an autonomous actor nor a master to whom the people must acquiesce. The function of government is to serve the people and to enhance the quality of life. The broad purpose of all constitutional limits on government power is to ensure that government does not stray from that role or abuse its power.

. . . This Court concludes that between 1960 and 1972 the right to due process . . . was sufficiently clear to lead a reasonable government official to the conclusion that forcing unwitting subjects to receive massive doses of radiation was a violation of due process.

In 1905, the Supreme Court upheld compulsory vaccinations for smallpox. In Jacobson v. Massachusetts, 197 U.S. at 29, 25 S.Ct. at 362-63, the Court first acknowledged the existence of "a sphere within which the individual may assert the supremacy of his own will" against governmental interference. Recognizing that the state's police power interests in legislating to protect the public health, safety, and welfare could justify interfering with the individual's sphere of autonomy, the Court held that the minimal invasion of a vaccination coupled with the state's need to prevent a smallpox epidemic were sufficient to overcome the individual's liberty interest. Importantly, the Court suggested that the results in the case would have been different if the vaccination would have seriously impaired the petitioner's health. . . .

In the Human Radiation Experiments, it is alleged that the individual and Bivens Defendants designed and implemented experiments to study the effect of massive doses of radiation on military personnel during a nuclear war. To facilitate their experiments, the individual and Bivens Defendants are alleged to have targeted low income and African-American cancer patients from Cincinnati General Hospital. Plaintiffs allege that the Defendants did not even explain to their decedents that experiments were being conducted, what the purposes of the experiments were, or that the high doses of radiation could result in their death, shorten their lives substantially, or cause burns, nausea, vomiting, or bone marrow failure.

The invasions of bodily integrity alleged in this case are more extreme than those at issue in [previous cases]. . . Unlike the case[s] of Jacobson. . ., the invasion of bodily integrity alleged to have occurred in this case had extreme consequences, among them the most permanent of all possible consequences. Thus, had this set of facts come before this Court in 1972, the Court would have found that Plaintiffs had stated a valid claim under the Due Process Clause of the Constitution. The right at issue and its contours were sufficiently well-defined by the Supreme Court prior to 1972 such that the individual and Bivens Defendants should have known that their conduct would violate the Constitution.

C. The Nuremberg Code

The preceding demonstrates that the constitutional law controlling the invasion of an individual's bodily integrity was clearly established between 1960 and 1972. Indeed, the prevailing law detailing the right was sufficiently clear that a reasonable official would have known that the Human Radiation Experiments violated constitutional law. Accordingly, that law provides an independent basis for the Plaintiffs' Section 1983 action. Nevertheless, it is impossible for the Court to ignore the historical context in which the Human Radiation Experiments were conducted.

After World War II, the United States and its allies were involved in a succession of criminal trials. The trials have commonly become known as the Nuremberg trials. Perhaps the best known Nuremberg trial involved the military officers of the Third Reich. . . .

The Nuremberg tribunal was asked to determine the culpability of twenty-three (23) German physicians under "the principles of the law of nations as they result from the usages established among civilized peoples, from the laws of humanity, and from the dictates of public conscience." The charges against the physicians included human experimentation involving nonconsenting prisoners. The experiments included studies of the limits of human tolerance to high altitudes and freezing temperatures. Medically-related experiments included inoculation of prisoners with infectious disease pathogens and tests of new antibiotics. Various experiments involving the mutilation of bone, muscle and nerve were also performed on nonconsenting prisoner subjects.

Throughout the trial, the question of what were or should be the universal standards for justifying human experimentation recurred. "The lack of a universally accepted principle for carrying out human experimentation was the central issue pressed by the defendant physicians throughout their testimony."

. . .

The final judgment of the court was delivered on July 19, 1947. The judgment has since become known as the "Nuremberg Code." The first provision of the Code states as follows:

The voluntary consent of the human subject is absolutely essential. This means that the person involved should have legal capacity to give consent; should be so situated as to be able to exercise free power of choice without the intervention of any element of force, fraud, deceit, duress, overreaching, or other ulterior form of constraint or coercion and should have sufficient knowledge and comprehension of the elements of the subject matter involved as to enable him to make an understanding and enlightened decision. This latter element requires that before the acceptance of an affirmative decision by the experimental subject there should be made known to him the nature, duration, and purpose of the experiment; the method and means by which it is to be conducted; all inconveniences and hazards reasonably to be expected; and the effects upon his health and person which may possibly come from his participation in the experiment.

The duty and responsibility for ascertaining the quality of the consent rests upon each individual who initiates, directs, or engages in the experiment. It is a personal duty and responsibility which may not be delegated to another with impunity. . .

Only five years later, in recognition of these principles, the Secretary of Defense directed that human experimentation for the Department of Defense could only be conducted where there was full and voluntary consent of the subject. The directive issued by the Secretary of Defense is a mirror of the Nuremberg Code. . . .Also in the mid-1950's, the Clinical Center of the National Institutes of Health ("NIH") adopted guidelines that applied to the use of human subjects in experimental medical research. The NIH Guidelines state:

The rigid safeguards observed at NIH are based on the so-called "ten commandments" of human medical research which were adopted at the Nuremberg War Crimes Trials after the atrocities performed by Nazi doctors had been exposed.

Every subject must give his full consent to any test, and he must be told exactly what it involves so that he goes into it with his eyes open. Among other things, the experiment must be designed to yield "fruitful results for the good of society," unnecessary "physical and mental suffering and injury" must be avoided, the test must be conducted by "scientifically qualified" persons, and the subject must be free to end it at any time he feels unable to go on. . . .

The Nuremberg Code is part of the law of humanity. It may be applied in both civil and criminal cases by the federal courts in the United States. At the very least, by the time the Human Radiation Experiments were designed, the Nuremberg Code served as a tangible example of conduct that "shocked the conscience," as contemplated in Rochin, supra. Rochin came only five years after the Nuremberg trials. Certainly Justice Frankfurter and the other members of the Court were influenced by the state-sponsored atrocities delineated in the Medical Case. Thus, even were the Nuremberg Code not afforded precedential weight in the courts of the United States, it cannot be readily dismissed from its proper context in this case. The individual and Bivens Defendants, as physicians and other health professionals, must have been aware of the Nuremberg Code, the Hippocratic Oath, and the several pronouncements by both world and American medical organizations adopting the Nuremberg Code. It is inconceivable to the Court that the individual and Bivens Defendants, when allegedly planning to perform radiation experiments on unwitting subjects, were not moved to pause or rethink their procedures in light of the forceful dictates of the Nuremberg Tribunal and the several medical organizations.. . .

The allegations in this case indicate that the government of the United States, aided by officials of the City of Cincinnati, treated at least eighty-seven (87) of its citizens as though they were laboratory animals. If the Constitution has not clearly established a right under which these Plaintiffs may attempt to prove their case, then a gaping hole in that document has been exposed. The subject of experimentation who has not volunteered is merely an object. The Plaintiffs in this case must be afforded at least the opportunity to present their case. As Justice O'Connor indicated in her dissent from United States v. Stanley, 483 U.S. 669, 107 S.Ct. 3054, 97 L.Ed.2d 550 (1987), [t]he United States military played an instrumental role in the criminal prosecution of Nazi officials who experimented with human beings during the Second World War ... and the standards that the Nuremberg Military Tribunals developed to judge the behavior of the defendants stated that the voluntary consent of the human subject is absolutely essential ... to satisfy moral, ethical, and legal concepts.... If this principle is violated, the very least society can do is to see that the victims are compensated, as best they can be, by the perpetrators. I am prepared to say that our Constitution's promise of due process of law guarantees this much.

The doctrine of qualified immunity does not insulate the individual and Bivens Defendants from liability for their deliberate and calculated exposure of cancer patients to harmful medical experimentation without their informed consent. No judicially-crafted rule insulates from examination the state-sponsored involuntary and unknowing human experimentation alleged to have occurred in this case. Accordingly, the individual and Bivens Defendants' motion to dismiss the substantive due process claim is DENIED.

V. THE SUBSTANTIVE RIGHT OF ACCESS TO COURTS AND PROCEDURAL DUE PROCESS. . .

As with the Court's analysis of Plaintiffs' substantive due process claims, here the Court must first determine whether the Plaintiffs have alleged the violation of a constitutional right under current law and, if so, determine whether the constitutional right was clearly established at the time of the alleged conduct.

. . .

In the Complaint, Plaintiffs claim that the individual Defendants intentionally did not explain the experiments' true nature and the risks for their subjects. Additionally, Plaintiffs claim that the individual Defendants failed to tell the patients that they were the subjects of experiments, funded by the Department of Defense, to study the effects of radiation on human beings in the event of a nuclear attack. Finally, Plaintiffs assert that the individual Defendants continued to conceal this information from Plaintiffs until press reports revealed the existence of the Human Radiation Experiments in 1994 and identified the names of some subjects of the Human Radiation Experiments.

The individual and Bivens Defendants contend that Plaintiffs' claim fails because the Sixth Circuit Court of Appeals explicitly and unequivocally held that fraudulent concealment claims, such as those made by Plaintiffs in this litigation, could not form the basis of a Section 1983 access to the courts claim. See Joyce v. Mavromatis, 783 F.2d 56 (6th Cir.1986).

. . .Indeed, the facts in this case are analogous to those in Ryland v. Shapiro, 708 F.2d 967 (5th Cir.1983). In Ryland, allegations of conduct by prosecutors in falsifying a death certificate and in covering up a murder for a period of 11 months were held to state a claim for deprivation of a claimant's right of access to the courts:

Conduct by state officers which results in delay in the prosecution of an action in state court may cause such prejudice.... Delay haunts the administration of justice. It postpones the rectification of wrong and the vindication of the unjustly accused. It crowds the dockets of the courts, increasing the costs for all litigants, pressuring judges to disposition of those causes in which all parties are diligent.... But even these are not the worst of what delay does. The most erratic gear in the justice machinery is at the place of fact finding, and possibilities for error multiply rapidly as time elapses between the original fact and its judicial determination.

. . . When the Human Radiation Experiments were conducted, the Plaintiffs' right of access to the courts was clearly established under the Fourteenth Amendment's Due Process Clause as well as the First Amendment's right to petition for redress of grievances. . . . Consequently, the Court finds that the Plaintiffs' constitutional right of access to the courts was clearly established at the time of the alleged misconduct so that a reasonable official should have known whether or not his conduct violated the law.

For the reasons set forth above, the individual and Bivens Defendants' motion to dismiss Plaintiffs' access to courts claim is DENIED.

B. Procedural Due Process

. . . In the Complaint, Plaintiffs allege that all of their claims have been substantially compromised by the conduct of the individual Defendants in concealing from Plaintiffs the true purpose and dangers of the Human Radiation Experiments. Plaintiffs allege that they have completely lost their ability to pursue a wrongful death claim. Plaintiffs assert that crucial evidence has been lost, including the subjects of the experiments themselves who may have witnessed the consent procedures, and also the percipient witnesses.

As was the case with Plaintiffs' access to courts claim, the Court finds that Plaintiffs have sufficiently alleged that their claims have been substantially compromised by the individual Defendants' conduct in concealing the true purpose and dangers associated with the Human Radiation Experiments. Likewise, as far back as 1882, the Supreme Court established that a cause of action is protected under the Due Process Clause. . . .Accordingly, the Court finds that these constitutional rights were clearly established at the time of the alleged conduct so that a reasonable official would have known that his conduct violated the law. In light of the preceding analysis, the individual and Bivens Defendants' motion to dismiss the Plaintiffs' procedural due process claim is DENIED.

. . .

VII. EQUAL PROTECTION

Plaintiffs have made a Section 1983 claim alleging that they have been denied equal protection of the laws under the Fourteenth Amendment of the Constitution. Unlike their defenses to Plaintiffs' other Section 1983 claims, the individual Defendants do not assert that the law of equal protection was not clearly established during the period of the Human Radiation Experiments. Rather, the individual Defendants argue that Plaintiffs have failed to adequately state an equal protection claim and thus move for a dismissal of that claim under Rule 12(b)(6) of the Federal Rules of Civil Procedure.

The Constitution guarantees that no state shall deprive any person "the equal protection of the laws." . . . Plaintiffs allege that the Human Radiation Experiments were directed predominantly at African-Americans. Plaintiffs also allege that the individual Defendants intentionally discriminated against them by purposefully targeting African-Americans as subjects. In an inartful passage of their Complaint, Plaintiffs assert that the disparity between the racial composition of the general population of patients at General Hospital vis-a-vis patients selected for the Human Radiation Experiments demonstrates that one purpose of the experiments was to subject African-Americans to high levels of radiation.

It is well-settled that facially neutral official acts can be administered in such a discriminatory fashion as to violate the Equal Protection Clause. . . .Plaintiffs in this action assert that like Castaneda and Yick Wo, the facially neutral Human Radiation Experiments were administered in such a way as to intentionally discriminate against African-Americans.

Disparate impact alone is not sufficient to state a valid equal protection claim. In Washington v. Davis, supra, and in *829 Village of Arlington Heights v. Metropolitan Housing Development Corp., 429 U.S. 252, 97 S.Ct. 555, 50 L.Ed.2d 450 (1977), the Supreme Court indicated that evidence of intent in addition to disparate impact (where the disparate impact was not extreme) was necessary to state an equal protection claim. To satisfy this additional pleading requirement, Plaintiffs assert that the predominance of African-Americans in the Human Radiation Experiments was not coincidental. Rather, Plaintiffs assert that African-American cancer patients were purposefully targeted as subjects for the Human Radiation Experiments. That allegation of intent, Plaintiffs contend, is sufficient to meet the pleading requirements of Washington and Arlington Heights.

The individual Defendants, on the other hand, contend that the Court need not examine the disparity in racial composition of the subject groups of the Human Radiation Experiments because Plaintiffs have failed to meet the threshold requirement that similarly situated persons were treated differently. Indeed, at oral argument, liaison counsel for the individual Defendants argued that the similarly situated persons at issue are the subjects of the Human Radiation Experiments. Thus, counsel contended, the Plaintiffs must demonstrate that African-American subjects were treated differently from the Caucasian subjects of the Human Radiation Experiments. Defense counsel's universe is simply too small. Plaintiffs allege that when the individual Defendants determined who would become subjects in the Human Radiation Experiments, they did so with racial animus. Obviously, then, the similarly situated group at issue is that universe of people from which the individual Defendants could have chosen their subjects. This fact reveals in part why the Court does not today dismiss the Plaintiffs' equal protection claim. The record in this case must be developed in order to determine what the universe of patients was and whether the racial composition of that group was similar to the racial composition of the subjects of the Human Radiation Experiments. The question of racial animus is also a fact-intensive question.

 . . .Here, Plaintiffs have pleaded that the subjects in the Human Radiation Experiments were predominantly African-American, and that the subjects for the experiments were chosen as a result of racial animus on the part of the individual Defendants. . . . Of course, if facts supporting this claim do not appear, the Court is confident that the parties will present this issue at summary judgment. Accordingly, the individual and Bivens Defendants' motion to dismiss this claim is DENIED.

. . .CONCLUSION

For all the reasons set forth herein, the individual and Bivens Defendants' motions to dismiss are GRANTED in part and DENIED in part. Plaintiffs have stated claims for violations of their constitutional rights of substantive due process, procedural due process, access to the courts, and equal protection as well as a claim for a violation of 42 U.S.C. § 1985. Thus, Defendants' motions to dismiss these claims are DENIED. . . .

IT IS SO ORDERED.

6.11.3. Population experimentation in biodefense

Nevin v. United States
696 F.2d 1229 (9th Cir. 1983)

Wrongful death action was brought under the Federal Tort Claims Act claiming that death occurred as result of Government's negligence in conducting simulated biological warfare attack on San Francisco in 1950. The United States District Court for the Northern District of California, Samuel Conti, J., concluded in part that Government was immune from suit, and appeal was taken. The Court of Appeals, Choy, Circuit Judge, held that chief chemical officer's decision to use particular strain of bacterium in simulated attack was made at the planning level and thus was exempt as discretionary function under the Tort Claims Act.

Vacated and remanded.

Norris, Circuit Judge, filed a dissenting opinion.

Purpose of discretionary function exemption under the Federal Tort Claims Act is to permit government to make planning level decisions without fear of suit. 28 U.S.C.A. § 2680(a).

Decision by chief chemical officer, who was responsible for final authorization of all test plans concerning biological warfare vulnerability, to use particular strain of bacterium in simulated biological warfare attack on San Francisco in 1950 was made at the planning level and thus decision to use particular strain of bacterium was exempt as a discretionary function under the Federal Tort Claims Act. 28 U.S.C.A. § 2680(a).

―――――――――

Whether discretionary function exemption under Federal Tort Claims Act applies is question of subject-matter jurisdiction. 28 U.S.C.A. § 2680(a).

Appeal from the United States District Court for the Northern District of California.

Before CHOY and NORRIS, Circuit Judges, and SMITH, District Judge.

CHOY, Circuit Judge:

Relatives of Edward Nevin appeal from a judgment in favor of the United States in this wrongful-death action brought under the Federal Tort Claims Act (the FTCA), 28 U.S.C. § 1346(b). They claim that Nevin died as a result of the Government's negligence in conducting a simulated biological warfare attack on the City of San Francisco in 1950. The district court concluded in part that the Government was immune from suit because its acts fell within the discretionary function exemption to the FTCA, 28 U.S.C. § 2680(a).

On appeal, the Nevins concede that the selection of the test site fell within the discretionary function exemption, but argue that the selection of the strain of bacterium used did not. Even assuming that we should isolate the selection of the strain of bacterium from the selection of the site, we conclude that the decision to use the particular strain was exempt as a discretionary function.

[1] The discretionary function exemption provides, in pertinent part, that the United States has not waived sovereign immunity on [a]ny claim ... based upon the exercise or performance or the failure to exercise or perform a discretionary function or duty on the part of a federal agency or an employee of the Government, whether or not the discretion involved be abused.

28 U.S.C. § 2680(a). The purpose of the exemption is to permit the government to make planning-level decisions without fear of suit. Dalehite v. United States, 346 U.S. 15, 32, 73 S.Ct. 956, 966, 97 L.Ed. 1427 (1953); Lindgren v. United States, 665 F.2d 978, 980 (9th Cir.1982).

[2] In this circuit, whether an act or omission falls within the exemption depends generally on whether that act or omission occurred at the planning level or the operational level of government. Weiss v. Lehman, 676 F.2d 1320, 1322 (9th Cir.1982), cert. denied, 459 U.S. 1103, 103 S.Ct. 725, 74 L.Ed.2d 953 (1983); Lindgren, 665 F.2d at 980. In making the determination, we have also considered the ability of the judiciary to evaluate the act or omission and whether the judicial evaluation would impair the effective administration of the government. Lindgren, 665 F.2d at 980 (citing Driscoll v. United States, 525 F.2d 136, 138 (9th Cir.1975)).

[3] There is ample evidence in the record to support the conclusion that the decision by the Chief Chemical Officer, General Anthony McAuliffe, to use the particular *1231 strain of bacterium was made at the planning level. It is undisputed that General McAuliffe was responsible for the final authorization of all test plans concerning biological warfare vulnerability. He made the decision to use San Francisco as the site. He personally approved the selection of serratia marcescens recommended by scientific and medical advisory personnel. That approval came only after General McAuliffe and one of his fellow officers conducted independent evaluations concerning the safety of the strain of bacterium. The final decision of whether to proceed with any given test or program rested with General McAuliffe and, as the district court noted, "although he tended to rely on his technical advisors he was not bound to do so.... General McAuliffe could have withheld his approval for the test for any reason, including the technical advice he was given or simply on his own judgment as to the inadvisability of conducting the test." Indeed, General McAuliffe himself rejected the plan to conduct a test using the same strain in the subways of New York.

In making the decisions concerning the testing, including which strain of bacterium to use, General McAuliffe had to weigh numerous factors, including concerns for national security, a need for secrecy, the possible risks of urban testing, and applicable medical concerns. As the Nevins admit, the higher the governmental rank involved in making any decision of this type, the more likely it is that political, social, military and economic factors were weighed. Upon careful reflection, we do not think that this court is equipped to weigh the type of factors involved in such a basic policy determination. In addition, our review would likely impair the effective administration of government programs believed to be vital to the defense of the United States at the time that they are conducted.

[4] In summary, none of the considerations we examine to determine the applicability of the discretionary function exemption calls for reversal of the district court's determination. Whether the discretionary function exemption applies, however, is a question of subject-matter jurisdiction. Lindgren, 665 F.2d at 983. We must, therefore, vacate the judgment of the district court and remand the case with instruction to dismiss the action for lack of subject-matter jurisdiction.

VACATED and REMANDED.

NORRIS, Circuit Judge, dissenting:

I cannot agree that General McAuliffe's decision to use a particular strain of bacterium in conducting a simulated biological attack on the City of San Francisco falls within the discretionary function exemption to the Federal Tort Claims Act, 28 U.S.C. § 2680(a) (1976).

That decision, in my view, was made at the operational, not the planning level of government. As appellant readily concedes, the decision to conduct a simulated attack on San Francisco was a planning decision that did fall within the exemption. It required the weighing of political, social and military factors and, as such, is a decision the judiciary is ill-equipped to review. But once that policy decision was made, its execution necessarily involved a myriad of decisions at the operational level which are not insulated from judicial review.FN1 The choice of bacterium was one such decision. 8 UK was chosen not on the basis of political*1232 or military concerns, but on the basis of medical and scientific ones. Care had to be exercised in selecting a bacterium that would not constitute a health hazard. Whether there was failure to exercise due care in making that decision is the type of question frequently subjected to judicial scrutiny. See United States v. DeCamp, 478 F.2d 1188 (9th Cir.), cert. denied 414 U.S. 924 (1973); Hendry v. United States, 418 F.2d 774, 783 (2d Cir.1969) ("[t]he judgments arrived at by the doctors are not different in complexity from those which courts are accustomed to entertain when tort suits are brought against private physicians.")

FN1. See S.A. Emprasa De Viacao Aerea Rio Grandense v. United States, 692 F.2d 1205, 1208 (9th Cir.1982) ("The discretionary function exemption was primarily intended to preclude tort claims arising from decisions by executives or administrators when such decisions require policy choices."); Miller v. United States, 583 F.2d 857, 866 (6th Cir.1978) ("The discretionary function exception does not insulate the Government from liability for all mistakes of judgment of its agents, but only for significant policy and political decisions, the types of governmental decisions which should not be circumscribed by customary tort standards."); Griffin v. United States, 500 F.2d 1059, 1066 (3d Cir.1974) ("Where the conduct of Government employees in implementing agency regulations requires only performance of scientific evaluation and not the formulation of policy, we do not believe that the conduct is immunized from judicial review as a 'discretionary function.' ")

I would hold that the district court had subject matter jurisdiction over plaintiff's action, but would affirm the judgment on the ground that the district court's finding that the bacteria used by the Army did not cause Nevin's death was not clearly erroneous.

CHAPTER SIX ENDNOTES

----

[1] Anti-Terrorism and Death Penalty Act of 1996,

[2] "I am a scientist. I am absolutely of no harm to anyone." Quoted at sentencing in 1997.

[3] 42 CFR § 72.

[4] 70 Fed. Reg. 13294, 13297 (March 18, 2005), Final Rule

[5] 61 Fed. Reg. 55190, Oct. 24, 1996.

[6] USA PATRIOT Act of 2001.

[7] U.S. Dept of Justice, Press Release, November 19, 2002.

[8] 42 CFR § 73.

[9] 61 FR 55190, Oct. 24, 1996, Final Rule.

[10] 61 FR 55190 (Oct. 24, 1996), Final Rule.

[11] *Serratia marcensens,* a usually harmless bacteria, has a bright red color.

[12] *Solid Waste Agency of Northern Cook County v. United States Army Corps of Engineers,* 531 U.S. 159, 172 (2001) (emphasis added).

[13] *Id.* at 172-73 (emphasis added).

Chapter Seven
Federal Statutes for Crimes of Bioterrorism

This chapter will discuss the federal criminal statutes which are applicable to bioterrorism and some of the weapons of mass destruction cases that would also be applicable to acts of bioterrorism. Pivotal cases in the development of the law in biosecurity are included here. Although it was never brought to trial nor was an indictment made, the Amerithrax investigation was a turning point in the development of the framework of biosecurity, bioterrorism and biosafety laws which have been passed and implemented since the anthrax attacks of the fall of 2001. However, the criminal procedure and the investigation include important aspects of investigating biocrimes, scientists and understanding the science. In fact, this section might have been included in Chapter Six on biological research regulation since almost all of the investigation centered in biological laboratories, and laws were passed based on the presumption that the Amerithrax crime originated in laboratories probably involving research scientists. However, since the focus of this discussion seems most appropriate to be on the criminal procedure --- specifically the use of search warrants in the Amerithrax investigation --- it has been included at the end of this chapter.

The Biological Weapons and Anti-Terrorism Act of 1989 was passed, in part, to satisfy our obligation under the Biological Weapons and Toxins Convention which entered into force on March 26, 1975, which requires state parties to the Convention to pass domestic legislation prohibiting bioterrorism. The statute is constructed with similar language in the Convention. This statute has been applied to cases involving the mailing of anthrax, for example. Since 1989, the statute has been amended broadening its scope, with the 1996 Anti-Terrorism and Death Penalty Act and in 2001 with the USA PATRIOT Act. The authority to pass the federal criminal statute is based on Constitutional Commerce Clause power of Congress. In the following cases, it is the Commerce Clause scope and application which is challenged in this statute in the pre-anthrax attacks period.

7.1. Biological Weapons and Anti-Terrorism Act of 1989
18 USCS §175
§175. Prohibitions with respect to biological weapons
(a) In general. Whoever knowingly develops, produces, stockpiles, transfers, acquires, retains, or possesses any biological agent, toxin, or delivery system for use as a weapon, or knowingly assists a

foreign state or any organization to do so, or attempts, threatens, or conspires to do the same, shall be fined under this title or imprisoned for life or any term of years, or both. There is extraterritorial Federal jurisdiction over an offense under this section committed by or against a national of the United States.

(b) Definition. For purposes of this section, the term "for use as a weapon" does not include the development, production, transfer, acquisition, retention, or possession of any biological agent, toxin, or delivery system for prophylactic, protective, or other peaceful purposes.

7.2. Anti-Terrorism and Effective Death Penalty Act of 1996
18 USCS §2332a (Supp. 2001)
§2332a. Use of certain weapons of mass destruction

(a) Offense against a national of the United States or within the United States. A person who, without lawful authority, uses, threatens, or attempts or conspires to use, a weapon of mass destruction (other than a chemical weapon as that term is defined in section 229F), including any biological agent, toxin, or vector (as those terms are defined in section 178)

(1) against a national of the United States while such national is outside of the United States;

(2) against any person within the United States, and the results of such use affect interstate or foreign commerce or, in the case of a threat, attempt, or conspiracy, would have affected interstate or foreign commerce; or

(3) against any property that is owned, leased or used by the United States or by any department or agency of the United States, whether the property is within or outside of the United States, shall be imprisoned for any term of years or for life, and if death results, shall be punished by death or imprisoned for any term of years or for life.

(b) Offense by national of the United State outside of the United States. Any national of the United States who, without lawful authority, uses, or threatens, attempts, or conspires to use, a weapon of mass destruction (other than a chemical weapon (as that term is defined in section 229F)) outside of the United States shall be imprisoned for any term of years or for life, and if death results, shall be punished by death, or by imprisonment for any term of years or for life.

(c) Definitions. For purposes of this section—

(1) the term "national of the United States" has the meaning given in section 101(a)(22) of the Immigration and Nationality Act (8 U.S.C. 1101(a)(22)); and

(2) the term "weapon of mass destruction" means—

(A) any destructive device as defined in section 921 of this title;

(B) any weapon that is designed or intended to cause death or serious bodily injury through the release, dissemination, or impact of toxic or poisonous chemicals, or their precursors;

(C) any weapon involving a disease organism; or

(D) any weapon that is designed to release radiation or radioactivity at a level dangerous to human life.

United States v. Wise
221 F.3d 140 (5th Cir. 2000)

OPINION District Judge LITTLE

Defendants-appellants Johnie Wise ("Wise") and Jack Abbott Grebe, Jr. ("Grebe") appeal the judgment of criminal conviction entered on 5 February 1999, in the United States District Court for the Southern District of Texas, Brownsville Division. Appellants argue that a number of errors occurred with regard to the trial, as a result of which this Court should find the evidence insufficient to sustain their conviction or, alternatively, reverse and remand for a new trial. We AFFIRM the judgment and the district court in all respects.

I. BACKGROUND
A. Facts of the Case

In March 1998, while shopping at a store in Harlingen, Texas called the "Bargain Barn," John Cain ("Cain"), a self-employed computer consultant, met owner John Roberts ("Roberts") and employee Oliver Dean Emigh ("Emigh"). During the course of conversation, Roberts told Cain that he was a member of the Republic of Texas ("ROT")[1] and often needed documents typed for ROT legal matters. Cain offered his assistance and returned to the Bargain Barn the next day to discuss computer-related topics with Roberts. Cain briefly met Johnie Wise, another ROT member, during the meeting.

Cain [an informant] eventually accepted the position of "Undersecretary of Trade and Commerce" for ROT. Between the April 29 meeting and Cain's next meeting with Agent Church on 20 May 1998, Wise and Grebe shared with Cain their angry sentiment that the "change in power" (referring to the re-establishment of Texas as a Republic, with its own government) was taking too long. They proposed having Emigh draft a letter to send out to the various government agencies previously mentioned. Not long thereafter, Wise and Grebe gave Cain a handwritten letter that laid out their plan, specifically targeting the IRS and the DEA. Wise and Grebe made some changes to that letter, and Cain typed the letter into the computer at their instruction.

On 20 May 1998, Cain met with Agent Church to describe the plan in greater detail and to deliver a copy of the letter. Agent Church told Cain that the FBI was interested in any information Cain received and that Agent Church was recommending the opening of an FBI investigation. Furthermore, he told Cain to get detailed information regarding the plan if Cain met again with Wise and Grebe.

A few days later, Wise gave Cain a third and final draft of the letter, titled "Declaration of War." Grebe was present and participated in making the changes. Cain typed the letter into the computer as instructed, printed several copies of the document, and saved it on a computer disk. Wise and Grebe asked Cain to find the e-mail addresses of the select government agencies and to send the letter anonymously via e-mail such that it would not be traced back to his computer. They discussed the idea of using a computer terminal at the Brownsville public library and transmitting the letter through the Anonymizer website so that if it were traced somehow, it would be traced to the library rather than to Cain.

Grebe later handed Cain another typed document, a follow-up letter to the first that was to be sent if the response to the first letter was deemed unsatisfactory.[2] If the response to the second letter in turn were deemed unsatisfactory, then the next step in the plan was to act upon the threat by actually infecting people with a biological agent. According to the plan, Wise was to procure the biological agent

---

[1] The Republic of Texas is an organization that is dedicated to removing all federal government operations from the State of Texas and re-establishing Texas as an independent nation.

[2] The second letter reads:

Dear Mr. Rossotti,

Your IRS employees and their families have been targeted for destruction by revenge. These people are extremely mad and will not accept the inequities any longer. Non-traceable, personal delivery systems have been developed to inject bacteria and/or viruses for the purpose of killing, maiming, and causing great suffering. Warn all concerned so that they may protect themselves and be made aware of this threat to themselves and their families. Good luck!

and to build the delivery device. Wise discussed the possibility of using such agents as botulism, rabies, and anthrax. According to Cain, Wise and Grebe urged Cain to send the Declaration of War e-mail because they thought he was taking too long to do so.

On 1 June 1998, Cain handed over to the FBI, who by now had opened an official investigation, a copy of the final draft of the Declaration of War and a copy of the Rossotti letter. Agent Church told Cain not to e-mail anything until he received proper approval. He again told Cain that the latter should obtain as much specific information as possible and notify the FBI if anything of an emergency nature arose.

The case became assigned to FBI Agent Franklin Sharkey ("Agent Sharkey"). Cain consented to Agent Sharkey's request to record their conversations. Subsequently, the FBI set up electronic surveillance and authorized Cain to send e-mails in an undercover investigation. The FBI rejected Cain's idea of using a public library computer and suggested instead that Cain use his home computer. On 11 June 1998, Cain called Wise and Grebe to tell them he was ready. They set the date and time for sending the Declaration of War for the following evening.

Grebe arrived at Cain's residence on 12 June 1998, and as planned, the Declaration of War was sent via e-mail to the United States Department of Justice, the DEA, the United States Treasury, the FBI, the United States Customs, and the Bureau of Alcohol, Tobacco, and Firearms....Cain called Wise to tell him that the Declaration of War had been sent. A tape recording of their conversation indicates that Wise was aware that the e-mails would be sent and was abreast of the situation overall.

After the first set of e-mails were sent, Cain continued to meet with Wise and Grebe....Grebe raised the notion of taking the next step, namely sending the follow-up letter to the Declaration of War. Moreover, both Wise and Grebe discussed who should be the first targeted victim, and they chose a Texas state judge whom Roberts purportedly disliked because she had not allowed ROT members to defend themselves pro se in her Texas state court....They planned to stalk her, learn her movements, and attack at the right moment. Wise suggested the use of rabies or botulism toxins for the delivery device and discussed ways to make botulism. Wise told the others that he already had purchased the parts to convert the Bic (R) lighters into delivery devices. After that meeting, Cain immediately called Agent Sharkey, who in turn advised Cain that the situation had become more serious now that a particular person was targeted....

3. Interstate Commerce Element

The third issue raised is whether the district court abused its discretion in refusing to charge the jury that the offense must have "substantially affected" interstate commerce. The district court gave the following jury instruction, in relevant part:

Title 18, United States Code, Section 2332a makes it a crime for anyone to threaten to use a weapon of mass destruction against any person within the United States and results of such use would have affected interstate or foreign commerce.

For you to find the Defendant guilty of this crime, you must be convinced that the government has proved each of the following beyond a reasonable doubt:

First: That the defendant intentionally and knowingly threatened to use a weapon or weapons of mass destruction;

Second: That the weapon or weapons of mass destruction were threatened to be used against persons within the United States as specifically alleged in Counts 2–8;

Third: That the results of such use would have affected interstate or foreign commerce.

(18 R., Attach. at 29–30.) In essence, Appellants argue that the district court erred in refusing to instruct the jury that a violation of 18 U.S.C. §2332a(a) requires a finding by them of a substantial effect on interstate commerce.

Section 2332a(a) provides in relevant part:

A person who, without lawful authority, uses, threatens, or attempts or conspires to use, a weapon of mass destruction...,including any biological agent, toxin, or vector (as those terms are defined in section 178)...against any person within the United States, and the results of such use affect interstate or foreign commerce or, in the case of a threat, attempt, or conspiracy, would have affected interstate or foreign commerce...shall be imprisoned for any term of years or for life....18 U.S.C. §2332a(a)(2).

Appellants were convicted on two counts of threatening to use a weapon of mass destruction, namely a biological agent and a weapon involving a disease organism, against persons within the United States. The statute on its face makes clear that, in the case of a threat, it applies where the results would have affected interstate or foreign commerce. The jury instruction in this case tracked the language of the statute by making as an essential element the government's proof beyond a reasonable doubt that the results of use of the weapon of mass destruction would have affected interstate or foreign commerce. The statute does not require, in the case of a threat, an actual or substantial effect on commerce; it requires only a showing that the use would have affected commerce. The jury instruction given by the court below, therefore, was proper.

In any event, the e-mails, which had been sent from Texas, were received by government agencies outside of Texas. For example, the FBI received the e-mails in California; the United States Customs received the e-mails at its website in Virginia; the ATF, the Secret Service, and the Office of Correspondence for the President all received the e-mails in Washington, D.C. The threat itself crossed state boundaries; therefore, it cannot be argued that an effect on interstate commerce is lacking in this case.

Appellants call into question the sufficiency of the evidence as to the effect on interstate commerce. Specifically, Appellants allege that the government failed to present any testimony or documentary evidence that the use of the weapon specified in the threat would have affected interstate commerce. As previously discussed, the e-mails, which had been sent by Appellants from Texas, were received by government agencies outside of Texas. The threat itself, therefore, crossed state boundaries. Since the IRS and the DEA are located outside of, and received the threat letters outside of, Texas, logic dictates that had Appellants actually carried out their threat, their action would have had consequences outside of Texas, where the IRS and the DEA are located. Viewing the evidence in the light most favorable to the jury's verdict, a rational trier of fact could have found that the interstate commerce element was satisfied in this case beyond a reasonable doubt....

III. CONCLUSION

The indictment sufficiently alleged the elements of an offense under 18 U.S.C. §2332a in charging that Appellants intentionally and knowingly threatened to use a weapon of mass destruction, in violation of 18 U.S.C. §2332a(a)(2) and (c)(2)(C), and 18 U.S.C. §2. The evidence fully supports the jury's verdict as to counts five and six of the indictment. The district court did not abuse its discretion in refusing to charge the jury that the offense "substantially affected" interstate commerce. The evidence supports the jury's finding that Appellants caused a threat to use a weapon of mass destruction to be communicated. Although the prosecutor made improper remarks during his closing argument, such remarks did not substantially affect the verdict. The district court did not abuse its discretion in denying Appellants' motion for judgment of acquittal based on the defense of entrapment. The district court properly declined to instruct the jury on the issue of spoliation. And finally, the district court did not abuse its discretion in allowing Agent Decker's expert opinion testimony. For these reasons, we deny the relief sought by Appellants and AFFIRM the district court's ruling and judgment in all respects.

AFFIRMED

————

The previous case was a successful conviction under 18 USCS §2332a (2001), finding the interstate commerce provision to be satisfied. Shortly after the U.S. Supreme Court decided *United States v. Lopez*, the Biological Weapons Act of 1989 was challenged as unconstitutional in the following case:

United States v. Baker
98 F.3d 330 (8th Cir. 1996)

OPINION by Circuit Judge McMillian

Douglas Allen Baker and Leroy Charles Wheeler appeal from final judgments entered in the District Court for the District of Minnesota, upon a jury verdict, finding each guilty of aiding and abetting the other in knowingly possessing a toxin for use as a weapon in violation of 18 U.S.C. §175, 2....

INTERSTATE OR FOREIGN COMMERCE NEXUS—LOPEZ DEFENSE

Next, both defendants argue 18 U.S.C. §175 is not a valid exercise of congressional power under the commerce clause in light of United States v. Lopez, 131 L. Ed. 2d 626, 115 S. Ct. 1624 (1995), because there is no substantial nexus between interstate or foreign commerce and the offense of possession of ricin for use as a weapon. In United States v. Lopez the Supreme Court held that Congress exceeded its authority under the commerce clause when it enacted the Gun-Free School Zones Act, which made it a federal offense knowingly to possess a firearm within 1000' of a school, because that activity had no substantial relation to interstate commerce. 115 S. Ct. at 1629–30. The statute, by its terms, had "nothing to do with commerce or any sort of economic enterprise," contained "no jurisdictional element which would ensure, through case-by-case inquiry, that the firearm possession in question affects interstate commerce, and there were no congressional findings that would have enabled the Court "to evaluate the legislative judgment that the activity in question substantially affected interstate commerce." Id. at 1630.

Defendants did not raise this issue in the district court and raise this issue for the first time on appeal. (Wheeler amended his brief on appeal to join Baker in raising this issue.) In pre-trial motions defendants argued the statute was unconstitutional because it was vague and overbroad. At sentencing Baker argued the statute was unconstitutional on several grounds but did not raise the commerce clause issue. The failure to raise the issue in the district court constitutes a waiver of the issue. E.g., United States v. Flaherty, 76 F.3d at 973 (failure to raise Lopez issue in district court resulted in waiver);...Although the Supreme Court decided Lopez on April 26, 1995, several months after defendants' trial in February 1995, this is not a case in which the law changed so dramatically and unexpectedly so as to excuse the failure to raise the issue in the district court. Lopez was argued to the Supreme Court on November 8, 1994, and the commerce clause arguments were widely known. Defendants were indicted in July 1994, the trial was held in February 1995, and Baker was sentenced on May 18, 1995, and Wheeler on June 1, 1995. Defendants could have raised the commerce clause arguments either at trial or at sentencing.

————

However, the interstate commerce clause argument was successful in the following case, where the court found that the facts of the case did not meet the requirements of a "substantial effect on interstate commerce". This indicates some question of the constitutionality of federal regulation of bioterrorism among the Circuit Courts.

In *Slaughter,* the incarcerated defendant is entitled to acquittal on the charge of violation of 18 U.S.C.S. 2332a(a)(2) for mailing letters containing a white powder and threatening that it contains anthrax to a prosecutor and to a television station, based upon a failure to prove that it had a substantial effect on interstate commerce.

United States v. Slaughter
116 F. Supp. 2d 688 (W.D. Va., 2000)

S. Catherine Dodson is a deputy state prosecutor in Norfolk, Virginia. In 1997, she was a supervisor in charge of the violent crime team, and in that capacity, she successfully prosecuted George Slaughter. Slaughter was sentenced to a lengthy state prison term.

On September 7, 1999, a letter for Dodson from Slaughter arrived at Dodson's office via the United States mail. The envelope was addressed to Catherine Dodson, had the return address of G. R. Slaughter at Red Onion State Prison, in Pound, Virginia, and was postmarked Bristol, TN/VA.

The letter itself was addressed to S. Catherine Dodson and signed by G. R. Slaughter. The letter stated that in the coming months, Slaughter would contact Dodson with instructions, and that if she failed to follow the instructions, members of her family would be killed. The letter also expressed, among other things, that Dodson would be killed if she went to the police and that Slaughter had found out the names and addresses of her family members. Dodson notified her boss, who in turn notified the police and the state department of corrections about the letter.

On October 18, 1999, Dodson received another letter at her office with Slaughter's return address via the United States mail. Dodson had been instructed to wait until an agent of the department of corrections arrived before opening the letter. The unopened letter was put in a transparency cover. The next day, department of corrections special agent James Leslie arrived and opened the letter. The envelope was addressed to S. Catherine Dodson, the return address was George Slaughter at Red Onion State Prison, and the postmark was Bristol TN/VA. Inside the envelope was a white powder. Agent Leslie smelled the white powder, then transferred it to a plastic envelope container.

The letter indicated that Slaughter wanted Dodson dead, even if it cost him his life. The letter claimed that the white powder was anthrax, stating, "guess what I got over the fence? I got enough anthrax to kill you with, and it can be done by mail. That powder you just dumped out of this letter is enough to kill at least 50,000 people. You'll think you have the flu tomorrow and the next day you'll be dead." At the end of the letter, the writer threatened that if he were ever released, he would dig up Dodson's grave and violate her corpse. The letter was signed George R. Slaughter.

Agent Leslie testified that he was "a little nervous" after the letter was read. None of the people present contacted the police or emergency medical help, and Leslie did not contact a doctor. The next day, Leslie took the powdery substance to a lab, and it was determined that the substance was not anthrax and was nontoxic.

Also in October, a third letter was sent through the United States mail to the Kentucky Educational Television station in Lexington, Kentucky. The envelope was addressed to 600 Cooper Drive, Lexington, Kentucky. The return address had Slaughter's name and address at Red Onion State Prison. The letter inside read:

Hello!
I just wanted you to know that you just opened a letter which contains enough anthrax to kill over 50,000 people. You have a nice day[]!

A mail room employee opened the letter because the envelope was not addressed to a specific person. A substance that looked like chalk dust spilled onto the counter. The employee brought the letter to his supervisor's attention. The mail room supervisor notified the postal inspector, who then notified the Federal Bureau of Investigation. The five people who had been near the letter were quarantined and no one was allowed to leave or enter the building. A variety [**6] of local fire trucks, police cars, and disaster and emergency response teams responded. After about five hours, the quarantine ended.

At trial, Leanne McCoy, the mailroom supervisor for Red Onion State Prison, testified that prisoners can send mail by handing it to a floor officer, who in turn takes it to an office until the afternoon mailbags come in. Alternatively, prisoners can put it into an outside mailbox on the way to the "chow hall." The outgoing mail is then put into mail bags and sent to the mail room. McCoy testified that the envelopes that carried the letters to Dodson bore the Red Onion State Prison disclaimer on the back. It is the prison's policy that the disclaimer is stamped onto all outgoing mail. McCoy also testified that all three envelopes were postmarked by the Bristol, Tennessee and Virginia, post office which handles the Red Onion State Prison mail.

The government also offered the testimony of Lieutenant Colonel John Rowe, M.D., an officer in the Army Medical Corps and an expert regarding anthrax. Col. Rowe described the manner in which anthrax infected humans, the effects of infection including mortality rates, and the ways anthrax can be manufactured. He also testified that in one case, the release of a gram of anthrax resulted in at least seventy-nine cases of inhalational anthrax, and that if the amount it took to fill a five-pound bag of sugar was disseminated efficiently, it would be enough to kill a million people. When asked about the effect of an amount that would fill up a regular envelope used for mail, Col. Rowe stated, "it could certainly kill somebody if they opened it up and aerosolized any of that powder. Because the amount that would be aerosolized verses the amount that would be inhaled, it would be easy to inhale [a lethal dose.]"

Finally, Col. Rowe also testified that if anthrax was used as a weapon, his agency would respond "in several different modalities." He stated that, "we would probably do the lab analysis on it for one thing, and then we would also send our physicians and other microbiologists out to respond to that." The scientists would be deployed from Fort Detrick in Maryland. In addition, a specialized team from the FBI would respond, including "some people" from an Army unit in Aberdeen, Maryland.

The government also presented the testimony of FBI special agent Tom Snapp, who interviewed Slaughter in prison after the letters had been received. He testified that Slaughter had admitted writing threatening letters to Dodson in order "to scare her."...

III. Sufficiency of the Evidence as to Interstate Commerce.

In counts one and three, Slaughter was charged with violating That statute, in relevant part, states that a person who "without lawful authority,...threatens...to use, a weapon of mass destruction...against any person within the United States, and the results of such...threat...would have affected interstate or foreign commerce..." shall be guilty of a crime against the United States.

Slaughter argues that the evidence that the government presented at trial was insufficient for a jury to find an effect on interstate or foreign commerce. In ruling on the motion, I must "allow the government the benefit of all reasonable inferences from the facts proven to those sought to be established."

Where Congress has written a statute to include an effect on interstate or foreign commerce as an element of the offense, it is necessary to perform a case-by-case analysis to determine whether the jurisdictional element is satisfied. Because the statute here includes such a jurisdictional element, the government need only show a minimal effect on interstate commerce.

However, in light of our federal system, "the government still must show that an effect on interstate commerce is reasonably probable." The Supreme Court has recently noted that the "regulation and punishment of intrastate violence that is not directed at the instrumentalities, channels, or goods involved in interstate commerce has always been the province of the States." *United States v. Morrison*, 529 U.S. 598, 146 L. Ed. 2d 658, 120 S. Ct. 1740, 1754 (2000).

In order for Congress to have regulatory power, where a statute targets noneconomic, violent criminal conduct, the conduct must have more than an aggregate effect on interstate commerce. The government must provide proof that each act prosecuted would have at least a minimal effect on interstate commerce. Thus, in this case, in order to sustain the jury's verdict, the government must have provided sufficient evidence for a jury to conclude that had Slaughter's threat been carried out, interstate commerce would have been affected.

The testimony at trial from Col. Rowe established that if the amount of anthrax in an envelope-sized container was released, it would be enough to "kill somebody." Col. Rowe also testified about the effects of a larger amount of anthrax. In addition, he stated that several military doctors and scientists would travel from Maryland to Virginia had the threatened use of anthrax been carried out.

In count one, the letter sent to Dodson, there was no evidence that the threatened use of anthrax would have affected a "tangible component of interstate commerce." Dodson is a state prosecutor, and the threatened use of a weapon of mass destruction was against her and some of her colleagues, not against a store, bank, leased vehicle, or other obvious component of interstate commerce. Slaughter's threat to Dodson would not have affected interstate commerce directly.

Similarly, there was no evidence that the use of anthrax threatened against the Kentucky Educational Television station would have affected a component of interstate commerce. No evidence was presented that the television station bought or sold interstate goods, broadcast to an interstate area, or had any other effect on interstate commerce. Thus, there was no evidence that the threatened use of anthrax had a direct effect on interstate commerce.[3]

The government may satisfy a statutory jurisdictional component indirectly if it presents evidence of "a reasonable probability that the defendant's actions would have the effect of depleting the assets of an entity engaged in interstate commerce." There is no evidence that the threatened uses of anthrax here would have affected interstate commerce under such a "depletion of assets" theory. The government did not introduce evidence that either Dodson or the television station lost any money due to the threats, nor that they engaged in interstate commerce.

The only evidence offered to show that the threatened use of anthrax would have affected interstate commerce was that an unspecified number of military doctors and scientists would have responded. The entire evidence in this regard, from Col. Rowe's testimony, is as follows:

Q And in the event that actually anthrax were to be, say, discovered and be used as a weapon, would your agency respond?

A Yes. We would probably respond in several different modalities. We would probably do the lab analysis on it for one thing, and then we would also send our physicians and other microbiologists out to respond to that.

Q Where would these different representatives from your agency come from location wise? What state?

A From Maryland, from Fort Detrick.

Q And does the FBI, to your knowledge, also have a response team for weapons of mass destruction?

A Domestic Emergency Support Team from the FBI would respond, and that would include some people from the Army's unit up in Aberdeen, Maryland.

The Fourth Circuit has held that an effect upon interstate commerce can be established by proof of probabilities. That is, the government does not have to prove that identifiable transactions in interstate commerce would be affected, but that there is a probability or likelihood of such an effect.

In this case, however, there was no evidence as to what probable effect the military personnel would have had on interstate commerce. The government did not introduce evidence that the military personnel would have had to bring or use supplies that had traveled in interstate commerce, or that they would have traveled in commercial carriers, lodged in hotels, or eaten at restaurants that engage in interstate commerce.

Federal criminal jurisdiction would be largely unrestrained if it were established under the facts of this case. If travel by a federal government employee to investigate possible criminal conduct alone established federal jurisdiction, then federal agencies would themselves control whether such jurisdiction existed.

It is possible that the use of a weapon of mass destruction, unlike other crimes, would be of such magnitude that every instance would require the response of specially trained government agents being dispatched across state lines to address the problem. In that case, the effect on interstate commerce

---

[3] The fact that the letters were mailed, and that one of them traveled from Virginia to another state, is of no moment, since the statute requires that the results of the threat would have affected interstate commerce, and not that the threat merely be communicated through interstate commerce.

caused by the agents' emergency travel would be a more direct result of the criminal activity than a federal agent that crossed state lines merely to investigate a crime. However, there was no evidence to indicate that the dispatch of the military units described by Col. Rowe would be a necessary result of the use of anthrax, or to demonstrate why these military units would travel to the scene of an anthrax infection.

Under this limited set of facts, there is insufficient evidence that the threatened use of anthrax would have affected interstate commerce to support a conviction under counts one and three. Accordingly, I will set aside the verdict as to those counts and enter a judgment of acquittal.

––––––––

Notes

1. In *Slaughter*, the prosecution argued only that the interstate commerce element was met because out-of-state scientists and law enforcers would respond to any anthrax threat. The court in dicta found that the federal criminal jurisdiction would be largely unrestrained if only these facts were sufficient to establish jurisdiction. However, in *Wise*, the court had no difficulty in finding the interstate commerce element was met because the letters were sent to the DEA and other federal agencies out of state.

2. April 2, 2001, the U.S. Supreme Court unanimously denied Writ of Certiorari in *Wise*.

––––––––

7.3. Cases from 9-11 under the Anti-Terrorism and Death Penalty Act of 1996

United States v. John Philip Walker Lindh
2002 LEXIS 12683 (E.D. Va., Alex. Div., July 11, 2002)

Honorable T. S. Ellis, III, United States District Judge.

MEMORANDUM OPINION

John Phillip Walker Lindh ("Lindh") is an American citizen who, according to the ten-count Indictment filed against him in February 2002, joined certain foreign terrorist organizations in Afghanistan and served these organizations there in combat against Northern Alliance and American forces until his capture in November 2001. In seven threshold motions, Lindh sought dismissal of certain counts of the Indictment on a variety of grounds, including lawful combatant immunity and selective prosecution. Lindh also sought dismissal, or alternatively, transfer of venue, arguing that he could not receive a fair trial in this district owing to pre-trial publicity. All motions were denied following extensive briefing and oral argument. See United States v. Lindh, Criminal No. 02-37-A (E.D. Va. June 17, 2002) (Order). Recorded here are the reasons underlying those rulings.

I.

The Indictment's allegations may be succinctly summarized. In mid-2001, Lindh attended a military training camp in Pakistan run by Harakat ul-Mujahideen ("HUM"), a terrorist group dedicated to an extremist view of Islam. After receiving several weeks of training, Lindh informed HUM officials that "he wished to fight with the Taliban in Afghanistan." Thus, in May or June 2001, he traveled from Pakistan into Afghanistan "for the purpose of taking up arms with the Taliban," eventually arriving at a Taliban recruiting center in Kabul, Afghanistan—the Dar ul-Anan Headquarters of the Mujahideen. On his arrival, Lindh presented a letter of introduction from HUM and advised Taliban personnel "that he was an American and that he wanted to go to the front lines to fight."

While at the Dar ul-Anan Headquarters, Lindh agreed to receive additional and extensive military training at an al Qaeda training camp. He made this decision "knowing that America and its citizens were the enemies of Bin Laden and al-Qaeda and that a principal purpose of al-Qaeda was to fight and kill Americans." In late May or June 2001, Lindh traveled to a bin Laden guest house in Kandahar, Afghanistan, where he stayed for several days, and then traveled to the al Farooq training camp, "an al Qaeda facility located several hours west of Kandahar." He reported to the camp with approximately twenty other trainees, mostly Saudis, and remained there throughout June and July. During this period, he participated fully in the camp's training activities, despite being told early in his stay that "Bin Laden had sent forth some fifty people to carry out twenty suicide terrorist operations against the United States and Israel." As part of his al Qaeda training, Lindh participated in "terrorist training courses in, among other things, weapons, orientating, navigation, explosives and battlefield combat." This training included the use of "shoulder weapons, pistols, and rocket-propelled grenades, and the construction of Molotov cocktails." During his stay at al Farooq, Lindh met personally with bin Laden, "who thanked him and other trainees for taking part in jihad." He also met with a senior al Qaeda official, Abu Mohammad Al-Masri, who inquired whether Lindh was interested in traveling outside Afghanistan to conduct operations against the United States and Israel. Lindh declined Al-Masri's offer in favor of going to the front lines to fight. It is specifically alleged that Lindh swore allegiance to jihad in June or July 2001.

When Lindh completed his training at al Farooq in July or August 2001, he traveled to Kabul, Afghanistan, where he was issued an AKM rifle "with a barrel suitable for long range shooting." Armed with this rifle, Lindh, together with approximately 150 non-Afghani fighters, traveled from Kabul to the front line at Takhar, located in Northeastern Afghanistan, where the entire unit was placed under the command of an Iraqi named Abdul Hady. Lindh's group was eventually divided into smaller groups that fought in shifts against Northern Alliance troops in the Takhar trenches, rotating every one to two weeks. During this period, Lindh "carried various weapons with him, including the AKM rifle, an RPK rifle he was issued after the AKM rifle malfunctioned, and at least two grenades." He remained with his fighting group following the September 11, 2001 terrorist attacks, "despite having been told that Bin Laden had ordered the [September 11] attacks, that additional terrorist attacks were planned, and that additional al Qaeda personnel were being sent from the front lines to protect Bin Laden and defend against an anticipated military response from the United States." Indeed, it is specifically alleged that Lindh remained with his fighting group from October to December 2001, "after learning that United States military forces and United States nationals had become directly engaged in support of the Northern Alliance in its military conflict with Taliban and al Qaeda forces."

In November 2001, Lindh and his fighting group retreated from Takhar to the area of Kunduz, Afghanistan, where they ultimately surrendered to Northern Alliance troops. On November 24, 2001, he and the other captured Taliban fighters were transported to Mazar-e-Sharif, and then to the nearby Qala-i-Janghi (QIJ) prison compound. The following day, November 25, Lindh was interviewed by two Americans—Agent Johnny Micheal Spann from the Central Intelligence Agency (CLA) and another government employee. Later that day, it is alleged that Taliban detainees in the QIJ compound attacked Spann and the other employee, overpowered the guards, and armed themselves. Spann was shot and killed in the course of the uprising and Lindh, after being wounded, retreated with other detainees to a basement area of the QIJ compound. The uprising at QIJ was eventually suppressed on December 1, 2001, at which time Lindh and other Taliban and al Qaeda fighters were taken into custody by Northern Alliance and American forces.

Following his capture, Lindh was interrogated, transported to the United States, and ultimately charged in this district with the following offenses in a ten-count Indictment:

(i) conspiracy to murder nationals of the United States, including American military personnel and other governmental employees serving in Afghanistan following the September 11, 2001 terrorist attacks, in violation of 18 U.S.C. §2332(b)(2) (Count One);

(ii) conspiracy to provide material support and resources to HUM, a foreign terrorist organization, in violation of 18 U.S.C. §2339B (Count Two);

(iii) providing material support and resources to HUM, in violation of 18 U.S.C. §2339B and 2 (Count Three);

(iv) conspiracy to provide material support and resources to al Qaeda, a foreign terrorist organization, in violation of 18 U.S.C. §2339B (Count Four);

(v) providing material support and resources to al Qaeda, in violation of 18 U.S.C. §2339B and 2 (Count Five);

(vi) conspiracy to contribute services to al Qaeda, in violation of 31 C.F.R. §595.205 and 595.204 and 50 U.S.C. §1705(b) (Count Six);

(vii) contributing services to al Qaeda, in violation of 31 C.F.R. §595.204 and 595.205 and 50 U.S.C. §1705(b) and 18 U.S.C. §2 (Count Seven);

(viii) conspiracy to supply services to the Taliban, in violation of 31 C.F.R. §545.206(b) and 545.204 and 50 U.S.C. §1705(b) (Count Eight);

(ix) supplying services to the Taliban, in violation of 31 C.F.R. §545.204 and 545.206(a) and 50 U.S.C. §1705(b) and 18 U.S.C. §2 (Count Nine); and

(x) using and carrying firearms and destructive devices during crimes of violence, in violation of 18 U.S.C. §924(c)(1)(A), 924(c)(1)(B)(ii) and 2 (Count Ten).

At issue are the following seven threshold motions to dismiss or transfer filed by the defense:

(i) motion to dismiss or, in the alternative, to transfer venue based on pre-trial publicity;

(ii) motion to dismiss Count One for failure to state a violation of the charging statute;

(iii) motion to dismiss Counts Six, Seven, Eight and Nine as lacking statutory authority;

(iv) motion to dismiss Counts Eight and Nine for selective prosecution;

(v) motion to dismiss Counts Two through Nine on freedom of association, overbreadth, and vagueness grounds;

(vi) motion to dismiss Counts Two, Three, Four and Five for failure to state a claim under the charging statute; and

(vii) motion to dismiss Count Ten on the ground that Lindh did not commit a crime of violence.

Each motion is separately addressed.

[This excerpt includes only the motion to dismiss for Count One, which applies to the charges made pursuant to the Anti-Terrorism and Death Penalty Act of 1996]

....The starting point in the analysis of Lindh's immunity claim is recognition that the President has unequivocally determined that Lindh, as a member of the Taliban, is an unlawful combatant and, as such, may not invoke lawful combatant immunity. On February 7, 2002, the White House announced the President's decision, as Commander-in-Chief, that the Taliban militia were unlawful combatants pursuant to GPW and general principles of international law, and, therefore, they were not entitled to POW status under the Geneva Conventions. This presidential determination, according to the government, is significant, indeed decisive, because the President, as the "Commander in Chief of the Army and Navy of the United States," n26 has broad constitutional power to issue such a determination. Moreover, in the current conflict, he has also been "authorized" by Congress "to use all necessary and appropriate force against those nations, organizations, or persons he determines planned, authorized, committed, or aided the terrorist attacks that occurred on September 11, 2001, or harbored such organizations or persons." Authorization for Use of Military Force, Pub. L. No. 107-40, §2, 115 Stat. 224 (2001). Thus, the government argues, the decision of the President to use force against the Taliban and al Qaeda, as endorsed by Congress, represents the exercise of the full extent of his constitutional presidential authority. It follows, the government contends, that the President's determination that Taliban members are unlawful combatants was made pursuant to his constitutional Commander-in-Chief and foreign affairs powers and is therefore not subject to judicial review or second guessing because it involves a quintessentially nonjusticiable political question.

This argument, while not without appeal, is ultimately unpersuasive. Because the consequence of accepting a political question argument is so significant—judicial review is completely foreclosed—courts must subject such arguments to searching scrutiny, for it is central to the rule of law in our constitutional system that federal courts must, in appropriate circumstances, review or second guess, and indeed sometimes even trump, the actions of the other governmental branches. At a minimum, this scrutiny requires careful consideration of whether the circumstances that trigger the application of the political question doctrine are present here. Thus, it is difficult to see, except at the highest level of abstraction, a textually demonstrable constitutional commitment regarding this issue. Moreover, it is difficult to see why the application of the GPW's lawful combatant immunity doctrine to Lindh's case involves a lack of judicially discoverable and manageable standards. Indeed, the contrary appears to be true. The presence of any remaining factors is also doubtful. To sum up briefly then, while it may be argued that some of the triggering circumstances for a political question are present to some degree here, others plainly are not and thus the government's political question argument is ultimately unpersuasive. Understandably and appropriately, therefore, courts have recognized that treaty interpretation does not implicate the political question doctrine and is not a subject beyond judicial review.

It is important to recognize that the deference here is appropriately accorded not only to the President's interpretation of any ambiguity in the treaty, but also to the President's application of the treaty to the facts in issue. Again, this is warranted given the President's special competency in, and constitutional responsibility for, foreign affairs and the conduct of overseas military operations. It is also crucial to be precise regarding the nature of the deference warranted. Conclusive deference, which amounts to judicial abstention, is plainly inappropriate. Rather, the appropriate deference is to accord substantial or great weight to the President's decision regarding the interpretation and application of the GPW to Lindh, provided the interpretation and application of the treaty to Lindh may be said to be reasonable and not contradicted by the terms of the treaty or the facts. It is this proviso that is the focus of the judicial review here of the President's determination that Lindh is an unlawful combatant under the GPW.

The GPW sets forth four criteria an organization must meet for its members to qualify for lawful combatant status:

i. the organization must be commanded by a person responsible for his subordinates;

ii. the organization's members must have a fixed distinctive emblem or uniform recognizable at a distance;

iii. the organization's members must carry arms openly; and

iv. the organization's members must conduct their operations in accordance with the laws and customs of war.

In the application of these criteria to the case at bar, it is Lindh who bears the burden of establishing the affirmative defense that he is entitled to lawful combatant immunity, i.e., that the Taliban satisfies the four criteria required for lawful combatant status outlined by the GPW. On this point, Lindh has not carried his burden; indeed, he has made no persuasive showing at all on this point. For this reason alone, it follows that the President's decision denying Lindh lawful combatant immunity is correct. In any event, a review of the available record information leads to the same conclusion. Thus, it appears that the Taliban lacked the command structure necessary to fulfill the first criterion, as it is manifest that the Taliban had no internal system of military command or discipline. As one observer noted, "there is no clear military structure with a hierarchy of officers and commanders while unit commanders are constantly being shifted around," and the Taliban's "haphazard style of enlistment...does not allow for a regular or disciplined army." Kamal Matinuddin, The Taliban Phenomenon: Afghanistan 1994–97 59 (1999). Thus, Lindh has not carried his burden to show that the Taliban had the requisite hierarchical military structure.

Similarly, it appears the Taliban typically wore no distinctive sign that could be recognized by opposing combatants; they wore no uniforms or insignia and were effectively indistinguishable from the rest of the population. The requirement of such a sign is critical to ensure that combatants may be distinguished from the non-combatant, civilian population. Accordingly, Lindh cannot establish the second criterion.

Next, although it appears that Lindh and his cohorts carried arms openly in satisfaction of the third criterion for lawful combatant status, it is equally apparent that members of the Taliban failed to observe the laws and customs of war. See GPW, art. 4(A)(2). Thus, because record evidence supports the conclusion that the Taliban regularly targeted civilian populations in clear contravention of the laws and customs of war, Lindh cannot meet his burden concerning the fourth criterion.

In sum, the President's determination that Lindh is an unlawful combatant and thus ineligible for immunity is controlling here (i) because that determination is entitled to deference as a reasonable interpretation and application of the GPW to Lindh as a Taliban; (ii) because Lindh has failed to carry his burden of demonstrating the contrary; and (iii) because even absent deference, the Taliban falls far short when measured against the four GPW criteria for determining entitlement to lawful combatant immunity.

The following is the indictment against the "shoe bomber", Richard Colvin Reid, who was charged, in part, under the Anti-Terrorism and Death Penalty Act of 1996. The counts relevant to a terrorist event—had this been a bioterrorist event—are included in this excerpt:

UNITED STATES DISTRICT COURT DISTRICT OF MASSACHUSETTS

United States of America v. Richard Colvin Reid a/k/a Abdul-Raheem a/k/a Abdul-Raheem, Abu Ibrahim)	) Criminal No. 42-10013-WGY) VIOLATIONS:) 18 U.S.C. §2332a(a)(1)) (Attempted Use of a Weapon of Mass) Destruction) 18 U.S.C. §2332

) (Attempted Homicide)
) 49 U.S.C. §46505(b)(3) and (c)
) (Placing Explosive Device on Aircraft)
) 49 U.S.C. §46506(1) and 18 U.S.C.
) §1113
) (Attempted Murder)
) 49 U.S.C. §46504
) (Interference with Flight Crew Members
)   and Attendants)
) 18 U.S.C. §924(c)
) (Using Destructive Device During and in
)   Relation to a Crime of Violence)
) 18 U.S.C. §1993(a)(1) & (8)
) (Attempted Wrecking of Mass
) Transportation Vehicle)

<u>Indictment</u>

COUNT ONE: (18 U.S.C. §2332(a)(1)—Attempted Use of Weapon of Mass Destruction)
The Grand Jury charges that:
1.   At all times relevant to this count brought under Title 18, United States Code, Chapter 113B—Terrorism, Al-Qaeda was a designated foreign terrorist organization pursuant to 8 U.S.C. §1189.
2.   At various times relevant to this count, Richard Colvin Reid received training from Al-Qaeda in Afghanistan.
3.   On or about December 22, 2001, at Paris, France, and on board American Airlines Flight 63 en-route from Paris, France to Miami, Florida, but landing at East Boston, Massachusetts, in the District of Massachusetts,
RICHARD COLVIN REID a/k/a Abdul-Raheem a/k/a Abdul Raheem, Abu Ibrahim, defendant herein, did, without lawful authority, attempt to use a weapon of mass destruction, to wit: a destructive device,

consisting of an explosive bomb placed in each of his shoes, against one and more than one national of the United States while such nationals were outside of the United States.

All in violation of Title 18, United States Code, Section 2332a(a)(1).

COUNT TWO: (18 U.S.C. §2332—Attempted Homicide)

The Grand Jury further charges that:

1. At all times relevant to this count brought under Title 18, United States Code, Chapter 113B—Terrorism, Al-Qaeda was a designated foreign terrorist organization pursuant to 8 U.S.C. §1189.

2. At various times relevant to this count, Richard Colvin Reid received training from al-Qaeda in Afghanistan.

3. On or about December 22, 2001, at Paris, France, and on board American Airlines Flight 63 en-route from Paris, France to Miami, Florida, but landing at East Boston, Massachusetts, in the District of Massachusetts,

RICHARD COLVIN REID a/k/a Abdul-Raheem a/k/a Abdul Raheem, Abu Ibrahim, defendant, herein, did, outside the United States, attempt to kill and to commit a killing that is a murder of one and more than one national of the United States, while such nationals were outside the United States.

All in violation of Title 18, United States Code, Section 2332(b)(1)....

COUNT FOUR: (49 U.S.C. §46506(1)—Attempted Murder)

The Grand Jury further charges that:

On or about December 22, 2001, at Paris, France, and on board American Airlines Flight 63 en-route from Paris, France to Miami, Florida, but landing at East Boston, Massachusetts, in the District of Massachusetts,

RICHARD COLVIN REID a/k/a Abdul-Raheem a/k/a Abdul Raheem, Abu Ibrahim, defendant herein, did, on an aircraft in the special aircraft jurisdiction of the United States, attempt to commit murder of one and more than one of the 183 other passengers and 14 crew members on board American Airlines Flight 63.

All in violation of Title 49, United States Code, Section 46506(1) and Title 18, United States Code, Section 1113...

A TRUE BILL

_____

Foreperson of the Grand Jury

_____

James B. Farmer
Chief, Criminal Division
DISTRICT OF MASSACHUSETTS; January 16, 2002 @ 12:20 pm
Returned into the District Court by the Grand Jurors and filed.

_____

Deputy Clerk

_____

Notes

1. October 4, 2002, John Walker Lindh was sentenced to 20 years in prison under a plea agreement. He had pled guilty to the two felony charges, but risked being found guilty on the remaining ten counts in the federal indictment had he proceeded to trial. The key evidence against Mr. Lindh included his own disclosures to military investigators and his CNN videotaped interview while in Afghanistan. Does this outcome have the effect of deterrence?

2. Richard Colvin Reid has admitted his guilt in the scheme to destroy an aircraft while in flight from France to the United States. He has characterized his action as an "act of war" and continues to state his allegiance to Osama bin Laden. Does the criminal law system of the United States adequately address the threat of terrorists, such as Richard Reid? What are the alternatives?

7.4. USA PATRIOT Act

The Uniting and Strengthening America by Providing Appropriate Tools Required to Intercept and Obstruct Terrorism Act, (USA PATRIOT Act), was signed into law on October 26, 2001, after favorable votes in the House 356 to 66, and in the Senate 98 to 1. This Act was in response to the 9-11 attacks and the startling acknowledgment that our intelligence about the terrorist plans was inadequate.

Civil rights groups, extreme right-wing groups, and libertarians opposed the new legislation as an assault on American freedoms. A final compromise with legislators, who were hesitant to pass the bill because of the potential for abuse by the government in the use of the new tools for surveillance and investigation, involved sunset clauses for some of the provisions, setting an expiration date for the year 2005.

7.4.1. New Federal Crimes

§802 Creates the crime of "domestic terrorism". The statute makes criminal "acts dangerous to human life that are a violation of the criminal laws" if these "appear to be intended...to influence the policy of a government by intimidation or coercion" within the "territorial jurisdiction of the United States." Opponents argue that this is too broad and will include environmental activists or other political activists, not related to terrorism.

7.4.2. Fourth Amendment Concerns

§213 Sneak and Peak Searches. This section allows the search of an area without notification to the person who is the subject of the search until after the search has been completed. Delay of notice of the execution of the warrant for a reasonable time is also permitted under this section. This section does not have an expiration clause.

Tracing internet "dialing, routing, addressing and signaling information" is permitted where a government agency seeks to obtain the information for an ongoing criminal investigation. The ability to collect this information includes the likelihood of the content of emails to be accessible through this system of surveillance.

§218 Probable cause requirement. Foreign intelligence surveillance with wiretaps and physical searches do not require a showing of probable cause, and there is no warrant requirement. Foreign intelligence information must be the "purpose" of the surveillance. This section allows the collection of criminal evidence where the collection of foreign intelligence is "a significant purpose" of the surveillance.

7.4.3. Sharing Information

The law provides for greater cooperation between domestic and foreign intelligence agencies for the purpose of intercepting and preventing terrorist activities. The FBI, CIA and INS, and other federal agencies can share information if it will "assist the official...in the performance of his official duties."

§203(a) permits disclosure of grand jury proceedings; §203(b) permits disclosure of recordings of telephone conversations and internet communications; and §203(c) permits the disclosure of foreign intelligence gathered in a criminal investigation.

7.4.4. Immigrants

§411 Definition of terrorism.

This section defines "terrorist activity" an "any crime that involves the use of a 'weapon or dangerous device (other than for mere personal monetary gain)." This broadens the definition from activity that was politically motivated, pre-meditated, and directed toward a civilian population.

§412 Attorney General's Power to Detain.

In questions of detention, due process "applies to all 'persons' within the United States, including aliens, whether their presence is lawful, unlawful, temporary, permanent." ***Zadvydas v. Davis***, 533 U.S. 678 (2001).

This section grants power to the Attorney General to detain immigrants where there are "reasonable grounds to believe" they are engaged in terrorist activities or other activities that are a threat to national security. A non-citizen can be held for as long as seven days without being charged with a criminal or immigration violation.

Prior to passage of the USA PATRIOT Act, in September 20, 2001, the Attorney General promulgated an interim regulation which allowed the detention of any non-citizen without a suspicion of a violation of a crime or immigration violation; whereas §412, requires a finding of "reasonable grounds to believe" that a non-citizen is engaged in terrorist activities that are a threat to the nation.

If the non-citizen is charged with a violation, the result is a mandatory detention and ineligibility for release until removal or until the Attorney General certifies that the non-citizen is no longer a threat. Criticism of §412 includes the lack of a requirement to provide the non-citizen with evidence on which the certification is based or to provide an opportunity to contest that evidence in an administrative procedure. Review is limited to a habeas corpus proceeding, and since they are civil in nature, no Sixth Amendment right to counsel attaches, and therefore no counsel is provided by the government to the non-citizen.

If removal is deemed "unlikely in the reasonable future" for example, because another country will not take the non-citizen, the non-citizen may be held for additional periods of six months "if the release of the alien will threaten the national security of the United States or the safety of the community or any person." The U.S. Supreme Court has spoken to the issue of detention periods of aliens in the context of a civil matter in the following case:

Zadvydas v. Davis
533 U.S. 678 (2001)

JUSTICE BREYER delivered the opinion of the Court.

When an alien has been found to be unlawfully present in the United States and a final order of removal has been entered, the Government ordinarily secures the alien's removal during a subsequent 90-day statutory "removal period," during which time the alien normally is held in custody.

A special statute authorizes further detention if the Government fails to remove the alien during those 90 days. It says:

"An alien ordered removed [1] who is inadmissible...[2] [or] removable [as a result of violations of status requirements or entry conditions, violations of criminal law, or reasons of security or foreign policy] or [3] who has been determined by the Attorney General to be a risk to the community or unlikely to comply with the order of removal, may be detained beyond the removal period and, if released, shall be subject to [certain] terms of supervision...." 8 U.S.C. §1231(a)(6) (1994 ed., Supp. V).

In these cases, we must decide whether this post-removal-period statute authorizes the Attorney General to detain a removable alien indefinitely beyond the removal period or only for a period reasonably necessary to secure the alien's removal. We deal here with aliens who were admitted to the United States but subsequently ordered removed. Aliens who have not yet gained initial admission to this country would present a very different question. See infra, at 12–14. Based on our conclusion that indefinite detention of aliens in the former category would raise serious constitutional concerns, we construe the statute to contain an implicit "reasonable time" limitation, the application of which is subject to federal court review.

We consider two separate instances of detention. The first concerns Kestutis Zadvydas, a resident alien who was born, apparently of Lithuanian parents, in a displaced persons camp in Germany in 1948. When he was eight years old, Zadvydas immigrated to the United States with his parents and other family members, and he has lived here ever since.

Zadvydas has a long criminal record, involving drug crimes, attempted robbery, attempted burglary, and theft. He has a history of flight, from both criminal and deportation proceedings. Most recently, he was convicted of possessing, with intent to distribute, cocaine; sentenced to 16 years' imprisonment; released on parole after two years; taken into INS custody; and, in 1994, ordered deported to Germany. See 8 U.S.C. §1251(a)(2) (1988 ed., Supp. V) (delineating crimes that make alien deportable).

In 1994, Germany told the INS that it would not accept Zadvydas because he was not a German citizen. Shortly thereafter, Lithuania refused to accept Zadvydas because he was neither a Lithuanian citizen nor a permanent resident. In 1996, the INS asked the Dominican Republic (Zadvydas' wife's country) to accept him, but this effort proved unsuccessful. In 1998, Lithuania rejected, as inadequately documented, Zadvydas' effort to obtain Lithuanian citizenship based on his parents' citizenship; Zadvydas' reapplication is apparently still pending.

The INS kept Zadvydas in custody after expiration of the removal period. In September 1995, Zadvydas filed a petition for a writ of habeas corpus under 28 U.S.C. §2241 challenging his continued detention. In October 1997, a Federal District Court granted that writ and ordered him released under supervision. *Zadvydas v. Caplinger*, 986 F. Supp. 1011, 1027-1028 (ED La.). In its view, the Government would never succeed in its efforts to remove Zadvydas from the United States, leading to his permanent confinement, contrary to the Constitution. Id. at 1027.

The Fifth Circuit reversed this decision. *Zadvydas v. Underdown*, 185 F.3d 279 (1999). It concluded that Zadvydas' detention did not violate the Constitution because eventual deportation was not "impossible," good faith efforts to remove him from the United States continued, and his detention was subject to periodic administrative review. Id. at 294, 297. The Fifth Circuit stayed its mandate pending potential review in this Court.

A statute permitting indefinite detention of an alien would raise a serious constitutional problem. The Fifth Amendment's Due Process Clause forbids the Government to "deprive" any "person...of...liberty...without due process of law." Freedom from imprisonment—from government custody, detention, or other forms of physical restraint—lies at the heart of the liberty that Clause protects. See *Foucha v. Louisiana*, 504 U.S. 71, 80, 118 L. Ed. 2d 437, 112 S. Ct. 1780 (1992). And this Court has said that government detention violates that Clause unless the detention is ordered in a criminal proceeding with adequate procedural protections, or, in certain special and "narrow" non-punitive "circumstances," Foucha, supra, at 80, where a special justification, such as harm-threatening mental illness, outweighs the "individual's constitutionally protected interest in avoiding physical restraint."

The proceedings at issue here are civil, not criminal, and we assume that they are nonpunitive in purpose and effect....

The Government argues that, from a constitutional perspective, alien status itself can justify indefinite detention, and points to *Shaughnessy v. United States ex rel. Mezei*, 345 U.S. 206, 97 L. Ed. 956, 73 S. Ct. 625 (1953), as support. That case involved a once lawfully admitted alien who left the United States, returned after a trip abroad, was refused admission, and was left on Ellis Island, indefinitely detained there because the Government could not find another country to accept him. The Court held that Mezei's detention did not violate the Constitution. Id. at 215–216.

Although Mezei, like the present cases, involves indefinite detention, it differs from the present cases in a critical respect. As the Court emphasized, the alien's extended departure from the United States required him to seek entry into this country once again. His presence on Ellis Island did not count as entry into the United States. Hence, he was "treated," for constitutional purposes, "as if stopped at the border." And that made all the difference.

V

The Fifth Circuit held Zadvydas' continued detention lawful as long as "good faith efforts to effectuate...deportation continue" and Zadvydas failed to show that deportation will prove "impossible." 185 F.3d at 294, 297. But this standard would seem to require an alien seeking release to show the absence of any prospect of removal—no matter how unlikely or unforeseeable—which demands more than our reading of the statute can bear. The Ninth Circuit held that the Government was required to release Ma from detention because there was no reasonable likelihood of his removal in the foreseeable future. But its conclusion may have rested solely upon the "absence" of an "extant or pending" repatriation agreement without giving due weight to the likelihood of successful future negotiations. Consequently, we vacate the decisions below and remand both cases for further proceedings consistent with this opinion.

It is so ordered.

JUSTICE SCALIA, with whom JUSTICE THOMAS joins, dissenting.

A criminal alien under final order of removal who allegedly will not be accepted by any other country in the reasonably foreseeable future claims a constitutional right of supervised release into the United States. This claim can be repackaged as freedom from "physical restraint" or freedom from "indefinite detention," ante, at 9, but it is at bottom a claimed right of release into this country by an individual who concededly has no legal right to be here. There is no such constitutional right.

Like a criminal alien under final order of removal, an inadmissible alien at the border has no right to be in the United States. In Shaughnessy v. United States ex rel. Mezei, 345 U.S. 206, 97 L. Ed. 956, 73 S. Ct. 625 (1953), we upheld potentially indefinite detention of such an inadmissible alien whom the Government was unable to return anywhere else. We said that "we [did] not think that respondent's continued exclusion deprives him of any statutory or constitutional right." While four members of the Court thought that Mezei deserved greater procedural protections (the Attorney General had refused to divulge any information as to why Mezei was being detained, id. at 209), no Justice asserted that Mezei had a substantive constitutional right to release into this country. And Justice Jackson's dissent, joined by Justice Frankfurter, affirmatively asserted the opposite, with no contradiction from the Court: "Due process does not invest any alien with a right to enter the United States, nor confer on those admitted the right to remain against the national will. Nothing in the Constitution requires admission or sufferance of aliens hostile to our scheme of government." Insofar as a claimed legal right to release into this country is concerned, an alien under final order of removal stands on an equal footing with an inadmissible alien at the threshold of entry: He has no such right.

––––––––––

7.5. Public Health Security and Bioterrorism Preparedness and Response Act of 2002, June 12, 2002

New criminal provisions were created and made a part of the Biological Weapons and Anti-Terrorism Act of 1989, 18 U.S.C. §175b, by making criminal the transfer of select agents to an unregistered person, punishable by fine or imprisonment for not more than 5 years, or both. Also made criminal is the possession of a biological agent or toxin or select agents, if the possessor is not registered to have those materials. These crimes are made punishable by fine or imprisonment for not more than 5 years, or both. (Subtitle D—Criminal Penalties Regarding Certain Biological Agents and Toxins, Sec. 231, Public Health Security and Bioterrorism Preparedness and Response Act of 2002.)

The definition of biological agent or toxin was expanded to include select agents, which are referenced in §212(a)(1) of the Agricultural Bioterrorism Protection Act of 2002. The new definition for biological agent "means any microorganism (including, but not limited to, bacteria, viruses, fungi, rickettsiae or protozoa), or infectious substance, or any naturally occurring, bioengineered or synthesized component of any such microorganism or infectious substance..." which now includes "synthesized" as a term which acknowledges advancing biotechnological capabilities in constructing weapons of mass destruction.

The definition of toxin was also expanded and "means the toxic material or product of plants, animals, microorganisms (including, but not limited to, bacteria, viruses, fungi, rickettsiae or protozoa), or infectious substances, or a recombinant or synthesized molecule, whatever their origin and method of production...". This expanded definition takes into account rapidly advancing biotechnology techniques, does not limit the mode of production, and does not limit the molecule to one created by recombinant technology, but includes synthesis of molecules.

7.6. Evidence and Planning for Use of Biological Weapons

The collection of evidence poses particular problems in the prevention of immediate public security. However, in the collection of evidence, protocols which ensure the admissibility of the evidence at trial against the defendant may slow the analysis of the substance. In addition, the admission of evidence in these cases raises some issues which are problematic in the context of bioterrorism.

United States v. Baker
98 F.3d 330 (8th Cir. 1996)

Judges: McMILLIAN, LAY and HANSEN, Circuit Judges. HANSEN, Circuit Judge, dissenting in part.
OPINION by Circuit Judge McMillian

Douglas Allen Baker and Leroy Charles Wheeler appeal from final judgments entered in the District Court for the District of Minnesota, upon a jury verdict, finding each guilty of aiding and abetting the other in knowingly possessing a toxin for use as a weapon in violation of 18 U.S.C.§175.2. The district court sentenced Baker and Wheeler each to 33 months imprisonment, 3 years supervised release and a special assessment of $ 50. For reversal, Baker argues the district court erred in denying his motion to sever and in admitting into evidence certain hearsay statements. For reversal, Wheeler argues the district court erred in admitting into evidence co-conspirator's statements. Both defendants also argue 18 U.S.C. §175 is unconstitutional, the district court erred in admitting into evidence certain documents, the evidence was insufficient to support the jury verdict, and the district court erred in denying their motion for jury selection from a particular division. For the reasons discussed below, we affirm Wheeler's conviction and sentence, but we reverse Baker's conviction and remand his case to the district court for further proceedings.

BACKGROUND FACTS

On May 21, 1992, Colette Baker, the wife of defendant Baker, went to the Pope County, Minnesota, sheriff's office. She appeared to be very nervous. She talked to the receptionist, Joan Holtberg. Colette Baker was carrying a small red coffee can. Inside the coffee can were a baby food jar containing a white powder, a fingernail polish bottle containing a greenish gel, a pair of rubber gloves, and a handwritten note.[4] Colette Baker took each of the items out of the coffee can and showed them to Holtberg. Colette Baker referred to the contents of the coffee can as "Maynard" and told Holtberg that she believed that the powder and gel were only dangerous if they were mixed together.

---

[4] The text of the note was as follows (minor misspelling corrected):
DOUG, Be extremely careful! After you mix the powder with the gel, the slightest contact will kill you! If you breathe the powder or get it in your eyes, you're a dead man. Dispose all instruments used. Always wear rubber gloves and then destroy them also.
Good hunting!!
P.S. Destroy this note!!

The sheriff's office turned over the coffee can and its contents to the FBI for analysis. The FBI found two of Wheeler's fingerprints inside one of the rubber gloves and one of his fingerprints on the bottom of the coffee can. The United States Army Medical Research Institute of Infectious Diseases identified the white powder as ricin. Ricin is a toxin derived from the castor bean plant and is extremely deadly. There is no known antidote for ricin poisoning. FBI special agent Thomas Lynch testified that the process for producing ricin from castor beans is relatively simple and is described in various publications which are commercially available. The baby food jar contained about .7 gram of 5% pure ricin, which, according to a government witness, was enough to kill 126 people. The greenish gel was a mixture of dimethyl sulfoxide (DMSO), a solvent which can penetrate the skin, and aloe vera gel, which is used in cosmetics and hair care products. According to Lynch, DMSO could be combined with ricin to carry the ricin through the skin; however, Lynch did not believe that DMSO would be an effective carrier unless the skin was broken and the ricin could enter the body through cuts or scratches.

Scott Loverink testified that he had known Wheeler since the late 1970s but had never met Baker. Loverink testified about conversations he had had with Richard Oelrich and Dennis Bret Henderson in the early 1990s about ordering castor beans through the mail, processing the castor beans into ricin, and using the ricin to kill people. According to Loverink, in the summer of 1991, Henderson told him that he (Henderson) had ordered some castor beans and had planted them in Wheeler's yard. Henderson also introduced Loverink to Oelrich. According to Loverink, Oelrich referred to "bureaucratic flu," identified various government employees as potential targets, and described the advantages of ricin over other poisons and how ricin could be used with DMSO to carry the ricin through the skin. Henderson also discussed how ricin could be used with DMSO and left in places where people would touch it.

According to Loverink, Oelrich and Henderson referred to ricin as "Maynard." Loverink did not initially know why they did so. However, Loverink later received copies of a newsletter called the CBA Bulletin and noticed that the newsletter contained advertisements for castor beans and instructions for making ricin which could be purchased from Maynard Campbell in Ashland, Oregon. Henderson told Loverink that was why they called ricin "Maynard."

Loverink testified that sometime during the summer of 1991, possibly in August, Henderson left a baby food jar containing ricin in his (Loverink's) workshop for about two weeks. Henderson explained to Loverink that he did not want to store it because there were small children around his house.

In July 1994 a federal grand jury charged Baker and Wheeler with one count of aiding and abetting one another in knowingly possessing a toxin, ricin, for use as a weapon, in violation of 18 U.S.C. §175, 2. Following their arrests, FBI special agent Daniel Lund interviewed them. According to Lund, Baker admitted possessing a powder he called "Maynard" two to three years before, but explained that he intended to use it as an insecticide by sprinkling it on cabbage plants in his garden (he did not do so). Baker denied receiving the powder from Henderson. Baker said that the powder was in a coffee can and that there were rubber gloves in the coffee can; he could not remember any specific instructions for its use except not to touch or inhale it or who had referred to the powder as "Maynard."

Lund also interviewed Wheeler. The interview was reduced to writing and Wheeler signed the written statement. The written statement was introduced into evidence at the trial (as Government Exhibit 12). Wheeler said that he was aware of a toxin called "Maynard" made from castor beans and that he had heard Oelrich, Henderson and Duane Baker, defendant Baker's father, discuss it. Wheeler had heard Oelrich and Henderson discuss mixing "Maynard" with DMSO and aloe vera and he also knew that DMSO is quickly absorbed into the skin. Wheeler knew about the advertisements for castor beans in the CBA Bulletin and that Oelrich had received the CBA Bulletin. Wheeler also knew that in April 1991 Oelrich had ordered castor beans from Maynard Campbell and that the castor beans had been sent to his (Wheeler's) house. Wheeler gave the castor beans to Henderson. According to Wheeler, Henderson processed the castor beans into ricin in his (Wheeler's) shed. Henderson wore rubber gloves and a face mask during the process. Wheeler described the ricin as a white powdery substance. Wheeler knew that it was a deadly poison and he had heard Oelrich and Henderson discuss using "Maynard" to kill people. Wheeler said that

Henderson put the powder in a baby food jar, which he (Henderson) then put inside a coffee can and stored in Wheeler's shed for several months.

[Footnote 3: There was some uncertainty about whether Baker intended to dismiss his appointed counsel and his appeal because, after the briefs had been filed, Baker submitted several pro se motions, including what was in effect a motion to voluntarily dismiss his appeal. We remanded the case to the district court for the limited purpose of holding an evidentiary hearing on this question. After conducting a telephone status conference with counsel and reviewing affidavits from Baker, the district court concluded that Baker did not want to dismiss his appointed counsel or his appeal and that therefore no evidentiary hearing was necessary. We appreciate the district court's prompt attention to this matter.]

BAKER—SEVERANCE

Baker argues that his case should not have been joined with Wheeler's and that the district court abused its discretion in denying his motion for severance. He argues that he was prejudiced by the joinder because the jury heard evidence that was admissible only against Wheeler, including co-conspirator's statements and Wheeler's inculpatory statement to the FBI.

Assuming for purposes of analysis that defendants were properly joined, Fed. R. Crim. P. 8(b) (defendants may be charged in the same indictment if they are alleged to have participated in the same act constituting an offense), we think this is the rare case in which severance should have been granted pursuant to Fed. R. Crim. P. 14 because there is a serious risk that the joint trial prevented the jury from making a reliable judgment about guilt or innocence. This is because evidence that the jury should not have considered against Baker and that would not have been admissible if Baker had been tried alone was admitted against Wheeler, Baker's co-defendant. Most of the evidence was properly admissible only against Wheeler. Baker and Wheeler were not charged with conspiracy. As discussed below, the conspiracy alleged involved Wheeler, Henderson and Oelrich, but not Baker. Co-conspirator's statements that the jury should not have considered against Baker and that would not have been admissible against Baker if Baker had been tried alone were admitted against Wheeler. As discussed below, the advertisements and the book cover, which were very prejudicial and highly inflammatory, were admissible against Wheeler only. In addition, Wheeler's inculpatory statement to the FBI was evidence that was probative of Baker's guilt (Wheeler's statement does not incriminate Baker on its face but arguably does so only when linked to other evidence) but was technically admissible only against Wheeler. Even though the issues and the evidence were relatively straight-forward, the risk of substantial prejudice from the spillover effect of the conspiracy evidence and the documents was too high to be cured by less drastic measures, such as the limiting instructions given by the district court. This is especially true in light of the extremely serious and admittedly sensational nature of the offense charged. Moreover, this is not the kind of case in which we can say, in light of the jury's verdict, that the jury was able to compartmentalize the evidence as it related to each defendant. Baker and Wheeler were charged together, in one count, with aiding and abetting the other in knowingly possessing ricin for use as a weapon.

For this reason, we reverse Baker's conviction and remand his case to the district court for further proceedings. We discuss the other issues raised by Baker and the issues raised by both defendants because they could become issues if Baker is retried.

BAKER—COLETTE BAKER'S STATEMENTS

Baker also argues the district court abused its discretion in admitting into evidence Colette Baker's statements to the sheriff's receptionist that the coffee can contained "Maynard" and that the contents were only dangerous if mixed together. Baker argues that these statements were inadmissible hearsay. We agree. These statements were made by the declarant (Colette Baker) out of court and were offered, through the testimony of the sheriff's receptionist, to prove the truth of the matters asserted therein, that is, that the coffee can contained "Maynard," the contents were only dangerous if mixed together, and, by reasonable inference, Baker's knowledge about the coffee can, its contents and its dangerousness. These statements do not fall within any of the hearsay exceptions and therefore were not admissible.

WHEELER—CO-CONSPIRATOR'S STATEMENTS

Wheeler argues the district court abused its discretion in admitting into evidence co-conspirator's statements made by Henderson and Oelrich. The co-conspirator's statements were admitted against Wheeler only. Wheeler argues there was no evidence that he was involved in a conspiracy with Oelrich and Henderson and that, even if there was evidence of a conspiracy, the statements were not made in furtherance of the conspiracy. He argues the evidence showed only that he associated with Oelrich and Henderson, knew about their activities and had listened to their conversations. We disagree.

[Fed. R. Evid.] 801(d)(2)(E) is the coconspirator exception to the hearsay rule. "As a general rule, statements made by a coconspirator in furtherance of the unlawful association...are properly admissible against all conspirators, whether or not a conspiracy is actually charged." Before admitting the disputed statements, the District Court must find by a preponderance of the evidence [and can consider the very hearsay statements sought to be admitted] that a conspiracy existed to which the declarant and the defendant were parties and that the statements were made in furtherance of the conspiracy.....

A statement that simply informs a listener of the declarant's criminal activities is not made in furtherance of the conspiracy; instead, the statement must "somehow advance the objectives of the conspiracy."

The co-conspirator's statements and other evidence, including Wheeler's inculpatory statement to the FBI, established by a preponderance of the evidence that Wheeler, Henderson and Oelrich were involved in a conspiracy to manufacture and knowingly possess ricin for use as a weapon. The evidence showed that Wheeler had heard Henderson and Oelrich and others discuss mixing ricin with DMSO and aloe vera gel and using it to kill people, including unspecified government officials; Wheeler knew that ricin was poisonous and dangerous to handle; castor beans ordered by Oelrich from Maynard Campbell were delivered to Wheeler's house; Wheeler gave the castor beans to Henderson; Henderson "processed" the castor beans in Wheeler's shed; and Henderson stored the ricin in Wheeler's shed for several months. Henderson's and Oelrich's statements were not merely informative; they attempted to involve Loverink in their criminal activities and succeeded in persuading Loverink to store the ricin in his workshop for two weeks. The district court did not abuse its discretion in admitting into evidence against Wheeler the co-conspirator's statements made by Henderson and Oelrich.

DOCUMENTS

Both defendants argue the district court erred in admitting into evidence certain documents, specifically, advertisements for castor beans from the CBA Bulletin (Gov't Exs. 6 (Mar. 1991), 7 (Apr. 1991)) and the cover of a book titled Silent Death (Gov't Ex. 13). Defendants argue that there was no evidence that they had in fact ever seen the advertisements or the book cover and that the documents were inflammatory and highly prejudicial. The advertisements and the book cover include the words "silent death" in a distinctive typeface and a skull-and-crossbones illustration. FBI special agent Lynch testified that the text of the advertisements incorporate references to the title of the book. The book itself was not admitted into evidence, and defense objections to questions about its contents were sustained.

The district court did not abuse its discretion in admitting these documents into evidence against Wheeler. The advertisements and the book cover were relevant and probative evidence of Wheeler's knowledge that ricin could be used as a weapon (or at least was advertised as such). The advertisements explained why Wheeler (and others) called the ricin "Maynard," showed how castor beans could be purchased by mail order from Maynard Campbell's Avenging Angel Supply, and described ricin (rather sensationally) as a "tool of justice" and as a "Silent Death for those who hate God, Freedom and this Republic!"

However, we do not think the documents should have been admitted against Baker. Unlike Wheeler, who had admitted knowing about the advertisements in the CBA Bulletin and about processing castor beans into ricin, there was no evidence that Baker had ever seen or knew about the advertisements, the CBA Bulletin, or the book, or that he was part of the conspiracy. The advertisements and the book cover, which provided a graphic nexus between castor beans, Maynard Campbell and the use of ricin as a weapon, can only have had an extremely prejudicial impact on the jury....

SUFFICIENCY OF THE EVIDENCE

Both defendants argue the evidence was insufficient to support the jury verdict. Baker does not dispute that he possessed the ricin; he argues there was insufficient evidence that he possessed the ricin for use as a weapon or aided and abetted another in possessing the ricin for use as a weapon. Wheeler does dispute the sufficiency of the evidence of possession. Wheeler argues there was insufficient evidence that he exercised any dominion or control over the ricin, possessed it for use as a weapon or aided and abetted another in possessing the ricin for use as a weapon and that he was merely an innocent bystander. We disagree.

"The standard of review of an appeal concerning the sufficiency of the evidence is very strict, and the verdict of the jury should not be overturned lightly. The jury's verdict must be upheld if there is an interpretation of the evidence that would allow a reasonable-minded jury to conclude guilt beyond a reasonable doubt."..."In reviewing the sufficiency of the evidence on appeal, the court views the evidence in the light most favorable to the government, resolving evidentiary conflicts in favor of the government, and accepting all reasonable inferences drawn from the evidence that support the jury's verdict." "A conviction may be based on circumstantial as well as direct evidence. The evidence need not exclude every reasonable hypothesis except guilt." Id. "If the evidence rationally supports two conflicting hypotheses, the reviewing court will not disturb the conviction."

We must determine whether the facts so viewed sufficiently proved the elements of aiding and abetting, which are: (1) that the defendant associated with the illegal activity; (2) that the defendant participated in it as something he or she wished to bring about; and (3) that the defendant sought by his or her actions to make the activity succeed.

We have reviewed the evidence and hold there was sufficient evidence to support the jury verdict that Baker knowingly possessed ricin for use as a weapon. The government showed that ricin is extremely toxic, deadly in extremely small quantities, and very difficult to detect, there is no known antidote, and has been popularized in various publications as a method to kill people. The handwritten note, which was addressed to "Doug" and found inside the coffee can, contained information about the dangerousness of the contents and the precautions to be used in handling it. Although there was no direct evidence that Baker had in fact read the note, the jury could have reasonably inferred that he had done so. The jury could have also inferred that the note was from Wheeler; Wheeler's fingerprints were found on rubber gloves inside the coffee can and on the coffee can itself. Baker admitted in his statement to the FBI that he knew that ricin was dangerous and had to be handled with extreme care. The jury could have found that Baker's statements that he intended to use ricin to kill garden pests and that he did not know who had given it to him were false.

We also hold the evidence was sufficient to support the jury verdict that Wheeler possessed ricin for use as a weapon or that he aided and abetted another in possessing ricin for use as a weapon. The evidence showed that Wheeler's fingerprints were found on the outside of the coffee can and in one of the rubber gloves found inside the coffee can. As noted above, the ricin, the handwritten note and the rubber gloves were found inside the coffee can. Wheeler admitted in his statement to the FBI that he knew that ricin was a deadly poison and had to be handled extremely carefully, that Oelrich had ordered the castor beans from Maynard Campbell, and that Henderson had processed the castor beans and stored them in his (Wheeler's) shed. In addition to the government's evidence about ricin's toxicity, there was also evidence that Wheeler had heard Henderson and Oelrich discuss using ricin to kill people. The jury could have reasonably inferred from the evidence that, had Wheeler been merely an innocent bystander, he would not have assisted Oelrich and Henderson or listened to their discussions about using ricin to kill people. "Jurors can be assumed to know that criminals rarely welcome innocent persons as witnesses to serious crimes and rarely seek to perpetrate felonies before larger-than-necessary audiences." (discussing mere presence/ innocent bystander defense).

Accordingly, we affirm Wheeler's conviction and sentence, but we reverse Baker's conviction and remand his case to the district court for further proceedings. Wheeler's motion to amend his brief on appeal is granted.

DISSENT by Circuit Judge Hansen, dissenting in part:

I respectfully dissent from that part of the court's opinion which reverses Douglas Allen Baker's conviction for the singular reason that the district court did not sever his trial from that of his co-defendant, Leroy Charles Wheeler. I concur in that part of the opinion which affirms Wheeler's conviction and sentence.

In my view, there is little reason to find this to be the rare case in which severance should have been granted. This was a single count indictment naming Wheeler and Baker as the only defendants; each was charged with aiding and abetting the other in knowingly possessing ricin for use as a weapon. The trial court went to some length to instruct the jury with respect to what evidence was admissible against which defendant, and to inform the jury that each defendant was to be judged only on that evidence which was admitted against that defendant.

I start with a proposition not mentioned in our court's opinion—that severance is a matter committed to the sound discretion of the district court, and it is only when the district court abuses that discretion and a defendant can clearly demonstrate "severe or compelling prejudice" resulting therefrom that the nonsevered defendant is entitled to a new trial. *United States v. Fregoso*, 60 F.3d 1314, 1328 (8th Cir. 1995) (internal quotations omitted).

"There is a preference in the federal system for joint trials of defendants who are indicted together." Joint trials promote efficiency and serve the interests of justice. A defendant seeking severance has the heavy burden of demonstrating that the joint trial will impermissibly infringe on his right to a fair trial. The appellant must demonstrate that the jury was unable to compartmentalize the evidence as it relates to the two defendants.

The court finds prejudice because evidence was presented to the jury against Wheeler which would not have been admissible if Baker were tried separately. But that happens in most every trial where there is more than one defendant, and limiting instructions are usually deemed sufficient to cure any risk of prejudice. See *Richardson*, 481 U.S. at 206–208. When Loverink testified for the government about the conspiracy, the court was very careful to tell the jury not once, but twice, that it could not use Loverink's testimony against Baker. The court relies on Zafiro, but Zafiro only says that a risk of prejudice "might" occur when such evidence is admitted. Our court's opinion grants relief without showing how the facts of this case turn "might occur" into "did occur." The court also finds prejudice because Wheeler's inculpatory statement (which the court agrees did not implicate Baker on its face but arguably does so when linked to other evidence) was admitted against Wheeler at the joint trial. The district court gave the jury the following instruction at the time the evidence about Wheeler's statement was offered:

THE COURT: Now, members of the Jury, I'm going to give you another instruction at this time concerning this witness' testimony relating to the certain statements alleged to have been made by the Defendants. You're about to hear testimony concerning statements made by the Defendants, as I said. You may consider the statement of defendant Wheeler only in the case against him and not in the case against defendant Baker. What that means is that you may consider defendant Wheeler's statement in the case against him, and for that purpose rely on it as much or as little as you think proper. But you may not consider or discuss that statement in any way when you are deciding if the Government has proved beyond a reasonable doubt its case against defendant Baker.

Such a procedure was expressly approved by the Supreme Court in *Richardson v. Marsh*, 481 U.S. at 211 (no Confrontation Claim violation when nontestifying codefendant's statement which has been redacted to eliminate the codefendant's name and any reference to the codefendant's existence is admitted at joint trial). In its final instructions the jury was told that it must give separate consideration to the evidence about each individual defendant and that each defendant was entitled to be treated separately. There is nothing in this record to indicate the jury failed to follow its instructions.

This was a simple, straightforward trial raising basic, noncomplex issues of possession and intent. The jury was only dealing with one count and two defendants. Only five witnesses were called by the government. The court's limiting instructions were clear, correct, and appropriately given. Our court reasons that relief should be granted in part because "this is not the kind of case in which we can say, in light of the jury's verdict that the jury was able to compartmentalize the evidence as it related to each defendant." The court's statement is true, but it is true in every case where there is but a single count and two defendants. Absent a finding of not guilty as to one of the two defendants, there is no way the jury's verdict proves or disproves its ability to compartmentalize the evidence. Because that is so, no inference either way can be drawn from this jury's verdict. The burden remains on the defendant to show "real prejudice."

Clearly, more evidence was presented against the defendant Wheeler than against the defendant Baker. But that in itself is no basis for finding that the trials should have been severed.

To the extent that our court relies on the district court's evidentiary error in admitting against Baker the advertisement for the castor beans from the CBA Bulletin and the book cover from Silent Death as proof that Baker suffered severe prejudice from the district court's denial of his severance motion, I believe the court's reliance to be misplaced. Granting Baker a separate trial would not have prevented the same error from occurring because there is no reason to believe that at a separate trial for Baker, the government would not have offered the documents against him or that the district court would not have let them in. The two issues of evidentiary error by the district court and a jury's ability or inability to compartmentalize the admitted evidence appear to me to be separate and independent, with neither impacting the other.

Because the defendant Baker has failed to carry his burden of demonstrating "real prejudice" caused by the joint trial (as opposed to evidentiary error), he has also failed to show that the district court abused its broad discretion in denying his Rule 14 severance motion. Consequently, I would affirm Baker's conviction and sentence.

Accordingly, I respectfully dissent.

7.7. Attorney-Client Confidentiality Policy and Regulation

In a controversial move, on October 31, 2001, the Bureau of Prisons, Department of Justice, promulgated a regulation permitting the monitoring of attorney-client communications if the Attorney General determines that unmonitored communication could result in death or serious bodily harm to others. These procedures are referred to as "SAM" or "special administrative measures" which involve modified attorney-client privilege, as described in the testimony below:

Viet D. Dinh, Assistant Attorney General, Office of Legal Policy, in testimony before the Committee on the Judiciary, U.S. Senate, on December 4, 2001, explained the new regulation:

"Since 1996, Bureau of Prisons regulations have subjected a very small group of the most dangerous federal detainees to 'special administrative measures,' if the Attorney General determine s that unrestricted communication with these detainees could result in death or serious bodily harm to others. Those measures include placing a detainee in administrative detention, limiting or monitoring his correspondence and telephone calls, restricting his opportunity to receive visitors, and limiting his access to members of the news media. The pre-existing regulations cut off all channels of communication through which detainees could plan or foment acts of terrorism, except one: communications through their attorneys. The new regulation closes this loophole.

This regulation permits the monitoring of attorney-client communications for these detainees only if the Attorney General, after having invoked the existing special administrative measures authority, makes the additional finding that reasonable suspicion exists that a particular detainee may use communications with attorneys to further or facilitate acts of terrorism. Only 12 of the approximately 158,000 inmates in federal custody would be eligible for monitoring.

In taking this action, the Department has included important procedural safeguards to protect the attorney-client privilege. First and foremost, the attorney and client will be notified in writing that their communication will be monitored pursuant to the regulation. Second, the regulation erects a "firewall" between the team monitoring the communications and the outside world, including persons involved with any ongoing prosecution of the client. Third, absent imminent violence or terrorism, the government will have to obtain court approval before any information from monitored communications is used for any purpose, including for investigative purposes. And fourth, no privileged information will be retained by the monitoring team; only information that is not privileged may be retained.

The Justice department has two objectives in the war on terrorism: to protect innocent American lives, and to safeguard the liberties for which America stands. We have enhanced our national security by immobilizing suspected terrorists before they are able to strike...."

Objections to the new regulations have come from defense attorneys and civil liberties groups. In testimony at the same hearing Michael Boyle, on behalf of the American Immigration Lawyers Association, objected to the new regulations to monitor attorney-client communications:

"...Despite government assertions that this broad authority will be applied in only a limited number of cases, nothing in the regulations prohibits it from being applied broadly. According to a summary published in the Federal Register, the monitoring will be conducted without a court order in any case the Attorney General certifies 'that reasonable suspicion exists to believe that an inmate may use communications with attorneys or their agents to facilitate acts of terrorism." Such certification will last for up to one year, and is not subject to judicial review. The new regulations also expand the definition of 'inmate' to cover anyone 'held as witnesses, detainees, or otherwise' by INS agents, US marshals or other federal authorities.

Other than vague and general assertions that these new measures are necessary to protect the public, the Department of Justice has failed to demonstrate the need for these rules to protect against attorneys who may help to facilitate future or ongoing criminal activity. Under existing law, federal authorities can seek appropriate remedies under the well-established 'crime-fraud' exception to attorney-client privilege. In a closed-door hearing before a federal judge, and in the absence of the offending attorney, the court can take immediate and effective actions, including ordering the monitoring of communications if necessary. Other options include removing the attorney from the case and prosecutors are always free to initiate criminal proceedings against attorneys where appropriate. These procedures ensure judicial review in the narrow band of cases where an attorney is abusing the attorney-client privilege, protect legitimate attorney-client communications, and ensure that authorities have the power to investigate and prevent criminal activity without obstruction..."

―――――――――

Dozens of Stewart's colleagues crowded the federal courtroom Tuesday as U.S. district Judge John G. Koeltl arraigned the 62-year-old Stewart. Prosecutors contend that she and three others helped Sheik Omar Abdel-Rahman pass messages to the media and to leaders of a terrorist organization he once led known as the Islamic Group....Stewart is accused primarily of violating a special administrative measure, known as a SAM, imposed on Adbel-Rahman, limiting his access to the mail, media, telephone and visitors to prevent him from further plotting against U.S. interests. Stewart was required to sign the SAM to continue contact with her client. She allegedly violated the measure by conspiring with Abdel-Rahman's interpreter to pass messages to an Islamic Group leader in New York and the former head of the London-based Islamic Observation Center. The indictment accuses Stewart of allowing discussions about whether the Islamic Groups should continue to comply with a cease-fire of terrorist activity in Egypt and then announcing to the media that Abdel-Rahman was withdrawing his support for the cease-fire....But during his announcement of the indictments, Attorney General John Ashcroft had a different assessment. He said inmates such as Abdel-Rahman were attempting to subvert the system of justice for terrorist ends. He mentioned that the al-Qaida training manual instructs recruits on how to continue terrorist operations from behind bars. Ashcroft said the Stewart case opens the door for federal officials to begin using his October 2001 administrative rule allowing for monitoring of conversations between Adbel-Rahman and his lawyers without the further need of court approval.

[Molly McDonough, "Lawyer Charged with Aiding Terrorists. Prosecution Claims Conspiracy to Violate Special Agreement Limiting Client's Access to Media," 1 ABA Journal & Report (April 12, 2002)].

United States v. Stewart
2002 U.S. Dist. LEXIS 10530

JOHN G. KOELTL, District Judge:

On April 8, 2002, Lynne Stewart, Esq. (the "defendant") was indicted for conspiring to provide material support or resources to designated foreign terrorist organizations in violation of 18 U.S.C. §2339B, providing such support and resources, conspiring to defraud the United States in violation of 18 U.S.C. §371, and making false statements to federal officers in violation of 18 U.S.C. §1001. The Indictment names three additional defendants. On that same day, the government obtained a warrant to search the defendant's law offices, which are part of a larger suite shared by her and four other criminal defense attorneys, for evidence and indicia of these alleged crimes. On April 9, 2002, agents entered the defendant's law offices and executed the warrant, seizing originals or copies of a number of documents, files, computers, diskettes and hard drives from her office and from the common areas of the suite.

The defendant now moves for the appointment of a neutral Special Master to review the items seized for privilege (including the applicability of any exceptions to any relevant privileges, such as the crime-fraud exception) and for responsiveness to the warrant so as to prevent the government from reviewing any materials that are either privileged or non-responsive. The government has placed the disputed materials under seal and has agreed not to review any of them until the Court decides this motion....

The defendant, Lynne Stewart, is a criminal defense attorney whose offices are located in New York County and who has represented numerous defendants or potential defendants in criminal cases.

One of these clients, Sheikh Abdel Rahman, was convicted in 1995 of engaging in a seditious conspiracy to wage a war of urban terrorism against the United States, which included the bombing of the World Trade Center in 1993 and a failed plot to bomb a number of New York City landmarks, including the United Nations, the FBI Building in lower Manhattan and the Lincoln and Holland tunnels. During his time in prison, Sheikh Rahman has allegedly remained one of the principal spiritual leaders of the so-called "Islamic Group" ("IG"), as well as a high-ranking member of jihad organizations based in Egypt and elsewhere.

Beginning in 1997, the Bureau of Prisons, acting at the direction of the Attorney General, placed Sheikh Rahman under Special Administrative Measures ("SAM's"), pursuant to 28 C.F.R. §501.3, which were allegedly designed to sharply curtail his ability to communicate with other members of the IG and with the media in order to protect "persons against the risk of death or serious bodily injury" that might otherwise allegedly result. After Sheikh Rahman's conviction and after these SAM's were put into effect, the defendant has continued to meet with the Sheikh and communicate with him on occasion, allegedly in her capacity as one of his attorneys.

Hence, the issue in this motion is whether, in view of the special circumstances of this case—including the search of the office of a criminal defense attorney who represents defendants unrelated to any of the allegations in this case and the seizure of at least computerized information belonging to lawyers who are also unrelated to this case, and who represent clients unrelated to this case—the Court, in the exercise of its discretion, should have a Special Master perform an initial review of the seized materials, as the defendant proposes, or should have a government privilege team do it, as the government proposes.

Finally, as both parties agree, this case is exceptional in that the documents seized on April 9, 2002 are likely to contain privileged materials relating not only to unrelated criminal defendants but also to the clients of attorneys other than the defendant, for whom there has been no showing of probable cause of criminal conduct. The privilege and responsiveness concerns raised by this class of materials are therefore exceptional, and the likely existence of materials that fall into this class speaks in favor of appointment of a Special Master.

In sum, this case presents a number of extraordinary circumstances that favor the appointment of a Special Master to perform an initial review of the materials for privilege and responsiveness. The government has raised a number of countervailing concerns, but none that cannot be accommodated within a reasonable set of procedures that is overseen by the Special Master in this case. Hence, the defendant's motion should be granted.

CONCLUSION

For the foregoing reasons:

1. Gary P. Naftalis is appointed as Special Master to review the documents seized in the April 9, 2002 search of the defendant's law office. The Special Master shall have the authority to review all documents and computer data seized to determine (a) whether the documents and data are responsive to the search warrant or fall within some valid exception to the warrant requirement, such as the plain view exception; (b) whether the materials are protected from disclosure because of attorney-client privilege, the work product doctrine, or any other relevant privilege; and (c) whether there are any valid exceptions to any applicable privileges, such as the crime-fraud exception. The government will pay the costs of the Special Master.

2. To expedite this review, the government is directed (without reviewing the substance of any documents or computer information) to make two copies of the entire set of documents and computer data that were seized, and, as promptly as possible, to transfer one complete set of copies to the Special Master. The government is directed to provide the defendant with one complete set of copies of the documentary materials seized and to return the two original hard drives to the defendant within this same time frame. The government should retain a complete set of the original documents and of the copies of

the computer materials for its records, although the government is directed to place these materials under seal and not to review them.

3. The Special Master is authorized to meet with the parties and to employ any procedures for review that may help ensure an accurate, impartial and expeditious review of the materials, such that all responsive and non-privileged materials are produced to the government as promptly as possible. To that end, the Special Master may direct the defendant to produce a privilege log within a reasonable time period. The Special Master may also meet with the parties at will and may avail himself of any aid or expertise that they may have, or any other sources of aid and expertise that he may need, in order to perform the review appropriately and in a manner that is consistent with the other concerns raised in this Opinion and Order. The parties are directed to work with the Special Master in good faith to expedite these proceedings and to ensure their integrity and accuracy.

4. The Special Master is directed to hand over to the prosecution any materials that the parties agree are responsive and not privileged (or fall within an exception to any relevant privilege) and to winnow down the class of computer materials that the government agrees it would not review in substance after a cursory review for responsiveness. With regard to the remaining documents, the Special Master is directed to issue a Report and Recommendation identifying any documents that are only arguably privileged or responsive and deciding any disputes between the parties concerning privilege or responsiveness. The parties may object to the Special Master's Report and Recommendation within seven (7) days of its issuance, and the Court will review these objections de novo. The Court reserves the right to employ any appropriate procedures at that point to decide any disputes between the parties.

––––––––––––––

Lynn Stewart was convicted in 2005 for communicating messages from her client, Sheikh Omar Abdel Rahman, to his followers in Egypt. Despite being under SAM restrictions because of the charges against Rahman that he had conspired to blow up specific New York City landmarks, she violated the terms of her representation. Rahman was convicted in 1995 and Stewart was sentenced to 10 years in prison. She was released before her term was completed, on January 2, 2014 from the Federal Medical Center Carswell, in Fort Worth, Texas, on compassionate release grounds that she was terminally ill with breast cancer. Judge Koehtlt signed the order once prison officials confirmed that she was expected to live less than 18 months.

7.8. Federal Sentencing Guidelines

The Federal Sentencing Commission is charged with establishing guidelines for criminal sentences in order to provide for more uniformity in sentencing. In cases involving biological weapons or bioterrorism, where the Sentencing Commission has not addressed the specific crime, the unique features of biological toxins and agents may require a departure from the guidelines. These departures permit several steps above the recommended sentencing guidelines.

The following case addresses the factors which can be considered in a departure from the guidelines in a case involving the possession of ricin, a highly poisonous toxin from the castor bean.

United States v. Leahy
169 F.3d 433 (7th Cir. 1999)

JUDGES: Before Coffey, Easterbrook, Kanne, Circuit Judges.
Opinion by Circuit Judge Kanne

Kanne, Circuit Judge. Thomas Leahy pleaded guilty to possession of a toxin for use as a weapon in violation of 18 U.S.C. §175(a) and was sentenced pursuant to the 1997 version of the United States Sentencing Guidelines Manual ("Sentencing Guidelines" or "U.S.S.G."). As part of a negotiated plea agreement with Leahy, the government agreed to recommend to the district court that U.S.S.G. §2K2.1, which covers the "Unlawful Receipt, Possession, or Transportation of Firearms or Ammunition," was the most "analogous" offense guideline because no guideline had been promulgated by the United States Sentencing Commission to cover violations of section 175(a) at the time of Leahy's sentencing. The district court accepted the government's recommendation. Although application U.S.S.G. §2K2.1 called for a guideline range of forty-one to fifty-one months, the district court determined that an upward departure was warranted because U.S.S.G. §2K2.1 did not adequately capture the seriousness of Leahy's offense. The district court then departed upward ten levels from the base offense level that otherwise would have been applicable to Leahy's offense under U.S.S.G. §2K2.1 and sentenced Leahy to 151 months in prison. Leahy now appeals this sentence.

Leahy's appeal raises difficult questions regarding the appropriateness and reasonableness of an upward departure in a case in which a district court applies an "analogous" guideline to an offense for which there is no directly applicable guideline. Leahy raises two issues in connection with his appeal: (1) whether it was appropriate for the district court to depart upward in this case; and (2) whether the extent of the resulting departure was reasonable. Because we agree with Leahy that the ten level upward departure was unreasonable in extent, we vacate Leahy's sentence and remand for resentencing.

I. History
A. Facts

On November 23, 1996, Thomas Leahy shot his step-son in the face with a handgun. Soon thereafter, local authorities arrested Leahy and the State of Wisconsin subsequently charged him with negligent use of a weapon and felon in possession of a weapon. During the course of the ensuing police investigation into the shooting, members of Leahy's family came forward and alerted both local and federal authorities of Leahy's possession and experimentation with dangerous chemical and biochemical materials.

Leahy's wife was the first to contact the authorities. She informed the investigating officers that Leahy possessed books and manuals regarding the making of poisons and had petri dishes in which she believed he was developing deadly concoctions. On several occasions, Leahy's wife provided authorities with items allegedly belonging to Leahy including: various insecticides, numerous unknown chemicals and materials, bags of castor beans, a spray bottle containing an unidentified liquid, gas masks and protective gear, assorted laboratory equipment, and several books and other scientific materials on the making of poisons and toxins.

When he was well enough, Leahy's step-son also made several reports to the authorities regarding his step-father's activities. Specifically, he told authorities that during the summer of 1996, Leahy showed him chemicals, poisons, and other similar materials he stored in a storage shed in Harvey, Illinois. He also reported that, on occasion, Leahy wore a gas mask and a white plastic gown around their home and that Leahy had shown him a large quantity of chemicals and biochemical materials he kept in the family's garage.

Members of Leahy's family also reported to local and federal authorities that Leahy had threatened to use the "poisons" he developed on several occasions. Leahy's wife stated that he told her two weeks before the shooting incident that he was going to poison his mother and murder his ex-wife. Leahy's step-son informed authorities that Leahy claimed to have used poisons in the past. Leahy's sister told authorities that Leahy often spoke of killing people, usually family and friends. On one occasion, Leahy told her that he was developing an airborne-type bacteria that could be delivered through the mail and used to kill his enemies. Leahy stated that he would put his "killer virus" on the edge of razor blades and affix the blades to envelopes to be mailed to his enemies. Leahy hoped his enemies would become infected by cutting their fingers when opening the envelopes.

Ultimately, authorities recovered two illegal substances from Leahy's home: ricin and a spray bottle containing a mixture of nicotine sulfate and dimelthyl sulfoxide ("DMSO"). Ricin is a toxin derived from the castor bean plant and is considered to be the second most deadly toxin known to man; a toxin for which there is no known antidote. When inhaled or ingested, in even a tiny amount, ricin dust is typically fatal. Equally as disconcerting, ricin is virtually impossible to trace as a cause of death. According to authorities, the amount (.67 grams) and purity (4.1 percent) of the ricin in Leahy's possession was enough to kill approximately 125 people.

Nicotine sulfate reportedly is marketed by chemical suppliers for use in a variety of insect poisons. If injected under the skin, a very small amount of nicotine sulfate can have a deadly effect. DMSO, a legal substance, has the ability to penetrate the skin on contact and enter the bloodstream. Applying DMSO contaminated with a toxin such as ricin or nicotine sulfate to a person's skin would have an effect similar to that of injecting the toxin directly with a syringe. According to authorities, given the amount and purity of nicotine sulfate/DMSO mixture in the spray bottle recovered from Leahy's home, as little as three sprays of this mixture could be lethal.

B. District Court Proceedings

A federal grand jury returned a one-count indictment charging Leahy with knowingly possessing a toxin, specifically, ricin, for use as a weapon in violation of 18 U.S.C. §175(a). In a superseding indictment, two new counts were added to the earlier indictment. Count 2 charged Leahy with knowingly possessing a toxin, specifically, nicotine sulfate, for use as a weapon. Count 3 charged Leahy with possessing a delivery system designed to deliver or disseminate a toxin for use as a weapon. All three counts of the superseding indictment charged offenses in violation of 18 U.S.C. §175(a).[5]

As part of a plea agreement, Leahy agreed to plead guilty to Count 1 of the superseding indictment, and the government agreed to dismiss the remaining charges. The government also agreed to inform both the district court and the probation office that U.S.S.G. §2K2.1 was the most "analogous" offense guideline because no guideline had been promulgated for violations of 18 U.S.C. §175(a). The government considered U.S.S.G. §2K2.1, which addresses the unlawful receipt, possession, or transportation of firearms, the most "analogous" guideline because the term "firearm" is defined to include a "destructive device," see 28 U.S.C. §5845(a), and the term "destructive device" is then defined to include poison gas devices, 26 U.S.C. §5845(f).[6] Reasoning that "ricin is poisonous," the government recommended that the district court utilize U.S.S.G. §2K2.1 in sentencing Leahy.

The probation office's presentence report ("PSR") similarly noted that no specific guideline had been expressly promulgated to cover violations of 18 U.S.C. §175(a). However, the PSR reached a conclusion contrary to the government's recommendation that U.S.S.G. §2K2.1 was the most "analogous" guideline to Leahy's offense. The PSR concluded that there was no "analogous" guideline for Leahy's offense because ricin is a toxin, not a destructive device or a poison gas. Therefore, the district court could

---

[5] Section 175(a) provides: Whoever knowingly develops, produces, stockpiles, transfers, acquires, retains, or possesses any biological agent, toxin, or delivery system for use as a weapon, or knowingly assists a foreign state or any organization to do so, or attempts, threatens, or conspires to do the same, shall be fined under this title or imprisoned for life or any terms of years, or both.

[6] A "Destructive device" is a type of firearm listed in 26 U.S.C. §5845(a) and is defined to mean: "(1) any explosive, incendiary, or poison gas (A) bomb, (B) grenade, (C) rocket having a propellant charge of more than four ounces, (D) missile having an explosive or incendiary charge of more than one-quarter ounce, (E) mine, or (F) similar device...." 26 U.S.C. §5845(f); see also U.S.S.G. §2K2.1 n.4 (quoting same language).

impose a sentence up to and including life in prison—the maximum statutory penalty for possession of a toxin under 18 U.S.C. §175(a).[7]

Notwithstanding its conclusion regarding the applicability of U.S.S.G. §2K2.1 to this case, the PSR calculated the guideline range to be applied under U.S.S.G. §2K2.1 in the event the district court elected to accept the government's recommendation. The PSR determined Leahy's initial base offense level to be twenty pursuant to U.S.S.G. §2K2.1(a)(4)(b). After subtracting three levels for acceptance of responsibility and adding a four level enhancement under U.S.S.G. §2K2.1(b)(5) for intent to use ricin as a weapon, the PSR calculated Leahy's total base offense level as twenty-one. With a criminal history category of II, the PSR determined the Guideline's imprisonment range to be forty-one to fifty-one months for Leahy's offense. However, the PSR recommended that the district court "depart upward significantly" if the court elected to apply U.S.S.G. §2K2.1 because the application of U.S.S.G. §2K2.1 did not "come close to capturing the seriousness of the offense" in this case.

At the sentencing hearing, the district court also recognized that there was no specific guideline applicable to violations of 18 U.S.C. §175(a). Contrary to the recommendation contained in the PSR, however, the district court concluded that the application of U.S.S.G. §2K2.1 by analogy was appropriate in this case. In support of its conclusion that U.S.S.G. §2K2.1 was "sufficiently analogous," the district court noted "that although ricin is a toxin as is set forth in the charge, nonetheless it has been used in the vernacular as being a poison and [is] commonly referred to as a poison in the less than legal jargon we are familiar with." The district court further reasoned that even though ricin is technically a toxin, not a poison, it is "perhaps more closely analogous to a poison gas than any other of the guidelines which can be found and examined." Therefore, the district court adopted the reasoning suggested by the government in the plea agreement and found that ricin was sufficiently analogous to poison gas devices to warrant application of U.S.S.G. §2K2.1.[8] Having selected U.S.S.G. §2K2.1 as the most "analogous" guideline, the

---

[7] In the absence of a "sufficiently analogous" guideline, the Sentencing Guidelines direct the district courts to fashion an "appropriate sentence" in accordance with the general provisions of 18 U.S.C. §3553(b). See U.S.S.G. §2X5.1 ("If there is not a sufficiently analogous guideline, the provisions of 18 U.S.C. §3553(b) shall control...").

Section 3553(b) provides, in relevant part, that: in the absence of an applicable sentencing guideline, the court shall impose an appropriate sentence, having due regard for the purposes set forth in subsection (a)(2). In the absence of an applicable sentencing guideline in the case of an offense other than a petty offense, the court shall also have due regard for the relationship of the sentence imposed to sentences prescribed by guidelines applicable to similar offenses and offenders, and to the applicable policy statements of the Sentencing Commission. 18 U.S.C. §3553(b). Subsection (a)(2) requires the sentencing court to consider: the need for the sentence imposed—(A) to reflect the seriousness of the offense, to promote respect for the law, and to provide just punishment for the offense; (B) to afford adequate deterrence to criminal conduct; (C) to protect the public from further crimes of the defendant; and (D) to provide the defendant with needed educational or vocational training, medical care, or other correctional treatment in the most effective manner. 18 U.S.C. §3553(a)(2).

[8] In adopting the recommendation set forth in the plea agreement, the district court also looked to United States v. Baker, 98 F.3d 330 (8th Cir. 1996)—the only other court to address the possession of ricin under the Sentencing Guidelines—for guidance. In Baker, a jury found the defendants guilty of aiding and abetting one another in knowingly possessing a toxin, ricin, for use as a weapon in violation of 18 U.S.C. §175. Id. at 335. Specifically, the defendants were found guilty of possessing about .7 grams of five percent pure ricin. Id. at 333.
The district court in Baker, presumably relying on U.S.S.G. §2K2.1, sentenced each defendant to thirty-three months imprisonment. Id. at 335. We say "presumably" because it appears the underlying district court

district court then found the probation office's initial calculation of the applicable guideline range of forty-one to fifty-one months "to be the appropriate level in this matter for purposes of sentencing."

After reaching these initial conclusions, the district court then opted to depart upward significantly from the guideline range provided in U.S.S.G. §2K2.1 because the aggravating circumstances existed in this case that were not adequately taken into account by the Sentencing Commission in formulating U.S.S.G. §2K2.1. The district court determined that a significant upward departure was necessary in this case because U.S.S.G. §2K2.1 depreciated the seriousness of Leahy's offense as it did not adequately address the possession of a toxin for use as a weapon. The district court found four specific aggravating circumstances warranted an upward departure in this case. These circumstances were: (1) the maximum penalty for possession of a toxin under 18 U.S.C. §175(a) is life whereas the maximum penalty for possession of a destructive device under 26 U.S.C. §5861 is only ten years; (2) the number of toxins possessed by Leahy (two); (3) the high toxicity of ricin, nicotine sulfate, and the mixture of nicotine sulfate and DMSO; and (4) the potential for mass homicides the toxins afforded.

Based on these aggravating factors, the district court increased Leahy's offense level by ten levels. To justify the extent of this departure, the district court first turned to 18 U.S.C. §2332a, which penalizes the use of "weapons of mass destruction," for guidance. This section provides, in relevant part, that:

A person who, without lawful authority, uses, threatens, or attempts or conspires to use, a weapon of mass destruction, including any biological agent, toxin, or vector (as those terms are defined in section 178)...shall be imprisoned for any term of years or for life, and if death results, shall be punished by death or imprisoned for any term of years or for life.

18 U.S.C. §2332a(a). The term "weapon of mass destruction" is defined, in part, as "any weapon that is designed or intended to cause death or serious bodily injury through the release, dissemination, or impact of toxic or poisonous chemicals, or their precursors." 18 U.S.C. §2332a(c). Although Leahy was never charged under 18 U.S.C. §2332a, the district court believed this section provided a better gauge for the proper sentence in this case as it is the section most related to the death that could have occurred if Leahy had been allowed to pursue his endeavors unchecked. However, the district court, having arrived at its conclusion that ricin is a potential "weapon of mass destruction," did not link the extent of the upward departure in this case to those guidelines specified as relating to the conduct prohibited by 18 U.S.C. §2332a.[9] Instead, the court relied upon U.S.S.G. §3A1.4, the Terrorism guideline, to justify the extent of the upward departure.

---

opinion is unpublished and the Eighth Circuit's opinion does not address any sentencing issues under the Sentencing Guidelines because the defendants did not challenge their sentences on appeal. However, a sentence of thirty-three months under the facts of that case does suggest that the district court did rely upon U.S.S.G. §2K2.1 in sentencing the defendants.

[9] After identifying the relevant statute of conviction (or in this case, the most analogous statute related to the charged offense conduct), the district court should have turned, as the Sentencing Guidelines direct, to the Statutory Index (Appendix A of the Sentencing Guidelines) to assist it in determining the applicable offense guideline section. See U.S.S.G. §1B1.1(a). The introduction to the Statutory Index explains that "this index specifies the guideline section or sections ordinarily applicable to the statute of conviction." U.S.S.G. app. A, at 417 (introduction). For violations of 18 U.S.C. §2332a, the Statutory Index refers us to U.S.S.G. §2A1.1 (First Degree Murder), 2A1.2 (Second Degree Murder), 2A1.3 (Voluntary Manslaughter), 2A1.4 (Involuntary Manslaughter), 2A1.5 (Conspiracy or Solicitation to Commit Murder), 2A2.1 (Assault with Intent to Commit Murder; Attempted Murder), 2A2.2 (Aggravated Assault), 2B1.3 (Property Damage or Destruction), and 2K1.4 (Arson; Property Damage by Use of Explosives). The district court did not look to any of these guidelines to justify the extent of the upward departure in this case. Instead, the district court

U.S.S.G. §3A1.4 calls for an upward adjustment of twelve levels and a Criminal History of VI "if the offense is a felony that involved, or was intended to promote, a federal crime of terrorism." A "federal crime of terrorism" is defined as an offense that is "calculated to influence or affect the conduct of government by intimidation or coercion, or to retaliate against government conduct" and is a violation of, among other provisions, 18 U.S.C. §175 (relating to biological weapons). See 18 U.S.C. §2332(b)(g)(5). However, because the district court recognized that Leahy did not engage in "an actual act or attempted act of terrorism," the court elected to depart upward only ten levels, rather than twelve, resulting in an adjusted base offense level of thirty-one. For this same reason, the district court also elected not to increase Leahy's Criminal History category. All told, the district court's upward adjustment resulted in a guideline range of 121 to 151 months. The district court then selected the maximum sentence within this range, a term of 151 months, to "reflect the seriousness of this offense, hold the defendant accountable for his conduct, promote general and specific deterrence, and protect the community from the defendant." Leahy now appeals the district court's upward departure in this case.

II. Analysis

A district court's decision to depart from the applicable sentencing guideline range is reviewed under an abuse of discretion standard....This Court employs a three-part approach in reviewing a district court's decision to depart upward from the applicable guideline range. First, we ask whether the grounds for the departure were appropriate. Second, we must ensure that the district court's factual findings regarding the departure were not clearly erroneous. Third, we consider whether the extent of the resulting upward departure was reasonable.

On appeal, Leahy challenges the district court's decision to depart upward from the base offense level for his conduct as proscribed by U.S.S.G. §2K2.1. Leahy first argues that the district court abused its discretion in departing upward from the guideline range of thirty-one to forty-one months provided by U.S.S.G. §2K2.1. Having made the determination that U.S.S.G. §2K2.1 was the most "analogous" guideline, Leahy contends that the district court should have sentenced him within that range. The primary thrust of Leahy's first challenge is that there were no grounds present in this case which took it outside of the "heartland" of cases covered by U.S.S.G. §2K2.1. As a result, the district court's decision to depart upward was erroneous.

Leahy's second challenge is that the ten level upward departure was unreasonable. Leahy submits that even if the factors relied upon by the district court were adequate grounds for a departure in this case, the district court nevertheless abused its discretion by departing upward ten levels. Specifically, Leahy contends that the district court erred in relying upon 18 U.S.C. §2332a and U.S.S.G. §3A1.4 as providing a basis for departing upward ten levels given the uncontested facts in this case.

Because we agree with Leahy that the district court erred in looking to U.S.S.G. §3A1.4 to determine the proper extent of the departure in this case, we will vacate Leahy's sentence and remand for resentencing.

A. The Grounds For Departure Were Appropriate

At the outset, we note that a district court must ordinarily impose a sentence falling within the applicable guideline range. A district court may depart from the applicable guideline range and sentence a defendant outside that range only if "the court finds 'that there exists an aggravating or mitigating circumstance of a kind, or to a degree, not adequately taken into consideration by the Sentencing Commission in formulating the guidelines that should result in a sentence different from that described.'" In other words, "in the absence of a characteristic or circumstance that distinguishes a case as sufficiently

---

looked to U.S.S.G. §3A1.4, a guideline that provides for victim-related adjustments stemming from acts of terrorism.

atypical to warrant a sentence different from that called for under the guidelines, a sentence outside the guideline range is not authorized."

In examining a district court's ability to depart from the applicable guideline range in a particular case, the Supreme Court in Koon explained that the Sentencing Commission intended "the sentencing courts to treat each guideline as carving out a 'heartland', a set of typical cases embodying the conduct that each guideline describes." That is, the Sentencing Commission "did not adequately take into account cases that are, for one reason or another, 'unusual.'" Thus, "when a court finds an atypical case, one to which a particular guideline linguistically applies but where conduct significantly differs from the norm, the court may consider whether a departure is warranted." Therefore, before a district court is permitted to depart in a given case, certain features of the case must be found "unusual" enough for it to fall outside the "heartland" of cases covered in the applicable guideline.

1.

Before we turn to look at whether the specific factors cited by the district court in this case were appropriate grounds for an upward departure, we first pause to consider whether any violation of 18 U.S.C. §175(a) can be said to fall within the "heartland" of cases under U.S.S.G. §2K2.1. As we previously stated, it is Leahy's contention that the district court, having made the determination that U.S.S.G. §2K2.1 was the appropriate guideline for this case, should have been compelled to sentence Leahy within the guideline range provided in U.S.S.G. §2K2.1. Relying primarily on the analysis employed by the government in suggesting that U.S.S.G. §2K2.1 was the most "analogous" guideline to the charged offense conduct, Leahy argues that U.S.S.G. §2K2.1 specifically contemplates the possession of ricin as being within its "heartland" of cases. That is, U.S.S.G. §2K2.1 covers "destructive devices," which are defined to include poison gas devices, grenades, rockets, and missiles. Leahy argues that his conduct, the "mere" possession of .67 grams of ricin, cannot be said to significantly differ from the norm "where the norm includes possession of poison gas rockets and or bombs."

...By implication, cases embodying conduct regulated by statutory provisions that are not referenced by a particular guideline logically cannot be found to fall within the "heartland" of that particular guideline.

...Therefore, the fact that U.S.S.G. §2K2.1 was not expressly promulgated to cover violations of 18 U.S.C. §175(a), we believe is sufficient, in and of itself, to take this case outside the "heartland" of cases covered by U.S.S.G. §2K2.1.

Our conclusion here does not nullify the directive contained in U.S.S.G. §2X5.1 to apply the most "analogous" guideline. Although each case would be by definition "unusual" and, therefore, a candidate for departure, the selection and application of the most "analogous" guideline still serves an important function within the framework of the Sentencing Guidelines—it provides the starting or reference point within the structure of the Guidelines for violations of statutory provisions the Sentencing Commission has not yet tied to a particular guideline or guidelines. And it is from that starting point that any subsequent departure by the sentencing court, whether upward or downward, must begin.

2.

In any event, notwithstanding the foregoing analysis, we believe sufficient grounds existed in this case to justify the district court's decision to depart. The district court departed upward from Leahy's adjusted base offense level, because in the district court's opinion U.S.S.G. §2K2.1 did not adequately reflect the seriousness of Leahy's conduct. Leahy contends that the district court erroneously departed because its decision to depart was not premised upon any factor encouraged as a basis for departure by the Sentencing Commission. We disagree with Leahy and conclude that there were appropriate grounds for departure in this case.

In Koon, the Supreme Court set forth the analytical framework to be utilized in determining whether an upward departure from the applicable guidelines range is appropriate. District courts are directed to ask:

1) What features of this case, potentially, take it outside the Guidelines' "heartland" and make of it a special, or unusual, case?

2) Has the Commission forbidden departures based on those features?

3) If not, has the Commission encouraged departures based on those features?

4) If not, has the Commission discouraged departures based on those features?

Koon, 518 U.S. at 95 (quoting United States v. Rivera, 994 F.2d 942, 949 (1st Cir. 1993)). The Supreme Court went on to explain the mechanics of applying this framework:

If the special factor is a forbidden factor, the sentencing court cannot use it as a basis for departure. If the special factor is an encouraged factor, the court is authorized to depart if the applicable Guideline does not already take it into account. If the special factor is a discouraged factor, or an encouraged factor already taken into account by the applicable Guideline, the court should depart only if the factor is present to an exceptional degree or in some other way makes the case different from the ordinary case where the factor is present. If a factor is unmentioned in the Guidelines, the court must, after considering the structure and theory of both relevant individual guidelines and the Guidelines taken as a whole, decide whether it is sufficient to take the case out of the Guidelines heartland. The court must bear in mind the Commission's expectation that departures based on grounds not mentioned in the Guidelines will be highly infrequent.

518 U.S. at 95–96 (citations and internal quotations omitted).

In justifying its decision to depart upward, the district court identified four factors it believed took this case out of the "heartland" of cases under U.S.S.G. §2K2.1. The factors relied upon by the district court were: (1) the maximum penalty for possession of a toxin under 18 U.S.C. §175(a) is life whereas the maximum penalty for possession of a destructive device is only ten years; (2) the number of toxins possessed by Leahy (two); (3) the high toxicity of ricin, nicotine sulfate, and the mixture of nicotine sulfate and DMSO; and (4) the potential for mass homicides ricin afforded. We believe these factors, when viewed cumulatively, provide an adequate basis in the record to support the district court's implicit finding that this case was "unusual" and that it warranted an upward departure under U.S.S.G. §5K2.0.

We begin by noting that the Sentencing Commission has not ruled out any of the factors cited by the district court as a forbidden factor.[10] Nor has the Commission found any of these factors to be a discouraged factor.[11] Instead several of the factors relied upon by the district court are arguably encouraged bases for upward departure under U.S.S.G. §5K2.6 and 5K2.14.

---

[10] The Sentencing Guidelines identify certain factors that can never be the basis for departure. These "forbidden factors" include race, sex, national origin, creed, religion, socio-economic status, drug or alcohol dependence, economic hardship, or lack of guidance as a youth. See U.S.S.G. §5H1.4, 5H1.10, 5H1.12, 5K2.12; see Koon, 518 U.S. at 93. Except for these "forbidden" factors, the Sentencing Guidelines do not "limit the kinds of factors, whether or not mentioned anywhere elsewhere in the guidelines, that could constitute grounds for departure in an unusual case."

[11] Discouraged factors include a defendant's age, education, family and community ties, employment record, and mental or emotional conditions. Generally, these factors are not relevant to the departure decision. ("If a special factor is a discouraged factor...the court should depart only if the factor is present to an exceptional degree or in some other way makes the case different from the ordinary case where the factor is present.").

Pursuant to U.S.S.G. §5K2.6, a district court may increase a defendant's sentence above the authorized guideline range if a "weapon or dangerous instrumentality was used or possessed" during the offense.[12] Leahy argues that U.S.S.G. §5K2.6 is not a proper basis for departure in this case because the use of ricin as a weapon is an encouraged factor already taken into account under U.S.S.G. §2K2.1 as a specific enhancement under U.S.S.G. §2K2.1(b)(5). That section provides, in part, that a district court should increase a defendant's offense level by four offense levels "if the defendant used or possessed any firearm or ammunition in connection with another felony offense." U.S.S.G. §2K2.1(b)(5). In this case, the district court imposed the four level enhancement provided in U.S.S.G. §2K2.1(b)(5) after concluding that Leahy had threatened to use the toxins he had developed on various family members on several occasions.[13] Thus, because the intent to use ricin is inherent in the offense covered by U.S.S.G. §2K2.1 and the four level enhancement provided in U.S.S.G. §2K2.1(b)(5), Leahy argues that it would be improper for the district court to depart upward under U.S.S.G. §5K2.6.

Leahy also claims not to remember making any of the threatening statements attributed to him. It appears that Leahy suffers from some form of mental illness for which he has periodically taken medication. Leahy claims that he had stopped taking his medication and that as a result his thinking may have become confused in the months preceding his arrest. Because of these "blackouts," Leahy contends that he cannot now remember making any threatening statements, although he does not dispute that some witnesses may attribute those statements to him.

At his plea hearing, however, Leahy admitted to possessing ricin and having the ingredients and instructions for its manufacture, admitted that he knew of ricin's deadly characteristics, admitted that he intended to use it as a weapon (regardless of whether he intended to use it to defend himself against real or imagined enemies), and acknowledged that he may well have made the threatening statements attributed to him. Thus, in the proceedings before the district court, Leahy acceded to the district court's characterization of these charges and cannot now be allowed to contest them.

Given the typical behavior of those who possess a "firearm" under U.S.S.G. §2K2.1, we believe Leahy's possession of a toxin can be appropriately characterized as "unusual" so as to remove it from the "heartland" of cases to which U.S.S.G. §2K2.1 applies. As an initial matter, we re-emphasize that U.S.S.G. §2K2.1 was not promulgated to cover weapons such as toxins, which suggests that this is not an ordinary case involving the use or threatened use of a firearm under U.S.S.G. §2K2.1(b)(5). In addition, a district court may take into account the "especially dangerous nature of a weapon" when considering an upward departure pursuant to U.S.S.G. §5K2.6. See United States v. Joshua, 40 F.3d 948, 951 (8th Cir. 1994). In the present case, the district court noted that ricin is extremely dangerous and that Leahy possessed enough ricin to kill approximately 125 people. Because of the high toxicity of the toxin involved in this case and the deadly consequences that could have resulted from its use, we believe the district court could have properly departed under U.S.S.G. §5K2.6....

---

[12] Specifically, section 5K2.6 provides: If a weapon or dangerous instrumentality was used or possessed in the commission of the offense the court may increase the sentence above the authorized guideline range. The extent of the increase ordinarily should depend on the dangerousness of the weapon, the manner in which it was used, and the extent to which its use endangered others. The discharge of a firearm might warrant a substantial increase.

[13] On appeal, Leahy also challenges the district court's finding that he threatened to use the toxins he developed on family members. Leahy claims that he never intended to use ricin as a weapon against any actual person. Instead, he claims that he created the ricin and nicotine sulfate to protect himself from imaginary enemies—against men he believed sought to poison him and his family and had obtained illegal entry into his house and tapped his telephone. In order to protect his home against unauthorized entry, Leahy developed the toxins to place on areas of his home, such as the doorknobs.

Similarly, under U.S.S.G. §5K2.14, a district court may depart upward if public health or safety is "significantly endangered" by the defendant's conduct.[14] We believe at least two of the factors cited by the district court would have provided a sufficient basis for a finding that Leahy's conduct posed a significant threat to public safety such as to justify an upward departure under U.S.S.G. §5K2.14. First, the district court referred to the high toxicity of the ricin possessed by Leahy as one factor underlying its decision to depart. Second, the district court expressed its concern about the "potential for mass homicides" the toxins possessed by Leahy afforded him. Relying, in part, on these factors the district court concluded that because the toxins possessed by Leahy were so dangerous, an upward departure was warranted in order to "protect the community from the defendant."

In a similar case, the Ninth Circuit concluded that a defendant's possession of homemade pipe bombs posed a significant threat to public safety warranting an upward departure under U.S.S.G. §5K2.14. See United States v. Loveday, 922 F.2d 1411 (9th Cir. 1991); accord United States v. Dempsey, 957 F.2d 831, 833-34 (11th Cir. 1992) (concluding that the defendant's possession of two homemade pipe bombs and one handmade grenade posed a significant risk to public safety warranting an upward departure under U.S.S.G. §5K2.14 because of the "diabolical" nature of the destructive devices)....Similarly, ricin is not detectible once disseminated, and there are no identifiable symptoms for those infected with the toxin. Clearly, ricin, like homemade bombs, is not a danger the Sentencing Commission had in mind when it formulated U.S.S.G. §2K2.1.

Another factor relied upon by the court in Loveday, which is also present in the instant case, is that the amateur construction of lethal devices, such as toxins, can contribute towards their instability. As the Ninth Circuit explained, when such devices are manufactured and stored in residences, they pose a danger to public safety not present in commercial firearms. Similarly, in the present case, Leahy produced ricin in a residential area apparently without concern for its accidental dissemination. Based on the dangerous nature of ricin and the circumstances surrounding Leahy's manufacture of it, we believe Leahy's conduct posed a significant threat to public safety and welfare and that a departure would have been warranted under U.S.S.G. §5K2.14. See United States v. Stumpf, (concluding that upward departure was justified under U.S.S.G. §5K2.14 when the defendant constructed highly volatile bombs in a residential area without regard to the safety of others).

In light of the foregoing considerations, we believe Leahy's conduct falls outside of the "heartland" of cases contemplated by the Sentencing Commission in formulating U.S.S.G. §2K2.1. Accordingly, we conclude that the district court did not abuse its discretion in departing upward from the applicable guideline range provided by U.S.S.G. §2K2.1....

C. The Extent Of The District Court's Upward Departure Was Unreasonable

Having determined that the grounds underlying the upward departure were appropriate and that the district court's factual findings were not clearly erroneous, we must now decide whether the district court's decision to depart upward ten levels was reasonable.

A district court's determination of the extent of an upward departure is by nature a discretionary decision. See United States v. Horton, 98 F.3d 313, 317 (7th Cir. 1996). However, while a district court's findings on the degree of departure are normally given deference, every departure from the Sentencing Guidelines must be "reasonable" in extent.

While this Court has approved of looking to an analogous sentencing guideline in measuring the extent of a departure, we must be mindful that the analogy selected is an appropriate one. Leahy claims

---

[14] Section 5K2.14 provides: If national security, public health, or safety was significantly endangered, the court may increase the sentence above the guideline range to reflect the nature and circumstances of the offense. U.S.S.G. §5K2.14.

the district court erred in looking to U.S.S.G. §3A1.4 for guidance in determining the extent of the upward departure and, as a result, the court's upward departure was unreasonable. Upon close review, we agree.

The reasoning we employed in Horton appears to be dispositive of this issue. In Horton, the defendant pleaded guilty to making a bomb threat against a federal building in violation of 18 U.S.C. §844(e). Id. at 314. The defendant made his threat one day after the bombing of the Alfred P. Murrah Federal Building in Oklahoma City, Oklahoma. Id. Although no explosive device was found, the bomb threat significantly disrupted the activities of the federal government. One hundred and twenty-three federal employees and many members of the public had to be evacuated from the building, an exhaustive multi-agency search for the bomb ensued, and as a result fourteen federal agencies remained closed until the following morning.

At sentencing, the government argued that the district court should consider an upward departure pursuant to because the defendant's threat resulted in a "significant disruption of a governmental function." The district court agreed and departed upward eight levels from the base offense level that otherwise would have been applicable to the defendant's offense. The court reasoned that such a departure would be appropriate given the grave nature and the unfortunate timing of the defendant's bomb threat. The district court arrived at its eight level upward departure by considering, in part, the six level enhancement provided in...the guideline provision that applies to threatening communications accompanied by "conduct indicating that the defendant intends to carry out such threat." While conceding that some level of upward departure pursuant to U.S.S.G. §5K2.7 may well have been warranted because the bomb threat did disrupt governmental functions, the defendant attacked the reasonableness of the extent of the upward departure imposed by the district court.

We agreed with the defendant in Horton that the extent of the departure was unreasonable concluding that the district court had erred in linking the extent of its upward departure to U.S.S.G. §2A6.1(b)(1). In order for the enhancement provided in U.S.S.G. §2A6.1(b)(1) to be an appropriate analogue for determining the extent of the upward departure in Horton, we reasoned that the defendant must have engaged in conduct beyond the bounds of making an empty threat because U.S.S.G. §2A6.1(b)(1) required the defendant to take some action that demonstrated his willingness to carry out his threat. Because the defendant "did not engage in any conduct that demonstrated an intent to plant an explosive device in the Federal Building," we concluded that the district court chose an inappropriate analogy for determining the extent of the upward departure. As a result, we found the extent of the resulting departure to be unreasonable....

In order for the district court's analogy to the Terrorism guideline to be appropriate, Leahy must have committed an offense "that involved, or was intended to promote, a federal crime of terrorism." See U.S.S.G. §3A1.4. The term "federal crime of terrorism" is defined as an offense that is "calculated to influence or affect the conduct of government by intimidation or coercion, or to retaliate against government conduct" and is a violation of, among other provisions, 18 U.S.C. §175 (relating to biological weapons). While Leahy did violate 18 U.S.C. §175(a), there is absolutely no evidence in the record that Leahy sought to influence or affect the conduct of the government. In fact, the district court itself readily concluded that Leahy did not engage or attempt to engage in any act of terrorism. The court stated that "because this is not an actual act [or] attempted act of terrorism, the Court elects to depart upward only ten levels...[and] for the same reason, the Court does not increase the Criminal History Computation." Thus, we must conclude here, as we did in Horton, that the district court, in selecting U.S.S.G. §3A1.4, chose an inappropriate analogy for determining the extent of the upward departure in this case. See also United States v. Baldwin, 5 F.3d 241, 242 (7th Cir. 1993) (finding it improper for the district court to depart upward under a guideline that required a dangerous weapon be "used or possessed in the commission of the offense" when there was no evidence that the defendant used or possessed a dangerous weapon during the offense of conviction). As a result, we must find the upward departure in this case to be unreasonable.

This conclusion is further supported when we look to those guidelines promulgated to cover offenses prohibited by 18 U.S.C. §2332a, which the district court initially relied upon in determining the extent of Leahy's upward departure before turning to U.S.S.G. §3A1.4. 18 U.S.C. §2332a, by its express terms, appears to cover more closely that conduct the district court seeks to attribute to Leahy. Section 2332a punishes the use, attempted use, or threatened use of a weapon of mass destruction, "including any biological agent, toxin, or vector." By comparison, section 175(a) punishes any person who develops, produces, or possesses any biological agent, toxin, or delivery system for use as a weapon. 18 U.S.C. §175(a). Thus, section 2332a punishes the use (or attempted or threatened use) of weapons of mass destruction while section 175(a) merely seeks to punish acquisition and possession of those same weapons.

While there was no evidence introduced in this case that Leahy actually used, or even attempted to use, the toxins against any person, there was some evidence that Leahy had threatened to use the toxins he had developed against various family members and friends. Because 18 U.S.C. §2332a purports to punish any person who "threatens" to use a weapon of mass destruction (including any toxin), arguably one of the guidelines promulgated to cover conduct prohibited by section 2332a could provide an appropriate analogy for an upward departure in this case as there was at least some evidence that Leahy engaged in that type of conduct.

As we have previously stated, the Sentencing Commission refers to a number of guidelines for violations of section 2332a including: U.S.S.G. §2A1.1 (First Degree Murder); 2A1.2 (Second Degree Murder); 2A1.3 (Voluntary Manslaughter); 2A1.4 (Involuntary Manslaughter); 2A1.5 (Conspiracy or Solicitation to Commit Murder); 2A2.1 (Assault with Intent to Commit Murder; Attempted Murder), 2A2.2 (Aggravated Assault); 2B1.3 (Property Damage or Destruction); and 2K1.4 (Arson; Property Damage by Use of Explosives). Because Leahy did not cause the death of any person, none of the guidelines that cover offenses resulting in actual death would be appropriate.

While neither of these guidelines, by their terms, appear to cover "threats," they are nevertheless useful because they illustrate that the district court's upward departure in this case had the effect of imposing a longer sentence upon Leahy than he likely would have received had he actually attempted to use the ricin against a person without killing them—an offense more serious than the mere possession or threatened use of a prohibited toxin. For example, under U.S.S.G. §2A2.1, the attempted murder guideline, Leahy's initial base offense level would be either twenty-eight or twenty-two, depending on whether the object of the offense would have constituted first degree murder. Assuming Leahy's hypothetical attempt resulted in no harm to the intended victim, Leahy's adjusted base offense level, after subtracting three levels for acceptance of responsibility, would be either twenty-five or nineteen. Even if Leahy's attempt had been partially successful, in that it resulted in some injury to the victim, under the specific offense characteristics provided in U.S.S.G. §2A2.1(b), Leahy's offense level could be increased, at most, by four levels, depending on the nature of the injury suffered by the victim. Thus, in a worst case scenario from Leahy's perspective, one in which Leahy attempts to murder someone and his attempt results in permanent injury, but not death, Leahy's offense level would be either twenty-nine or twenty-two.

Similarly, according to our calculations, Leahy's maximum potential base offense level under U.S.S.G. §2A2.2, the aggravated assault guideline, would be around twenty-five. As provided in U.S.S.G. §2A2.2(a), Leahy's initial base offense level for aggravated assault with a toxin would be fifteen. If we factor in possible specific offense characteristics: two levels under U.S.S.G. §2A2.2(b)(1) for an assault involving more than minimal planning, five levels under U.S.S.G. §2A2.2(b)(2) for the discharge of a firearm, and six levels for permanent bodily injury; Leahy's base level would be twenty-eight. After subtracting three levels for acceptance of responsibility, Leahy's adjusted base offense level would be twenty-five. Thus, even if we assume that Leahy's hypothetical aggravated assault involved more than minimal planning, that Leahy used ricin during the assault, and that the assault resulted in permanent injury to the victim, Leahy's adjusted base offense level would still be only twenty-five.

In comparison, the district court determined Leahy's adjusted base offense level for the possession of ricin in the present case to be thirty-one. Thus, we find it significant that Leahy could have attempted to use the toxin, even causing significant injury to a victim, and potentially have received a less severe sentence than that which the district court imposed for Leahy's conduct in possessing a toxin. Because these are the types of sentencing ranges Leahy could have received had he committed a more serious offense, a departure logically should not exceed these levels.

Accordingly, we conclude that the district court abused its discretion in departing upward ten levels.

III. Conclusion

Because there was no evidence showing that Leahy engaged in an actual act or attempted act of terrorism, we conclude that the district court, in selecting U.S.S.G. §3A1.4, chose an inappropriate analogy for determining the extent of the upward departure in this case. As a result, we hold that the district court abused its discretion in imposing a ten level upward departure. Therefore, we VACATE Leahy's sentence and REMAND for resentencing in accordance with this opinion.

In *United States v. Leahy*, the court found the district court abused its discretion by its upward departure from the sentencing guidelines by ten levels, it appears primarily because the court found that had Leahy actually committed the act of terrorism, rather than just threaten one, he would have received a lesser sentence.

In *United States v. Thomas Butler*, on appeal of his conviction and sentencing of 24 months, on March 10, 2004, where the federal district court had departed downward, rather than upward, for among other counts, conviction of illegally exporting plague without an export permit. The case involved a scientist at Texas Tech University who had triggered an investigation when he reported that he had 30 missing or stolen vials of plague from his office, presumptively to avert attention from his activities of working with *yersinia pestis* and his diversion of funds from his employer.

On December 1, 2003, the jury returned a verdict of guilty on 47 of 69 counts, the one carrying the highest possible sentence was the exportation of plague to Tanzania without an export permit. The government entered a " Motion for Upward Departure of Criminal Fine Under US Sentencing Guidelines by USA as to Thomas Campbell Butler," on March 4, 2004. However, the sentence was a downward departure.

His appeal of his conviction and sentencing to the 5th Circuit was curious in that the sentence was a downward departure, not the upward departure authorized by the sentencing guidelines. The following excerpt from the sentencing trial transcript evidences the impact of the support from other scientists and organizations on Judge Cummings in his decision for the downward departure:

> "Number two, as noted in trial and sentencing testimony, the defendant's research and discoveries have led to the salvage of millions of lives throughout the world. There is not a case on record that could better exemplify a great service to society as a whole that is substantially extraordinary and is outside of anything the United States Sentencing Commission could have formulated in their devising of the guidelines governing departures regarding educational and vocational skills, as shown in Section 5H1.2 of the guidelines; the employment record, as stated in 5H1.5; and military, civic, charitable, or public service; employment-related contributions; and record of prior good works as referred to in Section 5H1.11 of the guidelines. It should be noted that the record adequately reflects these contributions to be exceptional in nature.
>
> The court has therefore departed an additional three levels from the total offense level of 20, now finding that the total offense level is 17.

With a Criminal History Category of I, the guideline custody range now becomes 24 to 30 months, and I have assessed a sentence of 24 months' incarceration."

In fact, it was possible that the 5th Circuit could have remanded for consideration of an upward departure. However, the 5th Circuit confirmed the federal district court's conviction and sentencing of Thomas Butler.

The case had received worldwide attention due to the recognition of Thomas Butler as a published expert on plague for decades. The National Academies and Institute of Medicine convened the Humans Rights Committee to seek to help Dr. Butler find employment after he was required to forfeit his medical license and was prohibited from handling any select agent, including plague, because of his felony conviction. It was only the second time the committee had considered a case, having been formed primarily for foreign scientists seeking employment due to human rights issues.

Dr. Butler petitioned the U.S. Supreme Court on *certiorari* to hear his case, April 11, 2006. The petition for *certiorari* was denied on May 15, 2006. (*Butler v. United States*, Petition for Cert., No. 05-1308).

The case remains a stark reminder of the rapid shift in the legal framework for regulating potential bioweapons, as well as the heightened vigiliance for the enforcement of applicable laws, after the anthrax attacks. Scientists who formerly had been unaffected by criminal laws that addressed only intentional uses of bioweapons, were now well aware of the broad scope of both the new legal framework and the increased scrutiny on their activities.

7.9   The Amerithrax Case

On September 18, 2001 just seven days after the attacks of 9/11, the anthrax attacks' first victim came to light. In the weeks that followed, five people died and 17 or more people were injured, and thousands were treated for exposure to anthrax spores. These spores could be inhaled from opening the envelopes that served as the delivery device, or inhaled in the postal letter processing center or mailrooms across the country, through which they passed.

The investigation that followed is described by the U.S. FBI on their website as follows: "The ensuing investigation by the FBI and its partners—code-named "Amerithrax"—has been one of the largest and most complex in the history of law enforcement." An early suspect was Steven Hatfil, a scientist at USAMRIID, the U.S. Army research center for biodefense. He was ultimately exonerated, but not before years of search warrants, surveillance and searches had disrupted his life and his science career. In litigation against the government, Hatfil ultimately received a settlement. On June 27, 2008 a settlement was announced by the U.S. Justice Department for Steven Hatfil. His defamation litigation against the New York Times, columnist Nicholas D. Kristof and, separately, Vanity Fair, Reader's Digest, and Vassar College was ultimately dismissed at the appeals level, finding that he was a "public figure", therefore the publishers' free speech was protected. Litigation filed by the widow of the first victim of the anthrax attacked, Maureen Stevens, was suspended at the request of the government to pursue the investigation.

The Amerithrax investigation began to focus more and more Bruce E. Ivins, another scientist at USAMRIID, also using search warrants to find evidence to tie in the vast amount of circumstantial evidence held by the FBI which tended to point to Bruce Ivins as the perpetrator of the anthrax attacks. The primary evidence on which they relied was that the strain of anthrax in his possession matched the strain of anthrax used to perpetrate the attacks. In a review by the National Academies in an unpreceded review of an FBI investigation, their report tended to discredit the FBI's conclusion, finding that the mere possession of the strain of anthrax when 219 other people had access to it was not enough to conclude that Bruce Ivins was the perpetrator. The U.S. Dept of Justice and the FBI announced that the case was closed on February 19, 2010.[1]

When the case was closed and Bruce Ivins was announced as the likely perpetrator through the FBI and the U.S. Department of Justice making public many of the documents in the investigation, Maureen Stevens renewed her claim that the government had been negligent in allowing the anthrax to leave the government's laboratory. Afterall, they had just identified the perpetrator and he was a federal employee. This put the U.S. Department of Justice in a compromised (if not embarrassing) position, arguing that the government was not responsible, yet simultaneously announcing that a government scientist was the likely perpetrator. Maureen Stevens received a settlement of $2.5 million but with no admission of responsibility of the federal government.

The following journal article excerpt discusses the use of search warrants in this case which had a high degree of technical facts and evidence.

Grafft, Courtney (2012) "A Legal Analysis of the Search Warrants of the Amerithrax Investigation," *Journal of Biosecurity, Biosafety and Biodefense Law.* Vol. 3: Iss. 1, Article 6. DOI: 10.1515/2154-3186.1040

A Legal Analysis of the Search Warrants of the Amerithrax Investigation
Courtney Grafft

I. INTRODUCTION
One of the United States' most complex investigations in history stemmed from the 2001 anthrax attack letters. Filled with dead-ends, false leads, and flustered Federal Bureau of Investigation (FBI) agents and United States Postal Inspection officers who struggled with intricate scientific details, the "Amerithrax" investigation caused many to question the abilities of the U.S. foremost investigative entities. The specialized American bioweapons community remained in a constant state of paranoia from late 2001 to 2008, as more than 30,000 members of the American Society for Microbiology received a letter indicating the high probability "that one or more of you know" the anthrax killer.[2] Finally, in 2007, the Amerithrax Task Force formally announced its primary suspect, Dr. Bruce Ivins, a civilian bioweapons specialist at the United States Army Medical Research Institute for Infectious Diseases (USAMRIID). Only a few years before being identified, Dr. Ivins helped the Amerithrax officers sort through the complicated task of studying weaponized anthrax. Authorities constantly followed Dr. Ivins, and began a thorough inquiry. Investigative efforts ratcheted up in the Fall of 2007, when a series of warrants were issued to search Dr. Ivins' home, office, and vehicles. . . .

A. September 18, 2001
While the date is not as memorable as September 11, the events surrounding September 18, 2001, produced a subtle, yet similarly frightening and unknown crisis. One week after the attacks of September 11, letters containing anthrax spores were mailed to various U.S. media outlets and American politicians.8,[3] The first case of anthrax was not confirmed until October 4, 2001.9,[4] The next day, the spores used in the letters claimed its first victim, Robert Stevens, a photo editor at the tabloid magazine, the *Sun*.10,[5] The anthrax letters infected twenty-two people and ultimately caused the death of five people within a seven-week period.11,[6]
However, with the significant number of individuals, primarily U.S. postal workers, who also would have come in contact with these poisonous letters, the nation held its breath, hoping to avoid further reports of exposed individuals or anthrax-related deaths.12,[7] Additionally, the FBI struggled to figure out where to begin to find the culprit of such a malicious, unfocused biological strike.

B. The Investigation

Recognizing the fear and panic these anthrax letters were likely to cause, between twenty-five and thirty members of the FBI, United States Postal Inspection Office, federal prosecutors with the District of Columbia, and Department of Justice assembled as a "Task Force" to investigate the case.[13] At the outset of this process, the agencies involved could not have envisioned the missteps and false identifications that contributed to a relatively fruitless, yet expensive, seven-year investigation.[14] Perhaps the biggest and costliest mistake involved Dr. Steven Hatfill.

1. Steven Hatfill: A Costly Mistake

Once investigators focused on the possibility of the anthrax letters being a domestic terrorist attack, a likely profile of the perpetrator was developed.[15] In 2002, Attorney General John Ashcroft publicly announced that Dr. Steven Hatfill, a bioweapons expert with the Science Applications International Corporation (SAIC), had been identified as a "person of interest."[16] Once the Task Force recognized that Hatfill fit the perpetrator profile, they began prying into Hatfill's life to investigate his activities.[17] At a cursory glance, the FBI's identification of Hatfill as a likely domestic terrorist seemed reasonable. He was a specialist in the science of biowarfare, who had some questionable ties to military groups in Rhodesia and a few inaccuracies on his resume.[18] However, of the thirty total persons of interest identified by the FBI, Hatfill was the only one placed under continuous surveillance.[19]

Eventually, the FBI ruled out Hatfill as a suspect, but not before spending $250,000 of taxpayers' money for investigation actions, including draining a pond near Hatfill's home in June of 2003, which unfortunately yielded no results. As a result of his being named a suspect of domestic terrorism, Hatfill lost his researching job at SAIC and struggled to find employment elsewhere, considering his highly public investigation. After five years of enduring FBI probes, Hatfill filed a lawsuit against the Department of Justice and various media officials for violation of privacy. While publicly denying any liability, the government agreed to award Hatfill $5.82 million to settle his case. When adding up the settlement agreement amount and the cost of investigation, the taxpayer price tag for misidentifying Steven Hatfill as the anthrax mastermind is quite significant.

2. Amerithrax Villain Bruce Ivins

After the debacle surrounding the Hatfill investigation, the Amerithrax Task Force played their cards closer, at least in the beginning, with a second suspect, USAMRIID researcher, Dr. Bruce Ivins. Reports now say that authorities began considering Ivins as a possible suspect as early as September of 2005, at which time they pursued covert investigative techniques. Through testing of the attack letters' spores, scientists used genetic mutations of the anthrax, matching it to a flask labeled "RMR-1029." Ivins was asked twice by investigators to produce a viable, testable sample of the parent anthrax strain from RMR-1029. After contaminating the first sample by not following protocol and giving the wrong sample on the second attempt, investigators became suspicious and seized Ivins' flask. Utilizing the best known scientific methods, the FBI investigators claimed that Ivins' flask-anthrax was the origin of the anthrax spores found in the letters. According to the investigators, in addition to being one of the few individuals with access to that particular strain of anthrax, but Ivins also possessed the necessary skills to prepare the anthrax for use in the letters.

Over the course of three years, the Amerithrax Task Force collected substantial evidence linking Ivins to the 2001 crimes. Unfortunately, Dr. Ivins committed suicide in late July 2008, which prevented a full trial of the evidence to evaluate his involvement beyond a reasonable doubt. . . .

Although authorities ultimately conceded that Hatfill had zero involvement in the 2001 anthrax attacks, the search warrants, and accompanying affidavits, remained under seal for nearly three years after Hatfill was discounted as a person of interest.

a. The Right of the Courts to Seal Records

In 1978, the Supreme Court discussed the right of every court to control records which come under the court's review. Outside access to court records may be denied if the court determines that such access may be for an improper purpose.

The Ninth Circuit also claimed an inherent power to seal court documents in order to protect witnesses or prohibit interference with an ongoing investigation.60 The United States' Attorney's Office in Washington D.C. unsuccessfully moved for the court to seal certain search warrants used in the Hatfill investigation, claiming that release of the documents would hinder the investigation and have adverse consequences for Hatfill.

b. The Public Wins—Warrants are Released

While the circuit courts disagree, both a First Amendment right of access and a common law right of access have been recognized as applicable to search warrants and affidavits. More than two months after the release of the Ivins search warrants, a district judge ordered the Department of Justice to reveal the Hatfill warrants. In opposition to the order, the government argued not only that the ongoing investigation would be hindered, but Hatfill's privacy would be violated if the documents were unsealed. In defending his order, Judge Royce Lamberth stated, "The anthrax investigation was one of the most complex, timeconsuming and expensive investigations in recent history . . . [a]s a result, the American citizens have a legitimate interest in observing and understanding how and why the investigation progressed in the way that it did."

On November 25, 2008, search warrants relating to the Hatfill investigation were made available to the public. These warrants allowed for the search of a number of Hatfill's personal areas including, his apartment and basement storage and a rented storage locker. Additionally, warrants authorized the search of a Washington D.C. residence and a 1994 Toyota Corolla, each belonging to Hatfill's then-girlfriend, Peck Chegne. To demonstrate probable cause for these searches, the affidavit supporting the search warrants pointed to Hatfill's biological warfare expertise, his past dealings with the Rhodesian military, and his prescription for Cipro, a well-known antibiotic used for anthrax infections.

C. The Ivins Search Warrants

1. Warrants Released

While the media was forced to seek court approval for the release of documents surrounding the Steven Hatfill investigation, hundreds of pages of information containing evidence against Bruce Ivins was publically released without procedure a mere eight days after he committed suicide.69 In an interesting contrast with its stance surrounding the Hatfill investigation, the United States government moved to have portions of search warrant records in the Ivins investigation to be unsealed.70 On August 6, 2008, D.C. District Court judge, Royce Lamberth, granted the government's motion and ordered that redacted copies of the documents be made public record.

When questioned about the timing of the motion to unseal the Ivins documents, an unnamed official in the U.S. Attorney's Office cited the government's incumbent duty to release information to the public once the reason for keeping it sealed is no longer valid. The official further added that, due to the highly sensitive context of the Amerithrax investigation, the government sought to prevent the release of information describing the amount and type of evidence gathered against a suspect. After consulting with experts on the propriety of releasing investigation documents, the government thought it best to provide the victims and the public with as much information as possible. The released versions of the warrants and affidavits contained numerous redactions, primarily to protect the privacy of the Ivins family and names of witnesses.

After studying the Ivins investigation, taking into account the Steven Hatfill situation, one could surmise that the government may have wanted to release Ivins documents to persuade the public to view Dr. Bruce Ivins as the person solely responsible for the 2001 anthrax attacks.

Regardless of whether Ivins was aware of all the evidence gathered against him, three years of constant surveillance and public attention caused an unbelievable strain to an already troubled man. Perhaps the stress of investigation, combined with the rumors of a pending indictment, proved too much for Ivins as he committed suicide, thus closing the case on his own terms.

To date, there has been no [broad] public outcry against the government's investigation of Ivins, and the large amount of information gathered against him and described within the search warrants, diminished sympathetic claims of privacy-deprivation. Perhaps Ivins preferred death to the uncertainty and possible humiliation of a public trial. One thing is certain, because Ivins can never be tried before a court, or proven guilty beyond a reasonable doubt; the government's release of documents has left the public to draw its own conclusion.

CHAPTER SEVEN ENDNOTES

[1] Scott Shane, "F.B.I., Laying Out Evidence, Closes Anthrax Letters Case". *The New York Times.*,10 February 2010.

[2] Bob Cohen & Eric Nader, Dead Silence: Fear and Terror on the Anthrax Trail 8 (2009).

[3] Anne L. Clunan, R. Peter Lavoy & Susan B. Martin Eds., Terrorism, War or Disease? Unraveling the use of Biological Weapons 23 (Stanford Security Studies, 2008).

[4] Leonard A. Cole, The Anthrax Letters: A Bioterrorism Expert Investigates the Attacks that Shocked America 15 (2009).

[5] *Id.* at 1, 21-22.

[6] *Id.* at 184.

[7] *See id.* at 74.

Chapter Eight
National Defense and Bioterrorism:
The Military, Criminal Law and Biodefense

8.1.   History of Biodefense Research

The following excerpt from *Medical Aspects of Biological Warfare*, Jeffrey E. Stephenson, Ph.D. and Arthur O. Anderson, M.D., Medical Aspects of Biological Warfare, Chap. 24, "Ethical and Legal Dilemmas of Biodefense Research" (2006) at http://www.bordeninstitute.army.mil/published_volumes/biological_warfare/BW-ch24.pdf provides the military documentation and viewpoint of the history of biodefense research in the context of the ethical and legal aspects.

Introduction

The anthrax attacks of October 2001 made the nation acutely aware of not just the possibility of a large-scale biological weapons attack on US soil, but also has brought to the forefront concerns over the proper measures to be implemented to prepare for such biological warfare scenarios. It is evident that drugs and vaccines may be needed immediately to respond appropriately to emergency or battle situations. Government regulatory agencies, the pharmaceutical industry, and the armed services must work together more effectively so that vaccines and drugs that are not yet approved for marketing but have preclinical evidence of efficacy may be considered and used in the event of bioterrorist attacks or in times of war.

The pharmaceutical industry is not accustomed to responding to such situations; it is in the business of developing drugs to treat natural diseases afflicting patients of the civilian healthcare industry. Profit considerations and sustained business growth are, understandably, the primary objectives of pharmaceutical companies, so drugs are more likely to be developed for common rather than rare diseases. For such naturally occurring, often relatively common diseases, many potential test subjects are ready and willing to participate in drug safety and efficacy trials because of the possibility that the new drug might cure their diseases or help future patients.

This is not the case for products required as countermeasures against biological warfare agents. These infectious disease agents and toxins are usually found in areas of the world where humans have learned it is not safe to settle, or they occur in sporadic, small epidemics that kill everyone affected and fail to spread. In any case, there are rarely enough "naturally" occurring disease outbreaks of this kind to conduct clinical trials yielding substantial evidence of human clinical efficacy.

Over the past 60 years the conditions that must be met in order to use many of these drugs and vaccine products have become more restrictive. Until the approval of an animal efficacy rule and passage of the Project BioShield Act of 2004, Food and Drug Administration (FDA) regulations originating in the 1938 Food, Drug, and Cosmetic Act made emergent medical responses to bioterrorist attacks extremely complex by prohibiting use of investigational products until there was substantial evidence of human clinical efficacy. Gathering evidence in a scientifically valid clinical trial requires the participation of large numbers of subjects who have or are at risk of acquiring the disease, and accumulating these clinical observations takes a long time. Although some disease agents cause sporadic epidemics, others only infect individuals randomly when they happen upon a reservoir of contagion. Biowarfare attacks involving these uncommon agents would likely affect many people suddenly, permitting neither the opportunity to enroll enough subjects in a study nor the time for observation. Although FDA restrictions are meant to protect the public from possible harm, delaying use of potentially beneficial products until outcomes are known can be detrimental in the event of a widespread biowarfare attack. Throughout most of the 20th century and into the 21st century, successful animal studies followed by substantial evidence of efficacy from human clinical trials have been required before a drug could be approved for market. In an emergency, however, it may be beneficial to allow animal study evidence to suffice if the circumstances cannot permit valid human clinical trials.

Current regulations governing research related to biodefense development cover a wide swath of legal and ethical ground. However, the relationship between the military and the FDA is a complex one, partly because of the institutions' different missions. The FDA regulates the manufacture, testing, promotion, and commerce of medical products, and it makes a legal distinction between products that are approved and not approved for marketing. Products not approved for marketing are classified as investigational new drugs (INDs). FDA regulations specify what is necessary to change from the latter status to the former.

Because members of the armed services are at the greatest risk for biowarfare attack, it is prudent for the military to research and develop effective biological defenses that may also be used for treatment in the civilian population in an emergency. But in the military context, FDA regulations pose three significant legal hurdles to the military's ethical responsibility to protect military personnel. First, because diseases that are potential weapons, such as Ebola or Rift Valley fever, are both rare in nature and can be life threatening, it is immoral to conduct clinical trials to determine clinical efficacy because of the inherent risk to participants. Second, outside of clinical trials, the systematic use of INDs (as opposed to single use instances) in emergency life-threatening situations, is illegal. Third, it is illegal to systematically use licensed drugs in large numbers of persons for uses other than those indicated on the label. Ultimately, however, researchers must find ways to circumvent these limitations so that the FDA and Department of Defense (DoD) can fulfill their respective executive branch responsibilities while minimizing conflicts.

Federal regulations serve as practical and praiseworthy legal and ethical safeguards for the conduct of human subjects research. However, as detailed above, regulations governing the conduct of human subjects research can also have the unintended consequence of slowing the development and advancement of biodefense-related medicine. When the letter of the law is applied, the interests of military personnel may be lost in the shuffle, leaving the following ethical dilemma: on one hand, the military has the duty to adhere to regulations and obey the country's laws; on the other hand, the military has the duty to use all available means to protect its personnel and civilians and accomplish the mission at hand. Some way to bridge the two horns of this dilemma is needed; in particular, there must be a legal way to make protective drugs and vaccines available when the normally required clinical trials cannot be carried out.

This chapter will demonstrate ways to protect military personnel and possibly even the civilian population. The history of the development of biodefense in military medicine and the ethics of biomedical research will be covered. In addition, a summary of the evolution of regulations that influence or inform human subjects research, including research intended and designed in part to meet the needs of the military personnel, will be presented. Then an analysis and discussion of the conflict between regulatory requirements and adherence to ethical principles in the military setting will demonstrate three options the DoD might pursue in relation to the issues outlined. Some of the legislated solutions recently proposed or implemented will also be included.

OVERVIEW OF THE HISTORY OF BIODEFENSE DEVELOPMENT AND MEDICAL ETHICS

Advances in biomedical research have led to considerable breakthroughs in the treatment of diseases that military personnel face. Although the focus of this chapter is on biodefense, the history of research to protect military personnel from disease has frequently targeted naturally occurring diseases unfamiliar to US troops. The need for development of medical treatment in military settings has frequently been the impetus for conceptual breakthroughs in the ethics of human participation in research. Biomedical research involving human subjects in military research facilities must be conducted with oversight from an institutional review board (IRB), per 32 CFR 219.109.[1] Acknowledgment of ethical dimensions in biodefense research requires the cooperation of all military personnel. However, the ethical principles that serve as the foundations of current ethical practices in military medical research did not come about de novo, and neither did the biodefenses and protections. Military medical ethics standards evolved over centuries, often in tandem with or in reaction to biodefense needs, or in response to ethical lapses or controversies. At times the military has assumed the lead in establishing human subjects research ethics precedence.

Biodefense and Ethics in the 18th and 19th Centuries

In 1766, while still a general for England, George Washington and his soldiers were unable to take Quebec in the French and Indian War. In part this failure was due to smallpox outbreaks that affected his troops.[2] Later when Washington led Continental Army troops against the British, a smallpox epidemic reduced his healthy troop strength to half while the British troops, who had been variolated, were already immune to the spreading contagion. Troops were often gathered together from remote parts of the fledgling nation and placed into crowded camps, mingling with local civilian populations, which expanded variola transmission even further into vulnerable populations.[3] Washington proclaimed smallpox to be his "most dangerous enemy," and by 1777 he had all his soldiers variolated before beginning new military operations. In doing so, Washington fulfilled the ethical responsibility of ensuring the health of his military personnel, which in turn served to fulfill his professional responsibility as commander of a military force to preserve the nation. However, his actions were criticized by a public unfamiliar with the stakes or conditions weighing on this choice (Figure 24-1).

Fig. 8-1. George Cruikshank, Vaccination against Small Pox or Mercenary and Merciless spreaders of Death and Devastation driven out of Society! London, England: SW Fores, 1808. General George Washington was strongly criticized in the press because of the risks and his decision to go ahead with forced variolation despite concerns. A political cartoon, published in the 1800s, shows how critically forced variolation was seen by the public despite the Army's intent to benefit its soldiers.

Advances in military medicine and hygiene developed through experiences gained in battlefield medicine during the American Civil War were adapted as standards of medical care during the latter part of the 19th century. New medical schools such as Johns Hopkins sought advice about the most advanced patient care facilities, medical practices, and medical treatment lessons learned on the battlefield. The most direct evidence of the influence of military medicine on standard medical care practice is provided by John Shaw Billings.4 While serving in the office of the Army surgeon general, he designed the Johns Hopkins Hospital building, applying concepts he learned about the importance of hygiene, light, and ventilation while evaluating medical care in Civil War field hospitals. Billings also created an indexing system for medical publications that was used for the Army surgeon general's library and became the nidus of the National Library of Medicine. The Welch Medical Library at the Johns Hopkins University School of Medicine adopted this same system. Additionally, the Army ambulance system was developed during the Civil War because removing injured soldiers to field hospitals had a better outcome than treating soldiers in the field. Furthermore, soldiers suffering war wounds frequently died from infection. This lesson was not lost on military physicians. As the end of the war neared, the fledgling science of bacteriology and epidemiology became hot topics of battlefield military medical research. Surgical techniques and use of anesthesia and antiseptics became commonplace during the Civil War.5-7

The Civil War was also a testing ground for medical education. One lesson learned from the war was that many who served as military physicians did not have the skills needed to save lives in the battlefield. So the Army created its own medical school at what later became the old Walter Reed Army Institute of Research building. Those who created this school liked the training being done at Johns Hopkins, where some later became faculty. Later, civilian hospitals adopted the same surgical techniques and treatment methods. Johns Hopkins Medical School created new academic standards not found at "proprietary" medical schools. Thus, with the help and influence of military medical experience, Johns Hopkins set the stage for medical treatment in the modern era.

Surgeon General George Sternberg, who had been trained as a bacteriologist at Johns Hopkins Medical School, appointed Major Walter Reed, another Johns Hopkins medical trainee, to the Yellow Fever Commission in 1900. Reed used "informed consent" statements when he recruited volunteer subjects from among soldiers and civilians during the occupation of Cuba at the end of the Spanish-American War, and those statements could be considered "personal service contracts" (Figure 24-2). These documents clearly communicated the risks and benefits of participation, described the purpose of the study, provided a general timeline for participation, and stated that compensation and medical care would be provided. All of these are standard elements required in informed consent forms provided to research participants today. Even if the yellow fever statements did not directly influence the creation of other military or civilian informed consent documents, it is at least plausible to claim that documentation of informed consent from research participants in the military predates the practice in civilian medicine.

Biodefense, Ethics, and Research in the 20th Century

Ethical issues surrounding informed consent continued into the 20th century. At the same time, the importance of strategic research was emphasized, which influenced the growth of epidemiological and infectious disease research. A 1925 Army regulation (AR) promoting infectious disease research noted that "volunteers" should be used in "experimental" research.8 In 1932 the secretary of the Navy granted permission for experiments with divers, provided they were "informed volunteers."9

The importance of strategic medical research was not unwarranted. In 1939 Japanese scientists attempted to obtain virulent strains of yellow fever virus from Rockefeller University. The attempt was thwarted by vigilant scientists, but it did not take long before the threat of biological weaponry reached the War Department. In 1941 Secretary of War Henry L Stimson wrote to Frank B Jewett, president of the National Academy of Sciences, and asked him to appoint a committee to recommend actions. He wrote, "Because of the dangers that might confront this country from potential enemies employing what may be broadly described as biological warfare, it seems advisable that investigations be initiated to survey the present situation and the future possibilities."10 In the summer of 1942, the War Research Service was established, under George W Merck, Jr, in the civilian Federal Security Agency to begin development of the US biological warfare program with offensive and defensive objectives. On October 9, 1942, the full committee of the War Research Service endorsed the chairman's statement on the use of humans in research:

> Human experimentation is not only desirable, but necessary in the study of many of the problems of war medicine which confront us. When any risks are involved, volunteers only should be utilized as subjects, and these only after the risks have been fully explained and after signed statements have been obtained which shall prove that the volunteer offered his services with full knowledge and that claims for damage will be waived. An accurate record should be kept of the terms in which the risks involved were described.11

Despite the War Research Service's ethical commitment to adequately inform subjects of the risks involved in research, the statement includes an assertion of waiver of rights that is now considered unethical to include in military informed consent documents. The War Research Service also supported other experiments performed by civilian scientists that involved subjects whose capacity to give valid consent to participate was doubtful, including institutionalized people with cognitive disabilities.

Meanwhile, military involvement in the development of infectious diseases research was advancing. One of the military's clear successes was the progress it made against acute respiratory disease. Because of crowded living conditions and other physical stresses, acute respiratory disease had consistently been a cause of morbidity among soldiers and an increasing economic liability for the military. In the early 1950s military researchers under Maurice Hilleman at the Walter Reed Army Institute of Research identified seven distinct types of adenoviruses and created vaccines against them—the quick, successful development of medical countermeasures.

As the medical research community began preparing for biological threat and committing resources and time to attendant research, the undercurrent of doubts among human subjects research continued. It was not until Nazi war crimes became public that human subjects research issues came to the forefront of the dialogue on the role and value of science in society. Dr Andrew Ivy compiled 10 conditions that must be met for research involving human subjects for the Nuremberg Tribunal in December 1946. This document, now famously referred to as the "Nuremberg Code," was part of the Tribunal outcomes. In 1947 the Nuremberg Code was published in response to widespread knowledge of Nazi atrocities, including the unethical and traumatizing practices of Nazi doctors. The Nuremberg Code provided a clear statement of the ethical conditions to be met for humans as medical research subjects (Exhibit 24-1).

The DoD adopted all of the elements of the Nuremberg Code verbatim and added a prisoner-of-war provision.12 The Army included the code in directive Cs-385, which required that informed consent must be in writing, excluded prisoners of war from participation, and included a method for DoD compensation for research-related injuries sustained by participants. In 1962 Cs-385 became AR 70-25, *Use of Volunteers as Subjects of Research*,13 which regulated Army research until 1983.

In 1952 the Armed Forces Medical Policy Council noted that nonpathogenic biological warfare simulations conducted at Fort Detrick and at various locations across the United States showed that the population was vulnerable to biological attack. Additionally, experiments with virulent disease agents in animal models attested to the incapacitating and lethal effects of these agents when delivered as weapons. However, there was doubt among the council members that extrapolation of animal data to humans was valid, and human studies appeared necessary. Ad hoc meetings of scientists, Armed Forces Epidemiology Board advisors, and military leaders occurred at Fort Detrick during the spring of 1953.14,15 Thorough consideration of the ethical and legal basis for human subjects research resulted in the design of several prototype research protocols and creation of the US Army Medical Unit (Figures 24-3 and 24-4). This unit heavily invested in animal experimentation but aimed at modeling human infectious diseases to study pathogenesis and response to vaccines and therapeutics. Later, the US Army Medical Unit became the US Army Medical Research Institute of Infectious Diseases (USAMRIID).

In 1955 military research studies using human participants began in a program called CD-22 (Camp Detrick–22) that included soldier participants in a project called Operation Whitecoat. The participants were mainly conscientious objectors who were Seventh-day Adventists trained as Army medics. The program was designed to determine the extent to which humans are susceptible to infection with biological warfare agents. The soldier participants were exposed to actual diseases such as Q fever and tularemia to understand how these illnesses affected the body and to determine indices of human vulnerability that might be used to design clinical efficacy studies. In keeping with the charge in the Nuremberg Code to protect study participants, the US Army Medical Unit, under the direction of the Army surgeon general, carefully managed the project. Throughout the program's history from 1954 to 1973, no fatalities or long-term injuries occurred among Operation Whitecoat volunteers.

Operation Whitecoat serves as a morally praiseworthy model for the conduct of biodefense research involving human subjects. The process of informed consent was successfully implemented from the inception of Operation Whitecoat. Each medical investigator prepared a protocol that was extensively reviewed and modified to comply with each of the elements of the Nuremberg Code. After a committee determined whether ethical requirements and scientific validity were met, Army officials approved the protocol. Then potential volunteers were briefed as a group regarding the approved protocol, and they attended a project interview with the medical investigator in which the potential volunteers could ask questions about the study. Informed consent documents (Figure 24-5) were signed after an obligatory waiting period that ranged from 24 hours to 4 weeks, depending on the risk involved in the study. Volunteers were encouraged to discuss the study with family members, clergy, and personal physicians before making a final decision. By allowing volunteers sufficient time and opportunity to ask questions about risks, potential benefits, and the conduct of the study, this multistage informed consent process ensured that participation was voluntary. Soldiers were told that their participation in the research was not compulsory. Approximately 20% of those soldiers approached for participation in Operation Whitecoat declined. Review of Operation Whitecoat records of interviews with many of the volunteers and investigators revealed that the researchers informed participants that the research was scientifically valid and potentially dangerous, and that any harm to the participants would be minimized.

Approximately 150 studies related to the diagnosis, prevention, and treatment of various diseases were completed during Operation Whitecoat, including research on Q fever and tularemia infections and staphylococcal enterotoxins. Vaccines to be used against Venezuelan equine encephalitis, plague, tularemia, Rocky Mountain spotted fever, and Rift Valley fever were tested for evidence of safety in humans. However, scientists conducted animal studies before human subjects research. For instance, researchers exposed Operation Whitecoat volunteers to aerosolized Q fever organisms only after completion of animal safety and efficacy studies. The first exposure occurred on January 25, 1955, with the use of a 1-million-liter stainless steel sphere at Fort Detrick known as the "Eight Ball." This research device was designed to allow exposure of animals and humans to carefully controlled numbers of organisms by an aerosol route.

Research conducted during Operation Whitecoat also contributed to the development of equipment and procedures that established the standard for laboratory biosafety throughout the world. The ethical commitment to the safety of laboratory workers engaged with dangerous toxins, viruses, and diseases was manifested by the development of biological safety cabinets with laminar flow hoods, "hot suites" with differential air pressure to contain pathogens, decontamination procedures, prototype fermentors, incubators, refrigerated centrifuges, particle sizers, and various other types of specially fabricated laboratory equipment. Many of the techniques and systems developed at Fort Detrick to ensure worker safety while handling hazardous materials are now used in hospitals, pharmacies, and various manufacturing industries.

Operation Whitecoat was not the only example of US military involvement in human subjects research, and not all involvement in human subjects research reflects favorably on the US military. For example, the US military conducted unethical research involving LSD on uninformed human subjects from 1958 to 1964.16

Congress enacted the National Research Act of 1974 because federally funded researchers violated human subjects' rights, most famously in the Tuskegee syphilis experiments. This act immediately imposed rules for the protection of human subjects involved in research, requiring informed consent from subjects and review of research by institutional review boards. The act created the National Commission for the Protection of Human Subjects of Biomedical and Behavioral Research, which published the Belmont Report, a compilation of the principles implicit in ethical medical practices, in 1979. The commission also provided a schema for the formal review of research by standing committees. Belmont Report findings were incorporated into AR 70-25 in 1983.13

The ethical principles identified in the report, including the principles of respect for persons, beneficence, and justice, were compiled from a review of codes of conduct and standard medical and research ethics practices. Respect for persons refers to those practices whereby the right of individuals to make fully informed decisions is respected, and the need for protection of persons who are less able to exercise autonomy is recognized. Beneficence refers to the deliberate intention to do good and the assurance that participation in the research is more likely to result in good than in harm. Justice demands that the potential benefit and harm of the research be distributed fairly in society, which has typically been understood to mean that the research cannot solely assist or exploit any certain demographic.

In practice, these three principles yield the research requirements respectively for informed consent, risk/benefit analysis, and fair inclusion/exclusion criteria for participants. Much has been written about these principles, their flexibility and adequacy as guides, and their connection to philosophical foundations,17-19 and they remain appreciated as a practical approach to considering actions in biomedical contexts. The principles are secular but not incompatible with religious views, and they recognize the value of human individuals and the importance of collective benefits. The principles were incorporated into all federal institutions that fund research, including the DoD, as part of this common rule. Hence "common rule" became the catch phrase used to refer to the institution-wide incorporation of explicit ethical requirements as identified in the Belmont Report.

Success in incorporating ethical principles into human subjects research in the military in the early and mid 20th century was complemented by military researchers' numerous achievements in vaccine development with a variety of infections, including yellow fever (1900), typhoid fever (1911), pneumonia (1945), hepatitis A (1945), influenza (1957), rubella (1961), adenovirus (1952–1969), and meningitis (1966).3

The undersigned, Antonio Benino   *Antonio Benino*

being more than twenty-five years of age, native of Cerceda,

in the province of   Corima   , the son of Manuel Benino

and Josefa Castro   here states by these presents, being in

the enjoyment and exercise of his own very free will, that he consents

to submit himself to experiments for the purpose of determining the

methods of transmission of yellow fever, made upon his person by the

Commission appointed for this purpose by the Secretary of War of the

United States, and that he gives his consent to undergo the said ex-

periments for the reasons and under the conditions below stated.

The undersigned understands perfectly well that in case of the

development of yellow fever in him, that he endangers his life to a

certain extent but it being entirely impossible for him to avoid the

infection during his stay in this island, he prefers to take the

chance of contracting it intentionally in the belief that he will

receive from the said Commission the greatest care and the most skill-

ful medical service.

It is understood that at the completion of these experiments, with-

in two months from this date, the undersigned will receive the sum of

$100 in American gold and that in case of his contracting yellow fever

at any time during his residence in this camp, he will receive in addi-

tion to that sum a further sum of $100 in American gold, upon his re-

covery and that in case of his death because of this disease, the

Commission will transmit the said sum (two hundred American dollars)

to the person whom the undersigned shall designate at his convenience.

The undersigned binds himself not to leave the bounds of this camp

during the period of the experiments and will forfeit all right to the

benefits named in this contract if he breaks this agreement.

And to bind himself he signs this paper in duplicate, in the Experi-

mental Camp, near Quemados, Cuba, on the 26th day of November

nineteen hundred.

	The contracting party,
On the part of the Commission:	Antonio Benigno
Walter Reed	
Maj. & Surg., U.S.A.	

Fig. 8-1. (a) English translation of the yellow fever informed consent document. **(b)** Spanish version of the yellow fever informed consent documents. Major Walter Reed, who was appointed to the Yellow Fever Commission in 1900, used "informed consent" statements when he recruited volunteer subjects from among soldiers and civilians during the occupation of Cuba at the end of the Spanish-American War, which could be considered "personal service contracts." However, these documents clearly communicated the risks and benefits of participation, described the purpose of the study, provided a general timeline for participation, and stated that compensation and medical care would be provided. All of these are standard elements required in informed consent forms provided to research participants today.

The Nuremberg Code (1947)

1. The voluntary consent of the human subjects is absolutely essential.

This means that the person involved should have legal capacity to give consent; should be so situated as to be able to exercise free power of choice, without the intervention of any element of force, fraud, deceit, duress, overreaching, or other ulterior form of constraint or coercion; and should have sufficient knowledge and comprehension of the elements of the subject matter involved as to enable him to make an understanding and enlightened decision. This latter element requires that before the acceptance of an affirmative decision by the experimental subject there should be made known to him the nature, duration, and purpose of the experiment; the method and means by which it is to be conducted; all inconveniences and hazards reasonably to be expected; and the effects upon his health or person which may possibly come from his participation in the experiment. The duty and responsibility for ascertaining the quality of the consent rests upon each individual who initiates, directs or engages in the experiment. It is a personal duty and responsibility which may not be delegated to another with impunity.

2. The experiment should be such as to yield fruitful results for the good of society, unprocurable by other methods or means of study, and not random and unnecessary in nature.

3. The experiment should be so designed and based on the results of animal experimentation and a knowledge of the natural history of the disease or other problem under study that the anticipated results will justify the performance of the experiment.

4. The experiment should be so conducted as to avoid all unnecessary physical and mental suffering and injury.

5. No experiments should be conducted where there is an a priori reason to believe that death or disabling injury will occur; except, perhaps, in those experiments where the experimental physicians also serve as subjects.*

6. The degree of risk to be taken should never exceed that determined by the humanitarian importance of the problem to be solved by the experiment.

7. Proper preparations should be made and adequate facilities provided to protect the experimental subject against even remote possibilities of injury, disability, or death.

8. The experiments should be conducted only by scientifically qualified persons. The highest degree of skill and care should be required through all stages of the experiment of those who conduct or engage in the experiment.

9. During the course of the experiment the human subject should be at liberty to bring the experiment to an end if he has reached the physical or mental state where continuation of the experiment seems to him to be impossible.

10. During the course of the experiment the scientist in charge must be prepared to terminate the experiment at any stage, if he has probable cause to believe, in the exercise of the good faith, superior skill, and careful judgment required of him, that a continuation of the experiment is likely to result in injury, disability, or death to the experimental subject.

Fig. 8-2. The Nuremberg military tribunal's decision in the case of the *United States v Karl Brandt et al* includes what is now called the Nuremberg Code, a 10-point statement delimiting permissible medical experimentation on human subjects. According to this statement, human experimentation is justified only if the results benefit society, and only if carried out in accord with basic principles that "satisfy moral, ethical and legal concepts." Data source: Permissible medical experiments. In: *Trials of War Criminals before the Nuremberg Military Tribunals under Control Council Law No. 10*. Vol 2. Washington, DC: US Government Printing Office; 1946–1949.

IMPACT OF REGULATING AGENCIES ON STRATEGIC RESEARCH

The evolution of regulatory bodies overseeing human subjects research paralleled the evolution of military medical research ethics. These regulatory bodies influenced military research in positive and negative ways.

In 1901 in Missouri, 13 children died of tetanus after receiving horse serum contaminated by *Clostridium tetani* for treatment of diphtheria. In 1902 Congress enacted the Biologics Control Act (the Virus-Toxin Law), which gave the federal government authority to require standards for the production of biological products, including vaccines. The act contained provisions for establishing a board (including the surgeons general of the Navy, Army, and Marine Hospital Service) with the power to create regulations for licensing vaccines and antitoxins. Thereafter, only annually licensed, inspected facilities were permitted to produce biologics. This act marked the commencement of America's federal public health policy for biologics.

The 1938 Food, Drug, and Cosmetics Act regulated biologics through mid-century. For the first time, drug production had to meet standards for safety before receiving approval for marketing. The 1944 Public Health Service Act reinforced or expanded public health policy standards in two ways: (1) it became the mechanism containing explicit regulation of biologics, and (2) it created the FDA. Under its new authority, the FDA approved the influenza vaccine, chiefly on the strength of data provided by the Army.20

In 1962 Congress passed the FDA Kefauver-Harris Drug Amendments, which effectively launched the modern US drug regulatory system. These amendments stipulated an intense premarketing approval system, giving the FDA the power to deny approval for products with safety concerns. The amendments also required proof of human efficacy for all drugs and biologics, including vaccines.

The requirement for proof of efficacy of all medical countermeasures, premised on the principle of protecting the lives and other interests of human subjects, is a responsible action. But the Kefauver-Harris Drug Amendments also categorized the only available medical countermeasures against biological weapons as INDs, which created an ethical dilemma for the DoD. Compliance with the FDA regulations meant that the DoD either had to risk the deaths of human subjects in a valid clinical trial, or withhold potentially life-saving drugs or vaccines because they lacked substantial evidence of human clinical efficacy. (Of course, the drugs and vaccines in question would all require evidence of animal efficacy, unless no animal model of human disease could be found. Additionally, AR 70-25 [1962 and 1974]14 contained clauses [3c] that exempted biodefense research and testing if there was intent to benefit the research subject.) To resolve this issue, the DoD sought exceptions to these new regulations by negotiating memoranda of understanding (MOU) with the FDA in 1964, 1974, and 1987. The most recent MOU provided the FDA an assurance that the DoD would conduct clinical testing of biologics, categorized as INDs, under FDA regulations, including requirements for human subject informed consent, IRB review, and controlled clinical trials in medical research (see 21 CFR 50 and 56).21 The MOU states that the DoD will meet these requirements without jeopardizing responsibilities related to its mission of protecting national interests and safety.

CONFLICT BETWEEN REGULATIONS AND ETHICAL RESPONSIBILITIES

The military situation is unique. In the tension between the good of the individual and the good for the social organization, the latter justifiably holds greater weight in decision-making procedures in the military context. Members of the military have unique responsibilities, which include being fit for duty. The military organization also has responsibilities to its service members, including providing healthcare specific to the dangers encountered in battle zones.

Department of Defense/Food and Drug Administration Memorandum of Understanding (1987)

The 1991 Persian Gulf War brought into focus the inadequacy of the 1987 MOU and the conflicts between the duties of the two agencies. The DoD's mission is to protect the interests of the United States through use of military force. The DoD also recognizes its ethical responsibility to protect the health of military personnel. Thus, the DoD is doubly obligated to the mission and to service members. It is the responsibility of service members to keep themselves fit throughout the current mission and for future missions. When troops are threatened by biowarfare, in the absence of an approved biodefense product, one supported by preclinical data may be the only available option for troop protection. With a credible threat, the situation is similar to that of patients with an incurable disease who wish to try a potential remedy in advance of large clinical trials if it offers plausible expectation of some benefit. Such a product administered but proven ineffective would be analogous to sending troops to battle with faulty equipment. Such a product later proven unsafe would be analogous to friendly fire—perhaps an even more damaging situation for morale. Thus, the military requires a fine balance between necessity and caution. Proper biodefensive posture requires vaccination against credible threats. Vaccinations include licensed anthrax and smallpox vaccines and unlicensed vaccines for botulism toxin poisoning and a variety of encephalitides, including Venezuelan equine encephalitis, western equine encephalitis, and eastern equine encephalitis. Data for these unlicensed vaccines support human safety and efficacy,[22] even though efficacy has been demonstrated only in animals. Medical experts favor the use of these vaccines in protecting human beings when threat dictates. Because the vaccines are not licensed and will not, for ethical reasons, undergo the clinical efficacy trials required by FDA, they can only be used in an IND status.

Investigational New Drug Status of Vaccines

FDA considers any administration of an IND to a human to constitute research and authorizes the administration of an investigational product only in the context of a clinical research trial. Because the therapeutic benefit of the IND is unknown, FDA also requires informed consent. Administration of an IND requires specific and detailed recordkeeping measures. However, the recordkeeping requirements relate specifically to research, not to emergency or preventive measures connected to imminent risk of biological attacks on the battlefield. Collecting data from and recordkeeping for 100,000 soldiers would take exponentially longer than merely administering an unlicensed vaccine for treatment or prevention purposes. The consenting process alone for 100,000 individuals receiving an IND would take so long that strategic combat moves, such as immediate mobilization and deployment of a unit, would be impossible. Storing informed consent documents for 100,000 soldiers, and the accompanying logistical challenge of reconsenting soldiers if new risk information emerged during deployment, would also be daunting tasks. Furthermore, continuous data collection, as required by the FDA's good clinical practices (GCPs), is unfeasible and would effectively result in noncompliance problems, such as occurred during the Persian Gulf War. FDA regulations governing storage and distribution of INDs (21 CFR 312.57 and 59)[21] are rigid and restrictive, which would render any immunization schedule impossible in the field.

The FDA's commitment to protecting the citizenry from the unknown effects of medical treatments has thus resulted in two legal quandaries. First, the FDA permits the use of INDs, including the vaccines in question, for research purposes. However, the situation in war is not a research situation. Giving these products to military personnel before engagement in war for purposes of thwarting the onset of some horrific disease constitutes a treatment application of the product, not research. No benefit is believed to accrue to an individual receiving an IND. Thus, administration of IND vaccinations to military personnel in wartime does not constitute research, even though it is the only classification FDA permits for these unlicensed and untried vaccines. Continuing to categorize such vaccines and drugs as "investigational" also fails to inspire confidence in soldiers asked to receive the vaccine, even if there is limited evidence that the vaccine is not only safe but likely efficacious based on extrapolation from animal data. The label "investigational" does not communicate the strength of the data from animal studies that supports the safety and efficacy of the product. It creates the perception that soldiers at risk of losing their lives in combat are also being used as subjects of research, or "guinea pigs," despite the intent to use these products solely for the soldiers' protection.

The FDA requires informed consent from subjects receiving INDs. Consequently, subjects have the right to decide whether they will receive the IND, and soldiers understand that they cannot be required to take IND products. The requirement for informed consent is based on the Nuremberg Trial findings related to research in which benefits did not directly accrue to research participants. In the context of preventive treatment in a military conflict, the requirement for informed consent is a misapplication of a principle of research ethics. Enlisted and commissioned soldiers surrender much of their autonomy in matters of choice and accept the relinquishment of autonomy as a standard of military discipline. Specifically, one of the rights that military personnel forsake is the discretionary authority over their medical treatment. The requirement for informed consent threatens to put a divisive wedge between commander and subordinates, and such discord is counterproductive to military recruitment, retention, and mission accomplishment. One solution to this problem may be to move IND products to licensure either by animal efficacy rule or by BioShield emergency use authorization, with all of the attendant medical subject matter expert board review and input afforded to products going before the FDA.

In the first Persian Gulf War, the DoD was acutely concerned with protecting military personnel from harm related to biological weapons. Intelligence indicated that Iraq had not only used chemical weapons against humans in the past, but had also manufactured and stockpiled biological weapons that were believed to be ready for use. In documents sent to the FDA regarding implementing proper biodefense in military personnel against botulism, the DoD argued that waiver of informed consent was justified because a botulism vaccine (also referred to as the "pentavalent botulinum toxoid vaccine") was to be administered as protection of and not as research on military personnel. The FDA accepted this DoD argument and exempted the DoD from the data gathering and recordkeeping requirements typically required during the administration of INDs.

This decision had historic consequences. Some commentators characterized the FDA's accommodation of the DoD's wishes as unethical. This accusation resulted in changes in the relationship between the FDA and DoD after veterans claimed "Gulf War syndrome" injuries. Gulf War syndrome is a phrase used to capture the constellation of injury claims stemming from symptoms experienced by Gulf War veterans after the conflict, some of which have been attributed to anthrax and/or botulism vaccination. Despite repeated high visibility studies conducted by the Institute of Medicine of the National Academies of Science, no evidence of causal relation has been shown between these symptoms and receipt of vaccine. Most soldiers who received inoculations from the same lots of vaccine as those who claim illness did not experience any of the associated symptoms. Furthermore, the majority of claims of illness were associated with receipt of a vaccine involved the anthrax vaccination, which was an FDA-licensed product at the time of deployment for the first Persian Gulf War, rather than the botulism vaccination, which few soldiers received. Articles that summarize long-term outcomes after receipt of multiple vaccines, including those used during the Persian Gulf War, address the safety of these vaccines.[23-25] But even if the existence of a causal relationship between receipt of the vaccine and the manifestations of the Gulf War syndrome is accepted, the DoD's use of the vaccines to protect the force was an ethically supportable decision. It was an ethically supportable decision first and foremost because military intelligence indicated botulism was Iraq's biological weapon of choice, which meant there was a likelihood of its use during military operations. Any use of botulism by the Iraqi forces would place American soldiers directly in harm's way, but to an extent greater than would be faced during most traditional 20th century warfare. The DoD had an obligation to meet this extra threat, for the health of its soldiers, and for the benefit of the military mission. To meet this threat in as ethical a manner as possible, subject matter experts weighed in on risks and benefits of the use of the vaccine, and discussions between the DoD and FDA were held. That there may have been ill effects from the vaccine is an unintended consequence of the situation, the facts of which could not have been known beforehand, and which do not alter the ethically supportable dimensions of the decision-making process, the intentions, or even the execution of the plan to vaccinate soldiers.

Summary Points
Human Subjects Protections Regulations are Incompatible with Department of Defense Deployments

The immediacy of war preparations works against requirements of human subjects protection, including the requirement to solicit and obtain informed consent from subjects. Receipt of an IND drug must be voluntary. However, by definition, true force health protection (FHP) measures cannot be "voluntary." The voluntary nature of FDA-regulated research could undercut the effectiveness of FHP measures, which rely on universal compliance for their efficacy. FHP measures, which are necessary for success in war, are imposed to safeguard the soldiers' health. If left to the choice of individual soldiers, the health benefit to the soldier may be compromised. Military personnel, who have ceded part of their autonomy to the government as a condition of service, are obligated to accept command-directed protective measures in the United States (immunizations are voluntary in the United Kingdom and in most European militaries).

However, waiving the requirement for informed consent for receipt of INDs can undermine public trust and military morale. FDA requirement for informed consent for receipt of an IND is premised on the idea that administration of an IND is for research purposes, and the safety and efficacy of the drug are unknown. If countermeasures without medically significant contraindications were licensed for therapeutic purposes, this would lower the threshold for requiring informed consent. Licensure "for military use" would remove the stigma attached to use of an agent categorized as "investigational" for research purposes.

Realities of Deployment Conflict with Food and Drug Administration Regulations and Guidance

GCP data requirements support new product license applications, but GCP data collection does not serve the purposes of DoD military use of selected (unlicensed) medical products. The FDA enforces clinical data collection on IND products as a function of stringent protection of research integrity. Shortfalls in data management, such as missing data, missing vials, or missing forms, are inevitable during expediencies of real-time deployment and the exigencies of warfare, making it difficult for the DoD to meet FDA requirements. Protocol violations inevitably occur, even under ideal investigational circumstances, and even when researchers fully intend to strictly follow GCP requirements. Unforeseen circumstances encountered in war are unavoidable. Scientific misconduct, then, may be suspected when the realities of deployment work against traditional scripted research strategies. Ultimately force protection, not research, is the primary purpose of the military use of these countermeasures.

OPTIONS FOR FULFILLING MISSION AND ETHICAL RESPONSIBILITIES TO MILITARY PERSONNEL

Option 1: Continue to Use Investigational New Drug Products Without Full Compliance

The DoD can continue to use IND products, even though full compliance will not be achieved. GCP conflicts with the requirements of countermeasure use during wartime, as seen during the first Persian Gulf War. The ethical responsibility of the DoD to protect soldier health and welfare does not commit the DoD to creating marketable products. However, if the data gathered on these INDs during wartime are to be used for increasing product knowledge, then GCP restrictions should be relaxed for wartime military use. These changes would permit the DoD to contribute to research by adding to the data gathered before bringing INDs to market. DoD can choose to move forward with a particular IND product while doing its best to use the product according to FDA requirements, including adhering to GCP when practical.

Problems

Any relaxation of FDA standards could facilitate an impression of abuse of power by the DoD. Accusations of product approvals without sufficient consideration of safety issues could result in legal and economic fallout for the federal government. Most importantly, relaxing these standards, which the FDA has put in place to protect citizens, could result in a patient's injury or death.

Option 2: Negotiate for Accelerated Licensure

The DoD can negotiate with the FDA for assistance in hastening licensure of products required in contingencies or for FHP. If the DoD negotiates directly with the FDA, then drugs and vaccines could be given without the burden of research format and documentation. Epidemiological follow-up, not case report forms, would determine benefit, and decisions to retain or withdraw approval could be based on epidemiological analyses. The DoD could ask the FDA to waive IND requirements that cannot be practicably met in specific cases. Finally, the DoD and FDA could negotiate and agree to an updated MOU that permits the exemption of certain products for contingency use in protecting or treating soldiers.

Problems

The potential for DoD abuse of such power, or even the perception of abuse of such powers, will always be present.

Option 3: Institute Waiver of Informed Consent

Although considered a necessary condition for research to be ethical, the requirements for obtaining informed consent (21 CFR 50.20-.27, 32 CFR 219.116-.117, 45 CFR 46.116-.117)[21,26,27] are not absolute. If informed consent is unfeasible or contrary to the best interests of recipients (21 CFR 50),[21] such as in emergency situations or where the subject cannot give informed consent because of a medical condition and no representative for the subject can be found, the requirement can be waived. Executive Order 13139 and the Strom Thurmond National Defense Authorization Act of 1999 give the president of the United States the power to waive the requirement for informed consent for the administration of an unlicensed product to military personnel in connection with their participation in a particular operation.[28] The requirements are a formal request from the secretary of defense for such a waiver, based on evidence of safety and efficacy weighed against medical risks, and the requirement that a duly constituted institutional review board must approve the waiver, recordkeeping capabilities, and the information to be distributed to soldiers before receipt of the drug or vaccine.

One might argue that there is no need for a waiver of informed consent. If a soldier refuses receipt of a particular unlicensed product, he or she can be replaced by another soldier who is willing. But one does not have to search far for a scenario where waiver of informed consent might be warranted. The present day worries over recruitment and retention reflect this situation.

Problems

Some existing regulations conflict with the president's recent power to waive informed consent requirements for military personnel, including conflicts and limitations posed by Title 10 USC Section 980 (10 USC 980),29 AR 70-25.13 Title 10 USC 980 reads as follows:

Funds appropriated to the Department of Defense may not be used for research involving a human being as an experimental subject unless – (1) the informed consent of the subject is obtained in advance; or (2) in the case of research intended to be beneficial to the subject, the informed consent of the subject or a legal representative of the subjects is obtained in advance.30

10 USC 980 contains no provision for waiver of the requirement for informed consent, not even for the president, and neither of its two conditions for waiving the requirement would be met by a presidential waiver.

Chapter 3, section 1, paragraph (f) of AR 70-25 states that "voluntary consent of the human subject is essential. Military personnel are not subject to punishment under the Uniform Code of Military Justice for choosing not to take part as human subjects. No administrative sanctions will be taken against military or civilian personnel for choosing not to participate as human subjects."13 Thus, the Army's own regulations can be interpreted to conflict with a presidential waiver of consent, and if soldiers cannot be compelled to receive vaccines or drugs intended to fight diseases, the presidential waiver fails to accomplish its intent.

An additional problem with presidential waiver of informed consent is the requirement that such a waiver be posted for public review in the *Federal Register*. This requirement makes operational secrecy impossible, especially given the length of time some vaccines require to elicit adequate titers in recipients.

Also, public perception is a looming issue. If the requirement for informed consent is waived, even by the president, public backlash is not likely to be quiet or short lived. Public awareness of research subject abuse has grown, and the public is aware that informed consent is essential for the ethical use of products for which the FDA cannot claim knowledge of safety and efficacy. Public outrage directed at the military, and the subsequent erosion of trust between the government and the governed, is a risk that also must be considered.

CURRENT MOVEMENTS IN THE REGULATORY ENVIRONMENT

Further restricting the ability of the DoD to properly protect military personnel with vaccines with preclinical evidence of efficacy would not be the best solution to this legal and ethical dilemma. If the DoD were to eschew unlicensed products and the IND issue entirely, an argument could be made that military personnel would be at greater risk from infectious agents. However, several options are available to address this issue, some of which have seen dialogue or attention in the form of legislation.

The Public Health Security and Bioterrorism Preparedness and Response Act of 2002

The Public Health Security and Bioterrorism Preparedness and Response Act of 2002, also called the Bioterrorism Act, contains a provision to "fast track" certain products under the Federal Drug Act, including vaccines and other "priority countermeasures" eligible for accelerated approval, clearance, or licensing. Title II of the act also contains the kernel of what is known as "biosurety," which is a combination of biosafety, security, and personal reliability needed to safeguard select biological agents and toxins that could potentially be used in bioterrorism. Finally, this act approved the "animal efficacy rule."[30]

The Animal Efficacy Rule

Another regulatory response that reflects a positive move toward reducing conflicts in responsibilities between the FDA and DoD was the creation of an animal efficacy rule. A draft animal efficacy rule was prepared by the FDA commissioner's office and had been published for public comment 2 years before the terrorist attacks in fall 2001. The FDA recognized the acute need for an animal efficacy rule that would help make certain essential new pharmaceutical products available much sooner. These products, such as current IND vaccines, cannot be safely or ethically tested for effectiveness in humans because of the nature of the illnesses they are designed to treat.

The FDA amended its new drug and biological product regulations so that certain human drugs and biologics intended to relieve or prevent serious or life-threatening conditions may be approved for marketing based on evidence of effectiveness from appropriate animal studies when human efficacy studies are not ethical or feasible. The FDA took this action because it recognized the need for adequate medical responses to protect or treat individuals exposed to lethal or permanently disabling toxic substances or organisms. This new rule, part of FDA's effort to help improve the nation's ability to respond to emergencies, including terrorist events, will apply when adequate and well-controlled clinical studies in humans cannot be ethically conducted because the studies would involve administering a potentially lethal or permanently disabling toxic substance or organism to healthy human volunteers.

Under the new rule, certain new drug and biological products used to reduce or prevent the toxicity of chemical, biological, radiological, or nuclear substances may be approved for use in humans based on evidence of effectiveness derived only from appropriate animal studies and any additional supporting data. Products evaluated for effectiveness under the rule will be evaluated for safety under preexisting requirements for establishing the safety of new drug and biological products. The FDA proposed this new regulation on October 5, 1999, and the rule took effect on June 30, 2002. The advent of the animal efficacy rule shows the importance of animals in finding safe and effective countermeasures to the myriad of toxic biological, chemical, radiological, and nuclear threats.

Using animal surrogates to prove clinical efficacy is not a perfect solution, even though it is the only ethical and moral solution in the case of drugs and vaccines aimed at mitigating biowarfare or bioterrorism threats. To improve the validity of animal efficacy studies as models of human clinical efficacy, it is important to be rigorous in searches for the most optimal model that accurately mimics human disease. It is also necessary to draw precise comparisons between immune responses and drug kinetics in the animal surrogate and analogous responses in patients who participate in product safety but not clinical efficacy studies. Furthermore, because drugs approved by the animal efficacy rule may still not be "proven" efficacious in humans, postmarketing epidemiological studies are necessary to monitor outcomes. Finally, some diseases, such as dengue and smallpox, only affect human beings and do not affect animals. If animal efficacy data cannot be produced for a disease, the implication is that no vaccine could be created or used in human beings, which hardly seems a fitting solution.

BioShield Act of 2004

Perhaps the most promising solution to the current impasse is the BioShield Act of 2004, which President George W Bush outlined in his 2003 State of the Union address as a key legislative priority for his administration. Project BioShield is designed to speed the development and availability of medical countermeasures in response to bioweapons threats by accelerating and streamlining government research on countermeasures, creating incentives for private companies to develop countermeasures for inclusion in a national stockpile, and giving the government the ability to make these products quickly and widely available in a public health emergency to protect citizens from an attack using an unmodified select agent.

The BioShield Act of 2004 creates permanent funding for the procurement of medical countermeasures and gives the federal government the power to purchase available vaccines. The FDA and Department of Health and Human Services are tasked not only with determining that new vaccines and treatment measures are safe and efficacious, but also with the responsibility of making promising vaccines and treatment measures expeditiously available for emergency situations. The newly created FDA Emergency Use Authorization for Promising Medical Countermeasures provides one of the best ways of getting such products to those who might need them most, including military personnel. The legislation also requires the secretary of the Department of Health and Human Services to approve such emergency use measures, with the added requirement of FDA expert opinion that the benefits of the vaccine or treatment outweigh the risks involved in its application. Just such an emergency use of anthrax vaccine adsorbed (Biothrax, BioPort Corporation, Lansing, Mich) was approved by Health and Human Services Secretary Tommy G Thompson on January 14, 2005, authorizing its emergency use.

However, Project BioShield contains a provision that still conflicts with DoD discretionary authority over medical treatment for military personnel, continuing to require voluntary willingness to receive a vaccine or other treatment approved under the category of "emergency use." Although the language in the legislation refers specifically to "civilians," how this requirement will play out in the military setting, especially in wartime, is unclear. For maximum military effectiveness, a further stipulation in the legislation is required that the voluntary acceptance of treatment be waived in emergency situations, presumably on authority of the president of the United States with expert opinion from ethicists, legal scholars, and scientists. Additionally, there is no profit motive for private companies to engage in the research that this legislation aims to foster, and indemnification concerns also exist. There is no guarantee of efficacy of the theoretical drug or vaccine, and accountability measures should be created if the legislation is going to achieve its intended results.

The Turner Bill

Another bill (HR 4258 "Rapid Pathogen Identification to Delivery of Cures Act"), introduced by Congressman Jim Turner et alia on May 4, 2004, allows research and development of medical countermeasures and diagnostics to move at a quicker pace so that new products can rapidly be made available for emergencies. In addition, the Turner Bill provides for research and development of drugs and vaccines against genetically modified pathogens not accounted for in the Project BioShield legislation, which covered only countermeasures related to existing unmodified threat agents.

Project BioShield and the Turner Bill together establish an FDA emergency use authorization for critical biomedical countermeasures. The FDA may approve solely for emergency use a product not approved for full commercial marketing. For products that are near final approval but may not have met all the criteria, the FDA has created a streamlined IND process, with the animal efficacy rule playing a central role, for products designed to protect against or treat conditions caused by nuclear, chemical, or biological terrorism. Such a process was used to obtain FDA approval for pyridostigmine, which is licensed for use in treating myasthenia gravis but had not been approved for use against chemical warfare agents.

Biodefense and Pandemic Vaccine and Drug Development Act of 2005

In October 2005 Senator Richard Burr of North Carolina introduced the Biodefense and Pandemic Vaccine and Drug Development Act of 2005 (S 1873). This bill establishes the Biomedical Advanced Research and Development Agency as the lead federal agency for the development of countermeasures against bioterrorism. The new agency would report directly to the secretary of Health and Human Services. The bill provides incentives for domestic manufacturing of vaccines and countermeasures, and it gives broad liability protections to companies that develop vaccines for biological weapons. This bill may appear to settle the residual concerns left unresolved by Project BioShield, but it has raised additional controversy because of public perceptions that it is too favorable to the pharmaceutical industry and issues related to secrecy provisions.

Summary

This chapter has provided a view of the history of ethically conducted human subjects research in the military and has presented some of the problems that still exist among the distinct regulatory bodies that impact this research. The DoD has an ethical responsibility to protect military personnel, yet there is disagreement over how to best protect them against biochemical weapons attacks, in light of equal commitments to respecting agency autonomy and limiting government power over individual decisions regarding what constitutes one's own best interests. These issues and problems are not a mystery to those who confront them on a daily basis, and many thoughtful individuals are focusing their attention on resolving these dilemmas. Some progress is being made, at least in terms of productive dialogue and substantive attention to legislation that might impact research.

8.2.   The Military and Vaccinations
8.2.1. Courts-Martial

The military commanders are responsible for maintaining discipline, accomplishing their missions and protecting the welfare of their troops. The purpose of the military law system as stated in the Preamble to the Manual for Courts-Martial in the United States (2000 Edition) is "to promote justice, to assist in maintaining good order and discipline in the armed forces, to promote efficiency and effectiveness in the military establishment, and thereby to strengthen the national security of the United States."

The constitutional basis for Congress "to make Rules for the Government and regulation of the land and naval Forces," was the authority for the enactment of the Uniform Code of Military Justice. While Congress defines the crimes, the President establishes the procedures by which punishment is determined for violation of those crimes.

In the following testimony before the Subcommittee on Administrative Oversight and the Courts, Committee on the Judiciary, U.S. Senate, Major General, Michael J. Nardotti, Jr., U.S. Army-Retired, Former Judge Advocate General of the Army, 1993–1997, Gen. Nardotti explained differences between the military law system and the Article III federal court system: (http://judiciary.senate.gov/te120401f2-nardotti.htm) (site visited Aug. 10, 2002).

Several aspects of the military justice system differ from Article III courts in the pretrial, trial and post-trial phases: (1) Rights warnings against self-incrimination in the military are broader than those required in the civilian community and actually predated the requirement of the Miranda decision by many years. Rights advisement in the military is and has been mandated whether or not the interrogation occurs in a custodial session; (2) Right to counsel in the pretrial and trial phases in the military is broader than in the civilian community where counsel is appointed if the accused is indigent. Military counsel is provided regardless of ability to pay. Individually requested military counsel also may be provided if available. Civilian counsel may be appointed as well at the service members own expense; (3) In the pretrial investigation phase for felony prosecutions in the military, there is not the equivalent of a secret grand jury in which the defendant has no right to be present. An investigative hearing, which is routinely open, is conducted under Article 32 of the UCMJ to determine whether there are reasonable grounds to believe the accused service member committed the offense alleged. The accused service member has the right to be advised in writing of the charges, to attend the hearing with counsel, to examine the government's evidence, to cross examine witnesses, to produce witnesses, and to present evidence; (4) Pretrial discovery in the military is similar to that followed in federal criminal proceedings, but more broad. The government is required to disclose any evidence it will use in the sentencing phase of the proceeding if there is a conviction, or evidence that tends to negate the degree of guilt or reduce the punishment; (5) Unlawful command influence—an attempt by superior military authority to influence the outcome of a proceeding—is prohibited and is subject to criminal sanctions. There is no equivalent issue in federal proceedings; (6) In federal prosecution a jury of peers is selected at random. General courts-marital must have at least five members selected, as required by Article 25 of the UCMJ, based on "age, education, training, experience, length of service, and judicial temperament." Civilian jury and military court-martial panel members may be challenged for cause or peremptorily; (7) With respect to trial evidence, the rules in both forums—the Federal Rules of Evidence in federal courts and the Military rules of Evidence in courts-martial are almost identical. New Federal Rules of Evidence automatically become new Military Rules of evidence unless the President takes contrary action within 18 months; (8) The burden of proof for conviction in both forums is beyond a reasonable doubt; (9) For conviction or acquittal in federal prosecutions jurors must be unanimous. Otherwise, a hung jury results and the defendant may be retried. In courts-martial, except in capital cases, two-thirds of the panel must agree to convict. The first vote is binding. If more than one-third of the panel vote to acquit, then there is an acquittal. A hung jury and retrial on that basis in not possible in the military. In capital cases in courts-martial, a unanimous verdict is required for conviction; (10) Sentencing in federal courts is done by the judge alone, and sentencing guidelines for minimum and maximum sentences apply. In courts-martial, sentencing is decided by the court-martial panel members or by the military judge (if the accused service member chose to be tried by a military judge alone). There are maximum sentence limitations but no minimums. The accused service member is entitled to present evidence in extenuation and mitigation, including the testimony of witnesses on his or her behalf, and may make a sworn or unsworn statement for the court-martial's consideration. Two-thirds of the panel must agree for sentences of less than 10 years. Three-quarters of the panel must agree for sentences of 10 years or more. To impose capital punishment, the panel must unanimously agree to the findings of guilt, must unanimously agree to the existence of an "aggravating factor" required for a capital sentence, and must unanimously agree on the sentence of death. Capital punishment may not be imposed by a military judge alone; (11) In federal prosecutions, appeal is permissible, but mandatory in cases of capital punishment. There are two levels of appeal—the Circuit Courts of Appeal and the United States Supreme Court. In the military, appeal is automatic for sentences which include confinement of one year or more or a punitive (Bad Conduct or Dishonorable) discharge. There are three levels of appeal—the Courts of Criminal Appeals of the military services, the Court of Appeals of the Armed Forces, and the United States Supreme Court. Sentences which do not require automatic appeal may be appealed to the Judge Advocate General of the convicted member's service; (12) Appellate representation in federal prosecutions is provided if the convicted person is indigent. In the military, appellate representation is provided in all cases regardless of financial status.

This comparison of the relative handling of pretrial, trial, and post-trial matters, respectively, in Article III Federal courts and courts-martial is not exhaustive. It demonstrates, however, that even in accommodating the needs unique to the administration of military justice, courts-martial, in many important respects, compare very favorably, even though not identically, to process and procedures accorded in the Article III courts.

8.2.2. Military Commissions

Military Commissions are different from courts-martial and procedures are created for the particular military commission.

There has been a long history of military commissions in the United States. The U.S. Congress affirmed the use of military commissions in the Articles of War and in Articles 21 and 36 of the Uniform Code of Military Justice. The U.S. Supreme Court upheld the use of military commissions in **Ex Parte Quirin**, in 1942.

On September 29, 1780, the first of these commissions—a "Board of General Officers" was appointed to try Major John Andre, Adjutant-General to the British Army. The charge was that he had moved into American territory, in disguise and using a false name, to meet with General Benedict Arnold. The Board found that the facts charged were true, and that when captured Major Andre had in his possession papers containing intelligence for the enemy, and reported their conclusion that "Major Andre...ought to be considered as a Spy from the enemy, and that agreeably to the law and usage of nations...he ought to suffer death." Major Andre was hanged on October 2, 1780. [Proceedings of a Board of General Officers Respecting Major John Andre, Sept. 29, 1780, printed at Philadelphia in 1780, quoted in Ex Parte Quirin, 317 U.S. 1 (1942)]

During the Mexican War military commissions were created in a large number of instances for the trial of various offenses. See General Orders cited in 2 Winthrop, Military Law (2d ed. 1896) p. 1298, note 1.

During the aftermath of the Civil War, a military commission was appointed to try T.E. Hogg and others for "violations of the laws and usages of civilized war. Hogg was charged with "being commissioned, enrolled, enlisted or engaged" by the Confederate Government when he boarded a United States merchant steamer in the port of Panama in order to capture and convert the steamer into a Confederate vessel. Hogg and his cohorts boarded the steamer "in the guise of peaceful passengers". They were found guilty and sentenced to be hanged. The reviewing authority affirmed the judgments, but reduced the sentences to imprisonment for life and for various periods of years. Dept. of the Pacific, G. O. No. 52, June 27, 1865.

Another military commission after the Civil War was appointed to try Robert C. Kennedy, a Captain of the Confederate Army, who attempted to set fire to the City of New York and acted as a spy in violation of the law of war "in undertaking to carry on irregular and unlawful warfare."

On January 17, 1865, Kennedy was sentenced to be hanged and the sentence was confirmed upon review. Dept. of the East, G. O. No. 24, March 20, 1865.

Military commissions tried William Murphy, "a rebel emissary in the employ of and colleagued with rebel enemies," and convicted him of "violation of the laws and customs of war" for burning a United States steamboat and other property G. C. M. O. No. 107, April 18, 1866. Daniel Davis for "recruiting men within the lines," G. O. No. 397, Dec. 18, 1863; and Augustus A. Williams for "lurking about the posts, quarters, fortifications and encampments of the armies of the United States," although not "as a spy," Middle Dept., G. O. No. 34, May 5, 1864. For other cases of violations of the law of war punished by military commissions during the Civil War, see 2 Winthrop, Military Laws and Precedents (2d ed. 1896) 1310–11. Quoted in Ex Parte Quirin,

Ex Parte Quirin, was a review on habeas corpus of a military commission judgment, as a result of a thwarted attempt of terrorism by Germans, entering the United States as civilians from a submarine.

After the terrorist attack on the Pan Am jetliner over Lockerbie, Scotland in 1988, military commissions for the trial of those responsible was proposed. Scotland, however, was opposed to the death penalty was not interesting in participating in the military commission, so the United States did not move forward on the proposal. [Bumiller and Myers, "Senior Administration Officials Defend Military Tribunals for Terrorist Suspects," The New York Times (Nov. 15, 2001).

On November 13, 2001, President George W. Bush issued a military order, concerning the "Detention, Treatment, and Trial of Certain Non-Citizens in the War Against Terrorism," authorizing trial by military commission for a non-U.S. citizen upon the sole determination of the President of their association with terrorism. The order specified that the Secretary of Defense would develop procedural rules for the commissions but that the decisions of the military commissions would not be reviewable by any court. Art. 36, UCMJ specifically provides that the President has the power to determine what rules of procedure will apply, requiring the application of principles and rules generally recognized in criminal law. §5(c)(2) requires that the procedure provide "full and fair trials". §4(c)(4) provides that the President may conduct proceedings in secret at his option. The offenses covered in the order include "any and all offenses triable by military commission" §4(a); and "for violations of the laws of war" and for "violations of...other applicable laws" §1(e).

March 21, 2002, the Secretary of Defense announced procedures governing the use of military commissions related to the war on terrorism. These procedures include: access to the charges in his or her language; the presumption of innocence; proof of guilt beyond a reasonable doubt; the right to counsel (military and/or civilian); access to the prosecution's evidence; no double jeopardy; and no adverse inference form the defendant's failure to testify. A finding of guilt must be supported by at least a two-thirds majority of the commission. A unanimous vote for the death penalty. The admissibility of evidence can be determined by a majority vote of the commission. Review of the commission's decision is available from a three-member appellate panel and the panel may reverse on its own for clear errors of law.

Ex Parte Quirin
317 U.S. 1 (1942)

Prior History

MOTIONS FOR LEAVE TO FILE PETITIONS FOR WRITS OF HABEAS CORPUS; CERTIORARI TO THE UNITED STATES COURT OF APPEALS FOR THE DISTRICT OF COLUMBIA.

The applications, seven in number (ante, p. 1, n. 1), first took the form of petitions to this Court for leave to file petitions for writs of habeas corpus to secure the release of the petitioners from the custody of Brigadier General Albert L. Cox, U. S. A., Provost Marshal of the Military District of Washington, who, pursuant to orders, was holding them in that District for and during a trial before a Military Commission constituted by an Order of the President of the United States. During the course of the argument, the petitioners were permitted to file petitions for writs of certiorari, directed to the United States Court of Appeals for the District of Columbia, to review, before judgment by that Court, orders then before it by appeal by which the District Court for the District of Columbia had denied applications for leave to file petitions for writs of habeas corpus.

MR. CHIEF JUSTICE STONE delivered the opinion of the Court.

These cases are brought here by petitioners' several applications for leave to file petitions for habeas corpus in this Court, and by their petitions for certiorari to review orders of the District Court for the District of Columbia, which denied their applications for leave to file petitions for habeas corpus in that court.

The question for decision is whether the detention of petitioners by respondent for trial by Military Commission, appointed by Order of the President of July 2, 1942, on charges preferred against them purporting to set out their violations of the law of war and of the Articles of War, is in conformity to the laws and Constitution of the United States.

After denial of their applications by the District Court, 47 F.Supp. 431, petitioners asked leave to file petitions for habeas corpus in this Court. In view of the public importance of the questions raised by their petitions and of the duty which rests on the courts, in time of war as well as in time of peace, to preserve unimpaired the constitutional safeguards of civil liberty, and because in our opinion the public interest required that we consider and decide those questions without any avoidable delay, we directed that petitioners' applications be set down for full oral argument at a special term of this Court, convened on July 29, 1942. The applications for leave to file the petitions were presented in open court on that day and were heard on the petitions, the answers to them of respondent, a stipulation of facts by counsel, and the record of the testimony given before the Commission.

The following facts appear from the petitions or are stipulated. Except as noted they are undisputed.

All the petitioners were born in Germany; all have lived in the United States. All returned to Germany between 1933 and 1941. All except petitioner Haupt are admittedly citizens of the German Reich, with which the United States is at war. Haupt came to this country with his parents when he was five years old; it is contended that he became a citizen of the United States by virtue of the naturalization of his parents during his minority and that he has not since lost his citizenship. The Government, however, takes the position that on attaining his majority he elected to maintain German allegiance and citizenship, or in any case that he has by his conduct renounced or abandoned his United States citizenship. See Perkins v. Elg, 307 U.S. 325, 334; United States ex rel. Rojak v. Marshall, 34 F.2d 219; United States ex rel. Scimeca v. Husband, 6 F.2d 957, 958; 8 U. S. C. §801, and compare 8 U. S. C. §808. For reasons presently to be stated we do not find it necessary to resolve these contentions. After the declaration of war between the United States and the German Reich, petitioners received training at a sabotage school near Berlin, Germany, where they were instructed in the use of explosives and in methods of secret writing. Thereafter petitioners, with a German citizen, Dasch, proceeded from Germany to a seaport in Occupied France, where petitioners Burger, Heinck and Quirin, together with Dasch, boarded a German submarine which proceeded across the Atlantic to Amagansett Beach on Long Island, New York. The four were there landed from the submarine in the hours of darkness, on or about June 13, 1942, carrying with them a supply of explosives, fuses, and incendiary and timing devices. While landing they wore German Marine Infantry uniforms or parts of uniforms.

Immediately after landing they buried their uniforms and the other articles mentioned, and proceeded in civilian dress to New York City.

The remaining four petitioners at the same French port boarded another German submarine, which carried them across the Atlantic to Ponte Vedra Beach, Florida. On or about June 17, 1942, they came ashore during the hours of darkness, wearing caps of the German Marine Infantry and carrying with them a supply of explosives, fuses, and incendiary and timing devices. They immediately buried their caps and the other articles mentioned, and proceeded in civilian dress to Jacksonville, Florida, and thence to various points in the United States. All were taken into custody in New York or Chicago by agents of the Federal Bureau of Investigation. All had received instructions in Germany from an officer of the German High Command to destroy war industries and war facilities in the United States, for which they or their relatives in Germany were to receive salary payments from the German Government. They also had been paid by the German Government during their course of training at the sabotage school and had received substantial sums in United States currency, which were in their possession when arrested. The currency had been handed to them by an officer of the German High Command, who had instructed them to wear their German uniforms while landing in the United States.

The President, as President and Commander in Chief of the Army and Navy, by Order of July 2, 1942, appointed a Military Commission and directed it to try petitioners for offenses against the law of war and the Articles of War, and prescribed regulations for the procedure on the trial and for review of the record of the trial and of any judgment or sentence of the Commission. On the same day, by Proclamation, the President declared that "all persons who are subjects, citizens or residents of any nation at war with the United States or who give obedience to or act under the direction of any such nation, and who during time of war enter or attempt to enter the United States...through coastal or boundary defenses, and are charged with committing or attempting or preparing to commit sabotage, espionage, hostile or warlike acts, or violations of the law of war, shall be subject to the law of war and to the jurisdiction of military tribunals."

The Proclamation also stated in terms that all such persons were denied access to the courts.

Pursuant to direction of the Attorney General, the Federal Bureau of Investigation surrendered custody of petitioners to respondent, Provost Marshal of the Military District of Washington, who was directed by the Secretary of War to receive and keep them in custody, and who thereafter held petitioners for trial before the Commission.

On July 3, 1942, the Judge Advocate General's Department of the Army prepared and lodged with the Commission the following charges against petitioners, supported by specifications:

1. Violation of the law of war.

2. Violation of Article 81 of the Articles of War, defining the offense of relieving or attempting to relieve, or corresponding with or giving intelligence to, the enemy.

3. Violation of Article 82, defining the offense of spying.

4. Conspiracy to commit the offenses alleged in charges 1, 2 and 3.

The Commission met on July 8, 1942, and proceeded with the trial, which continued in progress while the causes were pending in this Court. On July 27th, before petitioners' applications to the District Court, all the evidence for the prosecution and the defense had been taken by the Commission and the case had been closed except for arguments of counsel. It is conceded that ever since petitioners' arrest the state and federal courts in Florida, New York, and the District of Columbia, and in the states in which each of the petitioners was arrested or detained, have been open and functioning normally.

Petitioners' main contention is that the President is without any statutory or constitutional authority to order the petitioners to be tried by military tribunal for offenses with which they are charged; that in consequence they are entitled to be tried in the civil courts with the safeguards, including trial by jury, which the Fifth and Sixth Amendments guarantee to all persons charged in such courts with criminal offenses. In any case it is urged that the President's Order, in prescribing the procedure of the Commission and the method for review of its findings and sentence, and the proceedings of the Commission under the Order, conflict with Articles of War adopted by Congress—particularly Articles 38, 43, 46, 50 H and 70—and are illegal and void.

The Government challenges each of these propositions. But regardless of their merits, it also insists that petitioners must be denied access to the courts, both because they are enemy aliens or have entered our territory as enemy belligerents, and because the President's Proclamation undertakes in terms to deny such access to the class of persons defined by the Proclamation, which aptly describes the character and conduct of petitioners. It is urged that if they are enemy aliens or if the Proclamation has force, no court may afford the petitioners a hearing. But there is certainly nothing in the Proclamation to preclude access to the courts for determining its applicability to the particular case. And neither the Proclamation nor the fact that they are enemy aliens forecloses consideration by the courts of petitioners' contentions that the Constitution and laws of the United States constitutionally enacted forbid their trial by military commission. As announced in our per curiam opinion, we have resolved those questions by our conclusion that the Commission has jurisdiction to try the charge preferred against petitioners. There is therefore no occasion to decide contentions of the parties unrelated to this issue. We pass at once to the consideration of the basis of the Commission's authority.

Congress and the President, like the courts, possess no power not derived from the Constitution. But one of the objects of the Constitution, as declared by its preamble, is to "provide for the common defense." As a means to that end, the Constitution gives to Congress the power to "provide for the common Defense," Art. I, §8, cl. 1; "To raise and support Armies," "To provide and maintain a Navy," Art. I, §8, cl. 12, 13; and "To make Rules for the Government and Regulation of the land and naval Forces," Art. I, §, cl. 14. Congress is given authority "To declare War, grant Letters of Marque and Reprisal, and make Rules concerning Captures on Land and Water," Art. I, §8, cl. 11; and "To define and punish Piracies and Felonies committed on the high Seas, and Offences against the Law of Nations," Art. I, §, cl. 10. And finally, the Constitution authorizes Congress "To make all Laws which shall be necessary and proper for carrying into Execution the foregoing Powers, and all other Powers vested by this Constitution in the Government of the United States, or in any Department or Officer thereof." Art. I, §8, cl. 18.

The Constitution confers on the President the "executive Power," Art. II, §1, cl. 1, and imposes on him the duty to "take Care that the Laws be faithfully executed." Art. II, §3. It makes him the Commander in Chief of the Army and Navy, Art. II, §2, cl. 1, and empowers him to appoint and commission officers of the United States. Art. II, §3, cl. 1.

The Constitution thus invests the President, as Commander in Chief, with the power to wage war which Congress has declared, and to carry into effect all laws passed by Congress for the conduct of war and for the government and regulation of the Armed Forces, and all laws defining and punishing offenses against the law of nations, including those which pertain to the conduct of war.

By the Articles of War, 10 U. S. C. §1471–1593, Congress has provided rules for the government of the Army. It has provided for the trial and punishment, by courts martial, of violations of the Articles by members of the armed forces and by specified classes of persons associated or serving with the Army. Arts. 1, 2. But the Articles also recognize the "military commission" appointed by military command as an appropriate tribunal for the trial and punishment of offenses against the law of war not ordinarily tried by court martial. See Arts. 12, 15. Articles 38 and 46 authorize the President, with certain limitations, to prescribe the procedure for military commissions. Articles 81 and 82 authorize trial, either by court martial or military commission, of those charged with relieving, harboring or corresponding with the enemy and those charged with spying. And Article 15 declares that "the provisions of these articles conferring jurisdiction upon courts martial shall not be construed as depriving military commissions...or other military tribunals of concurrent jurisdiction in respect of offenders or offenses that by statute or by the law of war may be triable by such military commissions...or other military tribunals." Article 2 includes among those persons subject to military law the personnel of our own military establishment. But this, as Article 12 provides, does not exclude from that class "any other person who by the law of war is subject to trial by military tribunals" and who under Article 12 may be tried by court martial or under Article 15 by military commission....

Citizenship in the United States of an enemy belligerent does not relieve him from the consequences of a belligerency which is unlawful because in violation of the law of war. Citizens who associate themselves with the military arm of the enemy government, and with its aid, guidance and direction enter this country bent on hostile acts, are enemy belligerents within the meaning of the Hague Convention and the law of war. Cf. Gates v. Goodloe, 101 U.S. 612, 615, 617-18. It is as an enemy belligerent that petitioner Haupt is charged with entering the United States, and unlawful belligerency is the gravamen of the offense of which he is accused.

All these are instances of offenses committed against the United States, for which a penalty is imposed, but they are not deemed to be within Article III, §2, or the provisions of the Fifth and Sixth Amendments relating to "crimes" and "criminal prosecutions." In the light of this long-continued and consistent interpretation we must conclude that §2 of Article III and the Fifth and Sixth Amendments cannot be taken to have extended the right to demand a jury to trials by military commission, or to have required that offenses against the law of war not triable by jury at common law be tried only in the civil courts.

We need not inquire whether Congress may restrict the power of the Commander in Chief to deal with enemy belligerents. For the Court is unanimous in its conclusion that the Articles in question could not at any stage of the proceedings afford any basis for issuing the writ. But a majority of the full Court are not agreed on the appropriate grounds for decision. Some members of the Court are of opinion that Congress did not intend the Articles of War to govern a Presidential military commission convened for the determination of questions relating to admitted enemy invaders, and that the context of the Articles makes clear that they should not be construed to apply in that class of cases. Others are of the view that—even though this trial is subject to whatever provisions of the Articles of War Congress has in terms made applicable to "commissions"—the particular Articles in question, rightly construed, do not foreclose the procedure prescribed by the President or that shown to have been employed by the Commission, in a trial of offenses against the law of war and the 81st and 82nd Articles of War, by a military commission appointed by the President.

Accordingly, we conclude that Charge I, on which petitioners were detained for trial by the Military Commission, alleged an offense which the President is authorized to order tried by military commission; that his Order convening the Commission was a lawful order and that the Commission was lawfully constituted; that the petitioners were held in lawful custody and did not show cause for their discharge. It follows that the orders of the District Court should be affirmed, and that leave to file petitions for habeas corpus in this Court should be denied.

8.2.3. Court Martial for Refusal of Vaccine

During Desert Storm in 1992, concerns were heightened upon finding that Saddam Hussein, leader of Iraq, had a biological weapons facilities and plans to deploy those weapons. The Pentagon distributed 300,000 doses of anthrax vaccine and 8.000 doses of botulin toxoid to U.S. forces in the Persian Gulf.

In 1995, the military began a review of a program of anthrax vaccination for troops. The military anthrax vaccination program was approved by Secretary of Defense, William S. Cohen, on December 15, 1997, after a two-year review. This review was based upon four factors: (1) supplemental testing to assure sterility, safety, potency, and purity of the vaccine stockpile; (2) implementation of a system for fully tracking anthrax immunizations; (3) approval of operational plans to administer the vaccine and communications plans to inform military personnel; and (4) review of medical aspects of the program by an independent expert. In May 18, 1998, William S. Cohen, Secretary of Defense, mandated anthrax vaccine for all troops with a memorandum to all Secretaries of the Military Departments.

The Subcommittee on National Security, Veterans Affairs, and International Relations of the House Government Reform Committee held hearings in 1999 on the legality of ordering soldiers to take the anthrax vaccination. The use of the vaccine on soldiers for inhalation anthrax defense differs from the original purpose of the vaccine when it was licensed, which was for use by personnel who worked around animals or tanning operations who might be exposed to dermal anthrax. Further, the GAO found that the vaccine currently used by the military differs from the molecule licensed by the FDA prior to 1970.

In 1996, the manufacturer of the anthrax vaccine applied for an investigational drug approval (IND) to modify the existing license.

Federal legislation was proposed in the 106th Congress to end the anthrax program, or to make it voluntary. The "Department of Defense Anthrax Vaccination Moratorium Act," proposed the suspension of the program; the "American Military Health Protection Act," H.R. 2543, made the vaccine voluntary; and H.R. 3460 proposed prohibiting the waiver of informed consent for an IND drug not yet licensed.

A federal class action lawsuit was filed against the federal government agencies and Bioport, manufacturer of the anthrax vaccine. Bates et al. v. Rumsfeld et al., No. 1:01cv00941, complaint filed (D.D.C., May 2, 2001). Sonnie Bates and John Buck claim the Anthrax Vaccine Absorbed is being administered involuntarily to members of the U.S. armed forces although it is still in experimental status as an investigational drug and unapproved for its intended use, and requires consent. The company, Bioport, has experienced some difficulties putting the military's vaccine program in jeopardy, according to Secretary Rumsfeld. In January 2002, Bioport was permitted by the FDA to release 500,000 doses of the anthrax vaccine.

June 28, 2002, the U.S. Defense Department announced that they would resume a program to vaccinate some military and civilian personnel against anthrax because the threat of anthrax still exists. "We continue to believe that the threat of anthrax being used against our armed forces is very real," said William Winkenwerder, the assistant secretary of defense for health affairs. The Department of Defense plans to set aside about half of the military's supply for stockpiling for civilian use in the event of a bioterrorist attack.

———————

Ponder v. Stone
54 M.J. 613; 2000 CCA LEXIS 243
UNITED STATES NAVY-MARINE CORPS COURT
OF CRIMINAL APPEALS
(November 29, 2000, Decided)

BEFORE R.B. LEO, Senior Judge, D.A. ANDERSON, Judge, K.J. NAUGLE, Judge. Judge ANDERSON and Judge NAUGLE concur.

OPINION:

Decision on Petition for Extraordinary Relief in the Nature of a Writ of Mandamus.

LEO, Senior Judge:

On 17 August 2000, the petitioner submitted a petition for extraordinary relief in the nature of a writ of mandamus and a stay of the proceedings below. The petitioner alleges that the military judge erred (1) by declaring, as a matter of law, that an order to receive the anthrax vaccination was lawful, (2) by granting the Government's motion to bar the petitioner from presenting any evidence before the court-martial members on the safety, efficacy, and necessity of the anthrax vaccine, and (3) by denying the petitioner's several motions relating to the lawfulness of the order. He requested that we reverse the military judge's rulings on these matters. On 18 August 2000, we granted the petitioner's preliminary requests for a stay of the proceedings and for the production of a transcript of the lower court proceedings pending our review of the petition. Having completed our review, we find that the petitioner has failed to establish that he has been denied a clear and indisputable right to challenge the lawfulness of the order as a result of the military judge's rulings on the motions. Accordingly, the petition is denied.

I. Background

The petitioner is charged with a violation of Article 90, Uniform Code of Military Justice, 10 U.S.C. §890, by willfully disobeying a lawful order from his superior commissioned officer on or about 12 January 2000, to receive the anthrax vaccine. The thrust of his complaint is that the military judge's rulings effectively deny him the right to present an affirmative defense to the charge against him. If the charge cannot be dismissed, his contention is that he should at the very least be allowed to introduce evidence on the merits showing that the order in question violates existing federal laws and regulations. [10 U.S.C. §1107; 50 U.S.C. §1520a; and Executive Order 13139 of September 30, 1999.]

The petitioner asserts that the current anthrax vaccine is both an investigational new drug [IND] and an experimental drug and that it is being used in a manner inconsistent with its original license of 1970 from the Food and Drug Administration [FDA]. Therefore, he argues, the order that he received was unlawful because, by law, he cannot be compelled to take the vaccine without his prior consent. In ruling in favor of the Government, the military judge held that the legal authority relied upon by the petitioner confers no individual legal rights enforceable at a court-martial.

When an accused is charged with willful disobedience of a lawful order under Article 90, UCMJ, the order is presumed to be lawful, unless it is patently illegal. MANUAL FOR COURTS-MARTIAL, UNITED STATES (1998 ed.), Part IV, P 14c(2)(a)(i). This presumption, however, is rebuttable. If the lawfulness of the order is challenged, it is normally an issue of law to be resolved by the military judge as an interlocutory matter. If the military judge determines that the presumption of lawfulness has not been rebutted, the issue is not put to the members. After receiving evidence and hearing argument from counsel, the military judge in this case ruled that the petitioner's order was lawful as a matter of law and stated that he would so instruct the court-martial members, thereby precluding the petitioner from putting the matter before the members as an issue of fact.

The petitioner had argued that, by statute, informed consent must be obtained by the Secretary of Defense from members of the Armed Forces before an IND or a drug unapproved for its applied use may be administered, unless the President waives this requirement. 10 U.S.C. §1107(f)(1). Similarly, he argued that informed consent must be obtained by the Secretary of Defense from any human subject of an experiment or a test directly related to protection against toxic chemicals or biological weapons and agents. 50 U.S.C. §1520a(c). Therefore, he wanted to introduce evidence showing that the anthrax vaccine was the type of drug requiring informed consent under both statutes.

Executive Order 13139, which implements 10 U.S.C. §1107, clearly states that the requirements it incorporated from the statute are for internal management only and confer no right enforceable by any party against the United States. E.O. 13139, §6(b). Additionally, Secretary of the Navy Instruction 6230.4 of 29 April 1998, which implements the Department's anthrax vaccination implementation program, states that the anthrax vaccine is a FDA-licensed product and not an IND requiring informed consent for its administration. This would imply that the vaccine is also not an experimental or test drug that would require informed consent under 50 U.S.C. §1520a(c). [T]he...anthrax immunization is mandatory and those refusing the vaccine are subject to disciplinary action. [According to the instruction, the DON AVIP is intended to be a force-wide protective measure against the biological anthrax agent, which is the primary biological weapons threat against U.S. naval forces today.] Under these circumstances, the petitioner has not shown that the military judge's ruling is so contrary to statute, settled case law, or valid military regulation as to deny him relief that is clearly and indisputably due him as a matter of right. Accordingly, we find that the issuance of an extraordinary writ at this time is neither necessary nor appropriate.

IV. Disposition

The petition for extraordinary relief in the nature of a writ of mandamus is denied without prejudice to the petitioner's right to raise the issue before this court in the normal course of appellate review. Our order of 18 August 2000 staying the proceedings below is hereby dissolved.

Judge ANDERSON and Judge NAUGLE concur.

Notes

1. The objection to the vaccine by the petitioner in *Ponder v. Stone*, was whether the vaccine was experimental and therefore required informed consent from the human subjects of the experimentation; or whether is was truly an FDA approved vaccine, as stated. If the FDA states that the drug is approved, and no longer experimental, can this be challenged? Administrative challenges of agency decisions receive Chevron deference, which makes it difficult to challenge a scientific agency's decision. See *Chevron v. Natural Resources Defense Council*, 467 U.S. 837 (1984).

2. The anthrax program has been expanded for civilian use. What legal authority would be required to make anthrax vaccine mandatory, or is it possible under the U.S. Constitution? Since anthrax is not communicable, would *Jacobson v. Massachusetts* be useful to compel vaccination for public safety purposes?

Boylan v. Matejka
770 N.E.2d 1266 (Ill. App. 2d, 2002)

OPINION: JUSTICE BOWMAN delivered the opinion of the court:

Plaintiff, Daniel Boylan, filed a complaint in the circuit court of Du Page County against Larry Matejka, in his capacity as executive director of the Illinois Student Assistance Commission, and the Illinois Student Assistance Commission (collectively the Commission) seeking review of the Commission's final decision denying Boylan's application for an Illinois Veteran Grant. On appeal, Boylan contends that the trial court erroneously upheld the Commission's determination that Boylan was ineligible for an Illinois Veteran Grant because he was not honorably discharged from the United States Navy.

The pertinent facts are not in dispute. Boylan began serving in the Navy on September 19, 1996. After completing nuclear training, he was assigned to the U.S.S. Dwight D. Eisenhower, a nuclear aircraft carrier. In September 1998, Boylan and all other crewmembers on the Eisenhower were told that they had to take an anthrax vaccine, pursuant to an order issued by the Secretary of Defense. When Boylan's captain ordered him to take the vaccine, Boylan refused because of concerns over the vaccine's efficacy and safety. As a result of his refusal, Boylan's rank was reduced by one grade, he was reassigned from nuclear technician duty to galley work, and he was restricted to the ship for 60 days.

In March 1999, Boylan's commanding officer recommended an administrative separation from the Navy for Boylan. According to Boylan's "Certificate of Release or Discharge from Active Duty" he received a "General (Under Honorable Conditions)" discharge. The commanding officer's report regarding Boylan's separation indicated that, in addition to refusing to take his anthrax vaccine, Boylan also failed to report at his restricted personnel musters on five occasions. The commanding officer's report contained the following comments about Boylan:

"MMFN Boylan has repeatedly refused to take his Anthrax vaccination. His continuing misconduct is incompatible with the Naval service. I have determined that MMFN Boylan has no potential for future service and should be separated with a General (Under Honorable Conditions) discharge by reason of misconduct due to a pattern of misconduct and misconduct due to commission of a serious offense."

Following his separation from the Navy, Boylan returned to Illinois, where he had resided prior to his Navy service. He applied for an Illinois Veteran Grant, which exempts eligible Illinois veterans from paying tuition and fees at State-controlled colleges, universities, and community colleges. The Commission denied Boylan's application on the ground that he was not honorably discharged from the Navy. Following an administrative hearing, the executive director of the Commission issued a final decision denying Boylan's application. Boylan filed a complaint in the circuit court for administrative review of the Commission's decision. The court entered an order upholding the Commission's decision. Boylan filed a timely notice of appeal from the circuit court's order, and this appeal ensued.

The issue before us is whether, under section 40 of the Higher Education Student Assistance Act (Act), a person who receives a general discharge from the armed forces under honorable conditions and who otherwise meets the requirements of section 40 is eligible for an Illinois Veteran Grant. This appears to be an issue of first impression.

Section 40 of the Act provides that an Illinois Veteran Grant shall be awarded to persons who, among other things, have been "honorably discharged" from the armed services. An "honorable discharge" and a "general discharge under honorable conditions" are two different things. The Department of the Navy personnel regulations define the three types of administrative discharges as follows:

"(1) Honorable. A separation from the naval service with honor. The issuance of an Honorable Discharge is contingent upon proper military behavior and performance of duty.

(2) Under Honorable Conditions (also termed General Discharge). A separation from the naval service under honorable conditions. The issuance of a discharge under honorable conditions is contingent upon military behavior and performance of duty which is not sufficiently meritorious to warrant an Honorable Discharge.

(3) Under Other Than Honorable Conditions (formerly termed Undesirable Discharge). A separation from the naval service under conditions other than honorable. It is issued to terminate the service of a member of the naval service for one or more of the reasons/basis listed in the Naval Military Personnel Manual, Marine Corps Separation and Retirement Manual and their predecessor publications." (Emphasis added.) 32 C.F.R. §724.109(a) (2002).

We conclude that section 40 of the Act is clear and unambiguous. When setting forth the eligibility requirements for an Illinois Veteran Grant, the legislature used the term "honorably discharged" rather than "discharged under honorable conditions." The meaning of the term "honorably discharged" is clear. Only those armed forces personnel who perform their duties and behave properly as defined by the armed forces may be honorably discharged. It is equally clear that an individual who receives a general discharge under honorable conditions has not been honorably discharged. If the legislature had desired to make Illinois Veteran Grants available to those who received a general discharge under honorable conditions, it could have so specified.

Last, we address Boylan's apparent contention that we should consider the reasons underlying his discharge from the Navy when determining whether he is eligible for an Illinois Veteran Grant. It is not this court's function to do so. Under section 40, only the characterization of an applicant's discharge is relevant; the reasons therefore are irrelevant and rightly so, for the Commission is not a military tribunal. Consequently, even though Boylan may have had valid reasons for disobeying his superiors, those reasons play no part in our determination.

Accordingly, for the reasons stated, we affirm the judgment of the circuit court of Du Page County.

Affirmed.

Notes

1. In Congressional hearings which questioned the legality of ordering soldiers to take the vaccine, Cong. Christopher Shays (R-4th) of Connecticut was an opponent of the vaccination program. In *United States v. Chadwell*, 36 C.M.R. 741 (1965) the defendant was court martialed for failure to accept a vaccination. The court did not accept a religious objection to an otherwise legal order to accept administration of the vaccine. Chadwell was a member of the Church of Christ whose doctrine precludes members from accepting any medical treatment including vaccines. Cong. Shays is a Christian Scientist, whose doctrine includes the refusal of all medical treatment including vaccines. Is this problematic for Cong. Shays to take part in an evaluation of the medical efficacy of the vaccine program, when his underlying beliefs reject the vaccine under any circumstances?

2. Evaluation of the reports of harmful effects of the anthrax vaccine that were submitted to the Vaccine Adverse Event Reporting System (VAERS) revealed six serious adverse events (AE) from vaccination from the military anthrax vaccine program. Approximately 400,000 U.S. military men and women have been inoculated against anthrax. Negative side effects caused by the vaccine are reported to VAERS, which documents adverse events from all vaccines. The committee members concluded, "At this time, ongoing evaluation of VAERS reports does not suggest a high frequency or unusual pattern of serious or other medically important AEs." Should the anthrax vaccination be continued? (Vaccine Weekly, July 31, 2002).

8.3.   Biological Espionage

Espionage in biosecurity is an important tool for criminalizing the transfer, delivery or communication that "is to be used to the injury of the United States or to the advantage of a foreign nation".

Art. 106e

Article 106a—Espionage

(a)

(1) Any person subject to this chapter who, with intent or reason to believe that it is to be used to the injury of the United States or to the advantage of a foreign nation, communicates, delivers, or transmits, or attempts to communicate, deliver, or transmit, to any entity described in paragraph (2), either directly or indirectly, anything described in paragraph (3) shall be punished as a court-martial may direct, except that if the accused is found guilty of an offense that directly concerns (A) nuclear weaponry, military spacecraft or satellites, early warning systems, or other means of defense or retaliation against large scale attack, (B) war plans, (C) communications intelligence or cryptographic information, or (D) any other major weapons system or major element of defense strategy, the accused shall be punished by death or such other punishment as a court-martial may direct.

(2) An entity referred to in paragraph (1) is—

(A) a foreign government;

(B) a faction or party or military or naval force within a foreign country, whether recognized or unrecognized by the United States; or

(C) a representative, officer, agent, employee, subject, or citizen of such a government, faction, party, or force.

(3) A thing referred to in paragraph (1) is a document, writing, code book, signal book, sketch, photograph, photographic negative, blueprint, plan, map, model, note, instrument, appliance, or information relating to the national defense.

(b)

(1) No person may be sentenced by court-martial to suffer death for an offense under this section (article) unless—

(A) the members of the court-martial unanimously find at least one of the aggravating factors set out in subsection (c); and

(B) the members unanimously determine that any extenuating or mitigating circumstances are substantially outweighed by any aggravating circumstances, including the aggravating factors set out under subsection (c).

(2) Findings under this subsection may be based on— (A) evidence introduced on the issue of guilt or innocence; (B) evidence introduced during the sentencing proceeding; or

(C) all such evidence. (3) The accused shall be given broad latitude to present matters in extenuation and mitigation.

(c) A sentence of death may be adjudged by a court-martial for an offense under this section (article) only if the members unanimously find, beyond a reasonable doubt, one or more of the following aggravating factors:

(1) The accused has been convicted of another offense involving espionage or treason for which either a sentence of death or imprisonment for life was authorized by statute.

(2) In the commission of the offense, the accused knowingly created a grave risk of substantial damage to the national security.

(3) In the commission of the offense, the accused knowingly created a grave risk of death to another person.

(4) Any other factor that may be prescribed by the President by regulations under section 836 of this title (Article 36)."

Elements.

(1) Espionage.

(a) That the accused communicated, delivered, or transmitted any document, writing, code book, signal book, sketch, photograph, photographic negative, blueprint, plan, map, model, note, instrument, appliance, or information relating to the national defense;

(b) That this matter was communicated, delivered, or transmitted to any foreign government, or to any faction or party or military or naval force within a foreign country, whether recognized or unrecognized by the United States, or to any representative, officer, agent, employee, subject or citizen thereof, either directly or indirectly; and

(c) That the accused did so with intent or reason to believe that such matter would be used to the injury of the United States or to the advantage of a foreign nation.

(2) Attempted espionage.

(a) That the accused did a certain overt act;

(b) That the act was done with the intent to commit the offense of espionage;

(c) That the act amounted to more than mere preparation; and

(d) That the act apparently tended to bring about the offense of espionage.

(3) Espionage as a capital offense.

(a) That the accused committed espionage or attempted espionage; and

(b) That the offense directly concerned (1) nuclear weaponry, military spacecraft or satellites, early warning systems, or other means of defense or retaliation against large scale attack, (2) war plans, (3) communications intelligence or cryptographic information, or (4) any other major weapons system or major element of defense strategy.

Explanation.

(1) Intent. "Intent or reason to believe" that the information "is to be used to the injury of the United States or to the advantage of a foreign nation" means that the accused acted in bad faith and with-out lawful authority with respect to information that is not lawfully accessible to the public.

(2) National defense information. "Instrument, appliance, or information relating to the national defense" includes the full range of modern technology and matter that may be developed in the future, including chemical or biological agents, computer technology, and other matter related to the national defense.

(3) Espionage as a capital offense. Capital punishment is authorized if the government alleges and proves that the offense directly concerned (1) nuclear weaponry, military spacecraft or satellites, early warning systems, or other means of defense or retaliation against large scale attack, (2) war plans, (3) communications intelligence or cryptographic in-formation, or (4) any other major weapons system or major element of defense strategy. See R.C.M. 1004 concerning sentencing proceedings in capital cases.

Lesser included offense. Although no lesser included offenses are set forth in the Code, federal civilian offenses on this matter may be incorporated through the third clause of Article 134.

Maximum punishment.

(1) Espionage as a capital offense. Death or such other punishment as a court-martial may direct. See R.C.M. 1003.

(2) Espionage or attempted espionage. Any punishment, other than death, that a court-martial may direct. See R.C.M. 1003.

[Manual for Court Martial, 2002, Chapter 4, Paragraph 30a]

Chapter Nine
Federal Law and Civil Issues Arising from Bioterrorism

9.1. Environmental Statutes

The federal environmental statutes have preempted state common law in the regulation of hazardous air and water pollutants, and provide a federal regulatory scheme for monitoring and cleaning up hazards to human health. The applicability of these environmental statutes to biological hazards was tested in the following case.

Smith v. Potter
2001 U.S. Dist. LEXIS 18625 (S.D.N.Y. Nov. 16, 2001)

Opinion by JOHN F. KEENAN, United States District Judge:

Background

This is an application for a preliminary injunction under 42 U.S.C. §6972, the Resource Conservation and Recovery Act ("RCRA"). Plaintiffs seek mandatory injunctive relief to compel the United States Postal Service ("USPS") to shut-down and decontaminate the Morgan Processing and Distribution Center ("Morgan"), to test the James A. Farley postal facility ("JAF"), and to test all "downstream" postal facilities that are serviced by Morgan.

By order of November 9, 2001, this Court denied the application to shut down Morgan, but directed that JAF be tested immediately. In that order, I stated that a full Opinion would follow and this is that Opinion.

Plaintiffs seek this relief because in October 2001 anthrax testing revealed the presence of anthrax spores on five pieces of mail-sorting equipment on the third floor in the south building of the Morgan Facility. Morgan is a building complex located between 28th and 30th Streets and 9th and 10th Avenues on the Westside of Manhattan. The south building runs from 28th to 29th Streets and has six work floors plus office space on the top floors.

Anthrax is a virulent infectious disease caused by the bacterium "bacillus anthracus." The bacillus can be carried in spores existing in powder form and can cause death. The anthrax contamination at Morgan likely came from anthrax-laced letters that were sent to Tom Brokaw at NBC News and The New York Post, which were processed at the Morgan Facility. Morgan is the largest central mail-processing facility in the New York City area and JAF is adjacent to Morgan and connected to it by tunnel.

Events of September 11, 2001 and thereafter recall a similar situation in our history. September 11, 2001, like December 7, 1941, "is a date that will live in infamy," and as we have learned since the 11th there is real concern amongst us for safety. Adding to our worries are the recent bioterrorist attacks involving anthrax-contaminated letters sent through the Nation's mail system. Tragically, four Americans have died from anthrax poisoning since September 11th and several others have become ill from it. Postal workers and others who handle our mail understandably are afraid. But what we cannot allow is for that fear to grow into unreasoned panic. For what we have to fear now, more than anything else, is panic. As President George W. Bush said in his speech to the Nation on November 8, 2001: "We will not give in to exaggerated fears or passing rumors. We will rely on good judgment and good, old common sense."

Life necessarily entails risks and the risk here is minimal compared to the harm that would be caused by shutting down the Morgan Facility. Morgan processes "over 13 million pieces of mail a day," according to Robert Daruk, its plant manager, and is the largest industrial facility in Manhattan.

The Court finds that the USPS has taken appropriate remedial measures to diminish any safety risk created by the presence of anthrax at the Morgan Facility. The USPS has properly responded to the presence of anthrax spores on the third floor in the Morgan Facility. Once anthrax was found in the mails, the USPS sought direction from the Centers for Disease Control and Prevention ("CDC"), a branch of the United States Department of Health and Human Services, as to the appropriate precautionary actions needed to protect the health and well-being of USPS employees and to reduce the risk of infection. As a result, the USPS provided postal workers with gloves and face masks, along with instructional safety talks. When contaminated mail appeared in New York, the USPS tested for anthrax in areas of those New York facilities through which the tainted letters passed. In addition, the USPS conducted anthrax testing of employees who worked on the processing and delivery routes along which the contaminated letters traveled. When anthrax spores were found on the third floor of Morgan, the USPS closed-down the affected area, again consulted with the CDC, and retained environmental clean-up specialists to clean 120,000 square feet of space. In consultation with the CDC, the USPS has provided and is now providing over 7000 postal workers in New York City with antibiotics that will prevent them from contracting anthrax while the affected area in the Morgan Facility is cleaned. This includes workers at Morgan.

From a public-health perspective, Dr. Stephen Ostroff, the Chief Epidemiologist in the Infectious Disease Center at the CDC, took the lead role in the investigation of the anthrax-tainted letters mailed to various New York media outlets. At the evidentiary hearing, Dr. Ostroff testified that, based on the scientific information available regarding these mailings (i.e., development of disease, time frames, etc.), the amount of anthrax "tracked through" Morgan does not "continue to pose an ongoing public health risk." Dr. Ostroff stated that if the postal workers were at risk of anthrax from processing the letters, such illness would have occurred during the time period immediately after the letters passed through the Morgan Facility, which was in mid-September. Because, among other factors, no New York postal worker contracted the disease during the five-week period before the CDC started its investigation of the Morgan-mail trail, [officials did not become aware of the anthrax in New York until October 12, 2001]. Dr. Ostroff concluded that the present risk to New York postal workers is "very, very low." Although Dr. Stellman disagreed in part with Dr. Ostroff, the Court accepts and credits the Ostroff testimony because he is the infectious disease specialist.

Thanks to the remedial actions employed, the continued operation of the Morgan Facility currently poses no imminent and substantial risk to health or the environment. Prudence required testing of JAF and the court on November 9, 2001 ordered such testing.

During the evidentiary hearing, postal officials agreed to implement the Court's directions as to how to better guarantee the safety of postal employees at Morgan. These instructions included relocating the glove and mask distribution site to the employee entrance, so this way workers will not have to traipse through the facility before obtaining protective gear. Also, the Court instructed the USPS to post an advisory at each employee time-clock station regarding the availability of prophylactic antibiotic treatment....

Conclusions of Law

The CDC is the federal agency responsible for protecting the public health of the country by providing leadership and direction in the prevention and control of diseases. As the D.C. Circuit has advised: "It is not the court's role to second-guess scientific judgments of" a governmental agency that is responsible for protecting public health. Indeed, the CDC is the type of public medical health agency to which courts should defer. The CDC is entitled to deference, but not an abdication of judicial responsibility. See American Mining Congress, 907 F.2d at 1187. Here, the CDC has studied and examined the situation and the status of the anthrax contamination at Morgan and, therefore, has met "its obligation to engage in reasoned decisionmaking." The CDC has reached the conclusion that there is no need to close Morgan....I do not have the medical knowledge or expertise to become a Monday morning quarterback here. The CDC is complying with its responsibilities under the law. So long as it does so the courts should not butt in and I decline to do so.

A. RCRA

Plaintiffs seek a preliminary injunction against the USPS under 42 U.S.C. §6972(a)(1)(B), the citizen-suit provision of RCRA, alleging that the USPS' response to the anthrax contamination has created an imminent and substantial danger to the public health and the environment. Congress has waived the federal government's sovereign immunity for purposes of citizen suits under RCRA by providing that a suit can be brought against any person, including the United States. See 42 U.S.C. §6972(a)(1)(B). Therefore, sovereign immunity does not preclude the plaintiffs from bringing a citizen suit under RCRA against the Postal Service, a federal agency.

RCRA is a comprehensive environmental statute designed to prevent the disposal of solid and hazardous wastes in ways that are harmful to the public health or the environment. To that end, RCRA regulates the generation, handling, treatment, storage, transportation, and disposal of solid and hazardous wastes. By enacting a citizen-suit provision under RCRA, Congress sought to increase enforcement of this legislation by authorizing affected citizens to bring suit against any RCRA offender whose solid waste handling practices may pose "an imminent and substantial endangerment to health or to the environment."

Despite the broad scope of the imminent-hazard citizen suit, a court must be cautious when considering the propriety of preliminary injunction relief under this provision. Indeed, an imminent and substantial danger for purposes of a RCRA claim does not exist "if the risk of harm is remote in time, speculative in nature, and de minimis in degree." According to the CDC, the anthrax contamination at Morgan does not pose a danger to employees or the community because, by mid-October, any danger had dissipated due to the passage of time. Also, the CDC found significant the fact that, thankfully, no postal worker in New York has fallen ill due to anthrax exposure. Therefore, this Court, defers to the CDC and, concludes that because the USPS implemented the CDC's recommended actions, including providing prophylactic antibiotic treatment, issuing protective gear to workers and sanitizing the affected areas, USPS' response to the anthrax contamination poses no imminent and substantial danger to the public or the environment.

The USPS argues that because anthrax does not constitute "a solid waste" under RCRA, that Act does not apply here. The Court, however, sees no need to decide this issue in view of the fact that there is no imminent and substantial danger present.
A status conference is set for December 7, 2001 at 10:00 A.M.
SO ORDERED.

Although the preliminary injunction failed for Smith, a second case was filed to challenge the cleanup after its completion. The court then addressed the applicability of RCRA and CERCLA in a bioterrorism context.

Smith v. Potter
2002 U.S. Dist. LEXIS 11878 (S.D.N.Y. July 1, 2002)

JOHN F. KEENAN, United States District Judge:
Before the Court are the following motions: (1) motion to dismiss the complaint, pursuant to Fed. R. Civ. P. 12(b)(1) for lack of subject matter jurisdiction and Fed. R. Civ. P. 12(b)(6) for failure to state a claim, filed on behalf of defendant, John E. Potter, Post Master General of the United States ("USPS"); and (2) motion to compel inspection and testing of the Morgan Processing and Distribution Center ("Morgan"), pursuant to Fed. R. Civ. P. 34, by plaintiffs, William M. Smith, New York Metro Area Postal Union and Dennis O'Neil ("Plaintiffs"). The motions are opposed and the Court heard oral argument on them on March 12, 2002. For the reasons stated herein, the Court grants the USPS's motion to dismiss the complaint in its entirety and denies as moot Plaintiffs' Rule 34 inspection motion.

Background

On or about September 20, 2001, mail contaminated with "bacillus anthracus," i.e., anthrax, was processed at the Morgan facility, the mail-processing center serving the New York metropolitan area. During processing of the tainted mail, anthrax spores were released at that site. See Compl. PP 20-21. The USPS first became aware of a potential threat of anthrax contamination at New York postal facilities on October 19, 2001 after the Centers for Disease Control ("CDC") advised that anthrax-tainted letters were mailed to various New York media outlets. See Declaration of Daniel S. Alter, dated January 11, 2002. Immediately thereafter, USPS officials arranged for anthrax testing at Morgan and postal facilities downstream of Morgan. This testing revealed the presence of anthrax spores on five pieces of mail-sorting equipment on the third floor in the south building of the Morgan facility. See id. As a result of the anthrax contamination, the USPS made available antibiotic prophylaxis (Cipro and Doxycycline) as well as protective gear to over 7,000 postal employees in New York. See id. at 95–96. The USPS, in conjunction with various other federal agencies, commenced cleanup operations, including closing down the affected area and retaining environmental specialists to assist in an anthrax removal project. Thus far, the USPS has incurred over $ 15 million in investigation and cleanup costs.

On October 29, 2001, Plaintiffs filed this suit by order to show cause, requesting a preliminary injunction and alleging that the USPS was conducting its New York City postal operations in violation of the Resource Conservation and Recovery Act ("RCRA"), 42 U.S.C. §6901, et seq., and New York State environmental laws on account of, among other things, the USPS's "handling, storage, treatment, transportation, or disposal of a hazardous waste." In their complaint, Plaintiffs also alleged a common law public nuisance cause of action, a claim that

Plaintiffs have since voluntarily dismissed pursuant to Fed. R. Civ. P. 41(a). See Notice of Voluntary Dismissal of Fifth Cause of Action (Public Nuisance), dated February 1, 2002.

In early November of 2001, an evidentiary hearing was conducted over several days in relation to Plaintiffs' preliminary injunction motion, which sought mandatory injunctive relief to compel the USPS to shut-down and decontaminate the Morgan facility, to test the James A. Farley postal facility ("JAF"), a post office immediately adjacent to the Morgan facility and connected to it by tunnel, and to test all "downstream" postal facilities serviced by Morgan. Upon consideration of the evidence adduced at the hearing, I denied Plaintiffs' preliminary injunction motion, finding that the USPS had instituted appropriate remedial measures to diminish any safety risk created by the presence of anthrax at the Morgan facility. Specifically, the Opinion and Order of November 9, 2001 held that: "Thanks to the remedial actions employed, the continued operation of the Morgan facility poses no imminent and substantial risk to health or the environment." Id. This holding was predicated, in part, on the fact that no New York postal worker contracted anthrax during the five-week period before the USPS learned of the possibility of anthrax contamination and prior to when the CDC began its investigation of the Morgan-mail trail. See id. To date, thankfully no New York postal worker has experienced any anthrax-related health problems as a result of the tainted mail that passed through the Morgan facility.

B. Imminent and Substantial Endangerment Claim (Count 1)

In count I of their complaint, Plaintiffs allege that operation of the Morgan facility poses an imminent and substantial danger to public health and the environment in violation of the citizen suit provision of 42 U.S.C. §6972(a)(1)(B) due to the USPS's handling of the anthrax contamination at that site. On this claim, Plaintiffs seek, among other things, injunctive relief requiring testing, cleaning, inspection and controlled operations of postal facilities. See Compl. PP C-F. Section 6972(a)(1)(B) permits a civil suit against any person or entity, including the United States, "who has contributed or who is contributing to the past or present handling, storage, treatment, transportation, or disposal of any solid or hazardous waste which may present an imminent and substantial endangerment to health or the environment." 42 U.S.C. §6972(a)(1)(B) (herein referred to as "imminent-hazard" claim).

Back in November of 2001, in opposing Plaintiffs' motion for a preliminary injunction, the USPS argued that Plaintiffs could not obtain RCRA relief because the anthrax found at the Morgan facility did not constitute "solid waste" as defined by the Act, 42 U.S.C. §6903 (27),[1] because it, the anthrax, had not been discarded within the meaning of the statute. In deciding the preliminary injunction motion, there was no need to reach the issue of whether the anthrax found at the postal plant constituted solid waste in view of the finding that no imminent and substantial endangerment to health or the environment existed so as to entitle Plaintiffs to an injunction pursuant to Section 6972(a)(1)(B). In spite of its initial position, the USPS now concedes that the anthrax discovered at Morgan does constitute "solid waste" as defined by RCRA.[2]

---

[1] RCRA defines the term "solid waste" as "any garbage, refuse sludge from a waste treatment plant, water supply treatment plant, or air pollution control facility and other discarded material, including solid, liquid, semisolid, or contained gaseous material resulting from industrial, commercial, mining, and agricultural operations, and from community activities..." 42 U.S.C. §6903(27).

[2] The USPS makes this concession with a caveat: "The Government does not maintain that anthrax, per se, is a 'solid waste' under RCRA, or that RCRA applies in every context in which anthrax may be present. Whether RCRA applies in any case involving

With respect to the imminent-hazard claim, the USPS argues that this claim is jurisdictionally barred under the RCRA/CERCLA[3] statutory scheme because, upon discovery of the anthrax at the Morgan facility, the USPS immediately initiated a CERCLA Section 104 removal action to eliminate the contamination. Section 113(h) of CERCLA precludes federal courts from exercising jurisdiction (subject to certain exceptions not applicable here) over actions that attack the adequacy of CERCLA Section 104 removal actions: "No Federal court shall have jurisdiction under Federal law...to review any challenges to removal or remedial action selected under section 104 of this title,...in any action except one of the following...." 42 U.S.C. §9613(h). Subsection 6972(b)(2)(B)(ii) of RCRA likewise provides:

> No action may be commenced under subsection (a)(1)(B) of this section if the [EPA] Administrator, in order to restrain or abate acts or conditions which may have contributed or are contributing to the activities which may present the alleged endangerment—

> (ii) is actually engaging in a removal action under section 104 of the Comprehensive Environmental Response, Compensation and Liability Act of 1980 [CERCLA].

Plaintiffs assert basically two arguments as to why the Section 113(h) bar does not preclude their RCRA claims: (1) the USPS's response to the anthrax contamination does not constitute a removal action under Section 104 of CERCLA since only the EPA, not the USPS, can conduct such an initiative; and (2) alternatively, that even if the USPS's response constitutes a removal action, Plaintiffs' claims are not barred in light of the timing of their lawsuit. Both arguments fail.

By its terms, Section 104 of CERCLA authorizes the President to initiate a removal action, but the President delegated to all Executive department heads the authority to undertake removal actions under the provisions of Section 104 in certain specified circumstances. In particular, the President delegated his statutory authority to conduct removal actions to "the heads of Executive departments and agencies," in non-emergency situations where there has been a release of a hazardous substance, pollutant, or contaminant "on or the sole source of [such] release is from any facility...under the jurisdiction, custody, or control of those departments and agencies." Exec. Order 12580, §2(e)(1), 52 Fed. Reg. 2923, 2924 (Jan. 23, 1987), 1987 WL 181273. n5 In this case, pursuant to the express authority delegated to him by the President in Executive Order 12580, the Postmaster General, head of the USPS (an Executive agency), took action in accord with Section 104 of CERCLA to cleanup the anthrax discovered at the Morgan facility, federal property within the jurisdiction and control of the USPS.

The EPA itself has recognized the result of this delegation of power, advising that it "will respond only to those public health or environmental emergencies that [a] Federal agency [with delegated Section 104 authority to conduct removal actions] cannot respond to in a timely manner."

---

anthrax requires a fact-specific analysis, which in turn considers whether the anthrax at issue has been 'discarded.'"

[3] "CERCLA" refers to the Comprehensive Environmental Response, Compensation and Liability Act, as amended by the Superfund Amendments and Reauthorization Act of 1986, 42 U.S.C. §9601–9675.

To the extent that Plaintiffs argue that the anthrax contamination presented an emergency situation outside the scope of the delegation of authority, this argument fails given that when officials first learned of the presence of anthrax, the situation posed no urgent health risk in light of the fact that five weeks had passed after the anthrax-laced letters passed through the Morgan facility. See Smith, 187 F. Supp. 2d at 96 ("Because, among other factors, no New York postal worker contracted the disease during the five-week period before the CDC started its investigation of the Morgan-mail trail, Dr. Ostroff concluded that the present risk to New York postal workers is 'very, very low.'" (footnote omitted)).

The anthrax testing and other investigative measures commenced by the USPS on October 21, 2001 qualifies as a removal action under Section 104. Even apart from this, the Court notes that Plaintiffs here cannot avoid dismissal of their RCRA claim by second-guessing the cleanup procedures commenced by the USPS, for such a tactic eviscerates the purpose of the Section 113(h) bar and flouts Congress's intent in enacting that ban in the first place—namely, to protect ongoing CERCLA cleanups from delay and interference occasioned by disputes over applicable environmental standards.

Next, Plaintiffs argue that even if the USPS response constitutes a removal action, Section 113(h)'s ban on challenges to ongoing CERCLA removal actions does not bar their RCRA claims given the timing of their suit. Specifically, Plaintiffs contend that the removal action either did not start till October 31, 2001, (two days after the date on which Plaintiffs filed their complaint, i.e., October 29, 2001) insofar as that is when the administrative record "references the first oral contact with a cleanup contractor," or as late as January 2002, when the USPS made the administrative record available to the public. Alternatively, Plaintiffs claim that the removal action is now over, and, therefore, the Section 113(h) bar does not apply in this case. Regardless of the version of Plaintiffs' chronology of the Section 104 removal action, their timing argument fails.

Because the plain language of Section 113(h) allows citizen suits challenging a removal action only after the cleanup is actually completed and given that Plaintiffs commenced this action during the pendency of a CERCLA removal action, Plaintiffs' imminent-hazard claim constitutes an improper challenge under Section 113(h). (CERCLA Section 113 bars challenges to removal or remedial actions "until completion of cleanup activities"). Based on the foregoing, the Court holds that Plaintiffs' Section 6972(a)(1)(B) imminent-hazard claim constitutes a Section 113(h)-barred challenge to the removal action at the Morgan facility, and, therefore, the Court grants the USPS's motion to dismiss that claim for lack of jurisdiction.

Conclusion

For the reasons set forth above, the Court grants the USPS's motion to dismiss the complaint in its entirety and denies as moot Plaintiffs' Rule 34 inspection motion. The Court orders this case closed and directs the Clerk of Court to remove it from the Court's active docket.

Notes

1. CERCLA defines "pollutant or contaminant" as: "any element, substance, compound, or mixture, including disease-causing agents, which after release into the environment and upon exposure, ingestion, inhalation, or assimilation into any organism, either directly from the environment or indirectly by ingestion through food chains, will or may reasonably be anticipated to cause death [or] disease." 42 U.S.C. §9601(33) (2002).

The CERCLA definition which includes "disease causing agents" is applicable to anthrax. What other cleanup issues might arise in cleaning up biological agents, as compared to chemical hazardous wastes?

2. Could the plaintiffs have succeeded in a RCRA citizen suit action on an "imminent and substantial endangerment" basis to compel cleanup if their suit had been instituted earlier?

RCRA provides that once a citizen suit has been initiated, the EPA has 60 days in which to commence the suit, and the citizen suit must be dropped. If EPA does not initiate the suit, the citizen suit may continue.

_____

9.2. Tort Claims against the Federal Government
9.2.1. Public Nuisance

Smith v. Potter
2001 U.S. Dist. LEXIS 18625 (November 16, 2001)

[facts in section 5.1]
B. Public Nuisance Cause of Action

In its opposition papers, the USPS argues that sovereign immunity bars the Plaintiffs' public nuisance cause of action. The public nuisance claim centers on allegations that "actions and omissions of the USPS with respect to the handling of anthrax have created a public nuisance because of the potential exposure of the general public to a deadly bacteria" The USPS argues that the Court should consider this theory relative to the injunction, even though the plaintiffs have not urged it on the injunction aspect of the case.

Congress has waived the Postal Services' sovereign immunity by providing that the Postal Service may "sue or be sued." But the scope of the waiver under Section 401(1) is limited with respect to tort claims. Specifically...any tort claim against the Postal Service is subject to the remedies and restrictions of the Federal Tort Claims Act ("FTCA"). "[The FTCA] shall apply to tort claims arising out of the activities of the Postal Services."

Money damages are the only form of relief permitted under the FTCA. Accordingly, Congress has not waived the government's sovereign immunity for tort claims, like the plaintiffs' public nuisance claim, that seek injunctive relief against the USPS. As such, the circumstances here mean that injunctive relief is not appropriate based on a public nuisance theory.

The application for a preliminary injunction is denied, but the Court directs that on November 26, 2001 by 1:00 P.M., I and the plaintiffs' counsel be supplied with a detailed report from the Government as to the then-existing status of the anthrax condition at Morgan as well as the clean-up. Should the status quo change between now and November 26, 2001, the Court is to be advised immediately.

_____

Notes
1. The Smith case voluntarily dropped its claim for public nuisance in its subsequent filing. Would public nuisance succeed against a private party?

2. Could the Emergency Planning and Community Right-to-Know Act of 1986 which requires local emergency planning committees (LEPCs) to utilize companies' inventories of toxic substances to make emergency plans for the community for release of hazardous substances. Would biological laboratories be required to disclose their biological agents to the LEPCs for inclusion in local emergency plans?

9.2.2. Federal Tort Claim Act

The Federal Tort Claims Act provides for citizens to sue the federal government for negligence of its employees for specified torts, thereby waiving sovereign immunity for this limited purpose. The standard for the act is that it must be "under circumstances where the United States, if a private person, would be liable to the claimant in accordance with the law of the place where the act or omission occurred." (28 U.S.C. §1346(b)). The liability of the act must be determined by the applicable law of the state or territory within which the act occurred.

The Federal Tort Claims Act, § 1346(b) (2000), provides that the district courts shall have exclusive jurisdiction of civil actions on claims against the United States, for money damages, for injury or loss of property, or personal injury or death caused by the negligent or wrongful act or omission of any employee of the Government while acting within the scope of his office or employment, under circumstances where the United States, if a private person, would be liable to the claimant in accordance with the law of the place where the act or omission occurred. § 1346(b)(1).

Sovereign immunity is not waived for assault, battery, false imprisonment, false arrest, malicious prosecution, abuse of process, libel, slander, misrepresentation, deceit, or interference with contract. However, in cases where the government employee is a law enforcement officer, sovereign immunity is waived for the torts of assault, battery, false imprisonment, false arrest, abuse of process, or malicious prosecution. (28 U.S.C. §2680(h)).

The exception to the character of the act, is that if the act is a "discretionary function" the action is barred. A discretionary function is established by a two part test. If an action or failure to act is based upon "an element of judgment or choice" (Gaubert, 499 U.S. 315, 322 (1991)) and if " the judgment is of the kind that the discretionary function exception was designed to shield in that if it involves considerations of 'social, economic, and political policy," then the action is a "discretionary function" and the action is barred. Gaubert, 499 U.S. 315, 322–23 (1991).

In a bioterrorism context, as seen in the previous case, **Smith v. Potter**, 2001 U.S. Dist. LEXIS 18625 (S.D.N.Y. Nov. 16, 2001), public nuisance is a tort for which the federal government has not waived its sovereign immunity and is thereby barred. However, negligence in the context of the FTCA is available to the plaintiff, and is a basis for a third-party claim against the federal government in **Morris v. Kaiser Foundation Health Plan** (Civ. No. PJM 02-1468 (D.Md. May 28, 2002).

In the third party action against the United States, the defendant and third-party plaintiff, Kaiser, alleges jurisdiction under the Federal Tort Claims Act and makes the following allegations in the complaint:

35. Notwithstanding these denials, if a finder of fact determines that the defendants and third party plaintiffs, or any of them, are liable to the plaintiffs, on any or all claims asserted by the plaintiffs, the defendants and third party plaintiffs are entitled to an adjudication that the United States of American is a joint tortfeasor, by reason of the negligence of unknown agents, servants, and employees of the agencies, departments of the third party defendant, the United States of America, which include, but are not limited to, the United States Postal Service, the United States Department of Health and Human Services, and the Centers for Disease Control, and any harm caused to the plaintiffs thereby.

36. At all times relevant to the matters asserted herein, the United States of America, by and through its agencies, departments, agents, servants and employees, owed a duty to the plaintiffs, to the defendants and third party plaintiffs, to state and local health departments, and to the public at large, (a) to use reasonable care in the preparation of all communications expected to be disseminated and relied upon by the general public concerning the transmission, prevention, diagnosis and treatment of inhalation anthrax; (b) to use reasonable care in the preparation of all communications expected to be disseminated and relied upon by health care providers concerning the transmission, prevention, diagnosis and treatment of inhalation anthrax; (c) to use reasonable care in the investigation and prompt identification of anthrax exposure or

contamination in facilities, including postal facilities, through which anthrax contaminated mail had been handled or processed; (e) to offer prophylaxis, testing, and treatment to federal employees who were at risk for anthrax exposure, based on what a prudent investigation would have disclosed and to provide a safe place to work; and (f) to otherwise act in a reasonable and prudent manner to assure prompt and effective diagnosis and treatment of persons who have been, or may have been, exposed to anthrax.

37. Notwithstanding the duties stated above, the United States of America, by and through its agencies, departments, agents, servants and employees, (a) failed to use reasonable care in the preparation of communications expected to be disseminated and relied upon by the general public concerning the transmission, prevention, diagnosis and treatment of inhalation anthrax; (b) failed to use reasonable care in the preparation of communications expected to be disseminated and relied upon by health care providers concerning the transmission, prevention, diagnosis and treatment of inhalation anthrax; (c) failed to use reasonable care in the investigation and prompt identification of anthrax exposure or contamination in public facilities, including postal facilities, through which anthrax contaminated mail had been handled or processed; (d) failed to use reasonable care in the preparation of communications expected to be disseminated and relied upon by the general public and by health care providers concerning exposure, contamination, and transmission of anthrax in public facilities, including postal facilities, through which anthrax contaminated mail had been handled or processed, (e) failed to timely offer prophylaxis, testing, and treatment to federal employees who were at risk for anthrax exposure, based on what a prudent investigation should have disclosed and did not provide a safe place to work; and (f) failed to otherwise act in a reasonable and prudent manner to assure prompt and effective diagnosis and treatment of persons who have been, or may have been, exposed to anthrax.

38. The plaintiffs, the defendants and third party plaintiffs, state and local health departments, and the public at large relied in fact, or reasonably could have relied on the negligent actions and omissions of the United States of America, by and through its agencies, departments, agents, servants and employees, as stated above.

In *Maureen Stevens v. United States*, 994 So.2d 1062 (Fla. 2008), the widow of the first victim of the anthrax attacks, sued the federal government for its negligence in securing the anthrax in its government laboratory, USAMRIID. The following opinion from the Florida Supreme Court which accepted a question on certiorari: Under Florida law, does a laboratory that manufactures, grows, tests or handles ultra-hazardous materials owe a duty of reasonable care to members of the general public to avoid an unauthorized interception and dissemination of the materials, and, if not, is a duty created where a reasonable response is not made where there is a history of such dangerous materials going missing or being stolen?

United States v. Stevens
994 So.2d 1062 (Fla. 2008)

Supreme Court of Florida.

Oct. 30, 2008. Background: Personal representative of estate of worker who died after inhaling anthrax allegedly stolen from private research facility and mailed to his employer brought wrongful death suit pursuant to Federal Tort Claims Act (FTCA) against the United States in federal court and against private research facility in state court. Research facility removed state case to federal court and suits were consolidated for discovery purposes. Government moved to dismiss for failure to state a claim and facility moved for judgment on the pleadings. The United States District Court for the Southern District of Florida, Nos. 03–81110–CV–DTKH and 04–80253–CV–DTK, Daniel T.K. Hurley, J., denied motions. Order denying motion to dismiss was certified for interlocutory appeal. The Court of Appeals, Kravitch, Circuit Judge, 488 F.3d 896, certified question of whether laboratory that handled ultrahazardous materials owed a duty of care to public. Holdings: The Supreme Court, Anstead, J., held that:

(1) no special relationship between laboratory and individual who committed crime of stealing anthrax, sending it through the mail, and killing the recipient was required to be shown, and
(2) laboratory owed a duty of reasonable care to members of the general public to avoid an unauthorized interception and dissemination of the ultrahazardous materials.

Question answered. Wells, J., dissented and filed opinion.

ANSTEAD, J. The United States Court of Appeals for the Eleventh Circuit has certified the following question of Florida law that is determinative of a cause pending in that court and for which there appears to be no controlling precedent: Under Florida law, does a laboratory that manufactures, grows, tests or handles ultra-hazardous materials owe a duty of reasonable care to members of the general public to avoid an unauthorized interception and dissemination of the materials, and, if not, is a duty created where a reasonable response is not made where there is a history of such dangerous materials going missing or being stolen? Stevens v. Battelle Mem'l Inst., 488 F.3d 896, 904 (11th Cir.2007). We have jurisdiction. See art. V, § 3(b)(6), Fla. Const. For the reasons that follow, we answer the first part of the certified question in the affirmative, and therefore, we need not address the second part.

PROCEEDINGS TO DATE
The Eleventh Circuit outlined the plaintiff's injuries and allegations:
In the fall of 2001, an unknown group or individual mailed letters containing Bacillus Anthracis ("anthrax") to recipients in Florida, New York, and Washington, D.C. One such letter was mailed to American Media, Inc. ("American Media") in Boca Raton, Florida where Robert Stevens ("Mr. Stevens") worked. Mr. Stevens became ill and died after inhaling the anthrax. As a result, two wrongful death suits were brought by Maureen Stevens, his wife, individually, as a personal representative of the estate of Mr. Stevens, and on behalf of their three children (collectively "Stevens"). Stevens sued the United States in federal court and Battelle Memorial Institute ("Battelle"), a private research facility, in state court, alleging that they were the source of the anthrax that killed Mr. Stevens. Battelle removed the state case to federal court and the two suits were consolidated for discovery purposes.
The complaint against the United States, brought pursuant to the Federal Tort Claims Act ("FTCA"), 28 U.S.C. §§ 1346(b), 2671 et seq., alleged that the origin of the strain of anthrax that killed Mr. Stevens could be traced to the United States Army Medical Research Institute for Infectious Diseases ("USAMRIID") at Fort Detrick, Maryland. The suit alleged further that the government knew it was utilizing an "ultra-hazardous" material requiring the highest degree of care in its handling, storage, use, and possession, and that, as early as 1992, samples of anthrax were missing from USAMRIID. The complaint stated that despite this knowledge, the government failed to provide adequate security for the handling or shipping of the materials, and, as a result, sometime before October 2001 anthrax was improperly intercepted either from USAMRIID or from another research facility to which the materials had been sent. The complaint does not describe the relationship between the government and the person who initially intercepted the

anthrax or between the government and the person who eventually mailed the anthrax to American Media.

The complaint against Battelle alleged that Battelle breached its duty of care to Mr. Stevens by failing to implement adequate security procedures at its facility. The suit alleged, inter alia, that Battelle failed to properly maintain the anthrax it was using for research, monitor employees who had access to the anthrax, or secure the facility from unauthorized access. The complaint also alleged that Battelle was negligent in its hiring practices because it failed to conduct background investigations prior to hiring individuals who would have access to anthrax. Finally, the complaint alleged negligent supervision of employees working with anthrax. As a result of these failings, the complaint alleged that anthrax was obtained and sent to American Media.

The government moved to dismiss the complaint, arguing that it could not be liable for any third party criminal activity allegedly occasioned by negligent security practices because it owed no duty of protection to Mr. Stevens, a stranger, and did not have a duty or ability to control the unidentified third party tortfeasor or tortfeasors responsible for intercepting and mailing the anthrax. Reiterating this argument, Battelle moved for judgment on the pleadings pursuant to Rule 12(c). Battelle also argued that Stevens could not satisfy the element of proximate cause. Stevens responded to these motions by arguing that the complaint did not allege a claim of failure to control or prevent the mailing of the anthrax by a third party criminal, but, rather, a claim of duty of care "whenever a human endeavor creates a generalized and foreseeable risk of harming others."

ANALYSIS

Preliminarily, we note that this case involves a claim of negligence, which we have explained consists of four components:

1. A duty, or obligation, recognized by the law, requiring the [defendant] to conform to a certain standard of conduct, for the protection of others against unreasonable risks.

2. A failure on the [defendant's] part to conform to the standard required: a breach of the duty

3. A reasonably close causal connection between the conduct and the resulting injury. This is what is commonly known as "legal cause," or "proximate cause," and which includes the notion of cause in fact.

4. Actual loss or damage Clay Elec. Coop., Inc. v. Johnson, 873 So.2d 1182, 1185 (Fla.2004) (quoting Prosser and Keeton on the Law of Torts § 30, at 164–65 (W. Page Keeton ed., 5th ed.1984)).

In certifying a question to this concept of foreseeability of harm to the circumstances alleged, which is a threshold question of law. See id. at 502–04. We have explained, where a person's conduct is such that it creates a "foreseeable zone of risk" posing a general threat of harm to others, a legal duty will ordinarily be recognized to ensure that the underlying threatening conduct is carried out reasonably. Id. at 503. We have also explained that as a general proposition the greater the risk of harm to others that is created by a person's chosen activity, the greater the burden or duty to avoid injury to others becomes. "Thus, as the risk grows greater, so does the duty, because the risk to be perceived defines the duty that must be undertaken." Id. at 503 (citing J.G. Christopher Co. v. Russell, 63 Fla. 191, 58 So. 45 (1912)).

In the instant case, we conclude that the district court appropriately turned to sections 302, 302A, and 302B of the Restatement for guidance in determining whether a duty exists under

Florida law.3 While we could "reinvent the wheel" and set out our own analysis as to the application of the principles of these sections to the circumstances alleged here, we acknowledge that we could not improve upon the district court's analysis. Because we agree with Judge Hurley's analysis, we adopt the portion of his order regarding the application of these sections to the certified question:

The duties described [in sections 302, 302A, and 302B of the Restatement] attach to acts of commission, which historically generate a broader umbrella of tort liability than acts of omission, which are the subject of §§ 315 and 314A. This distinction is expressed in Comment a, Section 302 of the Restatement of Torts (Second):

This section is concerned only with the negligent character of the actor's conduct, and not with his [or her] duty to avoid the unreasonable risk. In general, anyone who does an affirmative act is under a duty to others to exercise the care of a reasonable [person] to protect them against an unreasonable risk of harm to them arising out of the act. The duties of one who merely omits to act are more restricted, and in general are confined to situation[s] where there is a special relation between the actor and the other which gives rise to the duty. In this case, plaintiff alleges that the government generated, tested and handled deadly laboratory organisms, but failed to employ adequate security procedures during the commission of these acts. Thus, plaintiff contends, the government exposed the public to an unreasonable risk of contamination as a result of unauthorized interception and disbursement of lethal materials. In other words, the complaint effectively alleges the commission of affirmative acts (ownership and handling of biohazards), which, under Section 302b, give rise to a corresponding duty to protect all others exposed to any "unreasonable risk of harm" arising out of that activity.

Considered in conjunction with the further allegations of the complaint regarding the facility's history of missing samples of anthrax bacterium, hanta virus and ebola virus dating back to 1992, which the court must accept as true at this juncture, the court concludes that plaintiff's complaint states a potential claim under Section 302B of the Restatement (Second) of Torts (1965) against the government and will accordingly uphold the sufficiency of the complaint on this basis.

In doing so, the court draws from Florida case law precedent clearly recognizing that negligence liability may be imposed on the basis of affirmative acts which create an unreasonable risk of harm by creating a foreseeable opportunity for third party criminal conduct, even though there is no "special relationship" between the parties that independently imposes a duty to warn or guard against that misconduct. See e.g. Shurben v. Dollar Rent–A–Car, 676 So.2d 467 (Fla. 3d DCA 1996). In Shurben, a British tourist was accosted by unknown criminals while traveling in a rental car bearing a license plate designation easily recognized by knowledgeable criminals as the mark of a rental car. The consumer sued the rental agency in tort, contending that it should have realized criminals were targeting tourist car renters in certain areas of Miami and that a reasonable rental company would have understood that its customers would be exposed to unreasonable risk of harm if not protected against this risk. Although the rental agency and customer did not stand in any "special relation" toward each other, the Court concluded that the circumstances alleged stated a claim within the scope of Section 302B of the Restatement (Second) of Torts (1965), and sustained the plaintiff's complaint on this theory.

Similarly, taking the facts alleged in the complaint as true and reading them in the light most favorable to plaintiff here, the plaintiff's complaint may fairly be read to allege: (1) defendant knew or should have known of the risk of bioterrorism associated with lethal laboratory organisms under its ownership and control, particularly in light of its history of missing laboratory specimens dating back to 1992; (2) a reasonable medical research and testing laboratory operator in possession of those facts would understand that the public would be exposed to an unreasonable risk of harm unless it implemented adequate security procedures to guard against the risk of unauthorized interception of toxic materials from its laboratory; (3) the death of Mr. Stevens was a foreseeable consequence of the defendant's failure to use reasonable care in adopting and implementing security measures reasonably necessary to protect against the possibility of unauthorized interception and release of the biohazards under its control.

In the court's view, these allegations are sufficient to establish a duty of care under Section 302B of the Restatement (Second) of Torts (1965). . . .

In the instant case, we have no way of knowing whether Stevens will ultimately be able to prove a case against the defendants. However, we conclude that Stevens' allegations are sufficient to open the courthouse doors. The allegations assert that the government and Battelle have affirmatively chosen to work with an ultrahazardous substance that poses virtually unparalleled risk of injury to the general public if its security is not assured. . . .

CONCLUSION

We hold, therefore, consistent with the analysis set out above, that a laboratory that manufactures, grows, tests or handles ultrahazardous materials does owe a duty of reasonable care to members of the general public to avoid an unauthorized interception and dissemination of the materials. We answer the certified question in the affirmative and return this case to the Eleventh Circuit.

It is so ordered.

QUINCE, C.J., PARIENTE, and LEWIS, JJ., concur.

WELLS, J., dissents with an opinion.

CANADY and POLSTON, JJ., did not participate.

WELLS, J., dissenting. I dissent from the majority's answer to the certified question, which asks specifically: Under Florida law, does a laboratory that manufactures, grows, tests or handles ultra-hazardous materials owe a duty of reasonable care to members of the general public to avoid an unauthorized interception and dissemination of the materials, and, if not, is a duty created where a reasonable response is not made where there is a history of such dangerous materials going missing or being stolen? Stevens v. Battelle Mem'l Inst., 488 F.3d 896, 904 (11th Cir.2007) (emphasis added). The crux of the question concerns liability for injuries resulting from a defendant's work with ultrahazardous materials. The majority errs in answering this question on the basis of negligence law and this Court's decision in McCain v. Florida Power Corp., 593 So.2d 500 (Fla.1992). Contrary to the majority's analysis, liability for injuries resulting from ultrahazardous activities is controlled by application of section 519 of the Restatement of Torts (1938). Therefore, I would answer the certified question on the basis of section 519. . . .

Thus, in McCain, the Court did not expand the concept of duty to be a duty to protect the general public. Rather, the duty was to all persons "who foreseeably may come in contact with that equipment." Id. This limitation on the extent of a defendant's duty is similar to the extent of an actor's liability for injuries caused by ultrahazardous activities, which as stated above, extends only to persons the actor should know are likely to be harmed by the ultrahazardous activity.

In conclusion, in this case we are only to answer the certified question and not to decide whether the appellee stated a cause of action. My answer to the certified question would be that the laboratory owes a duty of care to those who operators of the laboratory should recognize are likely to be injured by contact with the ultrahazardous material.

———————

9.2.3. Privacy Act 5 U.S.C. §552a

An incident of 2007, causing global attention to Andrew Speaker for traveling for his honeymoon, despite the cautions from the CDC and local public health officials that he should not travel.   Those facts are disputed by Mr. Speaker. He filed an action against the U.S. Department of Health and Human Services, Centers for Diseases Control and Prevention, in the Northern District of Georgia federal court, claiming they had violated the Privacy Act, 5 U.S.C. §552a by "causing his name to be released" to the media and causing him harm, in July 2007. In 2009, the court dismissed his case for failure to state a claim upon which relief could be granted, a 12(b)(6) motion in favor of the government. *Speaker v. U.S. HHS, CDC,* 680 F. Supp. 2d 1369-70 (N.D. Ga. 2009).

The plaintiff"s burden to prove a Privacy Act violation at § 552a(g)(1)(D) requires: "(1) a violation of the CDC's record-keeping obligation in the form of a disclosure of his identity by any means of communication to any person or agency; and, (2) that the disclosure was intentional and willful. (3) the failure proximately caused an adverse effect on an individual; and (4) that individual suffered actual damages."

The federal district court offered a policy rationale for the court's reasoning in footnote number 14:

> "If the release at issue here were to constitute a Privacy Act violation as Speaker alleges, it would severely inhibit the reasonable and appropriate conduct of public health officials responding to possible public health emergencies. For example, if public health officials learned that a specific person, while on a business trip to new York attended a Broadway show nad that he had a highly contagious, fatal disease, under speaker's interpretation of the Privacy Act, public health officials would be prohibited from issuing an immediate public announcement, without disclosing the person's identity, that an infected person had attended the play, sat in a particular section, and traveled ina particular route in order to warn others attending the performance (and those with whom they came into contract) that their health was in serious danger and to seek immediate medical care."

Speaker filed a notice of appeal for the 11th Circuit, Federal Court of Appeals, and the opinion of the federal district court was reversed and remanded on October 22, 2010. *Speaker v. U.S. Dept. of Health and Human Services Centers for Disease,* 623 F.3d 1371, 1386 (11th Cir. 2010). The court reviewed the 12(b)(6) motion to dismiss, *de novo,* using a "plausible" standard and found:

> "Reading Speaker's Amended Complaint as a whole, we conclude that it
> both alleges the requisite statutory elements and marshals "enough facts
> to state a claim to relief that is plausible on its face."

The appeals court addressed each of the elements, two of which are of particular interest. Whether the disclosure was "made" or "caused to be made" by CDC was a distinction made by CDC and the district court in holding this element was not met, opining the disclosure must be "made" not "caused to be made". However, the 11th Circuit wrote this was too narrow of a reading and that this was sufficient to meet the standard, where further discovery would be required to prove this element:

> "The CDC's main argument here is that Speaker's Amended Complaint

impermissibly equivocated on the issue of whether the CDC itself disclosed his name. The CDC cites, in particular, Paragraph 82 of the Amended Complaint, which alleges that "the CDC caused personally identifiable information about Mr. Speaker to be improperly disclosed." Am. Compl. ¶ 82. The CDC, however, reads the Amended Complaint far too narrowly. Nothing in the transitive verb "cause" necessitates the intervention of a third party, as the CDC seems to imply."

The damages element alleged by Speaker included mental and emotional damages which the court found were excluded under the Privacy Act, however his pecuniary damages also alleged were enough to meet that element:

"Am. Compl. ¶ 114 (alleging that Speaker suffered "both pecuniary and non-pecuniary losses"); id. ¶ 115 (alleging that CDC disclosures "had a substantial economic and noneconomic impact upon his livelihood," including loss of prospective clients as an attorney); id. ¶ 116 (alleging "considerable economic and non-economic damage to his personal and professional reputation")."

Then, on March 14, 2012, on remand, the federal district court dismissed his case a second time, finding that "Plaintiff does not offer any direct evidence that any official from the CDC retrieved and intentionally or willfully disclosed his identity to the public and members of the media prior to when his identity was first reported by the AP on May 31, 2007."

Again, the court found there was not enough evidence alleged that would meet this "plausible" standard, and the presumption that the evidence had been destroyed by the person alleged to have released the information from CDC was not sufficient to rely upon for surviving a 12(b)(6) challenge. Further, Speaker alleged that CDC had an "agenda" to publicize his possible XDR-TB diagnosis as a way to attract attention to appeals for budget increases to combat the disease. For this proof, he offered an expert witness and an Institute of Medicine report citing the funding insufficient for the agency's statutory mandate to address XDR-TB. The court also rejected this allegation as insufficient to meet his burden that "the disclosure was intentional and willful."

Speaker appealed once again, this time it would be an appellate panel at the 11th Circuit that would hear his appeal. However, on September 17, 2012, in an unpublished opinion, *Speaker v. US Dep't of Health & Human Servs. Ctrs. for Disease Control & Prevention,* No. 12-11967, D. C. Docket No. 1:09-cv-01137-WSD (11th Cir. Sep. 14, 2012), the appellate panel upheld the federal district court's finding that his claim should be dismissed. The court held that:

"The district court ... correctly refused to draw the inference appellant draws from the destruction of email evidence," the appeals court said. As a result, "there is no basis for reversing the district court's decision."

Several other aspects of the case raised speculation as to how he might have contracted tuberculosis,, in particular his father-in-law was a microbiologist at CDC, involved in research of tuberculosis. The fact that Andrew Speaker was a tort lawyer, further suggested his was intelligent and aware of the circumstances. However, ultimately, the speculation about whether he had XDR-TB proved to be false, and he was ultimately diagnosed with MDR-TB, a form of tuberculosis that can be treated with at least one antibiotic; whereas, XDR-TB is resistant to all antibiotics.

9.3. Federal Labor Law

The following case is a motion for emergency injunctive relief to direct the postal service to expedite the arbitration of a safety grievance filed by the local union chapter regarding the safety of postal workers who may be exposed to anthrax, which may have been placed in mail received at the postal facility.

Because the parties had not exhausted their contractual remedies under the collective bargaining agreement for dispute resolution, the court could not hear the matter. Here, the court considered the motion for a preliminary injunction, and held that the plaintiff failed to produce evidence of irreparable harm. Although two postal workers in Washington, D.C. had died as a result of exposure to anthrax in the Brentwood postal facility, the court cited the lack of evidence of an actual threat, or evidence that any postal worker in Florida had suffered actual or imminent harm from exposure to anthrax.

Miami Area Local v. United States Postal Service
173 F. Supp. 2d 1322 (S.D. Fla. 2001)

JUDGES: PATRICIA A. SEITZ, UNITED STATES DISTRICT JUDGE.
OPINION:
ORDER DENYING PLAINTIFF'S MOTION FOR EMERGENCY INJUNCTIVE RELIEF

On Monday, October 29, 2001, Plaintiff Miami Area Local, American Postal Workers Union, AFL-CIO ["Miami Local"] filed a Motion for Emergency Injunctive Relief, requesting that the Court direct Defendant United States Postal Service ["USPS"] to expedite the arbitration of a safety grievance filed by the local union chapter of the American Postal Workers Union ["APWU"]. The Court conducted a preliminary hearing on this Motion on October 31, 2001, and took evidence and heard testimony from the parties from November 2, 2001 through November 9, 2001. After review of the record and the applicable law, the Court DENIES Miami Local's Motion for the reasons stated below.

PROCEDURAL AND FACTUAL BACKGROUND

In October of 2001, the United States struggled through the first widely-known bio-terrorist attack of the twenty-first century as law enforcement officers, scientists, postal workers, and ordinary citizens confronted a scourge of anthrax spores traced to letters apparently sent through the mail.[4] On October 5, 2001, medical authorities confirmed that Bob Stevens, an employee of American Media, Inc. ["AMI"], in Boca Raton, Florida, died after inhaling anthrax spores. Medical authorities later confirmed a second case of inhalation anthrax at AMI in Boca Raton, which was successfully treated. Throughout the month, law enforcement officers found anthrax-tainted correspondence on Capitol Hill and at numerous media outlets, and discovered anthrax linked to confirmed anthrax cases at the West Trenton post office and Hamilton Township mail center in New Jersey, the Brentwood mail center in the District of Columbia, and the mail

---

[4] USPS Management Instruction dated October 4, 1999 defines anthrax as: "an acute infectious disease caused by bacillus anthracis. Spores enter the body through open wounds, cuts, or mucous membranes (mouth, nose) or are inhaled or ingested. Humans usually get the disease by coming into contact with spores of infected animals (cattle, sheep, goats) or their products. It is probably not transmitted from person to person, and a person with anthrax is not contagious. Bacillus anthracis spores can cause disease in 2 to 60 days. Individuals who have been identified as having had an exposure to anthrax may be treated by medication."

center at the State Department headquarters. The Centers for Disease Control and Prevention ["CDC"] in Atlanta, Georgia, confirmed that there were sixteen cases of anthrax (and four anthrax-attributed deaths) in October. Anthrax felled two postal workers.[5] To date, investigators have found traces of anthrax spores at six postal facilities in the Postal Service's Central District of Florida. All of these facilities have been decontaminated.[6] No facilities in the Postal Service's Southern District have tested positive for anthrax, and no Florida postal workers have tested positive for exposure to anthrax. Although limited in scope, these unpredictable and grave attacks set the nation on edge.

On October 23, 2001, Miami Local n5 filed a Step 2 Grievance with USPS under the current Collective Bargaining Agreement ["CBA"] between national APWU and USPS. n6 In its grievance, Miami Local requested corrective action in the form of protective equipment, testing of all facilities and employees that may handle "suspicious mail," and paid administrative leave for hours lost due to suspicious mail or testing thereof. Six days later, on October 29, 2001, Miami Local filed the instant case, reiterating the charges raised in its grievance. In its Preliminary Injunction Motion, Miami Local requested an Order requiring arbitration on an expedited basis, stating that:

> There appears to be no policies which concern the [Miami Local] as...to matters concerning sweeps to determine if anthrax is present, testing of employees for anthrax, administrative leaves to employees for physical and psychological treatment, protective equipment such as gloves and face masks, and other health and safety matters, and such policies differ from location to location with no definitive policy for the jurisdiction of the [Miami Local]....

> Without immediate arbitration to resolve the above stated issues, irreparable harm will be done [to the Miami Local] and its members since postal workers will suffer actual and psychological damage due to anthrax.

(Pl.'s Compl. at 6). On November 2, 2001, the USPS responded to Miami Local's grievance, noting that "the relief the grievance requests, that window clerks be allowed to wear masks at the window, conflicts with [the] national policy that was developed in light of the obligations of Article 14 of the National Agreement (Safety and Health) in consultation and dialogue with the National APWU." Miami Local's grievance has been elevated to the national level because it involves an interpretive issue of general application. Because circumstances have evolved and most of the issues raised in the grievance have been resolved, on November 6, 2001, Miami Local stipulated that the only issues remaining before this Court are: (1) whether Miami Local is entitled to an Order, contrary to national policy, permitting window clerks to wear face masks when

---

[5] Funeral services were held for Thomas Morris Jr., on Oct. 26, 2001, and for Joseph Curseen Jr. on Oct. 27, 2001. Both worked at the Brentwood, D.C. postal sorting facility and died from inhalation anthrax.

[6] Of the six Florida facilities testing positive for anthrax, two are in Boca Raton (within the Miami Local's jurisdiction), and four are in West Palm Beach (outside of the Miami Local's jurisdiction). The Boca Raton facility is in the Postal Service's Central District of Florida. The remaining facilities in the Miami Local's jurisdiction are in the Postal Service's Southern District of Florida.

serving customers at the window pending arbitration; and (2) whether the Court may order arbitration on an expedited basis....

...The Court has no authority to dictate policy to the Postal Service or its employees. It is a basic principle of federal labor law that when a collective bargaining agreement provides a contractual means for dispute resolution, the parties must exhaust their contractual remedies before resorting to the courts.

Therefore, because the parties in this case have entered into a CBA that provides for a grievance-arbitration procedure, this Court must limit its inquiry to whether Miami Local has satisfied the four prerequisites for obtaining injunctive relief.

Standard of Review for Injunctive Relief

To obtain a preliminary injunction, Miami Local must prove: (1) that there is a substantial likelihood that it will prevail on the merits; (2) that there is a real threat of irreparable injury if the injunction is not granted; (3) that the threatened injury outweighs the threatened harm an injunction may impose on the defendant; *and* (4) that granting the preliminary injunction will not disserve the public interest.

1. Likelihood of Success on the Merits

To satisfy the likelihood of success on the merits prong, the Court need only find that the position the plaintiff will espouse in arbitration is "not frivolous and is sufficiently sound to prevent the arbitration from being a futile endeavor." The issue for the Court under this prong of the test is simply whether the matter is subject to arbitration. The Court cannot determine the propriety of either the Miami Local's grievance or the USPS' national window clerk mask policy, because these matters are exclusively reserved to the parties' arbitration process. The parties have stipulated that the face mask issue is subject to arbitration. Thus, the Court finds that Miami Local has satisfied this first prong.

2. Irreparable Injury

Miami Local must also establish that there is a real threat of irreparable injury if the injunction is not granted. To establish irreparable injury, Miami Local must prove that the injury it will suffer is "neither remote nor speculative, but actual and imminent." The possibility that Miami Local will obtain adequate relief at a later date, in the ordinary course of arbitration, weighs heavily against a claim of irreparable injury.

Miami Local's claim of irreparable injury is two-fold. First, it claims that the postal workers will suffer irreparable injury from the fear and stress that flows from not being permitted to wear masks at the window. Second, it claims that without arbitration on an expedited basis, the arbitration process will be a nullity.

As to its first claim, while it is true that there are window clerks who suffer from heightened levels of fear and stress because they are not permitted to wear masks while working at the window, the record is devoid of any evidence that their fear is based on an actual threat, or that any postal worker in Florida has suffered actual and imminent harm as a result of anthrax exposure. The CDC, the accepted medical authority, has indicated that there is no evidence at present that postal window clerks face an actual and imminent, or even an appreciable risk of contracting anthrax while servicing customers at the window.[7] Therefore, the Court finds that this first claim of injury alleged by Miami Local is both remote and speculative.

---

[7] According to the CDC, "persons working with or near machinery capable of generating aerosolized particles (e.g. electronic mail sorters) or at other work sites where such particles may

As to its second claim, given the speed at which all of the other issues raised in Miami Local's grievance have been resolved at the national level, the Court must conclude that it is more likely than not that the Postal Service and the national APWU will address the remaining face mask issue in the same expeditious manner. Therefore, the Court finds that Miami Local has failed to establish irreparable injury as to both of its claims.

3. Balancing of the Hardships and the Public Interest

Miami Local must also prove that the threatened injury outweighs the threatened harm an injunction may impose on the defendants. Miami Local suggests that an Order requiring expedited arbitration will cause no harm to the Postal Service because the parties have a common goal, namely the health and safety of postal workers. Miami Local asserts that its approach is pro-active, while the Postal Service's approach is re-active. However, this oversimplifies the complex nature of the threat which is one that faces all of the nation's postal workers and thus, is one of national scope and importance, requiring teamwork, concerted national planning, information sharing, and unified commitment of resources. In times of uncertainty and heightened fear, as even Miami Local's psychologist opined, a collaborative process, such as mediation, rather than the adversarial process involved in arbitration, is preferred.

The public has a substantial interest in having matters of national scope and importance dealt with on a national level. It is precisely in times such as these, that the Postal Service must utilize its limited resources in an efficient and effective manner. To force the Postal Service to address issues of national scope on a piecemeal and ad-hoc basis would hamper the unitary leadership and efficient use of resources that is required. Therefore, the Court finds that Miami Local has failed to establish that the threatened injury outweighs the threatened harm an injunction may impose on the defendants, and that granting the preliminary injunction will not disserve the public interest.

CONCLUSION

All of the parties, as well as this Court, recognize that this nation's postal workers have shown remarkable courage and dedication during these times of great uncertainty. The nation is indebted to them because without their combined efforts, the mail service on which the country depends for communication and commerce would cease. Thus, the parties' primary goals must be: (1) to protect the health and safety of all postal workers; (2) to allay any fears that the public might have as to the safety of our country's mail system; and (3) to maintain the efficient operation of the Postal Service. Amidst what many in the public perceived to be moments of crisis and chaos, the leadership within the USPS and the national APWU has remained calm, unified, and forthright in laying out policy and carrying out its procedures. All evidence indicates that the Postal Service and national APWU will continue their efforts to expeditiously address the concerns of all postal workers throughout the nation.

For the foregoing reasons, it is hereby

ORDERED that Plaintiff Miami Local's Motion for Emergency Injunctive Relief is DENIED.

DONE AND ORDERED in Miami, Florida, this 16th day of November, 2001.

————————

be generated should be fitted with [masks]...." (Def.'s Ex. 18). Dr. Wollschlaeger testified that window clerks are not subject to risk of inhalation anthrax because no means exists at the window, such as the "bellows" effect of a mail-processing machine, to disperse anthrax into the air in either a dangerous amount or in a manner sufficient for inhalation.

Chapter Ten
Private Causes of Action against Persons or Non-Governmental Entities
Concerning Issues in Bioterrorism

10.1. Introduction

This chapter addresses private actions which have been filed as a result of the 9-11 and anthrax attack events of 2001. The first part of this chapter considers the action involving the death of postal worker, Thomas Morris from inhalation anthrax; claims against the hospital who mis-diagnosed him; and third party claims against the federal government. The second postal worker, who had visited another hospital, who died as a result of inhalation anthrax in 2001, settled the claim.

The second part of this chapter addresses the action filed by survivors of the victims of the World Trade Center, Pentagon and Flight 93 crash in Pennsylvania against various individuals and corporate entities, and the Republic of Sudan. This chapter will focus on the claims against the private individuals and corporate entities. The legal bases for this action could also be legal bases for a claim against the operatives and funding entities of a biological attack against citizens and foreign nationals in the United States.

While the perpetrator of the anthrax attacks will have criminal charges, those who suffered or the estates of those who died will have claims in tort as well as statutory claims. However, proof of the source of the anthrax will continue to be problematic, as has been the case in the anthrax attacks of fall 2001, where distinguishing between strains of anthrax and that anthrax found in the victims of the anthrax attacks has not revealed the source of the anthrax. The following case addresses the difficult question of determining the source of anthrax, which is the issue on appeal to the Supreme Court of New Hampshire:

Bernard v. Whitefield Tanning Company
101 A. 439 (N.H. 1917)

OPINION:

The defendants, in support of their motion for a directed verdict, contend that the evidence of the plaintiff was not sufficient to warrant the verdict, because it could not be found on the evidence that the anthrax germs, which caused the damage to the plaintiff, came from the tannery while operated by them. The plaintiff owns and carries on a farm of one hundred acres situated on the northeast side of John's river in Dalton about five miles below the defendants' tannery. ...There is considerable water used in the various processes of tanning the hides, and all the waste runs into a sewer, which empties into John's river....

On June 10 the defendants received 1,000 China hides for tanning, and, from then to the bringing of this action, the tannery or some part of it was in continuous operation tanning these China hides. Anthrax is prevalent in China and many foreign countries. Under government regulations, if hides imported from Argentine are accompanied by a certificate of the American consul, stating that the animals from which the hides were taken were killed in abattoirs under government inspection, they are admitted. But if hides are imported from China, in order to be admitted, they must be accompanied by a certificate sworn to by the American consul, stating that they have been immersed for at least thirty minutes in a one to one thousand solution of bichloride of mercury, which is effective to kill both germs and spores. If such hides arrive here without the proper certificate, a government inspector sees that they receive the required immersion before they can be tanned. It appeared that anthrax germs in the spore form are very difficult to destroy, resisting drying, high temperatures and freezing; and that damp ground and muck holes furnish the best soil to promote the growth of the spores, and when such ground becomes infected it is likely to remain so for many years. There was evidence that the predecessors of the defendants in the tannery tanned domestic, country-gathered hides from the west and southwest, and that anthrax is more or less prevalent in the southern states in this country, and particularly in the Mississippi valley. The defendants urge that inasmuch as the evidence shows that the hides which they tanned before this suit was brought were all foreign hides admitted under government regulations, that it is very improbable that anthrax germs came from the tannery while operated by them, and that it is more probable, considering the ability of the germs to live in the soil, that the germs which did the injury came from the tannery when operated by those who preceded them, who tanned country-gathered hides and, therefore, that the jury could not find that they caused the pollution of the stream. This contention cannot be sustained. Whatever may be said in support of the defendants' position, it cannot be held as a matter of law that the jury were not justified in finding that the anthrax germs that killed the plaintiff's cows and inoculated his land came from the tannery in the summer of 1915. Previous to that summer the occupants of the plaintiff's farm had never had any trouble from cattle dying, and cattle did not suffer any ill effects from drinking the river water, when Bernard & Son and Obendorff & Adler were operating the tannery. Between the 5th and 10th of July, 1915, shortly before four of the plaintiff's cows died of anthrax, the water in John's river rose, due to heavy rains, and overflowed the plaintiff's low-lands in which his cows were pastured. And during the summer the water in the river had a strong odor and was filthy, and hair and pieces of flesh were floating on the water. The plaintiff had five cows die of anthrax in 1915. The four above stated died in July, and one died in December that had got out of the plaintiff's yard, and wandered down onto the low-lands and to the river. Some fifteen cattle along the course of John's river below the tannery contracted the disease of anthrax in the year 1915. The first creature died of it on June 22. There was no outbreak of the disease prior to that time. There were no known cases of the disease except on farms along the river below the tannery, and at places where meadow hay cut on the John's river intervale was being fed. The evidence disclosed that Amos Brown had cows taken sick with anthrax that were fed with hay that was cut in 1915 on a meadow, below the tannery, through which the river flows. Washings from this hay upon examination showed anthrax germs. An employee of the defendants testified that about the last of August or the first of September, 1915, he had a swelling on his neck starting with a pimple, that he went to a hospital, had it cut out, and the physician who did it sent the tissue to the state bacteriologist at Concord, who found that it contained anthrax germs.

The evidence above referred to is sufficient to warrant the finding of the jury that the anthrax which destroyed the plaintiff's property came from the defendants' tannery in the summer of 1915.

The evidence offered by the defendants tending to show that government inspection and disinfection of foreign hides was effectual to destroy anthrax germs and that the defendants in the management of their business relied upon such inspection and disinfection (which was excluded subject to exception) was competent and should have been admitted. It bore directly upon the question whether the pollution of the stream by anthrax germs was due to the defendants' want of care, which was one issue submitted to the jury. This error destroys the verdict.

As the defendants did not claim the right to put anthrax into the stream, the injury the plaintiff alleged arose not from a right which the defendants claimed but from their alleged negligence in the exercise of the right claimed by them. Whether they had the right to turn the refuse of the factory into the stream or not, as the damage complained of did not result from the exercise of that right, it is immaterial whether turning the general waste into the stream was reasonable or not. The submission of that issue to the jury might tend to confuse them and distract their attention from the real issue whether the presence of the anthrax in the stream was due to the defendants' fault. This issue was submitted as a part of the question of reasonable use, but at another trial the issue of negligence only should be submitted, unless the plaintiff proves damage from the exercise of the right which the defendants claim as appurtenant to their riparian ownership.

Exception sustained: new trial granted.

All concurred.

10.2. *Estate of Thomas L. Morris, Jr. v. Kaiser Foundation Health Plan v.United States*

Civ. No. PJM 02-1468, D.Md So.Div., (Filed March 28, 2002)

The original action was filed March 26, 2002 in the Circuit Court of Maryland for Prince Georges County, represented by attorneys Jimmy A. Bell and Johnnie L. Cochran, Jr. The widow, Mary R. Morris and their son, Thomas L. Morris, III are represented by William George Jepsen and Jimmy Bell. On April 23, 2002, the defendants filed a notice for removal of the case to federal district court and filed an amended complaint.

A nurse practitioner examined Morris and consulted with physician Karen McGibbon, in making their diagnosis. Alan Korff, nurse practitioner was named in the original complaint and Karen McGibbon was added as a defendant in the amended complaint.

On May 13, 2002, plaintiffs filed a second amended complaint that removed all of the Plaintiff's breach of contract and conspiracy claims.

The complaint filed with amendments in the federal district court, pleads the following facts and makes the following claims:

FACTUAL BASIS OF THE COMPLAINT

4. Plaintiffs are the estate of Thomas L. Morris, Jr., the surviving spouse, Mary R. Morris and the surviving child of the decedent, Thomas L. Morris, III.

5. Plaintiff Thomas L. Morris III, is a resident of Suitland, Maryland who resides at the address set forth in the caption above and resided at the same at all times material to this complaint.

6. Plaintiff Mary R. Morris, is a resident of Suitland, Maryland who resides at the address set forth in the caption above and resided at the same at all times material to this complaint.

7. Defendant Kaiser Permanente is a corporation with health care centers located in Maryland.

8. Plaintiffs Mary R. Morris and Thomas L. Morris III also bring this action as co-personal representatives of the estate of Thomas L. Morris Jr.

9. The factual circumstances rationally support claims of medical malpractice, wrongful death pursuant to Sections 3-901 through 3-904 of the Courts and Judicial Proceedings Article of Maryland Code Annotated and Maryland Rule 15-1001, loss of consortium, survival action for conscious pain and suffering against the Defendants.

10. Thomas L. Morris, Jr. is now deceased because he was not properly treated by the Defendants after he was exposed to Anthrax. A supportive and devoted husband and father, he worked for the United States Postal Service for 33 years and was 55 years old at the time of his death.

11. Thomas L. Morris Jr., was exposed to Anthrax while working, the Crew One shift, October 13, 2001 at the Brentwood Road Post Office in Washington, D.C., which is currently shut down indefinitely due to the deadly Anthrax contamination.

12. From as early as October 4, 2001 through October 17, 2001, the Center for Disease Control and the U.S. Department of Health and Human Services put out medical alert press releases on Anthrax. All of these medical alerts stated that when a person is exposed to Anthrax health care providers should treat them with antibiotics as a precautionary measure.

13. As reported on October 16, 2001 in the Washington Post, on October 15, 2001 about 50 Congressional employees were given antibiotics because they possibly were exposed to a letter contaminated by Anthrax that had been processed through the Brentwood post office. The Capitol Hill Anthrax incident was highly publicized and increased the public's awareness about the need to take precautionary measures in treating potential cases of Anthrax.

14. While Mr. Thomas Morris, Jr. was at work, a woman working in his vicinity found an envelope with powder in it, now known to be Anthrax. Mr. Morris was never told whether the substance in fact was Anthrax.

15. On October 18, 2001, Mr. Morris went to the Defendant Kaiser Permanente's Marlow Heights Medical Center because he was experiencing symptoms suggestive of an Anthrax infection. Specifically, Mr. Morris was experiencing difficulty breathing, chest constriction, body aches and a headache, all symptoms consistent with an Anthrax infection.

16. Mr. Morris explained to Alan Korff, the nurse practitioner, that he thought he may have been exposed to Anthrax because of what had happened while he was at work oat the Brentwood Post Office. However, Alan Korff after consulting with his supervising physician, Dr. Karen McGibbon, told Mr. Morris that he just had a virus. Mr. Korff told Mr. Morris to take fluids and a non-steroidal anti-inflammatory agent for his aches and pains. As the Journal of American Medical Association (JAMA) reported in a case study done on Mr. Morris's death from inhalation Anthrax, Mr. Morris was diagnosed as having a viral syndrome and was sent home. Consequently, Mr. Morris relied on the Defendant's employees/agents judgment and commend taking Tylenol for his pain.

17. Defendant Korff, acting as an employee/agent of Defendant Kaiser Permanente, took a culture, however, he never communicated to Mr. Morris the results.

18. On October 21, 2001, Mr. Morris was having severely labored breathing, and he called 911. He gave a detailed description of the events that occurred following his October 13, 2001 exposure to Anthrax. This description included the incidents at the post office, the symptoms he was experiencing that were consistent with Anthrax, as well as his visit to Defendant.

19. Unfortunately, due to the negligence and lack of care by Defendant Korff and his physician supervisors, Dr. McGibbon, both acting as employees/agents of Defendant Kaiser Permanente, Thomas L. Morris, Jr. passed away because of a delay in the diagnosis and a delay in the treatment of his Anthrax infection.

20. As a result of the Defendant's tortious actions and omissions, on October 18, 2001, Plaintiff Mary R. Morris, the widow of the decedent, has sustained loss of consortium, pecuniary loss, mental anguish, emotional pain and suffering, and loss of society, companionship, comfort, attention, advice and counsel. As a result of the same, Plaintiff Thomas L. Morris III, the only child of Thomas L. Morris, Jr. has sustained, mental anguish, emotional pain and suffering, pecuniary loss, loss of society, companionship, comfort, attention, advice and counsel. In addition, as co-personal representatives of the decedent's estate Plaintiffs bring a survival action for the decedent's pain and suffering. Plaintiffs also make claims of medical malpractice and ordinary negligence.

COUNT I
THOMAS L MORRIS, III
(WRONGFUL DEATH)

22. Defendant owed Thomas L. Morris Jr. a duty to use national, reasonable standard of medical care in examining and treating Mr. Morris.

23. By failing to exercise such reasonable care by not addressing Mr. Morris's potential exposure to Anthrax, by telling him to take a non-steroidal anti-inflammatory medicine (like Advil) for his illness and

by never giving Mr. Morris the results of his culture, Defendants Korff and McGibbon, both acting as employees/agents of Defendant Kaiser Permanente, breached the duties owed to Thomas L. Morris, Jr.

24. AS a direct and proximate result of Defendants' medical malpractice, breach of duties of ordinary care, for which Thomas L. Morris Jr. would have been able to maintain actions against Defendants and recover damages had he lived, Thomas L. Morris Jr. died from an Anthrax infection October 21, 2001.

25. AS a direct and proximate result of Defendant Korff's and Defendant McGibbon's negligence, both individually and collectively, which caused the death of Thomas L. Morris Jr. and while both Defendant Korff and Defendant McGibbon were acting as employees/agents of Defendant Kaiser Permanente, Thomas L. Morris III, surviving son of Thomas L. Morris Jr., sustained pecuniary loss, mental anguish, emotional pain and suffering, and loss of society, companionship, comfort, attention, advice and counsel.

[Morris, III asks for compensatory damages consistent with Maryland statute, pre-and post-judgment interest and the costs of litigation, etc.]

COUNT II
MARY R. MORRIS
(WRONGFUL DEATH)

[Count II is identical to Count I, except relative to Mary R. Morris]

COUNT III
MARY R. MORRIS
(LOSS OF CONSORTIUM)

[claims are the same]

44. AS a direct and proximate result of Defendant Korff's and Defendant McGibbon's negligence, both individually and collectively, which cased the death of Thomas L. Morris Jr. and while both Defendant Korff and Defendant McGibbon were acting as employees/agents of Defendant Kaiser Permanent, Defendants caused injury to the marital relationship of Plaintiff Mary Morris, the surviving widow of Thomas L. Morris, Jr., including loss of society, companionship, comfort, attention, advice, sexual relations and pecuniary loss.

[Compensatory damages of $1,000,000 are plead]

COUNT IV
ESTATE OF THOMAS L. MORRIS, JR.
(SURVIVAL ACTION)

50. By failing to exercise such reasonable care by not addressing Mr. Morris's potential exposure to anthrax, by telling him to take a non-steroidal anti-inflammatory medicine (like Advil) for his illness and by never giving Mr. Morris the results of his culture, Defendants Korff and McGibbon both acting as employees/agents of defendant Kaiser Permanent, were willfully and maliciously negligent and breached the duties owed to Thomas L. Morris Jr. As a direct and proximate result of Defendants' medical malpractice, breach of duties of ordinary care, for which Thomas L. Morris Jr. would have been able to maintain actions against Defendants and recover damages had he lived, Thomas L. Morris Jr. suffered tremendously and died from an Anthrax infection October 21, 2001.

51. Although seriously ill, due to his Anthrax infection, Thomas L. Morris was conscious and living after his visit to the Defendant, until the time of his death, three days later.

52. AS a direct and proximate result of the Defendant's willfully malicious and grossly negligent breach of duties owed to Mr. Thomas, he endured sever pain and suffering between the time of his visit to Kaiser Permanente's Marlow Heights Medical Center and the time of his death.

[Seeks $5,000,000 in compensatory damages; and $10,000,000 in punitive damages, etc.]

COUNT V
ESTATE OF THOMAS L. MORRIS, JR.
(ORDINARY NEGLIGENCE)

60. Defendants', Kaiser Permanente, and Defendants Korff and McGibbon, both being employees/agents of Defendant Kaiser Permanente, owed Thomas L. Morris,Jr. a duty to exercise ordinary care.

61. By failing to exercise such ordinary care, not specific for health care providers, and by not addressing Mr. Morris's potential exposure to Anthrax, by telling him to take a non-steroidal anti-inflammatory agent (like Advil) for his illness and by never giving Mr. Morris the results of his culture, Defendants' both individually and collectively, willfully and maliciously breached the duties of ordinary care owed to Thomas L. Morris, Jr.

62. Thomas L. Morris, Jr. died as a direct and proximate result of Defendant's negligent breach of duties ordinary care owed.

[Seeks compensatory damages of $2,000,000; and punitive damages of $10,000,000, etc.]

COUNT VI
ESTATE OF THOMAS L. MORRIS, JR.
(MEDICAL MALPRACTICE)

70. Mr. Morris was in no way contributorily negligent and relied upon the expertise of Defendant, Kaiser Permanente, and Defendants Korff and McGibbon, both being employees/agents of Defendant Kaiser Permanente.

71. Although seriously ill, due to his Anthrax infection, Thomas L. Morris was conscious and living after his visit to the Defendant until three days later.

72. As a direct and proximate result of Defendants' individual and collective willfully malicious negligent breach of duties owed to Mr. Morris, decedent Thomas L. Morris, Jr. sustained severe pain and suffering between the time of his Kaiser Permanente office visit and the time that he died.

[Seeks $5,000,000 in compensatory damages; and punitive damages of $10,000,000, etc.]

Notes

1. The Journal of the American Medical Association (JAMA) article which was referenced in the complaint, was published November 28, 2001, shortly after the anthrax deaths of the postal workers. The article describes a blood test which contained the anthrax bacillus gram-positive rods, 24 hours after the patient's admission—and the morning after his death the previous evening.

2. Why did the plaintiffs amend the complaint to omit the breach of contract and civil conspiracy claims?

3. Who would you anticipate should be selected to be expert witnesses and fact witnesses for the trial, should the case proceed to trial?

10.3 ***Burnett, et al. v. Al Baraka Investment and Dev. Corp., et al.,*** **Civ. No. ____**
         (D.D.C., Filed August 15, 2002)

The civil action filed by the families of the victims of the attacks on the World Trade Center, the Pentagon and the crash of flight 93, both citizens and foreign nationals, make their claim against 98 individuals and corporate entities, and the Republic of Sudan, which include three Saudi princes, seven banks and other international organizations, for hundreds of billions of dollars.

The families are represented by co-counsel, Allan Gerson, Washington, D.C., who represents relatives of the victims who died in 1988 on Pan Am 103, the aircraft which was blown up in flight by terrorists over Lockerbie, Scotland; and Ronald Motley, Mt. Pleasant, S.C., who represented attorneys general in 36 states in their successful lawsuit against the tobacco companies for deaths and injuries due to using tobacco.

The legal bases for their complaints are based upon the Foreign Sovereign Immunities Act (28 U.S.C. §1605(a)(2); §1605(a)(5); and §1605(a)(7) with Pub.L. 104-208, Div. A Title I §1605 note; Torture Victim Protection Act, Pub. L. 102-256, 106 Stat. 73 (reprinted at 28 U.S.C.A. §1350; and the Anti Terrorism Claims Act, 18 U.S.C. §2333 et. seq.(which provides for treble damages for U.S. Nationals), The Racketeer Influenced and Corrupt Organizations Act, 18 U.S.C. §1962(a), (c)-(d); The Alien Tort Claims Act; and common law actions in wrongful death, negligence, survival, negligent and/or intentional infliction of emotional distress, conspiracy, aiding and abetting, and punitive damages. Various international treaties are also cited in the complaint.

The following introduction of the complaint describes the plaintiffs' theory of the case:

INTRODUCTION

With the September 11 attacks on the United States, the once abstract and distant threat of terrorism has become a daily fact of life for every American. The ongoing threat of terrorism has been permanently lodged in the psyche of every civilized person in this nation. This new reality calls for action. In response to this act of barbarism, Plaintiffs herein respond with the collective voice of civilization, and ask for justice under the rule of law.

It is the tradition of a civilized nation to allow redress for wrongs through an appeal to the rule of law and justice. Law is at the foundation of civilization, thus it is particularly fitting that the rule of law responds to an attack of savagery. For it is the rule of law, and the voices of freedom, that separate civilization from barbarism and anarchy. The rule of law is a powerful weapon to be drawn upon in difficult times and to be forged in our defense. The United States system of justice and the American people have faced enemies more powerful than these terrorists and their sponsors, and will do so again. In doing so, Plaintiffs invoke the rule of law to hold those who promoted, financed, sponsored, or otherwise materially supported the acts of the barbarism and terror inflicted on September 11, 2001, accountable for their deeds. By taking vigorous legal action against the financial sponsors of terror, the Plaintiffs will force the sponsors of terror into the light and subject them to the rule of law.

This civil action seeks to hold those responsible for a more subtle and insidious form of terrorism, that which attempts to hide behind the facade of legitimacy. These entities, cloaked in a thin veil of legitimacy, were and are the true enablers of terrorism. The financial resources and support network of these Defendants—charities, banks, and individual financiers—are what allowed the attacks of September 11, 2001 to occur. Terrorists like Osama bin Laden and his al Qaeda network cannot plan, train and act on a massive scale without significant financial power, coordination and backing. Defendants herein, some of whom act in the shadows, are ultimately responsible for the damages caused by the actions of their terrorist agents and clients. On September 20, 2001, President George W. Bush addressed a joint session of Congress and made clear the Nation will fight the war on terrorism on all available fronts. The lines drawn on that day were diplomatic, military, political, legal and financial. The war on terrorism is also very personal to the Plaintiffs herein. Congress responded to the call to war by fashioning the Patriot Act of 2001, which strengthens the prior legal rights of individual citizens to pursue justice and punishment against the perpetrators of terror. Uniting and Strengthening America by Providing Appropriate Tools Required to Intercept and Obstruct Terrorism, (The USA Patriot Act, Title X, 2001). The Patriot Act itself was the culmination of decades of precedent setting judicial decisions and statutory enactments that gave individuals enlarged rights to seek redress and compensation for damages from the sponsors of terrorism. When viewed as a whole, these executive, legislative and judicial actions vastly empower individual victims of terrorism to seek, win and enforce justice. As one United States court recently stated, "[t]he only way to imperil the flow of money and discourage the financing of terrorist acts is to impose liability on those who knowingly and internationally supply the funds to the persons who commit the violent acts." Boim v. Quranic Literacy Institute, et al., 2002 WL 1174558 (7th Cir. Ill.).

Plaintiffs herein assert federal common law and statutory claims as available to victims' surviving spouses, children, siblings, parents, and legal representatives. In addition to common law causes of action, claims are brought pursuant to the Foreign Sovereign Immunities Act 28 U.S.C. §1605(a)(2); §1605(a)(5); and §1605 (a)(7) with Pub. L. 104-208, Div. A. Title I, §1605 note (West Supp.)(Flatow Amendment); Torture Victim Protection Act, Pub. La. 102-256, 106 Stat. 73 (reprinted at 28 U.S.C.A. §1350 note (West 1993); Alien Tort Claim Act, 28 U.S.C. §1350; and the Anti Terrorism Claims Act, 18 U.S.C. §2333, *et. seq.* This Complaint includes claims brought by both United States citizens and foreign nationals. Congress' enactment of these terrorist-related statutes set forth herein evidences legislative intent for accountability and provides these victims a forum for that accountability. In addition to compensation, these legal actions can also punish and deter future acts of terrorism.[1]

The USA Patriot Act of 2001 was enacted to "deter and punish terrorist acts in the United States and around the world, to enhance law enforcement investigatory tools, and for other purposes." USA Patriot Act of 2001, Title X, §1001. Congress, by enacting the USA Patriot Act, reinforced this legislative intention to enable victims the ability to deter and punish terrorists' acts in the United States and around the world. The Act makes this message clear: All Americans are united in condemning, in the strongest possible terms, the terrorists who planned and carried out the attacks against the United States on September 11, 2001, and in pursuing all those responsible for those attacks and their sponsors until they are brought to justice. USA Patriot Act of 2001, Title X, §1002 (emphasis added).

The armed forces of the United State have won a crushing initial victory, in what promises to be a long war on terror. The victims and families of the September 11 the attacks should also be able to play their part against the enemies that hide behind the cloak of legitimacy. The monetary lifeblood of the Defendants must be redirected to the ends of religious and political tolerance rather than be allowed to continue to sponsor and foster terror and butchery. The United States civil justice system is a necessary and crucial part of this endeavor. Osama bin Laden and his sponsors, promoters, financers, co-conspirators, aiders and abettors in the September 11, 2001, terrorist acts are fundamentally rooted in an illegitimate perversion of Islam. The charitable, financial, religious, and political networks that front terror— the Defendant banks, charities, financial and business institutions—are responsible for the death and injuries of September 11th, 2001. These Defendants, who aided, abetted, sponsored, conspired to sponsor, financed or otherwise provided material support to Osama bin Laden and al Qaeda must be held accountable.

The actions of certain members of the Saudi Royal family are implicated in the September 11th attacks, and are directly at issue in this case. Osama bin Laden is a naturalized Saudi Arabian whose family still has close ties to the inner circles of the monarchy. Royal denials notwithstanding, Saudi money has for years been funneled to encourage radical anti-Americanism as well as to fund the al Qaeda terrorists. Saudi Arabian money has financed terror while its citizens have promoted and executed it. It is no coincidence that immediately following the September 11th attacks, members of the bin Laden family were whisked away from the United States to Saudi Arabia, at a time when commercial aviation was shut down. Saudi Arabia's cash infusions to Muslim communities in America ensure that perverse fundamentalism takes hold in the United States. "The Saudis are active at every level of the terror chain,

---

[1] Moreover, the Victim's Compensation Fund is not a bar to terrorist suits. Kenneth Feinberg, Special Master for the Victim's Compensation Fund has stated publicly that Nations harboring terrorists, or promoting terrorism, can be sued by those participated in the Fund. The Department of Justice, Office of Attorney General has also reiterated victims' rights to pursue actions against terrorists: A claimant who files for compensation waives any right to file a civil action (or to be a party to an action) in any federal or state court for damages sustained as a result of the terrorist-related aircraft crashes of September 11, 2001, *except* for actions to recover collateral source obligations *or civil actions against any person who is a knowing participant in any conspiracy to hijack any aircraft or to commit any terrorist ac*t.

from planners to financiers, from cadre to foot-soldier, from ideologist to cheerleader," according to a briefing presented July 10, 2002 to the Defense Policy Board, a group of prominent intellectuals and former senior officials that advises the Department of Defense on policy. "Saudi Arabia supports our enemies and attacks our allies," continued the briefing, reportedly prepared by a Rand Corporation analyst. The group in power in Saudi Arabia blocks avenues of change, represses advocates of change, and promotes a culture of violence. This culture of violence is the prime enabler of terrorism. Wahhabism purports to loathe modernity, capitalism, human rights, religious freedom, and an open society—yet those in power live an extravagant, decadent lifestyle as they profess austerity and practice oppression. Ironically, the Defendants herein are the facilitators of terror who use our system while trying to destroy it.

A Short History of al Qaeda
We have not reached parity with them yet. We have the right to kill four million Americans—two million of them children—and to exile twice as many and wound and cripple hundreds of thousands. Furthermore, it is our right to fight them with chemical and biological weapons. America is kept at bay by blood alone...
Al Qaeda spokesman Suleiman Abu Gheith, June 12, 2002

In or around 1989, Osama bin Laden formed al Qaeda, which means "the Base" or "the Vanguard" in Arabic, into an international terrorist group with the aim of opposing non-Islamic governments with violence. Included in Bin Laden's edict was a call for the overthrow of those Islamic states that were considered to be too secular, or too beholden to the West, in the eyes of Osama bin Laden. Another founding goal of al Qaeda was to drive the American armed forces out of the Saudi Arabian peninsula and Somalia. The al Qaeda organization brought together a large number of Arab fighters that had fought in Afghanistan against Soviet invaders to defend their fellow Muslims. Up to five thousand Saudis, three thousand Yemenis, two thousand Algerians, two thousand Egyptians, four hundred Tunisians, three hundred Iraqis, two hundred Libyans, and numerous Jordanians served alongside the Afghans in attempting to oust the Russians. Osama bin Laden went to Afghanistan just after the Soviet invasion in 1979. He became a prime financier, recruiter, and military leader of the Mujahedeen groups. He advertised all over the Arab world for young Muslims to come fight in Afghanistan against the Soviets and set up recruiting offices all over the world, including in the United States and Europe. These recruiting offices were often run under the auspices of the Saudi charities which were taking donations from wealthy Saudi families and businessmen. These charities operated in the United States, Europe, Asia, Africa, and the Middle East. Charities became an essential part of the support system to Osama bin Laden, providing the financial resources that enabled them to wage war. The Saudi charitable institutions raised these funds in part through a system of Islamic tithing known as zakat. Zakat, as one of the pillars of Islam, calls for faithful Muslims to give a specified percentage on certain properties to certain classes of needy people. Cash funds held in possession for one year require a two and a half percent zakat payment to a charity which manages the donations. However, the intended recipients of the zakat were perverted as radical Islamic fundamentalist grew.

Osama bin Laden paid for the transportation of the new recruits to Afghanistan with some of his personal fortune, and set up camps there to train them. The Afghan government donated land and resources, while Osama bin Laden brought in experts from all over the world on guerilla warfare, sabotage, and covert operations. Within a little over a year, he had thousands of volunteers in training in his private military camps. After the defeat of the Soviets, these religiously radical and militaristic holy warriors spread out over the world to their countries of origin. Steeped in the bloody perversion of Jihad for many years, they were not inclined to let go of the militant life they had grown accustomed to during the war. Many took up the radical Islamic cause in their home countries with the aim of destabilizing and overthrowing the more secular Arab regimes, for not enforcing a "pure" form of Islam.

One thousand of Osama bin Laden's faithfuls returned to Algeria where they began a nine-year civil war. Those returning to Egypt joined the Gamaa Islamiya and the Egyptian Jihad groups determined to overthrow the government of that country. As many as two hundred of these radical fundamentalists settled in New York and New Jersey within the United States; some of these were later implicated in terrorist plots such as the 1993 World Trade Center bombing.[2] When Pakistan cracked down on its population of al Qaeda, many of them fled to Asia and joined radical Islamic groups in the Philippines such as the Abu Sayyaf group. Likewise, some returned to Central Asia to continue the fight against the Russians in Tajikistan, or to other areas such as Bosnia and Chechnya where Muslims were embroiled in conflicts. By this time, Osama bin Laden's funding network was in place, and served as a template for the creation and growth of the al Qaeda network. Osama bin Laden simply tapped into the same network formed through his Mujahedeen connections and incorporated those militant individuals and groups under the umbrella title al Qaeda.

After being "expelled" from Saudi Arabia in 1991, and allegedly "disowned" by his own family for his extremist actions, Osama bin Laden moved to Khartoum, the capital of Sudan. Here he continued to recruit former fundamentalist warriors into the ranks of al Qaeda and offer them employment. In addition to seasoned recruits, new volunteers to his radical cause were given military training and sponsorship in special camps set up there. Soon he had set up factories and farms established for the purpose of supplying jobs to those he had recruited. Osama bin Laden built roads and other infrastructure for the Sudanese government with his construction company, al-Hijrah Construction and Development Ltd. Osama bin Laden's money built the airport at Port Sudan, as well as a highway linking Khartoum to Port Sudan. These projects helped to establish and strengthen Osama bin Laden's relationship with the Sudanese regime. His import-export firm, Wadi Al-Aqiq, began doing brisk business. His Taba Investment Company Ltd. flourished while his agriculture company bought up huge plots of land. The Al-Shamal Islamic Bank, in which Osama bin Laden invested $50 million, helped finance all of these thriving companies, as well as the growing al Qaeda presence within Sudan. For five years, terrorist training activities fueled by these economic developments continued, while Osama bin Laden lived in Khartoum under the protection of the Sudanese regime. In 1996, the Sudanese government bowed to pressure from the United States and requested that Osama bin Laden leave the country. He moved back to Afghanistan as an honored guest of the Taliban. For the next five years, with the aiding and abetting of the Defendants herein, he continued to fund the terrorist training camps that filled the ranks of al Qaeda and served as bases from which to plan new attacks against America and the West. Soon after 1989, al Qaeda members began international terrorist attacks. The first such attack was against the United Nations forces in Somalia on October 3 and 4 of 1993, in which 18 American servicemen were killed. These terrorists used the military techniques learned in training camps of al Qaeda. Osama bin Laden and al Qaeda also plotted the first terrorist attacks against the World Trade Center in 1993, and a plan in 1995 (code named Project Bojinka) to blow up twelve American airliners simultaneously. The backup plan for Project Bojinka was to hijack planes and use them as missiles against prominent American landmarks such as the World Trade Center, the White House, and the CIA headquarters in Langley, Virginia. Al Qaeda was also involved in the Khowar towers bombing in Riyadh, Saudi Arabia in which five American servicemen were killed in November 1995. After this attack inside Osama bin Laden's native Saudi Arabia, a group of prominent Saudi's met in Paris where they conspired to pay off Osama bin Laden and his al Qaeda group to ensure that al Qaeda would never attack within the borders of the Saudi Kingdom again. This protection money served to safeguard Saudi Arabia, but also to enlarge the power of Osama bin Laden and al Qaeda. This plot served to embolden the terrorist leader and his ambition. In 1998, Osama bin Laden and al Qaeda orchestrated an attack on the United States embassies in the East African countries of Kenya and Tanzania. These explosions resulted in two-hundred ninety-one deaths and over five-thousand injuries. The attack

---

[2] An admitted al Qaeda operative Ramzi Yousef was convicted on murder and conspiracy charges for his role in the plot to topple the trade center's two 110-story towers to punish the United States for its support of Israel.

on the U.S.S. Cole in Yemen in October of 2000 then followed, with the brutal attacks on September 11th, 2001 thereafter. Osama bin Laden has publicly and proudly proclaimed direct responsibility for these multiple atrocities. These direct attacks on Americans intensified in 1998 after bin Laden issued this "fatwah," stating:

> We—with God's help—call on every Muslim who believes in God and wishes to be rewarded to comply with God's order to kill the Americans and plunder their money wherever and whenever they find it. We also call on Muslim ulema, leaders, youths, and soldiers to launch the raid on Satan's U.S. troops and the devil's supporters allying with them, and to displace those who are behind them so that they may learn a lesson.

These words provide a telling insight into how Osama bin Laden treats the world. Having not left the intellectual era of the crusades, in this world view the Middle East is the holy ground on which a battle of the three major religions should be waged. According to Islamic fundamentalist vision, a Judeo-Christian alliance has evolved which aims to conquer the holy places of Mecca, Medina, and Jerusalem. In this distortion of reality, this alliance is responsible for the violence surrounding Muslims throughout history and the modern world. In line with this world view, Osama bin Laden attempts to use terror to show his fellow Muslims that the "enemies" or infidels of Islam can be eliminated. Toward this end, Osama bin Laden has proclaimed his intention to obtain biological, chemical, and nuclear weapons to wage war. Terrorism is closely related to genocide, differing only in scope. The same legal rationale for holding those responsible for facilitating genocide in role of industrialists and bankers in Nazi Germany applies to financiers and perpetrators of international terrorism responsible for September 11th, 2001. Although this is a civil action for damages that draws upon specific United States statutory enactments aimed at civil remedies for international terrorism (as opposed to criminal complaint) it nevertheless draws upon the historic precedent and legacy of the Nuremberg Industrialists cases. See e.g., Trials of War Criminals before Nuremberg Military Tribunals Under Control Council Law #10 Nuremberg, October 1946–April 1949; Washington D.C.:GPO, 1949–1953; National Archives Record Group 238, M887. Those cases make clear that responsibility for genocide, and by implication its contemporary offshoot of massive terrorism, as exemplified by the attacks of September 11, rests not only with those who pull the trigger or plant the bomb or man the airplanes, but with those who facilitated those events through financial or other means. The legal challenge ahead is profound, but the Plaintiffs respectfully ask this Honorable Court to draw upon the many precedents in history and in law. Today's vehemence comes from a perversion of Saudi Arabia's sect of Islam, known as Wahabbism. Wahabbism is a fundamentalist Islamic sect founded by Mohammad Ibn Abdul-Wahhab in the 18th century. Abdul-Wahhab sought to rid Islam of the corruptions that he believed had crept into the religion from both within and without the Muslim world. His doctrine reverted to a strictly literal interpretation of the Koran which strove to directly implement the commands of the prophet Mohammed. Therefore, Wahhabism, in Abdul-Wahhab's view, became the sole source of legitimate Islamic thought and action. (However, Wahhab was not a direct descendent of the prophet Mohammad, raising serious questions about this legitimacy.) In direct contradistinction to the civilized Arab world—500 million strong—al Qaeda and its radical fringe refuse to move beyond ancient ideologies. The Wahhabi rebellions of the nineteenth and twentieth centuries establishing the power of the sect in Arabia were defined by their violence and brutality. As the sect took power, the Al Saud family united with the Wahhabi movement, eventually making it the "official" form of Islam practiced in Saudi Arabia. Hence, the intimate if tenuous relationship.

In recent decades, certain sects of Wahhabism have become even more virulent toward Western civilization, extolling the virtues of martyrdom for the sake of saving Islam. For example, inflammatory Khutbahs (sermons) given by the Khateeb (cleric) Salaah Al-Budair in the Mosques of Mecca and Medina in August 2001 warn of the imminent threat the West poses to Islamic civilization:

> Fellow Muslims! We are nowadays confronted with a relentless war waged by the materialistic western civilization and culture that burns its producers and afflicts them with calamities, misery, immorality, disruption, suicide, and all kinds of evils...it is a civilization that races towards creating

all means of trouble, disturbance, and destruction. Al-Budair also emphasizes the greatness of offering to die as a martyr: Today we Muslims and indeed the entire world can witness the greatness of martyrdom being illustrated in the uprising in Palestine in general and the Al-Aqsaa in particular. This kind of stance, which revives the magnitude and virtues of martyrdom in the heart of the Muslim nation, is exactly what we need at this time. It is vital that the Muslims exert every effort to spread the love for achieving martyrdom just like the pious early generations of Muslims did. We must continue on the same road that they were on, which is that of our Prophet, and indeed all the prophets before him, in order to support our religion and defeat our enemies. Revive the importance of martyrdom and reawaken the spirit of seeking it! Instill the virtues of it in the hearts and minds by all methods possible. Our country [Saudi Arabia] has set an example in supporting this and donating generously in its cause from all different sections of the community... Al-Budair finishes up these sermons by justifying the suicide bombings: The Jews are described in the Book of Allah as those who distort words and facts and quote them out of context and this is what they and their supporters from the tyrant regimes all over the world are currently doing. They use false terminology to misguide, confuse, and deceive. What your brothers are committing in Al-Aqsaa are not acts of mindless violence, but rather it is a blessed uprising to resist and curtail the Jewish oppression and aggression: this is a legal right which all religions, ideologies and international laws recognize. Nobody could deny this fact except the ignorant, arrogant, or evildoers.

Such are the perverse Wahabbi sermons as currently preached to inspire young men to join forces with Osama bin Laden in his war against the West. As the former head of counter-terrorism for the FBI and head of security for the World Trade Center at the time of the attacks, John O'Neill, said:

All the answers, everything needed to dismantle Osama bin Laden's organization can be found in Saudi Arabia. The hate-filled ideology of Al-Budair confirms O'Neill's judgment that the ideological and financial essence of al Qaeda, that led to the September 11th, 2001 terrorist attacks, stems from Saudi Arabia.

This Complaint is brought pursuant to Rule 42 of the Federal Rules of Civil Procedure, which allows consolidation where actions involve common questions of law or fact. The Plaintiffs herein—United States citizens and citizens of foreign nations—include mothers, fathers, wives, husbands, children, sisters and brothers of those killed or injured on September 11, 2001, from each attack, on all four of the doomed flights, at both Towers of the World Trade Center, inside the Pentagon, and in Shanksville, Pennsylvania. These Plaintiffs seek full, just, timely compensation and punitive damages as appropriate. Because of the enormity and sometimes complex nature of Defendants' collective and individual acts giving rise to liability, Plaintiffs herein have provided a detailed explanation of the facts currently known, which provide an abundant basis for this civil action.

––––––––––

The complaint included fifteen counts, with fourteen applying to all defendants and the last to the Republic of Sudan. For purposes of private actions, this part will focus on the first fourteen counts, which read as follows:

CLAIMS COUNT ONE
FOREIGN SOVEREIGN IMMUNITIES ACT

1113. Plaintiffs incorporate herein by reference the allegations contained in all preceding paragraphs.

1114. The actions of the foreign state defendant, Sudan, and the actions of its agencies and instrumentalities as described herein, forfeited their right to claim immunity of the Foreign Sovereign Immunities Act 28 U.S.C. §1605(a)(2), 1605(a)(5) and 1605(a)(7). Pursuant to 28 U.S.C. §1605(a)(7) and Pub. L. 104-208, Div. A, Title I, §101(c), 110 Stat. 3009-172 (reprinted at 28 U.S.C. §1605 note (West Supp.)), all defendants who are officials, employees or agents of the foreign state defendant are individually liable to the Plaintiffs for damages caused by their acts which resulted in the death and injury of the Plaintiffs.

1115. Foreign state defendant and the actions of its agencies and instrumentalities as described herein, conducted commercial activity that had a direct effect on the United States and is not immune pursuant to the Foreign Sovereign Immunities Act 28 U.S.C. §1605(a)(2).

1116. Foreign state defendant and the actions of its agencies and instrumentalities as described herein, is subject to liability from said acts resulting in personal injury and death in the United States caused by the tortuous act or omission of the foreign states, officials and employees while acting within the scope of his office and employment and thus have forfeited their right to claim immunity pursuant to 28 U.S.C. §1605(a)(5).

1117. Foreign state defendant and its agencies and instrumentalities designated as state a sponsors of terrorism as described herein, is subject to liability for said acts and provision of material support for said acts resulting in personal injury and death in the United States as a result of act of torture, extra judicial killing, and aircraft sabotage and have forfeited their right to claim immunity pursuant to the 1996 Anti Terrorism Effective Death Penalty Act codified as 28 U.S.C. §1605(a)(7).

1118. As a direct result and proximate cause of the conduct of the Foreign State Defendant and its agencies, instrumentalities, officials, employees and agents that violated the federal and common laws cited herein, all Plaintiffs suffered damages as set forth herein.

WHEREFORE, Plaintiffs demand judgment in their favor against the Foreign State Defendant, the Sudanese agents and Instrumentalities and each of their officials, employees and agents, jointly, severally, and/or individually, in an amount in excess of One Trillion Dollars($1,000,000,000,000) plus interest, costs, and such other monetary and equitable relief as this Honorable Court deems appropriate to compensate the Plaintiffs and deter the Defendants from ever again committing such terrorist acts.

COUNT TWO
TORTURE VICTIM PROTECTION ACT

1119. Plaintiffs incorporate herein by reference the allegations contained in the preceding paragraphs.

1120. The actions of the Defendants as described herein subjected the Plaintiffs to torture and extrajudicial killing within the meaning of the Torture Victim Protection Act, Pub.L. 102-256, 106 Stat. 73 (reprinted at 28 U.S.C.A. §1350 note (West 1993)).

1121. In carrying out these acts of extrajudicial killings and injury against the Plaintiffs, the actions of each Defendant were conducted under actual or apparent authority, or under color of law.

1122. As a direct result and proximate cause of the Defendants' violation of the Torture Victim Protection Act, Plaintiffs suffered damages as fully set forth herein.

WHEREFORE, Plaintiffs demand judgment in their favor against all Defendants, jointly, severally, and/or individually, in an amount in excess of One Trillion Dollars ($1,000,000,000,000) plus interest, costs, and such other monetary and equitable relief as this Honorable Court deems appropriate to prevent the Defendants from ever again committing the terrorist acts of September 11, 2001 or similar acts.

COUNT THREE
ALIEN TORT CLAIMS ACT

1123. Plaintiffs incorporate herein by reference the allegations contained in the preceding paragraphs.

1124. As set forth above, the Defendants, individually, jointly and severally, aided and abetted sponsored, materially supported, conspired to proximately cause the death and injury of the Plaintiffs through and by reason of acts of international terrorism. These terrorist activities constitute violations of the law of nations otherwise referred to as contemporary international law, including those international legal norms prohibiting torture, genocide, air piracy, terrorism and mass murder as repeatedly affirmed by the United Nations Security Council.

1125. As a result of the Defendants' sponsor of terrorism in violation of the law of nations and contemporary principles of international law, the Plaintiffs suffered injury and damages as set forth herein. Violations of the law of nations and of international agreements include but not limited to:

(1) The Universal Declaration of Human Rights, Dec. 10, 1958 G.A. Res 217A (III), U.N. Doc. A/810, at 71 (1948);

(2) The International Covenant of Political and Civil Rights, art. 6 (right to life), U.N. Doc. A/6316, 999 U.N.T.S. (1992);

(3) The Convention on the Prevention and Punishment of Crimes Against Internationally Protected Persons, Including Diplomatic Agents, 28 U.S.T. 1975, T.I.A.S. No. 8532 (1977), implemented in 18 U.S.C. §112;

(4) The General Assembly Resolutions on Measures to Prevent International Terrorism, G.A. Res. 40/61 (1985) and G.A. Res. 42/159 (1987);

(5) The Convention on the High Seas, arts. 14-22 (piracy), 13 U.S.T. 2312, T.I.A.S. No. 5200 (1962).

1126. Pursuant to 28 U.S.C. §1350, the Plaintiffs' herein who are estates, survivors and heirs of those killed or injured who were non-U.S. citizens or "aliens" at the time of their illegal death or injury are entitled to recover damages they have sustained by reason of the defendants' actions.

WHEREFORE, Plaintiffs who are estates, survivors and heirs of non U.S. citizens or 'aliens,' demand judgment in their favor against all Defendants, jointly, severally, and/or individually, in excess of One Trillion Dollars ($1,000,000,000,000), plus interest, costs, and such other monetary and equitable relief as this Honorable Court deems appropriate to compensate the victims, but prevent Defendants from ever again committing such terrorist acts.

COUNT FOUR
WRONGFUL DEATH

1127. Plaintiffs incorporate herein by reference the allegations contained in the preceding paragraphs.

1128. Plaintiffs herein—families of those killed on September 11, 2001. Bring this consolidated action for wrongful death proximately caused by the Defendants engaging in, sponsoring, financing, aiding and abetting and/or otherwise conspiring to commit acts of terror including the terrorist and attacks acts of September 11, 2001.

1129. Surviving family members are entitled to recover damages from Defendants for these wrongful deaths. These family members are entitled to all damages incurred as fair and just compensation for the injuries resulting from these wrongful deaths.

1130. The injuries and damages suffered by the Plaintiffs were proximately caused by the intentional, malicious, reckless, negligent acts of the defendants as described herein.

1131. As a direct and proximate result of the wrongful deaths of the decedents, their heirs and families have been deprived of future aid, income, assistance, services, comfort, companionship, affection and financial support.

1132. As a direct and proximate result of the defendants' acts of terrorism resulting in wrongful death, the heirs and families of the decedents suffer and will continue to suffer permanent wrongful, illegal acts, emotional distress, severe trauma, and permanent physical and psychological injuries.

1133. As a further result of intentional, malicious, reckless, negligent, wrongful, illegal acts, and tortuous conduct of the Defendants, the Plaintiffs have incurred actual damages including but not limited to medical expenses, psychological trauma, physical injuries, and other expenses and losses for which they are entitled to full recovery.

WHEREFORE, Plaintiffs demand judgment in their favor against all Defendants, jointly, severally, and/or individually, in an amount in excess of One Trillion Dollars ($1,000,000,000,000) plus interest, costs, and such other monetary and equitable relief as this Honorable Court deems appropriate to compensate and deter Defendants from ever again committing such terrorist acts.

COUNT FIVE
NEGLIGENCE

1134. Plaintiffs incorporate herein by reference the allegations contained in all preceding paragraphs.

1135. The banking and charity Defendants were under heightened duties as fiduciaries of banks and charities, as public servants endowed with the public's trust. All Defendants were under a general duty not to intentionally injure, maim or kill, commit criminal or tortuous acts, endanger lives, and engage in activity that would foreseeably lead to the personal injury and/or death of Plaintiffs.

1136. Defendants breached these duties, which was a proximate cause of the deaths and personal injuries inflicted by Plaintiffs on and since September 11, 2001.

WHEREFORE, Defendants are liable to Plaintiffs in an amount in excess of One Trillion Dollars ($1,000,000,000,000) plus interest, costs, and such other monetary and equitable relief as this Honorable Court deems appropriate to prevent Defendants from ever again committing the terrorist acts of September 11, 2001, or similar acts.

COUNT SIX
SURVIVAL

1137. Plaintiffs incorporate herein by reference the allegations contained in all preceding paragraphs.

1138. As a result of the intentional, malicious, reckless, conspiratorial and negligent acts of Defendants as described herein, those killed on September 11, 2001, were placed in a severe and prolonged extreme apprehension of harmful, offensive bodily contact, injury and assault. These Plaintiffs suffered severe, offensive, harmful, bodily contact, personal injury and battery; suffered extreme fear, terror, anxiety, emotional and psychological distress and trauma intentionally inflicted physical pain; they were mentally, physically and emotionally damaged, harmed, trapped, and falsely imprisoned prior to their deaths and injuries.

1139. As a result of Defendants' tortuous conduct, those killed suffered damages including extreme pain and suffering, severe trauma, fear, permanent physical and emotional distress, loss of life and life's pleasures, companionship and consortium, loss of family, career, earnings and earning capacity, loss of accretion to their estates, and other items of damages as set forth herein.

WHEREFORE, Plaintiffs demand judgment in their favor against all Defendants, jointly, severally, and/or individually, in an amount in excess of One Trillion Dollars ($1,000,000,000,000) plus interest, costs, and such other monetary and equitable relief as this Honorable Court deems appropriate to prevent Defendants from ever again committing such terrorist acts.

COUNT SEVEN
NEGLIGENT AND/OR INTENTIONAL INFLICTION OF
EMOTIONAL DISTRESS

1140. Plaintiffs incorporate herein by reference the averments contained in all preceding paragraphs.

1141. Defendants knew or should have known that their actions would lead to the killing of innocent persons; the defendants knew or should have known that the September 11, 2001 suicide hijackings and disaster would intentionally kill or injure innocent people, leaving devastated family members to grieve for their losses with ongoing physical, psychological and emotional injuries.

1142. The actions of Defendants were unconscionable with an intentional, malicious, and willful disregard for the rights and lives of the Plaintiffs.

1143. As a direct and proximate cause of Defendants' intended conduct and reckless disregard for human life, Plaintiffs have suffered and those surviving will forever in the future continue to suffer severe, permanent psychiatric disorders, emotional distress and anxiety, permanent psychological distress, and permanent mental injury and impairment causing ongoing and long-term expenses for medical services, and counseling and care.

1144. The conduct of Defendants was undertaken in an intentional manner to kill and injure innocent people. These acts and efforts culminated in the murder and maiming of innocent people, causing continuing, permanent emotional and physical suffering of the families and heirs of the decedents.

1145. Defendants, by engaging in this intentional, unlawful conduct, negligently and/or intentionally inflicted emotional distress upon the Plaintiffs.

WHEREFORE, Plaintiffs demand judgment in their favor against all Defendants, jointly, severally, and/or individually, in an amount in excess of One Trillion Dollars ($1,000,000,000,000) plus interest, costs, and such other monetary and equitable relief as this Honorable Court deems appropriate to prevent Defendants from ever again committing terrorist acts.

COUNT EIGHT
CONSPIRACY

1146. Plaintiffs incorporate herein by reference the averments contained in all preceding paragraphs.

1147. As set forth above, the defendants, unlawfully, willfully and knowingly combined, conspired, confederated, aided and abetted, tacitly and/or expressly agreed to participate in unlawful and tortuous acts pursuant to a common course of conduct, resulting in the death and injury of Plaintiffs.

1148. As set forth above, the defendants conspired with and agreed to provide material support, funding, sponsorship and/or resources to al Qaeda, Osama bin Laden, and the sponsors of terror.

1149. As set forth above, Defendants engaged in common, concerted and conspirational acts, efforts, transactions, and activities designed and intended to cause a terrorist attack on the United States, its citizens and society, and—attack those foreign citizens found within the United States, resulting in the harm to Plaintiffs, which was done pursuant to and furtherance of this common scheme.

1150. Defendants' concert of action and conspiracy to support and promote Osama bin Laden, and al Qaeda were a proximate cause of the September 11, 2001, terrorist attacks that killed and injured the Plaintiffs.1151. As a result of Defendants' concert of action and conspiracy to further terror, Plaintiffs have suffered damages as set forth herein.

WHEREFORE, Plaintiffs demand judgment in their favor against all Defendants, jointly, severally, and/or individually, in an amount in excess of One Trillion Dollars ($1,000,000,000,000) plus interest, costs, and such other monetary and equitable relief as this Honorable Court deems appropriate to prevent Defendants from ever again committing terrorist acts.

COUNT NINE
AIDING AND ABETTING

1152. Plaintiffs incorporate herein by reference the averments contained in all preceding paragraphs.

1153. As set forth above, Defendants knowingly and substantially assisted in the sponsorship of Osama bin Laden, al Qaeda and the September 11, 2001 terrorist attacks that killed and injured the Plaintiffs.

1154. At the time of such aiding and abetting, Defendants knew or should have known that its role was part of an overall and ongoing illegal and/or tortuous activity.

1155. As set forth above, the Defendants aided and abetted in concerted efforts, transactions, acts and activities designed to cause the attacks of September 11, 2001, on the United States, its citizens, foreign citizens, property and freedoms.

1156. That Defendants' aiding and abetting of terrorism through material sponsorship was a proximate cause of the September 11, 2001 terrorist attacks that killed and injured the Plaintiffs.

1157. As a result of the Defendants' aiding and abetting activities, Plaintiffs have suffered damages as set forth herein.

WHEREFORE, Plaintiffs demand judgment in their favor against all Defendants, jointly, severally, and/or individually, in an amount in excess of One Trillion Dollars ($1,000,000,000,000) plus interest, costs, and such other monetary and equitable relief as this Honorable Court deems appropriate to prevent Defendants from ever again committing terrorist acts.

COUNT TEN
18 U.S.C. §2333-TREBLE DAMAGES FOR U.S. NATIONALS

1158. Plaintiffs incorporate herein by reference the averments contained in all preceding paragraphs.

1159. As set forth above, Defendants, jointly, severally and proximately caused the deaths and injuries of Plaintiffs' person, property and business through and by reason of acts of international terrorism.

1160. As set forth above, Defendants provision of material support and assistance to Osama bin Laden, al Qaeda and the 9/11 terrorists from which they carried out terrorist attacks on the United States, including the September 11, 2001 terrorist attacks.

1161. As a result of Defendants' acts in furtherance of international terrorism, all Plaintiffs suffered damages as set forth herein.

1162. Pursuant to 18 U.S.C. §2333, et. seq., the estates, survivors and heirs of the decedents who are nationals of the United States are entitled to recover threefold the damages they have sustained and the cost of suit, including attorneys' fees.

WHEREFORE, Plaintiffs, who are nationals of the United States, demand judgment in their favor against all Defendants, jointly, severally, and/or individually, and demand treble damages in excess of Three Trillion Dollars ($3,000,000,000,000), plus interest, costs, and such other monetary and equitable relief as this Honorable Court deems appropriate to prevent Defendants from ever again committing such terrorist acts.

COUNT ELEVEN
VIOLATION OF THE RACKETEER INFLUENCED
AND CORRUPT ORGANIZATIONS ACT
18 U.S.C. §1962(a)

1163. Plaintiffs incorporate herein by reference the averments contained in all preceding paragraphs.

1164. Non Sovereign Defendants are each "persons" within the meaning of the Racketeer Influenced and Corrupt Organizations Act, 18 U.S.C. §1961, et seq. ("RICO").

1165. The Defendant charities, banks, and terrorists are each an "enterprise" within the meaning of RICO, the activities of which affect intrastate and foreign commerce.

1166. By virtue of the predicate acts described in this Complaint, including without limitations, engaging in the predicate acts of terrorism, murder, kidnapping, forgery, false use and misuse of passports, fraud and misuse of visas, laundering of monetary instruments, engaging in monetary transaction in improperly derived from unlawful activity, the use of interstate commerce, interstate transportation of terrorist property, and bringing in and harboring illegal aliens, and aiding and assisting illegal aliens in entering the United States. Osama bin Laden and al Qaeda, along with the Defendants herein, transferred received, and supplied financing and income that was designed, both directly and indirectly, from a pattern of racketeering activity in which each of them participated as a principal, and used and invested, both directly and indirectly, such income and the proceeds of such income, in establishing and operating terrorist enterprises in violation of 18 U.S.C. §1962(a).1167. As a direct and proximate result of Defendants' violation of 18 U.S.C. §1962(a), Plaintiffs suffered the loss of valuable property, financial services and support, and suffered other pecuniary damages in an amount to be determined at trial.

   WHEREFORE, Plaintiffs demand judgment in their favor against all Defendants, jointly, severally, and/or individually, in an amount in excess of One Trillion Dollars ($1,000,000,000,000) plus interest, costs, and such other monetary and equitable relief as this Honorable Court deems appropriate to prevent Defendants from ever again committing such terrorist acts.

COUNT TWELVE
VIOLATION OF THE RACKETEER INFLUENCED AND CORRUPT ORGANIZATIONS ACT
18 U.S.C. §1962(c)

   1168. Plaintiffs incorporate herein by reference the averments contained in all preceding paragraphs.

   1169. By virtue of the acts described in this Complaint, including without limitations, engaging in the predicate acts of terrorism, murder, kidnapping, forgery, false use and misuse of passports, fraud and misuse of visas, laundering of monetary instruments, engaging in monetary transaction in properly derived from unlawful activity. The use of interstate commerce, interstate transportation of terrorist property, bringing in and harboring illegal aliens, and aiding and assisting illegal aliens in entering the United States. Osama bin Laden and al Qaeda, along with the defendants herein, transferred, received and supplied financing and income that was designed, both directly and indirectly, from a pattern of racketeering activity in which each of them participated as a principal, and used and invested, both directly and indirectly, such income and the proceeds of such income, in establishing and operating terrorist enterprises, in violation of 18 U.S.C. §1962(c).1170. As a direct and proximate result of Defendants' violation of 18 U.S.C. §1962(c), Plaintiffs suffered the loss of valuable property, financial services and support, and suffered other pecuniary damages in an amount to be determined at trial.

   WHEREFORE, Plaintiffs demand judgment in their favor against all Defendants, jointly, severally, and/or individually, in an amount in excess of One Trillion Dollars ($1,000,000,000,000) plus interest, costs, and such other monetary and equitable relief as this Honorable Court deems appropriate to prevent Defendants from ever again committing such terrorist acts.

COUNT THIRTEEN VIOLATION OF RACKETEER INFLUENCED
AND CORRUPT ORGANIZATIONS ACT 18 U.S.C. §1962(d)

   1171. Plaintiffs incorporate herein by reference the averments contained in all preceding paragraphs.

   1172. By virtue of the acts described in this Complaint, including without limitations, engaging in the predicate acts of terrorism, murder, kidnapping, forgery, false use and misuse of passports, fraud and misuse of visas, laundering of monetary instruments, engaging in monetary transaction in properly derived from unlawful activity. The use of interstate commerce facilities in murder-for-hire, interstate transportation of terrorist property, bringing in and harboring illegal aliens, and aiding and assisting illegal aliens in entering the United States. Osama bin Laden and al Qaeda, along with the defendants herein transferred, received and supplied financing and income that was designed, both directly and indirectly, from a pattern of racketeering activity in which each of them participated as a principal, and used and invested, both directly and indirectly, such income and the proceeds of such income, in establishing and operating terrorist enterprises, in violation of 18 U.S.C. §1962(d).1173. As a direct and proximate result of Defendants' violation of 18 U.S.C. §1962(d), Plaintiffs suffered the loss of valuable property, financial services and support, and suffered other pecuniary damages in an amount to be determined at trial.

   WHEREFORE, Plaintiffs demand judgment in their favor against all Defendants, jointly, severally, and/or individually, in an amount in excess of One Trillion Dollars ($1,000,000,000,000) plus interest, costs, and such other monetary and equitable relief as this Honorable Court deems appropriate to prevent Defendants from ever again committing such terrorist acts.

COUNT FOURTEEN PUNITIVE DAMAGES

1174. Plaintiffs incorporate herein by reference the averments contained in all the preceding paragraphs.

1175. The actions of the defendants, acting in concert or otherwise conspiring to carry out, aid and abet these unlawful objectives of terror, were intentional, malicious, unconscionable, and in reckless disregard of the rights and safety of all Plaintiffs. Defendants, acting individually, jointly, and/or severally intended to carry out actions that would brutalize or kill the lives of the Plaintiffs.

1176. As a result of their intentional, malicious, outrageous, willful, reckless conduct, the defendants are individually, jointly and severally liable to all Plaintiffs for punitive damages.

WHEREFORE, Plaintiffs demand judgment in their favor against all Defendants, jointly, severally, and/or individually, in an amount in excess of One Trillion Dollars ($1,000,000,000,000) plus interest, costs, and such other monetary and equitable relief as this Honorable Court deems appropriate to prevent Defendants from ever again committing such terrorist acts.

Notes

1. If this were a biological attack, would these claims cover the types of damages? With insurance companies withdrawing terrorism coverage, and the possibility of the need to destroy contaminated personal property, would claims for personal property damage be additional claims in a biological attack?

2. In a biological attack, there is a possibility of adding victims in the attack who are not initially targeted by the terrorists, although it is foreseeable that there would be victims beyond the initial attack. Would that change the approach to the negligence claim?

3. As demonstrated in the introduction to this chapter, proving the source of the biological agent is problematic in demonstrating causation. In the 9-11 attacks, causation in the complaint is not a problem; however, in a biological attack, causation would require a statement of facts which would demonstrate causation in order to survive a F.R.C.P. 12(b)(6) motion to dismiss in federal court. How might you construct that language?

10.4 September 11th Victim Compensation Fund of 2001

This compensation fund was created by Title IV of Public Law 107–42, Air Transportation Safety and System Stabilization Act. "The Act authorizes compensation to any individual (or the personal representative of a deceased individual) who was physically injured or killed as a result of the terrorist related aircraft crashes on that day," 67 Fed. Reg. 11233- 11247 (Mar. 13, 2002).

The final rulemaking for administering the fund, acknowledged comments raised as to why victims of the anthrax attacks were also not compensated through this compensation fund, among other special groups. (at 11234). No compensation fund was created for victims of the anthrax attacks.

When the compensation fund was closed June 14, 2004, there were over 7,300 claims for death or physical injury, and 98% of the eligible families chose to accept the compensation rather than to litigate. Approximately $7 billion was awarded.

Chapter Eleven
Global Bioterrorism and Biosecurity Law

International law and bioterrorism includes international agreements between countries, as well as the comparison of other foreign countries' domestic laws that address bioterrorism to those of the United States. This chapter will first address international agreements between countries in part one, and then other countries' laws in comparison to those of the United States in part two.

"The maxim *salus populi suprema lex* is the law of all courts and countries. The individual right sinks in the necessity to provide for the public good. The only question has been, as to the extent of the powers that should be conferred for such purposes." *Haverty v. Bass*, 66 Me. 71 at 74 (1876). The interests of national security in times of war weigh heavily in favor of national security against civil rights. The approach to this balance varies between countries and their domestic laws addressing bioterrorism reflect these priorities.

11.1. A Global History of Law and Bioterrorism

In 1969, President Richard M. Nixon ended this nation's biological weapons program, and converted the work to a defensive program, stating:

"I have decided that the United States of America will renounce the use of any form of deadly biological weapons that either kill or incapacitate. Our bacteriological programs in the future will be confined to research in biological defense on techniques of immunization and on measures of controlling and preventing the spread of disease. I have ordered the Defense Department to make recommendations about the disposal of the existing stocks of bacteriological weapons."

"Mankind already carries in its own hands too many of the seeds of its own destruction. By the examples that we set today, we hope to contribute to an atmosphere of peace and understanding between all nations."

—Pres. Richard M. Nixon, November 1969

This leadership from the United States led to the negotiation of the Biological Weapons Convention of 1972, which prohibits any country from possessing or using biological weapons. By May 1997 the Convention had been ratified by 140 countries, and all major countries were included except

Israel. This international treaty initiated our international agreements to cease the production of biological weapons.

Although the Soviet Union signed the Biological Weapons Convention of 1972, a suspicious outbreak of anthrax in April 1979 in Sverdlovsk raised concerns that the Soviets might be engaged in biological weapons production. In 1980, the United States demanded an explanation from the Soviets. The Soviets gave the explanation that the anthrax outbreak was the result of consumption of contaminated black market meat. This explanation was accepted by the world community, but suspicions were high.

The Chemical and Biological Weapons Control Act of 1991 established a system of economic and export controls designed to prevent export of goods or technologies used in the development of chemical and biological weapons to designated nationals. Particular focus was on the prevention of trading between U.S. companies and Iraq, which was also under suspicion of producing biological weapons.

In 1992, the Soviet Union was dissolved, and it was discovered that a massive biological weapons production program, Biopreparat, was underway, in spite of the Soviet Union's participation in the Biological Weapons Convention of 1972. Yeltsin admitted in May 1992 that the Sverdlovsk anthrax outbreak was the result of military activities. From 1992 to 1993, a joint team of United States and Russian scientists conducted an investigation and determined that 68 civilians died from an accidental release of aerosolized anthrax bacteria from a military biological weapons facility in Sverdlovsk.

In 1993, President George H.W. Bush confronted Yeltsin with this information, and told President Yeltsin that he wanted the program stopped and the stockpiles destroyed. Yeltsin was vague about its existence but asked for a report from his staff, which was also, not surprisingly vague.

The Iraqis' biological weapons program was not fully discovered until after Desert Storm, although preparations had been made to inoculate United States troops against anthrax. It was not until 1995 that the Iraqis admitted that the plant production facility, Al-Hakam Single-Cell Protein Plant, which they had stated for years was a plant used to produce animal feed, was actually a biological weapons facility. Here they developed weapons and conducted tests on animals. They also admitted to the production of about 200 biological missiles and bomblets.

In 1996, the international community inaugurated negotiations to attempt to strengthen the Biological Weapons Convention by adding a monitoring protocol. In 2001, the Bush Administration announced that it rejected the draft Biological Weapons Convention protocol that those negotiations produced.

As a result of the Larry Wayne Harris case in the United States in 1995, the U.S. Congress passed the Anti-Terrorism and Effective Death Penalty Act of 1996. This statute expands the power of the United States to cover individuals and groups who attempt or even threaten to develop or use a biological weapon, and also broadens the definition of biological weapons to include engineered organisms. The statute includes the provision for the United States to identify terrorists groups, to deny access to financial institutions in the United States, and to withhold visas to those individuals and group members. Initially, the United States identified thirty such groups, which included the Abu Sayyaf Group of the Philippines, the Khmer Rouge of Cambodia, and the Japanese Red Army and the Aum Shinrikyo, both of Japan.

The international community was struck after September 11, 2001 with anthrax letters sent around the world. Letters were received in Brazil, Germany, Lithuania, and other parts of Europe following the receipt of anthrax letters in the United States.

Other countries responded to the anthrax attacks, but to the SARS outbreak, also required emergency public health responses in the context of domestic law and governmental organization. Germany created a national biosurveillance system, requiring all jurisdictions to uniformly report public health information that may indicate an emerging disease. Canada created the Public Health Agency, which provides a coordinated federal approach to public health. Unfortunately, the United States in their vigilance to protect state sovereignty have still been unable to agree on a uniform biosurveillance system. This has led to attempts by the CDC to collect health information through private sources, which in effect probably unconstitutionally gather state information that should be left to the discretion of the state to control under state public health powers.

The United States has invested more in biodefense research than any other country, and is a world leader in countermeasures to not only bioterrorism but also to other emerging infectious diseases. Between 2001 and the present, the United States Congress has passed multiple major federal statutes to address aspects of government organization, vaccines and countermeasures, preparedness and federal government response, biocrime law, and laboratory biosafety and biosecurity.

The SARS outbreak in the spring of 2003 was the first major threat of a pandemic since the last pandemic influenza in 1956, the Hong Kong Influenza. However, SARS presented a much more urgent case due to its highly infectious characteristics and fast spread through air transportation. In 2005, the World Health Organization issued the new version of the International Health Regulations, which requires member countries to report public health incidents of national importance immediately to the WHO to avoid the same delay in reporting that occurred with the SARS outbreak.

In July 2008, the FBI's sole suspect in the 2001 anthrax attacks emerged as a biodefense researcher at USAMRIID, Bruce Ivins, whose existence as a suspect and identity was announced only after his suicide. The formal announcement by the FBI concluded that Ivins was likely to be solely responsible for the deaths of five persons and injuries to others that resulted from the mailing of several anonymous letters, containing anthrax powder, to members of Congress and the media. Ivins committed suicide prior to formal charges being filed by the FBI.

11.2   World Health Organization
11.2.1. International Health Regulations

The publication of the 2005 International Health Regulations includes a regulatory history in the Foreword:

> A central and historic responsibility for the World Health Organization (WHO) has been the management of the global regime for the control of the international spread of disease. Under Articles 21(a) and 22, the Constitution of WHO confers upon the World Health Assembly the authority to adopt regulations "designed to prevent the international spread of disease" which, after adoption by the Health Assembly, enter into force for all WHO Member States that do not affirmatively opt out of them within a specified time period.
>
> The International Health Regulations ("the IHR" or "Regulations") were adopted by the Health Assembly in 1969[1], having been preceded by the International Sanitary Regulations adopted by the Fourth World Health Assembly in 1951. The 1969 Regulations, which initially covered six "quarantinable diseases" were amended in 1973[2] and 1981[3], primarily to reduce the number of covered diseases from six to three (yellow fever, plague and cholera) and to mark the global eradication.
>
> In consideration of the growth in international travel and trade, and the emergence or re-emergence of international disease threats and other public health risks, the Forty-eighth World Health Assembly in 1995 called for a substantial revision of the Regulations adopted in 1969[4]. In resolution WHA48.7, the Health Assembly requested the Director-General to take steps to prepare their revision, urging broad participation and cooperation in the process.
>
> After extensive preliminary work on the revision by WHO's Secretariat in close consultation with WHO Member States, international organizations and other relevant partners, and the momentum created by the emergence of severe acute respiratory

syndrome (the first global public health emergency of the twenty-first century[5], the Health Assembly established an Intergovernmental Working Group in 2003 open to all Member States to review and recommend a draft revision of the Regulations to the Health Assembly[6]. The IHR (2005) were adopted by the Fifty-eighth World Health Assembly on 23 May 2005. They entered into force on 15 June 2007.

The purpose and scope of the IHR (2005) are "to prevent, protect against, control and provide a public health response to the international spread of disease in ways that are commensurate with and restricted to public health risks, and which avoid unnecessary interference with international traffic and trade." The IHR (2005) contain a range of innovations, including: (a) a scope not limited to any specific disease or manner of transmission, but covering "illness or medical condition, irrespective of origin or source, that presents or could present significant harm to humans"; (b) State Party obligations to develop certain minimum core public health capacities; (c) obligations on States Parties to notify WHO of events that may constitute a public health emergency of international concern according to defined criteria; (d) provisions authorizing WHO to take into consideration unofficial reports of public health events and to obtain verification from State Parties concerning such events; (e) procedures for the determination by the Director-General of a "public health emergency of international concern" and issuance of corresponding temporary recommendations, after taking into account the views of an Emergency Committee; (f) protection of the human rights of persons and travellers; and (g) the establishment of National IHR Focal Points and WHO IHR Contact Points for urgent communications between State Parties and WHO.

By not limiting the application of the IHR (2005) to specific diseases, the Regulations intend to maintain their relevance and applicability for many years to come, even in the face of the continued evolution of diseases and of the factors determining their emergence and transmission.

The provisions in the IHR (2005) also update and revise many of the technical and other regulatory functions, including certificates applicable to international travel and transport, and requirements for international ports, airports, and ground crossings

ANNEX 2
DECISION INSTRUMENT FOR THE ASSESSMENT AND NOTIFICATION
OF EVENTS THAT MAY CONSTITUTE A PUBLIC HEALTH EMERGENCY
OF INTERNATIONAL CONCERN

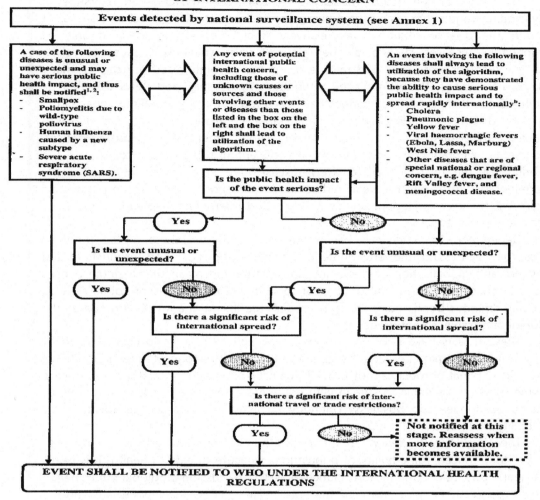

[1] As per WHO case definitions.
[2] The disease list shall be used only for the purposes of these Regulations.

43

Fig. 11.1 World Health Organization, Flowchart for reporting incidents of international concern

11.2.2 Global Public Health Security in the 21st Century: A WHO Report
    The World Health Organization in 2007 published a report titled Global Public Health Security in
the 21st Century. The message from the Director General outlines the goals of the report:

> The world has changed dramatically since 1951, when WHO issued its first set of
> legally binding regulations aimed at preventing the international spread of disease. At
> that time, the disease situation was relatively stable. Concern focused on only six
> "quarantinable" diseases: cholera, plague, relapsing fever, smallpox, typhus and yellow
> fever. New diseases were rare, and miracle drugs had revolutionized the care of many
> well-known infections. People travelled internationally by ship, and news travelled by
> telegram. Since then, profound changes have occurred in the way humanity inhabits the
> planet. The disease situation is anything but stable. Population growth, incursion into
> previously uninhabited areas, rapid urbanization, intensive farming practices,
> environmental degradation, and the misuse of antimicrobials have disrupted the
> equilibrium of the microbial world. New diseases are emerging at the historically
> unprecedented rate of one per year. Airlines now carry more than 2 billion passengers
> annually, vastly increasing opportunities for the rapid international spread of infectious
> agents and their vectors.
>
> Dependence on chemicals has increased, as has awareness of the potential
> hazards for health and the environment. Industrialization of food production and
> processing, and globalization of marketing and distribution mean that a single tainted
> ingredient can lead to the recall of tons of food items from scores of countries. In a
> particularly ominous trend, mainstay antimicrobials are failing at a rate that outpaces the
> development of replacement drugs.
>
> These threats have become a much larger menace in a world characterized by
> high mobility, economic interdependence and electronic interconnectedness. Traditional
> defenses at national borders cannot protect against the invasion of a disease or vector.
> Real time news allows panic to spread with equal ease. Shocks to health reverberate as
> shocks to economies and business continuity in areas well beyond the affected site.
> Vulnerability is universal.
>
> The *World Health Report 2007* is dedicated to promoting global public health
> security – the reduced vulnerability of populations to acute threats to health. This year's
> World Health Day, celebrated in April, launched WHO's discussion on global public health
> security. Around the world, academics, students, health professionals, politicians and the
> business community are engaged in dialogue on how to protect the world from threats
> like pandemic influenza, the health consequences of conflict and natural disasters, and
> bioterrorism.
>
> The *World Health Report 2007* addresses these issues, among others, in the
> context of new tools for collective defence, including, most notably, the revised
> International Health Regulations (2005). These Regulations are an international legal
> instrument designed to achieve maximum security against the international spread of
> diseases. They also aim to reduce the international impact of public health emergencies.
>
> The IHR (2005) expand the focus of collective defence from just a few
> "quarantinable" diseases to include any emergency with international repercussions for
> health, including outbreaks of emerging and epidemic-prone diseases, outbreaks of
> foodborne disease, natural disasters, and chemical or radionuclear events, whether
> accidental or caused deliberately.
>
> In a significant departure from the past, IHR (2005) move away from a focus on
> passive barriers at borders, airports and seaports to a strategy of proactive risk

management. This strategy aims to detect an event early and stop it at its source – before it has a chance to become an international threat.

Given today's universal vulnerability to these threats, better security calls for global solidarity. International public health security is both a collective aspiration and a mutual responsibility. As the determinants and consequences of health emergencies have become broader, so has the range of players with a stake in the security agenda. The new watchwords are diplomacy, cooperation, transparency and preparedness. Successful implementation of IHR (2005) serves the interests of politicians and business leaders as well as the health, trade and tourism sectors.

I am pleased to present the *World Health Report 2007* to our partners and look forward to the discussions, directions and actions that it will inspire.

Dr Margaret Chan
Director-General
World Health Organization

The report describes the evolution from geographically limited public health issues to today's threats to public health security because of inadequate investment in public health infrastructure; public health consequences of armed conflict; microbial evolution and antibiotic resistance; new and emerging infectious diseases such as human bovine spongiform encephalopathy and nipah virus; weather-related health emergencies; and other public health emergencies included radiological, chemical, or biological events. The anthrax letters in the United States and the SARS outbreak are also used as examples of the new problems the world faces. Thinking ahead, the report discusses planning for the next pandemic influenza, addressing extensively drug-resistant tuberculosis and its spread, and managing the spread of polio.

The report urges global cooperation as the first step towards managing these new threats to public health security, and the legally binding International Health Regulations issued in June 2005, are part of the strategy to achieve cooperation.

11.3. SARS Lessons

The facts of the SARS outbreak that presented the global community with the very real possibility of another pandemic that could threaten even political stability are summarized in this excerpt from an article by Dr. Mae-Wan Ho, "Bioterrorism and SARS," © 2003 Institute of Science in Society:

In March, Liu Jianlin, 64-year-old medical professor who was involved in treating patients, went from Guangdong to Hong Kong to attend a wedding. He was taken ill soon after arrival and admitted to hospital. He asked to be put into quarantine, but was ignored; nor did the hospital warn his contacts. As a result, nine guests in the hotel where he stayed caught the disease and carried it to Singapore, Canada, Vietnam and other hospitals in Hong Kong.

On 10 February, news of the disease was posted on ProMed, an international e-mail notification service for infectious diseases outbreaks. The next day, China informed the World Health Organisation (WHO), but refused to let the WHO team into Guangdong until early April. By 8 April, there were 2671 confirmed cases of SARS in 19 countries and 103 deaths.

A palpable sense of panic has gripped the health authorities around the world. "Mother nature is the ultimate terrorist," says an editorial in the journal Nature. "Powerless to stop the spread," says New Scientist magazine, whose editor decries the lack of international control when it comes to disease epidemics: "The international community has weapons inspectors poised to force entry into a country at the first hint that it may possess chemical weapons. But when it comes to disease, we have no international body empowered to take charge, even though the disease may be vastly more dangerous."

The following chart, Fig. 11.2, outlines the number of cases, deaths, recovered, and quarantined persons as a result of the worldwide outbreak of SARS.

Sars by country

	Cases	Deaths	Recovered (discharged)	Quarantined
China	1,807	79	1,140	-
Hong Kong	1,380	88	409	620
Singapore	178	14	104	467
Canada	306	14	27	thousands
Vietnam	68	5	53	-
United States	35	0	-	-
Taiwan	29	0	16	1,713
UK	6	0	3	-
Total	3,809	200		

NB: There have been cases in at least 17 other countries worldwide

Fig. 11.2 SARS by country

11.3.1.   Canada[7]

Canada, with its liberal system of civil rights, was one of the most severely affected among the common law countries. From the perspective of common law countries, the example of Canada provides insight into the kinds of governmental organization changes that were indicated after Canada's experience with SARS. The following is an assessment from within Canada of its experience and lessons learned from SARS.

SARS has illustrated that we are constantly a short flight away from serious epidemics. Strengthening the capacity of other nations to detect and respond to emerging infectious disease is a global responsibility for a country with Canada's resources and also a matter of enlightened self-interest. The Committee has recommended that the Government of Canada should build health R&D activities into its programs of international outreach. In particular, the new Canadian Agency for Public Health should have a mandate for greater engagement internationally in the emerging infectious disease field, and support projects to build capacity for surveillance and outbreak management in developing countries.

During the SARS epidemic, WHO facilitated collaboration among researchers, promulgated template case definitions, and issued various alerts. WHO established contact with affected countries and offered epidemiologic, laboratory, and clinical support. It also began issuing travel advisories for the first time, acting as a trans-national clearinghouse to assess the safety of international travel and, by extension, the effectiveness of outbreak management efforts in different countries.

In June at the WHO Global Meeting on SARS in Malaysia, it became clear that many countries had adopted their own case definitions for SARS. The Committee believes that further attention is needed to determine the respective roles of a body such as WHO and its member states in defining a new disease such as SARS.

Several Asian jurisdictions faced even greater challenges from SARS than did Canada. Many observers felt that Canadian officials failed to connect closely enough with officials in Hong Kong, Singapore, and China, and missed opportunities to learn from other countries.

Health Canada regularly transmitted information to WHO during the SARS outbreak, but data were limited during the early weeks of the outbreak owing to the absence of formal reporting processes among municipal, provincial, and federal governments. Protocols for data sharing must be established not only for more effective outbreak management, but to ensure that Canada can maintain the confidence of the international community during an outbreak.

Submissions to the Committee from the travel industry indicated significant gaps and inconsistencies with respect to information on SARS available to passengers and staff. The new agency must ensure that there is an effective communication strategy for infectious diseases with contact points for the travel industry.

On April 2, 2003, WHO issued a travel advisory recommending the postponement of all but essential travel to Hong Kong and China's Guangdong province. Previously, only individual countries had issued travel advisories. On April 23, 2003, WHO added Toronto, Beijing, and China's Shanxi province to the list of areas that travellers should avoid. The advice against non-essential travel to Toronto was scheduled to be in place for three weeks before reappraisal, but withdrawn on April 29 after Canadian protests. Controversy about the WHO travel advisory was augmented by inconsistency in categorization of Toronto between WHO and the US CDC, the weak evidence for the travel advisory criteria themselves, and limited warning from WHO of the forthcoming advisory. Assuming that WHO will continue issuing advisories, processes for developing evidence-based criteria and giving notice to affected countries must be developed by agreement among member states.

For many years, Health Canada's Travel Medicine Program has issued advisories to Canadians traveling abroad on risks such as disease outbreaks and natural disasters. Health Canada created its own scoring system to determine travel advice concerning countries affected by SARS, but its evidentiary basis appears no stronger than the contested WHO criteria. Moreover, travel advisories issued by Canada for Hong Kong were at times more severe than the WHO travel advice for Hong Kong. The Committee has therefore recommended that Canada's own practices in issuing travel advisories should be revisited, ideally in the context of a multilateral re-assessment of the basis, nature, goals, and impact of advice to travellers.

In 2002, Health Canada informed airport authorities that it would be transferring airport quarantine responsibilities to the Canada Customs and Revenue Agency. Customs staff were never trained to do the job. During the SARS outbreak, Health Canada amended the Quarantine Act Regulations to include SARS but only a tiny contingent of quarantine officers was on hand to enforce the new regulations. Airport authorities expressed concern about Health Canada's ability to mobilize knowledgeable quarantine staff to the airports, to provide logistical support, and to manage the relevant communications. In the case of cruise ships, Health Canada's protocols for screening, handling of suspected SARS cases, and decontaminating ships were not released until mid-June, after the outbreak had waned. The Committee has recommended that the Government of Canada ensure that an adequate complement of quarantine officers is maintained at all ports of entry, and that better collaboration with port authorities and personnel be established to clarify responsibilities in the event of a health threat.

Screening of incoming and outbound air passengers relied on information cards with screening questions and secondary assessments as needed, as well as a pilot project using thermal scanners in Toronto and Vancouver. As of August 27, 2003, an estimated 6.5 million screening transactions had occurred at Canadian airports to aid in the detection and prevention of SARS transmission. Roughly 9,100 passengers were referred for further assessment by screening nurses or quarantine officers. None had SARS. The pilot thermal scanner project screened about 2.4 million passengers. Only 832 required further assessment, and again none were found to have SARS. In other countries, the yields for airport screening measures were similarly low.

We have accordingly recommended that the Government of Canada should review its travel screening techniques and protocols with a view to ensuring that travel screening measures are based on evidence for public health effectiveness, while taking into account the financial and human resources required. While formal screening thus far appears relatively inefficient and ineffective, the Committee has recommended that the Government of Canada provide travelers in general with information about where and when health threats exist, including precautionary measures and first steps to take in case of suspected infection. A partnership with the travel industry would facilitate this process so that information could be provided at the time of bookings.

Conclusion

Long before SARS, evidence of actual and potential harm to the health of Canadians from weaknesses in public health infrastructure had been mounting but had not catalyzed a comprehensive and multi-level governmental response. SARS killed 44 Canadians, caused illness in hundreds more, paralyzed a major segment of Ontario's health care system for weeks, and saw in excess of 25,000 residents of the GTA placed in quarantine. Psychosocial effects of SARS on health care workers, patients, and families are still being assessed. However, the economic shocks have already been felt not only in the GTA, the epicenter of SARS, but across the country.

The National Advisory Committee on SARS and Public Health has found that there was much to learn from the outbreak of SARS in Canada - in large part because too many earlier lessons were ignored.

A key requirement for dealing successfully with future public health crises is a truly collaborative framework and ethos among different levels of government. The rules and norms for a seamless public health system must be sorted out with a shared commitment to protecting and promoting the health of Canadians. Systems-based thinking and coordination of activity in a carefully planned infrastructure are integral in public health because of its population-wide and preventive focus. They are also essential if we are to be effective in managing public health emergencies. Indeed, Canada's ability to contain an outbreak is only as strong as the weakest jurisdiction in the chain of P/T public health systems. Infectious diseases are an essential piece of the public health puzzle, but cannot be addressed in isolation, particularly since in local health units, the same personnel tend to respond to both infectious and non-infectious threats to community health. The Committee has accordingly recommended strategies that will reinforce all levels of the public health system as well as integrate the components more fully with each other.

The fiscal and strategic approaches set out in this report are consistent with international precedents and, we believe, the expectations of Canadians. Until now, there have been no federal transfers earmarked for local and P/T public health activities. Public health has instead been competing against personal health services for health dollars in provincial budgets, even as the federal government has increasingly earmarked its health transfers for personal health service priorities. Public health costs are modest – perhaps 2-3% of health spending, depending on how one defines numerators and denominators. The actual amount of new federal spending that the Committee has recommended would reach $700 million per annum by 2007 at the earliest. This is what F/P/T governments currently spend on personal health services in Canada between Monday and Wednesday in a single week.

The SARS story as it unfolded in Canada had both tragic and heroic elements. Although the toll of the epidemic was substantial, thousands in the health field rose to the occasion and ultimately contained the SARS outbreak in this country, notwithstanding systems and resources that were manifestly suboptimal. The challenge now is to ensure not only that we are better prepared for the next epidemic, but that public health in Canada is broadly renewed so as to protect and promote the health of all our present and future citizens.

———————————

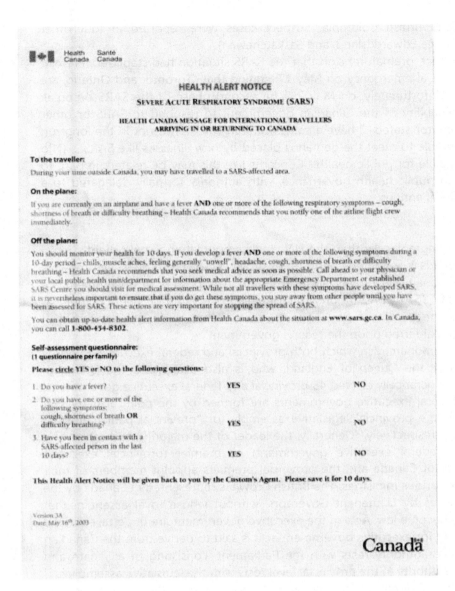

Fig. 11.3 Health Alert Notice (HAN) given to travelers immigrating into Canada during the SARS outbreak.

The U.S. Centers for Diseases Control and Prevention (CDC) commissioned a report on lessons-learned from the SARS incident. The following excerpt on the Canada case study provides more specific actions taken regarding the legal and governmental organization of Canada:

A. Canada

1. Introduction

Canada was among the countries hardest hit by SARS. Only the People's Republic of China, Hong Kong, and Taiwan had more probable SARS cases. Toronto was the Canadian city most affected the outbreak. The first (index) SARS case in Toronto was a 78-year-old woman, Mrs. K, who returned home to Toronto on February 23, 2003 from a trip to Hong Kong to visit relatives. Mrs. K, who was never hospitalized, died on March 5 after the onset of an illness later determined to be SARS.

Her son, Mr. T, became ill on February 27, was admitted to Scarborough Hospital (Grace Division) on March 7, and died on March 13. Transmission of SARS traceable to Mrs. K is thought to have included 224 other persons in Toronto alone. In all of Canada, there were 438 SARS cases, including 251 probable (1 active) and 187 suspect (0 active) cases. All of the probable cases were reported in two provinces,

Ontario, which includes Toronto, and British Columbia. Suspect cases were reported in four other provinces (Alberta, New Brunswick, Prince Edward Island, and Saskatchewan).

In an apparent (but in retrospect, premature) sign that the SARS situation had stabilized, Premier Eves of Ontario lifted the SARS provincial emergency on May 17, stating that "Toronto, and Ontario, are safe places to live, work and visit." Unfortunately, on May 23, the second phase of the SARS outbreak began. Opinions differ about the capability of the Canadian government to respond to SARS or other SARS-like outbreaks. As one commentator stated, "I have a concern about whether or not in the long run our public health-care system will be able to meet the demands placed by new illnesses like SARS.... [N]o one is directly accountable or responsible for public health." Concerns like this may be related, in part, to the decentralized nature of Canadian public health governance, with authority formally delegated to a multitude of federal, provincial, and local entities.

2. Political and Legal Systems

Canada is somewhat larger geographically than the U.S., but its population is only slightly more than a tenth the size of the U.S. Canada is a confederation of 13 provinces and territories, with powers delineated among the federal (or national) and provincial governments. The powers of government are established by the Constitution Act of 1867 ("Constitution Act"). Under the Constitution Act, a number of powers are exclusively reserved to the provincial governments; matters not exclusively vested with provincial governments are by default conferred upon the federal government.

Canada is also a constitutional monarchy in which both provincial and federal executive authority rests with the British Crown (currently the Queen of England, who is also designated the Queen of Canada), but which is exercised by democratically elected 45 provincial and federal executive governments (or "cabinets"). The provincial and federal executive governments are formed by the political party that wins the largest number of seats in the provincial legislative assembly (or "provincial parliament") or federal legislative House of Commons, respectively. Generally, the leader of the majority political party is designated as the Prime Minister (federal executive government) or premier (provincial executive government). Both the Prime Minister of Canada and the provincial premiers appoint members of their cabinets, who will in turn head up the various ministries. The British Crown is represented in Canada by the Governor General, and in the provinces by Lieutenant Governors, without whose royal assent neither federal nor provincial legislation may become law. Acts of the executive government are undertaken in the name of the Queen, although authority for executive government acts is said to derive from the Canadian people. At the federal level, legislative authority rests with the Parliament, consisting of a Senate and House of Commons, while legislative authority at the provincial level rests with the legislative assemblies.

The Canadian judicial system is divided into four different levels, including the provincial courts (which hear the majority of cases that come into the judicial system, and which often have more specific names based upon their subject matter jurisdiction); provincial and territorial superior courts (whose jurisdiction covers more serious crimes as well as appeals from the provincial courts, and which usually have subject matter divisions), as well as the Trial Division of the Federal Court (considered to be on the same level as the provincial and territorial superior courts but has jurisdiction for different issues, and is basically a superior court with civil jurisdiction); the provincial courts of appeal and the Federal Court of Appeal (whose jurisdiction includes appeals from the lower superior courts or Federal Court—Trial Division, respectively); and the Supreme Court of Canada, the final court of appeal from all other Canadian courts.

3. Public Health Structure and Laws
a. Federal level

The Constitution Act does not specifically address public health. However, the Constitution Act does provide for the national Parliament's exclusive legislative authority for matters of "Quarantine and the Establishment and Maintenance of Marine Hospitals." Pursuant to its authority, the federal government has enacted two statutes with significant public health implications, the Department of Health Act and the Quarantine Act.

The Department of Health Act establishes the executive branch's Department of Health, including the position of Minister of Health, and provides that the "powers, duties and functions of the Minister extend to and include all matters over which Parliament has jurisdiction relating to the promotion and preservation of the health of the people of Canada not by law assigned to any other department, board or agency of the Government of Canada." These powers, duties, and functions include, but are not limited to, the 46 following: "the protection of the people of Canada against risks to health and the spreading of disease"; "investigation and research into public health, including the monitoring of diseases"; "the protection of public health on railways, ships, aircraft and all other methods of transportation, and their ancillary services"; and "cooperation with provincial authorities with a view to the coordination of efforts made or proposed for preserving and improving public health."

The executive branch of the federal government, through the Governor in Council, is empowered to "make regulations that give effect to and carry out the objects" of the Department of Health Act; persons who "contravene" these regulations are "guilty of an offence punishable on summary conviction." The Department of Health Act further provides that neither the Minister nor any other officer or employee of the Department may exercise jurisdiction or control over the health authorities of the provinces. Consistent with the affirmative grant of the power to regulate, the Department of Health (now generally referred to as "Health Canada"), has the responsibility for administering a number of health laws and health related programs, including, for example, laws pertaining to food, drug, and medical device safety, regulation of tobacco products, the federal health insurance (Canada Health Act) program, control of hazardous workplace products, and reduction of the incidence of disease.

As part of its many ministerial responsibilities related to public health, the Department of Health has established the Population and Public Health Branch. The diverse activities of the branch include injury surveillance, prevention and control of sexually transmitted diseases, field epidemiology training, and biosafety. Within the branch is the Center for Emergency Preparedness and Response, charged with coordinating public health security issues by developing national emergency response plans, assessing public health emergency risks, developing federal rules for quarantine, and collaborating with other international, federal, and provincial agencies.

As a product of the constitutional structure of the Canadian government and contemporaneous but delineated authority among the federal, provincial, and local governments in matters related to public health, the legal authority for quarantine and isolation for purposes of public health may rest with federal, provincial, and/or municipal governments, depending upon the specific activity or context in which a public health issue is raised. For the federal government, the legal authority for quarantine and isolation appears limited to public health risks posed by travel or trade into or out of Canada, while for provincial and municipal governments, quarantine and isolation for purposes of public health are based on their broad police power over persons, businesses, or other entities that reside in or are located within their jurisdictions.

Canada's single most comprehensive law related to the control and prevention of contagious disease may be the Quarantine Act. The purpose of the Quarantine Act is to "prevent the introduction into Canada of infectious or contagious diseases. Under section 5 of the Quarantine Act, a duly designated quarantine officer is authorized to board any conveyance (air, train, motor vehicle, ship) arriving into or departing from 47 Canada to inspect for infectious or contagious diseases (enumerated on a schedule of diseases that included cholera, plague, smallpox, and yellow fever, and that now includes SARS), and to inspect persons arriving into Canada for "dangerous diseases" (discussed below). The Quarantine Act does not apply to persons who are not at a Canadian point of entry or departure.

Under section 8(1) of the Quarantine Act, a quarantine officer may request that a person arriving into or departing from Canada undergo a medical examination if the officer has reasonable grounds to believe that: such person is ill; may have or may be the carrier of an infectious or contagious disease; is infested with insects that may be carriers of an infectious or contagious disease; or has recently been in close proximity to a person who may have or may be the carrier of an infectious or contagious disease. Detention must take place in a designated quarantine station, hospital, or other place having suitable quarantine facilities or, for persons arriving into Canada on a vessel, on that vessel.

The period of detention may not to exceed the prescribed incubation period for the disease at issue. In lieu of detention, a quarantine officer may permit the person to proceed directly to his or her destination in Canada, but only if the person agrees in a signed writing to be placed under surveillance by a duly designated public health officer for the destination location for a period not exceeding the prescribed incubation period for the disease at issue.151

Under section 8(2), a quarantine officer may detain persons who refuse a quarantine officer's request to undergo a medical examination; persons who undergo the medical examination and who the quarantine officer suspects have an infectious or contagious disease; persons arriving into Canada who are unable to produce the requisite and satisfactory evidence of immunization for an infectious or contagious disease; or other persons at the port of entry who the quarantine officer believes on reasonable grounds have been in close proximity to a person fitting the description in section 8(1).

Persons detained pursuant to section 8(2) who are later determined by a quarantine officer to have an infectious or contagious disease may be detained "until the quarantine officer is satisfied that that person is not capable of infecting any other person with that [infectious or contagious] disease." Any person detained under section 8(2) must be immediately informed by the quarantine officer of the reason for the detention, and the person's right to appeal to the Deputy Minister of Health or his or her designate. Under section 13, a quarantine officer may detain—in a quarantine station, hospital or other place with suitable quarantine facilities, or, in the case of persons arriving into Canada on a vessel, on that vessel—any person arriving into or departing from Canada who the officer determines has an infectious or contagious disease. In line with the standard set forth for section 8(2) detentions with a later determination of disease, and unlike section 8(1) detentions (limited to the incubation period), section 13 detentions may continue "until the quarantine officer is satisfied that that person is not capable of infecting any other person with that [infectious or contagious] disease."

The detention procedure is somewhat different for cases involving a "dangerous disease," defined under the Quarantine Act as "any disease, other than a disease included 48 in the schedule, the introduction of which into Canada would, in the opinion of the quarantine officer concerned, constitute a grave danger to public health in Canada."

Under section 11, a quarantine officer may request that persons arriving in Canada undergo a medical examination where the quarantine officer believes on reasonable grounds that such persons may have or may be the carrier of a dangerous disease, or have recently been in close proximity to a person who may have or may be the carrier of a dangerous disease. A quarantine officer may detain—for a period of time not to exceed 14 days—any person described under section 11 who refuses the medical examination, or a person who undergoes the medical examination and who the quarantine officer suspects has a dangerous disease.

A quarantine officer who intends to detain a person under section 11 must, subject to the Minister of Health's approval, "make an order in prescribed form for the detention." For detentions longer than 48 hours, a quarantine officer must provide the detainee with a copy of the order, and inform the detainee of the right to a hearing.

Additionally, the Minister of Health must within 48 hours of the order make an application with notice in writing (with a copy served upon the detainee) to a judge of a superior court of the province in which the detainee is held, to confirm the quarantine officer's order of detention. The judge must hear the application within one day of the application, and must make an order to revoke, vary, or conform the detention order.

If the application is not made within the requisite 48-hour period, the quarantine officer must immediately release the detainee. In lieu of detention, a quarantine officer may permit the person described in section 11(1) to proceed directly to his or her destination in Canada, but only if the person agrees in writing to surveillance by a public health officer for the destination location for a period not exceeding 14 days; submits to being vaccinated against the dangerous disease; or both.   However, vaccination is not an option if it is apparent to the quarantine officer that the person should not be vaccinated, or if the quarantine officer has been informed that there are medical reasons not to vaccinate, and the quarantine officer is of the opinion that the person should not be vaccinated.

If required by a quarantine officer to enforce any provision under the Quarantine Act, "peace officers" must provide necessary assistance. Persons who violate any provision of the Quarantine Act or any regulation made under the Quarantine Act, for example, by failing to comply with any order of a quarantine officer made under the Act or failing to comply with the signed undertaking (in lieu of detention), is guilty of an offense punishable on conviction.

b. Provincial level

One of the exclusive powers of the provinces under the Constitution Act relates to public health. Provinces have authority over "[t]he Establishment, Maintenance, and Management of Hospitals, Asylums, Charities, and Eleemosynary Institutions in and for the Province, other than Marine Hospitals." Consistent with these constitutional powers, each of the provincial governments has enacted its own body of laws pertaining to public health. These laws operate independently of the laws of the other provinces.

For example, each of the provinces has enacted a statute to create a distinct provincial public health authority, as well as statutes or regulations that address specific public health matters.

Ontario, the epicenter of the SARS outbreak in Canada, enacted the Ministry of Health and Long-Term Care Act and the Health Protection and Promotion Act. The Ministry of Health and Long-Term Care Act provides for the establishment of a provincial Ministry of Health and the office of the Minister of Health. One of the functions of the Minister of Health is to "oversee and promote the health and the physical and mental well-being of the people of Ontario." The minister also has the power to enact regulations necessary to carry out the ministry's functions. These include regulations to "prescribe and govern the standards" for health care facilities and regulations to govern the establishment and use of, and the treatment provided in, facilities for tuberculosis diagnosis, surveillance and treatment, as well as "facilities for the diagnosis and surveillance of other respiratory diseases."

The Ministry of Health of Ontario has established a number of offices and programs to pursue its public health functions. Some of these offices and programs have responsibility for the regulation of hospitals, nursing homes, and medical laboratories.

Others are charged with carrying out health promotion and disease prevention activities. The ministry also provides or coordinates health insurance and drug benefits. Other Canadian provinces have similar ministries responsible for public health matters within their respective provinces and political subunits. In British Columbia, for example, the Health Act provides for the appointment of a provincial health officer and other staff as may be "necessary for the supervision and enforcement of this [Health] Act and the regulations." The Lieutenant Governor of Council is provided with the broad authority to make regulations for the "prevention, treatment, mitigation and suppression of disease," including regulations covering the isolation and quarantine, reporting by medical practitioners, and compulsory examination and treatment.

The Health Protection and Promotion Act, Ontario's most important source of public health authority, is intended to "provide for the organization and delivery of public health programs and services, the prevention of the spread of disease and the promotion and protection of the health of the people of Ontario." Under the Act, local boards of health are required to provide certain programs and services in health promotion, health protection, and disease and injury prevention. The Act provides for, among other things, the reporting of communicable diseases by physicians, hospital administrators, and school principals. It grants the provincial Minister of Health the authority to make regulations specifying diseases as communicable diseases. It authorizes the provincial Lieutenant Governor to make additional regulations governing the handling of bodies of persons who have died of a communicable disease and local medical officers to order isolation and treatment. It also addresses enforcement and penalties for persons who contravene an order or regulation.

Under the Health Protection and Promotion Act, a local medical officer of health (who must be a physician, has the requisite qualifications to hold the position, and is appointed by the Minister of Health) is vested with considerable authority with regard to communicable disease management. This authority may be executed through the use of a "written order," by which the medical officer of health may "require a person (or a class of persons) to take or to refrain from taking any action that is specified in the order in respect of a communicable disease." A medical officer of health's use of a written order to compel a person is discretionary, not obligatory. The use of a written order under these circumstances is conditioned upon reasonable and probable grounds, that (1) a communicable disease exists or may exist, or that there is an immediate risk of an outbreak of a communicable disease within the medical officer of health's jurisdiction; (2) the communicable disease presents a risk to the health of persons within the medical officer of health's jurisdiction; and (3) the requirements specified in the written order (to which requirements the person who is subject to the order must conform) are necessary to mitigate the health risk posed by the communicable disease.

A medical officer of health's written order may include isolation from other persons (note that the term "quarantine" is not used in the Health Protection and Promotion Act) and medical examination by a physician for purposes of determining communicable disease status. An order may also contain an instruction to act so as not to expose other persons to infection.179 For persons with a "virulent disease," care and treatment by a physician may be required. The Health Care Consent Act of 1996, which generally prohibits the administration of treatment in the absence of a patient's consent, does not apply to a physician's examination or care and treatment of a person pursuant to a written order.

A medical officer of health's written order may be directed to persons who reside or are present at or own or occupy certain premises or are engaged in or administer an enterprise or activity in a health unit served by the medical officer of health. An order may be directed to a class of persons instead of each member of a class of persons, but notice of the order must be provided to each class member where the provision of such a notice is practicable and can be carried out in a reasonable amount of time. If providing a written order to each individual is likely to cause a delay that could significantly increase the risk to the health of any person, then a general notice to the class may be provided through any "appropriate" communications media and posted at a location "most likely to bring the notice to the attention" of members of the class.

Parents or legal guardians must ensure compliance with orders directed to their children or wards who are less than 16 years of age. Orders must contain sufficient information so that members of the class understand that the order is directed to them, including: the reason for the order; the terms or requirements of the order, including the period within, by or for which compliance with the order is required; and information about where inquiries about the order may be directed, such as information about how to request a hearing. Persons to whom an order is directed, including members of a class who are the subject of an order, have a right to a hearing by the Board of Health under whose jurisdiction the medical officer of health's order was issued, but must request such a hearing in writing within 15 days of receiving the order. The Act provides additional details related to hearings, including requirements for extending a hearing, matters of evidence, and the appeal process.

In addition to serving an order, a medical officer of health may also require others to act with regard to a person who is the subject of the medical officer of health's order.

For example, a medical officer of health may direct persons who also work for or who are agents of the board of health for the medical officer of health's jurisdiction to take such actions as the medical officer of health may determine are necessary, if the "medical officer of health is of the opinion, [based] upon reasonable and probable grounds, that a communicable disease exists" and the person who is the subject of the order (1) has refused to comply or is not complying with an order; (2) is not likely to promptly comply with an order; (3) cannot be readily identified or located and as a result the order would not be promptly carried out; or (4) requests the assistance of the medical officer of health.

Special provisions may apply where persons fail to comply with orders with regard to the specifically enumerated virulent diseases. These circumstances would include a person's: (1) failure to isolate himself or herself and remain in isolation from other persons; (2) failure to submit to a medical examination; (3) failure to place himself or herself under the care and treatment of a physician; or (4) failure to conduct himself or herself in such a manner as to avoid exposing another person to infection. In such a case, a medical officer of health may apply to the Ontario Court of Justice for an order that the person be taken into custody and detained in a hospital or other facility; be examined by a physician to determine if the person is infected with a virulent disease; and, if found to be infected, be treated for the disease. It is interesting to note that a judge may not name a specific hospital or other facility in an order unless the court is satisfied that the hospital or facility is able to provide the requisite detention, care, and treatment. Applications to the court automatically stay or halt proceedings regarding the same matter before the Board of Health until the judge has disposed of the application.

An order made pursuant to section 35 of the Act provides "any person" (which term is not further defined or clarified) with the authority to locate and apprehend a person who is the subject of the order, or to deliver such a person to a hospital or facility named in the order. The order may also be provided to a law enforcement agency for purposes of locating, apprehending, and delivering the person who is the subject of the order. Without specifically indicating the class of persons to whom such authority is granted (but presumably meaning health care providers), an order issued under section 35 also provides the authority to "detain," "care for," "examine," and "treat the person" subject to the order consistent with "generally accepted medical practice."

The period of detention and treatment specified in an order may not exceed four months. However, if, upon motion by the medical officer of health, a court is satisfied that a person continues to be infected by a virulent disease and that the person's discharge would present "a significant risk to the health of the public," a judge of the Ontario Superior Court may by order extend a period of detention and treatment, including subsequent periods of detention and treatment, for up to four months. The Act provides that a person detained based upon a court order shall be released upon receipt of a medical officer of health's certificate authorizing release, and such a certificate must be issued as soon as the medical officer of health is "of the opinion that the person is no longer infected with a virulent disease or that release will not present a significant risk to public health." As with a written order prepared by a medical officer of health, the Health Care Consent Act, which generally prohibits the administration of treatment in the absence of a patient's consent, does not apply to a court order made under section 35.

An order issued by a judge of the Ontario Court of Justice may be appealed to the Ontario Superior Court of Justice; however, the appeal does not stay (or halt) the lower court's order unless a judge of the Superior Court of Justice so decides. In turn, a decision on a question of law made by the Superior Court of Justice may be appealed by any party to the lower court proceeding to the Ontario Court of Appeal, but no leave for the appeal may be granted unless a judge of the Court of Appeal determines that granting a leave is "essential in the public interest or for the due administration of justice."

Finally, the Health Protection and Promotion Act provides sanctions. Any person who fails to obey an order made under the Act, or otherwise contravenes a regulation promulgated under the Act, is guilty of an offense, and is liable upon conviction to a fine of not more than $5000 (Canadian) for every day or part of a day on which the offense occurs or continues.

British Columbia, the Canadian province with the second highest number of probable or suspect SARS cases (n=50, with 4 probable cases and 46 suspect cases), had many fewer SARS cases than did Ontario. No other province had any probable SARS cases. Alberta, New Brunswick, Prince Edward Island, and Saskatchewan had among them a dozen or so suspect cases.204 Because of the similarity of these provinces' public health laws to those of Ontario, we have omitted any discussion of these provinces' legal authority for quarantine and isolation. Nonetheless, each of the Canadian provinces' laws on matters related to public health, including regulations, provide provincial and local public health officials with the means to isolate and essentially quarantine persons with certain communicable diseases within their respective jurisdictions.

c. Local level

Local governments below the provincial level, such as municipal governments, may also be authorized by provincial law under certain conditions to act in the interest of public health. For example, the government of Ontario, under the Municipal Act, 2001, provides that "a municipality may regulate matters not specifically provided for by this [Municipal] Act or any other Act for purposes related to the health, safety and well-being of the inhabitants of the municipality." This is done largely through the use of "bylaws" passed by municipal (city) councils, sometimes upon the advice of municipal executive officers or entities. However, the Municipal Act only came into force on January 1, 2003, and it is not clear that any municipality in Ontario has taken action pursuant to this statute.

Other relevant law empowers specific municipalities. The City of Toronto Act, in addition to establishing the powers of the various governmental entities of the City of Toronto, provides for the establishment of Toronto's Board of Health and its jurisdiction, which is deemed a board of health established under Ontario's Health Protection and Promotion Act. The City of Toronto Act also requires the Toronto City Council to establish the Board's size through by-law and provide the Board with the staff, including public health nurses, necessary to carry out its functions. Those functions are established in the Health Protections and Promotion Act.208

4. SARS Response
a. Amendments to laws and guidance documents

On June 12, 2003, SARS was added to the Quarantine Act's schedule of infectious and contagious diseases, together with an established incubation period, thereby bringing SARS cases within the ambit of federal public health authority. As described above, the Act provides the Minister of Health with a multitude of powers related to the control of infectious disease. One important means of exercising public health authority in the wake of the SARS outbreak was to develop, coordinate, and provide specific guidance for both public and private entities, including public health workers and health professionals, in identifying and managing SARS cases and related health matters within their jurisdictions. At the federal level, the Department of Health has developed a large number of guidance documents intended to assist both public and private entities respond to specific SARS-related health matters. These include the following: definition of persons under SARS investigation; definition of a SARS case; interim guidelines for public health authorities in the management of probable and suspect SARS cases; definitions of geo-linked persons for hospital surveillance for SARS; public health protocol for persons meeting the "geo-linked person" definition; recommended laboratory testing for probable SARS cases and SARS contact cases; advisory for laboratory biosafety; guidelines for health care providers in the identification, diagnosis, and treatment of adults with SARS; guidelines for the use of respirators (masks) among health care workers; and recommendations and guidelines for public health officials for managing probable or suspect SARS cases among air travelers.

On April 1, 2003, British Columbia amended its Health Act Communicable Disease Regulation by means of an order-in-Council, adding SARS to the regulation's schedule of reportable communicable diseases. The province of Newfoundland and Labrador has a similar Communicable Diseases Act, and has also recently added SARS to the regulation's schedule of communicable diseases. By most appearances, the different provincial and local governments' responses have been proportionate to the prevalence of SARS cases within their respective jurisdictions, with little evidence of formal government activity in provinces or municipalities with no SARS cases. In contrast to other provincial and local governments—with the exception of British Columbia and to a lesser extent Alberta—only Ontario and the municipality of

Toronto have had to invoke their public health authority in a significant and large-scale manner to respond to the SARS outbreak within their jurisdictions.

There are many examples of efforts to provide guidance at the provincial and federal levels. In Ontario, the Ministry of Health and Long Term Care developed and distributed: a memorandum to hospital administrators regarding reportable disease requirements, including the reporting of SARS cases; a screening tool for all patients entering health care facilities, including a Chinese language version; a clinical decision guide for community clinicians in the diagnosis of SARS; directives and procedures for community health care agencies and other health care providers; and transition directives and procedures for acute care facilities, addressing matters such as screening, protective equipment, visitors, and physical plant. Other, extensive SARS-related information was made available to health professionals and the public through provincial and municipal government web sites, including web sites for the Ontario Ministry of Health, the Municipality of Toronto's Board of Health, and Toronto's Department of Community and Neighbourhood Services (which subsumes Toronto's Public Health Service).

In British Columbia, the Office of the Provincial Health Officer and a provincial SARS Scientific Committee developed and distributed: guidelines for managing SARS cases in acute care settings; a list of frequently asked questions together with detailed answers about SARS; and guidelines for infection control in the use of respiratory equipment. Similar to Ontario, other SARS-related information was made available by both provincial and municipal governments in British Columbia to health professionals and the public through web sites, including web sites for the British Columbia Ministry of Health Planning, the British Columbia Centre for Disease Control, and Vancouver Coastal Health (the municipality of Vancouver's public health authority, including the Vancouver Health Board).

b. Use of quarantine and isolation

On March 25, 2003, in the face of a rising number of SARS cases in the Toronto area, the Ontario government took the critical step of designating SARS as a reportable, communicable, and virulent disease under the province's Health Protection and Promotion Act, which authorized public health authorities to issue orders to detain and isolate persons for purposes of preventing SARS transmission. Eventually, about 30,000 persons in Toronto were quarantined. That number is similar to the number of persons who were quarantined due to the SARS outbreak in Beijing, China, but for the latter the number of probable SARS cases (2,500) was ten times larger than Toronto's (about 250).

Health facilities. The first use of isolation in Toronto occurred early in the SARS outbreak, when the physician treating the index case's son, Mr. T, had Mr. T placed in hospital isolation for suspected tuberculosis (at no time before Mr. T's death was his SARS established) and requested that other family members isolate themselves at home as they, too, might be at risk for tuberculosis infection. Unfortunately, these control measures occurred too late to contain the spread of SARS in Toronto. Mr. T, who had entered Scarborough Hospital through the emergency department, was left in the emergency department for 18-20 hours despite a physician's hospital admission order, and only later admitted to the hospital's Intensive Care Unit (ICU). When he was finally examined by a physician, a tuberculosis isolation order was issued and Toronto Public Health was notified as a routine matter of a possible tuberculosis case. During Mr. T's long wait in the Scarborough Hospital emergency department for admission to the ICU and his short time in the ICU before tuberculosis was suspected, other patients and staff were exposed to SARS. At the time there was no indication that these individuals were at risk of contracting or spreading any communicable disease, let alone SARS.

When tuberculosis was ruled out and public health officials and physicians began to understand the implications of Mr. T's case, steps were taken to remove other members of Mrs. K's family, some of whom were reporting illness, to negative pressure isolation rooms in other area hospitals. These steps undoubtedly limited the spread of SARS. Combining the information from the WHO's international health alert for atypical pneumonia with reports of the Scarborough Hospital cases, both Toronto Public Health and provincial public health authorities activated their emergency response plans.

A "Code Orange" (which required all area hospitals to go into emergency mode) was issued, under which area hospitals were required to suspend non-essential services, limit visitors, issue protective equipment for staff, and establish special isolation units for "potential SARS patients." Asymptomatic contacts of SARS patients were not isolated within health facilities, but were asked to adhere to a 10-day home quarantine.

The risk of acquiring SARS was greatest for persons (staff, patients, and visitors) within rather than outside of health care facilities, including doctors' offices; health care workers accounted for over 40% of all SARS patients in Toronto. Tragically, the early SARS patients who were seen in health care facilities were simply not identified in time to implement more rigorous infection control procedures. Moreover, it is not clear that health care workers were always provided with uniform or consistent advice or guidelines regarding the quarantine or isolation of persons with or suspected of having SARS, that adequate protective equipment was provided to health care workers within these hospital or clinic settings, or that health care administrators or workers were diligent about adhering to infection control precautions or procedures. Concerns about a lack of uniform guidance for quarantine were expressed by an ad hoc Scientific Advisory Committee of volunteer experts, which found that "different public health units seemed to have different thresholds for the use of quarantine."

Directives issued by Ontario health authorities instructed hospitals to isolate all patients with fever and respiratory symptoms in the hospital or in the hospital emergency department until SARS had been ruled out. Most hospitals took special precautions for inpatients with respiratory symptoms suggestive of infectious diseases. In Phase I of the Toronto SARS outbreak (March 13-25, 2003), over 20 Toronto area hospitals admitted and cared for SARS patients. No single facility was designated as a "SARS hospital," because both provincial and Toronto area officials feared that such a step would overwhelm the facility so designated. For this reason, capacity for SARS clinical management, including isolation of SARS patients and adequate infection control measures, was built into multiple facilities throughout the Greater Toronto area. Two hospitals (Sunnybrook and Woman's) in the Greater Toronto area appeared to carry the largest volume of SARS patients during Phase I. Unfortunately, many of these two hospitals' physicians with relevant expertise or experience in SARS clinical management were themselves ill or in quarantine. Despite the hospitals' requests for staff support, other Toronto area hospitals were either unable or unwilling to provide assistance. Needed support was obtained only after provincial authorities retained a private placement agency to help with recruitment of health care workers.

In Phase II of the Toronto SARS outbreak (May 23-June 30, 2003), four hospitals (later termed the SARS Alliance) were designated as SARS facilities. The "Code Orange" described above for Toronto area hospitals was later extended to all Ontario hospitals, meaning they, too, were required to suspend non-essential services, limit visitors, create isolation units for SARS patients, and issue protective equipment (gowns, masks, and goggles) for exposed staff. Some concern was expressed over whether the Code Orange was justified or overly broad.

Airports, ports and other entry points. No persons in transit into or out of Canada were actually quarantined or isolated, although clearly the federal government has the authority to take such measures in appropriate cases. In 2002, Health Canada transferred its airport quarantine responsibilities to the Canada Customs and Revenue Agency, but at the time of the SARS outbreak, neither Health Canada nor the Customs and Revenue Agency appeared prepared to discharge their quarantine responsibilities under the federal Quarantine Act Regulations, which soon after the SARS outbreak in Canada had been amended to include SARS. For ships, particularly cruise ships, Health Canada's protocol for handling SARS cases was not released until mid-June, after the SARS outbreak had begun to fade.

SARS screening for airline passengers took place at Canadian airports, but this screening relied primarily upon information cards that were distributed to and completed by both incoming and outbound passengers. In-person screening questions and secondary assessments were conducted only as needed. Thermal scanners were used in a pilot project at the Toronto and Vancouver (British Columbia) airports. As of August 27, 2003, 6.5 million screening transactions had taken place at Canadian airports, with about

9,100 passengers referred for further SARS assessment by screening nurses or quarantine officers. None of the passengers who underwent further assessment was found to meet the criteria for a probable or suspect SARS case. The pilot thermal scanner screened 2.4 million passengers, with 832 referred for further assessments, and none met the criteria for a probable or suspect SARS case.

Workplace and home quarantine. In Toronto, home and workplace quarantines were often imposed for what were definitive "contact" cases, meaning cases in which persons were known to have been in close physical proximity to a probable SARS case with inadequate or no protection from possible exposure. Contact cases included family and household members of SARS patients, hospital visitors and other non-SARS patients within hospitals who may have been exposed to SARS patients, health care staff who provided treatment to SARS patients without adequate protective equipment, and persons at workplaces who may have been exposed to co-workers with SARS. Provided they were timely identified and contacted, these persons were urged to remain at home for a 10-day period, with monitoring, usually by telephone, by a local public health worker.

5. Coordination Issues

It should be noted that once the provincial emergency was declared by the Ontario Prime Minister's office, provincial authorities assumed the lead for delivery of all main SARS messages to the public. However, this public information function was often delegated by provincial authorities to the Toronto municipal government. One concern among some commentators was that there were too many "talking heads," including government officials, whose opinions on the SARS outbreak appeared to diverge. According to these critics, there often appeared to be no coherent official or governmental communications strategy aimed at "dispelling the sense of deepening crisis" posed by the SARS outbreak. Interestingly, one of the most apt characterizations of the capacity of the federal and provincial governments to work collectively in their response to the SARS outbreak was provided by the Canadian federal government: Only weak mechanisms exist in public health for collaborative decision making or systematic data sharing across governments. Furthermore, governments have not adequately sorted out their roles and responsibilities during a national health crisis. The SARS outbreak has highlighted many areas where inter-jurisdictional collaboration is suboptimal; so far from being seamless, the public health system showed a number of serious gaps.

Given the acknowledged deficiencies in cross-jurisdictional coordination in the response to the SARS outbreak, it is quite likely that the coordination with the international community and the U.S. with respect to the SARS outbreak could likewise be considered suboptimal. As the report further noted, it "is unlikely that most other provinces [aside from Ontario] are in a better position, and the federal capacity to support one or more provinces facing simultaneous health crises is limited."

6. Public Reaction

The federal, provincial, and local governments used a variety of means to convey up-to-date information regarding the SARS outbreak to the public, as well as to health professionals. Features of the public health education and communication measures taken by the government generally and by public health authorities specifically included regular updates to their own websites. Additionally, Toronto Public Health established a SARS Hotline. Hotline staff, primarily public health nurses, provided callers with health information and counseling and case and contact identification, and the recognition and follow-up of emerging issues in SARS-affected institutions and communities. At the height of the outbreak the Hotline had 46 staff on the day shift and 34 staff on the evening shift, including individuals with special language skills. The Hotline received over 300,000 calls between March 15 and June 24, 2003, with a peak of 47,567 calls in a single day. Most calls were complex, with three or more issues identified per call, including self reports of illness or SARS contact, needed access to emergency supplies of food, masks, and other supplies, and concerns about loss of income, loss of housing, and business failure. In addition, the agency convened local community meetings and conducted other community outreach to address specific concerns in schools, workplaces, and among community groups.

Toronto Public Health translated updated SARS information into 14 languages and posted this information on the City of Toronto's official web site. Both Health Canada and the Ontario Ministry of Health also set up and maintained web sites for the dissemination of SARS-related information for members of the public and health professionals. In British Columbia, SARS-related information was made available to both the public and health professionals through web sites for the British Columbia Ministry of Health Planning, the British Columbia Centre for Disease Control, and the Vancouver Coastal Health authority.

Both federal (the Quarantine Act) and provincial laws (e.g., Ontario's Health Protection and Promotion Act, British Columbia's Health Act) regarding quarantine and/or isolation authorize—and may even require—law enforcement agencies to assist public health authorities to effect the quarantine and/or isolation of persons subject to quarantine orders. During the SARS outbreak in Toronto, law enforcement personnel were used to enforce the quarantine of patients with SARS at area hospitals, serve orders as needed, and conduct "spot checks" on persons who were quarantined. On at least one occasion, law enforcement personnel were also used to investigate and try to apprehend and charge a person who broke quarantine and subsequently infected a co-worker, but the person died from the illness. Almost all persons who were asked to submit to quarantine did so voluntarily. In only 27 cases was a written order mandating quarantine issued under Ontario's Health Protection and Promotion Act.

Certain actions taken by the federal and provincial governments may have had the effect of increasing public acceptance of SARS-control measures. For example, the federal government has amended its employment insurance regulations under the Employment Insurance Act to remove the waiting period for sickness benefits for certain persons placed under SARS quarantine, as well as to remove the requirement that certain persons under SARS quarantine obtain a medical certificate as a condition of receiving sickness benefits. The federal government also provided special employment insurance coverage for health care workers who were unable to work because of SARS and who were not otherwise eligible for benefits under the government's Employment Insurance Act, as well as tax and mortgage payment relief to persons who were facing difficulties making tax or mortgage payments because of SARS. The Ontario government enacted the SARS Assistance and Recovery Strategy Act, which provides certain qualified persons with unpaid leave in the event the person is unable to work due to a SARS-related event, such as being under individual medical investigation or having to provide care for or assistance to a person due to a SARS-related matter.

7. Current Situation

The use of quarantine and isolation measures in Toronto cannot be characterized as a uniform, coordinated (and perhaps optimal) response to the SARS outbreak, which is not surprising given the highly decentralized way in which public health functions in Canada are organized. The recently released federal Canadian government report mentioned earlier, Learning from SARS: Renewal of Public Health Canada, appears to confirm this, stating, "[t]he SARS experience illustrated that Canada is not adequately prepared to deal with a true pandemic." The report suggests comprehensive, large-scale reorganization of public health systems within Canada, including the prospect of establishing a national, federal public health agency with the requisite authority to respond to disease outbreaks and emergencies similar to SARS, and with appropriate linkages to other government departments and agencies engaged in public health activities. However, concerning public health activities at the local level, it is argued by officials of Toronto Public Health that at least with respect to Toronto, the "isolation of people who were symptomatic with SARS (i.e., "cases") served to protect the public from infection by separating those who were ill from those who were well." The same might be said of the quarantine of persons who were not symptomatic with SARS but who may have been at increased risk of acquiring or transmitting SARS.

11.3.2   China

As described in the introduction to this section, SARS originated in the Guangdong region of China, and quickly escalated to a global outbreak.

The chart below, Fig. 11.4, describes the timing of China's disclosure of the SARS outbreak in relation to the number of new cases:

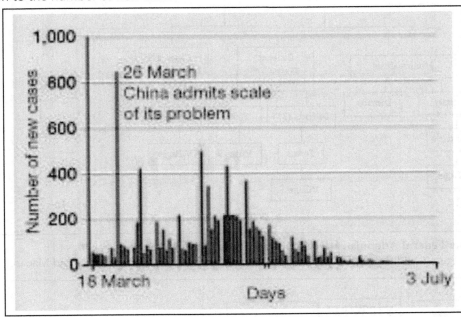

Fig. 11.4
Number of new cases in relation to disclosure by China

China has a civil law system of government, largely driven by codes, not judicial interpretations of cases and laws, like common law countries. Because of China's largely decentralized national government, as depicted in the organizational chart in Fig. 11.5, below, communication and coordination was a difficult, if not impossible, process in terms of a rapid response from China during the fast-moving SARS outbreak. The four major cities are the primary sources of regulation for their populations, and a weak, central government does not coordinate or make uniform many regulatory requirements, which left China in a weak position for mounting a national response to the outbreak.

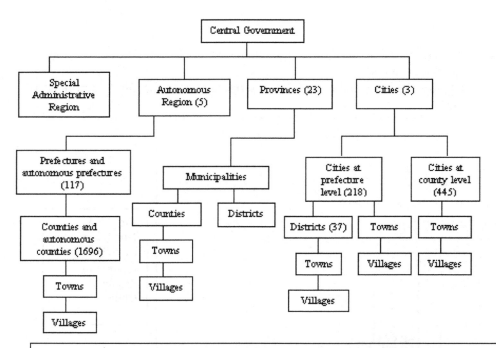

Fig. 11.5   China Federal Administrative Civil Law Organization. Four cities: Cities (4): Tianjin, Shanghai Chongqing and Beiging; Two Special Administrative Regions: Hong Kong and Macao.

Fig. 11.6 Typical political cartoons during the SARS outbreak. China was criticized for waiting to tell the international community about the SARS outbreak, and this is one of several political cartoons which followed. This probably led the WHO to develop significant changes in the International Health

The U.S. Centers for Diseases Control and Prevention (CDC) commissioned a report on lessons-learned from the SARS incident. The following excerpt from the report outlines the actions taken by China:

B. China (People's Republic of China)

1. Introduction

The first case of what was reported among scientists as "atypical pneumonia," later determined through blood and other diagnostic tests done in 2003 to be severe acute respiratory syndrome (SARS), occurred in China in Guangdong Province on November 22, 2002, in the city of Foshan. The second case occurred in the city of Heyuan on December 17, 2002. The third case was in Zhongshan on December 26, 2002. The first official report to public health officials of an atypical pneumonia was not made until January 21, 2003. It is not clear if any report was sent to the central government as this was near the time of the Chinese New Year. At this point, over half the clinically recognized cases (13) in Zhongshan were among health care workers. The further development of the SARS epidemic in China will be described in Section 4 below.

To learn from the use of quarantine and isolation in the PRC during the outbreak of SARS, it is necessary to understand the legal structure supporting the public health system. Three contextual factors are especially significant. First, the population density of the PRC has a dramatic impact on living conditions. As of 2001, the population of the PRC was nearly 1.2 billion people living in a land area about the size of Canada that has, by comparison, 31.5 million people. From a public health perspective, this population density means that most individuals in the PRC live in multiple-family dwellings. Beijing, where over 50% of the cases of SARS were reported, has a population of nearly 13 million. As a result, "When one talks about China, the numbers will always appear large, particularly to Westerners raised in the United States."

Second, the legal system of modern China is closer to the legal systems of France, Italy, or Germany than the common law-based legal systems of the United States, Canada, and England. In addition, the legal structure governing public health in the PRC was refined under a peculiar form of socialism that is undergoing change. Drawing "lessons learned" from the PRC requires an understanding of comparative law, an admittedly under-developed area in American legal education and public health law practice.

Third, globalization, particularly over the past quarter of a century, has caused the legal system and the public health infrastructure of the PRC to change. Under the socialist regime led by Mao Tse-tung, the PRC made considerable efforts to deal with the conditions leading to the spread of infectious diseases such as cholera. From 1946-1976, life expectancy increased from 35 years to 68 years without any appreciable increase in per capita income. Market-oriented reforms during the 1980s and 1990s led to increased wealth and some dramatic improvements in health status. For instance, during the 1990s, the infant mortality rate in urban areas dropped from 17.3 to 11.8 per 1,000. Health status has also improved in rural areas, although the rural population suffers from general disadvantage vis-à-vis the urban population. For example, between 1991 and 2000, the drop in the infant mortality rate in rural areas was from 58.0 to 37.7. At the same time, these market-oriented reforms have also led to income inequalities comparable to the United States that translate into insecure or inadequate access to health care for much of the population. The percentage of employment-based health insurance declined from 68% to 53% in urban areas from 1993-1998. In rural areas, insurance coverage that had been based on a collectivist economy nearly collapsed in the 1980s. Only 8% of the rural population had health insurance by 1998. While gains in health status and wealth have enhanced the capacity of the PRC to deal effectively with many infectious diseases, it now faces the challenge of dealing with chronic conditions among its population.

2. Political and Legal Systems

In the case of the PRC, familiarity with recent changes in the legal culture is key to understanding the current political and legal situation. There was no formal organization of lawyers in the PRC as recently as 1959. The Ministry of Justice had been abolished, and those few law schools remaining open following various political upheavals after 1949 could best be characterized as state sponsored schools of political administration. The few students enrolled in these so-called law schools received very little in the way of professional legal training because law was viewed, at the time, as irrelevant to the future of the PRC. The reestablishment of legal institutions was part of the economic, political, and cultural transformation taking place in the PRC in the 1980s.

The government began to reassemble the legal system in 1979. The Ministry of Justice was re-established and law schools were re-opened. Over 20 universities and institutes offered some form of four-year undergraduate legal training by 1982. A massive codification project paralleled the re-opening and redevelopment of law schools. A seven-year process of discussion and study involving jurists and political officials led to the adoption of a Code of Civil Procedure in 1986. A host of new substantive codes were enacted: the Marriage Law (1980); Economic Contract Law (1981); Trademark Law (1982); Patent Law (1984); and Inheritance Law (1985). The basic public health statute that provided the framework for the response to SARS, the Prevention and Treatment of Infectious Disease Law, discussed in detail in Section 3, was enacted in 1989.

International law was a major focus of legal scholars and legal reforms during the early 1980s. A planning conference on the study of law listed international law as a priority area for China in March 1979. Not a single article on international law was published in China in 1979; over 100 articles were published by 1984, and 20 senior Chinese jurists collaborated in publishing a definitive textbook on international law in 1981. This build up of legal capacity was important as the PRC began in the 1980s to participate in international institutions such as the International Monetary Fund and the World Bank. An indication of China's growing reliance on law and legal institutions during 1980s to deal with its future, as well as forces outside of China, is illustrated by the negotiations with Great Britain over the future of Hong Kong in 1983 and 1984.

The government of the PRC rests on a four-fold division at each of three hierarchical levels: national or central government, provincial government, and local 62 units. This structure has significant impact on how political and legal authority is distributed and implemented. This method of organizing governmental functions should be understood on its own terms, with no assumption that there are precise equivalents in China to the familiar legislative, executive, and judicial functions. The importance of this point will become clear in the analysis of the government's exercise of control over the movement of persons, goods, animals, and the provisions of services in the name of public health.

The national government consists of four institutions—the National People's Congress (NPC), the State Council, the Supreme People's Court, and the Supreme People's Procuratorate—that are woven into a system of authority by provisions of the Constitution and statutes of the PRC. The NPC theoretically has ultimate legislative authority, including the power to amend the Constitution. This body, consisting of approximately 2,000 representatives, only meets once a year for two or three weeks.

During these yearly sessions, the NPC can enact basic statutory provisions governing the country. The Standing Committee has the authority to "amend" laws enacted by the NPC and to enact other forms of legislation, but not to amend the Constitution. As a subsidiary body of the NPC, the Standing Committee's legislative enactments are likely to be in accordance with the prevailing wishes of the NPC. The major codes of the 1980s were enacted through a combination of actions by the Standing Committee and the NPC. The Standing Committee enacted the Prevention and Treatment of Infectious Disease Law in 1989.

The State Council, headed by the Premier, is the major administrative arm of the central government. The various ministries, such as the ministries of Health, Justice, and Public Security, are part of the State Council. Within the framework of statutes enacted by the NPC or the Standing Committee, these ministries have the authority to enact regulations governing their respective areas of responsibility.

Judicial authority is lodged in the Supreme People's Court in two forms. First is the power to interpret what the law means in a particular case before the court. Second is the power to give advisory opinions to provide guidance to lower courts. On the one hand, some advisory opinions might limit the authority of lower courts to act, and thus remove constraints on individual actions. On the other hand, this advisory power could be used to strengthen the power of state entities, as was the case during the SARS outbreak (see Section 4 below).

There are no provisions in the Constitution specifically authorizing courts to protect the "rights" of individuals against the state. An individual's ability to challenge a state ruling or action is governed by statutory enactments, rather than constitutional documents. Under the Administrative Procedure Law enacted by the NPC in 1989, courts can examine the legality of certain administrative actions. Article 2 of that statute specifically provides for a citizen or a legal corporation to challenge a concrete action of a governmental body, but the citizen or the corporation cannot challenge the administrative regulations.

The Procuratorate, the fourth institution in the PRC system, was re-established by the Constitution of 1982 as an independent entity for supervising a number of governmental functions: (1) prosecuting crimes; (2) supervising the police and prisons; (3) representing the government in civil and administrative matters; (4) protecting the right of individuals to lodge complaints against state officials who violate the law as well as deal with citizen accusations against fellow citizens; and (5) appealing sentences and verdicts in criminal cases. Conceptually, the Procuratorate is viewed as being independent of the Ministry for Public Security, the major law enforcement agency or police, for instance, and must carefully investigate before it acts. In theory, the Procuratorate collaborates with other agencies, such as the police, even though the Procuratorate has responsibility for determining the legality of the actions of those agencies. The authority to prosecute crimes is thus not an executive function, as it might be viewed in a common law system, but a purely legal function. The broad public functions of the Procuratorate in the government allowed it to participate along with the Supreme People's Court in an important ruling during the SARS outbreak.

These four institutions share legal authority at the central level based on the theory that the law is embodied in certain specific legislative enactments, be they statutes or constitutional provisions. Individual rights as such are given appropriate legal protection by ensuring that government action adheres to legal requirement. Thus, the notion of equality of all citizens before the law exists in the Chinese legal system, supported by a formal constitutional provision, section 2 of Article 33. The use of governmental authority to constrain the movement of individuals, goods, or animals is thus mediated by a balance of power between four institutions—with the fourth branch, the Procuratorate—having an obligation to work with the other three institutions.

The four-part division of political and legal authority is reproduced at the next level of government—the provincial level. (For convenience, the level of government directly responsible to the central government is called the "provincial level" because the PRC's 23 provinces are the principal entities at this level. But it is important to note that four municipalities— Tianjin, Shanghai, Chongqing, and Beijing—have the same legal authority as any one of the 23 provinces, and thus have their own legislative, judicial, administrative, and procuracy units. Furthermore, the five autonomous regions—Inner Mongolia, Tibet, Xinjiang, Guangxi, and Ningxia—have a greater degree of control than the 23 provinces or the four municipalities, but nonetheless are thought of as being at the same level vis-à-vis the central government. The relationship among these various units is hierarchical with authority flowing from the central government downwards. Finally, the two special administrative units of Hong Kong and Macao have greater authority than the provinces.

The local level consists of entities akin to counties and cities within the provinces, and within the cities, districts. Essentially, the horizontal structure of administrative agencies, legislative bodies, courts, and the Procuratorate is replicated at the local level. Some of the People's Congresses at the local level appear to have legislative authority. Certain big cities clearly have legislative authority, including the capitals of the provinces, for example, the capital of Guangdong province, Guangzhou. Some special economic zones, such as Shenzhen, Zhuhai, Xiamen, and those big cities approved by the State Council, also have legislative authority. Thus, when asking the question of what regulations might be in place to control infectious diseases, one should consider the level of regulations—central, provincial, or local.

3. Public Health Structure and Laws

The first principle underlying the structure of the Law on Prevention and Treatment of Infectious Disease of 1989 (Prevention and Treatment Law266) is that prevention and control methods are disease-specific. Article 3 classifies diseases into three basic categories: Type A, the most deadly of infectious diseases historically in China, which includes pestilence and cholera; Type B, which includes serious infectious diseases, such as hepatitis, dysentery, typhoid fever and paratyphoid, AIDS, gonorrhea, syphilis, poliomyelitis, epidemic encephalitis B; and Type C, which includes tuberculosis, measles, leprosy, influenza, mumps, and rubella. Not surprisingly, when there is an A or B type epidemic, Articles 24 and 26 of the law provide for the use of emergency measures including the quarantine of people, goods, and transportation vehicles and the declaration of epidemic zones with special control measures. At the most basic level, the first question for public health law analysis in the PRC is: what type of infectious disease is in need of control or prevention measures?

The second principle underlying the Prevention and Treatment Law is that the infectious disease categories are dynamic and subject to change. Thus, Article 3 also provides mechanisms for changing the classification of a particular infectious disease. The State Council as a whole can change the classification of Type A diseases without having to go back to a legislative body. The Ministry of Health, an agency within the State Council, has the authority to change the classifications of types B and C diseases. This built-in flexibility implies that for new infectious diseases, the question is: which instrument of government has the legal authority to classify the infectious disease? More important, the legislation is based on the assumption that the relationship among the three tiers of government is hierarchical. Thus, national legislation can impose duties on provincial and local health departments without encountering problems of federalism. The general rules found in Chapter 1 contain specific provisions (in Article 7) making all units of government and all individuals subject to inspection and verification of infectious diseases by public health authorities. Furthermore, under the same provisions, any individual or unit of government can report violations of the Prevention and Treatment Law or any regulations adopted under the Law's authority. These broad obligations under the public health law are constrained by the system of disease classification and the provisions for actually announcing the existence of an epidemic.

The remaining chapters contain provisions on the prevention of diseases (Chapter 2); the mechanisms for reporting epidemic situations (Chapter 3); the control measures that can be taken (Chapter 4); the supervision of those measures (Chapter 5); penalties for violations (Chapter 6); and authority to adopt implementing regulations (Chapter 7). Health care workers and those engaged in disease prevention are required to report infectious diseases to local health departments in accordance with the Ministry of Health's regulations. Local public health officials are required to report the existence of the infectious disease to the local government and the higher levels of health administration. Both health care workers and public health officials are prohibited from giving false information or concealing information regarding infectious diseases.

Violations of any of these reporting and disclosure obligations can lead to a variety of sanctions under Article 39. Once this information has been reported to the central government, the Ministry of Health can either announce the existence of an epidemic or authorize officials at lower levels to make the announcement. This level of detail for how public health information should flow is an example of the legal system's adaptation to the complex hierarchical and horizontal political structure.

Quarantine and isolation of individuals with various types of infectious diseases, and those suspected of having those diseases, are authorized in Article 24. There are specific provisions allowing the local government to restrict assemblies, to close factories, stores, and schools, and to temporarily confiscate residential dwellings in the event of a properly declared emergency or epidemic. Provincial governments have the authority to stop the movement of goods and people during a declared outbreak. The law even has provisions dealing with human resource requirements during an outbreak (Article 27), the handling of corpses infected with diseases (Article 28), and for requiring pharmaceutical companies to supply medicine in a timely fashion (Article 29). A host of prevention measures are outlined in Chapter 2 (Articles 9-20) that include everything from vaccination to sewage and designation of special hospitals for the treatment of infectious diseases.

This elaborate set of provisions for prevention and control of infectious diseases also contains measures for enforcement, ranging from administrative penalties (Articles 32-34 in Chapter 5) to fines and criminal sanctions (Articles 35-39 in Chapter 6). Article 40 allows the Ministry of Health and, by implication, its counterparts at the two lower levels of government, to engage in ongoing development of public health measures by an explicit provision authorizing the enactment of implementing regulations. There have been several implementing regulations over the past decade that provide a sense of the range of regulatory activity at the central level of government. The Ministry of Health issued regulations on the prevention and treatment of tuberculosis in 1991, and on statistical reporting in 1992. In general, the regulations provide a modernized legal infrastructure for implementing public health measures. Whether the existing public health law structure was adequate to deal with a deadly infectious agent of unknown origins such as SARS remains open to debate. It is clear that a host of public health laws were adopted in response to SARS. On the one hand, one could surmise that political leadership in the PRC, perhaps in response to international pressure, considered the existing laws inadequate. On the other hand, the existing public health laws provided the infrastructure for contact tracing and other control measures that helped to stop the spread of SARS in China. It is thus possible that emerging microbial infections require a new approach to public health law in China and elsewhere that builds on, but moves beyond, established measures.

Legal analysis with respect to China should not be limited to the national level. A few provinces, such as Sichuan (1985), had some form of public health measures even before 1989.274 With the passage of the Prevention and Treatment Law in 1989, more provinces (Hebei, Jiangsu, and Heilongjiang) enacted regulations on infectious disease control. Other provincial level governments, such as the city of Tianjin, issued a special notice on epidemic situations requiring any citizen or public health staff member to report an outbreak of a disease of unknown origin. Shanghai passed the Punishment for Supervision of Infectious Diseases Prevention and Treatment Law in 1995 (amended and reissued in 1997); this provincial law sets the administrative punishment for violations of the national law. Finally, at the local level, a few cities passed measures in the 1990s designed to implement the Prevention and Treatment Law: Guangzhou City of Guangdong Province; Hefei and Bangbu City of Anhui Province; Guiyang of Guizhou Province; Qingdao Municipality of Shandong Province; and Huhehote of Inner Mongolia.

Given the size of China, provincial and local measures to support public health measures exist in only a small percentage of the total number of provinces and local units. It is impossible to determine if this small percentage is a function of lack of interest on the part of lower levels of government or the effective "preemption" of the field by the Prevention and Treatment Law. The latter explanation seems most plausible, because the hierarchical legal structure allows for the central government to impose obligations on local officials and the basic public health statute is relatively recent. It cannot be determined at this time whether this hierarchical and horizontal method of authorizing legal authority has enough flexibility for an infectious disease outbreak in modern China that now includes a major world transportation hub—Hong Kong.

4. Response to SARS
According to WHO, by July 14, 2003, there were reported cases of SARS in nearly every province and autonomous region in the PRC. Only Hainan Province, Guizhou Province, Yunnan Province, Qinghai Province, Xinjiang, and Tibet Autonomous Regions did not report cases of SARS. Among those 26

provinces, Beijing, Guangdong Province, Shanxi Province, Inner Mongolia Autonomous Region, Hebei Province, and Tianjin were the most heavily affected areas. It is important to avoid "hindsight bias" in understanding the development and spread of SARS in China.

The investigation into the Zongshan outbreak led to several hypotheses by January 21, 2003. First, the outbreak was caused by an unknown pathogen, probably of a viral nature. Second, the disease was infectious, and family members and health care workers who had contact with an infected person were at the greatest risks. Scientists investigating the outbreak in Zongshan recognized the importance of documenting how to treat and prevent the spread of the disease and recommended that a case reporting system for the unknown disease be established.

Chinese scientists continued to engage in various methods of contact tracing and epidemiological studies in Guangdong Province. On January 31, 2002, the eve of the Chinese New Year, the first case of the unknown illness outside of the hospital setting appeared in the city of Guangzhou. Apparently this patient had visited Zongshan during the holiday travel period and was later determined to have infected more than 100 people before precautionary measures could be taken. When this patient was admitted to a hospital on January 31, over 30 members of the medical staff were infected within 24 hours. When the patient was transferred to another hospital from February 1-8, he infected 26 members of that hospital staff before being transferred to the Guangzhou Infectious Disease Hospital, where apparently some precautions were taken to deal with a person with an infectious disease. In the meantime, 19 family members and relatives of the patient became infected. Between November 16, 2002 and February 9, 2003, there were 305 cases, later classified as SARS according to WHO standards, with five deaths.

At the peak of the outbreak there were 50 new SARS cases reported on February 9, 30 reported on February 12, and five reported on February 19, 2003. It is possible that the declining figures were caused by precautions starting to arrest the spread of the disease. Scientists from the University of Hong Kong began an investigation into the outbreak in Guangdong Province on February 11, 2003. (At about the same time, one of the physicians who had treated patients with the unknown illness in Guangdong Province made a trip to Hong Kong in order to attend a wedding.) The research team started by asking whether there had been some type of transfer of the avian influenza (H5N1) virus to humans as in 1997. The team obtained 18 patient samples on February 12, and an additional 22 patient samples on February 18. These early efforts focusing on the H5N1 influenza virus led to the isolation of the influenza virus in one Hong Kong family and in one of the later-determined SARS patients from Guangdong Province. Although the scientists conducting the Guangdong Province investigation readily admit they failed to isolate the coronavirus, their efforts contributed to the work being done in Hong Kong and elsewhere. These collaborative efforts eventually led to the isolation of the coronavirus in cell cultures from a nurse, hospital clerk, and physician.

Once the viral nature of the symptoms health care workers had been treating was established, the investigation turned to determining where this new coronavirus—a family of infections common among several domestic and wild animals and in humans— came from. The isolation of the genome of the virus through international scientific collaboration played an important role in the ability to work backwards from cases to the source(s). The following facts about the early cases supported the hypothesis that the virus originated in some wild animals: early cases developed independently, in five different cities in Guangdong Province; early patients were more likely to report living near agricultural markets, so called "wet markets," where wild and domestic animals are slaughtered and sold as food; and 39% (9 of 23) of the early cases were individuals employed as food handlers in these markets.

Accordingly, eight different species of live domestic and wild animals being sold in markets in Shenzhen, a city in Guangdong Province, were tested on May 7, 2003. Two of the species were found to contain the same virus as the human patients. Thus, this laboratory work in China, in conjunction with the work coordinated by the WHO, established a baseline of scientific knowledge about the disease, and more importantly what was not known about the disease. With this growing level of knowledge (and uncertainty) about the nature of SARS, the Chinese were able to establish a number of specific control measures restricting the movement of individuals, goods, and animals in the spring of 2003. Meanwhile, the disease had spread through the country, with Beijing having more than 5,000 cases of SARS.

The legal and political response to the spread of SARS was primarily national in scope. After April 2003, a number of agencies within the State Council took actions to control the spread of SARS. From a legal perspective, the most significant of these actions was the Ministry of Health's approval of the listing of SARS as an infectious disease on April 8, 2003.280 As a result of this action by the Ministry of Health, all the provisions of the Prevention and Treatment Law could be used to control the spread of SARS through Decree 84 from the Ministry of Health. That notice informed all public health departments and related agencies throughout the country of the listing of SARS and ordered the following four measures: (1) local governments should inspect and report the number of SARS cases on a daily basis and all medical institutions should take control measures when encountering patients suspected of having SARS; (2) SARS patients and those suspected of having SARS should be isolated for treatment and those having close contacts with either patients or suspects should be monitored; (3) the control measures under Article 24 of the Prevention and Treatment Law were authorized as necessary; (4) use of communication and education to achieve compliance with control measures was also authorized. Given the vertical integration of health departments, this action by the Ministry of Health was the legal authority for all the measures taken to control SARS, including the use of quarantine and isolation.

After this notice and authorization, a number of other actions were taken by the central government. The Ministries of Health, Finance, Railway, and Transportation and Civil Aviation took steps on April 12, 2003 to prevent the spread of SARS through the country's transportation system. A government-issued notice instructed various governmental units to cooperate in order to prevent the spread of SARS through the transportation system. The local governments, for instance, were instructed to establish quarantine stations at railway stations and airports for people suspected of having SARS. The transportation agencies were instructed to enact emergency procedures for handling SARS patients and those suspected of having SARS. Public health agencies were to provide the necessary training of the medical staffs and technical support to the local governmental and transportation officials. Once a person with SARS was discovered in a vehicle or transportation station, those facilities and vehicles were to be disinfected immediately after the person or persons were removed. Furthermore, the operators of the transportation systems were to discourage people with SARS from traveling and train their respective staffs about ways of preventing the spread of SARS. The State Council enacted regulations for the Handling of Public Health Emergencies (Public Health Emergencies) on May 9, 2003. This ordinance differed conceptually from the Prevention and Treatment Law, which sought to classify infectious diseases into three categories. The Public Health Emergencies ordinance recognizes that public health situations can arise unexpectedly from mass food or occupational poisoning and other sources, and that diseases of unknown etiology exist. Once an emergency as defined in the ordinance exists, the State Council and the provincial and local government must develop a coordinated approach to handling the emergency.

Provisions in the new ordinance referring specifically to "diseases of unknown origins" appear to reflect some of the "lessons learned" from the prior five months in China and elsewhere. For instance, provincial and local governments were required to report the possible occurrence of infectious diseases of unknown origin to the central public health administration within one hour under Article 19. Health care institutions were required to report to the appropriate level of government under Article 20. Local government units were directed to investigate these reports under Article 22, as well as fulfilling their own obligations under Article 19. Other provisions of the new ordinance require any unit of government or person to report the neglect of disease reporting duties by various instrumentalities of government under Article 24, as well as the neglect of obligations to provide timely information about the emergencies under Article 25.

This highly detailed set of provisions for dealing with emergencies, ideally based on the best scientific information available, is reinforced by a long list of sanctions for violations by public officials in Articles 45-52. Failures of local public health officials to carry out their duties could lead to demotions or dismissals and to criminal charges in some limited circumstances. Similar provisions establish possible sanctions for officials at the higher levels of government for dereliction of duties under the new ordinance. Health care and sanitation officials had a separate provision that allowed for the revocation of their licenses to practice as well as job sanctions and possible criminal sanctions (Article 50). Finally, there were sanctions for failure to report and cooperate on the part of officials, and sanctions applicable to any person who spreads rumors, raises prices, or misleads customers during an emergency (Article 52).

The Ministry of Health used its authority under the ordinance on Public Health Emergencies and the Treatment and Prevention Law to take two important steps. First, the Ministry issued a complex set of regulations dealing with the prevention and treatment of SARS. The effect of this regulation was to establish SARS, an infectious disease of unknown origins, as one of the statutory infectious diseases for which control measures are permissible. In addition to the measures regarding sanitation, there are several provisions dealing with health education and what is called "propaganda." In this context, the term "propaganda" should be understood to be closer to its archaic meaning of "a group or movement organized for the spreading of ideas; a particular doctrine of systems of principles." There is thus an entire chapter of the regulations (Articles 9-13) on reporting of SARS through the hierarchy of the government and the obligations on units of government and individuals to report information in a timely fashion and not to falsify any information about SARS. These legal obligations are perhaps necessary in such a vast government with a massive population and are the backbone of the Prevention and Control Measures in Chapter III (Articles 14-22) and the Treatment Measures in Chapter 4 (Articles 23-29). Under the former, health care institutions are required to adopt control measures as soon as suspected cases of SARS appear at those facilities. Under the latter, health care facilities are required to treat without regard to the prospect of payment from a SARS patient or a person suspected of having SARS.288 These prevention and control measures, special treatment measures, and communication obligations for SARS are reinforced by the sanctions in Chapter 4 (Articles 35-39).

Second, the Ministry of Health issued a set of standards on May 8, 2003, for defining persons with close contacts with SARS patients and thus subject to prevention and control measures. For instance, the standards for airplanes are different from the standards for trains, buses, railroads, and ships. For airplanes, passengers within a certain number of rows are defined as having close contact, whereas on a ship, those sharing the same cabin are defined as having close contact. There are specific provisions for medical staffs, schools, cohabitants of SARS patients, and relatives and friends. The quarantine periods for those defined as having close contact is 14 days since the last contact with a patient or a suspected patient. The notice provides a legal basis for what is called "collective quarantine" if the contact occurs after the patient demonstrates symptoms. If the contact occurred before symptoms appeared, the person could be quarantined at home. More significant are provisions for keeping records of those having contact with SARS patients in the transportation system and instructions to individuals with contacts with SARS patients to reduce their contacts with others and to take their temperature twice a day.

The Ministry of Health joined with the Ministry of Civil Affairs, Ministry of Agriculture, National Development and Reform Commission, and National Population and Family Planning Commission to issue some special regulations for dealing with SARS in rural areas on May 20, 2003. These provisions, for instance, authorized the quarantining of entire villages in order to prevent the spread of the disease to other villages or towns, as occurred in Hebei Province from April 21 to May 13. It is impossible to determine how effective such a quarantine order was, but a ruling by the Supreme People's Procuratorate and Supreme People's Court allowed for the use of the police to enforce such quarantine orders.

On May 15, 2003, the Supreme People's Procuratorate and the Supreme People's Court issued a judicial interpretation of how criminal law could be used by prosecutors and police to enforce the prevention and control measures established for emerging infectious diseases such as SARS. The form of the ruling will appear to lawyers trained in a common law tradition as a set of regulations or codes, but given the statutory power of the Supreme Court and the inter-institutional role of the Purcuractory, the ruling establishes specific guidelines for when particular provisions of the criminal code can be used. For instance, infected persons or those suspected of having the disease who refuse voluntary isolation or quarantine can be sentenced to up to 10 years in prison under Article 114 of the Criminal Code if their spread of the pathogen is viewed as purposeful and endangers the public health. Even more stringent punishments are authorized for those who sell fake prevention drugs or violate the national standards of medical production during an epidemic. Persons who obstruct state officials or Red Cross staff engaged in prevention and control activities, such as quarantine or forced isolation, can be imprisoned for up to three years.

The controversial portion of Article 9, authorizing the death penalty in some instances, must be understood in the context of the statute. Under Article 9, individuals who gather to engage in "beating, smashing, or looting" while measures to prevent and control the spread of an emerging infectious disease such as SARS are in place are subject to penalties increasing in severity with the seriousness of the offense. The ring leaders of such "rioting" could be subject to the death penalty if their behavior otherwise constituted "capital murder" under the criminal code. In other words, a person instigating a riot on a train quarantined during an epidemic might be sentenced to death if that person had destroyed property and used a gun to rob and kill someone during the disturbance. The more important point to remember is that this ruling provides guidance to prosecutors and the police for how to use the existing criminal code to enforce the public health measures taken to control and prevent the spread of SARS. The number of instances in which law enforcement was actually involved in enforcement of the quarantine and isolation articles is difficult to determine without direct access to data in the PRC. The enactment of regulations for emerging infections in May 2003 could represent an entirely new approach to public health law that creates some uncertainty as to how the various legal rules operate in practice. The PRC may have adopted a two-tier approach towards control and prevention. Were SARS to reemerge in the PRC, one would expect the May 2003 regulations to apply. Once the nature of the disease and its cure and treatment are well established, the State Council and the Health Ministry might then classify the disease under the Prevention and Treatment Law of 1989.

By the end of May 2003, the central government had taken a number of steps to ensure that quarantine and isolation could be used to combat the spread of SARS. The ruling from the Procuratorate and Supreme Court provided guidance to law enforcement officials on how to use the criminal law as a tool to enforce public health measures adopted by various state officials. Acting first through the ministries under the State Council, all levels of government were, in theory, engaged in a systematic approach to control and prevent the outbreak of SARS.

It is perhaps not surprising that the provinces did little in terms of issuing formal regulations regarding SARS, given the exhaustive nature of the central government's response. Beijing—a municipality directly under the Central Government in the PRC—did enact a number of regulations consistent with the national ordinances enacted by the State Council in the spring of 2003. These include more detailed provisions for controlling the spread of SARS by restricting the movement of patients and suspected patients and establishing rules for quarantine and isolation measures for individuals coming in and out of the city. Beijing, which had over 47% of all the cases of SARS in the country, also used its provincial authority to designate certain areas as isolation areas for SARS. According to the statistics provided by the Supervision Office of SARS Prevention and Control of Beijing City, 30,173 persons were isolated and quarantined in 18 districts (counties) through June 21, 2003. Among them, 12,131 persons were isolated or quarantined collectively and 18,042 persons were isolated or quarantined individually. From April 22 to the end of October 2003, four hospitals were isolated as seriously affected zones, People's Hospital, Dongzhimen Hospital, Luhe Hospital of Tongzhou, and Herbalist Doctors' Hospital. Seven residential communities and buildings were totally isolated; two were residential buildings of the Beijing Science and Technology Research Institute, and the others were the residential community of People's Hospital, Xita Building #29 of National Economics and Finance University (a student dormitory), the students' residential building # ABC of Beifang Jiaotong University (now Beijing Jiaotong University), the residential courtyard #15 of Dongsishitiao, Gonghua Residential Community #1 section 2 of Shahe, and a residential community of Yanhua Corporation located in Pangshan District. Also, seven construction sites were isolated: Jinggang Mansion construction site at Dongcheng District, Zhonghua Jiayuan construction site at Xuanwu District, alteration construction of Dewai Road at Xicheng District, Xiyuan construction site at Chongwen District, Yunchao Jiayuan construction site at Tongzhou District, Huguangshanshe construction site of the Second Engineering Bureau of China Irrigation and Electricity Company and Beimei Taidu (North American Attitude) construction project.

The Jinggang Mansion construction site was the first quarantined place in Beijing, from April 22 to May 18, 2003, affecting 399 persons in succession. People's Hospital, affiliated with Peking University, was isolated on April 24, 2003, and was the first unit isolated as a whole in Beijing, with 1,563 persons affected. According to news reports, the decision to isolate was made by the Xicheng District Government.302 A city like Beijing has the authority to set up districts or counties within the city with legislative, judicial, and other units of government.

By contrast, another city directly under the central government, Shanghai, used isolation and quarantine on an individual basis. In addition, it is worth noting that Shanghai provided some mechanism for compensating those quarantined who were not in fact infected with SARS. The Shanghai Labor and Social Security Bureau issued a notice that the suspected patients or people having close contact with patients who were quarantined or received medical examinations and later were found not to be SARS patients were to be treated as if they had worked during the quarantine period and were entitled to the wages and benefits for that period. If the employers failed to provide the wages and benefits, the quarantined employees could sue the employer in the Labor Arbitration Commission. A few other cities enacted local measures, but the central government was the main source of new legal measures to control SARS.

5. Coordination Issues

The nature of SARS as a global threat caused two extraordinary events in the PRC. First, WHO took the unusual step in April 2003 of publicly challenging the PRC's report of the number of SARS cases in Beijing, even though in the past the WHO had refrained from criticizing member states. This public rebuke led to greater cooperation by the PRC. By late April, political leaders in the Communist Party had declared war on SARS and several public officials, including the Mayor of Beijing and the Minister of Health, were removed from their Communist Party positions.

Second, in early May, the PRC allowed a WHO team to provide assistance with the SARS outbreak in Taiwan. Early in the outbreak, the United States provided assistance to Taiwan because China had blocked WHO assistance. The visit by the WHO team was the first visit by any representatives of any UN-affiliated organization since the PRC took Taiwan's UN seat 30 years before. China's willingness to bend its traditional notions of sovereignty in the face of the epidemiological facts and international political pressures was probably significant in its ability to stop the spread of the disease.

It is significant for a strictly legal analysis that China had no obligation under the WHO treaty to report anything regarding SARS to WHO. Technically, the PRC's obligation was to report only three diseases—cholera, plague, and yellow fever. But international political and economic realities led the PRC to institute massive isolation and quarantine and other measures to contain the spread of SARS. Despite rapid advances in the scientific understanding of the SARS virus, the PRC used traditional public health measures of isolation and quarantine on a massive scale to contain the disease.

6. Public Reaction

How public health officials in the PRC communicated information about SARS became a matter of considerable international media attention during the spring of 2003. The term "cover-up" may or may not be appropriate for the actions of PRC officials, but it is clear that government and public health officials in the PRC were not in control of how the general public in the PRC or the international community was supplied with essential public health information. With the growth of the Internet and mobile phone communication within and outside of China, official announcements about the extent of the SARS outbreaks often followed non-governmental release of information to the media and WHO. The globalization and open communication needed to modernize the economy had a major effect on the government of the PRC to change the way it dealt with and reported about the SARS epidemic.

Although press reports document resistance to some of the measures implemented by the government, it is too early to determine the ultimate legal resolution of the prosecutions brought in many cases. The following selected case studies may provide the basis for researching the impact of these new SARS-based regulations for dealing with emerging pathogens while also providing a glimpse of how public health measures were enforced in the PRC.

Inner Mongolia

Li Song was a doctor in the emergency room of Railway Hospital of Linhe City, Bayanchuoer Meng, Inner Mongolia. He was infected with SARS while studying in a hospital in Beijing in the spring of 2003. He received treatment for several days in Beijing and returned to Linhe City on March 27, 2003. He was the first SARS patient in Linhe City, where he was treated in the individual clinic managed by his father; he was later transferred to Ba Meng Hospital on March 30. Ba Meng Hospital suspected that he was a SARS patient and isolated him for treatment. On April 8, Dr. Li, well aware of his disease, forced his way out of the Isolation Ward and went to the public area for eight hours. Dr. Li also violated the provisions for isolation and went out of the isolation ward. Because of Dr. Li's behavior, many of his relatives became infected; his parents and wife died. On May 1, 2003, the People's Procuracy of Linhe City arrested Li Song, after investigation for violation of Article 114 (endangering public security with dangerous means) and Article 330 (violating infectious disease prevention and treatment) of the Criminal Law. There is no report of the outcome of the prosecution.

Hebei Province

On April 24, 2003, the people's government of Xiong County, Baoding City of Hebei Province set up a SARS medical inspection (quarantine) station in Xiongfeng Hotel of Guzhuang. In the afternoon of April 25, some villagers in Guzhuang assembled in the Hotel and obstructed the work of the government. A few people even set fires to and smashed government vehicles. On May 1, the public security bureau of Xiong County arrested six individuals on the basis of warrants issued by the Xiong County People's Procuracy. On May 15, the Xiong County Court ruled that their conduct constituted the crime of group distribution of social orders, arson, and willfully damaging public and private properties, and sentenced them to fixed-term imprisonments for periods ranging from one to five years.

On May 3, 2003, Zhuozhou Municipality government dispatched a construction team to remodel Tongji Hotel in Dashiqiao Village of Shuangta District into a SARS quarantine station. Immediately after the construction began, some inhabitants of Dashiqiao village started obstructing the construction and hurt one construction worker. When the policemen arrived, villagers beat the policemen and damaged several police vehicles; nine villagers were later arrested on the basis of warrants issued by Zhuozhou Municipality People's Procuracy.

On May 3, 2003, three individuals of Baimiao Village, Xuanhua District of Zhangjiakou District, Hebei Province led a crowd of nearly 300 villagers in obstructing the construction of a SARS hospital in the village. On June 8, the three leaders were convicted of the crime of obstructing the state official's work and sentenced to fixed-term imprisonments of 1.5 years, one year, and six months respectively.

Jiangsu Province

A resident of Ganyu County of Jiangsu Province returned from Beijing to Ganyu County on April 25, 2003. He was quarantined until May 6, 2003. The staff at the quarantine and isolation station told him explicitly that he would be quarantined at home for another few days. On May 10, 2003, he was found going out in violation of the quarantine regulation. When some government officials were trying to persuade him to go back, he threatened an official with a pair of scissors. The Ganyu County Court found that the individual obstructed state officials from carrying out their duties and disturbed the SARS prevention and treatment work. He was convicted and sentenced to a fixed term imprisonment of 10 months.

Beijing

On May 1, 2003, a taxi driver drove his taxi back to Miyun County, Beijing from Huairou County, Beijing. He refused to wait in the line to be examined and disinfected at the SARS prevention and disinfection station, located on the "border" of Huairou and Miyun, and injured the policeman who was examining him. The Miyun County Court found that the taxi driver did not comply with the instructions, refused to disinfect the taxi that he drove, and obstructed the state officials from carrying out their duties with force. On June 4, 2003, he was convicted and sentenced to a fixed-term imprisonment of six months.

Dujiangyan City

Six individuals, residents of Dujiangyan City of Sichuan Province, were dissatisfied with the fact that their houses were located in the People's Hospital of Dujiangyan, which belonged to an Isolation Region of Dujiangyan City. They spread disparaging words about the government and induced the public to obstruct the construction work at the hospital, which resulted in a three-hour traffic jam in the city and an economic loss of 14,000 Yuan and aroused the public's dread of SARS. They were charged with the crime of defiance and affray. They were convicted and sentenced to fixed-term imprisonments of 1 year, 8 months, and 2-3 months detention respectively.

Some Chinese legal scholars have questioned the legality of the new measures taken by the Ministry of Health to control SARS under the Prevention and Treatment of Infectious Diseases Law of 1989. The basis of these objections is that the statute limits the use of certain types of control measures to Type A diseases or a limited number of Type B diseases. Since only the State Council, rather than the Ministry of Health, can add to the Type A diseases, these critics have argued that the new regulations issued by the Ministry of Health are illegal. Until the SARS crisis, it is likely that very little scholarly attention was devoted to Chinese public health law. In any event, these criticisms have not impeded the implementation of the measures. Newspaper accounts of the use of quarantine and isolation in the SARS crisis indicate that the government treated the regulations as legitimate and acted accordingly.

7. Current Situation

In China, the SARS notification system came back into effect on September 19, 2003 after it was stopped on August 16, 2003, when there were no more SARS patients in China. Since September 15, 2003, the major hospitals across the country have begun using the SARS case reporting system, which can report just-detected SARS patients or suspected patients to the Center for Disease Control of China and the Ministry of Health. Each province has submitted its preliminary plan for SARS prevention and control to the Ministry of Health. In addition, the state will allocate 11 billion Yuan to establishing a public health emergency treatment system. Different prevention measures have been taken in various provinces and cities. For example, Beijing adopted a preliminary plan for SARS prevention and control on August 28, 2003. Shanghai Bureau of Health issued an urgent notice providing that every suspected case is to be treated as SARS before being ruled out as SARS and summarizing six alerting situations for SARS so that officials can decide whether to trigger the SARS emergency handling system in a timely manner.

11.3.3. Hong Kong

The U.S. Centers for Diseases Control and Prevention (CDC) commissioned a report on lessons learned from the SARS incident. The following excerpt from the report outlines the actions taken by Hong Kong:

C. Hong Kong

1. Introduction

In March 2003, a physician who had been treating patients for atypical pneumonia at a hospital in Guangzhou traveled to Hong Kong and stayed in room 901 of the Metropole Hotel. It is thought that he was the first to transmit the SARS virus in Hong Kong. Seven others staying on the same floor of the hotel also became infected with SARS. This index patient was transferred to the Prince of Wales Hospital, where it is believed he spread the disease to nearly 100 hospital workers.

Another widespread outbreak of the virus occurred in April at the Amoy Gardens Apartment Complex where nearly 130 residents were diagnosed with SARS. An additional 241 residents, free from symptoms of the virus, were quarantined for 10 days. The source of the virus is thought to have been a visitor to the Amoy Gardens who had previously received treatment at the Prince of Wales Hospital. These two incidents and the continued threat of the spread of the SARS virus led to a range of responses by the Hong Kong government. In the case of Hong Kong, understanding of the response to SARS rests in part on knowledge of the complicated political and legal relationship between Hong Kong and China. That relationship is addressed in the section that follows.

2. Political and Legal Systems

Located at the southeastern tip of China, Hong Kong is a Special Administrative Region of the People's Republic of China. On July 1, 1997, after 150 years of British rule, the PRC assumed sovereignty over Hong Kong, according to the Joint Declaration of 1984 between China and Great Britain. Under the Joint Declaration, Hong Kong's special status will be protected for a period of 50 years from the transfer of power. This has led to the development of a government structure referred to as "one country, two systems."

Under the current division of power, the central government of the PRC exercises authority over foreign affairs and defense. Annex III to what is referred to as the "Basic Law," a constitutional document developed in connection with the transfer of sovereignty, details the laws that can be applied to Hong Kong. Authority over other areas of government rests with the Special Administrative Region. For example, the Special Administrative Region is responsible for maintaining public order in Hong Kong. This arrangement allows for Hong Kong to retain a legal system based on English common law for internal affairs and certain external affairs, as well as its non-socialist economic system.

The government of the Hong Kong Special Administrative Region is broken down into two levels, central and district. At the central level, authority is shared by the Chief Executive, the Executive Council, and the Legislative Council. The Basic Law states that the Chief Executive is accountable to the Central People's Government (the government of the PRC) and the Hong Kong Special Administrative Region. This dual responsibility is reflected in numerous aspects of the position. The Chief Executive is selected by the Election Committee, a committee made up of residents of Hong Kong, but appointed by the Central People's Government. The Chief Executive's charge to implement the Basic Law and legislation emerging from the Legislative Council is complemented by a charge to implement directives from the Central People's Government. The Chief Executive not only implements; he or she has the power to make decisions about government policies, issue executive orders, and nominate or appoint other officials. The Chief Executive oversees a number of secretaries who head bureaus, including the Secretary of Health, Welfare, and Food, and the Secretary of Security. The Executive Council is appointed by the Chief Executive and advises the Chief Executive on important policy decisions. The Legislative Council is responsible for legislating, monitoring the administration, and overseeing fiscal matters such as taxation and public expenditures. The Legislative Council is also charged with receiving and handling complaints from Hong Kong residents. At the district level, Hong Kong has 18 district councils whose duties include advising the government on district-level issues; setting priorities for their district; and performing environmental, cultural, and community activities for their districts.

As noted above, the legal system created during British occupation will remain largely undisturbed until 2047. A legacy of British rule is a strong commitment to the rule of law. The website for the Hong Kong Special Administrative Region discusses the concept and proclaims: "The Rule of Law begins with individuals and their right to seek protection from the courts where justice is administered by impartial judges." Structurally, members of the judiciary are independent of both the executive and legislative branches, and judgments made in courts in Mainland China are not binding on Hong Kong. Further, the Basic Law lays out fundamental rights to individuals which include the right to equality before the law; freedom of speech, of the press, and publication; freedom of association, of assembly, of processions, and of demonstration; and the right and freedom to form and join trade unions, and to strike; freedom of movement; freedom of conscience; and freedom of religious belief.

3. Public Health Structure and Laws

The Department of Health, under the Secretary for Health, Welfare, and Food, is the government's health advisor and the government agency with authority to execute health-related policies and regulations. The department provides a range of health promotion and prevention services as well as treatment and rehabilitation services. The Hospital Authority is responsible for all public hospitals in Hong Kong. It currently manages a head office, 43 public hospitals/institutions, 47 specialist outpatient clinics and 13 general outpatient clinics. The Hospital Authority is independent of the Department of Health, but like the Department of Health is accountable to the Secretary for Health, Welfare, and Food.

In July 2000, Hong Kong established the Disease Prevention and Control Division within the Department of Health. The mission of this division is to create and implement strategies for surveillance, prevention, and control of communicable and noncommunicable diseases. The division carries out this mission by developing intervention programs, conducting research and evaluation, and identifying health needs in the community. The division is also constructing a public health information system, with completion anticipated by the end of 2003. This system will collect, coordinate, analyze, and disseminate health information. It is intended to improve the division's ability to develop policies, allocate resources, and plan, implement and evaluate services and programs. The division also regularly conducts surveillance on 27 statutorily notifiable diseases and other infections of public health concern. The division works closely with the Hospital Authority, other government departments, and health professionals and authorities in other countries.

4. Response to SARS

The Quarantine and Prevention of Disease Ordinance provides a framework for the quarantine and prevention of infectious diseases relevant to the public. It is the basis for the Prevention of the Spread of Infectious Diseases Regulations. Under Regulation 4, medical professionals must report suspected cases of notifiable diseases to the Director of Health. Legal authority for quarantine and isolation is found in Chapter 141 of the Prevention of the Spread of Diseases Regulations. Persons arriving from infected places other than by sea and air may be medically inspected or examined by a health officer (Ch. 141, sec. 21). Additionally, Section 22 allows any vessel arriving in Hong Kong to be visited by a health officer. A health officer has the discretionary authority to detain in a quarantine station any person seeking to land in Hong Kong who upon arrival is found to have an infectious disease (Ch. 141, sec. 38). The Commissioner of Police is directed to furnish assistance to any health officer for the purpose of enabling the exercise of these powers (Ch. 141, sec. 42).

On March 27, 2003, the First Schedule of the Quarantine and Prevention of Disease Ordinance was amended to include SARS on the list of infectious diseases. Another order was issued to amend the

Prevention of the Spread of Infectious Diseases Regulations in 2003 to include SARS in the notification form for the reporting of infectious diseases. Surveillance has been enhanced through distribution of a clear case definition to all health care providers, active case contacting, and prompt laboratory investigation of virus samples. Use of current technology, such as the Internet, an e- SARS database, and a Major Incident Investigation and Disaster Support System (MIIDSS) has facilitated prompt case investigation and contact tracing. MIIDSS allows linkage of the contact person, location, and event.

The government of Hong Kong also broadened and strengthened existing quarantine and isolation laws, and various agencies have been aggressive in using the powers granted under these laws. Initially, visitors were allowed in hospitals where SARS patients were housed, which resulted in spread to the community. This led to a policy of isolation of patients. Visitors were prohibited from entering SARS wards and visitation to non-SARS wards was severely restricted and closely monitored. Also, special training in infection control was provided to hospital staff and all hospital employees were required to wear protective gear. Four medical centers were designated as treatment facilities for SARS patients.

The government also instituted home quarantine for households of individuals with SARS. Further, close contacts of confirmed SARS patients were placed under a 10-day home quarantine and monitored by public health nurses through telephone and unannounced home visits. As an alternative to home quarantine, some close contacts were placed in isolation camps outside the city of Hong Kong. The camps were holiday villages run by the Leisure Department of the government.

As noted in the introduction, the second major SARS outbreak in Hong Kong occurred at the Amoy Gardens housing complex. This was the first instance in which the government issued a quarantine order for an entire housing complex. Residents were not permitted to leave the complex without written permission from a Department of Health officer. At first, the Hong Kong government resorted to the use of barricades and tape to prevent residents from leaving. Hundreds of residents of the Amoy Gardens were eventually relocated to isolation camps. Residents of Amoy Gardens who were under the 10-day quarantine were provided with three meals a day and with emotional and psychological support through a special hotline established by the Home Affairs Department. Additional services were also available by calling a hotline set up by the Social Welfare Department. Others under home quarantine were also provided with home treatment and assistance with provision of daily necessities including financial assistance.

Because of their increased vulnerability to infection, the elderly received heightened attention. Residential care homes were given special support in the form of written guidelines for infection control, training for caregivers, and a requirement that all residents recently discharged from the hospital be placed in isolation at the facility for 10 days. The government also closed schools and universities for three weeks. When students and teachers were permitted to return, they were asked to wear surgical masks and continue temperature screens on a daily basis.

Compliance with home quarantine was enforced by interdepartmental teams of police and officials from immigration, social welfare, home affairs, and the health department. Hong Kong imposed strict penalties for breaking quarantine orders. Penalties for violations include fines of HKD$2,500 plus HKD$250 for every day the offense continues. (HKD=1.29 USD.) Increased penalties apply to subsequent offenses. If a second offense occurs within one year, imprisonment may result in lieu of or in addition to the fine. Additionally, an individual may be stopped and detained by any health officer or police officer and if his or her name and address are not provided, he or she may be arrested.

Other measures taken to control SARS involved travelers and those crossing borders. Screening, monitoring, and quarantining of vessels and arriving and departing individuals was instituted at seaports and airports. In mid-March, shortly after the initial outbreak of SARS, the government set up medical posts at all border points and began to require that all incoming visitors complete a health declaration. By April, health control measures at border points were increased to include temperature checks for all airport passengers and travelers by land, train, and sea. Additionally, infrared devices were installed throughout points of entry in Hong Kong to assist with temperature screening. On April 17, 2003, the Director of

Health, under the authority of Chapter 141 of the Prevention of the Spread of Diseases Regulations, granted immigration officers and members of the auxiliary medical service or civil aid service the power "to stop and detain any person seeking to leave Hong Kong in contravention of Regulation 27A...and remove the person to an infectious disease hospital...." Under Regulation 27A, persons cannot leave Hong Kong without receiving prior written permission from a health officer. Further, the Director of Health authorized any "member of the civil aid service on duty to take the body temperature of any person arriving in Hong Kong or leaving Hong Kong." Medical practitioners or health officers are also authorized to perform medical examinations on anyone entering or leaving Hong Kong to curtail the spread of SARS. Hong Kong International Airport is one of the busiest in the world and a hub for many airlines, and therefore it was an important site for control efforts. All in-bound, out-bound, and transit passengers had to undergo temperature checks. In-bound and transit passengers had to complete a health declaration stating whether they had fever, cough, shortness of breath or breathing difficulties, and they were required to list all countries and cities they visited within 10 days of their arrival in Hong Kong. Passengers with no fever or other symptoms were permitted to proceed to immigration. Passengers with no fever but other symptoms were advised to consult with a physician and permitted to proceed to immigration. Passengers with a fever were taken for a medical examination; if the examination revealed a suspicion of SARS, they were transported to a hospital selected by the Hospital Authority. Out-bound passengers were asked by airline employees about fever and contact with persons having SARS. Passengers with fever were sent to an airport medical clinic and were not permitted to proceed unless a certificate declaring them "fit for travel" was issued by a physician. Those with close contact with a SARS patient were sent to the Airport Health Authority. Hong Kong International Airport also implemented preventive health measures in terminals, including frequent air filter replacement, cleaning of courtesy and pay phones, daily cleaning of check-in counters, and sealing of drinking fountains.

In Hong Kong, infection control efforts backed by the threat of force were complemented by voluntary measures. A public education program was aimed at increasing awareness of SARS symptoms and recommending prompt medical treatment for anyone experiencing any symptoms of SARS, and included elements such as a SARS information hotline. Additionally, authorities in Hong Kong provided residents with disinfectant to use in their homes. The Hygiene Declaration of 2003 was the basis for a broad-based educational campaign. The strategy under the declaration was location specific and addressed hygiene standards and measures in various categories and settings, such as the home, food supply, medical, school, industrial, hotel, and sewage. The objectives included setting standards and renewing a culture of public hygiene, instilling a sense of individual responsibility for hygiene, and improving the image of Hong Kong internationally. Health and hygiene promotional materials addressing basic sanitary measures to reduce the spread of infectious disease include: "Health Advice for People Who Have Been in Contact with SARS Patients;" "Wearing Mask;" "Flush Toilet Properly;" and "Make Sure the Trap is Not Dry."

Hong Kong also established multi-disciplinary response teams composed of those with expertise in public health, building management, and environmental issues. The role of the teams was two-fold: investigating buildings and drainage and other systems, and taking remedial actions including disinfection, pest control, and cleansing. The response to SARS was supported by large allocations of funds including: HKD$200 million for infectious disease prevention, public health, and treatment of disease; HKD$200 million for training and support for the welfare of health care workers; HKD$1.3 billion to strengthen public health work and research on infectious disease; and HKD$500 million to establish a CDC-type organization. As result of the impact that SARS had on employment, the Chief Executive has announced plans for a HKD$715 million job package to create over 30,000 short-term jobs and training opportunities.

5. Coordination Issues

The Hospital Authority established a Central Task Force on Infection Control on SARS to make decisions regarding a range of professional and technical issues. This group of experts also provided assistance in the implementation of hospital control measures and the enforcement of such measures. A Central Task Force on Supplies was established to track the need for hospital supplies, oversee distribution of supplies, and assess the needs of various hospitals for protective gear and other precautionary items. The SARS outbreak at the Amoy Gardens Housing Complex required the coordination of numerous government agencies. The Department of Health led the investigation in conjunction with eight other governmental entities.

Another example of coordination was the government's use of various media outlets to provide broad outreach. Television, radio, the Internet, and public presentations provided updated information for residents of as well as travelers to Hong Kong. Radio and television announcements and billboards indicated how to wash hands properly, put on gloves, and wear masks. The mass-transit railway system joined with the medical faculty of the University of Hong Kong to implement a campaign on how to combat the disease, distributing informational brochures produced by the Department of Health and answering questions for the public. The campaign ran for two days at six of the busiest transit stations.

Looking beyond its borders, the Hong Kong government participated in a meeting with the Shenzhen municipal government. Shenzhen is the main transit point between Hong Kong and Mainland China. The meeting was intended as a forum for the exchange of experiences and ideas regarding border control points and the prevention of SARS. Each government agreed to install infrared imaging at the Lowu control point and each side agreed to screen incoming passengers. Both governments also agreed to hold regular meetings to exchange information.

An international group of experts was selected to review the Hong Kong government's work in containing SARS. Experts from the United Kingdom, United States, Australia, Hong Kong, and China comprised the committee that was charged with making recommendations for the improvement of Hong Kong's public health and medical systems. In addition, Hong Kong recognized that to effectively control communicable diseases collaboration was required with China, neighboring countries, WHO, and other international bodies.

6. Public Reaction

As noted above, the government of Hong Kong used public education as one of the key means for preventing the spread of SARS as well as to inform the public about individual responsibility in containing the spread of the virus. Still, broad-based educational campaigns were not sufficient to ease public fears. Government officials addressed public concerns about contamination, especially in large housing complexes, by making public the names of all buildings in which SARS cases were confirmed. There is also some evidence of resistance to government policies, especially in the area of quarantine. After the Amoy Gardens housing complex was quarantined, police discovered that more than half of the apartments were empty with residents having breached the 10-day quarantine order issued by the Secretary for Health, Welfare, and Food. In order to locate the residents who left Amoy Gardens during the quarantine period, the police department formed a task force.

To some degree, the harsh effects of quarantine were mitigated by a law, the Occupational Safety and Health Ordinance, that obligated employers to make reasonable efforts to protect the health and safety of employees. This obligation is quite general, but it may have implications for the SARS epidemic. Some legal experts maintain that under the Employment Ordinance, "where an employee has contracted the disease, he or she should be granted sick leave by the employer," meaning the employee is entitled to receive payment of four-fifths of normal wages during the leave period. Additionally, the government recommended that employers not terminate employees during sick leave and that employers not dismiss employees because they had an affected family member.

Additional information bearing on the public reaction to SARS and to government control efforts comes from an AC Nielsen Poll comparing the impact of SARS on Hong Kong and Singapore. The survey found that 35% of Hong Kong residents cancelled or postponed travel plans due to concerns about the SARS outbreak. When respondents were asked "What have you done to protect yourself/family from contracting the SARS virus?" 65% of respondents said that they wore a mask, 58% had adopted a more cautious approach toward personal hygiene, and 34% were avoiding crowded areas. The findings of this survey indicate that approximately 56% of Hong Kong residents found the SARS virus to be of most concern as compared to such things as the economy, unemployment, war in Iraq, and personal health.

7. Current Situation

It is too soon to tell how effective Hong Kong's strategies have been in combating the spread of SARS. However, on June 23, 2003, WHO removed Hong Kong from the list of areas with a recent transmission. According to Professor Lee Shiu Hung of Hong Kong University, many of the measures taken (e.g., contact tracing, wearing of masks, strict personal hygiene measures, and temperature screening) were effective in raising the public awareness, but enforcement of some measures was an issue. Professor Hung suggests that because the disease spread so rapidly, preparedness was an issue with shortages of masks and other protective gear for health workers, inadequate control measures, and poor communication with the public leading to panic. Hong Kong suffered serious economic losses linked to SARS. During the height of the outbreak, nearly 60,000 restaurant and hotel workers lost their jobs or were put on unpaid leave. The Standard & Poor's Rating Agency estimated that SARS could cut Hong Kong's gross domestic product as much as 1.5%.

A memo issued by the Secretary of Health, Welfare, and Food on the day WHO removed Hong Kong from the list announced the need to prepare for future outbreaks. The need to strengthen the public health system and the management of infectious diseases was acknowledged, with "$200 million allocated for treatment of diseases, strengthening infection control, and public education." Three committees were established to address certain issues based on the experience with SARS. One committee was to work on overall cleaning campaigns and environmental improvements at housing complexes, another on developing plans and programs for economic redevelopment including promoting tourism, and a third on promoting community involvement in improving the physical, social, and economic environments of the city.

The international group of experts published its findings in a lengthy report. The report delineated some of the shortcomings in Hong Kong's response to the SARS epidemic. One problem identified was the inadequate communication between the Hospital Authority, the Department of Health, and university health experts. Additionally, the report concluded that health care workers were not trained appropriately and facilities were not adequately equipped to deal with the outbreak. Hong Kong has, however, developed a response mechanism to be better prepared if such an event occurs again. The Hospital Authority established a three-stage SARS warning system to allow hospitals and outpatient facilities to detect SARS patients early and monitor the spread of the disease. Other plans include providing over 1,000 isolation beds in public hospitals and ensuring a three-month supply of protective clothing and equipment for medical professionals.

11.3.4. Singapore

Singapore has a civil law tradition, requiring little judicial intervention in the application of codes and regulatory requirements, in particular quarantine and isolation requirements. Singapore was one of the most successful countries in the Asian region, in terms of rapidly gaining control over the SARS outbreak, which can probably be largely attributed to the strict quarantine and isolation requirements.

Fig 11.7 Singapore Ministry of Health depiction of SARS cases by date of onset.

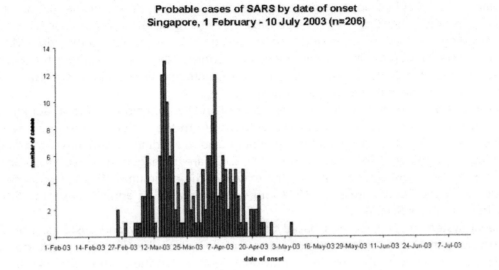

Probable cases of SARS by date of onset
Singapore, 1 February - 10 July 2003 (n=206)

Source: Ministry of Health, Singapore

The U.S. Centers for Diseases Control and Prevention (CDC) commissioned a report on lessons learned from the SARS incident. The following excerpt from the report outlines the actions taken by Singapore:

D. Singapore

1. Introduction

Singapore is a city-state located in Southeast Asia with a population just slightly over 4 million. Singapore's population is largely made up of descendents of Chinese, Malaysian, and Indian immigrants. Although English is the official language of administration, numerous languages are spoken in Singapore, including Mandarin, Malay, and Tamil. Singapore was first confronted with the SARS virus on March 14, 2003, when the Ministry of Health was informed that six persons at Tan Tock Seng Hospital/ Communicable Disease Center (Tan Tock Seng) were admitted with atypical pneumonia. By the time the epidemic subsided, Singapore had a total of 238 cases of SARS with 32 deaths. Three index cases were identified, all of whom had stayed at the Metropole Hotel in Hong Kong during the time that a SARS-infected person was a guest. Singapore found five SARS cases to be responsible for transmitting SARS to a larger than expected number of persons. These people were named "superspreaders" and the fact that SARS could be spread to a large number of persons by one patient strengthened the government's decision to take prompt and strong measures in containing the disease. Additionally, health officials in Singapore found evidence that casual contact, such as encounters in elevators, taxis, and hallways, had resulted in contagion. Although most secondary spread of SARS was initially hospital-related, no additional nosocomial cases were observed after March 22 in Tan Tock Seng (the date when this hospital was designated the official SARS hospital) or after April 17 in other hospitals.

The country's actions and responses to SARS were widely publicized as a result of Singapore's stringent and comprehensive approach to controlling the epidemic. Of greater relevance here, the country's ability to initiate rapid and sweeping public health and legal measures was facilitated by Singapore's political and legal systems and, more particularly, its existing public health structures and laws.

2. Political and Legal Systems

Singapore's governmental structure is based on the British Westminster system, consisting of a democratically elected Parliament of 84 members, a Prime Minister who is appointed by the President, an elected President, and a Cabinet appointed by the President. The President and the Cabinet are vested with executive authority. The Cabinet is responsible for the general direction and control of the government, including the administration of the affairs of state. It is responsible to the Prime Minister, and includes the ministers of Community Development and Sports, Defense, Education, the Environment, Finance, Foreign Affairs, Health, Home Affairs, Information, Communications and the Arts, Law, Manpower, National Development, Trade and Industry, and Transport.

At the local level, community development councils (CDCs) function as a local administration of each district. CDCs were implemented to devolve authority from the national housing authority to the local level and are responsible for "initiating, planning and managing community program[me]s to promote community bonding and social cohesion." CDCs are managed by a council consisting of anywhere from 12 to 80 members and includes the mayor of the community. CDCs are governed by the Community Development Council Rules of 1997 and were in charge of administering the SARS Home Quarantine Order Allowance Scheme.

The legal system of Singapore is based on English common law and customs. The Singapore Constitution provides the basis for the country's laws and delineates the functions of the governmental organs including the judiciary. It also sets forth individual rights within the context of the authority of the state.

3. Public Health Structure and Laws

The Ministry of Health enforces strict sanitation and public health regulations. As a result, the health conditions and health infrastructure of Singapore are comparable to some developed countries. The country has a broad-based system for surveillance of communicable diseases requiring that all infectious diseases reported to the Quarantine and Epidemiology Department of the Ministry of Environment be investigated. The Ministry of Health also has surveillance responsibilities as part of its disease outbreak prevention capacities.

The Ministry of Health's mission is to "promote good health and reduce illness; to ensure that Singaporeans have access to good and affordable healthcare that is appropriate to needs; and to pursue medical excellence." Singapore provides public health services for its residents through three ministries— Ministry of Health, Ministry of the Environment, and Ministry of Manpower-- as well as the private sector. Health care services are provided through a dual system of delivery. The public system is managed by the government and the private system is provided by private health facilities and providers. Residents can choose between the two systems for their care and are provided with some level of subsidization for the public health care system. The majority of primary health services in Singapore are provided by the private sector, whereas the majority of the hospital care is provided by the public sector. Emergency services are provided through the Accident and Emergency Departments at public hospitals. Public hospitals and clinics receive subsidies from the government and the private sector is subject to regulation by way of licensing through the Ministry of Health. There is no free health care in Singapore, and individuals are expected to provide co-payments for services. Patients can choose among different levels of service but have to pay more out-of-pocket for the higher level of care. Additionally, the government requires all working people to contribute 6-8% of their income into the Medisave account that can be used to cover the cost of hospitalization by individuals or their immediate family. In addition to Medisave, Medishield provides catastrophic illness insurance and Medifund provides coverage for the indigent so that no patient can be denied care by a public hospital for inability to pay. Singapore bases its authority to quarantine and isolate individuals on two key pieces of legislation, the Infectious Disease Act and the Environmental Public Health Act as amended in 2002.

The Infectious Disease Act was enacted in 1976 to control and prevent the spread of scheduled infectious diseases. The Act is administered jointly by the Ministry of Health and the Ministry of the Environment. It allows for medical examinations and treatment, surveillance, and investigation of infectious diseases. It also requires physicians to report specified infectious diseases to government authorities. According to the Ministry of Health's official website: The Act empowers the Director of Medical Services to order the treatment of premises or vessels, destruction and disposal of infected food, animals, water and corpses, closure of food establishments if the establishment is suspected to be the source of or responsible for the transmission of infectious disease, or the prohibition of meetings and public entertainment if such gatherings are likely to increase the spread of the infectious disease.

Under the Infectious Disease Act, Chapter 137, the Minister of Health and the Minister of the Environment are empowered to declare an area to be an outbreak area in Singapore and elsewhere if a dangerous infectious disease could be introduced into Singapore. The Act allows for certain amendments by the relevant public officials. Section 69 states that the "appropriate Minister may, from time to time, by notification in the Gazette, amend any of the Schedules."

The Environmental Health Act is administered by the Director-General of Public Health who is appointed by the Minister of the Environment. The Environmental Public Health Act regulates, among other things, food stalls and vendors. More specifically, under Part IV of the Act:

(1) The Director-General [of Public Health] may require any person to whom a license has been issued under this Part . . . or any assistant or employee of the licensee or any applicant for a license under this Part to submit to medical examination. (2) If such licensee, assistant, employee or applicant is suffering from or is suspected to be suffering from an infectious disease or is suspected to be a carrier thereof, the Director-General may require him to undergo treatment. (3) The Director-General may require treatment to be obtained at any hospital as he may think fit. (4) The Director-General may require any licensee or any assistant or employee of the licensee to submit to immunization against any infectious disease. (5) Every licensee shall ensure that his assistant or any person employed by him is immunized against any infectious disease as required by the Director-General. (6) The Director-General may, at any time, revoke or suspend any license issued under this Part if − (a) the licensee is suffering from an infectious disease; (b) the licensee knowingly employs any person who is suffering from or suspected to be suffering from an infectious diseases; obtained at any hospital as he may think fit . . . . Under Part X of the Act, the Director-General may direct the immediate execution of any act which in the Director General's opinion is necessary for public health or the safety of the public. The Environmental Public Health Act has had a tremendous impact on curbing the spread of such infectious diseases as cholera, salmonella, and typhoid by requiring street vendors to move indoors.

4. Response to SARS

Singapore relied upon the Infectious Disease Act-- as amended in 2002-- and the Environmental Public Health Act in its effort to stem the spread of SARS. Both the Ministry of Health and the Ministry of the Environment were instrumental in educating the public and in enforcing isolation and quarantine measures.

In March 2003 the Minister of Health exercised the authority to amend the schedules to the Infectious Disease Act. The Minister of Health, in a statement in support of his action, remarked that SARS presented "an unprecedented public health crisis." One of the key amendments was to include SARS on the list of First, Second, Fifth and Sixth Scheduled Infectious Diseases. In fact, SARS is the first disease to be listed in the Fifth Schedule, which addresses diseases in relation to the control of occupation, trade, or business. It is also the first disease listed in the Sixth Schedule, which allows information to be disclosed by the Director of Medical Services to a person to enable him to take steps to prevent the spread of disease.

The process for issuing these amendments was expedited through Parliament with the use of a Certificate of Urgency, a special condition allowed for by the Constitution that makes it possible for vital legislation to be passed in one rather than two Parliamentary sittings. The amendments were made within five categories: home quarantine orders, quarantine of premises, prevention of persons acting irresponsibly in a manner leading to the spread of infectious disease, compliance with disease control measures, and the handling of corpses when SARS is the suspected cause of death. The Infectious Disease Act, as amended, gives the Minister of Health the power to quarantine any premises for the purpose of controlling or preventing the spread of any infectious disease; to make it an offense to refuse to cooperate with disease control measures or to provide false information and to allow for compounding of fines for offenses; to address disposal of a deceased's remains when SARS is the suspected cause of death and to allow for post-mortem examinations of persons suspected of being a carrier or contact of an infectious disease; to allow for medical examination of persons if they are suspected of carrying an infectious disease; to allow disclosure of information to any person necessary to assist in the prevention of the spread of disease; to make the process of issuing home quarantine orders clearer, allowing for home quarantine of suspect cases, contacts, or carriers of an infectious disease; and to make it an offense for someone to "act irresponsibly" by exposing others to infection by his presence in a public place, with the exception of seeking medical treatment. SARS is the first disease under this new civic responsibility provision allowing for a finding of irresponsibility for being in a public place while knowingly suffering from an infectious disease.

On March 24, 2003, the Ministry of Health used its power under the Infectious Disease Act to quarantine persons to prevent the spread of SARS. The Ministry of Health developed a mechanism for obtaining home quarantine orders under Section 15(2) of the Infectious Disease Act. Home quarantine was mandatory for 10 days for contacts of all probable and suspected cases of SARS and contacts of pneumonia patients who might turn out to be SARS cases. Persons recovering from SARS or who had been treated for SARS were required to undergo a mandatory 14-day home quarantine.

Discharged patients under home quarantine also were subject to check by hospital workers every day and were required to undergo a medical examination at Tan Tock Seng at the end of the quarantine period. Persons with chronic diseases who were treated for a condition other than SARS in a hospital where SARS patients were treated were also served home quarantine orders as these patients could have SARS and present with atypical symptoms. Additionally, all patients discharged from a hospital where a SARS patient had been treated were monitored via telephone for 21 days.

During home quarantine persons were required to permit an electronic camera to be placed in their home and to be able to be contacted at all times. The Ministry of Health contracted with CISCO, Singapore's leading commercial security firm, to serve the quarantine orders, install ePic web cameras in homes of those under quarantine, and provide some of the enforcement of home quarantine. CISCO was initially established as a statutory board of the Ministry of Home Affairs to provide guard and escort services for commercial and industrial organizations. Persons under home quarantine were required to answer all calls from Ministry of Health officials, officers of CISCO, or persons acting on behalf of the Director of Medical Services. Persons under home quarantine were called randomly and directed to turn on the web cameras to verify their presence at home. This measure was in part taken in reaction to persons breaking home quarantine despite increased monetary penalties and the threat of jail time, as described below. Random checks were also permitted under home quarantine. Persons under home quarantine were only allowed to come into contact with family members and others living in their household, healthcare workers under orders of the Director of Medical Services, CISCO officers, persons carrying out a statutory order or function, persons needing access to the house to complete any official work, and any other person with authorization from the Director of Medical Services. The home quarantine order issued by the Ministry of Health provided detailed instructions on what was required and what was prohibited during home quarantine, including information on keeping good hygiene practices at home, numbers to call for help, what to do if SARS symptoms develop, and when to wear a mask.

Quarantined persons were given a SARS toolkit and required to check and record their temperature twice a day. During home quarantine, all children under 18 also had to stay home. Persons under home quarantine were given the option of having their children stay somewhere else for the duration of the quarantine so they could continue to attend school.

Quarantined persons could also choose to stay at government facilities for a cost of SGD $25 per day.[1] Staying at government facilities would also allow household children to continue going to school. A number of penalties were put in place through the amended Infectious Disease Act for breaking a home quarantine order. The Ministry of Health put together a form addressing the breach of home quarantine orders. The form specified that the breach of a home quarantine order is an offense under Section 15(3)b of the Infectious Disease Act; that anyone discovered breaking a home quarantine order will be required to wear an electronic monitoring tag at all times for the remainder of the home quarantine period; that the employer or person in quarantine will not be eligible for the Home Quarantine Allowance (discussed below under "Public Reaction"); and that a second violation of the quarantine order could result in detention and isolation in a hospital or other government assigned location. Additionally, a person could be arrested without a warrant for breaking an order, and a first offense was punishable by a fine up to SGD $10,000 and/or imprisonment for six months. Subsequent offenses could be punished by fines up to SGD $20,000 and/or imprisonment for up to one year.

On April 20, 2003, the Minister of Health closed the Pasir Panjang Wholesale Centre for 15 days after a SARS infected worker failed to stay in place while a special ambulance was called to transport him to the hospital. Approximately 2400 merchants at the Wholesale Centre were put on home quarantine and contact tracing was initiated with approximately 1200 quarantine orders served to persons who might have been exposed to SARS at the Wholesale Centre. Additionally, the Ministry of Health advised those who might have been exposed at the Centre but did not receive quarantine orders to stay at home.

Following this closure, news accounts document that the Health Ministry asked all market associations in Singapore to initiate temperature screenings of hawkers, and as of April 28, 2003, all hawkers and food vendors were required to have their temperatures checked twice daily. National Environmental Agency officers were responsible for conducting these temperature screens and providing hawkers and food vendors with kits that included thermometers, record cards, informational brochures, and "fever-free" stickers.

The general approach of the government of Singapore to SARS was "detect, isolate, and contain." An underlying theme in government actions in response to SARS was that of social and civic responsibility on the part of residents of Singapore. Under this general approach the government engaged in a wide range of activities, including identifying cases as early as possible, isolating patients, tracing and monitoring contacts, and adopting and enforcing stringent infection control measures for health care workers and others in settings where the risk of transmission was high. It also launched a number of public education campaigns, which will be discussed under "Public Reaction" below.

Concerning early identification of cases, Singapore adopted a case definition for SARS that was more comprehensive than the WHO case definition. Notification of suspect cases within 24 hours by email/fax by doctors was mandatory. Doctors and hospitals were in turn notified of cases through circulars and the MedAlert system, a computerized messaging and information database. According to the Director of Medical Services of the Ministry of Health, "intrahospital transmission is the most important amplifier of SARS infection." On March 22 the government selected Tan Tock Seng as the sole hospital for suspected and probable SARS cases. When a probable SARS case was identified, that person was admitted for isolation and observation. In addition, all acute public hospitals made preparations for creation of additional isolation facilities for SARS patients. When patients were released from a hospital where a SARS case had been treated, they were placed under telephone surveillance for 21 days. Additionally, as noted above, all discharged SARS patients were placed under mandatory home quarantine for 14 days. Fever clinics were also set up at the various polyclinics in Singapore.

All persons having household, social, hospital, and work-related contacts with a SARS case during the 10 days of the incubation period (prior to symptom onset), as well as from the time of symptom onset to hospital admission, were identified and monitored under home quarantine. Contacts of SARS cases were called daily by National Environmental Agency officers. All contacts with possible SARS symptoms were immediately brought to Tan Tock Seng for evaluation.

Other infection control measures included stringent temperature checks of all hospital staff and patients, use of protective gear (gloves, gowns, goggles, N95 or similar respirator) throughout all health care facilities, and isolation of staff working with SARS patients. All health care workers had temperature checks twice a day beginning April 9, 2003. No visitors were allowed at public health care institutions, except that one visitor was permitted in pediatric and obstetric cases. Other patients were allowed contact with family and friends through videoconferencing. Compliance with infection control measures was audited. The government also instituted hospital quarantine when clusters of health care workers or patients with fevers were identified in a particular work area. A dedicated ambulance transported suspected and probable SARS cases to the hospital. This ambulance was also used to transport persons on home quarantine who developed SARS symptoms and persons coming from ports of entry with symptoms. Temperature checks were also instituted at points of entry (e.g., airport thermal screeners) and community places and events. Persons returning from SARS-affected countries with no symptoms were advised to monitor their health for 10 days, including twice-daily temperature checks. Employers were allowed to impose a mandatory 10-day leave of absence for those returning from a SARS-affected country.

According to the Director of Medical Services, the government actions with the most success during the SARS outbreak include the containment of hospital infections and prevention of community infections. In his view, the most effective measures for containing hospital infections were designating one hospital as the SARS hospital, conducting temperature screens of all health care workers and patients, isolating staff caring for SARS patients, limiting and in most cases prohibiting hospital visitation, and enforcing use of protective gear in all health care facilities. Because Singapore's SARS cases were first identified in the hospital setting, keeping SARS out of the community was key to preventing its spread. Strategies considered most effective in this area include a strong surveillance system, contact tracing, and enforcement of quarantine with penalties. The surveillance system encompassed measures such as mandatory reporting of all suspected SARS cases by physicians within 24 hours, concentration of SARS cases at one hospital, monitoring fever clusters in hospitals and nursing homes, and temperature screens at community locales and events and all ports of entry.

5. Coordination Issues

On March 15, 2003, the Ministry of Health set up a task force to monitor the SARS situation and take prompt, appropriate action. The task force was chaired by the Director of Medical Services and members included various experts from the National Environmental Agency and hospitals. In practice, the response to SARS in Singapore was orchestrated by a number of the ministries. The Ministry of Health conducted telephone surveys with health care providers to assess their level of knowledge with respect to infection control. Health care workers were kept continually appraised of the situation and case definitions via the MedAlert system. The Ministry of Environment raised standards of public health and hygiene.

Action extended well beyond the two lead agencies under the Infection Control Act. The Ministry of National Development and Housing, the Housing and Development Board, and the Town Councils instituted measures to improve cleanliness in housing estates. The Ministry of Education implemented a four-pronged approach to SARS: Contain, Safeguard, Screen, and Isolate. The Ministry of Education instituted prevention and control measures at schools that included the closure of all primary and secondary schools and junior colleges and institutes from March 27 to April 6, 2003. The Ministry of Education further worked with the Ministry of Health in drafting its response measures to the isolated SARS case identified in September 2003. The Ministry of Education and the Ministry of Community

Development and Sport instituted preventive procedures—such as temperature screening-- for child care centers and kindergartens. The Ministry of Defense instituted precautionary measures. The Ministry of Manpower amended the Workmen's Compensation Act to include SARS as a disease for which workers would be compensated and imposed a10-day quarantine on all Work Permit and Employment Pass workers entering Singapore from SARS-affected areas. The Ministry of Home Affairs allowed illegal immigrants to receive medical care at polyclinics and announced they would not be prosecuted.

Also of note, the government of Singapore has committed SGD $230 million in an economic relief package to help businesses recover from the SARS outbreak. The relief package included money for the tourism and other tourism-related industries, and for the transportation sector. The government also committed some funds for the health care sector through contributions to a "Courage Fund." The Courage Fund is a public private partnership set up in April 2003 to provide financial assistance to SARS victims in the health care sector. The Courage Fund collected a total of SGD $28 million. The Fund provided money to healthcare workers who had treated SARS patients. As of October 27, 2003, SGD $5.5 million had been given to approximately 2,500 health care workers in Singapore. On July 1, 2003, the Minister of Health announced that Singapore's government had spent SGD$300 million on SARS-related efforts. This amount does not include the SGD$230 million relief package.

International coordination and collaboration was also essential to Singapore's success in controlling SARS. From the beginning of the outbreak, laboratories in Singapore worked with WHO to identify and gain knowledge about the SARS virus. Singapore has also collaborated with laboratories in the U.S. Centers for Disease Control and Prevention.

In addition to collaborating with WHO and the CDC, Singapore reached an agreement with Malaysia to cooperate in preventing the spread of SARS in eight particular areas through the formation of the Joint Cross-Border Health Committee. The focus of the agreement was to encourage the exchange of medical information relevant to the prevention of SARS. The areas of focus included: epidemiology; laboratory investigations; public health measures; infection control practices; contact tracing and quarantine measures; aircraft and other vessels; citizens hospitalized with SARS; and status updates on SARS cases. Malaysia and Singapore have thus far held four bilateral meetings on SARS. Both countries have agreed to expand cooperation on preventive measures for other infectious diseases.

6. Public Reaction

Public reaction to SARS control efforts in Singapore has been shaped by an extensive public education campaign initiated early on in the SARS outbreak. The Ministry of Health provided general advice to the public regarding symptoms and the need to seek immediate medical attention. Additionally, the Prime Minister delivered a number of public speeches on "Fighting SARS Together" and the civic duty and responsibility of Singaporeans to behave responsibly and abide by government measures. SARS toolkits were distributed by the Peoples' Associations' Constituency SARS Task Force to all residents of Singapore (containing digital thermometer, two surgical masks, and instruction pamphlets in four languages). The Ministry of Health instituted a policy of releasing daily press statements to update the public on the status of the outbreak and established a SARS hotline. The government also created an official SARS website with regular updates.

A unique feature of the public outreach effort in Singapore was the development of a dedicated channel for SARS information by the Ministry of Home Affairs. Media rivals joined together to launch the SARS Channel—a public service project running SARS information 12 hours a day (the other 12 hours consist of repeat programming). All programs were offered in the various languages spoken in Singapore. The government also supported several campaigns aimed at improving hygiene and sanitation. As information suggesting that SARS could be spread through mouth and nose excretions became available, the government began a campaign against spitting, with monetary fines for spitting in public. The Singapore Tourism Board's COOL Singapore Campaign was launched at least in part to recognize and reward "best practices to ensure rigorous precautionary measures are being taken against SARS in tourist establishments."

The potentially harsh economic effects of quarantine were mitigated by a Home Quarantine Order Allowance Scheme. According to the official Singapore government SARS website, the program was administered by the Community Development Councils and was intended to defray the costs of home quarantine for self-employed persons and small businesses (those with 50 employees or less) that had to close as a result of SARS. The allowance because available on April 30, 2003, but all persons issued a home quarantine order either before or after this date were eligible. Self-employed persons and employers were the only ones allowed to submit an application for the allowance. Employees of small businesses were required to submit their forms to their employers first. Unemployed persons, those in large businesses, and persons arriving in Singapore on new work passes put in home quarantine were not eligible for the allowance. The allowance consisted of a flat SGD$70 for self-employed persons, and daily salary up to SGD $70 for employees of small businesses closed down due to SARS and the absence of employees due to home quarantine. The government advised employers that the home quarantine period should be treated as paid hospital leave for their employees under the Employment Act. The allowance was given to self-employed persons in two installments: one at the beginning of the quarantine period and the second upon completion. Employers were given the allowance for their employees at the end of the period. The government set aside SGD$5 million for the Home Quarantine Order Allowance Scheme program, and as of June 17, the government had spent SGD $1.2 million. The expectation was that many of those under home quarantine would not claim the allowance because they were unemployed, retired, or worked at home.

All individuals under home quarantine were offered assistance with grocery shopping, hotline numbers to call in case of emergencies or questions, and free transportation by a dedicated SARS ambulance should they develop SARS symptoms. The government provided all persons seeking treatment for SARS, including foreigners, with subsidized care at hospitals. The government also provided unspecified financial assistance to workers at the Pasir Panjang Wholesale Market.

According to news reports, a total of 26 people broke quarantine. The government established special facilities for quarantine violators to spend the remainder of their quarantine period. In at least some cases, penalties were imposed. For example, one man was jailed for six months for twice leaving his home during the home quarantine period.

A Gallup Poll conducted on April 2 and 3, 2003, surveyed 512 Singapore residents age 15 and above through face-to-face random sampling. The poll found that the majority of people in Singapore acquired their information about SARS through television and newspaper accounts. Peoples' knowledge about SARS was high. Although the satisfaction with government responses was also high, fear regarding the spread of SARS was widespread. The survey also inquired about behavioral changes during the SARS outbreak, revealing that more than half of the respondents avoided or minimized visits to crowded public places, one-fourth followed stringent personal hygiene measures, and 7% instituted self-imposed home quarantine.

In addition to the Gallup Poll, an AC Nielsen Poll was conducted to compare responses to SARS in Hong Kong and Singapore. The findings of this survey indicate that approximately 45% of Singapore residents found the SARS virus to be of most concern as compared to such things as the economy, unemployment, war in Iraq, and personal health. It also showed that 38% of respondents cancelled or deferred travel plans as a result of the SARS outbreak.

7. Current Situation

On May 31, 2003, WHO removed Singapore from its list of SARS-affected areas. The last reported case of SARS was on May 11, 2003, and the last probable SARS patient was discharged from the hospital on June 6, 2003. No more suspected cases were admitted. On July 1, 2003, the Ten Tock Seng Hospital Emergency Department resumed its regular operation. Prior to July 1, the hospital was only treating SARS cases. Additionally, on June 13 the SARS hotline decreased operation to office hours, on July 10 the SARS Channel stopped running, and on July 25 the Ministry of Health discontinued daily SARS press releases.

Other measures discontinued since Singapore was removed from the WHO list include temperature screening in workplaces and buildings, at schools, childcare centers, and other children's centers, food centers and markets, student hostels and tourism establishments, and government buildings. Hospitals discontinued temperature screening on August 1, 2003. Temperature monitoring of hospital staff and patients will continue indefinitely and arriving air, land, and sea travelers will still be screened. Outbound travelers, though, will not be subject to temperature checks.

Post-outbreak assessments have shown the impact of SARS on Singapore's economy to be great. Visitors to the city-state fell by as much as 75%; hotel occupancy fell from an average of 75% to a low of 25%; and the Singapore stock market declined sharply both from the initial outbreak and the isolated case identified in September.

In early September, Singapore was shocked to identify a SARS case almost two months after WHO declared SARS to be under control and four months after Singapore's last case. The patient was a young laboratory technician working in the National Environmental Health Institute laboratories. He was quickly sent to Tan Tock Seng for isolation. Additionally, 25 of the patient's close contacts, including a provider of traditional Chinese medicine, were put under home quarantine. Despite confirmation from Singapore's Ministry of Health that this was a SARS case, and its treatment of the patient and his contacts as SARS cases and contacts, WHO did not find this case to be in line with the agency's new guidelines. WHO's new guidelines require at least two SARS cases to be identified in the same hospital in order to meet the post-outbreak case definition. The patient was, however, confirmed to be infected with the SARS coronavirus through two separate tests. At WHO's urging, the Singaporean government sent samples to the CDC in Atlanta for analysis, where the presence of the SARS virus was confirmed.

The Ministry of Health put together a review panel headed by a WHO expert to investigate the new case. A Ministry of Health press release stated that the panel found that the most probable source of infection was the affected individual's work at the Environmental Health Institute laboratories. As a precaution, the laboratories were closed for a night and disinfected and all staff that had been in contact with the patient were asked to voluntarily place themselves in home quarantine. The government did not, however, issue home quarantine orders for all the staff that self-quarantined. Panel recommendations included the implementation of a national legislative framework for "ensuring international standards in bio-safety" in laboratories throughout the country. Additionally, experts in biosafety from the CDC and WHO were sent to Singapore at the government's request to examine the laboratories where the patient worked. WHO has issued a statement since the new case was identified specifying that Singapore is a safe travel destination and that travelers from Singapore pose no additional risk.

Intragovernmental as well as international cooperation was again evident during this latest SARS case. Singapore's early communication and seeking of advice and expertise from WHO and the CDC are consistent with the country's record of open communication and cooperation. Additionally, the Ministry of Health worked with the Ministry of Education, the Singapore Tourism Board, as well as other agencies and entities in the nation to educate the public and coordinate necessary actions to prevent a second wave of SARS cases. Despite taking numerous precautionary measures, such as issuing 25 home quarantine orders, and openly announcing the case, the government of Singapore has declared this to be a case of low public health risk and definitely not an outbreak because it was limited to a single case, no contacts have fallen ill, and all necessary protective measures have been taken at the hospitals where the patient was treated.

———————

11.3.5. Taiwan

The U.S. Centers for Diseases Control and Prevention (CDC) commissioned a report on lessons learned from the SARS incident. The following excerpt from the report outlines the actions taken by Taiwan:

E. Taiwan (Republic of China)

1. Introduction

The first suspected SARS case was a businessman who traveled to the Guangdong province of China in early February, returning to Taiwan through Hong Kong two weeks later. The man was not hospitalized until March 8, 2003, and his wife was later diagnosed with pneumonia. Taiwan took prompt action, receiving assistance from the U.S. CDC. Although some Taiwanese researchers claim that their research with respect to the SARS virus was slowed by their exclusion from WHO, Taiwan was able to respond to the epidemic through a variety of mechanisms comparable to those recommended by WHO.

Taiwan is a small island located off the southeastern coast of Mainland China. In 1949, the Chinese national government fled to Taiwan when the Communist party took over China. Since that time, China has refused to recognize the Taiwanese government, considering Taiwan to be a "renegade province." Due to the strained relationship with China, Taiwan has no seat on the United Nations and has been denied membership in WHO since 1972, when the People's Republic of China was admitted to the U.N. This exclusion from WHO became significant during the SARS epidemic.

As of November 2002, Taiwan's total population was 22.51 million. Taiwan is densely populated and trails only Bangladesh in this category. Kaohsiung City is Taiwan's most crowded urban area, with approximately 9,827 persons per square kilometer; Taipei City had 9,720 persons per square kilometer at the time of the last census. Reflecting two major waves of immigration from Mainland China, one associated with famine in the sixteenth century and the other associated with defeats suffered by the Kuomintang (or Nationalist Party) at the hands of communist forces in the late 1940s, the Han Chinese form the largest ethnic group in Taiwan, making up roughly 98% of the population. Taiwan's population also includes nearly 60 non-Han minorities, including several groups of indigenous peoples. In 1949, after the Kuomintang established a capital in Taiwan, Mandarin became the official language. However, recent "social pluralization" has been accompanied by a growing emphasis on native languages. The Ministry of Education is currently drafting a language equality law aimed at preserving 14 major languages and dialects: Mandarin, Taiwanese, Hakka, and 11 indigenous languages. The draft law encourages both the government and private sectors to provide multilingual services.

2. Political and Legal Systems

Taiwan's official name is the Republic of China (ROC). Article 1 of the *Constitution of the Republic of China* states: "The Republic of China, founded on the Three Principles of the People, shall be a democratic republic of the people, to be governed by the people and for the people." The Three Principles of the People were first articulated by Kuomintang leader Sun Yat-sen and are usually translated as nationalism, democracy, and people's livelihood.

The government of the ROC is divided into three levels, the central, provincial/municipal, and county/city levels, each with specifically defined powers. The central government is composed of the Office of the President, the National Assembly, and five governing branches referred to as Yuans. The Yuans include the Executive Yuan, the Legislative Yuan, the Judicial Yuan, the Examination Yuan, and the Control Yuan.

The President is the head of the executive branch of government. On March 23, 1996, Taiwan held its first direct presidential election with selection of a winner based on a plurality of the popular vote. The inauguration of President Chen Shui-bian of the Democratic Progressive Party on May 20, 2000, representing an end to the Kuomintang's 50-year hold on the presidency, was an event of considerable national importance. Among other things, the President has the power to appoint the president of the

Executive Yuan (known as the Premier) and, with the consent of the Legislative Yuan, the president, vice president, and the grand justices of the Judicial Yuan; the president, vice president, and members of the Examination Yuan; and the president, vice president, auditor-general, and members of the Control Yuan. The Executive Yuan consists of various ministries and departments, including the Department of Health.

Changes in the constitutional framework, culminating with amendments promulgated on April 25, 2000, terminated the sitting National Assembly and established a unicameral legislative system. The National Assembly is now a non-standing body, and most of its functions have been transferred to the Legislative Yuan. The Legislative Yuan consists of representatives who serve for three years and are eligible for reelection. It presently has 225 members. Of these, 168 are elected from the special municipalities, counties, and cities in the ROC (at least one member from each county and city), eight from the plains and mountain aborigines, eight from ROC citizens residing abroad, and 41 from the nationwide constituency.

The main responsibilities of the Legislative Yuan include deliberating and voting on legislation, budgets, emergency declarations, and other issues of national importance. The Legislative Yuan operates through full sessions, committees, and its secretariat. The first session lasts from February to the end of May, and the second from September to the end of December. When necessary, a session may be extended. If the Legislative Yuan disagrees with an important policy of the Executive Yuan, it may, by resolution, request the Executive Yuan to alter it. The Executive Yuan may, with the approval of the President, request reconsideration. If after reconsideration one-half of the attending members of the Legislative Yuan uphold the original resolution, the Premier must either abide by the resolution or resign from office.

The Council of Grand Justices interprets the Constitution and unifies the interpretation of laws and ordinances. Under the Constitution of the ROC, the law cannot restrict Constitutional freedoms except under very limited circumstances such as when public order may be threatened. "Restrictions on constitutional freedoms are valid only if contained in legislation necessary to prevent restrictions against the freedom of others, to respond to emergencies, to maintain social order, or to enhance social interest. In any case, arrest, trial, and punishment must be implemented strictly in accordance with proper legal procedures. If human rights are violated by the government, the victims are entitled to compensation by the state."

The ROC court system consists of three levels: district courts, which hear civil and criminal cases at the first level; high courts at the intermediate level that hear appeals; and the Supreme Court at the highest appellate level, which reviews judgments by lower courts for compliance with pertinent laws or regulations. A separate system exists for administrative litigation. Any person who claims that his rights or legal interests are violated by an unlawful administrative action rendered by a government agency may institute administrative proceedings before one of three high administrative courts, with the possibility of appealing questions of law to the Supreme Administrative Court.

The Control Yuan is responsible for monitoring the government and carrying out the audit function. It was formerly a parliamentary body, with its members elected by provincial and municipal councils. Constitutional amendments in May 1992 transformed it into a quasi-judicial organization composed of the president, vice president, and 27 other members. The Examination Yuan is responsible for the civil service system. The second level of government, the provincial/municipal, also has administrative responsibilities. At present, only two provincial governments are operational – the Taiwan Provincial Government and the Fuchien Provincial Government. Taiwan is the only province completely under the effective control of the ROC; the Fuchien Provincial Government has delegated most of its powers to county governments. The Taiwan Provincial Government has jurisdiction over the 16 counties in Taiwan and most of the cities with the exception of Taipei and Kaohsiung. These two cities are considered to be special municipalities and are under the direct jurisdiction of the central government. The third level of government is the local level. The local level of government encompasses five cities and 16 counties.

3. Public Health Structure and Laws

From 1948 to 1972, WHO assisted Taiwan in developing the foundation of its public health structure. In 1972, the People's Republic of China was admitted to the United Nations forcing Taiwan out of WHO. To date, Taiwan's efforts to reverse its exclusion from WHO have not been successful, which has been an issue of heightened concern to Taiwan during the SARS outbreak. However, Taiwan has continued to enhance and expand its public health structure. In fact, Taiwan presently has one of the highest life expectancies in Asia.

Medical care expenditures account for 5.4% of the Gross Domestic Product of Taiwan and the physician to individual ratio is 1/750. There are 700 hospitals; 17,000 clinics as well as 43 acute beds/10,000 persons. To further enhance public health, in 1995 Taiwan established a universal health insurance system providing equal access to care for the entire population. Under this system, more than 96% of the population is covered by National Health Insurance and 96% of public and private medical care institutions have a contract with the National Health Insurance.

Health care policies for Taiwan are developed by the Department of Health, which is part of the Executive Yuan. There are many subordinate agencies of the Department of Health including the Center for Disease Control, the Bureau of Health Promotion, the National Health Insurance Bureau, and the National Bureau of Controlled Drugs. The Department of Health has five key goals or areas of responsibility: (1) health insurance; (2) health promotion; (3) epidemic prevention; (4) consumer protection; and (5) international cooperation.

One facet of the public health infrastructure of Taiwan is a communicable disease surveillance network comprised of over 450 doctors reporting weekly on a range of infectious diseases. Information from the network is made available to other physicians in a monthly publication, *Epidemiology Bulletin*. Prior to the SARS epidemic, Taiwan had established six disease surveillance centers and quarantine stations to control and prevent the spread of communicable diseases. The Department of Health is responsible for oversight of the nation's quarantine stations and substations.

The Law on the Control of Communicable Diseases and the Regulations

Governing Quarantine make up the major body of Taiwanese public health law relevant to the control of epidemics. The law provides a range of measures that may be adopted by all levels of the government and describes measures to be taken by hospitals and medical personnel, the allocation of funds for actions taken pursuant to the law, and a range of penalties that may be imposed for violation of the law.

Article 1 of the law expresses its purpose: to "curtail the occurrence, infection and spread of infectious diseases." The law lists a number of diseases that must be reported. Four categories of infectious diseases are addressed including "Type 4 Infectious Diseases," a catch-all which includes "[a]ny other infectious disease or emerging infectious disease which has been reckoned by central governing agency as necessary may be added to the list."

The law gives the governing authorities of Taiwan at the central and local levels wide latitude to curb the spread of infectious disease. Under Article 7, "Individuals who are infected with the antigen of an infectious disease and those suspected of probable infection who are regarded as infected patients, are bound...to undergo prescribed treatment and preventive measures." The law further requires that affected areas be disinfected. Additionally, the law grants local governing agencies discretionary authority in the event of an epidemic outbreak to ban or prohibit schools, meetings, banquets, or other types of group activities; limit the access to specific venues and place a limit on the number of persons that can be accommodated; and restrict part or all transportation to a diseased controlled area.

The law also specifically addresses the issue of quarantine as a preventive measure. Article 26 authorizes government agencies at all levels to quarantine and set up interim quarantine facilities. Article 27 addresses quarantine for inbound and outbound travel, providing that "an international harbor and terminal quarantine may be conducted on a paid basis on all inbound and outbound transportation vehicles and the personnel and good on board...." The specifics of quarantine at ports are addressed more thoroughly in the Regulations Governing Quarantine.

The Regulations Governing Quarantine were first promulgated by the Ministry of Health on June 28, 1930, and have been amended many times. The regulations were developed pursuant to Article 27 of the Law on the Control of Communicable Diseases. Article 18 of the regulations allows for the quarantine and isolation of passengers on vessels and aircraft. It provides that "the passengers . . . on board shall be kept in custody; and without permission of the quarantine authorities, shall not be in contact with other persons or commodities." Passengers who have been transferred ashore to isolation are handled in the same manner.

4. Response to SARS

To confront the threats posed by SARS, Interim Regulations on SARS Control were developed by the Department of Health based on the Law on the Control of Communicable Diseases and Regulations Governing Quarantine. The Interim Regulations were designed to strengthen control during the SARS outbreak. A variety of quarantine and isolation measures were undertaken in Taiwan to curb the spread of SARS.

Initially, Taiwan refused to impose health screening at immigration checkpoints, and quarantine measures were more lax than in other affected areas. Effective April 28, however, a mandatory 10-day quarantine was imposed on anyone arriving from Hong Kong, Mainland China, and other SARS-infected areas as designated by WHO. Taiwan's measures were more stringent than the WHO recommendations issued on May 15. Those from SARS-affected areas were required to wear masks prior to boarding for departure for Taiwan and were not permitted to board if they did not do so. Passengers arriving in Taiwan from an area unaffected by SARS, but with a change of planes in a SARS-infected area, were not subject to home quarantine if they had a normal temperature reading, but they were subject to enhanced monitoring. Arriving passengers were required to complete a SARS survey form and wear a surgical mask before deplaning. Providing misinformation on the survey form is considered to be actionable under the law. Temperature screening of all passengers was performed, and passengers were issued a "Notice of Compulsory Quarantine for Special Epidemic Prevention." Passengers had the choice of undergoing quarantine at an airport transit hotel, at home, or at an employer-designated compulsory quarantine location.

If they selected quarantine at a transit hotel, passengers were provided with transportation on a chartered vehicle. The hotel notified Taiwan's Center for Disease Control, and it monitored those under quarantine according to the regulations detailed in the quarantine notice. Individuals were free to leave if they did not exhibit any symptoms after 10 days of quarantine.

Those opting for home quarantine, referred to as Level B Home Quarantine, were asked to avoid public transportation and had to come to the public health office within 24 hours. The office then assumed responsibility for monitoring the individual. If the quarantined individual went outside of the quarantine area (with permission) the individual had to wear a mask at all times and was prohibited from using any public transportation. After 10-days, if no symptoms developed the individual was released from supervision. Those individuals who chose to be quarantined at an employer designated site were provided with room and board by the employer. The employer was responsible for monitoring the individual. Those employees under mandatory quarantine could not come in contact with employees not subject to quarantine, and all sites designated for quarantine needed to have good ventilation and not be connected to a central air-conditioning system.

Quarantine could also be mandated when a person was in close contact with someone diagnosed with SARS. This is referred to as Level A Home Quarantine. These individuals could not leave their home without prior written approval from a health authority. If such authority was granted, the designated health authority was responsible for arranging for transportation for the individual. Very specific guidelines were issued with respect to the actions that must and must not be taken while under compulsory home quarantine. For example, masks had to be worn to protect others, and if fever or respiratory symptoms occurred, the individual was required to seek medical attention immediately and provide details of all recent contacts. No matter what the level of quarantine, all persons subject to quarantine orders had to take and record their temperature two or three times daily.

In May 2003, the Department of Health published a review of the penalties imposed for violation of the Communicable Disease Control Act in an effort to tighten control over the spread of SARS. According to the Government Information Office, the purpose of enforcing home quarantine was three-fold: (1) managing and supervising persons under home quarantine; (2) providing supportive services to those subject to home quarantine; and (3) communicating with those under quarantine and implementing community education.

On May 6, 2003, the SARS Contingency Committee, Department of Health/Taiwanese CDC, published a list of common violations of SARS-related laws or regulations and their subsequent penalties. The list pertained to infractions by the general public, medical staff, and healthcare facilities. It included: refusing, avoiding or hindering compliance with health screening measures, the execution of spot-checks by health authorities on passenger or cargo transportation, or the enforcement of home or group quarantine, failure to comply with an isolation treatment order or violation of instructions from the health authorities during the quarantine period and/or entering a designated isolation area without authorization; physician failure to report SARS cases within the time period designated by law; healthcare institution failure to inform referring hospitals of the health condition of the referred patient, deliver proper care to patients with infectious diseases, and prevent infection, and/or turning people away without reason; medical personnel failure to adopt proper infection control while caring for patients, risking the spread of infection; failure to place the body of a deceased SARS patient in a closed coffin and cremate the body within 24 hours; refusal to work upon the request of the governments' use of empty buildings, equipment, vehicles, ships, airplanes, etc. for disease control purposes; suspecting infection with SARS but failing to abide by government orders, risking the spread of disease to others; and violation of the inspection and importation regulations regarding the control of infectious diseases or spreading a virus in a manner that puts the public in danger.

Penalties for these violations include fines ranging amounts from NT $1,000 to NT $500,000 (US $15,000)[8] and/or prison terms up to a maximum of three years. For example, providing inaccurate information on a SARS survey form is punishable by fines NT $60 to NT $300,000 according to Article 41 of the Law of Communicable Diseases Control and by incarceration for up to two years in accordance with Article 192 of the Criminal Code of the ROC. Additionally, the Cabinet in Taipei City Government will punish medical personnel and institutions who do not cooperate with quarantine orders by imposing fines anywhere from NT $60,000 to NT $240,000. Currently, medical personnel are required to report suspect cases of SARS within 24 hours. Other penalties may include fines, jail time, and/or revocation of a medical license.481

Other enforcement measures were also instituted. For example, violators of quarantine were assigned a site for compulsory group quarantine (in addition to fines and imprisonment). Home quarantine was enforced through the use of web-based cameras at the height of the outbreak. Additionally, because of the widespread panic of health care workers and the refusal of some to work with SARS patients or in facilities treating SARS patients, health officials considered firing staff nurses who refused to work and revoking licenses of many freelance nurses the hospitals often use as a way to save money. The Health Department fined three physicians NT $90,000 (US $2600) and three hospitals NT $1.5 million (US $43,000) each for covering up or delaying the reporting of possible SARS cases.

Health care institutions at risk of penalties provided incentives for health care workers to accept risks related to caring for actual or suspected SARS patients. During the height of the epidemic nearly 160 health care workers resigned for fear of contracting SARS. (It is worth noting that at least some resigned in the belief that hospital infection control measures were inadequate.) Because so many doctors and nurses were resigning, hospitals were offering "danger pay" to those working in SARS wards.

5. Coordination Issues

At the central government level, the Taiwanese Center for Disease Control took several actions to control the SARS epidemic, including activating its Disease Outbreak

Emergency Operations Center; conducting surveillance to detect probable cases of SARS; following WHO guidelines and reporting to WHO; investigating and evaluating reported cases of SARS; issuing guidelines and recommendations on clinical measures, laboratory testing, quarantine, isolation, infection control, and exposure management; strengthening airport quarantine; coordinating and providing support to local health authorities for local control centers; and educating members of the public on how to protect themselves. At the central government level, the agency called for intersectoral cooperation among various departments and subdepartments of the Executive Yuan, specifically, the Council of Labor Affairs, the Mainland Affairs Council, the Civil Aeronautics Administration, the Ministry of Transportation, the Ministry of Communications, and the Government Information Office.

Coordination of the various levels of government was no easy task in Taiwan. Because of an adversarial relationship between the President and the mayor of Taipei, coordination of efforts was quite difficult according to some reports. The Department of Health and the local governments required support from the Ministry of Defense, the National Health Insurance Bureau, the Center for Disease Control, and the Taipei city government to establish fever screening stations.

Despite strained relations with WHO due to tensions with the PRC, Taiwan participated in the global WHO SARS conference held in Kuala Lumpur. Before that meeting, the United States sent a team from the CDC to assist Taiwanese government health officials. Additionally, on May 3, 2003, Mainland China provided permission for two investigators from WHO to visit Taiwan. The investigators, however, were prohibited from contacting Taiwanese government officials. An example of regional coordination was the invitation from the Taiwanese SARS Contingency Committee to Vietnamese representatives to share their experiences in dealing with SARS.

6. Public Reaction

The government of Taiwan recognized a need to educate members of the public to ensure that they would have an understanding of SARS, thus enabling them to prevent the spread of the epidemic. In addition to conveying messages of good personal hygiene, the government also stressed the need for quarantine as a mechanism for epidemic prevention. To accomplish this widespread education, the government emphasized the need for local governments to bring together health and social welfare personnel to provide lists of lectures and offer promotional materials and enhance education of teachers, students and other school personnel as well as the community.

The priority of public education was especially high given numerous complaints about panic-inducing reports in the news. The Government Information Office called for non-government media outlets to exercise restraint in coverage of the epidemic. Additionally, the Premier ordered the Government Information Office to "monitor exaggerated or false SARS-related reports, clarify any false reports and demand that corrections are made" to ease the public's concerns. To quell public fears about the spread of SARS, the Department of Health developed a news program entitled "SARS Front-line." The program was intended to provide the public with accurate information about SARS, inform the public about government policies relevant to the prevention of SARS, and educate the public about protective measures. The show, hosted by an epidemiologist, aired during the evening news.

Taiwan implemented a number of other measures to protect the rights of those affected by isolation and quarantine and minimize resistance. For example, guest workers who were quarantined were paid salaries and had their jobs secure and medical bills were paid by the Taiwanese government. Additionally, families of workers who died from SARS at work were entitled to up to 45 months of salary, subject to approval by Taiwanese insurers and humanitarian aid. For those under home quarantine the government provided a range of assistance. Subjects were called at home and provided with as much psychological support as possible, and home care was provided to family members affected by home quarantine. Economic assistance, including stipends, was provided to those receiving a notice of home quarantine, complying with the regulations, and found to be uninfected with SARS. Those who completed the quarantine period were paid an amount equivalent to nearly US$150. In some cases, other assistance was provided. "The additional assistance needs of persons under home quarantine will be evaluated and provided for through the use of public resources or by conveying such requirements to the competent authorities."

To determine compliance with home quarantine orders, the Department of Health conducted a telephone survey of 100 individuals under quarantine. The survey indicated that 85% of respondents were at home when called and 70% were found to have never left their homes.

7. Current Situation

Enforcement of Taiwan's regulations with respect to SARS took a political toll - -both the Minister of Health and the director of the Center for Disease Control were forced to resign following allegations that their responses to the SARS outbreak were too slow, in particular in infection control measures in hospitals. One theory on the resignation of the Minister of Health is that he did not respond to the city government's call to declare SARS an infectious disease, resulting in less stringent measures being taken by medical personnel, which led to the spread of the virus within the health care setting.

A report by the U.S. CDC published in *Morbidity and Mortality Weekly Reports* reviewed the quarantine measures instituted in Taiwan to prevent the spread of SARS. The report indicated that only a small percentage (0.2%) of those quarantined were fined for violation of a quarantine order. Very few of those under quarantine were later diagnosed with probable or suspected SARS, and far fewer actually had a confirmed diagnosis of SARS. The report concluded that "more study is needed to determine whether the logistics and costs of quarantine warrants its use."

Similar analysis by the Department of Health no doubt led to its September announcement of its plans to modify the SARS quarantine policy. The new approach adopted by the Taiwanese Center for Disease Control is "no fever, no quarantine." This action was taken based upon the fact that during the SARS outbreak, more than 95,000 people were placed under quarantine and only 12 were found to be potential SARS cases, with only two being confirmed cases of SARS. The enormous cost of such an approach led to the modification. Under the new plan, arriving passengers to Taiwan will be hospitalized for observation for three days if they are found to be running a fever. In addition to modification of quarantine measures, Taiwan also announced SARS prevention measures in preparation for a resurgence. These include infection control measures for health care facilities and oversight of medical supplies, as well as better coordination of government agencies. For example, during the height of the flu season, individuals with fever will be diagnosed in a hospital to ensure that they are not suffering from SARS before they will be permitted to board an airplane.

11.3.6. Vietnam[9]
University of Louisville (CDC Report)
F. Socialist Republic of Vietnam
1. Introduction

Vietnam, located on the Indochinese Peninsula in southeast Asia, is a country with a rich and tumultuous history. It is a predominantly mountainous country with challenging topography—only 20% of the country is level land—and seven distinct geographical areas.486 Seventy-five percent of Vietnam's almost 80 million inhabitants live in rural areas. The main urban centers are Hanoi (capital) and Ho Chi

Minh City. Vietnamese is the official language, with a significant French language presence and a number of Chinese dialects and tribal languages also spoken.

On February 28, 2003, Vietnam reported its first case of SARS. A Chinese-American businessman coming from southern China was admitted to the Hanoi French Hospital. A WHO infectious disease expert, Dr. Carlo Urbani, was contacted. Dr. Urbani promptly alerted the Vietnamese government of the disease and eventually coined the term "Severe Acute Respiratory Syndrome." The SARS epidemic in Vietnam was primarily hospital-based and all cases were traced to the initial index case. The hospital, a small 60-bed facility, immediately isolated the patient and staff working in the ward. Five of the physicians in the ward died of SARS. The rest remained in self-imposed quarantine to prevent the spread of SARS.

The last SARS patient was released on May 2, 2003, bringing the total of all SARS patients in Vietnam to 68, with five fatalities between January 11, 2003 and June 7, 2003. The last probable SARS case was reported on April 28. Vietnam's clinical management of SARS patients was somewhat different from other countries. Because of the newness of the disease, each country evaluated cases to ascertain various important disease characteristics, such as incubation period, mode of transmission, and type and severity of symptoms. In Vietnam, the incubation period was found to be 4-5 days, as opposed to the 10 days cited by WHO. Additionally, all cases in Vietnam could be traced to the initial index case mentioned above. After the index case, all new cases were nosocomial and limited to hospital staff. Vietnam was the first country to contain the spread of the SARS virus and to be pronounced SARS-free by the World Health Organization.

The experience of Vietnam with SARS is particularly interesting because of Vietnam's limited resources relative to the other affected countries.

2. Political and Legal Systems

Vietnam has survived various invasions and conquests culminating in its declaration of independence in 1945 and thus becoming the first independent republic in southeast Asia. In 1954, however, the Geneva Accords divided Vietnam into a Communist north and a U.S.-supported south prompting a long, drawn-out war with U.S. involvement until the 1973 Paris Peace Agreement. In 1975, the country reunified and was renamed the Socialist Republic of Vietnam. Today, Vietnam is governed by a single party, the Communist Party, but like China it has changed significantly in recent years. In 1986, the Vietnamese government announced a new strategy of *doi moi*—or renovation—committing itself to both internal reforms and expanded external relationships. As a result, Vietnam has adopted market-oriented policies, creating a socialist market-economy under state management. This shift has, in turn, affected its political structure by way of the country's increasing participation in the international economy.

The country is divided into 53 provincial administrative units, which are in turn further divided into districts and communes. The government is divided into four levels: the central level, the provincial and urban authorities, the urban precincts and rural districts, and the urban wards and rural communes. The primary governing body in Vietnam at the central level is the unicameral National Assembly, the country's legislature. The National Assembly was established in 1992 when the country's Constitution was rewritten. The National Assembly is charged with electing the President, the Prime Minister, the Chief Procurator of the Supreme People's Court, and the Chief Procurator of the Supreme People's Office of Supervision and Control. Further, the National Assembly has both constitutional and legislative power and is charged with making both domestic and foreign policy, including addressing matters of social and economic welfare and national defense and security. The National Assembly is composed of 498 members elected by popular vote. The National Assembly membership is open to both Communist Party members and nonmembers, although in practice, approximately 90% of the members belong to the Communist Party. The President serves as the representative of Vietnam internationally and is the commander in chief of the armed forces. The Prime Minister is the head of the executive arm of the National Assembly and carries out the political, social, cultural, economic, national security and foreign duties of the government assisted by five deputy prime ministers and the cabinet. Vietnam currently has 17 ministries and nine state committees.

The main judicial institutions in Vietnam are the Supreme People's Court and the Supreme People's Procuracy. The Supreme People's Court is Vietnam's highest court and its responsibilities include "organization and implementation of all stages of judicial work, including hearing appeals, reviewing judgments, supervising the implementation of sentences passed by lower-level courts; the organization and conducting of professional training of judges, jurors and other court staff; providing professional guidance for drafting legal documents as requested by the National Assembly; providing professional guidance to local courts; and carrying out a review of judicial practice." The Supreme People's Procuracy is responsible for enforcing adherence to the law by all ministries, other entities of the government, social organizations, and all citizens, and has the power to initiate public prosecution. Other judicial bodies include the People's Courts, military tribunals, and other tribunals set up by the National Assembly for special situations.

Although local government is subordinate to and controlled by the central government, each local administrative unit has a People's Council which serves as its legislative body and a People's Committee which serves as its executive body. People's Committees are charged with maintaining law and order, carrying out budgetary policies, implementing policies from higher administrative levels, and developing socio-economic plans. People's Councils are responsible for implementing basic social services and issuing plans and decisions. Provincial and district level administrative units also have People's Courts and People's Procuraries.

Vietnam's legal system is based on Communist legal theory and the French civil law system. The 1992 Constitution guarantees all citizens fundamental rights including freedom of speech, press, demonstration, assembly, association, belief, religion and nonbelief, equal rights between men and women, and rights to education and health care. The 1992 Constitution also emphasizes the importance of the "law-based state" and making the law the "primary regulatory instrument." In addition to the Constitution, Vietnam has a total of 90 laws and ordinances. Laws in Vietnam "tend to be phrased in broad and general terms," meaning ministries and local agencies must develop implementing regulations and guidelines without clear legislative guidance.

An important feature of Vietnam's Constitution is a stress on the responsibilities as well as rights associated with citizenship. Article 51 of the 1992 Constitution states: "[A] citizen's rights are inseparable from his duties. The State guarantees the rights of the citizen; the citizen must fulfill his duties to the State and society. The citizen's rights and duties are determined by the Constitution and the law." In Article 61 a statement that all citizens are "entitled to a regime of health protection" is complemented by a statement that all citizens have the duty to "observe all regulations on disease prevention and public hygiene."

3. Public Health Structure and Laws

The government of Vietnam provides health care to its citizens through a network of state-run facilities at the various government levels: central, provincial, district, and commune. The Ministry of Health provides health care management at the central level and is also in charge of delineating policy at all levels. The Provincial and District Health Bureaus provide health care management at their respective levels. The situation varies at the commune level, with some communes receiving health care administration from the district level and others relying solely on the staff at the commune health stations. The commune level receives financial support from the Ministry of Health. All levels of health care are under the control of the central government and the People's Committees at the appropriate level. However, the Ministry of Health has little to no control over budgetary issues at the provincial level as such issues are decided by the Provincial People's Committees.

Vietnam's health infrastructure has grown tremendously in the past decades. In 1945, there were 47 hospitals in the country, by the late 1970s there were about 713 hospitals, and today there are approximately 800 hospitals. Although these hospitals are predominantly government-owned, the

Ministry of Health only controls about 18% of them. Some of the other hospitals are controlled by the Ministry of Defense and the Ministry of the Interior and are intended for use by government officials and the central leadership. In addition, many hospitals at the district level are supported by Overseas Development Aid. A more recent development, particularly in larger cities, is the inclusion of private, for-profit clinics within publicly-owned hospitals. Despite this growth, however, "hospital services are still limited" by Western standards. Vietnam's predominantly rural population poses a great challenge to access to health care services. To address this challenge, Vietnam has developed a vast community health care network. District health centers and district hospitals are now available in all districts and most communes have a health center as well. According to the World Bank, approximately 97% of the rural population has access to a public health center within their commune.

Recently, private health care was made legal, although the central government still maintains some control over prices. There are approximately 11,000 medical facilities, and the ratio of physicians to population is one physician/1,000 persons. Because Vietnam is largely a poor country, it depends on international aid to the Ministry of Health for much of its health expenditures. Traditional medicine plays a significant role in Vietnam's health care services and it is a goal of the central government to "promote and develop" traditional medicine.

The public health legislation in Vietnam, the "Law on People's Health Protection," was approved by the National Assembly in 1989.

4. Response to SARS

Although the SARS epidemic did not prompt any amendments to the Law on People's Health Protection, the Departments of Health Legislation, Preventive Medicine, and HIV/AIDS Control under the Ministry of Health are considering possible changes to the legislation in light of the events surrounding the SARS epidemic.

The Vietnamese government's response to SARS was prompt and included public acknowledgement of the epidemic from the outset. The use of isolation and quarantine was a key measure to the containment of the spread of SARS. The Law on People's Health Protection governs public health practice in Vietnam, but the specific procedures for quarantine and isolation are not available and it has not been possible to access the actual legislation. The Ministry of Health enforces quarantine and isolation; the Health Quarantine Service is housed in the Ministry of Health. Ministries and other government agencies are allowed to issue ordinances and regulations. It is possible that the authority for quarantine and isolation comes from a regulation or ordinance issued by the Ministry of Health and/or from the Law on People's Health Protection. Because details regarding the legislative authority is not known for quarantine and isolation in Vietnam, no detailed information on enforcement is available.

The government of Vietnam took the approach that "SARS is a political challenge" when handling the containment of the epidemic. Even before the first case in Vietnam the government took action based on reports of cases of atypical pneumonia in southern China. Soon after the reports began appearing, the Ministry of Health alerted hospitals and officials in the provinces bordering China about the possibility of SARS entering Vietnam through its borders.

Vietnam's efforts to contain SARS included identification of persons with SARS, their movements and contacts; isolation of SARS patients in hospitals; protection of medical staff treating these patients; identification and isolation of suspected SARS cases; exit screening of international travelers; and reporting and sharing information with other authorities and/or governments. For example, the Ministry of Health developed preventive guidelines, "Ten Measures for Prevention Against SARS," that were distributed to communities and to local medical workers. The 10 guidelines were: (1) Minimize close contact with patients. If contact is necessary, use protective gear such as gloves and masks. (2) Isolate source of disease. Sterilize, clean disease area with Chlormin B. Sterilize all used equipment, garments, etc. (3) Understand the symptoms of the disease to identify early, accurately and completely the death of patients and cases of people who are ill but without symptoms. Then organize the isolation and treatment immediately. Control each individual, each family. (4) Do not gather or have meetings, unless necessary, in an area where SARS is suspected. (5) Set up isolation areas in hospitals or clinics that have patients in treatment. Circulate air in schools and hospital rooms. Increase space between working areas. (6) Use antibiotics or a combination of antibiotics to treat respiratory problems. (7) Patients with respiratory symptoms need to be observed and treated immediately. (8) All clinics, preventive clinics, Pasteur Institute, hospitals for infectious disease, and emergency rooms need to be prepared for any situation. (9) Promote daily personal hygiene; hygiene for nose and throat using antibacterial liquid, use a combination of antibiotics to protect the respiratory system. (10) Apply all procedures to prevent an epidemic; report cases according to the Order dated December 6, 2002 from the Health Department.

These guidelines were supplemented by a number of training initiatives. The Ministry of Health and the Vietnam National Administration of Tourism (VNAT) joined together to provide a training course for tourism agencies and others in the tourism industry on ways to prevent SARS. The VNAT also established a SARS Steering Committee to coordinate actions to prevent, detect, and control SARS. The committee worked with the media to inform travelers and was charged with setting both short- and long-term plans for the tourism industry to deal with SARS. The Ministry of Public Health was asked by the Prime Minister to begin training courses at the local level to educate people in border areas and other high-risk areas in the prevention of SARS. In early May, the National SARS Steering Committee held a training workshop for the six northern border provinces to discuss ways to prevent SARS from re-entering the country from China. In May 2003, a two-day workshop for health workers, police, soldiers, and border guards on SARS detection, treatment, and quarantine was held in Quang Ninh province, which borders China. Further, many local governments held training for medical and health workers on the prevention and control of SARS.

Vietnam implemented strict quarantine and isolation measures from the beginning of the SARS outbreak. The Ministry of Health posted on its website the definitions of SARS suspicious cases and SARS cases consistent with information from WHO. The Ministry also made available information sheets for those who had close contacts and social contacts of SARS patients or anyone who had been in a SARS-affected country. These sheets provided information on voluntary isolation at home (10 days and under monitoring by local health workers) and for monitoring only. Family members of SARS patients and others who had close contacts with SARS patients were located and monitored by health workers. The Ministry of Health set up six SARS Mobile Teams to detect, prevent, and treat SARS cases. These teams were composed of physicians, nurses, medical workers, and drivers. The teams were equipped with medicines and the necessary vehicles to transport and isolate SARS cases.

The government selected two hospitals for isolation of SARS cases—the Hanoi French Hospital and the Tropical Medicine Institute of the Bach Mai Hospital. On March 11, the Hanoi French Hospital stopped admitting new patients and prohibited visitors from entering to prevent the spread of SARS. Two other hospitals were prepared to serve as isolation centers should the need arise. The Military Hygiene and Epidemiology Institute assisted the Hanoi French Hospital in sterilizing its grounds to prevent the spread of SARS within the hospital. Vietnam imposed more stringent hospital discharge requirements than those recommended by WHO. The Ministry of Health issued discharge protocols that went beyond WHO guidelines by requiring that patients be without a fever for five days; have clinical improvement; have normal blood examinations; have stable and improved chest x-rays; and have at least seven days in convalescence. Vietnam also followed different screening, diagnosing, treating, and discharging guidelines than other countries. The Tropical Medicine Institute maintained contact with all discharged patients for up to a month after being discharged from the hospital.

All 61 provinces and cities designated at least one quarantine area. SARS Prevention Boards were set up in six northern provinces and at the port city of Haiphong. The boards were headed by the chairmen of the People's Committees. These boards worked closely with the Ministry of Health, border guards, police, immigration, and quarantine agencies. Part of each province's budget was reallocated to purchase necessary medical equipment. Additionally, northern provinces received help from special medical teams created by the Ministry of Health. Although no SARS cases were reported in Ho Chi Minh City, the city also set up a SARS control board, and preventive measures were taken at the city's medical centers.

Because of Vietnam's expansive border with China, restrictions on entry or travel were particularly significant. It is estimated that approximately 5,000 persons travel between China and Vietnam on a daily basis. Seven of the 68 cases of SARS in Vietnam were from the northern provinces; the rest of the SARS cases were from a single city, Hanoi. The government instituted stringent control of border entry points and maintained them even after WHO declared Vietnam SARS free. The Prime Minister ordered the implementation of emergency epidemic prevention committees and doubled the personnel of the quarantine forces in the northern provinces bordering China. The Ministry of Foreign Affairs set up checkpoints at all ports of entry. Infrared thermal imagers were installed at airports, and temperature screenings were implemented at all borders and airports for those entering the country. Anyone with a temperature above 38C was placed under mandatory quarantine. Persons returning to Vietnam from a SARS-affected area were given the option to register to self-quarantine at home and undergo supervision by local medical clinic workers, or at a medical center. Quarantine stations were also set up at border checkpoints, airports, seaports, and at 54 local hotels.

As an added measure to controlling entry points, the Health Department required that medical preventive centers at border provinces report daily by fax on the number, nationality, and status of arrivals to the Epidemic Prevention Agency. In late March, the Ministry of Health issued an Arrival/Departure medical card used to screen for SARS symptoms or exposures of all arriving and departing travelers by all air, land, and sea entry ports. Vietnamese citizens from SARS affected areas completed health forms and had to provide health certificates from the country of origin and had to undergo a 10-day mandatory quarantine at a local medical clinic. Foreigners from affected areas completed health forms and had to provide health certificates and were required to have regular health checks and provide addresses and telephone numbers during their stay in Vietnam. On March 19, 2003, the Health Department issued a letter to all local health departments dealing with infectious diseases to follow a set of 11 measures issues by the government. Among these, local health departments were asked to work closely with the Customs Department and police in enforcing SARS measures; assign medical personnel to handle passengers from airplanes and buses; notify all passengers of SARS symptoms and distribute Arrival/Departure Medical Forms to all travelers; send information, including case definition, on SARS symptoms to all ports of entry; distribute "Ten Measures for Prevention Against SARS" to all travelers; and report immediately to the Health Department on all issues relating to SARS. In late March 2003, the Airport Authority set up a task force to monitor all flights coming and going from SARS-affected areas. Persons who wanted to leave Vietnam were given a health examination and issued a health declaration if no symptoms or fever were present. If the person had any symptoms or fever he or she would not be allowed to travel and would be placed on mandatory observation and be treated medically as needed.

Some of the more extreme measures included the government's quarantine of 2,000 Vietnamese students evacuated from China for 10-14 days upon their return to Vietnam, and the northern province of Quang Ninh's decision to turn away all Chinese visitors seeking to enter the province in late April. In the latter case, an exception was made for Chinese traders contingent upon a clean health exam conducted by Vietnamese health workers prior to entry.

The national government provided a substantial amount of financial support, equivalent to US $5.3 million, for medicine, disinfectant, equipment, and other necessary supplies to combat the SARS outbreak. Additionally, the northern province of Ninh Binh, which borders China, spent a substantial amount of money (VN $1.3 billion) on equipment, medicine, and protective gear for health workers. The Finance Ministry allocated VN $30 billion for the prevention of SARS. The majority of the money was spent on medical equipment. Also, the Ministry of Finance provided licensing support for the Vietnam-Russia Medical Centre to develop masks that could prevent the transmission of SARS under WHO guidelines.

Personnel participating in the prevention of the spread of SARS and the treatment of SARS patients received a government allowance of five times the amount normally given to health care workers, as authorized by an order issued by the Treasury Department. Funds for this increase were paid by each medical institution later to be reimbursed by the Health Department upon receiving the complete reports.

5. Coordination Issues

On March 19, after an emergency central government meeting to discuss SARS, an Inter-Governmental Steering Committee (IGSC) on SARS headed by the Health Minister and reporting directly to the Deputy Prime Minister was established. The committee was charged with educating the public, monitoring SARS patients, ensuring isolation of SARS patients, and providing for coordination within the government on SARS issues. The committee included members from the Ministries of Foreign Affairs, Civil Aviation, Culture and Information, Public Security, National Defense, Finance, and Transport. The IGSC was subdivided into four subcommittees: surveillance and containment; clinical management; information, education, and communication (IEC); and logistics. The IGSC met on a daily basis from March 19 to mid-April and produced a number of recommendations for the Ministry of Health. Additionally, in the weeks following the inception of the national IGSC task force, local task forces were implemented in 38 out of the 61 provinces and cities of Vietnam. Also on a local level, SARS Prevention Boards established in six northern provinces and one port city worked closely with the Ministry of Health, border guards, police, immigration, and quarantine agencies.

Officials at the provincial level were required to report daily with updates on SARS. All localities were told to immediately isolate suspected SARS cases and send them via a special ambulance to one of the two designated hospitals. Other examples of coordination or cooperation within the government include the coordinated detection and quarantine activities undertaken at border points by the Ministry of Health, Public Security, Finance, Transportation, Agriculture, and Rural Development. These multiministerial groups were called Quarantine Forces. The Ministry of Health and the VNAT coordinated activities directed at tourists and travelers and education for those working at entry points, as described in more detail above.

Throughout the SARS outbreak the government of Viet Nam presented an image of continued cooperation between the Ministry of Health, Ministry of Foreign Affairs, Ministry of Transportation, Ministry of National Defense, and the General Organization of Customs. Details on the level of coordination and cooperation and the ease with which this cooperation took place are not available from sources not affiliated with the central government. The central government of Vietnam worked closely with WHO from the outset of the epidemic. The Hanoi French Hospital informed the Ministry of Health of the first case of atypical pneumonia on March 5. That same day the Hanoi Health Service was sent to investigate. A few days later, on March 9, the first meeting was held with WHO experts. As noted in the introduction to this case study, it was in fact a WHO official, Dr. Carlo Urbani, who named SARS after examining the patient at the Hanoi French Hospital. In early April, more experts from WHO were sent to Vietnam to assist the government in handling the SARS outbreak. The IGSC served to coordinate communication efforts between the government and international experts, including the WHO representatives.

Vietnam also received technical assistance from Singapore, Japan, and the World Bank. Additionally, the Asian Development Bank reallocated US $6.17 million to help in the fight against SARS. Vietnam also received technical and financial support and assistance from the CDC in the United States, Malaysia, France, and Australia. In addition to providing technical assistance, the Japanese government donated thousands of masks, protective suits, and gloves to Vietnam for use by health workers. Vietnam worked with Taiwan to protect the safety and health of Vietnamese workers in Taiwan. The Taiwanese government's regulations provide for guest workers who were suspected of having an infectious disease to be quarantined based upon the guidance of health authorities. Under the regulations, workers would be guaranteed their jobs and would continue to be paid their salaries while in quarantine. Additionally, the Taiwanese government assured families of guest workers that if a guest worker died of SARS while working in Taiwan they would receive up to 45 months of salary, contingent upon approval by the Taiwanese government and availability of government and humanitarian aid funds.

6. Public Reaction

Vietnamese officials concluded at the end of the SARS outbreak that the epidemic was a political challenge necessitating both political and technical measures. They also considered SARS an ethical challenge that required a great degree of transparency of action to the public and the media. The Prime Minister acknowledged the SARS outbreak on national television and through other mass media outlets on March 14.568 Along with the announcement of the SARS outbreak, measures for prevention were disseminated via television and other media. Written information was made available in Vietnamese and English from the Ho Chi Minh City Health Department. Daily information was provided to the public through mass media and an intensive information, education and communication campaign.

Residents of Vietnam could access information on SARS by calling a hotline or checking a website set up by the Municipal Centre for Health Education and Communications. In Ho Chi Minh City, telephone hotlines were set up to provide the community with ongoing information. The hotlines were available during working hours, with health professionals available for information after hours. In order to minimize the personal burden of SARS and to encourage people to seek medical treatment when they experienced SARS symptoms, the government of Vietnam announced that SARS treatment would be free of charge for citizens and foreigners alike. All patients seeking treatment for respiratory system infections would be exempt from paying medical fees.

7. Current Situation

As the second country to experience a SARS case and the first to contain the disease, Vietnam has been cited by many as a success. Health authorities in Vietnam considered the early detection, isolation, and quarantine efforts taken by the government from the outset to be the keys to Vietnam's success in containing SARS. Additionally, the government's transparency, public acknowledgement of the epidemic, and early cooperation with WHO are often cited as reasons for Vietnam's rapid containment of SARS.

Even after Vietnam was removed from WHO's list of SARS-affected countries, the Health Minister reiterated the importance of maintaining preventive measures. As of late April, health checks at entry points were recommended but no longer mandatory; all travelers were still required to complete health forms; all major border points and ports maintained their quarantine facilities in function; and temperature screens were still in place at airports. The quarantine period was reduced from 14 days to 10 days once Vietnam was taken off the SARS affected areas list by WHO.

According to the Vice-Minister of Health of Vietnam, reflecting on his country's experience, the International Health Regulations should be revised promptly by WHO to provide member states with specific guidelines on issues relating to quarantine. Vietnam is also an advocate for an increase in sharing of scientific information, strengthening of the existing disease outbreak alert and response system at the regional and global levels, and the establishment of a regional referral laboratory capable of diagnosing emerging diseases.

After the outbreak was brought under control, several sources, including WHO and the U.S. CDC, touted Vietnam's efforts in both the management of the disease itself and the peripheral logistics associated with a much publicized and scrutinized epidemic of a new communicable disease. The fact that Vietnam is both a communist nation and a poor country, make its success in the management of SARS all the more impressive to the industrialized world.

11.4   International Police Organizations and Bioterrorism
11.4.1.   INTERPOL and Bioterrorism

INTERPOL, or the International Criminal Police Organization, was created in 1923 to facilitate cross-border police cooperation. The organization is governed by a constitution and has 187 member countries. Article 2 of the constitution states the organization's goals:

Article 2:
Its aims are:
(1) To ensure and promote the widest possible mutual assistance between all criminal police authorities within the limits of the laws existing in the different countries and in the spirit of the 'Universal Declaration of Human Rights';
(2) To establish and develop all institutions likely to contribute effectively to the prevention and suppression of ordinary law crimes.

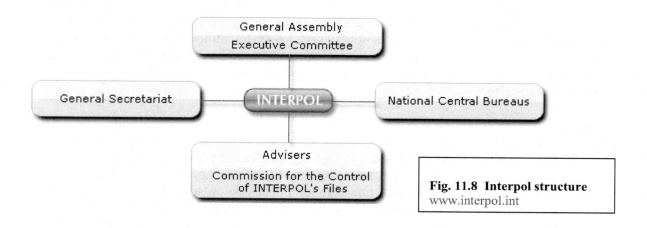

Fig. 11.8 Interpol structure
www.interpol.int

In 2005, INTERPOL began the development of a specialized group of expertise to address the threat of bioterrorism. The following is the fact sheet developed by INTERPOL describing this mission:

FACT SHEET: Bioterrorism:
Growing threat
The possibility of terrorist attacks using biological agents represents a growing concern for law enforcement bodies, governments and public health officials around the world. Biological agents (for instance, bacteria, viruses and fungi) are significantly easier to handle and transport than nuclear or conventional weapons. They are difficult to detect and symptoms from exposure may not appear for hours or days.

Many law enforcement officials believe that recent trends in terrorism show a heightened interest in the use of weapons of mass destruction such as biological weapons. It is relatively easy to acquire biological materials, and biological weapons are an effective means of instilling widespread fear among the public. There have been numerous historical events involving the use or threatened use of toxins and pathogens and there is clear evidence that, in recent times, a number of individuals and terrorist organizations have carried out research into, or attempted to acquire, biological agents and toxins.

For example, in Malaysia, an individual was arrested for terrorist activities related to the militant group Jemaah Islamiyah. Based on interrogations of two captured suspects, the individual was part of a plan to obtain biological agents and develop them into weapons. A raid on the office in Kabul, Afghanistan, of two Pakistani nuclear scientists uncovered documents indicating an interest in anthrax, including calculations related to the aerial dispersal of the material by balloon. The men are believed to have had contact with Al Qaeda.

Co-ordinated response

In April 2004, the United Nations Security Council adopted Resolution 1540, which highlighted the serious threat posed by biological weapons to international peace and security, and urged greater national and international co-ordination to strengthen the global response. Recognising the imminent dangers from this form of crime was the first step in countering the threat, and now it is vital to provide the tools which will enable the relevant agencies to take preparatory measures.

INTERPOL's Bioterrorism Prevention Unit has developed a programme to build national and international capacity to counter the threat, focusing mainly on bioterrorism-prevention police training.

Its main aims are to:
- raise awareness of the threat
- develop police training programmes
- strengthen efforts to enforce existing legislation
- promote the development of new legislation
- provide useful tools for police bio-related investigations
- encourage co-operation between countries and agencies

The unit was created in 2004 with financial support from the US-based Sloan Foundation. Further funding from the Sloan Foundation, US State Department and a grant from the Canadian government have helped sustain the programme.

Capacity building

The first INTERPOL Global Conference on Bioterrorism, held in March 2005, was a major event that brought together some 500 senior police officers, counter-terrorism specialists, national and international governmental and non-governmental agencies, scientists and other academics to share expertise and experience in all areas of bioterrorism. Following the conference, INTERPOL established a number of key initiatives:
- *Training sessions* – theoretical and practical activities for law enforcement agencies
  o Regional training workshops in Chile, Singapore, South Africa, Oman and Ukraine have brought together hundreds of experts.
  o 'Train-the-trainer' sessions help to enhance the capacity of national police forces to develop their own training capabilities and response units. They also highlight the need for increased collaboration among national agencies in areas such as law enforcement, public health, customs and prosecution. In 2007-2008 train-the-trainer sessions were organized in Egypt, Kenya, Peru, the Philippines and Romania.
  o International table-top exercises, assessing national capabilities for preventing bio-crimes and helping to identify issues critical to a co-ordinated response, were organized in France and Malaysia in 2007 and 2008.
- *Training materials* – guidelines and web resources
  o The online Bioterrorism Prevention Resource Centre aims to enhance knowledge-sharing and co-operation between public health officials, customs and law enforcement bodies

and international organizations. Its objective is to assess the vast amount of bioterrorism-related data that is increasingly available, and provide links to the most useful websites.

o   A Bioterrorism Incident Pre-Planning and Response Guide with specific instructions and investigative guidelines has been published in all four INTERPOL languages (Arabic, English, French and Spanish), and is available on INTERPOL's public website.

11.4.2.   Europol[10]

The European Police Office is the European law enforcement organization whose aim is to improve the cooperation between the European Union States member states' authorities in order to combat terrorism, drug traffic, and international crime.[11] The Europol headquarters are in Hague in the Netherlands. The Europol Convention agreed to in 1995 came into force in 1998. Europol has the same goals as Interpol

Regarding terrorism, Europol is frequently requested to support investigations in member states by providing operational and strategic analysis on site. Moreover, Europol, through its databases and exchange programs enables the member States to exchange and share sensitive intelligence in terrorist investigations. It also participates in forums and initiates some programs. These programs provide in part some basis for decision-making in member states but also and more necessary, at an EU level.

Europol has relations with third partners, which increase and strengthen more every year in order to facilitate the mutual cooperation between member states and their authorities. Indeed, in order to fight against terrorism effectively, Europol cooperates and works with several third party countries and organizations by signing cooperation agreements. Europol and INTERPOL have intensified their relations since 2007. The two organizations started an exchange program allowing their officers to obtain a greater awareness of their counterpart organization and to promote cooperation. INTERPOL and Europol representatives have participated in several operational working meetings at the premises of both organizations.

In 2001, the European National Assembly adopted a text allowing Europol's director to sign a cooperation agreement with INTERPOL. This agreement has been sign the 5th of November by both the Secretary General of INTERPOL and the Director of Europol. The joint initiative contains four articles. In this light, an exchange program between the two organizations has been implemented: this program consists of five officers from each organization who will meet each year for two weeks to discuss the common areas where issues can arise.

In 2007, Europol opened an liaisons office at the INTERPOL headquarters in order to strengthen the collaboration between the two police organizations. The liaison office provides additional communications support for ongoing projects and analysis of crime and criminal data between the INTERPOL General Secretariat in Lyon (France) and Europol's base in The Hague. The two organizations also started to discuss a "roadmap" in 2005. This "roadmap" identifies common areas where Interpol and Europol can work together and enhance their cooperation; those areas are child abuse, drug traffic and terrorism.

M Noble, Secretary General of INTERPOL, said "There are many areas where Interpol and Europol can work effectively together for the benefit of law enforcement in our member countries and Interpol will continue to develop links and share information to ensure this is done as efficiently as possible." Furthermore, M. Razel, Europol's director, stated: "Bilateral meetings between officers from our two organizations are of the highest importance and it is also essential that those in charge of the organizations meet in order to ensure that we complement each other's work and that we have a common agreement on our strategies in the fight against international organized crime and terrorism". Those statements emphasize that the two organization's need to work together in order to make their work easier and more efficient, and that the strategy of collaboration is essential to struggle against organized crime.

11.4.3.   European Commission[12]

The European Commission is the board of Europe, the executive body of the European Union that has the right to initiate legislation. It operates at the very heart of the European Union, acting as the source of policy initiatives, drafting legislation and overseeing the implementation of any treaties. Its 20 commissioners are chosen from the 15 European Union member countries.

After the anthrax attacks in the United States, the Council and the Commission of the EU developed a program in order to coordinate and support the public health preparedness, response capacity, and planning of the Member States against biological and chemical agents attacks.

Subsequently, the Health Security Committee (HSC) has been created as an informal cooperation and coordination body concentrated on the exchange of information on health–related threats from acts of terrorism or any deliberate release of biological or other agents. The HSC consists of the representatives of the EU Member States, representatives of Directorate – General for Health and Consumers, and other relevant Commission services and agencies (e.g. ECDC, EMEA) and holds regular meetings twice a year. Then, the Health Council agreed (in February 2007) on transitional prolongation and extension of the mandate of the Health Security Committee focusing on three domains: (1) public health preparedness and response to chemical, biological and radio nuclear (CBRN) attacks; (2) generic preparedness and response for public health emergencies, and (3) influenza preparedness and response.

In the international context, the European Commission has been closely cooperating with the WHO and the G7 states (USA, Canada, UK, France, Germany, Italy, Japan, and Mexico) in an effort to ensure an optimal and coordinated level of global preparedness and response to the potential threats to public health. In this context, the Global Health Security Initiative (GHSI) was set up in November 2001, under the leadership of the former U.S. Department of Health and Human Services (HHS). It was envisaged as an informal group to fill a gap for like-minded countries to address health issues of the day, such as global health security.

The major achievements of the GHSI are: strengthening smallpox preparedness and response; improving international communications and risk management; testing and enhancing laboratory capabilities; advancing global pandemic influenza preparedness and response; preparing against chemical and radiological threats; sharing information

Although only four EU Member States are members of the GHSI, the Commission will assure that results of GHSI work will be made available through the Health Security Committee to all Member States.

11.5   International Travel: Extremely Drug Resistant Tuberculosis (XDR-TB) and U.S. Citizen, Andrew Speaker

In 2007, Andrew Speaker, a U.S. citizen living in Fulton County, Georgia, received worldwide attention when he left the United States on his honeymoon, despite the meetings with the CDC cautioning him that he may have XDR-TB. Speaker was not quarantined nor ordered to stay in the United States, so he left on an odessey that brought him back to the United States under the scrutiny of the world's news media and public health authorities.

The CDC was called to testify before both the U.S. House of Representatives and the U.S. Senate to explain why this incident had become a global event, and to investigate what, if anything, had been done by the federal government that might have led to the event. The following graphic from The New York Times, charts the dates and the course that Andrew Speaker and his bride took for their honeymoon.

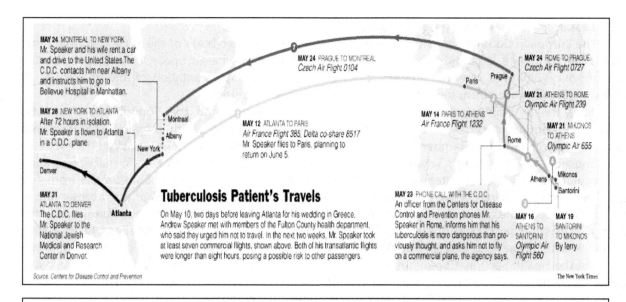

Fig. 11.1 "Tuberculosis Patient's Travels," The New York Times, June 2, 2007, at
http://www.nytimes.com/2007/06/02/health/02tick.html?scp=607&sq=prague&st=nyt&_r=0

The following narrative is based on a timeline produced as a result of the Congressional Hearings, showing the conflicting testimony between Speaker and CDC Officials and Fulton County Officials who argue they warned Speaker not to travel. Speaker heard it differently, and did not believe they were telling him not to travel. Here is a narrative of the account from the Congressional findings:

Andrew Speaker discovered through an unrelated medical appointment that he had evidence of tuberculosis in one lung, and subsequent testing proved this suspicion correct.[13] Speaker, had been tested by a private physician, who, under state and federal law was required to report the disease, did so, and the local and state public health authorities became involved with supervising his care. The next step required that Speaker be tested for multi-drug resistant tuberculosis (MDR-TB), a much more resistant and dangerous form of tuberculosis, which proved positive. [14] After some months, the local and state public health authorities failed to institute directly observed therapy, except to ask his fiancée to make sure that he took his prescribed drugs. On Friday, May 11, because the local and state public health authorities learned that Speaker planned to take a trip abroad for a wedding, a meeting with Speaker was held with a representative from the Centers for Diseases Control and Prevention when they discussed his medical condition and discouraged his travel.[15]   He was scheduled to depart the next day, May 12, for France, which he did.[16]   On the same day, May 11, Fulton County officials attempted to deliver an order to Speaker's home, but he could not be located.[17] CDC was made aware of his departure out of the country on May 21st, and notified the Customs and Border Patrol in Atlanta, Georgia on May 22nd.[18] When CDC notified the Office of Health Affairs, Department of Homeland Security, there was confusion about whether to release his name to the agencies,[19] and CDC did not release his name to DHS until five hours[20] before he returned to the United States.

Speaker was contacted through an informal network by CDC at his hotel in Italy and was advised not to travel, not to board a commercial craft, to check into a hospital in Italy, and to contact the public health authorities in Italy to advise them of his medical diagnosis, which by then, had changed to a diagnosis of Extensively Drug Resistant tuberculosis (XDR-TB),[21] a much rarer and more deadly form of tuberculosis which is resistant to all of the antibiotics used to treat tuberculosis.

It was learned on May 24th, that Speaker did not take this advice from CDC, and had checked out of his hotel in Rome.[22] Instead, he booked a return flight from Prague, Czechoslovakia to Montreal,

Canada, for May 25th. He boarded a flight in Prague with his wife, and traveled to Montreal, Canada, admittedly to avoid detection by flying directing to the United States.[23] From Montreal, he rented a car and crossed the U.S.-Canadian border, when a Customs and Border Patrol officer decided to unilaterally override the system to allow Andrew Speaker and his wife to enter the country, although he was blocked from entering the United States.[24] CDC notified WHO of Speaker's travel on May 25th.[25] After crossing the border, Speaker drove south, toward his home, Georgia, when he was located by cell phone by CDC,[26] who had been notified that he had crossed the border into the United States. CDC advised Speaker to go to a specific hospital in New York, and to check himself into their care. Speaker, did so, and was hand-delivered a quarantine order restricting his movement for three days.[27] During the following eight days, Speaker was transferred to a hospital in Denver, Colorado for treatment, and a quarantine order was issued by the Denver Health Authority Public Health Department,[28] where Speaker underwent treatment for his XDR-TB.

The Speaker case raised concerns on the Hill, and hearings were held by both the U.S. House of Representatives[29] and the U.S. Senate.[30] A CDC representative, during one press interview on May 30th, described the "covenant of trust" that the agency has with patients who are on the honor system of following medical restrictions for the protection of the public's health, saying that "there is not much it can do when someone breaks the trust while overseas."[31] The case was complicated by the fact that Speaker's father-in-law was a CDC research scientist who worked in the field of tuberculosis research, which led CDC to conduct an investigation of his role in the incident. [32] Nine plaintiffs who were on the flight from Prague with Speaker, filed an action against Speaker in the Quebec Provincial Court, claiming money damages for their losses, exposure to a potentially deadly disease, and consequential pain and hardship his actions have caused them.[33]

The following essay makes the case for a global public health commons where an global public health commons doctrine can be derived from the "covenant of trust" and clarified by international law.

The case for a global public health commons:
based on the "covenant of trust" and clarified by international law
Victoria Sutton

The "Covenant of Trust" Doctrine

This is a universal society preference --- to subordinate the individual interest for the good of the whole. But that is measured by giving more weight to the constitutional protection of individual liberty and freedom when weighed against the threat to the public's health, when those risks are not imminent. When the state's interest increases, the weight given to individual liberty is diminished. In the increasingly accessible global commons, it might be suggested that the state interest is increasing with our responsibility not to spread infectious diseases to other countries.

The "covenant of trust" doctrine has grown into its current state, due to the explosion in constitutional due process, during the last forty years. This due process, which requires that the person whose liberty is being limited, be afforded the opportunity procedurally for a hearing to challenge this limitation, but also the least restrictive means possible, limiting liberty only to the extent required to protect the public's health. Over the last 30 years, local and state public health authorities were less and less likely to be granted judicial orders, restricting the liberty of an individual, simply for medical treatment, if the individual promised to adhere to the medical protocol recommended. In fact, courts began requiring increasing evidence of non-compliance on the part of the individual, often not just once, but perhaps requiring multiple instances of noncompliance before ordering isolation or quarantine. Hence, the broadening of the "covenant of trust," resulted.

Is there a place in the law for the "covenant of trust" in the now broader community which extends to the global commons? Has the "covenant of trust' outlived its colonial-era quaintness? The idea of a "covenant of trust" within our domestic jurisdictions where there was little chance of escape of the police powers of the state, allowed the "covenant of trust" to operate in a world that moved slowly by ship or by horse, and communications took weeks and months to accomplish. In that same context, there was no responsibility felt to accrue to the city ports who freely and perhaps hopefully allowed infected people to leave, thereby directly infecting people at the next port-of-call. Should we, as a federal government, consider our biosecurity and biodefense laws in the context of our role in the global commons rather than solely as our role of protectorate of the public's health within our state jurisdictions? Specifically, should we rethink our reliance on the legal principles of solely keeping people out of our country, with its roots in the principle that domestic laws will not have extra-territorial jurisdiction without several very high threshold tests being met, so therefore, we cannot control individuals who escape our jurisdictional control?[34] In the same sense of our responsibilities to the global commons, should we revisit our reliance on the "convenant of trust" with individuals who can seriously damage international relations with a simple violation of that "covenant of trust", simply by boarding a flight and shedding infection throughout the global commons? No longer do countries ignore the responsibilities of the offending country that fails to detain or fails to notify the global community that an infected individual has left the control of the domestic laws of that country. It was only recently, in 2003, that the world cast a judgmental eye toward China which had delayed notification to the World Health Organization (WHO) about the emergence of the new and highly-infectious and deadly virus, SARS, and the subsequent travel of people from the infected region to all parts of the world, causing infections in many of these destination countries.

Failures of China to be a responsible global citizen in the protection of the public's health in the global commons, furthered the will to implement and shape the new International Health Regulations (IHR) which provide for a coordinating mechanism for notification and response to public health emergencies. Implementation of the IHR may require us to re-examine the "covenant of trust" in our international relationships under the IHR in our relationships with other countries in the global commons.

An International Relational Ethic and International Law for Biosecurity

The new global commons require that we as a nation extend our traditional legal foundation to not just the government's response to is citizens within its jurisdictional boundaries, but also a responsibility not to harm others outside of that jurisdiction.

It was only in 2003 (a mere four years earlier), that the world took a dim view of China's failure to curtail travel out of its Guangdong district to other parts of the world, spreading the highly contagious SARS disease. Further criticism of China's silence followed, knowing that China could have warned the rest of the world of the possibility of contagion from its country. Should the United States also take responsibility for the lack of clarity in Speaker's instructions, resulting in his travels abroad, potentially exposing others to a serious disease?

There are three essential ethical principles of international relational ethics which are relevant for biosecurity and biodefense: "(1) the inherent worth and dignity of individuals; (2) the community defined public good; and (3) authentic relationships."[35] The focus on individuals maintains the aspect of human rights and the balance of public interests with the individual interests in health. The community defined public good, signals how the balancing of individual rights will be weighted against the public good, which may change over time or with circumstances. Our weighing of individual rights against the biosecurity and national security interest of not doing harm to others outside of our jurisdiction may be shifting. It is the second, the community defined public good, which is challenged by the "covenant of trust" doctrine, and its failure in the Speaker case.

The third principle recognizes that it is the relationships between countries themselves which holds the most promise for ethical behavior by governments   There is support in foreign relations law, which indicates four principles of international law apply in this case. First, there is state responsibility, defined in the Restatement of Foreign Relations Law, comment d, that "A state is responsible . . . for its own activities and those of individuals . . . under its jurisdiction. The state may be responsible, for instance, not enacting necessary legislation, for not enforcing is laws against persons acting in its territories."[36]

Second, the UN Charter includes as one of its purposes "to achieve international cooperation in solving international problems of an economic, social, cultural or humanitarian character . . ."[37] An international legal principle, the duty to cooperate, is established by the 1970 UN Declaration of Principles on International Law, which states that states have a duty to cooperate with each other.[38]

Third, the duty to provide prior notification and to consult in good faith[39] requires that nations provide prior notification to any state regarding potential damage that might occur to a shared natural resource. While this is applicable to shared natural resources and commonly applied to matters involving the natural environment, how much more critical are the human resources of a country?

Fourth, the international legal principle, the "protective principle" which recognizes the right of a sovereign state to prescribe law, regulates conduct outside its territory for the purpose of protecting national security.[40]

A laissez-faire form of international relations that has been the normative approach to international law, will likely give way to the pressures of the duties and obligations of one country to another in the area of public health in the global commons.

In the global community, where diseases do not recognize jurisdictional boundaries, and travel freely with their human or non-human hosts; it is imperative that a biosecurity ethic emerges from these experiences. Reinstating my call for an international framework convention on an international ethic in biosecurity and biodefense from 2005,[41] I recommend that the WHO convene a working group to discuss basic principles of a global public health global commons ethic. Further, the United States should offer a meeting venue. We must re-examine our duty to other countries and other humans in the world as a starting point.

Conclusion

The International Health Regulations (IHR 2005) clarified the trigger for reporting an incident that meets the threshold for a Public Health Emergency of International Concern (PHEIC) to the WHO and to other nations who might be affected by a public health issue. The U.S. should avoid appearances of failures to disclose public health threats, such as the failure to disclose by China in the 2003 SARS incident which resulted in the deaths of people throughout the world as a result of the spread of SARS through air transportation.

An immediate effort to acknowledge these issues and propose solutions so that an incident such as this cannot be repeated should be undertaken by the United States. Further, the United States should propose to host the first such meeting and take the lead in demonstrating our interest in being a world partner in protecting global health. Allowing this incident to languish without taken corrective action could damage our credibility with other sovereign nations in the public health global commons.

11.6. International Agreements
11.6.1. Geneva Convention of 1925
The first attempt to limit biological weapons was through the 1925 Geneva Convention. Originally, the Convention banned the use of chemical weapons in war, but the provision was extended to include biological weapons.
11.6.2. Biological Weapons Convention of 1972[42]
The following report was produced by the international committee of the NATO Parliamentary Assembly concerning biological weapons, April 16, 1999.[43]

I. Introduction
. . . The purpose of this Report is to analyse the evidence of the proliferation of biological weapons, to assess th threat related to them, both in the context of a award and with regard to terrorism,

and to try to outline the different responses put forward by Western countries and the international community at large.

2. In theory, the acquisition and development of biological agents for offensive military purposes has been forbidden since the 1972 Biological and Toxin Weapons Convention (BWC). However, unlike the Non-Proliferation Treaty and the Chemical Weapons Convention, the BWC does not provide for any verification measures. In consequence, the number of countries suspected of conducting germ warfare programmes has doubled since 1972....

3. . . . . In 1995, the Japanese cult Aum Shinrikyo released a chemical agent in the Tokyo underground, killing twelve and injuring thousands of people. It was the first time that a terrorist group had resorted to weapons of mass destruction against the civilian population on a large scale. The attack made a huge impact on public opinion and policy makers, who realised the extreme vulnerability of our societies to bioterrorism.

II. Biological Weapons, A New Problem?
A. Definitions

5. A biological weapon could be defined as the association of any infectious agent combined with any means of delivery (artillery shells, bombs, missiles, aerosols...) In order to inflict harm upon others.

6. Warfare agents fall into two categories: living micro-organisms, and toxins. The living biological warfare agents include: bacteria, causing anthrax, the plague or tularaemia; viruses, responsible for diseases such as smallpox, yellow fever or Ebola; rickettsiae causing Q fever; and fungi, acting primarily on crops and responsible for potato blights for example. Toxins are the non-living products of plants or micro-organisms and include for example ricin and botulinum toxin. They can also be produced by chemical synthesis. Biotechnological techniques can be used to produce biological warfare agents in large quantities, and it is said that genetic engineering could improve their stability and resistance to vaccines and existing treatments. Some scientists even argue that, in the near future, genetically modified agents could attack specific ethnic groups.

B. Historical Background and the First Treaties

9....in the 1960s, some countries concluded that biological agents offered no advantages in offensive military operations and renounced such programmes. The United Kingdom was one of the first to do so, followed in 1969 by the decision of the US government to renounce unilaterally "the use of biological agents and weapons and all other methods of biological warfare". The United States was to confine its research to "defensive measures, such as immunization and safety measures". France dismantled its programme in 1972.

10. The first attempt of the international community to limit the threat of biological warfare was the signature of the 1925 Geneva Convention. The Convention banned the use of poison gas in war, and the provision was extended to include bacteriological agents as well. However, the Biological and Toxin Weapons Convention signed on 10 April 1972, was the first comprehensive document dealing exclusively with this threat. The Convention entered into force in 1975 and to date has been ratified by 141 countries, among which Iraq, Iran, Libra, North Korea, Indian, Pakistan, the Russian Federation and China. Significant cases of national that have signed but not ratified are Egypt and Syria. The BWC prohibits the development, production, stockpiling, and acquisition of biological agents or toxins that "have no justification for prophylactic, protective or other peaceful purposes" (Article I), as well as any weapons or means of delivery for such agents or toxins. According to the treaty, member states were required to destroy or divert to peaceful purposes all agents, weapons, equipment and means of delivery within nine months of the treaty's entry into force (Article 3).

C. Evolution of the Biological Weapons Concern

11. Because it was prepared in the context of the Cold War, the 1972 Convention did not provide for any co-operative verification provisions....In cases of proven or suspected non-compliance, member states were supposed to make complaints to the United Nations Security Council. Under these conditions, it is not surprising that many countries have violated the Convention and that biological warfare techniques have proliferated. Several US sources have estimated that more than 10 countries have developed offensive biological warfare programmes over the last two decades, although there is no hard evidence pointing at these countries. The first suspicions about Soviet non-compliance emerged in 1979 when 68 people died following an outbreak of anthrax in Sverdlovsk. At the time, Soviet officials blamed the consumption of contaminated meat, but many started having doubts about USSR compliance with the Convention. In 1992, President Yeltsin finally admitted that the outbreak of anthrax was due to an accident at a military facility and that the USSR had been conducting covert biological weapons research programmes for decades. Unlike the United States, the USSR adopted a strategic approach based on the ground that biological weapons could play a central military role. The Soviets funded a massive programme known as Biopreparat, which reportedly employed as many as 25,000 people at 18 major facilities. According to some defectors such as Vladimir Pasechnik and Ken Alibek, it is suspected that the Russian scientists created, among others, genetically modified strains of plague and anthrax. President Yeltsin officially renounced Russia's biological weapons programme in April 1992. In order to respond to the inadequacies of the BWC, some verification measures were adopted outside the Convention. In September 1992, Russia agreed to take part in a trilateral agreement with the United Kingdom and the United States to initiate data exchanges and site visits at military and private sector biological facilities.

12. Over the last 25 years, perceptions regarding biological weapons have changed significantly. Policy makers, who in 1972 did not take the threat of a biological attack seriously, now consider it to be a realistic threat to security. Scientific technical advances in biotechnology and genetics could be used for biological warfare purposes. DNA techniques might be used to change the genetic structure of a micro-organism, thus allowing it to overcome human immunity, or to make a micro-organism resistant to antibiotics and even easier to produce or store. Biotechnology has thus given biological weapons a greater potential utility. Moreover, the numerous violations of the 1972 Convention have demonstrated the limits of an agreement which has been unable to contain the proliferation of biological techniques. Iraq, Iran, Syria, India and China are reported to possess some sort of biological arsenal. It is feared that biological weapons, which are easier to make and more destructive than nuclear or chemical weapons, could become the weapon of choice for "rogue" governments or terrorist groups. To conclude, it could be argued that, although biological weapons have been developed in the past, they now represent virtually a new problem.

13. In summary, biological weapons have been with us for a long time. In the context of the Cold War they were largely intended as a deterrent. Since the end of the Cold War, because of the factors listed above, they are more of a menace because of their attraction as relatively cheap and easy-to-produce offensive weapons, either in a local war or in the hands of terrorists....

III. Risks of Proliferation and Bioterrorism
B. The Risks of Proliferation
1. An overview of the proliferation problem
17. According to many sources, the number of countries conducting offensive biological research has doubled since the signature of the 1972 Convention. It is estimated that up to 10 countries now possess offensive biological programmes despite the existence of the Convention. Suspected proliferators are concentrated in areas of conflict such as the Middle East (Iran, Iraq, Libya) and include Asian countries such as Taiwan and North Korea. Some of these countries are openly opposed to Western policies and culture and, due to the nature of the arms concerned, are reluctant to supply any information. Hard evidence is, therefore, difficult to come by.

18. An obvious source of concern is the attempt by some countries to approach and recruit Russian scientists who have worked for the Russian germ warfare programme. Iran, which has powerful reasons to want such weapons, is said to be one of them. Most Iranians believed that Iraq used biological weapons against them in the 1980s, and neighbouring countries such as Syria and Israel are suspected of possessing germ arsenals. According to some sources, Iraq is helping Libya to develop a covert germ programme under the guise of a medical facility. Strong doubts still persist about China, which is believed to have maintained a biological programme in the 1980s, even though Presidents Clinton and Jiang reaffirmed their strong support for the complete elimination of biological weapons in June 1998.

C. The Threat of Bioterrorism...

23. Biological weapons are attractive for terrorists for a variety of reasons. They are extremely toxic, highly lethal and destructive. Sheer terror associated with these weapons could easily lead to scenes of panic and social upheaval. The time lag between the attack and the appearance of disease reduces the chances of the offenders being apprehended. Furthermore, biological agents can be produced quite easily and cheaply....

25. The taboo associated with the use of weapons of mass destruction was broken in 1995 by the Japanese religious sect Aum Shinrikyo. It was the first large-scale use of a lethal chemical agent by a terrorist group on a civilian population. The group released sarin gas in the Tokyo underground killing 12 people and injuring more than 5,000. The impurity of the gas and the poor system of dispersion saved thousands of people, but one could just imagine the consequences if the attack had been better planned. It was later proved that the sect had been working on biological agents as well, and it even claimed to have poured a slurry of anthrax spores from the roof of a building in a residential area in 1993. In addition, an attempt to release a lethal toxin in the underground was also reported. On both occasions, the attacks went unnoticed and failed to harm anyone for technical reasons....

26....[A]nalysts disagree about measures that can be undertaken to respond to such a threat.

IV. Responses to the Threat
A. Strengthening the 1972 Biological and Toxin Weapons Convention

27. The proliferation of weapons of mass destruction in general is a major concern for the international community. During the Cold War, attention focused on nuclear weapons, and the response to this threat was primarily viewed in terms of deterrence. Due to the nature of biological weapons, traditional responses may not prove useful...

28. Since the inadequacies of the BWC Convention are partly responsible for the proliferation of biological weapons, an international consensus has now been reached on the necessity to reform and strengthen it. In September 1998, Presidents Clinton and Yeltsin released a joint statement urging the successful conclusion of the negotiations to strengthen the Convention by the adoption of a legally binding protocol at the earliest possible date. States are currently engaged in talks on the adoption of this additional protocol, which would respond to some of the past inadequacies.

29. According to the 1972 Convention, member states had to participate every five years in review conferences in order to consider issues of concern. Over the last twenty years, controversy has focused primarily on compliance and verification measures. At the second review conference in September 1986, BWC members agreed on a number of modest confidence-building measures (CBMs), such as the exchange of data related to biological activities permitted under the treaty. The 1991 review conference, which also adopted some additional CBMs, appointed an Ad Hoc Group of Governmental Experts, the so-called VEREX, to study verification possibilities from a scientific standpoint. By doing so, member states reacted to growing concerns over the risks of proliferation and acknowledged the inadequacy of the 1972 Convention. VEREX concluded that the best way to monitor the BWC would be to combine off-site measures, including the declaration of vaccine production facilities and laboratories and the description of biological weapons defence programmes with on-site measures, meaning the authorisation of short-

notice inspections. The group identified 21 potential verification measures that could make the BWC a more efficient instrument. Although considered in 1994 at a special BWC meeting, the parties failed to adopt any of them. Nevertheless, they agreed on the creation of a new working group, the Ad Hoc Group whose task it would be to draft verification measures which would be incorporated into a legally binding protocol to the BWC.

31. Countries disagree on the verification measures that should be adopted. Most European countries are in favour of allowing random or "non-challenge" inspections, namely to allow inspectors to make visits, at short notice, to any factory or laboratory in the signatory countries. Worried that it will expose its biotechnology industry, the United States rejects this idea categorically and only agrees to allow "challenge" inspections.[44] Countries could call for an inspection only if there was evidence of a violation of the Convention. It is a controversial position if one considers the lessons learned from the Iraqi experience. UNSCOM has claimed that random visits were crucial to its work, and the United States has constantly put pressure on Iraq to allow the mission to carry out its work. In January 1998, President Clinton announced that he would support limited non-challenge inspections to clarify unclear declarations, but he categorically rejected random inspections....

37. Since the evolution of the threat is perceived differently by Western countries, it is not surprising to note a great discrepancy between countries at the time of allocating resources and setting priorities. The United States, the United Kingdom and Canada are taking more initiatives than any other country, have even signed a trilateral research agreement and are pursuing their collaborative efforts. They focus on detecting the presence of biological agents in the battlefield. The UK Defence Evaluation and Research Agency (DERA) has just released a vehicle-mounted Prototype Biological Detection System, which is to be part of a more advanced biological detection system. During the Gulf War, the United Kingdom was considered to be the leader in the field of deploying detection systems. Other countries, like France, are also currently trying to develop their own detection systems. The French Integrated System of Biological Agents Detection (Systèème intéégréé de déétection des agents biologiques) should enter into service by the year 2005.[45]

38. Other defence measures include better training and preparation of armed forces, the development of reliable protective equipment, and a better medical response. In the medical field, most of the work has concentrated on developing vaccines. The United Kingdom for example is said to be conducting research on bubonic plague, anthrax, botulinum toxin and pneumonia. In December 1997, the United States announced that they would undertake an extensive anthrax vaccination programme for all US military personnel. According to the US Department of Defense, 14 other vaccines are in preparation and could be approved by the Food and Drug Administration in the near future. The vaccination programme, which is also followed in the United Kingdom, is highly controversial. In fact, many experts point out that the vaccine would only protect against one particular strain of the biological agent, and could therefore be totally ineffective on all the others. Other countries, like France, have decided to concentrate their efforts on prevention, research, and preparation of antidotes.

C. Responding to the Terrorist Threat

40. In March 1999, a US expert on biological warfare gave another clear indication of the degree of vulnerability faced by public institutions and cities at large. He managed to smuggle powdered anthrax into the Pentagon and the State Department without being detected, which must have been most embarrassing for the US authorities as a major lapse in security. In general, experts are quite pessimistic about finding really efficient measures that would reduce the risks to the minimum. The lack of preparation of countries to respond to this particular risk is now being addressed seriously, especially in the United States where it is considered as a matter of high priority.

41. The best solution would be to combine a number of measures. When dealing with counter-terrorism strategy, the first priority should be to work on pre-emption, that is to say the ability to prevent terrorist attacks before they occur. Intelligence agencies would need to monitor closely the activities of

potentially dangerous groups; greater exchange of information and co-operation policies between countries would be needed. Co-operation should include countries which do not belong to the Western sphere but whose help would be vital to create an efficient information network. Attention should also focus on keeping track of exports of biological agents and toxins. Even if most of the products are dual-use, a clear control over imports, exports or any exchange of material could make their acquisition by terrorist groups more difficult. The issue of the dispersion of Russian know-how should be seriously addressed as well. The Americans have already developed some forms of exchange between scientists, joint research projects and sponsored programmes in order to tackle the "brain-drain" problem and convert laboratories and institutes which used to work for the Russian germ warfare programme to civilian use.

42. To make pre-emption work, participating states should be able to rely on their own domestic laws too. The production, development or possession of biological agents should be recognised as a major crime by most nations: the 1972 Convention already stated that the countries should take all necessary measures to make the treaty prohibitions binding on its citizens. Out of 141 signatory countries, only 40 have adopted such enforcement laws.[46] The United States waited until 1989 to pass the Biological Weapons Antiterrorism Act. Before it was enacted, it was not illegal for any citizen to possess or produce biological agents as long as it was not serving criminal purposes.

43. Some countries also believe in the necessity to develop civil defence strategies, among them Sweden, Switzerland or Israel. One could look at the Israeli experience regarding the protection of civilians: in 1991, before the Gulf War, the state distributed gas masks and antidote kits. However, this approach has its limits: logistically, the distribution of material was possible because of the size of the country and because they had enough time available. Since it is not possible to predict if and when an attack will occur, particular attention should be given to medical and post exposure treatment.

44. Because of the delayed effects of a covert biological weapon attack, defensive measures might prove difficult. The terrorist attack in the Tokyo underground really served as a wake-up call for city disaster planners. In 1996, the US Department of Defense created the Domestic Preparedness Programme, which decided to spend more than $ 40 million to train and evaluate emergency personnel in 120 cities. The first conclusions of the simulation programme confirmed the lack of preparedness of first-aid rescuers, and medical personnel in general. They concluded that the first step should be to develop effective disease surveillance in order to be able to identify the epidemic as early as possible and that efforts should focus on training, stockpiling vaccines and drugs, and providing rapid reaction....

––––––––––

The Iraqi case[47]

19. An insight into the recent Iraqi crisis might prove useful to understand the proliferation concerns of the international community. After the Gulf War, UN Security Council Resolution 687 created the United Nations Special Commission (UNSCOM)) to oversee the destruction of Iraq's weapons of mass destruction.[48] For years, Iraq denied possessing any biological weapons even though UNSCOM had collected "conclusive evidence that Iraq was engaged in an advanced military biological research programme". It proved that Iraq had bought equipment useful for the production of biological weapons. Some details started to appear in 1995, and Iraq finally admitted the existence of a biological warfare programme from 1975 to 1991. Following the defection of General Hussein Kamel, who was overseeing the Iraqi biological weapons programme, Iraq provided UNSCOM with inside information and confirmed the doubts of the international community. Iraq denied the weaponisation of biological agents but declared the production of 19,000 litres of botulinum toxin and 8,500 litres of anthrax. Baghdad also claimed to have destroyed its arsenal in 1991 but failed to provide UNSCOM with credible and sufficient evidence. Later, Iraqi officials admitted to have deployed to operational delivery units weapons containing three types of biological agents: anthrax, botulinum toxin and aflatoxin.[49]

20. Under Resolution 687, Iraq was supposed to provide UNSCOM with complete disclosures of military programmes and allow "unconditional and unrestricted access to all areas".[50] However, the UN mission has been constantly confronted with Iraq's lack of co-operation, the delivery of false or incomplete information, the disappearance of equipment which the mission had to inspect and even the denial of access to certain sites. Under these conditions, as Mr. Richard Butler, Chairman of UNSCOM, pointed out in his report to the UN Secretary General in December 1998, "it has not been possible to verify Iraq's claims with respect to the nature and magnitude of its proscribed weapons programmes and their current disposition". The fear is that the country might retain some stock of biological agents, and restart production of anthrax within weeks.[51]

11.7   Organizational Responses to Biodefense from other Countries

Canada and Gernany were the two countries to enact significant government organizational changes in response to the anthrax attacks and the SARS outbreak. The United States instead took the direction of creating a Department of Homeland Security, and skirted the difficult issue of constitutional federalism, which would have required taking significant state sovereign authority from the states over public health matters. It went largely unnoticed that the Department of Homeland Security took authority to protect the American people against terrorism of every kind including agroterrorism, but no authority over bioterrorism. In a more direct approach to public health governance, Canada created a new governmental agency with the specific mandate to protect public health, and Germany created a national biosurveillance system to achieve a uniform reporting system for more rapid outbreak detection.

11.7.1 Canada's Department of Public Health[52]

On February 2, 2004, the Governor General and Commander-in-Chief of the Canadian Forces, the representative of the Queen of England, announced in a "Speech from the Throne" the support of the appointment of a Chief Officer for Public Health and a new organization to address public health threats:

> Canadians also want to be protected from emerging threats to their health, from global epidemics to contaminated water. Safeguarding the health of Canadians is a top priority of this Government.
>
> The shock of SARS demonstrated vividly our vulnerability to infectious diseases that may be incubated anywhere on earth.
>
> Diseases such as SARS and the recent avian flu pose threats which increased global mobility can only make worse.
>
> The Government will therefore take the lead in establishing a strong and responsive public health system, starting with a new Canada Public Health Agency that will ensure that Canada is linked, both nationally and globally, in a network for disease control and emergency response.
>
> The Government will also appoint a new Chief Public Health Officer for Canada - and undertake a much-needed overhaul of federal health protection through a Canada Health Protection Act.
>
> Strengthening our social foundations also means improving the overall health of Canadians - starting with health promotion to help reduce the incidence of avoidable disease. The Government will work with all of its partners to that end, following the age-old prescription that prevention is the best cure.

The description of the Public Health Agency as it appears on the government website is as follows:[53]

11.7.2 German's National Biosurveillance System

SurvNet@RKI – a multistate electronic reporting system for communicable diseases[54]
(Berlin, Germany)

ABSTRACT

In 2001 Germany implemented a new electronic reporting system for surveillance of notifiable infectious diseases (SurvNet@RKI). The system is currently being used in all 431 local health departments (LHD), the 16 state health departments (SHD) and the Robert Koch-Institut (RKI), the national agency for infectious disease epidemiology. The SurvNet@RKI software is written in MS Access 97 and Visual Basic and it supports MS Access as well as MS SQL Server database management systems as a back-end. The database is designed as a distributed, dynamic database for 73 reporting categories with more than 600 fields and about 7000 predefined entry values. An integrated version management system documents deletion, undeletion, completion and correction of cases at any time and entry level and allows reproduction of previously conducted queries. Integrated algorithms and help functions support data quality and the application of case definitions. RKI makes the system available to all LHDs and SHDs free of charge. RKI receives an average of 300,000 case reports and 6240 outbreak reports per year through this system. A public web-based query interface, SurvStat@RKI, assures extensive and timely publication of the data. During the 5 years that SurvNet@RKI has been running in all LHDs and SHDs in Germany it has coped well with a complex federal structure which makes this system particularly attractive to multinational surveillance networks. The system is currently being migrated to Microsoft C#/.NET and transport formats in XML. Based on our experiences, we provide recommendations for the design and implementation of national or international electronic surveillance systems.

Introduction

In January 2001 a new law for the prevention and control of infectious diseases (Infektionsschutzgesetz, IfSG) was enacted in Germany. This has resulted in a modernisation of the national surveillance system for notifiable infectious diseases. In order to assure information flow between local, state and federal institutions we developed a new electronic reporting system (SurvNet@RKI) as the technical backbone of the new surveillance system. While various evaluations of the German surveillance system have already been published elsewhere, this report intends to present and critically discuss the technical aspects of the software and database architecture for electronic data transfer within the surveillance system. The objective of this paper is to present technical solutions developed in Germany which could be applicable in surveillance systems of other countries or international networks.

Methods

Background and requirements

Germany is a federal republic with 16 states (Bundesländer) and 439 counties (Stadt-/Landkreise). Typically, there is one local health department (LHD) per county, responsible for managing single cases and outbreaks of infectious diseases and carrying out necessary prevention and control activities. The IfSG defines 47 pathogens and 14 diseases that laboratories and clinicians, respectively, have to notify to the local health department. LHD complete and verify the case information based on national case definitions. These cases are then transmitted on a single case basis to the state health departments (SHD) and from there to the Robert Koch-Institut (RKI), the central national agency for infectious disease epidemiology. A requirement analysis revealed the need for an electronic reporting system with the following functional and non-functional features:

The system capacity needed to be sufficient for over 300 000 reported cases per year with 25 to 60 variables per case entered by 431 LHDs throughout the country. The system needed to take issues of data security of privacy-related patient data as well as specific additional requirements of individual states into account. For economic reasons the software had to run on common hardware without the need for additional software licenses and expensive back-end systems. As permanent internet connection was not available in all LHDs, the system needed to be operable offline as well. The system should incorporate reporting of complex outbreaks and be flexible enough to adapt quickly to unexpected changes caused by new emerging diseases (e.g., SARS).

In July 2000 the two legislative houses of representatives in Germany (Bundestag and Bundesrat) ratified the IfSG to be enacted by 1 January 2001. Within 6 months the RKI developed the electronic reporting system for the national surveillance system.

Software design

The architecture of the system was designed in-house at the RKI. However, a major part of the programming was done by an external IT company. The newly developed system was called SurvNet@RKI

The data flow is depicted in the figure. The front-end of SurvNet@RKI is written in MS Access 97 and Visual Basic. Depending on the data volume it supports MS Access as well as MS SQL Server database management systems as a back-end. Adding or removing reporting categories, fields or allowed values do not require changes to the programme structure, which is based on the fractal® concept of picoware GmbH. SurvNet@RKI allows the reproduction of previously conducted queries and analyses by means of an integrated version management system: Any updates of a data record (case or outbreak) result in the creation of a complete new record in the database that is marked as valid beginning at the time when the record was created.   The old record's validity period ends at that time. As shown above the data replication is organised by the transmission of transport files in a format specified by the RKI. The transmission format is text-based and allows the representation of complex data with possibly multiple nominations of a field. Online help functions provide additional information for the user (for example, the disease-specific case definition). Integrated algorithms that follow the national case definitions assure that case records are exported only if the case confirmation criteria are met.

Deletion is integrated into in the transport process by activation of a marker which makes retrieval of previously deleted records possible.

FIGURE

Data flow in the German computerized reporting system

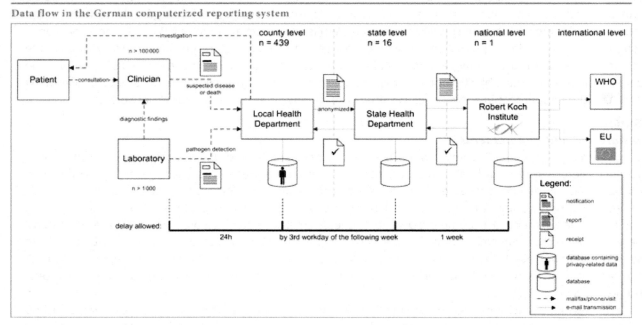

Data base design and management

The database is designed as a dynamic, relational database that currently consists of 73 reporting categories with more than 600 fields and about 7000 predefined entry values in look-up fields. All criteria formulated in the national case definitions are integrated into the data entry forms in order to facilitate application of and compliance with case definitions.

Furthermore, each record representing a case of an infectious disease can belong to one or more groups of cases representing an outbreak. The version management described above is also applied to outbreak records.

Results
Software design

The RKI provided the commercial software manufacturers with the final technical specifications for electronic case reporting in October 2000 and released its own software programme, SurvNet@RKI, in December 2000, free of charge. The new system was implemented nationwide on 1 January 2001. Within a few weeks, almost all LHDs were reporting at least weekly through the new system [2]. All state health departments use SurvNet@RKI Among the 431 LHDs in 2005, 112 (26%) use SurvNet@RKI while 319 (74%) use one of five different commercially available software programmes for public health administration which include a case reporting module based on the specifications published by RKI. Public health nurses at the LHD enter the data into the reporting software and complete the records according to findings of subsequent investigations. When outbreaks occur, the LHD (or the SHD or the RKI) creates an electronic outbreak record, which groups the affected case reports and holds additional data regarding the outbreak, such as modes of transmission and evidence for this information. At least once a week each LHD creates a transport file containing all changes since the last export. Those data are automatically extracted by the system. Any information subject to data privacy remains physically in the database of the LHD. The transport file is sent via email to the SHD, where the data is imported into SurvNet@RKI, which in turn generates a confirmation file that is sent back to the LHD, also via email. In all SHD and in those LHD that use SurvNet@RKI changes and additions in field definitions and database structure are usually executed within one month after publication of the new specifications. New versions of SurvNet@RKI are fully downward compatible, which ensures that data generated by older software versions can still be imported and handled.

Data base design and management

The RKI receives an average of 300 000 reported cases per year. Thirty six per cent of the case reports are completed or corrected during the investigation process and are therefore transmitted in two or more different versions, which are all retrievable in the database. This results in a total of 490 000 datasets sent to the RKI each year. Based on the complex record versioning system, datasets are never frozen at any given deadline but can be continuously corrected, completed, deleted and undeleted if necessary. Historical case counts can therefore be performed for any state of knowledge in the past, which facilitates the generation of epidemiological reports and comparison of data.

Eight per cent of the fields in SurvNet@RKI, such as reporting week and year, are mandatory fields, and must be filled in ore the record cannot be saved. About 10% of the fields undergo an integrated plausibility algorithm (for example, the order of the timestamps for date of birth, onset of illness and date of diagnosis). This will generate error messages when data has not been entered or is in conflict with entries in other fields. Case reports of disease with a yearly incidence of approximately less than 1 case per 100 000 population undergo a manual quality control procedure at the RKI before they are released for publication; these cases made up 0.89% of the mean number of yearly reports (n= 1 212 482) from 2001-2004. Most data quality indicators have improved significantly over the past four years, but show variations depending on the state where the data is generated and the kind of software used to enter and manage the data at the LHD.

Development effort

The estimated cost for the development of the initial software prototype adds up to one year full time equivalent (FTE) for an IT scientist, one year full time equivalent for a medical epidemiologist and EURO 50 000 worth of external programming work. Furthermore, an estimated amount of 1 FTE for an IT scientist and 0.5 FTE medical epidemiologist in addition to EURO 60 000 for programming done externally been invested each year for maintenance and further improvement of the system. This comes to a total of approximately EURO 170 000 for the initial development, plus EURO 150 000 per year for improvements and maintenance. It does not include the actual epidemiological work for data quality control, system evaluation, scientific interpretation of the data, and the training of external users of the system.

Data release and publication

The national surveillance data collected at RKI are published periodically or whenever required by RKI staff or external scientists. In order to improve data quality, implausibilities are fed back to the SHD, and are forwarded from there to the appropriate LHD requesting validation or correction. SurvStat@RKI, a web-based query interface, allows interested users to perform analyses on the national data. Each spring following the reporting year, RKI releases an annual epidemiological report of over 170 pages. Germany contributes more case reports than any other country to the European Basic Surveillance Network, which is facilitated by the ability of SurvNet@RKI to automatically translate the German raw data to the European data formats. RKI also reports surveillance data electronically to the World Health Organization and to various dedicated surveillance networks of the EU.

Outbreaks detected

Interlinked with the reported individual cases, RKI receives an average of 6240 outbreak reports per year, which generally have been primarily identified and investigated by the LHD. On average, 2047 (33%) of these outbreaks have five or more cases. In addition to assessing outbreaks detected at the LHD level, SurvNet@RKI has also been able to report outbreaks and clusters that were not identifiable at the SHD or LHD level because of their rather diffuse geographical distribution. Examples for such outbreaks are an outbreak of Salmonella Agona from contaminated aniseed, an international outbreak of Salmonella Oranienburg due to German chocolate and a large outbreak of hepatitis A among German tourists returning from a hotel in Egypt.

In 2003 SurvNet@RKI has also been adopted for internal use in the German Armed Forces, contributing to a better information exchange between civil and military health departments as shown in a large outbreak of epidemic conjunctivitis.

Discussion

SurvNet@RKI has proved to be a powerful reporting system for cases and outbreaks of notifiable infectious diseases.

Many national surveillance systems rely on or are moving towards electronic reporting systems (such as NEDSS in the United States, CIDR in Ireland, and SMINet in Sweden). In comparison to these systems SurvNet@RKI provides some features of database and communication architecture that make the system particularly useful for surveillance networks of multiple states or countries and for environments in which requirements of data security and limitations to data sharing usually create major obstacles.

SurvNet@RKI addresses these challenges by using a physically distributed database characterised by a highly standardised core database and variable branch subsets. Another remarkable, and to our knowledge unique, feature is the tight integration of case reporting and outbreak reporting.

During the five years that the system has been running in all Germany's LHDs and SHDs, it has coped well with a complex federal structure, which generally complicates or even impedes efficient information exchange between administrative levels.

We believe a key to the success of SurvNet@RKI was the very strong cooperation of epidemiologists from LHDs, SHDs and RKI, the in-house IT staff and the external company. The costs have been kept low.

However, we also experienced difficulties in implementing necessary changes rapidly throughout the country, particularly because manufacturers of commercial software at the LHD level took a long time to implement the changes, and in some cases were unable to implement the specifications at all. This puts LHDs who use such software programmes at a significant disadvantage, because the majority of the system changes aim to reduce the workload at the LHD level and to avoid data entry errors.

The use of MS Access 97 with Visual Basic programming proved to be an effective basis for finalising a stable prototype within a very short time. However, now after approximately five years of experience, recurring changes and amendments have resulted in a complexity of the system that is becoming hard to maintain with the current platform. For similar projects we recommend the use of professional development environments, object-oriented approaches, and data exchange technologies that are better at supporting team development, code reuse and change management.

We are currently migrating SurvNet@RKI to a new platform that better meets those requirements. It will be re-implemented in Microsoft C#/.NET. The former transport file format specification will be replaced by an XML schema. This allows, for instance, the manufacturers of third-party products to test their export files against the specification eliminating a frequent error source. The user interface will be multilingual.

In the framework of a federal government initiative (BundOnline 2005) to foster e-government solutions, we intend to develop an interface for the most commonly used laboratory software systems in order to enable laboratories to report automatically in electronic format to the respective LHDs.

Recommendations

Based on our findings and experience in designing and implementing SurvNet@RKI, we have come up with the following recommendations for future developments of multistate electronic reporting systems:

- Adhere to the best practices in software engineering. We recommend following an agile development process to keep costs low. Staff the team with both IT specialists and epidemiologists.
- The number of fields per case needs to be kept to a minimum. In contrast to the general tendency

to expand the amount of data, revisions of the system should always aim to reduce complexity of the database. The more experience available on the quality of the incoming data and on its actual contribution to epidemiological conclusions, the easier it will be to keep the database simple.

- Drop-down menus presenting the choice of data field entries need to be formulated in clear, concise language that can be understood without advanced medical knowledge.
- Transport and interface formats should be based on XML.
- Software development should not be completely outsourced from the institution that will be in charge of the system. First, the epidemiological expertise needs to be included into the process from the beginning on, which is more efficiently done if the software design is done in-house as well. Second, maintenance and improvement of the system requires in-house IT expertise, otherwise sustainability is at risk or may become costly.
- Cooperation with multiple peripheral software manufacturers may result in difficulties of rapidly implementing a system on a nationwide basis. If feasible, a one-stop-shop approach, where the same software is used by all users, is likely to avoid such complications.
- Sufficient resources need to be planned for to train the users of the software. This task has to be seen as part of a continuous maintenance effort, due to the large number of staff involved nationwide, the fluctuation and rotation within the staff and the changes in the system itself.

The particular characteristic of giving great importance to data security and privacy concerns, the flexibility of the underlying data structures, and adaptability to federal administrative structures combine to make SurvNet@RKI particularly attractive to multinational surveillance networks like the EU-wide infectious disease surveillance hosted by the European Centre for Disease Prevention and Control (ECDC), since it would allow participating member states to basically use their existing national systems and connect to the universal interface of SurvNet@RKI. Having proven itself able manage complex outbreaks reports from many independent states, SurvNet@RKI may also be the appropriate platform for the management of the complex data that the new International Health Regulations now require all states to report.

Liberty Dies by Inches: German Counter-Terrorism Measures and Human Rights, Part 1 of 2

By Verena Zöller "I believe there is no trade-off to be made between human rights and terrorism. Upholding human rights is not at odds with battling terrorism: on the contrary, the moral vision of human rights – the deep respect for the dignity of each person – is among our most powerful weapons against it."

A. Human Rights After September 11

On February 5, 2004 Abdelghani Mzoudi walked free from court in Hamburg, Germany. The Moroccan engineering student had been suspected of aiding and abetting the planning of the heinous terrorist attacks on the World Trade Center and the Pentagon of September 11, 2001 and of being a member of a terrorist organization. Even though the court expressed discomfort with its judgement, not being entirely convinced of Mzoudi's innocence, it acquitted him due to the lack of sufficiently compelling evidence. The main problem was that the crucial testimony of an alleged co-plotter, Ramzi Binalshib, had been withheld by the United States. Subsequently, Bundesgerichtshof (Germany's highest court of appeal) basically on the same grounds ordered a retrial for Mounir el-Mossadaq, who had been the first person to be convicted in relation to the 9/11 attacks. He had been sentenced to 15 years of prison for accessory to murder on more than 3,000 counts.

While the rulings are deplorable if Mzoudi and el-Mossadaq in fact are guilty and certainly there should be no doubt that persons involved in terrorist acts must be brought to justice, there is a positive note on the case from a human rights perspective: In spite of the gravity of the accusations and strong political pressure the court upheld rules of due process and the fundamentally important presumption of innocence. In the tensioned climate since 9/11 this attitude is not self-evident. In response to the tragic events, many States felt a need to re-evaluate their security and introduced legislative measures putting them in a stronger position to combat terrorism. While some of these measures certainly may be necessary and proportionate, others give raise to severe human rights concerns. As the UN Secretary General stated, human rights are in danger of becoming "collateral damage" in the so-called war on terrorism. In evaluating counter-terrorism measures with reference to human rights, the focus of academic writing and NGOs has mainly been on the United States, where some violations of international and human rights law are most obvious, as exemplified by the Guantanamo detention camp. But little work has been done to revisit legislative and operational measures in other countries.

Soon after 9/11 Germany came into the spotlight, as it became known that the attacks had at least partly been planned and prepared in Hamburg. Concern was raised about the country being a 'safe haven' for terrorists and possible 'sleepers' hiding behind an unsuspicious façade. In this climate the Government rushed through counter-terrorism legislation. On November 9, 2001, Parliament adopted the so-called "Security Package I," containing urgent measures addressing the perceived security threat. Terrorismusbekämpfungsgesetz ("Security Package II") promptly followed suit in December 2001. The new legislation basically amends a number of existing laws, mainly regarding the powers of the security authorities. Furthermore, changes concern the Strafgesetzbuch (Criminal Code), the Asylgesetz (Asylum Act) and the Ausländergesetz (Foreigners Act). The focus of this law is on prevention rather than on repression; it is supposed to ensure that terrorist activities are detected early on and that Germany does not provide a 'safe haven' for foreigners involved in terrorist activities.

As in other countries around the globe, legislative and operational measures raised concern about their compatibility with national and international human rights obligations. Many feel that the new, security-driven laws compromise long-standing civil and political rights and freedoms. The necessity and desirability of bringing persons to justice who are involved in terrorist acts remains unquestioned. Nevertheless, counter-terrorism measures must be under strict scrutiny regarding their conformity with international human rights standards.

This essay shall evaluate measures introduced in Germany, mainly under Security Packages I & II. As they amended a variety of existing legislation, not all facets can be covered. Thus, some of the most important aspects shall be analysed with regards to the respective affected groups of persons: all persons living in Germany, foreigners living in Germany and asylum seekers. Efforts against the financing of terrorism, although important, will not be covered as they form a whole sphere on their own. Moreover, it is not within the scope of the essay to take all relevant human rights instruments into consideration. Therefore, preference shall be given to the European Convention on Human Rights (ECHR), the International Covenant on Civil and Political Rights (ICCPR) and the 1951 Refugee Convention.

Before turning to this evaluation, some general thoughts on the concepts of liberty and security are necessary to establish the context of counter-terrorism measures in democratic societies. Secondly, an overview over Germany's international obligations in combating terrorism and protecting its citizens shall be given. Thirdly, problems arising from the vague use of the term 'terrorism' will be looked at. Finally, some of the new measures shall be analysed with respect to Germany's international human rights obligations.

B. Liberty and Security in a Democratic Society

Any debate on counter-terrorism measures must be seen in the light of the correlation of liberty and security. Although these are often said to be antagonistic, the modern democratic State embraces both: while ensuring as much security to its citizens as deemed necessary, it grants as much liberty as possible. Both elements are crucial in democratic systems, as security cannot be ensured without civil liberty. This view is reflected in many human rights instruments, which protect liberty and security of the person in one single paragraph. An interference with one of them will always affect the other. Hence, the State must ensure a prudent balance of the two. In the tradition of post-enlightenment philosophy and French and American Revolutions, liberal democracies strongly emphasised liberty. Hobbesinian thinking of the guarantee of security as the State's foremost duty has been overcome by the conviction that a good order must allow citizens to develop their lives and ideas as free as possible. When Rousseau said, "man is born free, and everywhere he is in chains", he did not advocate a lawless state of nature, but a political system built on the free will of its citizens. The concept of the State's exclusive right to resort to force to ensure security and the rule of law – illustrated in Hobbes' Leviathan – has been upheld in European constitutional history. But it must be controlled be its people; and it must not interfere with their right to freedom and personal development – as long as these don't threaten the order of the state or violate the rights of others. German philosophers Kant and Hegel both placed individual liberty at the heart of the State. This idea of everyone's free development within the democratic State is reflected in art. 2(1) of the Grundgesetz (German Basic Law):

"Everyone has the right to free development of his personality insofar as he does not violate the rights of others or offend against the constitutional order or against morality."

The Federal Republic of Germany, as it emerged out of the Third Reich dictatorship, was conscious about the importance to control state power and guarantee personal freedom. Fundamental civil rights and liberties, such as the right to privacy and the rights to freedom of expression, association and assembly are core elements of freedom and condition sine qua non for the healthy functioning of democracy. Throughout the terrorist threat posed by violent left-wing groups during the seventies and eighties, most prominently the Red Army Faction (RAF), this conviction was not severely compromised. The logic of RAF terrorist action was to force the State to make intensive use of its powers in order to ensure the rule of law and suppress terrorist opposition, thereby debunking itself as illiberal and loosing legitimacy. This logic eventually did not gain momentum. While some civil rights were restricted by the widely protested against Notstandsgesetzgebung (emergency law), three so-called anti-terrorism acts and the Kontaksperrengesetz (contact ban law) allowing for solitary confinement, overall the primacy of civil rights persisted. The impossibility to guarantee absolute security within the democratic order was accepted. Nevertheless, during this period Germany laid the legal foundations for combating terrorist action.

This sense of proportionality seems to have faded away during the 1990s. In 1998, the Government introduced a law on widely extended eavesdropping in private homes with the purpose of combating organized crime and terrorism – the latter explanation being particularly interesting, because at the time Germany did not face any particular terrorist threat. This law is so far-reaching that it led to the resignation of the Minister of Justice, who subsequently challenged it before courts. After a long judicial fight, only recently the Supreme Court declared the law in wide parts unconstitutional. This example shows that already in the 1990s an increasing emphasis was placed on security – probably in response to the loss of stability in the international order and the spread of organized crime from the former Soviet countries. Still, this development is surprising in the light of the young history of public surveillance through the STASI in the Democratic Republic of Germany.

After the heinous attacks of September 11, the fragile balance between liberty and security was tipped even more towards the latter. The new counter-terrorism legislation is clearly security-driven. While in many respects it builds upon the legislation introduced in the 1970s, the official justifications do not refer back to the history of terrorism in Germany but only to a new dimension of 'international terrorism'. However, it remained unclear what characterized this 'new dimension' – all the more because European societies have had to live – and actually managed – with terrorist activities for a long time. The mere scale of the 9/11 attacks can hardly serve as a satisfactory explanation. Rather, as Lepsius points out, the perception derives from the fact that this time it was not identifiable individuals but a globally operating 'obscure' network who was responsible for the attacks. This perceived new quality of a threat to security seemed to justify a new quality of measures with a focus on preventive action. But the equation that a restriction of civil liberties will provide for a higher level of security is highly problematic. As was submitted, during the 1980s in German public law the concept of a basic right to security equal to the other constitutional civil rights and liberties emerged. This concept entails two problems: First, as Lepsius showed, contrary to the constitutional basic rights, security is not defined on a normative level. It can only be defined on a factual basis, that is in connection with specific threats and thereby specific criminal activities – which is difficult when operating with categories of diffuse networks instead of individual perpetrators. Thus, the factual character of security can't be balanced against the normative character of the basic rights, as it should be done within the German constitutional system. But security seems to have become a value as such that prevails over other basic rights. Secondly, even the factual level of security is questionable: It basically is defined negatively through the absence of a specific threat. But as the threat remains obscure as long as it does not translate into activities, it is mainly a question of perception. The assumption that the State can guarantee absolute positive security, i.e. no criminal or terrorist actions actually occur, is a pure fiction – not only in open societies but also in autocratic States, as the bombings in Saudi Arabia and Morocco showed. While certainly a high level of security is desirable, societies have to accept that they have to live with a certain extent of threat and danger. Moreover, this conception of security is rather one-dimensional, focused on threats to life and limb. It neglects the dimension of security of individuals within the legal system, i.e. from arbitrary actions of the State, which is on the utmost important foundations of the democratic State. If this dimension of legal certainty is neglected, citizens loose both freedom and security.

Critics complained that there was no sufficient time for parliamentary and public debate and that the Government used the opportunity to adopt legislation, which had already been planned before 9/11 September but had lacked politic support. This 'opportunity' is rooted in the inherent logic of terrorist attacks: the indefinite risk of further attacks forces governments to react – primarily to prevent more attacks, but also to appear strong and active in a situation of crisis. The security of its citizens momentarily becomes the utmost function of the State, while the citizens are more willing to accept restrictions of their liberty. This situation may not be problematic as long as the measures taken are proportionate to the security threat. Proportionality may include a strict focus on the legitimate aim of the measures – the prevention of further attacks – and a temporary factor, i.e. it may be necessary to revisit the measures when the perceived security threat has lowered. Otherwise, there may be a clash with fundamental human rights norms. And if societies allow human rights to be impaired in the name of the fight against terrorism, they threaten exactly what they claim to fight for: the democratic order on the basis of the freedom of its citizens.

C. International Obligations to Combat Terrorism and Related Human Rights Obligations

When analysing the compatibility of counter-terrorism measures with human rights it is important to bear in mind that Germany has not only obligations under human rights instruments which may collude with anti-terrorism legislation. Also, it undertook a variety of international obligations to combat terrorism. Among the most important are:

Eleven out of twelve UN Conventions covering several specific terrorist offences;
the 1977 European Convention on the Suppression of Terrorism and the 1957 European Convention on Extradition; several Security Council resolutions, most prominently resolution 1373 of 28.09.2001; the EU Council Framework Decision on Combating Terrorism of 19.09.2001 and the Council Framework Decision on an European Arrest Warrant of 07.08.2002; numerous bilateral agreements related to terrorism.

Furthermore, it is important to mention Germany's obligations under human rights treaties to protect citizens from terrorist acts, e.g. bombings or hostage taking. Especially relevant are the right to life under art. 6 ICCPR and art. 2 ECHR, the right to liberty and security of the person (art 5 ECHR, art. 9 ICCPR) as well as the protection from torture and inhuman and degrading treatment (art. 3 ECHR, art. 7 ICCPR). Also, the protection of property under art. 1 of the first Protocol to the European Convention is of some importance. These provisions not only put the State under a negative obligation not to arbitrarily interfere with those rights, but also under a positive duty to protect its citizens from interference of third parties. Thus, Germany has an obligation under international human rights law to secure life, liberty and property of the people within its territory as well as to protect them from ill-treatment.

These obligations have to be borne in mind in order to avoid rash judgements on counter-terrorism legislation. In this context, it shall be sufficient to observe that the Counter Terrorism Committee (CTC), established by the Security Council after 9/11, did not criticise Germany of not satisfactorily fulfilling any core obligations. Germany reported to the CTC fist in December 2001 and pursuant in October 2002 and June 2003. The additional information requested by the Committee related to quite detailed questions, indicating that there are no major deficiencies. Therefore it shall be assumed that no crucial additional measures are necessary.

D. Lack of Clarity in the Legal Concept Of Terrorism
I. International level: no agreed definition of terrorism
The major problem surrounding the issue of terrorism on the international level is the failure to agree on a definition of the term. The central disagreements arise from key questions such as the actors involved, the precise nature of the acts, and the issue of State terrorism. With the increasing international tensions after the events of 11 September a solution to the problem is even less likely to be found. Moreover, the term is increasingly used within simplistic and polarized rhetoric making certain groups of people, such as minorities, migrants and prisoners, even more vulnerable to marginalisation of their human rights. Some scholars expressed doubt about the legal significance of "terrorism", but in fact it is used as a legal concept on the domestic and international level and thus, the need of a definition can hardly be called into question.

II. Domestic level: terrorist offences in the Criminal Code
This lack of an internationally agreed upon definition is mirrored on the national level. Neither the 1970s acts nor the new legislation provide for a clear definition of the term. The most relevant provision is article 129a of the German Criminal Code, introduced in 1976. It penalizes the formation of terrorist organizations as well the support of or recruitment for it.

1. Terrorist organizations
Article 129a specifies the notion of terrorist organizations through listing a number of crimes as their objectives or activities, inter alia murder, manslaughter and kidnapping/hostage taking, causing of explosion and interference in public operations. Not all these crimes are typically considered to be terrorist offences in terms of a certain scale: Terrorist offences should reach a certain degree of severity because they justify extraordinary investigational measures and harsh punishment. More restrictive concepts of terrorism only include the use of serious violence against persons. Thus, the notion of terrorist organisations is very broad in comparison to the national definitions of other States. As regards the formal question what constitutes an organization – terrorist or of other nature – jurisprudence has clarified that it should have at least three members and should be intended to exist over a certain duration of time. Moreover, the fact that the individual members subordinate their wills under the common objective of the organization is critical.

2. Objective Element
Also, the objective elements of the criminalized acts are problematic. Article 129a criminalizes the formation of a terrorist organization as well as being a ringleader or supporting or recruiting for it. Especially critical is the notion of 'support' as it may entail a wide range of actions (or their omission) but is not further specified in the criminal code. Basically, it may manifest itself in financial, practical/logistical or written and oral support. Thus, the courts are left with the interpretation and jurisprudence provided for some degree of clarification. Accordingly, financial and logistical support largely come within the scope of the provision. Less clarity exists with regard to support through words, but it may be considered that many respective acts, such as solidarity manifestations or printing documentaries with statements of terrorist organizations are protected as freedom of expression under art. 5 Grundgesetz. Nevertheless, a coherent

clarification would be strongly desirable. It should be added that under article 138 Criminal Code there exists a duty to inform if a person has knowledge the planning or execution of certain specified crimes, including the crimes under article 129a.

3. Subjective Element

Furthermore, article 129a does not set out any subjective requirement, i.e. terrorist intention. Most national definitions entail an intention to create a climate of terror and fear within the population and the advancement of political, religious or other ideological goals. The silence on any subjective element obscures the distinction to the offence of forming a criminal organization. This is critical because of the more extensive investigation powers, such as solitary confinement and widespread phone tapping, as well as more severe punishment coming along with 129a. The newly introduced article 129b extends the provisions of 129a to terrorist organisations abroad but does not add to its clarity.

The annual reports of the Federal Office for the Protection of the Constitution describe terrorism as "the persistent struggle for political goals, which are to be attained with the help of attacks against the physical integrity, life, and property of other persons, in particular through serious criminal offences as defined in article 129a para. 1 of the Criminal Code, or through other offences, which serve as preparation for such crimes." While this definition is more comprehensive, including the subjective element, it certainly has no legal status and is thus not applicable in criminal proceedings.

III. Requirement of clarity of law in international human rights law

From the perspective of human rights law this vagueness poses a problem because international norms require domestic law to be precise and foreseeable. This principle should be upheld even more so in the case of a provision of criminal law, which entails severe punishment, grants the State wide investigating powers and requires a low threshold of suspicion. The importance of certainty of national law was pointed out by the European Court. It uses the question whether the law is precise and foreseeable as part of the test whether an interference of the State was "prescribed by law" in relation to the claw back clauses in articles 8-11. In the Sunday Times case, the Court stated:

A norm cannot be regarded as 'law' unless it is formulated with sufficient precision to enable the citizen to regulate his conduct: he must be able – if needed with appropriate advice – to foresee to a degree that is reasonable in the circumstances, the consequences which a given action may entail.

The Court upheld this approach in a number of cases. Furthermore, the requirement of clarity in criminal legislation follows from the prohibition of retrospective legislation under art. 7 of the Convention. According to Kokkinakis v Greece, an individual must know from the wording of the relevant provision what acts and omissions will make him liable. Nevertheless, the Court accepted that criminal law cannot be absolutely precise in order to avoid excessive rigidity and to keep pace with changing circumstances. Moreover, it recognized "the gradual clarification of the rules of criminal liability through judicial interpretation from case to case, provided that the resulting development is consistent with the essence of the offence and could reasonably be foreseen." Thus, while establishing a general rule of precision and foreseeability, the Court gives States considerable leeway and accepts a certain degree of vagueness.

The Human Rights Committee (HRC) addressed the question of clarity of law in relation to State interference with the art. 17 protection of privacy. In General Comment 16 the Committee stated: "[R]elevant legislation must specify in detail the precise circumstances in which such interferences may be permitted." Several States were asked to adopt more precise legislation regulating these matters.

The question if article 129a would withstand scrutiny of the European Court or the Human Rights Committee is rather speculative. Given the wide margin of appreciation States are granted in questions of national security, these bodies might find sufficient clarity in the provision. Nevertheless, as German jurisprudence only clarifies the matter to a certain degree, more precision would be strongly desirable – especially for the element of 'support' and with regards to an inclusion of an element of intention, in order to strengthen the distinction to criminal organizations. This appears even more important in the light of new article 129b, which extends the criminal act to organizations abroad, as the new provision may mainly have implications for non-nationals who are less familiar with the German legal system. The same holds true for certain newly introduced provisions of the Associations Act, the Aliens Act and the Asylum Procedure Act, which exclusively apply to foreigners and are interpreted in the light of article 129a.

Liberty Dies by Inches: German Counter-Terrorism Measures and Human Rights, *Part 2 of 2*
By Verena Zöller

E. Counter-Terrorism Measures

The principal international body monitoring the measures taken by all States is the Counter Terrorism Committee (CTC) established by Security Council resolution 1373. The Committee's mandate is to monitor the implementation of resolution 1373 and to increase the capability of States to fight terrorism. All States are obliged to report to the CTC. Germany first did so in December 2001 and, judging from the follow-up questions of the Committee, the report was carefully analysed. However, the scrutiny of the CTC only extends to whether it regards the measures taken sufficient and appropriate to combat terrorism. It does not consider their conformity with human rights law. Thus, the reports provide an overview of the measures in place but are silent about their compatibility with human rights standards.

As can be seen from the Germany's report, counter-terrorism measures are wide-ranging. Security Packages I and II amended 19 different statutes and six statutory orders. In the following some of the most important measures shall be reviewed regarding their accordance with Germany's human rights obligations. The selection was made with a view to cover all different groups of affected persons. Also included are the eavesdropping law and grid search, both introduced before 9/11, firstly because of their importance and secondly to illustrate a certain continuity.

I. Measures potentially affecting all persons present in Germany
1. The right to privacy: surveillance and data protection in human rights instruments
The most wide-ranging measures in that they potentially affect all persons on German territory mainly concern issues of surveillance and therefore pose a problem with the right to privacy as guaranteed in art. 17 ICCPR and art. 8 ECHR. International jurisprudence left no doubt that measures of surveillance and data collection/processing fall within the scope of the right to privacy.

Art. 8 of the European Convention guarantees the right to respect for private and family life, home and correspondence. Paragraph 2 sets out the circumstances when an interference by the State with these rights is legitimate. European case law on surveillance and data protection is extensive. The leading case *Klass v Germany* concerned a 1960s law on surveillance of mail and telecommunications. The Court pointed out that the restriction of free communication constituted a direct interference with art. 8. Also in terms of data collection the Court repeatedly affirmed the applicability of art 8, stating that the storing of information relating to a person's private life as well as the release of such information falls within the scope of the right to privacy. Moreover, in *Niemitz v Germany* the Court pointed out that the private life includes the ability to establish relationships with others, and in *Halford v UK* it concluded that professional and business activities may fall within the notion of private life.

Thus, the right to privacy under the European Convention protects citizens from arbitrary gathering, storage and release of personal data. However, as art. 8 is no absolute right this cannot mean that the State is prohibited from performing such activities at all. In Klass the necessity of some degree of surveillance was explicitly accepted: "Democratic societies nowadays find themselves threatened by highly sophisticated forms of espionage and by terrorism, with the result that the State must be able, in order to effectively counter such threats, to undertake secret surveillance of subversive elements operating within its jurisdiction." Thus, the State enjoys a certain but not unlimited discretion, subject to art. 8(2): The measures have to be prescribed by law, have a legitimate aim, such as national security, be necessary in a democratic society and strictly proportionate. As laid out in Klass, a crucial factor for proportionality are sufficient safeguards to ensure that the measures are not carried out in an excessive or arbitrary manner.

The ICCPR protects from "arbitrary or unlawful interference with privacy, family, home or correspondence." Unlike the ECHR, the Covenant does not contain a claw back clause. But still art. 17 is no absolute right –there may be interference as long as it is not arbitrary or unlawful. Case law provides for an inclusion of data protection. As the European Court, the HRC includes the ability of individuals to develop relationships with others. The issue of surveillance measures is addressed in General Comment 16, para 8: "Surveillance, whether electronic or otherwise, interceptions of telephonic, telegraphic and other forms of communication, wire-tapping and recording of conversations should be prohibited." Despite this strict language, the concluding comments to various State reports make it clear that surveillance measures are permissible when strictly controlled and overseen by independent, preferably judicial, bodies.

The Comment also elaborates on the necessity of data protection guarantees. It clarifies that "the competent public authorities should only be able to call for such information relating to an individual's private life the knowledge of which is essential in the interests of society." The Committee demands some safeguards, e.g., personal data must not get into the hands of persons not authorised by law and individuals must have the possibility to inquire about stored information and to rectify incorrect data. However, these seem to be less far-reaching than under the European Convention. For example, they don't address the manner of information gathering or the issue of non-excessive use. Thus, while the HRC addressed the issue with greater clarity through a General Comment, one may argue that the actual protection is less far-reaching than under the ECHR. Nevertheless, it must be ascertained that both treaties provide for clear protection against unlawful or arbitrary surveillance as well as personal data collection and use.

2. Eavesdropping and phone-tapping

Telecommunications surveillance for investigational purposes and crime prevention is not a recent phenomenon but plays a major role in combating terrorism. In Europe, today only Italy, the Netherlands and Switzerland make more use of phone interception than Germany. Recent records show a considerable increase by 80% between 1996 and 2001. The biggest leap by 75% in 1996 is hard to explain. A ministerial statement, linking it to the increased use of mobile phones is questionable, as the big rise in mobile phone users occurred only from 1999 on.

In the Klass case, the European Court found that German legislation did not violate art. 8 of the Convention and showed itself largely satisfied with the safeguards in place. Inter alia, surveillance is only permissible if "the establishment of the facts by any other method is without prospects of success or considerably more difficult." The application for a surveillance order must be in written form and give reasons for their necessity and measures must be reported to a parliamentary supervisory body. After discontinuation the intercepted person is to be notified unless notification would impair the long-term goals of surveillance. Thus, after cessation legal remedy becomes available.

However, as a recent report by the Max-Planck-Institute revealed, these safeguards are not satisfactorily respected. First of all, the unexplained increase in phone-tapping since mid-1990s suggests that the measure is being used excessively, i.e. not as last resort. The fact that only 25% of all cases lead to an investigational success calls proportionality into question. 66,5% of convicted persons were sentenced to less than five years of detention, indicating that the measure often relates to less serious crimes, mostly drug-related. Moreover, 73% of persons subjected to phone-tapping were not notified after discontinuation and thus had no access to legal remedy. While the reasons for this lax practice are not entirely clear, there is a strong suggestion that it may be due to a lack of resources. Hence, while the law as such is accordance with human rights standards, its implementation is to be criticized. Largely, the safeguards set out by the European Court and the HRC are not sufficiently respected. In conclusion, the compatibility of surveillance practice in Germany with the right to privacy and – with regards to notification – the right to a legal remedy as guaranteed by art. 13 ECHR and art. 2(3a) ICCPR is highly questionable.

If the same holds true for the above-mentioned 1998 Großer Lauschangriff[68] (eavesdropping law) has to be awaited until a similar report becomes available in summer 2004. However, the findings may not be of major relevance anymore: The law was in large parts declared unconstitutional in March 2004. It had amended art. 13 Grundgesetz (inviolability of the home) and the Criminal Procedure Act, allowing for 'acoustic surveillance' of private homes in cases of explicitly listed grave crimes. It provided for similar safeguards as mail and telecommunications surveillance. The Constitutional Court did not challenge the amendment of art. 13 Grundgesetz, as it does not interfere with human dignity (Art. 1) and the basic principles of the State order (art. 20). However, it found parts the implementation as laid down in the Criminal Procedure Act disproportionate with a view to the guarantees of human dignity and the inviolability of the home, i.e. eavesdropping must be conducted in such a way not endangering the protection of human dignity. Hence, it is not allowed when the suspect is around persons of his confidence, such as close friends, family, lawyers, doctors and clergy, and when the rights of third parties would be violated. Respective evidence may not be used before the courts. Moreover, the Court declared the list of crimes as too extensive, as more than twenty offences do not entail a sentence of at least five years of detention and thus do not reach the threshold of severity. Finally, it regarded the regulations regarding notification as insufficient. Although the law must be rectified until June 2005, it is safe to say that German surveillance practice at least since the mid-1990s was in violation with the internationally guaranteed right to privacy.

3. Extension of powers of the security authorities

While the above-described surveillance partly could be analysed in relation to the actual practice, this is not the case for the newly introduced measures as there is no data available yet. Thus, the view on the legislation as such must suffice. In respect of the right to privacy, one of the most important features of the second Security Package is the extension of the powers of the two intelligence services, namely the Bundesverfassungsschutz (Office for the Protection of the Constitution) and the Bundesnachrichtendienst (Federal Intelligence Service). Before 2001 the Office for the Protection of the Constitution could gather and evaluate information on endeavours directed against the free democratic order, national security, an impairment of the administration as well as activities of an intelligence nature and activities which, by the use of force, endanger the external interests of Germany. Security Package II extended this list to include "endeavours that are directed against the idea of international understanding (art. 9(2) Grundgesetz), especially against the peaceful co-existence of people (art.26(1) Grundgesetz)." While based in the Constitution, these principles are relatively vague for legitimating intelligence action. However, the actual measures allowed for are even more concerning. Both intelligence services are given the authority to request information about individuals suspected to engage in the above-mentioned activities from various financial service institutions, postal service providers, telecommunications services and aviation companies. Moreover, the possibilities of data exchange between all major institutions involved in crime prevention and investigation have been extended, i.e. apart from the intelligence services mainly the Bundeskriminalamt (Federal Office of Criminal Investigation) and the Bundesgrenzschutz (Federal Border Guard).

Again, the question is if these amendments are compatible with data protection under privacy rights. Basically, the same safeguards as for other surveillance measures apply. Nevertheless, the law greatly extends the list of institutions private information can be requested from, and thereby the type of information that may be gathered. Furthermore, the grounds for request do not seem to be sufficiently precise. In the Malone case, the European Court has reiterated the need for clarity in legislation in relation to surveillance measures. Thus, while there are safeguards in place, the new powers may amount to a violation of privacy rights because of their mere scope. Moreover, the enhancement of data exchange obscures the separation between intelligence and police, rooted in the historical experiences from the

Third Reich and the GDR. Also, this exchange may endanger the principle that collected data may only be used for the purpose it was collected for – this requirement may be difficult to control when data come from a variety of sources. Thus, strict scrutiny must be maintained supervising the application of the new measures. On a positive note, the provisions contain a sunset clause, requiring them to be reviewed after five years.

II. Measures affecting foreigners living in Germany

In the aftermath of September 11 many NGOs reported on increasing xenophobia in Germany, especially against Muslims or persons with an Arab appearance. Complaints ranged from vandalism and bomb threats against mosques, to verbal abuse, discrimination and violent attacks. While German politicians condemned intolerance and hostility towards Muslims, critics made counter-terrorism measures partly responsible for creating prejudice. Indeed, a great part targets foreigners, either wishing to enter or living in Germany. Regarding the latter, there are problems with various human rights: again, the right to privacy, but also freedom of religion and the prohibition of discrimination. In the following, two measures shall be evaluated: the so-called grid search and the ban of extremist religious foreigner's associations.

1. Rasterfahndung (Grid search)

Rasterfahndung is a method of systematic screening of personal data which initially was used rather unsuccessfully to search members of the RAF. It was taken up again after it became known that three of the 9/11 terrorists had been living in Germany. Practically, the data of individuals are systematically compared and screened for certain criteria presumed to be characteristics of criminals. The purpose is to identify 'sleepers' of Islamist terror organizations. While basically the criteria are not publicly known, they seem to include affiliation with Islam, male, between 18 and 40 years old and university studies in natural science and technical subjects. As a result, allegedly thousands of Muslims have had their data screened and many subsequently had their houses searched, sometimes in the middle of the night, have been arrested and interrogated. Some individuals reported on police brutality. Supposedly only within the first four months in Hamburg data of more than 30,000 male students had been screened and 140 persons were interrogated at police stations. Relatively new is the use for preventive purposes, i.e. independent of a concrete suspicion of persons having committed a crime. Universities, health and social insurance agencies, employers and other institutions were asked to provide information on individuals, which clearly poses a problem to data protection and the right to privacy as it requires no degree of suspicion in relation to a concrete offence but just a very abstract danger and involves no safeguards. Rasterfahndung puts a considerable number of persons under a general suspicion, denying the fundamental presumption of innocence as laid out in and art. 14(2) of the ICCPR. Thus, the inference with the right to privacy can hardly be called proportionate - even more so in the light of the poor investigational success rate.

Furthermore, it gives rise to an issue of discrimination under art. 14 ECHR and articles 2(1) and 26 ICCPR on the basis of race or national origin and religion. The protection from discrimination under the European Convention is the weakest one: Article 14 is not considered a freestanding right, i.e. it can only be violated in conjunction with another Convention right – in this case privacy. According to such reasoning, not only the right to privacy was violated, but also it was done so in a discriminatory way. The affected persons were singled out, inter alia, on the grounds of race or national origin and religion. The Court often has been reluctant to address article 14 even if it had found a violation of another provision. However, in recent years it seems to have taken the question of discrimination somewhat more serious if it is considered to be "a fundamental aspect of the case." The protection against discrimination in art. 26 ICCPR thus is much stronger, as the Covenant considers it a right on its own. The protection under art 2(1) is limited to the rights set forth in the Covenant. Hence, just as for the ECHR, it has to be seen in connection with the right to privacy. However, as the Committee pointed out, not all distinction on one of the grounds constitutes discrimination. If the differentiation is based on objective and reasonable criteria it is not prohibited. Nevertheless, it is questionable if the distinction for the purpose of Rasterfahndung, mainly on the basis of personal characteristics of a few persons who committed terrorist crimes, can be justified.

The practice of Rasterfahndung has widely been criticised on all these grounds on the national level, but apart from the highest court in the Federal State Hessen judiciary upheld it. It has not come under review of the Constitutional Court.

2. Ban of extremist religious associations

One of the first measures in September 2001 within Security Package I was the abolition of the so-called "religious privilege," under which religious or ideological associations were not subject to the Vereinsgesetz (Act Governing Private Associations) and thus could not be prohibited accordingly. Hence, now religious associations may be banned – in accordance with art. 9(2) Grundgesetz – under art. 3(1) of the law when their endeavours are directed against the Criminal Code, the constitutional order or against the idea of international understanding. Associations of foreigners, i.e. when the majority of members or executive members are non-nationals (excluding EU nationals), additionally may be prohibited on grounds listed in art. 14(2). These include activities directed against peaceful co-existence of Germans and foreigners or foreigners among each other, or against Germany's obligations under international law, incitement to violence or support of organisations abroad which plan or support attacks against persons or property. The aim of this more restrictive approach towards foreigner's associations is the prevention of extremist activities. It has to be emphasised that the abolition of the religious privilege applies not only to foreigner's associations, but certainly these are subjected to more extensive prohibition grounds. Among scholars it had been debated if the abolition violated freedom of thought, conscience and religion, on the international level protected under art. 9 ECHR and art. 18 ICCPR. But religious associations are not prohibited as such; they are just subjected to the same rules as other private associations. While it may be argued that religious groups need somewhat greater protection than is guaranteed under freedom of associations, it is hard to see why they should be able to engage in activities related to the prohibitions grounds of articles 3 and 14(2). The activities indicated there are by no means necessary for the exercise of religious freedom.

Thus, the question would rather be if there were an issue of discrimination in that more prohibition grounds apply to foreigner's associations and thus their right to freedom of association is more restricted. There appears to be an underlying assumption that foreigner's associations are more likely to engage in organized crime and terrorism, as such are the justifications for art. 14(2). Freedom of association is one of the core principles in a democratic society. It helps to guarantee the healthy functioning of democracy and is especially important for groups which don't constitute a majority. However, in art. 16 the European Convention limits freedom of association under art. 11: It grants State Parties the right to restrict political activities of aliens. It is not very clear why the limitations laid out in art. 11(2) should not be sufficient to control political activities by non-nationals and accordingly, the Court has never considered the provision. As early as 1977 the Parliamentary Assembly has recommended its removal. Hence, while art. 16 certainly can't be ignored, it does not have a very strong standing and runs counter developments in international law. Accordingly, the ICCPR does not know such a restriction of political activities of foreigners. Freedom of association under art. 22 as all rights equally applies to nationals and non-nationals – subject to the restrictions set forth in para 2. Thus, the distinction regarding prohibition grounds under German law on the basis of nationality, while justifiable under the ECHR, is clearly questionable in terms of universal human rights standards and may well be called discriminatory.

In practice, since the abolition of the religious privilege the Ministry of Interior prohibited several Muslim associations: the Turkish Islamic group Kalifstaat (Caliphate State) along with 19 connected associations. The objective of the Kalifstaat was said to be the overthrow of the Turkish secular State and its replacement by a system based on the Shari'a. The ban was confirmed by the Federal Administrative Court on the ground that the group contravened the principles of democracy, the rule of law and human dignity. The leader of Kalifstaat, Metin Caplan, was sentenced to four years imprisonment because of incitement to murder. Furthermore, the association Al-Aqsa was prohibited because of financial support of Hamas and Hizb ut-Thahir al-Islami (Islamic Liberation Party) was banned for propagating violence and anti-Semitism. On the basis of the facts, these bans appear to be justified and by no means disproportionate. All these organizations fall within the scope of art. 3 of the Associations Act.

III. Measures affecting asylum seekers

The concern about foreigners engaging in terrorist activities is also illustrated by the numerous changes in aliens and asylum law through Security Package II. The amendments are to ensure that data about foreigners who wish to enter are available to all relevant institutions, including the Federal Criminal Office and that potential terrorists are not granted stay permit or can be expelled. These measures involve some critical aspects, especially the extension of expulsion grounds and the restriction of the right to non-refoulement.

1. Extension of expulsion grounds

According to Security Package II, persons now can be expelled when they threaten the democratic order or national security, pursue political aims by violent means or publicly incite violence, are member of an organisation which supports international terrorism or support such an organisation, make false or incomplete statements regarding their contacts to persons or organisations who are suspected of supporting international terrorism.

It can be argued that these new grounds fall within the scope of art. 32 of the 1951 Refugee Convention, allowing for expulsion on grounds of national security and public order. Accordingly, the provision was not criticised as such. The basic problem arises out of the vague language of the new text. As elaborated above, the term 'terrorism' lacks precise definition in German law and so does the concept of 'support'. Thus, the competent authorities are left with the decision which organisations can be called terrorist. But this decision is especially critical for asylum-seekers, as they are frequently engaged in opposition movements against repressive governments. The issue leads back to the bonmot "one person's terrorist is another person's freedom fighter": It often is a question of digression where legitimate opposition ends and terrorism begins, especially in cases of internal conflict. Furthermore, information about alleged terrorist activity will often come from the country of origin. This results in a conflict of interest between the asylum seeker and his home country and may put him at risk in case of return.

2. Restriction of non-refoulement

Under art. 33 of the 1951 Convention refugees are guaranteed not to be sent back to territories where their life would be threatened. Thus, even if a refugee falls under the art. 32 grounds of expulsion, the State is not allowed to send him or her to an unsafe country (including third countries). However, the protection is not absolute: it does not apply where there are reasonable grounds to believe the person to be a threat to national security or when he has been convicted for a particularly serious crime (art. 33(2)). Art. 51 of the German Aliens Act reflects this provision. Moreover, Germany is bound by the prohibition to sent someone back when he is in danger to be tortured under the art. 3 jurisprudence of the ECHR and art. 3 of the Convention against Torture (CAT). The leading case of the European Convention is Soering, who could not be extradited to the United States because there he faced death row. The principle was re-affirmed in several other cases. In Chahal, the Court indicated that national security had no application in art. 3 cases as the prohibition of torture is an absolute, non-derogable right. Hence, the prohibition of no-refoulement under the ECHR is even stronger than under the 1951 Convention. A prominent example of non-refoulement is the case of Kalifstaat leader Kaplan: An extradition request by Turkey so far has been refused, as Turkey has not guaranteed that Kaplan will not face the death penalty.

Nevertheless, Security Package II restricted non-refoulement by inserting the exclusion grounds of art. 1(F) 1951 Convention into art. 51 of the Aliens Act. This runs counter the system of the Refugee

Convention, as both articles apply to different groups of people: the art.33(2) exception from non-refoulement concerns persons already recognized as refugees, while art. 1(F) applies to persons who are in the process of having their refugee claim considered. Thus, German law obscures the distinction between these groups, which is of high importance for a fair asylum procedure. The principle of 'inclusion before exclusion',[102] providing that before a person is excluded from refugee status his well-founded fear of prosecution under art. 1(A) must be considered, may not be respected. The inclusion of art. 1(F) in the grounds for expulsion extends this category because it uses the exclusion grounds without the context of art. 1(A). Thus, it may be possible to deport an asylum seeker before first assessing his claim for refugee status. Moreover, both articles require different standards of proof. Thus, by integrating both articles in one provision, the higher standard of art. 33 may be applied to art. 1(F). This leads to an unfair procedure not in line with the Convention. However, even if a refugee qualifies for expulsion under art. 51 of the Aliens Act, he still should be protected from refoulement under the ECHR and CAT.

In conclusion, German refugee law – much criticised for not respecting international standards for a long time – was made even more restrictive through counter-terrorism legislation. It remains to be noted that much of the law governing aliens and refugees will be changed with the new Immigration Act, currently discussed between government and opposition in the Federal Council. Presumably a good deal of the envisaged improvements for refugees will not survive these negotiations – even more so as now they take place under the shadow of the recent terrorist attacks in Madrid.

F. Conclusion

Since the introduction of the emergency law in 1967 Germany has had a long history of countering terrorist threats, from inside and outside the country. The two Security Packages of 2001 built on a considerable body of legislation. After left-wing terrorism had faded by the late 1980s, the mid-1990s witnessed a new wave in security driven State activity. Hence, the measures after 9/11 were not an isolated reaction to the attacks in the United States, which seem to have been more the trigger than the actual reason. This is in any event true for measures which were taken up again, as the Rasterfahndung, and the provisions of Security Package I, which was put together rather speedily. The rush in which legislation was pushed through did not allow for thorough discussion and fortifies the assumption that 9/11 provided the opportunity to get things approved which previously had lacked political support. In contrast to measures already in place, the focus of the Security Packages is rather on prevention than on repression.

As exemplified by the analysed measures, the main concerns for human rights are:

(1) The vagueness of many provisions, which opens the door to broad interpretations and leaves individuals in uncertainty of which conduct is actually prohibited. This imprecision poses a problem mainly wherever a definition of terrorism, terrorist organisation or support of the latter is involved, but also where powers of security authorities are extended through the broad language of constitutional principles. The legislator should consider clarifying the respective provisions.

(2) Interferences with the right to privacy, which used to enjoy an unprecedented strong protection under German law due to the history of the Third Reich and the GDR. The awareness of the fundamental importance of privacy rights seems to be fading away. As exemplified by the practice of the eavesdropping law, scrutiny must be given to the law as such and its actual implementation.

(3) The measures disproportionately aim at foreigners, who are restricted in their civil rights and freedoms and their rights as refugees. This gives not only rise to concern about discrimination, but also fosters a climate of xenophobia. By further undermining the principles of the 1951 Convention, the rights of a group needing special protection are endangered.

On a positive note, despite increasing 'islamophobia' in the Western world, freedom of religion has not been considerably restricted, although the ongoing debate about female teachers wearing the

Islamic headscarf should be noted. However, this debate has not the dimension it currently takes in France. Another positive aspect is that an independent judiciary reviews legislation and does not give in to political pressure, as shown in the Hamburg trials and the refusal to extradite Metin Kaplan.

But it also has to be noted that Germany not only introduced far-reaching national legislation, but also pushes for additional measures within the European Union – for good or for worse. For example, the introduction of Rasterfahndung on the European level was suggested. Furthermore, Germany advocated the European Arrest Warrant. After the tragic bombings in Madrid one week ago, the Minister of Interior was one of the first calling for an emergency meeting to discuss further measures.

In conclusion, while surely not all measures pose problems with respect to human rights obligations, there is an ongoing effort to introduce security driven legislation, on the national and European level without thoroughly considering human rights implications. As in many countries, human rights seem to be regarded as hampering the fight against terrorism – which is not only a misperception but also a serious mistake in the strategy against terrorism.

11.8   Approaches to Biosecurity and Biodefense Law in Other countries

11.8.1.   Former Soviet Union

In 1979, unknown to almost every human on earth, a biological weapons plant in Sverdlovsk, Soviet Union, accidentally released weaponized anthrax, which became airborne, creating a plume that floated over Chkalovskiy, the working class section of Sverdlovsk.

In the early days of the outbreak at Sverdlovsk, which occurred April 7 or 8, 1979, the investigation of the incident revealed a militaristic approach implemented by the local public health authority:

> At the emergency meeting, Dr. Babich...called for suggestions for identifying the disease. One person suggested plague. Another thought it could be smallpox. Everyone rejected cholera as the answer; the symptoms and fast progress of the mystery disease were markedly different. Arenskiy [described as a mid-level public health official concerned with tuberculosis, at the time of the outbreak] remembers pointing out recent cattle cases he'd heard of and putting his bet on anthrax.
>
> The group recognized that, whatever the disease was, it could be highly contagious as well as fatal...So it instituted what Arenskiy called 'a military approach,' for which Babich outlined three goals. The first was to get sick patients to a quarantined hospital ward. They agreed that all adults and older children taken ill should go to Hospital 40, to the infectious disease division. Young children and infants would go to Hospital 4, to its pediatric infectious diseases unit. The morgue conditions and the burials had to be sanitary and segregated. Second, the medical personnel, especially the nurses and primary physicians, had to be warned to take appropriate precautions when treating infected patients. Third, the neighborhoods most affected by the disease had to be canvassed and warned of the danger of contamination. Then the group gave the unknown disease a code number...and arranged for notices to be sent to medical stations to transport patients to the two designated hospitals.[55]

According to the account, the local public health response was already in place when the Moscow officials arrived, and it was the local authority that made the decisions concerning the transport of suspected victims, segregated burial, and house-tohouse checking in Chkalovskiy. As for any military involvement during the response, the 'military sat silently within their compounds.' A wife, Dayanova, describes what happened when public health authorities took her husband by ambulance to Hospital 40, on May 6, 1979. That evening, after a call to the hospital, she was told to come. Upon arrival she found her husband gone from his room and a posted sign directing the staff to burn the clothes and linens. When she asked where was her husband, she received a reply to go to the morgue. Upon her arrival at the morgue she found her husband in the middle of an autopsy. His body was never returned. A mother, after her son was taken to Hospital 40, describes what happened in their home: "Strangers invade and begin scrubbing the walls of his room. 'Our house was disinfected....The bed linens were taken away.'" No more than ten miles separated Chkalovskiy and Sverdlovsk, but there were no newspapers, radio or television stations. There was no word-of mouth between the center of the city and the northern, working class area of Chkalovskiy. A scientist, Dr. Donald Ellis, who had arrived for professional collaboration in the field of physics, spoke and read Russian, yet he knew nothing of the events.

Jeanne Guillemin, *Anthrax—An Investigation of a Deadly Outbreak* (1999).

A militaristic approach, no public information, and a rising mortality rate, in a communistic government that addressed the outbreak of an unknown biological agent with secrecy as a priority, saving lives was a secondary concern, while civil rights of any of the citizens was not even contemplated. In the Sverdlovsk case, with the Soviet Union's extensive public health system, it still took six days to learn that an anthrax release had occurred and nine days to confirm the diagnosis, during which time many victims were already dead or close to death.

The recent anthrax terrorist attack in the United States raised public consciousness of a new theater of war, not previously contemplated in our lifetimes. The use of anthrax to terrorize Americans, followed the September 11, 2001 attack, making indistinguishable American's fears about the threat of various kinds of terrorism. Our response to these attacks has been the passage of the USA PATRIOT Act of 2001 which has allowed for greater surveillance activities of law enforcement officers and for the unprecedented sharing of information between the FBI and the CIA. The use of anthrax has also given rise to concerns about the use of quarantine, which was implemented in a number of instances during this outbreak, although anthrax is not among the contagious biological agents. The anthrax attack has given rise to the concern that smallpox may be used as a biological weapon, and on November 23, 2001, the Centers for Diseases Control issued its guidance for a smallpox protocol in the event of its appearance among the population.

The Soviet Union's local public health authorities responded to the anthrax outbreak utilizing a similar protocol for response, except within a governmental framework devoid of civil rights considerations. While the public health approach may have been performed optimally, where national security was the overarching concern, unconstrained by civil rights; public health, civil rights and national security under the U.S. Constitution must be examined, balancing these interests prior to an emergency in a bioterrorism attack, in order to avoid any similarity to the de-humanizing Sverdlovsk incident.

Russian Federation.

In January 2002, a Russian court ruled on the fate of five Russian followers of the Japanese cult, Aum Shinrikyo, who were implicated in a scheme to commit terrorist actions in Tokyo and Aomori, Japan.

Prosecutors asked for prison terms of between five and eight years for five defendants: Dmitry Sigachev, Boris Tupeiko, Dmitry Voronov, and Alexander Shevchenko, from Moscow, and Alexei Yurchuk, from the eastern Primorye region. The defendants were charged with terrorism, possession of illegal arms, and smuggling.

After a one-hour trial, Dmitriy Sigachev, the leader, was sentenced to eight years in prison and to have property worth 100 minimum monthly wages confiscated R20,000 (roughly equivalent to 650 U.S. dollars). The sentence is to be served in a high security prison. Three other defendants received sentences of between six and three years, and one was committed to a mental institution.

11.8.2. Japan

In World War II, Japan had a bioweapons development program and utilized a large number of human subjects in Unit 731. The testimony from the victims of the experimentation that followed the end of the War were remarkable in the level of torture and inhumane treatment that they received, including vivisection of humans. The United States allowed the exclusion of the testimony and records of experimentation from the trial of the defendants in exchange for these documents.

During this period, Japan allegedly engaged in biological warfare against China dropping plague-infested fleas over the cities of Ningbo and Quzhou in Zhejiang province. In 1997, Konen Tsuchiya, attorney representing victims of Unit 731 and victims of the attacks, filed a class action against the Japanese government asking for reparations. No resolution or settlement has been forthcoming.

Japan passed the Anti-Subversive Activities Law in 1952, which allows the government to disband a group if it has been engaged in "subversive activities for political purposes."

The Independent Commission for Public Security judges the propriety of the disbandment proceedings initiated by the agency under the Anti-Subversive Activities Law.

The Aum Shinrikyo, the cult responsible for the sarin gas attack in the Tokyo subway in 1995, was so adjudged by the Public Safety Commission. During the proceeding phase of arguments, the Public Security Investigation Agency insisted, and the cult denied, that there was a likelihood that the cult "will engage in violent subversive activities in the future," which is the definition under the law to determine whether disbandment proceedings can take place. No evidence was produced by either side.

Through a majority decision, the seven-member commission, rejected the disbandment request in 1997, finding that the cult did not satisfy the legal requisite for disbandment—a clear danger of engaging as an organization in violent subversive activities repeatedly and continuously in the future. The Commission almost certainly relied upon the fact that almost all of the criminal suspects belonging to the AUM cult, had been arrested and were on or awaiting trial. In addition, there exists controversy over constitutional rights which guarantee the freedom to assemble, and the Anti-Subversive Activities Act.

Prosecutors asked for death sentences for four of the five former Aum Shinrikyo members who allegedly released the gas in the subway system. Shoko Asahara, the main leader of Aum Shinrikyo, was charged with multiple murders and, if convicted, is likely to be sentenced to death. On July 1998, the first of 20 defendants was convicted. A three-judge panel gave only a life sentence to Hyashi, after considering evidence of his deep remorse, for confessing his participation in the attack, for turning himself into the police, and for informing the police that the cult had conducted the sarin gas attack.

In September 1999, Yokoyama, 35, one of the five current and former Aum Shinrikyo members to have been charged with carrying out the sarin nerve gas attack on the Tokyo subway system received a life sentence.

In November 1999, the Japanese Parliament passed a law that created two measures designed to give the Japanese government increased controls over the Aum Shinrikyo doomsday cult. These laws were supported by both the political opposition and the Japanese government. Under the new legislation, the Japanese government is permitted to track the activities of organizations that in the past ten years have committed "indiscriminate mass murders." Authorities are allowed to keep such groups under surveillance for up to three years and the police can conduct searches at any time. These organizations must also submit reports of their activities every three months. Any violations of these requirements can result in the closing of the organization's facilities for up to six months. The second of the two measures permits the Japanese government to confiscate the violating organization's property and use it to help compensate victims of the offending organization.

On Dec. 27, 1999, the Public Security Investigation Agency, utilizing the new law, again asked the Public Security Commission to permit it to monitor the cult through the use of on-the-spot inspections and requiring the cult to regularly submit reports on its members and activities.

Again, the Commission refused to disband the organization.

In May 2000, the Aum Shinrikyo made a commitment to pay some 4.1 billion yen (37.6 million dollars) in compensation to victims of the 1995 sarin gas attack on the Tokyo subway system and other crimes committed by Aum Shinrikyo, according to the cult's bankruptcy administrator.

11.8.3. France

On July 22, 2001, the French Parliament passed a new law allowing the French government to disband organizations whose leaders commit crimes. This law identifies cults that among other criteria, employ "techniques to alter thinking." The French government appointed a commission which identified 172 such cults, all of which are candidates for disbandment if their leaders commit crimes.

11.8.4. Israel

Following the SARS outbreak, several countries sought to install infra-red heat detection equipment in airports to scan for travelers with fevers, which might indicate they were infected with SARS. While this works well for diseases where fever is a symptom of the onset of the disease, it is almost useless for pandemic influenza where a period of contagion precedes the presence of fever by days.

The following is a press release from Israel, announcing the new equipment:

PRESS RELEASE:
Karmiel, Israel May 8, 2003[56]

1.   Press Release OPGAL announces the release of its FDA - FEVER DETECTING SYSTEM, now entering use in several major international airports. Opgal is contributing to the world health community's effort to stop the spread of SARS by adapting its uncooled thermal imaging systems and cameras for the detection of individuals who may be infected with SARS. OPGAL, a leader in the development of thermal imaging technology, announced today the release of its Fever Detector & Alarm (FDA) system, a complete integrated remote sensing system designed to detect persons who may be suffering from elevated body temperature.

The system is based on Opgal's sophisticated Uncooled Infra-Red Thermal Imaging technology that can detect differences in temperature as small as 0.2C. SARS is characterized by a fever of over 100.4oF (38C), so that the Fever Detector & Alarm (FDA) System can easily detect individuals who have elevated temperatures.

The Fever Detector & Alarm (FDA) System consists of an uncooled highly sensitive infrared Thermal Camera integrated with customized software, sophisticated algorithms . The system screens real-time thermal images, to detect individuals passing through its field of view, whose body temperature exceeds a pre-set threshold. The individual is designated on the display, and an audible alarm is heard. The specific person can then be further evaluated. "We offer a system that can be rapidly deployed in airports, train stations and other transportation hubs without any special infrastructure requirements." says OPGAL's CEO Dadi Lapidoth. "Because the system does not require a one-on-one person check, passenger flow is not obstructed. We are sure that this product will be extremely useful in keeping flow of transportation, and other public gathering to perform as normal as possible under the threat of the spread of SARS". Over the past few weeks, before the system was officially released to the market, Opgal has sold hundreds of its IR Cameras to different system integrators, to be implemented as part of their own application as SARS Fever Detectors. Founded in 1983 and owned by Rafael and the Elbit Group, OPGAL is a leading manufacturer of thermal and optical imaging products for use in public safety, paramilitary, navigation, and search and rescue applications. OPGAL has long-standing experience with thermal imaging technologies and aims at high commercial visibility by setting up strategic partnerships with appropriate companies.

11.8.5   South Africa

Project Coast was developed during the height of the apartheid years in South Africa, led by director Wouter Basson, who was acting on behalf of the South African government despite their membership in the UN BWC. The purpose of Project Coast was "to develop biological and chemical weapons to control, poison and kill people within and outside South Africa." It started in 1981 and officially ended in 1995. Allegations were made by the London-published South African anti-conscription journal, Resister, that claimed that the South African Police were part of research to develop a biological "race weapon, to which black people would be more susceptible than whites."[57] Many of the allegations involved poisonings using botulinum toxin, cholera, yellow fever virus, and salmonella. Evidence showed that in 1989, the Head of Research of Project Coast developed a list of biological agents formulated, and provides the list to the South African Police.

In 1997, the project 's director, Dr. Wouter Basson, was arrested by the narcotics division of the South African Police Service for allegedly selling the street drug Ecstasy. Upon a search of his home, documents relating to Project Coast were discovered and seized by the National Intelligence Agency, and turned over to the Truth and Reconciliation Commission (TRC) and the Attorney General.

The TRC began an investigation and heard testimony from scientists who had worked in the "front" companies of the project, as well as the managers and directors. This was followed by a criminal case filed against Dr. Wouter Basson for his involvement in the project in the Pretoria High Court in October 1999. On April 11, 2002, Judge Hartzenberg found Basson not guilty of any charges filed against him.

Commey Pusch, "Dr Death' walks free," (South Africa), *The New African*, May 1, 2002[58]

The champagne was on ice and barbecue flames alight even before Dr Wouter Basson, popularly known as "Dr Death", walked into the Pretoria high court on 11 April to hear the final verdict in a marathon trial that had lasted two-and-a- half years, starting from October 1999.

The state's bill was R20m (R9.5m of it being legal fees for Basson, borne by the South African Defence Force). Close to 200 witnesses testified on behalf of the stare. Basson called only one witness -- himself, in his own defence.

And the verdict: not guilty on all charges -- 46 charges! And so he was free to walk again. Giving his famous "Diablo wink", Basson embraced his mother and his lawyer amidst spontaneous applause from a courtroom packed with well-wishers and old apartheid veterans, including the former defence minister, Magnus Malan, and the former surgeon general, General Knobel, who had earlier on testified for the state. Basson said nothing to the press but rather made a hasty exit through the back door, to prepare for the evening party that was to come.

Basson had to answer 46 charges out of an original 67 (300 pages of indictment), relating to apartheid era crimes, which included 18 of murder, conspiracy to murder, assault and intimidation. And in addition, he faced 24 counts of fraud and theft, possession of drugs and being in possession of classified documents.

Particularly gruesome was a conspiracy to poison 200 SWAPO fighters in Namibia who were allegedly murdered using muscle relaxants and their bodies dumped into the sea by a special aircraft purchased for that purpose. Judge Willie Hartzenberg discharged Basson on that charge even before the case had started, on the grounds that it happened outside South Africa. Several of the original charges were soon to follow suit, like dominoes.

The result came as no surprise to the prosecution which immediately applied for leave to appeal even before reading the text. The judge apparently was planning to take a long leave soon after the judgement. The application will be heard on 29 April.

To the prosecution, the case was decided right at the beginning when Judge Hartzenberg, even before all the evidence had been led, said it would not take much to convince him that Basson was innocent on fraud related charges. The state proceeded to apply for him to step down for a new judge, but he refused.

A great part of the case became a showdown between the chief prosecutor Anton Ackerman and Judge Hartzenberg. Tempers frayed to such an extent that Ackerman opted to discontinue arguing the case, giving way to his junior counsel to see to its completion.

South African law does not have a jury system, and the state has the right to appeal against the decision of a judge who sits at a trial, with or without assessors. The jury system was done away with in 1966, and a jury system in a racially polarised South Africa will most likely be unable to deliver justice.

The state's key contention will be that Judge Hartzenberg was patently biased. And the appeal court, on the record of the trial, will decide whether to accept or set aside the judgement and find any appropriate remedy.

The judgement

In his judgement, the judge called the state's case "fragmented and confusing", and that it was largely superficial, hoping to convince the court of Basson's guilt in a manner which fell far short of the standard "beyond reasonable doubt".

Judge Hartzenberg further added that the state seemed to have decided what the truth was and had urged the court not to believe anything that contradicted the state's version of the truth.

On the fraud charges, he said the state expected Basson to give an account of every single cent that was spent on the South African Defence Force's secretive chemical and biological warfare programme. He moved on to reject every aspect of the state's evidence, a good portion of his judgement based on who and what he believed.

At the end of it all, he believed what Basson told the court in his defence even though he had not called a single witness to corroborate his story. It was Basson's right, as long as after cross-examination his answers were found to be reasonably possibly true.

And Basson took II advantage of the rules of the criminal procedure and ran his case close to that of the state to sow reasonable doubt. In effect, he mixed truth with what the prosecution called "lies" and cleverly "cooked up" answers for every question, which even though might not be plausible could at the same time be reasonably possibly true.

But neither did the judge opt to call material witnesses to clear up crucial issues, which he was entitled to do with an open mind. Rather, Judge Hartxenberg refused to listen to possible key witnesses, including Roger Buffham, a former British secret service agent, branding him a liar on the basis of a sworn affidavit.

At the end of the day, the judge did more for the defence than the defence counsel himself who basically rehashed the judge's points in the course of the trial.

The trial

The trial also called into question the Anglo-American adversarial system of justice, where the role of the judge is limited to that of an umpire in a contest between two gladiators, the state and the defence, in contrast to the European continental system where the judge is deeply involved in questioning all parties concerned to arrive at the truth.

The ANC resolved apartheid not as a conqueror, and the position of weakness from which it negotiated the new South Africa has meant serious concessions which has translated into several prominent people involved in heinous crimes walking free, even when brought to trial in front of their own.

Also of disturbing proportions is the trend of judges from the old apartheid order who use judicial somersaulting and bags of tricks to acquit their kith and kin. Even when overwhelmingly guilty, accused brothers escape with a slap on the wrist. The appeal court will shed light on whether Judge Harrzenberg followed this trend.

While Magnus Malan (also acquitted in a celebrated multiple murder trial dating from 1996), the old generals of the SADF and apartheid sympathisers celebrated, the ANC seethed. The white opposition Democratic Alliance "accepted the court's ruling".

Malan told The Guardian (of London): "We warned them two-and-a-half years ago that they were going to lose, and still they wasted money instead of looking at the poverty in our country."

The New National party, the final metamorphosed version of the National Party that ruled apartheid South Africa, was understandably guarded in its reactions. "A bit of a shock, considering how much the case has cost," said Sheila Camerer, the party's justice spokeswoman.

Calling the acquittal outrageous, Smuts Ngonyama, the ANC spokesman warned: "This is not the end of the case, it cannot be the end of the case."

Sipho Ngwema, the prosecution authority's spokesman, added: "We have said the judge must stand down because he was biased. In that context, what we saw today came as no surprise at all."

Jubilee South Africa, the apartheid debt and reparations task team, called the ruling "a travesty of justice." Neville Gabriel, its spokesperson said: "It is a shameful day for truth and justice in post-apartheid South Africa. Basson's case represents all that was despicable about the corrupted apartheid system and the continued impunity of apartheid criminals in the new South Africa, while apartheid's victims continue to suffer in poverty, joblessness, and the failure to ensure reparations."

Jubilee South Africa further expressed alarm that conflicting statements have emerged from South Africa's departments of justice and national intelligence about who has custody of missing Truth and Reconciliation Commission (TRC) files relating to chemical and biological weapons, and the murder of Dulcie September.

"It is highly irregular that the National Intelligence Agency had access to the files. We demand an explanation of this from both relevant government departments," Jubilee South Africa said.

"Similarly," it continued, "reports that Swiss Secret Service chief, Peter Regli, destroyed documents relating to his dealings with the likes of Basson demonstrate that the victims cannot rely on goodwill to ensure that the truth is known and that justice is delivered.

"We, therefore, demand the immediate release of all apartheid-era archive material for public scrutiny -- both in South Africa and in countries implicated in the Basson trial, especially Switzerland -- so that the truth may be told about the past and that the healing process of victims of apartheid can be advanced."

In particular, Jubilee South Africa demanded that:

(1) Swiss military and bank archives be immediately opened to researchers so as to fully understand the nature of Swiss-apartheid South Africa financial and military links.

(2) The missing TRC documents be immediately restored to South Africa's national archives under the custody of the Department of Justice.

(3) An independent audit of the files be conducted to ensure that all original documentation remains intact.

11.8.6. Cuba

The relationship between the United States and Cuba has been characterized by exchanges of suspicion regarding the use and the capabilities for the use of biological weapons.

On June 5, 2002, the United States Congress has held hearings to hear evidence as to whether Cuba is conducting an offensive biological weapons program, perhaps in collaboration with the former Soviet Union.[59]

The hearing was called as a result of a statement made by first by Undersecretary John Bolton and the "Assistant Secretary of State for Intelligence and Research, who will be testifying briefly. It is true that

Mr. Ford touched upon this subject in March of this year in the course of testimony before this committee on the subject of biological weapons. Mr. Ford spent a minute or two and 4 lines of his testimony on this matter. He said at that time, and I quote him: 'The United States believes that Cuba has at least a limited developmental offensive biological warfare research and developmental effort. Cuba has provided dual-use biotechnology to rogue states. We are concerned that such technology could support BW programs in those states. We call on Cuba to cease all BW-applicable cooperation with rogue states and to fully comply with all of its obligations under the Biological Weapons Convention.[60]

Assistant Secretary Ford was referenced by Senator Dodd when he stated, "Now, that is why I stand behind Under Secretary Bolton's remarks, which are consistent with Mr. Ford's, which says that Cuba "has at least a limited offensive biological research and development effort," and furthermore "that Cuba has provided dual-use biotechnology to rogue states." So it is certainly a fact, not fiction, that Cuba has a capability to pursue biological weapons."

In Assistant Secretary Ford's oral testimony, in conclusion, he said,

> "What then can I say about the evidence for our assessment? The nature of biological weapons makes it difficult to procure clear, incontrovertible proof that a country is engaged in illicit biological weapons research, production, weaponization, and stockpiling. Cuba's sophisticated denial and deception practices make our task even more difficult. That said, we have a sound basis for our judgment that Cuba has at least a limited developmental offensive biological warfare research and development effort. I am prepared to discuss the evidence we do have in a closed session or leave behind a classified statement for the record.
>
> Thank you, Mr. Chairman."

11.8.6.1.   UN Petition Against the U.S. for Bioterrorism

Cuban Allegations of U.S. Biological Warfare and the UN BWC Consultative Process of Resolution[61]

. . . In 1997, the Cuban government alleged that the United States had already, in 1962, deployed the Newcastle disease virus against its poultry industry. A more likely reason why a Newcastle disease occurred is that, due to poor manufacturing practices or lack of quality control, the Cuban manufacturer produced a faulty vaccine that contained virulent viruses that caused the outbreak.

On June 1, 1964, a communiqué issued over Fidel Castro's name accused the United States of having sent balloons carrying bacteriological cultures over Cuban territory. No claim for damages was made. Since the Cubans have provided no information about this alleged event, it cannot be analyzed.

Cuba blamed African Swine Fever (ASF) outbreaks in 1971 and 1980 on the United States as part of what I call an "allegation package." The outbreaks caused enormous damage to Cuban agriculture. The 1971 outbreak, for example as controlled only after the Cuban government slaughtered over 740,554 pigs. The 1980 outbreak led to the slaughter of 297,137 pigs. The United States had nothing to do with either outbreak, however; the first was caused when a commercial aircraft that departed from a country in which ASF was endemic brought the virus to Cuba in contaminated meat. The second time, the virus was imported by Haitian refugees who, together with their household animals, foundered on the Cuban coast as they were trying to sail to Florida.

Devastating tobacco blue mold epidemics affected Cuba during 1979 and 1980. Castro stated that these epidemics destroyed 25 percent of Cuba's tobacco crop in 1979 and almost 90 percent in 1980. Cuban officials have frequently alleged, as part of the "allegation package," that the United States was responsible for introducing the blue mold disease into Cuba. However, blue mold spores probably arose from a primary inoculum source in the Caribbean region itself and were carried into Cuba by winds that prevail in the Caribbean Sea.

Surgarcane rust disease affected many Caribbean countries, including Cuba, in 1979. As part of its "allegation package," Cuban officials assert that the United States was responsible for the introduction of sugar cane rust. Rather than being an incident of biological warfare, however, the most likely explanation is that rust spores, which had been conveyed from the Cameroon Republic in west Africa to the Dominican Republic, subsequently spread by prevailing winds to other Caribbean countries, including Cuba.

In 1980, dengue fever (DF) appeared in Cuba, and by the time the outbreak ended in 1981, 344,203 Cubans had contracted the disease. Of these, 10,312 developed dengue hemorrhagic fever (DHF), and 158 died. On July 26, 1981, as part of the "allegation package," Castro claimed that the CIA had introduced DF. The most likely explanation for the outbreak, however, is that Cuban soldiers or health workers who had served in Africa or the Indochina peninsula, where DF is endemic, brought a DF virus strain endemic to those regions back to Cuba with them.[62]

Soon after Acute Hemorrhagic Conjunctivitis (AHC) was first reported in Cuba in 1981, the Cuban government alleged that it resulted from a U.S.-instigated biological attack. The most likely explanation for the AHC outbreak is that Cuban soldiers or health workers had brought the AHC virus (as well as the DF virus in 1980), when they returned home after having served in African or Asian countries where the disease is endemic.

When epidemic optic and peripheral neuropathy first appeared in 1992, Cuban officials asserted that it was caused by "enemy action." In fact, it resulted from the lack of folic acid in the Cuban diet. After the Cuban government provided the vitamin supplements to its population in May 1993, the outbreak abated and then disappeared.

In the beginning of 1997, the Cuban government alleged that the United States was responsible for having introduced the insect pest Thrips palmi (commonly called thrip or thrips) onto the island in 1996. Since this allegation had important international repercussions, it is discussed in detail below.

The Cuban government has continued indicting the United States as a biological aggressor since 1997. Most noteworthy, Cuban labor unions and other organizations brought suits in Cuban courts against the U.S. government twice, in 1999 and 2000, seeking damages for alleged attacks by the United States. The first was adjudicated in the plaintiff's favor and awarded them $181 billion in damages. Added to the 11 allegations discussed above, Cuba claimed that the United States carried out attacks that utilized or caused bovine nodular pseudodermatosis (1981), ulcerative mammalititis of cows (1989), black sigatoka of plantain (1990), black plant louse of citrus trees (1992), citrus leafminer of citrus trees (1993), rabbit viral disease (1993), borer worm of coffee (1995), varroasis of bees (1996), ulcerative disease of trout and tilapia (1996), and rice mite (1997). The suit was adjudicated in plaintiffs' favor in April 2000. The U.S. government did not contest either suit.

In 2004, as part of its campaign to refute allegations made by certain Bush administration officials that Cuba supported a BW research and development program, the Cuban government invited the Center for Defense Information (CDI) to organize a visit to its biotechnological facilities. A member of the CDI group, Jonathan Tucker, subsequently reported that Cuban government officials addressing the group had claimed that "more than a dozen covert releases of infectious-disease-agents" had been "carried out by the CIA, beginning with Operation Mongoose during the 1960s." Tucker further quoted the assertion of Jesus Bermudez Cutino, president of the Cuban Center on Studies for Defense Information, that:

"Cuban scientists have proved that the strains responsible for these outbreaks had been artificially modified in the laboratory, or were not indigenous to the Americas, indicating that they had been artificially introduced." Neither Cutino, nor any other Cuban officials, provided the group with scientific data to back up these claims.. . . [With regard to the allegation of the thrips palmi infestation, an insect that feeds on my types of agricultural crops, which scars or kills plants and fruits,] [O]n December 26, 1996, the Cuban Ministry of Foreign Affairs asked for the U.S. Interest Section in Havana to clarify the S2R's actions [a U.S. aircraft over Cuba]. The United States explained the pilot of the S2R aircraft had seen the

Cuban aircraft below him, and that it had appeared to be climbing. To warn the Cuban aircraft of his presence, he had used the aircraft's smoke generator to generate smoke for visual effect. The U.S. reply did not satisfy the Cuban government. Thus on April 29, 1997, the Cuban government wrote the UN Secretary-General, claiming that, "There is reliable evidence that Cuba has once again been the target of biological aggression." It requested that is complaint be considered by a consultative meeting of BWC state parties.

> Two BWC articles address compliance concerns; of most relevance is Article V:
> The States Parties to this Convention undertake to consult one another and to cooperate in solving any problems which may arise in relation to the objective of, or in the application of the provisions of, the Convention. Consultation and cooperation pursuant to this article may also be undertaken through appropriate international procedures within the framework of the United Nations and in accordance with its Charter.

Article V's "undertaking to consult . . . and to cooperate" has been termed ambiguous and imprecise, and therefore attempts have been made to clarify it at review conferences of the BWC (held every five years). At the first review conference of the BWC (known as RevCom1) in March 1980, the British delegation proposed that any state party could request that "a consultative meeting open to all State Parties be convened at the expert level." This concept of a "consultative meeting" was refined a RevCom2 in 1986, RevCom3 in 1991, and RecCom4 in 1996. IN the end, a mechanism was created that allowed for the rapid convening of a consultative meeting in the event that one or more state parties had concerns that another state party had violated the BWC; it further allowed for any of the involved parties, or the consultative meeting itself, to request specialized assistance to help resolve technical issues.

The 1997 consultative meeting . . . was held August 25-27, 1997, in Geneva. Delegates appointed Ambassador Ian Soutar of the United Kingdom as the Chairman; together with six vice-chairmen (these were the representatives of Brazil, Canada, Iran, Netherlands, Nigeria, and Russia), formed the meeting's Bureau. The United States was represented by Ambassador Donald Mahley; Deputy Minister of Foreign Affairs Maria Florez represented Cuba. The United States and Cuba each made a formal presentation and took questions; each also distributed written materials to all members of the consultative meeting. Ambassador Soutar then invited state parties to submit "observations" on the presentations, which the Bureau would consider when attempting to clarify and resolve issues related to the Cuban allegation.

By the deadline of September 27, 1997, 11 states parties had offered observations. Australia, Canada, Denmark, Germany, Hungary, Japan, Netherlands and New Zealand found no causal link between the U.S. overflight and the Thrips infestation. Two others, China and Vietnam, argued that the technical complexity of the issue and the lack of detailed information made it impossible to reach a clear verdict. North Korea alone concluded that the U.S. aircraft had dispersed thrips over Cuba. Reflecting this lack of consensus, the "finding of fact" in the Bureau's report was inconclusive: "due inter alia to the technical complexity of the subject and the passage of time, it has not proved possible to reach a definitive conclusion with regard to the concerns raised by the Government of Cuba.

11.9. Ports of Entry to the United States

In addition to the CDC's authority to quarantine based on interstate commerce within the United States, the CDC also has the authority to conduct inspections for any carrier at a U.S. port for international commerce and travel that might pose a threat of the introduction of a communicable disease. The following regulation, authorized by 42 U.S.C. §264, provides for the process for carrying out that authority:

§71.31 General provisions.

(a) Upon arrival at a U.S. port, a carrier will not undergo inspection unless the Director determines that a failure to inspect will present a threat of introduction of communicable diseases into the United States, as may exist when the carrier has on board individual(s) reportable in accordance with §71.21 or meets the circumstances described in §71.42.

(b) The Director may require detention of a carrier until the completion of the measures outlined in this part that are necessary to prevent the introduction or spread of a communicable disease....

The continuation of the regulation provides for actions to prevent the spread of communicable diseases, but requires a belief that an arriving person is infected or has been exposed to specific diseases, as well as any other unknown disease:

§71.32 Persons, carriers, and things.

(a) Whenever the Director has reason to believe that any arriving person is infected with or has been exposed to any of the communicable diseases listed in paragraph (b) of this section, he/she may detain, isolate, or place the person under surveillance and may order disinfection or disinfestation as he/she considers necessary to prevent the introduction, transmission, or spread of the listed communicable diseases.

(b) The communicable diseases authorizing the application of sanitary, detention, and/or isolation measures under paragraph (a) of this section are: cholera or suspected cholera, diphtheria, infectious tuberculosis, plague, suspected smallpox, yellow fever, or suspected viral hemorrhagic fevers (Lassa, Marburg, Ebola, Congo-Crimean, and others not yet isolated or named).

(c) Whenever the Director has reason to believe that any arriving carrier or article or thing on board the carrier is or may be infected or contaminated with a communicable disease, he/she may require detention, disinsection, disinfection, disinfestation, fumigation, or other related measures respecting the carrier or article or thing as he/she considers necessary to prevent the introduction, transmission, or spread of communicable diseases.

The regulation of aircraft at ports of entry provide for disinfection for insect-borne communicable diseases, but no other diseases, and the responsibility is on the air carrier or pilot for private craft:

§71.44 Disinsection of aircraft.

(a) The Director may require disinsection of an aircraft if it has left a foreign area that is infected with insect-borne communicable disease and the aircraft is suspected of harboring insects of public health importance.

(b) Disinfection shall be the responsibility of the air carrier or, in the case of aircraft not for hire, the pilot in command, and shall be subject to monitoring by the Director.

The CDC has authority, however, to detain passengers who are risks to the public health:

§71.33 Persons: Isolation and surveillance.

(a) Persons held in isolation under this subpart may be held in facilities suitable for isolation and treatment.

(b) The Director may require isolation where surveillance is authorized in this subpart whenever the Director considers the risk of transmission of infection to be exceptionally serious.

(c) Every person who is placed under surveillance by authority of this subpart shall, during the period of surveillance:

(1) Give information relative to his/her health and his/her intended destination and report, in person or by telephone, to the local health officer having jurisdiction over the areas to be visited, and report for medical examinations as may be required;

(2) Upon arrival at any address other than that stated as the intended destination when placed under surveillance, or prior to departure from the United States, inform, in person or by telephone, the health officer serving the health jurisdiction from which he/she is departing.

(d) From time to time the Director may, in accordance with section 322 of the Public Health Service Act, enter into agreements with public or private medical or hospital facilities for providing care and treatment for persons detained under this part.

In order to carry out these duties, the regulations further require the provision of facilities by the airports:

§71.47 Special provisions relating to airports: Office and isolation facilities.

Each U.S. airport which receives international traffic shall provide without cost to the Government suitable office, isolation, and other exclusive space for carrying out the Federal responsibilities under this part.

There is an exemption, however, for mail under the authority of the U.S. government or any other government, which may remain a risk for introduction of a biological agent into the U.S.:

§71.43 Exemption for mails.

Except to the extent that mail contains any article or thing subject to restrictions under subpart F of this part, nothing in the regulations in this part shall render liable to detention, disinfection, or destruction any mail conveyed under the authority of the postal administration of the United States or of any other Government.

In a 2007 thesis from the Naval War College, the following assessment of biological threats through the U.S. Port system was made:

Abstract: . . . Although seaport security receives considerable policy attention in other areas of risk management, such as radiological detection, public health investments are relatively neglected. Effective, sustainable approaches to building interagency collaboration could prove to be an indispensable homeland security initiative to prepare for a bioterrorism attack or other infectious disease incidents.

The International Outreach and Coordination Strategy identified human smuggling networks and bioterrorism attacks as threats to the maritime domain. The strategy further states that a bioterrorism attack would most likely be perpetrated by a small, sophisticated group and be exceedingly difficult to detect. The Central Intelligence Agency analysis agrees that a bioterrorism attack by a small, sophisticated group is a high probability event. An attack perpetrated by international crewmen during a rapid turnover port visit is a viable biosecurity threat. The National Plan to Achieve Maritime Domain Awareness, the National Strategy for Maritime Security and the International Outreach and Coordination Strategy consider undocumented immigration as a security threat, but fail to recognize the risk of the intentional or unintentional introduction of a disease of public health significance into the United States.

Three possible scenarios of illnesses on-board a marine vessel, that would require notification are (1) an ill traveler is reported to the CDC before the boarded vessel enters the port; (2) an ill traveler is identified during screening processes; or (3) a traveler develops an illness while in port and under the supervision of port staff.

Fig. 11.8 Port Illness Notification Flowchart and Responsible Agencies (from Annette L. Neu, Master's Thesis, **BUILDING COLLABORATIVE CAPACITY FOR BIOSECURITY AT THE GEORGIA, (March 2007).**

Communication flow model is shown in Figure 10 with immediate no all core agencies required for any level of activation.

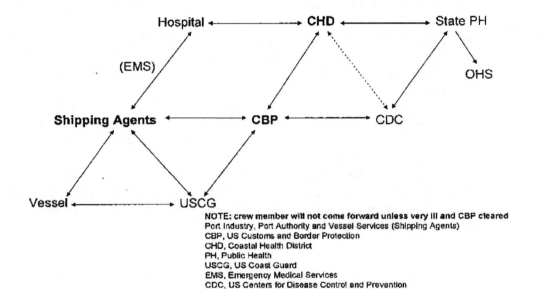

Illness Notification Web

NOTE: crew member will not come forward unless very ill and CBP cleared
Port Industry, Port Authority and Vessel Services (Shipping Agents)
CBP, US Customs and Border Protection
CHD, Coastal Health District
PH, Public Health
USCG, US Coast Guard
EMS, Emergency Medical Services
CDC, US Centers for Disease Control and Prevention
OHS, GA Office of Homeland Security
NOTE: USCG only inspects a fraction of vessel that fall under security matrix

11.10. International Criminal Court

The concept of an international criminal court arose with the unsuccessful attempt to establish such a tribunal after the First World War. However, following the Second World War, the Nuremberg and Tokyo war crimes tribunals provided the basis for efforts to create a permanent court. The first proposal for such a court was made with the adoption of the 1948 Convention on the Prevention and Punishment of the Crime of Genocide.

It was not until 1992 that the United Nations General Assembly began again to establish an international criminal court, directing the International Law Commission to draft a statute. The Security Council then in 1993 and 1994 established tribunals for the former Yugoslavia and Rwanda, respectively.

On July 17, 1998, the United Nations Diplomatic Conference established a permanent International Criminal Court with power to exercise its jurisdiction over persons for the most serious crimes of international concern. Those crimes are genocide, crimes against humanity, war crimes, as well as the crime of aggression. The statute was passed with a non-recorded vote of 120 in favor, 7 against, and 21 abstentions.

But those crimes do not include the use of biological weapons. Punishments do not include the death penalty. Prior to the adoption of the Statute, the Committee of the Whole of the Conference rejected attempts by India and the United States to introduce amendments to the draft Statute. One of those amendments would have "added to the list of weapons whose use is considered a serious violation of the laws and customs of international armed conflict language referring to 'weapons of mass destruction, i.e. nuclear, chemical and biological weapons.'" The non-action motion was proposed by Norway, supported by Malawi and Chile, and adopted by a vote of 114 in favor to 16 against, with 20 abstentions.

Specific comments made in explanation of the vote included several statements of widespread disappointment that the use of weapons of mass destruction was not made an international crime.

"India....What is worse, the Statute does not list any weapon of mass destruction among those whose use is banned as a war crime."

"United States...Including crimes of terrorism...will not help the fight against those crimes. The problem is not one of prosecution, but of investigation, and the Court will not be well equipped to do that."

"Sri Lanka...We...regret it had to abstain because the crime of terrorism was not included in the Statute."

"Turkey...wanted to have seen the crime of terrorism included in the Statute under crimes against humanity...For war crimes, it would have been better to have language stating that the future Court will not have anything to do with internal matters of States, as those actions it must take to root out terrorism."

"Singapore...To our dismay, chemical and biological weapons have been inexplicably dropped."

"Cuba...It regrets that destructive weapons of mass destruction were not included in the Statute."

"Egypt...It had stated time and again the need for inclusion of the use of weapons of mass destruction such as nuclear weapons."

"Bangladesh...It regrets that the Conference has not been able to deal with the issue of weapons of mass destruction."

"International Committee of the Red Cross (ICRC)...The exclusion of weapons of mass destruction from the Statute is hard to understand."[63]

The following is an excerpt from the German Law Journal, discussing the European perspective on international bioterrorism and the public international law tools to address it:[64]

Kerstin Wolny (Erlangen) exceeded the European dimension in her presentation on "Bioterrorism as a Challenge for Public International Law". She explained that so far, the general focus in public international law had been on prevention. In 1975, the Biological Weapons Convention[8] was concluded and in 2001, a protocol to the Convention was proposed but has not yet entered into force. However, the general problem was that these instruments were solely state-directed. With respect to biological weapons though, non-state actors formed a threat equal to that of states. Therefore, her proposal was to use international criminal law in order to fill the gap. In this context, she explored the possibilities of prosecuting acts of bioterrorism before the International Criminal Court (ICC) in The Hague. The problem here is that the Court's jurisdiction is limited to four categories of crimes: aggression, war crimes, crimes against humanity and genocide (Art.5 (1) ICC Statute). As for the crime of aggression, it can be perpetrated only by states; besides, the ICC Statute is imperfect in so far as it leaves the definition of this category to future developments (Art.5 (2) ICC Statute). If an act of bioterrorism is committed in times of war, it could in principle be regarded as a war crime within the meaning of Art.8 ICC Statute. This result, however, is rebutted by the fact that when the ICC Statute was concluded, the States Parties wanted to exclude both atomic and biological weapons from the scope of this provision. Wolny's solution was that under certain conditions, acts of bioterrorism may form a crime against humanity (Art.7 ICC

Statute). In particular, she argued that this provision had an objective different from that of war crimes. Therefore, the fact that bioterrorism could not be regarded as a war crime was not decisive for the interpretation of crimes against humanity. In the debate, she was confronted with the observation that according to Art.32 of the Vienna Convention on the Law of Treaties, the preparatory work of a treaty and the circumstances of its conclusion are merely supplementary means of interpretation where the meaning is ambiguous or obscure. Therefore, the question was raised whether in juridical terms, it was at all possible to take into account the states' will to exclude biological weapons from the scope of Art.8 ICC Statute. In her answer, Wolny underlined that the ICC mainly depended on the cooperation of the States Parties; therefore, it was dangerous to ignore their will.

CHAPTER ELEVEN ENDOTES
_____

ENDNOTES 11.2

[1] See WHO Official Records, No. 176, 1969, resolution WHA22.46 and Annex I.
[2] See WHO Official Records, No. 176, 1969, resolution WHA22.46 and Annex I.
[3] See document WHA34/1981/REC/1 resolution WHA34.13; see also WHO Official Records, No. 217, 1974, resolution WHA27.45, and resolution EB67.R13, Amendment of the International Health Regulations (1969).
[4] See resolution WHA48.7.
[5] See resolution WHA56.29.
[6] See resolution WHA56.28.
ENDNOTES 11.3.1

[7] *Learning from SARS - Renewal of Public Health in Canada - Executive Summary.* International Aspects of SARS at http://www.phac-aspc.gc.ca/publicat/sars-sras/naylor/index.html. [Note: this document was published by Health Canada prior to the announcement of the establishment of the Public Health Agency of Canada on September 24, 2004. Any reference to Health Canada should be assumed to be to the Public Health Agency of Canada.]
ENDNOTES 11.3

[8] At current (2010) exchange rates, NT $1 is roughly equivalent to US $0.03. "NT" stands for New Taiwan dollar.
[9] Excerpt from: *Quarantine and Isolation: Lessons Learned from SARS,* A Report to the Centers for Disease Control and Prevention, Mark A. Rothstein, JD, Institute for Bioethics, Health Law & Policy.

[10] Acknowledgment to Marie Laure Capela, International Center Fellow, for the research and drafting of this section
[11] Information from Europol website: www.europol.europa.eu/
[12] Acknowledgement to Marie Laure Capela, International Center Fellow, for the research and drafting of this section.
Endnotes for 11.5

[13] David Brown, "Man With Rare TB Easily Eluded Safeguards," *The Washington Post,* p. A03 (May 31, 2007). At http://www.washingtonpost.com/wp-dyn/content/article/2007/05/30/AR2007053001962.html
[14] David Brown, "Man With Rare TB Easily Eluded Safeguards," *The Washington Post,* p. A03 (May 31, 2007). Available at: http://www.washingtonpost.com/wp-dyn/content/article/2007/05/30/AR2007053001962.html
[15] *Man knew he had TB before flying to Europe.* (May 30, 2007). Available at http://www.cnn.com/2007/HEALTH/conditions/05/30/tb.flight/index.html
[16] *Man knew he had TB before flying to Europe.* (May 30, 2007). Available at http://www.cnn.com/2007/HEALTH/conditions/05/30/tb.flight/index.html
[17] *Man knew he had TB before flying to Europe.* (May 30, 2007). Available at http://www.cnn.com/2007/HEALTH/conditions/05/30/tb.flight/index.html .
[18] Department of Homeland Security Committee staff briefing with Department of Homeland Security officials (TSA, CMO, and CBP), June 4, 2007, fn 27, at http://homeland.house.gov/SiteDocuments/20070606160848-79812.pdf
[19] Department of Homeland Security Committee staff briefing with Department of Homeland Security

officials (TSA, CMO, and CBP), June 4, 2007, fn 40, at
http://homeland.house.gov/SiteDocuments/20070606160848-79812.pdf

[20] Department of Homeland Security Committee staff briefing with Department of Homeland Security officials (TSA, CMO, and CBP), June 4, 2007, fn 40, 46, at
http://homeland.house.gov/SiteDocuments/20070606160848-79812.pdf

[21] Testimony, Julie Gerberding, U.S. House of Representatives, Committee on Homeland Security, "The XDR-TB Tuberculosis Incident: A Poorly Coordinated Federal Response with Homeland Security Implications," June 6, 2007. Available at: http://homeland.house.gov/SiteDocuments/20070606125418-21114.pdf

[22] http://homeland.house.gov/SiteDocuments/20070606125418-21114.pdf

[23] ABC, "Exclusive: TB Patient Asks Forgiveness but Defends Travel," June 1, 2007 at
http://www.abcnews.go.com/GMA/OnCall/story?id=3231184&page=1 .

[24] Lawrence K. Altman, The New York Times, "Agent at Border, Aware, Let In Man With TB," June 1, 2007 at
http://www.abcnews.go.com/GMA/OnCall/story?id=3231184&page=1 .

[25] http://homeland.house.gov/SiteDocuments/20070606125418-21114.pdf

[26] Center for Disease Control and Prevention, *Update on CDC Investigation Into People Potentially Exposed to Patient With Extensively Drug-Resistant TB.*," May 30, 2007 at
http://www.cdc.gov/od/oc/media/transcripts/t070530.htm .

[27] Department of Health and Human Services, Centers for Disease Control and Prevention, Order for Provisional Quarantine and Medical Examination, May 24, 2007, at
http://www2a.cdc.gov/phlp/dailynews/default.asp?specific=402 .

[28] Department of Health and Human Services, Centers for Disease Control and Prevention, Order Pursuant to Section 361 of the Public Health Service Act Rescinding Movement Restrictions, June 2, 2007, at
http://www2a.cdc.gov/phlp/dailynews/default.asp?specific=402 .

[29] Hearing, U.S. House of Representatives, Committee on Homeland Security, "The XDR Tuberculosis Incident: A Poorly Coordinated Federal Response to an Incident with Homeland Security Implications," June 6, 2006, available at http://homeland.house.gov/hearings/index.asp?ID=56 .

[30] U.S. Senate, Committee on Appropriations, Subcommittee on Labor, Health and Human Services, and Related Agencies, June 6, 2006. Audio of hearing available at: http://appropriations.senate.gov/labor.cfm .

[31] CBC News, Wed., May 30, 2007, at http://www.cbc.ca/health/story/2007/05/30/tb-flight.html .

[32] Associated Press, "Father-in-Law of TB patient to be investigated," (June 3, 2007) at
http://www.msnbc.msn.com/id/19004955/ .

[33] "Canadians on flight with TB-infected man file suit," (July 12, 2007) at
http://www.ctv.ca/servlet/ArticleNews/story/CTVNews/20070712/TB_lawsuit_070712/20070712?hub=TopStories .

[34] Factors for extra-territorial jurisdiction require that a clear, express intent be evident from Congress and that this application not infringe on the sovereign authority of any other sovereign nation.

[35] L. Fast, R.C. Neufeldt, and L. Schirch, "Toward Ethically Grounded Conflict Interventions: Reevaluating Challenges in the 21st Century," *International Negotiation: A Journal of Theory and Practice* 7 (2002): 185-207.

[36] Restatement (Third) of Foreign Relations Law §601, Comment d.

[37] United Nations Charter, Art. 1.3.

[38] 1970 UN Declaration of Principles on International Law Concerning Friendly Relations and Cooperation Among States in Accordance with the Charter of the United Nations, U.N.G.A. Res. 2625 (Oct. 24, 1970),

[39] Principle 6, 1978 UNEP Principles on Shared Natural Resources.

[40] Restatement (Third) of Foreign Relations Law § 402.

[41] Sutton, "A Multidisciplinary Approach to an Ethic of Biodefense and Bioterrorism," 33 *Journal of Law, Medicine and Ethics* 310-322 (Summer 2005).

———

[42] 26 March 2000 marked the 25th Anniversary of the entry into force of the Biological Weapons Convention. This agreement was the first multilateral disarmament treaty banning an entire category of weapons of mass destruction. However, the BWC is not a legally-binding instrument. What are the consequences for a country which does not comply with the Convention? The next section addresses that question.

[43] "Biological Weapons: the Threat of the New Century?" NATO Parliamentary Assembly, Science and Technology Committee, Sub-committee on the Proliferation of Military Technology, Draft Interim Report, Mr. Michael Mates (United Kingdom) Rapporteur (16 April 1999) http://www.naa.be/publications/comrep/1999/as135stcmt-e.html.

[44] The United States objected to the inspections. President Clinton agreed to limited non-challenge inspections to clarify unclear declarations, but categorically rejected random inspections in order to protect the United States's biotechnology industry. In 2001, President Bush also rejected the inspection protocol proposed for the Biological Weapons Convention. Is this a reasonable position for the United States?

[45] While France is pursuing strategies of prevention and surveillance, the United States and the United Kingdom are pursuing research on vaccines, as a priority for addressing the threat of bioterrorism. Sweden, Switzerland and Israel have pursued civil defense strategies. How are these approaches different from chemical and nuclear threat preparations?

[46] The report notes that only 40 countries of the 141 signatories have adopted enforcement laws in compliance with the 1972 Convention which specifies that the production, development or possession of biological agents should be recognized as a major crime by most nations. Why did the United States wait until 1989 to pass the Biological Weapons and Anti-Terrorism Act?

[47] Biological Weapons: the Threat of the New Century? NATO Parlimentary Assembly Science and Technology Committee, Sub-committee on the Proliferation of Military Technology Draft Interim Report, Mr. Michael Mates (United Kingdom) Rapporteur, 16 April 1999. http://www.naa.be/publications/comrep/1999/as135stcmt-e.html

[48] As a result of the Gulf War in 1991, the United Nations appointed an inspection team to enter Iraq and inspect the country for biological weapons facilities. The appointment of the inspection team, a temporary group, was modeled after the chemical weapons inspection teams under the Chemical Weapons Convention. Since this inspection activity was not under the authority of the Biological Weapons Convention, why not just rely upon the United Nations to do inspections when there is a suspicion of development of biological weapons?

[49] A Full, Final and Complete Disclosure (FFCD) is required by the Security Council resolutions 687 (1991) and 707 (1991) which documents a complete disclosure of Iraq's programs of weapons of mass destruction. Until August 1995, the Iraqi's did not include information on its biological weapons program. At that time, the facility called the Al-Hakam Single Cell Protein Plant, which had previously been claimed as an animal feed production facility was disclosed as a biological weapons facility.

[50] In late 1997, Iraq requested a forum for disclosure of the biological weapons program through UNSCOM. The first two meetings were held in early 1998 to evaluate the chemical and missiles programs. Then, from March 20–27, 1998, a team of international scientists assembled by the United Nations Special Commission (UNSCOM) met with Iraqi weapons experts at the Vienna International Center to evaluate the "Full, Final and Complete Disclosure" (FFCD) of the Iraqi biological weapons programme. The international

team consisted of 18 scientists from 15 countries. The Iraqi delegation consisted of 10 weapons experts. The group produced a consensus evaluation to the UNSCOM Executive Chair.

ENDNOTES 11.7

[52] Speech from the Throne to Open the Third Session of the 37th Parliament of Canada (February 2, 2004) http://www.pco-bcp.gc.ca/index.asp?lang=eng&page=information&sub=publications&doc=sft-ddt/2004_1_e.htm.

[53] The Public Health Agency was created by legislation passed by the Parliament of Canada, Bill C-5 Public Health Agency of Canada Act, April 26, 2006 at http://www2.parl.gc.ca/Content/LOP/LegislativeSummaries/39/1/c5-e.pdf.

[54] D Faensen, H Claus, J Benzler, A Ammon, T Pfoch, T Breuer, G Krause, Robert Koch-Institut, SurvNet@RKI – a multistate electronic reporting system for communicable diseases, Berlin, Germany, indexed in MedLine as: Euro Surveill 2006;11(4):100-3. Published online April 2006.

ENDNOTES 11.8

[55] Jeanne Guillemin, *Anthrax—An Investigation of a Deadly Outbreak,* 113–4 (1999).

[56] For more information please contact: Tzvika Avigdor, Vice President for Marketing Phone: +972-4-9953931, E-mail: avigdor@opgal.com Web Site: www.opgal.com

[57] United Nations, Gould and Folb, *Project Coast: Apartheid's Chemical and Biological Warfare Programme, pg. 61,* UNIDIR/2002/12 (2002).

[58] Commey Pusch, "Dr Death' Walks Free," (South Africa), *The New African,* May 1, 2002COPYRIGHT 2002 IC Publications Ltd. Copyright 2002 Gale, Cengage Learning. All rights reserved. http://www.thefreelibrary.com/'Dr+Death'+walks+free.+(South+Africa)-a085881522

[59] *Cuba's Pursuit of Biological Weapons: Fact or Fiction?* Hearing Before The U.S. Senate, Foreign Relations Committee, chaired by Sen. Joseph Biden. S. Hrg. 107-736.

[60] Hearing, U.S. Cong., Comm. On Foreign Relations, June 5, 2002, Sen. Dodd statement.

[61] Raymond A. Zilinskas, "Cuban Allegations of U.S. Biological Warfare, False Allegations and Their Impact on Attribution from Terrorism, War, or Disease?: Unraveling the Use of Biological Weapons," edited by Anne L. Clunan, Peter R. Lavoy and Susan B. Martin (2008).

[62] It bears noting that Cuba periodically has experienced DF outbreaks throughout its history; for example, particularly sever DF outbreaks occurred in 1977, 1997, and 2002. However, the United States has not been accused of causing them.

ENDNOTES 11.10

[63] From Press Release, L/2889 20 July 1998, "UN Diplomatic Conference Concludes in Rome." The use of prisoners for "biological experiments" is made criminal and punishable by the International Criminal Court.
[64] Excerpt from: Rome Statute For The International Criminal Court, reprinted in The Statute of the International Criminal Court: A documentary History, art. 8(2)(ii) (M. Cherif Basssiouni ed. 1998).

Chapter Twelve
The Future of Biosecurity Law

The threat of emerging infectious diseases, bioterrorism, and failures of biosecurity are threats that we as a society must learn to address through the rule of law in order to preserve order and provide for the best human public health and emergency response. The biotechnology revolution of the 20th century and the continuing progress in biotechnology applications will feature largely in our arsenal of technological responses to these threats. However, for any of these defenses and measures of biosecurity to be utilized in our society, the rule of law must be precisely crafted to address the need for balancing freedoms and privacy with the need for preserving governmental order and public safety.

In *Law and Bioterrorism*, the predecessor to this volume published in 2003, a similarly-placed chapter on the future of bioterrorism suggested that genetics technologies, First Amendment restrictions on publishing biodefense research, internet publishing of information useful to bioterrorists, laboratory biosecurity, and vaccine development might be replaced by countermeasures that focus on broad spectrum immunity and changing drug approval processes in the Food and Drug Administration.

Since 2003, the regulatory aspect of laboratory biosecurity has developed into a growing subject of oversight and consideration. Legislation was proposed in subsequent years to amend and renew the program of laboratory biosafety and biosecurity regulation. The National Academies were asked to review the program and make recommendations for its improvement, and universities have experienced significant changes to comply with the new regulatory framework for laboratories that house specific biodefense research.

The restrictions on publication of biodefense research were relaxed and withdrawn as a restriction by the Department of the Treasury, and a community volunteer standard among scientific journals developed a dual-use test for authors. This new standard allowed editors to reject any article that they deemed contained information that was not outweighed by its scientific merit. In three specific controversial articles that questioned whether they should be published, all three articles were published. This appears to be a workable standard, and has not resulted in a test of the constitutional protection of free speech as this book goes to press.

This chapter raises a few new issues that may be of serious consequence in the coming years, including: the rapid development of nanotechnologies, the continuing use of the internet for communication among terrorists and purchasing of supplies and equipment, and the international shifting response to the international treaty after reaching a stalemate in the United

Nations forum to move forward to provide better oversight for potential state-sponsored biological weapons programs.

12.1.   Genetics, Synthetic Genomics, and Bioterrorism

In November 2009, *Gen Engineering News* reported that five nanotechnology companies had formed a consortium to develop a common set of principles for ensuring biosecurity in the gene synthesis industry.   The five companies (Blue Heron Biotechnology, DNA2.0, GeneArt, GenScript, and Integrated DNA Technologies) created the International Gene Synthesis Consortium (IGSC).

> Their "Harmonized Screening Protocol for Gene Sequence & Customer Screening to Promote Biosecurity" establishes five core components that each IGSC company will apply to promote the safe use of synthetic genes:
>
> (1) Gene Sequence Screening: The complete DNA sequence of every synthetic gene order is to be screened against a regulated pathogen database developed by the consortium and one or more of the internationally coordinated sequence reference databanks. Amino acid sequences of possible translation products for each synthetic gene ordered will also be screened. All orders originating in the U.S. will also be screened against the U.S. Select Agent lists.
>
> (2) Gene Customer Screening: A complete screening of each potential gene-synthesis customer will be conducted to establish identity and clearance for delivery of genes ordered in accordance with national guidelines.
>
> (3) Record Keeping: The IGSC companies will keep all screening, customer, and order records for at least eight years.
>
> (4) Order Refusal & Reporting: IGSC firms reserve the right to refuse to fill any order and to notify authorities upon identifying potentially problematic orders.
>
> (5) Regulatory Compliance: IGSC companies comply with all applicable laws and regulations governing the synthesis, possession, transport, export, and import of gene synthesis and other products.

The CEO of Blue Heron Technologies was quoted as saying,

> It quickly became apparent to us when we started that gene synthesis not only had many potential benefits to biomedical research but also potential dangers . . . Many companies and individuals would be able to gain access to potentially lethal pathogens where they otherwise would not have been able to. In thinking about the implications of gene synthesis, we wanted to make sure that we were not enabling any nefarious use of DNA.

[*Genetic Engineering and Biotechnology News*, "Gene-Synthesis Firms Set Up Biosecurity Protocol" (Nov. 18, 2009).]

Whether the federal government adopts these guidelines or develops others is a topic of discussion in working groups within the federal government.   There are currently no federal government regulations specifically designed for synthetic biology.

12.2.   Nanotechnologies and Bioterrorism and Biodefense

Nanotechnologies that involve biological materials or that interface with biological materials or human tissues are often referred to as nanobiotechnologies. Despite calls from non-profit groups and "think tanks" such as the Woodrow Wilson Public Policy Foundation, no clear path to a regulatory framework has emerged in the federal government.   Even though the risks are potentially as high as laboratories that work at higher biosafety levels, such as BSL-3 and BSL-

4 laboratories, there is no equivalent regulation to the Select Agent Regulations in the nanobiotechnology industry. The reason for this is two-fold: first, there is reluctance on the part of the federal government to impose regulations on an emerging technological field too early because it would likely constrain or redirect the field in directions that might not be as advantageous or economically profitable to industry and society; and second, nanotechnology remains largely misunderstood, along with its risks, and there is no one federal agency that is charged with its regulation, leading to a piecemeal approach to nanotechnology regulation.

The regulation of these technologies, in particular laboratory safety levels, will likely be considered for federal regulation in the next three to seven years. A laboratory accident or disaster would move this date closer.

12.3. International responses: the Biological Weapons Convention shifts from a monitoring protocol of the Biological Weapons Convention to Biosecurity Codes of Conduct

The Biological Weapons Convention was signed in 1972 and entered into force in 1975. With 163 state parties to the Convention, 13 signatories, and 19 states, not parties, the Biological Weapons Convention has been a success in terms of participation. However, the BWC has been weak in terms of verification and enforcement, since it lacks any mechanism within the "four corners" of the treaty. The convention allows for meetings of the parties to amend or add to the BWC, but there was stalemate when an inspection protocol, similar to the Chemical Weapons Convention inspection protocol, was proposed, which led to coalitions taking hard stands in the negotiations. This ultimately has not led to any progress in talks among the parties.

The United Nations is the administrative and institutional center for the BWC, and it is here that meetings and communications between the parties takes place. The direction of the BWC meetings changed in 2005, when it became evident that a stalemate had been reached in moving forward with the inspection protocol, and when the growth in biological laboratories began to shift the focus of the risk from purely intentional acquisition and use of biological weapons, to issues of securing laboratory supplies of biological materials, ensuring that accidental releases from these growing number of laboratories was adequately addressed in the context of the biological weapons convention.

While the safety aspect would typically fall squarely within the jurisdictional purview of the World Health Organization, the combined threat of biosafety and biosecurity engaged the joint collaborative efforts of the two United Nations organizations to address this global challenge: the World Health Organization with the Biological Weapons Convention directorate.

Utilizing other existing legal instruments, such as the UN 1540 mechanism in combination with the BWC in order to require inspections of suspected state programs in bioterrorism, was used in the inspection of Iraq after Saddam Hussein the itinerate dictator had refused to fully cooperate with disclosure. The use of the UN 1540 mechanism in collaboration with the World Health Organization and the BWC directorate as directed by the United Nations member states will be utilized as the primary process for addressing threats of state programs in biological weapons for the next ten to twenty years.

12.4. The World Wide Web and Bioterrorism

After the attacks of 9/11 on the World Trade Center and the Pentagon by terrorists, it became clear that the internet had played a key role in communication, making purchases, transferring funds—utilizing the freedoms they wanted to destroy. A study conducted from January 1998 to May 2005 searched for internet sites of terrorist organizations listed on the U.S. State Department list of terrorist organizations, and more than 4,300 sites were found serving terrorists and their suppliers and followers.[1]

The use of the internet for bioterrorism purposes has been examined for buying biological processing equipment, pharmaceuticals, personal protective equipment, and anything that would be needed to set up a full-scale laboratory for the development of biological weapons. These communications are not going to cease, and they will not grow less sophisticated in their ability to go undetected.

Online genetic libraries that can be used to search and build new organisms or chimeras are accessible via the internet, and the DNA codes developed from these libraries can be downloaded to a device that can put together the DNA code from biological materials, all available for purchase on the world wide web. This can be done by a graduate student in microbiology or an advanced high school student. There should be a tracking system to identify which computer IP address is requesting certain DNA combinations that would raise a "red flag" for their construction. However, since these databases are used by scientists for research, this would mean that all of their research would be tracked and unnecessarily monitored. However, if tracking all downloaded genetic codes for developing organisms proved to be the optimum way to prevent maleficent use of them, then the burden on the scientist would probably be considered negligible against the benefit to the public health of society.

12.5   Domestic response: a new way of thinking

The Hurricane Katrina disaster demonstrated the lack of coordination between federal and state authorities in responding to an immediate emergency that developed into a longer-term public health emergency. This brought focus on a negative aspect of federalism that has served the U.S. government so well, the balancing and dividing of governmental powers.

In times of an emergency that pose a national security threat, the Constitution is clear about shifting authority to the federal government from state government. However, in domestic disasters or public health emergencies, a national security threat is not so evident as to make the constitutional shift in power a clear indication. This led to delay on the part of the state government of Louisiana in relinquishing any control of governmental functions in the hours and days immediately following the disaster in New Orleans. The federal government response units were "sidelined" while the constitutional determinations were made, which included a never-presented draft to the Governor of Louisiana to relinquish the governors powers to the federal government so that a federal response could be implemented. This petition was never presented, and so such a conflict has not yet been adjudicated. It is likely that this scenario may present itself again in the United States, and decisions about the proper balance of powers and the time to shift that power between state and federal governments will once again be in the forefront of constitutional jurisprudence.

12.6   Biodiplomacy

The future of biosecurity law will almost certainly be dominated by the development of strategies to use diplomacy rather than force in the control of biological threats, which are unique in their ubiquity, use, storage, distribution, transportation, and dual use aspects. Because of the unique factors of biological organisms, which can be used for both beneficial and malevolent purposes, the need for a new strategy of *biodiplomacy* is critical.

Definition: A rare form of diplomacy, but becoming more common; used to address the issues of biological weapons prohibition, verification, and confidence-building between nations, and the issues unique to biological materials, not limited to their inherent self-propagating quantities; used to address the opportunities for dual use research, where either maleficent or beneficent purposes could be the objective of the identical research. Calls for biodiplomacy also arise from the biotechnology revolution, which has presented growing challenges of balancing the need to regulate with the need to allow development of one of the most important scientific fields to develop in the last century, biotechnologies.

What is the magnitude of the biological threat which would require a specialized form of diplomacy such as biodiplomacy?

Twelve factors have contributed to the significant increase in the magnitude of the global biological threat and the need for a biodiplomacy strategy: (1) the biotechnology revolution beginning in the early 1970s; (2) the explosion in international air travel, increasing 400% since the 1960s; (3) the simplicity of the biotechnology to clone new organisms to include toxin producing genes; DNA engineering of all types and the isolation of bioregulators which affect human physiological function; (4) emerging infection diseases have increased; (5) the growing loss of our arsenal against diseases with antibiotic resistant organisms; (6) state sponsored and rogue utilized bioweapons programs; (7) the success and notoriety of the anthrax attacks in the fall of 2001; (8) the increase in biodefense research from $300,000 to $24 billion since 2001; (9) the accidental release of organisms from laboratories which have increased since 2001, due to the great need to expand laboratory infrastructure and resources to do research in this growing global biological threat; (10) global climate change which is shifting not only the ecologies which support specific diseases, but will be causing the shifting of populations of humans due to flooding and drought, perhaps the largest factor in global climate change to precipitate a global biological threat; (11) the transport of biological clinical samples in a pandemic, or for research and the lack of biosecurity for these shipments; and (12) poorly conceived regulatory frameworks or gaps in international law which exacerbate the risks of global biological risks.

Existing traditional legal structures have failed to provide the kind of regulatory oversight and enforcement that was intended, and new biodiplomatic processes have been utilized. For example, the United Nations process for filing complaints regarding the use of biological weapons has never been used. However within the United Nations system, the consultative process has been the choice of nations in resolving disputes. Cuba, for example has brought twenty-two complaints of the use of biological terrorism by the United States, without utilizing the formal process. Why has this mechanism never been used, and why has the consultative method been utilized? Failing to assess the international politics of filing formal complaints, the process for making formal complaints has all but ensured that no one will ever file a complaint, giving rise to the need for biodiplomatic approaches.

The Biological Weapons Convention lacks an inspection and verification protocol, which has led to the development of confidence building measures after failing to reach an agreement on an inspection protocol. Confidence Building Measures is an example of biodiplomacy, where the parties share information about their biosafety and biosecurity programs in order to build confidence in their capabilities and capacities to keep such materials and processes secure.

The use of the UN 1540 mechanism has been the result of biodiplomatic efforts to respond to a gap in the Biological Weapons Convention which lacks a verification mechanism. The UN 1540 mechanism was utilized in the inspection of the Iraq biological weapons program after significant intelligence led the UN member states to conclude that there was still such a program underway in Iraq.

Incidents where biodiplomacy has been utilized in the 21st Century demonstrate the importance of this approach.

The SARS pandemic in 2003 was a wakeup call when China failed to notify the world that an unusually virulent and unusually contagious illness had emerged in Guangdong and the infected individuals were leaving the China. This was a call to action for the World Health Organization and its members to address this gap in global public health.

On the eve of the effective date of the World Health Organization's International Health Regulations (2005) which would be effective in June 2007; the United States through a series of biodiplomatic failures, allowed Andrew Speaker, a tuberculosis patient who had been advised not to travel outside of the United States, to visit multiple countries potentially exposing hundreds of people traveling on airlines to a potentially deadly strain of tuberculosis.

After the International Health Regulations became effective, Libya reported an outbreak of swine flu in 2008 which gave Egypt and an excuse to engage in what many saw as a political backlash for Libya when Egypt closed its border to Libya and slaughtered all of the swine in Egypt. Russia also put up a trade barrier to U.S. produced pork upon notification of the presence of swine flu in the U.S., although there was no evidence that eating pork would transmit the swine flu.

In 2009, a greatly successful biodiplomatic process emerged when Mexico reported the presence of swine flu to the World Health Organization upon the discovery of the first cases. This led to tremendous political capital for Mexico and assistance from the WHO and member countries, but Mexico also suffered greatly from the plummet in tourism which lasted through the year and into 2010.

The WHO Biodiplomacy in Assisting in Mass Gatherings Preparations has led to the development of a new group of experts to assist with planning mass gatherings such as sports events (e.g., the Olympics) or religious events (e.g., the Hajj, the Muslim annual pilgrimage to Mecca and Medina in Saudi Arabia); all of who are engaged in biodiplomacy to advise the host countries and coordinating committees on the most effective preparation public health emergencies.

These recent examples of global biosecurity events and practices and the biodiplomatic responses to them, ensure that the field of biodiplomacy is an important one for global biosecurity in the 21st century.

CHAPTER TWELVE ENDNOTE

---

[1] Gabriel Weimann, *Terror on the Internet: The New Arena, The New Challenges* p. 5 (2006).

CPSIA information can be obtained
at www.ICGtesting.com
Printed in the USA
LVOW04s1020090118
562378LV00015B/303/P

9 780983 802495